THE CARTOON HISTORY OF THE UNIVERSE

Volumes 1~7

Larry Gonick

DOUBLEDAY

NEW YORK · LONDON · TORONTO · SYDNEY · AUCKLAND

PUBLISHED BY DOUBLEDAY
A DIVISION OF BANTAM DOUBLEDAY DELL PUBLISHING GROUP INC.
666 FIFTH AVENUE, NEW YORK, NEW YORK 10103

DOUBLEDAY AND THE PORTRAYAL OF AN ANCHOR WITH A DOLPHIN ARE TRADEMARKS OF DOUBLEDAY, A DIVISION OF BANTAM DOUBLEDAY DELL PUBLISHING GROUP, INC.

LIBRARY OF CONGRESS CATALOGING-IN-PUBLICATION DATA

GONICK, LARRY.
THE CARTOON HISTORY OF THE UNIVERSE.
VOLUMES 1-7 / LARRY GONICK.
P. CM.
INCLUDES BIBLIOGRAPHICAL REFERENCES.
1. WORLD HISTORY — CARICATURES AND CARTOONS.
I. TITLE.
D21.1 G66 1990 89-27397
902.07 — dc20 CIP

ISBN 0-385-26520-4

PRINTED IN THE UNITED STATES OF AMERICA
SEPTEMBER 1990
6 8 10 11 9 7 5

TO LISA

THE CARTOON
HISTORY
OF THE
UNIVERSE

·INTRODUCTION·

THIS CARTOON HISTORY IS THE OUTCOME OF MY NINE YEARS AT HARVARD, WHERE I STUDIED MATHEMATICS—
YES...
NINE YEARS THE MATH DEPARTMENT SCOFFED AT MY THEORIES! BUT WHAT DO THEY KNOW ABOUT TIME TRAVEL? SNORT!! MOST MATHEMATICIANS CAN'T TELL A SECOND HAND FROM A SECOND BASE!! WE PARTED WAYS IN 1972...
AFTER I DROPPED OUT, I BUILT THIS: MY TIME MACHINE! LET'S HEAR 'EM SCOFF NOW!
YOU SEE? SIMPLE! JUST A PILE OF OLD HISTORY BOOKS! GAD, BUT THAT MUSTY SMELL IS BRACING!!
IF I READ THE RIGHT BOOKS AND CONCENTRATE HARD ENOUGH, THE MACHINE TRANSPORTS ME—IN MY IMAGINATION —ANYWHERE IN THE PAST THAT I WANT!
HMM—ANOTHER OVERDUE LIBRARY BOOK!
FOR YOU IT'S EVEN EASIER— ALL YOU HAVE TO DO IS KEEP READING! BUT HANG ON TIGHT! I'VE SET THE CONTROLS FOR THE TIME BEFORE TIME BEGAN...
HEH HEH HEH...

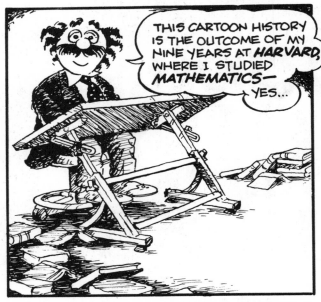

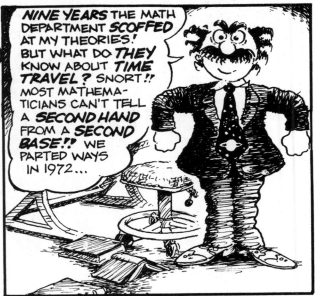

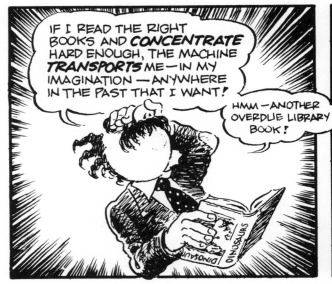

THE CARTOON HISTORY OF THE UNIVERSE

VOLUME 1.

THE EVOLUTION OF EVERYTHING

BEFORE TIME BEGAN, THE ENTIRE UNIVERSE WAS PRESSED TOGETHER IN ONE HOT LUMP. THEN CAME...

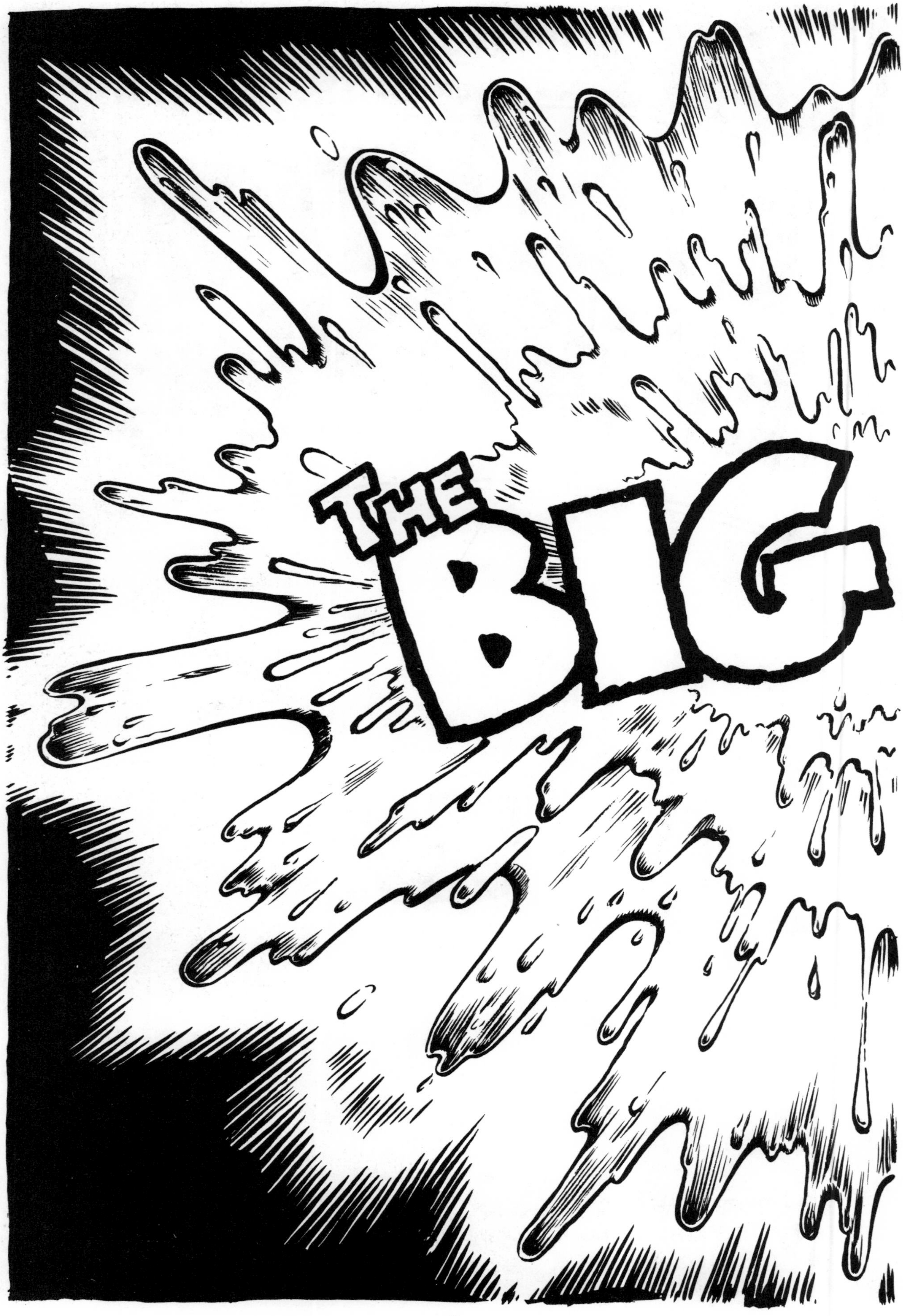
THE BIG

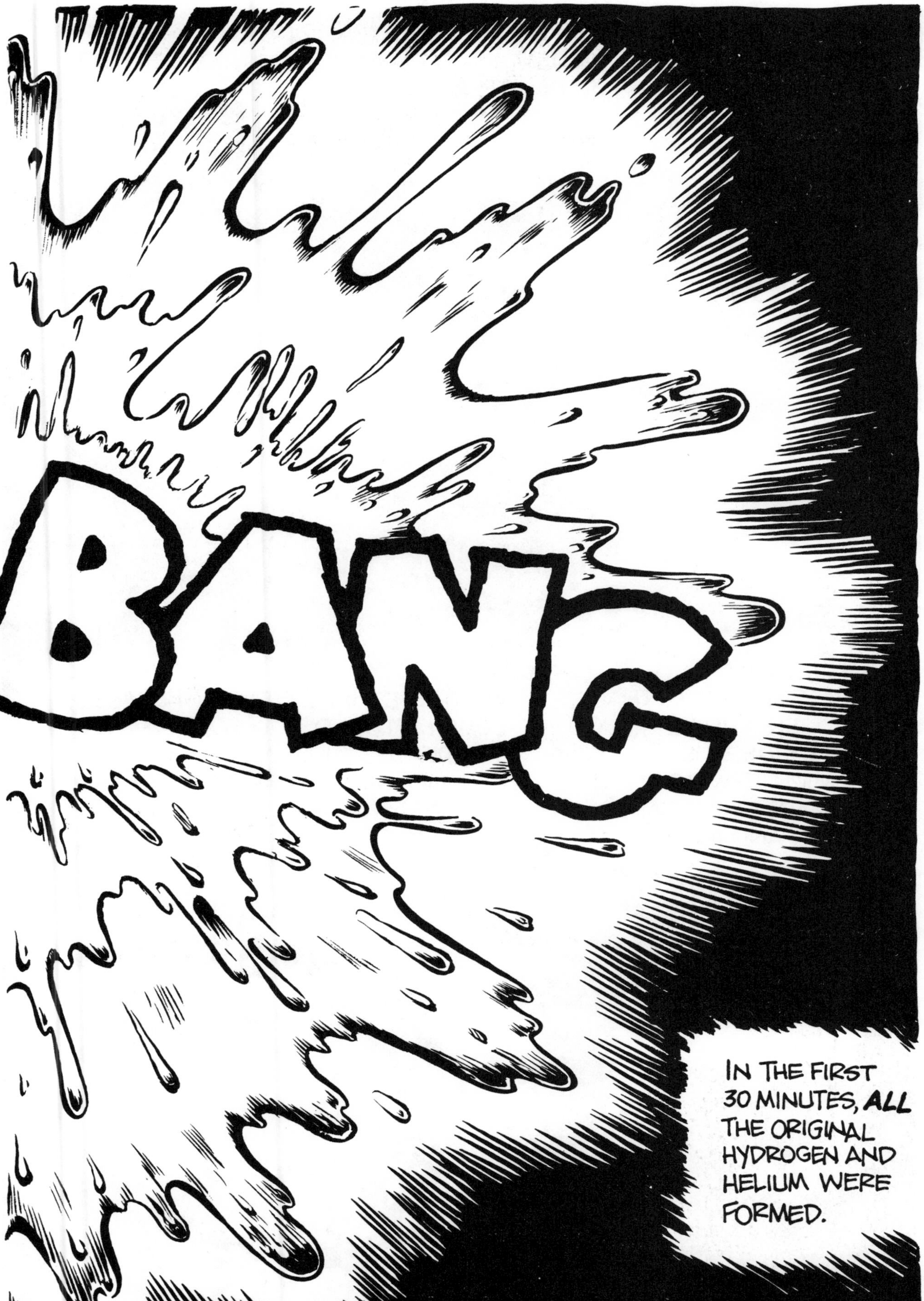
BANG
IN THE FIRST 30 MINUTES, ALL THE ORIGINAL HYDROGEN AND HELIUM WERE FORMED.

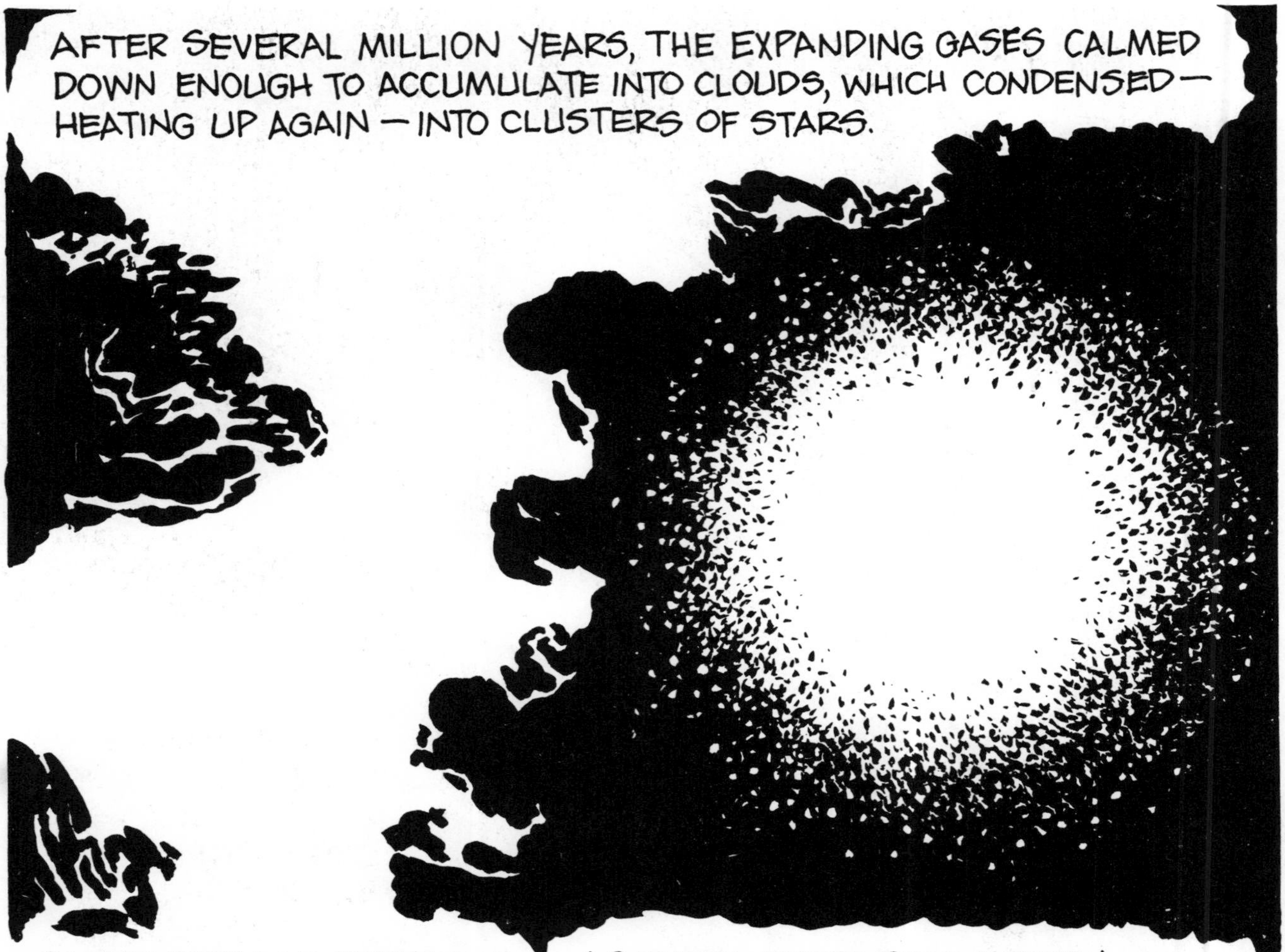
AFTER SEVERAL MILLION YEARS, THE EXPANDING GASES CALMED DOWN ENOUGH TO ACCUMULATE INTO CLOUDS, WHICH CONDENSED—HEATING UP AGAIN—INTO CLUSTERS OF STARS.

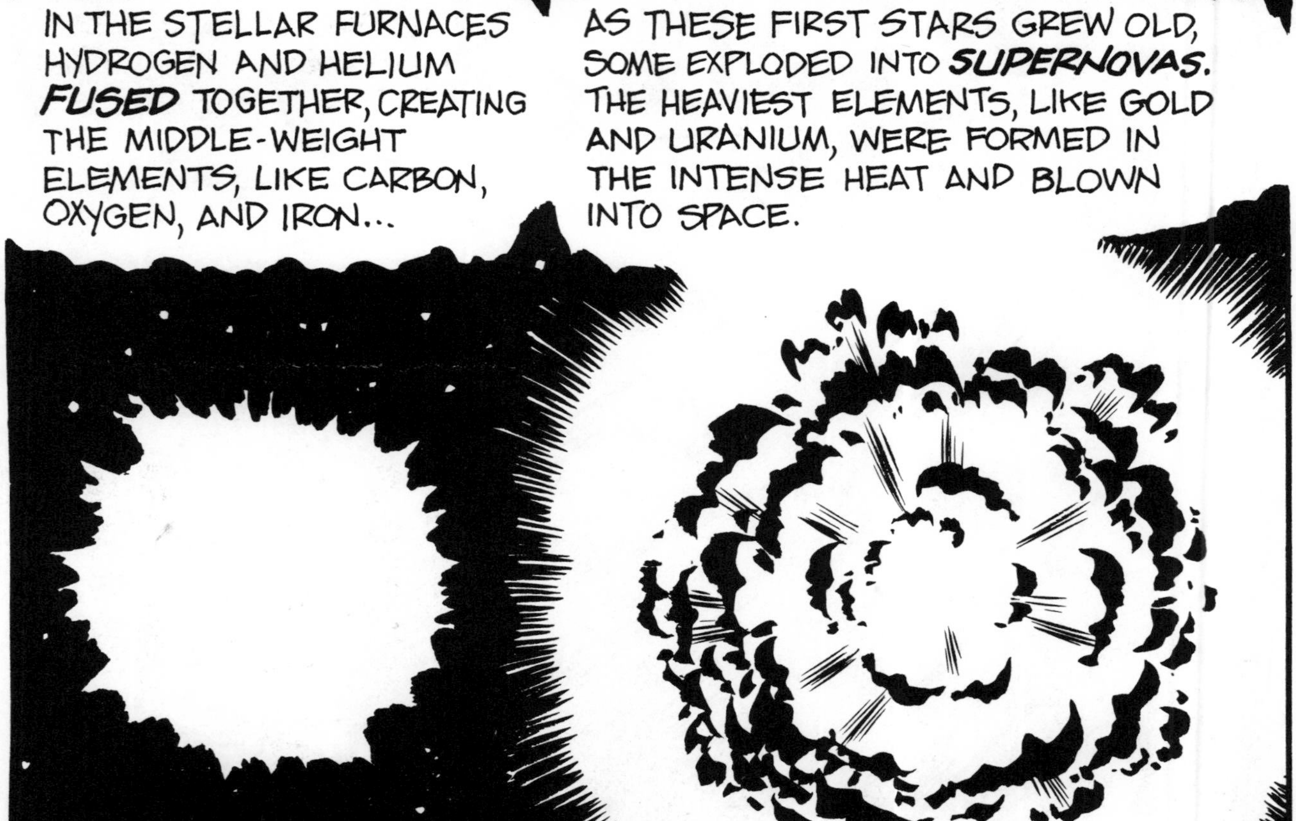
IN THE STELLAR FURNACES HYDROGEN AND HELIUM ***FUSED*** TOGETHER, CREATING THE MIDDLE-WEIGHT ELEMENTS, LIKE CARBON, OXYGEN, AND IRON...
AS THESE FIRST STARS GREW OLD, SOME EXPLODED INTO ***SUPERNOVAS.*** THE HEAVIEST ELEMENTS, LIKE GOLD AND URANIUM, WERE FORMED IN THE INTENSE HEAT AND BLOWN INTO SPACE.

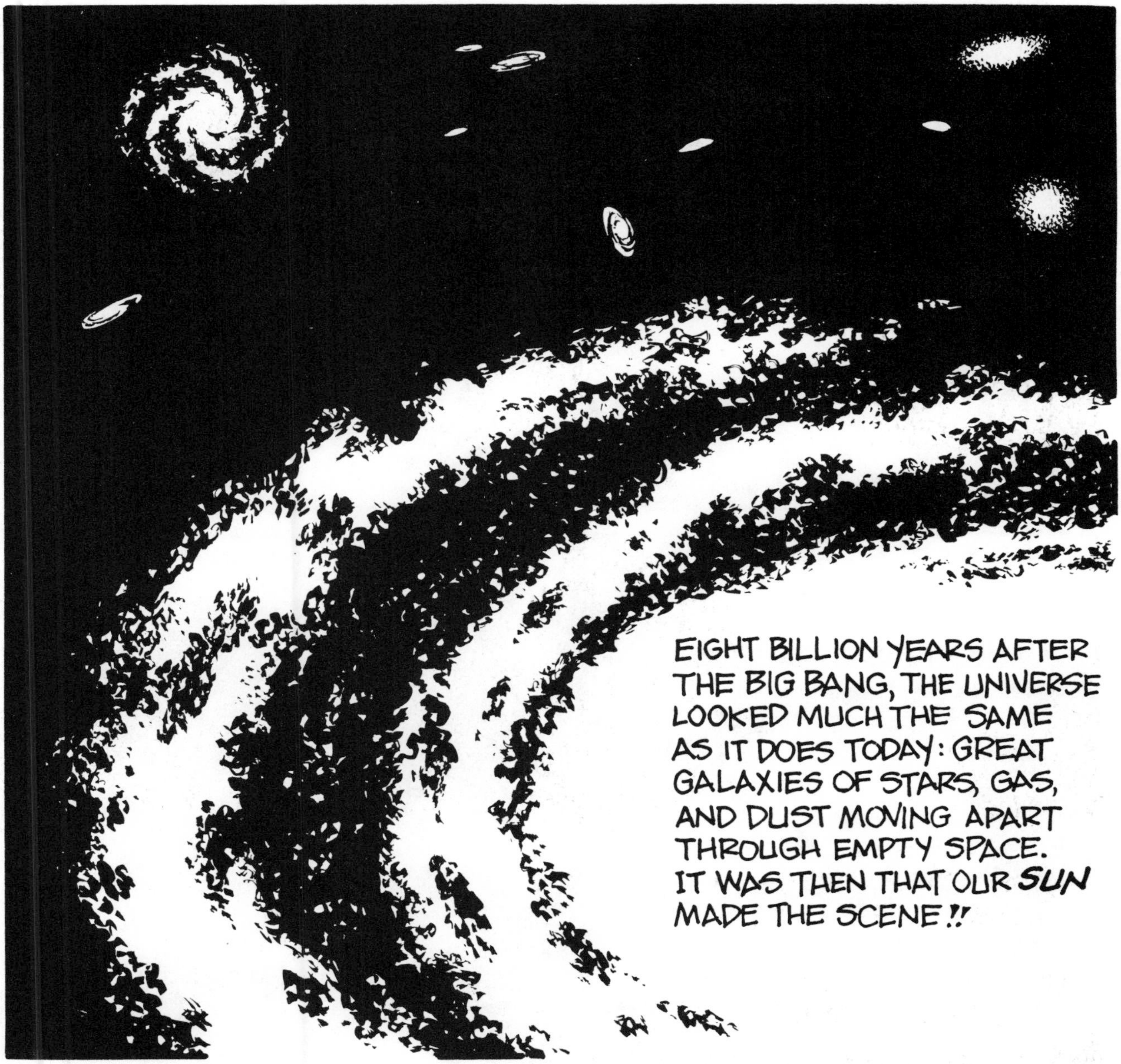
EIGHT BILLION YEARS AFTER THE BIG BANG, THE UNIVERSE LOOKED MUCH THE SAME AS IT DOES TODAY: GREAT GALAXIES OF STARS, GAS, AND DUST MOVING APART THROUGH EMPTY SPACE. IT WAS THEN THAT OUR SUN MADE THE SCENE!!

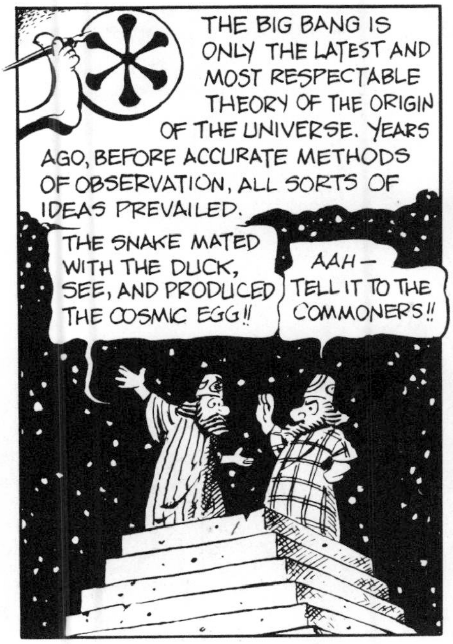
THE BIG BANG IS ONLY THE LATEST AND MOST RESPECTABLE THEORY OF THE ORIGIN OF THE UNIVERSE. YEARS AGO, BEFORE ACCURATE METHODS OF OBSERVATION, ALL SORTS OF IDEAS PREVAILED.
THE SNAKE MATED WITH THE DUCK, SEE, AND PRODUCED THE COSMIC EGG!!
AAH— TELL IT TO THE COMMONERS!!

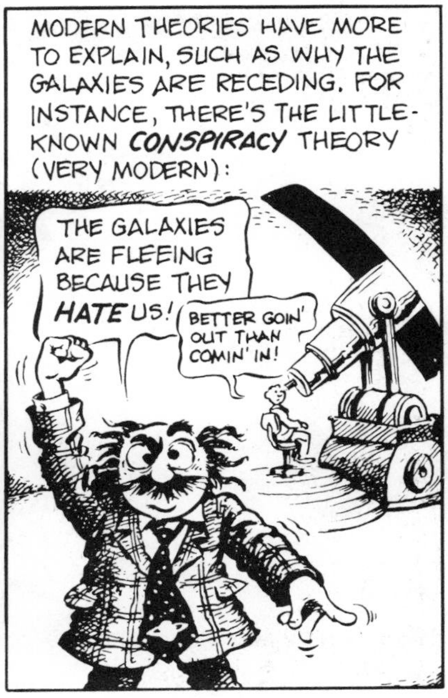
MODERN THEORIES HAVE MORE TO EXPLAIN, SUCH AS WHY THE GALAXIES ARE RECEDING. FOR INSTANCE, THERE'S THE LITTLE-KNOWN CONSPIRACY THEORY (VERY MODERN):
THE GALAXIES ARE FLEEING BECAUSE THEY HATE US!
BETTER GOIN' OUT THAN COMIN' IN!

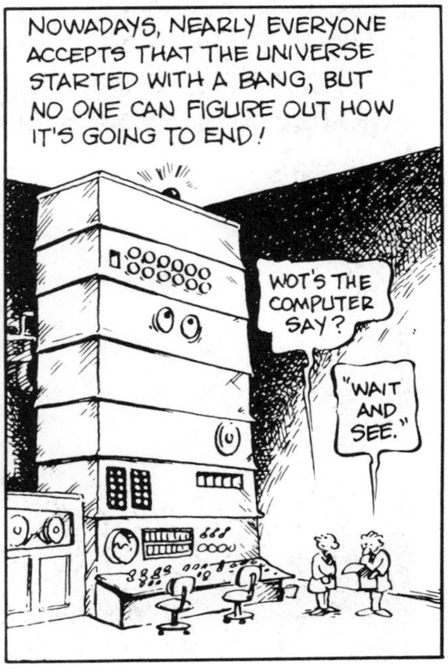
NOWADAYS, NEARLY EVERYONE ACCEPTS THAT THE UNIVERSE STARTED WITH A BANG, BUT NO ONE CAN FIGURE OUT HOW IT'S GOING TO END!
WOT'S THE COMPUTER SAY?
"WAIT AND SEE."

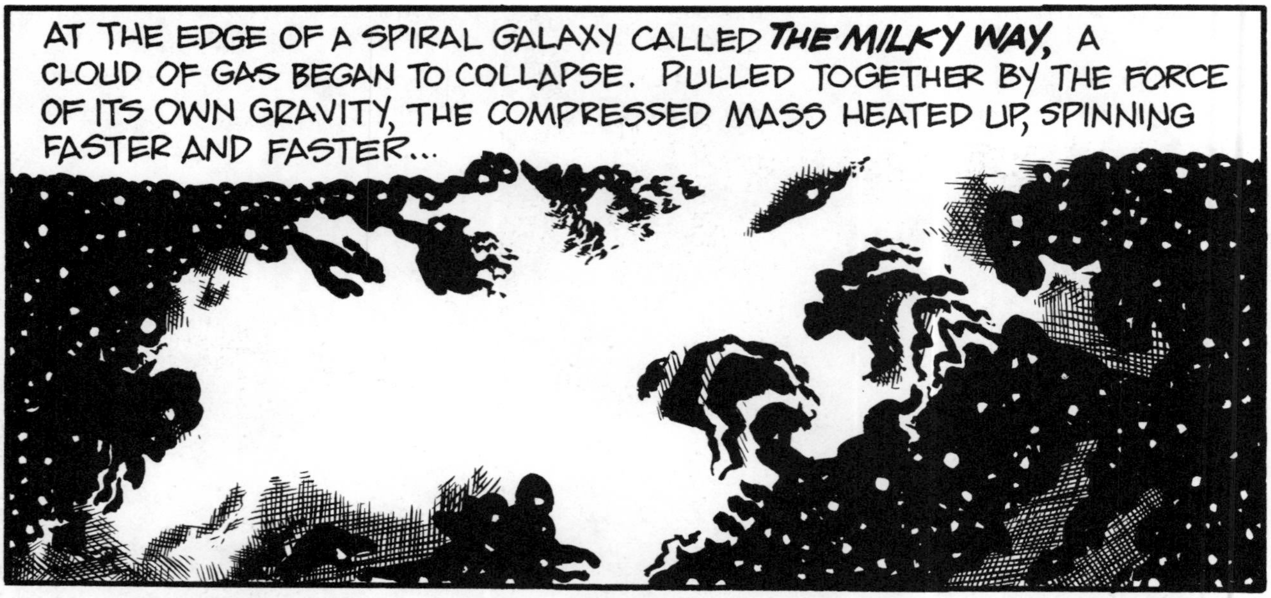
AT THE EDGE OF A SPIRAL GALAXY CALLED **THE MILKY WAY**, A CLOUD OF GAS BEGAN TO COLLAPSE. PULLED TOGETHER BY THE FORCE OF ITS OWN GRAVITY, THE COMPRESSED MASS HEATED UP, SPINNING FASTER AND FASTER...

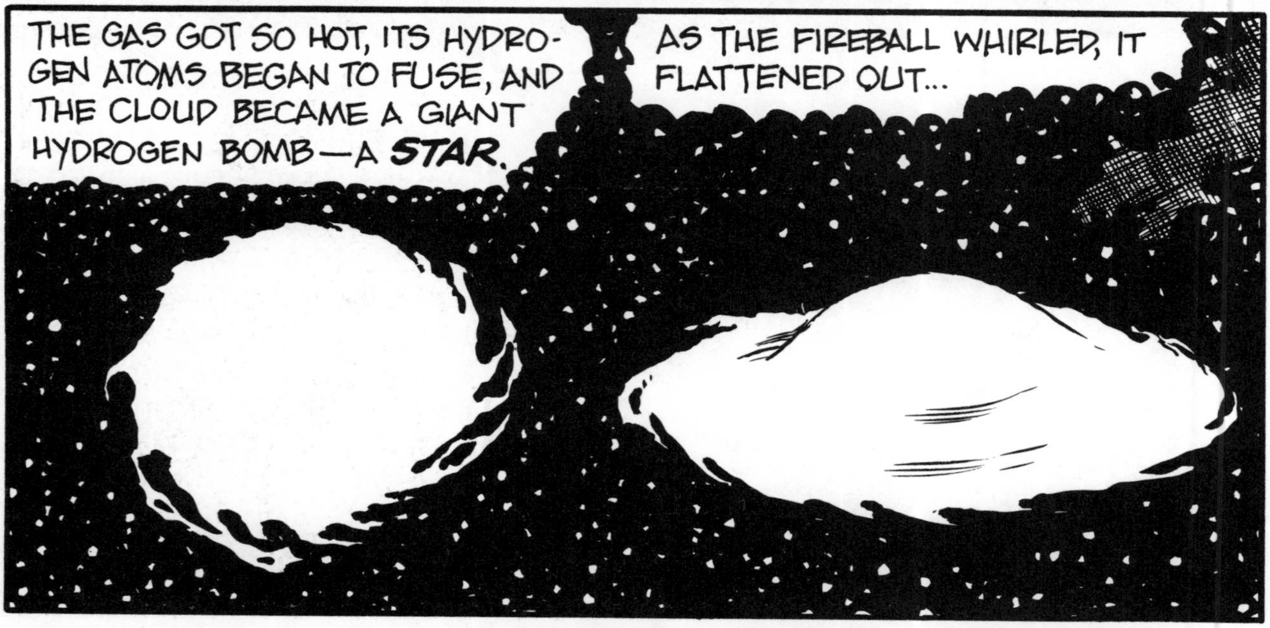
THE GAS GOT SO HOT, ITS HYDROGEN ATOMS BEGAN TO FUSE, AND THE CLOUD BECAME A GIANT HYDROGEN BOMB—A **STAR**.
AS THE FIREBALL WHIRLED, IT FLATTENED OUT...

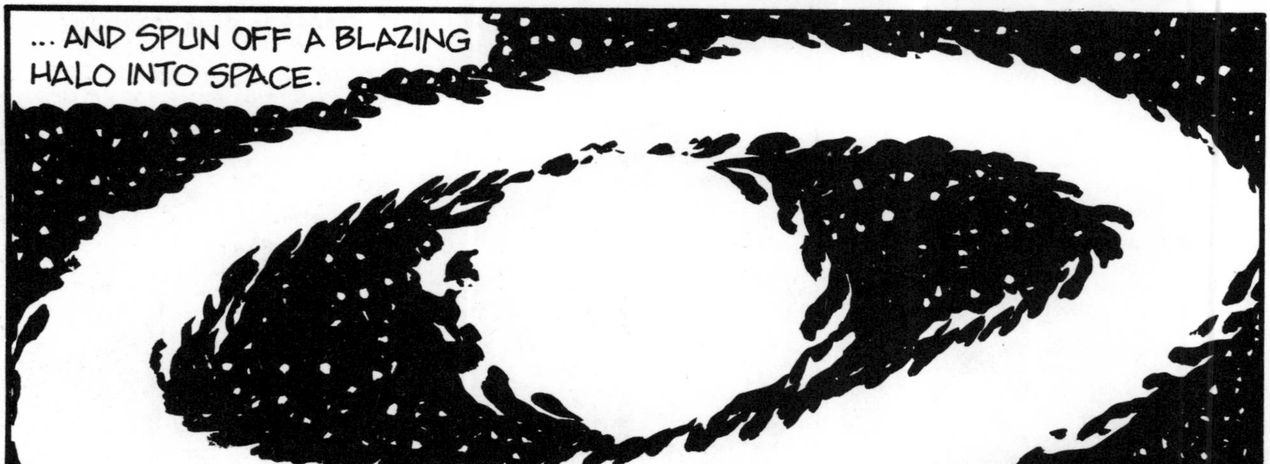
... AND SPUN OFF A BLAZING HALO INTO SPACE.

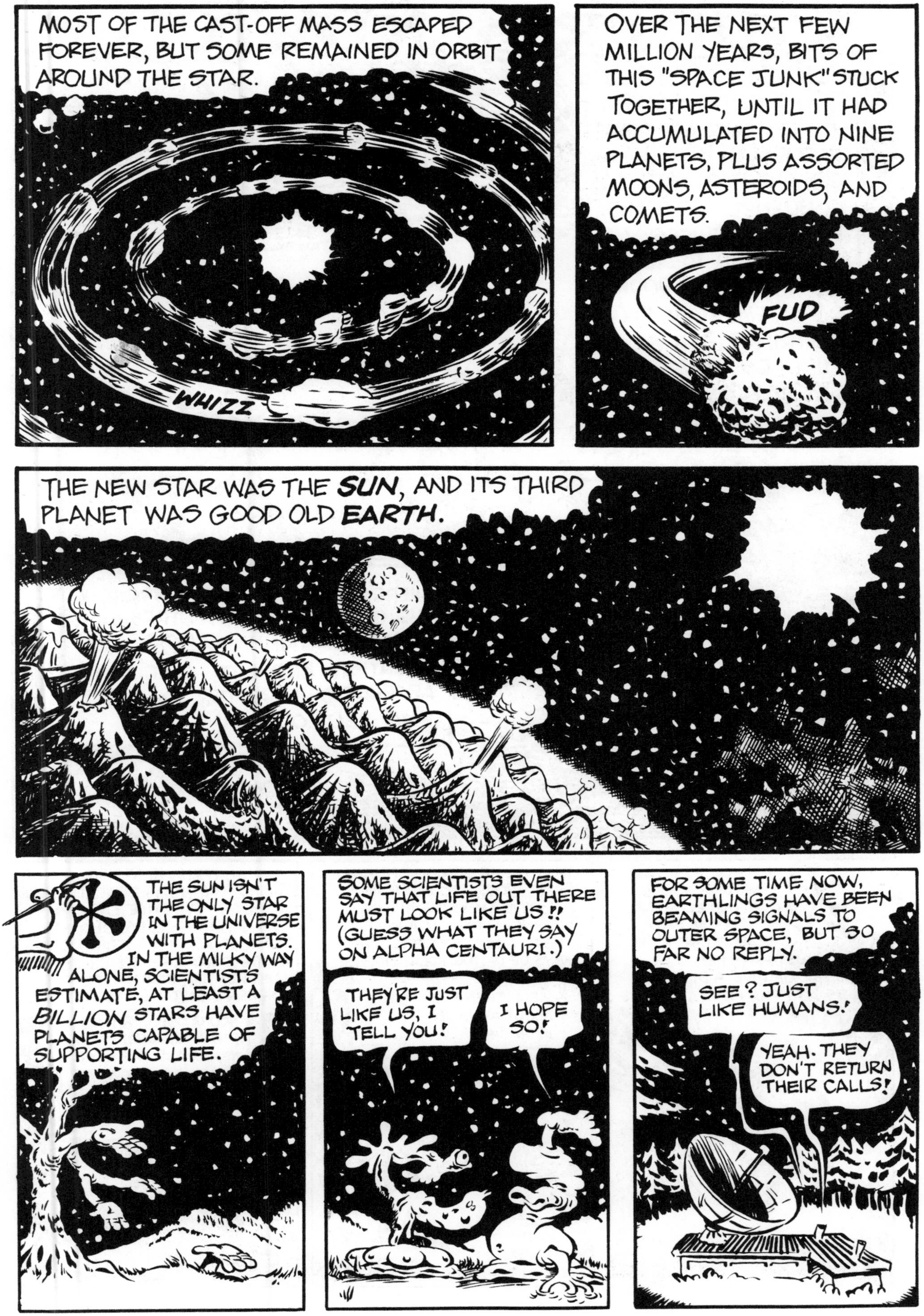
MOST OF THE CAST-OFF MASS ESCAPED FOREVER, BUT SOME REMAINED IN ORBIT AROUND THE STAR.
WHIZZ
OVER THE NEXT FEW MILLION YEARS, BITS OF THIS "SPACE JUNK" STUCK TOGETHER, UNTIL IT HAD ACCUMULATED INTO NINE PLANETS, PLUS ASSORTED MOONS, ASTEROIDS, AND COMETS.
FUD
THE NEW STAR WAS THE **SUN**, AND ITS THIRD PLANET WAS GOOD OLD **EARTH**.
THE SUN ISN'T THE ONLY STAR IN THE UNIVERSE WITH PLANETS. IN THE MILKY WAY ALONE, SCIENTISTS ESTIMATE, AT LEAST A *BILLION* STARS HAVE PLANETS CAPABLE OF SUPPORTING LIFE.
SOME SCIENTISTS EVEN SAY THAT LIFE OUT THERE MUST LOOK LIKE US!! (GUESS WHAT THEY SAY ON ALPHA CENTAURI.)
THEY'RE JUST LIKE US, I TELL YOU!
I HOPE SO!
FOR SOME TIME NOW, EARTHLINGS HAVE BEEN BEAMING SIGNALS TO OUTER SPACE, BUT SO FAR NO REPLY.
SEE? JUST LIKE HUMANS!
YEAH. THEY DON'T RETURN THEIR CALLS!

SOUP OR SANDWICH?

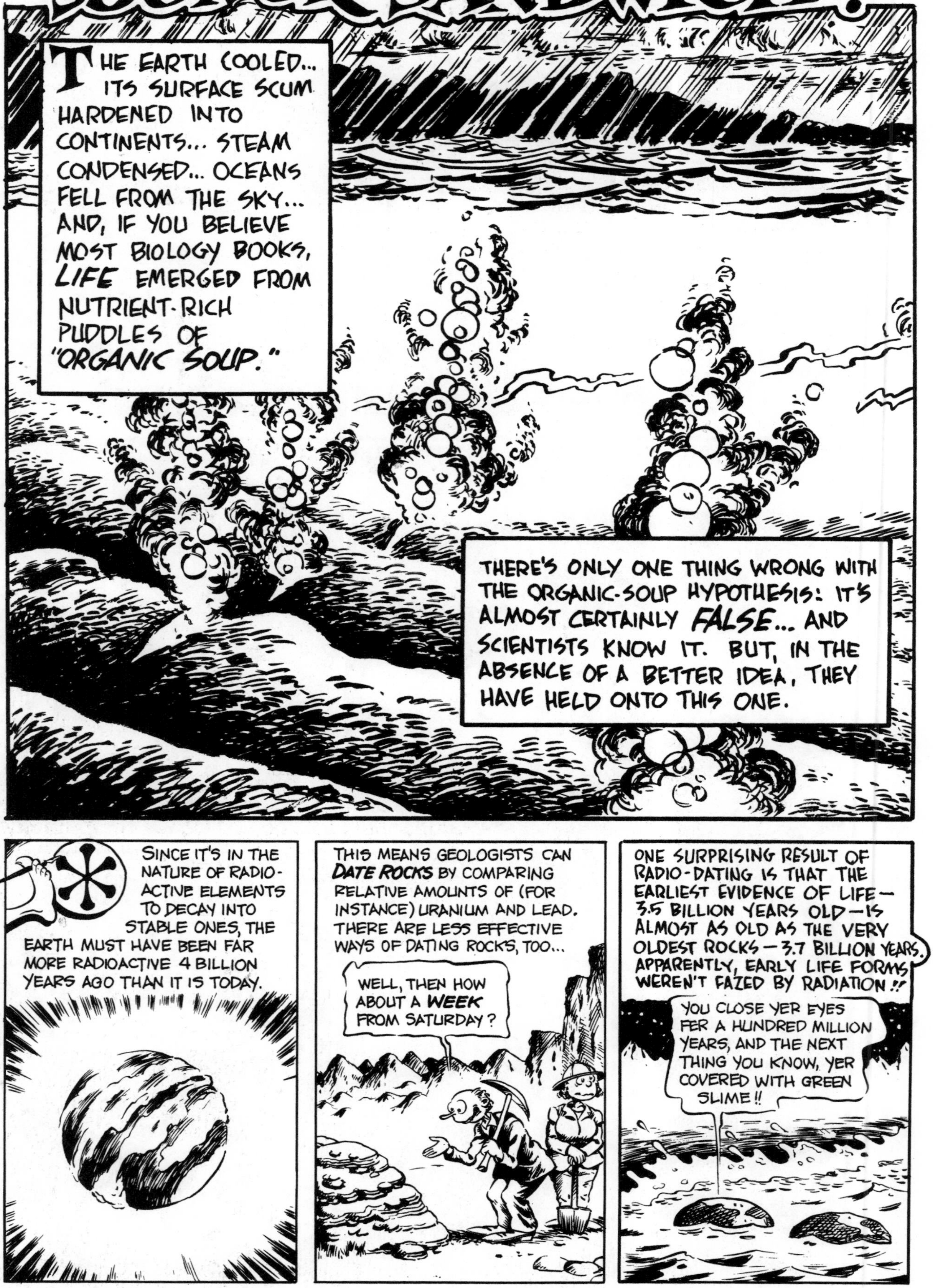
THE EARTH COOLED... ITS SURFACE SCUM HARDENED INTO CONTINENTS... STEAM CONDENSED... OCEANS FELL FROM THE SKY... AND, IF YOU BELIEVE MOST BIOLOGY BOOKS, *LIFE* EMERGED FROM NUTRIENT-RICH PUDDLES OF "*ORGANIC SOUP.*"
THERE'S ONLY ONE THING WRONG WITH THE ORGANIC-SOUP HYPOTHESIS: IT'S ALMOST CERTAINLY *FALSE*... AND SCIENTISTS KNOW IT. BUT, IN THE ABSENCE OF A BETTER IDEA, THEY HAVE HELD ONTO THIS ONE.
SINCE IT'S IN THE NATURE OF RADIO-ACTIVE ELEMENTS TO DECAY INTO STABLE ONES, THE EARTH MUST HAVE BEEN FAR MORE RADIOACTIVE 4 BILLION YEARS AGO THAN IT IS TODAY.
THIS MEANS GEOLOGISTS CAN ***DATE ROCKS*** BY COMPARING RELATIVE AMOUNTS OF (FOR INSTANCE) URANIUM AND LEAD. THERE ARE LESS EFFECTIVE WAYS OF DATING ROCKS, TOO...
WELL, THEN HOW ABOUT A ***WEEK*** FROM SATURDAY?
ONE SURPRISING RESULT OF RADIO-DATING IS THAT THE EARLIEST EVIDENCE OF LIFE— 3.5 BILLION YEARS OLD—IS ALMOST AS OLD AS THE VERY OLDEST ROCKS—3.7 BILLION YEARS. APPARENTLY, EARLY LIFE FORMS WEREN'T FAZED BY RADIATION!!
YOU CLOSE YER EYES FER A HUNDRED MILLION YEARS, AND THE NEXT THING YOU KNOW, YER COVERED WITH GREEN SLIME!!

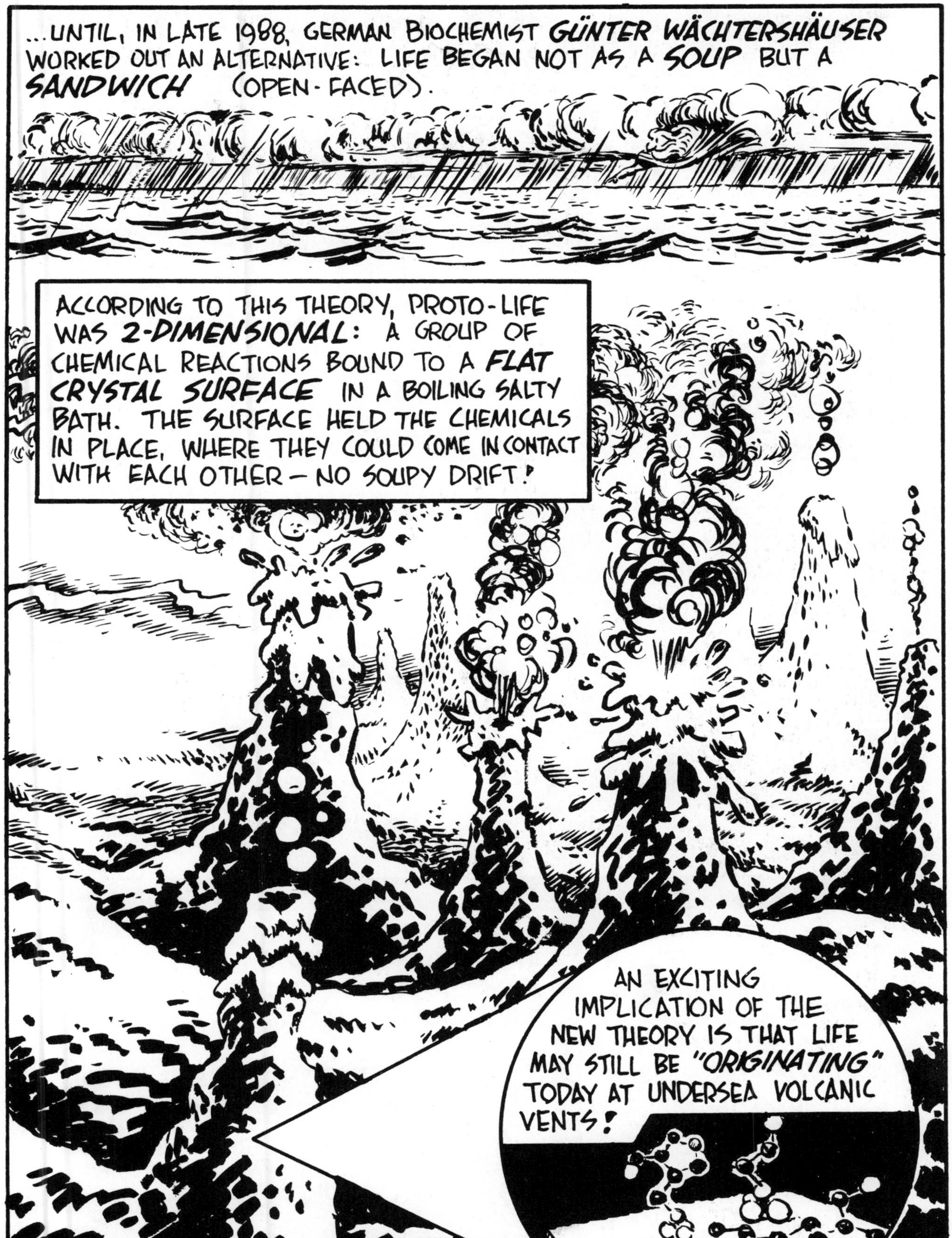
...UNTIL, IN LATE 1988, GERMAN BIOCHEMIST GÜNTER WÄCHTERSHÄUSER WORKED OUT AN ALTERNATIVE: LIFE BEGAN NOT AS A SOUP BUT A SANDWICH (OPEN-FACED).
ACCORDING TO THIS THEORY, PROTO-LIFE WAS 2-DIMENSIONAL: A GROUP OF CHEMICAL REACTIONS BOUND TO A FLAT CRYSTAL SURFACE IN A BOILING SALTY BATH. THE SURFACE HELD THE CHEMICALS IN PLACE, WHERE THEY COULD COME IN CONTACT WITH EACH OTHER — NO SOUPY DRIFT!
AN EXCITING IMPLICATION OF THE NEW THEORY IS THAT LIFE MAY STILL BE "ORIGINATING" TODAY AT UNDERSEA VOLCANIC VENTS!

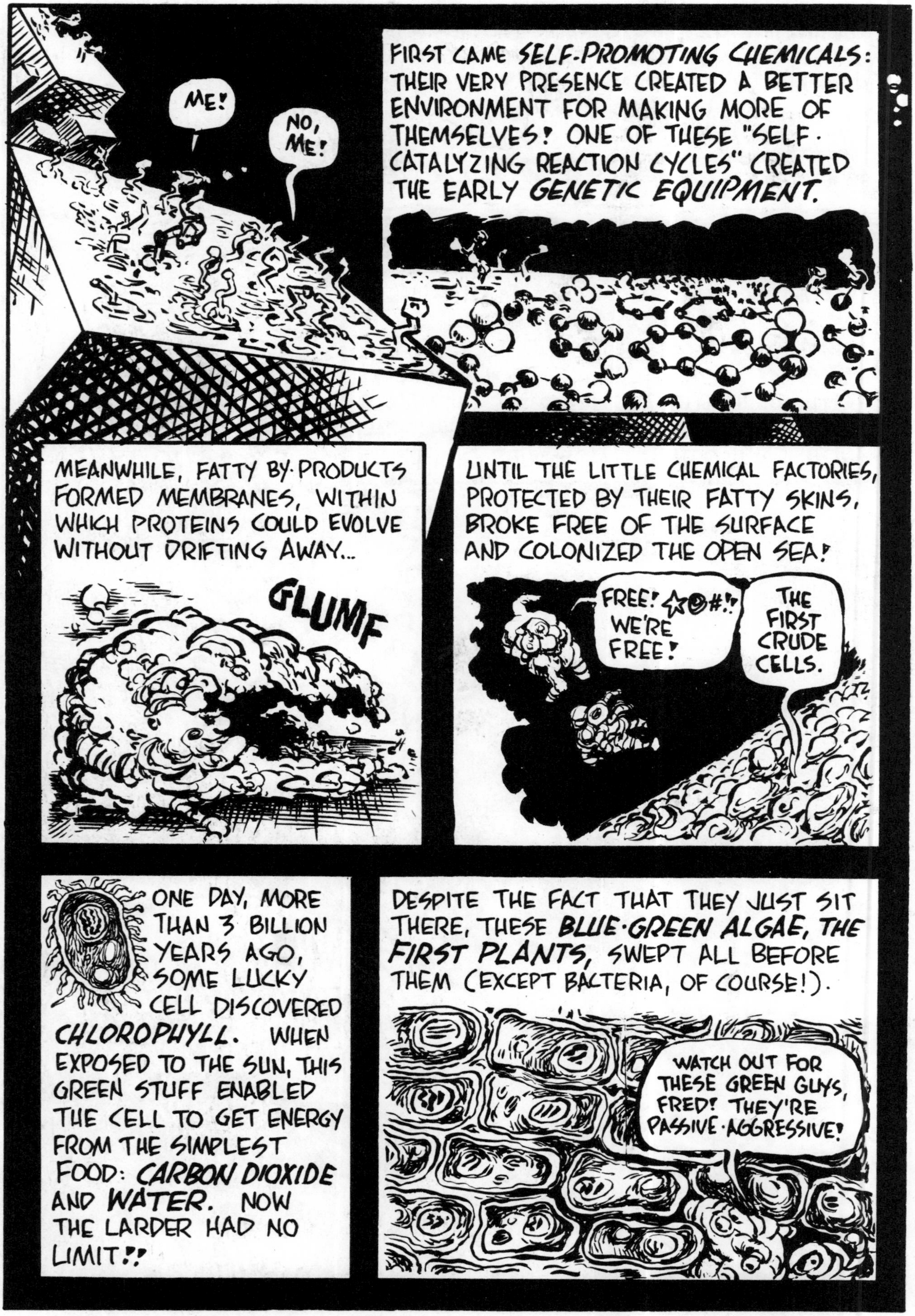
ME!
NO, ME!
FIRST CAME SELF-PROMOTING CHEMICALS: THEIR VERY PRESENCE CREATED A BETTER ENVIRONMENT FOR MAKING MORE OF THEMSELVES! ONE OF THESE "SELF-CATALYZING REACTION CYCLES" CREATED THE EARLY GENETIC EQUIPMENT.
MEANWHILE, FATTY BY-PRODUCTS FORMED MEMBRANES, WITHIN WHICH PROTEINS COULD EVOLVE WITHOUT DRIFTING AWAY...
GLUMF
UNTIL THE LITTLE CHEMICAL FACTORIES, PROTECTED BY THEIR FATTY SKINS, BROKE FREE OF THE SURFACE AND COLONIZED THE OPEN SEA!
FREE! ☆@#!! WE'RE FREE!
THE FIRST CRUDE CELLS.
ONE DAY, MORE THAN 3 BILLION YEARS AGO, SOME LUCKY CELL DISCOVERED CHLOROPHYLL. WHEN EXPOSED TO THE SUN, THIS GREEN STUFF ENABLED THE CELL TO GET ENERGY FROM THE SIMPLEST FOOD: CARBON DIOXIDE AND WATER. NOW THE LARDER HAD NO LIMIT!!
DESPITE THE FACT THAT THEY JUST SIT THERE, THESE BLUE-GREEN ALGAE, THE FIRST PLANTS, SWEPT ALL BEFORE THEM (EXCEPT BACTERIA, OF COURSE!).
WATCH OUT FOR THESE GREEN GUYS, FRED! THEY'RE PASSIVE-AGGRESSIVE!

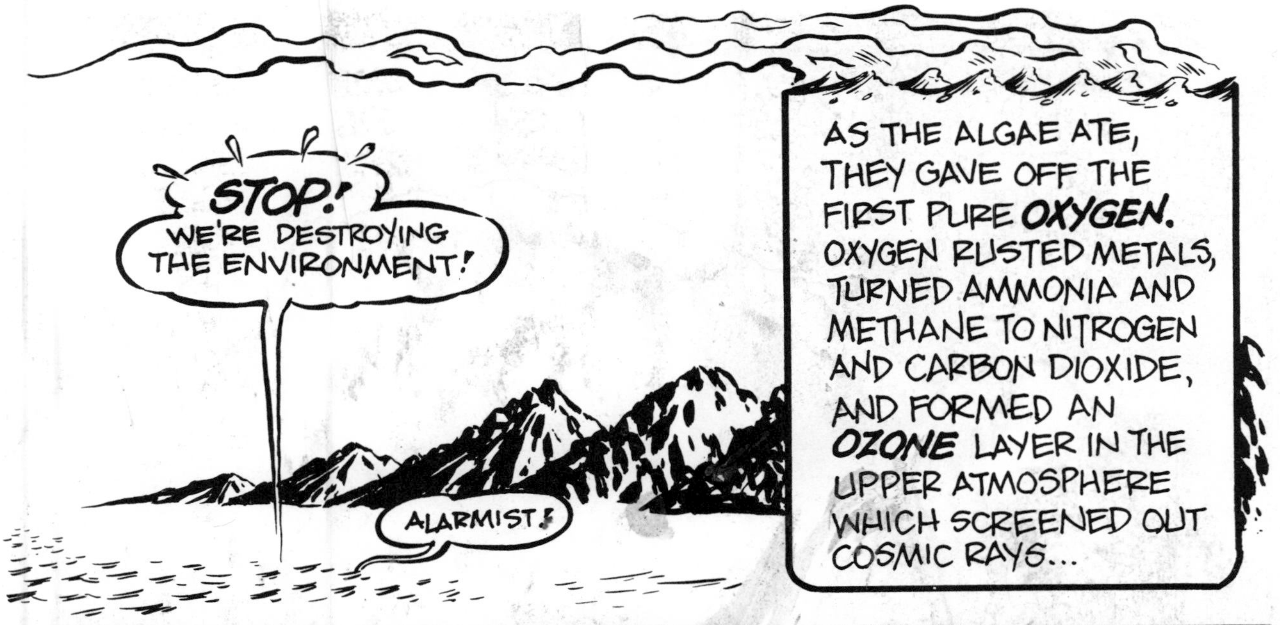
STOP! WE'RE DESTROYING THE ENVIRONMENT!
AS THE ALGAE ATE, THEY GAVE OFF THE FIRST PURE OXYGEN. OXYGEN RUSTED METALS, TURNED AMMONIA AND METHANE TO NITROGEN AND CARBON DIOXIDE, AND FORMED AN OZONE LAYER IN THE UPPER ATMOSPHERE WHICH SCREENED OUT COSMIC RAYS...
ALARMIST!

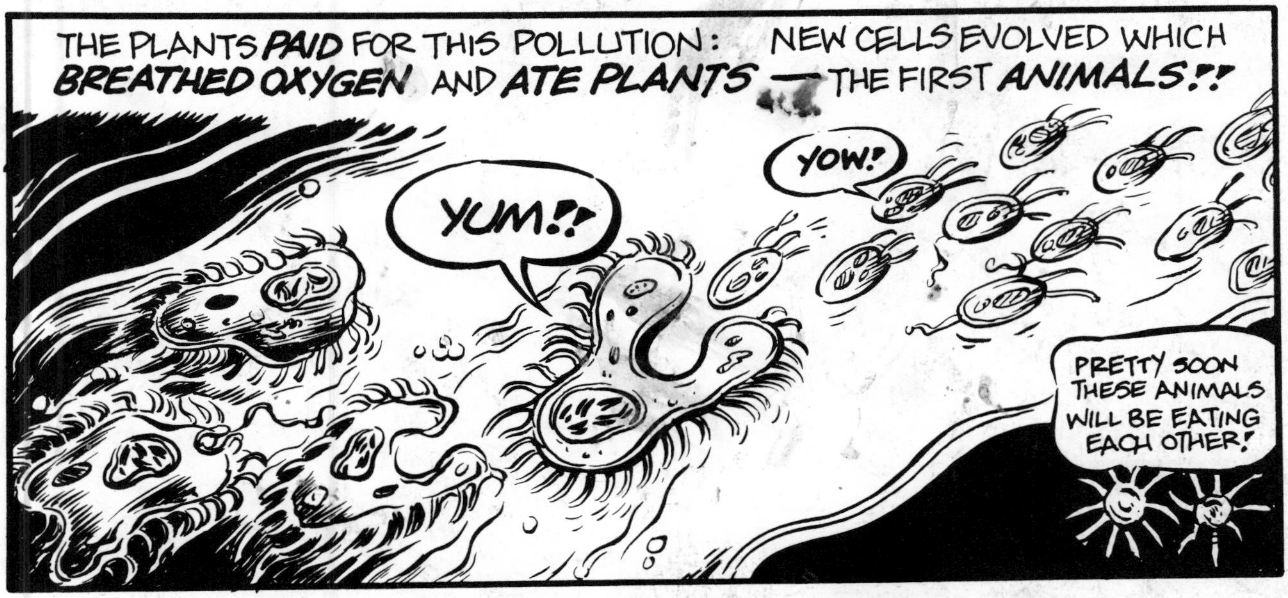
THE PLANTS PAID FOR THIS POLLUTION: NEW CELLS EVOLVED WHICH BREATHED OXYGEN AND ATE PLANTS — THE FIRST ANIMALS!!
YUM!!
YOW!
PRETTY SOON THESE ANIMALS WILL BE EATING EACH OTHER!

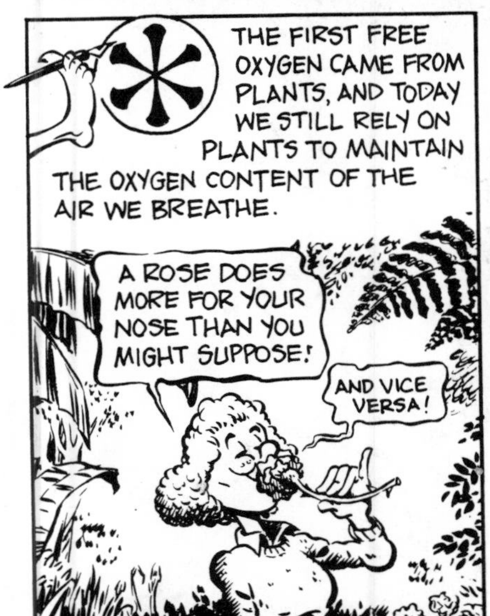
THE FIRST FREE OXYGEN CAME FROM PLANTS, AND TODAY WE STILL RELY ON PLANTS TO MAINTAIN THE OXYGEN CONTENT OF THE AIR WE BREATHE.
A ROSE DOES MORE FOR YOUR NOSE THAN YOU MIGHT SUPPOSE!
AND VICE VERSA!

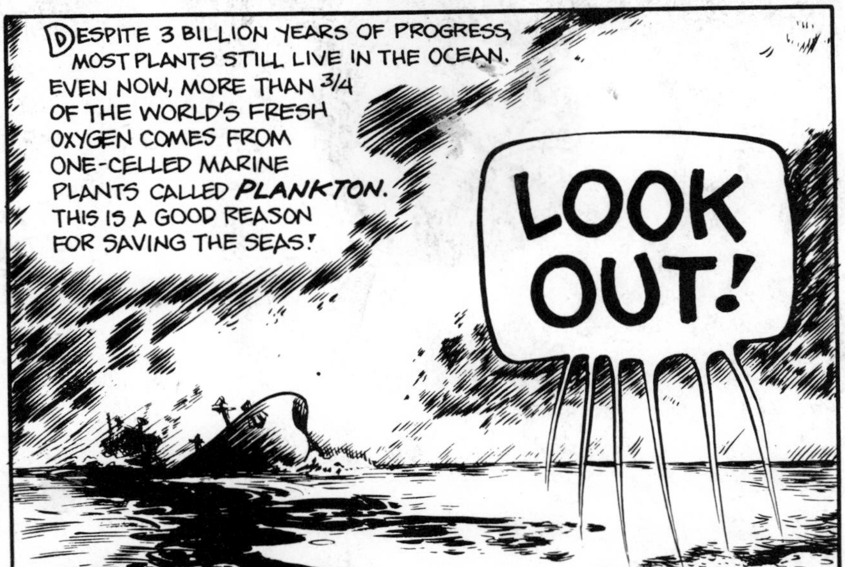
DESPITE 3 BILLION YEARS OF PROGRESS, MOST PLANTS STILL LIVE IN THE OCEAN. EVEN NOW, MORE THAN 3/4 OF THE WORLD'S FRESH OXYGEN COMES FROM ONE-CELLED MARINE PLANTS CALLED PLANKTON. THIS IS A GOOD REASON FOR SAVING THE SEAS!
LOOK OUT!

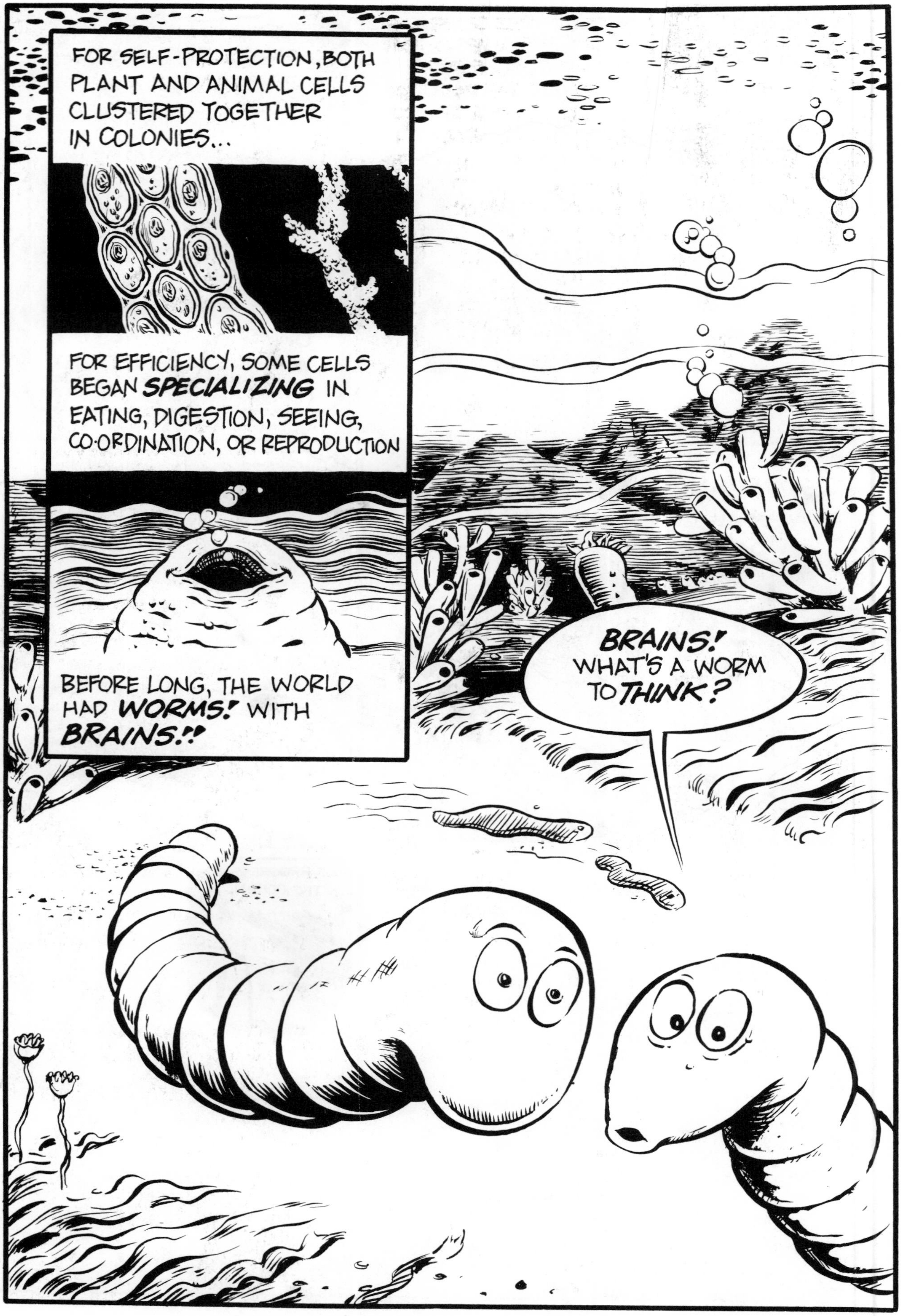
FOR SELF-PROTECTION, BOTH PLANT AND ANIMAL CELLS CLUSTERED TOGETHER IN COLONIES...
FOR EFFICIENCY, SOME CELLS BEGAN **SPECIALIZING** IN EATING, DIGESTION, SEEING, CO-ORDINATION, OR REPRODUCTION
BEFORE LONG, THE WORLD HAD **WORMS!** WITH **BRAINS!?**
BRAINS! WHAT'S A WORM TO **THINK?**

A DIGRESSION ON EVOLUTION!

SINCE THE TIME OF THE ALGAE, ORGANISMS HAVE COMPETED FOR RESOURCES, BUT DON'T GET THE IDEA THAT EVOLUTION IS A SIMPLE *WAR* OF ALL AGAINST ALL, IN WHICH THE WEAK PERISH AND ONLY THE STRONG SURVIVE! *NO!!*

FROM THE VERY BEGINNING OF LIFE, ONE OF THE MOST SUCCESSFUL SURVIVAL STRATEGIES HAS BEEN *CO·OPERATION!!*

FIRST OF ALL, DIFFERENT STRANDS OF NUCLEIC ACID HAD TO TEAM UP INTO *CHROMOSOMES* TO STORE ALL THE INFORMATION NEEDED TO RUN A LIVING CELL.

WOW!

IT IS BELIEVED THAT MODERN CELLS, WHICH ARE HIGHLY COMPLEX, EVOLVED FROM *CO·OPERATIVE ARRANGEMENTS* AMONG EARLIER, SIMPLER CELLS...

HOWZIT GOIN' AT YOUR END OF THE PROTOPLASM?

I'VE BEEN WORRIED ABOUT LOSING MY *INDIVIDUALITY.*

HEY, IT'S TOO LATE NOW, JACK!

ZRT

ZNP

OUR OWN CELLS CARRY MYSTERIOUS LITTLE GLOBS CALLED *MITO·CHONDRIA* WHICH HAVE *THEIR OWN GENETIC MATERIAL.*

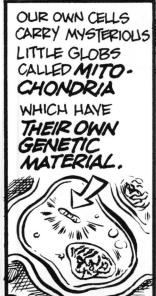

I NEVER KNOW IF I'M TAKING MY MITOCHONDRIA FOR A WALK, OR VICE VERSA...

THEN, SINGLE CELLS COLLABORATED TO MAKE THE HIGHER LIFE FORMS, AND AS FOR THE *HIGHER LIFE FORMS—* WELL, HAVEN'T YOU HEARD OF THE *BEES* AND THE *FLOWERS?!*

ON WITH THE STORY!

THE ORIGIN OF SEX

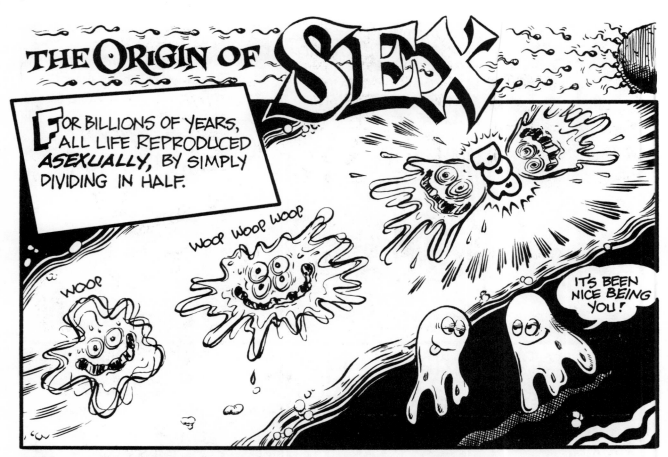

FOR BILLIONS OF YEARS, ALL LIFE REPRODUCED **ASEXUALLY**, BY SIMPLY DIVIDING IN HALF.

WOOP

WOOP WOOP WOOP

PPP

IT'S BEEN NICE BEING YOU!

ALL OFFSPRING WERE EXACTLY LIKE THEIR PARENT (EXCEPT FOR MUTANTS).

WOOP WOOP WOOP

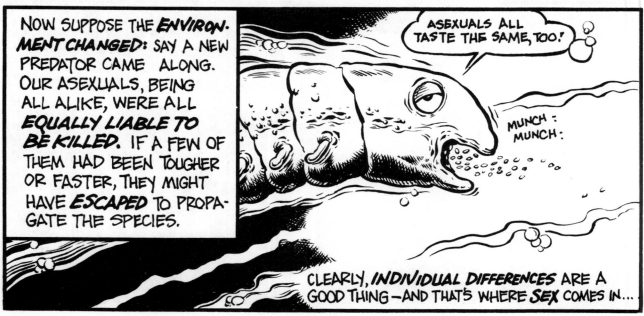

NOW SUPPOSE THE **ENVIRON-MENT CHANGED:** SAY A NEW PREDATOR CAME ALONG. OUR ASEXUALS, BEING ALL ALIKE, WERE ALL **EQUALLY LIABLE TO BE KILLED.** IF A FEW OF THEM HAD BEEN TOUGHER OR FASTER, THEY MIGHT HAVE **ESCAPED** TO PROPA-GATE THE SPECIES.

ASEXUALS ALL TASTE THE SAME, TOO!

MUNCH : MUNCH :

CLEARLY, **INDIVIDUAL DIFFERENCES** ARE A GOOD THING — AND THAT'S WHERE **SEX** COMES IN...

16

SEX IS A **GENETIC** WAY OF CREATING AND TRANSMITTING INDIVIDUAL DIFFERENCES WITHIN A POPULATION...

ALSO A WAY TO SELL COMIC BOOKS!

SEX HAS BEEN AROUND A LOT LONGER THAN **SEXUAL REPRODUCTION**— EVER SINCE THE FIRST TWO STRANDS OF NUCLEIC ACID GOT **CLOSE** ENOUGH TO FORM A CHROMOSOME AND SOMETHING **DIFFERENT.**

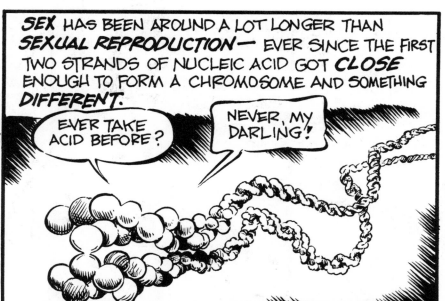

EVER TAKE ACID BEFORE?

NEVER, MY DARLING!

IN FACT, SEX ORIGINALLY WAS JUST THE **OPPOSITE** OF REPRODUCTION. **REPRODUCTION** MEANT ONE CELL SPLITTING IN TWO, BUT **SEX** MEANT TWO CELLS **JOINING** FOR A WHILE TO PLAY WITH EACH OTHERS' **GENES.** SEX **DELAYED** REPRODUCTION!!

I'M ONLY DOING THIS, ANITA, BECAUSE I WANT YOUR DESCENDANTS TO BE AN IMPROVEMENT ON YOU!

EGOTIST!

BACTERIA, TINIER THAN THE SMALLEST CELL, ARE THEMSELVES LIKE A FOOTNOTE TO LIFE. YET SCIENTISTS HAVE RECENTLY DISCOVERED THAT BACTERIA, TOO, CAN HAVE SEX.

BUT NOT TONIGHT, O.K.? I HAVE A VIRUS!

THE EXPERIMENT: TWO STRAINS OF THE GONORRHEA-CAUSING BACTERIUM **GONOCOCCUS,** ONE RESISTANT TO PENICILLIN AND THE OTHER NOT, WERE COMBINED IN A DISH.

ALL RIGHT!

AFTER A TIME, **ALL** THE GONOCOCCI COULD RESIST PENICILLIN. IT TURNED OUT THE BACTERIA HAD PAIRED OFF, AND THE RESISTANT ONES HAD **MODIFIED THE GENES** OF THE OTHERS — A SMALL BUT SOPHISTICATED ACT OF SEX!!

MY GOD! IT'S AN ORGY!!

SEXUAL **REPRODUCTION,** THE REGULAR USE OF SEX IN THE REPRODUCTIVE PROCESS, BEGAN AS A **PERVERSION** OF ORDINARY REPRODUCTION. WHO KNOWS WHY?

I WAS UNDER A LOT OF STRESS, SEE, AND..

SOME CELL, INSTEAD OF DIVIDING INTO **TWO** REGULAR CELLS, SPLIT INTO **FOUR** **HALF-CELLS** CALLED **GAMETES.**

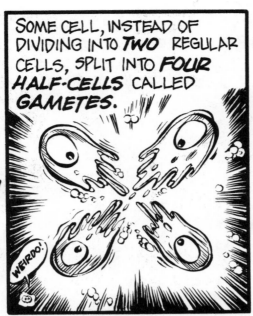

WEIRDO!

SINCE THESE **GAMETES** HAD ONLY **HALF** A SET OF **GENES,** THEY EXPERIENCED —

THE URGE TO MERGE !!

GOOSH!

AND THAT WAS IT.

THAT WAS IT?

YES, BY SPLITTING INTO GAMETES AND RECOMBINING, THE CELL HAD FOUND A WAY TO **REPRODUCE** AND **SHUFFLE ITS GENES** AT THE SAME TIME.

WITH **TWO** PARENTS, IT WORKED EVEN BETTER, AS THE OFFSPRING COMBINED FEATURES OF BOTH:

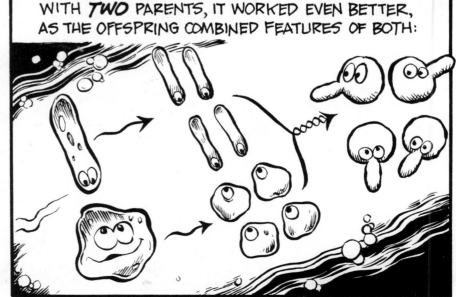

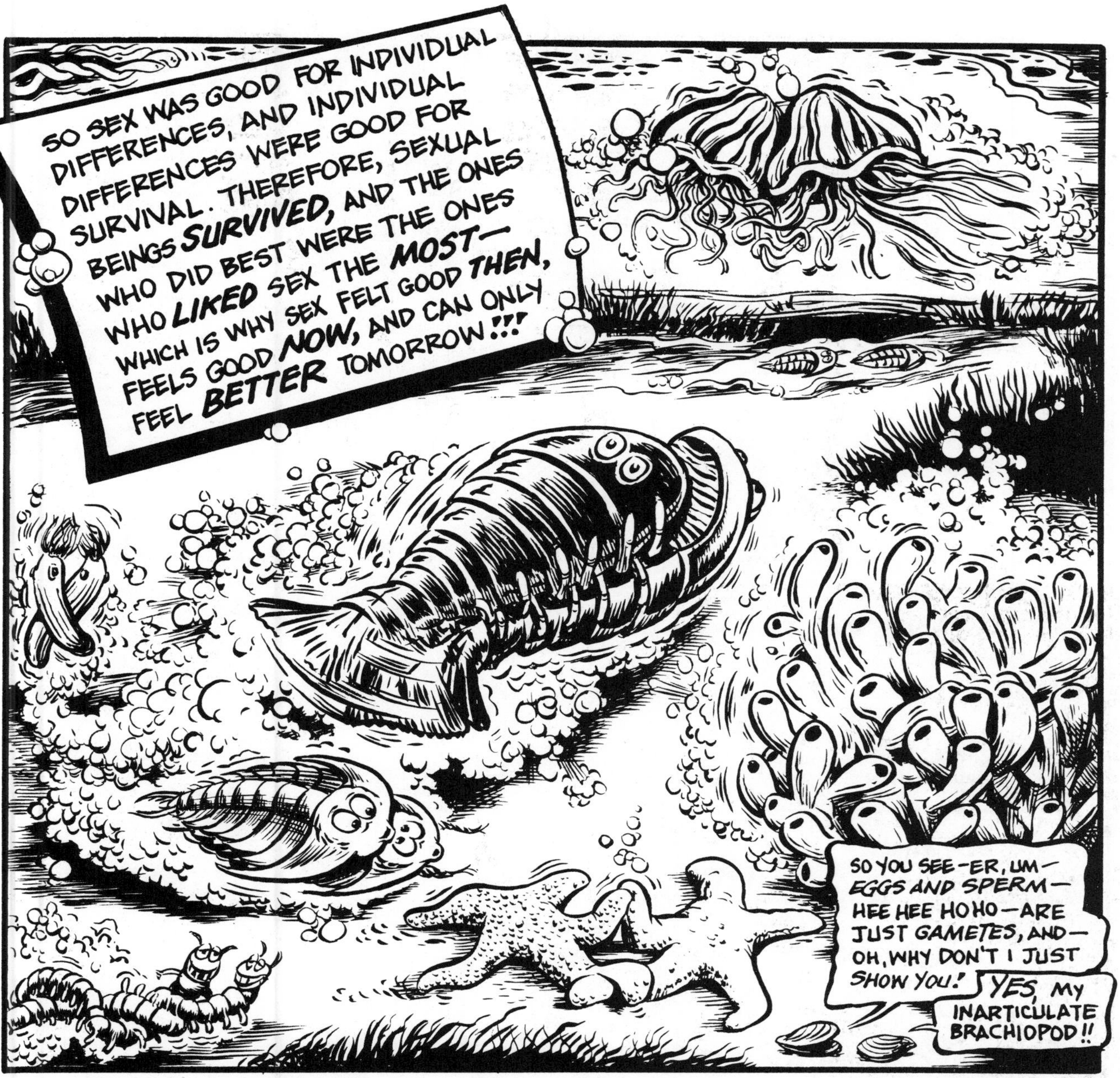
SO SEX WAS GOOD FOR INDIVIDUAL DIFFERENCES, AND INDIVIDUAL DIFFERENCES WERE GOOD FOR SURVIVAL. THEREFORE, SEXUAL BEINGS SURVIVED, AND THE ONES WHO DID BEST WERE THE ONES WHO LIKED SEX THE MOST— WHICH IS WHY SEX FELT GOOD THEN, FEELS GOOD NOW, AND CAN ONLY FEEL BETTER TOMORROW!!!
SO YOU SEE-ER, UM- EGGS AND SPERM- HEE HEE HO HO-ARE JUST GAMETES, AND- OH, WHY DON'T I JUST SHOW YOU!
YES, MY INARTICULATE BRACHIOPOD!!

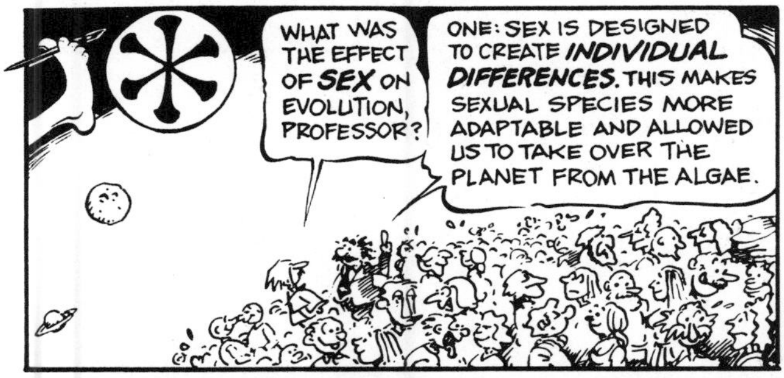
WHAT WAS THE EFFECT OF SEX ON EVOLUTION, PROFESSOR?
ONE: SEX IS DESIGNED TO CREATE INDIVIDUAL DIFFERENCES. THIS MAKES SEXUAL SPECIES MORE ADAPTABLE AND ALLOWED US TO TAKE OVER THE PLANET FROM THE ALGAE.

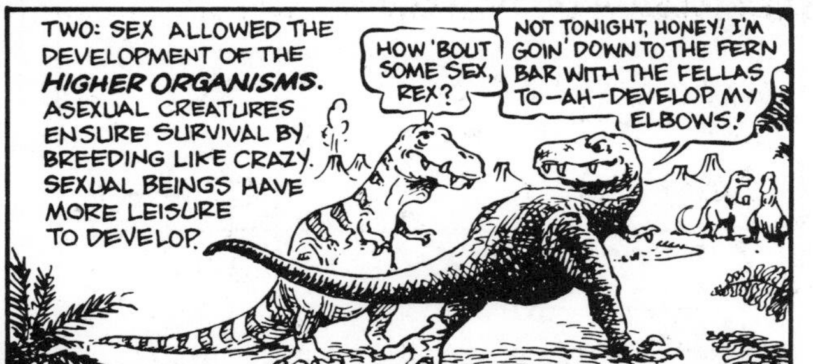
TWO: SEX ALLOWED THE DEVELOPMENT OF THE HIGHER ORGANISMS. ASEXUAL CREATURES ENSURE SURVIVAL BY BREEDING LIKE CRAZY. SEXUAL BEINGS HAVE MORE LEISURE TO DEVELOP.
HOW 'BOUT SOME SEX, REX?
NOT TONIGHT, HONEY! I'M GOIN' DOWN TO THE FERN BAR WITH THE FELLAS TO-AH-DEVELOP MY ELBOWS!

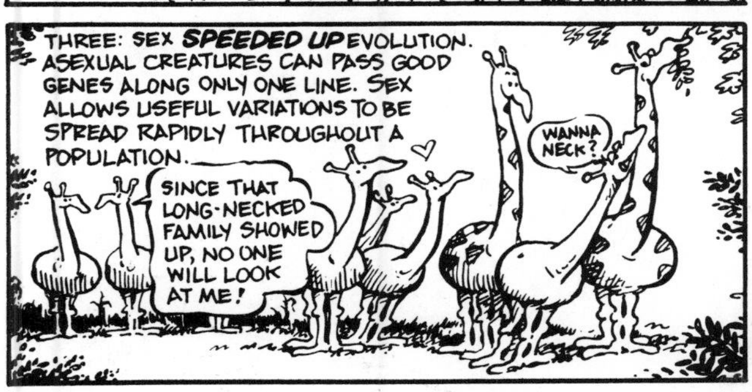
THREE: SEX SPEEDED UP EVOLUTION. ASEXUAL CREATURES CAN PASS GOOD GENES ALONG ONLY ONE LINE. SEX ALLOWS USEFUL VARIATIONS TO BE SPREAD RAPIDLY THROUGHOUT A POPULATION.
WANNA NECK?
SINCE THAT LONG-NECKED FAMILY SHOWED UP, NO ONE WILL LOOK AT ME!

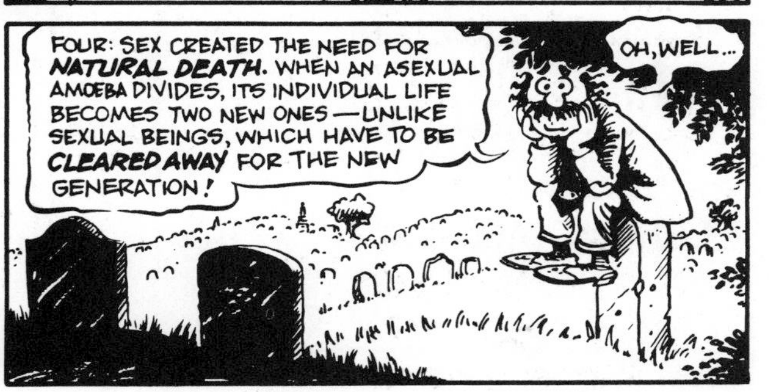
FOUR: SEX CREATED THE NEED FOR NATURAL DEATH. WHEN AN ASEXUAL AMOEBA DIVIDES, ITS INDIVIDUAL LIFE BECOMES TWO NEW ONES—UNLIKE SEXUAL BEINGS, WHICH HAVE TO BE CLEARED AWAY FOR THE NEW GENERATION!
OH, WELL...

MODERN TIMES

ERAS	PERIODS	DURATION (MILLIONS)	YEARS AGO (MILLIONS)
CENOZOIC	**QUATERNARY** THE WEIRDEST MAMMAL OF THEM ALL.	3	3
	TERTIARY WEIRD MAMMALS	65	68
MESOZOIC	**CRETACEOUS** T. REX VS. THE FLOWERS	72	140
	JURASSIC BIRDY AND BRONTY	65	205
	TRIASSIC TINY MAMMALS	25	230
PALEOZOIC	**PERMIAN** WEIRD REPTILES	55	285
	CARBONIFEROUS THE FUTURE IS COAL-BLACK	65	350
	DEVONIAN FISH AND FOREST	60	410
	SILURIAN ON THE BEACH	20	430
	ORDOVICIAN "NO FISHIN'"	70	500
	CAMBRIAN LIFE IS HARD	100	600

PRE-CAMBRIAN TIME LASTED 4 BILLION YEARS

THANKS PARTLY TO SEX, LIFE REALLY BEGAN TO FLOURISH ABOUT 600 MILLION YEARS AGO!
SINCE THEN, THE FOSSIL RECORD HAS BEEN COMPLETE ENOUGH TO PERMIT THIS CLASSIFICATION OF THE EARTH'S "RECENT HISTORY!"
MARSUPIALS
PRIMATES
CATS, DOGS, BEARS
DOLPHINS & WHALES
TITANO-THERES
BIRDS
TURTLES
DINOSAURS
FLYING REPTILES
ARCHAEOPTERYX
THECODONTS
TINY MAMMALS
MAMMAL-LIKE REPTILES
BUGS
"STEM" REPTILES
SCORPIONS
SHARKS
AMPHIBIANS
RAY-FINNED FISH
LOBE-FINS
CRABS
STARFISH
ARMORED FISH
SNAILS
FISHOIDS
EURYPTERIDS
TRILOBITES
MOLLUSCS
SPONGES & CORALS
WORMS
PROTOZOA

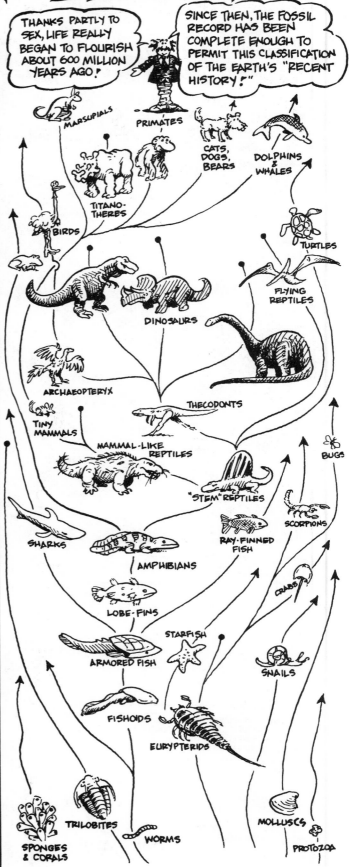

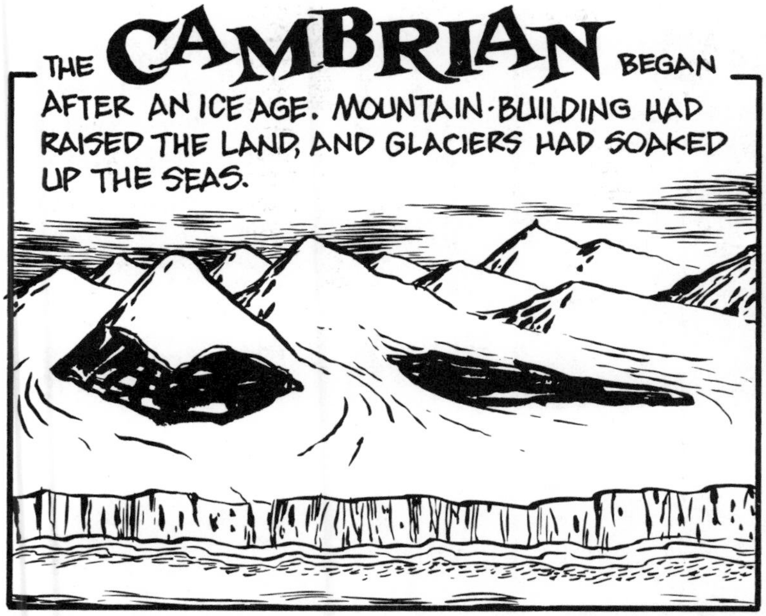
THE CAMBRIAN BEGAN
AFTER AN ICE AGE. MOUNTAIN-BUILDING HAD RAISED THE LAND, AND GLACIERS HAD SOAKED UP THE SEAS.

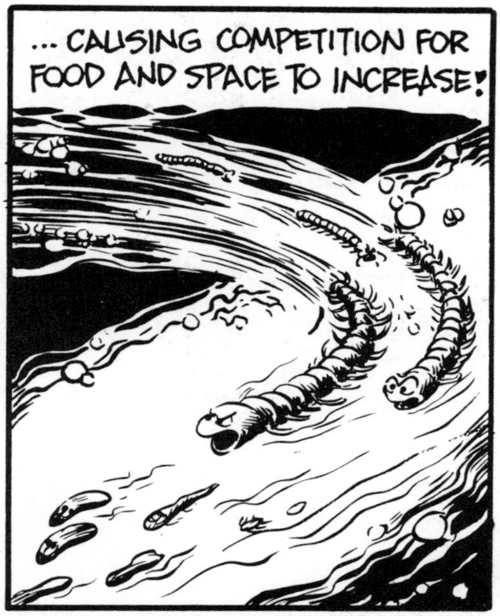
...CAUSING COMPETITION FOR FOOD AND SPACE TO INCREASE!

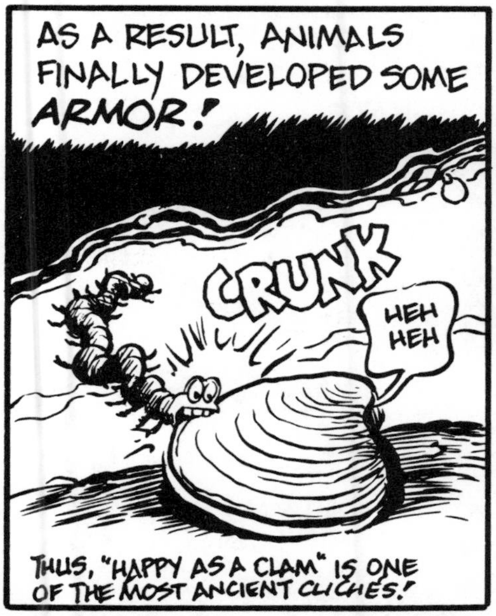
AS A RESULT, ANIMALS FINALLY DEVELOPED SOME ARMOR!
CRUNK
HEH HEH
THUS, "HAPPY AS A CLAM" IS ONE OF THE MOST ANCIENT CLICHÉS!

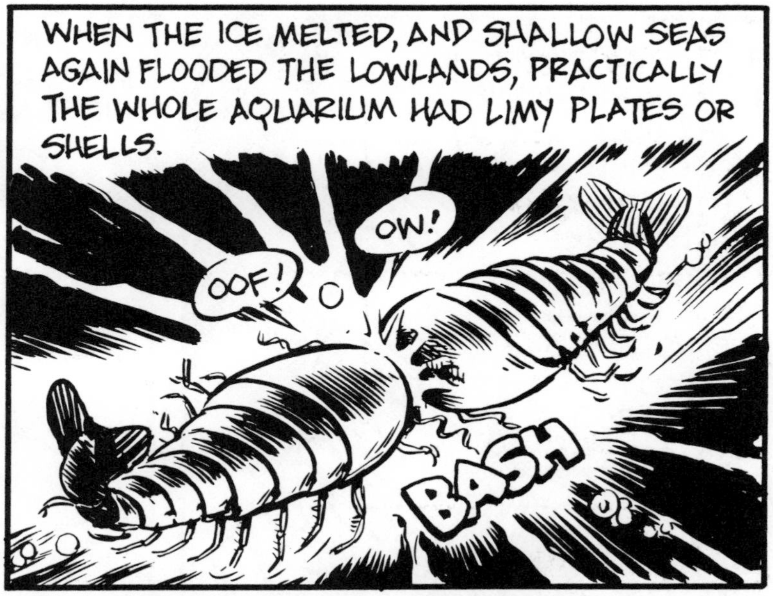
WHEN THE ICE MELTED, AND SHALLOW SEAS AGAIN FLOODED THE LOWLANDS, PRACTICALLY THE WHOLE AQUARIUM HAD LIMY PLATES OR SHELLS.
OOF!
OW!
BASH

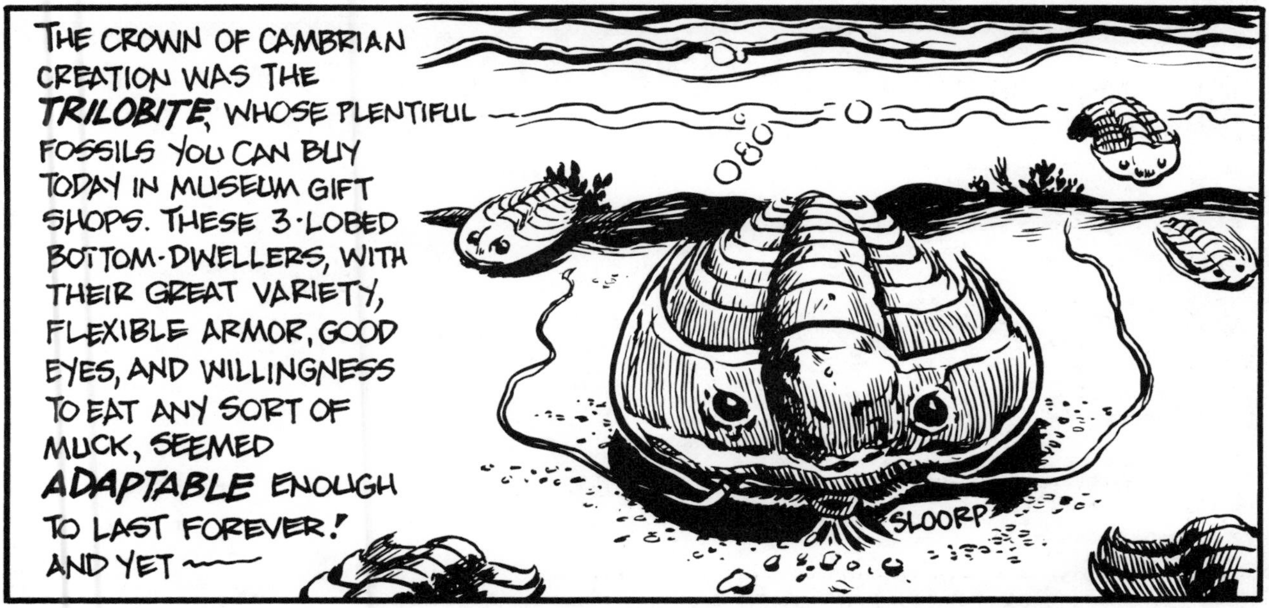
THE CROWN OF CAMBRIAN CREATION WAS THE TRILOBITE, WHOSE PLENTIFUL FOSSILS YOU CAN BUY TODAY IN MUSEUM GIFT SHOPS. THESE 3-LOBED BOTTOM-DWELLERS, WITH THEIR GREAT VARIETY, FLEXIBLE ARMOR, GOOD EYES, AND WILLINGNESS TO EAT ANY SORT OF MUCK, SEEMED ADAPTABLE ENOUGH TO LAST FOREVER! AND YET ~~
SLOORP

THE ORDOVICIAN

ALREADY PRODUCED A CHANGE WHICH WAS TO PUT TRILOBITES OUT OF THE SWIM — AND IT WASN'T THIS GIANT SHELL-SQUID (WHO WAS ONLY PASSING THRU).

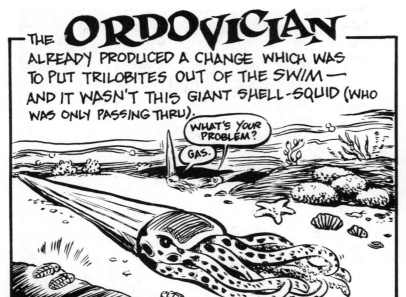

WHAT'S YOUR PROBLEM?

GAS.

A SMALL, SOFT, WORMY ANIMAL BEGAN TO DEVELOP AN INTERNAL STIFFENING ROD, CALLED A **NOTOCORD**, RUNNING ALONG ITS CENTRAL NERVE.

?

THE NOTOCORD EVOLVED INTO A FLEXIBLE SEQUENCE OF CARTILAGE UNITS, WHICH PROTECTED THE CENTRAL NERVOUS SYSTEM WITHOUT ANY CUMBERSOME ARMOR.

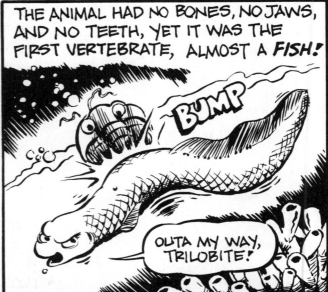

THE ANIMAL HAD NO BONES, NO JAWS, AND NO TEETH, YET IT WAS THE FIRST VERTEBRATE, ALMOST A *FISH!*

BUMP

OUTA MY WAY, TRILOBITE!

SILURIAN

IN THE BRIEF BUT WILD SILURIAN, THE JAWLESS FISH SHARED THE SEAS WITH *EURYPTERIS*, A 7-FOOT *SEA SCORPION*, SO THEY HAD TO GROW ARMOR AFTER ALL — OR ELSE VERY FAST FINS!!

GET 'EM, EURYPTY!

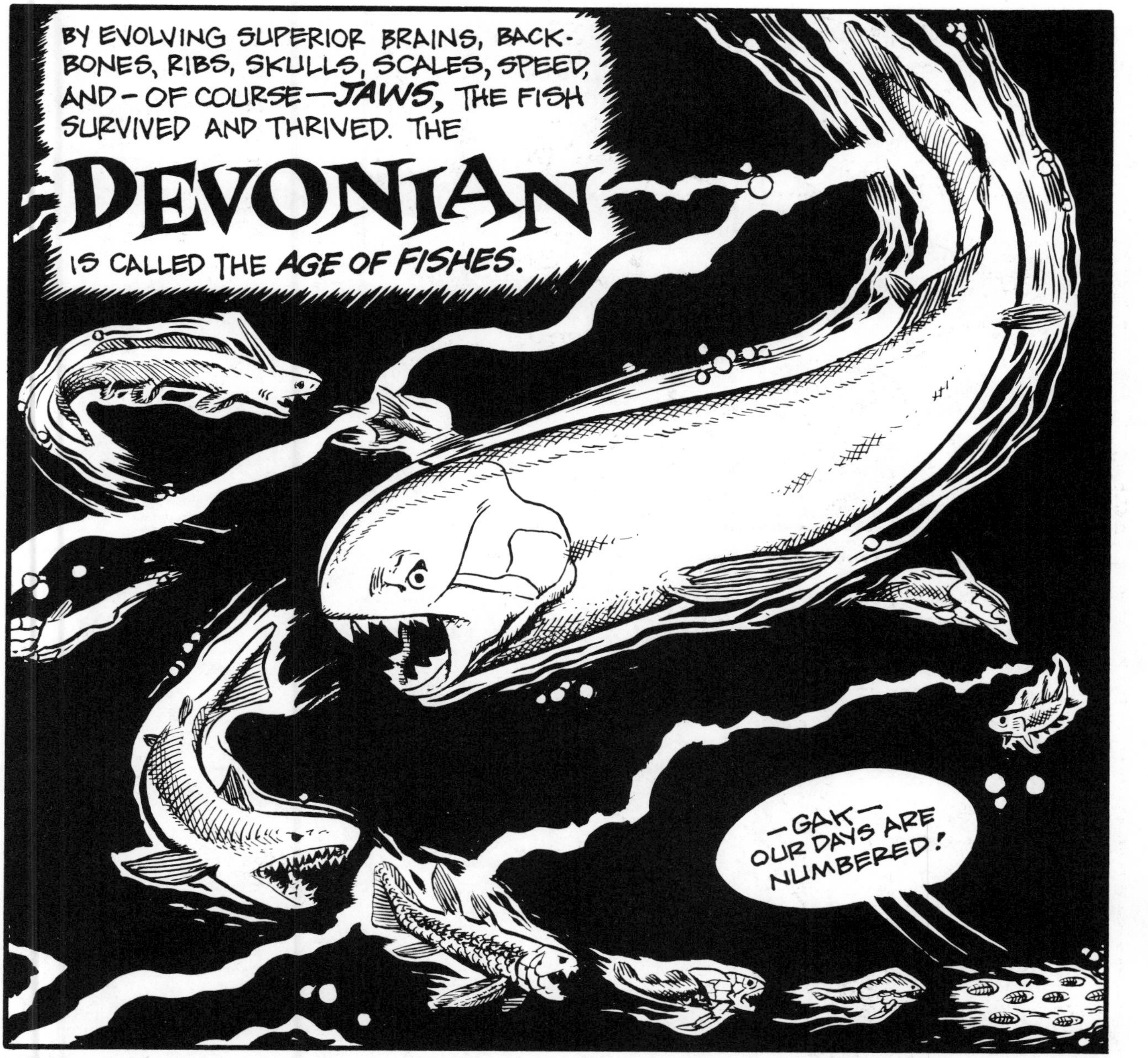
BY EVOLVING SUPERIOR BRAINS, BACKBONES, RIBS, SKULLS, SCALES, SPEED, AND—OF COURSE—*JAWS*, THE FISH SURVIVED AND THRIVED. THE
DEVONIAN
IS CALLED THE *AGE OF FISHES*.
—GAK— OUR DAYS ARE NUMBERED!
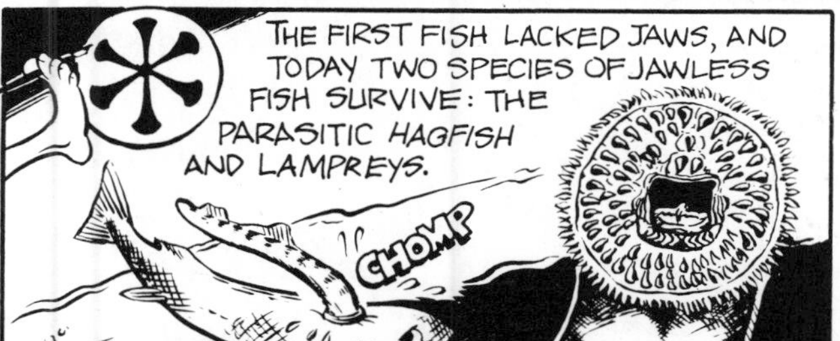
THE FIRST FISH LACKED JAWS, AND TODAY TWO SPECIES OF JAWLESS FISH SURVIVE: THE PARASITIC *HAGFISH* AND LAMPREYS.
CHOMP
LAMPREY MOUTH
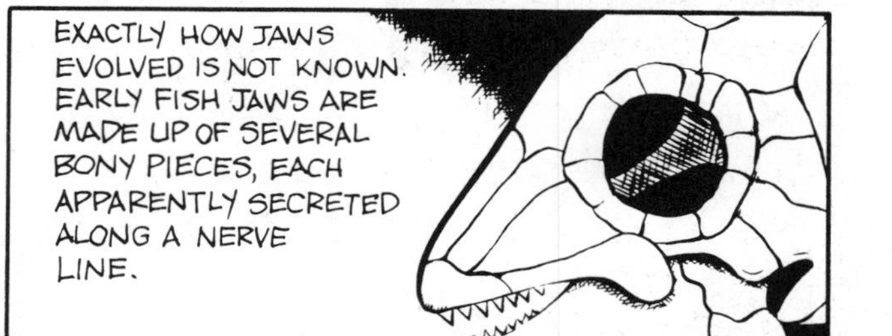
EXACTLY HOW JAWS EVOLVED IS NOT KNOWN. EARLY FISH JAWS ARE MADE UP OF SEVERAL BONY PIECES, EACH APPARENTLY SECRETED ALONG A NERVE LINE.
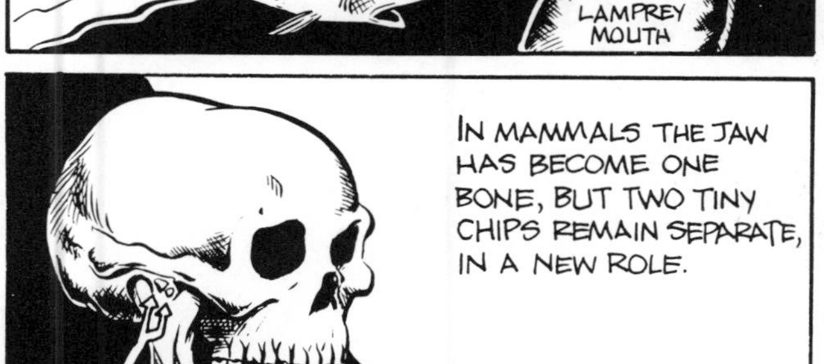
IN MAMMALS THE JAW HAS BECOME ONE BONE, BUT TWO TINY CHIPS REMAIN SEPARATE, IN A NEW ROLE.
MALLEUS & INCUS
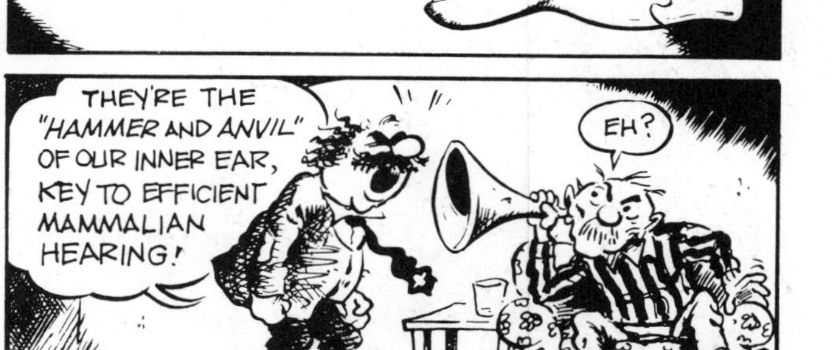
THEY'RE THE *"HAMMER AND ANVIL"* OF OUR INNER EAR, KEY TO EFFICIENT MAMMALIAN HEARING!
EH?

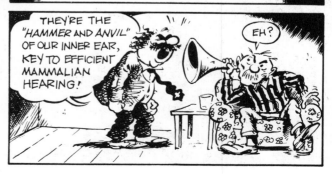

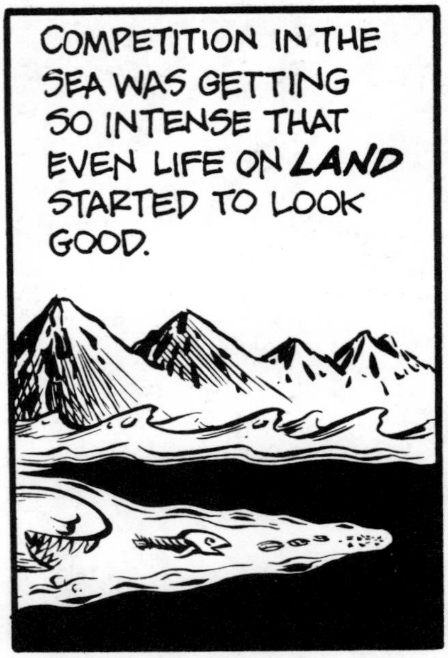
COMPETITION IN THE SEA WAS GETTING SO INTENSE THAT EVEN LIFE ON ***LAND*** STARTED TO LOOK GOOD.

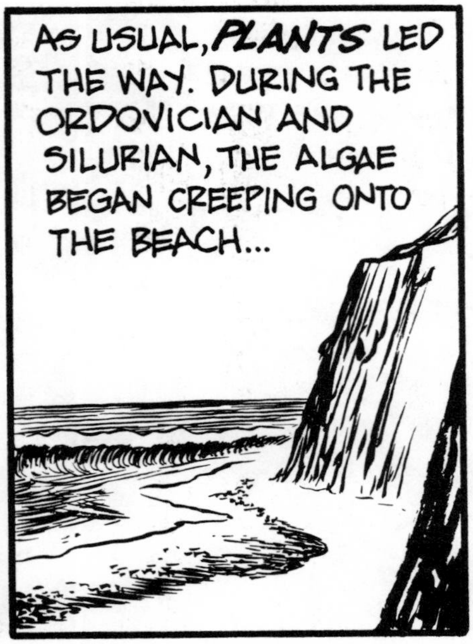
AS USUAL, ***PLANTS*** LED THE WAY. DURING THE ORDOVICIAN AND SILURIAN, THE ALGAE BEGAN CREEPING ONTO THE BEACH...

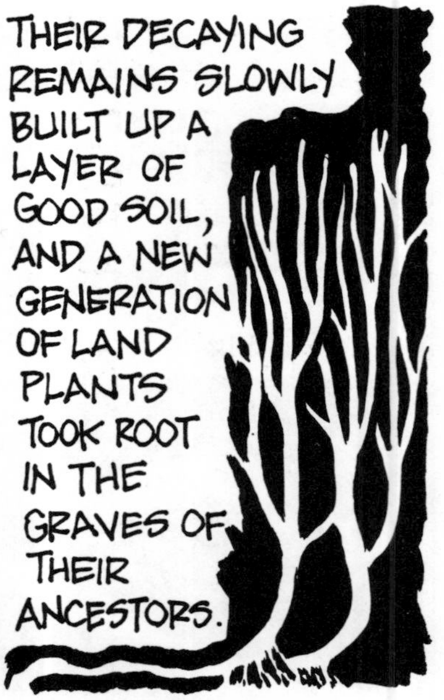
THEIR DECAYING REMAINS SLOWLY BUILT UP A LAYER OF GOOD SOIL, AND A NEW GENERATION OF LAND PLANTS TOOK ROOT IN THE GRAVES OF THEIR ANCESTORS.

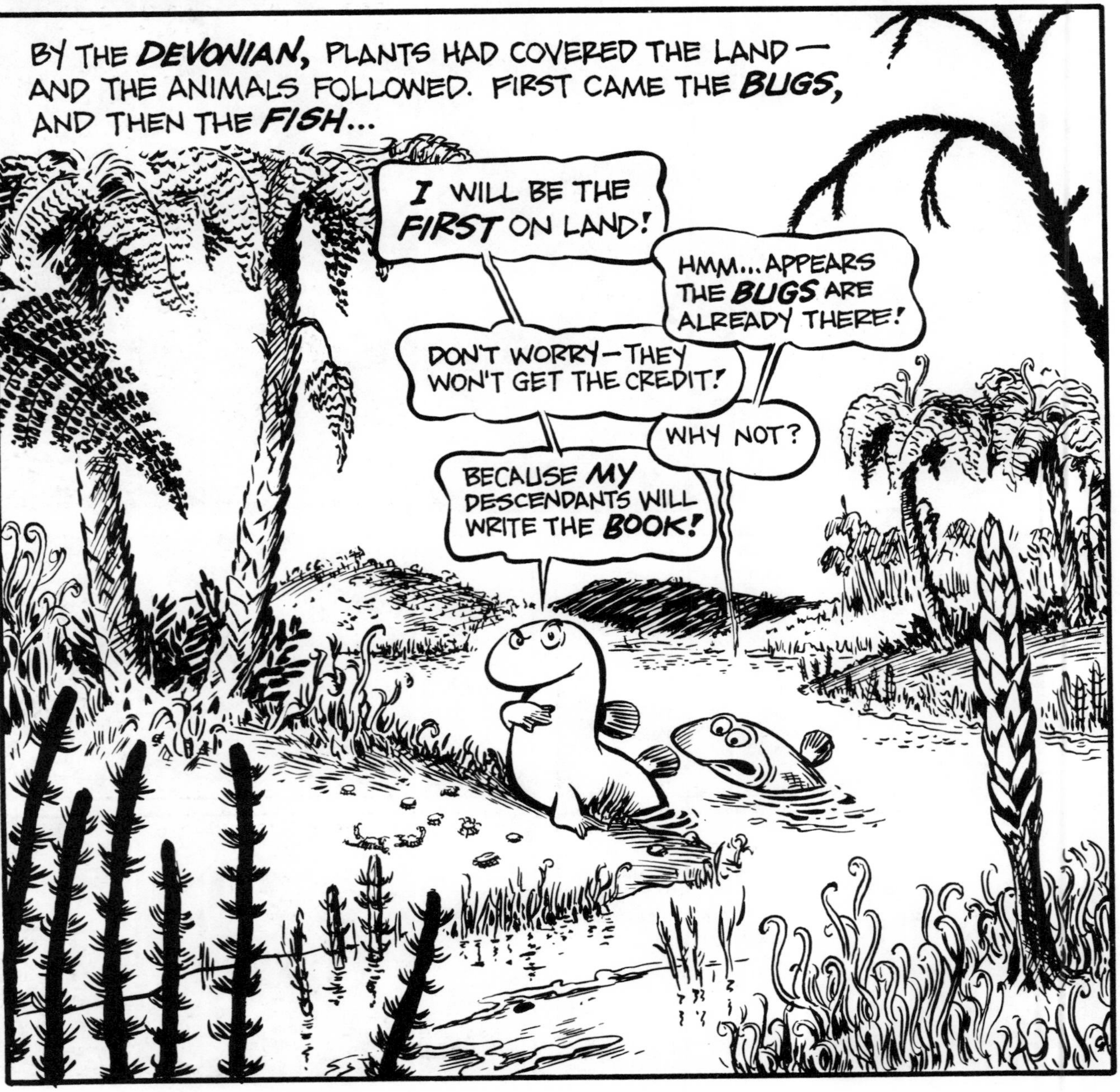
BY THE ***DEVONIAN,*** PLANTS HAD COVERED THE LAND — AND THE ANIMALS FOLLOWED. FIRST CAME THE ***BUGS,*** AND THEN THE ***FISH***...
I WILL BE THE ***FIRST*** ON LAND!
HMM... APPEARS THE ***BUGS*** ARE ALREADY THERE!
DON'T WORRY — THEY WON'T GET THE CREDIT!
WHY NOT?
BECAUSE ***MY*** DESCENDANTS WILL WRITE THE ***BOOK!***

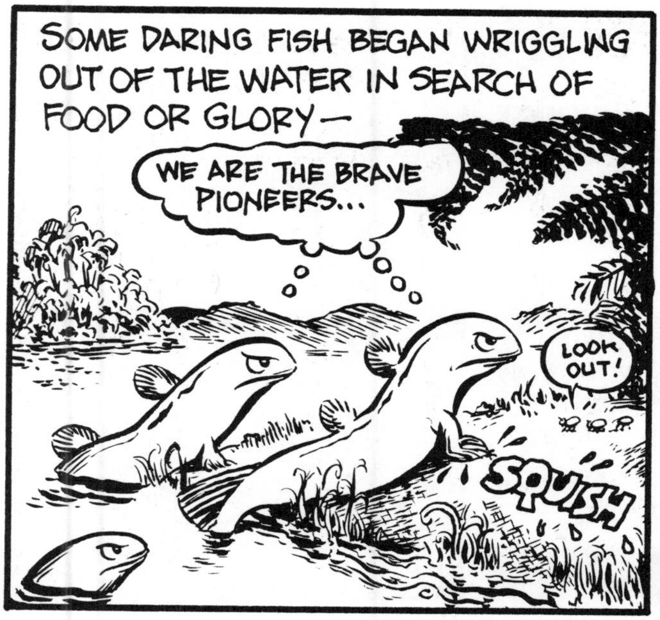
SOME DARING FISH BEGAN WRIGGLING OUT OF THE WATER IN SEARCH OF FOOD OR GLORY—
WE ARE THE BRAVE PIONEERS...
LOOK OUT!
SQUISH

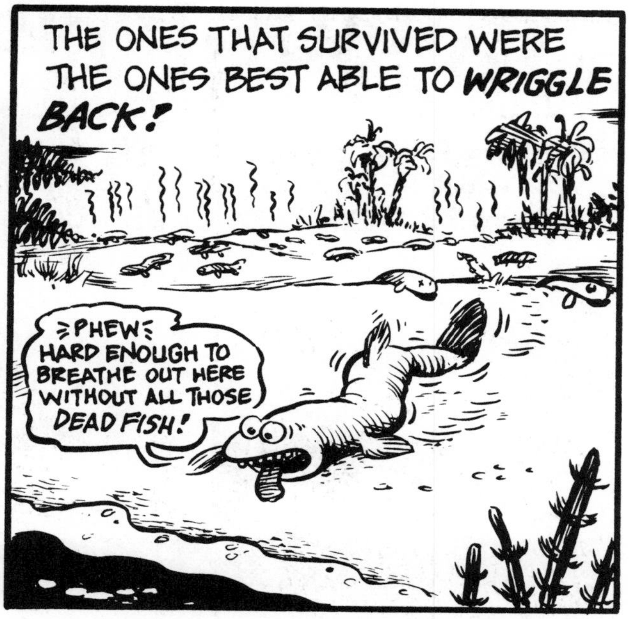
THE ONES THAT SURVIVED WERE THE ONES BEST ABLE TO WRIGGLE BACK!
PHEW
HARD ENOUGH TO BREATHE OUT HERE WITHOUT ALL THOSE DEAD FISH!

SO NATURE SELECTED IN FAVOR OF A STRONG SET OF FINS... WHICH GRADUALLY EVOLVED INTO ***LEGS.*** FOR BREATHING PURPOSES THE LAND-FISH ADAPTED ITS ***AIR BLADDER,*** ORIGINALLY USED IN THE WATER FOR BUOYANCY, INTO ***LUNGS...***

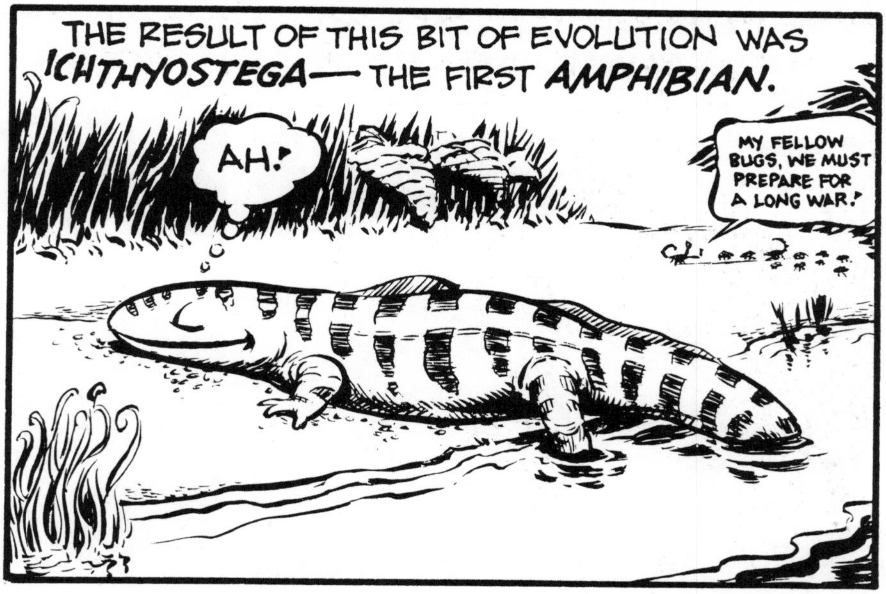
THE RESULT OF THIS BIT OF EVOLUTION WAS ICHTHYOSTEGA— THE FIRST AMPHIBIAN.
AH!
MY FELLOW BUGS, WE MUST PREPARE FOR A LONG WAR!

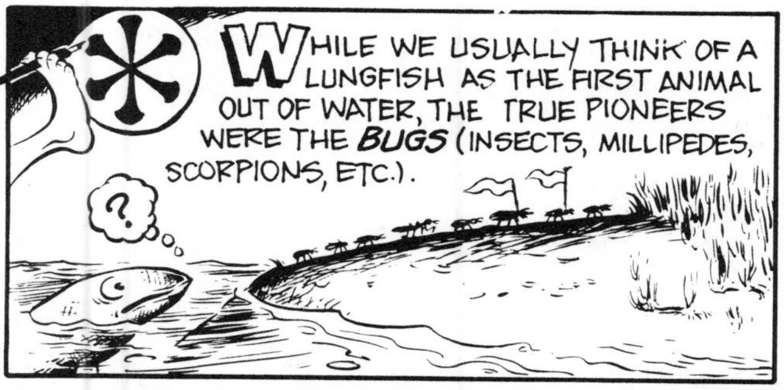
*
WHILE WE USUALLY THINK OF A LUNGFISH AS THE FIRST ANIMAL OUT OF WATER, THE TRUE PIONEERS WERE THE BUGS (INSECTS, MILLIPEDES, SCORPIONS, ETC.).
?

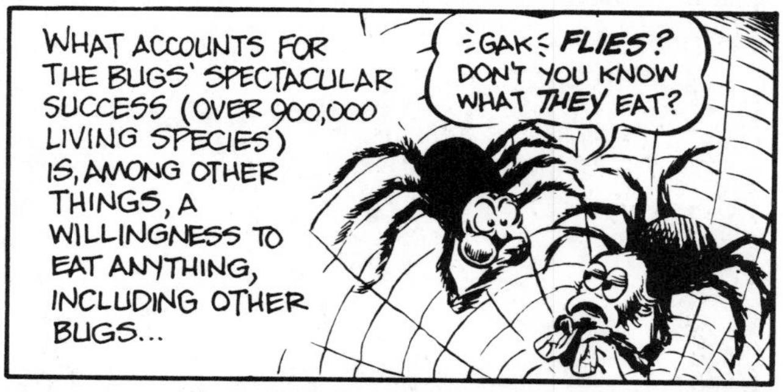
WHAT ACCOUNTS FOR THE BUGS' SPECTACULAR SUCCESS (OVER 900,000 LIVING SPECIES) IS, AMONG OTHER THINGS, A WILLINGNESS TO EAT ANYTHING, INCLUDING OTHER BUGS...
GAK FLIES? DON'T YOU KNOW WHAT THEY EAT?

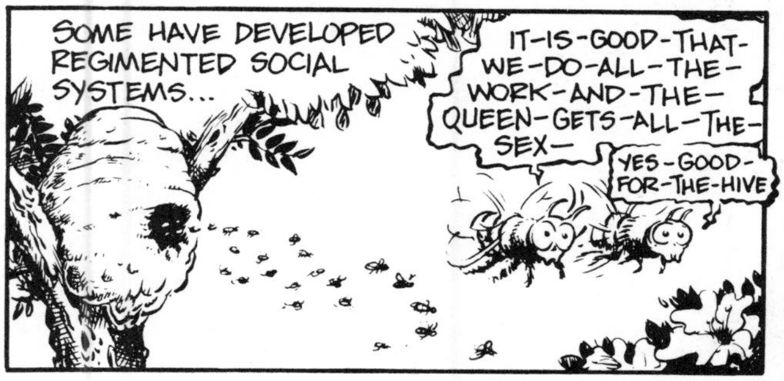
SOME HAVE DEVELOPED REGIMENTED SOCIAL SYSTEMS...
IT-IS-GOOD-THAT-WE-DO-ALL-THE-WORK-AND-THE-QUEEN-GETS-ALL-THE-SEX—
YES-GOOD-FOR-THE-HIVE

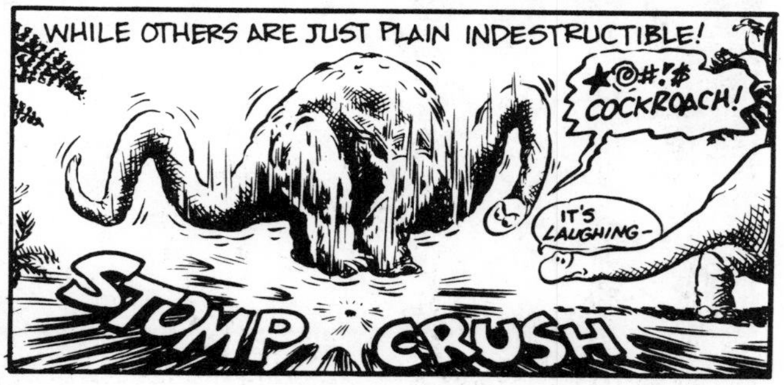
WHILE OTHERS ARE JUST PLAIN INDESTRUCTIBLE!
★@#!$ COCKROACH!
IT'S LAUGHING—
STOMP
CRUSH

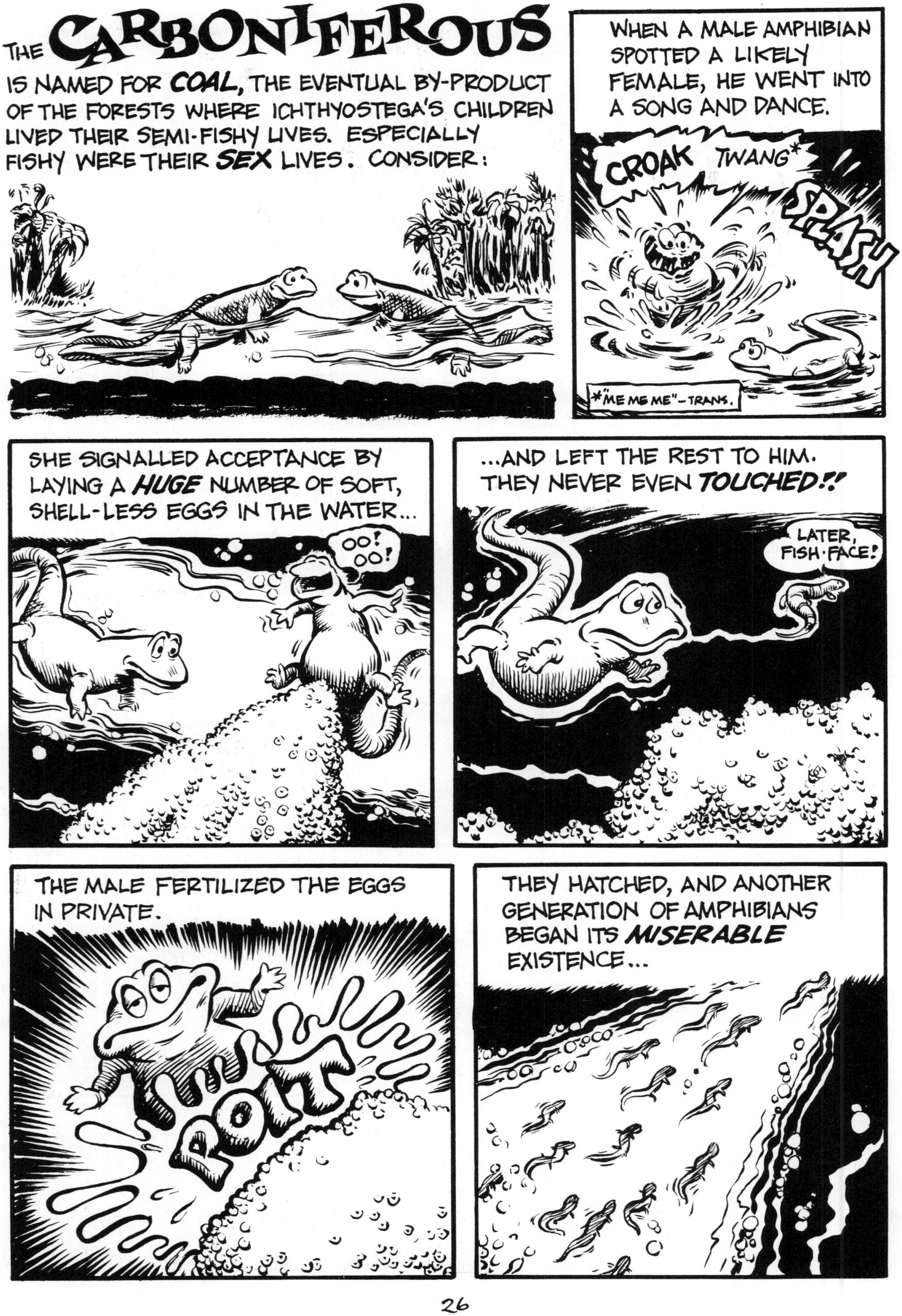

THE CARBONIFEROUS
IS NAMED FOR COAL, THE EVENTUAL BY-PRODUCT OF THE FORESTS WHERE ICHTHYOSTEGA'S CHILDREN LIVED THEIR SEMI-FISHY LIVES. ESPECIALLY FISHY WERE THEIR SEX LIVES. CONSIDER:
WHEN A MALE AMPHIBIAN SPOTTED A LIKELY FEMALE, HE WENT INTO A SONG AND DANCE.
CROAK TWANG*
SPLASH
*"ME ME ME"–TRANS.
SHE SIGNALLED ACCEPTANCE BY LAYING A HUGE NUMBER OF SOFT, SHELL-LESS EGGS IN THE WATER...
OO! OO!
...AND LEFT THE REST TO HIM. THEY NEVER EVEN TOUCHED!?!
LATER, FISH·FACE!
THE MALE FERTILIZED THE EGGS IN PRIVATE.
POIT
THEY HATCHED, AND ANOTHER GENERATION OF AMPHIBIANS BEGAN ITS MISERABLE EXISTENCE...

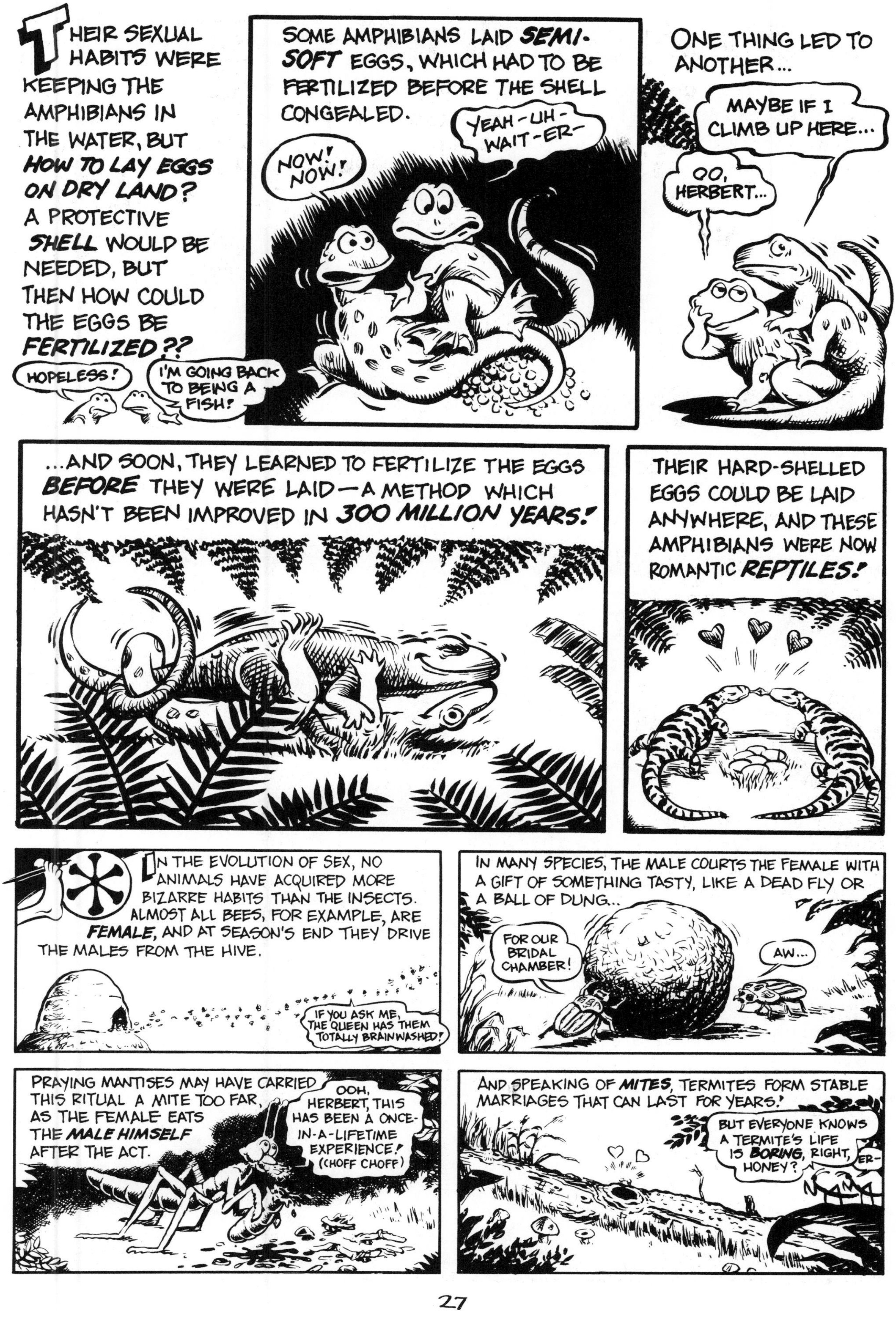
THEIR SEXUAL HABITS WERE KEEPING THE AMPHIBIANS IN THE WATER, BUT HOW TO LAY EGGS ON DRY LAND? A PROTECTIVE SHELL WOULD BE NEEDED, BUT THEN HOW COULD THE EGGS BE FERTILIZED??
HOPELESS!
I'M GOING BACK TO BEING A FISH!
SOME AMPHIBIANS LAID SEMI-SOFT EGGS, WHICH HAD TO BE FERTILIZED BEFORE THE SHELL CONGEALED.
NOW! NOW!
YEAH-UH-WAIT-ER-
ONE THING LED TO ANOTHER...
MAYBE IF I CLIMB UP HERE...
OO, HERBERT...
...AND SOON, THEY LEARNED TO FERTILIZE THE EGGS BEFORE THEY WERE LAID—A METHOD WHICH HASN'T BEEN IMPROVED IN 300 MILLION YEARS!
THEIR HARD-SHELLED EGGS COULD BE LAID ANYWHERE, AND THESE AMPHIBIANS WERE NOW ROMANTIC REPTILES!
IN THE EVOLUTION OF SEX, NO ANIMALS HAVE ACQUIRED MORE BIZARRE HABITS THAN THE INSECTS. ALMOST ALL BEES, FOR EXAMPLE, ARE FEMALE, AND AT SEASON'S END THEY DRIVE THE MALES FROM THE HIVE.
IF YOU ASK ME, THE QUEEN HAS THEM TOTALLY BRAINWASHED!
IN MANY SPECIES, THE MALE COURTS THE FEMALE WITH A GIFT OF SOMETHING TASTY, LIKE A DEAD FLY OR A BALL OF DUNG...
FOR OUR BRIDAL CHAMBER!
AW...
PRAYING MANTISES MAY HAVE CARRIED THIS RITUAL A MITE TOO FAR, AS THE FEMALE EATS THE MALE HIMSELF AFTER THE ACT.
OOH, HERBERT, THIS HAS BEEN A ONCE-IN-A-LIFETIME EXPERIENCE! (CHOFF CHOFF)
AND SPEAKING OF MITES, TERMITES FORM STABLE MARRIAGES THAT CAN LAST FOR YEARS!
BUT EVERYONE KNOWS A TERMITE'S LIFE IS BORING, RIGHT, HONEY?
ER-

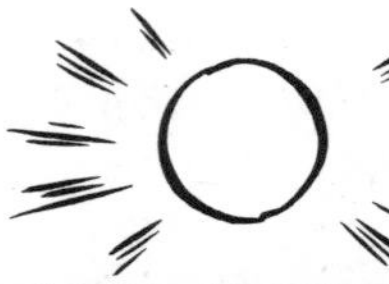

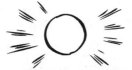

ANOTHER PROBLEM FACED BY REPTILES WAS ***REGULATING BODY HEAT.*** THIS IS HARDER ON LAND, WHERE TEMPERATURES FLUCTUATE MORE THAN IN THE WATER.

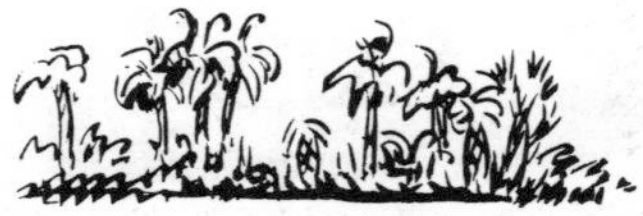

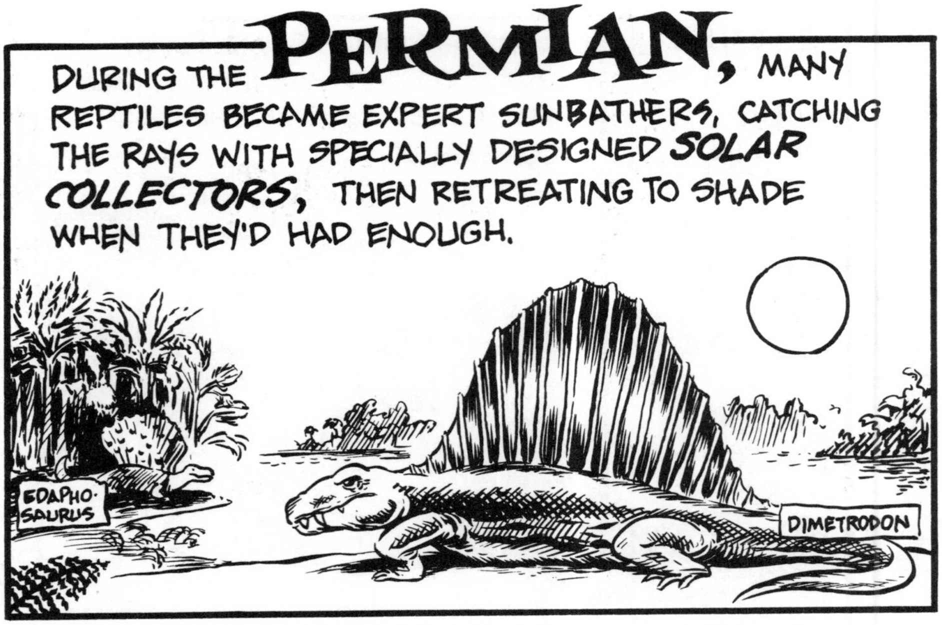
DURING THE PERMIAN, MANY REPTILES BECAME EXPERT SUNBATHERS, CATCHING THE RAYS WITH SPECIALLY DESIGNED SOLAR COLLECTORS, THEN RETREATING TO SHADE WHEN THEY'D HAD ENOUGH.
EDAPHO-SAURUS
DIMETRODON

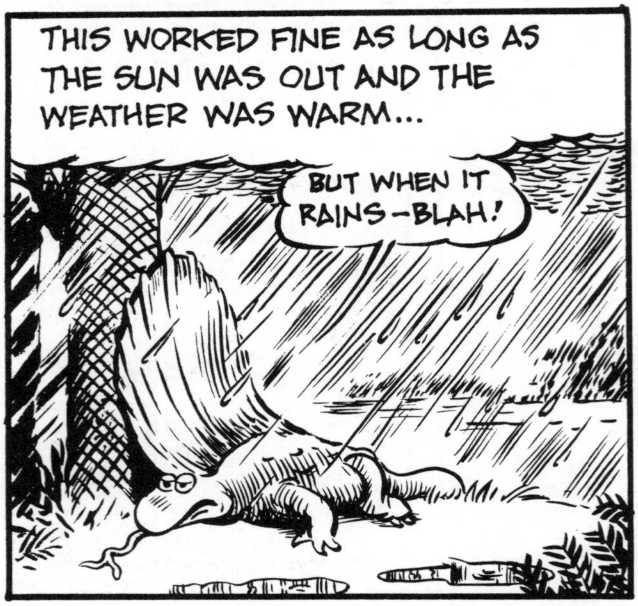
THIS WORKED FINE AS LONG AS THE SUN WAS OUT AND THE WEATHER WAS WARM...
BUT WHEN IT RAINS—BLAH!

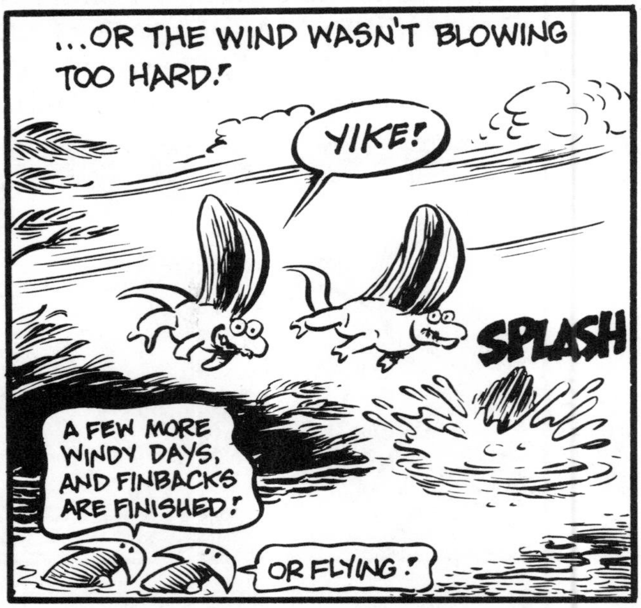
...OR THE WIND WASN'T BLOWING TOO HARD!
YIKE!
SPLASH
A FEW MORE WINDY DAYS, AND FINBACKS ARE FINISHED!
OR FLYING!

MEANWHILE, IN COOL PERMIAN SOUTH AFRICA, OTHER REPTILES, THE ***THERAPSIDS,*** WERE LEARNING TO GENERATE HEAT ***INTERNALLY,*** BY BURNING THEIR FOOD FASTER...

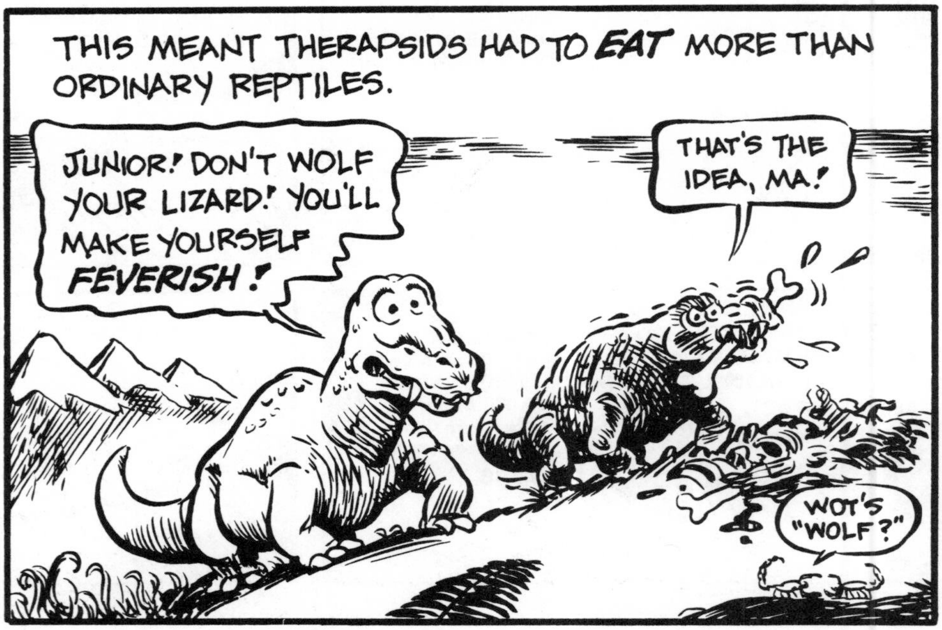
THIS MEANT THERAPSIDS HAD TO EAT MORE THAN ORDINARY REPTILES.
JUNIOR! DON'T WOLF YOUR LIZARD! YOU'LL MAKE YOURSELF FEVERISH!
THAT'S THE IDEA, MA!
WOT'S "WOLF?"

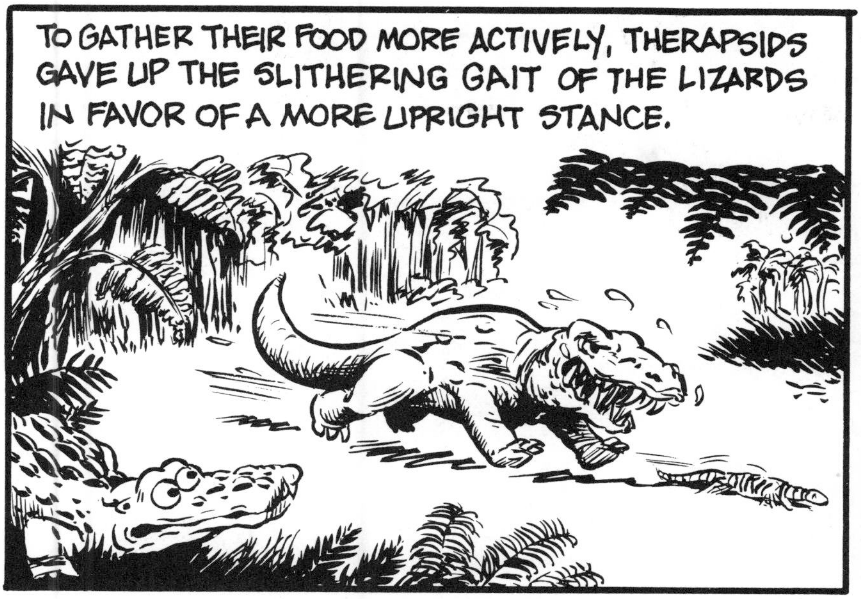
TO GATHER THEIR FOOD MORE ACTIVELY, THERAPSIDS GAVE UP THE SLITHERING GAIT OF THE LIZARDS IN FAVOR OF A MORE UPRIGHT STANCE.

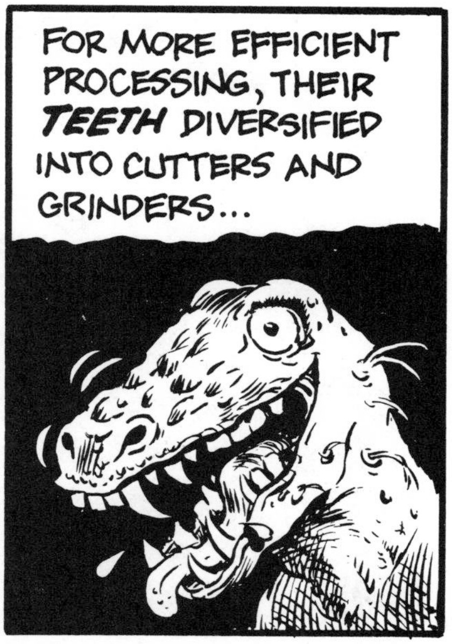
FOR MORE EFFICIENT PROCESSING, THEIR ***TEETH*** DIVERSIFIED INTO CUTTERS AND GRINDERS...

HAIR PROBABLY STARTED AS THERAPSID SIDE-WHISKERS, USED TO EXTEND THE SENSE OF TOUCH, AND THEN SPREAD OVER THE BODY LATER, AS A WAY TO KEEP WARM.

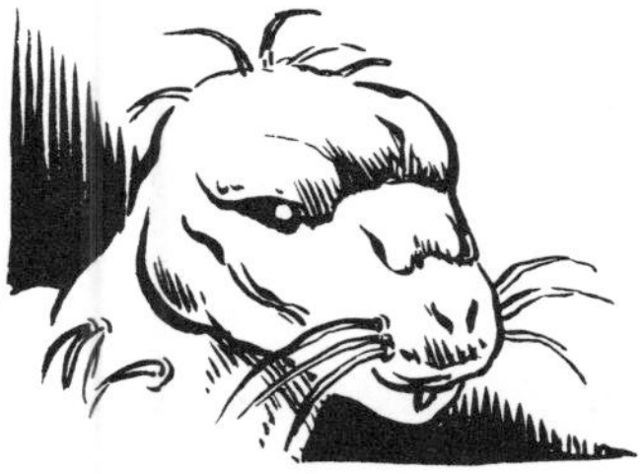

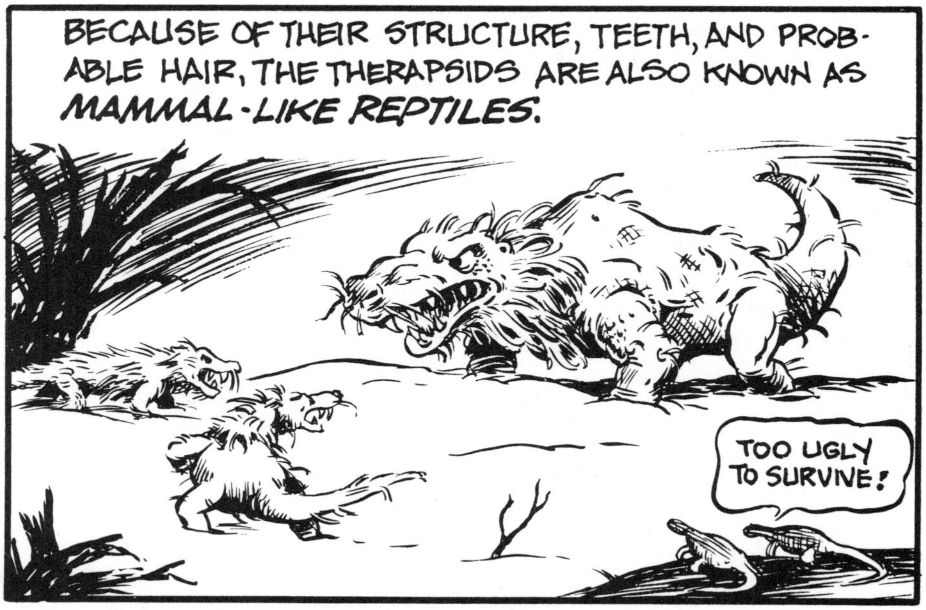
BECAUSE OF THEIR STRUCTURE, TEETH, AND PROBABLE HAIR, THE THERAPSIDS ARE ALSO KNOWN AS ***MAMMAL-LIKE REPTILES.***
TOO UGLY TO SURVIVE!

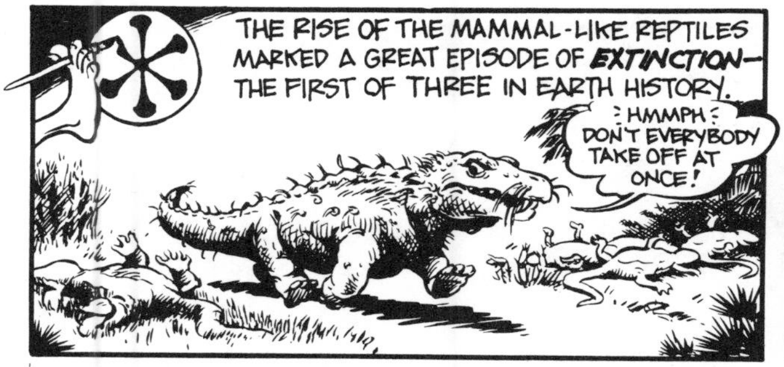
THE RISE OF THE MAMMAL-LIKE REPTILES MARKED A GREAT EPISODE OF ***EXTINCTION***— THE FIRST OF THREE IN EARTH HISTORY.
HMMPH DON'T EVERYBODY TAKE OFF AT ONCE!

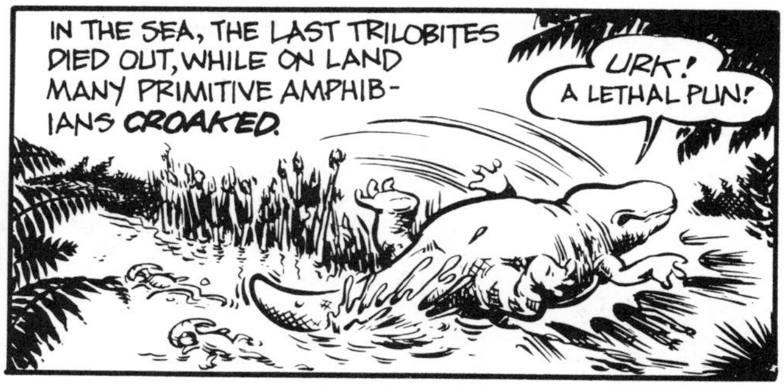
IN THE SEA, THE LAST TRILOBITES DIED OUT, WHILE ON LAND MANY PRIMITIVE AMPHIBIANS ***CROAKED.***
URK! A LETHAL PUN!

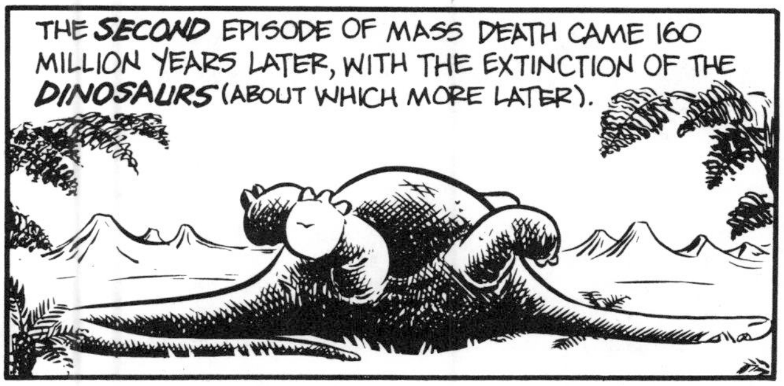
THE ***SECOND*** EPISODE OF MASS DEATH CAME 160 MILLION YEARS LATER, WITH THE EXTINCTION OF THE ***DINOSAURS*** (ABOUT WHICH MORE LATER).

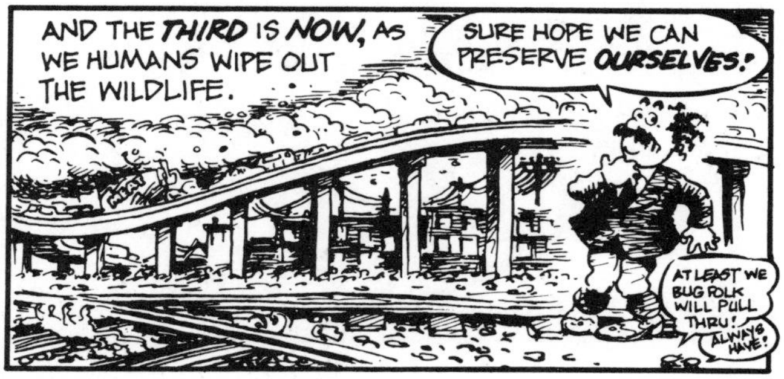
AND THE ***THIRD*** IS ***NOW,*** AS WE HUMANS WIPE OUT THE WILDLIFE.
SURE HOPE WE CAN PRESERVE ***OURSELVES!***
AT LEAST WE BUG FOLK WILL PULL THRU!
ALWAYS HAVE!

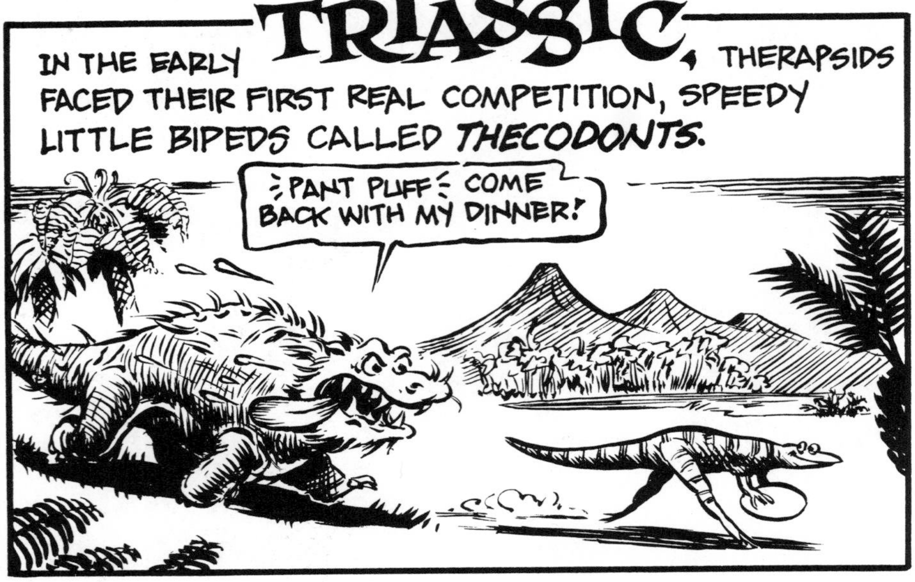
IN THE EARLY TRIASSIC, THERAPSIDS FACED THEIR FIRST REAL COMPETITION, SPEEDY LITTLE BIPEDS CALLED *THECODONTS.*
PANT PUFF COME BACK WITH MY DINNER!

DESCENDED FROM AQUATIC REPTILES WHOSE LONG HIND LEGS WERE ADAPTED FOR SWIMMING, THECODONTS FOUND LONG LEGS TO BE HANDY ON LAND, TOO!

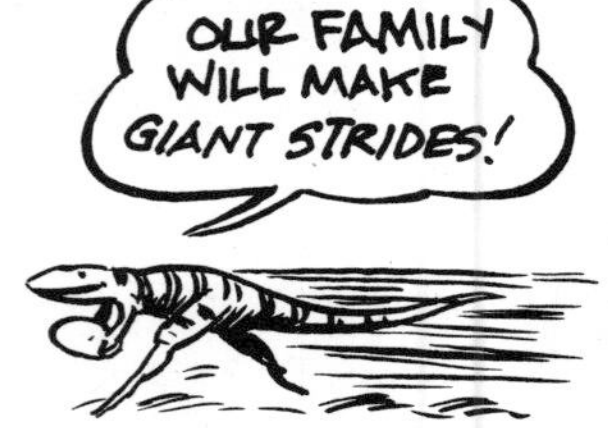
OUR FAMILY WILL MAKE *GIANT STRIDES!*

ONLY TWICE IN EARTH HISTORY HAS A QUADRUPED STOOD UP ON TWO LEGS, AND BOTH TIMES THE EXPERIMENT WAS A FANTASTIC SUCCESS (FOR THE ANIMAL THAT TRIED IT, ANYWAY)...

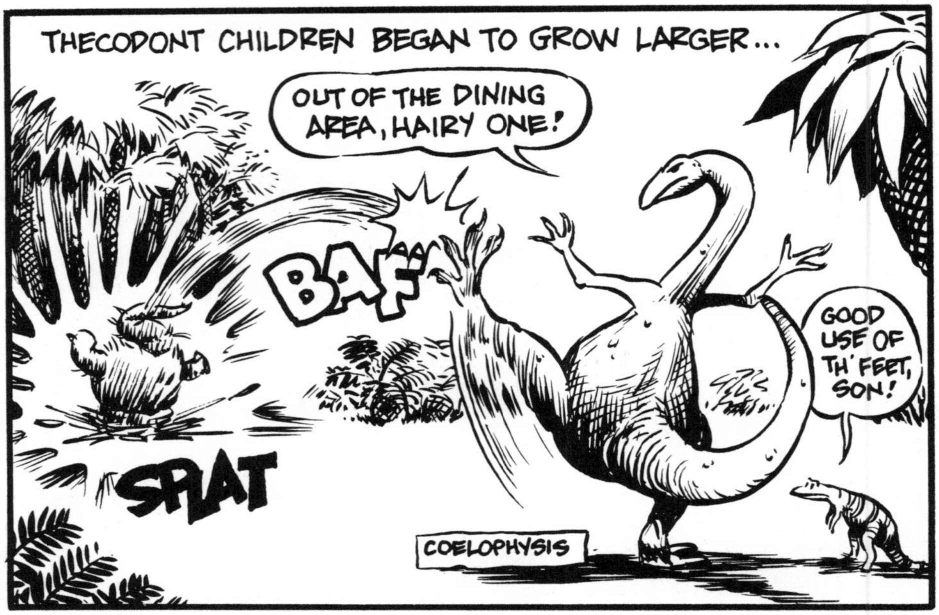
THECODONT CHILDREN BEGAN TO GROW LARGER...
OUT OF THE DINING AREA, HAIRY ONE!
BAF
GOOD USE OF TH' FEET, SON!
SPLAT
COELOPHYSIS

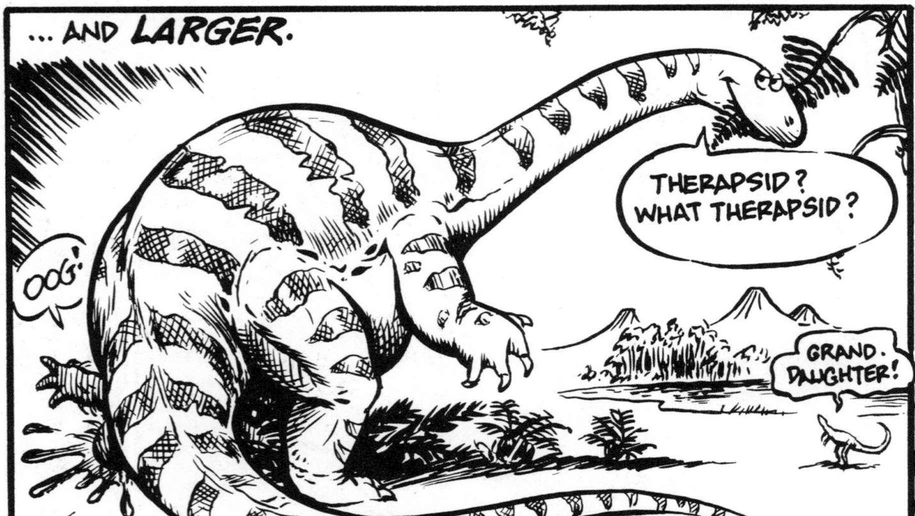
... AND *LARGER.*
THERAPSID? WHAT THERAPSID?
OOG!
GRAND. DAUGHTER!
PLATEOSAURUS

UNABLE TO COMPETE WITH SUCH MONSTERS, THE LARGER THERAPSIDS DIED OUT. ONLY A FEW VERY SMALL TYPES SURVIVED TO EVOLVE INTO THE FIRST ***MAMMALS.***

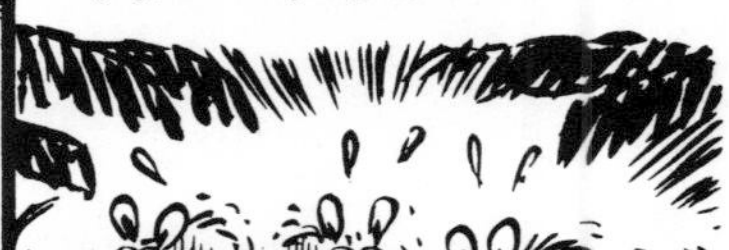

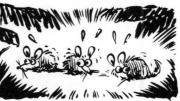

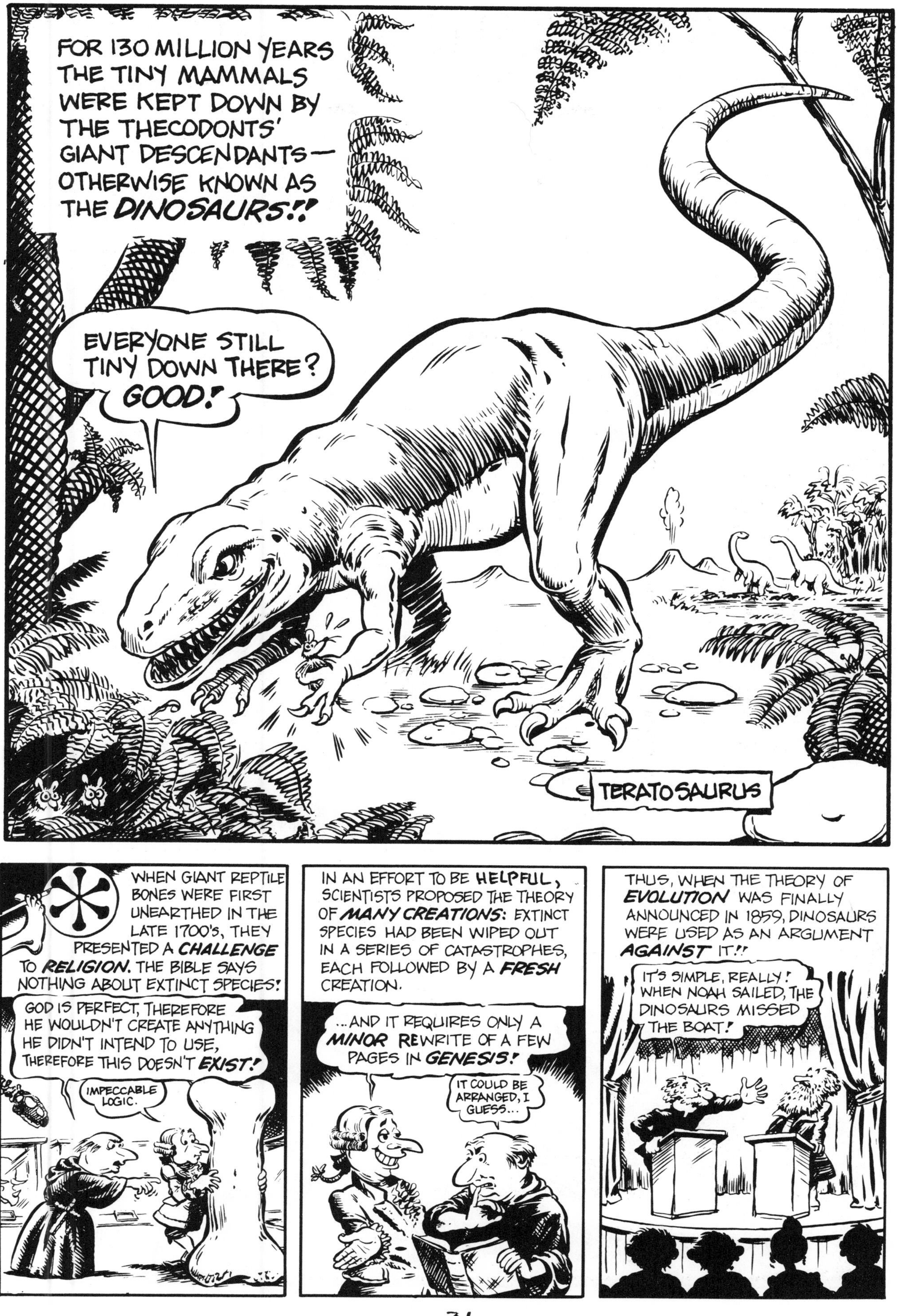

FOR 130 MILLION YEARS THE TINY MAMMALS WERE KEPT DOWN BY THE THECODONTS' GIANT DESCENDANTS— OTHERWISE KNOWN AS THE DINOSAURS!!
EVERYONE STILL TINY DOWN THERE? GOOD!
TERATOSAURUS
WHEN GIANT REPTILE BONES WERE FIRST UNEARTHED IN THE LATE 1700'S, THEY PRESENTED A CHALLENGE TO RELIGION. THE BIBLE SAYS NOTHING ABOUT EXTINCT SPECIES!
GOD IS PERFECT, THEREFORE HE WOULDN'T CREATE ANYTHING HE DIDN'T INTEND TO USE, THEREFORE THIS DOESN'T EXIST!
IMPECCABLE LOGIC.
IN AN EFFORT TO BE HELPFUL, SCIENTISTS PROPOSED THE THEORY OF MANY CREATIONS: EXTINCT SPECIES HAD BEEN WIPED OUT IN A SERIES OF CATASTROPHES, EACH FOLLOWED BY A FRESH CREATION.
...AND IT REQUIRES ONLY A MINOR REWRITE OF A FEW PAGES IN GENESIS!
IT COULD BE ARRANGED, I GUESS...
THUS, WHEN THE THEORY OF EVOLUTION WAS FINALLY ANNOUNCED IN 1859, DINOSAURS WERE USED AS AN ARGUMENT AGAINST IT!!
IT'S SIMPLE, REALLY! WHEN NOAH SAILED, THE DINOSAURS MISSED THE BOAT!

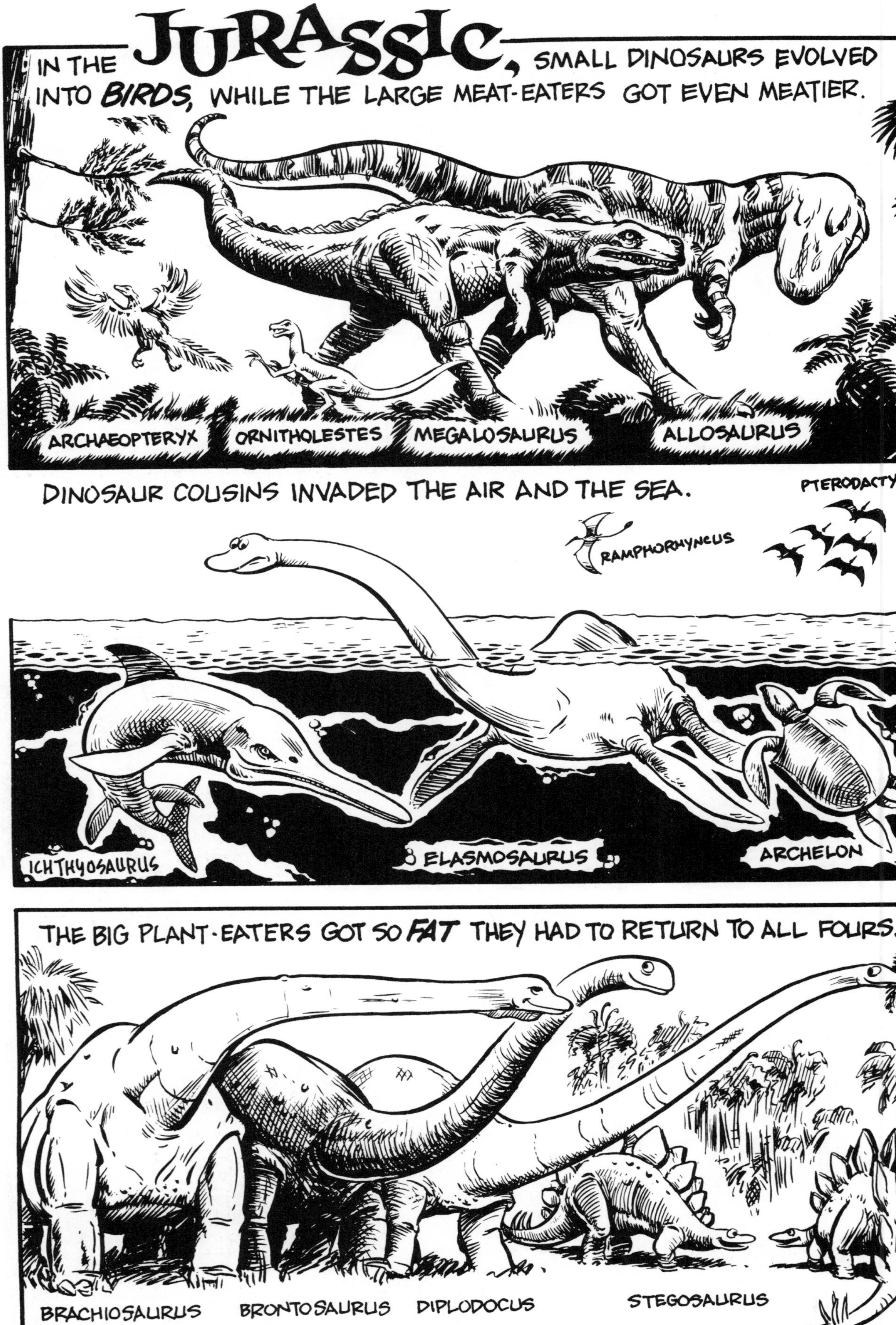
IN THE JURASSIC, SMALL DINOSAURS EVOLVED INTO BIRDS, WHILE THE LARGE MEAT-EATERS GOT EVEN MEATIER.
ARCHAEOPTERYX
ORNITHOLESTES
MEGALOSAURUS
ALLOSAURUS
DINOSAUR COUSINS INVADED THE AIR AND THE SEA.
RAMPHORHYNCUS
PTERODACTYL
ICHTHYOSAURUS
ELASMOSAURUS
ARCHELON
THE BIG PLANT-EATERS GOT SO FAT THEY HAD TO RETURN TO ALL FOURS.
BRACHIOSAURUS
BRONTOSAURUS
DIPLODOCUS
STEGOSAURUS

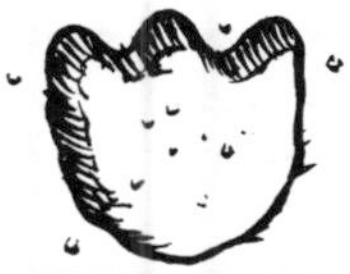

BECAUSE BRONTOSAURS OFTEN WALKED IN MUD, THEY LEFT BEHIND ***FOSSIL FOOTPRINTS,*** WHICH HAVE GIVEN US GLIMPSES OF ***ACTUAL EPISODES*** OF BRONTOSAURIAN LIFE. HERE ARE THREE:

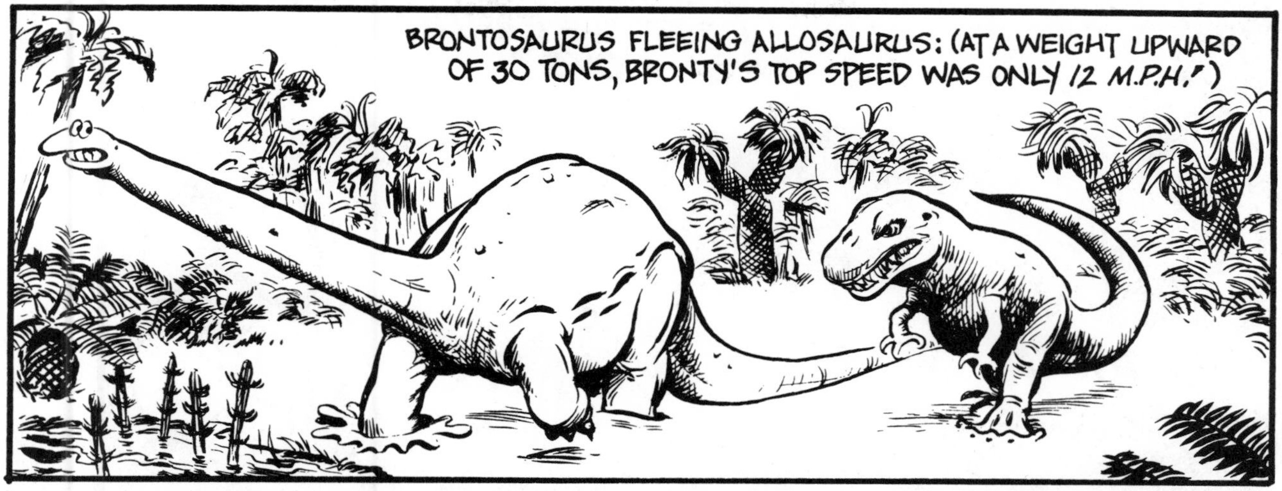
BRONTOSAURUS FLEEING ALLOSAURUS: (AT A WEIGHT UPWARD OF 30 TONS, BRONTY'S TOP SPEED WAS ONLY *12 M.P.H.!*)

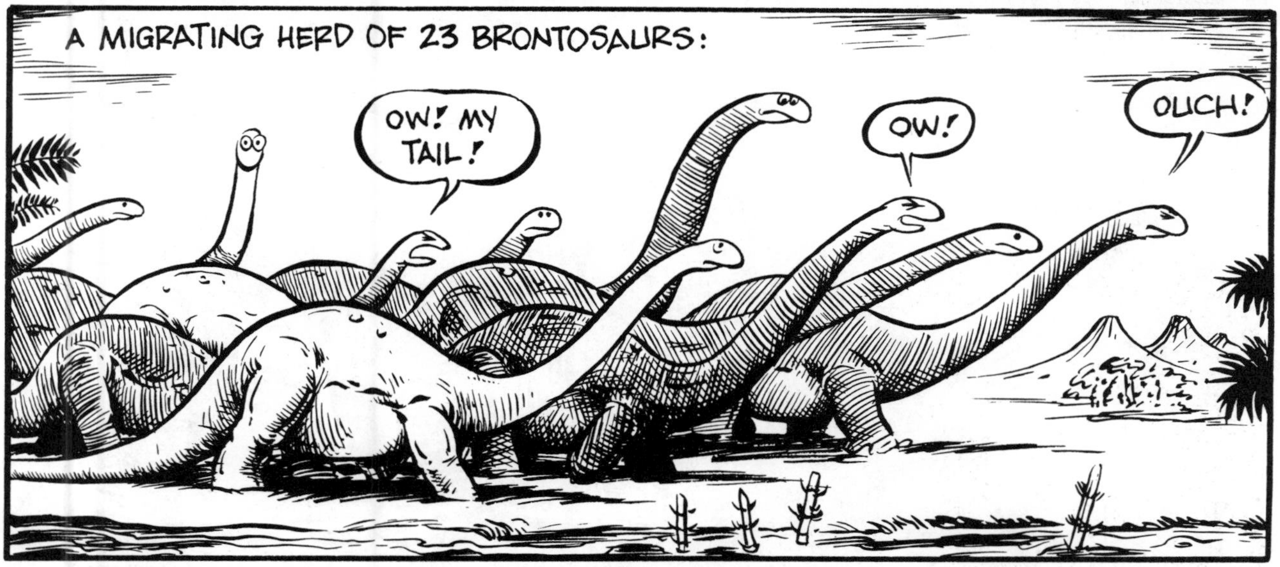
A MIGRATING HERD OF 23 BRONTOSAURS:
OW! MY TAIL!
OW!
OUCH!

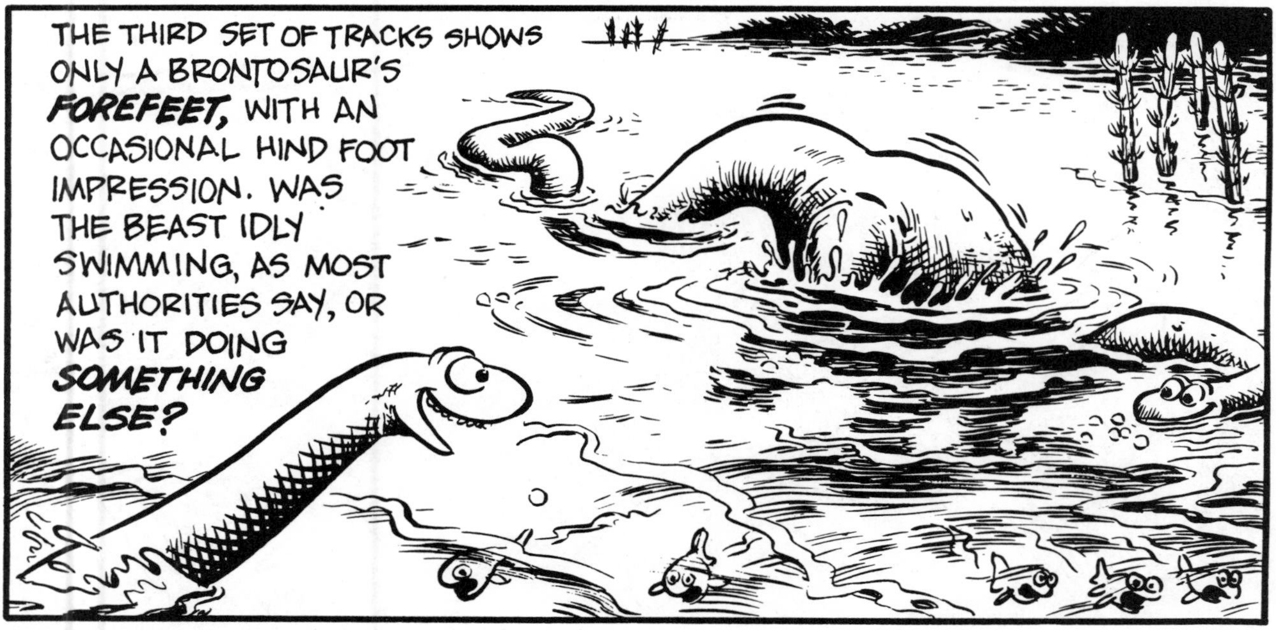
THE THIRD SET OF TRACKS SHOWS ONLY A BRONTOSAUR'S ***FOREFEET,*** WITH AN OCCASIONAL HIND FOOT IMPRESSION. WAS THE BEAST IDLY SWIMMING, AS MOST AUTHORITIES SAY, OR WAS IT DOING ***SOMETHING ELSE?***

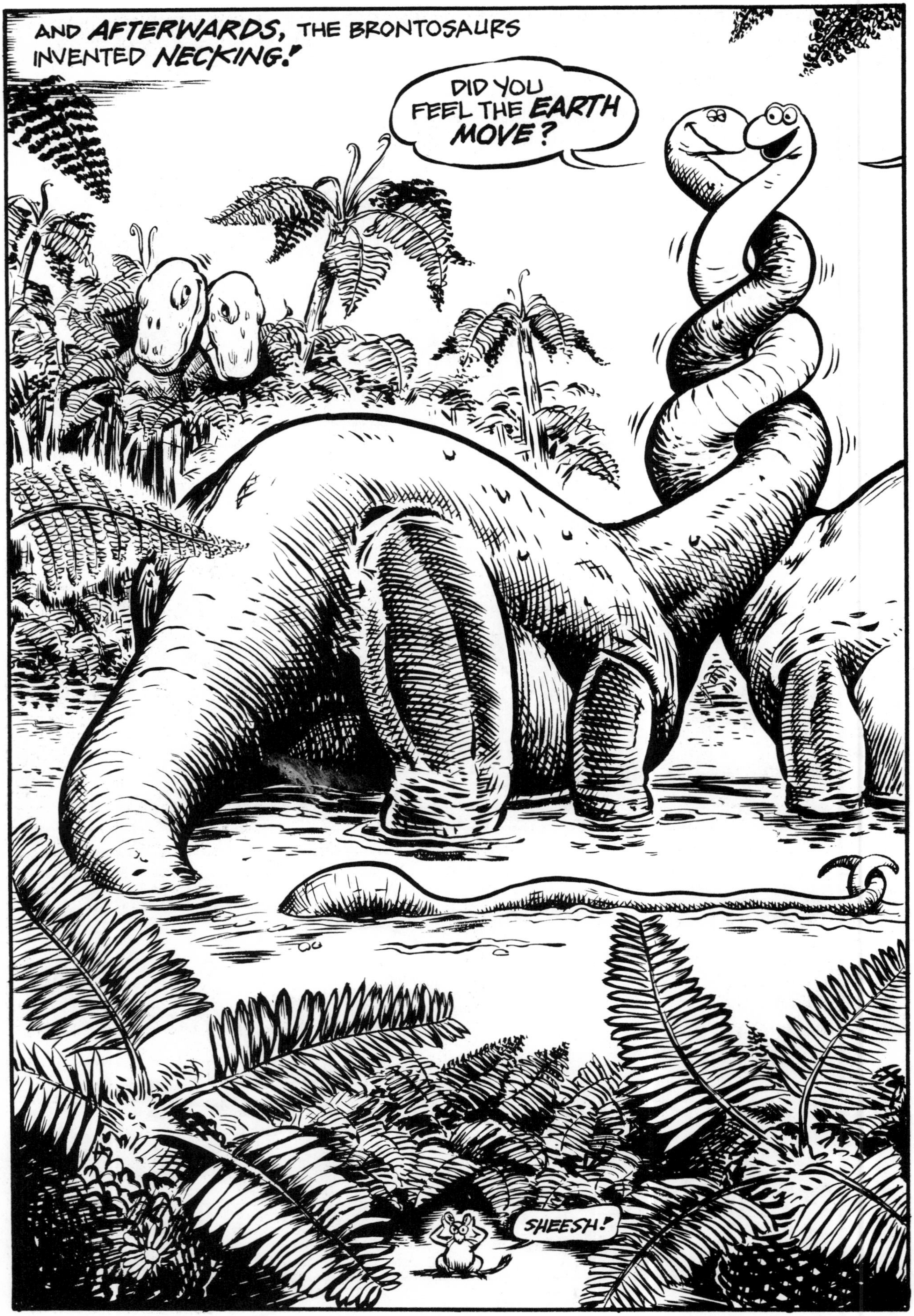
AND AFTERWARDS, THE BRONTOSAURS INVENTED NECKING!
DID YOU FEEL THE EARTH MOVE?
SHEESH!

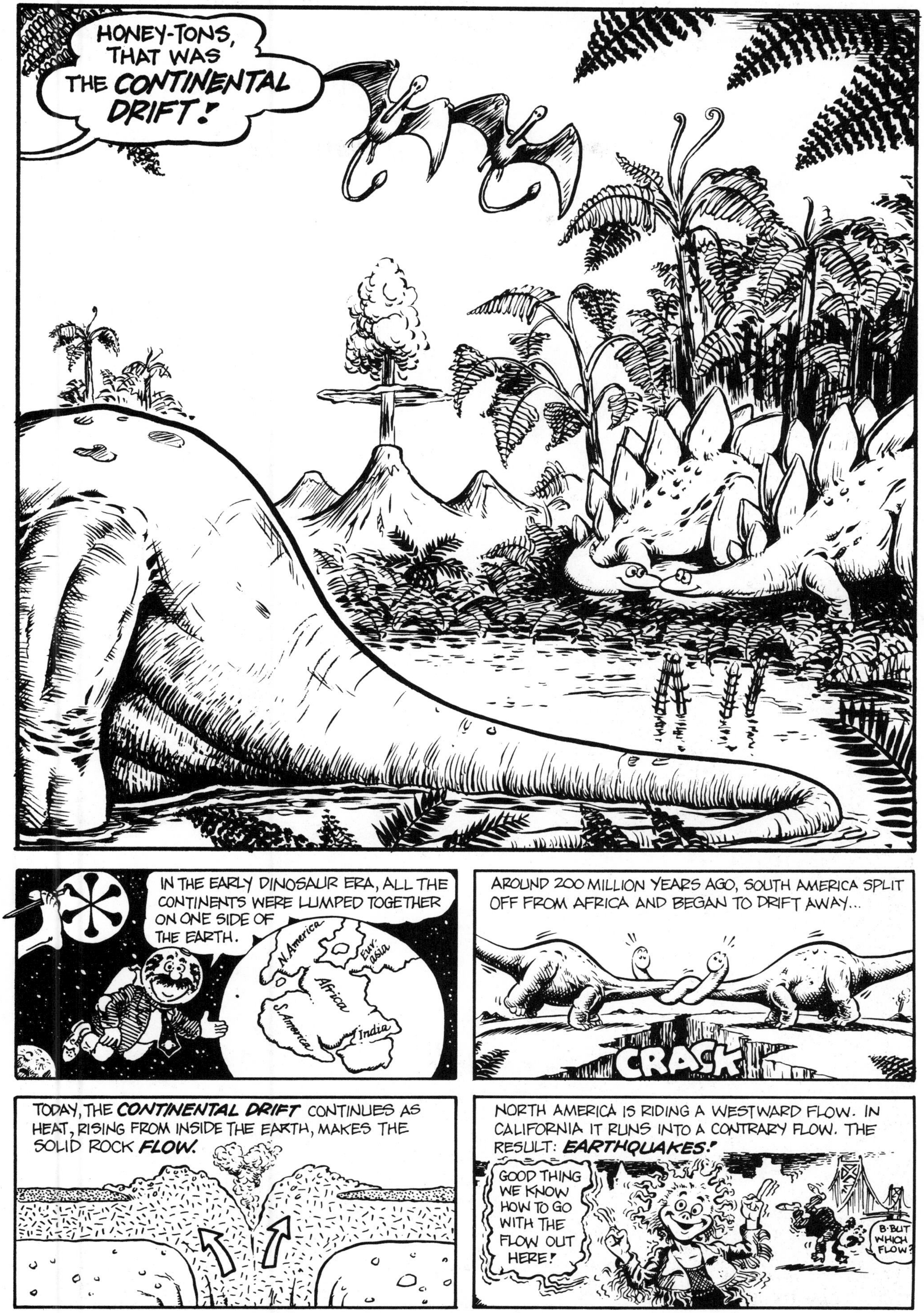
HONEY-TONS, THAT WAS THE CONTINENTAL DRIFT!
IN THE EARLY DINOSAUR ERA, ALL THE CONTINENTS WERE LUMPED TOGETHER ON ONE SIDE OF THE EARTH.
N. America
Eur. asia
Africa
S. America
India
AROUND 200 MILLION YEARS AGO, SOUTH AMERICA SPLIT OFF FROM AFRICA AND BEGAN TO DRIFT AWAY...
CRACK
TODAY, THE CONTINENTAL DRIFT CONTINUES AS HEAT, RISING FROM INSIDE THE EARTH, MAKES THE SOLID ROCK FLOW.
NORTH AMERICA IS RIDING A WESTWARD FLOW. IN CALIFORNIA IT RUNS INTO A CONTRARY FLOW. THE RESULT: EARTHQUAKES!
GOOD THING WE KNOW HOW TO GO WITH THE FLOW OUT HERE!
B-BUT WHICH FLOW?

CRETACEOUS

THE CROWDED CRETACEOUS WAS THE HEIGHT OF THE DINOSAUR ERA. IN THIS SCENE, THE GIANT ***TYRANNOSAURUS REX*** EYES SOME ***DUCKBILLS*** WHILE HIS COUSIN ***GORGOSAURUS*** FLEES FROM A RAMPAGING HERD OF ***TRICERATOPS.*** SPECTATORS INCLUDE TWO ARMORED ***ANKYLOSAURS,*** AN AIRBORNE ***PTERANODON,*** AND SOME DISTANT ***TITANOSAURS. STRUTHIOMIMUS*** ("OSTRICH-MIMIC") IGNORES THE WHOLE SITUATION!

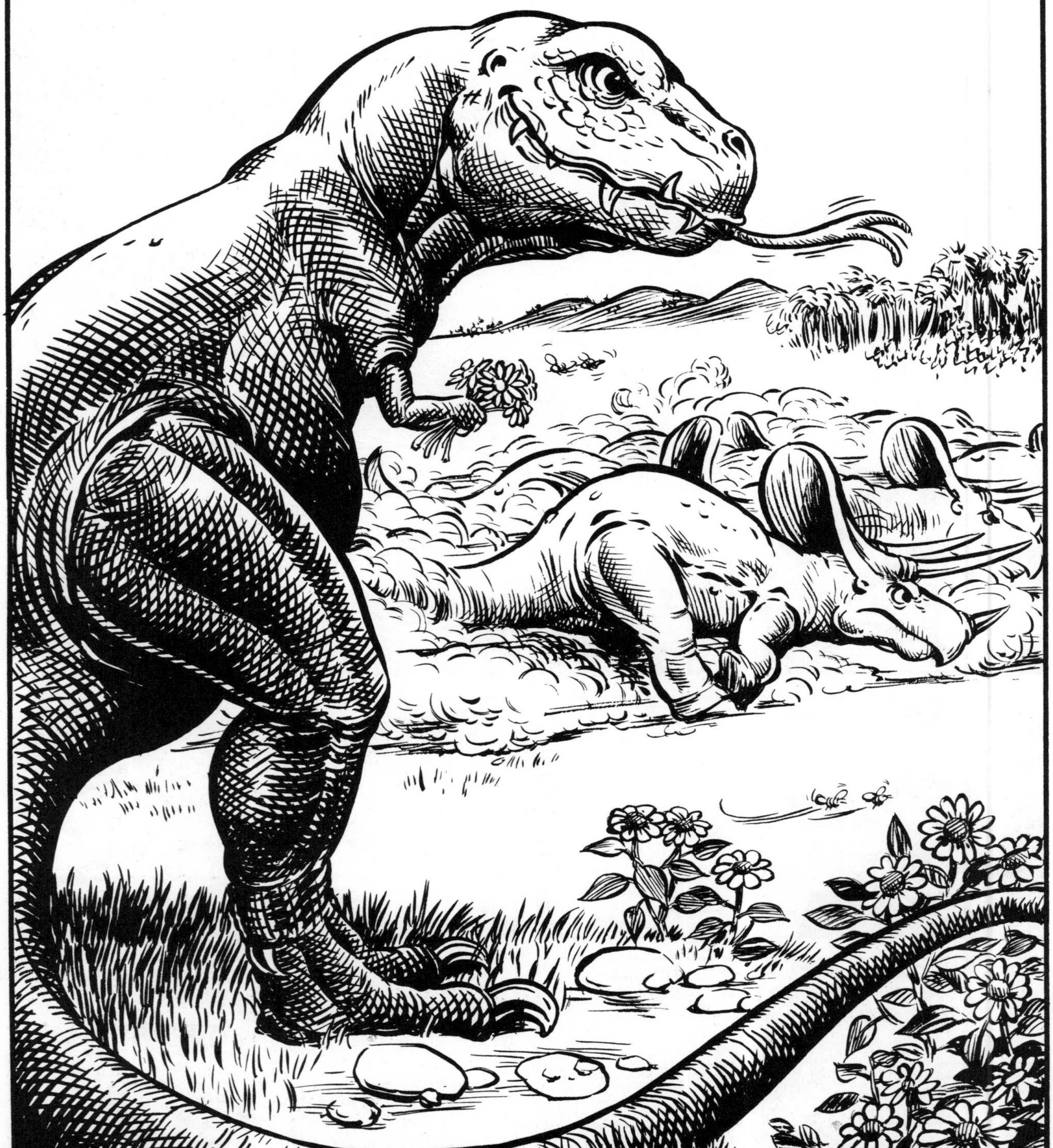

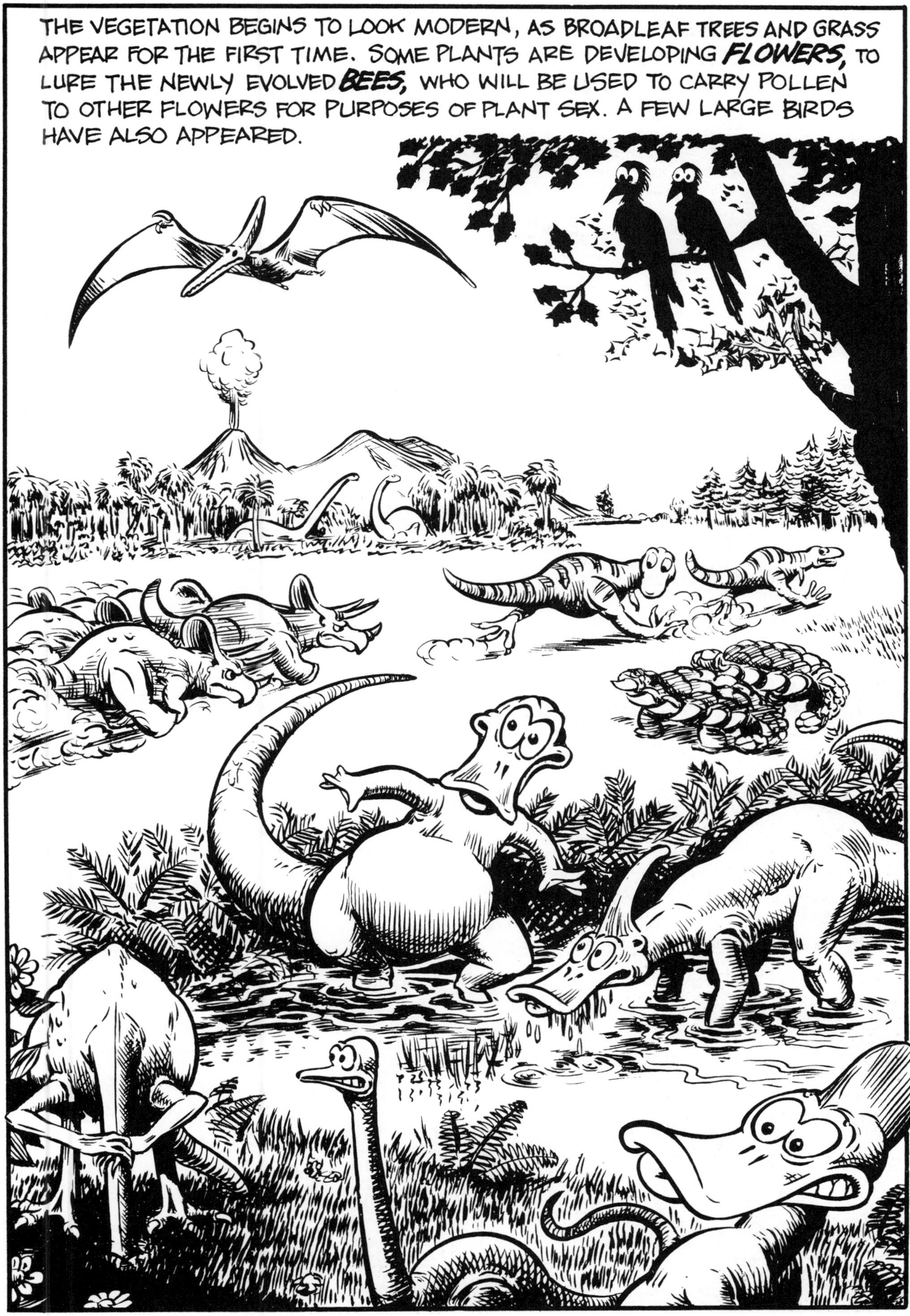
THE VEGETATION BEGINS TO LOOK MODERN, AS BROADLEAF TREES AND GRASS APPEAR FOR THE FIRST TIME. SOME PLANTS ARE DEVELOPING ***FLOWERS,*** TO LURE THE NEWLY EVOLVED ***BEES,*** WHO WILL BE USED TO CARRY POLLEN TO OTHER FLOWERS FOR PURPOSES OF PLANT SEX. A FEW LARGE BIRDS HAVE ALSO APPEARED.

SUDDENLY, AROUND 70 MILLION YEARS AGO, FOR REASONS THAT ARE STILL UNCLEAR, THE WORLD COOLED RAPIDLY.

IN THE OCEAN, ENTIRE POPULATIONS OF ONE-CELLED PLANKTON PERISHED, SETTING OFF AN *ECOLOGICAL CATASTROPHE.*

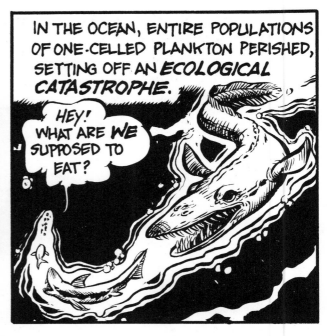

HEY! WHAT ARE *WE* SUPPOSED TO EAT?

WITH THE BASIS OF THE FOOD CHAIN GONE, MANY FAMILIES OF SEA LIFE WERE WIPED OUT, INCLUDING VARIOUS FISH, SHELLFISH, AND ALL THE GREAT SEA REPTILES...

ON LAND THE DEVASTATION WAS EQUALLY WIDESPREAD. AS PLANTS DIED OUT, ALL ANIMALS BEGAN TO SUFFER, ESPECIALLY THE GIANTS.

THE UNDERNOURISHED DINOSAURS, LIKE POISONED BIRDS, LAID EGGS WITH THINNER AND THINNER SHELLS. THE EMBRYOS, UNABLE TO DRAW ENOUGH CALCIUM FROM THEIR EGG-SHELLS TO DEVELOP BONES, WERE TOO WEAK TO HATCH...

AFTER 130 MILLION YEARS OF DOMINANCE, THE DINOSAURS HAD FINALLY LEFT THE WORLD TO THEIR OLD COMPETITORS, THE ***TINY MAMMALS.***

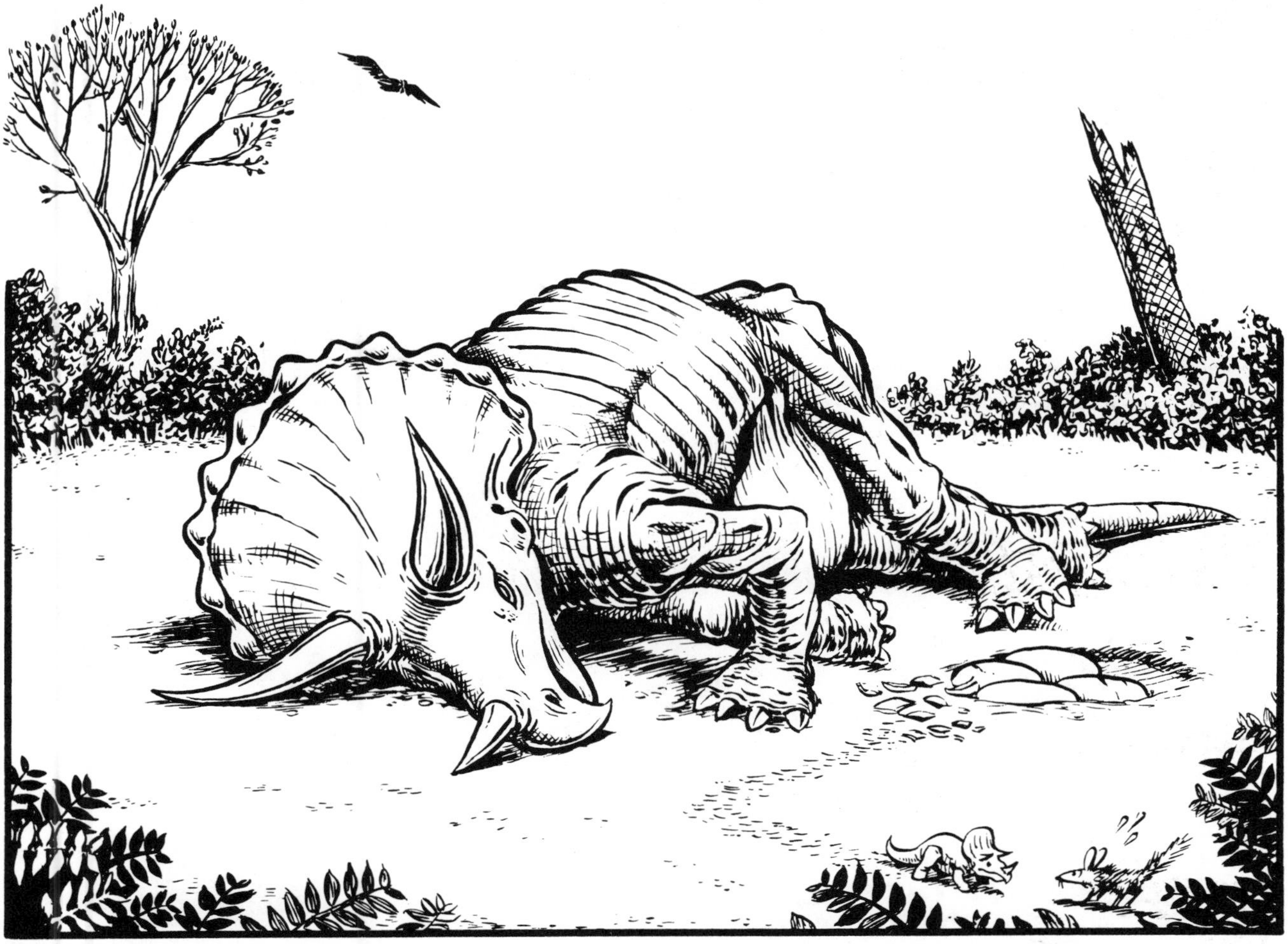

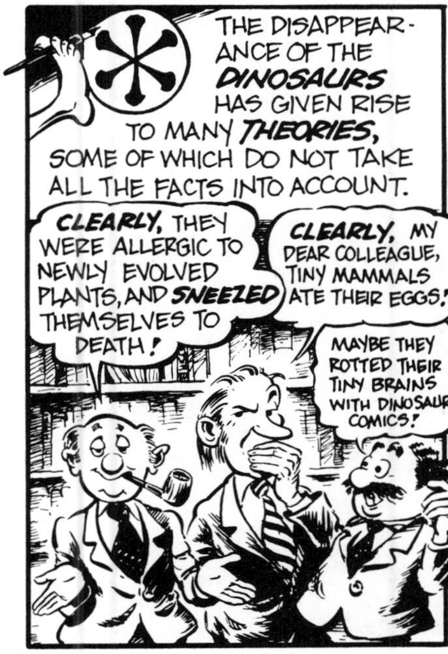
THE DISAPPEARANCE OF THE DINOSAURS HAS GIVEN RISE TO MANY THEORIES, SOME OF WHICH DO NOT TAKE ALL THE FACTS INTO ACCOUNT.
CLEARLY, THEY WERE ALLERGIC TO NEWLY EVOLVED PLANTS, AND SNEEZED THEMSELVES TO DEATH!
CLEARLY, MY DEAR COLLEAGUE, TINY MAMMALS ATE THEIR EGGS!
MAYBE THEY ROTTED THEIR TINY BRAINS WITH DINOSAUR COMICS!

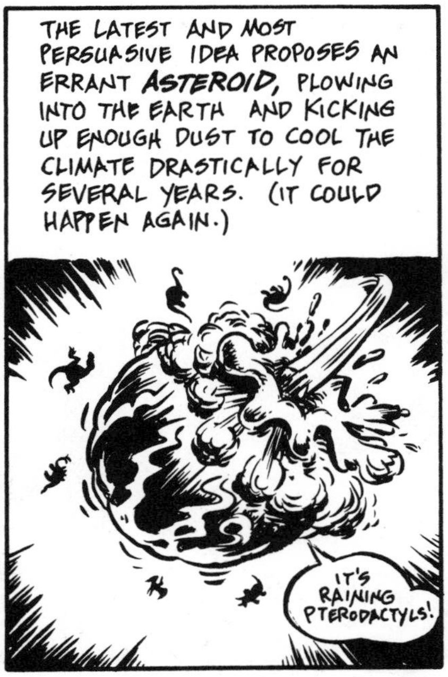
THE LATEST AND MOST PERSUASIVE IDEA PROPOSES AN ERRANT ASTEROID, PLOWING INTO THE EARTH AND KICKING UP ENOUGH DUST TO COOL THE CLIMATE DRASTICALLY FOR SEVERAL YEARS. (IT COULD HAPPEN AGAIN.)
IT'S RAINING PTERODACTYLS!

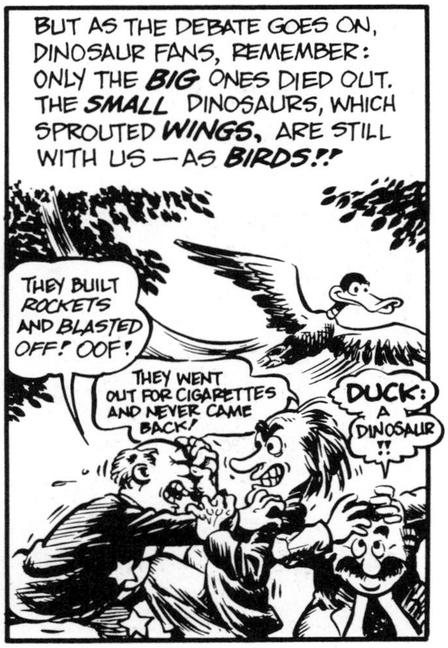
BUT AS THE DEBATE GOES ON, DINOSAUR FANS, REMEMBER: ONLY THE BIG ONES DIED OUT. THE SMALL DINOSAURS, WHICH SPROUTED WINGS, ARE STILL WITH US — AS BIRDS!?
THEY BUILT ROCKETS AND BLASTED OFF! OOF!
THEY WENT OUT FOR CIGARETTES AND NEVER CAME BACK!
DUCK: A DINOSAUR !!

· THE AGE OF MAMMALS ·

EPOCHS OF THE TERTIARY PERIOD (SEE P. 20.)		
EPOCH	DURA-TION (MILLIONS)	YEARS AGO
		3
PLIOCENE	15	
		18
MIOCENE	12	
		30
OLIGOCENE	11	
		41
EOCENE	22	
		63
PALEOCENE	5	
		68
CRETACEOUS PERIOD		

THE TINY MAMMALS SCURRIED OUT OF THE SHADOWS, RACING TO TAKE THE PLACES VACATED BY THE DINOSAURS.

CHIRP

GO UNDERGROUND, FRED!

SOME WENT FOR THE *PLAINS*, DODGING THE 8-FOOT *"TERROR CRANE"* DIATRYMA.

OTHERS CHASED INSECTS INTO THE *AIR*.

AIEEEP

THUD

STILL OTHERS DEVELOPED A TASTE FOR FISH AND TRIED TO *SWIM*.

WOULD YOU PLEASE DROWN AND STOP SCARING THE FISH?

...WHILE OUR ANCESTORS, THE *PRIMATES*, JUST STAYED IN THE TREES, WHERE THEY HAD ALWAYS BEEN!

—ER— WHAT'S THE RUSH?

CRASH CRUNCH CHEW MANGLE

40

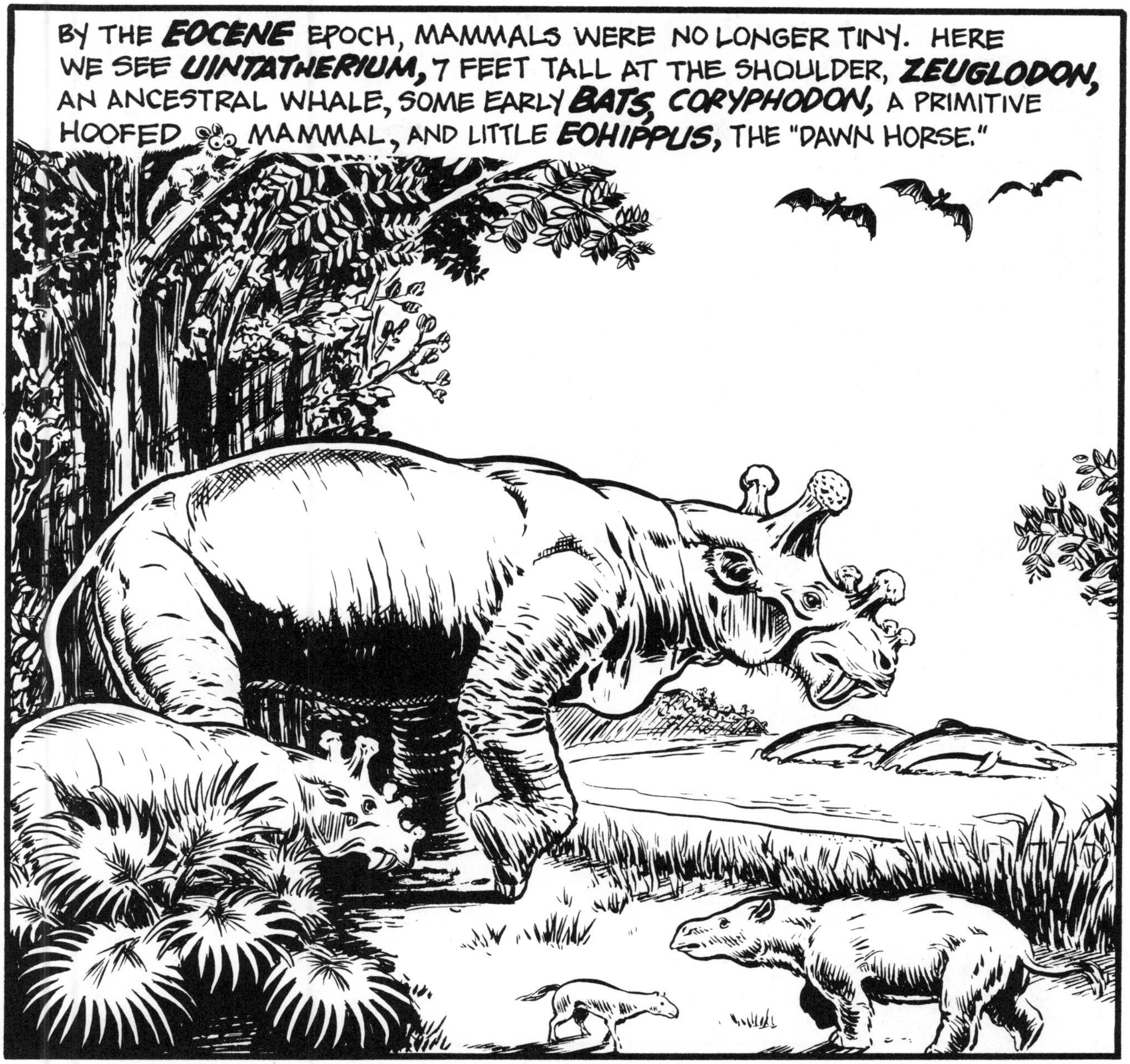
BY THE EOCENE EPOCH, MAMMALS WERE NO LONGER TINY. HERE WE SEE UINTATHERIUM, 7 FEET TALL AT THE SHOULDER, ZEUGLODON, AN ANCESTRAL WHALE, SOME EARLY BATS, CORYPHODON, A PRIMITIVE HOOFED MAMMAL, AND LITTLE EOHIPPUS, THE "DAWN HORSE."

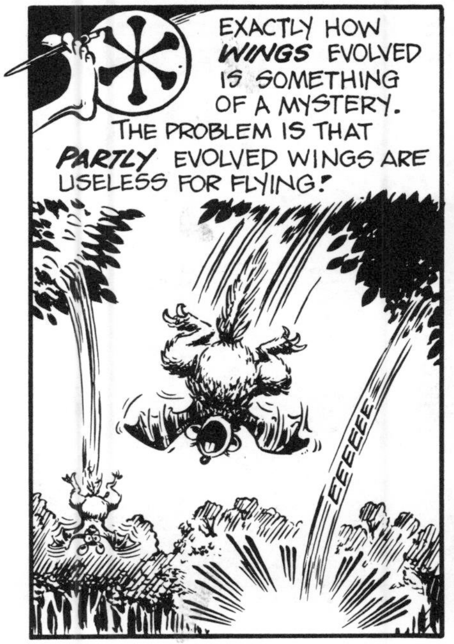
EXACTLY HOW WINGS EVOLVED IS SOMETHING OF A MYSTERY. THE PROBLEM IS THAT PARTLY EVOLVED WINGS ARE USELESS FOR FLYING!

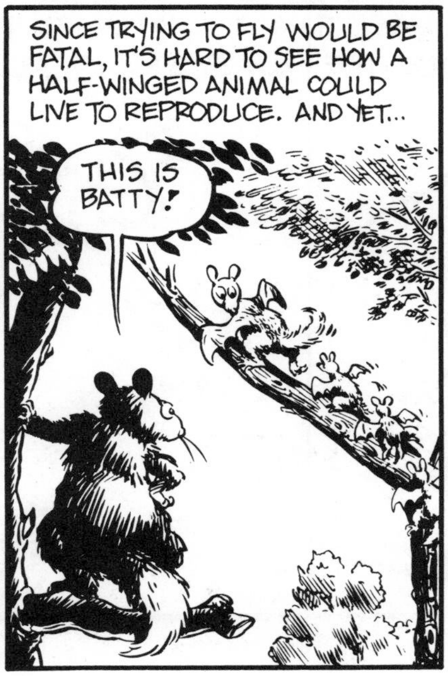
SINCE TRYING TO FLY WOULD BE FATAL, IT'S HARD TO SEE HOW A HALF-WINGED ANIMAL COULD LIVE TO REPRODUCE. AND YET...
THIS IS BATTY!

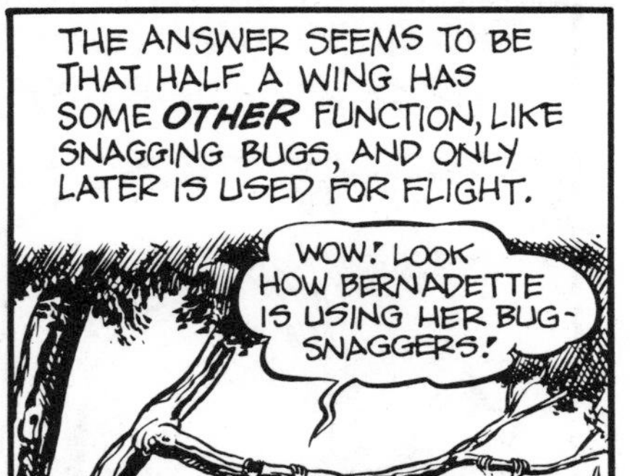
THE ANSWER SEEMS TO BE THAT HALF A WING HAS SOME OTHER FUNCTION, LIKE SNAGGING BUGS, AND ONLY LATER IS USED FOR FLIGHT.
WOW! LOOK HOW BERNADETTE IS USING HER BUG-SNAGGERS!

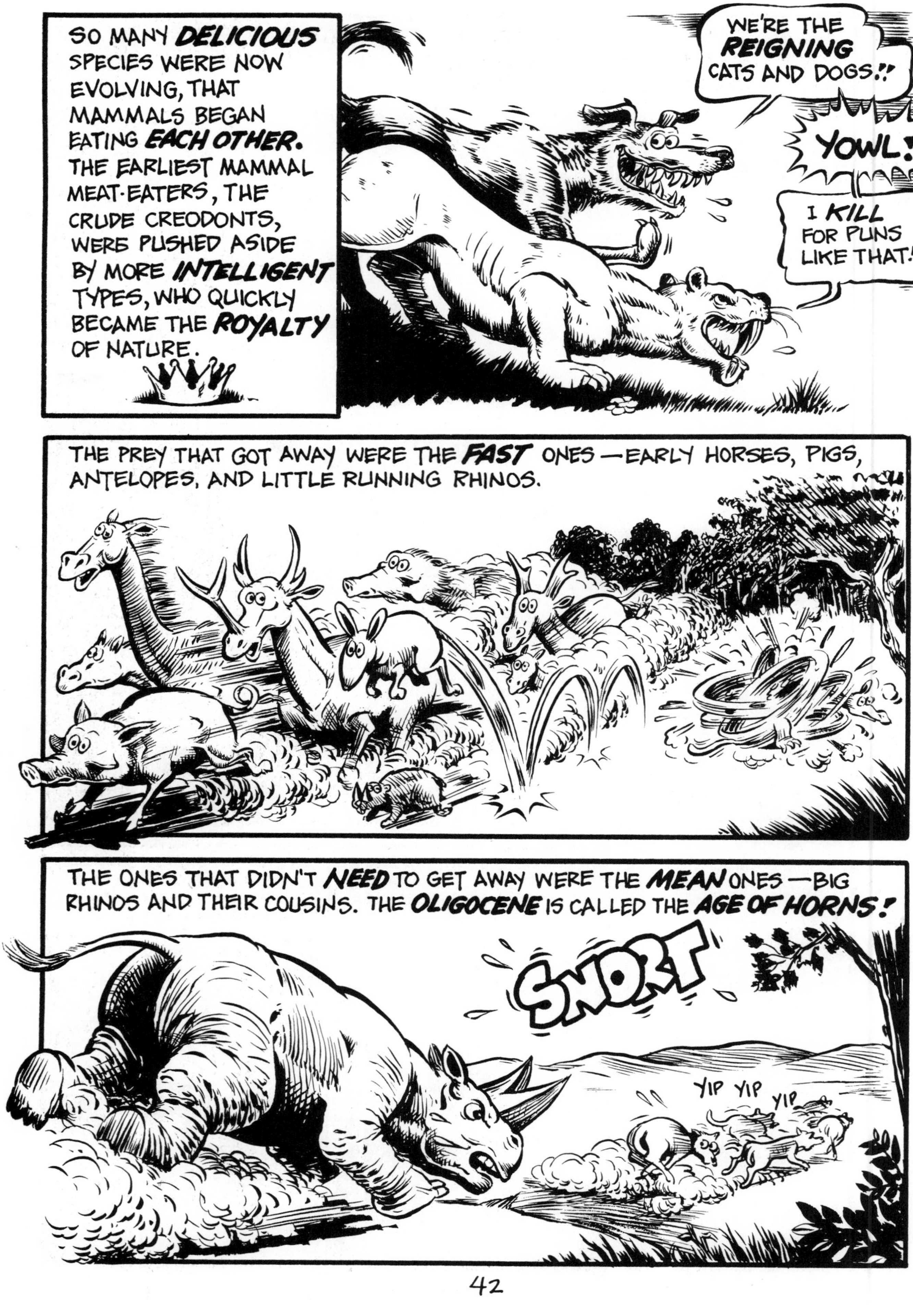
SO MANY DELICIOUS SPECIES WERE NOW EVOLVING, THAT MAMMALS BEGAN EATING EACH OTHER. THE EARLIEST MAMMAL MEAT-EATERS, THE CRUDE CREODONTS, WERE PUSHED ASIDE BY MORE INTELLIGENT TYPES, WHO QUICKLY BECAME THE ROYALTY OF NATURE.
WE'RE THE REIGNING CATS AND DOGS!!
YOWL!
I KILL FOR PUNS LIKE THAT!
THE PREY THAT GOT AWAY WERE THE FAST ONES—EARLY HORSES, PIGS, ANTELOPES, AND LITTLE RUNNING RHINOS.
THE ONES THAT DIDN'T NEED TO GET AWAY WERE THE MEAN ONES—BIG RHINOS AND THEIR COUSINS. THE OLIGOCENE IS CALLED THE AGE OF HORNS!
SNORT
YIP YIP YIP

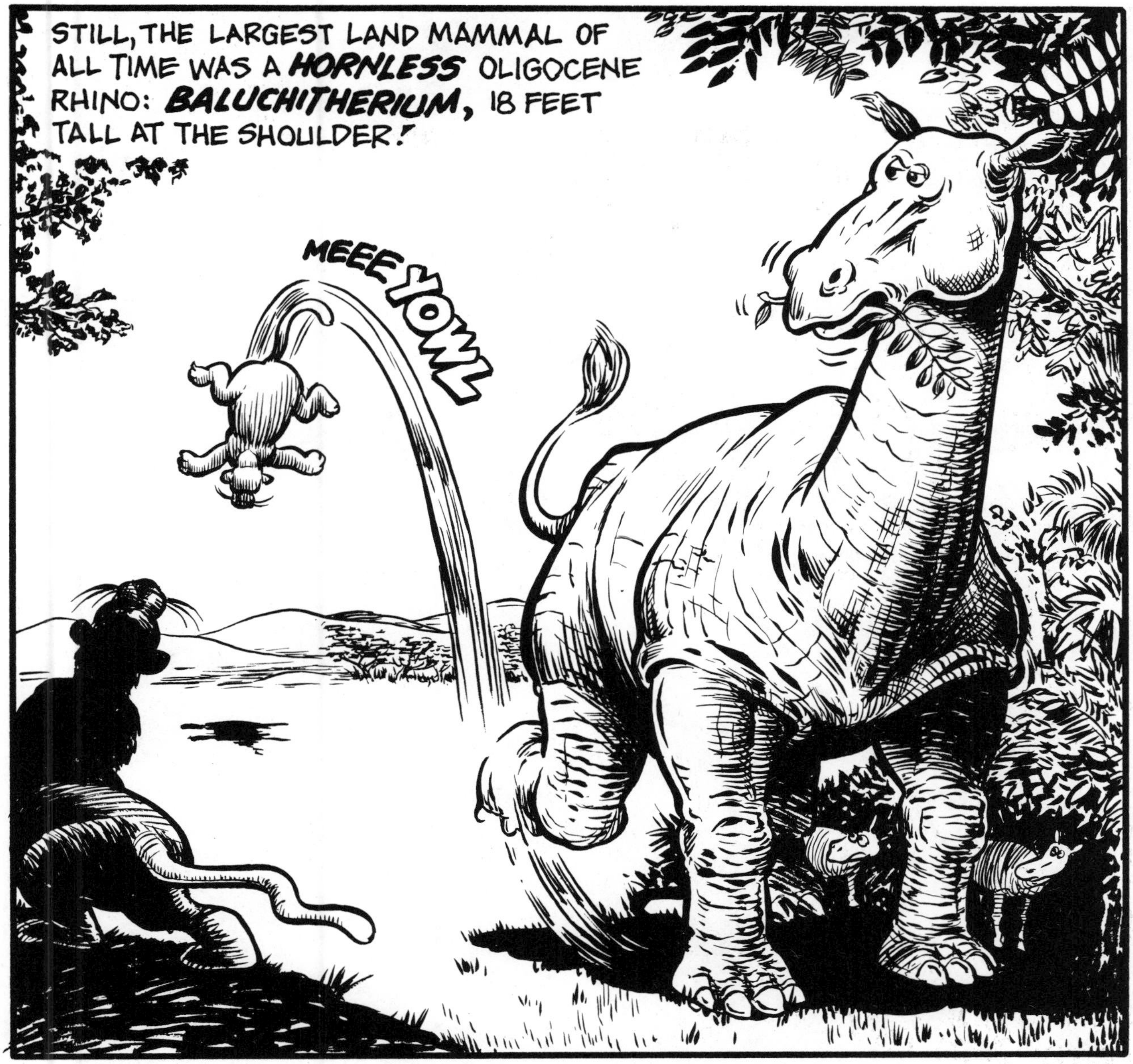
STILL, THE LARGEST LAND MAMMAL OF ALL TIME WAS A **HORNLESS** OLIGOCENE RHINO: **BALUCHITHERIUM**, 18 FEET TALL AT THE SHOULDER!
MEEE YOWL

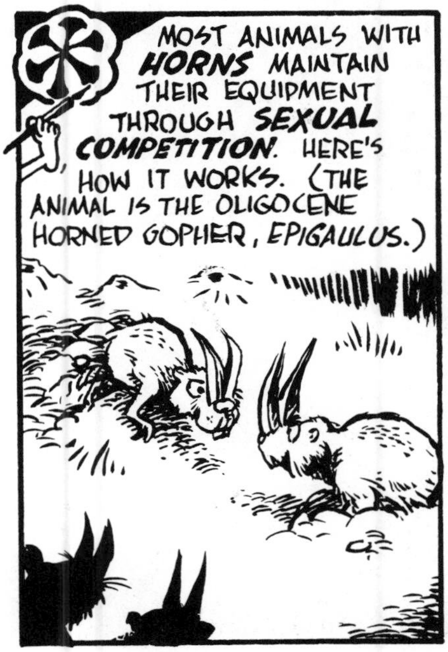
MOST ANIMALS WITH **HORNS** MAINTAIN THEIR EQUIPMENT THROUGH **SEXUAL COMPETITION**. HERE'S HOW IT WORKS. (THE ANIMAL IS THE OLIGOCENE HORNED GOPHER, *EPIGAULUS*.)

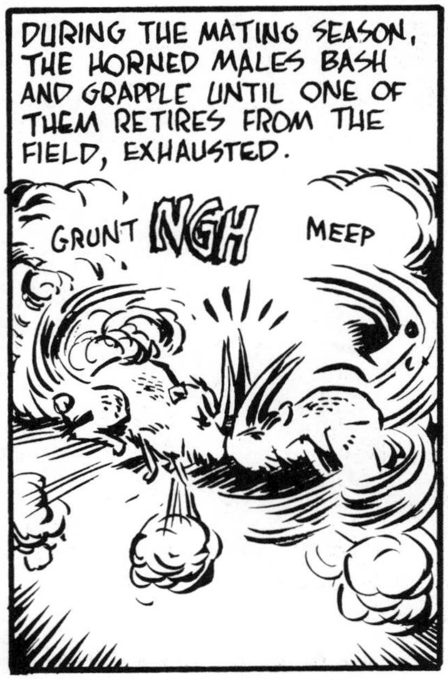
DURING THE MATING SEASON, THE HORNED MALES BASH AND GRAPPLE UNTIL ONE OF THEM RETIRES FROM THE FIELD, EXHAUSTED.
GRUNT
NGH
MEEP

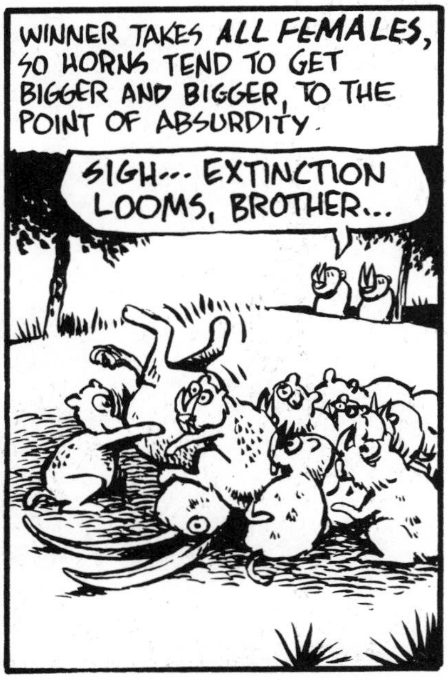
WINNER TAKES **ALL FEMALES**, SO HORNS TEND TO GET BIGGER AND BIGGER, TO THE POINT OF ABSURDITY.
SIGH... EXTINCTION LOOMS, BROTHER...

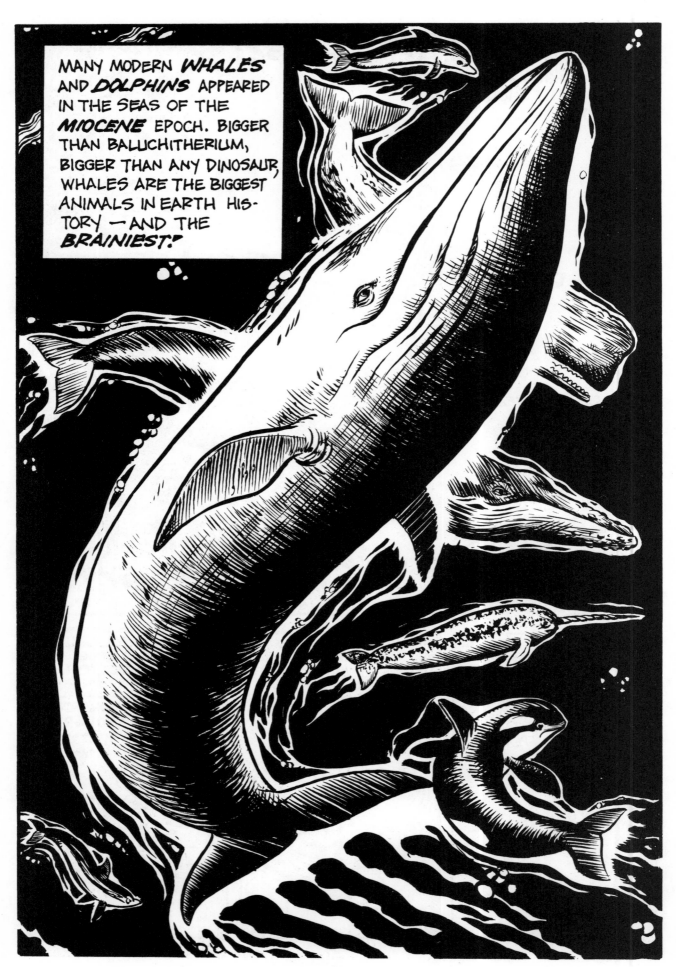

MANY MODERN *WHALES* AND *DOLPHINS* APPEARED IN THE SEAS OF THE *MIOCENE* EPOCH. BIGGER THAN BALUCHITHERIUM, BIGGER THAN ANY DINOSAUR, WHALES ARE THE BIGGEST ANIMALS IN EARTH HISTORY — AND THE *BRAINIEST!*

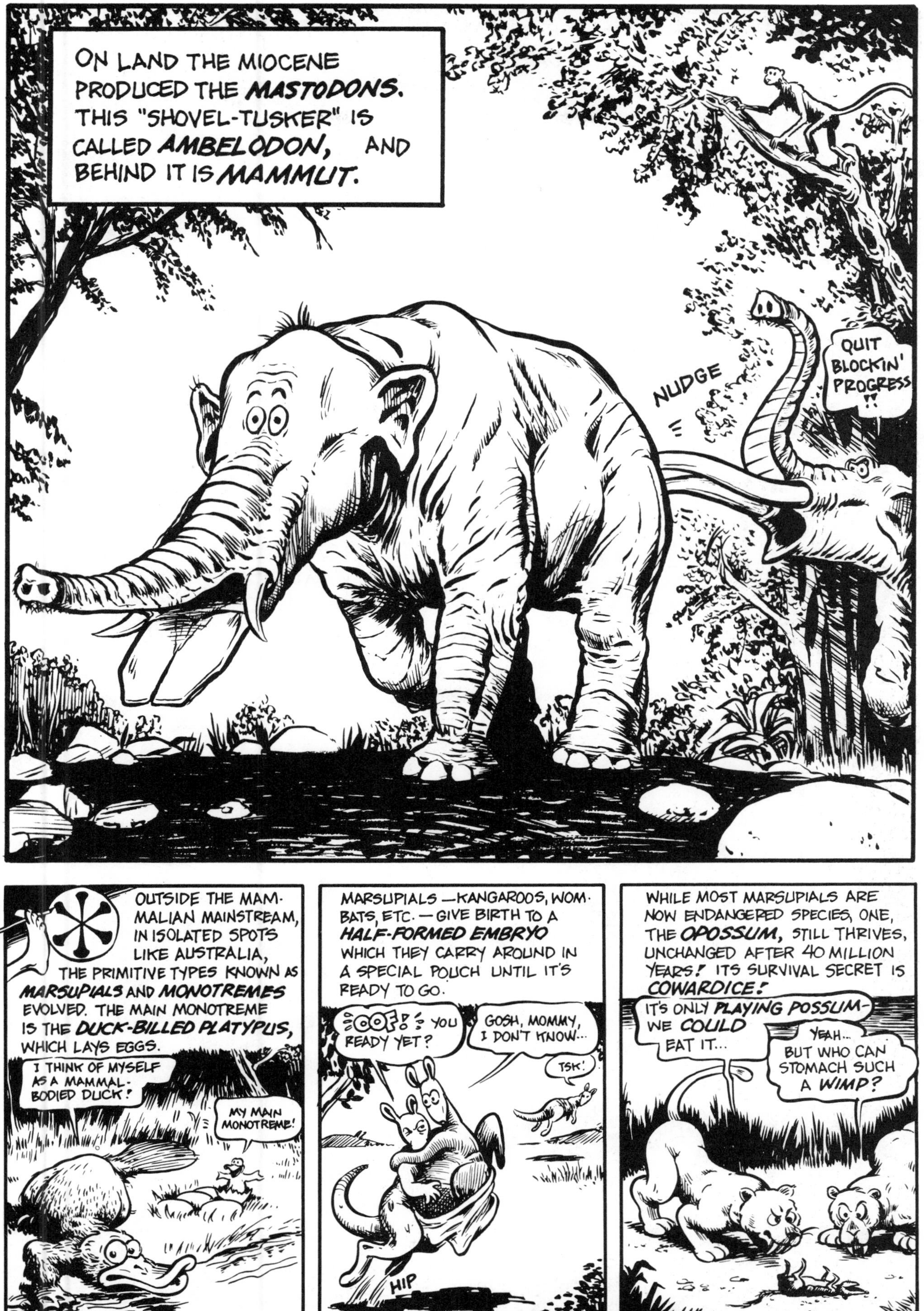
ON LAND THE MIOCENE PRODUCED THE MASTODONS. THIS "SHOVEL-TUSKER" IS CALLED AMBELODON, AND BEHIND IT IS MAMMUT.
NUDGE
QUIT BLOCKIN' PROGRESS!!
OUTSIDE THE MAMMALIAN MAINSTREAM, IN ISOLATED SPOTS LIKE AUSTRALIA, THE PRIMITIVE TYPES KNOWN AS MARSUPIALS AND MONOTREMES EVOLVED. THE MAIN MONOTREME IS THE DUCK-BILLED PLATYPUS, WHICH LAYS EGGS.
I THINK OF MYSELF AS A MAMMAL-BODIED DUCK!
MY MAIN MONOTREME!
MARSUPIALS —KANGAROOS, WOMBATS, ETC. — GIVE BIRTH TO A HALF-FORMED EMBRYO WHICH THEY CARRY AROUND IN A SPECIAL POUCH UNTIL IT'S READY TO GO.
OOF! YOU READY YET?
GOSH, MOMMY, I DON'T KNOW...
TSK!
HIP
WHILE MOST MARSUPIALS ARE NOW ENDANGERED SPECIES, ONE, THE OPOSSUM, STILL THRIVES, UNCHANGED AFTER 40 MILLION YEARS! ITS SURVIVAL SECRET IS COWARDICE!
IT'S ONLY PLAYING POSSUM- WE COULD EAT IT...
YEAH... BUT WHO CAN STOMACH SUCH A WIMP?

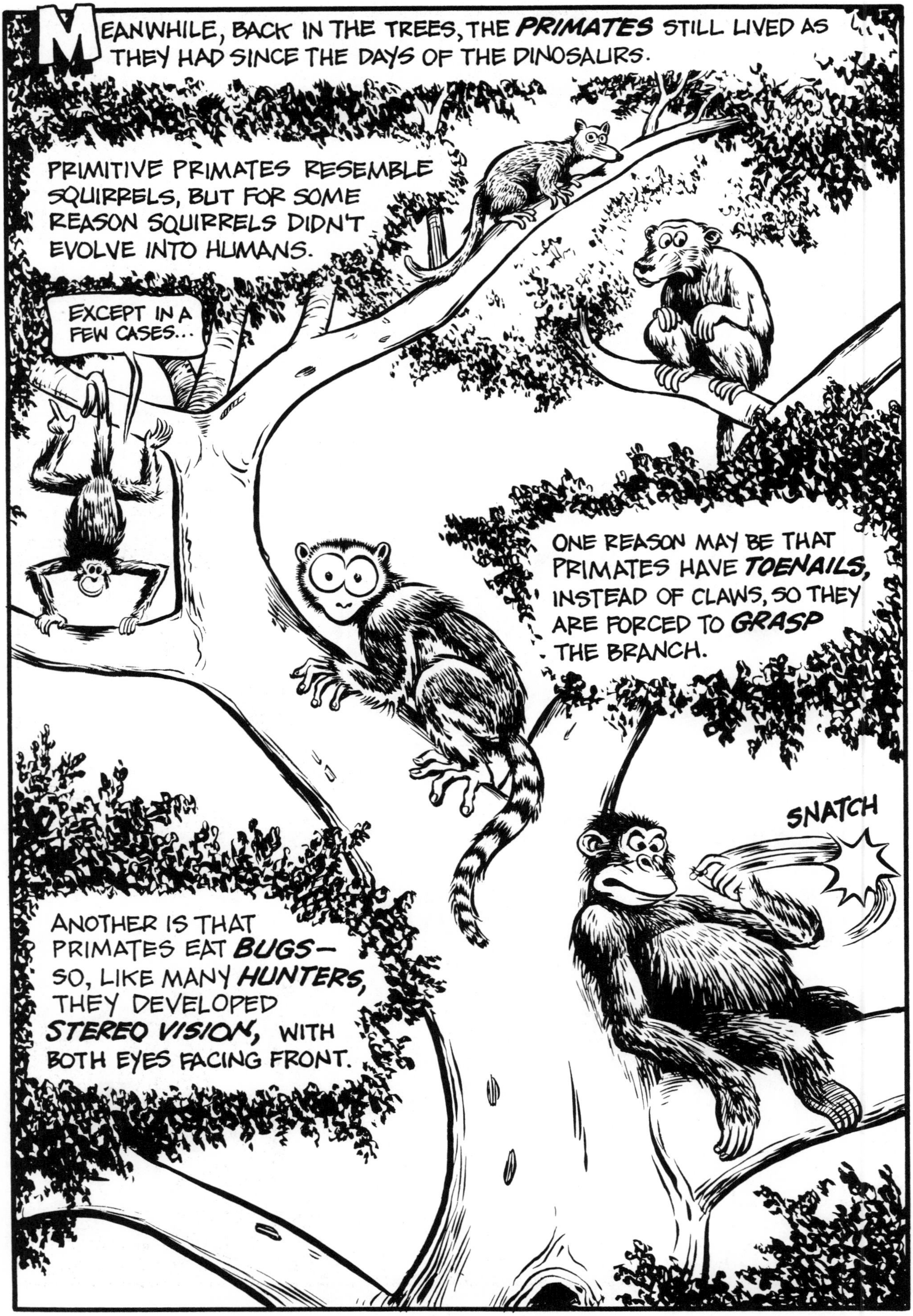
MEANWHILE, BACK IN THE TREES, THE PRIMATES STILL LIVED AS THEY HAD SINCE THE DAYS OF THE DINOSAURS.
PRIMITIVE PRIMATES RESEMBLE SQUIRRELS, BUT FOR SOME REASON SQUIRRELS DIDN'T EVOLVE INTO HUMANS.
EXCEPT IN A FEW CASES...
ONE REASON MAY BE THAT PRIMATES HAVE TOENAILS, INSTEAD OF CLAWS, SO THEY ARE FORCED TO GRASP THE BRANCH.
SNATCH
ANOTHER IS THAT PRIMATES EAT BUGS— SO, LIKE MANY HUNTERS, THEY DEVELOPED STEREO VISION, WITH BOTH EYES FACING FRONT.

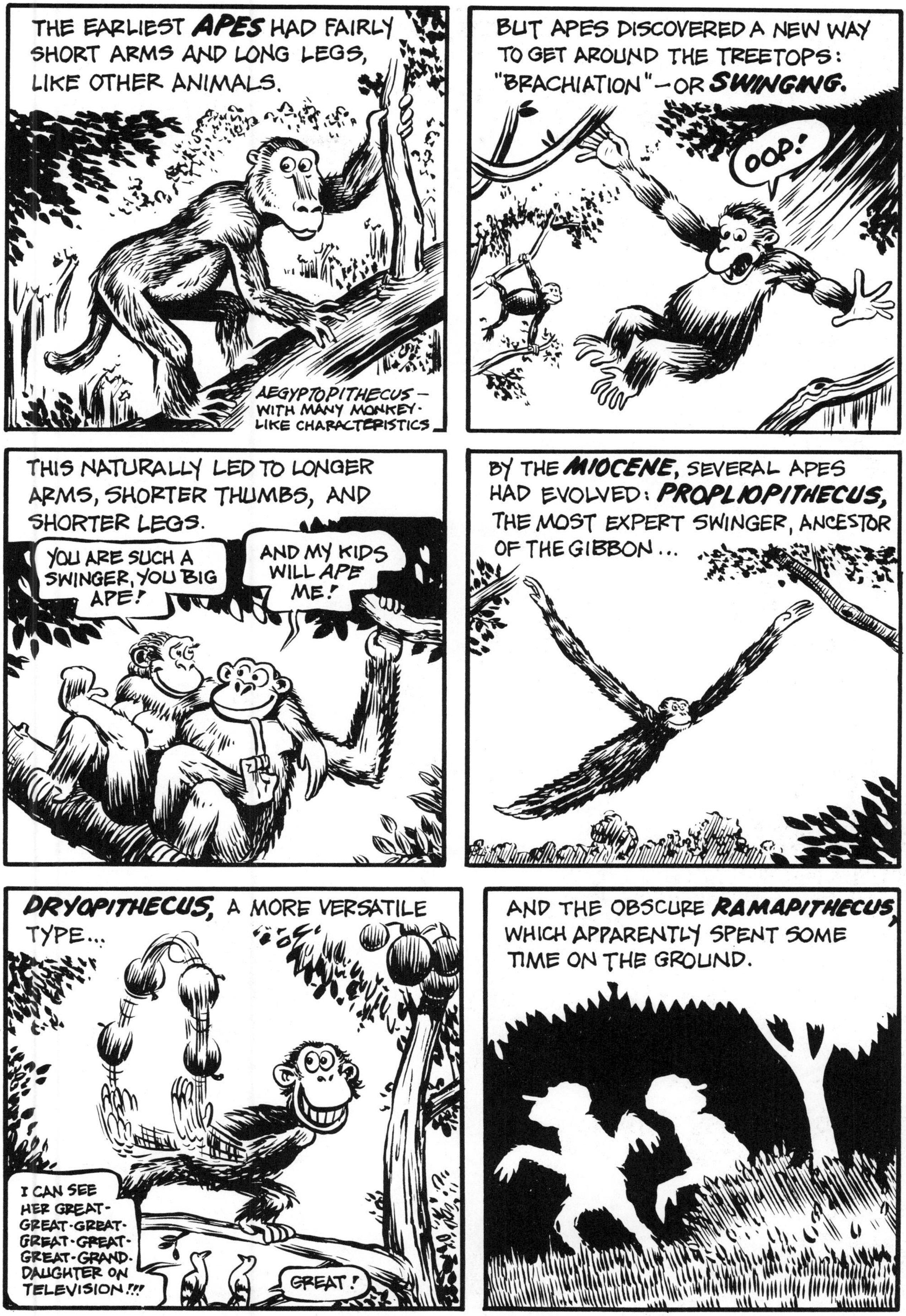
THE EARLIEST APES HAD FAIRLY SHORT ARMS AND LONG LEGS, LIKE OTHER ANIMALS.
AEGYPTOPITHECUS— WITH MANY MONKEY-LIKE CHARACTERISTICS
BUT APES DISCOVERED A NEW WAY TO GET AROUND THE TREETOPS: "BRACHIATION"—OR SWINGING.
OOP!
THIS NATURALLY LED TO LONGER ARMS, SHORTER THUMBS, AND SHORTER LEGS.
YOU ARE SUCH A SWINGER, YOU BIG APE!
AND MY KIDS WILL APE ME!
BY THE MIOCENE, SEVERAL APES HAD EVOLVED: PROPLIOPITHECUS, THE MOST EXPERT SWINGER, ANCESTOR OF THE GIBBON...
DRYOPITHECUS, A MORE VERSATILE TYPE...
I CAN SEE HER GREAT-GREAT-GREAT-GREAT-GREAT-GREAT-GRAND-DAUGHTER ON TELEVISION!!!
GREAT!
AND THE OBSCURE RAMAPITHECUS, WHICH APPARENTLY SPENT SOME TIME ON THE GROUND.

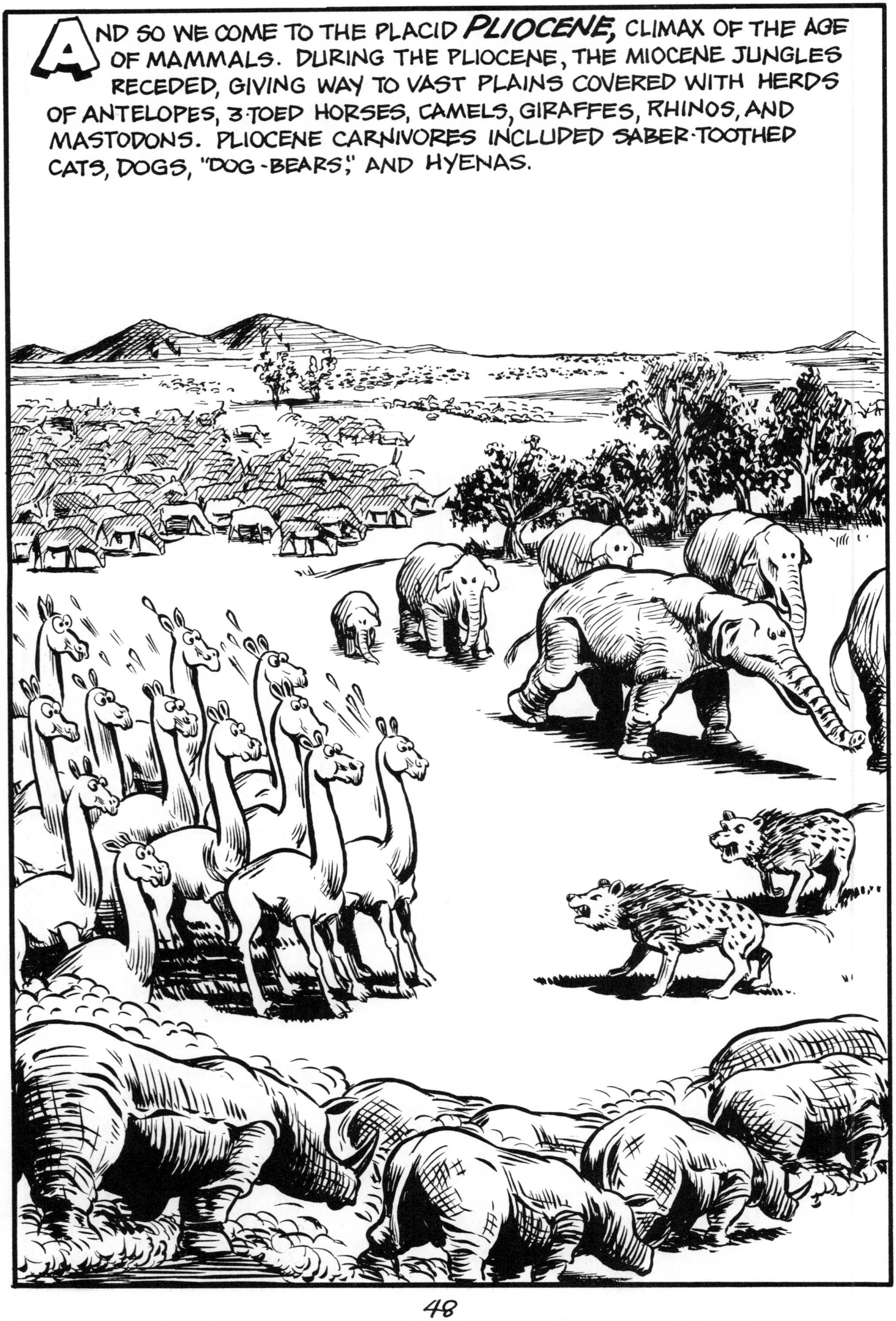
AND SO WE COME TO THE PLACID *PLIOCENE,* CLIMAX OF THE AGE OF MAMMALS. DURING THE PLIOCENE, THE MIOCENE JUNGLES RECEDED, GIVING WAY TO VAST PLAINS COVERED WITH HERDS OF ANTELOPES, 3-TOED HORSES, CAMELS, GIRAFFES, RHINOS, AND MASTODONS. PLIOCENE CARNIVORES INCLUDED SABER-TOOTHED CATS, DOGS, "DOG-BEARS," AND HYENAS.

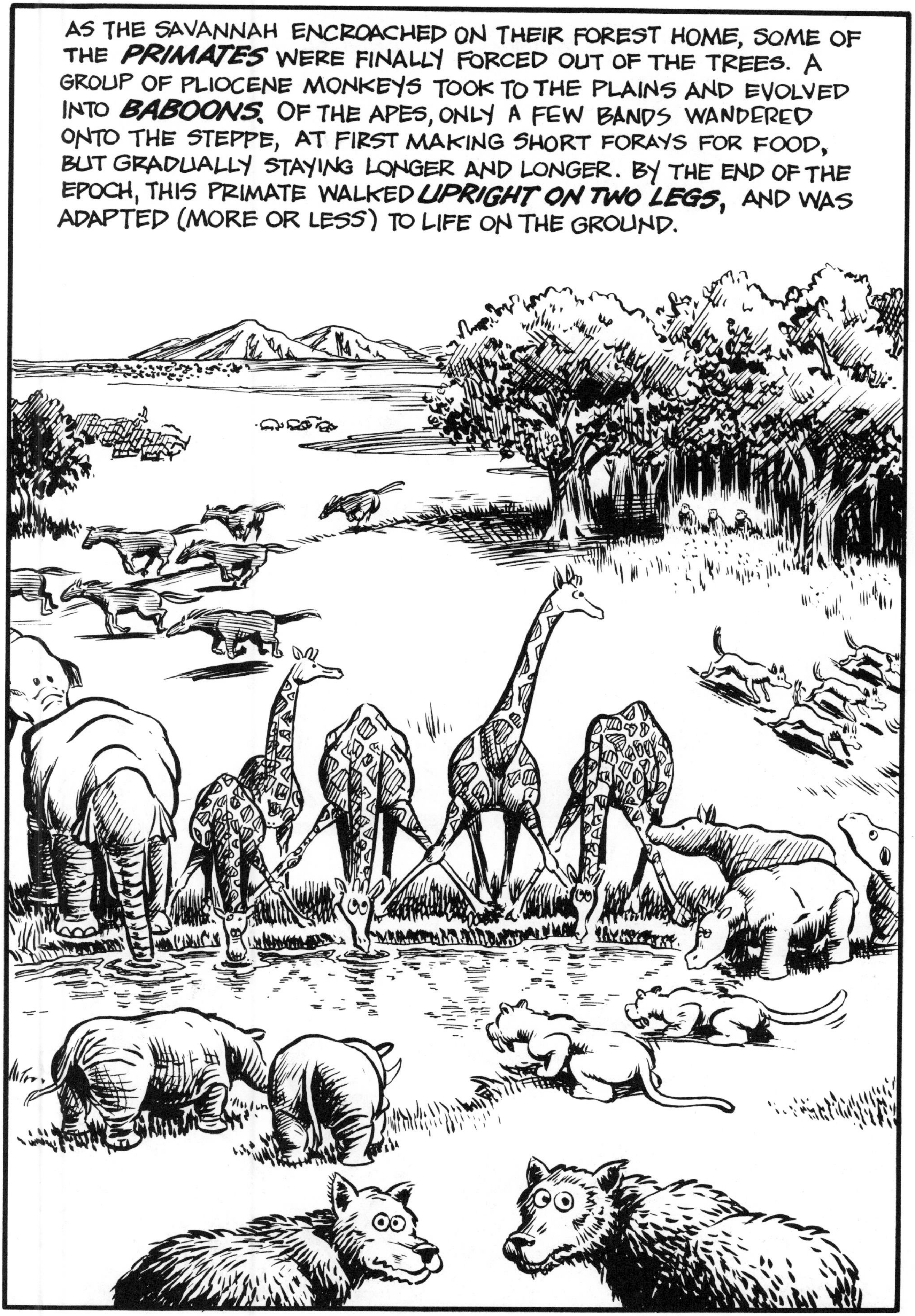
AS THE SAVANNAH ENCROACHED ON THEIR FOREST HOME, SOME OF THE PRIMATES WERE FINALLY FORCED OUT OF THE TREES. A GROUP OF PLIOCENE MONKEYS TOOK TO THE PLAINS AND EVOLVED INTO BABOONS. OF THE APES, ONLY A FEW BANDS WANDERED ONTO THE STEPPE, AT FIRST MAKING SHORT FORAYS FOR FOOD, BUT GRADUALLY STAYING LONGER AND LONGER. BY THE END OF THE EPOCH, THIS PRIMATE WALKED UPRIGHT ON TWO LEGS, AND WAS ADAPTED (MORE OR LESS) TO LIFE ON THE GROUND.

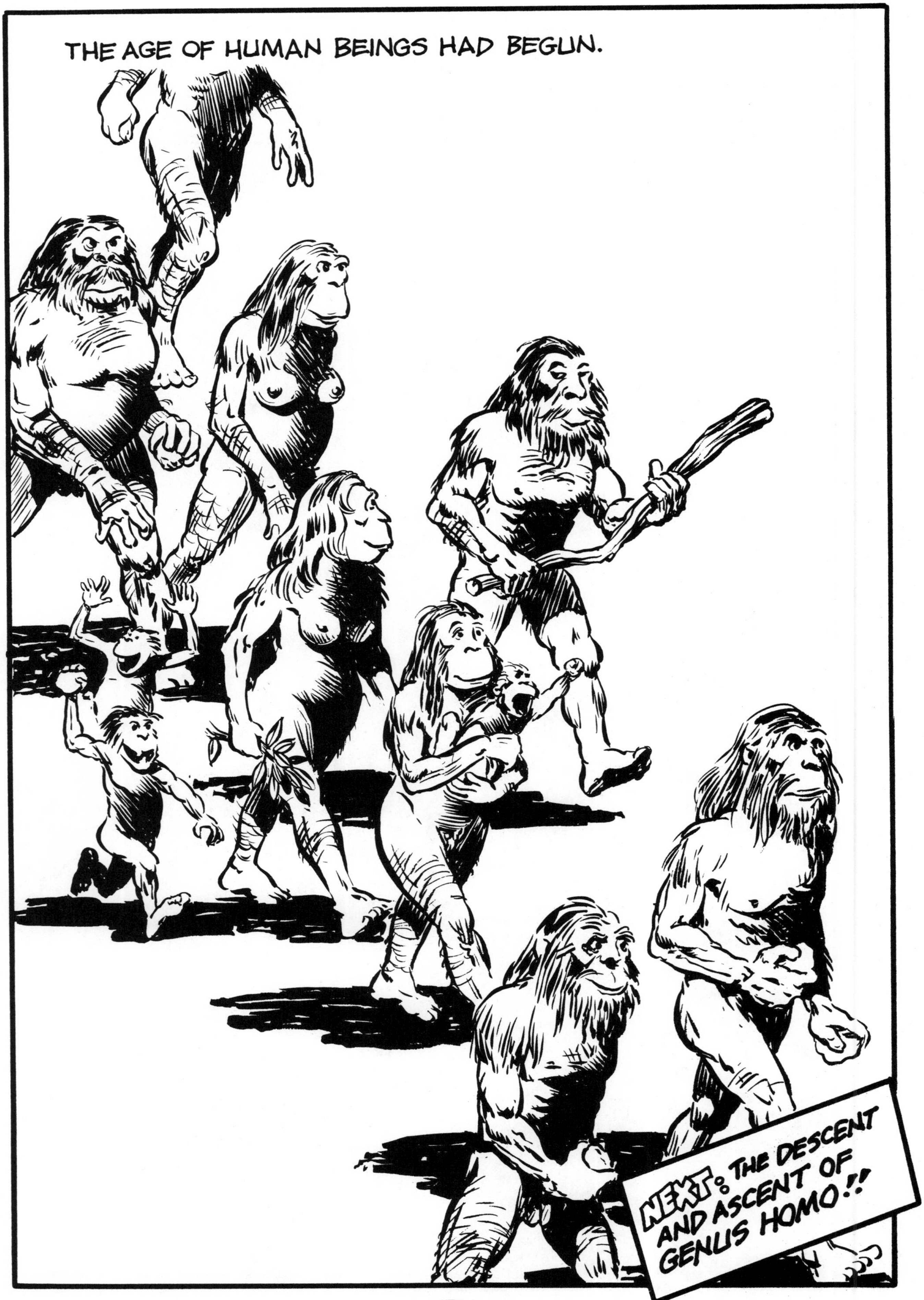
THE AGE OF HUMAN BEINGS HAD BEGUN.
NEXT: THE DESCENT AND ASCENT OF GENUS HOMO!!

INTRODUCTION

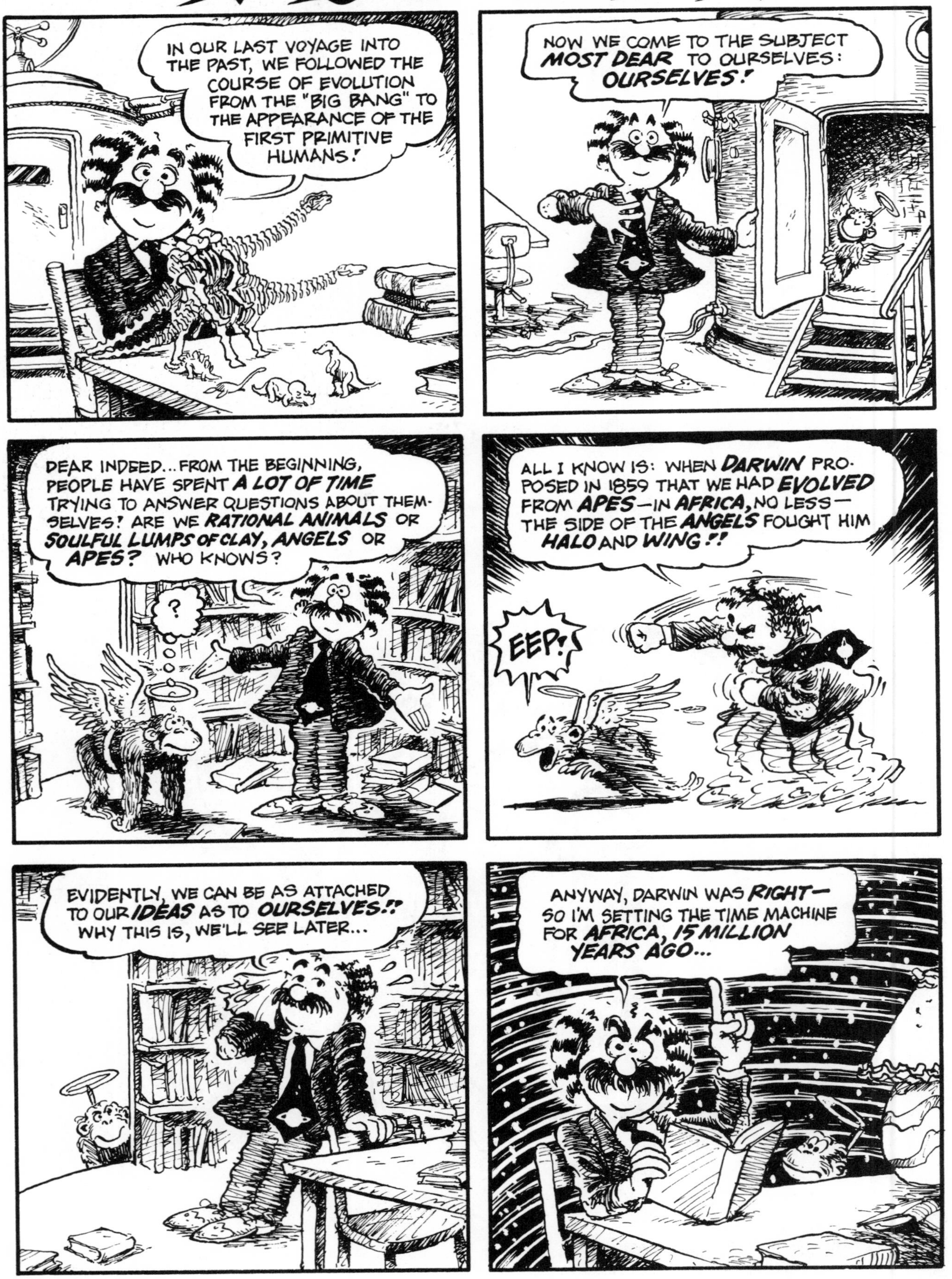
IN OUR LAST VOYAGE INTO THE PAST, WE FOLLOWED THE COURSE OF EVOLUTION FROM THE "BIG BANG" TO THE APPEARANCE OF THE FIRST PRIMITIVE HUMANS!
NOW WE COME TO THE SUBJECT MOST DEAR TO OURSELVES: OURSELVES!
DEAR INDEED... FROM THE BEGINNING, PEOPLE HAVE SPENT A LOT OF TIME TRYING TO ANSWER QUESTIONS ABOUT THEM-SELVES! ARE WE RATIONAL ANIMALS OR SOULFUL LUMPS OF CLAY, ANGELS OR APES? WHO KNOWS?
?
ALL I KNOW IS: WHEN DARWIN PRO-POSED IN 1859 THAT WE HAD EVOLVED FROM APES—IN AFRICA, NO LESS—THE SIDE OF THE ANGELS FOUGHT HIM HALO AND WING!!
EEP!
EVIDENTLY, WE CAN BE AS ATTACHED TO OUR IDEAS AS TO OURSELVES!? WHY THIS IS, WE'LL SEE LATER...
ANYWAY, DARWIN WAS RIGHT—SO I'M SETTING THE TIME MACHINE FOR AFRICA, 15 MILLION YEARS AGO...

THE CARTOON HISTORY OF THE UNIVERSE

VOLUME 2

STICKS AND STONES

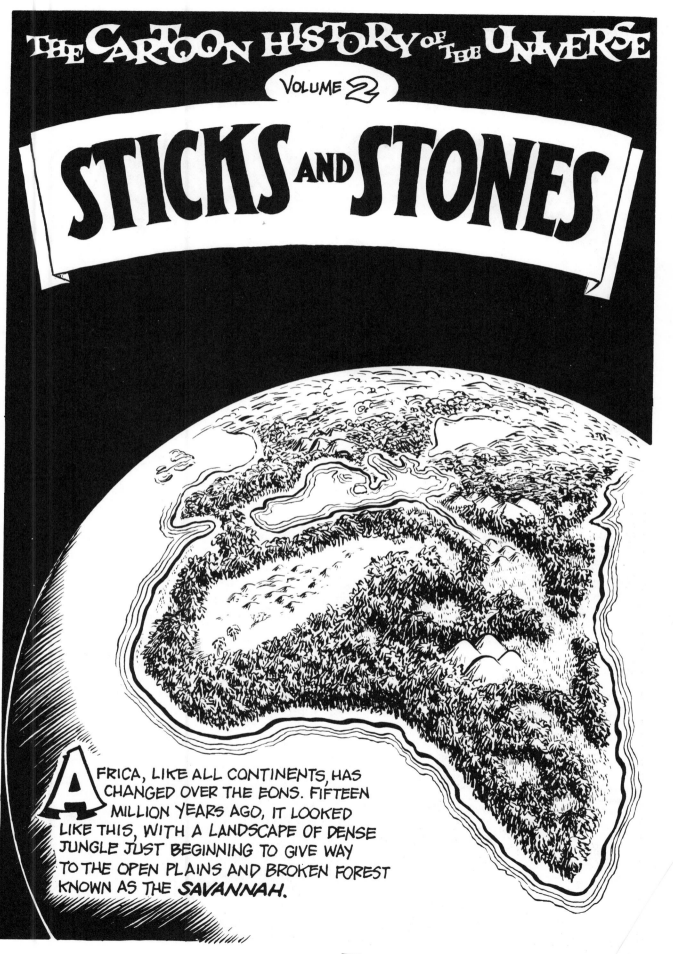

AFRICA, LIKE ALL CONTINENTS, HAS CHANGED OVER THE EONS. FIFTEEN MILLION YEARS AGO, IT LOOKED LIKE THIS, WITH A LANDSCAPE OF DENSE JUNGLE JUST BEGINNING TO GIVE WAY TO THE OPEN PLAINS AND BROKEN FOREST KNOWN AS THE *SAVANNAH.*

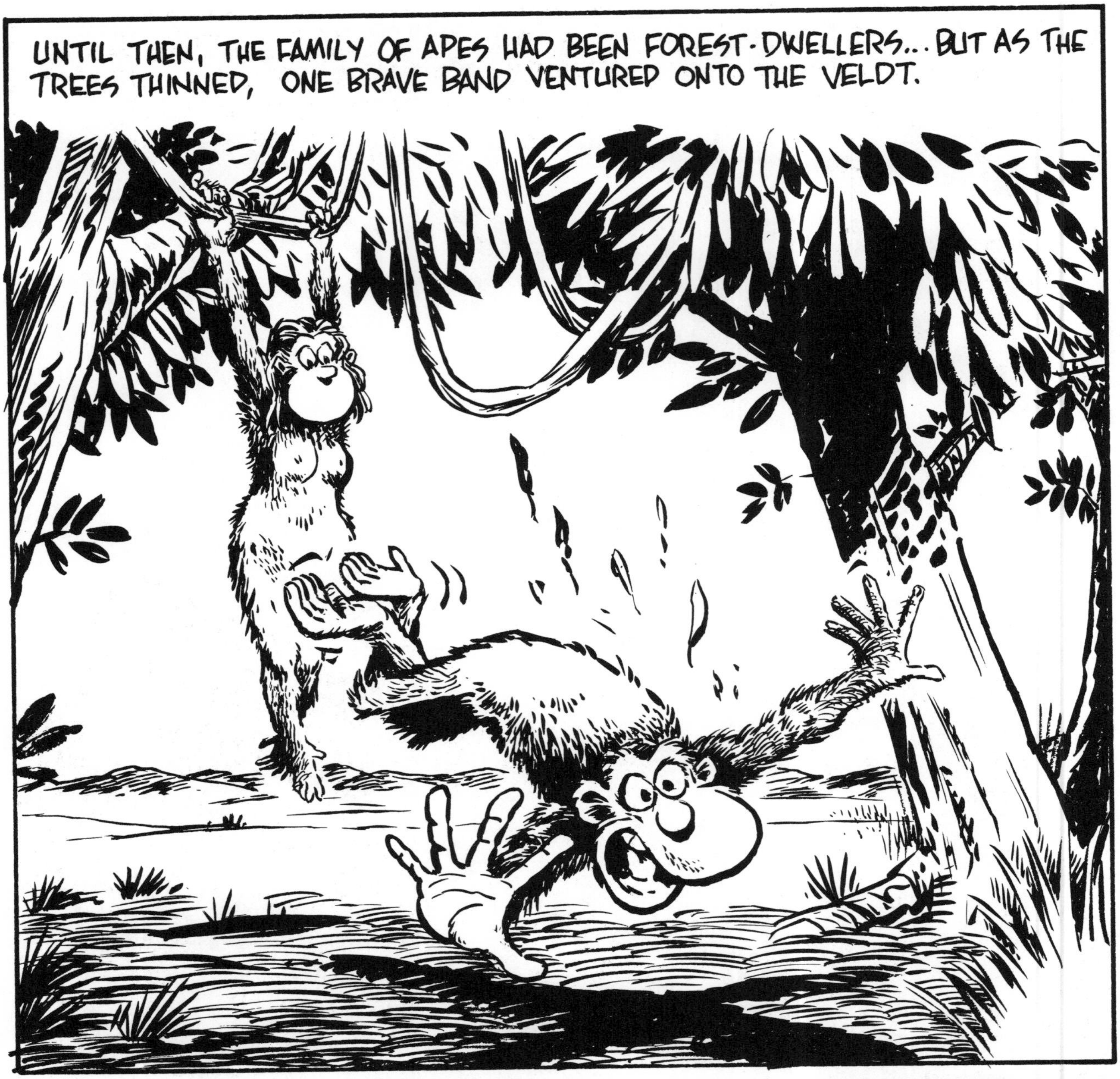
UNTIL THEN, THE FAMILY OF APES HAD BEEN FOREST-DWELLERS... BUT AS THE TREES THINNED, ONE BRAVE BAND VENTURED ONTO THE VELDT.

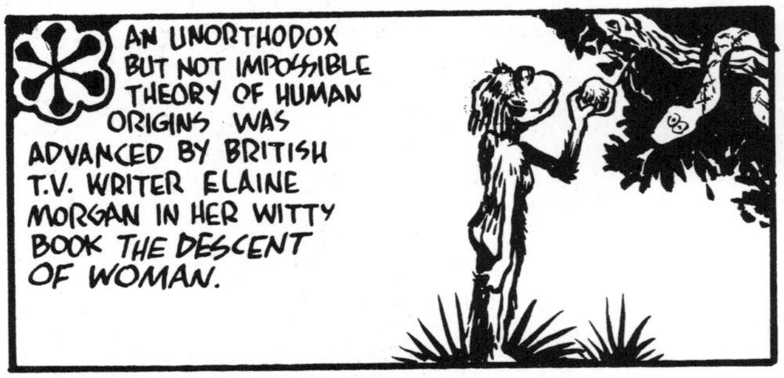
AN UNORTHODOX BUT NOT IMPOSSIBLE THEORY OF HUMAN ORIGINS WAS ADVANCED BY BRITISH T.V. WRITER ELAINE MORGAN IN HER WITTY BOOK *THE DESCENT OF WOMAN.*

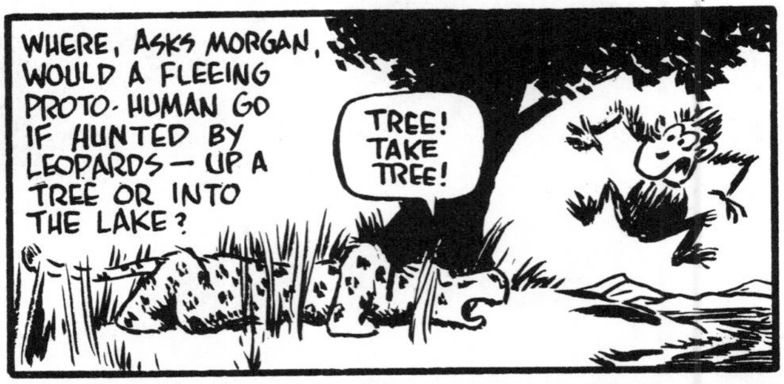
WHERE, ASKS MORGAN, WOULD A FLEEING PROTO-HUMAN GO IF HUNTED BY LEOPARDS — UP A TREE OR INTO THE LAKE?
TREE! TAKE TREE!

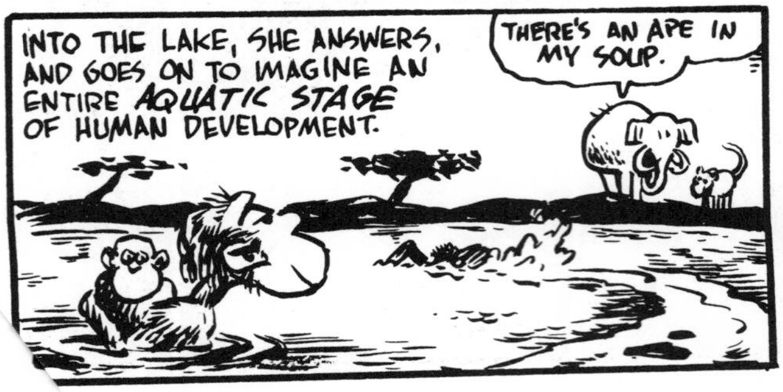
INTO THE LAKE, SHE ANSWERS, AND GOES ON TO IMAGINE AN ENTIRE *AQUATIC STAGE* OF HUMAN DEVELOPMENT.
THERE'S AN APE IN MY SOUP.

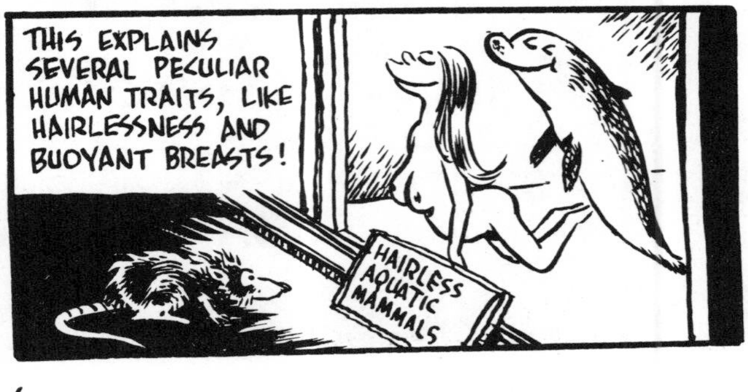
THIS EXPLAINS SEVERAL PECULIAR HUMAN TRAITS, LIKE HAIRLESSNESS AND BUOYANT BREASTS!
HAIRLESS AQUATIC MAMMALS

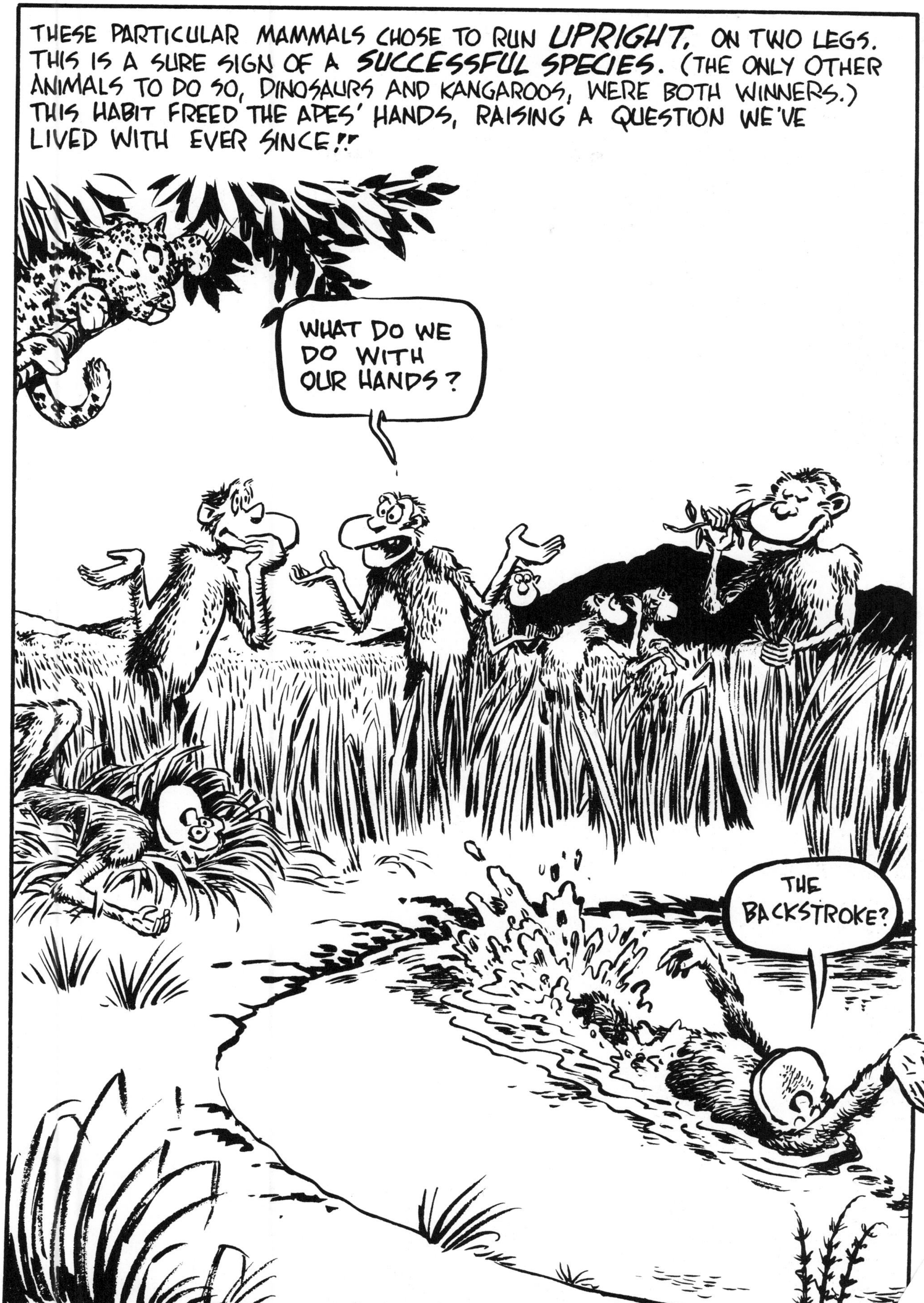
THESE PARTICULAR MAMMALS CHOSE TO RUN UPRIGHT, ON TWO LEGS. THIS IS A SURE SIGN OF A SUCCESSFUL SPECIES. (THE ONLY OTHER ANIMALS TO DO SO, DINOSAURS AND KANGAROOS, WERE BOTH WINNERS.) THIS HABIT FREED THE APES' HANDS, RAISING A QUESTION WE'VE LIVED WITH EVER SINCE!!
WHAT DO WE DO WITH OUR HANDS?
THE BACKSTROKE?

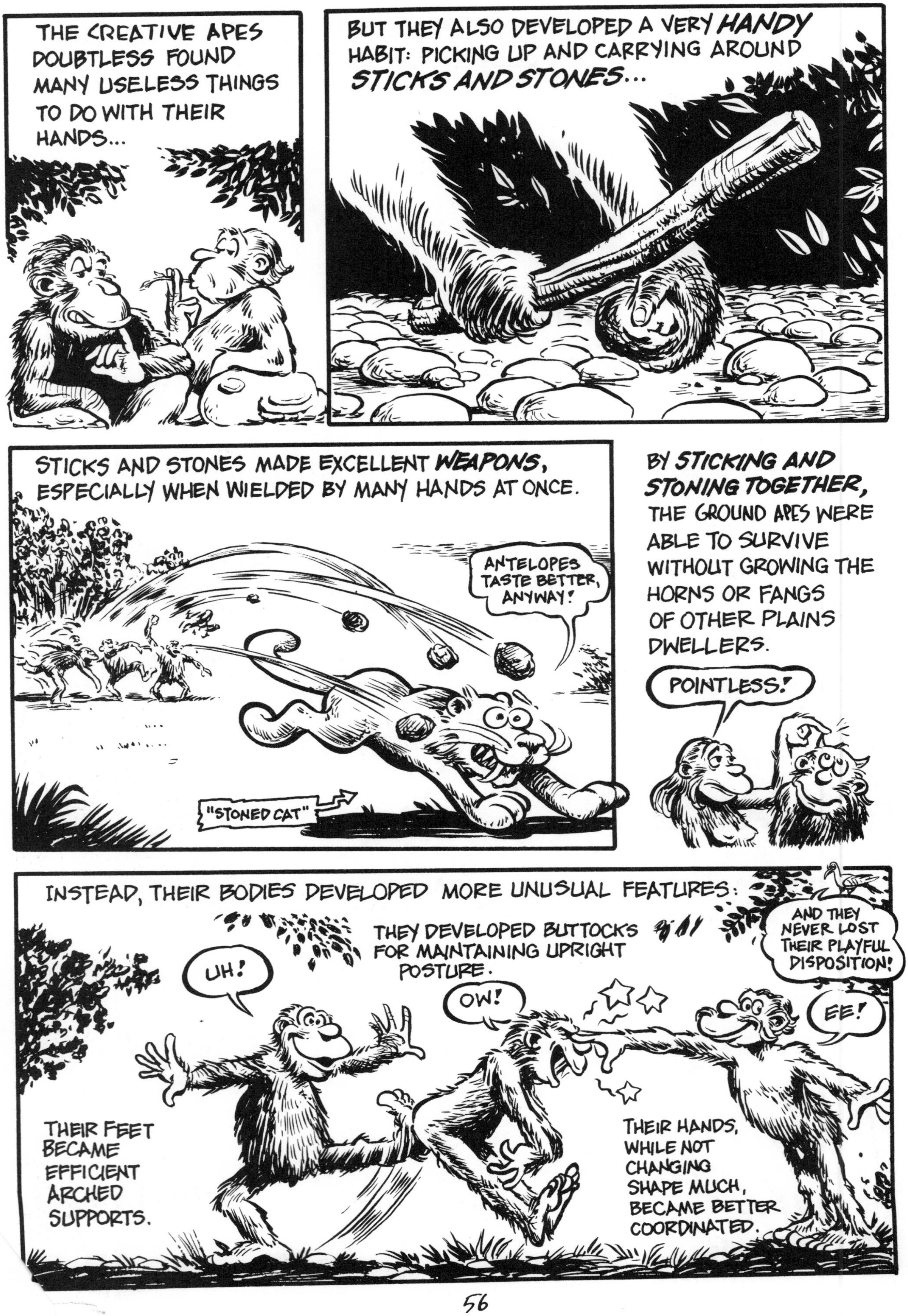
THE CREATIVE APES DOUBTLESS FOUND MANY USELESS THINGS TO DO WITH THEIR HANDS...
BUT THEY ALSO DEVELOPED A VERY HANDY HABIT: PICKING UP AND CARRYING AROUND STICKS AND STONES...
STICKS AND STONES MADE EXCELLENT WEAPONS, ESPECIALLY WHEN WIELDED BY MANY HANDS AT ONCE.
ANTELOPES TASTE BETTER, ANYWAY!
"STONED CAT"
BY STICKING AND STONING TOGETHER, THE GROUND APES WERE ABLE TO SURVIVE WITHOUT GROWING THE HORNS OR FANGS OF OTHER PLAINS DWELLERS.
POINTLESS!
INSTEAD, THEIR BODIES DEVELOPED MORE UNUSUAL FEATURES:
UH!
THEY DEVELOPED BUTTOCKS FOR MAINTAINING UPRIGHT POSTURE.
OW!
AND THEY NEVER LOST THEIR PLAYFUL DISPOSITION!
EE!
THEIR FEET BECAME EFFICIENT ARCHED SUPPORTS.
THEIR HANDS, WHILE NOT CHANGING SHAPE MUCH, BECAME BETTER COORDINATED.

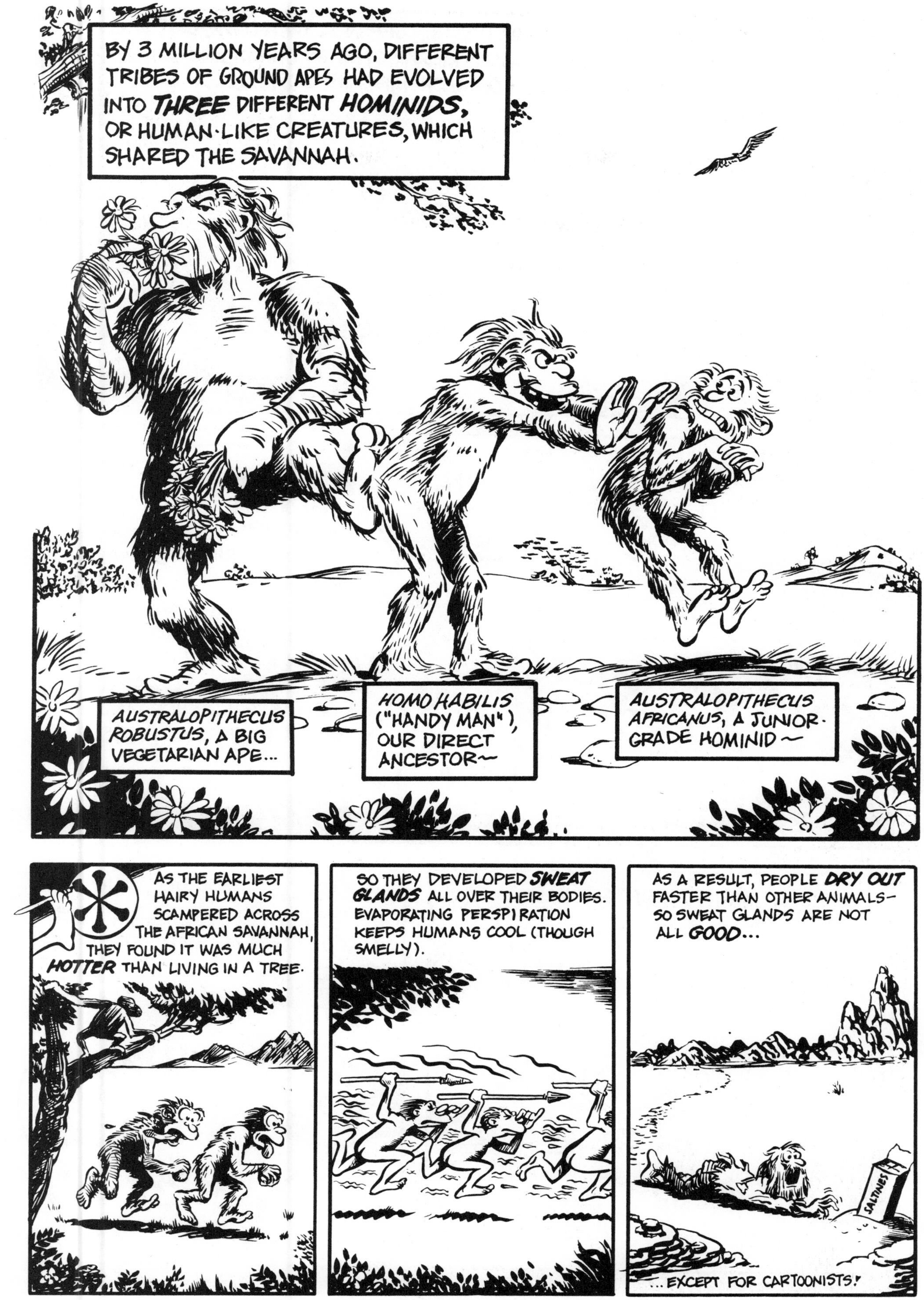
BY 3 MILLION YEARS AGO, DIFFERENT TRIBES OF GROUND APES HAD EVOLVED INTO THREE DIFFERENT HOMINIDS, OR HUMAN-LIKE CREATURES, WHICH SHARED THE SAVANNAH.
AUSTRALOPITHECUS ROBUSTUS, A BIG VEGETARIAN APE...
HOMO HABILIS ("HANDY MAN"), OUR DIRECT ANCESTOR~
AUSTRALOPITHECUS AFRICANUS, A JUNIOR-GRADE HOMINID~
AS THE EARLIEST HAIRY HUMANS SCAMPERED ACROSS THE AFRICAN SAVANNAH, THEY FOUND IT WAS MUCH HOTTER THAN LIVING IN A TREE.
SO THEY DEVELOPED SWEAT GLANDS ALL OVER THEIR BODIES. EVAPORATING PERSPIRATION KEEPS HUMANS COOL (THOUGH SMELLY).
AS A RESULT, PEOPLE DRY OUT FASTER THAN OTHER ANIMALS- SO SWEAT GLANDS ARE NOT ALL GOOD...
SALTINES
...EXCEPT FOR CARTOONISTS!

WHAT GAVE *HABILIS* THE EDGE, IT APPEARS, WAS ITS ***COOPERATIVE SOCIAL LIFE***...

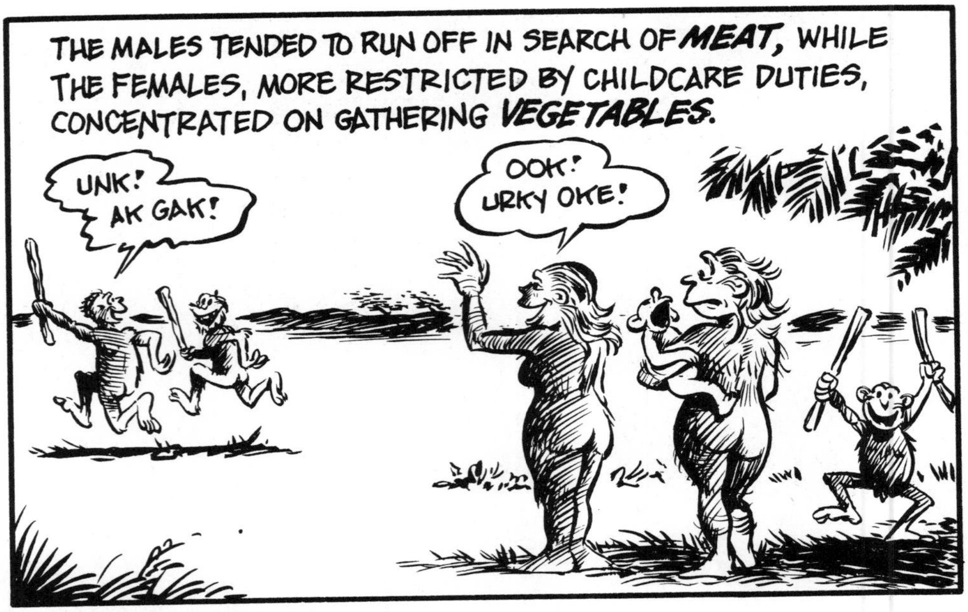
THE MALES TENDED TO RUN OFF IN SEARCH OF MEAT, WHILE THE FEMALES, MORE RESTRICTED BY CHILDCARE DUTIES, CONCENTRATED ON GATHERING VEGETABLES.
UNK! AK GAK!
OOK! URKY OKE!

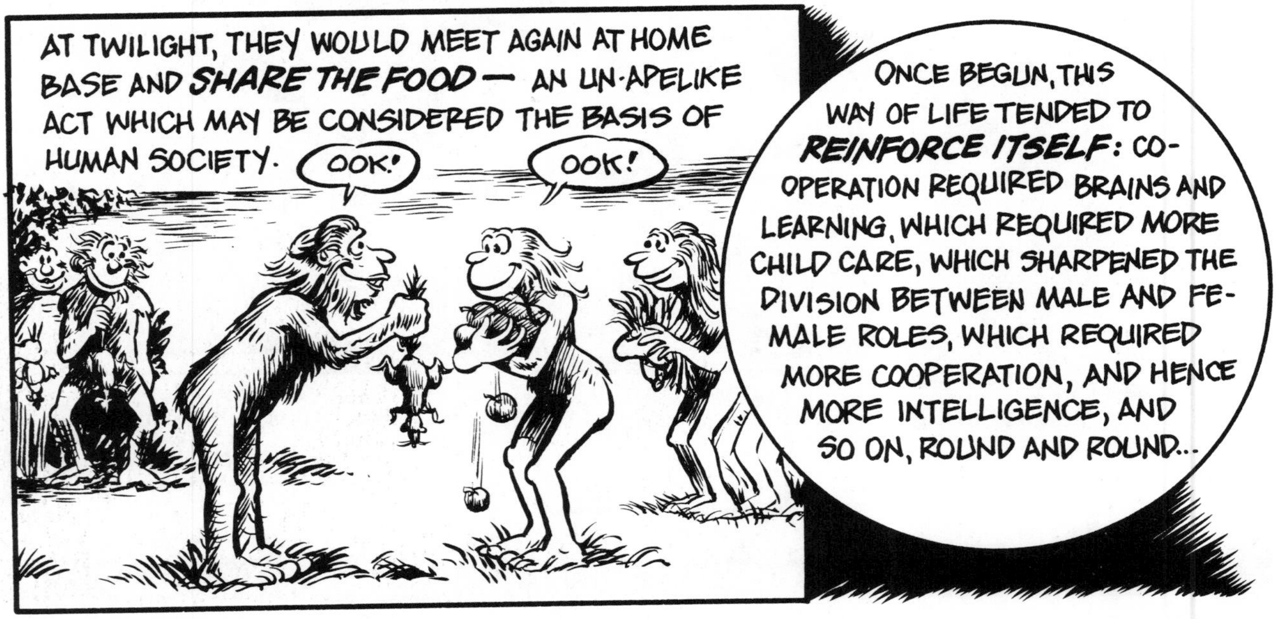
AT TWILIGHT, THEY WOULD MEET AGAIN AT HOME BASE AND SHARE THE FOOD — AN UN-APELIKE ACT WHICH MAY BE CONSIDERED THE BASIS OF HUMAN SOCIETY.
OOK!
OOK!
ONCE BEGUN, THIS WAY OF LIFE TENDED TO REINFORCE ITSELF: CO-OPERATION REQUIRED BRAINS AND LEARNING, WHICH REQUIRED MORE CHILD CARE, WHICH SHARPENED THE DIVISION BETWEEN MALE AND FE-MALE ROLES, WHICH REQUIRED MORE COOPERATION, AND HENCE MORE INTELLIGENCE, AND SO ON, ROUND AND ROUND...

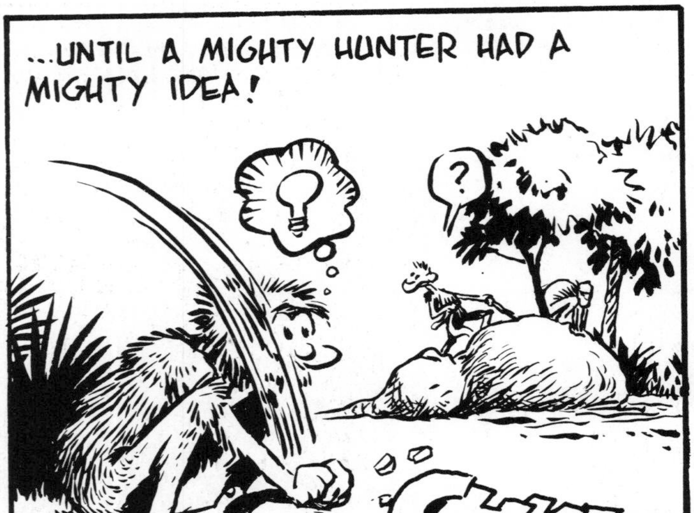
...UNTIL A MIGHTY HUNTER HAD A MIGHTY IDEA!
?
CHUK

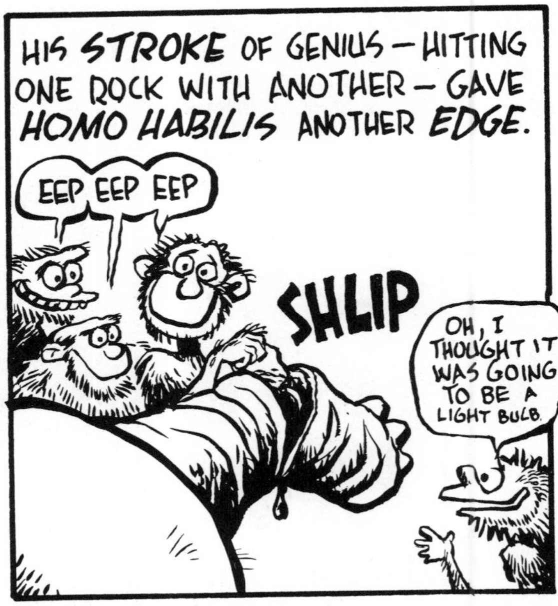
HIS STROKE OF GENIUS — HITTING ONE ROCK WITH ANOTHER — GAVE HOMO HABILIS ANOTHER EDGE.
EEP EEP EEP
SHLIP
OH, I THOUGHT IT WAS GOING TO BE A LIGHT BULB.

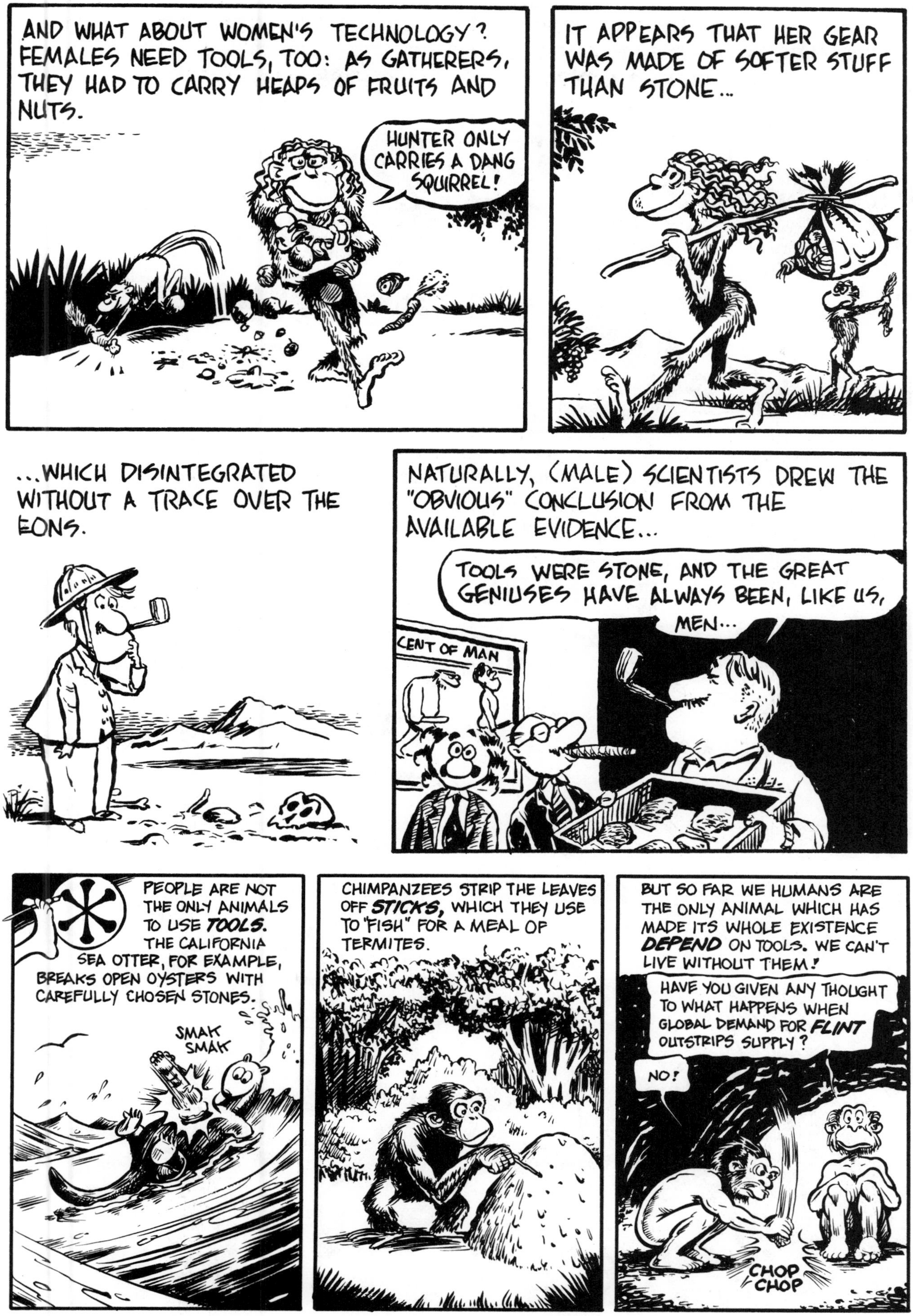
AND WHAT ABOUT WOMEN'S TECHNOLOGY? FEMALES NEED TOOLS, TOO: AS GATHERERS, THEY HAD TO CARRY HEAPS OF FRUITS AND NUTS.
HUNTER ONLY CARRIES A DANG SQUIRREL!
IT APPEARS THAT HER GEAR WAS MADE OF SOFTER STUFF THAN STONE...
...WHICH DISINTEGRATED WITHOUT A TRACE OVER THE EONS.
NATURALLY, (MALE) SCIENTISTS DREW THE "OBVIOUS" CONCLUSION FROM THE AVAILABLE EVIDENCE...
TOOLS WERE STONE, AND THE GREAT GENIUSES HAVE ALWAYS BEEN, LIKE US, MEN...
CENT OF MAN
PEOPLE ARE NOT THE ONLY ANIMALS TO USE TOOLS. THE CALIFORNIA SEA OTTER, FOR EXAMPLE, BREAKS OPEN OYSTERS WITH CAREFULLY CHOSEN STONES.
SMAK SMAK
CHIMPANZEES STRIP THE LEAVES OFF STICKS, WHICH THEY USE TO "FISH" FOR A MEAL OF TERMITES.
BUT SO FAR WE HUMANS ARE THE ONLY ANIMAL WHICH HAS MADE ITS WHOLE EXISTENCE DEPEND ON TOOLS. WE CAN'T LIVE WITHOUT THEM!
HAVE YOU GIVEN ANY THOUGHT TO WHAT HAPPENS WHEN GLOBAL DEMAND FOR FLINT OUTSTRIPS SUPPLY?
NO!
CHOP CHOP

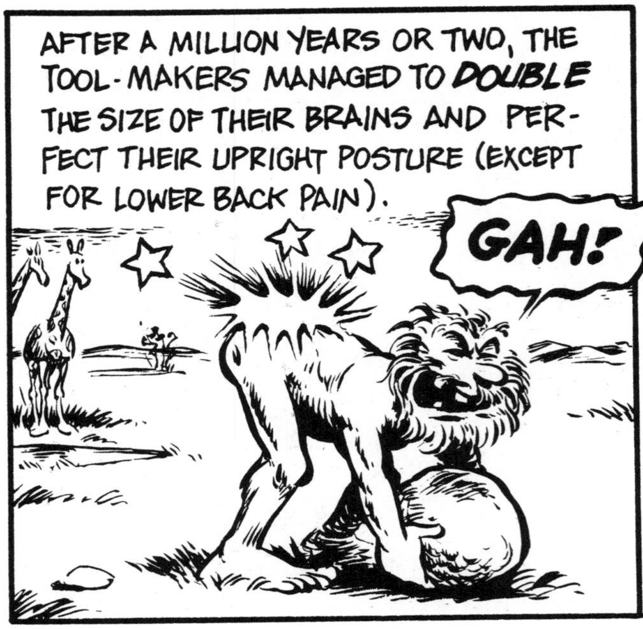
AFTER A MILLION YEARS OR TWO, THE TOOL-MAKERS MANAGED TO ***DOUBLE*** THE SIZE OF THEIR BRAINS AND PERFECT THEIR UPRIGHT POSTURE (EXCEPT FOR LOWER BACK PAIN).
GAH!

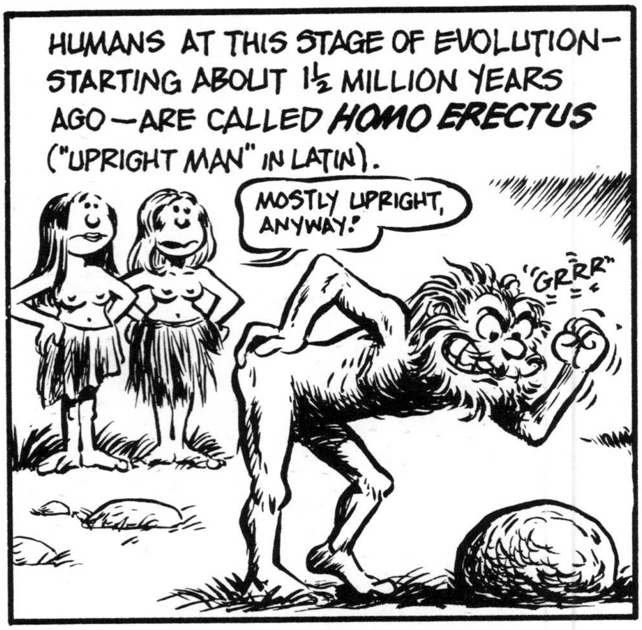
HUMANS AT THIS STAGE OF EVOLUTION—STARTING ABOUT 1½ MILLION YEARS AGO—ARE CALLED ***HOMO ERECTUS*** ("UPRIGHT MAN" IN LATIN).
MOSTLY UPRIGHT, ANYWAY!
"GRRR"

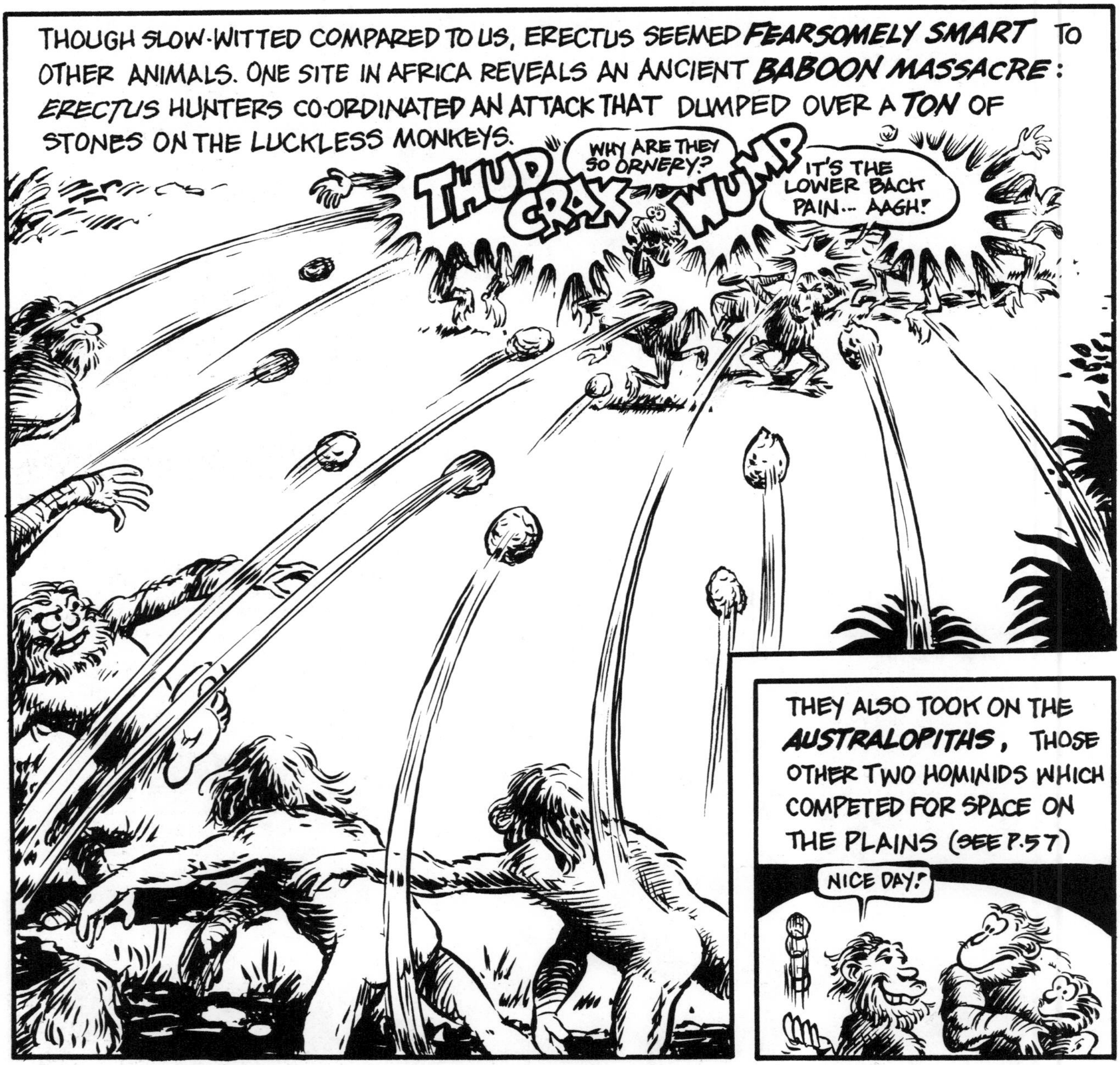
THOUGH SLOW-WITTED COMPARED TO US, ERECTUS SEEMED ***FEARSOMELY SMART*** TO OTHER ANIMALS. ONE SITE IN AFRICA REVEALS AN ANCIENT ***BABOON MASSACRE***: *ERECTUS* HUNTERS CO-ORDINATED AN ATTACK THAT DUMPED OVER A ***TON*** OF STONES ON THE LUCKLESS MONKEYS.
THUD
CRAX
WHY ARE THEY SO ORNERY?
WUMP
IT'S THE LOWER BACK PAIN... AAGH!
THEY ALSO TOOK ON THE ***AUSTRALOPITHS***, THOSE OTHER TWO HOMINIDS WHICH COMPETED FOR SPACE ON THE PLAINS (SEE P.57)
NICE DAY!

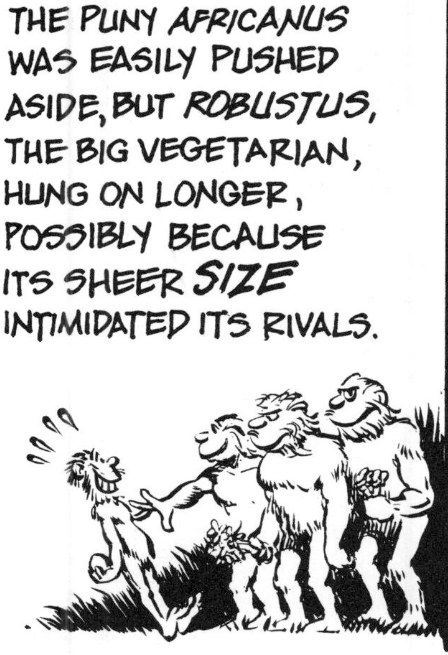
THE PUNY AFRICANUS WAS EASILY PUSHED ASIDE, BUT ROBUSTUS, THE BIG VEGETARIAN, HUNG ON LONGER, POSSIBLY BECAUSE ITS SHEER SIZE INTIMIDATED ITS RIVALS.

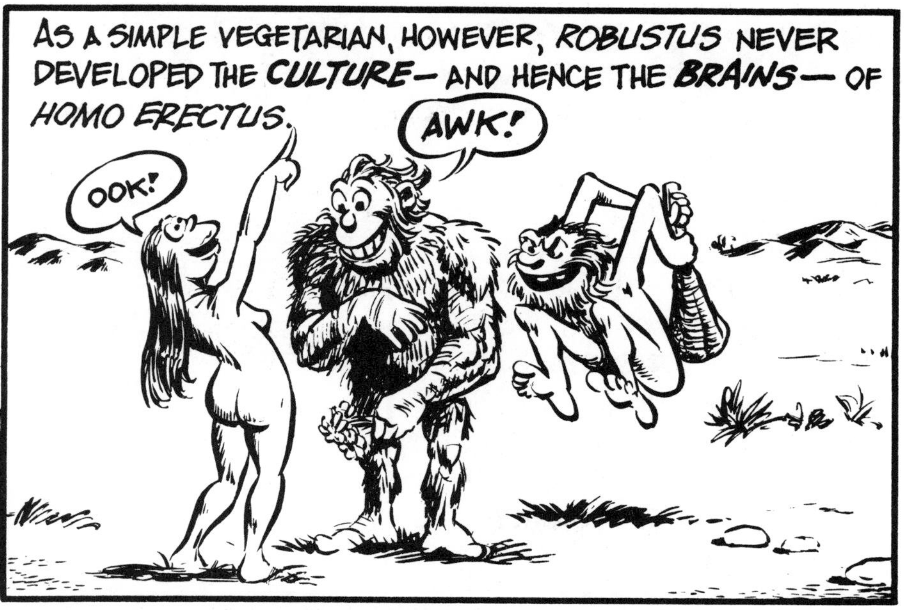
AS A SIMPLE VEGETARIAN, HOWEVER, ROBUSTUS NEVER DEVELOPED THE CULTURE— AND HENCE THE BRAINS— OF HOMO ERECTUS.
OOK!
AWK!

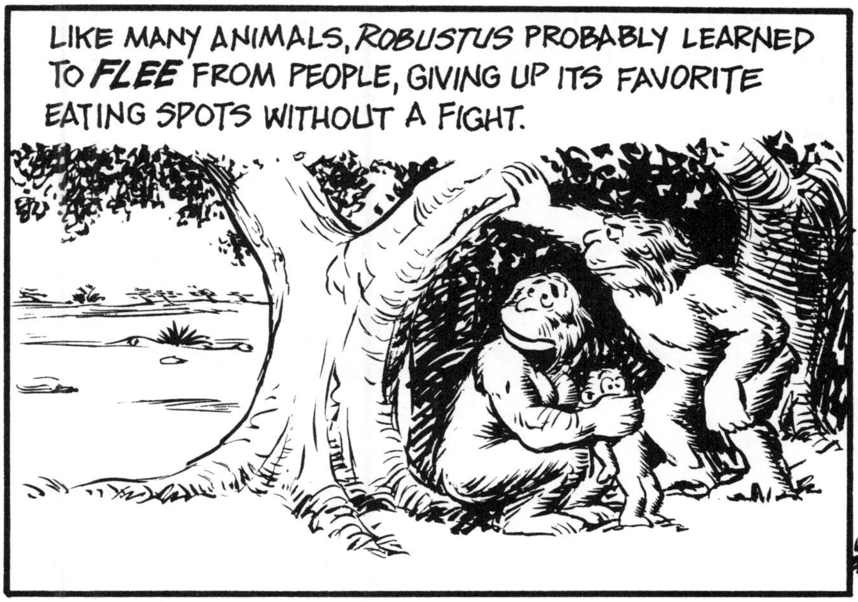
LIKE MANY ANIMALS, ROBUSTUS PROBABLY LEARNED TO FLEE FROM PEOPLE, GIVING UP ITS FAVORITE EATING SPOTS WITHOUT A FIGHT.

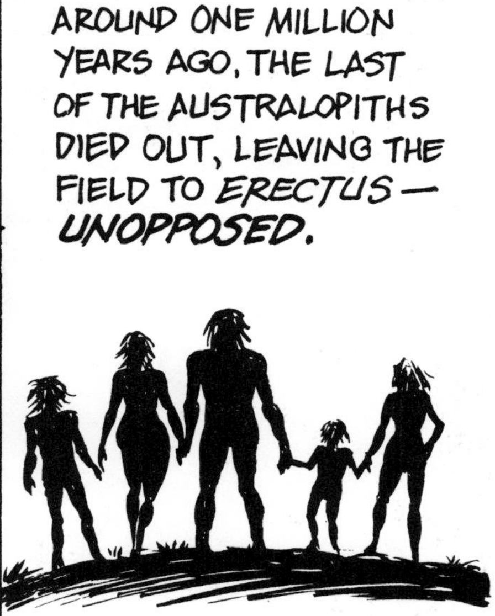
AROUND ONE MILLION YEARS AGO, THE LAST OF THE AUSTRALOPITHS DIED OUT, LEAVING THE FIELD TO ERECTUS— UNOPPOSED.

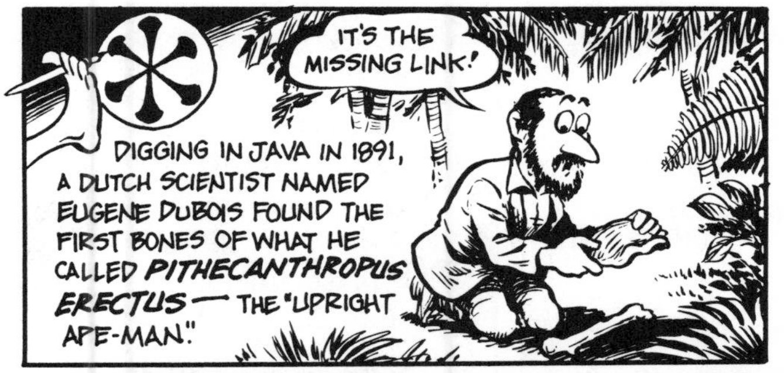
IT'S THE MISSING LINK!
DIGGING IN JAVA IN 1891, A DUTCH SCIENTIST NAMED EUGENE DUBOIS FOUND THE FIRST BONES OF WHAT HE CALLED PITHECANTHROPUS ERECTUS— THE "UPRIGHT APE-MAN."

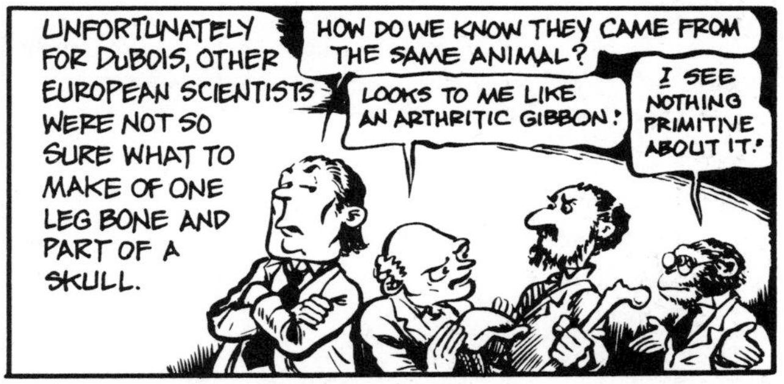
UNFORTUNATELY FOR DUBOIS, OTHER EUROPEAN SCIENTISTS WERE NOT SO SURE WHAT TO MAKE OF ONE LEG BONE AND PART OF A SKULL.
HOW DO WE KNOW THEY CAME FROM THE SAME ANIMAL?
LOOKS TO ME LIKE AN ARTHRITIC GIBBON!
I SEE NOTHING PRIMITIVE ABOUT IT!

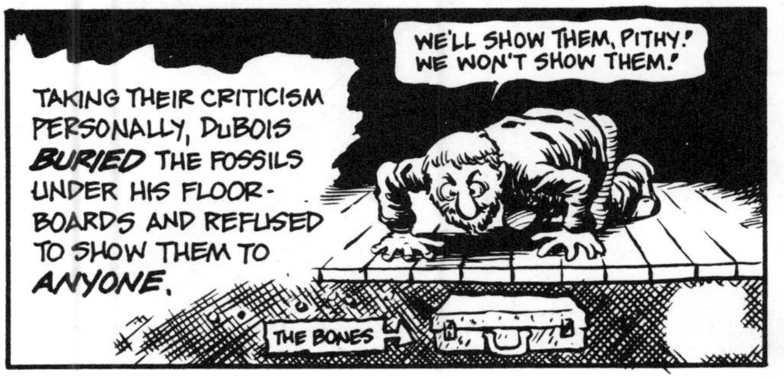
TAKING THEIR CRITICISM PERSONALLY, DUBOIS BURIED THE FOSSILS UNDER HIS FLOOR-BOARDS AND REFUSED TO SHOW THEM TO ANYONE.
WE'LL SHOW THEM, PITHY! WE WON'T SHOW THEM!
THE BONES

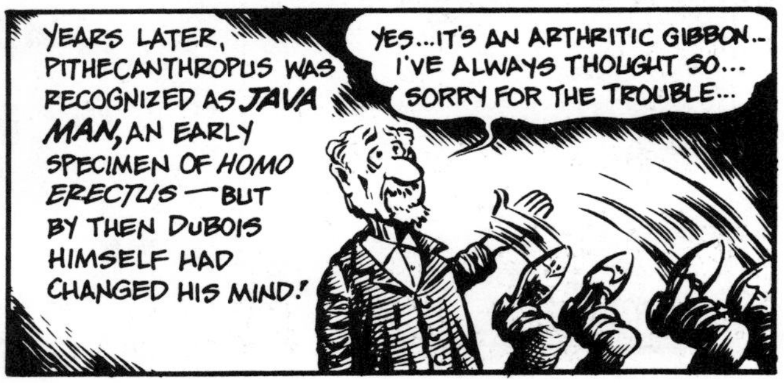
YEARS LATER, PITHECANTHROPUS WAS RECOGNIZED AS JAVA MAN, AN EARLY SPECIMEN OF HOMO ERECTUS— BUT BY THEN DUBOIS HIMSELF HAD CHANGED HIS MIND!
YES...IT'S AN ARTHRITIC GIBBON... I'VE ALWAYS THOUGHT SO... SORRY FOR THE TROUBLE...

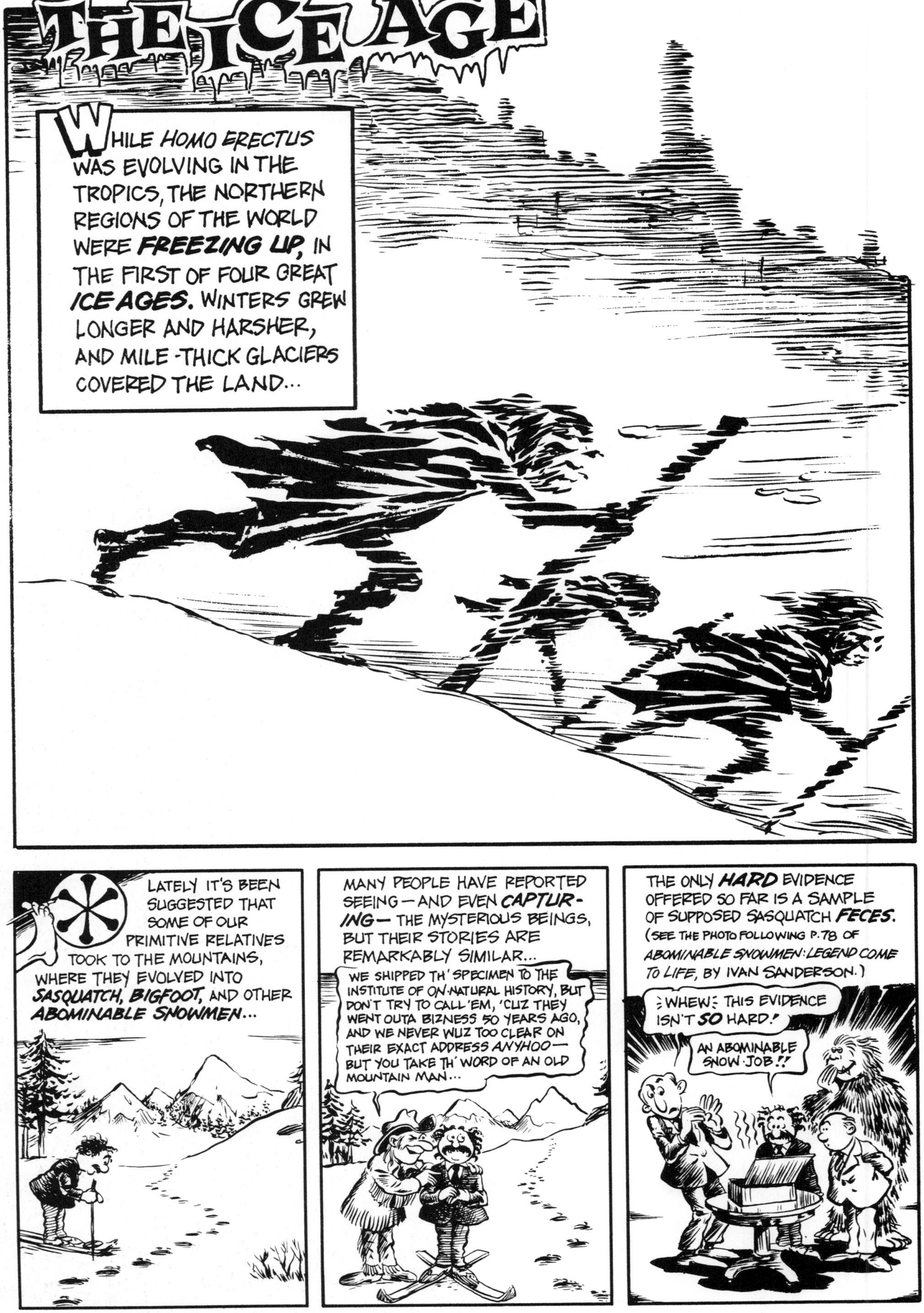
THE ICE AGE
WHILE HOMO ERECTUS WAS EVOLVING IN THE TROPICS, THE NORTHERN REGIONS OF THE WORLD WERE FREEZING UP, IN THE FIRST OF FOUR GREAT ICE AGES. WINTERS GREW LONGER AND HARSHER, AND MILE-THICK GLACIERS COVERED THE LAND...
LATELY IT'S BEEN SUGGESTED THAT SOME OF OUR PRIMITIVE RELATIVES TOOK TO THE MOUNTAINS, WHERE THEY EVOLVED INTO SASQUATCH, BIGFOOT, AND OTHER ABOMINABLE SNOWMEN...
MANY PEOPLE HAVE REPORTED SEEING—AND EVEN CAPTURING—THE MYSTERIOUS BEINGS, BUT THEIR STORIES ARE REMARKABLY SIMILAR...
WE SHIPPED TH' SPECIMEN TO THE INSTITUTE OF ON-NATURAL HISTORY, BUT DON'T TRY TO CALL 'EM, 'CUZ THEY WENT OUTA BIZNESS 50 YEARS AGO, AND WE NEVER WUZ TOO CLEAR ON THEIR EXACT ADDRESS ANYHOO—BUT YOU TAKE TH' WORD OF AN OLD MOUNTAIN MAN...
THE ONLY HARD EVIDENCE OFFERED SO FAR IS A SAMPLE OF SUPPOSED SASQUATCH FECES. (SEE THE PHOTO FOLLOWING P. 78 OF ABOMINABLE SNOWMEN: LEGEND COME TO LIFE, BY IVAN SANDERSON.)
WHEW! THIS EVIDENCE ISN'T SO HARD!
AN ABOMINABLE SNOW-JOB!!

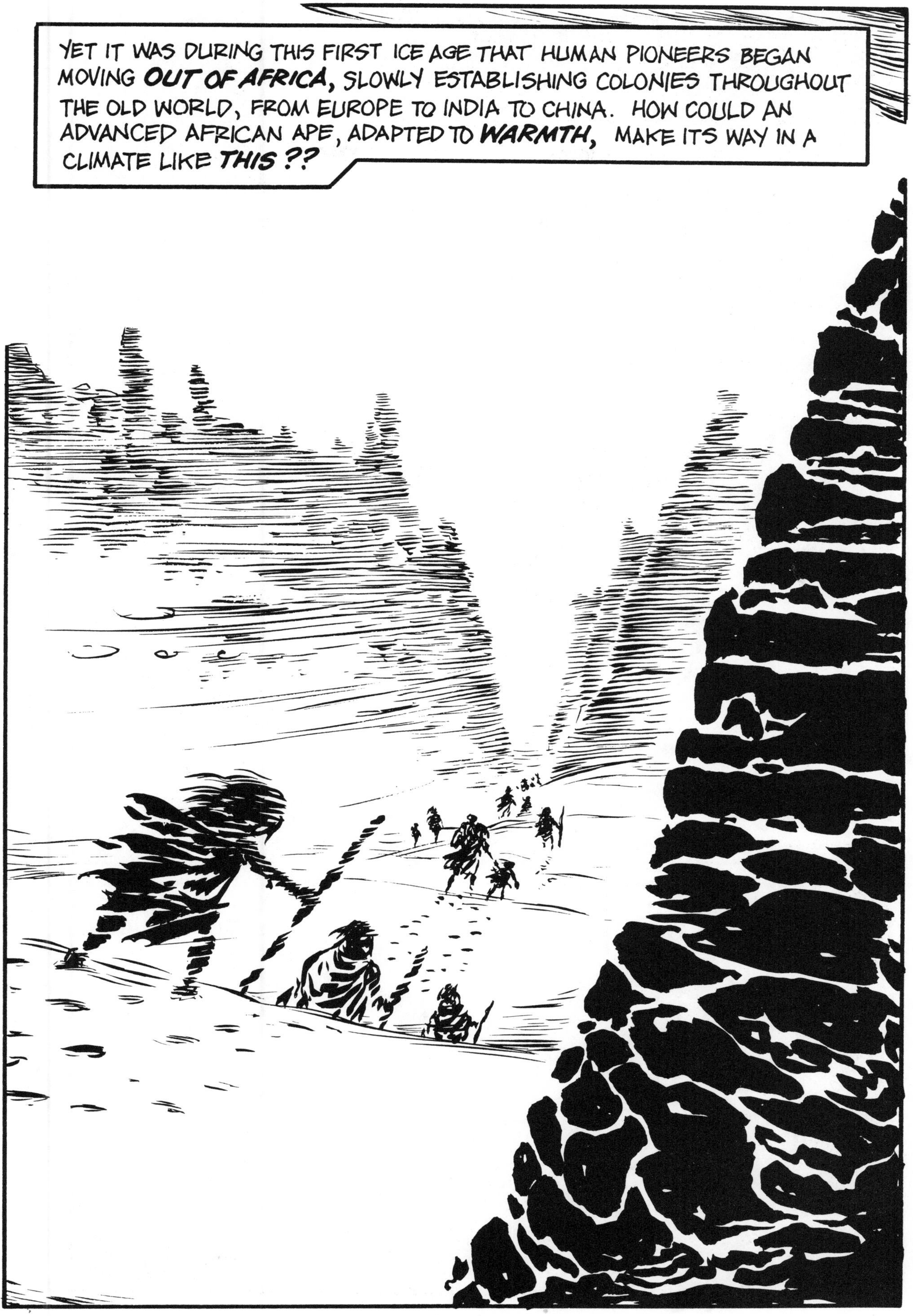
YET IT WAS DURING THIS FIRST ICE AGE THAT HUMAN PIONEERS BEGAN MOVING **OUT OF AFRICA**, SLOWLY ESTABLISHING COLONIES THROUGHOUT THE OLD WORLD, FROM EUROPE TO INDIA TO CHINA. HOW COULD AN ADVANCED AFRICAN APE, ADAPTED TO **WARMTH**, MAKE ITS WAY IN A CLIMATE LIKE **THIS**??

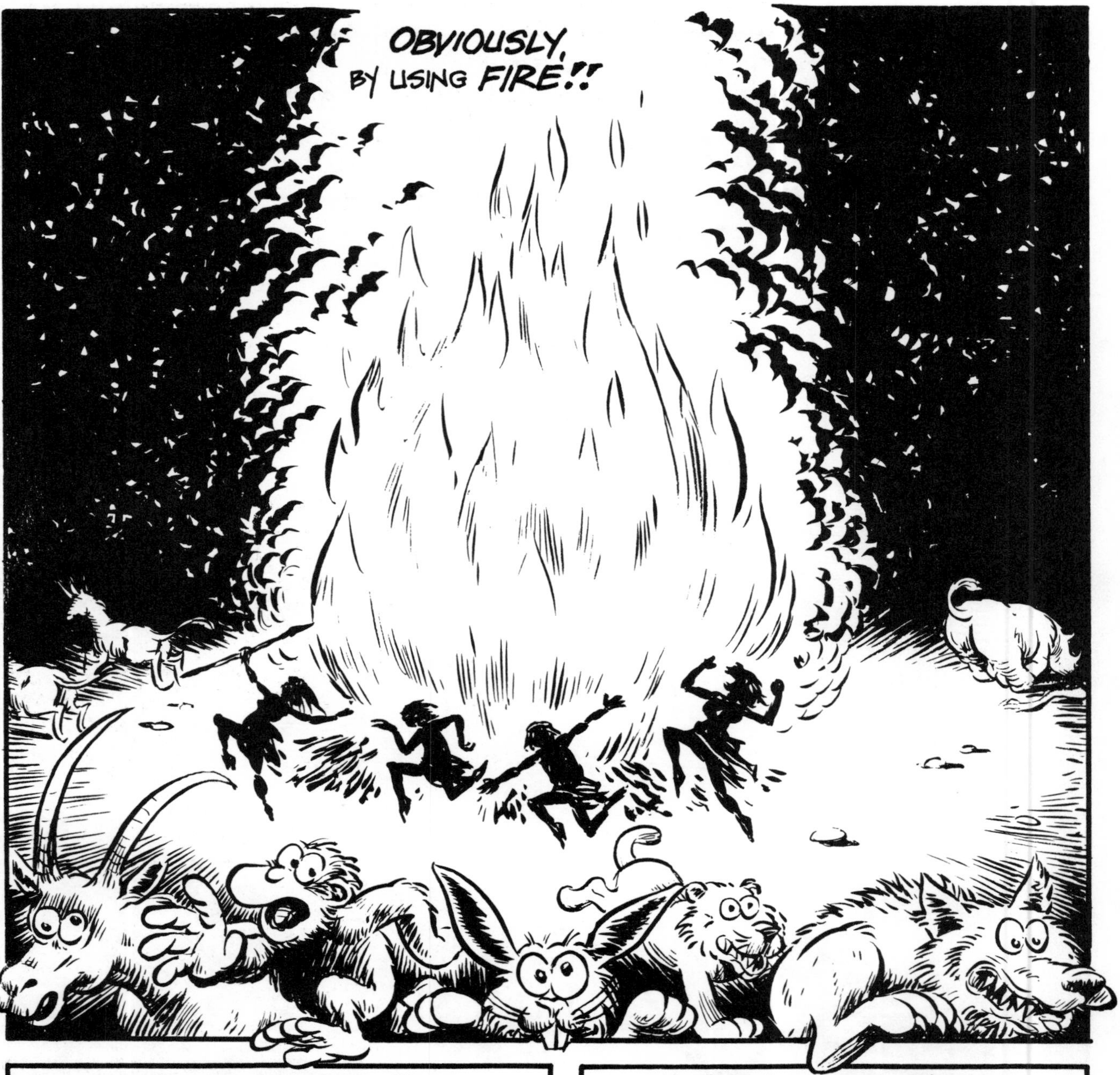
OBVIOUSLY, BY USING FIRE!!

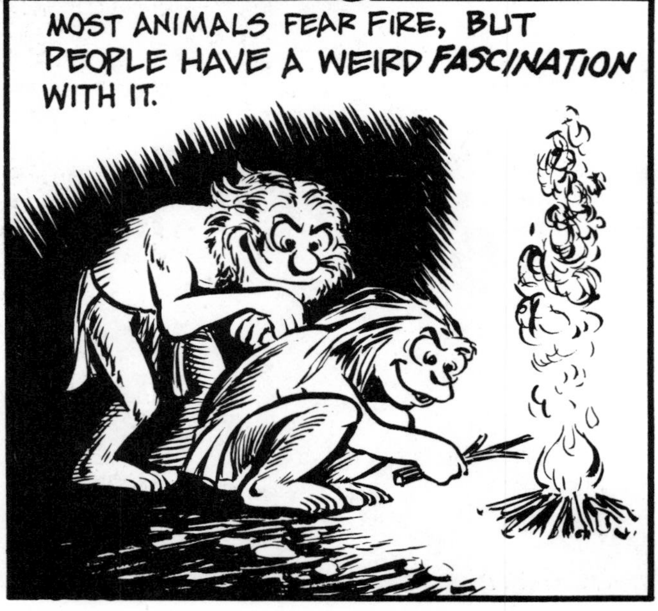
MOST ANIMALS FEAR FIRE, BUT PEOPLE HAVE A WEIRD FASCINATION WITH IT.

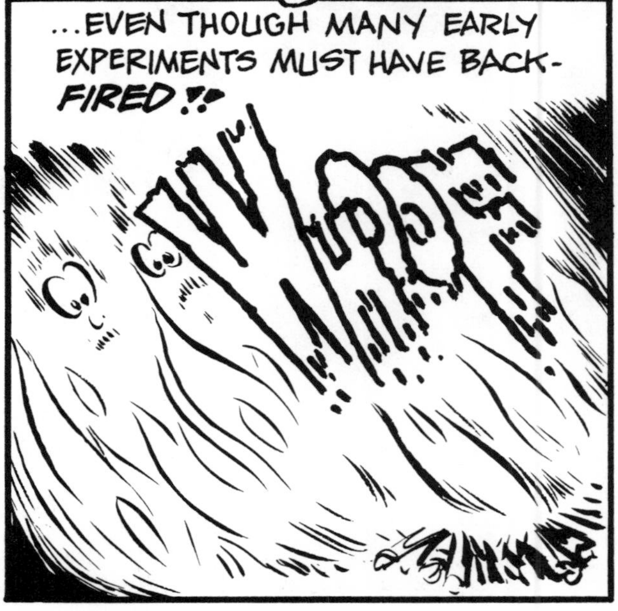
...EVEN THOUGH MANY EARLY EXPERIMENTS MUST HAVE BACK-FIRED!!

THE FIRST FIRE-USERS PROBABLY "CAPTURED" NATURAL FIRE, TAKING IT HOME AND KEEPING IT "ALIVE" FOR ***GENERATIONS***. (ONE BED OF ASHES IN A CHINESE CAVE IS ***22 FEET DEEP.***) HOWEVER IT WAS USED, FIRE ***CHANGED PEOPLE'S LIVES...***

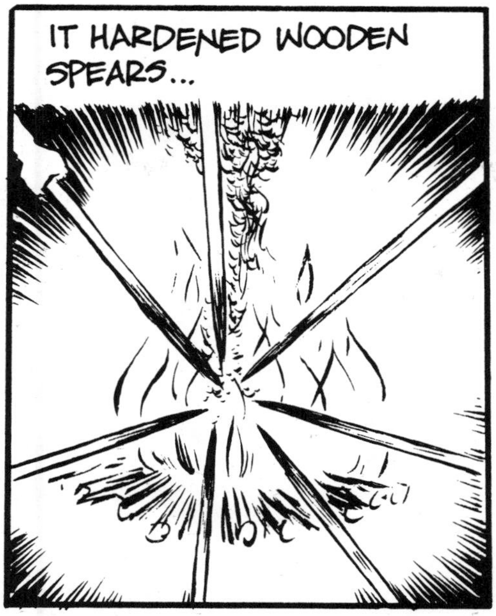
IT HARDENED WOODEN SPEARS...

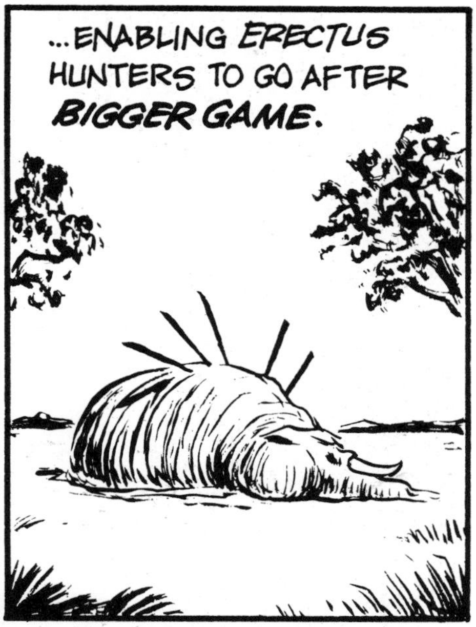
...ENABLING *ERECTUS* HUNTERS TO GO AFTER ***BIGGER GAME.***

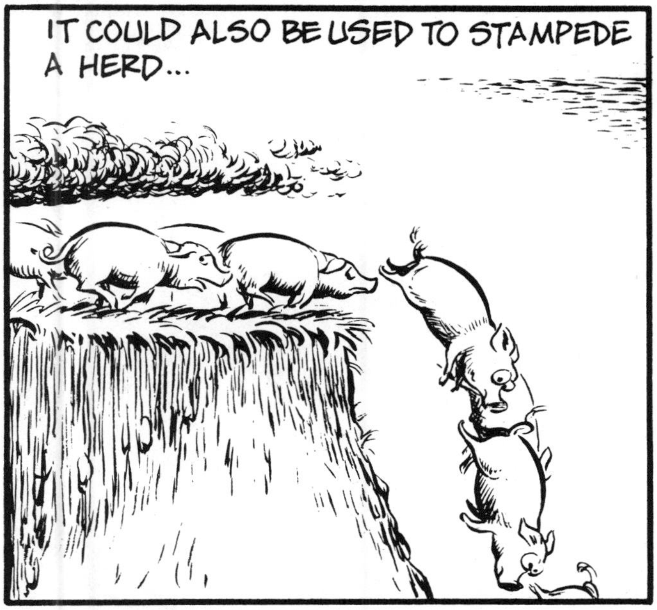
IT COULD ALSO BE USED TO STAMPEDE A HERD...

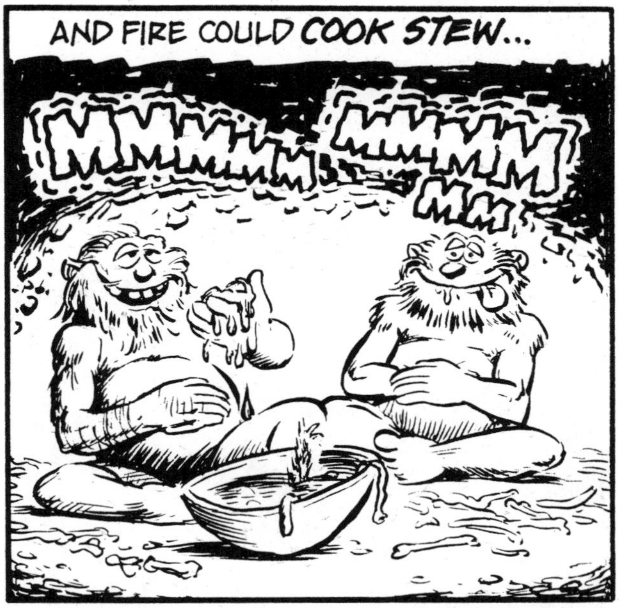
AND FIRE COULD ***COOK STEW...***
MMMMMM
MMMMM MM

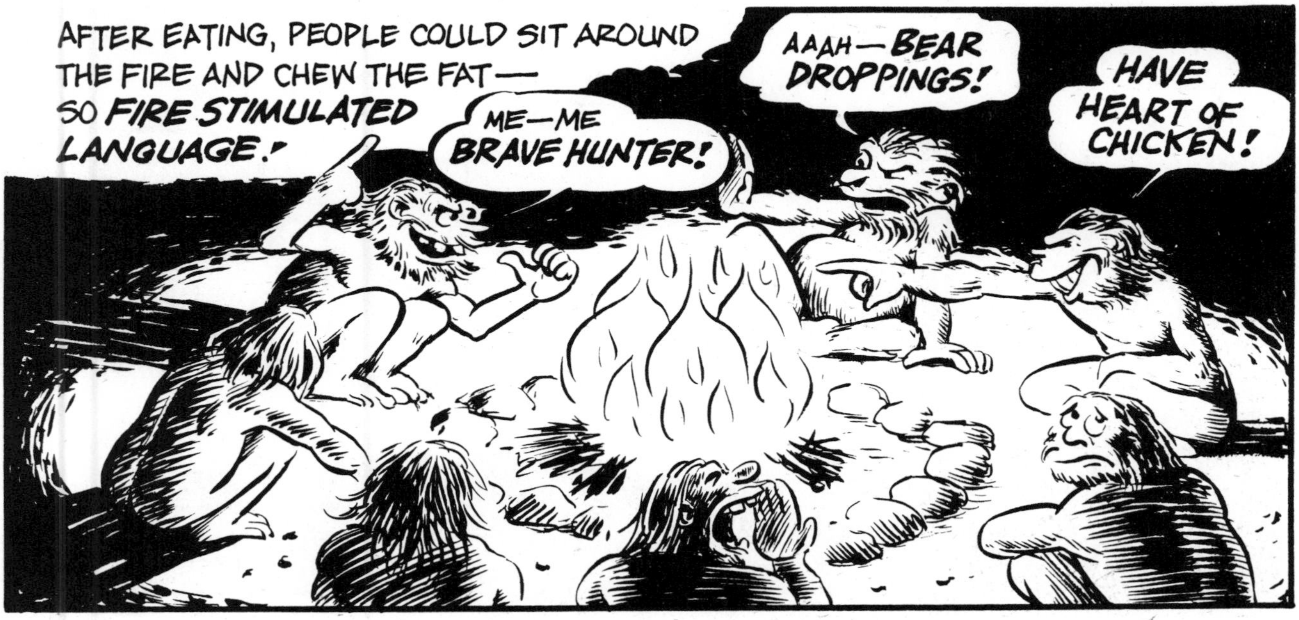
AFTER EATING, PEOPLE COULD SIT AROUND THE FIRE AND CHEW THE FAT— SO ***FIRE STIMULATED LANGUAGE.***
ME—ME BRAVE HUNTER!
AAAH—BEAR DROPPINGS!
HAVE HEART OF CHICKEN!

ALL HIGHER ANIMALS COMMUNICATE BY SOUNDS AND GESTURES, BUT ONLY HUMANS, (AS FAR AS WE KNOW) HAVE DEVISED A ***SYMBOL SYSTEM*** REQUIRING THEM CONSCIOUSLY TO ***NAME THINGS***.

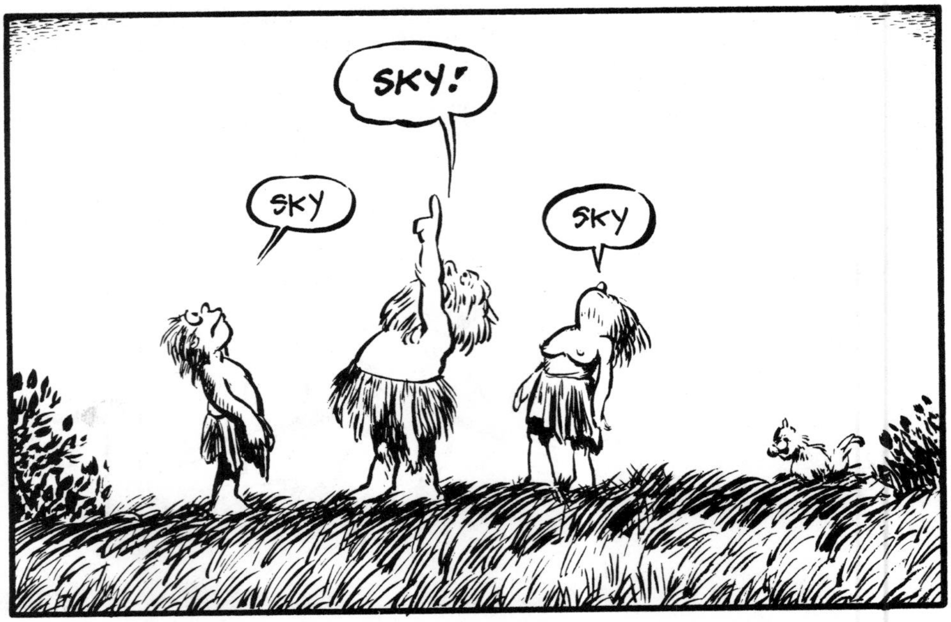
SKY!
SKY
SKY

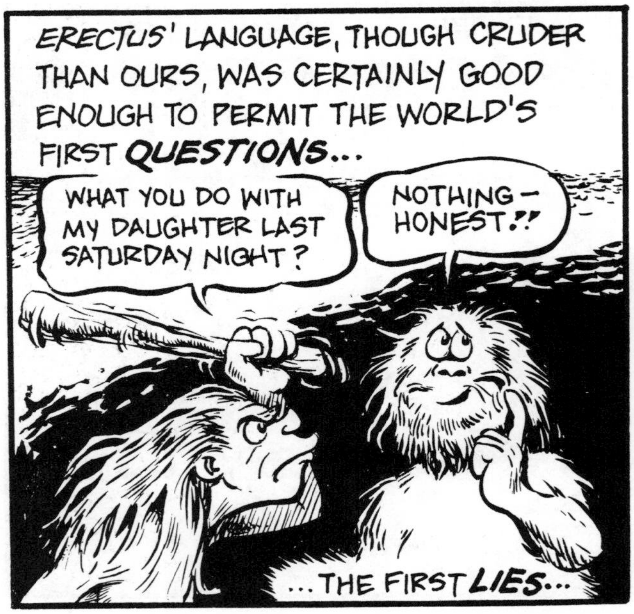
ERECTUS' LANGUAGE, THOUGH CRUDER THAN OURS, WAS CERTAINLY GOOD ENOUGH TO PERMIT THE WORLD'S FIRST QUESTIONS...
WHAT YOU DO WITH MY DAUGHTER LAST SATURDAY NIGHT?
NOTHING — HONEST!?
...THE FIRST LIES...

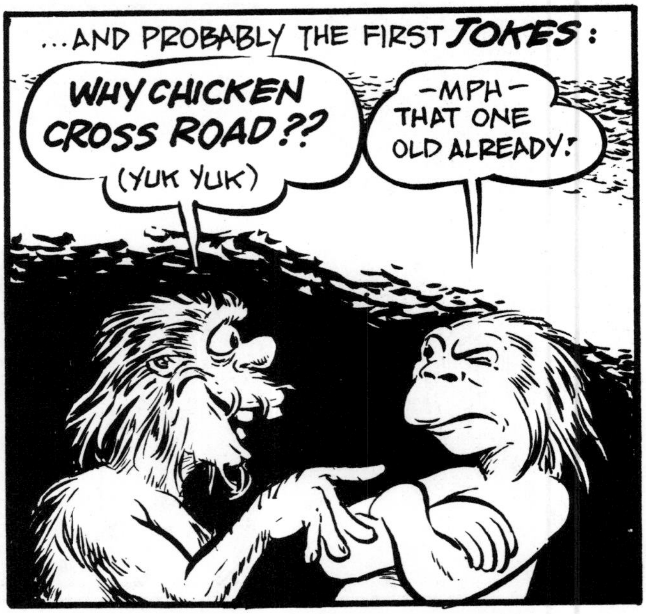
...AND PROBABLY THE FIRST JOKES:
WHY CHICKEN CROSS ROAD?? (YUK YUK)
—MPH— THAT ONE OLD ALREADY!

LANGUAGE ALSO ALLOWS PEOPLE TO CONSTRUCT SENTENCES WHICH MAY OR MAY NOT HAVE ANYTHING TO DO WITH THE ***REAL WORLD***.

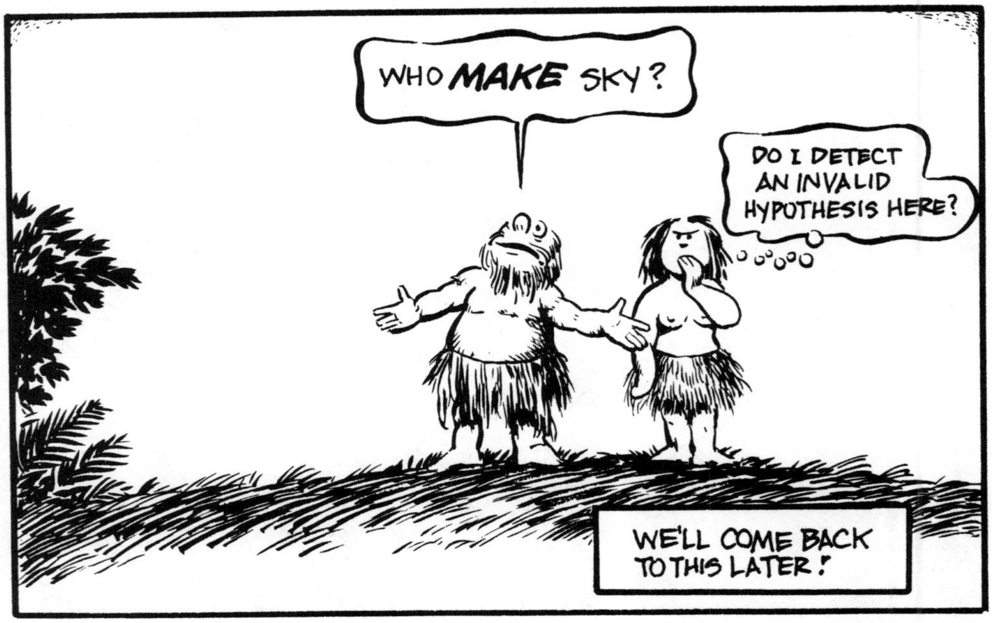
WHO MAKE SKY?
DO I DETECT AN INVALID HYPOTHESIS HERE?
WE'LL COME BACK TO THIS LATER!

AS PEOPLE CAME TO REALIZE THE POWER OF SYMBOLS, THEY BEGAN TO DEVISE ***RITUALS***— ACTS PERFORMED NOT FOR THEIR OWN SAKE, BUT FOR THEIR ***SYMBOLIC VALUE***. ONLY TWO OF *ERECTUS'* RITUAL PRACTICES ARE KNOWN...

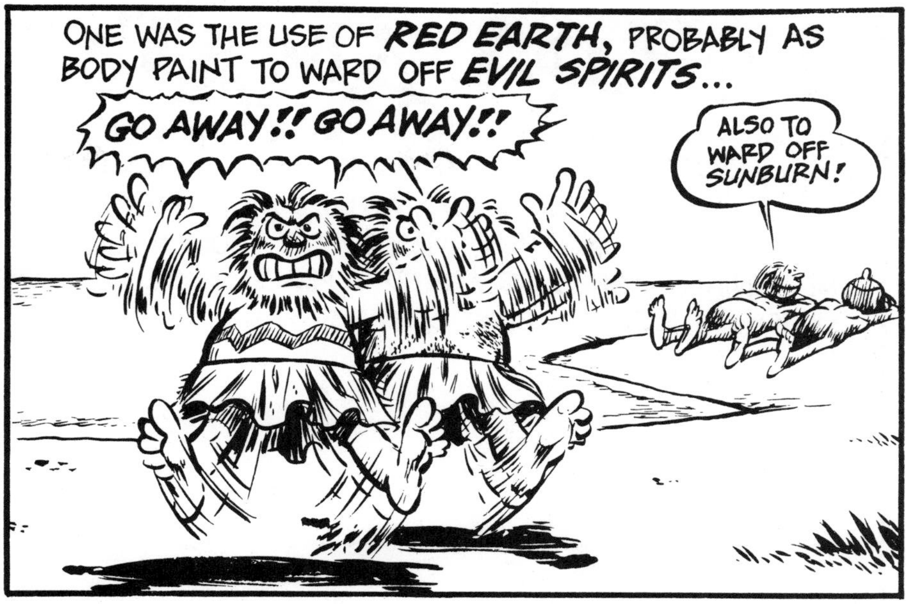
ONE WAS THE USE OF RED EARTH, PROBABLY AS BODY PAINT TO WARD OFF EVIL SPIRITS...
GO AWAY!! GO AWAY!!
ALSO TO WARD OFF SUNBURN!

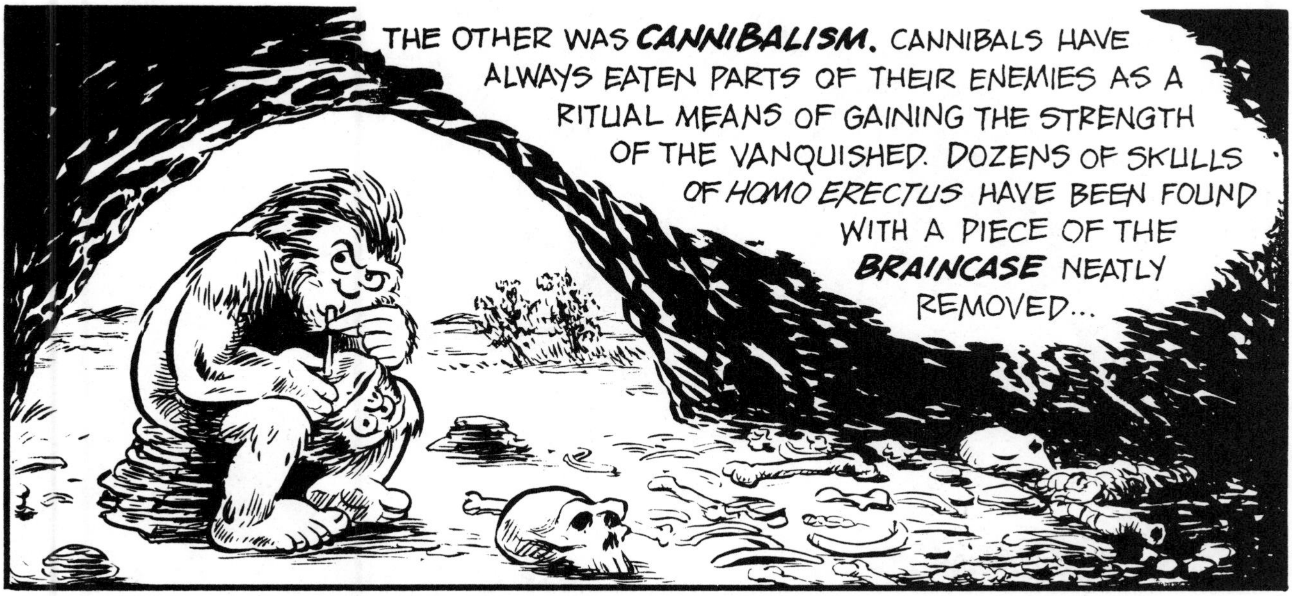
THE OTHER WAS CANNIBALISM. CANNIBALS HAVE ALWAYS EATEN PARTS OF THEIR ENEMIES AS A RITUAL MEANS OF GAINING THE STRENGTH OF THE VANQUISHED. DOZENS OF SKULLS OF HOMO ERECTUS HAVE BEEN FOUND WITH A PIECE OF THE BRAINCASE NEATLY REMOVED...

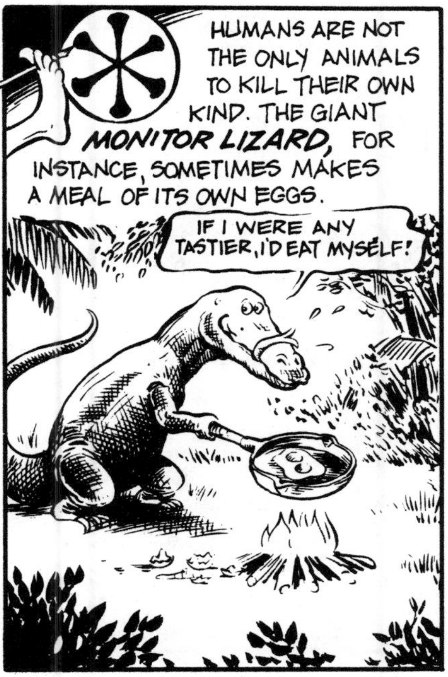
HUMANS ARE NOT THE ONLY ANIMALS TO KILL THEIR OWN KIND. THE GIANT MONITOR LIZARD, FOR INSTANCE, SOMETIMES MAKES A MEAL OF ITS OWN EGGS.
IF I WERE ANY TASTIER, I'D EAT MYSELF!

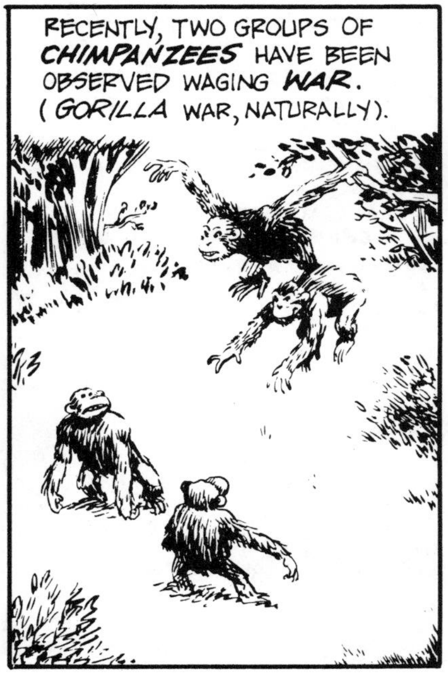
RECENTLY, TWO GROUPS OF CHIMPANZEES HAVE BEEN OBSERVED WAGING WAR. (GORILLA WAR, NATURALLY).

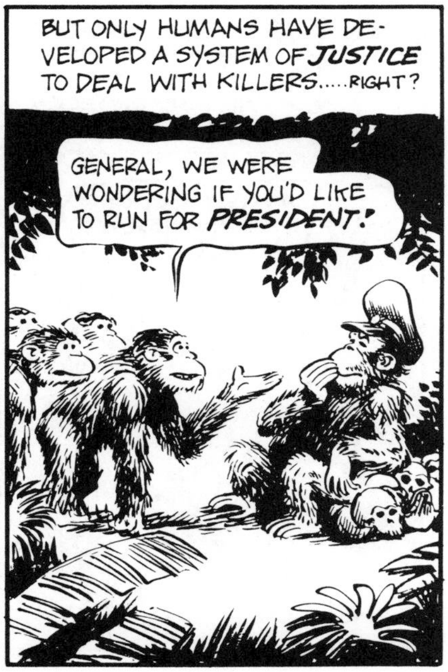
BUT ONLY HUMANS HAVE DEVELOPED A SYSTEM OF JUSTICE TO DEAL WITH KILLERS.....RIGHT?
GENERAL, WE WERE WONDERING IF YOU'D LIKE TO RUN FOR PRESIDENT!

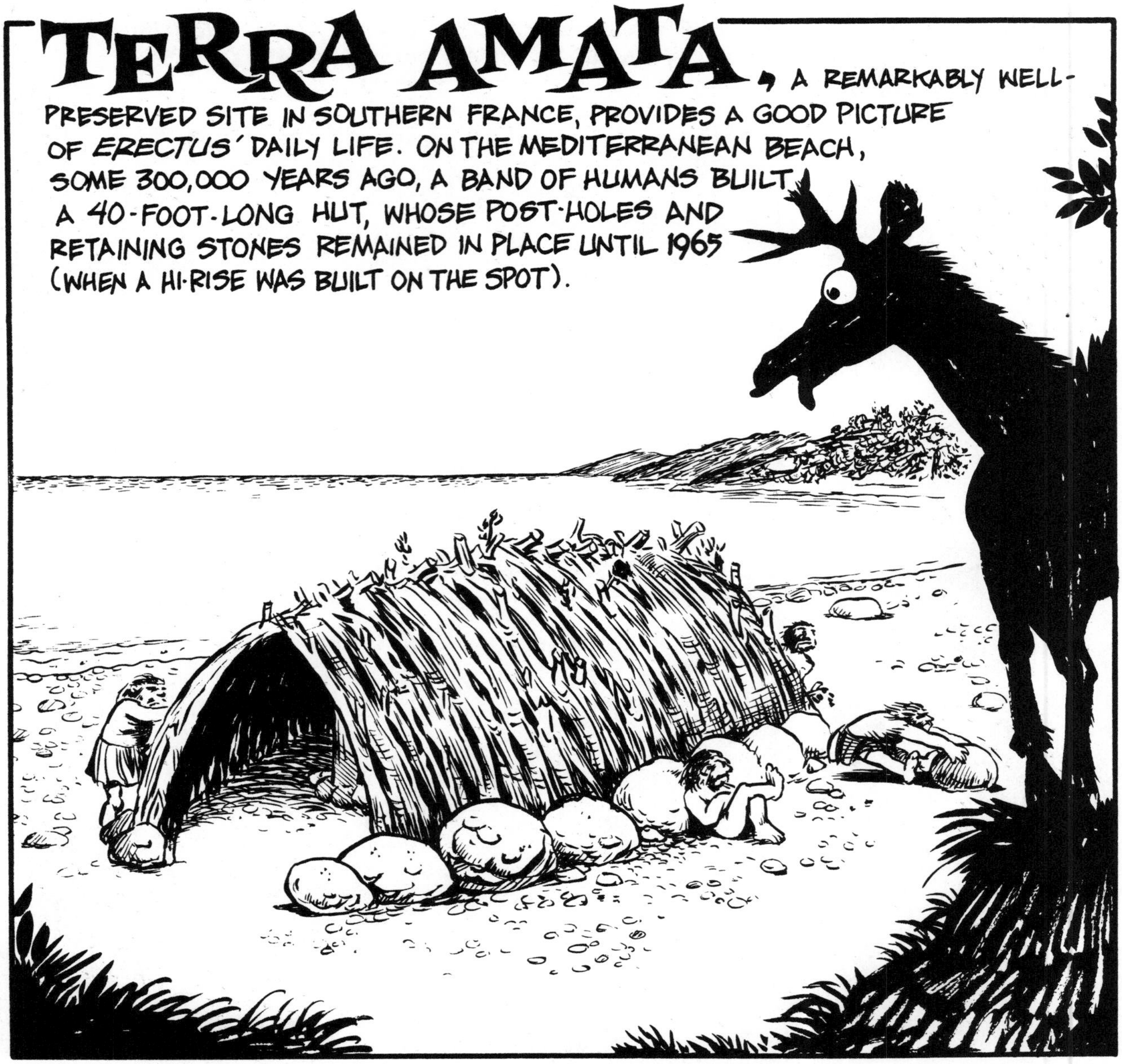
TERRA AMATA, A REMARKABLY WELL-PRESERVED SITE IN SOUTHERN FRANCE, PROVIDES A GOOD PICTURE OF *ERECTUS'* DAILY LIFE. ON THE MEDITERRANEAN BEACH, SOME 300,000 YEARS AGO, A BAND OF HUMANS BUILT A 40-FOOT-LONG HUT, WHOSE POST-HOLES AND RETAINING STONES REMAINED IN PLACE UNTIL 1965 (WHEN A HI-RISE WAS BUILT ON THE SPOT).

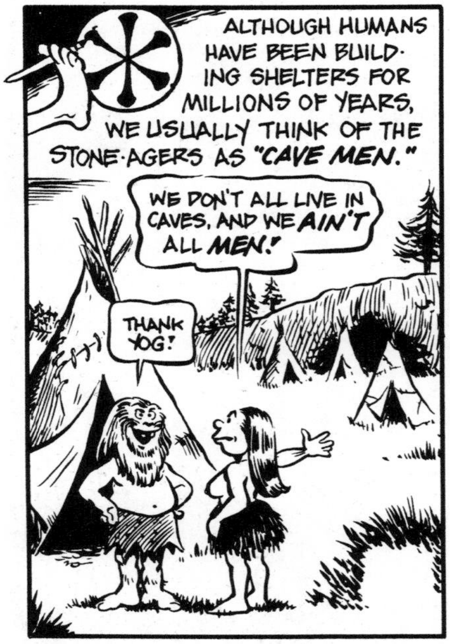
ALTHOUGH HUMANS HAVE BEEN BUILDING SHELTERS FOR MILLIONS OF YEARS, WE USUALLY THINK OF THE STONE-AGERS AS "CAVE MEN."
WE DON'T ALL LIVE IN CAVES, AND WE AIN'T ALL MEN!
THANK YOG!

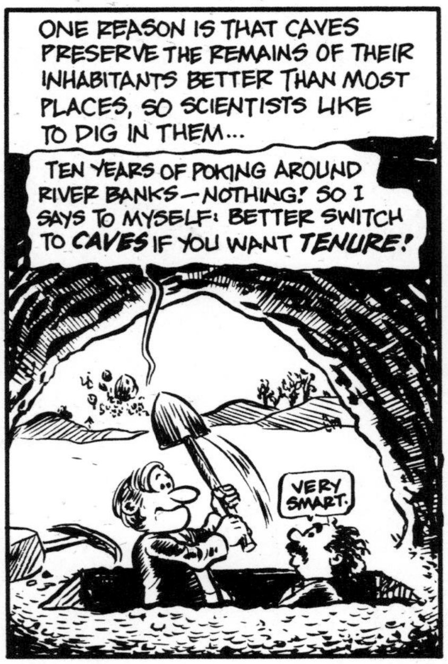
ONE REASON IS THAT CAVES PRESERVE THE REMAINS OF THEIR INHABITANTS BETTER THAN MOST PLACES, SO SCIENTISTS LIKE TO DIG IN THEM...
TEN YEARS OF POKING AROUND RIVER BANKS—NOTHING! SO I SAYS TO MYSELF: BETTER SWITCH TO CAVES IF YOU WANT TENURE!
VERY SMART.

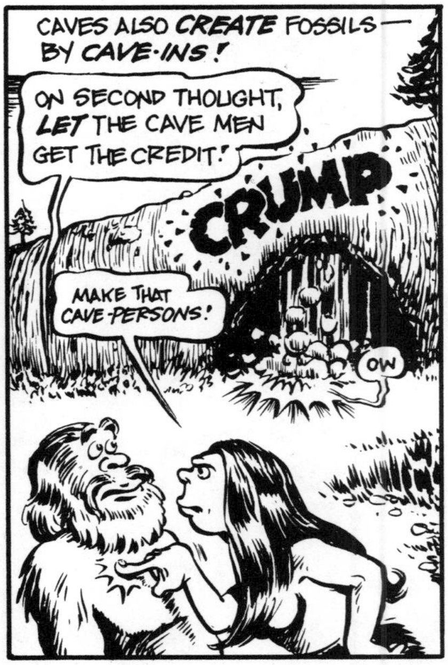
CAVES ALSO CREATE FOSSILS—BY CAVE-INS!
ON SECOND THOUGHT, LET THE CAVE MEN GET THE CREDIT!
CRUMP
MAKE THAT CAVE-PERSONS!
OW

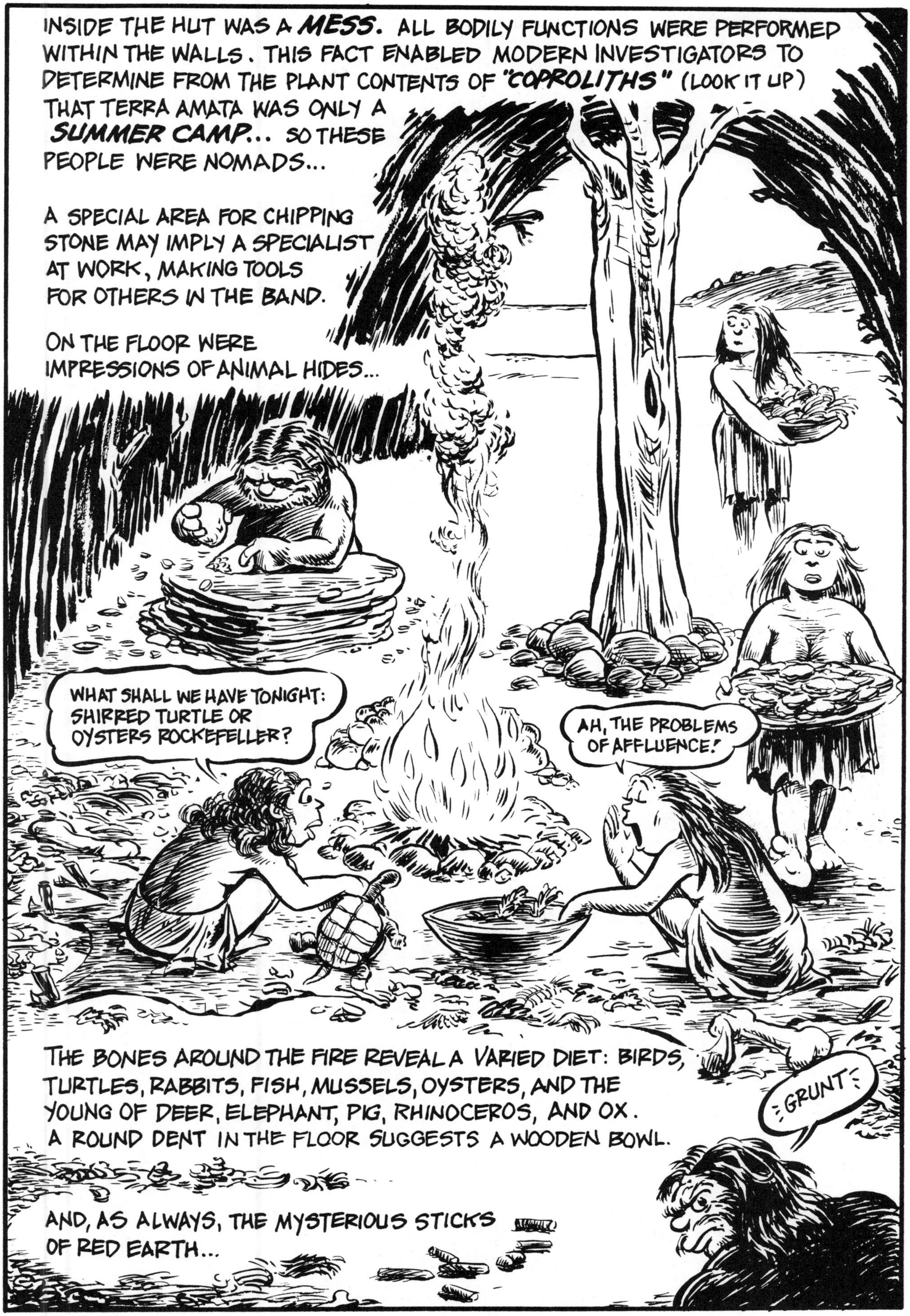
INSIDE THE HUT WAS A MESS. ALL BODILY FUNCTIONS WERE PERFORMED WITHIN THE WALLS. THIS FACT ENABLED MODERN INVESTIGATORS TO DETERMINE FROM THE PLANT CONTENTS OF "COPROLITHS" (LOOK IT UP) THAT TERRA AMATA WAS ONLY A SUMMER CAMP... SO THESE PEOPLE WERE NOMADS...
A SPECIAL AREA FOR CHIPPING STONE MAY IMPLY A SPECIALIST AT WORK, MAKING TOOLS FOR OTHERS IN THE BAND.
ON THE FLOOR WERE IMPRESSIONS OF ANIMAL HIDES...
WHAT SHALL WE HAVE TONIGHT: SHIRRED TURTLE OR OYSTERS ROCKEFELLER?
AH, THE PROBLEMS OF AFFLUENCE!
THE BONES AROUND THE FIRE REVEAL A VARIED DIET: BIRDS, TURTLES, RABBITS, FISH, MUSSELS, OYSTERS, AND THE YOUNG OF DEER, ELEPHANT, PIG, RHINOCEROS, AND OX. A ROUND DENT IN THE FLOOR SUGGESTS A WOODEN BOWL.
GRUNT
AND, AS ALWAYS, THE MYSTERIOUS STICKS OF RED EARTH...

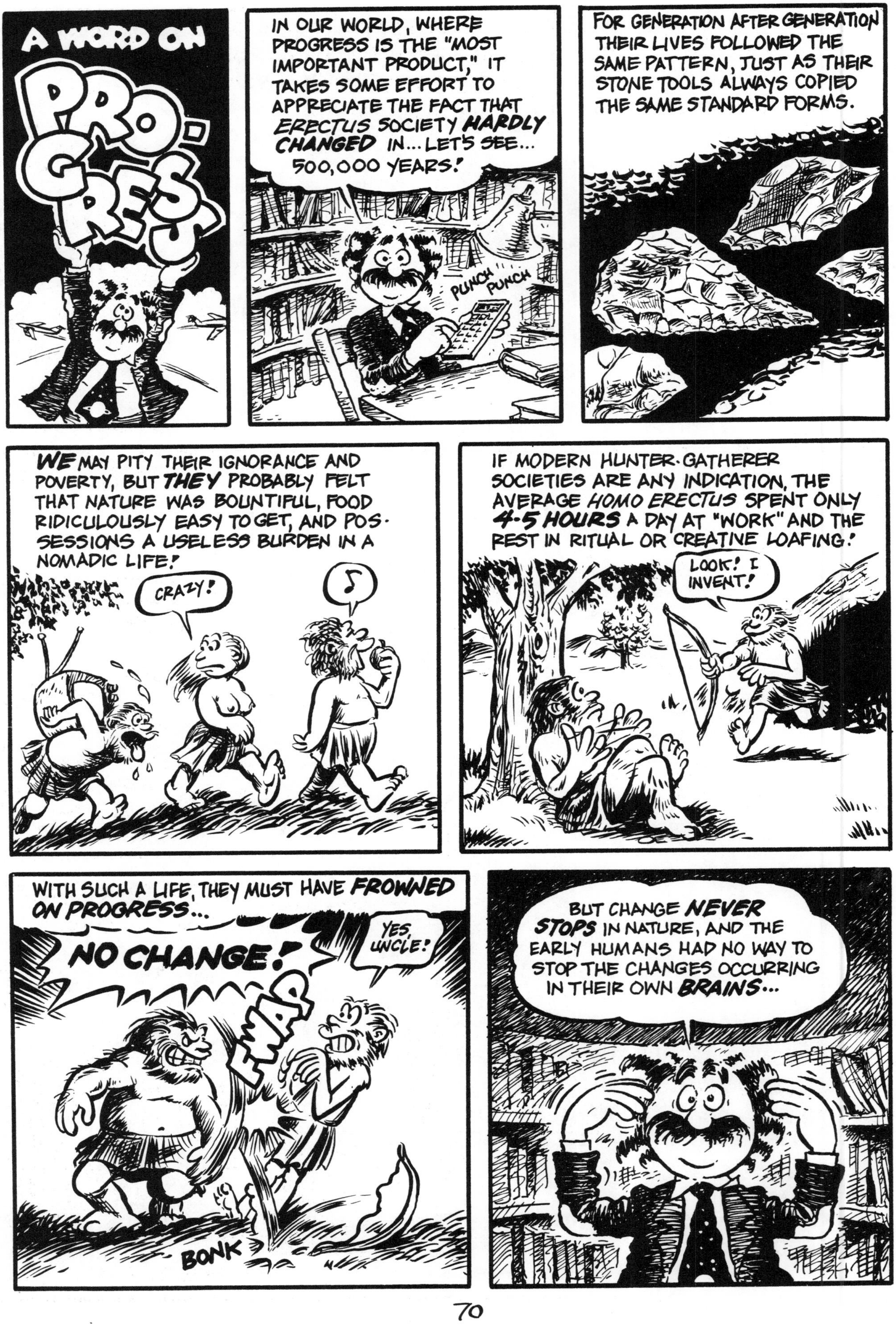
A WORD ON
PRO-GRES
IN OUR WORLD, WHERE PROGRESS IS THE "MOST IMPORTANT PRODUCT," IT TAKES SOME EFFORT TO APPRECIATE THE FACT THAT ERECTUS SOCIETY HARDLY CHANGED IN... LET'S SEE... 500,000 YEARS!
PUNCH PUNCH
FOR GENERATION AFTER GENERATION THEIR LIVES FOLLOWED THE SAME PATTERN, JUST AS THEIR STONE TOOLS ALWAYS COPIED THE SAME STANDARD FORMS.
WE MAY PITY THEIR IGNORANCE AND POVERTY, BUT THEY PROBABLY FELT THAT NATURE WAS BOUNTIFUL, FOOD RIDICULOUSLY EASY TO GET, AND POSSESSIONS A USELESS BURDEN IN A NOMADIC LIFE!
CRAZY!
♪
IF MODERN HUNTER-GATHERER SOCIETIES ARE ANY INDICATION, THE AVERAGE HOMO ERECTUS SPENT ONLY 4-5 HOURS A DAY AT "WORK" AND THE REST IN RITUAL OR CREATIVE LOAFING!
LOOK! I INVENT!
WITH SUCH A LIFE, THEY MUST HAVE FROWNED ON PROGRESS...
NO CHANGE!
YES, UNCLE!
FWAP
BONK
BUT CHANGE NEVER STOPS IN NATURE, AND THE EARLY HUMANS HAD NO WAY TO STOP THE CHANGES OCCURRING IN THEIR OWN BRAINS...

IN ANY WORLDWIDE POPULATION, VARIATIONS BEGIN TO APPEAR...

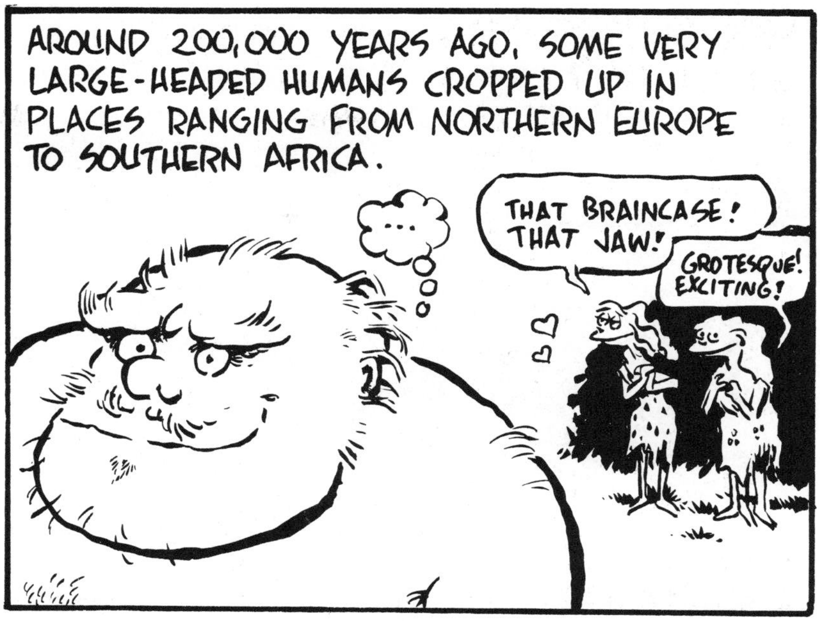
AROUND 200,000 YEARS AGO, SOME VERY LARGE-HEADED HUMANS CROPPED UP IN PLACES RANGING FROM NORTHERN EUROPE TO SOUTHERN AFRICA.
...
THAT BRAINCASE! THAT JAW!
GROTESQUE! EXCITING!

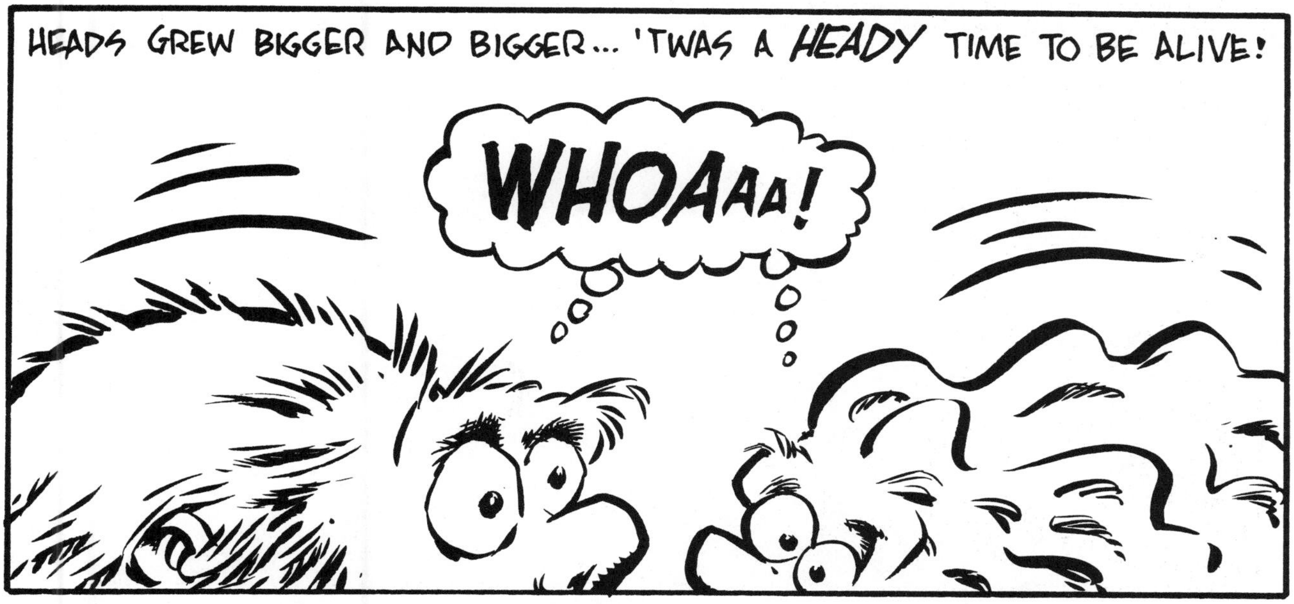
HEADS GREW BIGGER AND BIGGER... 'TWAS A *HEADY* TIME TO BE ALIVE!
WHOAAA!

...UNTIL, IN MOST OF THE WORLD, PEOPLE HAD EVOLVED INTO A BIG-HEADED, LOWBROW FORM OF ***OUR OWN SPECIES, HOMO SAPIENS***— "MAN THINKING."

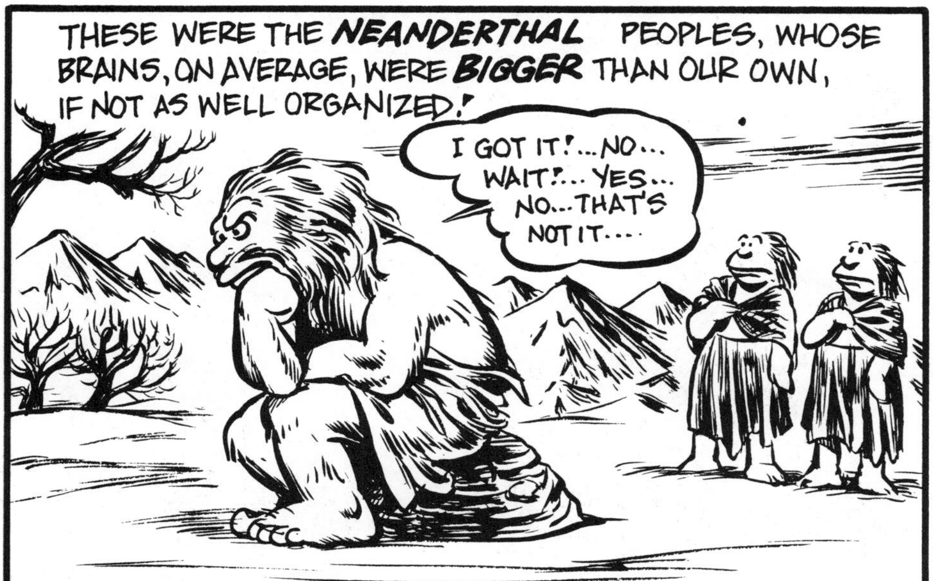
THESE WERE THE ***NEANDERTHAL*** PEOPLES, WHOSE BRAINS, ON AVERAGE, WERE ***BIGGER*** THAN OUR OWN, IF NOT AS WELL ORGANIZED!
I GOT IT!... NO... WAIT!... YES... NO... THAT'S NOT IT....

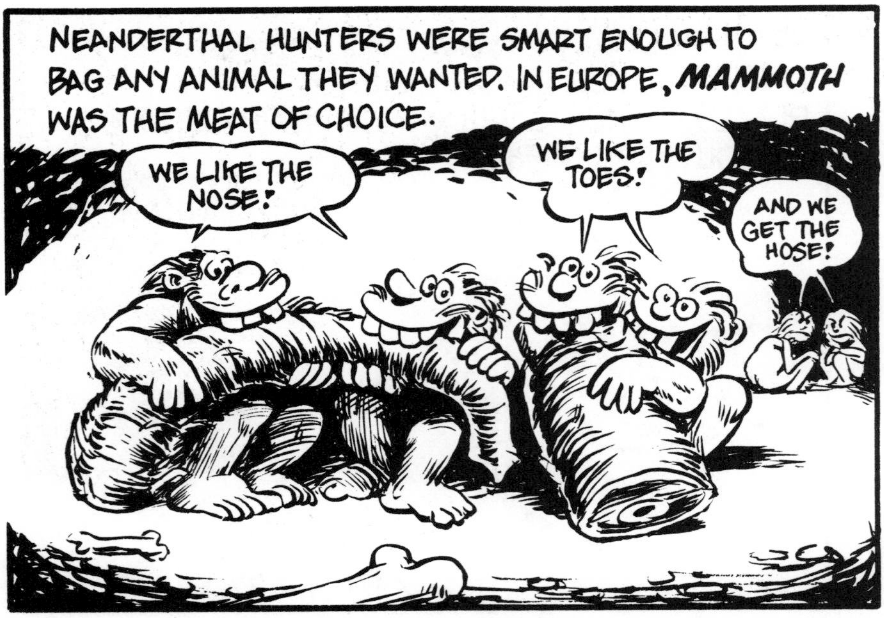
NEANDERTHAL HUNTERS WERE SMART ENOUGH TO BAG ANY ANIMAL THEY WANTED. IN EUROPE, ***MAMMOTH*** WAS THE MEAT OF CHOICE.
WE LIKE THE NOSE!
WE LIKE THE TOES!
AND WE GET THE HOSE!

THEY ADVANCED THE ART OF STONEWORKING. RATHER THAN CHIPPING A ROCK INTO A TOOL, THE NEANDERTHALS WOULD ***PREPARE*** A ***"CORE"*** STONE AND KNOCK OFF ***PRE-SHAPED FLAKES,*** WHICH WERE WORKED INTO DAGGERS, SCRAPERS, ETC...

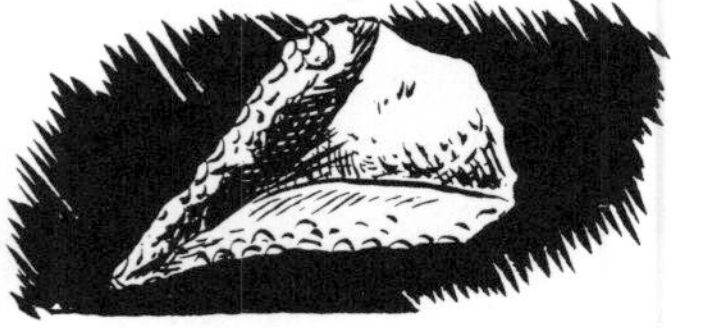

NEANDERTHALS ALSO CONSIDERED THE ***MYSTERIES*** OF THE WORLD. WHILE WE CAN NEVER KNOW EXACTLY WHAT THEY BELIEVED, A FEW TRACES OF ***NEANDERTHAL MAGIC*** HAVE BEEN UNCOVERED...

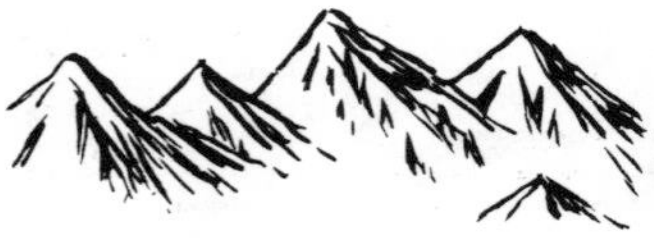

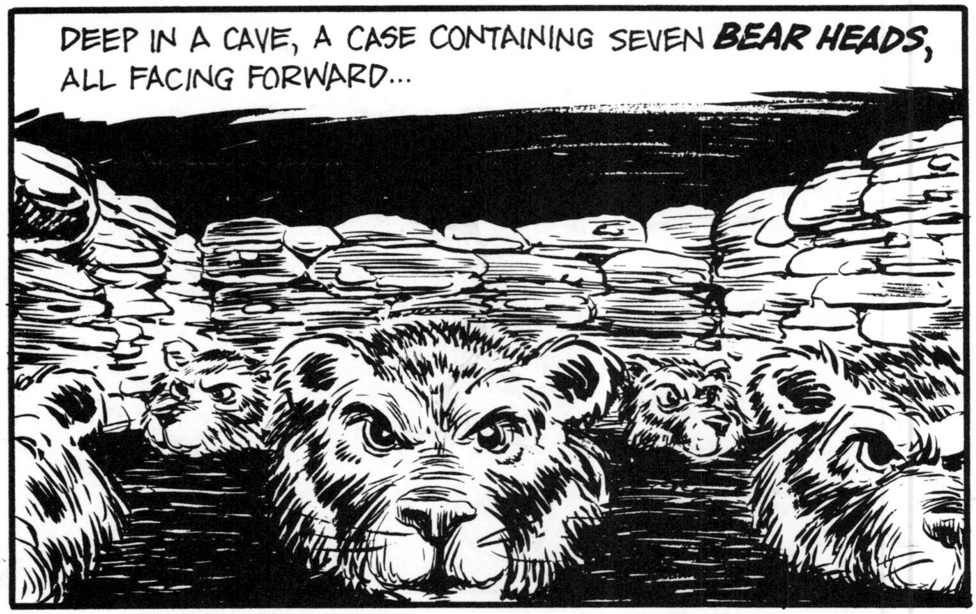
DEEP IN A CAVE, A CASE CONTAINING SEVEN ***BEAR HEADS,*** ALL FACING FORWARD...

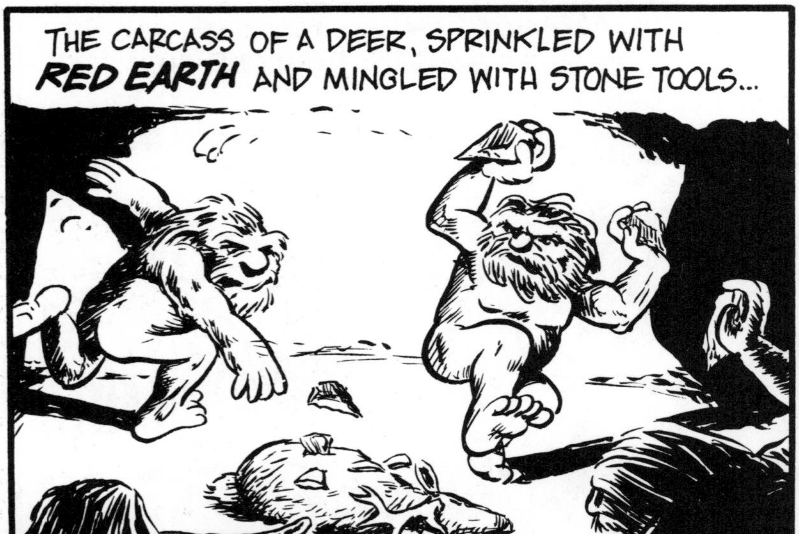
THE CARCASS OF A DEER, SPRINKLED WITH ***RED EARTH*** AND MINGLED WITH STONE TOOLS...

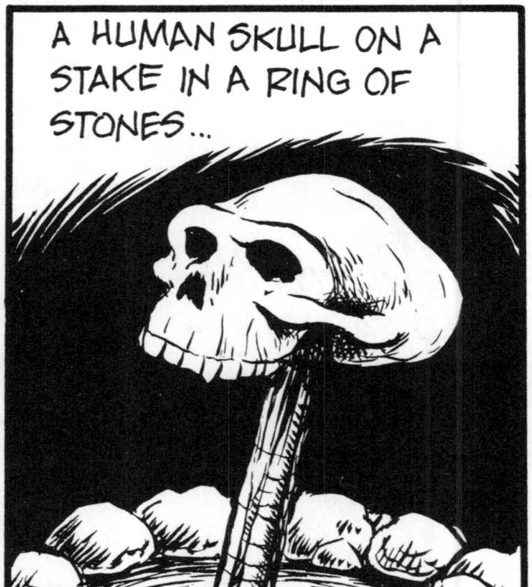
A HUMAN SKULL ON A STAKE IN A RING OF STONES...

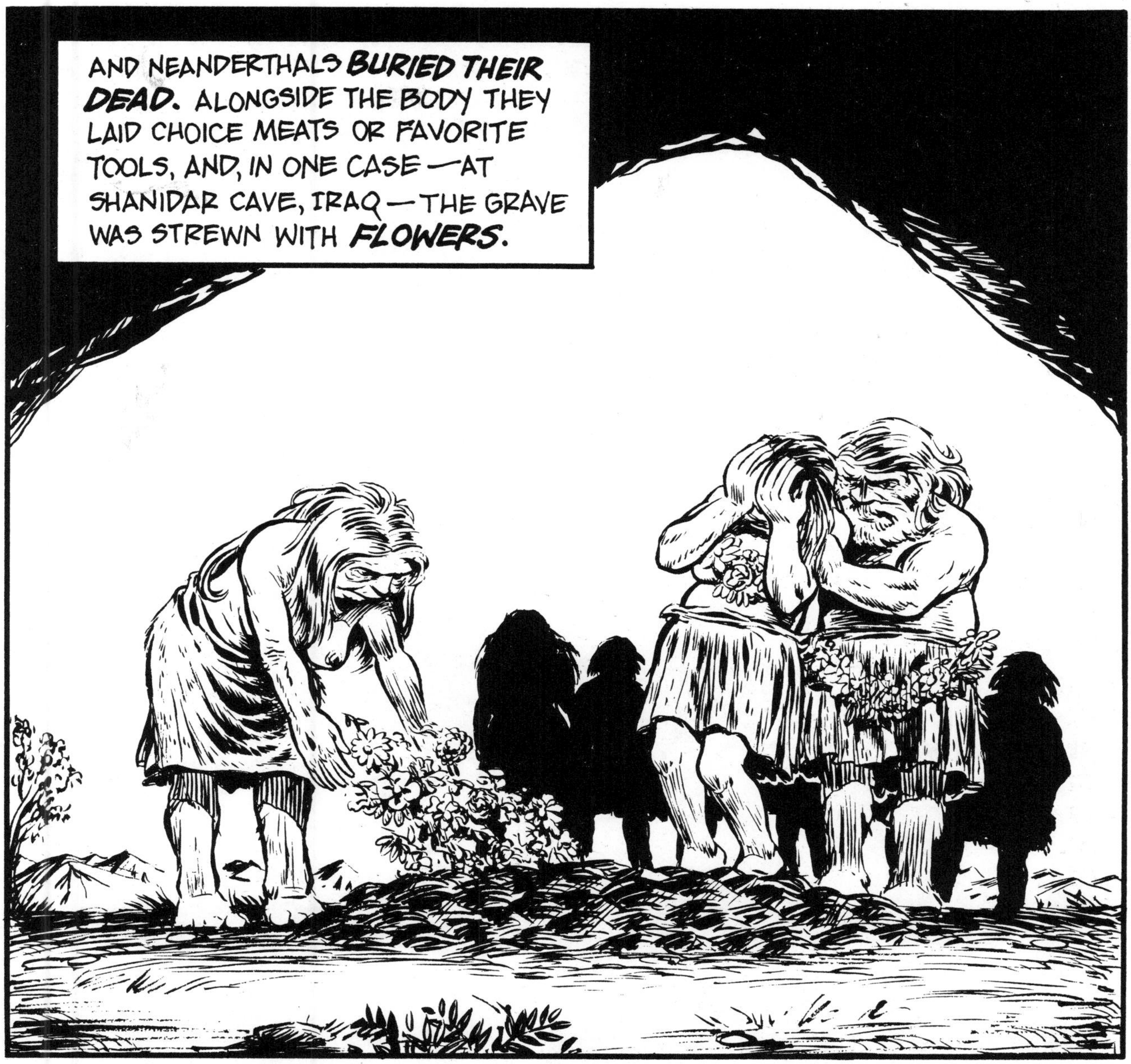
AND NEANDERTHALS BURIED THEIR DEAD. ALONGSIDE THE BODY THEY LAID CHOICE MEATS OR FAVORITE TOOLS, AND, IN ONE CASE—AT SHANIDAR CAVE, IRAQ—THE GRAVE WAS STREWN WITH FLOWERS.

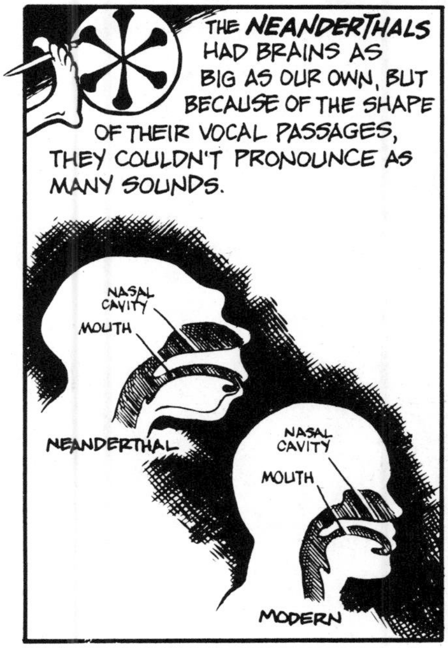
THE NEANDERTHALS HAD BRAINS AS BIG AS OUR OWN, BUT BECAUSE OF THE SHAPE OF THEIR VOCAL PASSAGES, THEY COULDN'T PRONOUNCE AS MANY SOUNDS.
NASAL CAVITY
MOUTH
NEANDERTHAL
NASAL CAVITY
MOUTH
MODERN

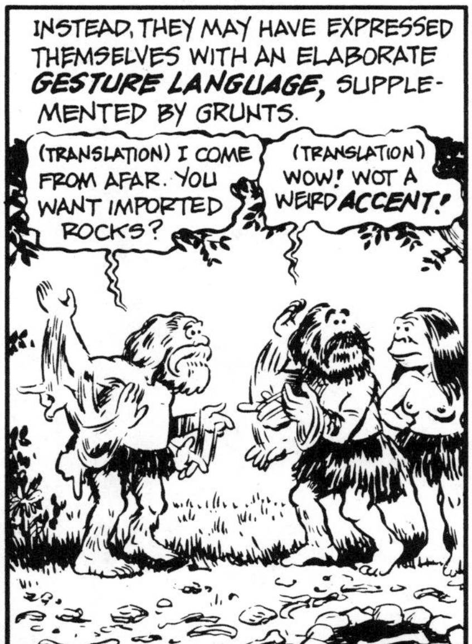
INSTEAD, THEY MAY HAVE EXPRESSED THEMSELVES WITH AN ELABORATE GESTURE LANGUAGE, SUPPLEMENTED BY GRUNTS.
(TRANSLATION) I COME FROM AFAR. YOU WANT IMPORTED ROCKS?
(TRANSLATION) WOW! WOT A WEIRD ACCENT!

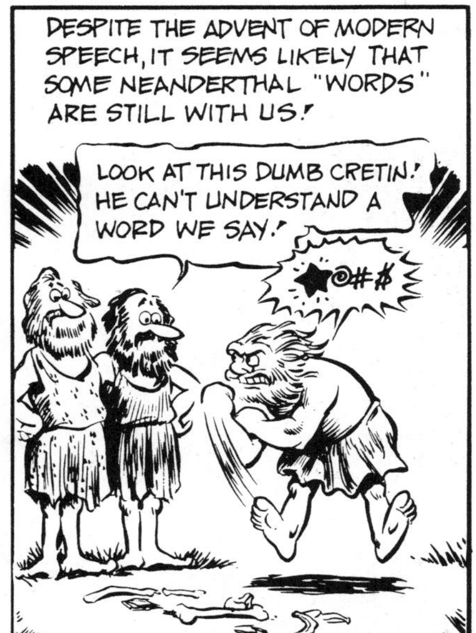
DESPITE THE ADVENT OF MODERN SPEECH, IT SEEMS LIKELY THAT SOME NEANDERTHAL "WORDS" ARE STILL WITH US!
LOOK AT THIS DUMB CRETIN! HE CAN'T UNDERSTAND A WORD WE SAY!
★@#$

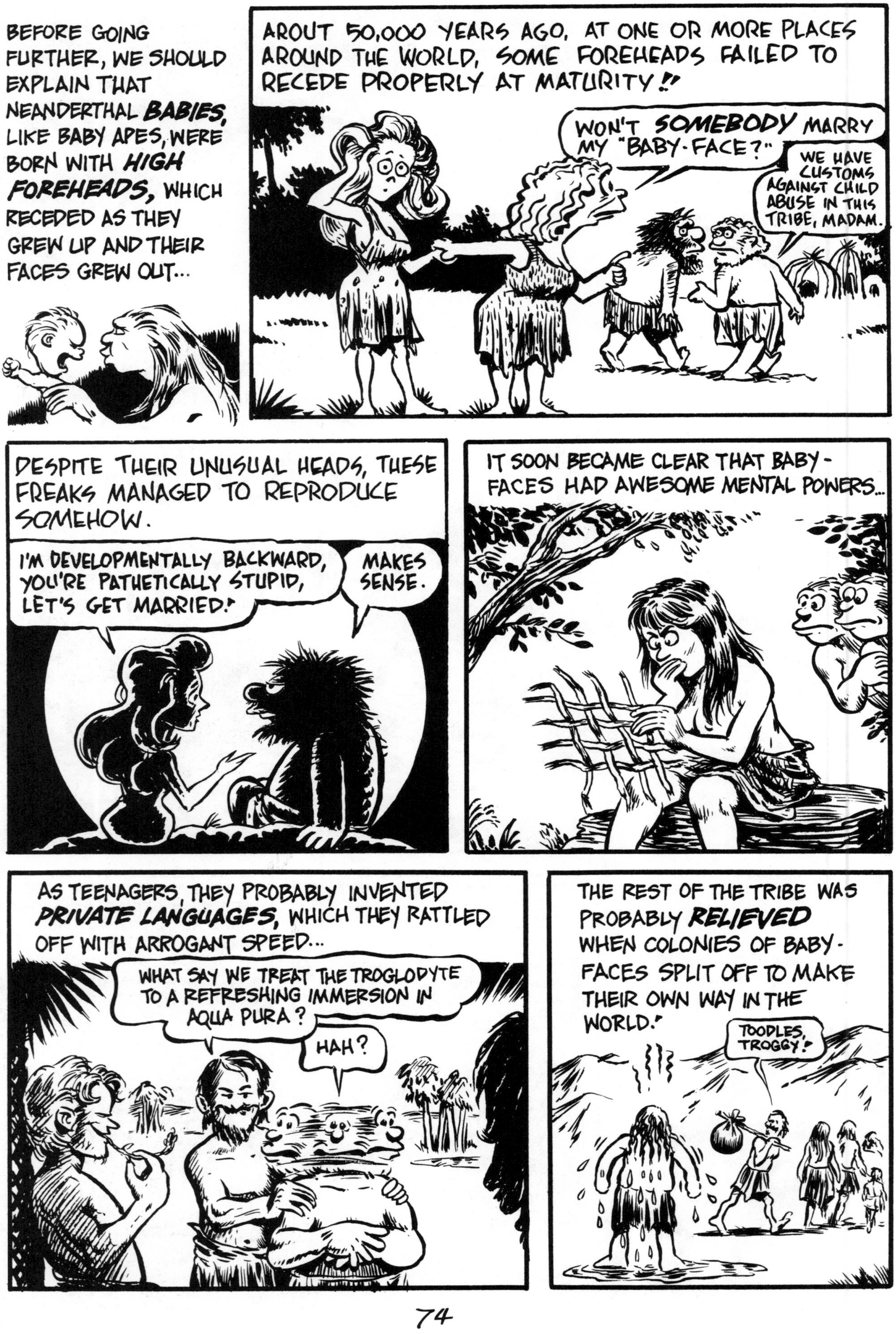
BEFORE GOING FURTHER, WE SHOULD EXPLAIN THAT NEANDERTHAL **BABIES**, LIKE BABY APES, WERE BORN WITH **HIGH FOREHEADS**, WHICH RECEDED AS THEY GREW UP AND THEIR FACES GREW OUT...
ABOUT 50,000 YEARS AGO, AT ONE OR MORE PLACES AROUND THE WORLD, SOME FOREHEADS FAILED TO RECEDE PROPERLY AT MATURITY!!
WON'T **SOMEBODY** MARRY MY "BABY-FACE?"
WE HAVE CUSTOMS AGAINST CHILD ABUSE IN THIS TRIBE, MADAM.
DESPITE THEIR UNUSUAL HEADS, THESE FREAKS MANAGED TO REPRODUCE SOMEHOW.
I'M DEVELOPMENTALLY BACKWARD, YOU'RE PATHETICALLY STUPID, LET'S GET MARRIED!
MAKES SENSE.
IT SOON BECAME CLEAR THAT BABY-FACES HAD AWESOME MENTAL POWERS...
AS TEENAGERS, THEY PROBABLY INVENTED **PRIVATE LANGUAGES**, WHICH THEY RATTLED OFF WITH ARROGANT SPEED...
WHAT SAY WE TREAT THE TROGLODYTE TO A REFRESHING IMMERSION IN AQUA PURA?
HAH?
THE REST OF THE TRIBE WAS PROBABLY **RELIEVED** WHEN COLONIES OF BABY-FACES SPLIT OFF TO MAKE THEIR OWN WAY IN THE WORLD!
TOODLES, TROGGY!

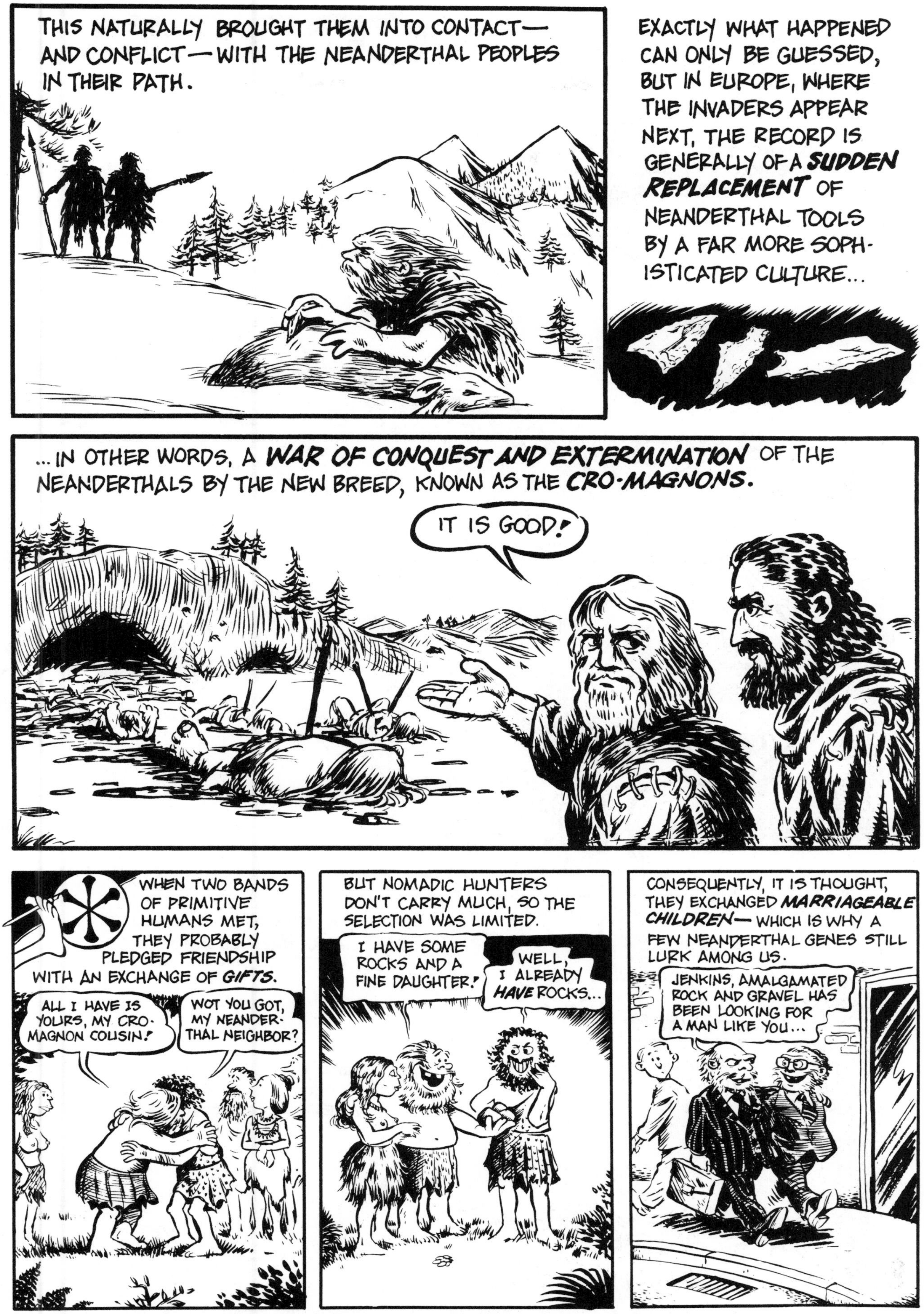
THIS NATURALLY BROUGHT THEM INTO CONTACT— AND CONFLICT—WITH THE NEANDERTHAL PEOPLES IN THEIR PATH.
EXACTLY WHAT HAPPENED CAN ONLY BE GUESSED, BUT IN EUROPE, WHERE THE INVADERS APPEAR NEXT, THE RECORD IS GENERALLY OF A **SUDDEN REPLACEMENT** OF NEANDERTHAL TOOLS BY A FAR MORE SOPHISTICATED CULTURE...
...IN OTHER WORDS, A **WAR OF CONQUEST AND EXTERMINATION** OF THE NEANDERTHALS BY THE NEW BREED, KNOWN AS THE **CRO-MAGNONS.**
IT IS GOOD!
WHEN TWO BANDS OF PRIMITIVE HUMANS MET, THEY PROBABLY PLEDGED FRIENDSHIP WITH AN EXCHANGE OF *GIFTS*.
ALL I HAVE IS YOURS, MY CRO-MAGNON COUSIN!
WOT YOU GOT, MY NEANDERTHAL NEIGHBOR?
BUT NOMADIC HUNTERS DON'T CARRY MUCH, SO THE SELECTION WAS LIMITED.
I HAVE SOME ROCKS AND A FINE DAUGHTER!
WELL, I ALREADY *HAVE* ROCKS...
CONSEQUENTLY, IT IS THOUGHT, THEY EXCHANGED **MARRIAGEABLE CHILDREN**— WHICH IS WHY A FEW NEANDERTHAL GENES STILL LURK AMONG US.
JENKINS, AMALGAMATED ROCK AND GRAVEL HAS BEEN LOOKING FOR A MAN LIKE YOU...

CRO-MAGNO
OF THE

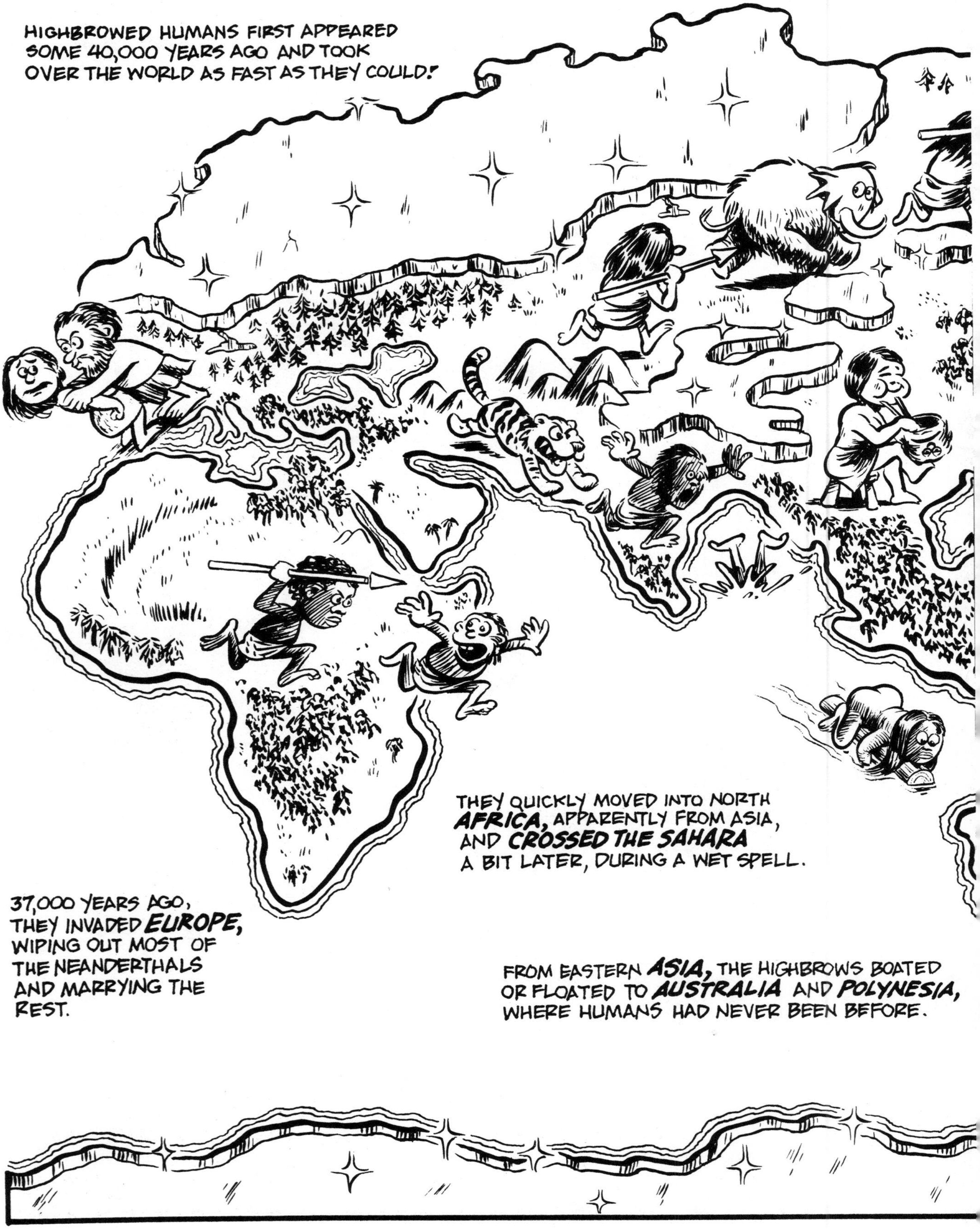
HIGHBROWED HUMANS FIRST APPEARED SOME 40,000 YEARS AGO AND TOOK OVER THE WORLD AS FAST AS THEY COULD!
THEY QUICKLY MOVED INTO NORTH **AFRICA,** APPARENTLY FROM ASIA, AND **CROSSED THE SAHARA** A BIT LATER, DURING A WET SPELL.
37,000 YEARS AGO, THEY INVADED **EUROPE,** WIPING OUT MOST OF THE NEANDERTHALS AND MARRYING THE REST.
FROM EASTERN **ASIA,** THE HIGHBROWS BOATED OR FLOATED TO **AUSTRALIA** AND **POLYNESIA,** WHERE HUMANS HAD NEVER BEEN BEFORE.

N CONQUEST
WORLD

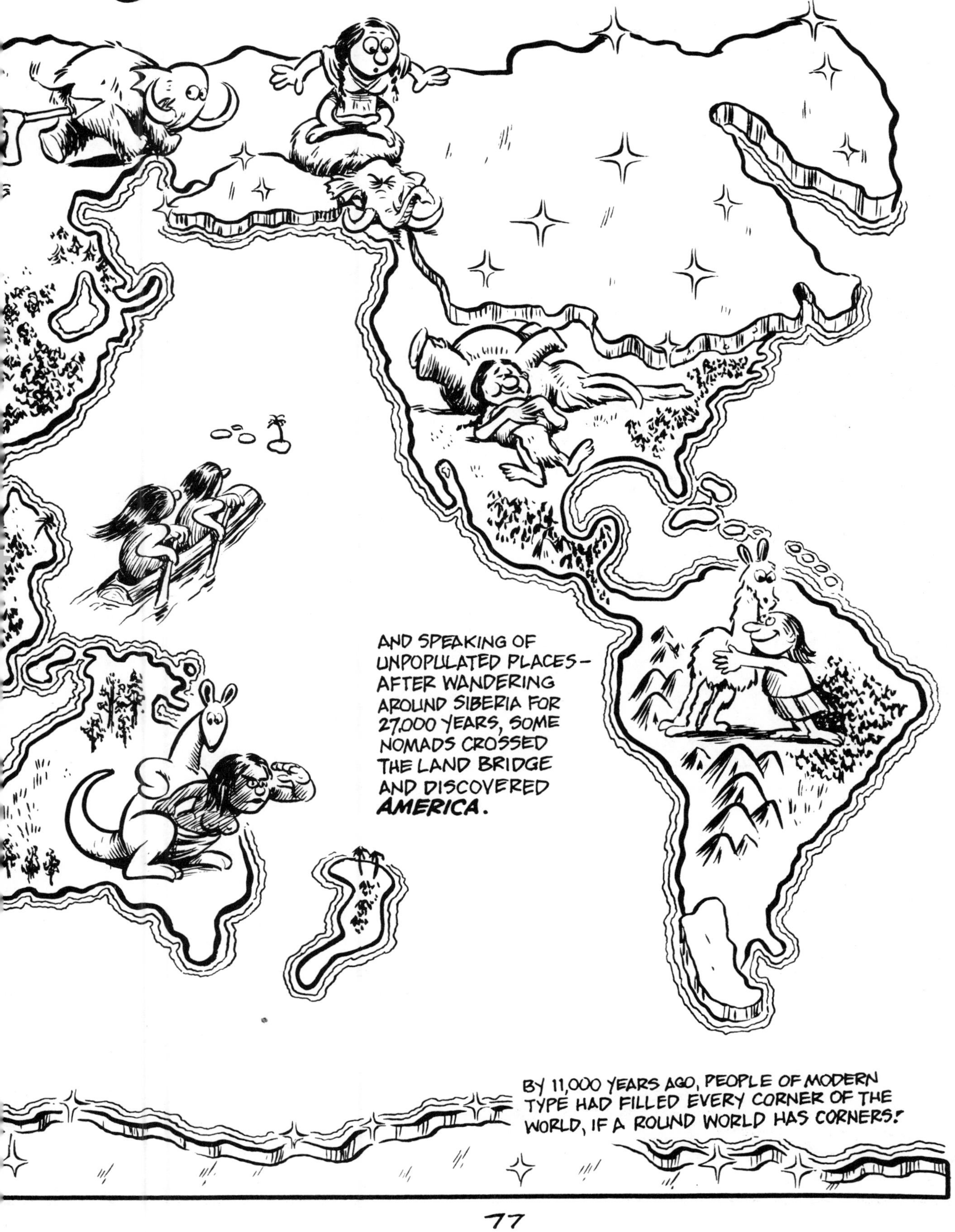
AND SPEAKING OF UNPOPULATED PLACES— AFTER WANDERING AROUND SIBERIA FOR 27,000 YEARS, SOME NOMADS CROSSED THE LAND BRIDGE AND DISCOVERED ***AMERICA***.
BY 11,000 YEARS AGO, PEOPLE OF MODERN TYPE HAD FILLED EVERY CORNER OF THE WORLD, IF A ROUND WORLD HAS CORNERS.*

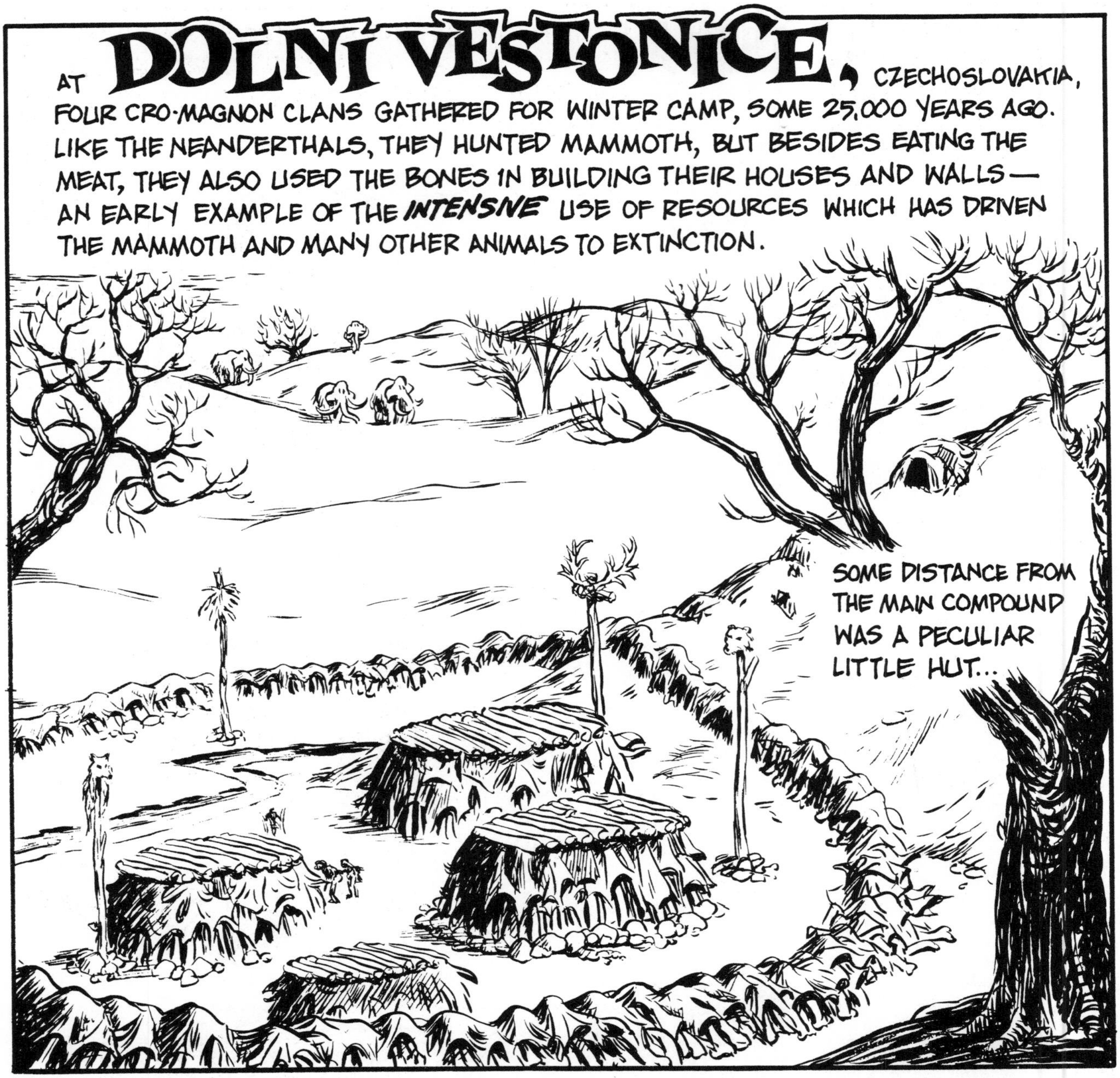
AT DOLNI VESTONICE, CZECHOSLOVAKIA,
FOUR CRO-MAGNON CLANS GATHERED FOR WINTER CAMP, SOME 25,000 YEARS AGO. LIKE THE NEANDERTHALS, THEY HUNTED MAMMOTH, BUT BESIDES EATING THE MEAT, THEY ALSO USED THE BONES IN BUILDING THEIR HOUSES AND WALLS— AN EARLY EXAMPLE OF THE *INTENSIVE* USE OF RESOURCES WHICH HAS DRIVEN THE MAMMOTH AND MANY OTHER ANIMALS TO EXTINCTION.
SOME DISTANCE FROM THE MAIN COMPOUND WAS A PECULIAR LITTLE HUT...

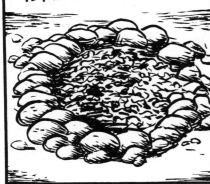

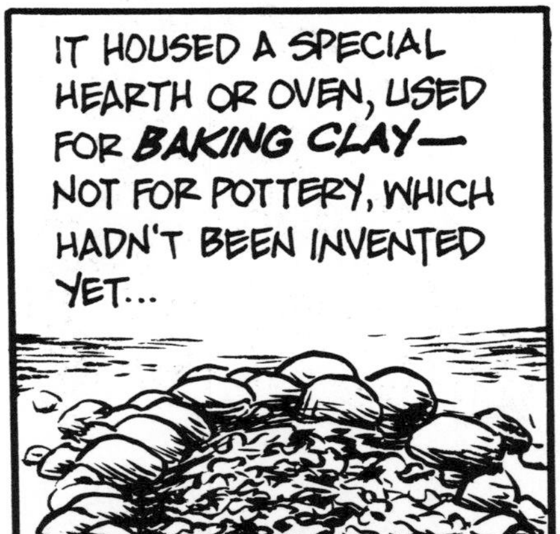
IT HOUSED A SPECIAL HEARTH OR OVEN, USED FOR *BAKING CLAY*— NOT FOR POTTERY, WHICH HADN'T BEEN INVENTED YET...

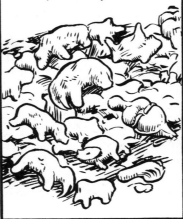

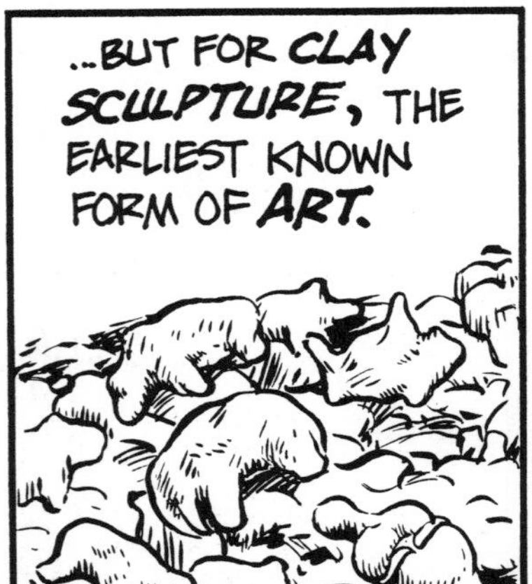
...BUT FOR *CLAY SCULPTURE*, THE EARLIEST KNOWN FORM OF *ART*.

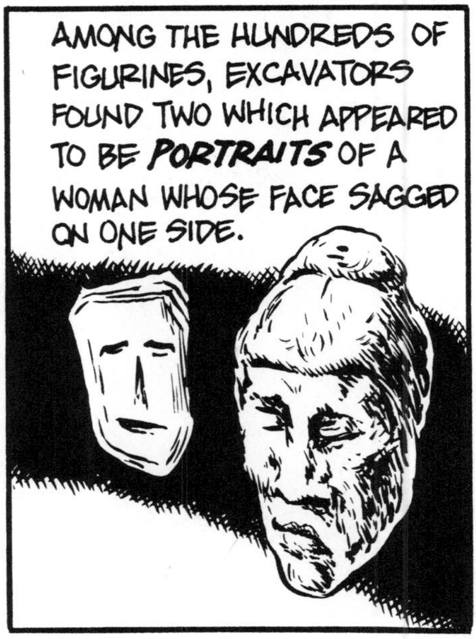
AMONG THE HUNDREDS OF FIGURINES, EXCAVATORS FOUND TWO WHICH APPEARED TO BE *PORTRAITS* OF A WOMAN WHOSE FACE SAGGED ON ONE SIDE.

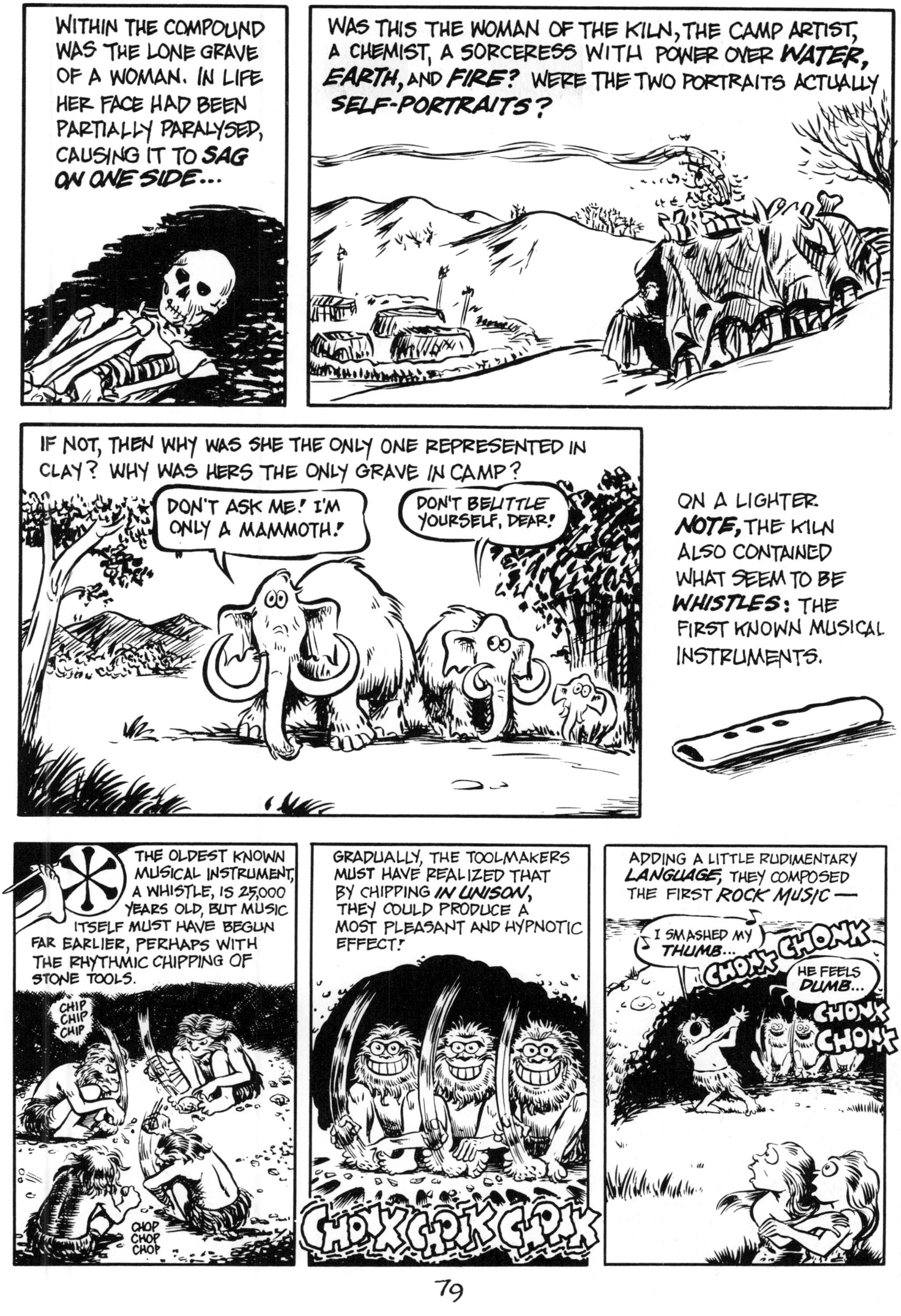
WITHIN THE COMPOUND WAS THE LONE GRAVE OF A WOMAN. IN LIFE HER FACE HAD BEEN PARTIALLY PARALYSED, CAUSING IT TO SAG ON ONE SIDE...
WAS THIS THE WOMAN OF THE KILN, THE CAMP ARTIST, A CHEMIST, A SORCERESS WITH POWER OVER WATER, EARTH, AND FIRE? WERE THE TWO PORTRAITS ACTUALLY SELF-PORTRAITS?
IF NOT, THEN WHY WAS SHE THE ONLY ONE REPRESENTED IN CLAY? WHY WAS HERS THE ONLY GRAVE IN CAMP?
DON'T ASK ME! I'M ONLY A MAMMOTH!
DON'T BELITTLE YOURSELF, DEAR!
ON A LIGHTER NOTE, THE KILN ALSO CONTAINED WHAT SEEM TO BE WHISTLES: THE FIRST KNOWN MUSICAL INSTRUMENTS.
THE OLDEST KNOWN MUSICAL INSTRUMENT, A WHISTLE, IS 25,000 YEARS OLD, BUT MUSIC ITSELF MUST HAVE BEGUN FAR EARLIER, PERHAPS WITH THE RHYTHMIC CHIPPING OF STONE TOOLS.
CHIP CHIP CHIP
CHOP CHOP CHOP
GRADUALLY, THE TOOLMAKERS MUST HAVE REALIZED THAT BY CHIPPING IN UNISON, THEY COULD PRODUCE A MOST PLEASANT AND HYPNOTIC EFFECT!
CHOK CHOK CHOK
ADDING A LITTLE RUDIMENTARY LANGUAGE, THEY COMPOSED THE FIRST ROCK MUSIC—
I SMASHED MY THUMB...
CHONK CHONK
HE FEELS DUMB...
CHONK CHONK

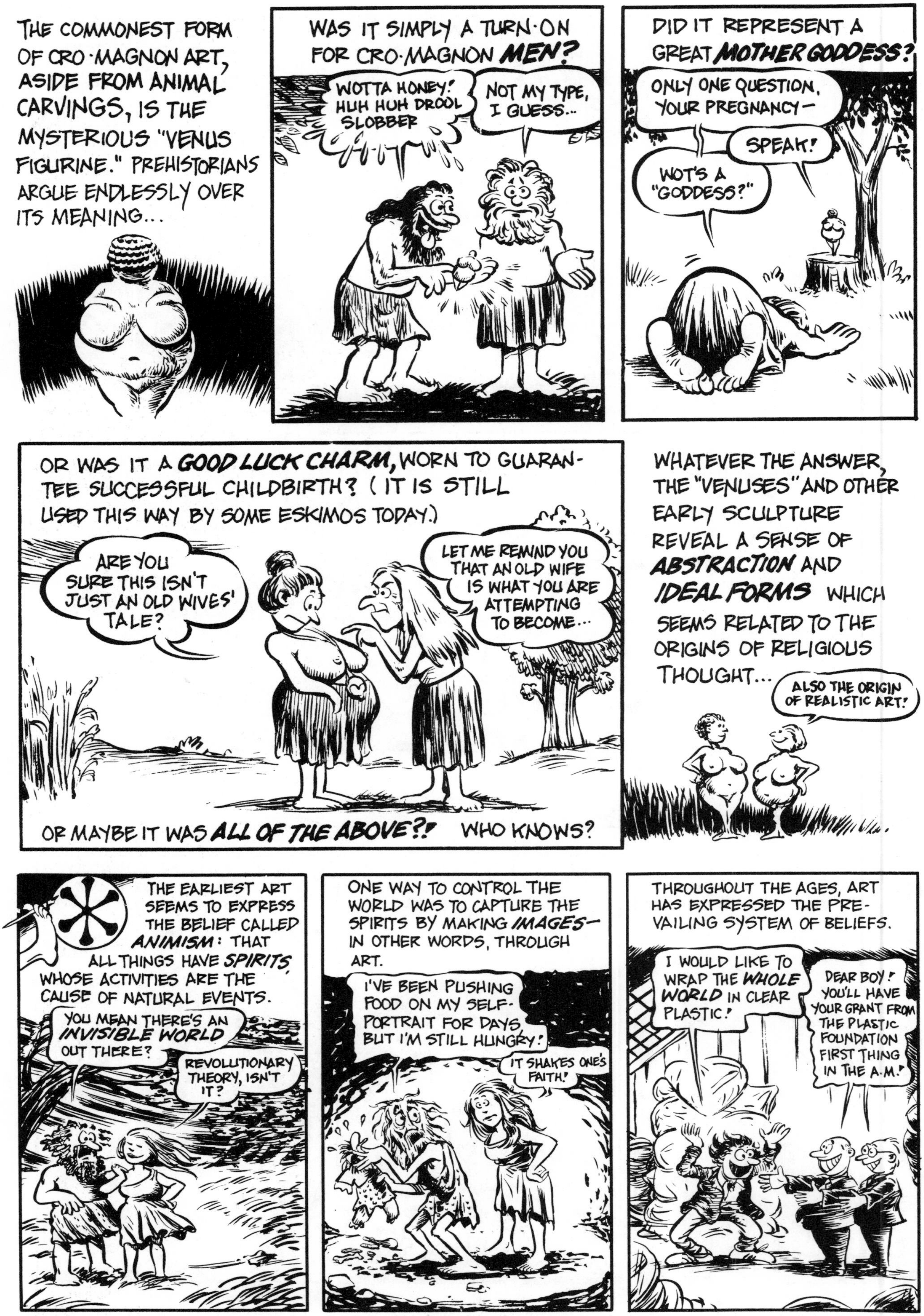

THE COMMONEST FORM OF CRO·MAGNON ART, ASIDE FROM ANIMAL CARVINGS, IS THE MYSTERIOUS "VENUS FIGURINE." PREHISTORIANS ARGUE ENDLESSLY OVER ITS MEANING...
WAS IT SIMPLY A TURN·ON FOR CRO·MAGNON MEN?
WOTTA HONEY! HUH HUH DROOL SLOBBER
NOT MY TYPE, I GUESS...
DID IT REPRESENT A GREAT MOTHER GODDESS?
ONLY ONE QUESTION, YOUR PREGNANCY—
SPEAK!
WOT'S A "GODDESS?"
OR WAS IT A GOOD LUCK CHARM, WORN TO GUARANTEE SUCCESSFUL CHILDBIRTH? (IT IS STILL USED THIS WAY BY SOME ESKIMOS TODAY.)
ARE YOU SURE THIS ISN'T JUST AN OLD WIVES' TALE?
LET ME REMIND YOU THAT AN OLD WIFE IS WHAT YOU ARE ATTEMPTING TO BECOME...
OR MAYBE IT WAS ALL OF THE ABOVE?! WHO KNOWS?
WHATEVER THE ANSWER, THE "VENUSES" AND OTHER EARLY SCULPTURE REVEAL A SENSE OF ABSTRACTION AND IDEAL FORMS WHICH SEEMS RELATED TO THE ORIGINS OF RELIGIOUS THOUGHT...
ALSO THE ORIGIN OF REALISTIC ART!
THE EARLIEST ART SEEMS TO EXPRESS THE BELIEF CALLED ANIMISM: THAT ALL THINGS HAVE SPIRITS, WHOSE ACTIVITIES ARE THE CAUSE OF NATURAL EVENTS.
YOU MEAN THERE'S AN INVISIBLE WORLD OUT THERE?
REVOLUTIONARY THEORY, ISN'T IT?
ONE WAY TO CONTROL THE WORLD WAS TO CAPTURE THE SPIRITS BY MAKING IMAGES— IN OTHER WORDS, THROUGH ART.
I'VE BEEN PUSHING FOOD ON MY SELF-PORTRAIT FOR DAYS, BUT I'M STILL HUNGRY!
IT SHAKES ONE'S FAITH!
THROUGHOUT THE AGES, ART HAS EXPRESSED THE PREVAILING SYSTEM OF BELIEFS.
I WOULD LIKE TO WRAP THE WHOLE WORLD IN CLEAR PLASTIC!
DEAR BOY! YOU'LL HAVE YOUR GRANT FROM THE PLASTIC FOUNDATION FIRST THING IN THE A.M.!

ANCIENT ***PAINTING*** IS KNOWN FROM FRANCE, SPAIN, AND THE SOUTHERN SAHARA.

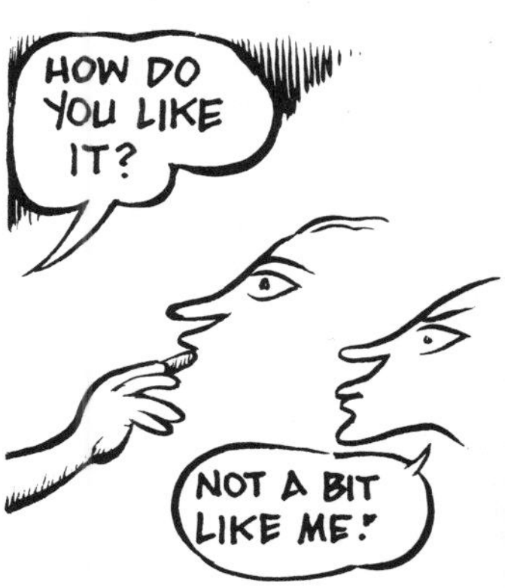
HOW DO YOU LIKE IT?
NOT A BIT LIKE ME!

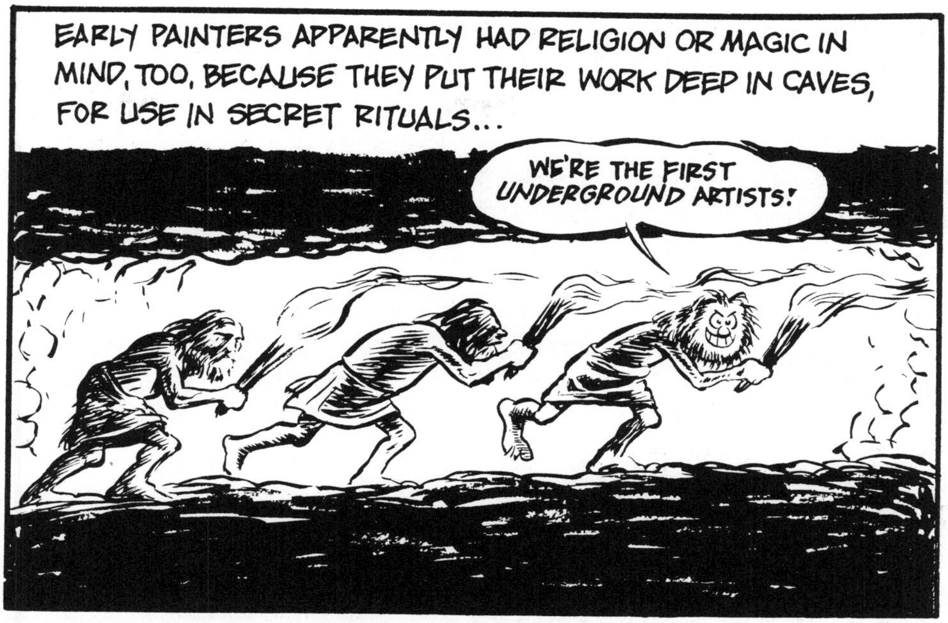
EARLY PAINTERS APPARENTLY HAD RELIGION OR MAGIC IN MIND, TOO, BECAUSE THEY PUT THEIR WORK DEEP IN CAVES, FOR USE IN SECRET RITUALS...
WE'RE THE FIRST *UNDERGROUND* ARTISTS!

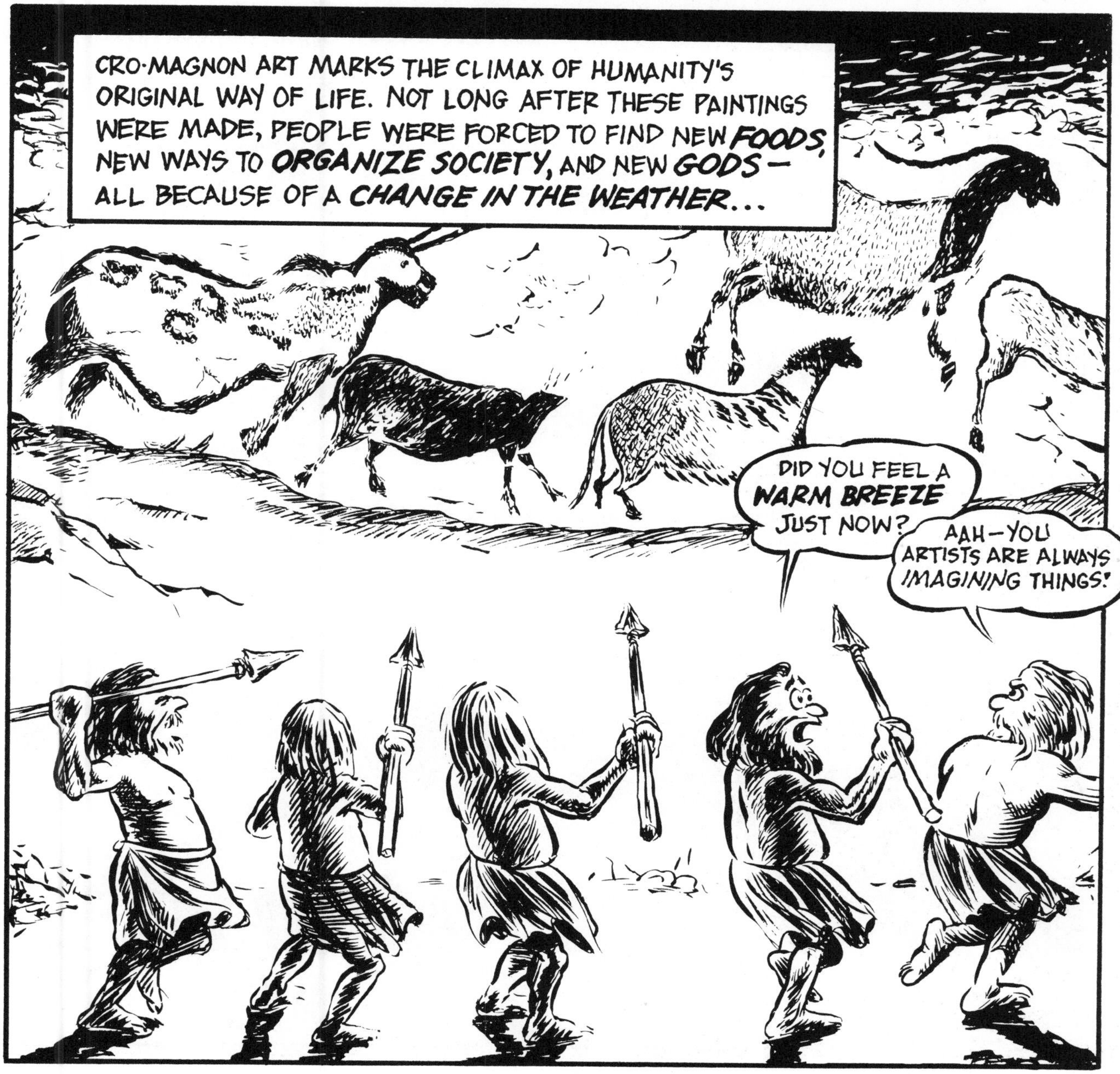
CRO-MAGNON ART MARKS THE CLIMAX OF HUMANITY'S ORIGINAL WAY OF LIFE. NOT LONG AFTER THESE PAINTINGS WERE MADE, PEOPLE WERE FORCED TO FIND NEW ***FOODS,*** NEW WAYS TO ***ORGANIZE SOCIETY,*** AND NEW ***GODS*** — ALL BECAUSE OF A ***CHANGE IN THE WEATHER***...
DID YOU FEEL A **WARM BREEZE** JUST NOW?
AAH—YOU ARTISTS ARE ALWAYS *IMAGINING* THINGS!

END OF AN AGE

AROUND 12,000 YEARS AGO, THE EARTH'S CLIMATE BEGAN TO **WARM** AGAIN, MELTING THE GLACIERS AND BRINGING AN END TO THE LAST **ICE AGE**. THIS SOUNDS NICE, BUT—

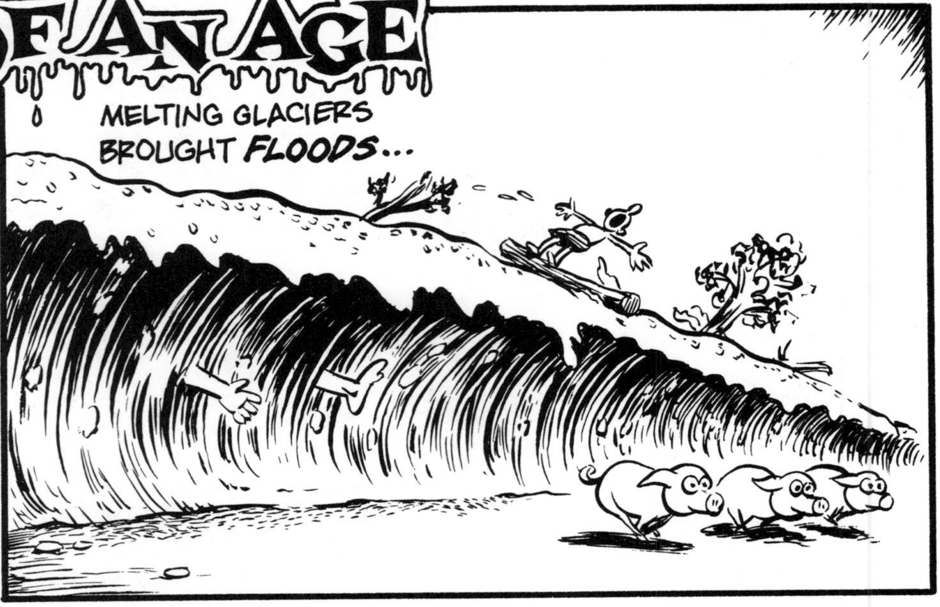

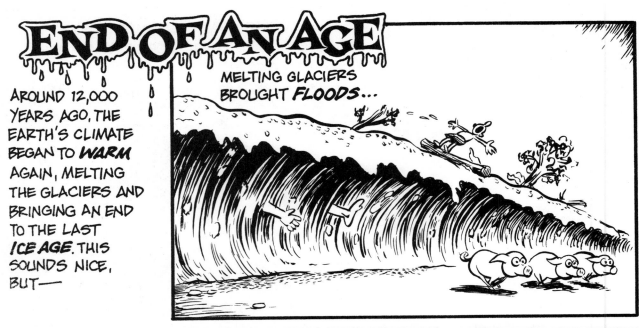

MELTING GLACIERS BROUGHT **FLOODS**...

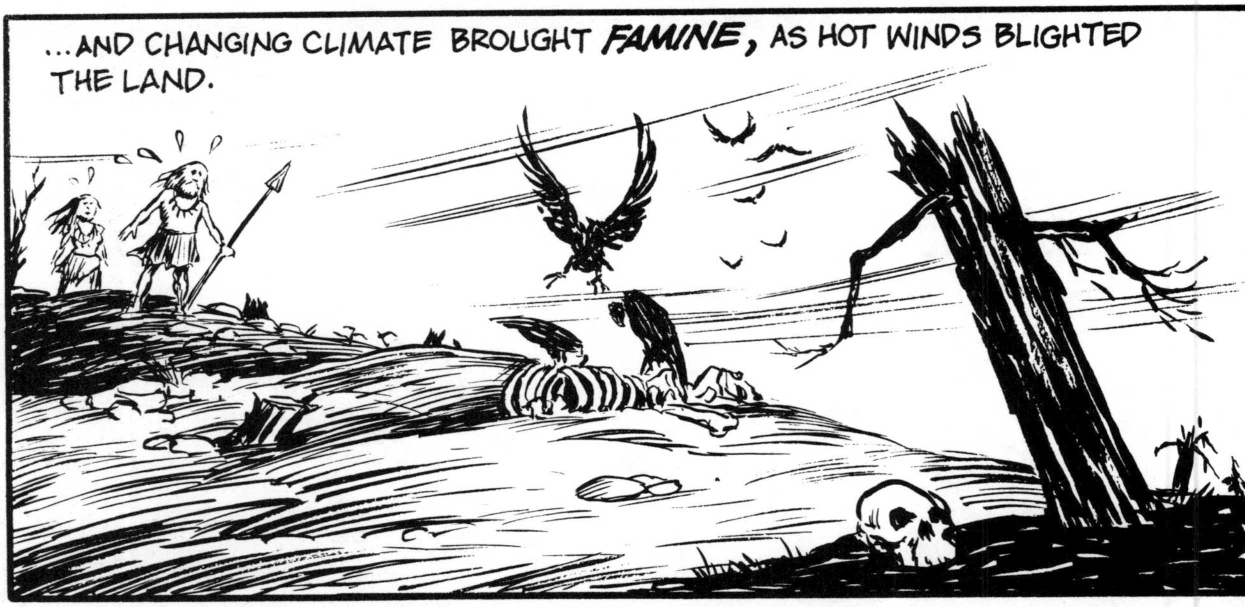

...AND CHANGING CLIMATE BROUGHT **FAMINE**, AS HOT WINDS BLIGHTED THE LAND.

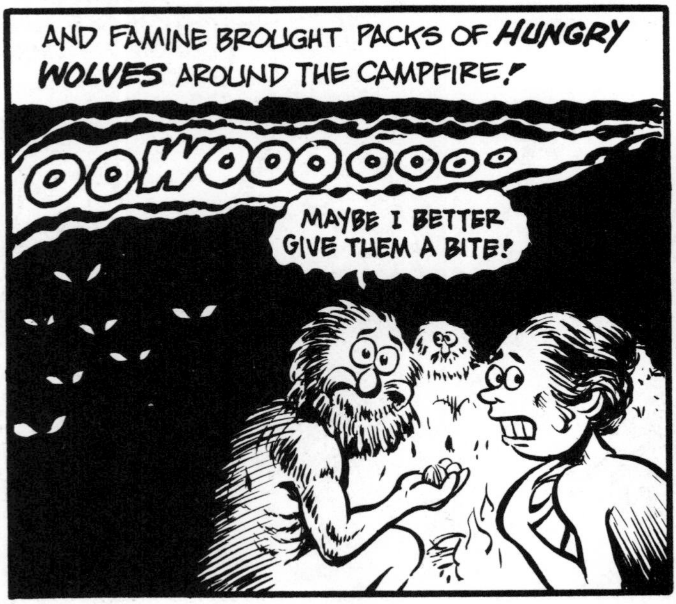

AND FAMINE BROUGHT PACKS OF **HUNGRY WOLVES** AROUND THE CAMPFIRE!
OOWOOOOOOO
MAYBE I BETTER GIVE THEM A BITE!

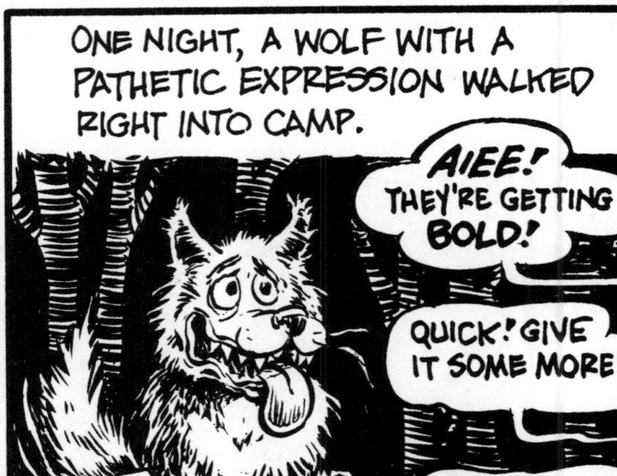

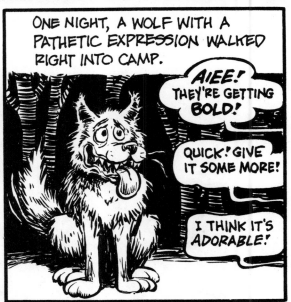

ONE NIGHT, A WOLF WITH A PATHETIC EXPRESSION WALKED RIGHT INTO CAMP.
AIEE! THEY'RE GETTING BOLD!
QUICK! GIVE IT SOME MORE!
I THINK IT'S ADORABLE!

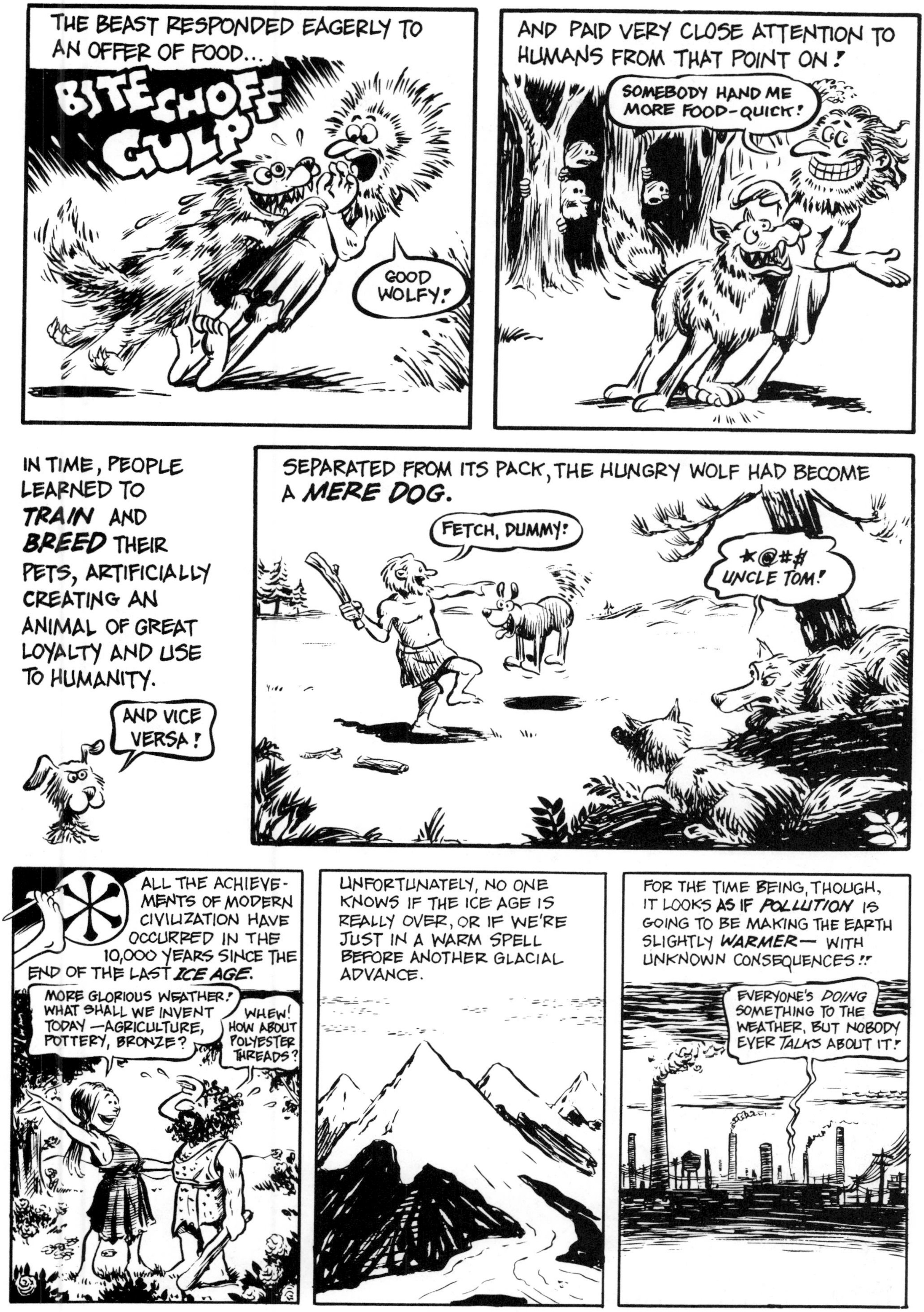
THE BEAST RESPONDED EAGERLY TO AN OFFER OF FOOD...
BITE CHOFF GULP
GOOD WOLFY!
AND PAID VERY CLOSE ATTENTION TO HUMANS FROM THAT POINT ON!
SOMEBODY HAND ME MORE FOOD-QUICK!
IN TIME, PEOPLE LEARNED TO TRAIN AND BREED THEIR PETS, ARTIFICIALLY CREATING AN ANIMAL OF GREAT LOYALTY AND USE TO HUMANITY.
AND VICE VERSA!
SEPARATED FROM ITS PACK, THE HUNGRY WOLF HAD BECOME A MERE DOG.
FETCH, DUMMY!
*@#$ UNCLE TOM!
ALL THE ACHIEVEMENTS OF MODERN CIVILIZATION HAVE OCCURRED IN THE 10,000 YEARS SINCE THE END OF THE LAST ICE AGE.
MORE GLORIOUS WEATHER! WHAT SHALL WE INVENT TODAY —AGRICULTURE, POTTERY, BRONZE?
WHEW! HOW ABOUT POLYESTER THREADS?
UNFORTUNATELY, NO ONE KNOWS IF THE ICE AGE IS REALLY OVER, OR IF WE'RE JUST IN A WARM SPELL BEFORE ANOTHER GLACIAL ADVANCE.
FOR THE TIME BEING, THOUGH, IT LOOKS AS IF POLLUTION IS GOING TO BE MAKING THE EARTH SLIGHTLY WARMER— WITH UNKNOWN CONSEQUENCES!!
EVERYONE'S DOING SOMETHING TO THE WEATHER, BUT NOBODY EVER TALKS ABOUT IT!

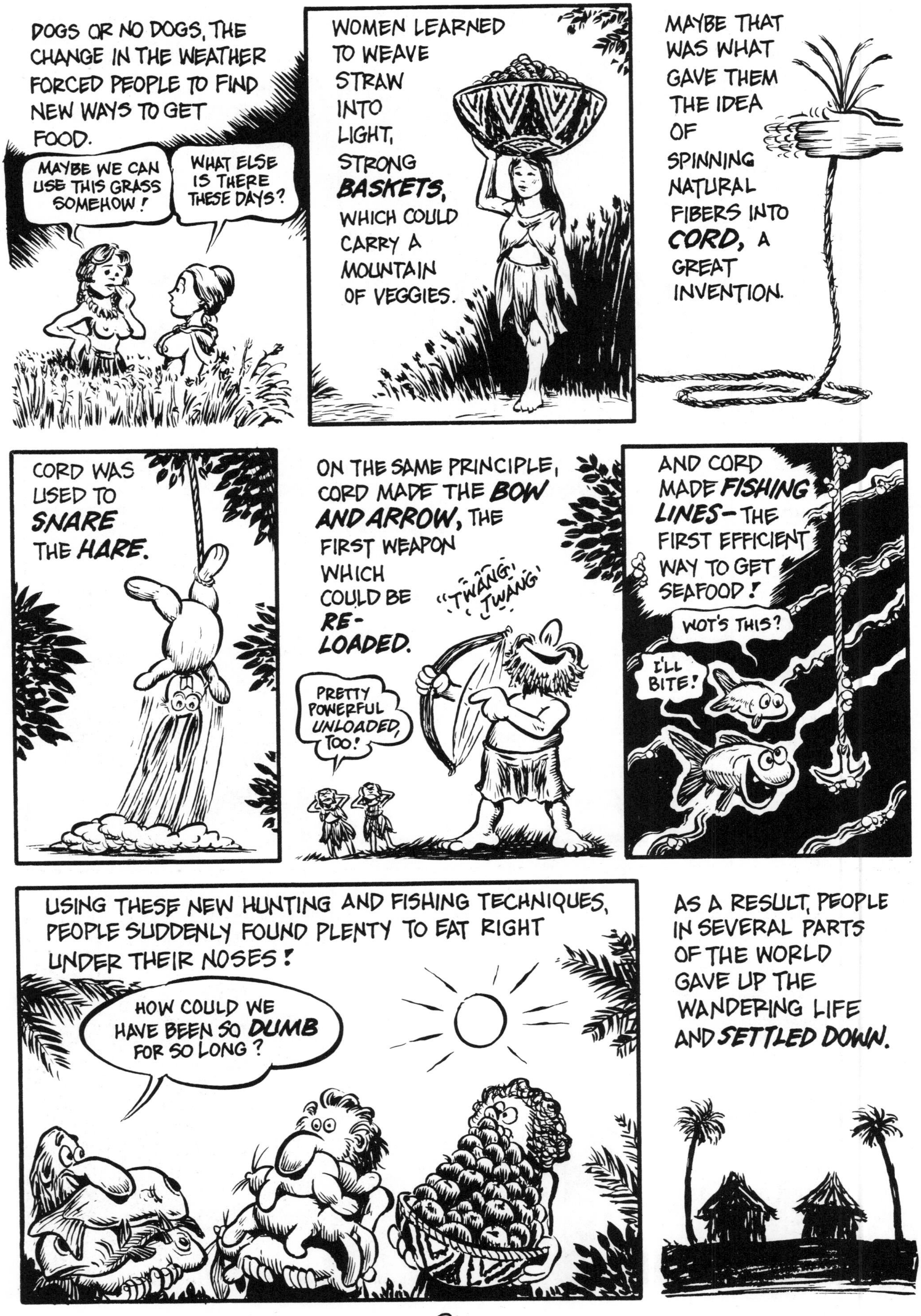
DOGS OR NO DOGS, THE CHANGE IN THE WEATHER FORCED PEOPLE TO FIND NEW WAYS TO GET FOOD.
MAYBE WE CAN USE THIS GRASS SOMEHOW!
WHAT ELSE IS THERE THESE DAYS?
WOMEN LEARNED TO WEAVE STRAW INTO LIGHT, STRONG BASKETS, WHICH COULD CARRY A MOUNTAIN OF VEGGIES.
MAYBE THAT WAS WHAT GAVE THEM THE IDEA OF SPINNING NATURAL FIBERS INTO CORD, A GREAT INVENTION.
CORD WAS USED TO SNARE THE HARE.
ON THE SAME PRINCIPLE, CORD MADE THE BOW AND ARROW, THE FIRST WEAPON WHICH COULD BE RE-LOADED.
"TWANG TWANG"
PRETTY POWERFUL UNLOADED, TOO!
AND CORD MADE FISHING LINES— THE FIRST EFFICIENT WAY TO GET SEAFOOD!
WOT'S THIS?
I'LL BITE!
USING THESE NEW HUNTING AND FISHING TECHNIQUES, PEOPLE SUDDENLY FOUND PLENTY TO EAT RIGHT UNDER THEIR NOSES!
HOW COULD WE HAVE BEEN SO DUMB FOR SO LONG?
AS A RESULT, PEOPLE IN SEVERAL PARTS OF THE WORLD GAVE UP THE WANDERING LIFE AND SETTLED DOWN.

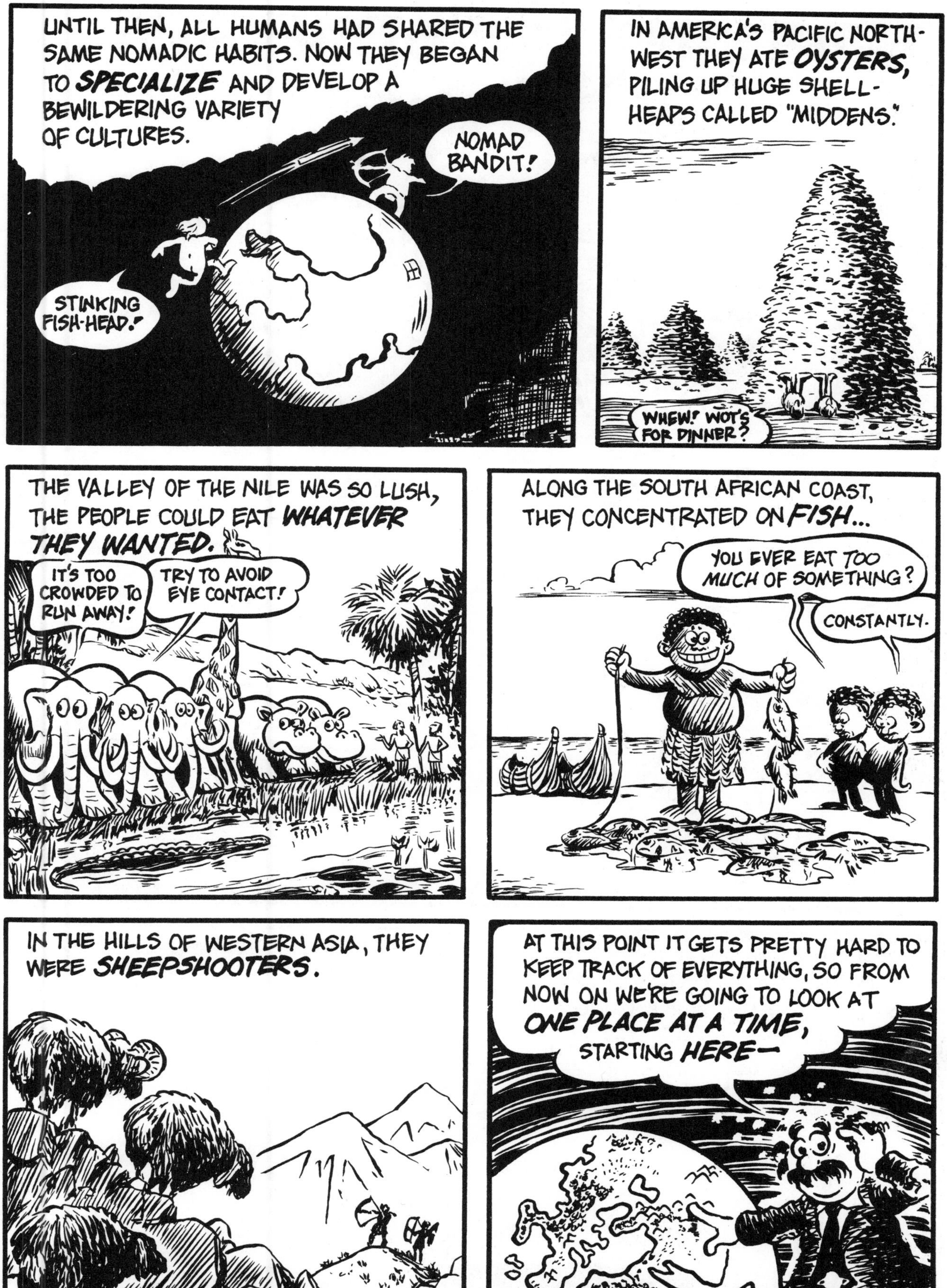
UNTIL THEN, ALL HUMANS HAD SHARED THE SAME NOMADIC HABITS. NOW THEY BEGAN TO SPECIALIZE AND DEVELOP A BEWILDERING VARIETY OF CULTURES.
NOMAD BANDIT!
STINKING FISH-HEAD!
IN AMERICA'S PACIFIC NORTH-WEST THEY ATE OYSTERS, PILING UP HUGE SHELL-HEAPS CALLED "MIDDENS."
WHEW! WOT'S FOR DINNER?
THE VALLEY OF THE NILE WAS SO LUSH, THE PEOPLE COULD EAT WHATEVER THEY WANTED.
IT'S TOO CROWDED TO RUN AWAY!
TRY TO AVOID EYE CONTACT!
ALONG THE SOUTH AFRICAN COAST, THEY CONCENTRATED ON FISH...
YOU EVER EAT TOO MUCH OF SOMETHING?
CONSTANTLY.
IN THE HILLS OF WESTERN ASIA, THEY WERE SHEEPSHOOTERS.
AT THIS POINT IT GETS PRETTY HARD TO KEEP TRACK OF EVERYTHING, SO FROM NOW ON WE'RE GOING TO LOOK AT ONE PLACE AT A TIME, STARTING HERE—

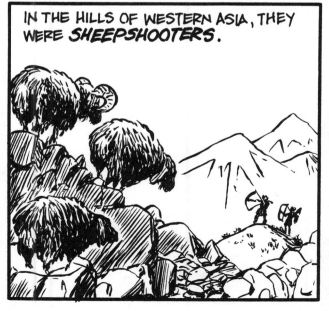

IN THE HILLS OF WESTERN ASIA

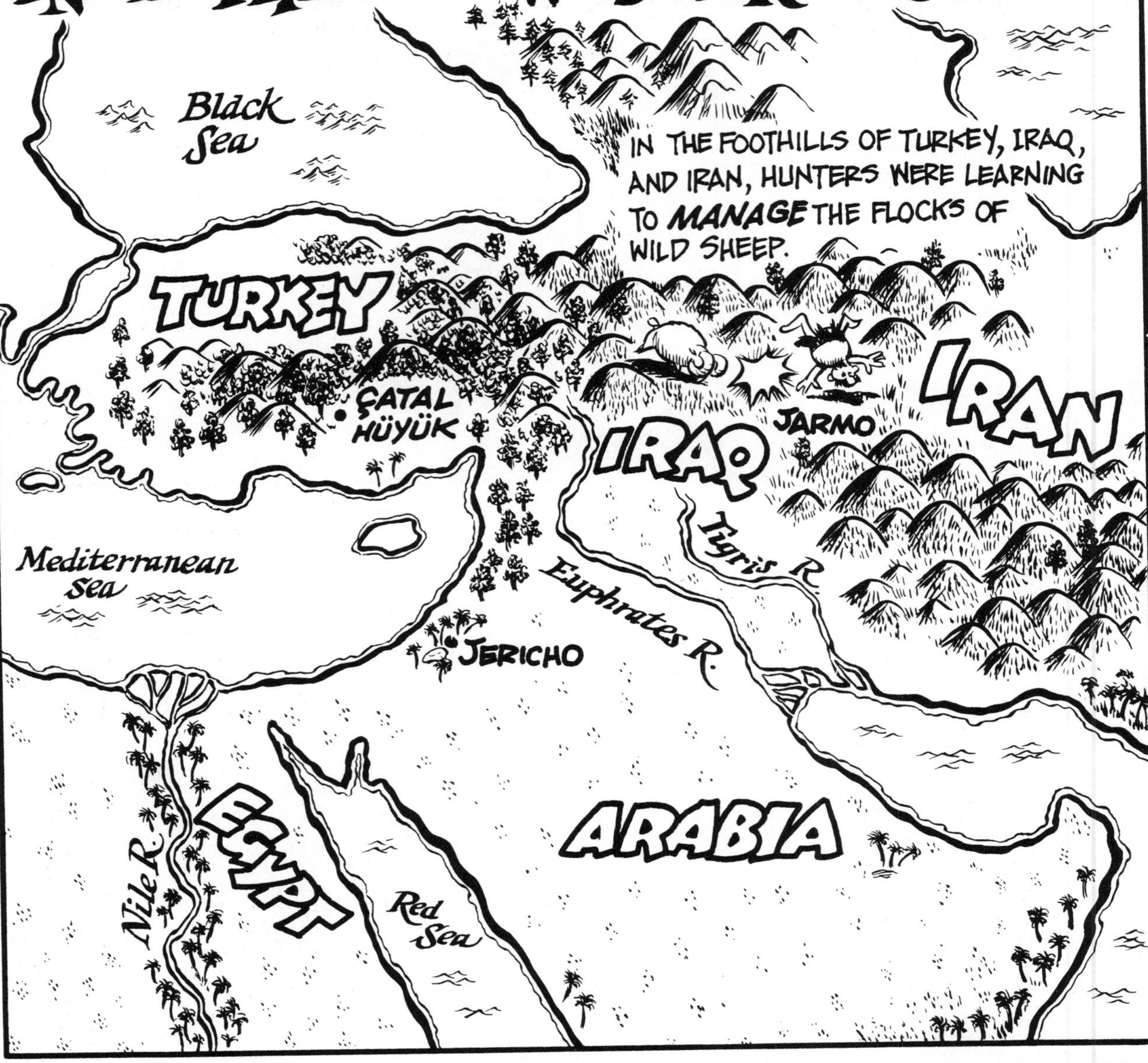
IN THE FOOTHILLS OF TURKEY, IRAQ, AND IRAN, HUNTERS WERE LEARNING TO *MANAGE* THE FLOCKS OF WILD SHEEP.
Black Sea
TURKEY
ÇATAL HÜYÜK
JARMO
IRAN
IRAQ
Tigris R.
Mediterranean Sea
Euphrates R.
JERICHO
EGYPT
ARABIA
Nile R.
Red Sea

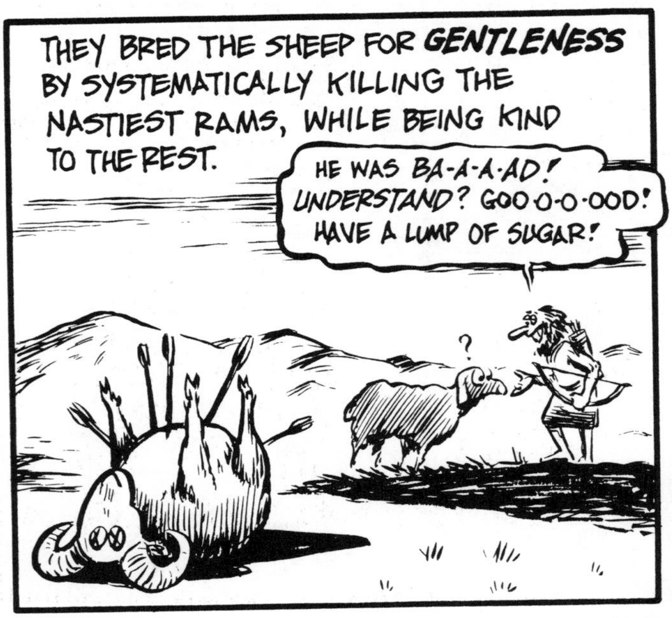
THEY BRED THE SHEEP FOR *GENTLENESS* BY SYSTEMATICALLY KILLING THE NASTIEST RAMS, WHILE BEING KIND TO THE REST.
HE WAS BA-A-A-AD! UNDERSTAND? GOO-O-O-OOD! HAVE A LUMP OF SUGAR!
?

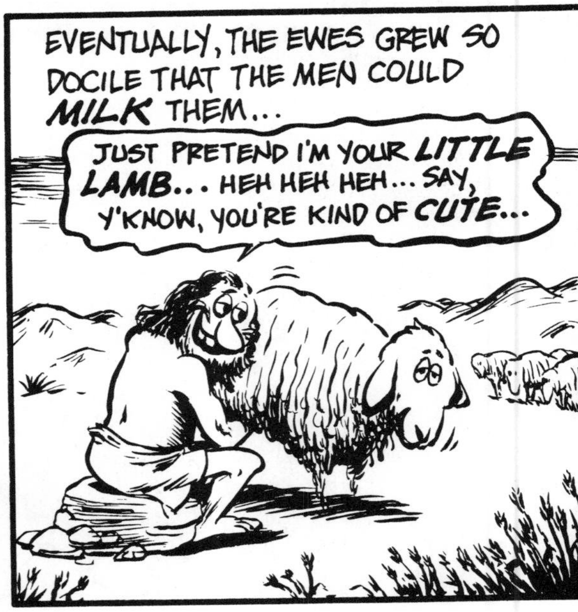
EVENTUALLY, THE EWES GREW SO DOCILE THAT THE MEN COULD *MILK* THEM...
JUST PRETEND I'M YOUR *LITTLE LAMB*... HEH HEH HEH... SAY, Y'KNOW, YOU'RE KIND OF *CUTE*...

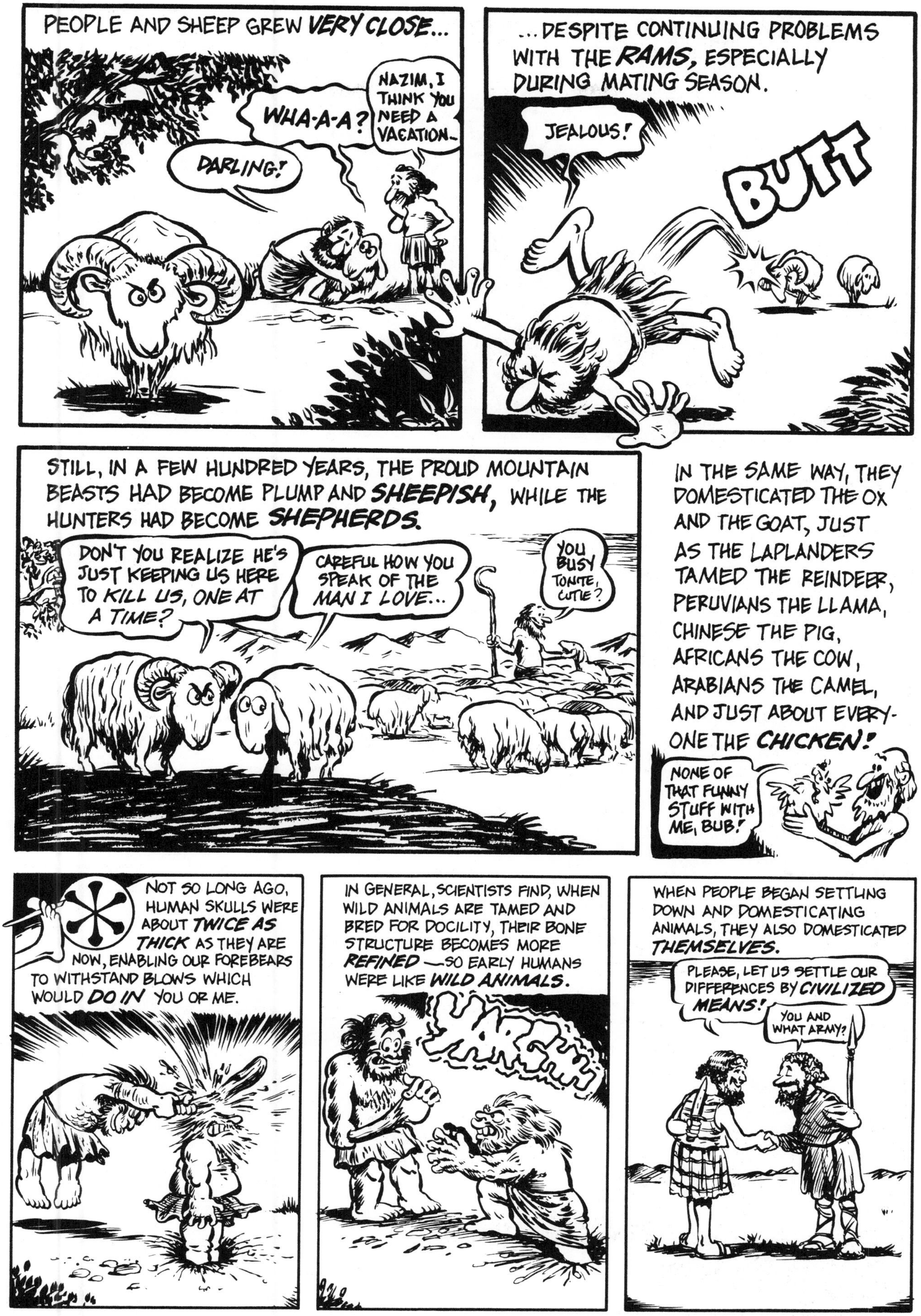
PEOPLE AND SHEEP GREW VERY CLOSE...
WHA-A-A?
NAZIM, I THINK YOU NEED A VACATION...
DARLING!
...DESPITE CONTINUING PROBLEMS WITH THE RAMS, ESPECIALLY DURING MATING SEASON.
JEALOUS!
BUTT
STILL, IN A FEW HUNDRED YEARS, THE PROUD MOUNTAIN BEASTS HAD BECOME PLUMP AND SHEEPISH, WHILE THE HUNTERS HAD BECOME SHEPHERDS.
DON'T YOU REALIZE HE'S JUST KEEPING US HERE TO KILL US, ONE AT A TIME?
CAREFUL HOW YOU SPEAK OF THE MAN I LOVE...
YOU BUSY TONITE, CUTIE?
IN THE SAME WAY, THEY DOMESTICATED THE OX AND THE GOAT, JUST AS THE LAPLANDERS TAMED THE REINDEER, PERUVIANS THE LLAMA, CHINESE THE PIG, AFRICANS THE COW, ARABIANS THE CAMEL, AND JUST ABOUT EVERY-ONE THE CHICKEN!
NONE OF THAT FUNNY STUFF WITH ME, BUB!
NOT SO LONG AGO, HUMAN SKULLS WERE ABOUT TWICE AS THICK AS THEY ARE NOW, ENABLING OUR FOREBEARS TO WITHSTAND BLOWS WHICH WOULD DO IN YOU OR ME.
IN GENERAL, SCIENTISTS FIND, WHEN WILD ANIMALS ARE TAMED AND BRED FOR DOCILITY, THEIR BONE STRUCTURE BECOMES MORE REFINED —SO EARLY HUMANS WERE LIKE WILD ANIMALS.
WHEN PEOPLE BEGAN SETTLING DOWN AND DOMESTICATING ANIMALS, THEY ALSO DOMESTICATED THEMSELVES.
PLEASE, LET US SETTLE OUR DIFFERENCES BY CIVILIZED MEANS!
YOU AND WHAT ARMY?

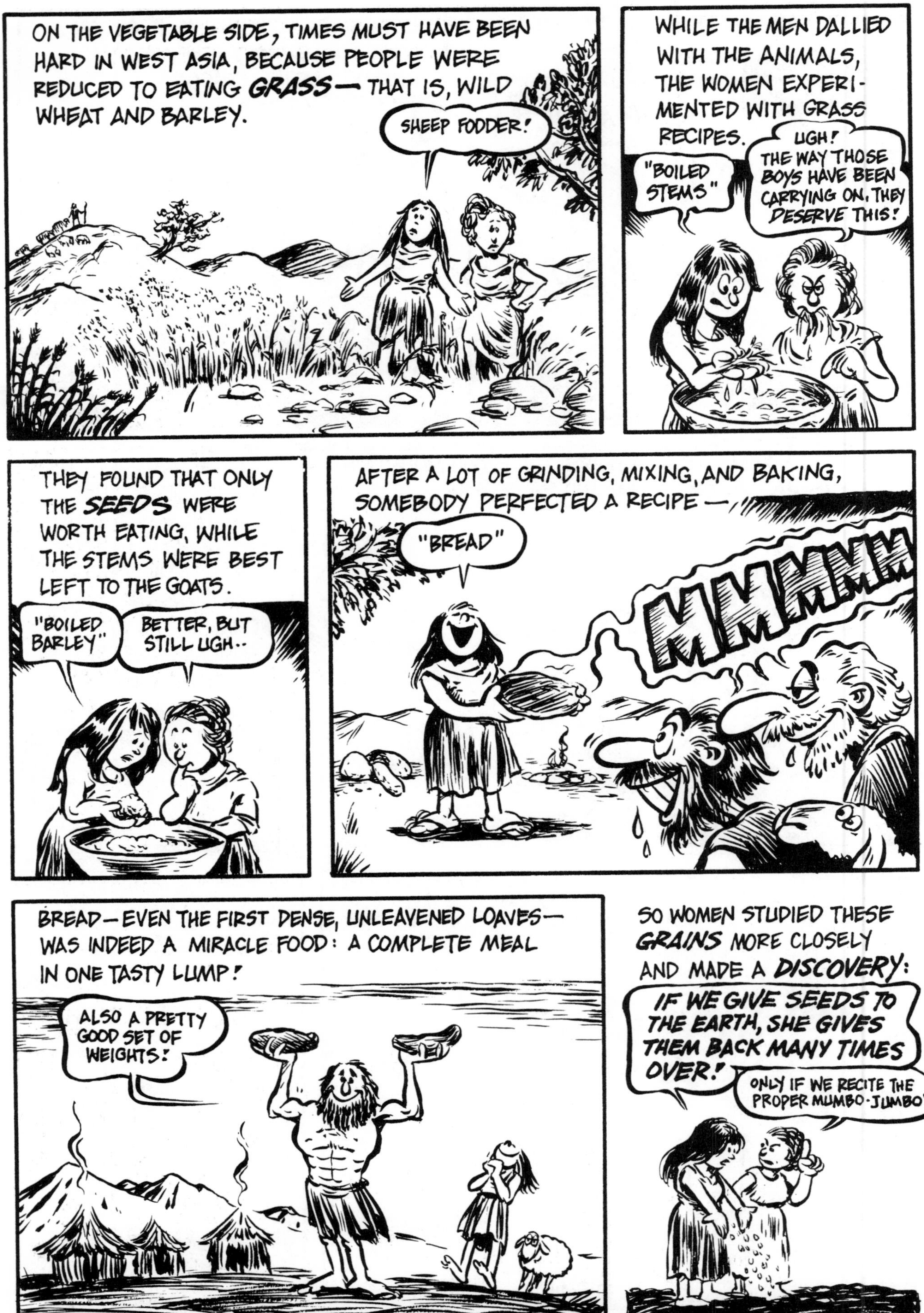
ON THE VEGETABLE SIDE, TIMES MUST HAVE BEEN HARD IN WEST ASIA, BECAUSE PEOPLE WERE REDUCED TO EATING GRASS— THAT IS, WILD WHEAT AND BARLEY.
SHEEP FODDER!
WHILE THE MEN DALLIED WITH THE ANIMALS, THE WOMEN EXPERIMENTED WITH GRASS RECIPES.
"BOILED STEMS"
UGH! THE WAY THOSE BOYS HAVE BEEN CARRYING ON, THEY DESERVE THIS!
THEY FOUND THAT ONLY THE SEEDS WERE WORTH EATING, WHILE THE STEMS WERE BEST LEFT TO THE GOATS.
"BOILED BARLEY"
BETTER, BUT STILL UGH..
AFTER A LOT OF GRINDING, MIXING, AND BAKING, SOMEBODY PERFECTED A RECIPE—
"BREAD"
MMMMM
BREAD—EVEN THE FIRST DENSE, UNLEAVENED LOAVES—WAS INDEED A MIRACLE FOOD: A COMPLETE MEAL IN ONE TASTY LUMP!
ALSO A PRETTY GOOD SET OF WEIGHTS!
SO WOMEN STUDIED THESE GRAINS MORE CLOSELY AND MADE A DISCOVERY:
IF WE GIVE SEEDS TO THE EARTH, SHE GIVES THEM BACK MANY TIMES OVER!
ONLY IF WE RECITE THE PROPER MUMBO-JUMBO!

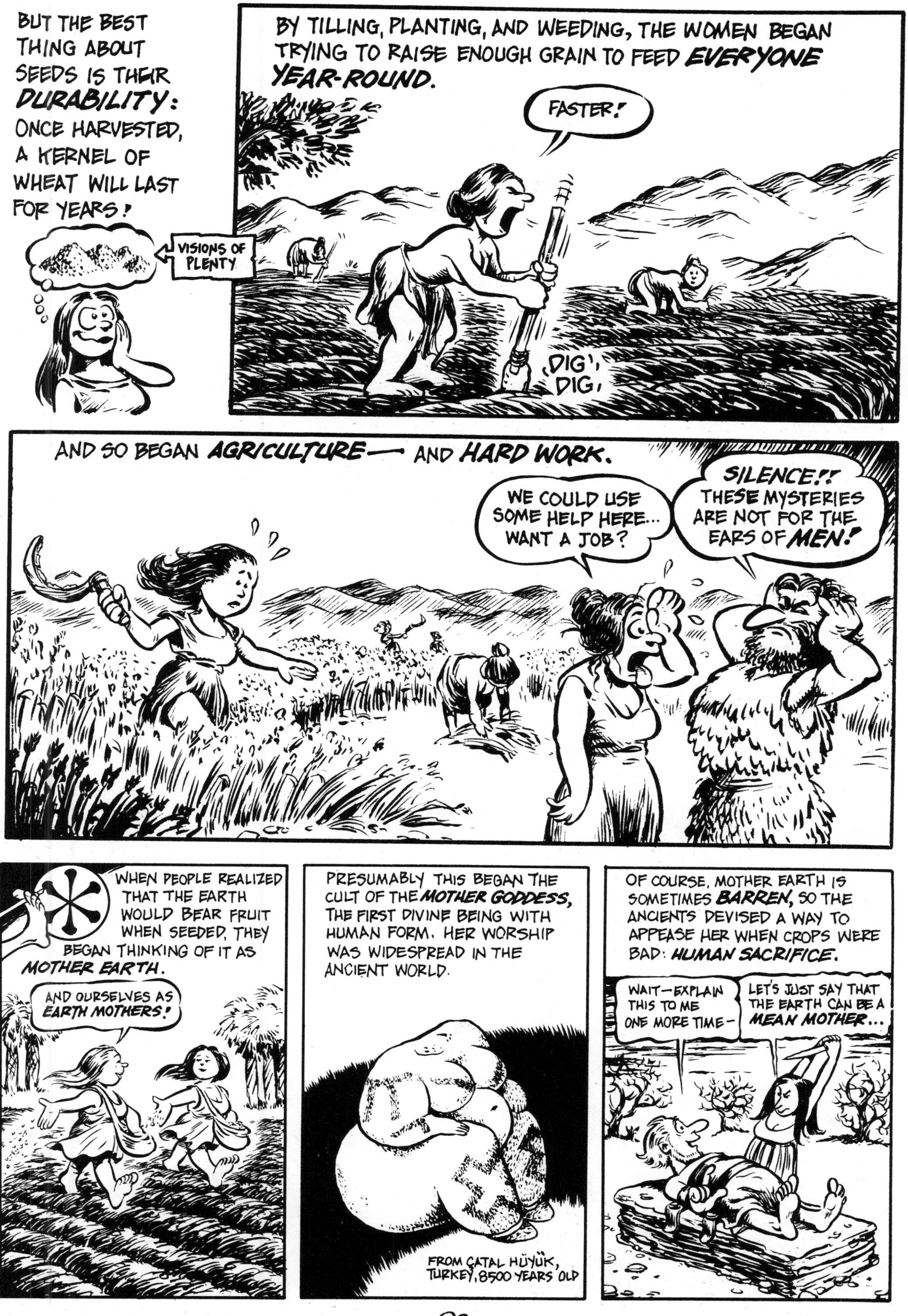

BUT THE BEST THING ABOUT SEEDS IS THEIR DURABILITY: ONCE HARVESTED, A KERNEL OF WHEAT WILL LAST FOR YEARS!
VISIONS OF PLENTY
BY TILLING, PLANTING, AND WEEDING, THE WOMEN BEGAN TRYING TO RAISE ENOUGH GRAIN TO FEED EVERYONE YEAR-ROUND.
FASTER!
DIG, DIG,
AND SO BEGAN AGRICULTURE— AND HARD WORK.
WE COULD USE SOME HELP HERE... WANT A JOB?
SILENCE!! THESE MYSTERIES ARE NOT FOR THE EARS OF MEN!
WHEN PEOPLE REALIZED THAT THE EARTH WOULD BEAR FRUIT WHEN SEEDED, THEY BEGAN THINKING OF IT AS MOTHER EARTH.
AND OURSELVES AS EARTH MOTHERS!
PRESUMABLY THIS BEGAN THE CULT OF THE MOTHER GODDESS, THE FIRST DIVINE BEING WITH HUMAN FORM. HER WORSHIP WAS WIDESPREAD IN THE ANCIENT WORLD.
FROM ÇATAL HÜYÜK, TURKEY, 8500 YEARS OLD
OF COURSE, MOTHER EARTH IS SOMETIMES BARREN, SO THE ANCIENTS DEVISED A WAY TO APPEASE HER WHEN CROPS WERE BAD: HUMAN SACRIFICE.
WAIT—EXPLAIN THIS TO ME ONE MORE TIME—
LET'S JUST SAY THAT THE EARTH CAN BE A MEAN MOTHER...

ALTHOUGH THE EARLY FARMERS DIDN'T GIVE UP HUNTING AND GATHERING RIGHT AWAY, THEY FOUND THAT PRODUCING ***FOOD*** ALSO PRODUCED ***NEEDS.***

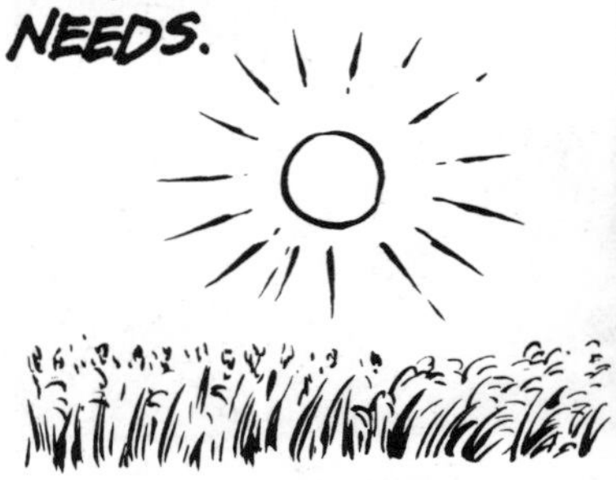

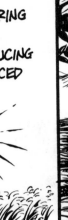

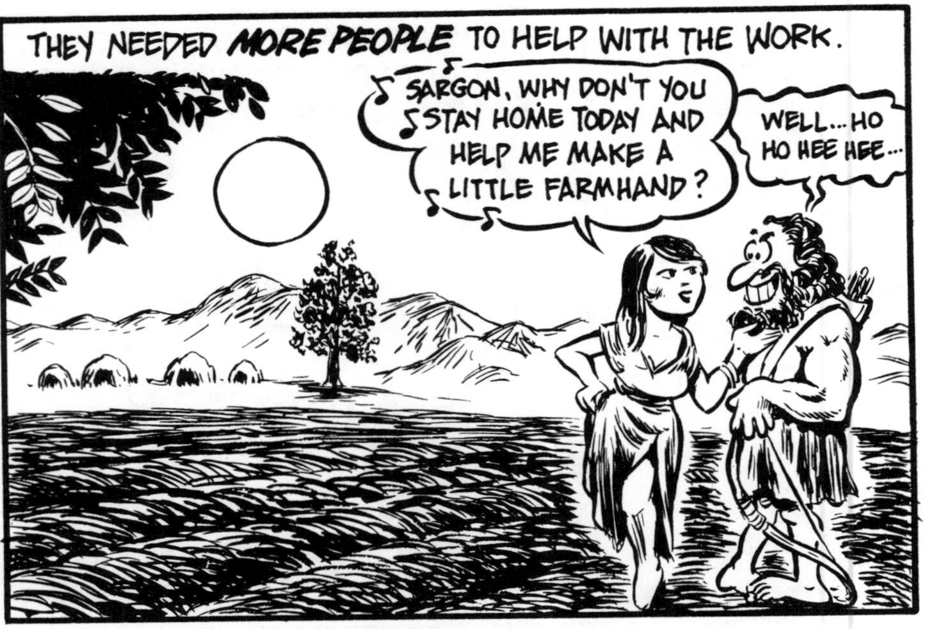
THEY NEEDED MORE PEOPLE TO HELP WITH THE WORK.
SARGON, WHY DON'T YOU STAY HOME TODAY AND HELP ME MAKE A LITTLE FARMHAND?
WELL... HO HO HEE HEE...

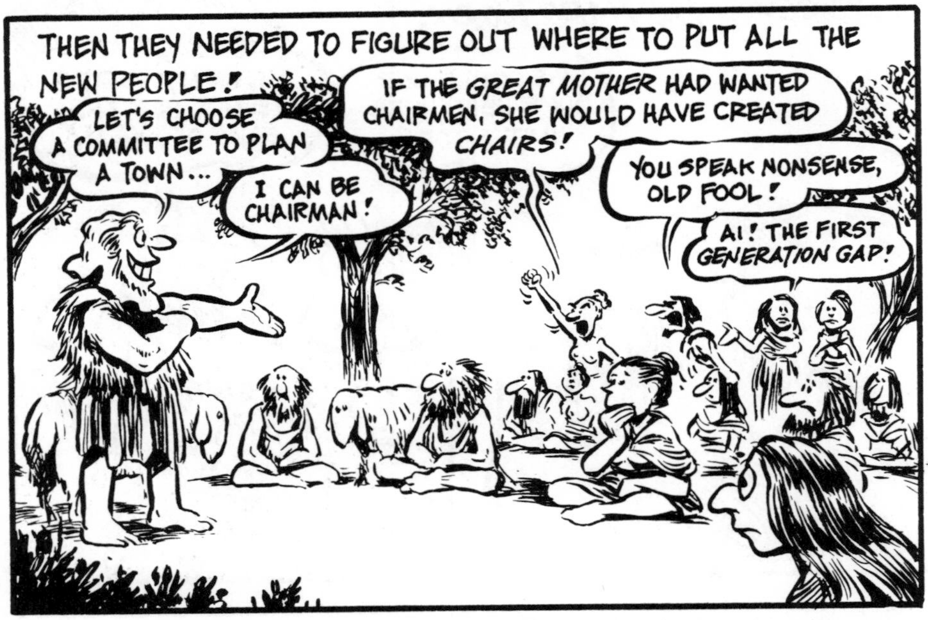
THEN THEY NEEDED TO FIGURE OUT WHERE TO PUT ALL THE NEW PEOPLE!
LET'S CHOOSE A COMMITTEE TO PLAN A TOWN...
I CAN BE CHAIRMAN!
IF THE GREAT MOTHER HAD WANTED CHAIRMEN, SHE WOULD HAVE CREATED CHAIRS!
YOU SPEAK NONSENSE, OLD FOOL!
AI! THE FIRST GENERATION GAP!

AS THE FARMERS BUILT THE EARLY VILLAGES AT JARMO AND ÇATAL HÜYÜK (SEE MAP, P. 86.), THEY CREATED ***MORE*** NEEDS: BUILDING MATERIALS, SEWAGE DISPOSAL, HEAT, ETC. ETC...

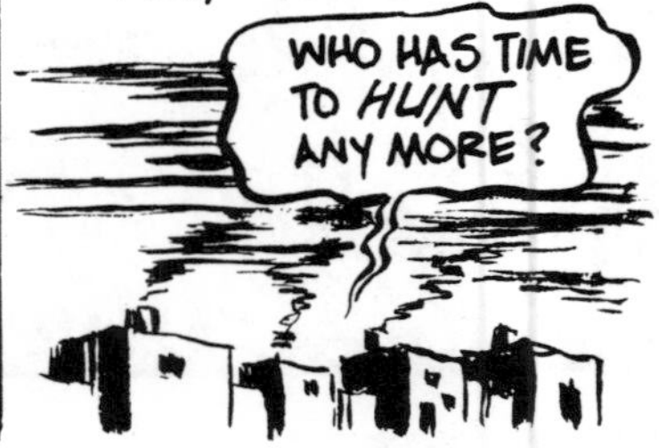
WHO HAS TIME TO HUNT ANY MORE?

TO USE THE ***WOOL*** FROM THEIR SHEEP, THEY INVENTED ***SPINNING*** AND ***WEAVING*** ON THE ***LOOM***. TO STORE THE GRAIN, THEY DEVELOPED ***POTTERY***.

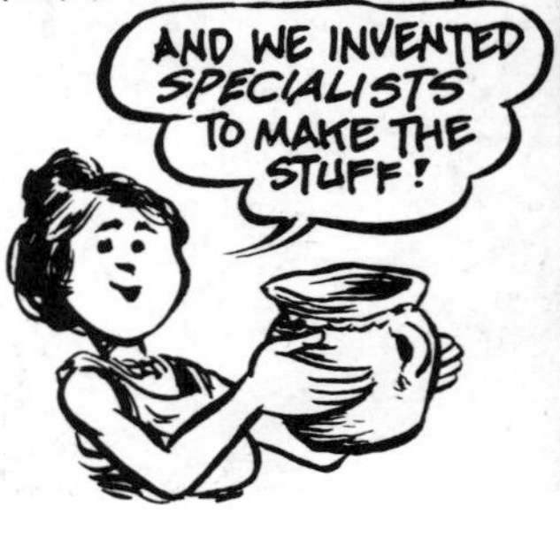
AND WE INVENTED SPECIALISTS TO MAKE THE STUFF!

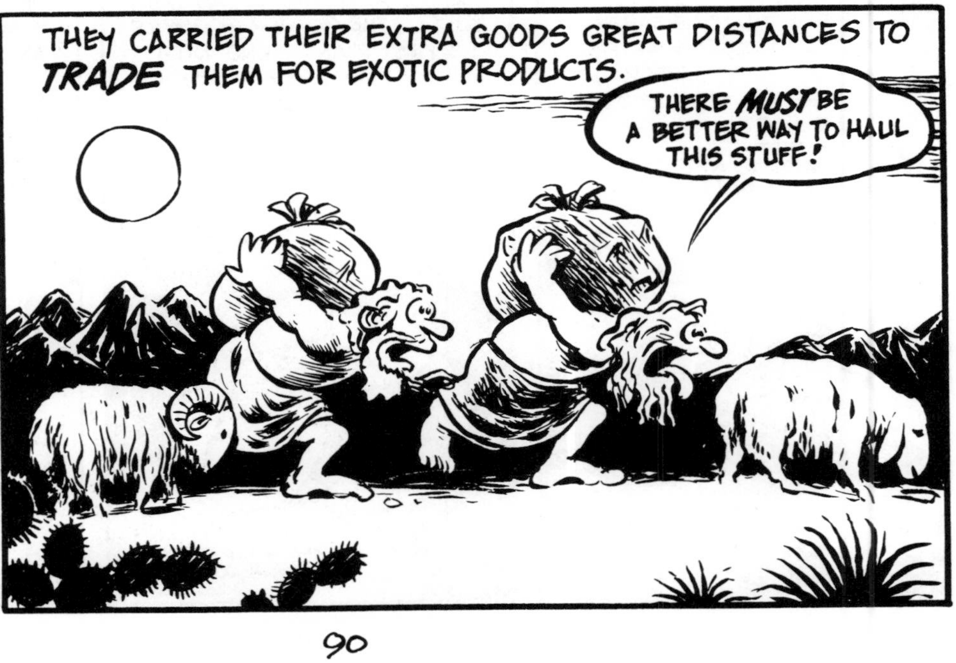
THEY CARRIED THEIR EXTRA GOODS GREAT DISTANCES TO TRADE THEM FOR EXOTIC PRODUCTS.
THERE MUST BE A BETTER WAY TO HAUL THIS STUFF!

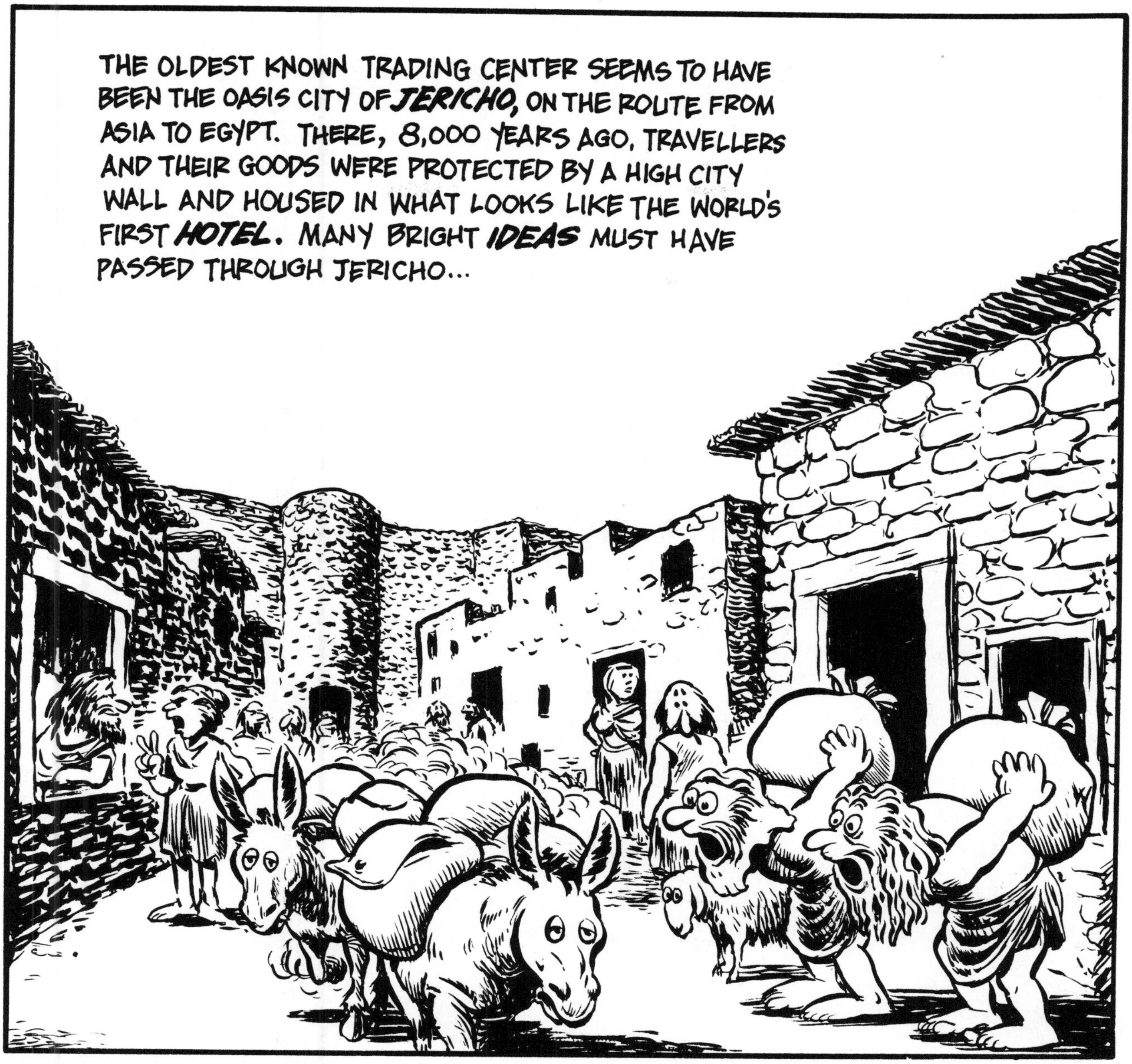
THE OLDEST KNOWN TRADING CENTER SEEMS TO HAVE BEEN THE OASIS CITY OF JERICHO, ON THE ROUTE FROM ASIA TO EGYPT. THERE, 8,000 YEARS AGO, TRAVELLERS AND THEIR GOODS WERE PROTECTED BY A HIGH CITY WALL AND HOUSED IN WHAT LOOKS LIKE THE WORLD'S FIRST HOTEL. MANY BRIGHT IDEAS MUST HAVE PASSED THROUGH JERICHO...

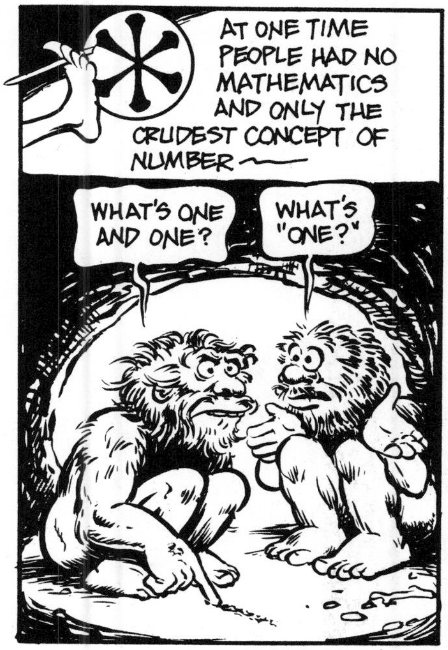
AT ONE TIME PEOPLE HAD NO MATHEMATICS AND ONLY THE CRUDEST CONCEPT OF NUMBER ~
WHAT'S ONE AND ONE?
WHAT'S "ONE?"

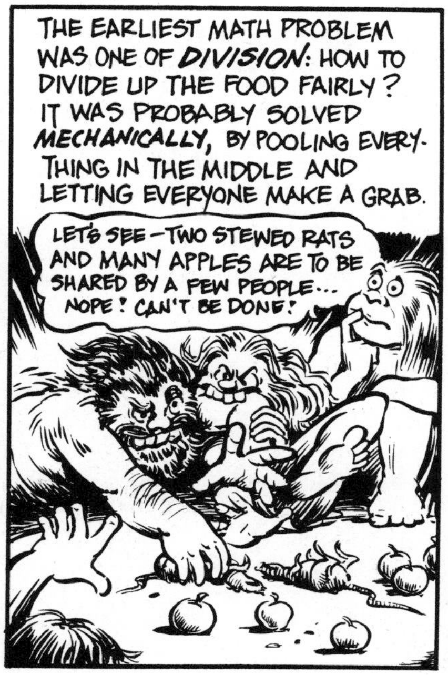
THE EARLIEST MATH PROBLEM WAS ONE OF DIVISION: HOW TO DIVIDE UP THE FOOD FAIRLY? IT WAS PROBABLY SOLVED MECHANICALLY, BY POOLING EVERYTHING IN THE MIDDLE AND LETTING EVERYONE MAKE A GRAB.
LET'S SEE — TWO STEWED RATS AND MANY APPLES ARE TO BE SHARED BY A FEW PEOPLE... NOPE! CAN'T BE DONE!

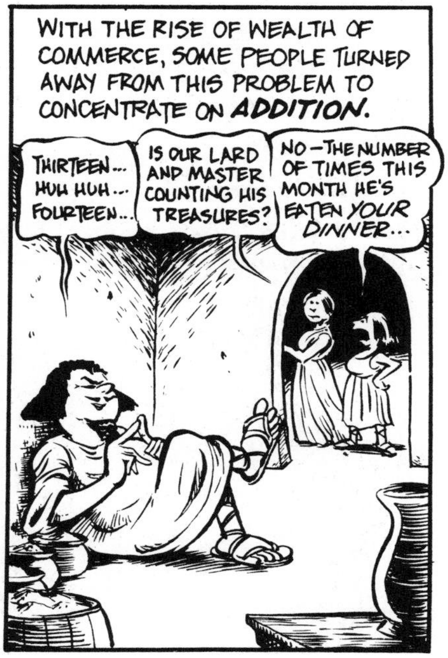
WITH THE RISE OF WEALTH OF COMMERCE, SOME PEOPLE TURNED AWAY FROM THIS PROBLEM TO CONCENTRATE ON ADDITION.
THIRTEEN... HUH HUH... FOURTEEN...
IS OUR LARD AND MASTER COUNTING HIS TREASURES?
NO — THE NUMBER OF TIMES THIS MONTH HE'S EATEN YOUR DINNER...

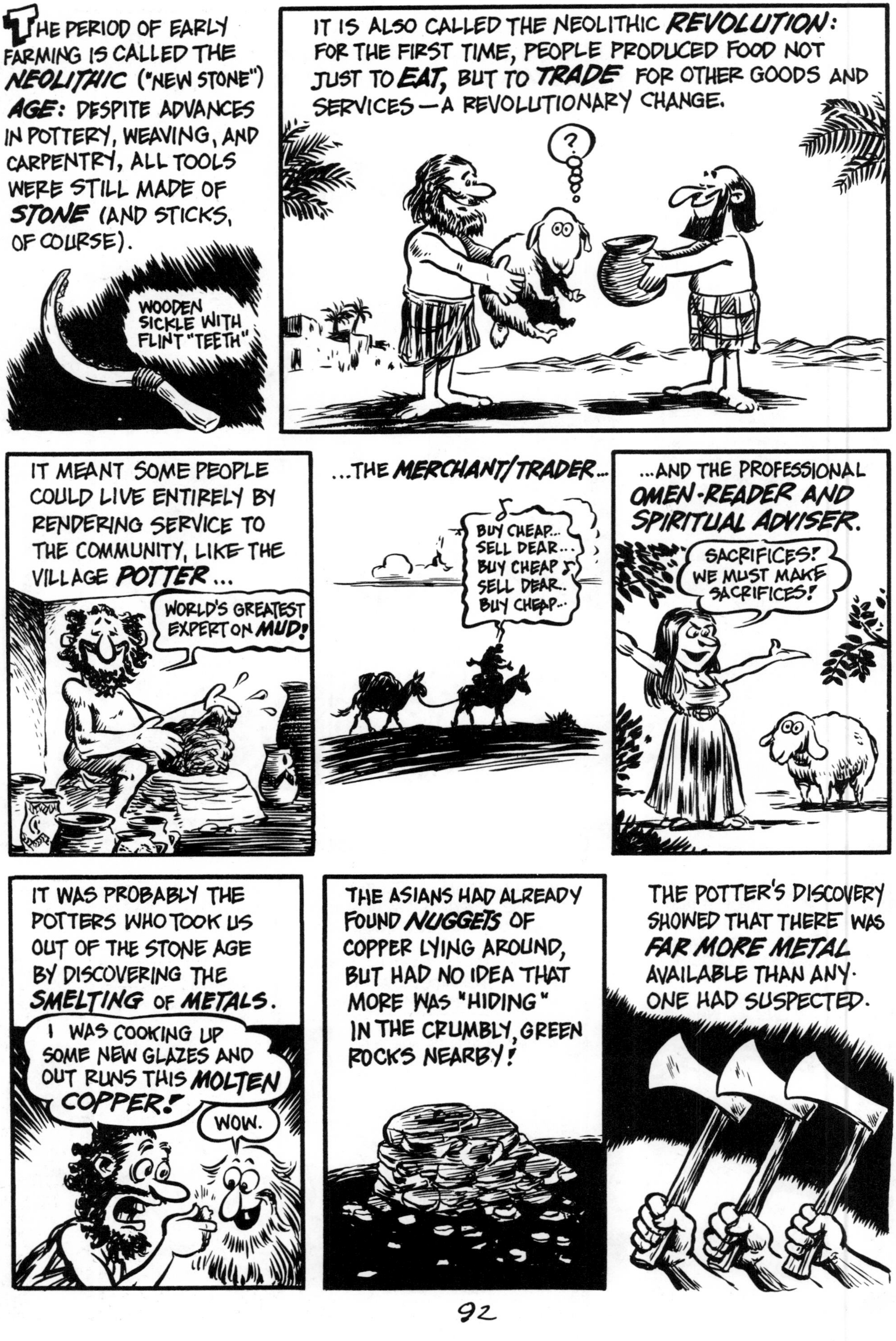
THE PERIOD OF EARLY FARMING IS CALLED THE NEOLITHIC ("NEW STONE") AGE: DESPITE ADVANCES IN POTTERY, WEAVING, AND CARPENTRY, ALL TOOLS WERE STILL MADE OF STONE (AND STICKS, OF COURSE).
WOODEN SICKLE WITH FLINT "TEETH"
IT IS ALSO CALLED THE NEOLITHIC REVOLUTION: FOR THE FIRST TIME, PEOPLE PRODUCED FOOD NOT JUST TO EAT, BUT TO TRADE FOR OTHER GOODS AND SERVICES—A REVOLUTIONARY CHANGE.
?
IT MEANT SOME PEOPLE COULD LIVE ENTIRELY BY RENDERING SERVICE TO THE COMMUNITY, LIKE THE VILLAGE POTTER...
WORLD'S GREATEST EXPERT ON MUD!
...THE MERCHANT/TRADER...
BUY CHEAP... SELL DEAR... BUY CHEAP SELL DEAR.. BUY CHEAP...
...AND THE PROFESSIONAL OMEN-READER AND SPIRITUAL ADVISER.
SACRIFICES! WE MUST MAKE SACRIFICES!
IT WAS PROBABLY THE POTTERS WHO TOOK US OUT OF THE STONE AGE BY DISCOVERING THE SMELTING OF METALS.
I WAS COOKING UP SOME NEW GLAZES AND OUT RUNS THIS MOLTEN COPPER!
WOW.
THE ASIANS HAD ALREADY FOUND NUGGETS OF COPPER LYING AROUND, BUT HAD NO IDEA THAT MORE WAS "HIDING" IN THE CRUMBLY, GREEN ROCKS NEARBY!
THE POTTER'S DISCOVERY SHOWED THAT THERE WAS FAR MORE METAL AVAILABLE THAN ANYONE HAD SUSPECTED.

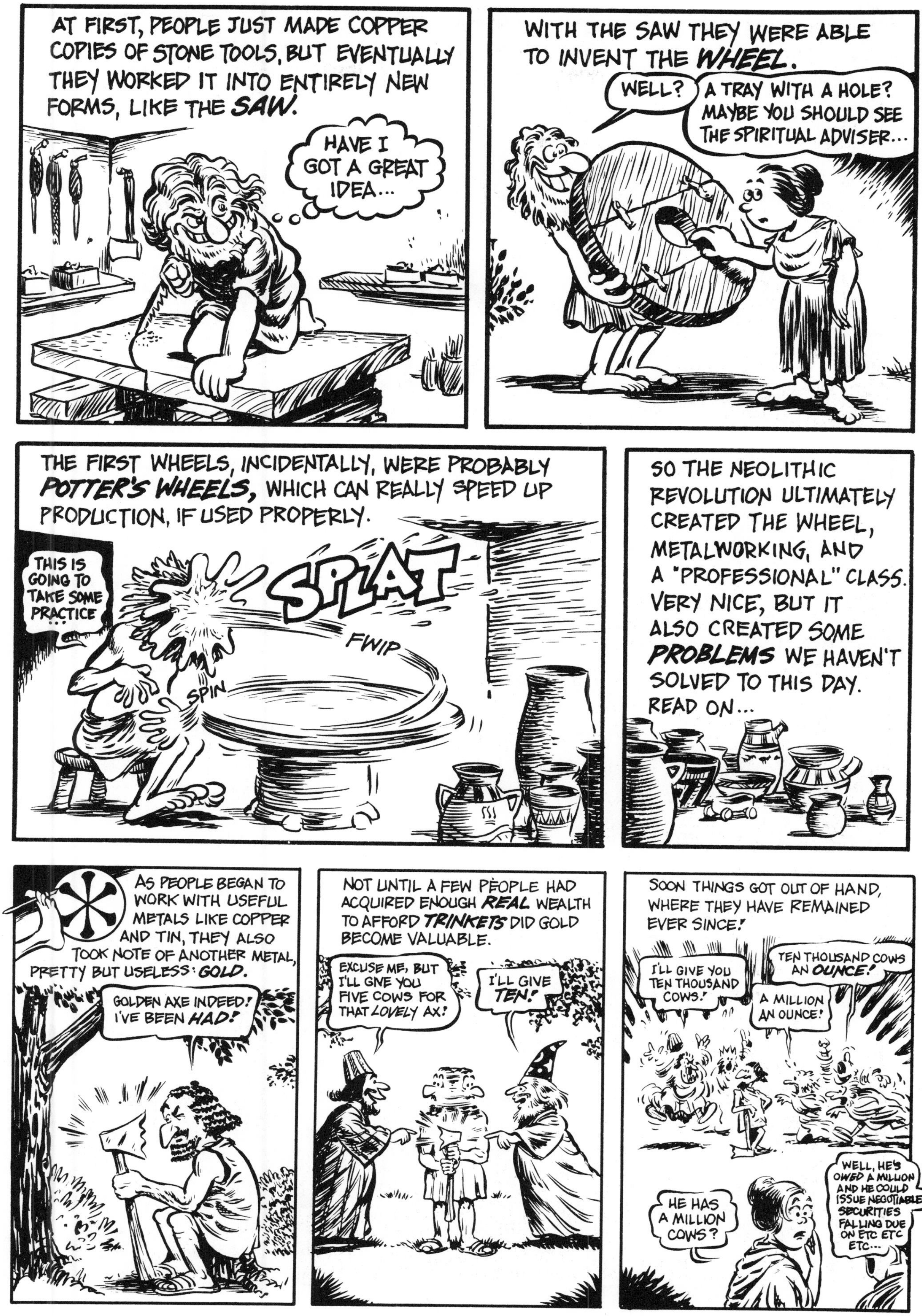

AT FIRST, PEOPLE JUST MADE COPPER COPIES OF STONE TOOLS, BUT EVENTUALLY THEY WORKED IT INTO ENTIRELY NEW FORMS, LIKE THE SAW.
HAVE I GOT A GREAT IDEA...
WITH THE SAW THEY WERE ABLE TO INVENT THE WHEEL.
WELL?
A TRAY WITH A HOLE? MAYBE YOU SHOULD SEE THE SPIRITUAL ADVISER...
THE FIRST WHEELS, INCIDENTALLY, WERE PROBABLY POTTER'S WHEELS, WHICH CAN REALLY SPEED UP PRODUCTION, IF USED PROPERLY.
THIS IS GOING TO TAKE SOME PRACTICE...
SPLAT
FWIP
SPIN
SO THE NEOLITHIC REVOLUTION ULTIMATELY CREATED THE WHEEL, METALWORKING, AND A "PROFESSIONAL" CLASS. VERY NICE, BUT IT ALSO CREATED SOME PROBLEMS WE HAVEN'T SOLVED TO THIS DAY. READ ON...
AS PEOPLE BEGAN TO WORK WITH USEFUL METALS LIKE COPPER AND TIN, THEY ALSO TOOK NOTE OF ANOTHER METAL, PRETTY BUT USELESS: GOLD.
GOLDEN AXE INDEED! I'VE BEEN HAD!
NOT UNTIL A FEW PEOPLE HAD ACQUIRED ENOUGH REAL WEALTH TO AFFORD TRINKETS DID GOLD BECOME VALUABLE.
EXCUSE ME, BUT I'LL GIVE YOU FIVE COWS FOR THAT LOVELY AX!
I'LL GIVE TEN!
SOON THINGS GOT OUT OF HAND, WHERE THEY HAVE REMAINED EVER SINCE!
I'LL GIVE YOU TEN THOUSAND COWS!
TEN THOUSAND COWS AN OUNCE!
A MILLION AN OUNCE!
HE HAS A MILLION COWS?
WELL, HE'S OWED A MILLION AND HE COULD ISSUE NEGOTIABLE SECURITIES FALLING DUE ON ETC ETC ETC...

CHIEFS AMONG MEN

WHATEVER THE BENEFITS OF A SETTLED LIFE, IT ALSO ***DESTROYED*** ANCIENT TRADITIONS OF FAMILY AND GOVERNMENT. WHAT WERE THESE TRADITIONS?

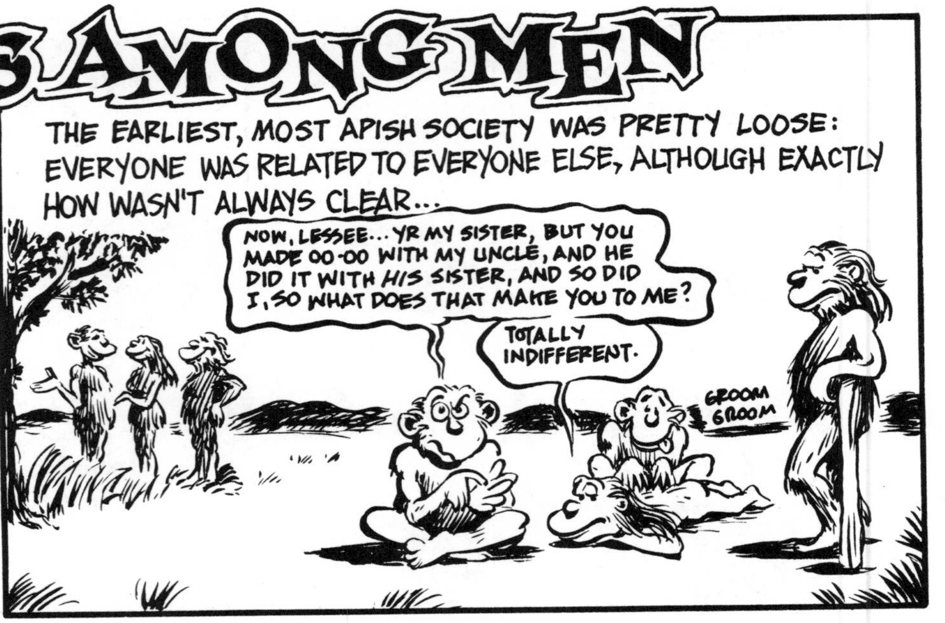
THE EARLIEST, MOST APISH SOCIETY WAS PRETTY LOOSE: EVERYONE WAS RELATED TO EVERYONE ELSE, ALTHOUGH EXACTLY HOW WASN'T ALWAYS CLEAR...
NOW, LESSEE... YR MY SISTER, BUT YOU MADE OO-OO WITH MY UNCLE, AND HE DID IT WITH HIS SISTER, AND SO DID I, SO WHAT DOES THAT MAKE YOU TO ME?
TOTALLY INDIFFERENT.
GROOM GROOM

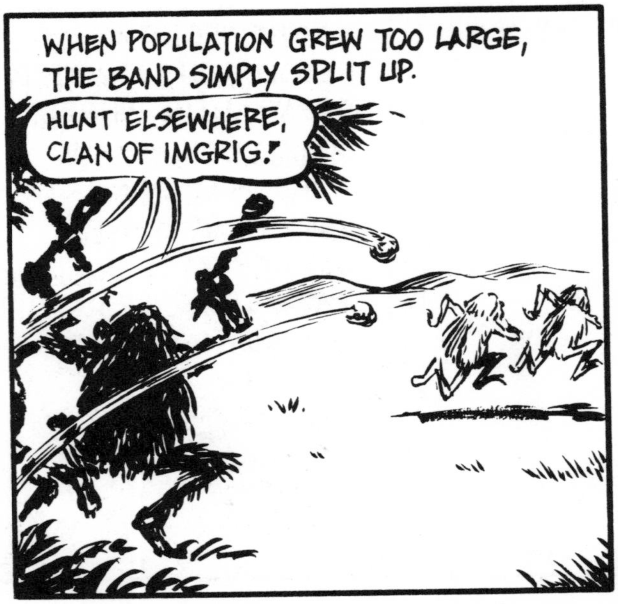
WHEN POPULATION GREW TOO LARGE, THE BAND SIMPLY SPLIT UP.
HUNT ELSEWHERE, CLAN OF IMGRIG!

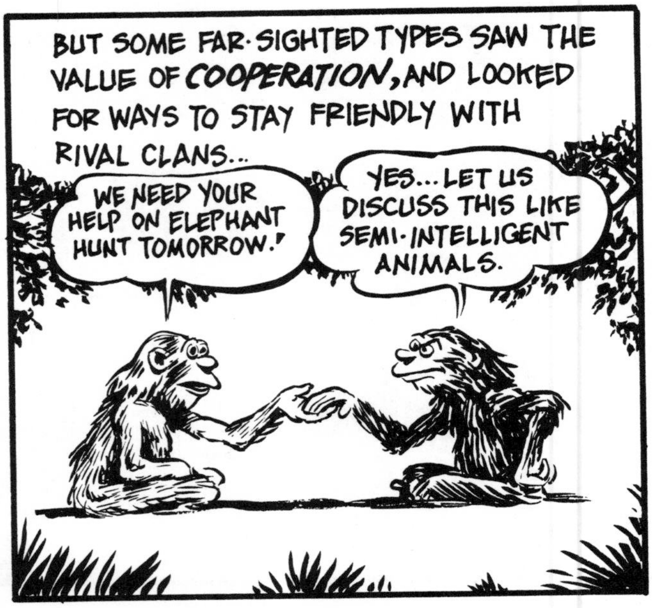
BUT SOME FAR-SIGHTED TYPES SAW THE VALUE OF COOPERATION, AND LOOKED FOR WAYS TO STAY FRIENDLY WITH RIVAL CLANS...
WE NEED YOUR HELP ON ELEPHANT HUNT TOMORROW!
YES... LET US DISCUSS THIS LIKE SEMI-INTELLIGENT ANIMALS.

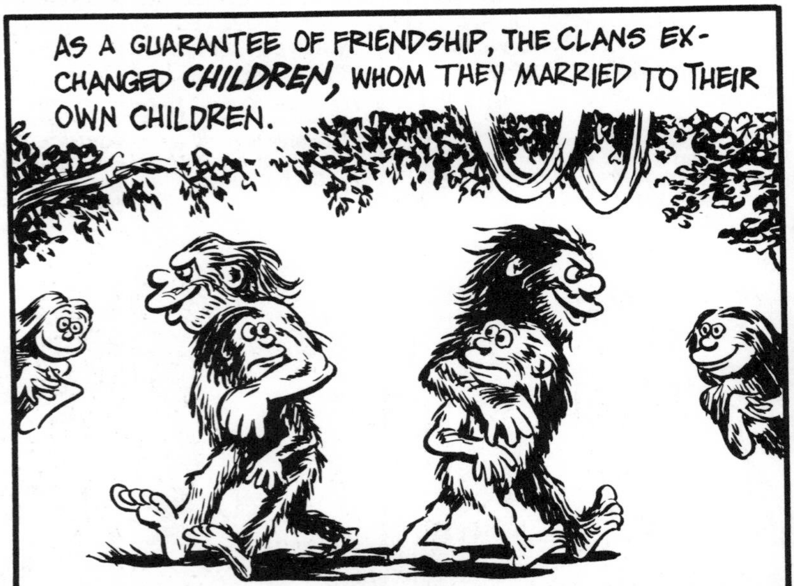
AS A GUARANTEE OF FRIENDSHIP, THE CLANS EX-CHANGED CHILDREN, WHOM THEY MARRIED TO THEIR OWN CHILDREN.

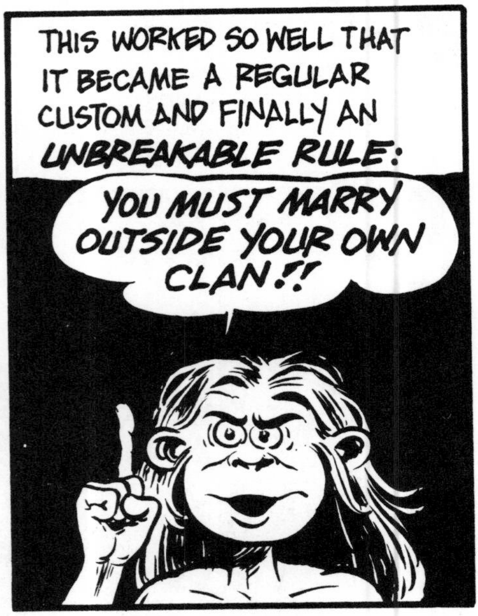
THIS WORKED SO WELL THAT IT BECAME A REGULAR CUSTOM AND FINALLY AN UNBREAKABLE RULE:
YOU MUST MARRY OUTSIDE YOUR OWN CLAN!!

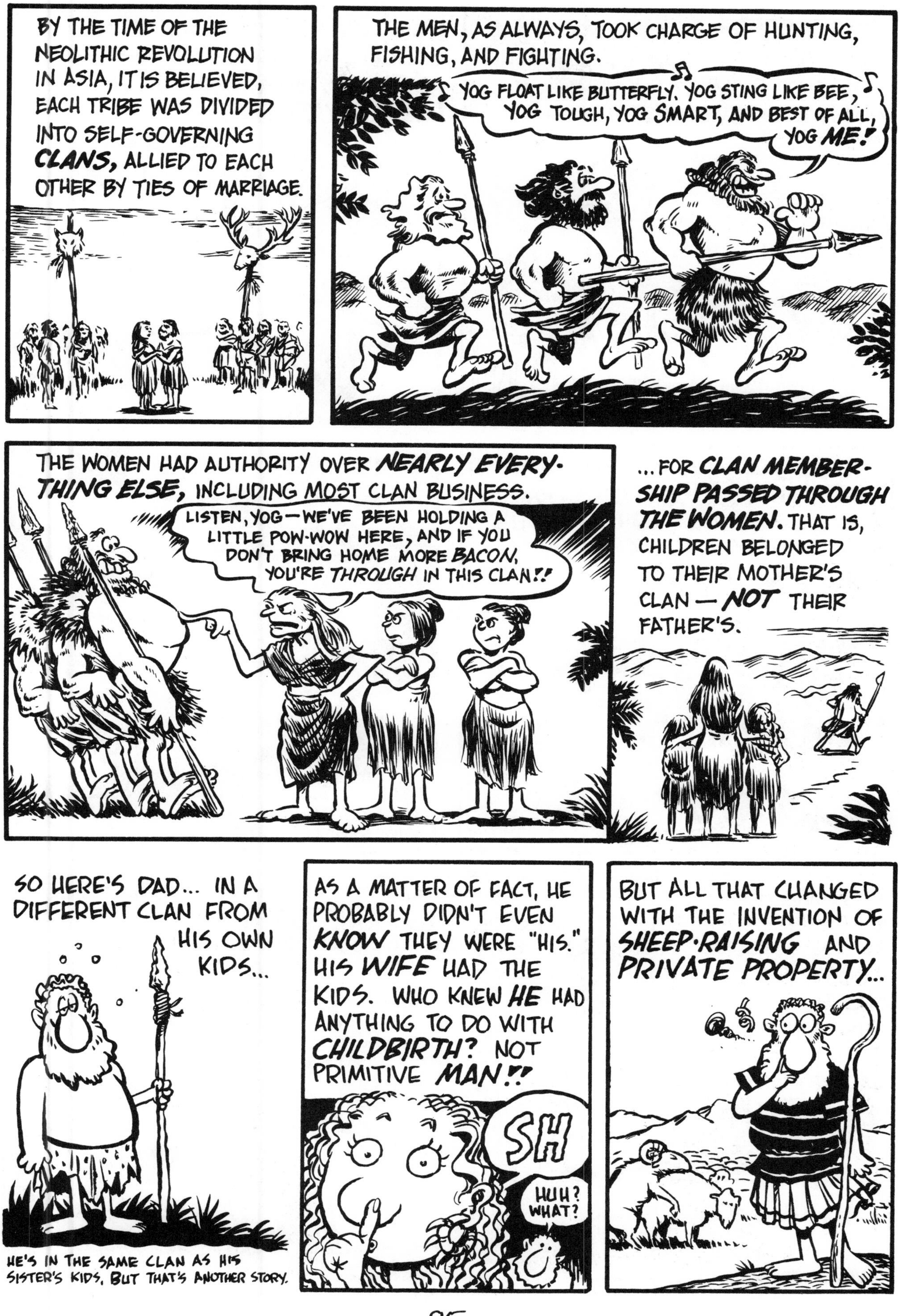
BY THE TIME OF THE NEOLITHIC REVOLUTION IN ASIA, IT IS BELIEVED, EACH TRIBE WAS DIVIDED INTO SELF-GOVERNING **CLANS,** ALLIED TO EACH OTHER BY TIES OF MARRIAGE.
THE MEN, AS ALWAYS, TOOK CHARGE OF HUNTING, FISHING, AND FIGHTING.
YOG FLOAT LIKE BUTTERFLY. YOG STING LIKE BEE, YOG TOUGH, YOG SMART, AND BEST OF ALL, YOG **ME!**
THE WOMEN HAD AUTHORITY OVER **NEARLY EVERYTHING ELSE,** INCLUDING MOST CLAN BUSINESS.
LISTEN, YOG—WE'VE BEEN HOLDING A LITTLE POW-WOW HERE, AND IF YOU DON'T BRING HOME MORE *BACON,* YOU'RE *THROUGH* IN THIS CLAN!!
...FOR **CLAN MEMBERSHIP PASSED THROUGH THE WOMEN.** THAT IS, CHILDREN BELONGED TO THEIR MOTHER'S CLAN—**NOT** THEIR FATHER'S.
SO HERE'S DAD... IN A DIFFERENT CLAN FROM HIS OWN KIDS...
HE'S IN THE SAME CLAN AS HIS SISTER'S KIDS. BUT THAT'S ANOTHER STORY.
AS A MATTER OF FACT, HE PROBABLY DIDN'T EVEN **KNOW** THEY WERE "HIS." HIS **WIFE** HAD THE KIDS. WHO KNEW **HE** HAD ANYTHING TO DO WITH **CHILDBIRTH?** NOT PRIMITIVE **MAN!!**
SH
HUH? WHAT?
BUT ALL THAT CHANGED WITH THE INVENTION OF **SHEEP-RAISING** AND **PRIVATE PROPERTY...**

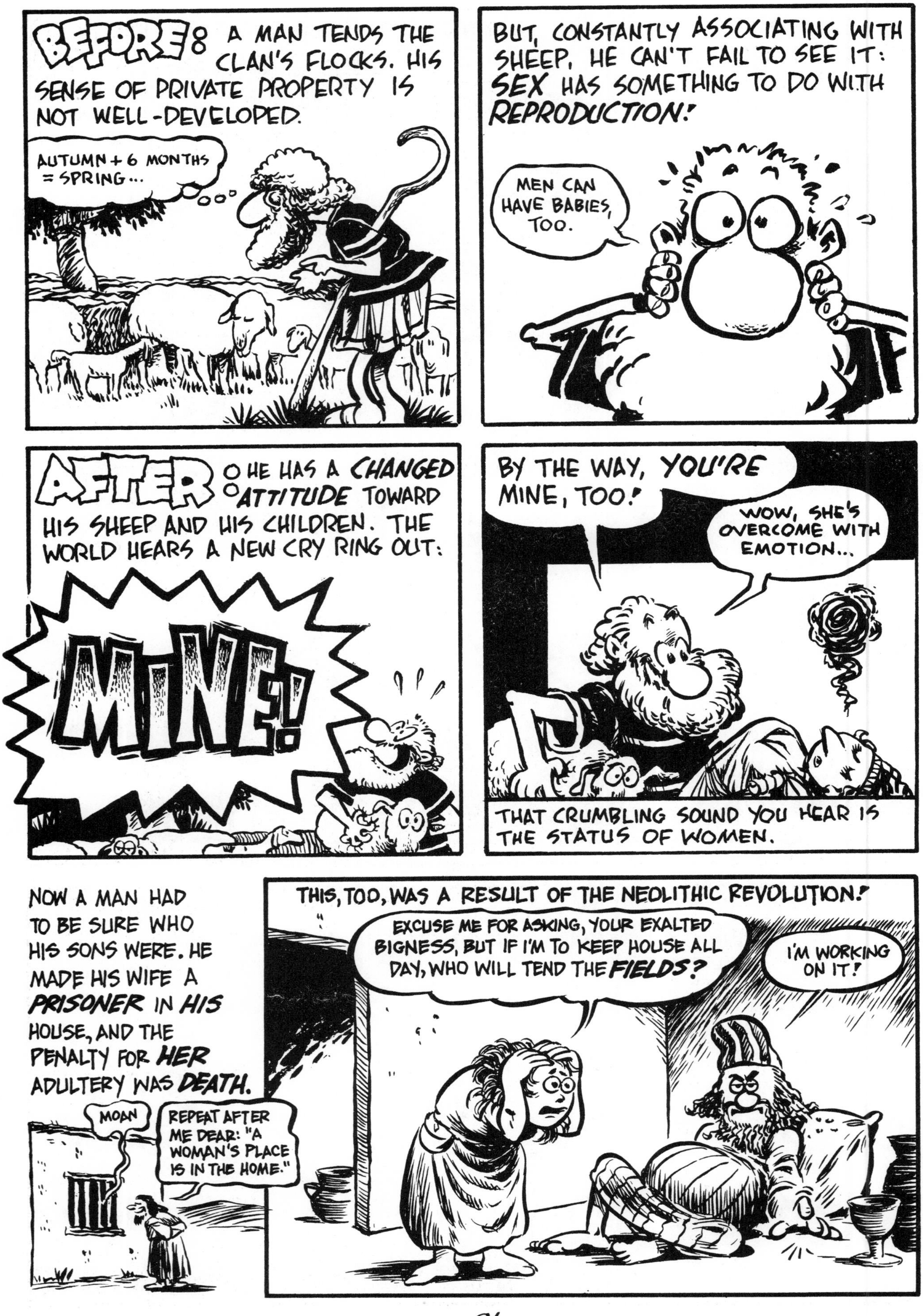

BEFORE: A MAN TENDS THE CLAN'S FLOCKS. HIS SENSE OF PRIVATE PROPERTY IS NOT WELL-DEVELOPED.
AUTUMN + 6 MONTHS = SPRING...
BUT, CONSTANTLY ASSOCIATING WITH SHEEP, HE CAN'T FAIL TO SEE IT: SEX HAS SOMETHING TO DO WITH REPRODUCTION!
MEN CAN HAVE BABIES, TOO.
AFTER: HE HAS A CHANGED ATTITUDE TOWARD HIS SHEEP AND HIS CHILDREN. THE WORLD HEARS A NEW CRY RING OUT:
MINE!
BY THE WAY, YOU'RE MINE, TOO!
WOW, SHE'S OVERCOME WITH EMOTION...
THAT CRUMBLING SOUND YOU HEAR IS THE STATUS OF WOMEN.
NOW A MAN HAD TO BE SURE WHO HIS SONS WERE. HE MADE HIS WIFE A PRISONER IN HIS HOUSE, AND THE PENALTY FOR HER ADULTERY WAS DEATH.
MOAN
REPEAT AFTER ME DEAR: "A WOMAN'S PLACE IS IN THE HOME."
THIS, TOO, WAS A RESULT OF THE NEOLITHIC REVOLUTION!
EXCUSE ME FOR ASKING, YOUR EXALTED BIGNESS, BUT IF I'M TO KEEP HOUSE ALL DAY, WHO WILL TEND THE FIELDS?
I'M WORKING ON IT!

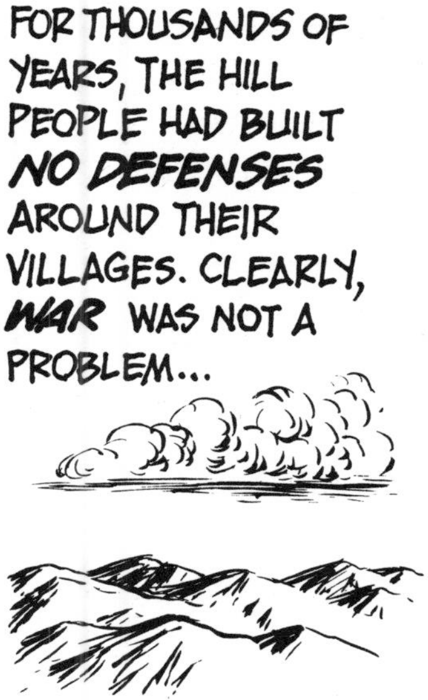
FOR THOUSANDS OF YEARS, THE HILL PEOPLE HAD BUILT NO DEFENSES AROUND THEIR VILLAGES. CLEARLY, WAR WAS NOT A PROBLEM...

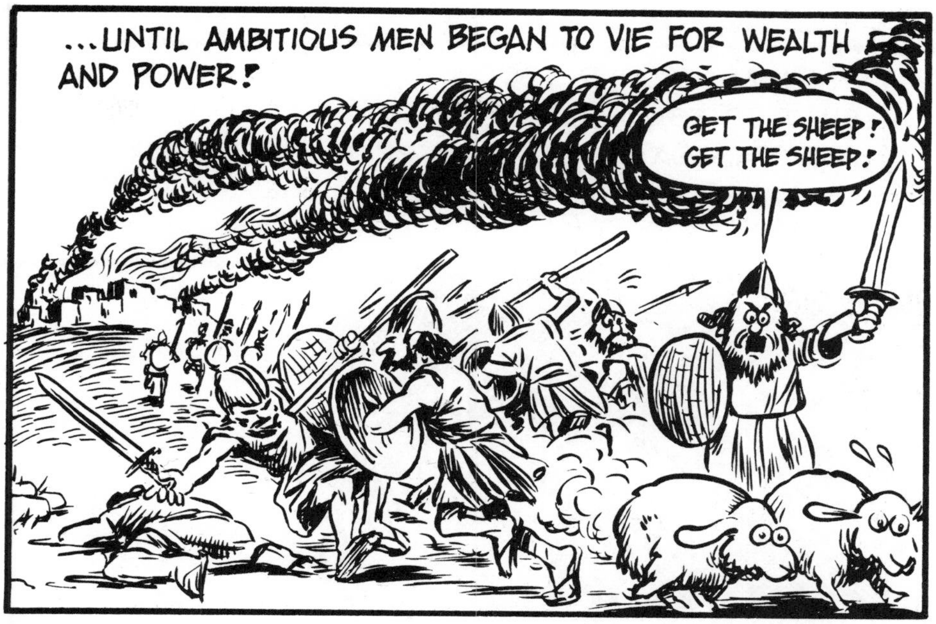
...UNTIL AMBITIOUS MEN BEGAN TO VIE FOR WEALTH AND POWER!
GET THE SHEEP! GET THE SHEEP!

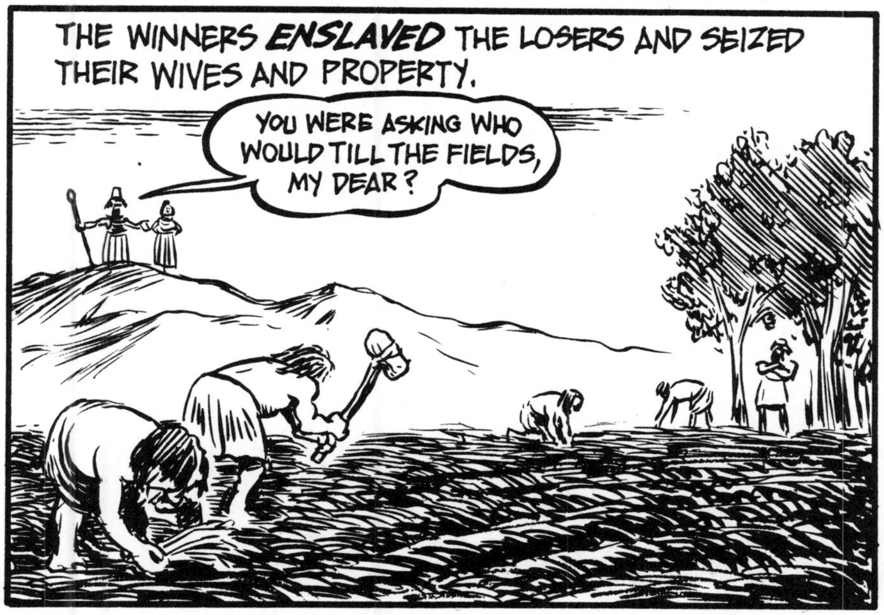
THE WINNERS ENSLAVED THE LOSERS AND SEIZED THEIR WIVES AND PROPERTY.
YOU WERE ASKING WHO WOULD TILL THE FIELDS, MY DEAR?

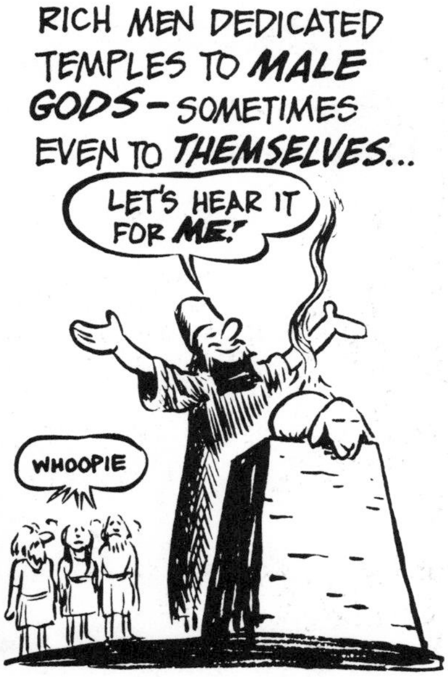
RICH MEN DEDICATED TEMPLES TO MALE GODS – SOMETIMES EVEN TO THEMSELVES...
LET'S HEAR IT FOR ME!
WHOOPIE

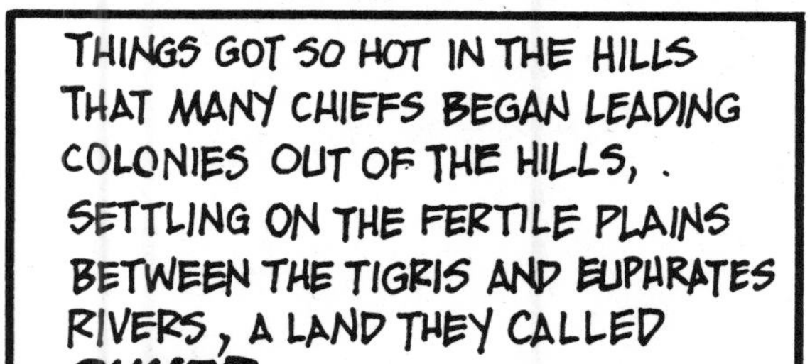
THINGS GOT SO HOT IN THE HILLS THAT MANY CHIEFS BEGAN LEADING COLONIES OUT OF THE HILLS, SETTLING ON THE FERTILE PLAINS BETWEEN THE TIGRIS AND EUPHRATES RIVERS, A LAND THEY CALLED SUMER.

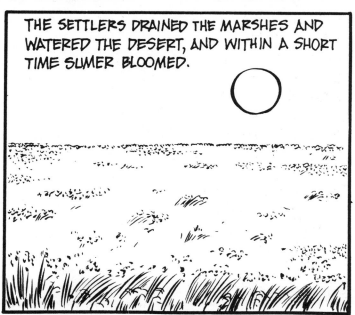

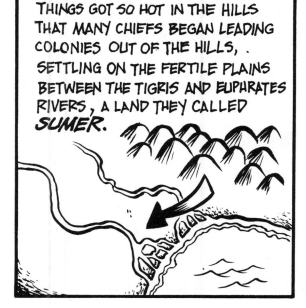

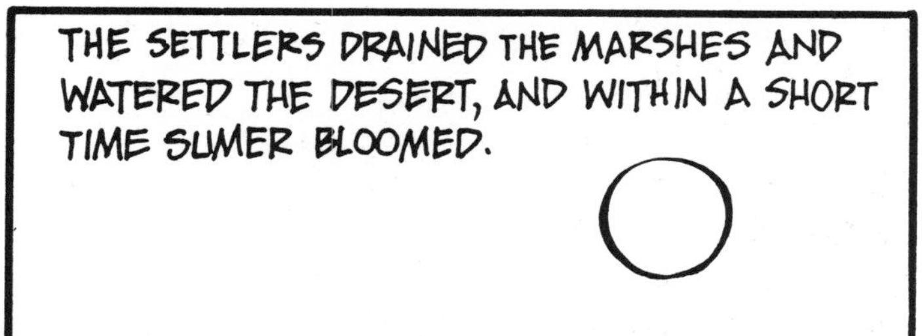
THE SETTLERS DRAINED THE MARSHES AND WATERED THE DESERT, AND WITHIN A SHORT TIME SUMER BLOOMED.

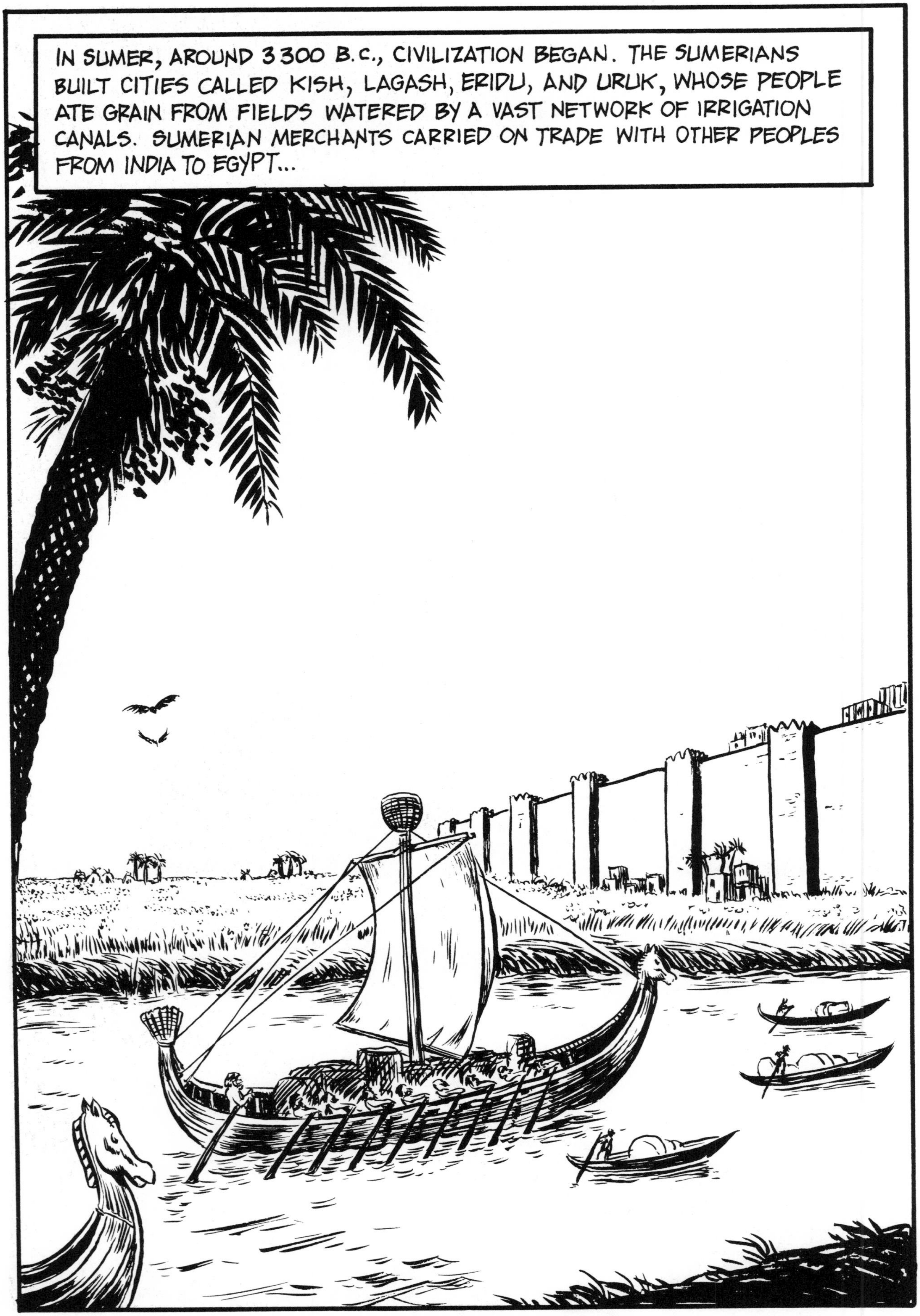
IN SUMER, AROUND 3300 B.C., CIVILIZATION BEGAN. THE SUMERIANS BUILT CITIES CALLED KISH, LAGASH, ERIDU, AND URUK, WHOSE PEOPLE ATE GRAIN FROM FIELDS WATERED BY A VAST NETWORK OF IRRIGATION CANALS. SUMERIAN MERCHANTS CARRIED ON TRADE WITH OTHER PEOPLES FROM INDIA TO EGYPT...

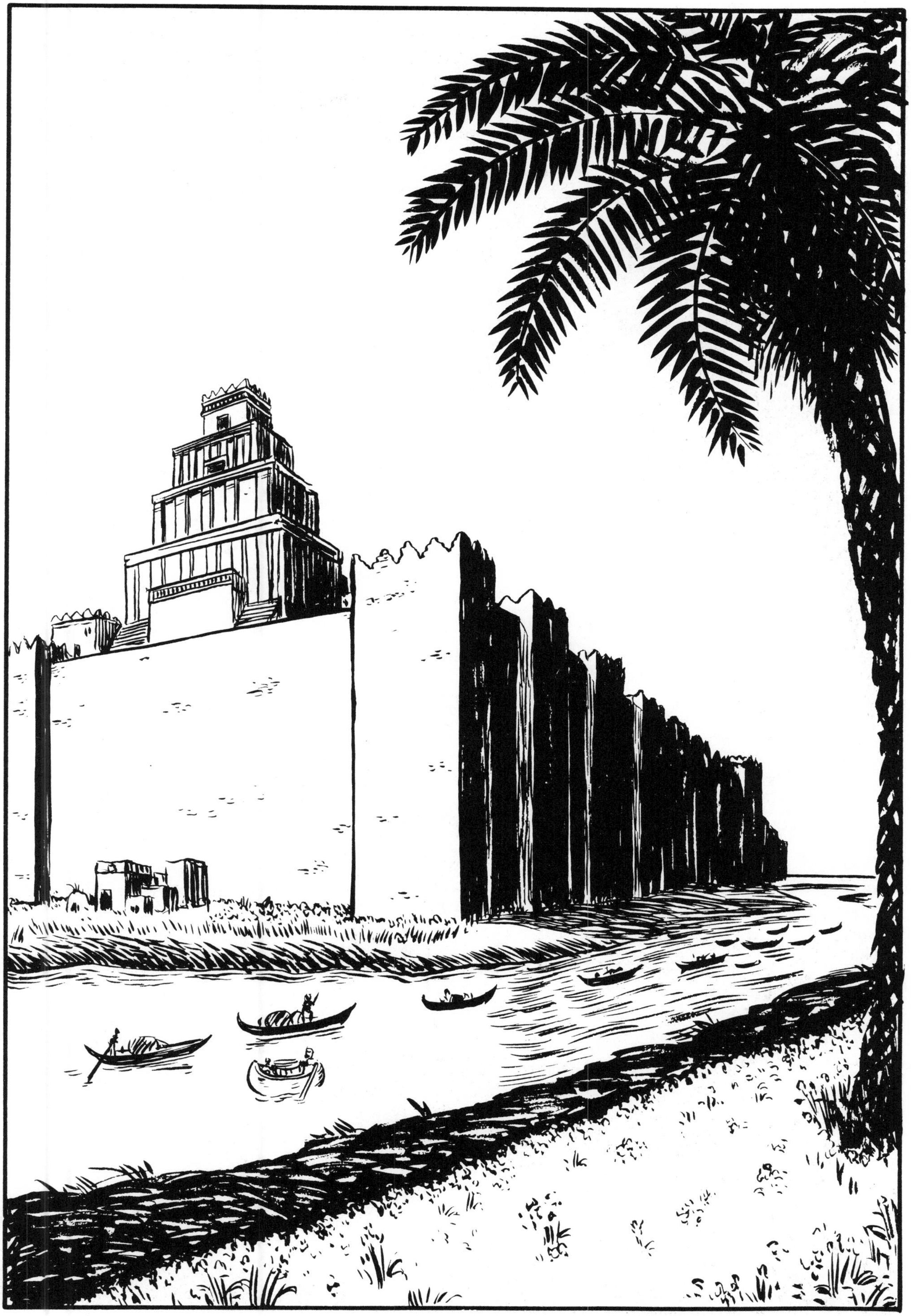

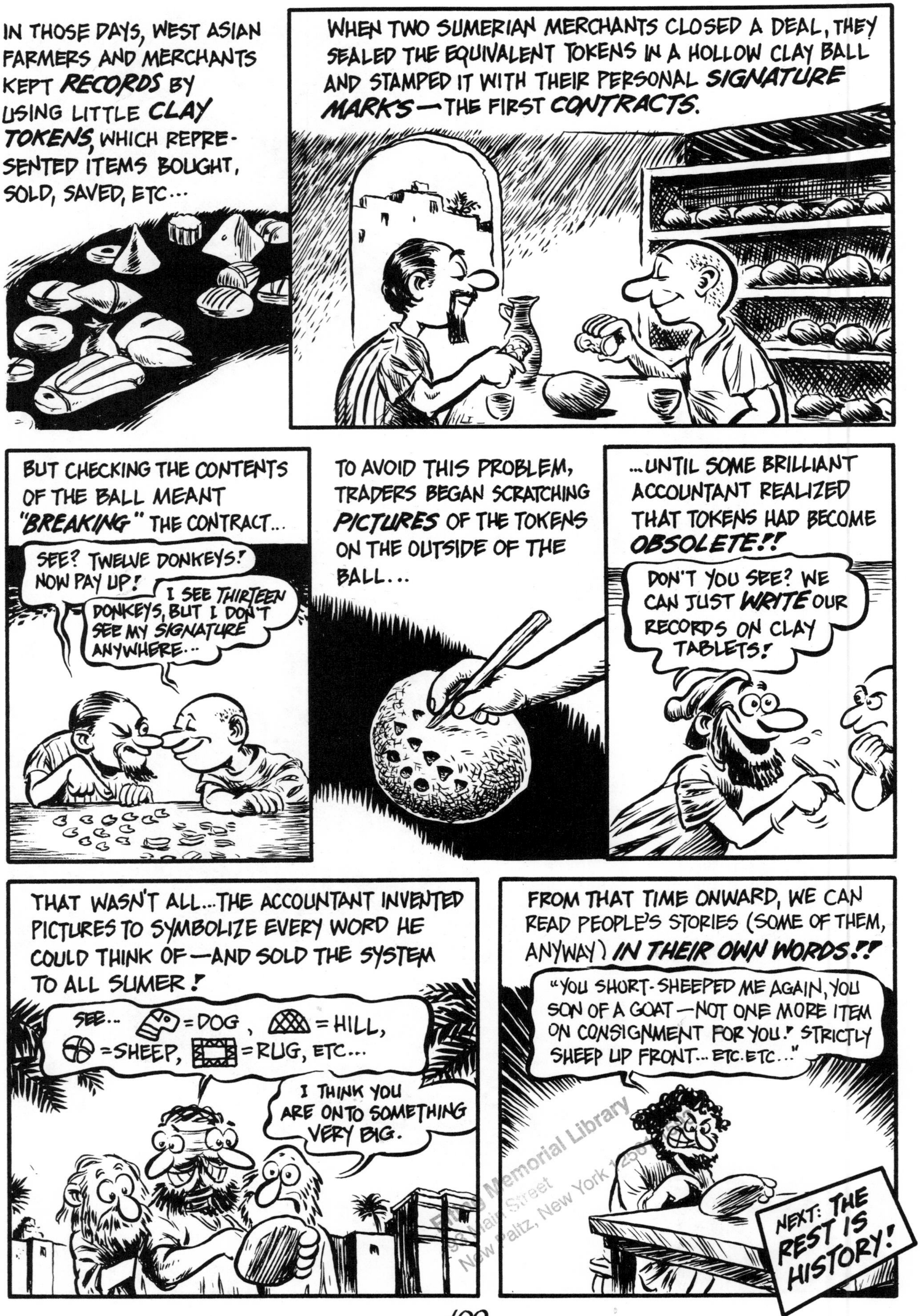
IN THOSE DAYS, WEST ASIAN FARMERS AND MERCHANTS KEPT **RECORDS** BY USING LITTLE **CLAY TOKENS**, WHICH REPRESENTED ITEMS BOUGHT, SOLD, SAVED, ETC...
WHEN TWO SUMERIAN MERCHANTS CLOSED A DEAL, THEY SEALED THE EQUIVALENT TOKENS IN A HOLLOW CLAY BALL AND STAMPED IT WITH THEIR PERSONAL **SIGNATURE MARKS**—THE FIRST **CONTRACTS**.
BUT CHECKING THE CONTENTS OF THE BALL MEANT "**BREAKING**" THE CONTRACT...
SEE? TWELVE DONKEYS! NOW PAY UP!
I SEE *THIRTEEN* DONKEYS, BUT I DON'T SEE MY *SIGNATURE* ANYWHERE...
TO AVOID THIS PROBLEM, TRADERS BEGAN SCRATCHING **PICTURES** OF THE TOKENS ON THE OUTSIDE OF THE BALL...
...UNTIL SOME BRILLIANT ACCOUNTANT REALIZED THAT TOKENS HAD BECOME **OBSOLETE!!**
DON'T YOU SEE? WE CAN JUST **WRITE** OUR RECORDS ON CLAY TABLETS!
THAT WASN'T ALL...THE ACCOUNTANT INVENTED PICTURES TO SYMBOLIZE EVERY WORD HE COULD THINK OF—AND SOLD THE SYSTEM TO ALL SUMER!
SEE... =DOG, =HILL, =SHEEP, =RUG, ETC...
I THINK YOU ARE ONTO SOMETHING VERY BIG.
FROM THAT TIME ONWARD, WE CAN READ PEOPLE'S STORIES (SOME OF THEM, ANYWAY) **IN THEIR OWN WORDS!!**
"YOU SHORT-SHEEPED ME AGAIN, YOU SON OF A GOAT—NOT ONE MORE ITEM ON CONSIGNMENT FOR YOU! STRICTLY SHEEP UP FRONT... ETC. ETC..."
NEXT: THE REST IS HISTORY!

·INTRODUCTION·

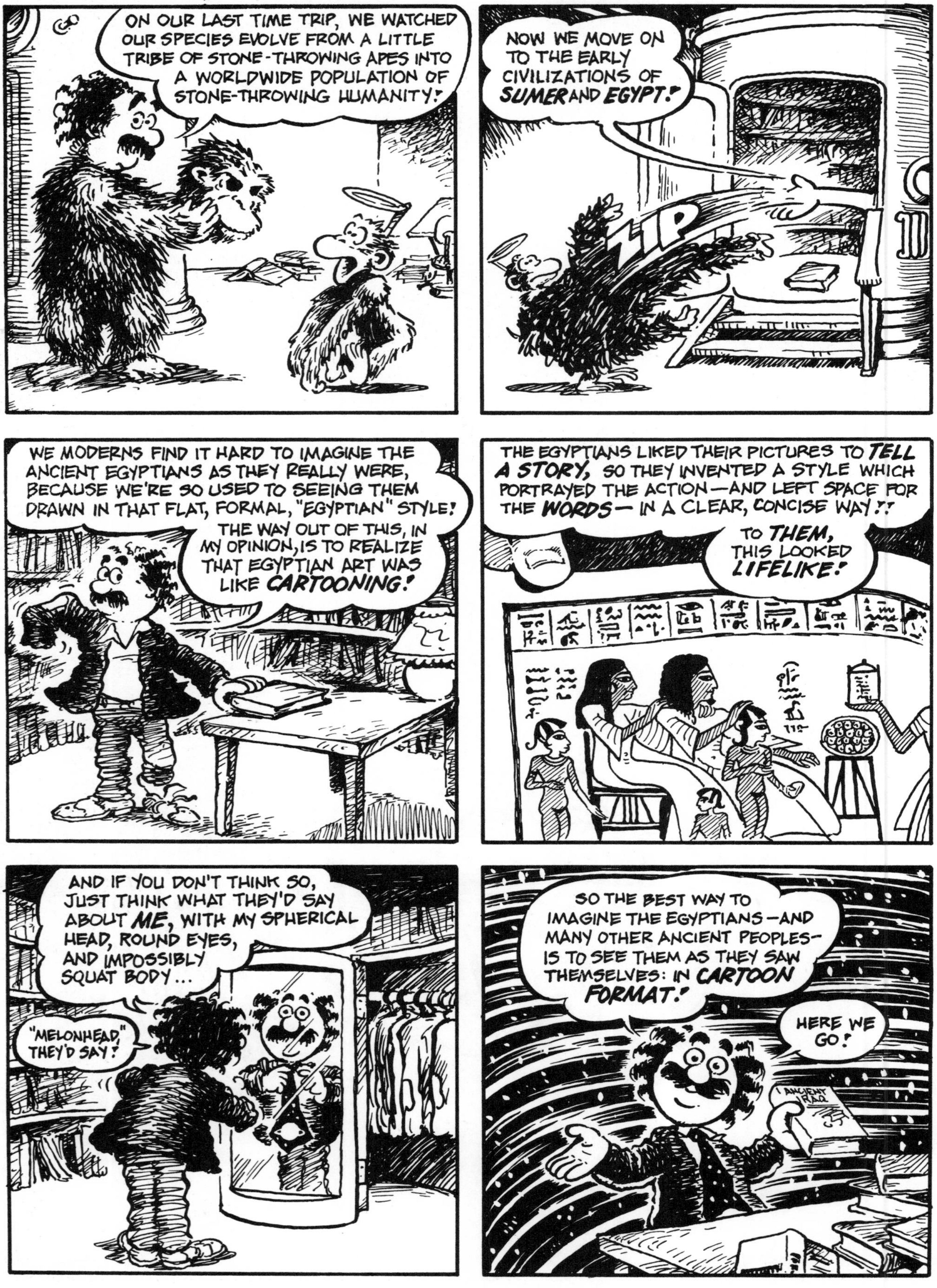
ON OUR LAST TIME TRIP, WE WATCHED OUR SPECIES EVOLVE FROM A LITTLE TRIBE OF STONE-THROWING APES INTO A WORLDWIDE POPULATION OF STONE-THROWING HUMANITY!
NOW WE MOVE ON TO THE EARLY CIVILIZATIONS OF **SUMER** AND **EGYPT**!
ZIP
WE MODERNS FIND IT HARD TO IMAGINE THE ANCIENT EGYPTIANS AS THEY REALLY WERE, BECAUSE WE'RE SO USED TO SEEING THEM DRAWN IN THAT FLAT, FORMAL, "EGYPTIAN" STYLE!
THE WAY OUT OF THIS, IN MY OPINION, IS TO REALIZE THAT EGYPTIAN ART WAS LIKE **CARTOONING**!
THE EGYPTIANS LIKED THEIR PICTURES TO **TELL A STORY**, SO THEY INVENTED A STYLE WHICH PORTRAYED THE ACTION—AND LEFT SPACE FOR THE **WORDS**—IN A CLEAR, CONCISE WAY!!
TO **THEM**, THIS LOOKED **LIFELIKE**!
AND IF YOU DON'T THINK SO, JUST THINK WHAT THEY'D SAY ABOUT **ME**, WITH MY SPHERICAL HEAD, ROUND EYES, AND IMPOSSIBLY SQUAT BODY...
"MELONHEAD," THEY'D SAY!
SO THE BEST WAY TO IMAGINE THE EGYPTIANS—AND MANY OTHER ANCIENT PEOPLES—IS TO SEE THEM AS THEY SAW THEMSELVES: IN **CARTOON FORMAT**!
HERE WE GO!
ANCIENT IRAQ

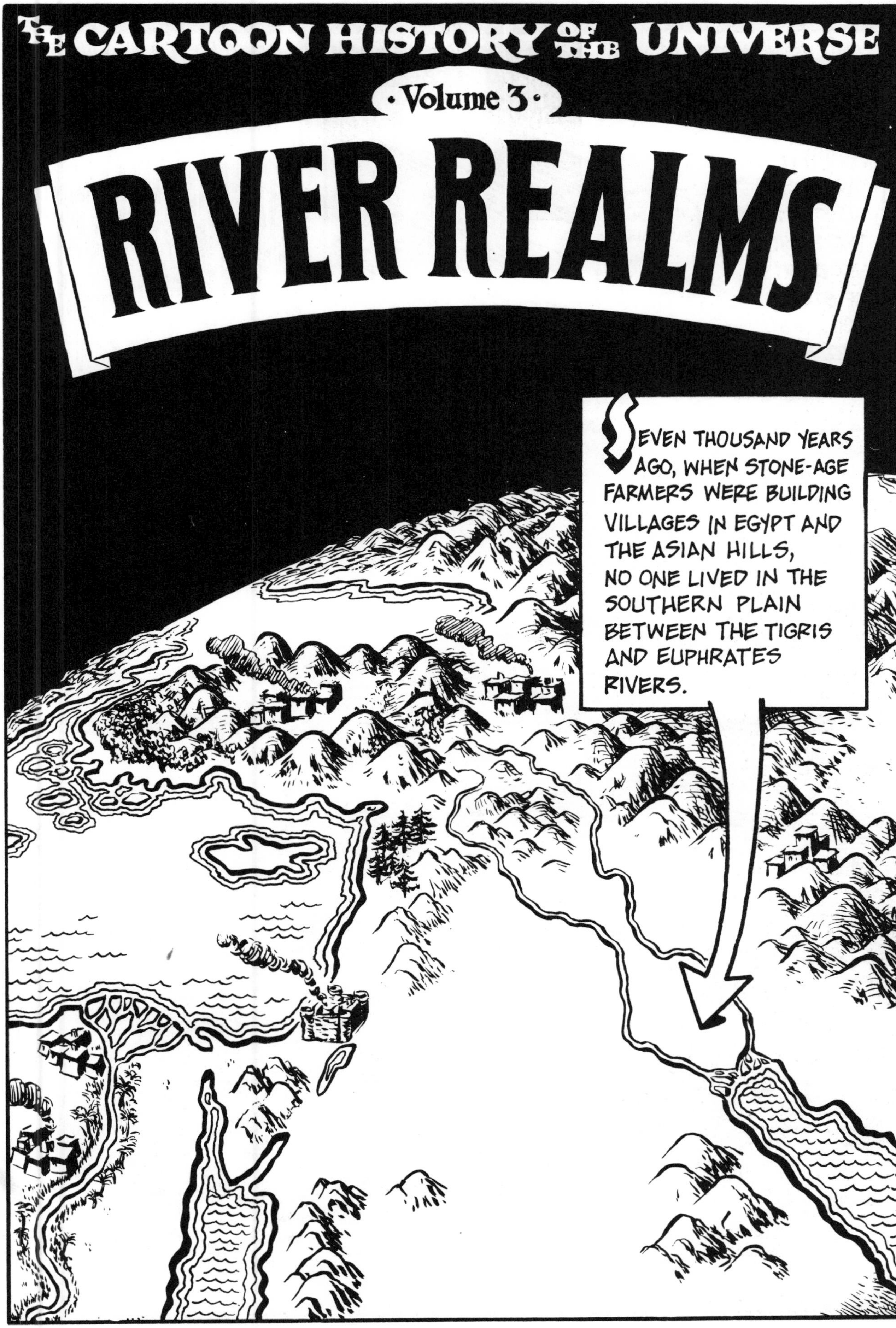
THE CARTOON HISTORY OF THE UNIVERSE
·Volume 3·
RIVER REALMS
SEVEN THOUSAND YEARS AGO, WHEN STONE-AGE FARMERS WERE BUILDING VILLAGES IN EGYPT AND THE ASIAN HILLS, NO ONE LIVED IN THE SOUTHERN PLAIN BETWEEN THE TIGRIS AND EUPHRATES RIVERS.

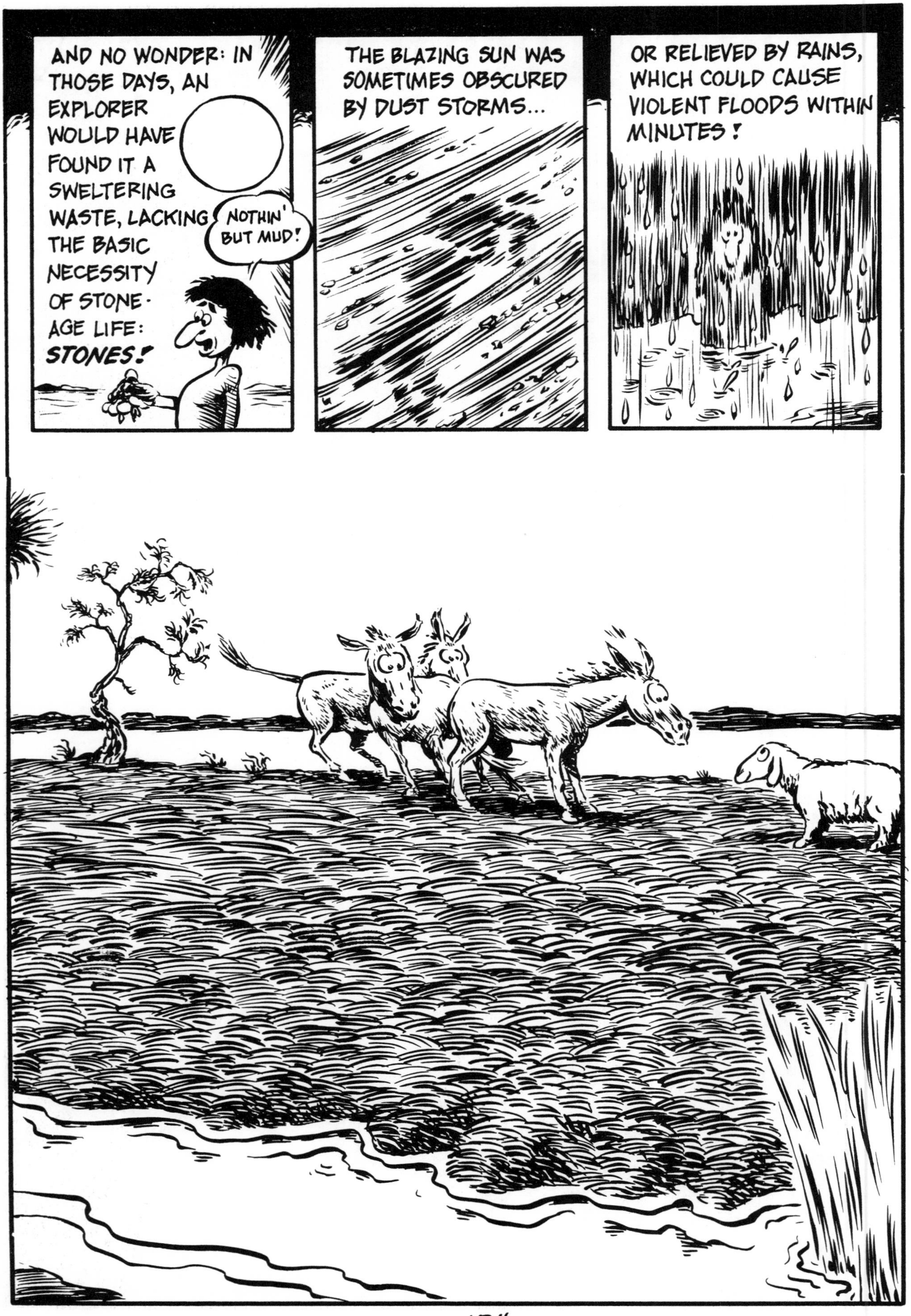
AND NO WONDER: IN THOSE DAYS, AN EXPLORER WOULD HAVE FOUND IT A SWELTERING WASTE, LACKING THE BASIC NECESSITY OF STONE-AGE LIFE: **STONES!**
NOTHIN' BUT MUD!
THE BLAZING SUN WAS SOMETIMES OBSCURED BY DUST STORMS...
OR RELIEVED BY RAINS, WHICH COULD CAUSE VIOLENT FLOODS WITHIN MINUTES!

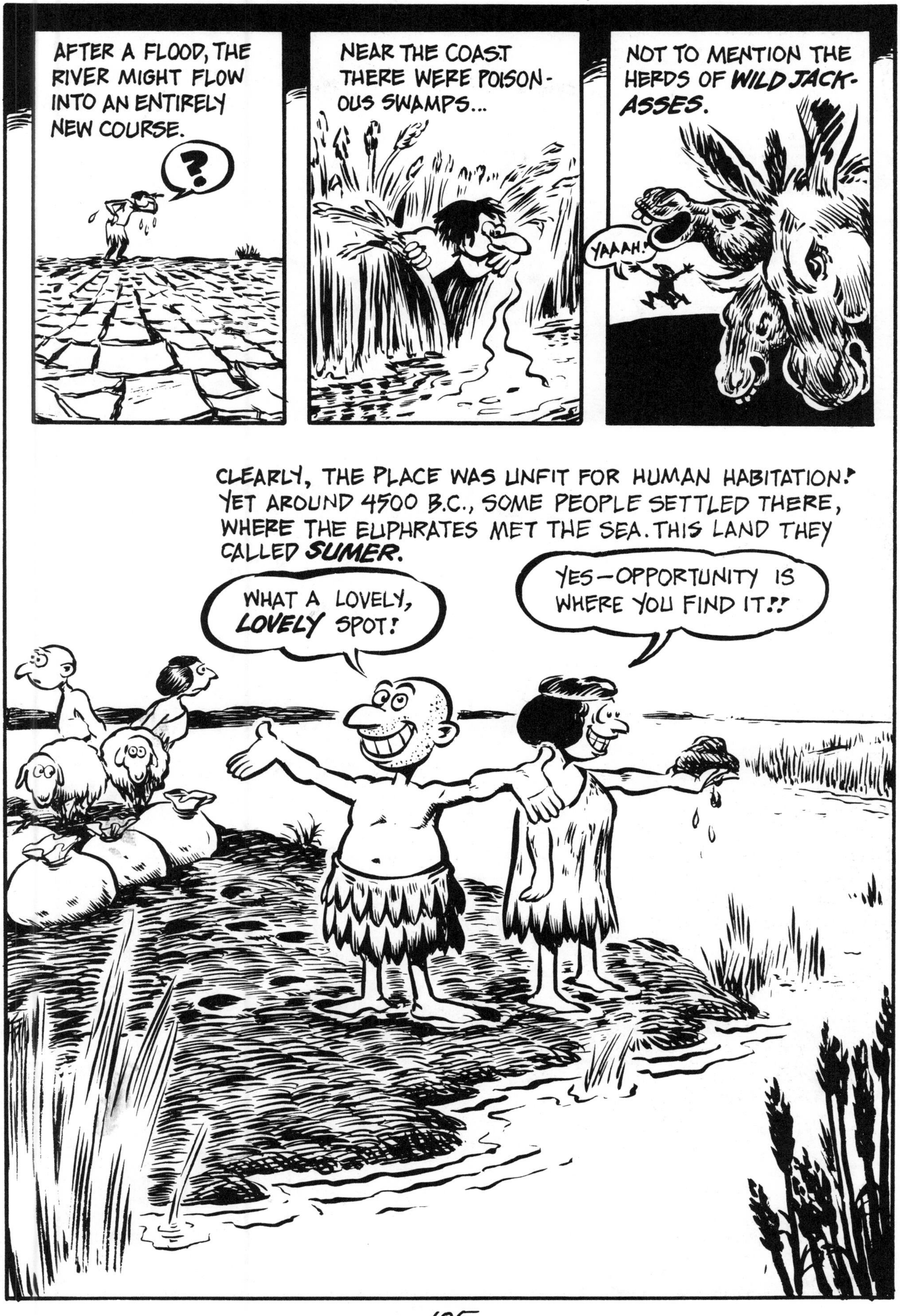

AFTER A FLOOD, THE RIVER MIGHT FLOW INTO AN ENTIRELY NEW COURSE.
?
NEAR THE COAST THERE WERE POISON-OUS SWAMPS...
NOT TO MENTION THE HERDS OF **WILD JACK-ASSES**.
YAAAH!
CLEARLY, THE PLACE WAS UNFIT FOR HUMAN HABITATION! YET AROUND 4500 B.C., SOME PEOPLE SETTLED THERE, WHERE THE EUPHRATES MET THE SEA. THIS LAND THEY CALLED **SUMER**.
WHAT A LOVELY, **LOVELY** SPOT!
YES—OPPORTUNITY IS WHERE YOU FIND IT!!

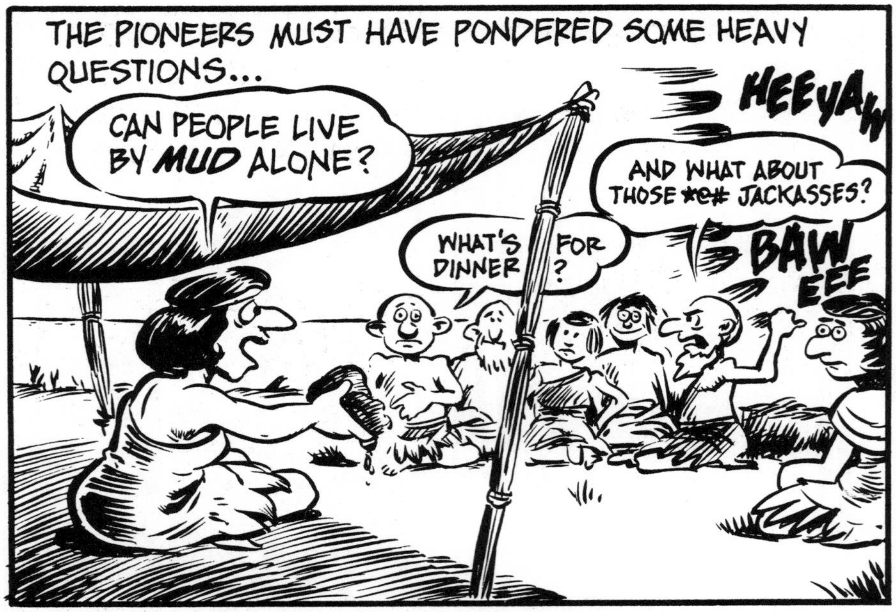
THE PIONEERS MUST HAVE PONDERED SOME HEAVY QUESTIONS...
CAN PEOPLE LIVE BY MUD ALONE?
HEEYAW
AND WHAT ABOUT THOSE *@# JACKASSES?
WHAT'S FOR DINNER?
BAW EEE

THE MUD WAS A SNAP: WHEN BAKED, IT TURNED ***STONY HARD,*** SO BESIDES POTTERY IT WAS GOOD FOR MAKING SICKLES, AXES, HAMMERS, AND EVEN ***NAILS.*** MIXED WITH STRAW AND DRIED IN THE SUN, IT MADE DECENT BRICKS.

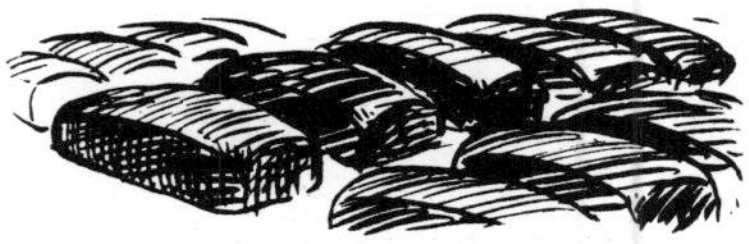

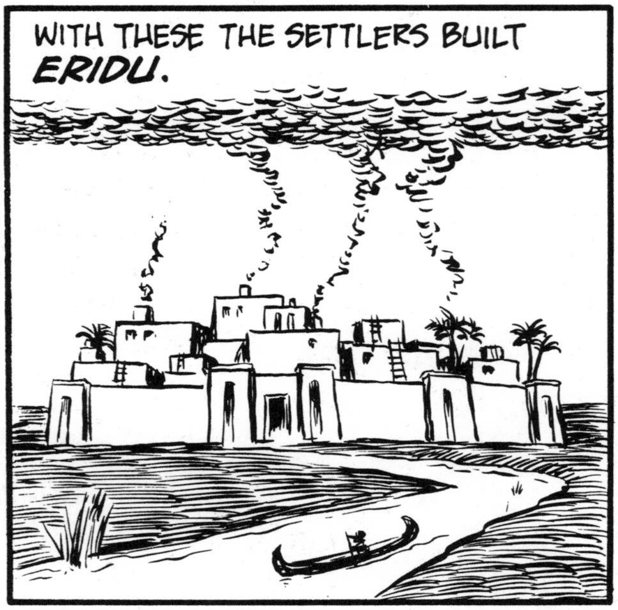
WITH THESE THE SETTLERS BUILT ERIDU.

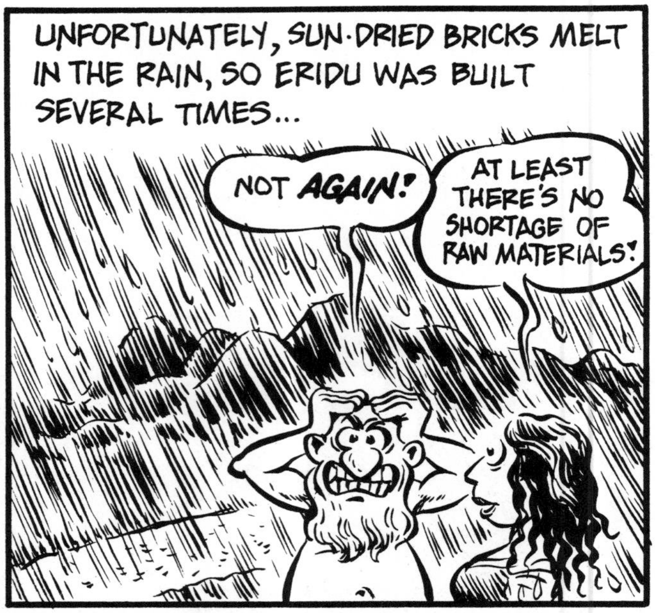
UNFORTUNATELY, SUN-DRIED BRICKS MELT IN THE RAIN, SO ERIDU WAS BUILT SEVERAL TIMES...
NOT AGAIN!
AT LEAST THERE'S NO SHORTAGE OF RAW MATERIALS!

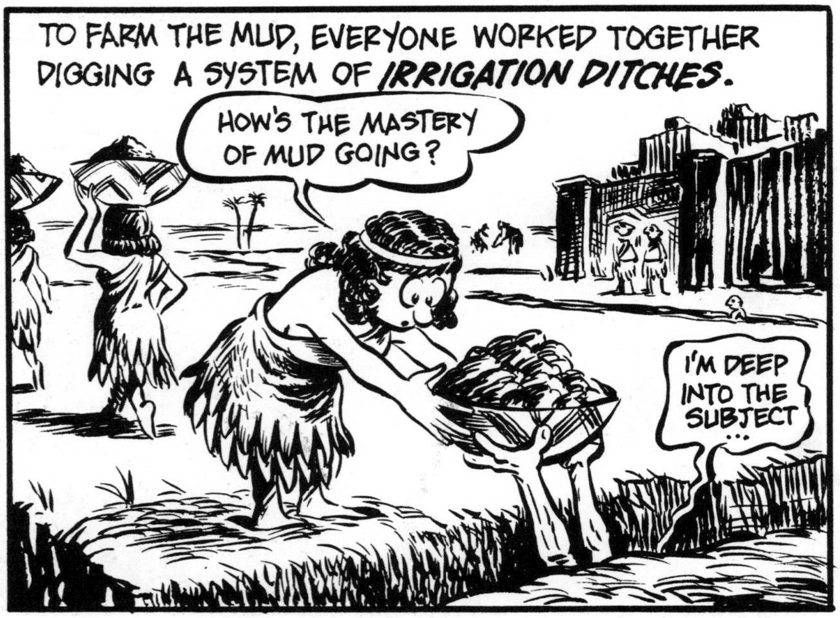
TO FARM THE MUD, EVERYONE WORKED TOGETHER DIGGING A SYSTEM OF IRRIGATION DITCHES.
HOW'S THE MASTERY OF MUD GOING?
I'M DEEP INTO THE SUBJECT...

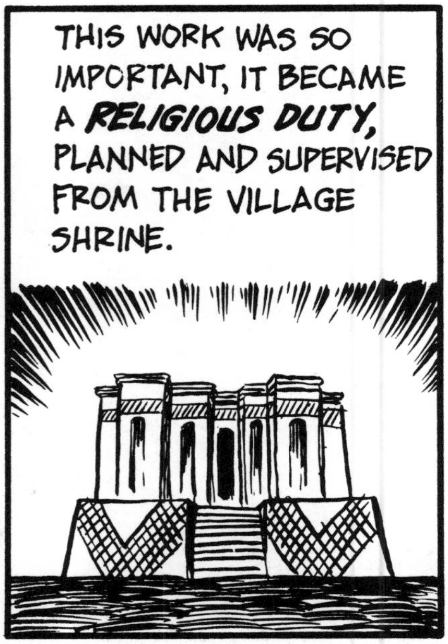
THIS WORK WAS SO IMPORTANT, IT BECAME A RELIGIOUS DUTY, PLANNED AND SUPERVISED FROM THE VILLAGE SHRINE.

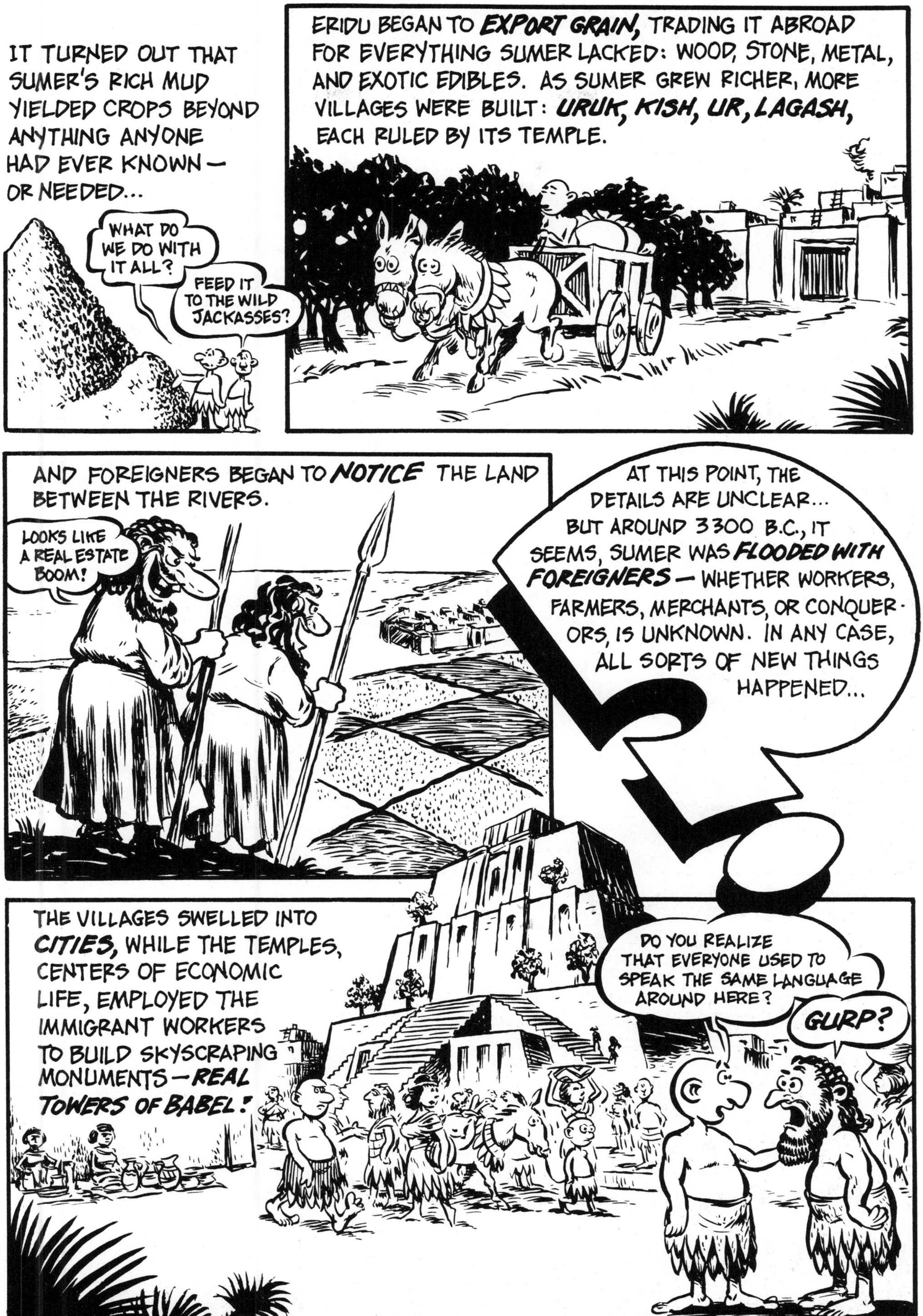
IT TURNED OUT THAT SUMER'S RICH MUD YIELDED CROPS BEYOND ANYTHING ANYONE HAD EVER KNOWN — OR NEEDED...
WHAT DO WE DO WITH IT ALL?
FEED IT TO THE WILD JACKASSES?
ERIDU BEGAN TO EXPORT GRAIN, TRADING IT ABROAD FOR EVERYTHING SUMER LACKED: WOOD, STONE, METAL, AND EXOTIC EDIBLES. AS SUMER GREW RICHER, MORE VILLAGES WERE BUILT: URUK, KISH, UR, LAGASH, EACH RULED BY ITS TEMPLE.
AND FOREIGNERS BEGAN TO NOTICE THE LAND BETWEEN THE RIVERS.
LOOKS LIKE A REAL ESTATE BOOM!
AT THIS POINT, THE DETAILS ARE UNCLEAR... BUT AROUND 3300 B.C., IT SEEMS, SUMER WAS FLOODED WITH FOREIGNERS — WHETHER WORKERS, FARMERS, MERCHANTS, OR CONQUER-ORS, IS UNKNOWN. IN ANY CASE, ALL SORTS OF NEW THINGS HAPPENED...
THE VILLAGES SWELLED INTO CITIES, WHILE THE TEMPLES, CENTERS OF ECONOMIC LIFE, EMPLOYED THE IMMIGRANT WORKERS TO BUILD SKYSCRAPING MONUMENTS — REAL TOWERS OF BABEL!
DO YOU REALIZE THAT EVERYONE USED TO SPEAK THE SAME LANGUAGE AROUND HERE?
GURP?

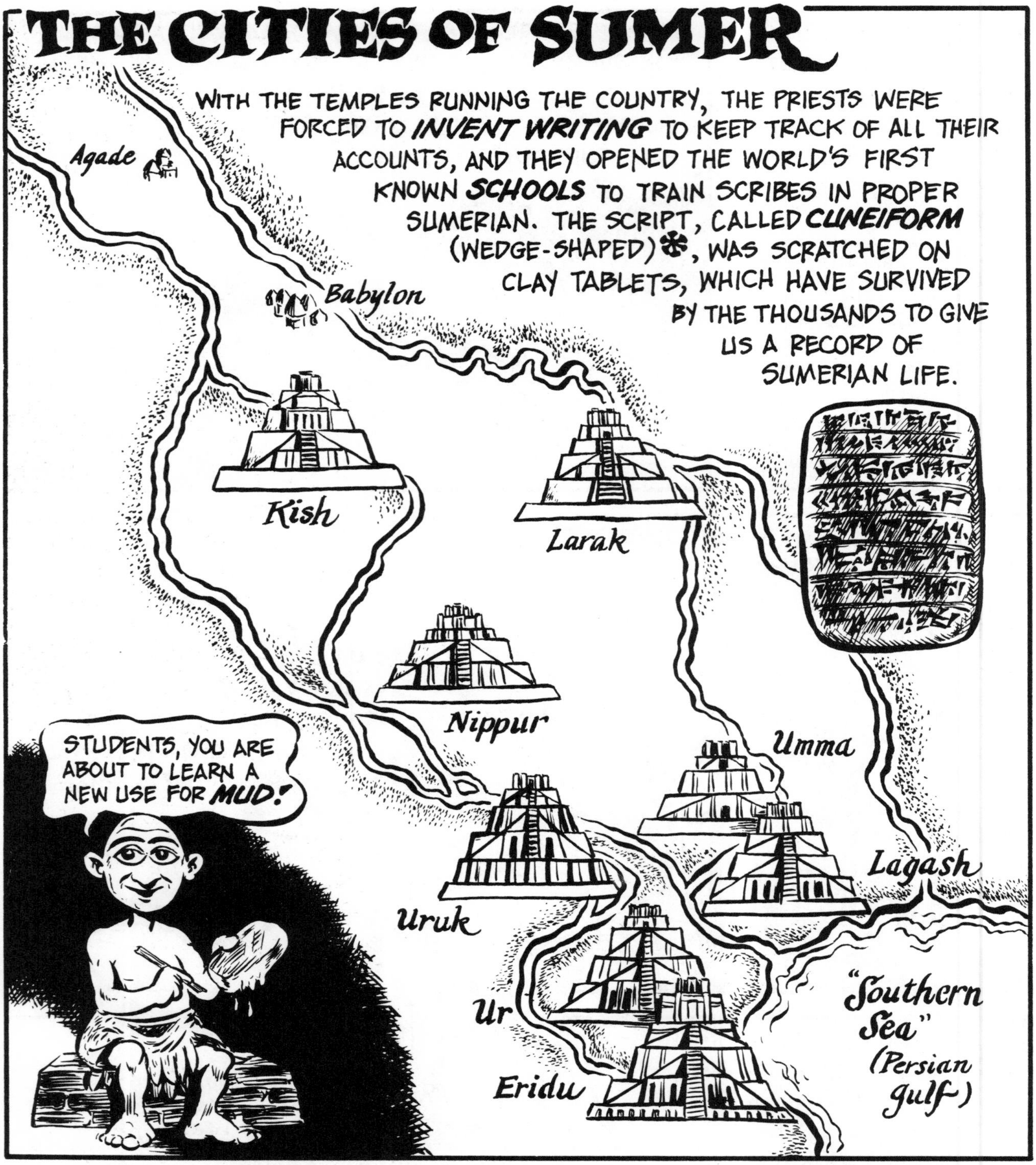
THE CITIES OF SUMER
WITH THE TEMPLES RUNNING THE COUNTRY, THE PRIESTS WERE FORCED TO ***INVENT WRITING*** TO KEEP TRACK OF ALL THEIR ACCOUNTS, AND THEY OPENED THE WORLD'S FIRST KNOWN ***SCHOOLS*** TO TRAIN SCRIBES IN PROPER SUMERIAN. THE SCRIPT, CALLED ***CUNEIFORM*** (WEDGE-SHAPED)*, WAS SCRATCHED ON CLAY TABLETS, WHICH HAVE SURVIVED BY THE THOUSANDS TO GIVE US A RECORD OF SUMERIAN LIFE.
Agade
Babylon
Kish
Larak
Nippur
Umma
Uruk
Lagash
Ur
Eridu
"Southern Sea" (Persian gulf)
STUDENTS, YOU ARE ABOUT TO LEARN A NEW USE FOR ***MUD!***

* BETWEEN THE EARLIEST PICTOGRAPHIC WRITING AND THE LATER CUNEIFORM SCRIPT CAME A MIDDLE STAGE, IN WHICH THE PICTOGRAPHS WERE TURNED ON THEIR SIDES.

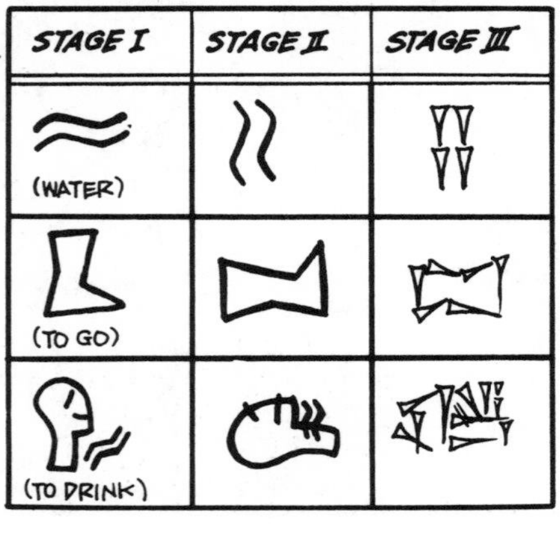
STAGE I
STAGE II
STAGE III
(WATER)
(TO GO)
(TO DRINK)

THE REASON WAS THAT THE SUMERIANS ORIGINALLY WROTE IN COLUMNS ON WET CLAY, STARTING AT THE UPPER RIGHT. THIS CAUSED THEM TO ***SMUDGE*** WHAT THEY HAD ALREADY WRITTEN, SO THE SCRIBES DECIDED TO TURN EVERYTHING SIDEWAYS— ***INCLUDING THE SCRIPT!***

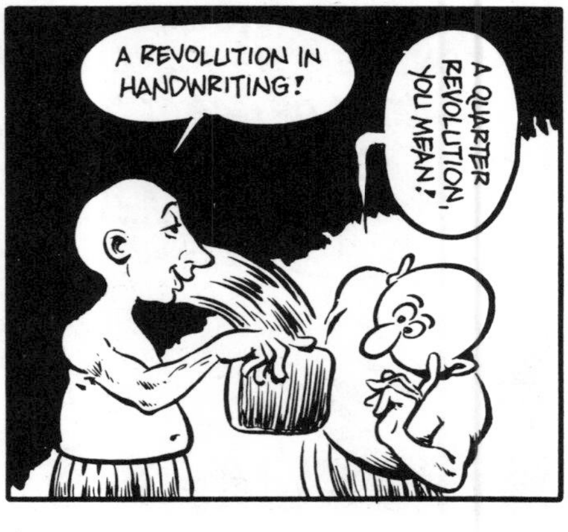
A REVOLUTION IN HANDWRITING!
A QUARTER REVOLUTION, YOU MEAN!

BESIDES SCRIBES, EACH TEMPLE ALSO EMPLOYED BRICKLAYERS, CARPENTERS, BUTCHERS, METALWORKERS, FISHERMEN, BAKERS, BREWERS, POTTERS, PLOWMEN, SHEPHERDS, OXHERDS, SWINEHERDS, SPINNERS, WEAVERS, JEWELLERS, HAIRDRESSERS, EVEN PROSTITUTES— ANY OF WHOM MIGHT BE DRAFTED TO DO DITCH-DIGGING...

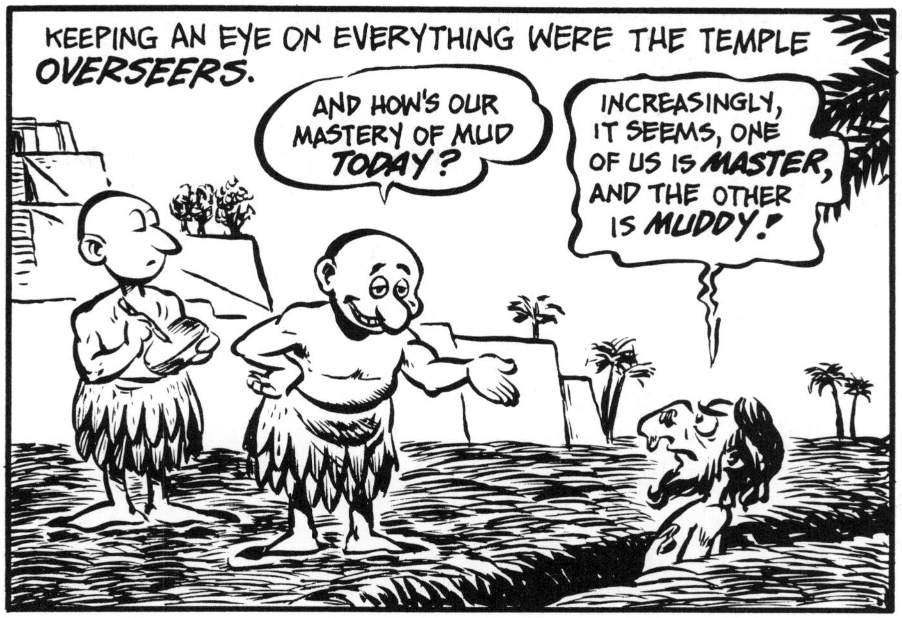
KEEPING AN EYE ON EVERYTHING WERE THE TEMPLE ***OVERSEERS.***
AND HOW'S OUR MASTERY OF MUD ***TODAY?***
INCREASINGLY, IT SEEMS, ONE OF US IS ***MASTER,*** AND THE OTHER IS ***MUDDY!***

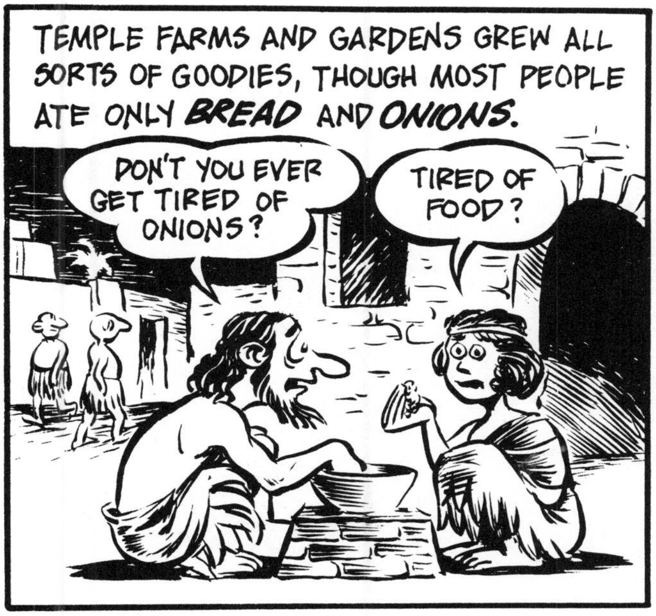
TEMPLE FARMS AND GARDENS GREW ALL SORTS OF GOODIES, THOUGH MOST PEOPLE ATE ONLY ***BREAD*** AND ***ONIONS.***
DON'T YOU EVER GET TIRED OF ONIONS?
TIRED OF FOOD?

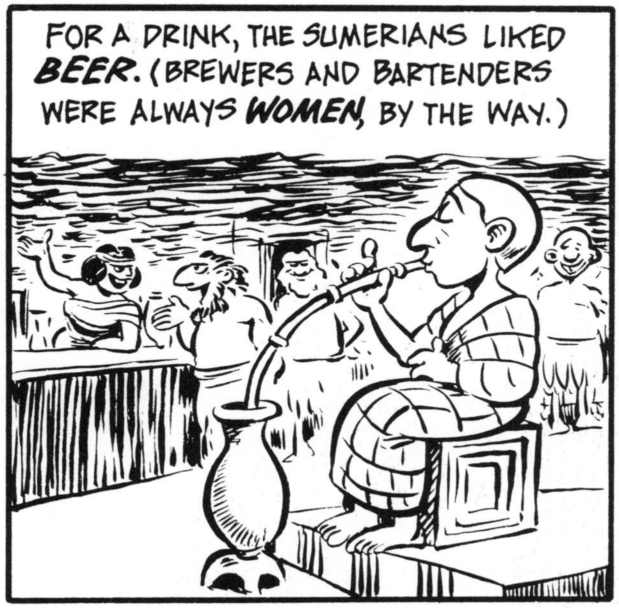
FOR A DRINK, THE SUMERIANS LIKED ***BEER.*** (BREWERS AND BARTENDERS WERE ALWAYS ***WOMEN,*** BY THE WAY.)

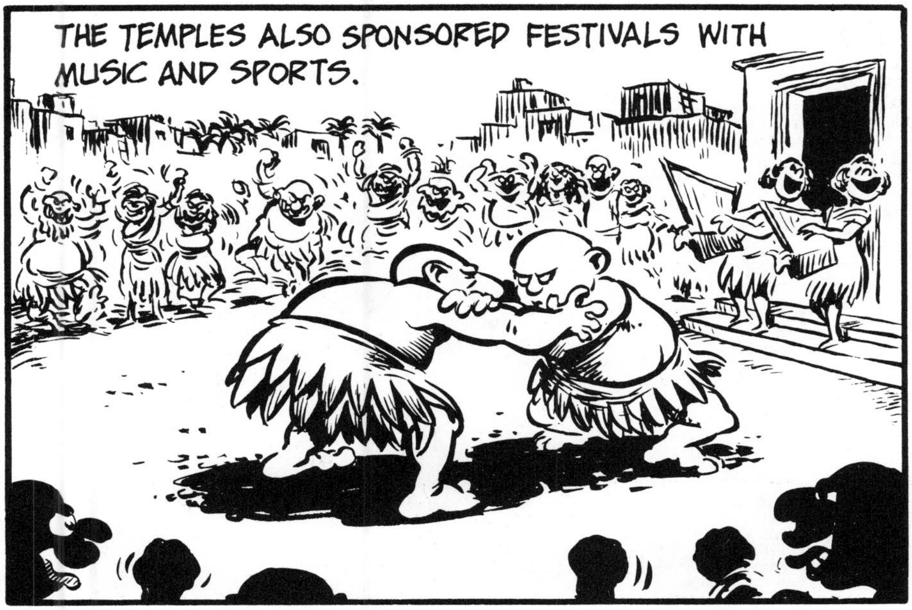
THE TEMPLES ALSO SPONSORED FESTIVALS WITH MUSIC AND SPORTS.

PRESIDING OVER ALL WAS THE ***EN,*** THE HIGH PRIESTESS OR PRIEST. STRANGE TO SAY, THIS OFFICIAL WAS ***ELECTED***— THAT IS, UNTIL THE "AGE OF HEROES."

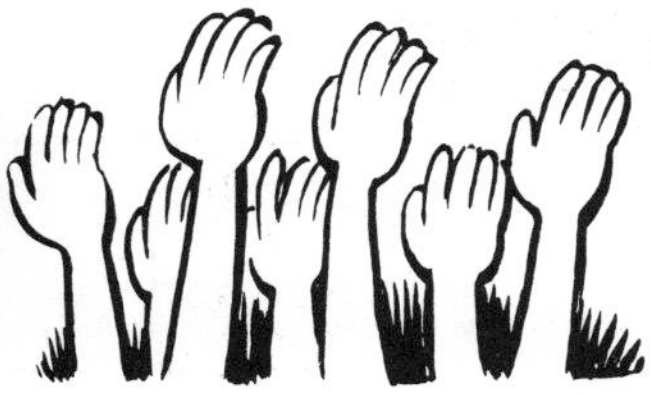

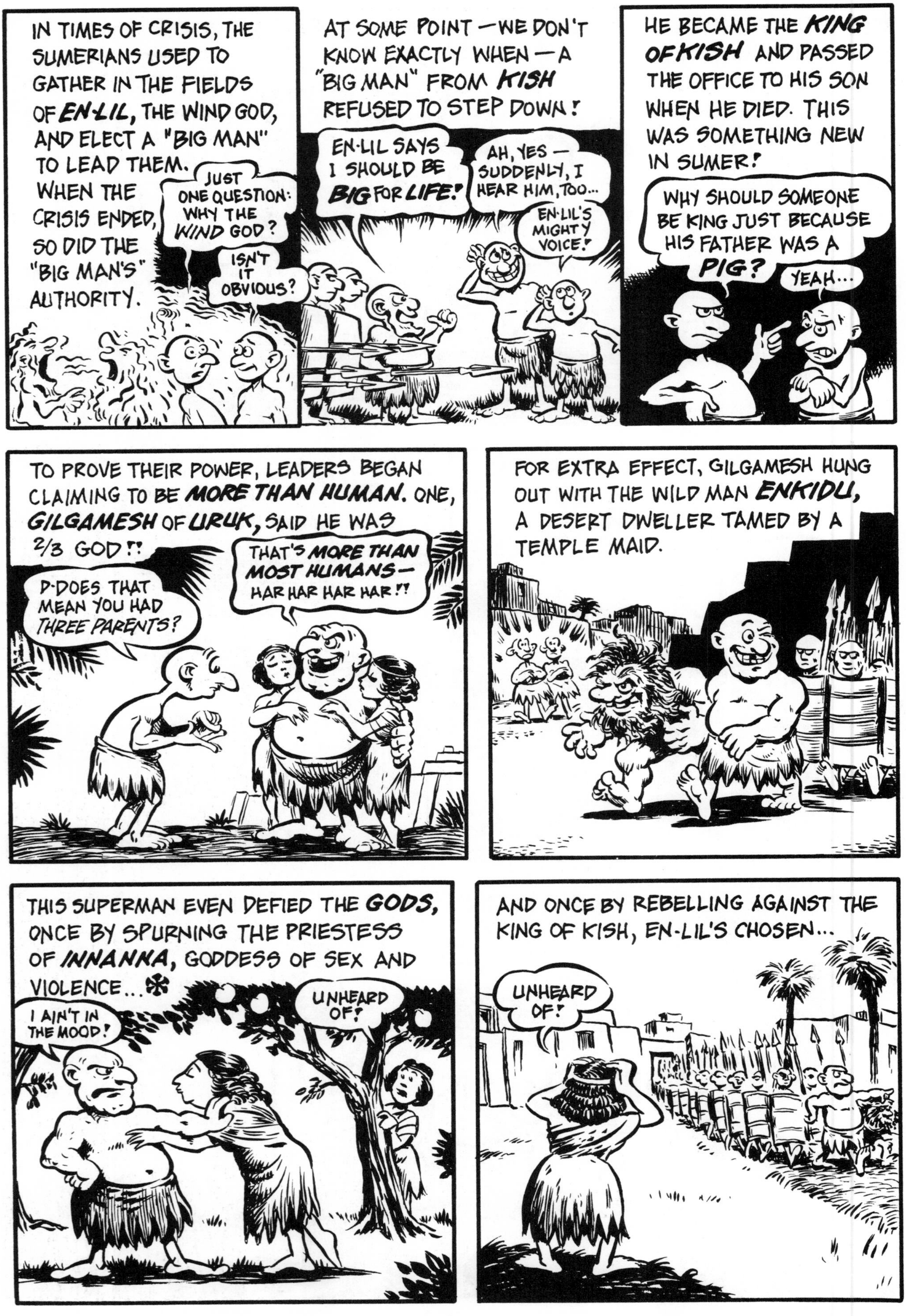
IN TIMES OF CRISIS, THE SUMERIANS USED TO GATHER IN THE FIELDS OF EN-LIL, THE WIND GOD, AND ELECT A "BIG MAN" TO LEAD THEM. WHEN THE CRISIS ENDED, SO DID THE "BIG MAN'S" AUTHORITY.
JUST ONE QUESTION: WHY THE WIND GOD?
ISN'T IT OBVIOUS?
AT SOME POINT — WE DON'T KNOW EXACTLY WHEN — A "BIG MAN" FROM KISH REFUSED TO STEP DOWN!
EN-LIL SAYS I SHOULD BE BIG FOR LIFE!
AH, YES — SUDDENLY, I HEAR HIM, TOO...
EN-LIL'S MIGHTY VOICE!
HE BECAME THE KING OF KISH AND PASSED THE OFFICE TO HIS SON WHEN HE DIED. THIS WAS SOMETHING NEW IN SUMER!
WHY SHOULD SOMEONE BE KING JUST BECAUSE HIS FATHER WAS A PIG?
YEAH...
TO PROVE THEIR POWER, LEADERS BEGAN CLAIMING TO BE MORE THAN HUMAN. ONE, GILGAMESH OF URUK, SAID HE WAS 2/3 GOD!!
D-DOES THAT MEAN YOU HAD THREE PARENTS?
THAT'S MORE THAN MOST HUMANS— HAR HAR HAR HAR!!
FOR EXTRA EFFECT, GILGAMESH HUNG OUT WITH THE WILD MAN ENKIDU, A DESERT DWELLER TAMED BY A TEMPLE MAID.
THIS SUPERMAN EVEN DEFIED THE GODS, ONCE BY SPURNING THE PRIESTESS OF INNANNA, GODDESS OF SEX AND VIOLENCE...*
I AIN'T IN THE MOOD!
UNHEARD OF!
AND ONCE BY REBELLING AGAINST THE KING OF KISH, EN-LIL'S CHOSEN...
UNHEARD OF!

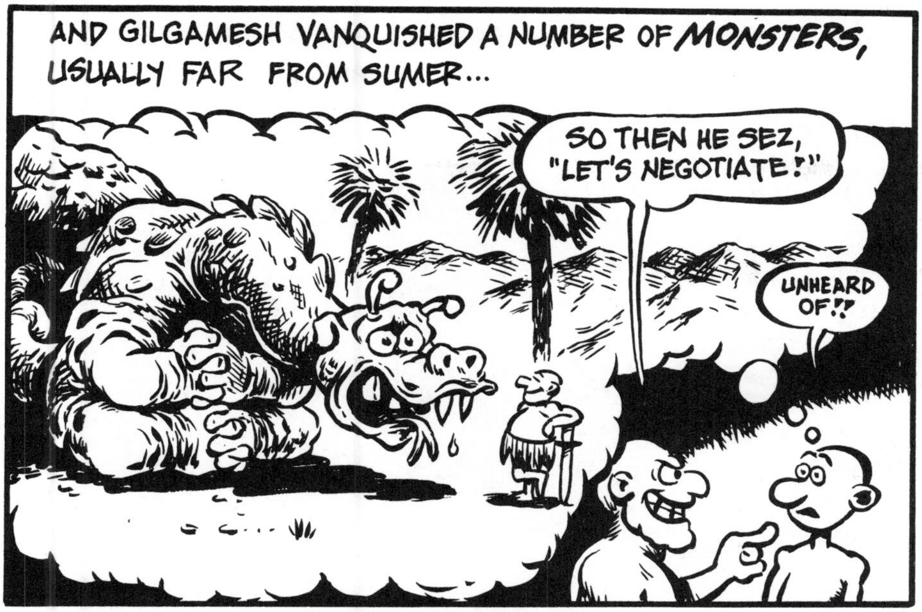
AND GILGAMESH VANQUISHED A NUMBER OF MONSTERS, USUALLY FAR FROM SUMER...
SO THEN HE SEZ, "LET'S NEGOTIATE!"
UNHEARD OF!?

IN REALITY, THESE DRAGONS WERE PROBABLY ***FOREIGN TRIBES***, WHOM THE KING HAD PLUNDERED FOR TIMBER, GOLD, AND SLAVES. THE EXPLOITS OF GILGAMESH WERE SUNG BY THE POETS, AND IN TIME HE BECAME THE MOST FAMOUS HERO OF SUMER'S ***HEROIC AGE*** (AROUND 2700 B.C.).

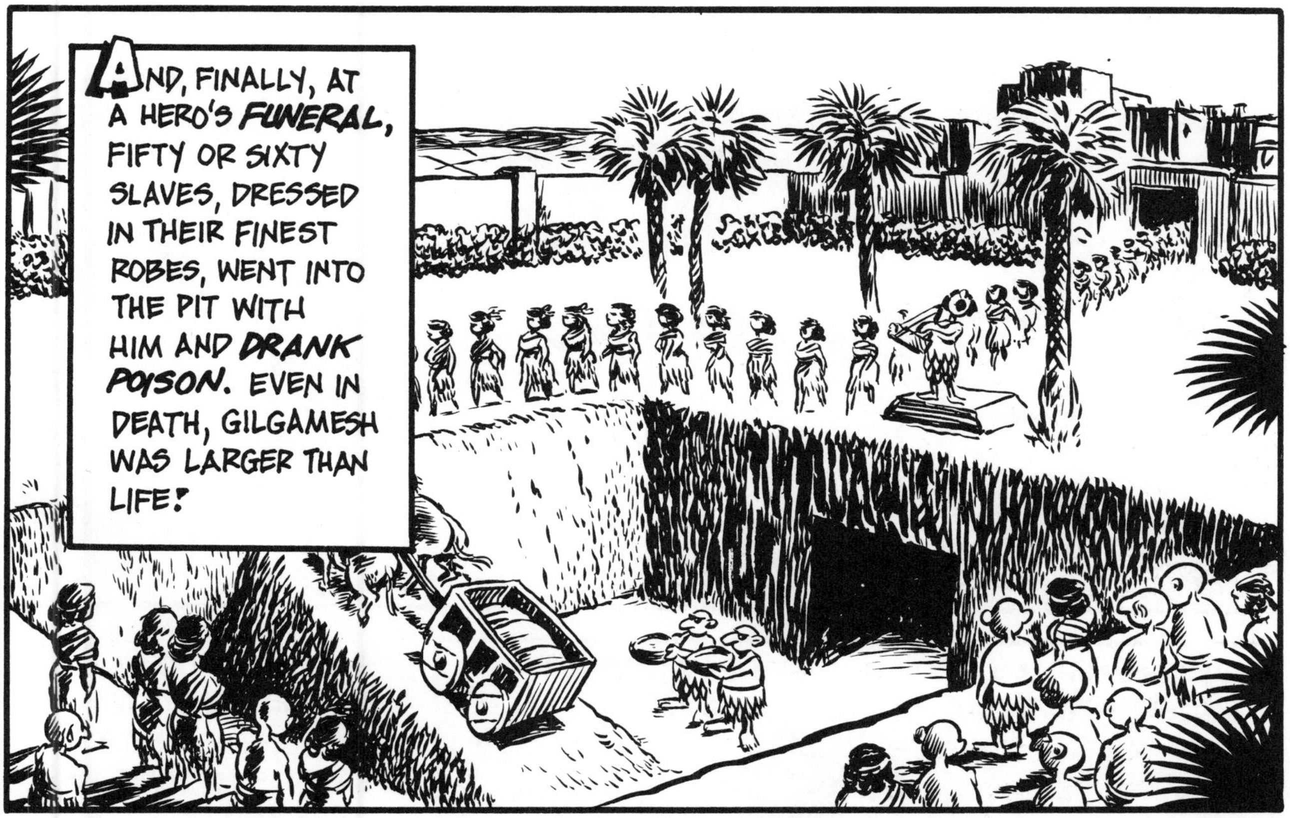
AND, FINALLY, AT A HERO'S FUNERAL, FIFTY OR SIXTY SLAVES, DRESSED IN THEIR FINEST ROBES, WENT INTO THE PIT WITH HIM AND DRANK POISON. EVEN IN DEATH, GILGAMESH WAS LARGER THAN LIFE!

LIKE MANY FARMING PEOPLES, THE SUMERIANS WORSHIPPED FERTILITY AND SEXUALITY. EVERY SPRING, THE HIGH PRIESTESS OF THE GODDESS ***INNANNA*** ENACTED THE ***"SACRED MARRIAGE"*** WITH THE KING ON A SPECIAL BED ATOP THE TEMPLE. A GENERAL ORGY FOLLOWED DOWN-STAIRS, EXPERTS SAY.

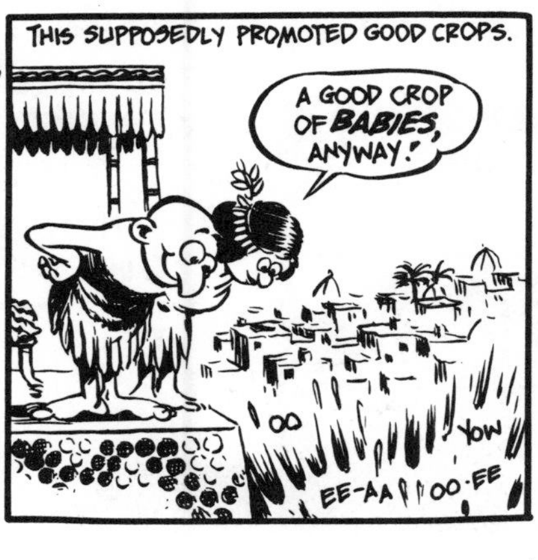
THIS SUPPOSEDLY PROMOTED GOOD CROPS.
A GOOD CROP OF BABIES, ANYWAY!
OO
YOW
EE-AA! OO-EE

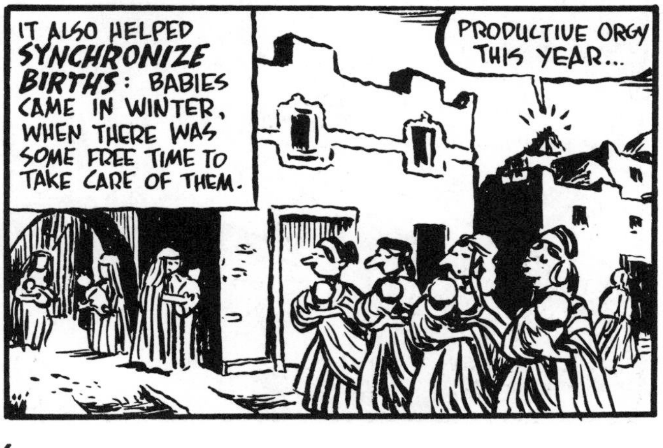
IT ALSO HELPED SYNCHRONIZE BIRTHS: BABIES CAME IN WINTER, WHEN THERE WAS SOME FREE TIME TO TAKE CARE OF THEM.
PRODUCTIVE ORGY THIS YEAR...

IN THE LAND OF MUD, IT WAS ONLY NATURAL FOR PEOPLE TO **FIGHT** OVER **WATER**, WHICH IS MUD'S MORE EXPENSIVE INGREDIENT...

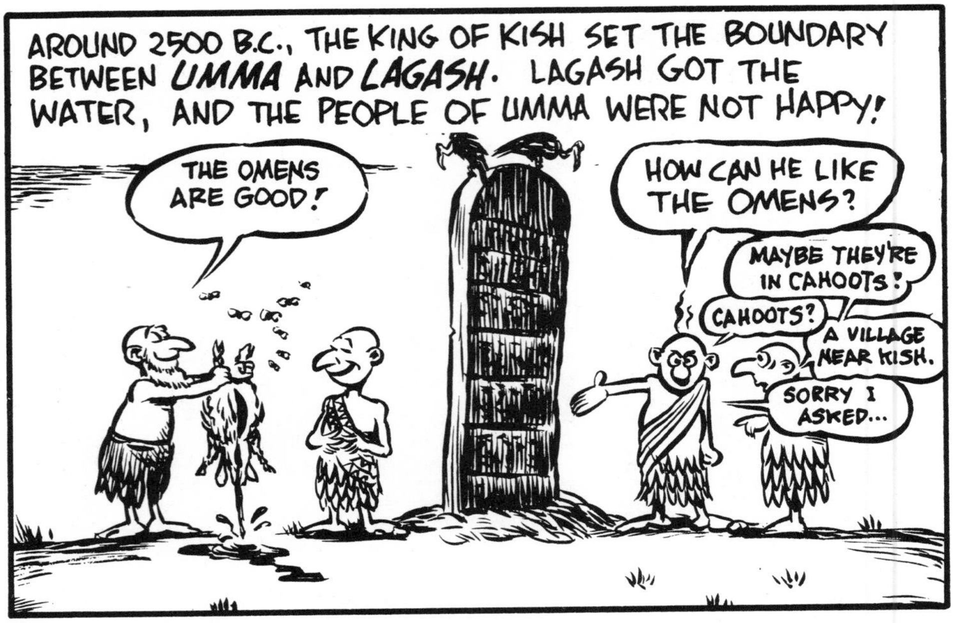
AROUND 2500 B.C., THE KING OF KISH SET THE BOUNDARY BETWEEN UMMA AND LAGASH. LAGASH GOT THE WATER, AND THE PEOPLE OF UMMA WERE NOT HAPPY!
THE OMENS ARE GOOD!
HOW CAN HE LIKE THE OMENS?
MAYBE THEY'RE IN CAHOOTS!
CAHOOTS?
A VILLAGE NEAR KISH.
SORRY I ASKED...

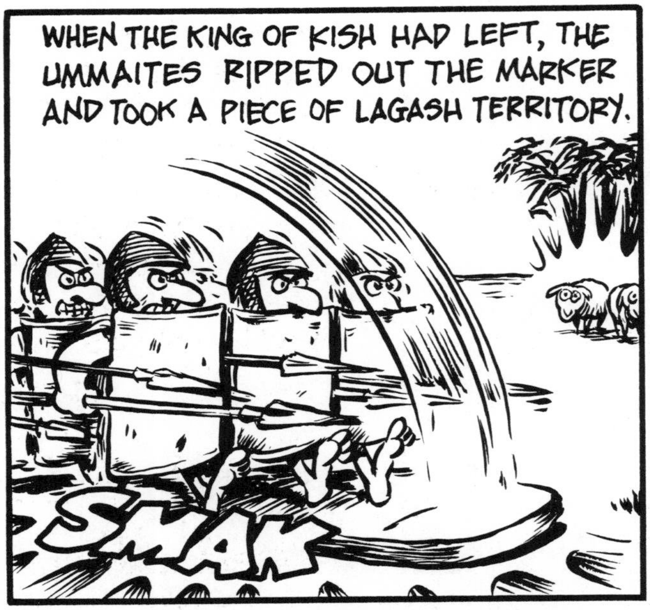
WHEN THE KING OF KISH HAD LEFT, THE UMMAITES RIPPED OUT THE MARKER AND TOOK A PIECE OF LAGASH TERRITORY.
SMAK

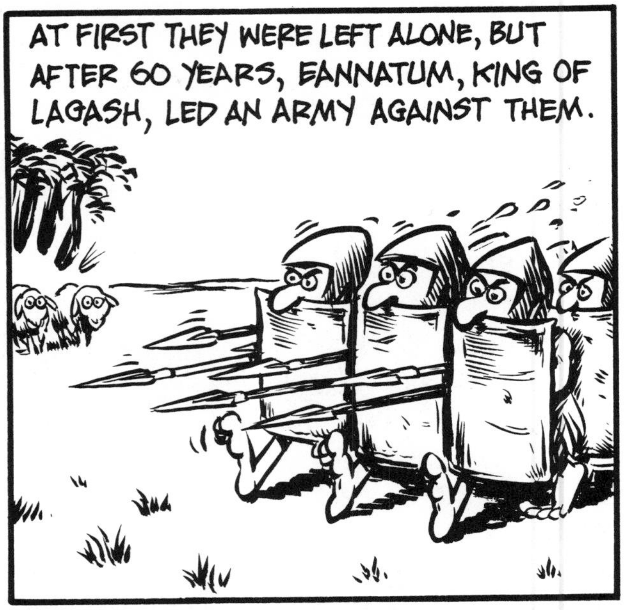
AT FIRST THEY WERE LEFT ALONE, BUT AFTER 60 YEARS, EANNATUM, KING OF LAGASH, LED AN ARMY AGAINST THEM.

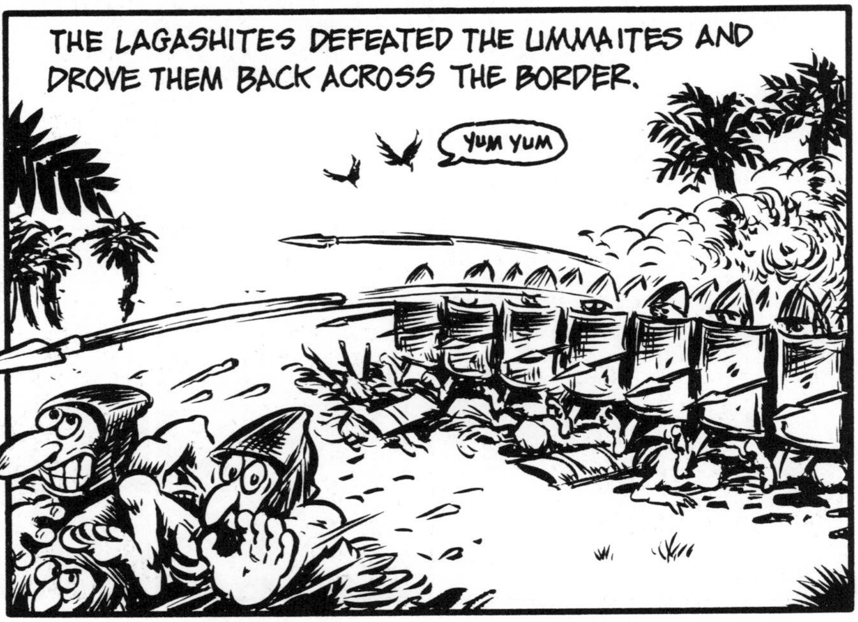
THE LAGASHITES DEFEATED THE UMMAITES AND DROVE THEM BACK ACROSS THE BORDER.
YUM YUM

EANNATUM THEN OFFERED UMMA THE USE OF THE DISPUTED LAND — AS LONG AS THEY PAID **RENT** FOR THE PRIVILEGE. AGAIN THE KING OF UMMA WAS DISPLEASED!!

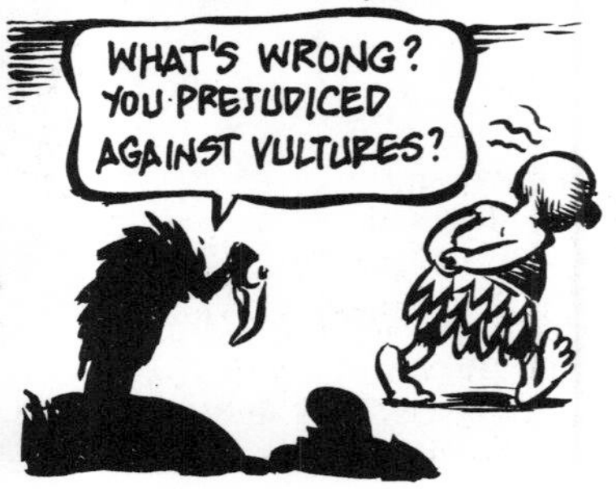
WHAT'S WRONG? YOU PREJUDICED AGAINST VULTURES?

WITHIN ANOTHER GENERATION, UMMA WAS ON THE MARCH AGAIN.

THIS TIME THE LAGASHITES DROVE THEIR FOES ALL THE WAY BACK TO THE GATES OF UMMA.

WHEN THEY WERE FINISHED WEARING EACH OTHER OUT, A *THIRD* KING, *IL OF ZABALAM,* SWEPT DOWN WITH *HIS* ARMY, TRASHED LAGASH AND CONQUERED UMMA.

AFTER CHECKING THE OMENS ✳, IL AND THE KING OF LAGASH CAME TO TERMS: UMMA COULD STILL USE THE WATER, BUT WITHOUT PAYMENT—MAKING UMMA THE CLEAR WINNER—OR WAS IT ZABALAM?

WE VULTURES NEVER LOSE!

THE MESOPOTAMIANS USED MANY *MAGICAL* METHODS TO UNDERSTAND THE WORLD — SUCH AS READING THE FUTURE FROM THE SHAPE AND COLOR OF A *SHEEP'S LIVER.*

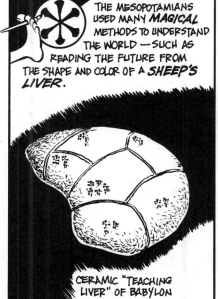

CERAMIC "TEACHING LIVER" OF BABYLON

THEY ALSO DEVELOPED THE PRACTICE OF *ASTROLOGY* TO DETERMINE SUCH MATTERS AS WHETHER OR NOT THE KING SHOULD CHANGE HIS CLOTHES.

IT'S FORTY DAYS AND FORTY NIGHTS ALREADY! I CAN'T STAND MYSELF!

THE STARS AREN'T MELLOW ENOUGH YET, SIRE, SO KEEP YOUR SHIRT ON...

FOR SOME REASON, ASTROLOGY HAS SURVIVED, WHILE LIVEROLOGY PERISHED LONG AGO. IT *MIGHT* HAVE BEEN OTHERWISE, THOUGH...

WHAT'S THE *LIVERSCOPE* FOR TODAY?

"DON'T LOSE SLEEP OVER JAUNDICED SHEEP"

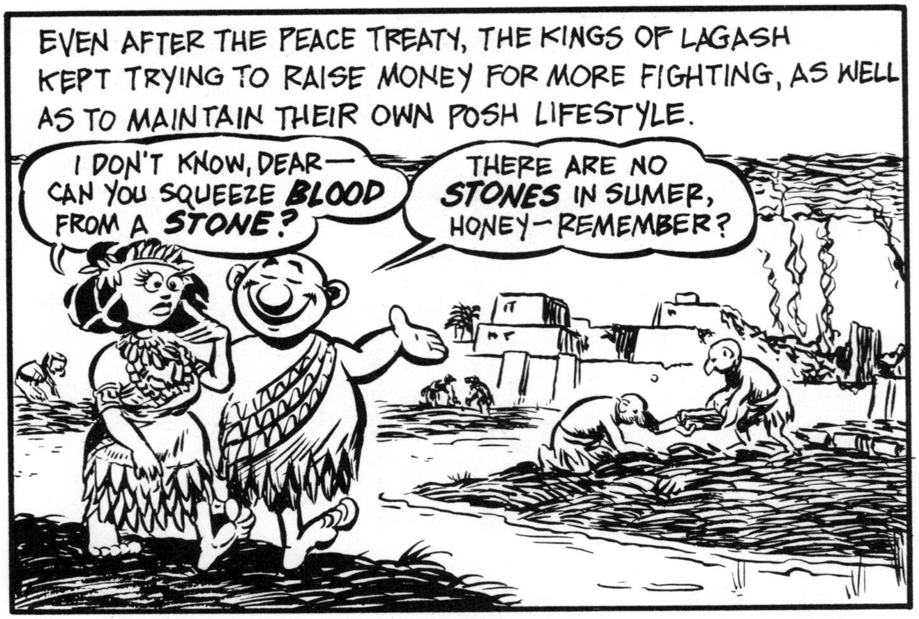
EVEN AFTER THE PEACE TREATY, THE KINGS OF LAGASH KEPT TRYING TO RAISE MONEY FOR MORE FIGHTING, AS WELL AS TO MAINTAIN THEIR OWN POSH LIFESTYLE.
I DON'T KNOW, DEAR— CAN YOU SQUEEZE **BLOOD** FROM A **STONE**?
THERE ARE NO **STONES** IN SUMER, HONEY—REMEMBER?

THE KING'S MEN TOOK TEMPLE LANDS AND PLANTED THEM WITH THE KING'S ONIONS; THE ROYAL BOAT INSPECTORS SEIZED PEOPLE'S BOATS; AND NATURALLY **TAXES** WENT UP.

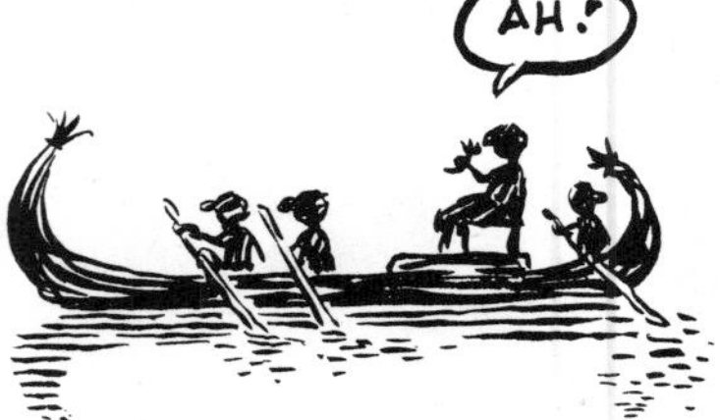
AH!

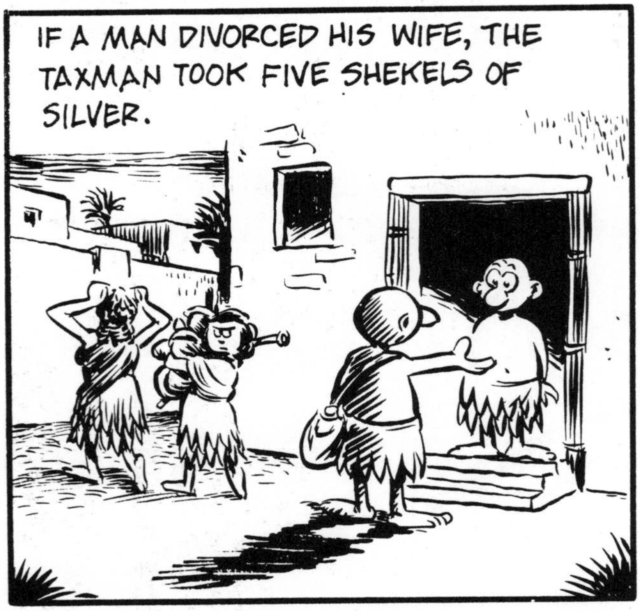
IF A MAN DIVORCED HIS WIFE, THE TAXMAN TOOK FIVE SHEKELS OF SILVER.

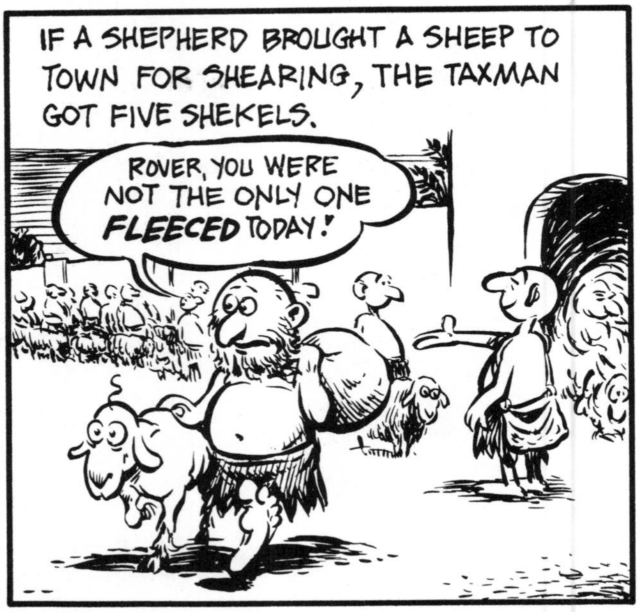
IF A SHEPHERD BROUGHT A SHEEP TO TOWN FOR SHEARING, THE TAXMAN GOT FIVE SHEKELS.
ROVER, YOU WERE NOT THE ONLY ONE **FLEECED** TODAY!

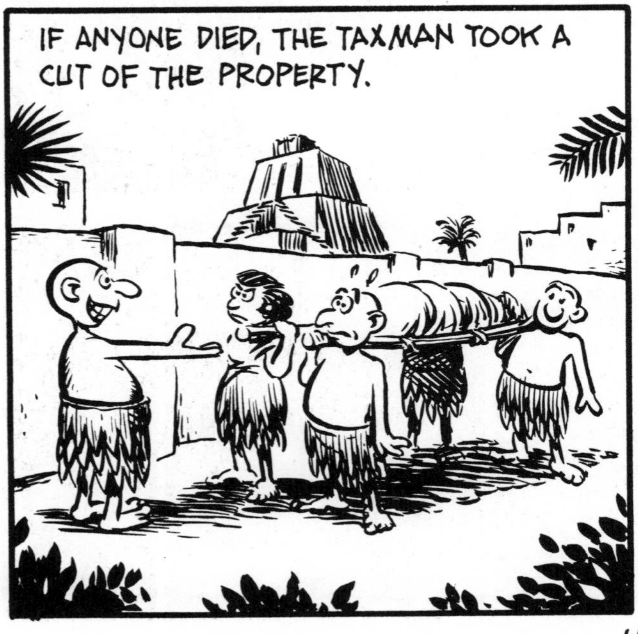
IF ANYONE DIED, THE TAXMAN TOOK A CUT OF THE PROPERTY.

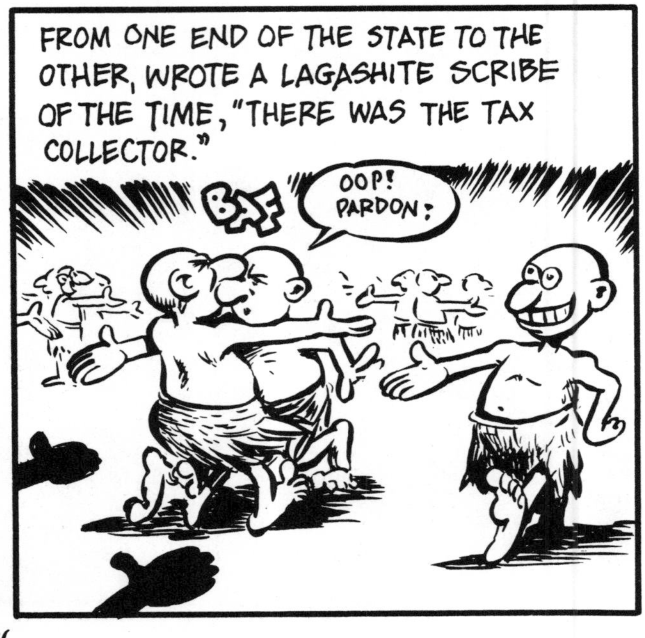
FROM ONE END OF THE STATE TO THE OTHER, WROTE A LAGASHITE SCRIBE OF THE TIME, "THERE WAS THE TAX COLLECTOR."
BAF
OOP! PARDON!

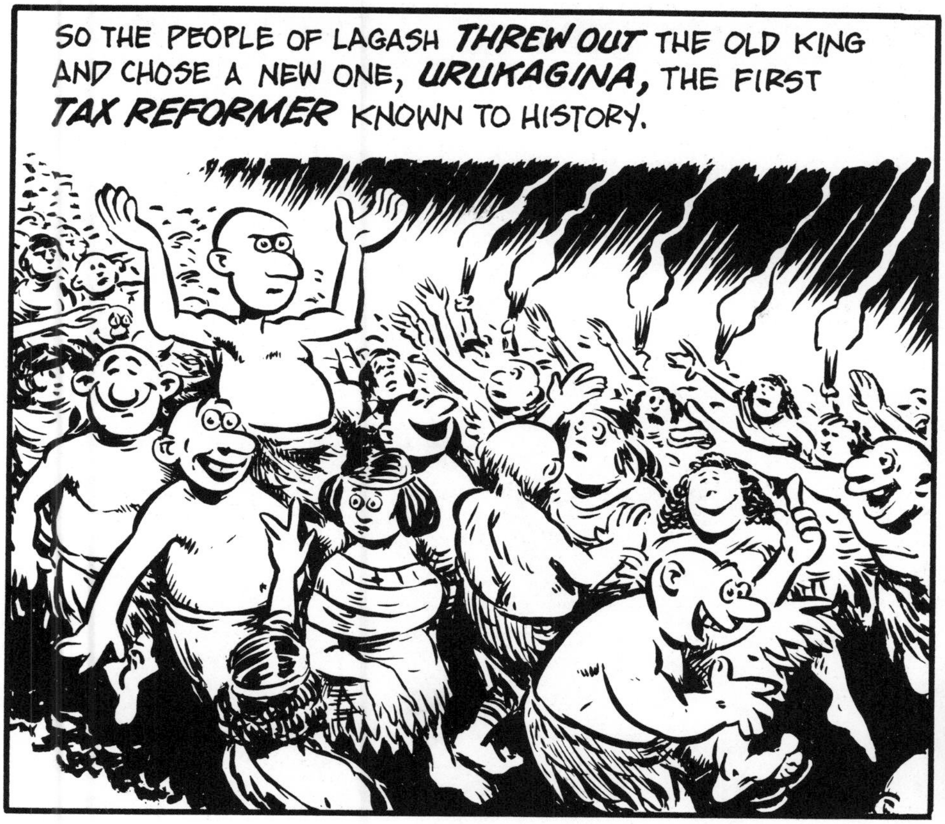
SO THE PEOPLE OF LAGASH **THREW OUT** THE OLD KING AND CHOSE A NEW ONE, **URUKAGINA,** THE FIRST **TAX REFORMER** KNOWN TO HISTORY.

URUKAGINA CUT TAXES AND FIRED THE COLLECTORS, RESTORED TEMPLE PROPERTY, AND PASSED MANY LAWS PROTECTING WIDOWS, ORPHANS AND THE POOR FROM THEIR GREEDY AND MORE POWERFUL NEIGHBORS. ✻ THE TAX CUTS, HOWEVER, CREATED A **NEW** PROBLEM:

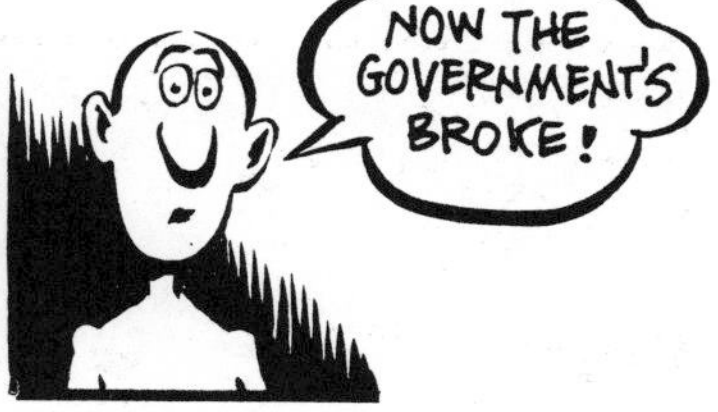
NOW THE GOVERNMENT'S BROKE!

WHEN LAGASH WAS INEVITABLY ATTACKED AGAIN BY THE UMMAITES, URUKAGINA WAS TOO PEACEABLE OR TOO POOR TO RESIST THEM. AFTER JUST 8 YEARS, THE REFORMER WENT DOWN CURSING:

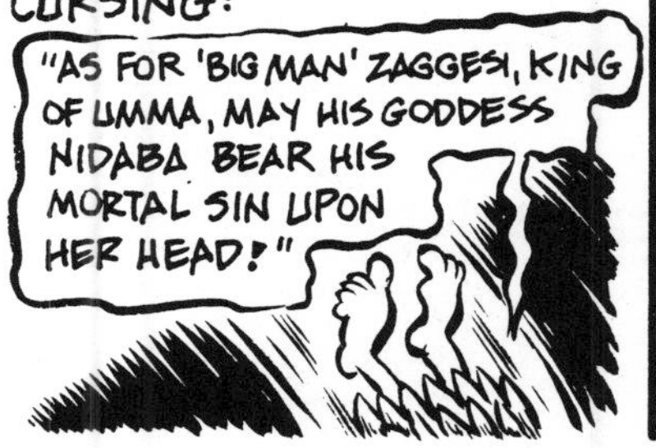
"AS FOR 'BIG MAN' ZAGGESI, KING OF UMMA, MAY HIS GODDESS NIDABA BEAR HIS MORTAL SIN UPON HER HEAD!"

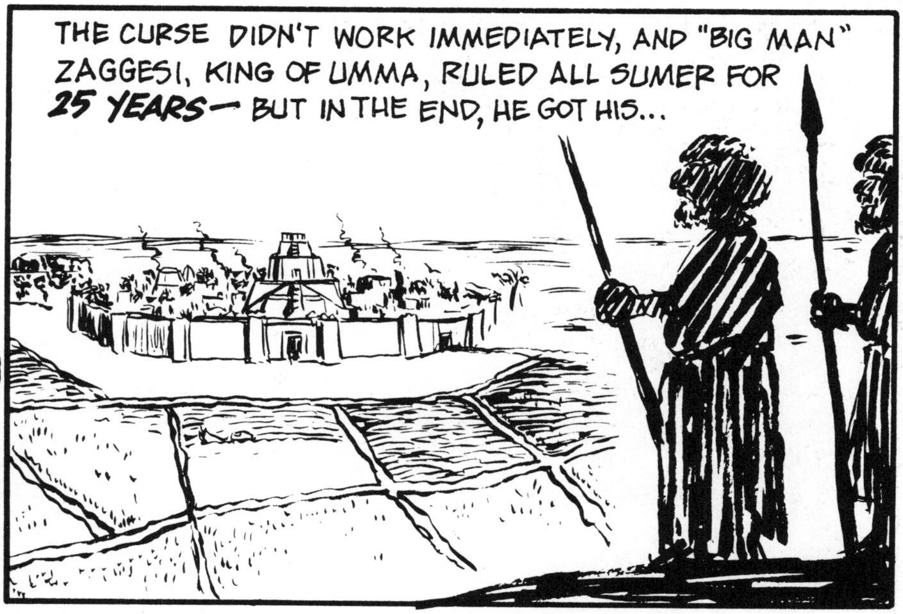
THE CURSE DIDN'T WORK IMMEDIATELY, AND "BIG MAN" ZAGGESI, KING OF UMMA, RULED ALL SUMER FOR **25 YEARS**— BUT IN THE END, HE GOT HIS...

✻ IN EARLY SUMERIAN TIMES, A WOMAN OF WEALTH SOMETIMES TOOK MORE THAN ONE **HUSBAND.** WE KNOW THIS BECAUSE, AROUND 2400 B.C., THE REFORMER URUKAGINA **BANNED** THE PRACTICE IN NO UNCERTAIN TERMS:

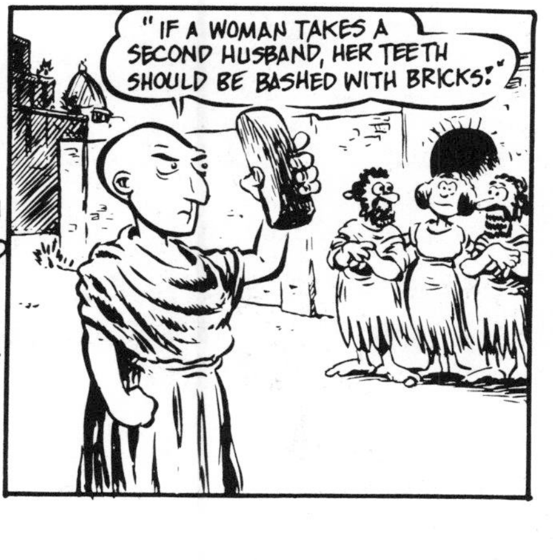
"IF A WOMAN TAKES A SECOND HUSBAND, HER TEETH SHOULD BE BASHED WITH BRICKS!"

AS MEN GAINED MORE AND MORE OF THE WEALTH AND POWER, WOMEN'S STATUS DECLINED EVEN FURTHER, UNTIL THE SAYING HAD BECOME: "IF A WIFE **CONTRADICTS** HER HUSBAND, HER TEETH SHOULD BE BASHED WITH BRICKS."

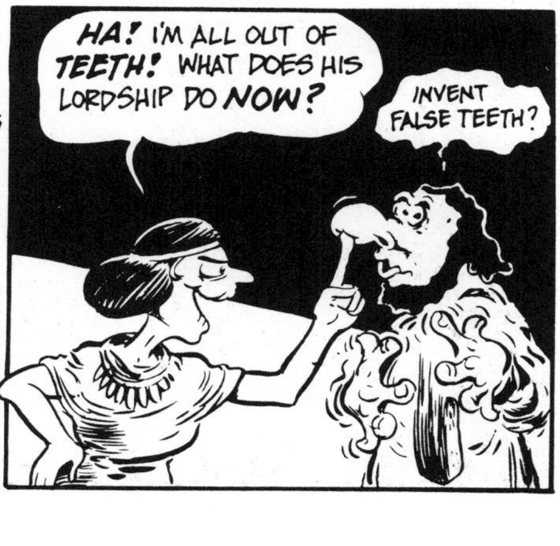
HA! I'M ALL OUT OF **TEETH!** WHAT DOES HIS LORDSHIP DO **NOW?**
INVENT FALSE TEETH?

THE SWORD OF SARGON

NORTH AND WEST OF SUMER, IN AN ARC EXTENDING FROM THE CITY OF ***KISH,*** THROUGH THE NORTHERN TIGRIS-EUPHRATES PLAIN TO THE COAST OF ***CANAAN,*** LIVED THE ***SEMITES,*** A GROUP OF PEOPLES WHO SPOKE LANGUAGES RELATED TO MODERN ARABIC AND HEBREW. FROM THE EARLIEST DAYS, SEMITES HAD ALSO SETTLED IN SUMER AND MINGLED FREELY WITH THE SUMERIANS.

Canaan
SEMITES
Agade
Kish
Ur
Arabia
Egypt

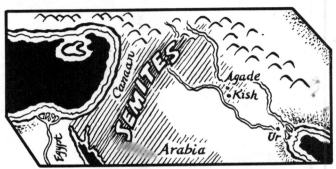

AROUND 2370 B.C., A YOUNG SEMITIC OFFICER, ***SARGON OF AGADE,*** LED A REVOLT WHICH TOPPLED THE KING OF KISH.

NEXT HE LED HIS FOLLOWERS NORTH, CONQUERING CITIES AND BUILDING HIS ARMY, BEFORE FINALLY TURNING SOUTH AGAINST SUMER. IN A DECISIVE BATTLE, SARGON'S FORCES DEFEATED THE COMBINED SUMERIAN ARMIES, LED BY—NONE OTHER THAN ***"BIG MAN" ZAGGESI.*** ZAGGESI WAS MARCHED TO KISH IN A DOG COLLAR, WHILE SARGON WASHED HIS SWORD IN THE SOUTHERN SEA.

TH' CURSE CAME TRUE!
SILENCE, DOG!

SARGON'S ***54-YEAR*** REIGN MARKED THE FIRST TIME IN SEVEN CENTURIES THAT A NON-SUMERIAN HAD RULED SUMER.

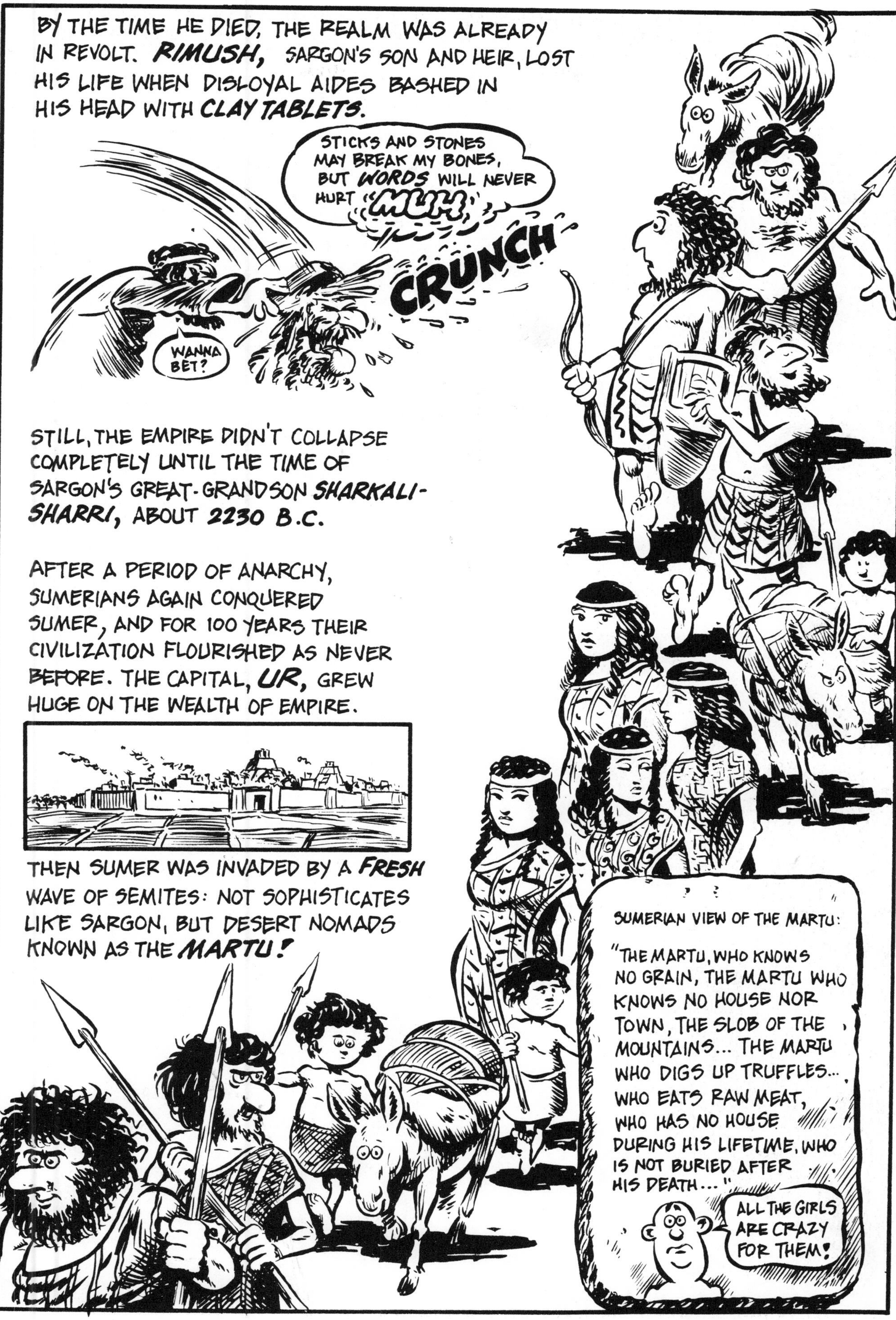
BY THE TIME HE DIED, THE REALM WAS ALREADY IN REVOLT. RIMUSH, SARGON'S SON AND HEIR, LOST HIS LIFE WHEN DISLOYAL AIDES BASHED IN HIS HEAD WITH CLAY TABLETS.
STICKS AND STONES MAY BREAK MY BONES, BUT WORDS WILL NEVER HURT "MUH
CRUNCH
WANNA BET?
STILL, THE EMPIRE DIDN'T COLLAPSE COMPLETELY UNTIL THE TIME OF SARGON'S GREAT-GRANDSON SHARKALI-SHARRI, ABOUT 2230 B.C.
AFTER A PERIOD OF ANARCHY, SUMERIANS AGAIN CONQUERED SUMER, AND FOR 100 YEARS THEIR CIVILIZATION FLOURISHED AS NEVER BEFORE. THE CAPITAL, UR, GREW HUGE ON THE WEALTH OF EMPIRE.
THEN SUMER WAS INVADED BY A FRESH WAVE OF SEMITES: NOT SOPHISTICATES LIKE SARGON, BUT DESERT NOMADS KNOWN AS THE MARTU!
SUMERIAN VIEW OF THE MARTU:
"THE MARTU, WHO KNOWS NO GRAIN, THE MARTU WHO KNOWS NO HOUSE NOR TOWN, THE SLOB OF THE MOUNTAINS... THE MARTU WHO DIGS UP TRUFFLES... WHO EATS RAW MEAT, WHO HAS NO HOUSE DURING HIS LIFETIME, WHO IS NOT BURIED AFTER HIS DEATH..."
ALL THE GIRLS ARE CRAZY FOR THEM!

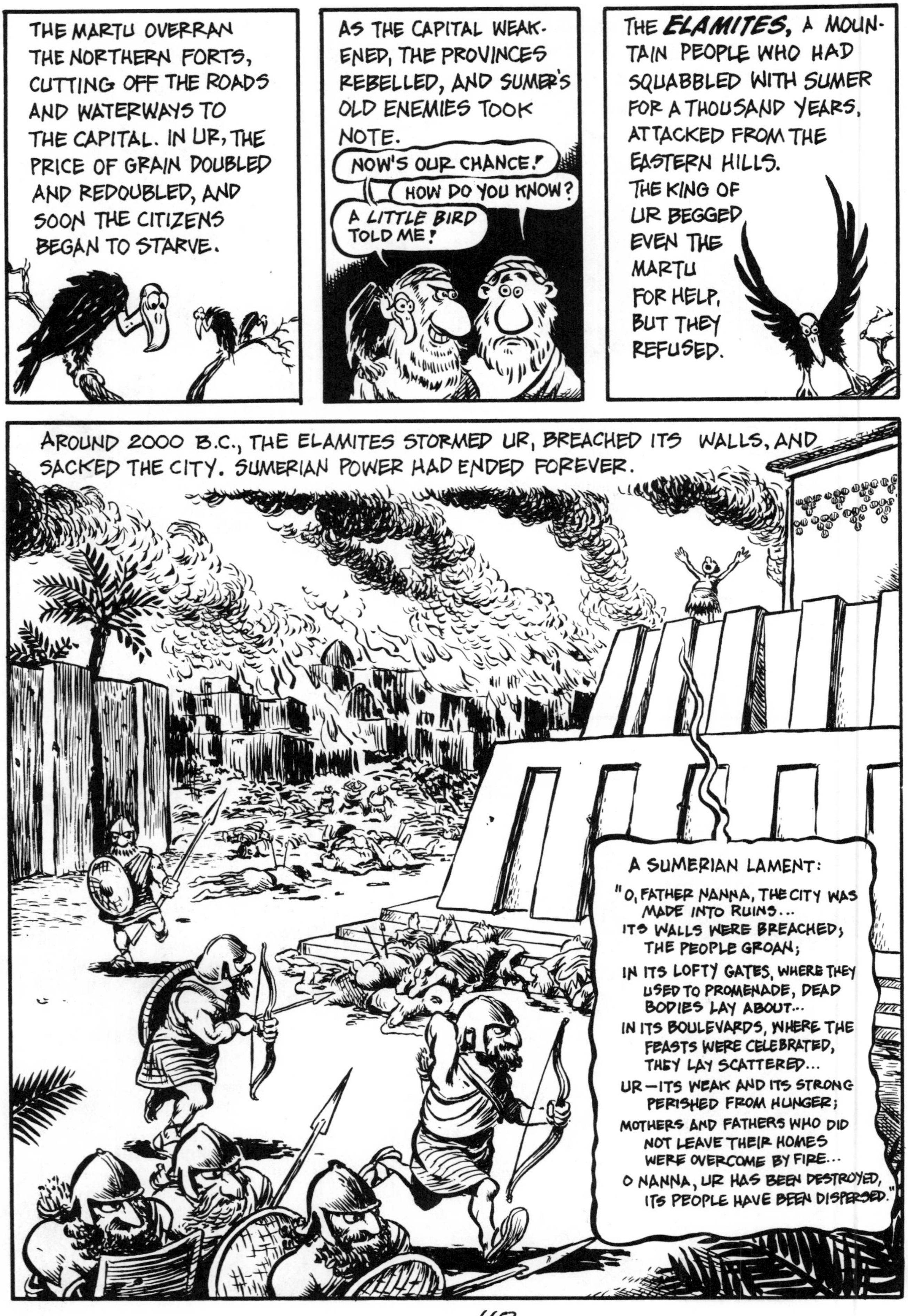
THE MARTU OVERRAN THE NORTHERN FORTS, CUTTING OFF THE ROADS AND WATERWAYS TO THE CAPITAL. IN UR, THE PRICE OF GRAIN DOUBLED AND REDOUBLED, AND SOON THE CITIZENS BEGAN TO STARVE.
AS THE CAPITAL WEAK-ENED, THE PROVINCES REBELLED, AND SUMER'S OLD ENEMIES TOOK NOTE.
NOW'S OUR CHANCE!
HOW DO YOU KNOW?
A LITTLE BIRD TOLD ME!
THE ELAMITES, A MOUN-TAIN PEOPLE WHO HAD SQUABBLED WITH SUMER FOR A THOUSAND YEARS, ATTACKED FROM THE EASTERN HILLS.
THE KING OF UR BEGGED EVEN THE MARTU FOR HELP, BUT THEY REFUSED.
AROUND 2000 B.C., THE ELAMITES STORMED UR, BREACHED ITS WALLS, AND SACKED THE CITY. SUMERIAN POWER HAD ENDED FOREVER.
A SUMERIAN LAMENT:
"O, FATHER NANNA, THE CITY WAS MADE INTO RUINS...
ITS WALLS WERE BREACHED; THE PEOPLE GROAN;
IN ITS LOFTY GATES, WHERE THEY USED TO PROMENADE, DEAD BODIES LAY ABOUT...
IN ITS BOULEVARDS, WHERE THE FEASTS WERE CELEBRATED, THEY LAY SCATTERED...
UR—ITS WEAK AND ITS STRONG PERISHED FROM HUNGER;
MOTHERS AND FATHERS WHO DID NOT LEAVE THEIR HOMES WERE OVERCOME BY FIRE...
O NANNA, UR HAS BEEN DESTROYED, ITS PEOPLE HAVE BEEN DISPERSED."

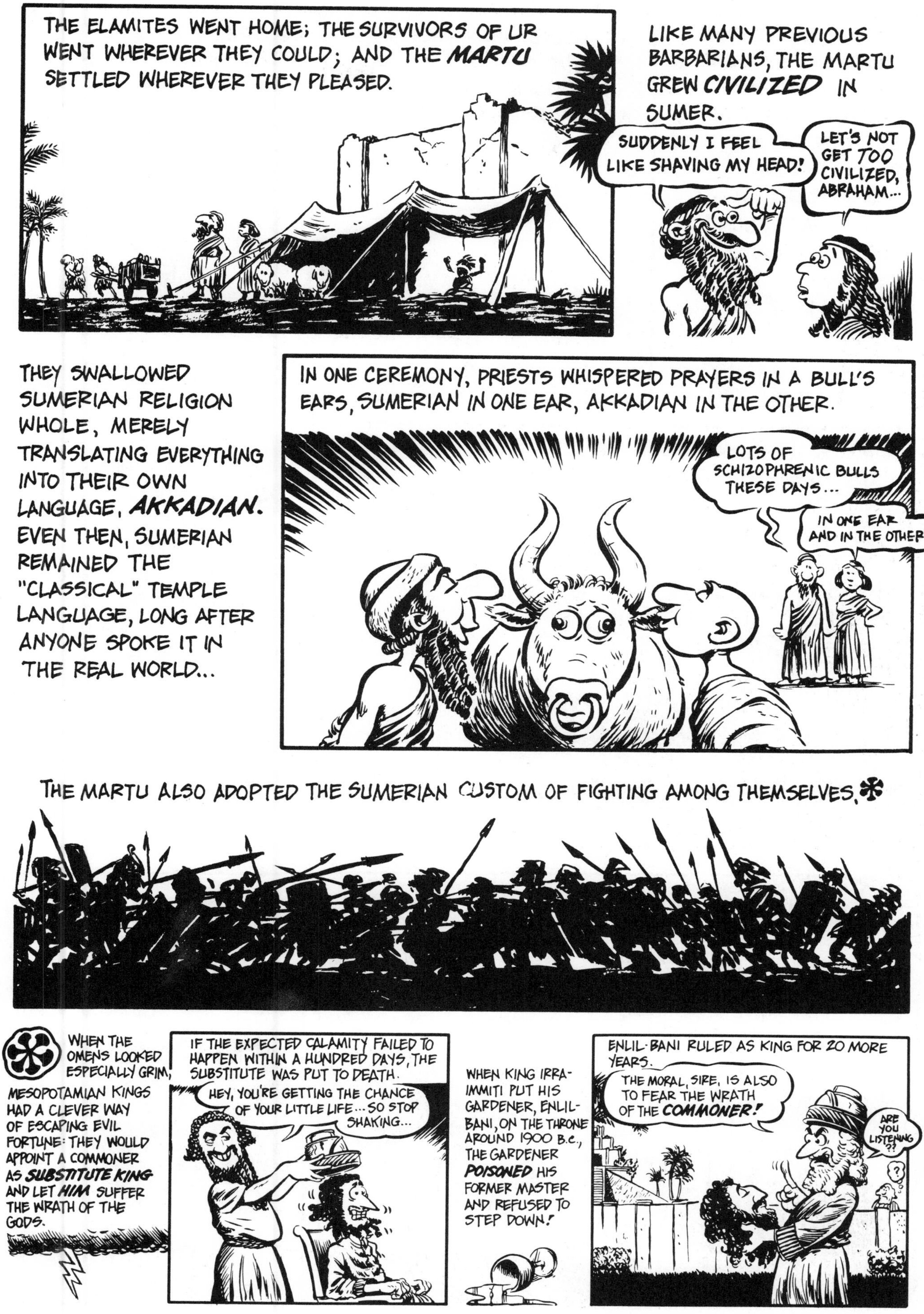
THE ELAMITES WENT HOME; THE SURVIVORS OF UR WENT WHEREVER THEY COULD; AND THE MARTU SETTLED WHEREVER THEY PLEASED.
LIKE MANY PREVIOUS BARBARIANS, THE MARTU GREW CIVILIZED IN SUMER.
SUDDENLY I FEEL LIKE SHAVING MY HEAD!
LET'S NOT GET TOO CIVILIZED, ABRAHAM...
THEY SWALLOWED SUMERIAN RELIGION WHOLE, MERELY TRANSLATING EVERYTHING INTO THEIR OWN LANGUAGE, AKKADIAN. EVEN THEN, SUMERIAN REMAINED THE "CLASSICAL" TEMPLE LANGUAGE, LONG AFTER ANYONE SPOKE IT IN THE REAL WORLD...
IN ONE CEREMONY, PRIESTS WHISPERED PRAYERS IN A BULL'S EARS, SUMERIAN IN ONE EAR, AKKADIAN IN THE OTHER.
LOTS OF SCHIZOPHRENIC BULLS THESE DAYS...
IN ONE EAR AND IN THE OTHER!
THE MARTU ALSO ADOPTED THE SUMERIAN CUSTOM OF FIGHTING AMONG THEMSELVES.✱
✱ WHEN THE OMENS LOOKED ESPECIALLY GRIM, MESOPOTAMIAN KINGS HAD A CLEVER WAY OF ESCAPING EVIL FORTUNE: THEY WOULD APPOINT A COMMONER AS SUBSTITUTE KING AND LET HIM SUFFER THE WRATH OF THE GODS.
IF THE EXPECTED CALAMITY FAILED TO HAPPEN WITHIN A HUNDRED DAYS, THE SUBSTITUTE WAS PUT TO DEATH.
HEY, YOU'RE GETTING THE CHANCE OF YOUR LITTLE LIFE... SO STOP SHAKING...
WHEN KING IRRA-IMMITI PUT HIS GARDENER, ENLIL-BANI, ON THE THRONE AROUND 1900 B.C., THE GARDENER POISONED HIS FORMER MASTER AND REFUSED TO STEP DOWN!
ENLIL-BANI RULED AS KING FOR 20 MORE YEARS.
THE MORAL, SIRE, IS ALSO TO FEAR THE WRATH OF THE COMMONER!
ARE YOU LISTENING??
?

AS USUAL, THE FEUDING WAS STOPPED BY A NEW ***EMPIRE-BUILDER,*** THE GREAT GENERAL AND STATESMAN ***HAMMURABI*** OF ***BABYLON,*** WHOSE REIGN BEGAN AROUND 1790 B.C.

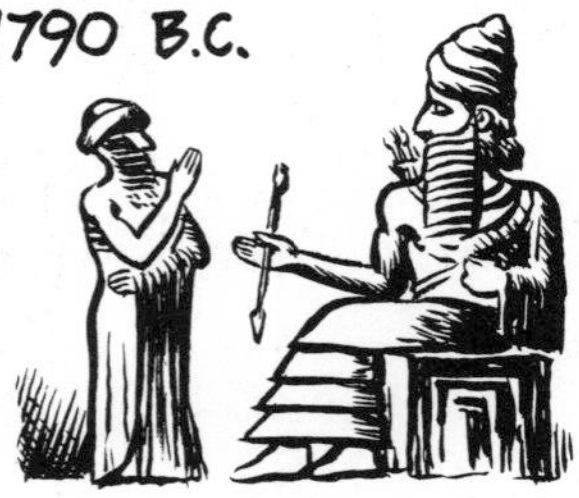

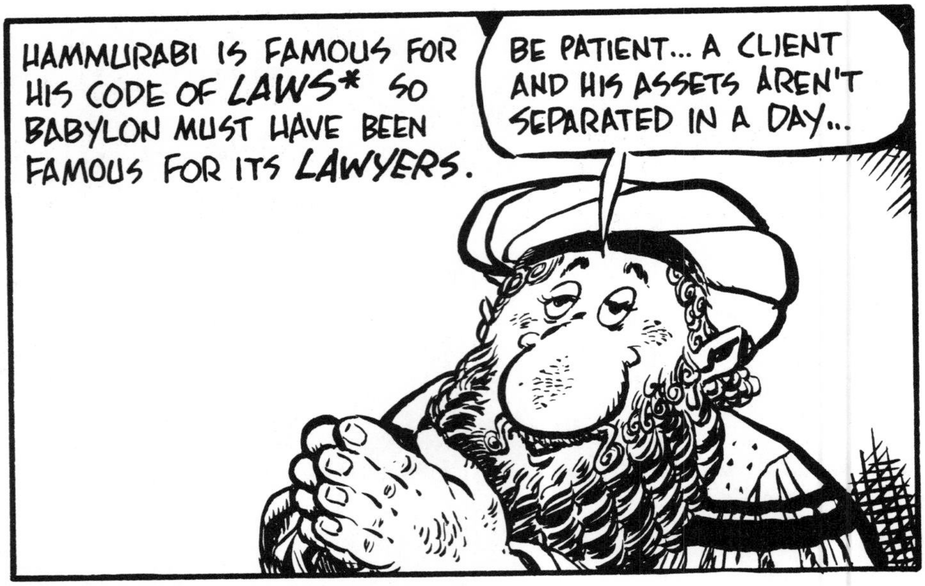
HAMMURABI IS FAMOUS FOR HIS CODE OF LAWS* SO BABYLON MUST HAVE BEEN FAMOUS FOR ITS LAWYERS.
BE PATIENT... A CLIENT AND HIS ASSETS AREN'T SEPARATED IN A DAY...

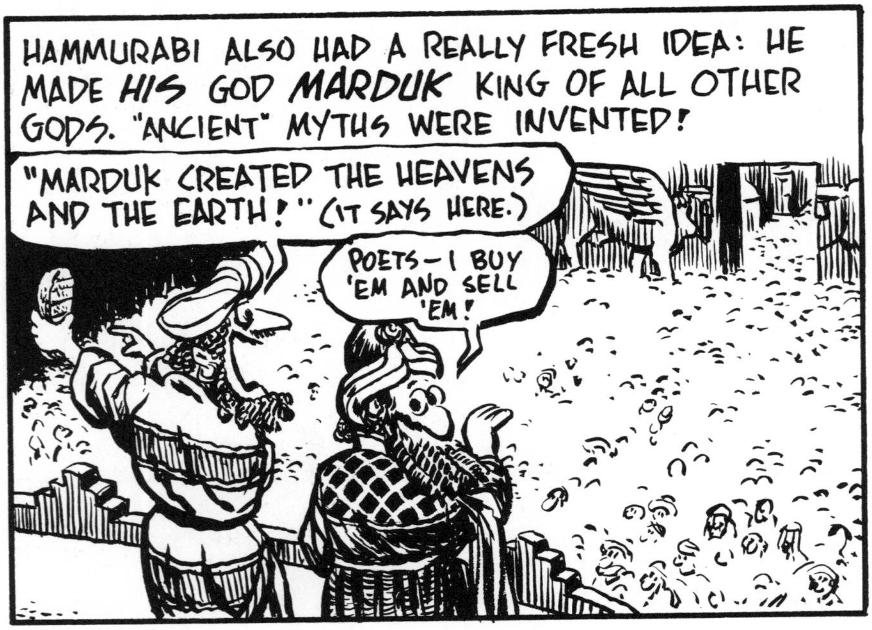
HAMMURABI ALSO HAD A REALLY FRESH IDEA: HE MADE HIS GOD MARDUK KING OF ALL OTHER GODS. "ANCIENT" MYTHS WERE INVENTED!
"MARDUK CREATED THE HEAVENS AND THE EARTH!" (IT SAYS HERE.)
POETS— I BUY 'EM AND SELL 'EM!

HAMMURABI BUILT HIS CAPITAL INTO THE GREATEST CITY BETWEEN EGYPT AND INDIA, A CENTER OF ART, SCIENCE, AND COMMERCE. FOR THE NEXT THOUSAND YEARS, THE LAND BETWEEN THE RIVERS WAS KNOWN AS ***BABYLONIA,*** A LAND WE MUST NOW PREPARE TO LEAVE FOR A TIME...

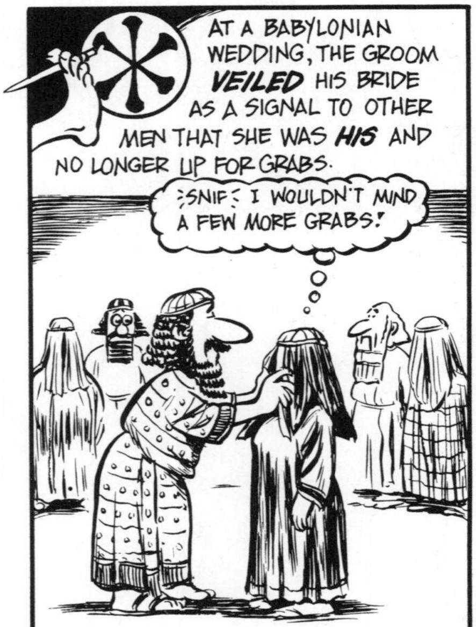
AT A BABYLONIAN WEDDING, THE GROOM VEILED HIS BRIDE AS A SIGNAL TO OTHER MEN THAT SHE WAS HIS AND NO LONGER UP FOR GRABS.
SNIF I WOULDN'T MIND A FEW MORE GRABS!

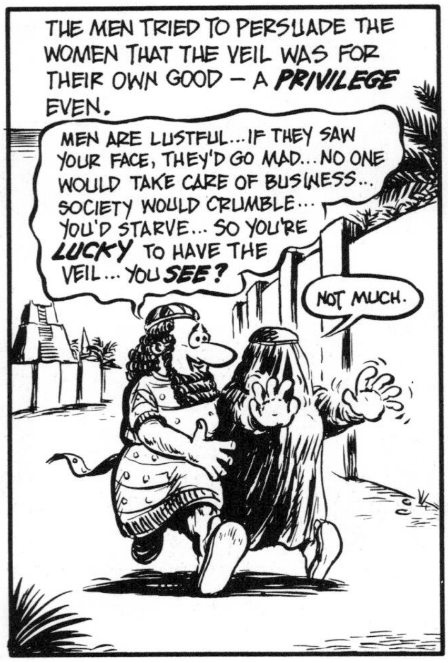
THE MEN TRIED TO PERSUADE THE WOMEN THAT THE VEIL WAS FOR THEIR OWN GOOD — A PRIVILEGE EVEN.
MEN ARE LUSTFUL... IF THEY SAW YOUR FACE, THEY'D GO MAD... NO ONE WOULD TAKE CARE OF BUSINESS... SOCIETY WOULD CRUMBLE... YOU'D STARVE... SO YOU'RE LUCKY TO HAVE THE VEIL... YOU SEE?
NOT MUCH.

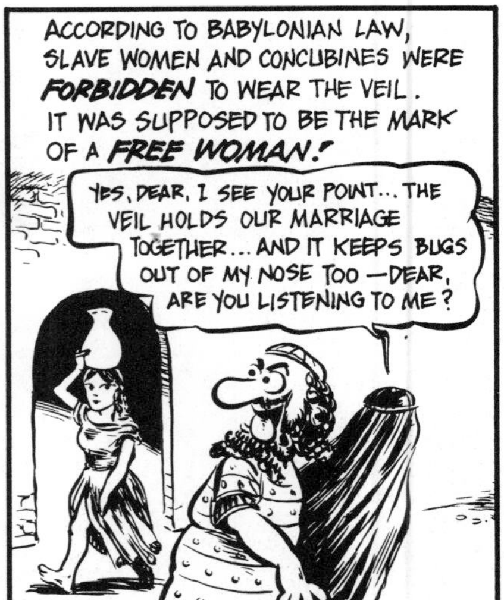
ACCORDING TO BABYLONIAN LAW, SLAVE WOMEN AND CONCUBINES WERE FORBIDDEN TO WEAR THE VEIL. IT WAS SUPPOSED TO BE THE MARK OF A FREE WOMAN!
YES, DEAR, I SEE YOUR POINT... THE VEIL HOLDS OUR MARRIAGE TOGETHER... AND IT KEEPS BUGS OUT OF MY NOSE TOO —DEAR, ARE YOU LISTENING TO ME?

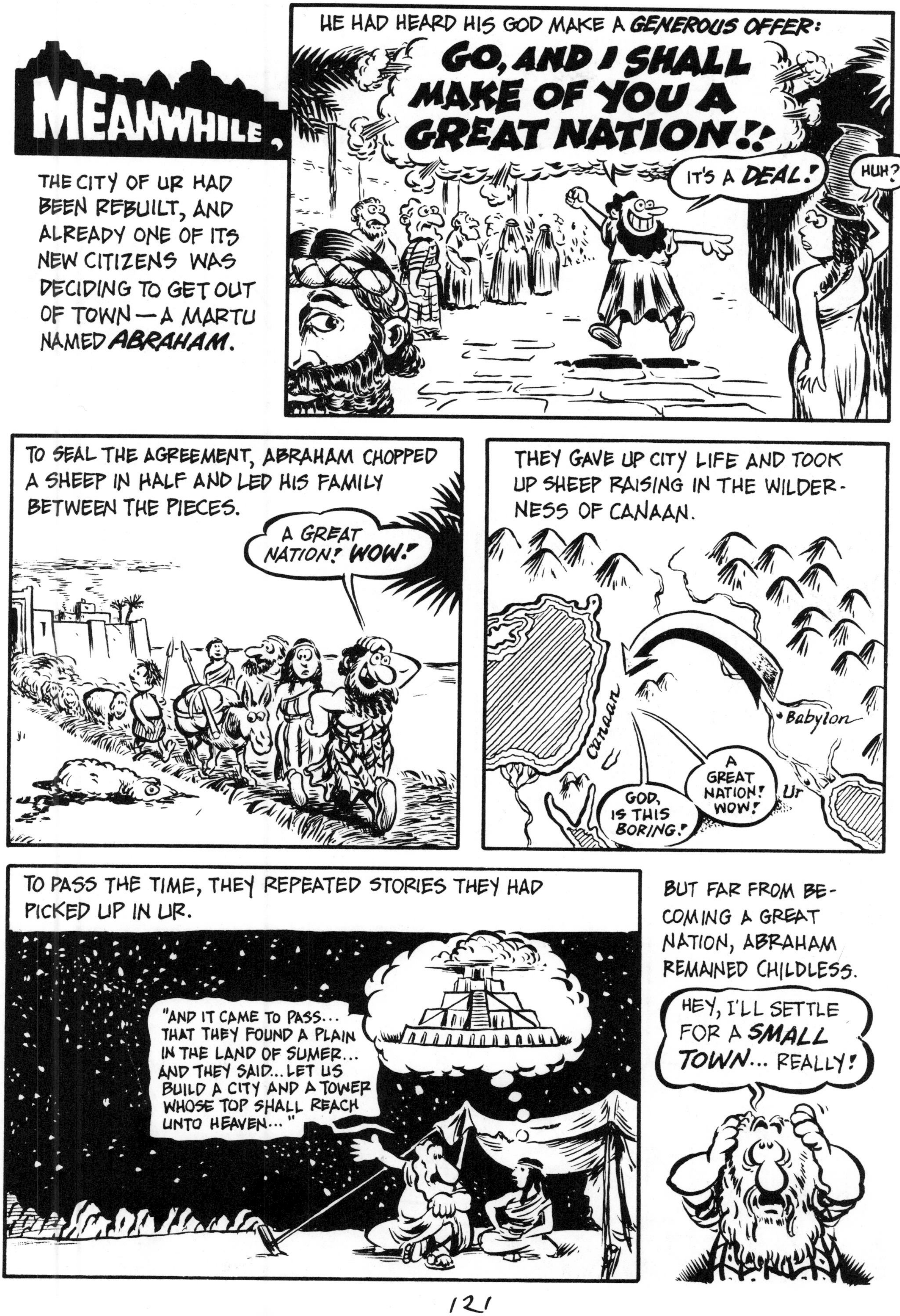
MEANWHILE,
THE CITY OF UR HAD BEEN REBUILT, AND ALREADY ONE OF ITS NEW CITIZENS WAS DECIDING TO GET OUT OF TOWN — A MARTU NAMED ABRAHAM.
HE HAD HEARD HIS GOD MAKE A GENEROUS OFFER:
GO, AND I SHALL MAKE OF YOU A GREAT NATION!!
IT'S A DEAL!
HUH?
TO SEAL THE AGREEMENT, ABRAHAM CHOPPED A SHEEP IN HALF AND LED HIS FAMILY BETWEEN THE PIECES.
A GREAT NATION! WOW!
THEY GAVE UP CITY LIFE AND TOOK UP SHEEP RAISING IN THE WILDERNESS OF CANAAN.
Canaan
Babylon
Ur
GOD, IS THIS BORING!
A GREAT NATION! WOW!
TO PASS THE TIME, THEY REPEATED STORIES THEY HAD PICKED UP IN UR.
"AND IT CAME TO PASS... THAT THEY FOUND A PLAIN IN THE LAND OF SUMER... AND THEY SAID... LET US BUILD A CITY AND A TOWER WHOSE TOP SHALL REACH UNTO HEAVEN..."
BUT FAR FROM BECOMING A GREAT NATION, ABRAHAM REMAINED CHILDLESS.
HEY, I'LL SETTLE FOR A SMALL TOWN... REALLY!

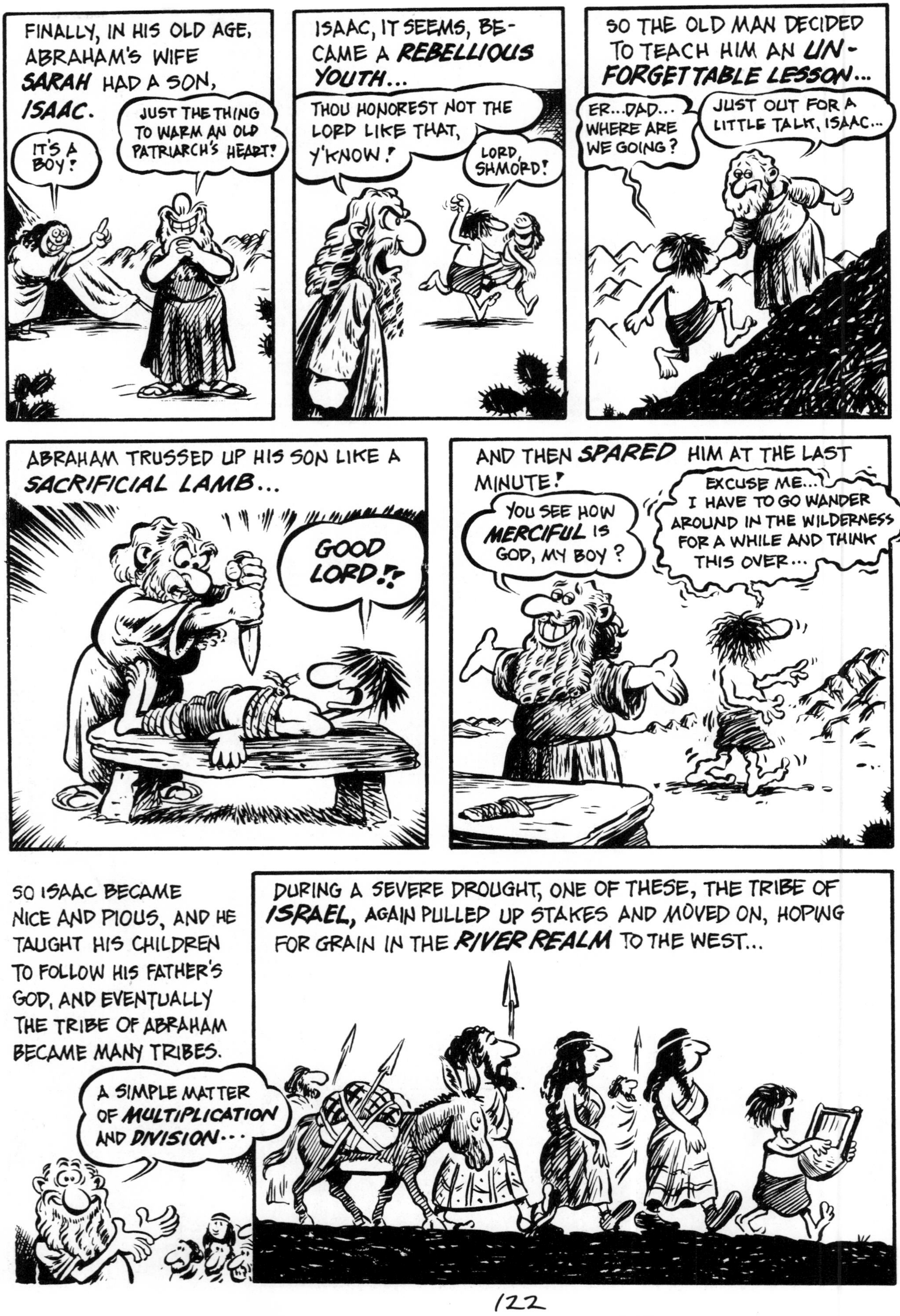
FINALLY, IN HIS OLD AGE, ABRAHAM'S WIFE SARAH HAD A SON, ISAAC.
IT'S A BOY!
JUST THE THING TO WARM AN OLD PATRIARCH'S HEART!
ISAAC, IT SEEMS, BECAME A REBELLIOUS YOUTH...
THOU HONOREST NOT THE LORD LIKE THAT, Y'KNOW!
LORD, SHMORD!
SO THE OLD MAN DECIDED TO TEACH HIM AN UNFORGETTABLE LESSON...
ER...DAD... WHERE ARE WE GOING?
JUST OUT FOR A LITTLE TALK, ISAAC...
ABRAHAM TRUSSED UP HIS SON LIKE A SACRIFICIAL LAMB...
GOOD LORD!?!
AND THEN SPARED HIM AT THE LAST MINUTE!
YOU SEE HOW MERCIFUL IS GOD, MY BOY?
EXCUSE ME... I HAVE TO GO WANDER AROUND IN THE WILDERNESS FOR A WHILE AND THINK THIS OVER...
SO ISAAC BECAME NICE AND PIOUS, AND HE TAUGHT HIS CHILDREN TO FOLLOW HIS FATHER'S GOD, AND EVENTUALLY THE TRIBE OF ABRAHAM BECAME MANY TRIBES.
A SIMPLE MATTER OF MULTIPLICATION AND DIVISION...
DURING A SEVERE DROUGHT, ONE OF THESE, THE TRIBE OF ISRAEL, AGAIN PULLED UP STAKES AND MOVED ON, HOPING FOR GRAIN IN THE RIVER REALM TO THE WEST...

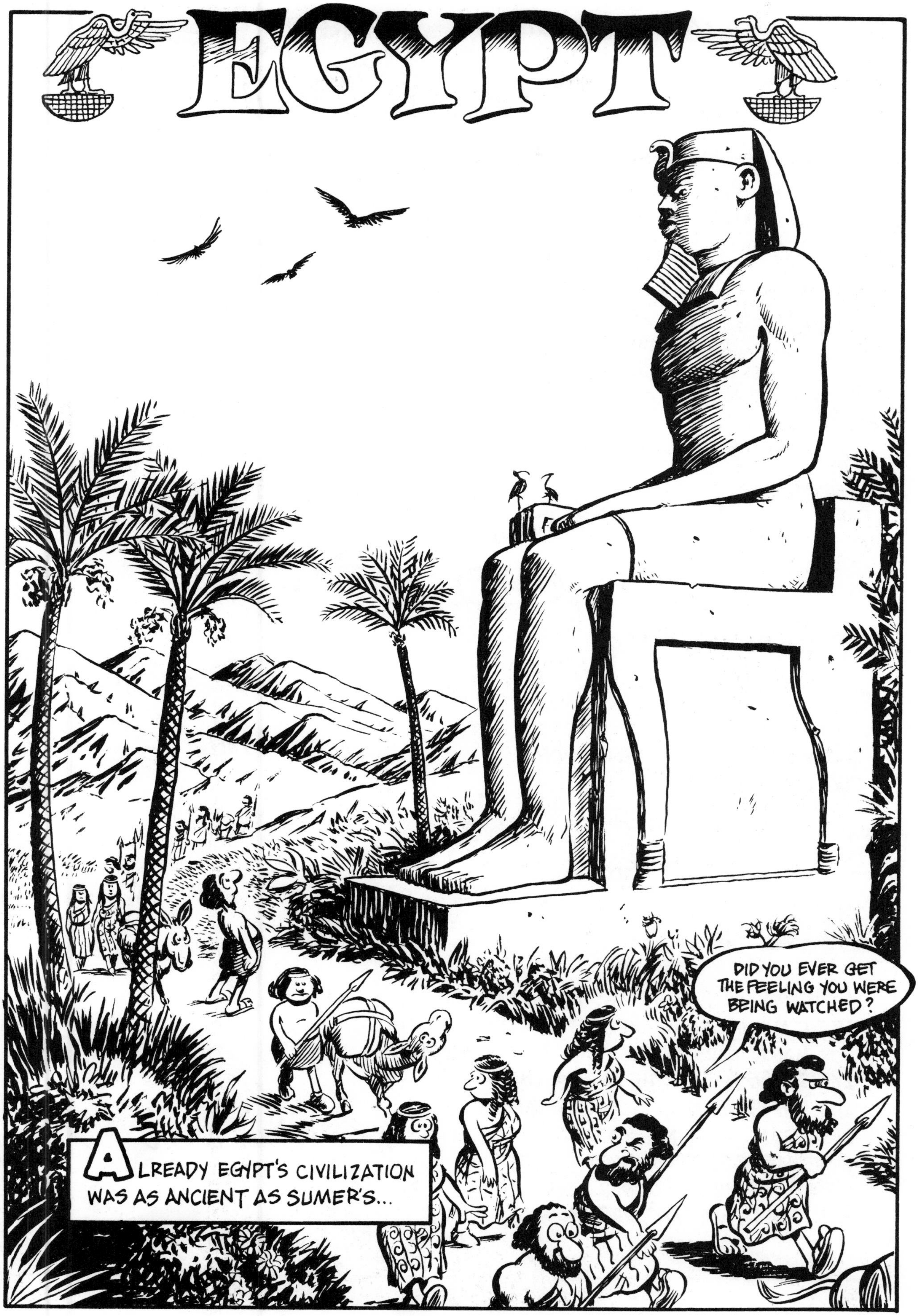

EGYPT
DID YOU EVER GET THE FEELING YOU WERE BEING WATCHED?
ALREADY EGYPT'S CIVILIZATION WAS AS ANCIENT AS SUMER'S...

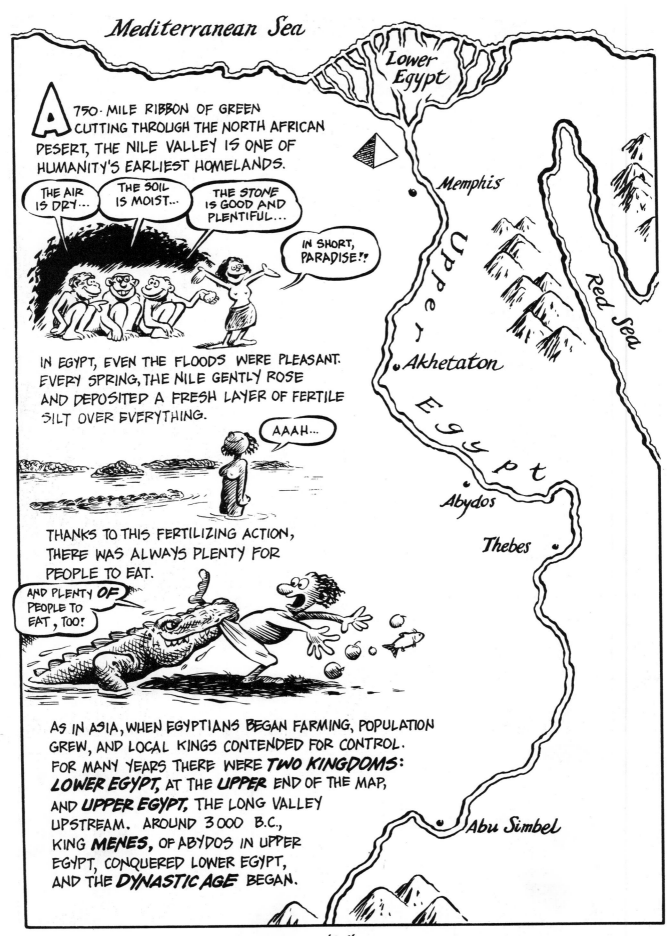

Mediterranean Sea

Lower Egypt

Memphis

Upper Egypt

Akhetaton

Red Sea

Abydos

Thebes

Abu Simbel

A 750-MILE RIBBON OF GREEN CUTTING THROUGH THE NORTH AFRICAN DESERT, THE NILE VALLEY IS ONE OF HUMANITY'S EARLIEST HOMELANDS.

THE AIR IS DRY...

THE SOIL IS MOIST...

THE STONE IS GOOD AND PLENTIFUL...

IN SHORT, PARADISE!?

IN EGYPT, EVEN THE FLOODS WERE PLEASANT. EVERY SPRING, THE NILE GENTLY ROSE AND DEPOSITED A FRESH LAYER OF FERTILE SILT OVER EVERYTHING.

AAAH...

THANKS TO THIS FERTILIZING ACTION, THERE WAS ALWAYS PLENTY FOR PEOPLE TO EAT.

AND PLENTY OF PEOPLE TO EAT, TOO!

AS IN ASIA, WHEN EGYPTIANS BEGAN FARMING, POPULATION GREW, AND LOCAL KINGS CONTENDED FOR CONTROL. FOR MANY YEARS THERE WERE TWO KINGDOMS: LOWER EGYPT, AT THE UPPER END OF THE MAP, AND UPPER EGYPT, THE LONG VALLEY UPSTREAM. AROUND 3000 B.C., KING MENES, OF ABYDOS IN UPPER EGYPT, CONQUERED LOWER EGYPT, AND THE DYNASTIC AGE BEGAN.

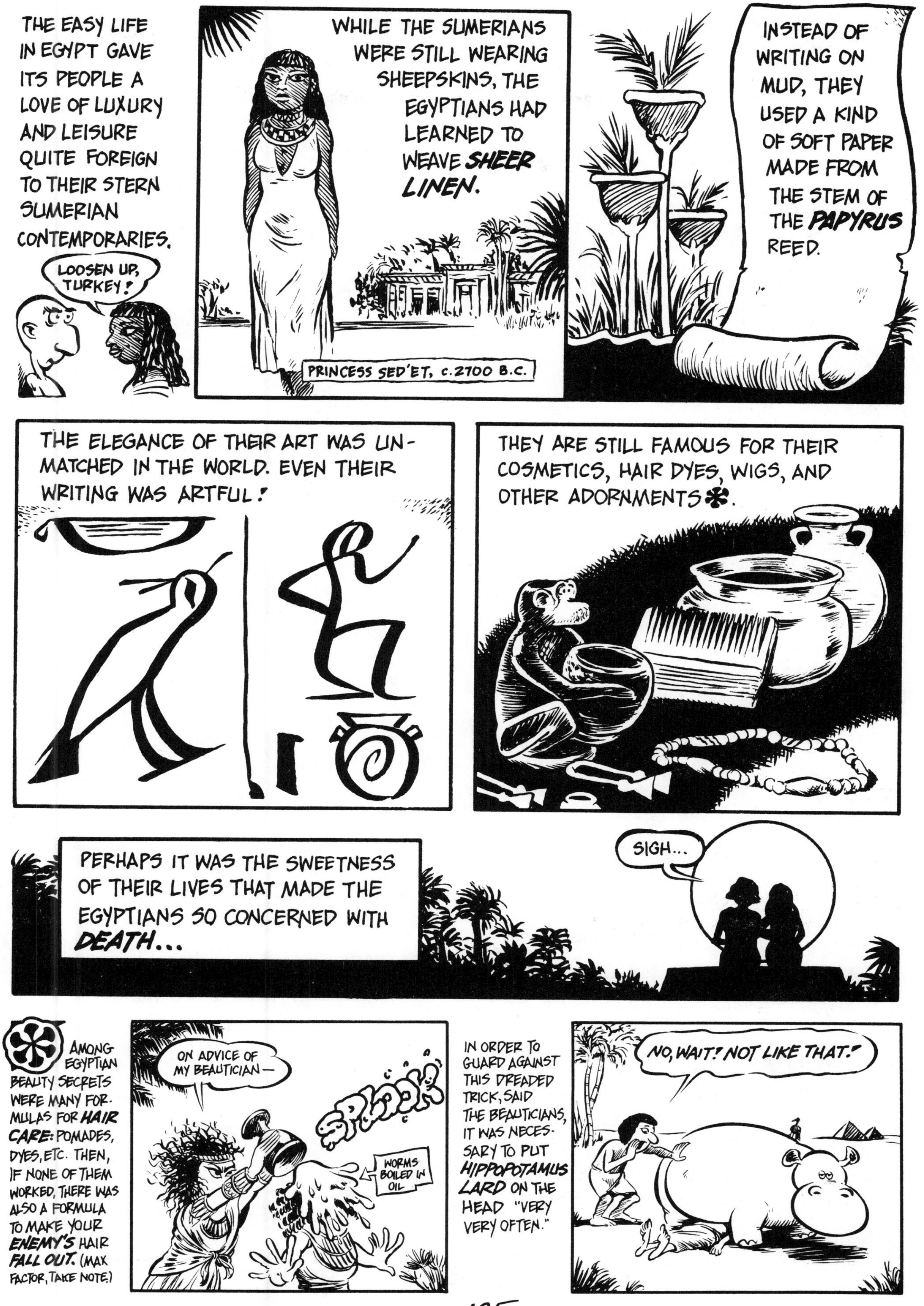
THE EASY LIFE IN EGYPT GAVE ITS PEOPLE A LOVE OF LUXURY AND LEISURE QUITE FOREIGN TO THEIR STERN SUMERIAN CONTEMPORARIES.
LOOSEN UP, TURKEY!
WHILE THE SUMERIANS WERE STILL WEARING SHEEPSKINS, THE EGYPTIANS HAD LEARNED TO WEAVE SHEER LINEN.
PRINCESS SED'ET, C.2700 B.C.
INSTEAD OF WRITING ON MUD, THEY USED A KIND OF SOFT PAPER MADE FROM THE STEM OF THE PAPYRUS REED.
THE ELEGANCE OF THEIR ART WAS UN-MATCHED IN THE WORLD. EVEN THEIR WRITING WAS ARTFUL!
THEY ARE STILL FAMOUS FOR THEIR COSMETICS, HAIR DYES, WIGS, AND OTHER ADORNMENTS*.
PERHAPS IT WAS THE SWEETNESS OF THEIR LIVES THAT MADE THE EGYPTIANS SO CONCERNED WITH DEATH...
SIGH...
* AMONG EGYPTIAN BEAUTY SECRETS WERE MANY FOR-MULAS FOR HAIR CARE: POMADES, DYES, ETC. THEN, IF NONE OF THEM WORKED, THERE WAS ALSO A FORMULA TO MAKE YOUR ENEMY'S HAIR FALL OUT. (MAX FACTOR, TAKE NOTE.)
ON ADVICE OF MY BEAUTICIAN—
SPLOOSH
WORMS BOILED IN OIL
IN ORDER TO GUARD AGAINST THIS DREADED TRICK, SAID THE BEAUTICIANS, IT WAS NECES-SARY TO PUT HIPPOPOTAMUS LARD ON THE HEAD "VERY VERY OFTEN."
NO, WAIT! NOT LIKE THAT!

PILE ON THE NILE

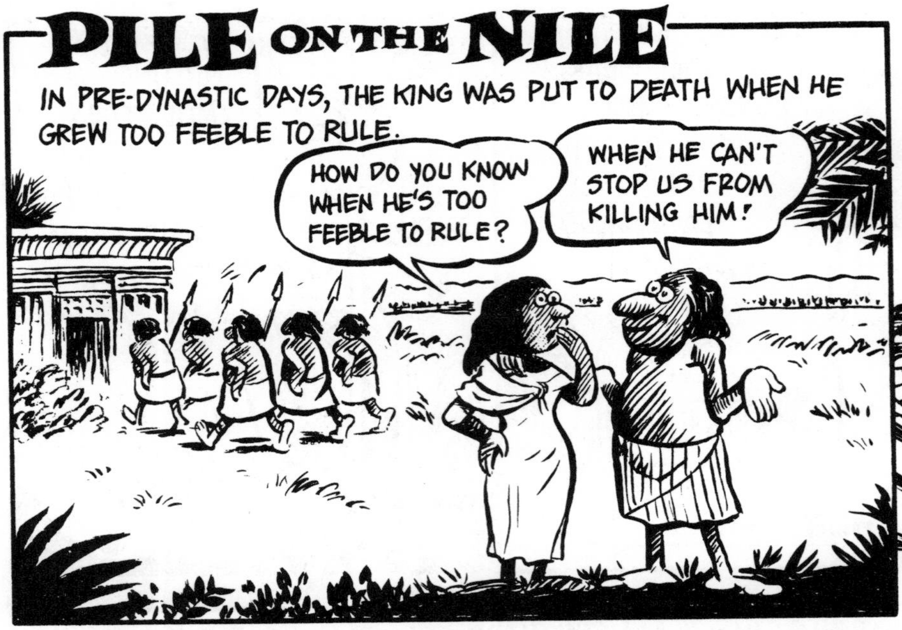
IN PRE-DYNASTIC DAYS, THE KING WAS PUT TO DEATH WHEN HE GREW TOO FEEBLE TO RULE.
HOW DO YOU KNOW WHEN HE'S TOO FEEBLE TO RULE?
WHEN HE CAN'T STOP US FROM KILLING HIM!

THE PRIESTS COMFORTED THE MONARCH WITH THE THOUGHT THAT HE WOULD ***LIVE AFTER DEATH.***

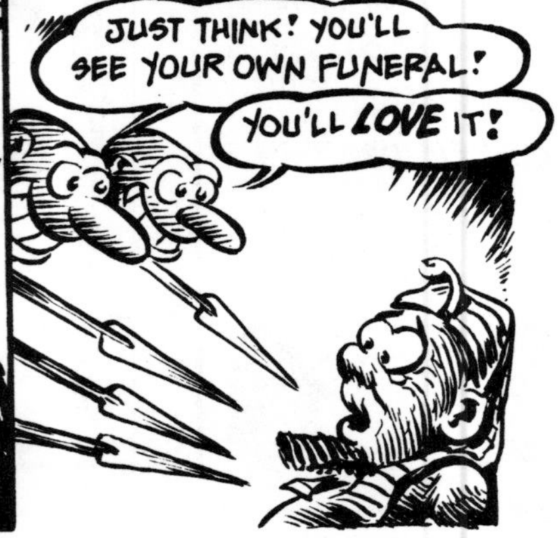
JUST THINK! YOU'LL SEE YOUR OWN FUNERAL!
YOU'LL ***LOVE*** IT!

TO EASE THE TRANSITION OF POWER, THEY ALSO KILLED ALL OF HIS ***SERVANTS.***

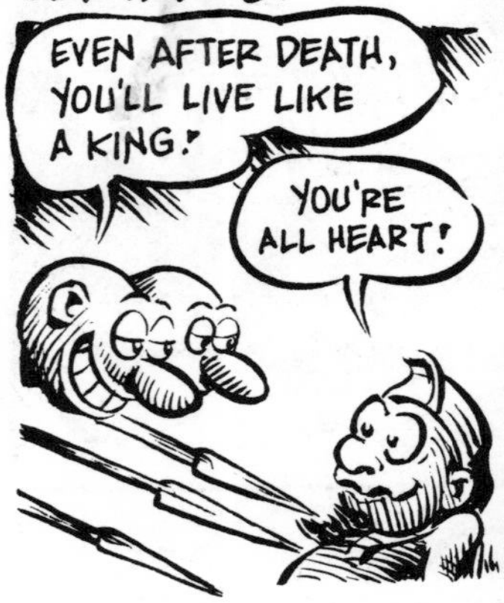
EVEN AFTER DEATH, YOU'LL LIVE LIKE A KING!
YOU'RE ALL HEART!

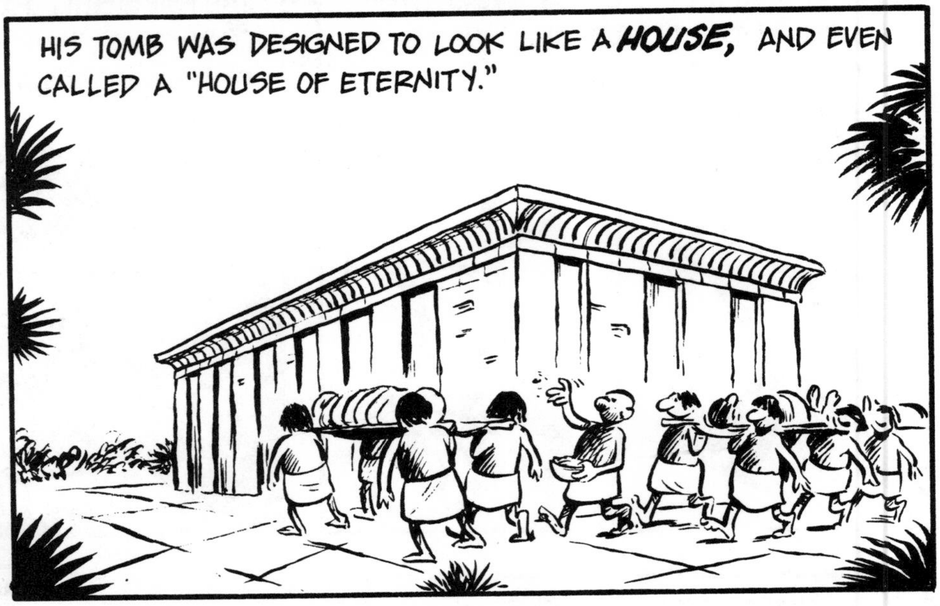
HIS TOMB WAS DESIGNED TO LOOK LIKE A ***HOUSE,*** AND EVEN CALLED A "HOUSE OF ETERNITY."

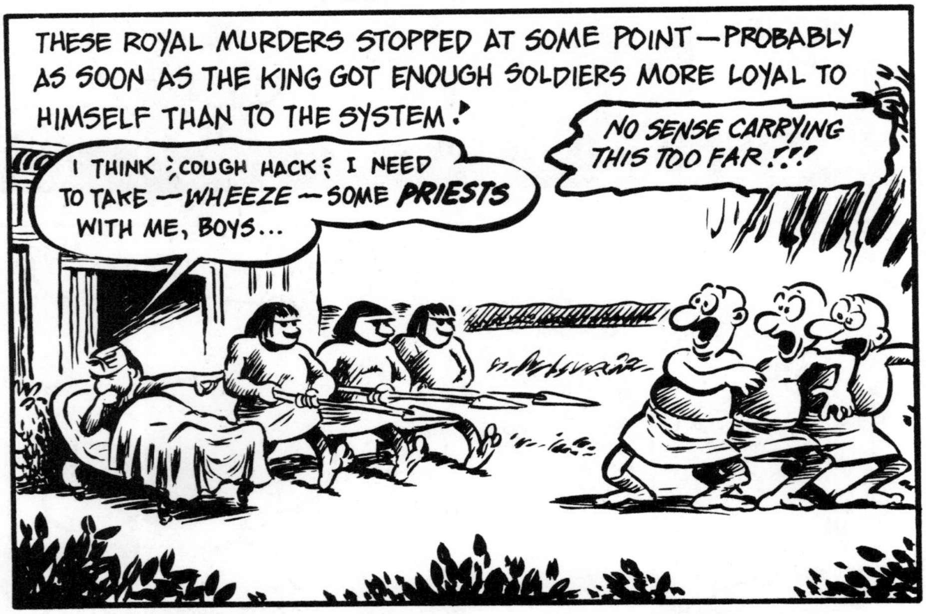
THESE ROYAL MURDERS STOPPED AT SOME POINT—PROBABLY AS SOON AS THE KING GOT ENOUGH SOLDIERS MORE LOYAL TO HIMSELF THAN TO THE SYSTEM!
I THINK ;COUGH HACK; I NEED TO TAKE —*WHEEZE*— SOME ***PRIESTS*** WITH ME, BOYS...
NO SENSE CARRYING THIS TOO FAR!!!

THE PRIESTS REPLACED THE ***REAL*** MURDER WITH A ***RITUAL*** CALLED THE HEB-SED. THEN, WHEN THE KING FINALLY DIED, THEY FILLED HIS GRAVE WITH ***PAINTINGS*** AND ***STATUES*** OF SERVANTS, INSTEAD OF THE REAL THING.

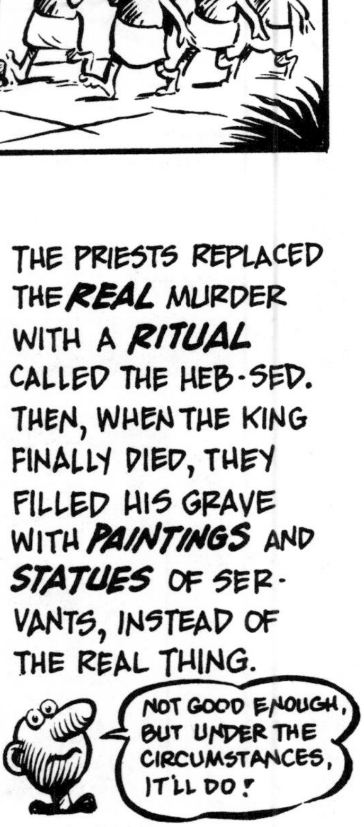
NOT GOOD ENOUGH, BUT UNDER THE CIRCUMSTANCES, IT'LL DO!

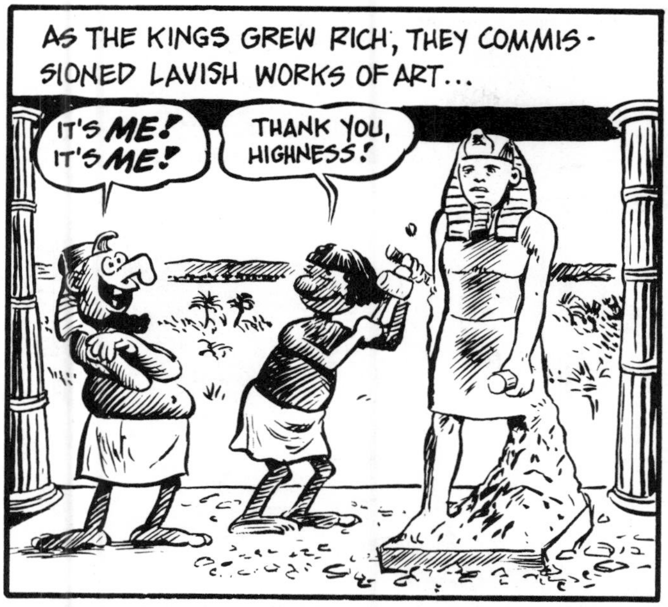
AS THE KINGS GREW RICH, THEY COMMISSIONED LAVISH WORKS OF ART...
IT'S **ME!** IT'S **ME!**
THANK YOU, HIGHNESS!

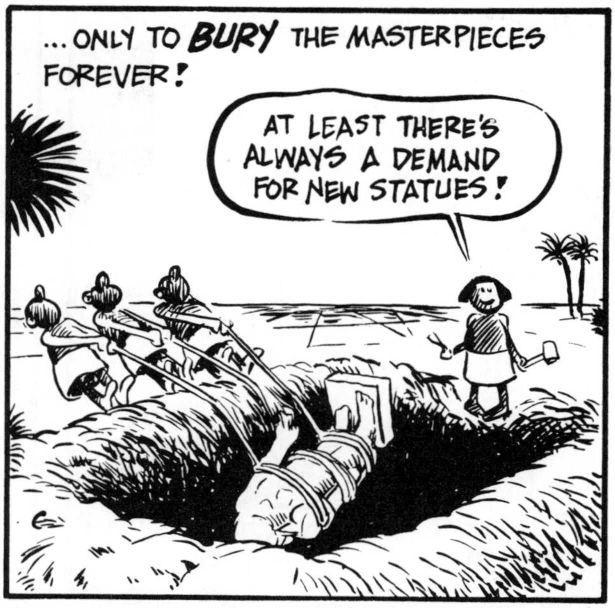
...ONLY TO **BURY** THE MASTERPIECES FOREVER!
AT LEAST THERE'S ALWAYS A DEMAND FOR NEW STATUES!

WELL, NOT REALLY FOREVER... AS SOON AS THE PICKINGS GOT FANCY ENOUGH, ***TOMB ROBBERS*** WENT TO WORK...

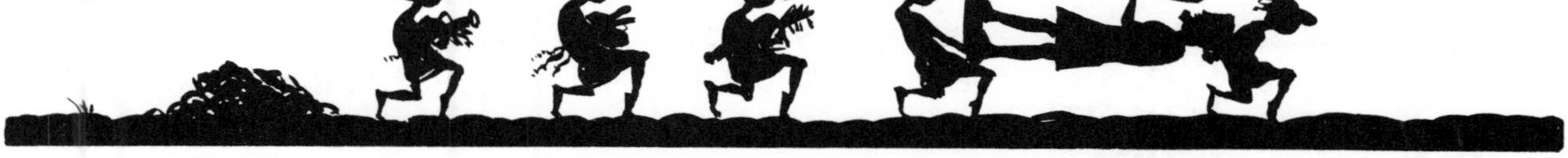

TO PROTECT THE RICHES, KING AND ART WERE SUNK DEEPER INTO THE EARTH, AND THE SHAFT WAS COVERED WITH A HEAP OF STONES, WHICH IN TURN WAS COVERED BY THE "HOUSE."

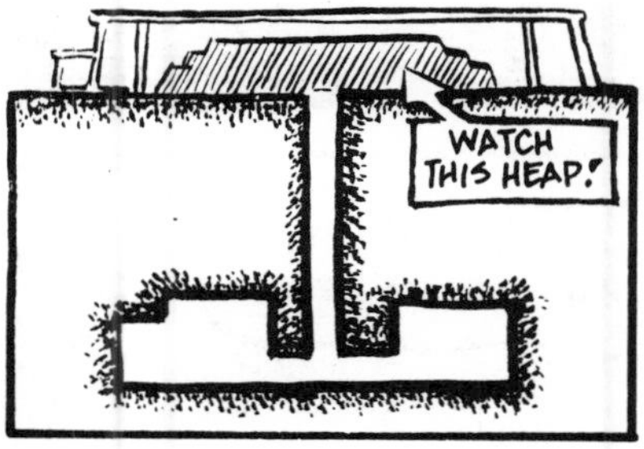
WATCH THIS HEAP!

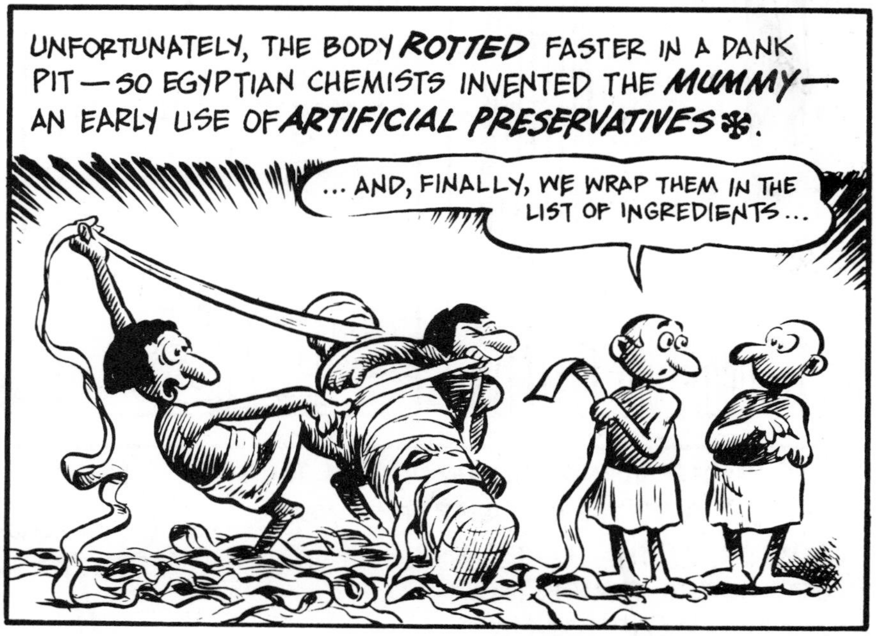
UNFORTUNATELY, THE BODY ***ROTTED*** FASTER IN A DANK PIT—SO EGYPTIAN CHEMISTS INVENTED THE ***MUMMY***—AN EARLY USE OF ***ARTIFICIAL PRESERVATIVES*** ❋.
...AND, FINALLY, WE WRAP THEM IN THE LIST OF INGREDIENTS...

❋ EGYPTIAN EMBALMERS HAD THREE DIFFERENT WAYS TO MAKE ***MUMMIES,*** RANGING FROM A SIMPLE PICKLING TO ELABORATE SURGICAL PROCEDURES, COMBINED WITH PICKLING.

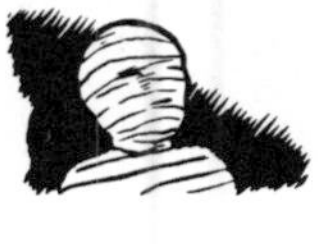

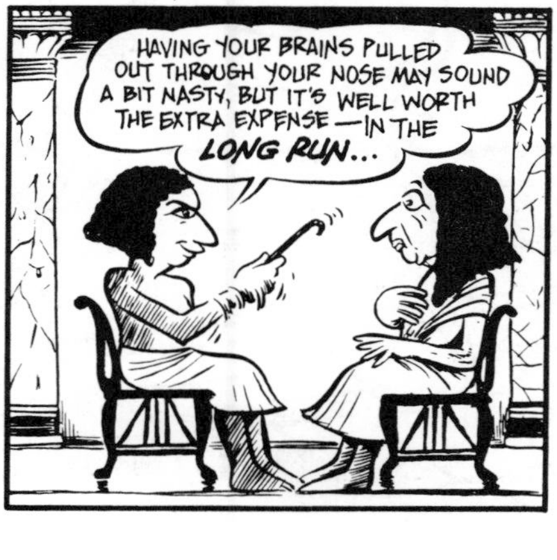
HAVING YOUR BRAINS PULLED OUT THROUGH YOUR NOSE MAY SOUND A BIT NASTY, BUT IT'S WELL WORTH THE EXTRA EXPENSE—IN THE ***LONG RUN...***

ORDINARILY, MUMMIFICATION WAS BEGUN JUST AFTER DEATH, BUT IF THE BODY WAS THAT OF A NOBLEWOMAN, THE FAMILY WOULD LET IT ***RIPEN*** A FEW DAYS FIRST—TO DISCOURAGE ANY AMOROUS EMBALMERS!

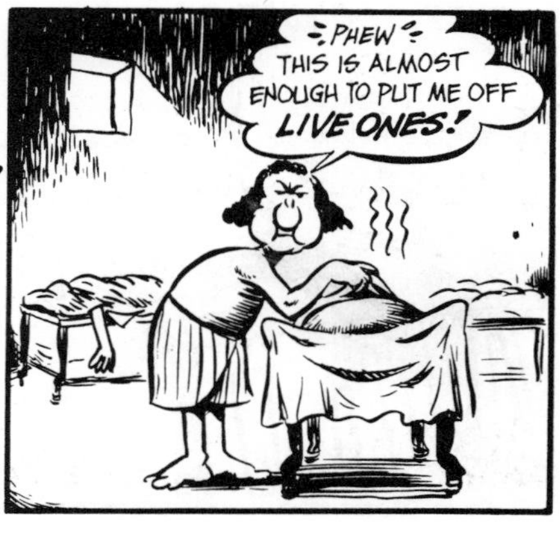
PHEW
THIS IS ALMOST ENOUGH TO PUT ME OFF ***LIVE ONES!***

MEANWHILE, ABOVE GROUND, THE KING'S ADMINISTRATORS WERE ALSO GETTING RICH AND FURNISHING FINE TOMBS FOR THEIR FAMILIES.

SOMEDAY, SON, ALL THIS WILL BE YOURS!

AROUND 2700 B.C., KING **ZOSER** ASKED HIS ARCHITECT, **IMHOTEP,** FOR A TOMB WHICH WOULD DISPLAY HIS SUPERIOR STATUS.

SOMETHING BETTER THAN EVERY PTAH, DICK, AND HATHOR!

IMHOTEP DESIGNED A TOMB OF **STONE,** INSTEAD OF BRICK, THE USUAL MATERIAL OF TOMBS.

BENEATH THE TOMB AND ITS TEMPLES, HE PLANNED ONE OF THE MOST COMPLICATED NETWORKS OF UNDERGROUND TUNNELS EVER BUILT.

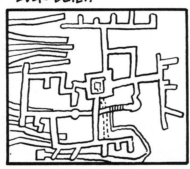

HE DRAFTED THOUSANDS OF WORKERS DURING THE **FLOOD SEASON,** NORMALLY THEIR VACATION TIME.

TRULY, PHARAOH IS SUPREME NOW!

TOO *@#$ SUPREME, IF YOU ASK ME!

AND IMHOTEP TURNED THE TRADITIONAL TOMB **INSIDE OUT:** THE OLD HEAP OF STONES CAME OUT OF THE "HOUSE" AND BECAME THE CENTERPIECE: A **STEPPED PYRAMID** OVER 200 FEET TALL!?

OO! THIS IS SO PRETTY, I'M ALMOST HAPPY TO BE DEAD!

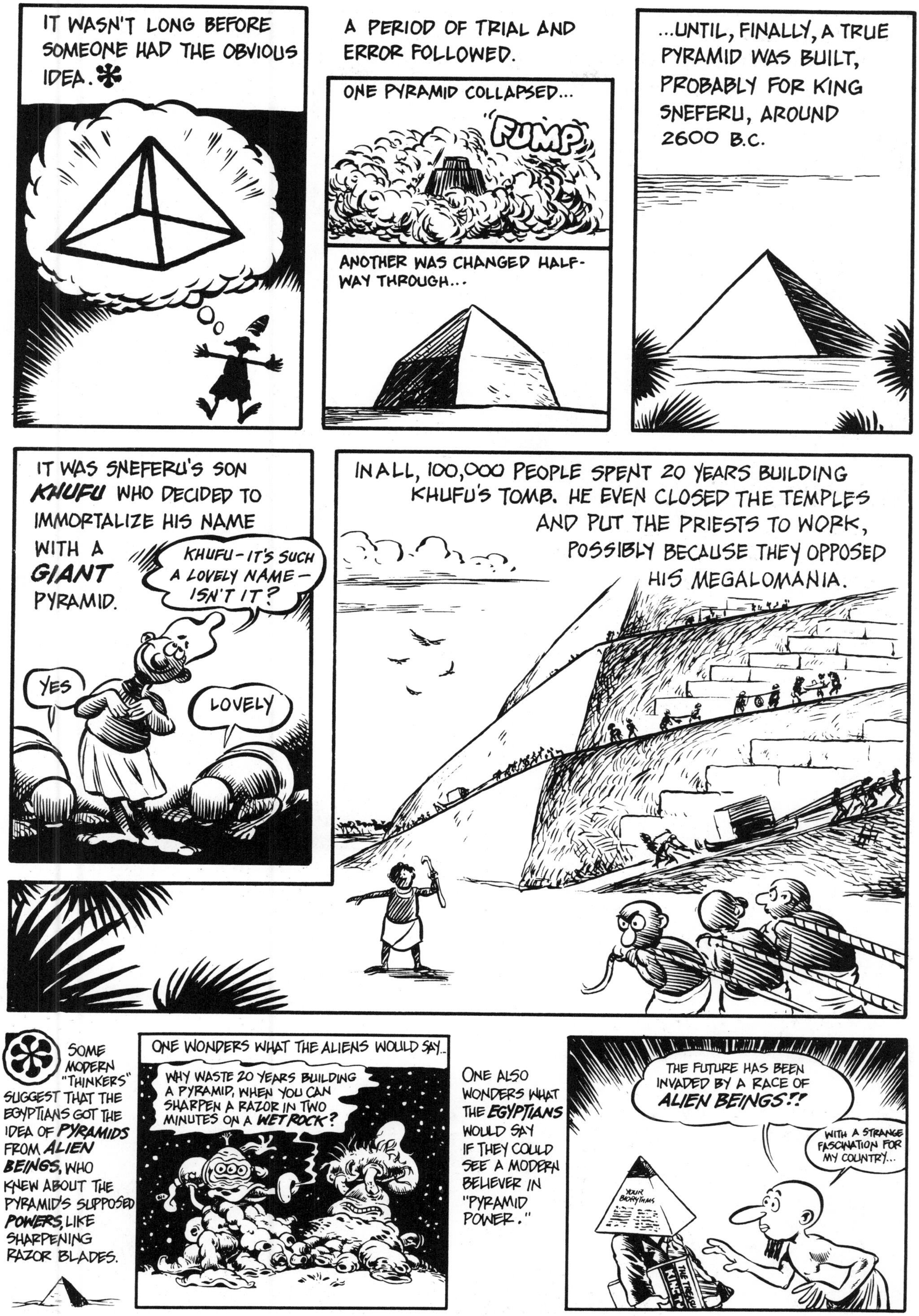
IT WASN'T LONG BEFORE SOMEONE HAD THE OBVIOUS IDEA. ✻
A PERIOD OF TRIAL AND ERROR FOLLOWED.
ONE PYRAMID COLLAPSED...
FUMP
ANOTHER WAS CHANGED HALF-WAY THROUGH...
...UNTIL, FINALLY, A TRUE PYRAMID WAS BUILT, PROBABLY FOR KING SNEFERU, AROUND 2600 B.C.
IT WAS SNEFERU'S SON KHUFU WHO DECIDED TO IMMORTALIZE HIS NAME WITH A GIANT PYRAMID.
KHUFU - IT'S SUCH A LOVELY NAME - ISN'T IT?
YES
LOVELY
IN ALL, 100,000 PEOPLE SPENT 20 YEARS BUILDING KHUFU'S TOMB. HE EVEN CLOSED THE TEMPLES AND PUT THE PRIESTS TO WORK, POSSIBLY BECAUSE THEY OPPOSED HIS MEGALOMANIA.
✻ SOME MODERN "THINKERS" SUGGEST THAT THE EGYPTIANS GOT THE IDEA OF PYRAMIDS FROM ALIEN BEINGS, WHO KNEW ABOUT THE PYRAMID'S SUPPOSED POWERS, LIKE SHARPENING RAZOR BLADES.
ONE WONDERS WHAT THE ALIENS WOULD SAY...
WHY WASTE 20 YEARS BUILDING A PYRAMID, WHEN YOU CAN SHARPEN A RAZOR IN TWO MINUTES ON A WET ROCK?
ONE ALSO WONDERS WHAT THE EGYPTIANS WOULD SAY IF THEY COULD SEE A MODERN BELIEVER IN "PYRAMID POWER."
THE FUTURE HAS BEEN INVADED BY A RACE OF ALIEN BEINGS?!
WITH A STRANGE FASCINATION FOR MY COUNTRY...
YOUR BIORYTHMS

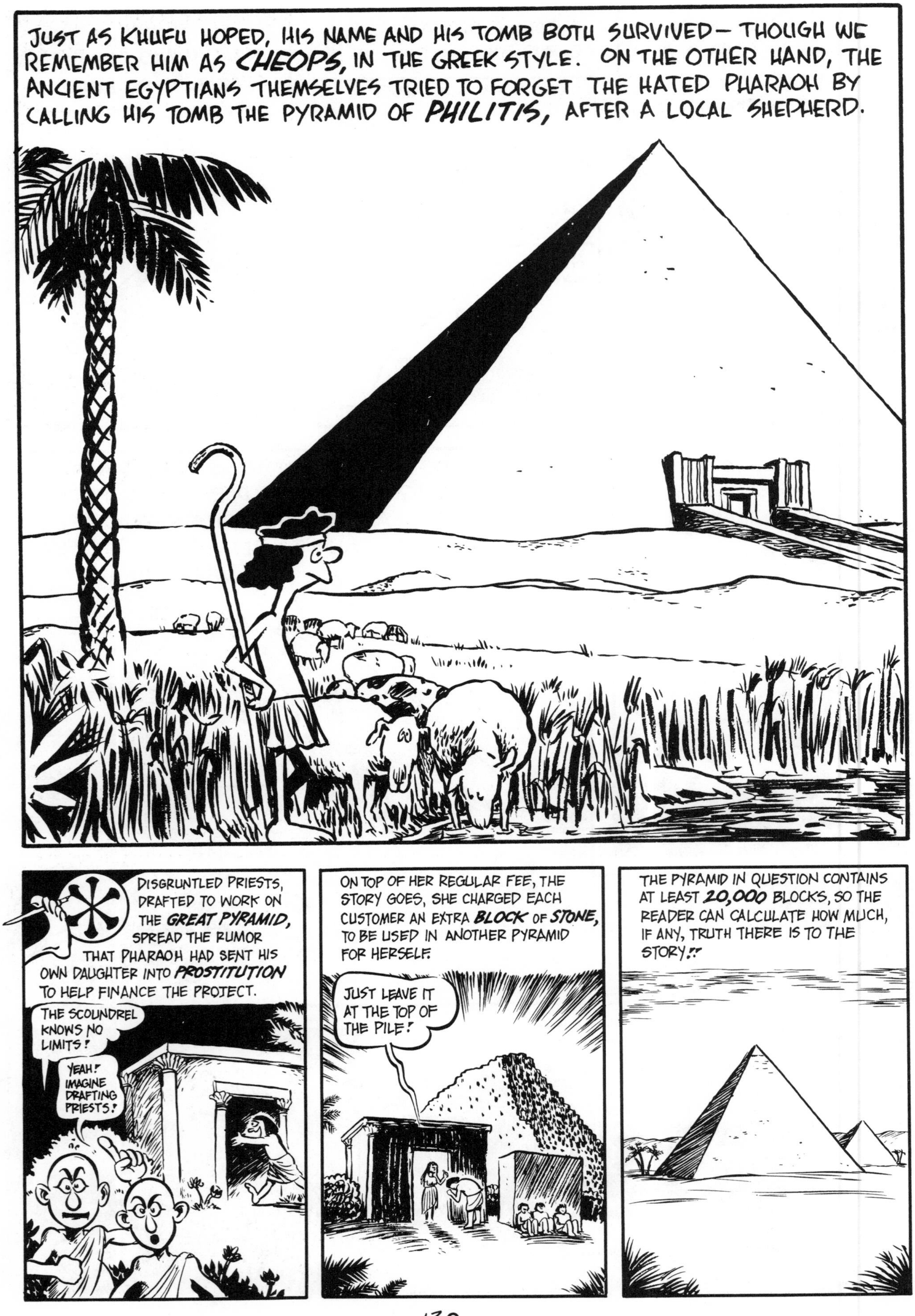
JUST AS KHUFU HOPED, HIS NAME AND HIS TOMB BOTH SURVIVED— THOUGH WE REMEMBER HIM AS CHEOPS, IN THE GREEK STYLE. ON THE OTHER HAND, THE ANCIENT EGYPTIANS THEMSELVES TRIED TO FORGET THE HATED PHARAOH BY CALLING HIS TOMB THE PYRAMID OF PHILITIS, AFTER A LOCAL SHEPHERD.
DISGRUNTLED PRIESTS, DRAFTED TO WORK ON THE GREAT PYRAMID, SPREAD THE RUMOR THAT PHARAOH HAD SENT HIS OWN DAUGHTER INTO PROSTITUTION TO HELP FINANCE THE PROJECT.
THE SCOUNDREL KNOWS NO LIMITS!
YEAH! IMAGINE DRAFTING PRIESTS!
ON TOP OF HER REGULAR FEE, THE STORY GOES, SHE CHARGED EACH CUSTOMER AN EXTRA BLOCK OF STONE, TO BE USED IN ANOTHER PYRAMID FOR HERSELF.
JUST LEAVE IT AT THE TOP OF THE PILE!
THE PYRAMID IN QUESTION CONTAINS AT LEAST 20,000 BLOCKS, SO THE READER CAN CALCULATE HOW MUCH, IF ANY, TRUTH THERE IS TO THE STORY!?

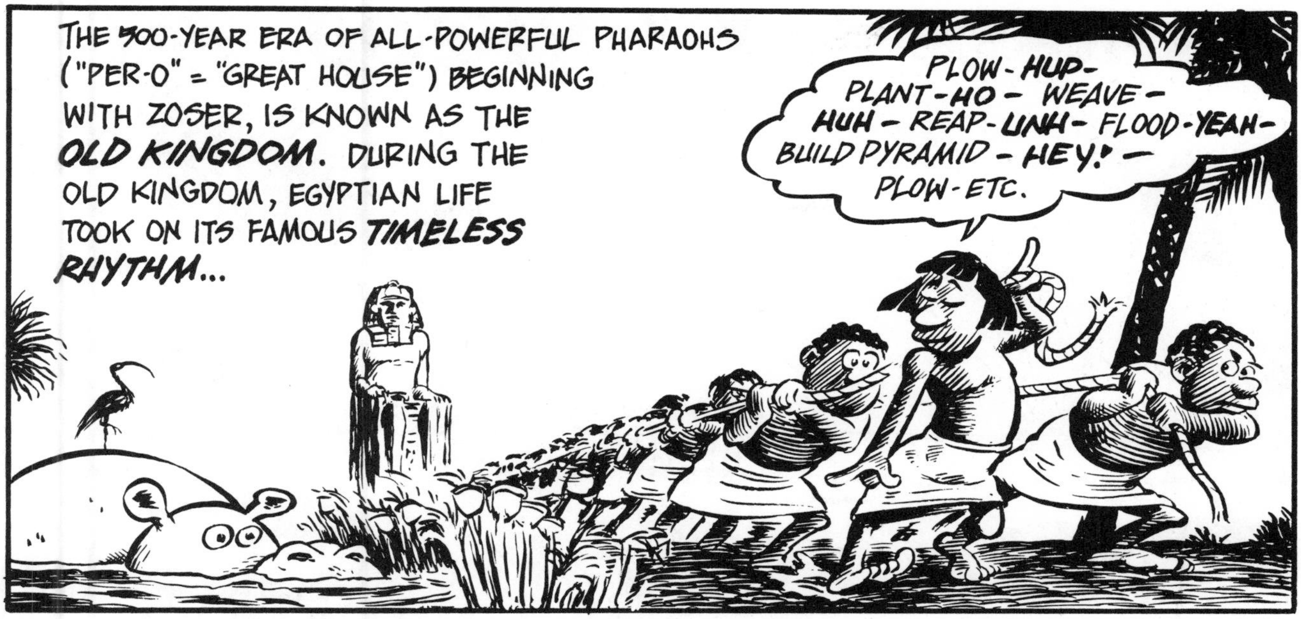
THE 500-YEAR ERA OF ALL-POWERFUL PHARAOHS ("PER-O" = "GREAT HOUSE") BEGINNING WITH ZOSER, IS KNOWN AS THE **OLD KINGDOM**. DURING THE OLD KINGDOM, EGYPTIAN LIFE TOOK ON ITS FAMOUS **TIMELESS RHYTHM**...
PLOW-HUP-PLANT-HO-WEAVE-HUH-REAP-UNH-FLOOD-YEAH-BUILD PYRAMID-HEY!-PLOW-ETC.

MEANWHILE, AS ALREADY NOTED, LOCAL GOVERNORS WERE COMPETING WITH PHARAOH FOR A SHARE OF THE COMMON PEOPLE'S LABOR. (IN EGYPT THE WORD FOR "TAXES" MEANT "LABOR.") AROUND 2200 B.C., A REVOLUTION TOPPLED THE KING AND INTRODUCED THE ***FIRST INTERMEDIATE PERIOD.***

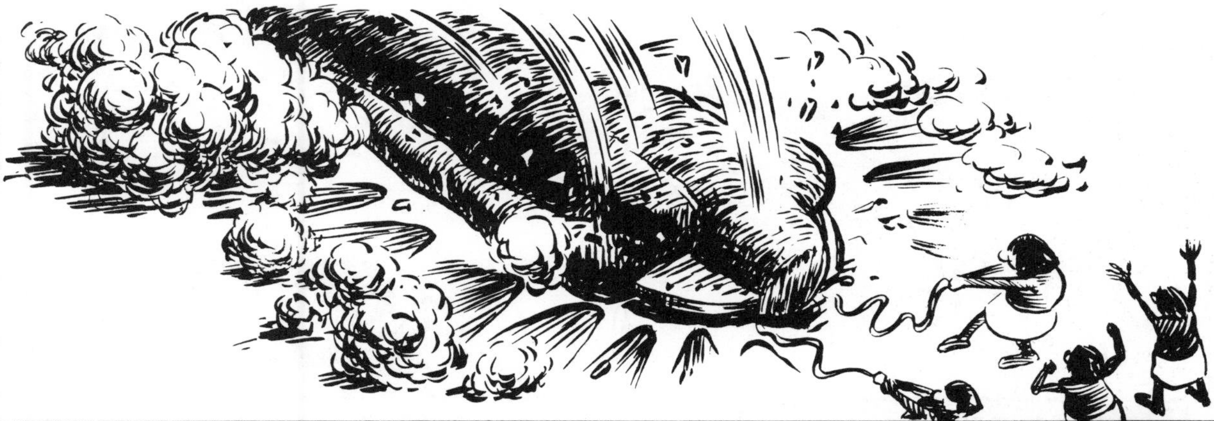

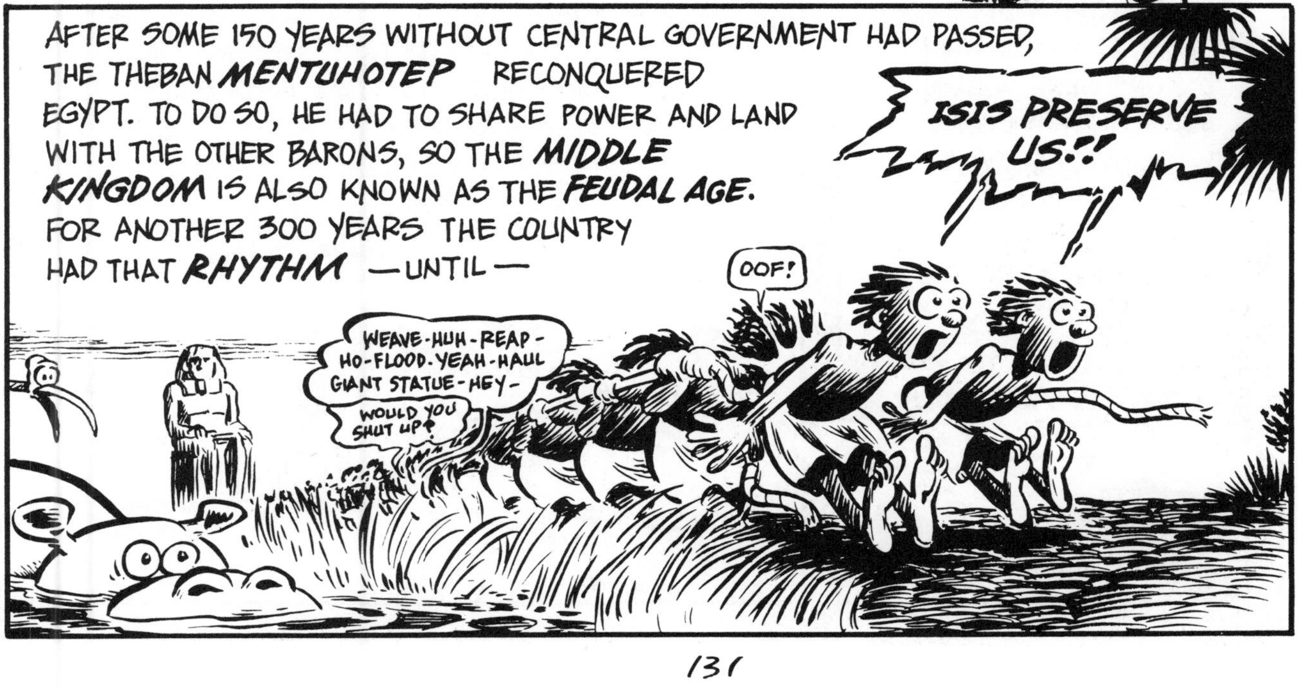
AFTER SOME 150 YEARS WITHOUT CENTRAL GOVERNMENT HAD PASSED, THE THEBAN **MENTUHOTEP** RECONQUERED EGYPT. TO DO SO, HE HAD TO SHARE POWER AND LAND WITH THE OTHER BARONS, SO THE **MIDDLE KINGDOM** IS ALSO KNOWN AS THE **FEUDAL AGE**. FOR ANOTHER 300 YEARS THE COUNTRY HAD THAT **RHYTHM** —UNTIL—
ISIS PRESERVE US?!
OOF!
WEAVE-HUH-REAP-HO-FLOOD-YEAH-HAUL GIANT STATUE-HEY-
WOULD YOU SHUT UP?

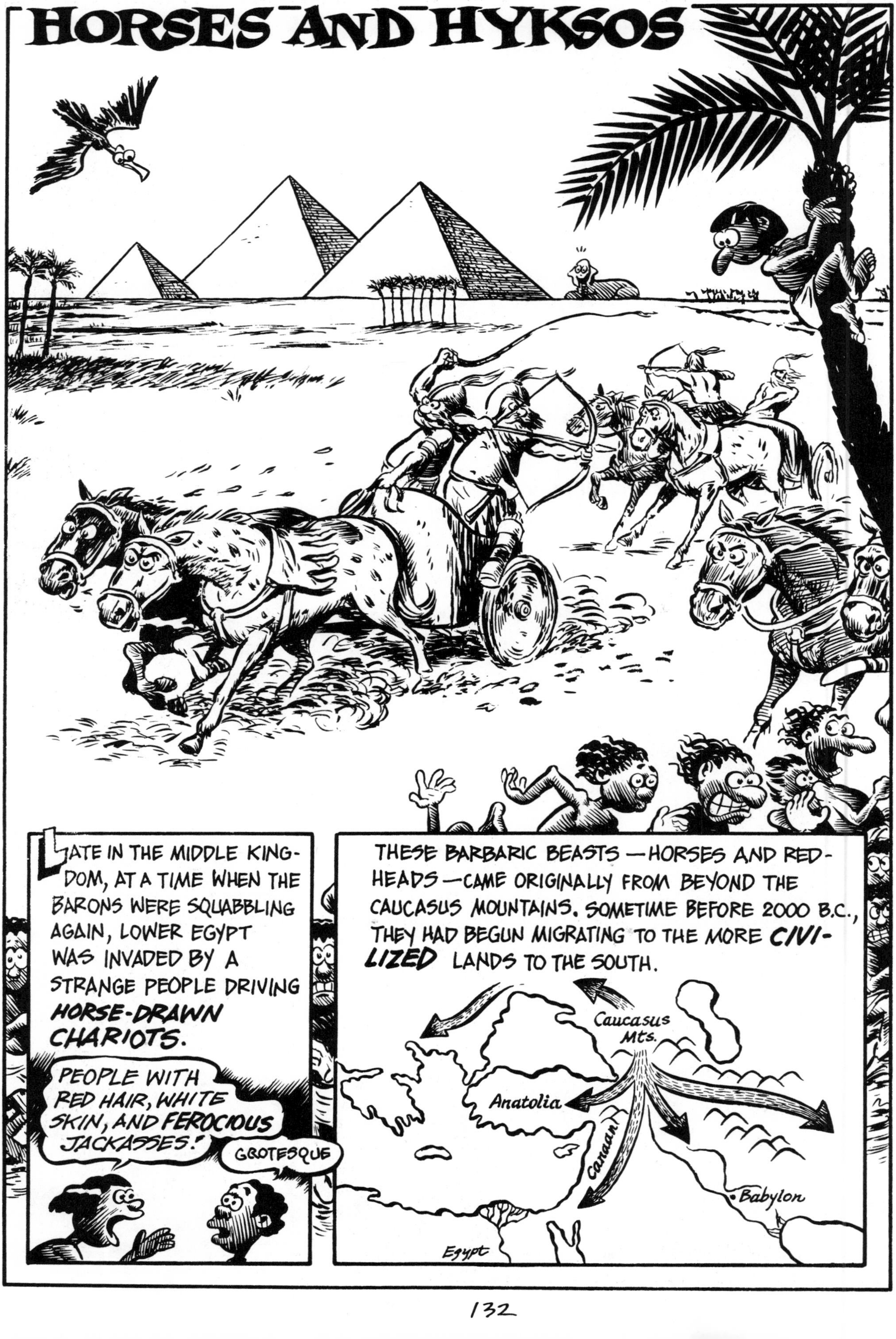

HORSES AND HYKSOS
LATE IN THE MIDDLE KINGDOM, AT A TIME WHEN THE BARONS WERE SQUABBLING AGAIN, LOWER EGYPT WAS INVADED BY A STRANGE PEOPLE DRIVING HORSE-DRAWN CHARIOTS.
PEOPLE WITH RED HAIR, WHITE SKIN, AND FEROCIOUS JACKASSES!
GROTESQUE
THESE BARBARIC BEASTS —HORSES AND REDHEADS—CAME ORIGINALLY FROM BEYOND THE CAUCASUS MOUNTAINS. SOMETIME BEFORE 2000 B.C., THEY HAD BEGUN MIGRATING TO THE MORE CIVILIZED LANDS TO THE SOUTH.
Caucasus Mts.
Anatolia
Canaan
Babylon
Egypt

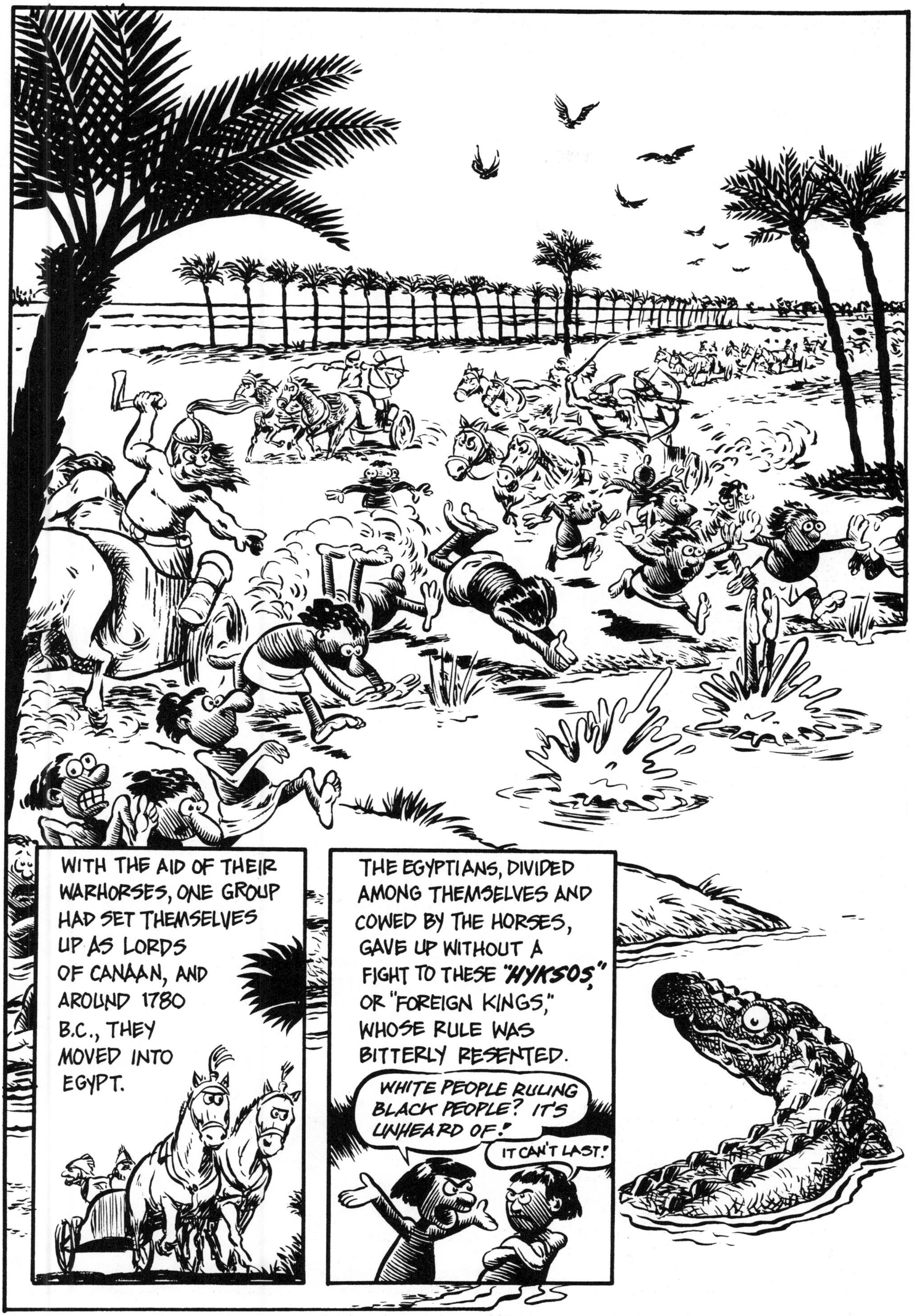
WITH THE AID OF THEIR WARHORSES, ONE GROUP HAD SET THEMSELVES UP AS LORDS OF CANAAN, AND AROUND 1780 B.C., THEY MOVED INTO EGYPT.
THE EGYPTIANS, DIVIDED AMONG THEMSELVES AND COWED BY THE HORSES, GAVE UP WITHOUT A FIGHT TO THESE "HYKSOS," OR "FOREIGN KINGS," WHOSE RULE WAS BITTERLY RESENTED.
WHITE PEOPLE RULING BLACK PEOPLE? IT'S UNHEARD OF!
IT CAN'T LAST!

TWO HUNDRED YEARS OF HYKSOS RULE TAUGHT THE EGYPTIANS A VALUABLE LESSON.

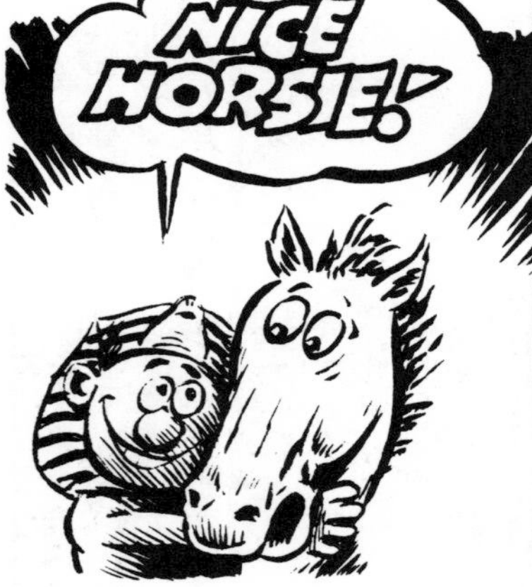
NICE HORSIE!

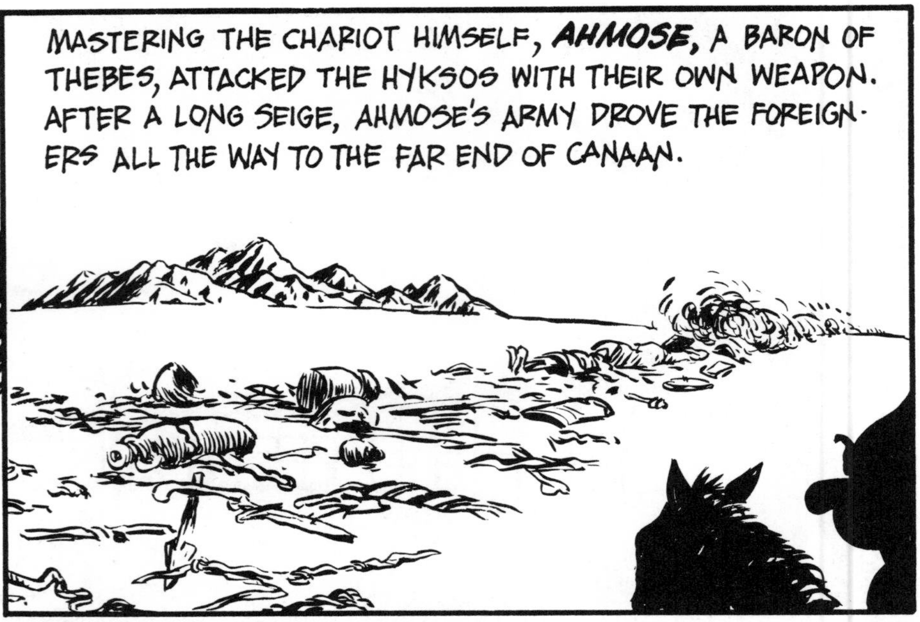
MASTERING THE CHARIOT HIMSELF, AHMOSE, A BARON OF THEBES, ATTACKED THE HYKSOS WITH THEIR OWN WEAPON. AFTER A LONG SEIGE, AHMOSE'S ARMY DROVE THE FOREIGN-ERS ALL THE WAY TO THE FAR END OF CANAAN.

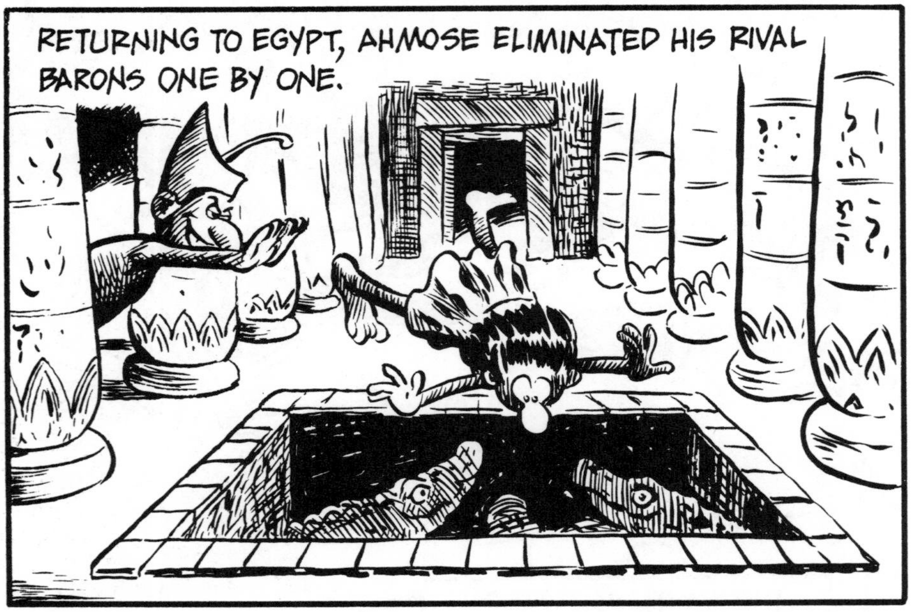
RETURNING TO EGYPT, AHMOSE ELIMINATED HIS RIVAL BARONS ONE BY ONE.

AT THIS POINT, APPARENTLY, OCCURRED AN EPISODE OF ***ANTI-SEMITISM,*** DURING WHICH THE TRIBES OF ISRAEL—AND PROBABLY OTHER SEMITES IN EGYPT — WERE ENSLAVED AS FELLOW-TRAVELLERS OF THE HYKSOS.

AHMOSE AND HIS SUCCESSOR, AMENHOTEP I, BUILT UP THEBES, ESTABLISHED A STATE RELIGION, AND TRAINED A MODERN STANDING ARMY TO MAINTAIN PHARAOH'S POWER AT HOME AND ABROAD.

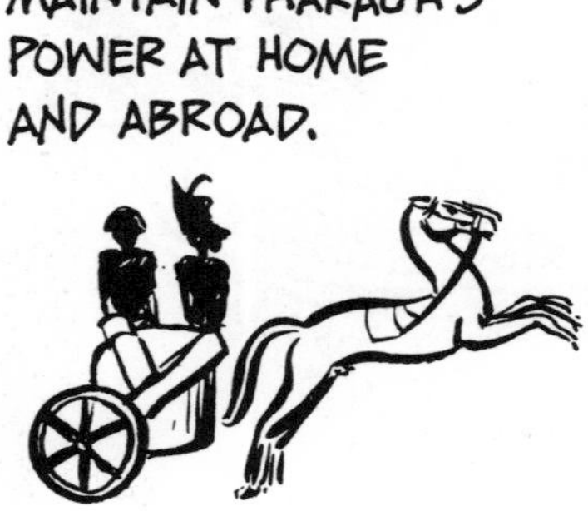

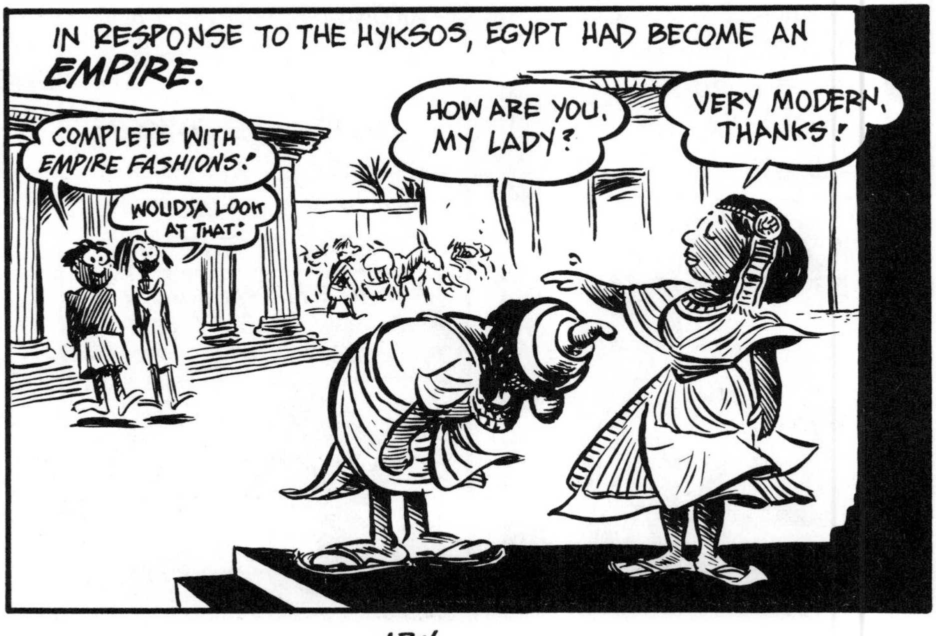
IN RESPONSE TO THE HYKSOS, EGYPT HAD BECOME AN EMPIRE.
COMPLETE WITH EMPIRE FASHIONS!
WOUDJA LOOK AT THAT!
HOW ARE YOU, MY LADY?
VERY MODERN, THANKS!

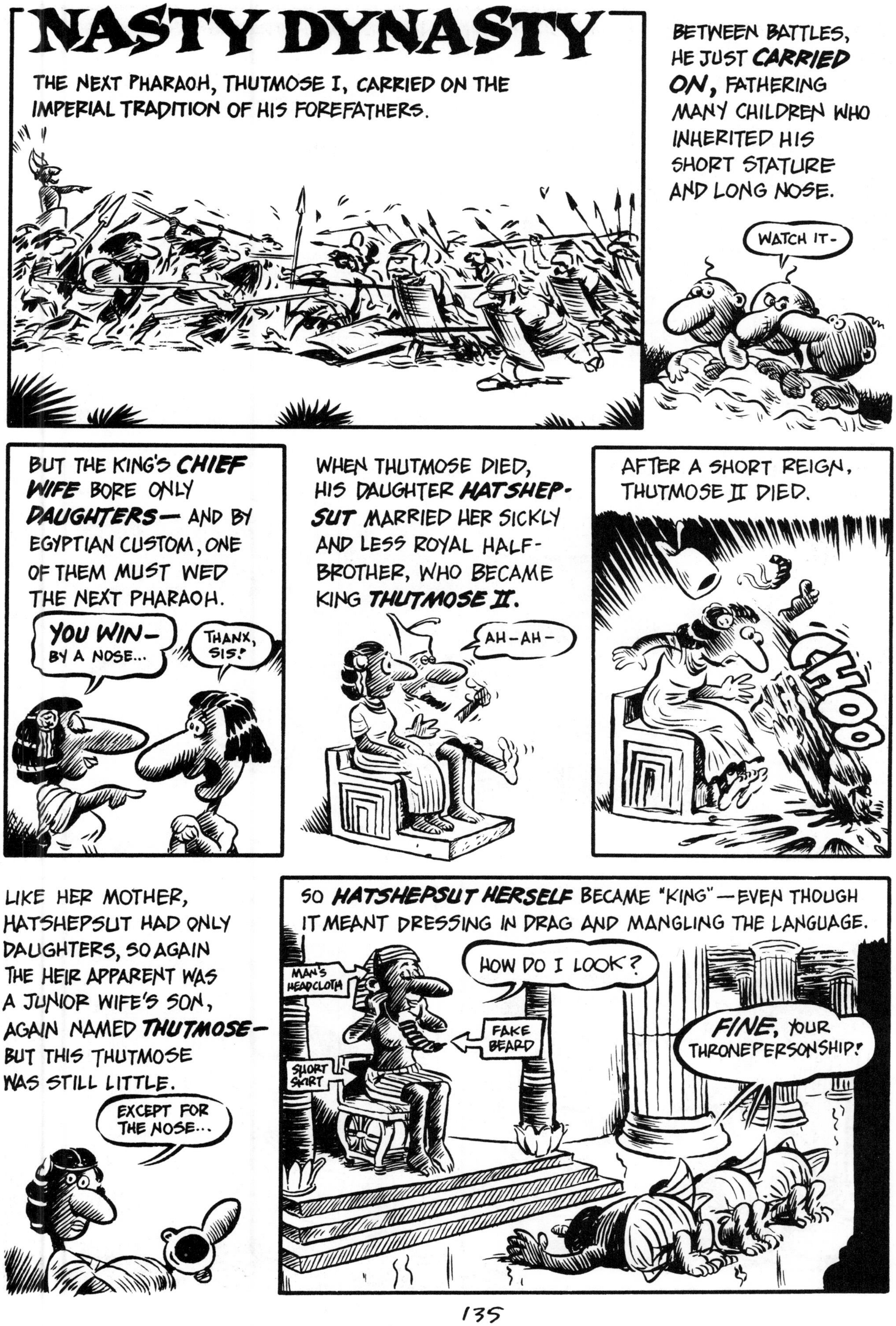
NASTY DYNASTY
THE NEXT PHARAOH, THUTMOSE I, CARRIED ON THE IMPERIAL TRADITION OF HIS FOREFATHERS.
BETWEEN BATTLES, HE JUST **CARRIED ON,** FATHERING MANY CHILDREN WHO INHERITED HIS SHORT STATURE AND LONG NOSE.
WATCH IT-
BUT THE KING'S **CHIEF WIFE** BORE ONLY **DAUGHTERS**— AND BY EGYPTIAN CUSTOM, ONE OF THEM MUST WED THE NEXT PHARAOH.
YOU WIN— BY A NOSE...
THANX, SIS!
WHEN THUTMOSE DIED, HIS DAUGHTER **HATSHEPSUT** MARRIED HER SICKLY AND LESS ROYAL HALF-BROTHER, WHO BECAME KING **THUTMOSE II.**
AH-AH-
AFTER A SHORT REIGN, THUTMOSE II DIED.
CHOO
LIKE HER MOTHER, HATSHEPSUT HAD ONLY DAUGHTERS, SO AGAIN THE HEIR APPARENT WAS A JUNIOR WIFE'S SON, AGAIN NAMED **THUTMOSE**— BUT THIS THUTMOSE WAS STILL LITTLE.
EXCEPT FOR THE NOSE...
SO **HATSHEPSUT HERSELF** BECAME "KING"—EVEN THOUGH IT MEANT DRESSING IN DRAG AND MANGLING THE LANGUAGE.
MAN'S HEADCLOTH
HOW DO I LOOK?
FAKE BEARD
SHORT SKIRT
FINE, YOUR THRONEPERSONSHIP!

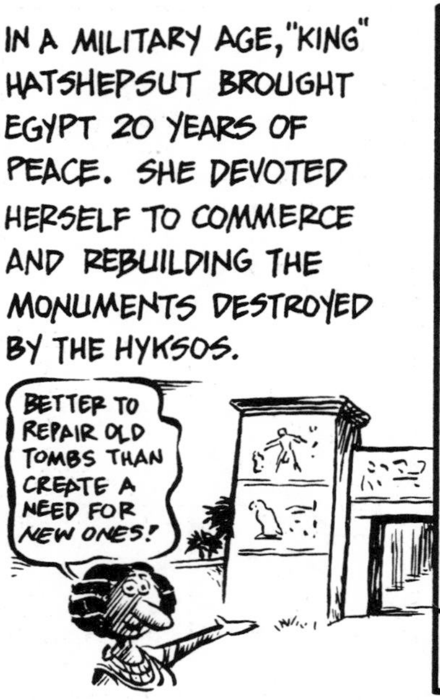
IN A MILITARY AGE, "KING" HATSHEPSUT BROUGHT EGYPT 20 YEARS OF PEACE. SHE DEVOTED HERSELF TO COMMERCE AND REBUILDING THE MONUMENTS DESTROYED BY THE HYKSOS.
BETTER TO REPAIR OLD TOMBS THAN CREATE A NEED FOR *NEW ONES!*

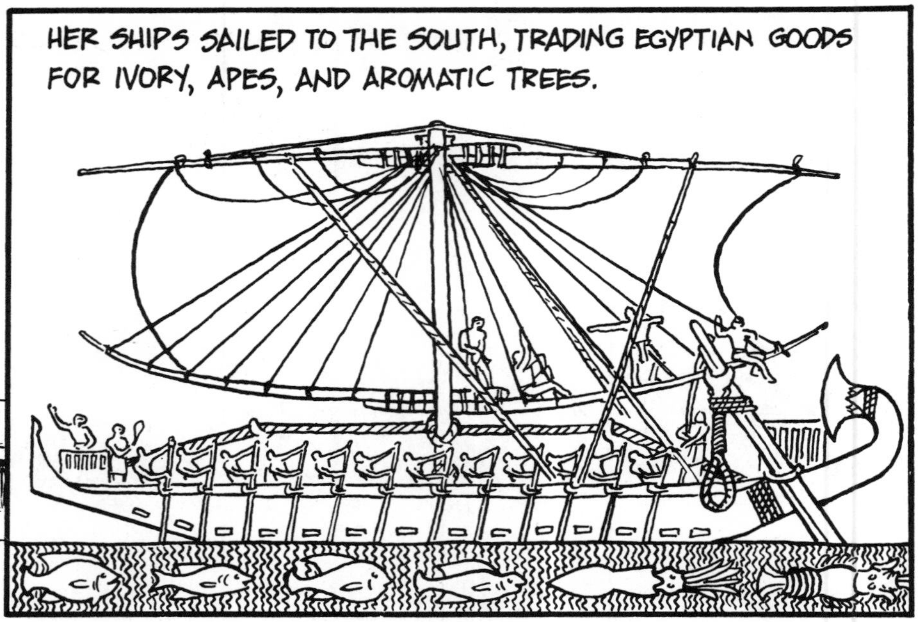
HER SHIPS SAILED TO THE SOUTH, TRADING EGYPTIAN GOODS FOR IVORY, APES, AND AROMATIC TREES.

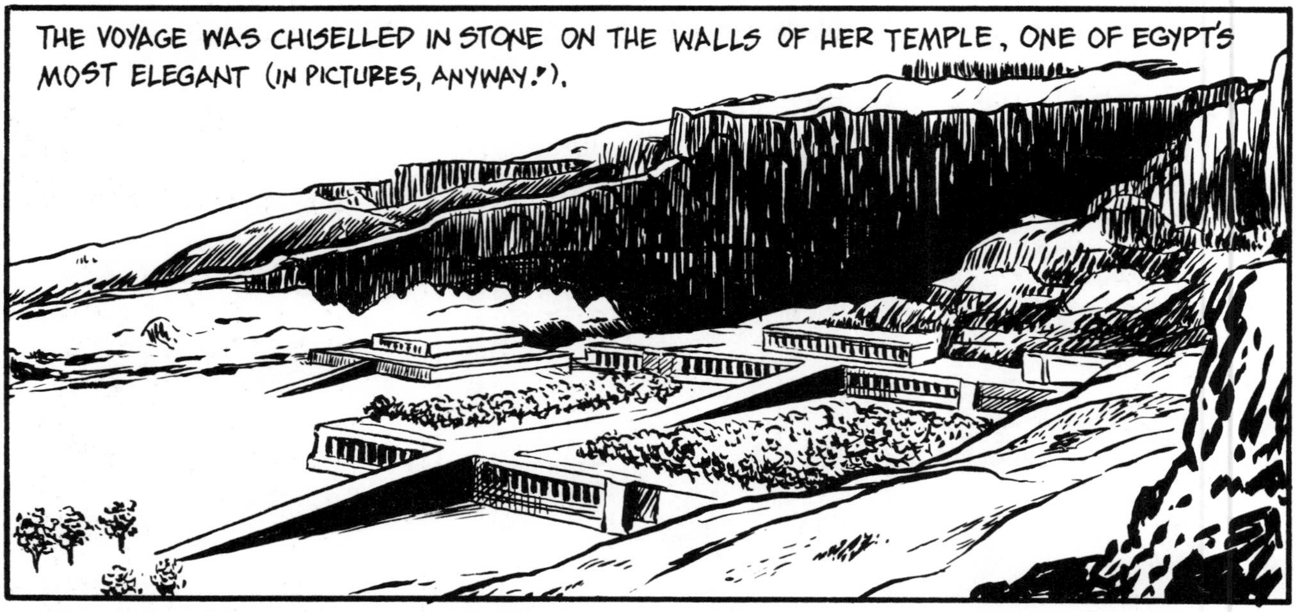
THE VOYAGE WAS CHISELLED IN STONE ON THE WALLS OF HER TEMPLE, ONE OF EGYPT'S MOST ELEGANT (IN PICTURES, ANYWAY!).

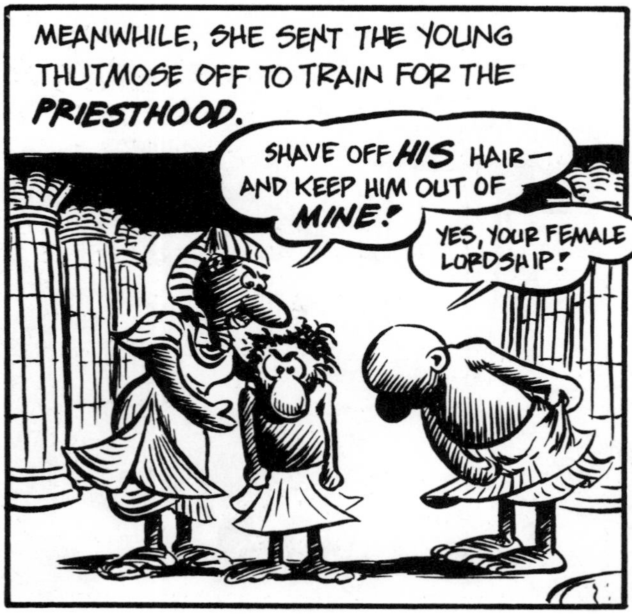
MEANWHILE, SHE SENT THE YOUNG THUTMOSE OFF TO TRAIN FOR THE ***PRIESTHOOD.***
SHAVE OFF ***HIS*** HAIR— AND KEEP HIM OUT OF ***MINE!***
YES, YOUR FEMALE LORDSHIP!

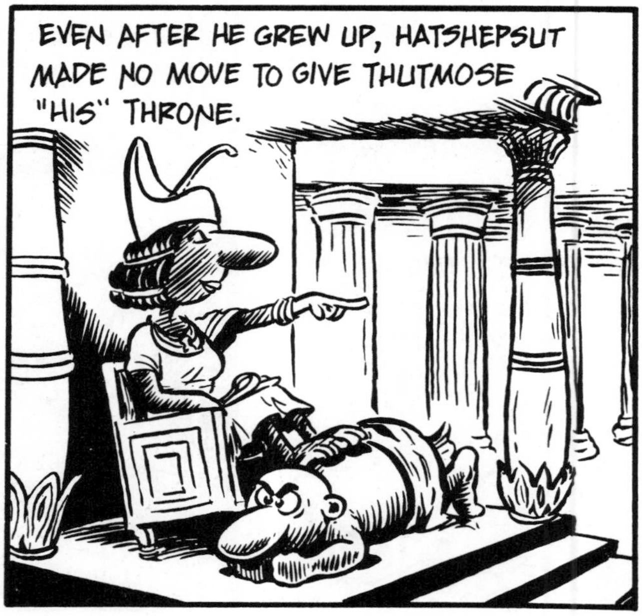
EVEN AFTER HE GREW UP, HATSHEPSUT MADE NO MOVE TO GIVE THUTMOSE "HIS" THRONE.

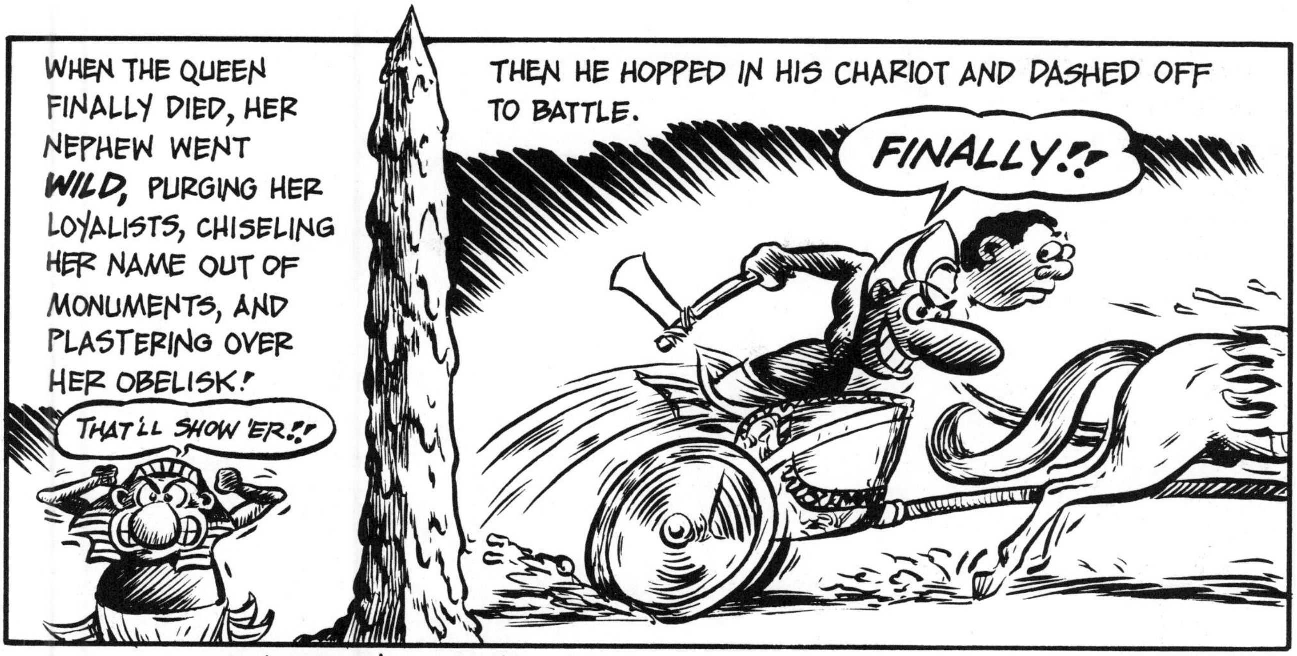
WHEN THE QUEEN FINALLY DIED, HER NEPHEW WENT **WILD**, PURGING HER LOYALISTS, CHISELING HER NAME OUT OF MONUMENTS, AND PLASTERING OVER HER OBELISK!
THAT'LL SHOW 'ER!!
THEN HE HOPPED IN HIS CHARIOT AND DASHED OFF TO BATTLE.
FINALLY!!

TRUE TO HIS GRANDFATHER'S MEMORY, THUTMOSE III SPENT HIS REMAINING 30 YEARS AT **WAR**, ESPECIALLY AGAINST HIS ARCH ENEMY, THE KING OF KADESH (A CITY IN CANAAN)✽.

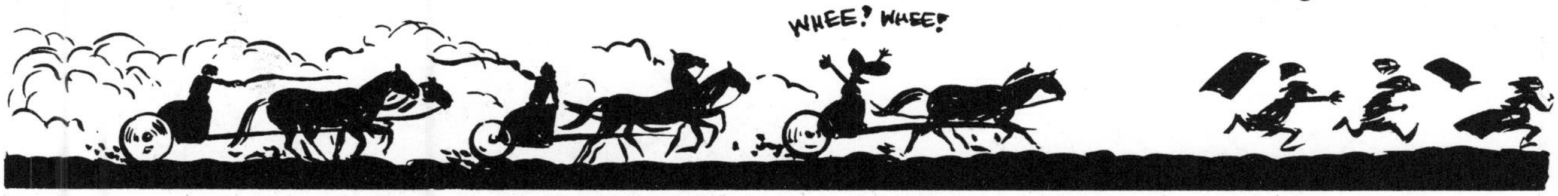
WHEE! WHEE!

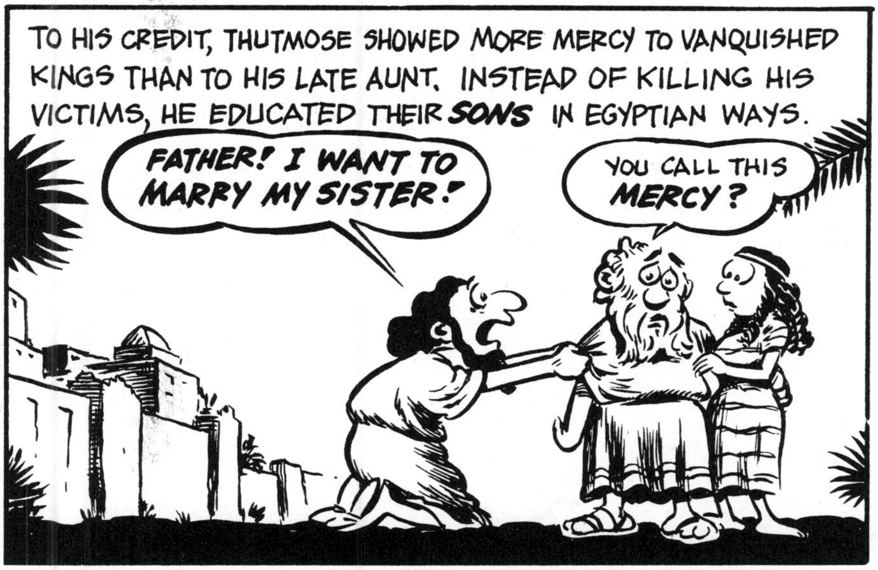
TO HIS CREDIT, THUTMOSE SHOWED MORE MERCY TO VANQUISHED KINGS THAN TO HIS LATE AUNT. INSTEAD OF KILLING HIS VICTIMS, HE EDUCATED THEIR **SONS** IN EGYPTIAN WAYS.
FATHER! I WANT TO MARRY MY SISTER!
YOU CALL THIS **MERCY**?

MOST HISTORIANS, PREFERRING EXCITING, WARLIKE KINGS TO DULL, PEACEFUL ONES, REFER TO THE LITTLE IMPERIALIST AS "THUTMOSE THE GREAT," BUT I'D RATHER THINK OF HIM AS **THUTMOSE, THE NASTIEST OF A NASTY DYNASTY!**

✽ WHENEVER A NEW WEAPON IS INVENTED, MILITARY MEN LOOK FOR NEW WAYS TO DEFEND THEMSELVES. IN 1500 B.C., THE SUPERWEAPON WAS THE **CHARIOT**, AND NO ONE COULD FIGURE OUT HOW TO STOP IT!

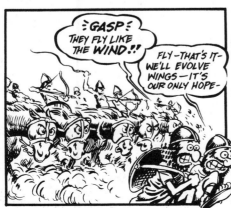

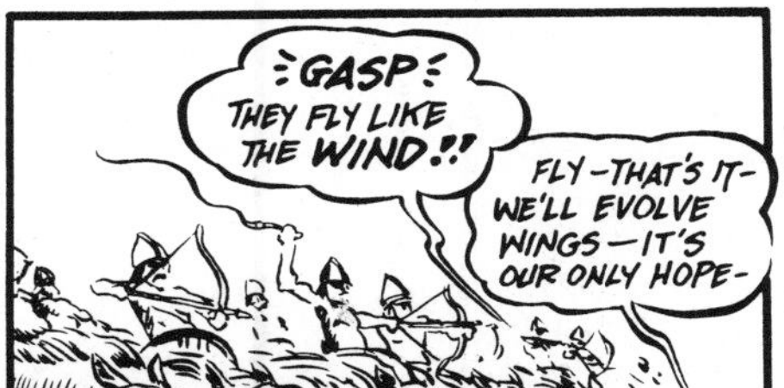
GASP
THEY FLY LIKE THE **WIND**!!
FLY—THAT'S IT—WE'LL EVOLVE WINGS—IT'S OUR ONLY HOPE-

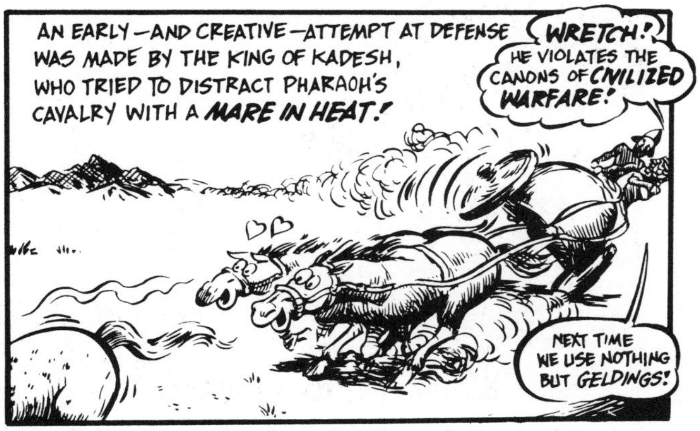
AN EARLY—AND CREATIVE—ATTEMPT AT DEFENSE WAS MADE BY THE KING OF KADESH, WHO TRIED TO DISTRACT PHARAOH'S CAVALRY WITH A **MARE IN HEAT**!
WRETCH! HE VIOLATES THE CANONS OF **CIVILIZED WARFARE**!
NEXT TIME WE USE NOTHING BUT GELDINGS!

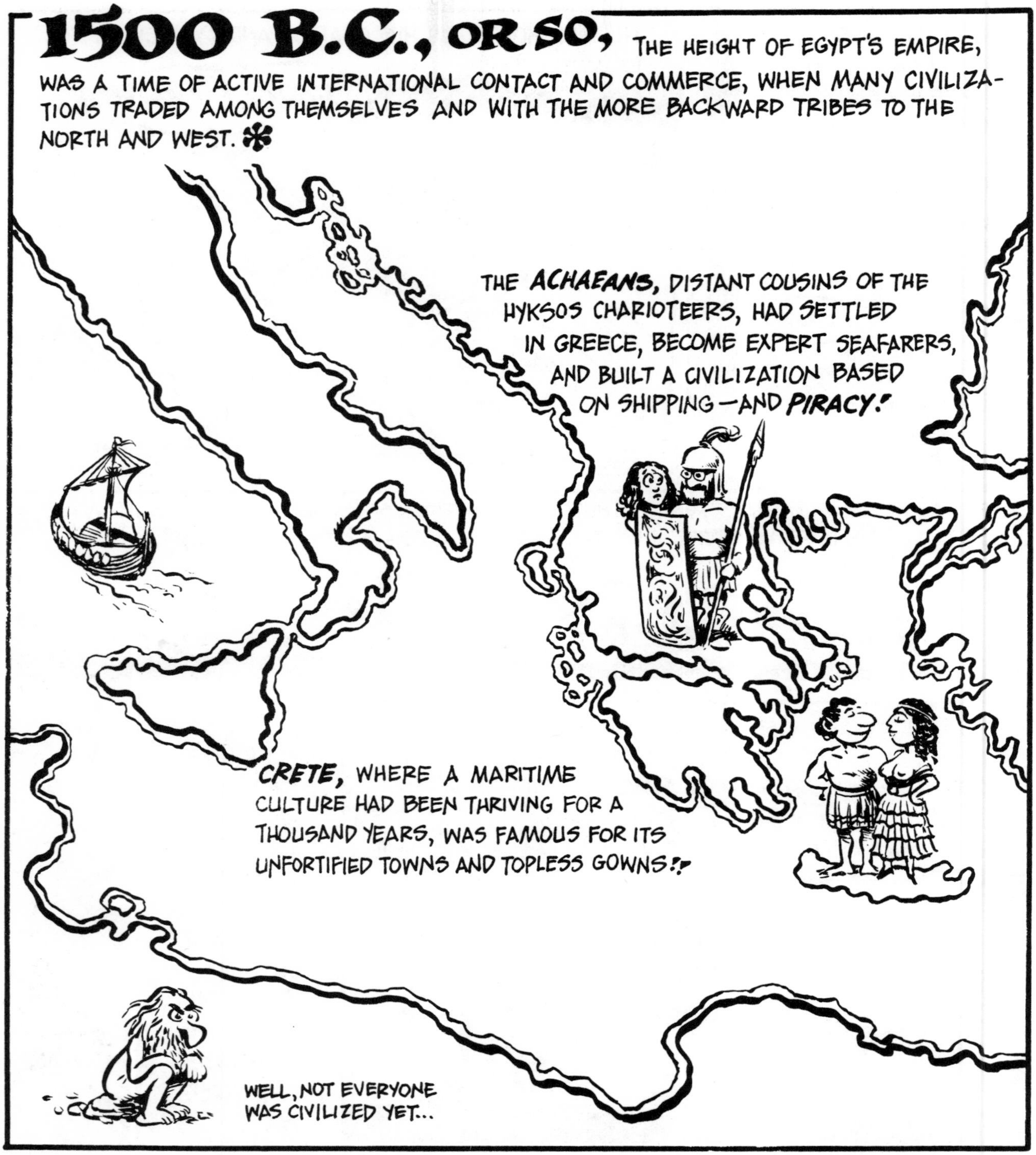
1500 B.C., OR SO, THE HEIGHT OF EGYPT'S EMPIRE, WAS A TIME OF ACTIVE INTERNATIONAL CONTACT AND COMMERCE, WHEN MANY CIVILIZATIONS TRADED AMONG THEMSELVES AND WITH THE MORE BACKWARD TRIBES TO THE NORTH AND WEST. ✽
THE ACHAEANS, DISTANT COUSINS OF THE HYKSOS CHARIOTEERS, HAD SETTLED IN GREECE, BECOME EXPERT SEAFARERS, AND BUILT A CIVILIZATION BASED ON SHIPPING—AND PIRACY!
CRETE, WHERE A MARITIME CULTURE HAD BEEN THRIVING FOR A THOUSAND YEARS, WAS FAMOUS FOR ITS UNFORTIFIED TOWNS AND TOPLESS GOWNS!!
WELL, NOT EVERYONE WAS CIVILIZED YET...

✽ BY 1500 B.C., MEDITERRANEAN METALLURGISTS KNEW THAT TIN, WHEN ALLOYED WITH COPPER, MADE A MUCH HARDER METAL, ***BRONZE.*** THE BRONZE-WORKERS TRAVELLED AS FAR AS BRITAIN AND SCANDINAVIA TO TRADE THEIR WARES FOR AMBER AND SLAVES.

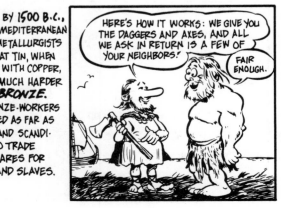

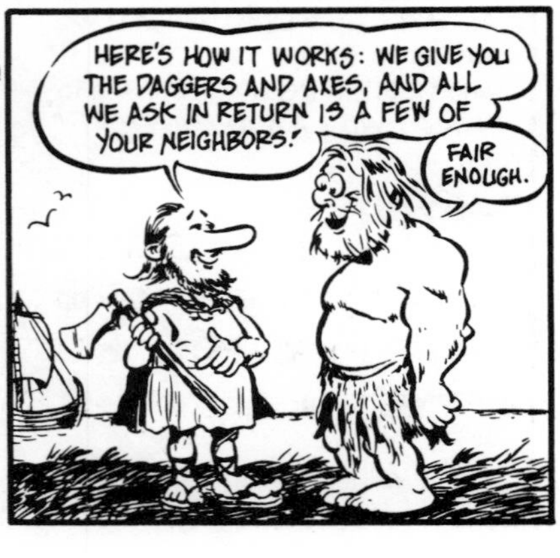
HERE'S HOW IT WORKS: WE GIVE YOU THE DAGGERS AND AXES, AND ALL WE ASK IN RETURN IS A FEW OF YOUR NEIGHBORS!
FAIR ENOUGH.

THEY WERE ALSO LOOKING FOR NEW SOURCES OF ***TIN,*** A FAIRLY RARE METAL. WHEN THEY FOUND IT, ONE PRESUMES, THEY DID THEIR BEST TO GET THE ORE ***DIRT CHEAP...***

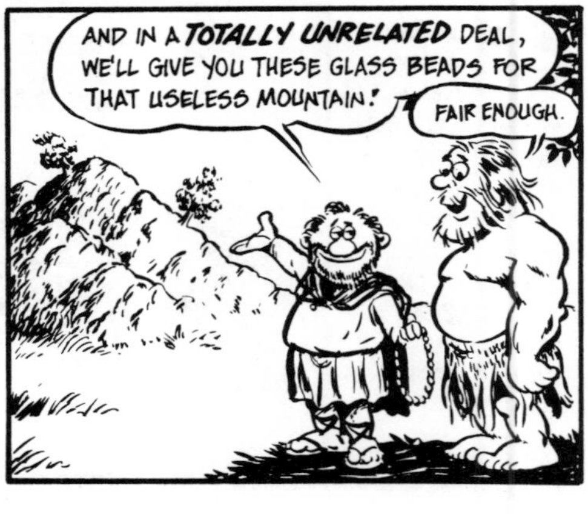
AND IN A TOTALLY UNRELATED DEAL, WE'LL GIVE YOU THESE GLASS BEADS FOR THAT USELESS MOUNTAIN!
FAIR ENOUGH.

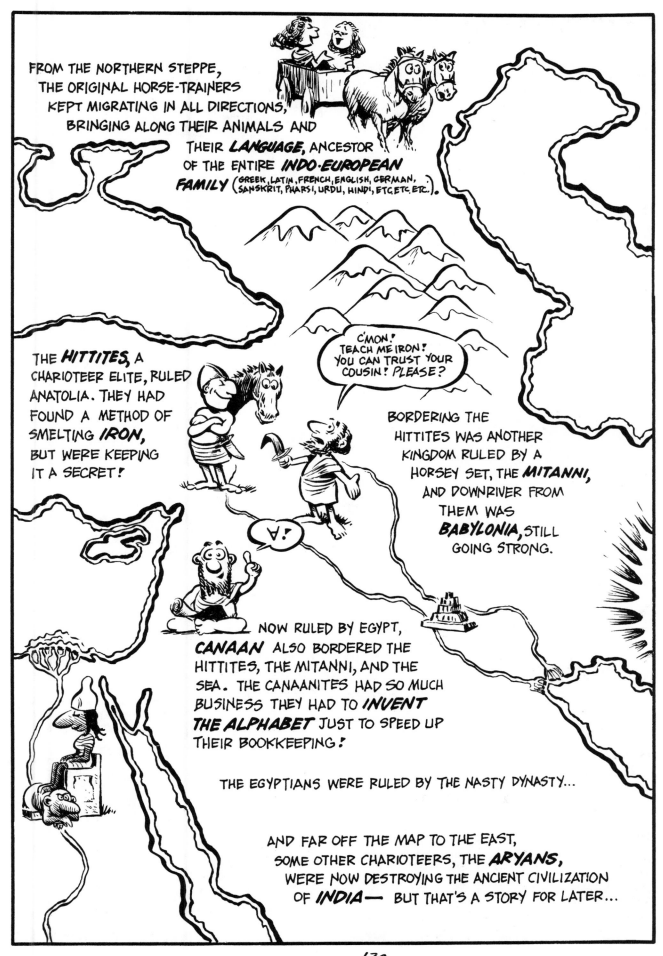

FROM THE NORTHERN STEPPE, THE ORIGINAL HORSE-TRAINERS KEPT MIGRATING IN ALL DIRECTIONS, BRINGING ALONG THEIR ANIMALS AND THEIR *LANGUAGE*, ANCESTOR OF THE ENTIRE *INDO-EUROPEAN FAMILY* (GREEK, LATIN, FRENCH, ENGLISH, GERMAN, SANSKRIT, PHARSI, URDU, HINDI, ETC ETC ETC.).

THE *HITTITES*, A CHARIOTEER ELITE, RULED ANATOLIA. THEY HAD FOUND A METHOD OF SMELTING *IRON*, BUT WERE KEEPING IT A SECRET!

C'MON! TEACH ME IRON! YOU CAN TRUST YOUR COUSIN! PLEASE?

¡A!

BORDERING THE HITTITES WAS ANOTHER KINGDOM RULED BY A HORSEY SET, THE *MITANNI*, AND DOWNRIVER FROM THEM WAS *BABYLONIA*, STILL GOING STRONG.

NOW RULED BY EGYPT, *CANAAN* ALSO BORDERED THE HITTITES, THE MITANNI, AND THE SEA. THE CANAANITES HAD SO MUCH BUSINESS THEY HAD TO *INVENT THE ALPHABET* JUST TO SPEED UP THEIR BOOKKEEPING!

THE EGYPTIANS WERE RULED BY THE NASTY DYNASTY...

AND FAR OFF THE MAP TO THE EAST, SOME OTHER CHARIOTEERS, THE *ARYANS*, WERE NOW DESTROYING THE ANCIENT CIVILIZATION OF *INDIA*— BUT THAT'S A STORY FOR LATER...

TUT·ANKH·WHO?

THE EMPIRE RAN SMOOTHLY UNDER THREE MORE PHARAOHS, WHO KEPT PEACE WITH FOREIGN KINGS BY RESPECTING THEIR GODS AND MARRYING THEIR DAUGHTERS.

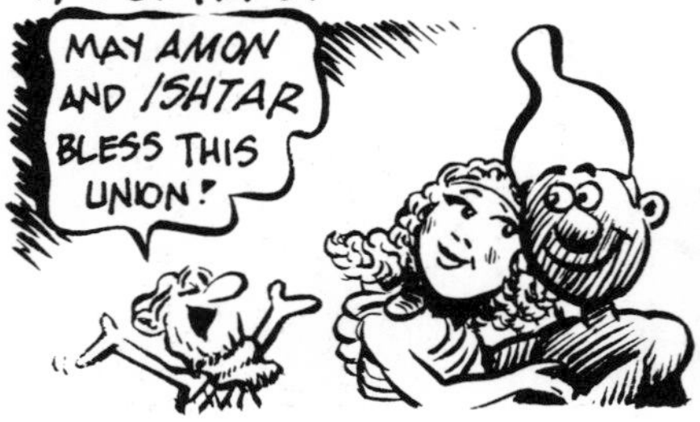

MAY *AMON* AND *ISHTAR* BLESS THIS UNION!

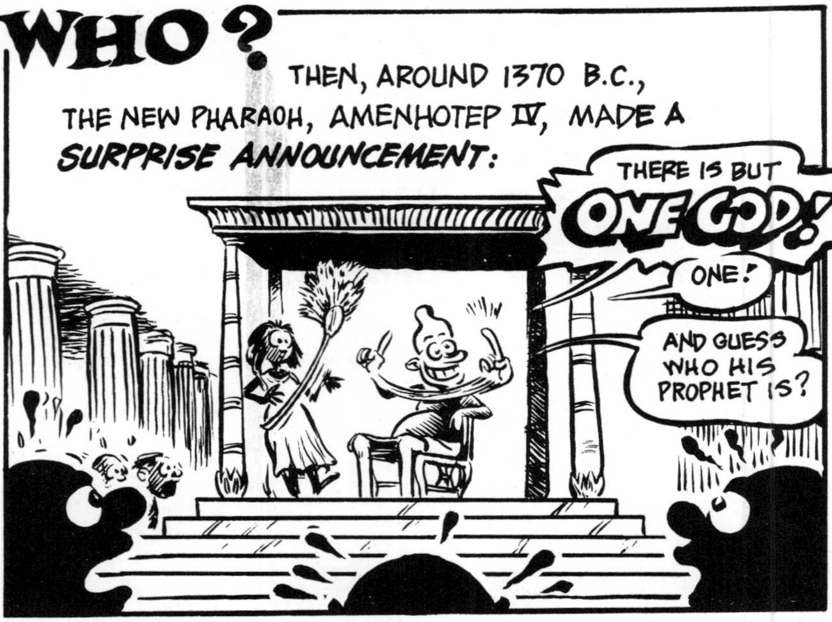

THEN, AROUND 1370 B.C., THE NEW PHARAOH, AMENHOTEP IV, MADE A ***SURPRISE ANNOUNCEMENT***:
THERE IS BUT **ONE GOD!**
ONE!
AND GUESS WHO HIS PROPHET IS?

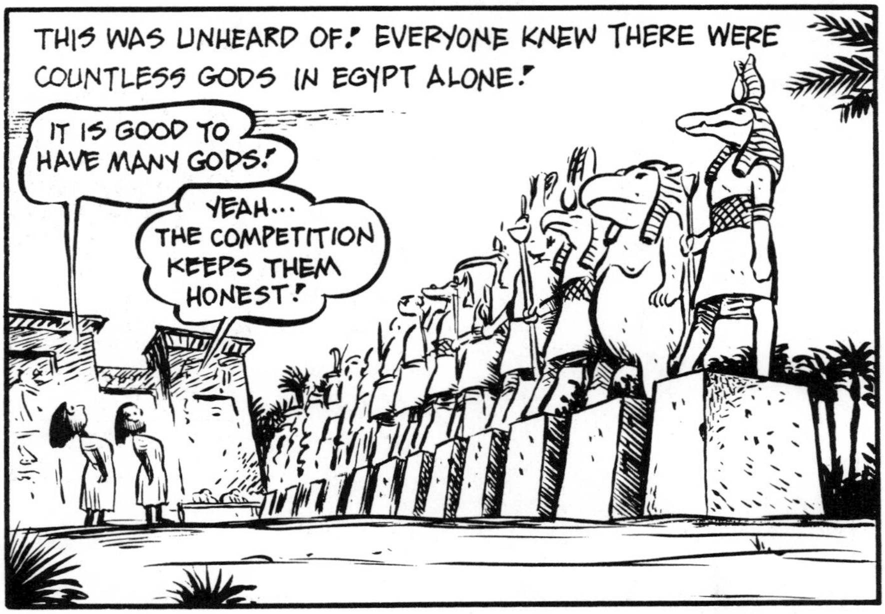

THIS WAS UNHEARD OF! EVERYONE KNEW THERE WERE COUNTLESS GODS IN EGYPT ALONE!
IT IS GOOD TO HAVE MANY GODS!
YEAH... THE COMPETITION KEEPS THEM HONEST!

WHEN AHMOSE I HAD FIRST CONQUERED THE EMPIRE, HOWEVER, HE HAD PUT ALL GODS UNDER THE TEMPLE OF ***AMON***, A THEBAN DEITY. SUBSIDIZED BY THE KINGS, AMON'S TEMPLES GREW RICH, AND HIS PRIESTS INVENTED NEW WAYS TO MAKE THEM ***RICHER***, LIKE SELLING FAVORS IN THE AFTERLIFE...

FOR A GOOD SHOW THEY EVEN HAD STATUES OF AMON, OPERATED BY HIDDEN GIZMOS, WHICH ***MOVED*** AND ***SPOKE***. PERHAPS SUCH FRAUDS DISGUSTED THE NEW PHARAOH.

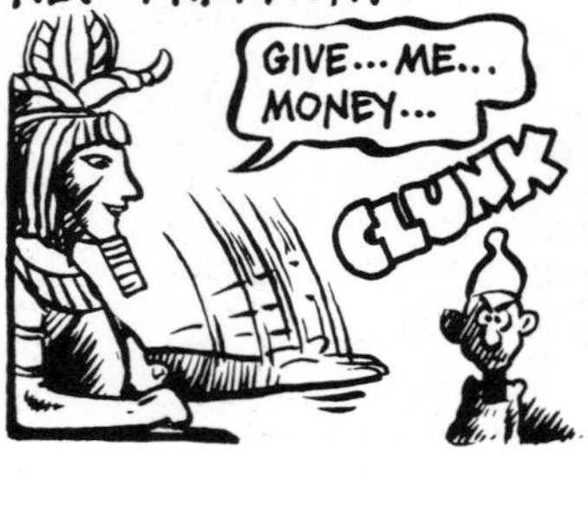

GIVE... ME... MONEY...
CLUNK

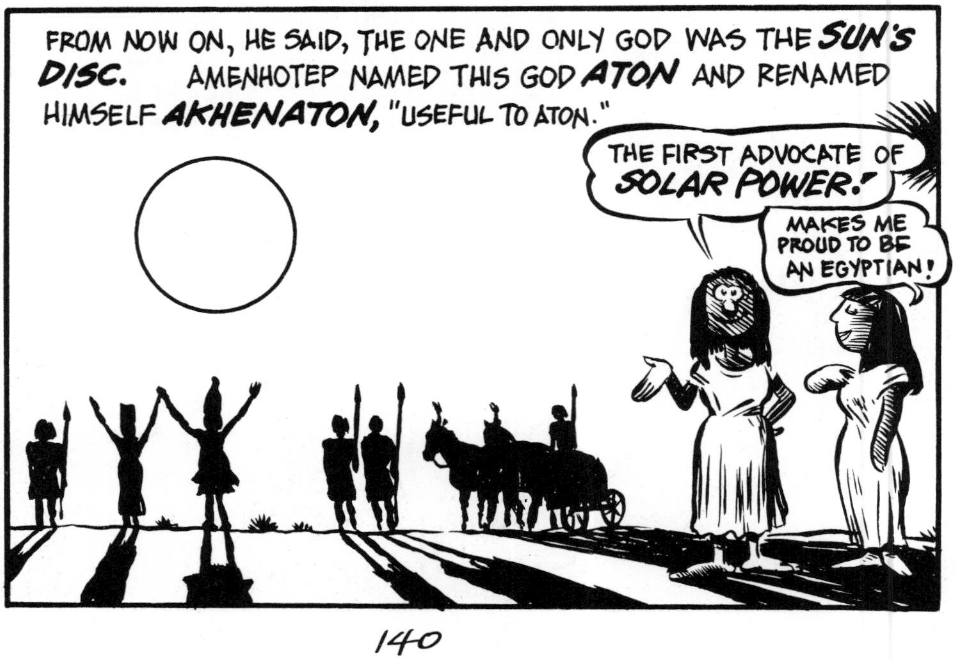

FROM NOW ON, HE SAID, THE ONE AND ONLY GOD WAS THE ***SUN'S DISC***. AMENHOTEP NAMED THIS GOD ***ATON*** AND RENAMED HIMSELF ***AKHENATON***, "USEFUL TO ATON."
THE FIRST ADVOCATE OF ***SOLAR POWER!***
MAKES ME PROUD TO BE AN EGYPTIAN!

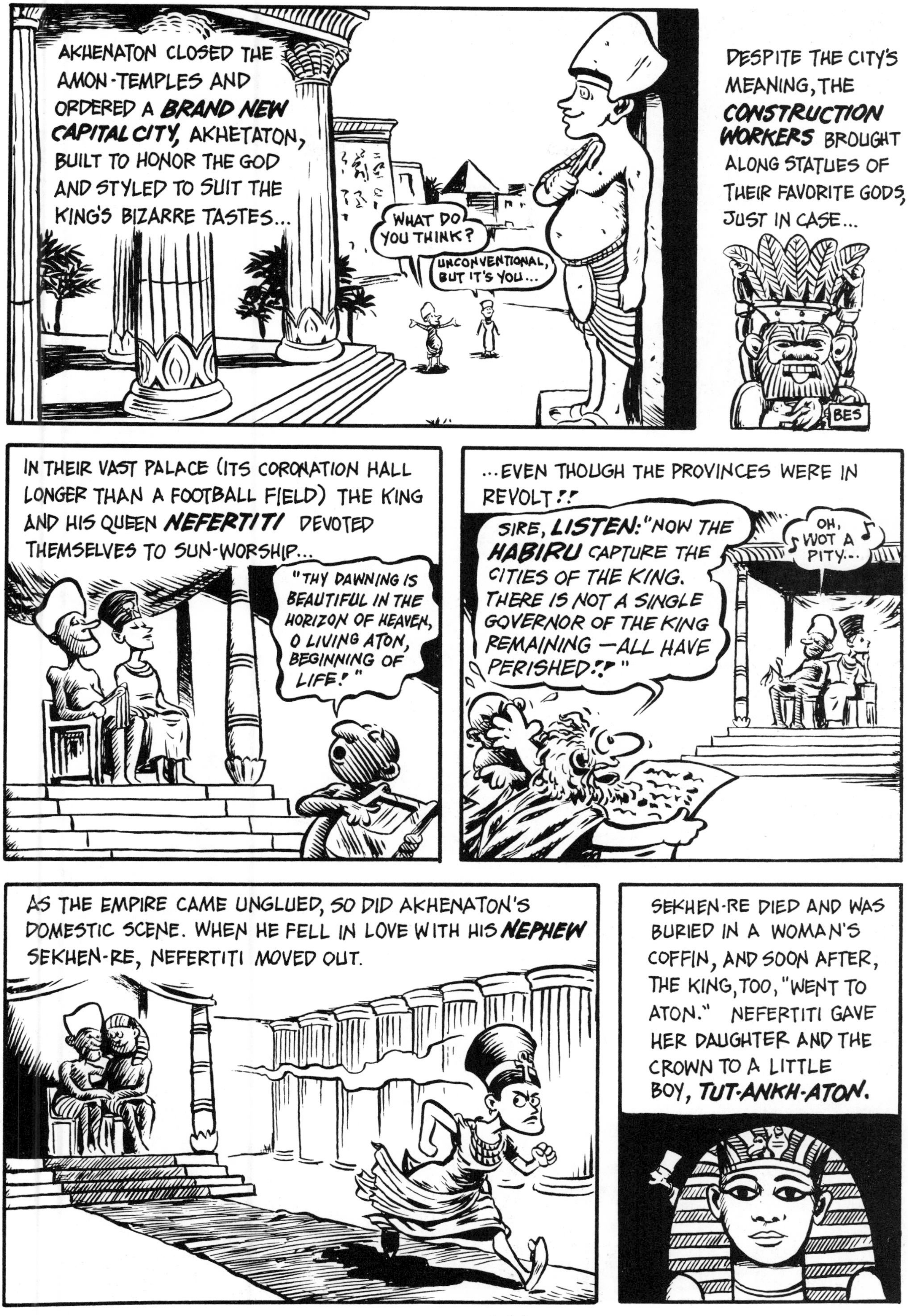
AKHENATON CLOSED THE AMON-TEMPLES AND ORDERED A **BRAND NEW CAPITAL CITY,** AKHETATON, BUILT TO HONOR THE GOD AND STYLED TO SUIT THE KING'S BIZARRE TASTES...
WHAT DO YOU THINK?
UNCONVENTIONAL, BUT IT'S YOU...
DESPITE THE CITY'S MEANING, THE **CONSTRUCTION WORKERS** BROUGHT ALONG STATUES OF THEIR FAVORITE GODS, JUST IN CASE...
BES
IN THEIR VAST PALACE (ITS CORONATION HALL LONGER THAN A FOOTBALL FIELD) THE KING AND HIS QUEEN ***NEFERTITI*** DEVOTED THEMSELVES TO SUN-WORSHIP...
"THY DAWNING IS BEAUTIFUL IN THE HORIZON OF HEAVEN, O LIVING ATON, BEGINNING OF LIFE!"
...EVEN THOUGH THE PROVINCES WERE IN REVOLT!!
SIRE, **LISTEN:** "NOW THE ***HABIRU*** CAPTURE THE CITIES OF THE KING. THERE IS NOT A SINGLE GOVERNOR OF THE KING REMAINING — ALL HAVE PERISHED!!"
♪ OH, WOT A PITY... ♪
AS THE EMPIRE CAME UNGLUED, SO DID AKHENATON'S DOMESTIC SCENE. WHEN HE FELL IN LOVE WITH HIS ***NEPHEW*** SEKHEN-RE, NEFERTITI MOVED OUT.
SEKHEN-RE DIED AND WAS BURIED IN A WOMAN'S COFFIN, AND SOON AFTER, THE KING, TOO, "WENT TO ATON." NEFERTITI GAVE HER DAUGHTER AND THE CROWN TO A LITTLE BOY, **TUT-ANKH-ATON.**

THE FAMOUS BOY-KING BECAME A PAWN OF THE OLD GUARD, AND **AMON** WAS RESTORED.

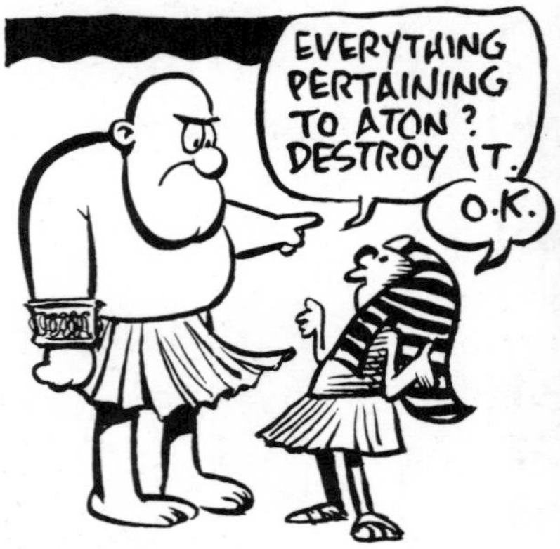
EVERYTHING PERTAINING TO ATON? DESTROY IT.
O.K.

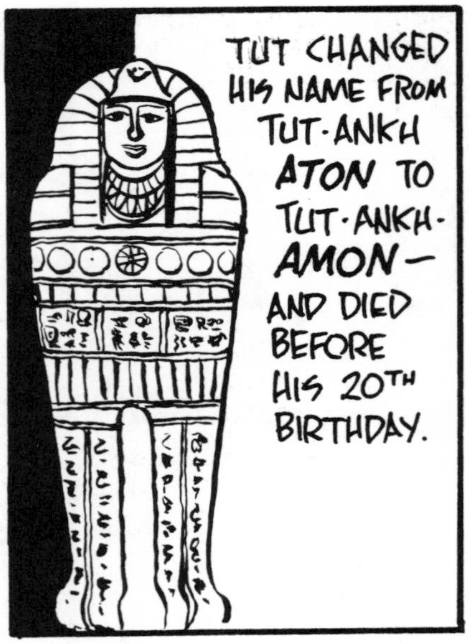
TUT CHANGED HIS NAME FROM TUT-ANKH **ATON** TO TUT-ANKH-**AMON**— AND DIED BEFORE HIS 20TH BIRTHDAY.

THEN, AN AMAZING THING—TUT'S WIDOW, QUEEN ***ANKH-ESEN-AMON***, SECRETLY WROTE TO THE HITTITE KING ***SHUBILULLIAMA***, OFFERING TO MARRY ONE OF HIS SONS, MAKING A ***HITTITE PHARAOH***. DOESN'T THIS HINT THAT ONE OF ANKH'S PARENTS, NEFERTITI, OR AKHENATON, MAY HAVE BEEN HITTITE... THAT THE ATON RELIGION WAS A WAY OF RECONCILING THE GODS OF TWO EMPIRES???

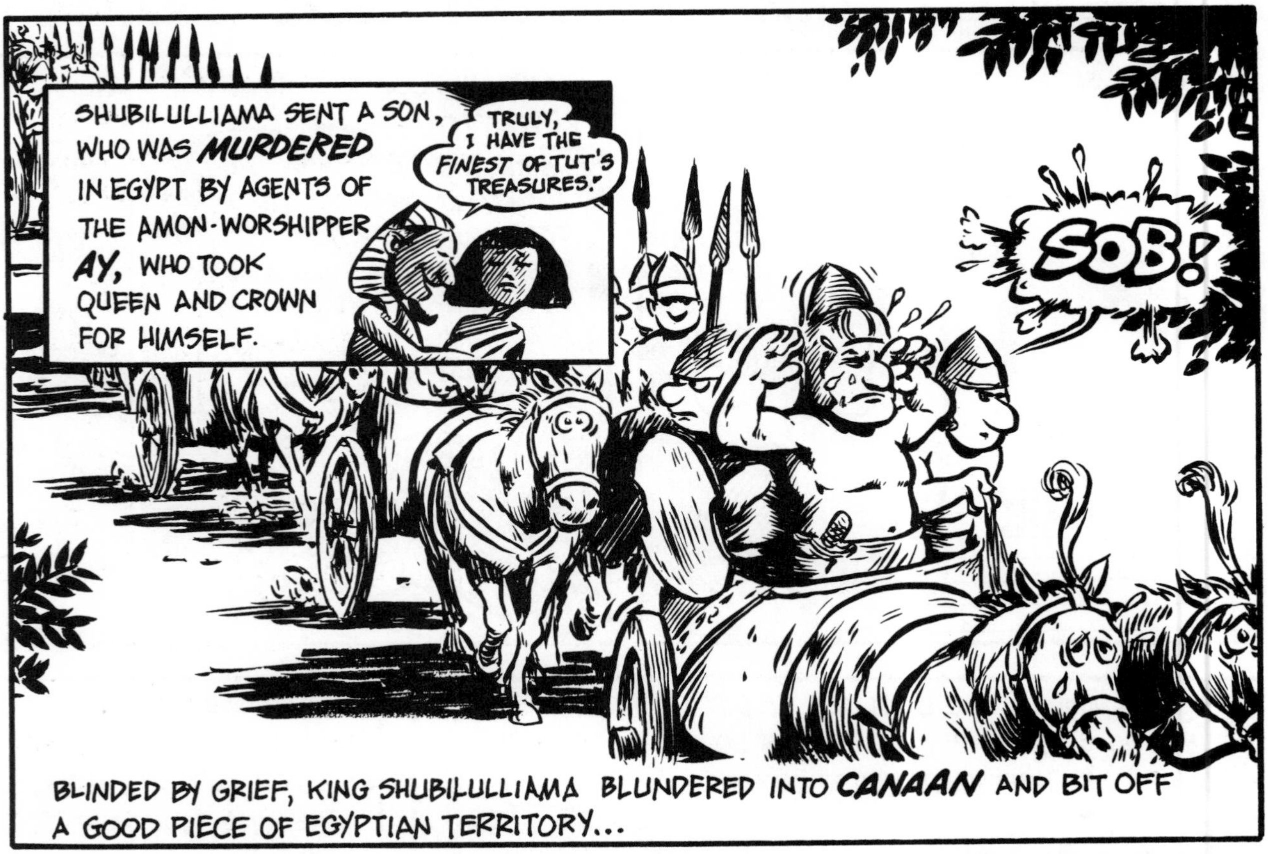
SHUBILULLIAMA SENT A SON, WHO WAS ***MURDERED*** IN EGYPT BY AGENTS OF THE AMON-WORSHIPPER ***AY,*** WHO TOOK QUEEN AND CROWN FOR HIMSELF.
TRULY, I HAVE THE ***FINEST*** OF TUT'S TREASURES!
SOB!
BLINDED BY GRIEF, KING SHUBILULLIAMA BLUNDERED INTO ***CANAAN*** AND BIT OFF A GOOD PIECE OF EGYPTIAN TERRITORY...

WHILE THE PHARAOHS WORSHIPPED THE SUN, EGYPTIAN COMMONERS PREFERRED THE CULT OF ***OSIRIS***. ACCORDING TO LEGEND, KING OSIRIS WAS CUT TO BITS BY HIS UGLY BROTHER ***SET***. OSIRIS' WIDOW ***ISIS*** FOUND ALL THE PIECES EXCEPT THE GENITALS (WHICH A FISH HAD EATEN) AND MAGICALLY RESTORED OSIRIS TO LIFE. DESPITE THE MISSING ITEM, ISIS SOMEHOW CONCEIVED A SON ***HORUS***, WHO AVENGED THE MURDER.

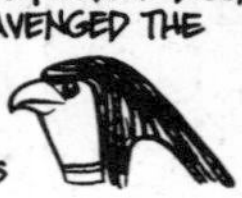
HORUS

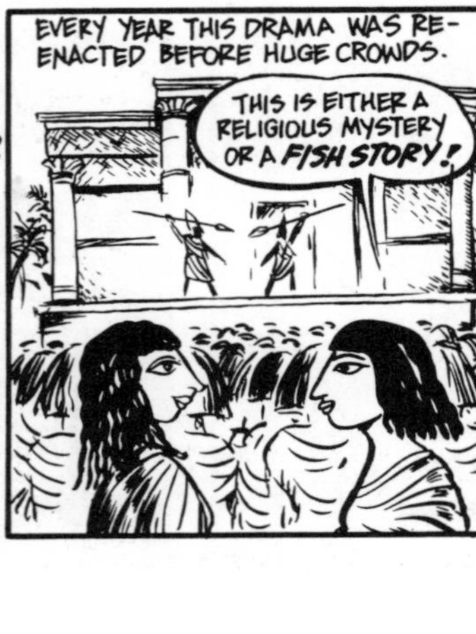
EVERY YEAR THIS DRAMA WAS RE-ENACTED BEFORE HUGE CROWDS.
THIS IS EITHER A RELIGIOUS MYSTERY OR A ***FISH STORY!***

OSIRIS BECAME ***JUDGE OF THE DEAD***. IF THE DEAD ONE'S SOUL WAS PURE ENOUGH, IT SURVIVED TO LABOR IN OSIRIS' FIELDS, AND IF NOT, IT WAS ***EATEN*** BY A HIDEOUS DEMON. (SOME CHOICE!)

THIS IS THE FIRST KNOWN USE OF THE ***AFTERLIFE*** AS A REWARD FOR ***GOOD BEHAVIOR***...

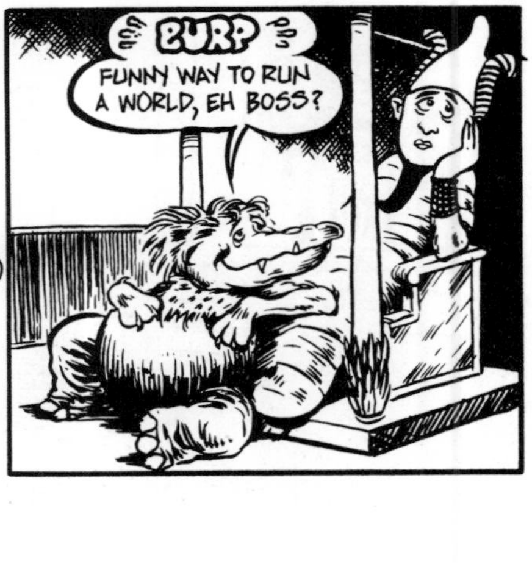
BURP
FUNNY WAY TO RUN A WORLD, EH BOSS?

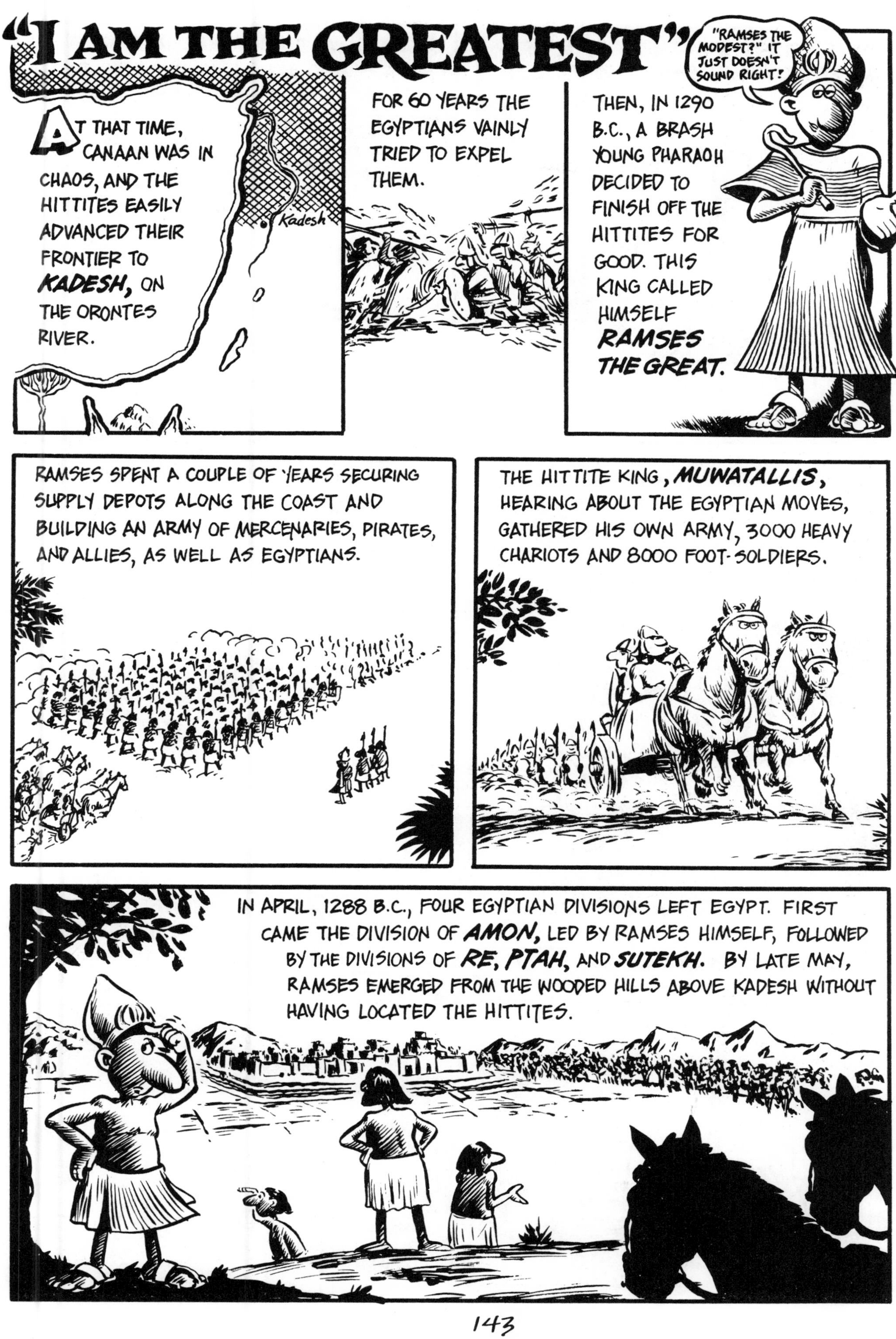
"I AM THE GREATEST"
"RAMSES THE MODEST?" IT JUST DOESN'T SOUND RIGHT!
AT THAT TIME, CANAAN WAS IN CHAOS, AND THE HITTITES EASILY ADVANCED THEIR FRONTIER TO KADESH, ON THE ORONTES RIVER.
Kadesh
FOR 60 YEARS THE EGYPTIANS VAINLY TRIED TO EXPEL THEM.
THEN, IN 1290 B.C., A BRASH YOUNG PHARAOH DECIDED TO FINISH OFF THE HITTITES FOR GOOD. THIS KING CALLED HIMSELF RAMSES THE GREAT.
RAMSES SPENT A COUPLE OF YEARS SECURING SUPPLY DEPOTS ALONG THE COAST AND BUILDING AN ARMY OF MERCENARIES, PIRATES, AND ALLIES, AS WELL AS EGYPTIANS.
THE HITTITE KING, MUWATALLIS, HEARING ABOUT THE EGYPTIAN MOVES, GATHERED HIS OWN ARMY, 3000 HEAVY CHARIOTS AND 8000 FOOT-SOLDIERS.
IN APRIL, 1288 B.C., FOUR EGYPTIAN DIVISIONS LEFT EGYPT. FIRST CAME THE DIVISION OF AMON, LED BY RAMSES HIMSELF, FOLLOWED BY THE DIVISIONS OF RE, PTAH, AND SUTEKH. BY LATE MAY, RAMSES EMERGED FROM THE WOODED HILLS ABOVE KADESH WITHOUT HAVING LOCATED THE HITTITES.

AS IT HAPPENED, MUWATALLIS' HORSES AND MEN WERE *RIGHT BEHIND THE CITY.*

PHARAOH WAS FURTHER FOOLED BY SOME NOMADS WHO WERE FRIENDLY WITH THE FOE.

HITTITES? NEVER HEARD OF 'EM!!

WHATEVER THEY ARE, THEY SURELY AREN'T HIDING RIGHT BEHIND THE CITY AT THIS VERY MOMENT!

GREAT! ALMOST AS GREAT AS RAMSES HIMSELF!

ALTHOUGH THEY'D BEEN MARCHING ALL DAY, RAMSES AND THE *AMON* DIVISION HURRIED ON TOWARD KADESH, LEAVING THE REST OF THE ARMY BEHIND.

SIRE, IS THIS WISE?

SILENCE! *INTUITION* IS ONE OF RAMSES' *GREATEST* QUALITIES!

AS THE COLUMN ADVANCED, THE HITTITES CIRCLED AROUND KADESH, KEEPING THE CITY BETWEEN THEMSELVES AND THE EGYPTIANS.

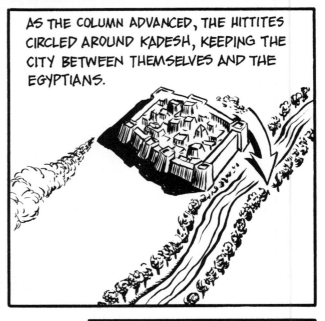

EVEN WHEN RAMSES REACHED THE WALLS, HE STILL HAD NO IDEA HIS ENEMY HAD BEEN THERE, THOUGH THERE *MUST* HAVE BEEN *EVIDENCE.*

≷SNIF≷ THIS SMELLS LIKE A GOOD PLACE TO MAKE CAMP!

AS THE HITTITES MASSED FOR THE ATTACK, THE DIVISION OF AMON WAS MAKING CAMP, AND THE DIVISION OF *RE* WAS STRAGGLING UP THE ROAD BEHIND.

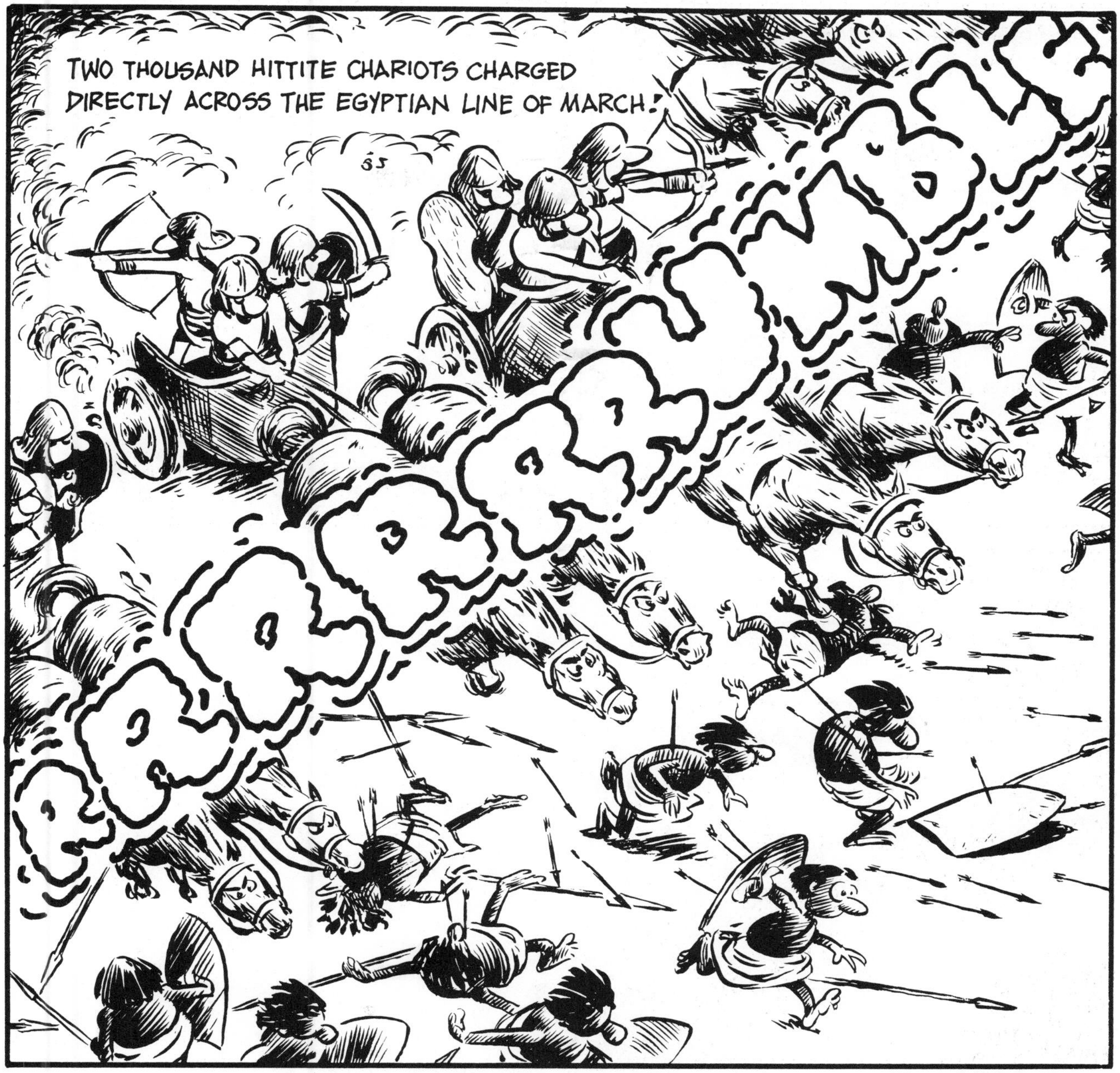
TWO THOUSAND HITTITE CHARIOTS CHARGED DIRECTLY ACROSS THE EGYPTIAN LINE OF MARCH!
RRRRRRUMBLE

AFTER CHOPPING THE DIVISION OF RE TO BITS, THE HITTITES SURROUNDED THE CAMP OF RAMSES, WHO FINALLY REALIZED WHAT WAS HAPPENING!

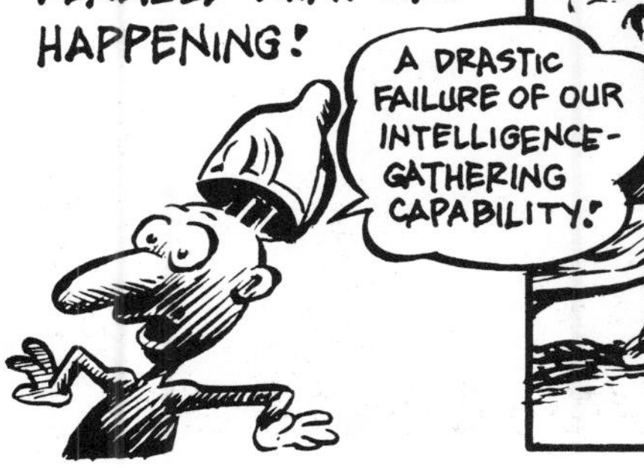
A DRASTIC FAILURE OF OUR INTELLIGENCE-GATHERING CAPABILITY!

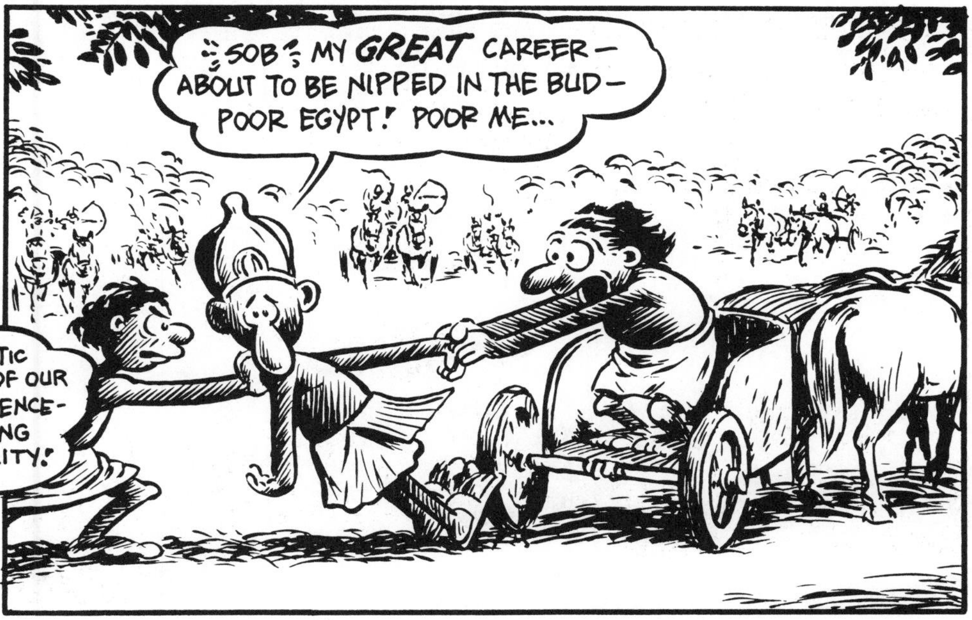
SOB MY GREAT CAREER— ABOUT TO BE NIPPED IN THE BUD— POOR EGYPT! POOR ME...

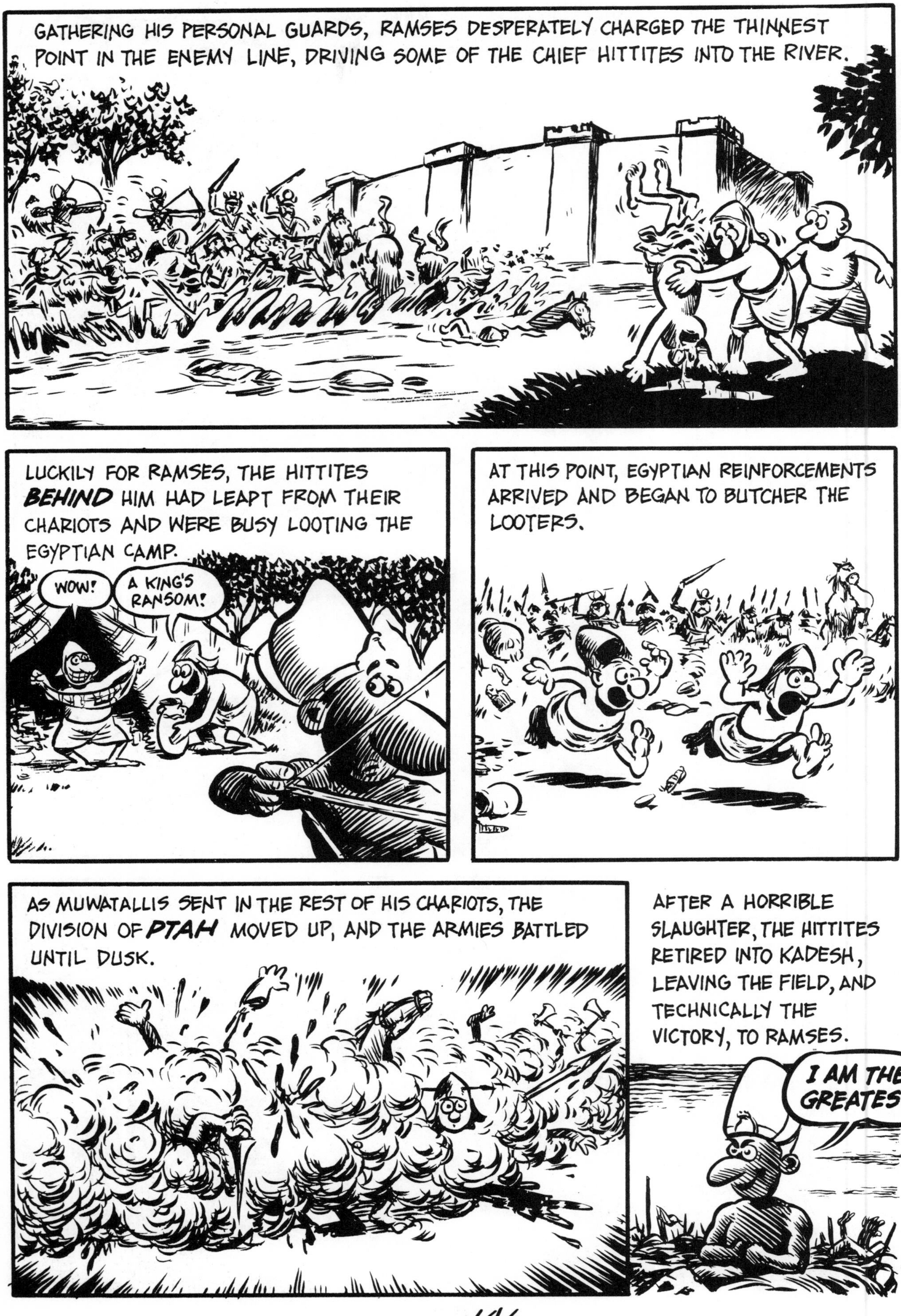
GATHERING HIS PERSONAL GUARDS, RAMSES DESPERATELY CHARGED THE THINNEST POINT IN THE ENEMY LINE, DRIVING SOME OF THE CHIEF HITTITES INTO THE RIVER.
LUCKILY FOR RAMSES, THE HITTITES BEHIND HIM HAD LEAPT FROM THEIR CHARIOTS AND WERE BUSY LOOTING THE EGYPTIAN CAMP.
WOW!
A KING'S RANSOM!
AT THIS POINT, EGYPTIAN REINFORCEMENTS ARRIVED AND BEGAN TO BUTCHER THE LOOTERS.
AS MUWATALLIS SENT IN THE REST OF HIS CHARIOTS, THE DIVISION OF PTAH MOVED UP, AND THE ARMIES BATTLED UNTIL DUSK.
AFTER A HORRIBLE SLAUGHTER, THE HITTITES RETIRED INTO KADESH, LEAVING THE FIELD, AND TECHNICALLY THE VICTORY, TO RAMSES.
I AM THE GREATEST!

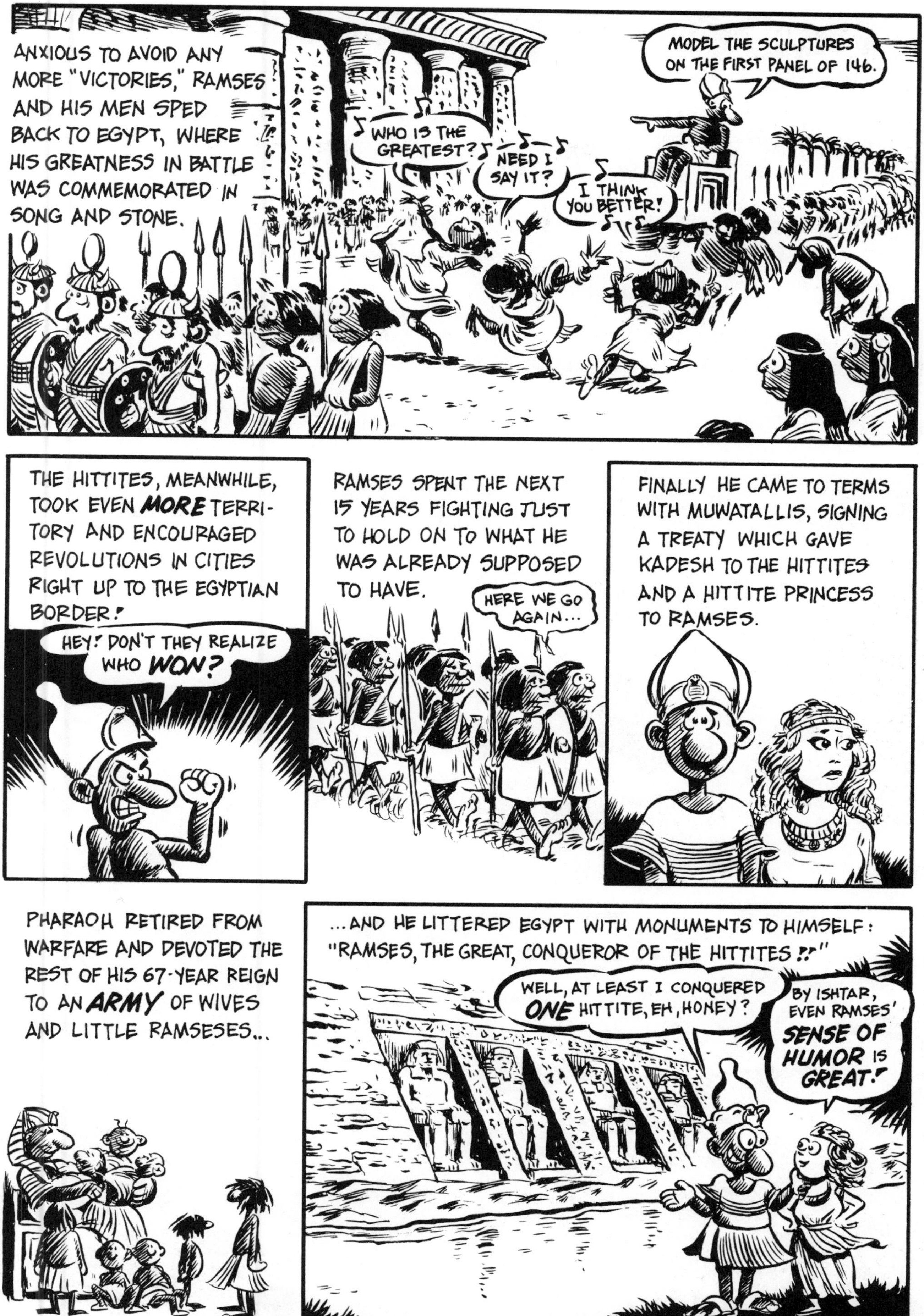
ANXIOUS TO AVOID ANY MORE "VICTORIES," RAMSES AND HIS MEN SPED BACK TO EGYPT, WHERE HIS GREATNESS IN BATTLE WAS COMMEMORATED IN SONG AND STONE.
WHO IS THE GREATEST?
NEED I SAY IT?
I THINK YOU BETTER!
MODEL THE SCULPTURES ON THE FIRST PANEL OF 146.
THE HITTITES, MEANWHILE, TOOK EVEN MORE TERRITORY AND ENCOURAGED REVOLUTIONS IN CITIES RIGHT UP TO THE EGYPTIAN BORDER!
HEY! DON'T THEY REALIZE WHO WON?
RAMSES SPENT THE NEXT 15 YEARS FIGHTING JUST TO HOLD ON TO WHAT HE WAS ALREADY SUPPOSED TO HAVE.
HERE WE GO AGAIN...
FINALLY HE CAME TO TERMS WITH MUWATALLIS, SIGNING A TREATY WHICH GAVE KADESH TO THE HITTITES AND A HITTITE PRINCESS TO RAMSES.
PHARAOH RETIRED FROM WARFARE AND DEVOTED THE REST OF HIS 67-YEAR REIGN TO AN ARMY OF WIVES AND LITTLE RAMSESES...
...AND HE LITTERED EGYPT WITH MONUMENTS TO HIMSELF: "RAMSES, THE GREAT, CONQUEROR OF THE HITTITES!!"
WELL, AT LEAST I CONQUERED ONE HITTITE, EH, HONEY?
BY ISHTAR, EVEN RAMSES' SENSE OF HUMOR IS GREAT!

1200 B.C., OR SO, BEGAN A DARK AGE FOR THE MEDITERRANEAN WORLD.

WITH THE DEATH OF RAMSES IN 1225, THE PHARAOHS RETREATED FROM INTERNATIONAL POLITICS INTO SPLENDID SELF-ABSORPTION. WITHIN 300 YEARS, EGYPT FELL TO FOREIGN RULE. (THESE DECLINES CAN TAKE TIME!)

BEYOND THE EUPHRATES, THE MITANNI WERE UNDER ATTACK BY AN UPSTART KINGDOM CALLED ***ASSYRIA***, AND THE MULTI-SIDED STRUGGLE FOR POWER CONTINUED AS USUAL.

THE HITTITE EMPIRE, WEAKENED BY FIGHTING WITH EGYPT, COLLAPSED WITHIN 50 YEARS OF THE PEACE TREATY, AS HOSTILE TRIBES ATTACKED FROM ALL SIDES AT ONCE.

TO THE WEST, THE GREEKS WERE BESEIGING THE CITY OF ***TROY*** IN A LONG WAR THAT WOULD SEND REFUGEES SAILING ALL OVER THE MEDITERRANEAN.

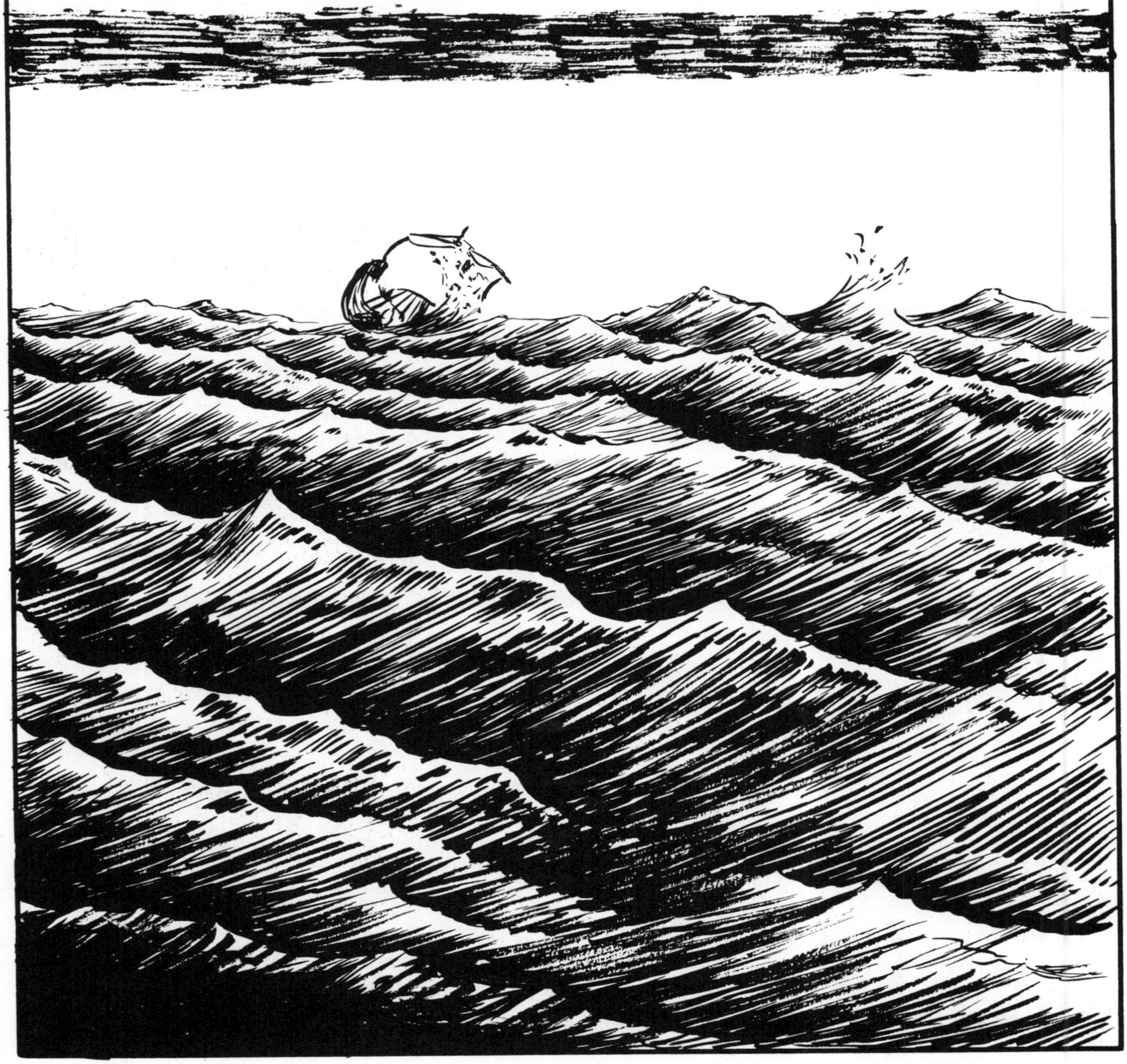

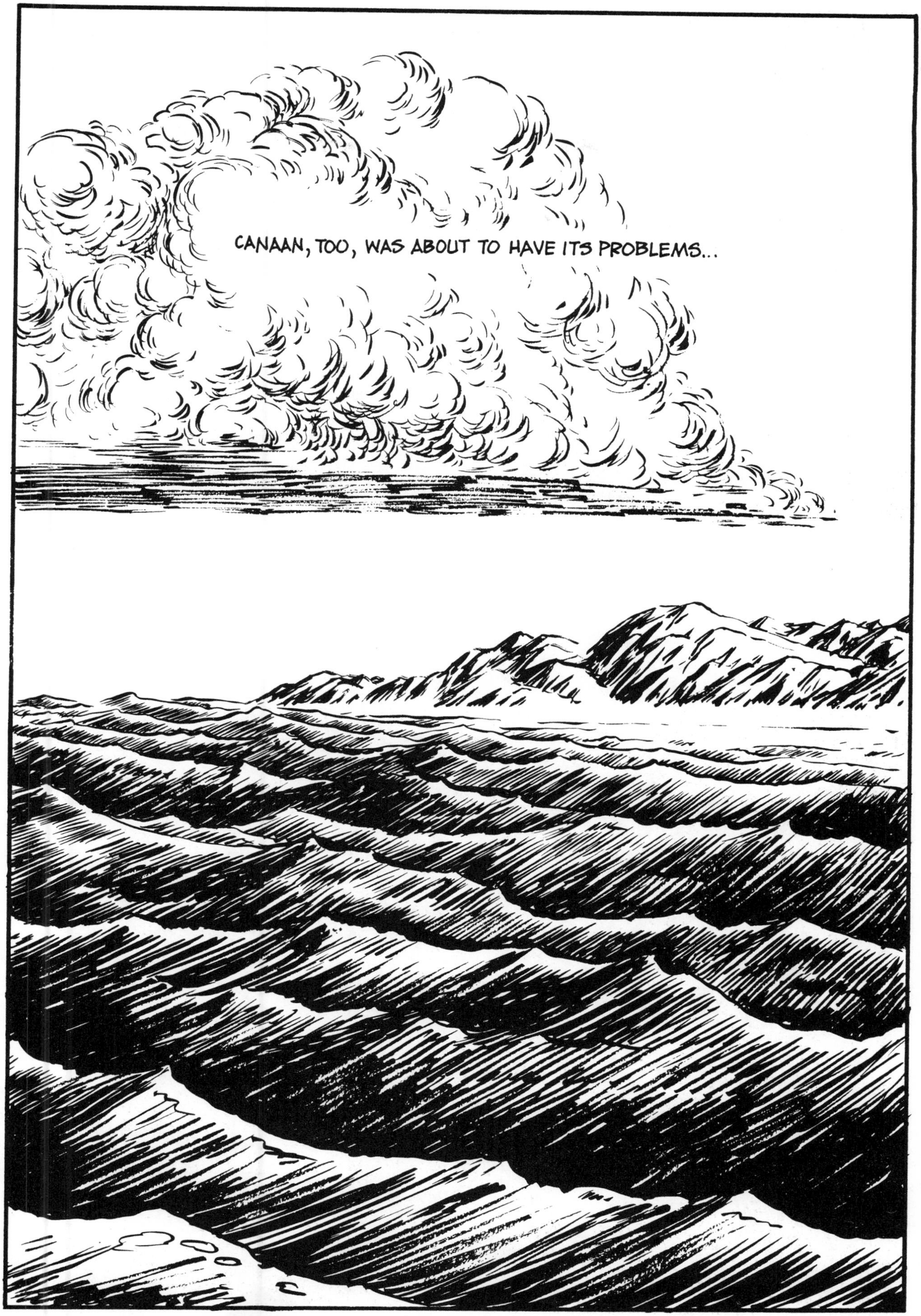
CANAAN, TOO, WAS ABOUT TO HAVE ITS PROBLEMS...

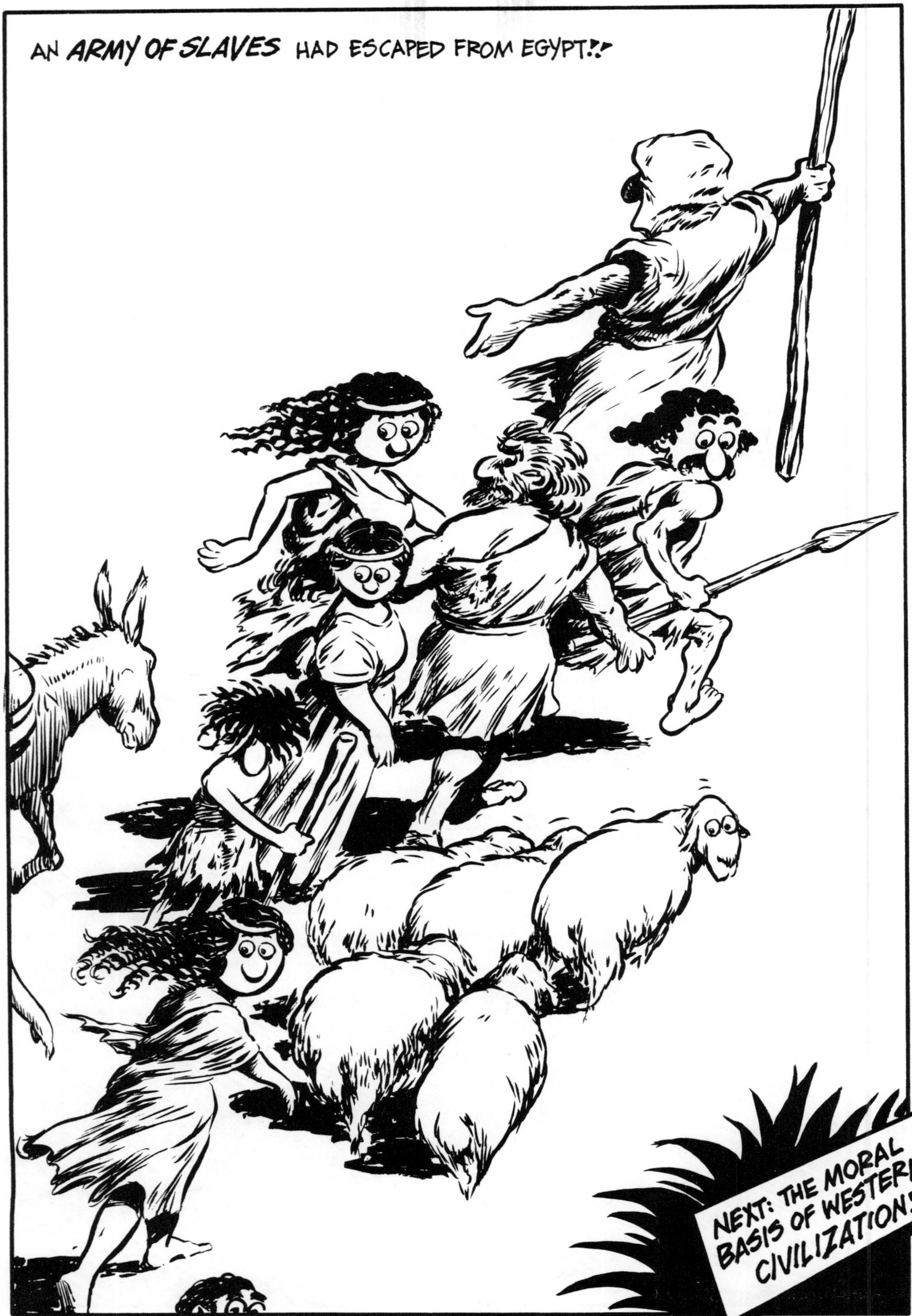

AN ARMY OF SLAVES HAD ESCAPED FROM EGYPT!!
NEXT: THE MORAL BASIS OF WESTERN CIVILIZATION!

IN THE LAST VOLUME, THE TIME MACHINE SHOWED US THE EARLY CIVILIZATIONS OF SUMER AND EGYPT, AND WE NOTED SOME NOMADS MOVING BACK AND FORTH BETWEEN THE TWO.

NOW WE'LL SEE WHAT HAPPENED TO THESE TRIBES WHEN THEY ESCAPED FROM EGYPT AND BEGAN TO WORSHIP A GOD WHO, DESPITE SOME EARLY SETBACKS, HAS HAD *QUITE* A SUCCESSFUL CAREER.

FAMILIAR AS THIS GOD IS, ODDLY ENOUGH, WE DON'T REALLY KNOW HIS *NAME.* THE HEBREW SCRIBES WROTE ONLY THE CONSONANTS: "YHWH," AND LATER THEY DECIDED THAT ANYONE WHO SPOKE THE WORD WOULD BE STRUCK BY *LIGHTNING* — SO WHO CAN SAY IF THEY CALLED HIM *YAHWEH, YEHOWAH,* OR EVEN *YAHU-WAHU?*

ZZOK

YAHU-WAHU?

≶MOAN≷ THE THINGS YOU GOTTA PUT UP WITH IN THIS BUSINESS...

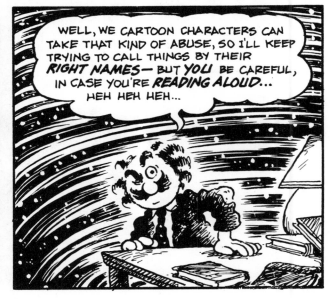

WELL, WE CARTOON CHARACTERS CAN TAKE THAT KIND OF ABUSE, SO I'LL KEEP TRYING TO CALL THINGS BY THEIR *RIGHT NAMES* — BUT *YOU* BE CAREFUL, IN CASE YOU'RE *READING ALOUD...* HEH HEH HEH...

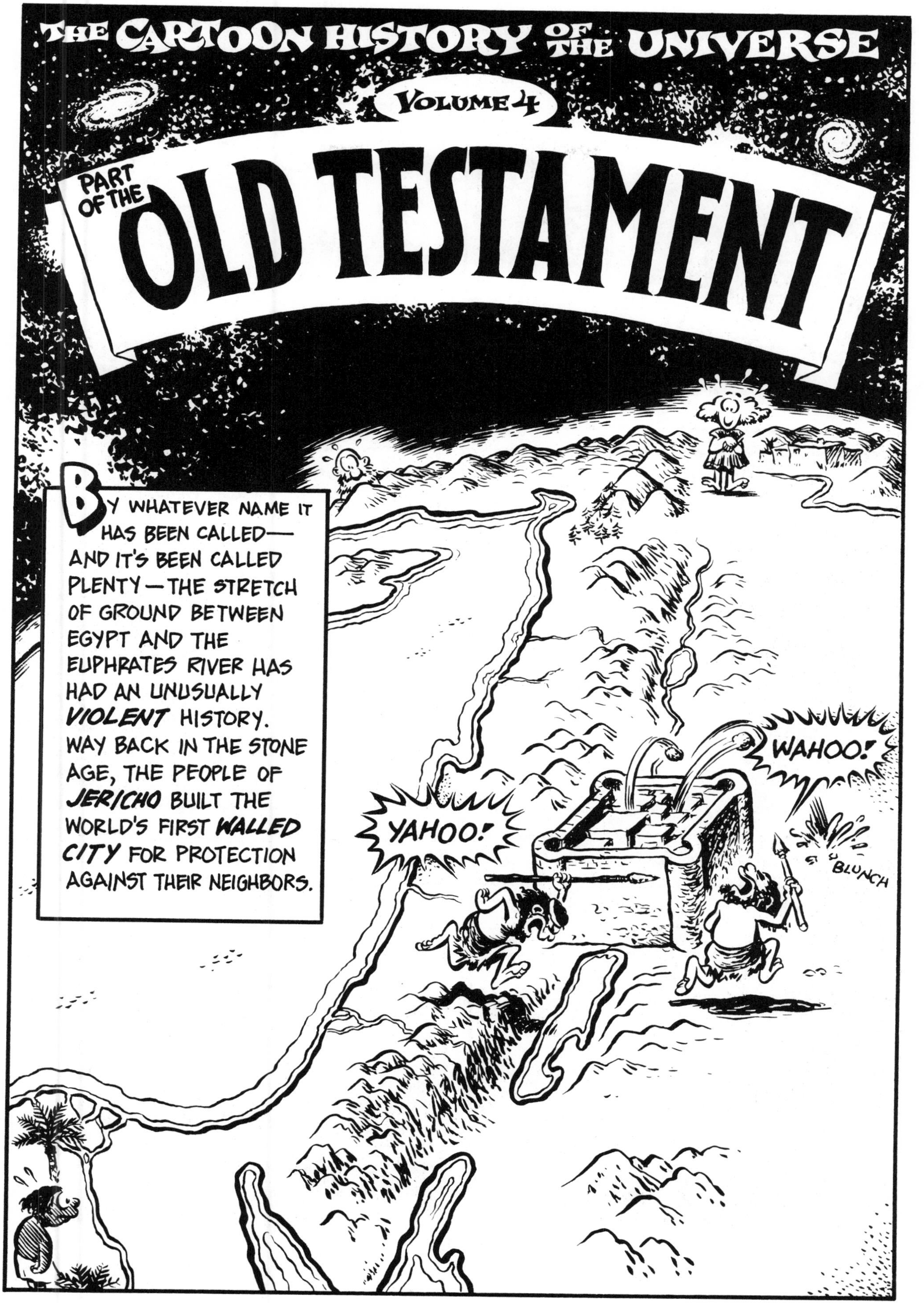
THE CARTOON HISTORY OF THE UNIVERSE
VOLUME 4
PART OF THE OLD TESTAMENT
BY WHATEVER NAME IT HAS BEEN CALLED— AND IT'S BEEN CALLED PLENTY—THE STRETCH OF GROUND BETWEEN EGYPT AND THE EUPHRATES RIVER HAS HAD AN UNUSUALLY VIOLENT HISTORY. WAY BACK IN THE STONE AGE, THE PEOPLE OF JERICHO BUILT THE WORLD'S FIRST WALLED CITY FOR PROTECTION AGAINST THEIR NEIGHBORS.
YAHOO!
WAHOO!
BLUNCH

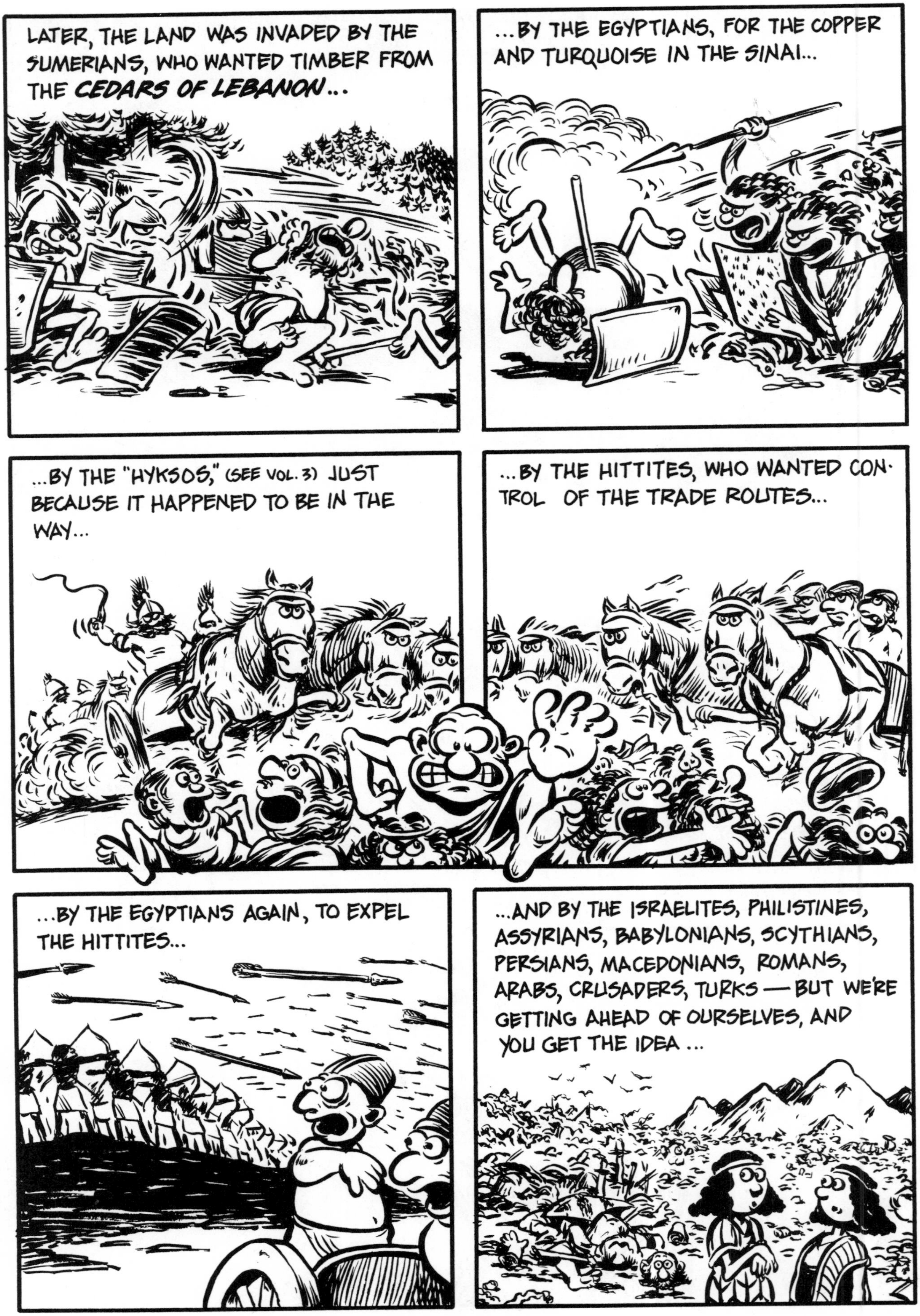
LATER, THE LAND WAS INVADED BY THE SUMERIANS, WHO WANTED TIMBER FROM THE ***CEDARS OF LEBANON***...
...BY THE EGYPTIANS, FOR THE COPPER AND TURQUOISE IN THE SINAI...
...BY THE "HYKSOS," (SEE VOL. 3) JUST BECAUSE IT HAPPENED TO BE IN THE WAY...
...BY THE HITTITES, WHO WANTED CONTROL OF THE TRADE ROUTES...
...BY THE EGYPTIANS AGAIN, TO EXPEL THE HITTITES...
...AND BY THE ISRAELITES, PHILISTINES, ASSYRIANS, BABYLONIANS, SCYTHIANS, PERSIANS, MACEDONIANS, ROMANS, ARABS, CRUSADERS, TURKS — BUT WE'RE GETTING AHEAD OF OURSELVES, AND YOU GET THE IDEA ...

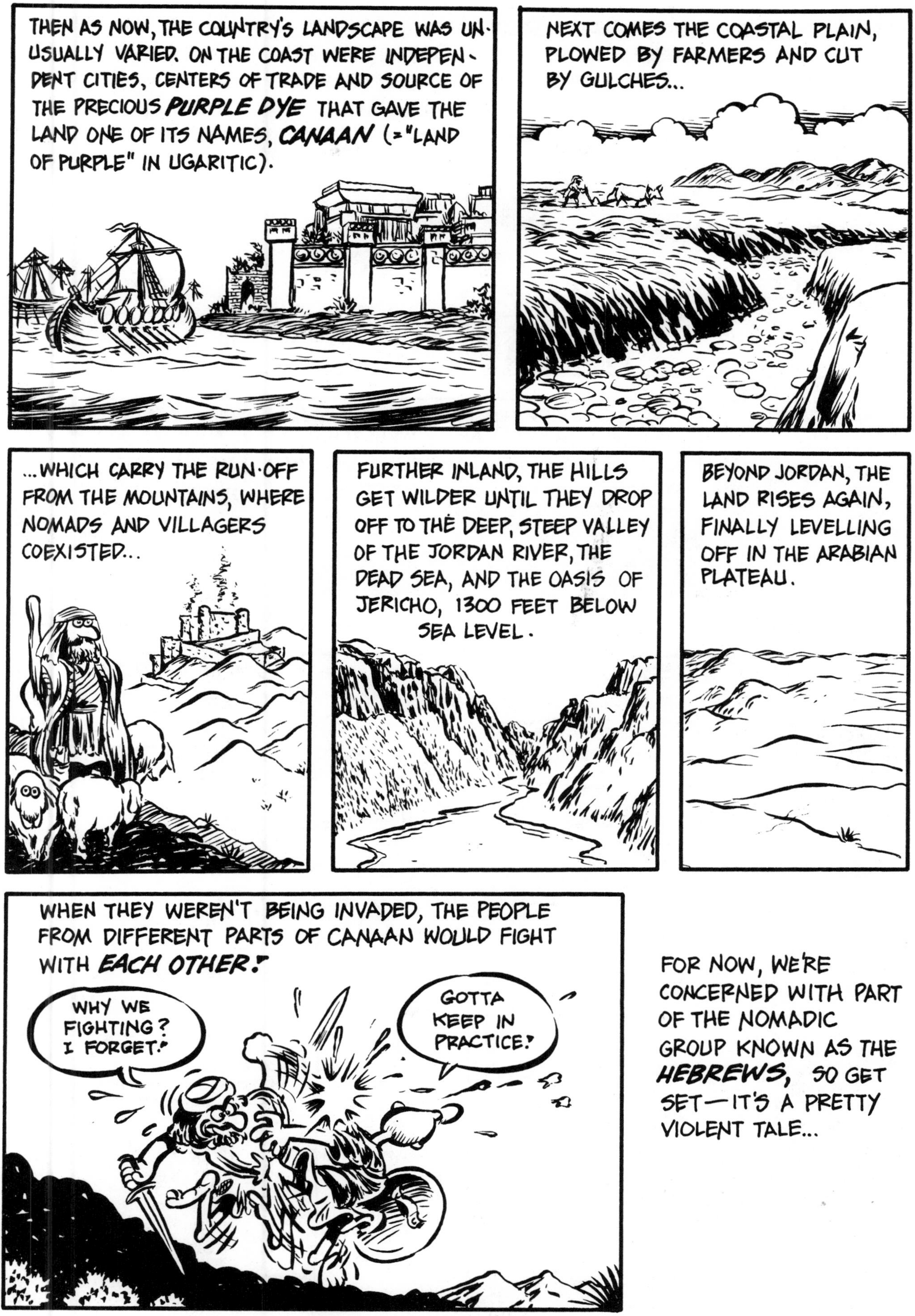
THEN AS NOW, THE COUNTRY'S LANDSCAPE WAS UNUSUALLY VARIED. ON THE COAST WERE INDEPENDENT CITIES, CENTERS OF TRADE AND SOURCE OF THE PRECIOUS PURPLE DYE THAT GAVE THE LAND ONE OF ITS NAMES, CANAAN (="LAND OF PURPLE" IN UGARITIC).
NEXT COMES THE COASTAL PLAIN, PLOWED BY FARMERS AND CUT BY GULCHES...
...WHICH CARRY THE RUN-OFF FROM THE MOUNTAINS, WHERE NOMADS AND VILLAGERS COEXISTED...
FURTHER INLAND, THE HILLS GET WILDER UNTIL THEY DROP OFF TO THE DEEP, STEEP VALLEY OF THE JORDAN RIVER, THE DEAD SEA, AND THE OASIS OF JERICHO, 1300 FEET BELOW SEA LEVEL.
BEYOND JORDAN, THE LAND RISES AGAIN, FINALLY LEVELLING OFF IN THE ARABIAN PLATEAU.
WHEN THEY WEREN'T BEING INVADED, THE PEOPLE FROM DIFFERENT PARTS OF CANAAN WOULD FIGHT WITH EACH OTHER!
WHY WE FIGHTING? I FORGET!
GOTTA KEEP IN PRACTICE!

FOR NOW, WE'RE CONCERNED WITH PART OF THE NOMADIC GROUP KNOWN AS THE **HEBREWS,** SO GET SET—IT'S A PRETTY VIOLENT TALE...

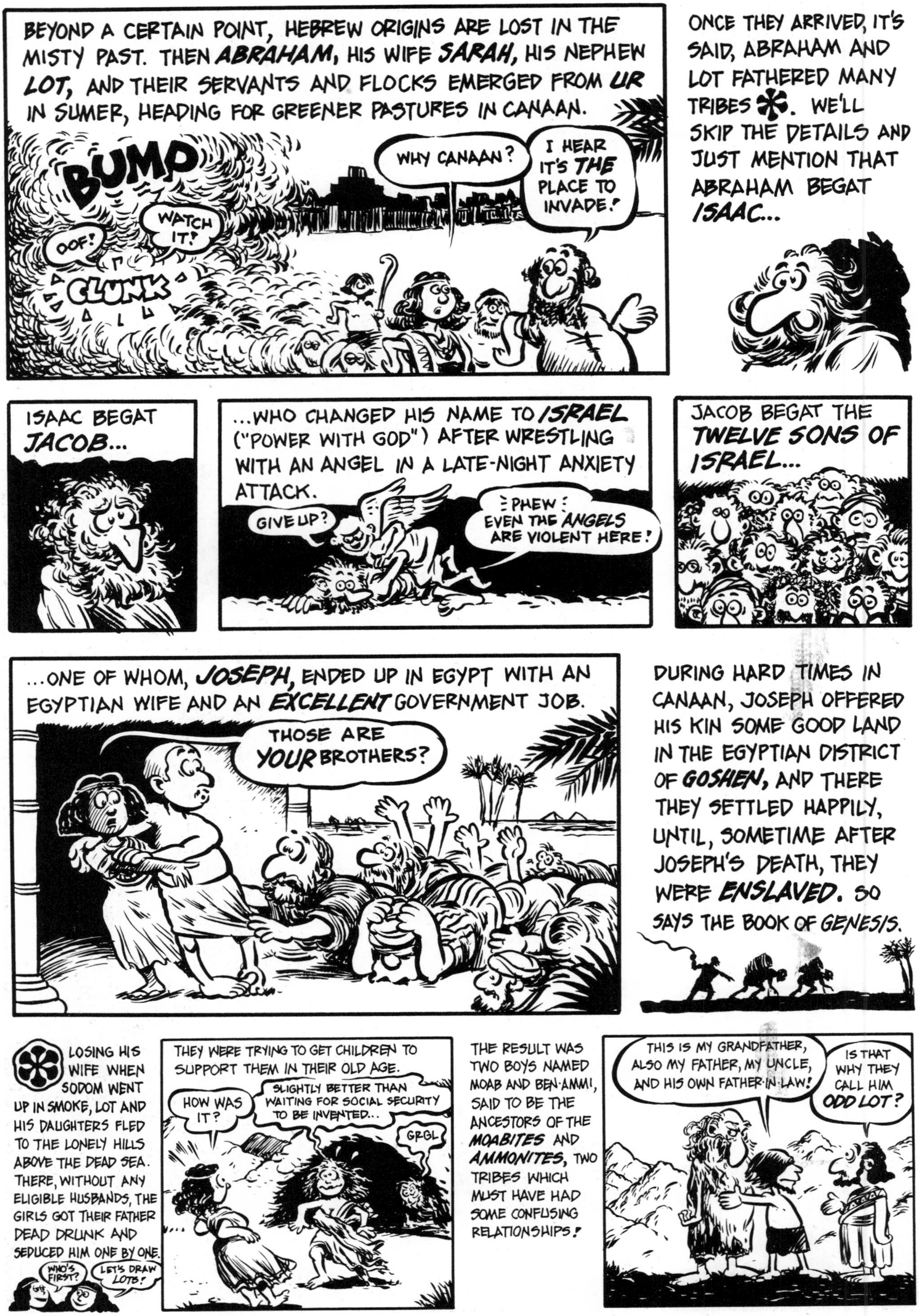
BEYOND A CERTAIN POINT, HEBREW ORIGINS ARE LOST IN THE MISTY PAST. THEN ABRAHAM, HIS WIFE SARAH, HIS NEPHEW LOT, AND THEIR SERVANTS AND FLOCKS EMERGED FROM UR IN SUMER, HEADING FOR GREENER PASTURES IN CANAAN.
BUMP
WATCH IT!
OOF!
CLUNK
WHY CANAAN?
I HEAR IT'S THE PLACE TO INVADE!
ONCE THEY ARRIVED, IT'S SAID, ABRAHAM AND LOT FATHERED MANY TRIBES ✻. WE'LL SKIP THE DETAILS AND JUST MENTION THAT ABRAHAM BEGAT ISAAC...
ISAAC BEGAT JACOB...
...WHO CHANGED HIS NAME TO ISRAEL ("POWER WITH GOD") AFTER WRESTLING WITH AN ANGEL IN A LATE-NIGHT ANXIETY ATTACK.
GIVE UP?
PHEW EVEN THE ANGELS ARE VIOLENT HERE!
JACOB BEGAT THE TWELVE SONS OF ISRAEL...
...ONE OF WHOM, JOSEPH, ENDED UP IN EGYPT WITH AN EGYPTIAN WIFE AND AN EXCELLENT GOVERNMENT JOB.
THOSE ARE YOUR BROTHERS?
DURING HARD TIMES IN CANAAN, JOSEPH OFFERED HIS KIN SOME GOOD LAND IN THE EGYPTIAN DISTRICT OF GOSHEN, AND THERE THEY SETTLED HAPPILY, UNTIL, SOMETIME AFTER JOSEPH'S DEATH, THEY WERE ENSLAVED. SO SAYS THE BOOK OF GENESIS.
✻ LOSING HIS WIFE WHEN SODOM WENT UP IN SMOKE, LOT AND HIS DAUGHTERS FLED TO THE LONELY HILLS ABOVE THE DEAD SEA. THERE, WITHOUT ANY ELIGIBLE HUSBANDS, THE GIRLS GOT THEIR FATHER DEAD DRUNK AND SEDUCED HIM ONE BY ONE.
WHO'S FIRST?
LET'S DRAW LOTS!
THEY WERE TRYING TO GET CHILDREN TO SUPPORT THEM IN THEIR OLD AGE.
HOW WAS IT?
SLIGHTLY BETTER THAN WAITING FOR SOCIAL SECURITY TO BE INVENTED...
GRGL
THE RESULT WAS TWO BOYS NAMED MOAB AND BEN-AMMI, SAID TO BE THE ANCESTORS OF THE MOABITES AND AMMONITES, TWO TRIBES WHICH MUST HAVE HAD SOME CONFUSING RELATIONSHIPS!
THIS IS MY GRANDFATHER, ALSO MY FATHER, MY UNCLE, AND HIS OWN FATHER-IN-LAW!
IS THAT WHY THEY CALL HIM ODD LOT?

DOUBLE EXODUS

A FEW THINGS THE BIBLE ***DOESN'T*** MENTION ALSO HELP TO UNDERSTAND MATTERS:

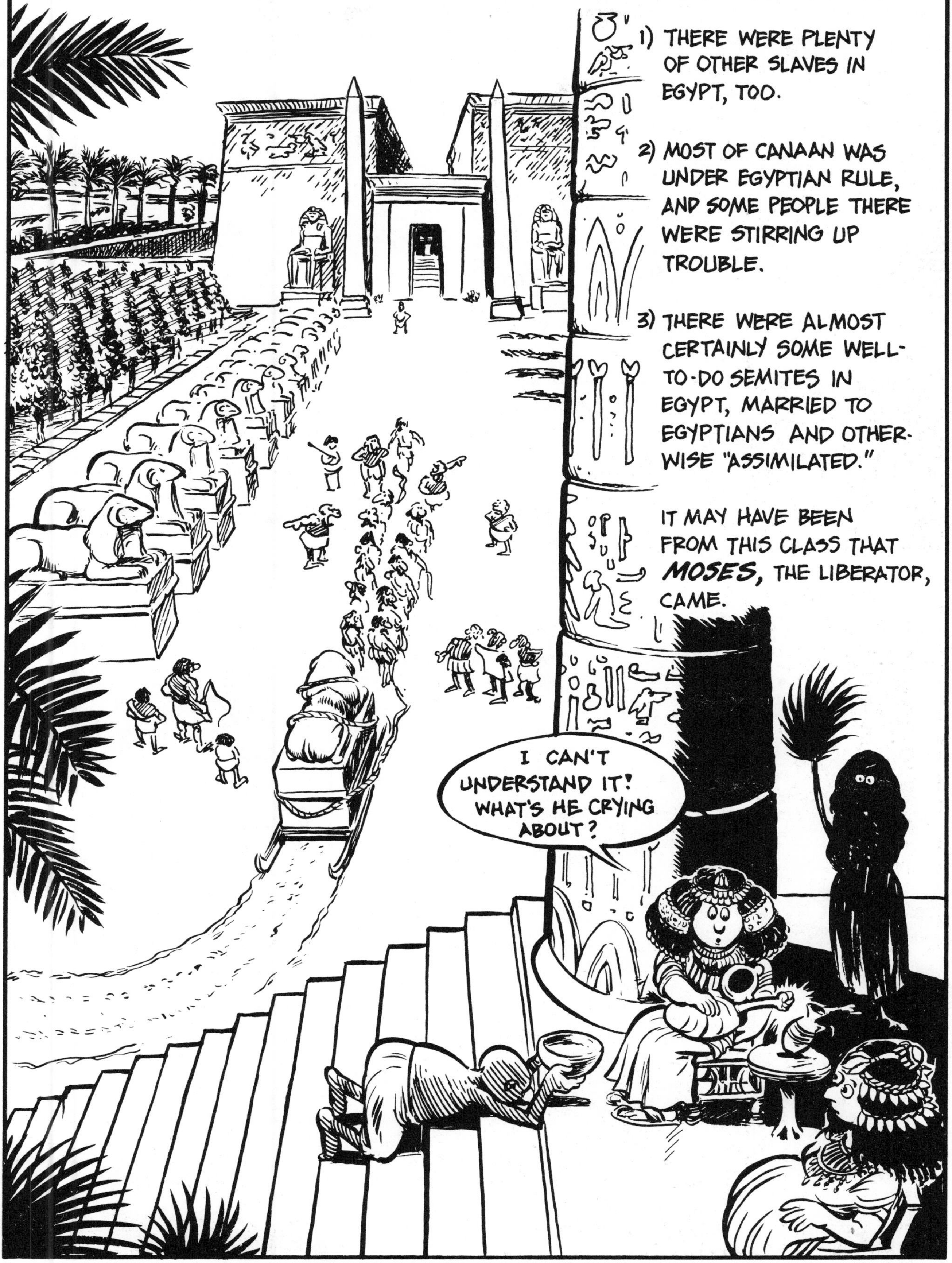

1) THERE WERE PLENTY OF OTHER SLAVES IN EGYPT, TOO.
2) MOST OF CANAAN WAS UNDER EGYPTIAN RULE, AND SOME PEOPLE THERE WERE STIRRING UP TROUBLE.
3) THERE WERE ALMOST CERTAINLY SOME WELL-TO-DO SEMITES IN EGYPT, MARRIED TO EGYPTIANS AND OTHERWISE "ASSIMILATED."
IT MAY HAVE BEEN FROM THIS CLASS THAT ***MOSES,*** THE LIBERATOR, CAME.
I CAN'T UNDERSTAND IT! WHAT'S HE CRYING ABOUT?

WE MAY WELL DOUBT THE STORY OF MOSES' BIRTH ✻, BUT THIS MUCH SEEMS CERTAIN: "MOSES" IS AN EGYPTIAN NAME; MOSES WAS RAISED IN COURT AS AN EGYPTIAN; AND HE MUST HAVE HAD FORMAL, "COOL" EGYPTIAN MANNERS. LET'S IMAGINE HIM, THEN, AS ***HALF EGYPTIAN,*** A BIT OF A LONER, WITH A LOT OF REPRESSED ANGER, WHICH HE COULDN'T ALWAYS CONTROL.

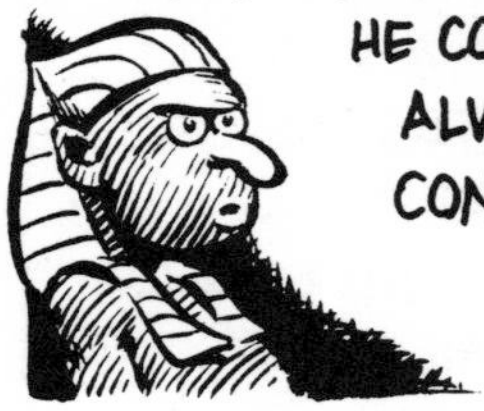

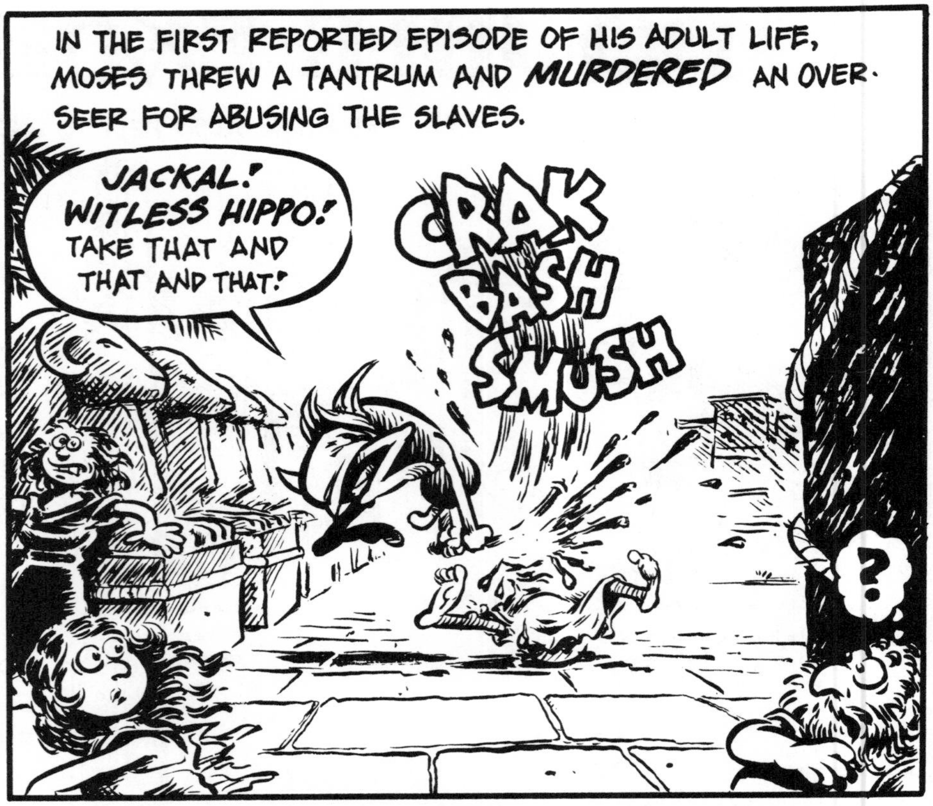
IN THE FIRST REPORTED EPISODE OF HIS ADULT LIFE, MOSES THREW A TANTRUM AND MURDERED AN OVERSEER FOR ABUSING THE SLAVES.
JACKAL! WITLESS HIPPO! TAKE THAT AND THAT AND THAT!
CRAK BASH SMUSH
?

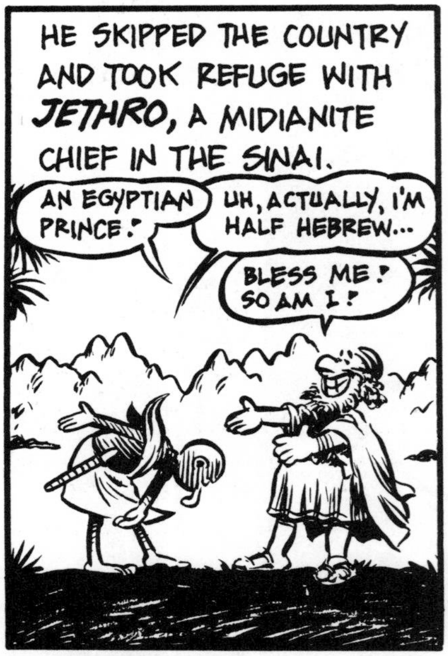
HE SKIPPED THE COUNTRY AND TOOK REFUGE WITH JETHRO, A MIDIANITE CHIEF IN THE SINAI.
AN EGYPTIAN PRINCE!
UH, ACTUALLY, I'M HALF HEBREW...
BLESS ME! SO AM I!

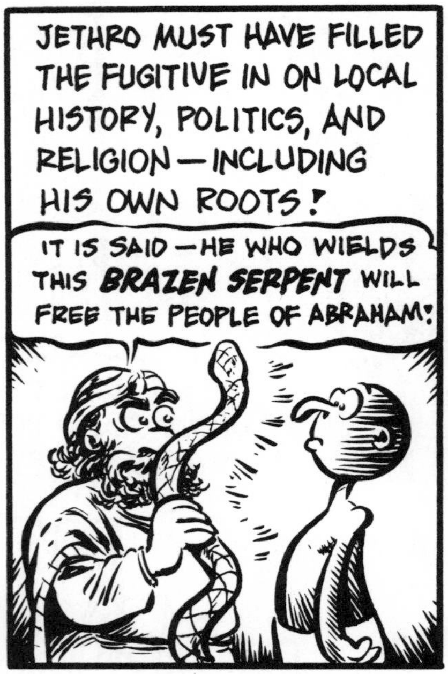
JETHRO MUST HAVE FILLED THE FUGITIVE IN ON LOCAL HISTORY, POLITICS, AND RELIGION—INCLUDING HIS OWN ROOTS!
IT IS SAID—HE WHO WIELDS THIS BRAZEN SERPENT WILL FREE THE PEOPLE OF ABRAHAM!

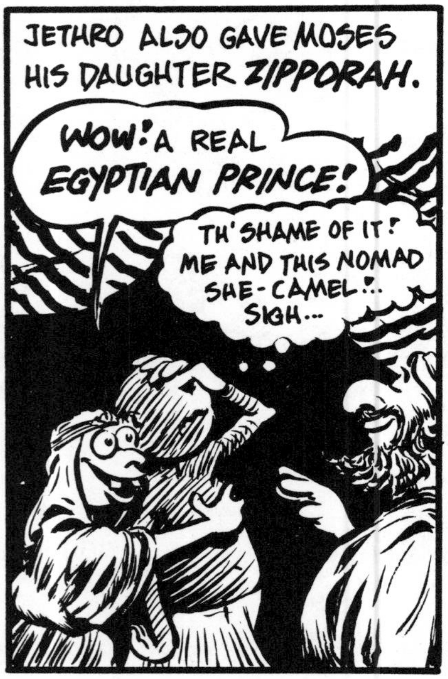
JETHRO ALSO GAVE MOSES HIS DAUGHTER ZIPPORAH.
WOW! A REAL EGYPTIAN PRINCE!
TH' SHAME OF IT! ME AND THIS NOMAD SHE-CAMEL!.. SIGH...

✻ WE'VE ALL HEARD HOW THE BABY MOSES WAS CAST ADRIFT ON THE NILE, BUT BEFORE BELIEVING IT, WE SHOULD CONSIDER THAT THE ABANDONED-BABY-WHO-BECOMES-KING THEME ALSO APPEARS IN THE LIVES OF SARGON OF AKKAD, OEDIPUS REX, CYRUS OF PERSIA, ROMULUS + REMUS, AND OTHERS. MANY SCHOLARS BELIEVE THE STORY WAS INVENTED BY "OFFICIAL BIOGRAPHERS" TO GIVE THESE PRINCES THE RIGHT PARENTS.

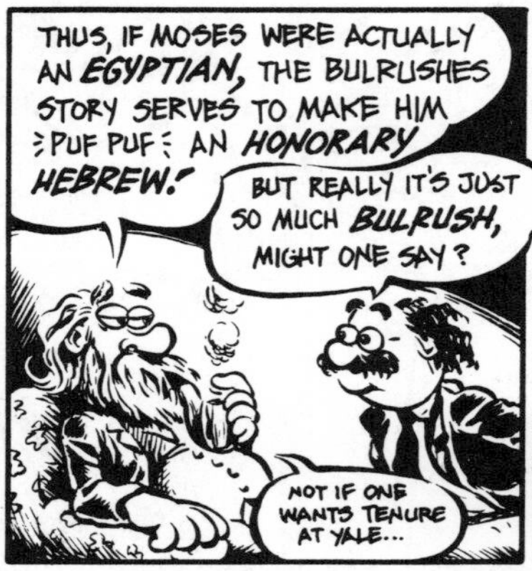
THUS, IF MOSES WERE ACTUALLY AN EGYPTIAN, THE BULRUSHES STORY SERVES TO MAKE HIM ≥PUF PUF≤ AN HONORARY HEBREW!
BUT REALLY IT'S JUST SO MUCH BULRUSH, MIGHT ONE SAY?
NOT IF ONE WANTS TENURE AT YALE...

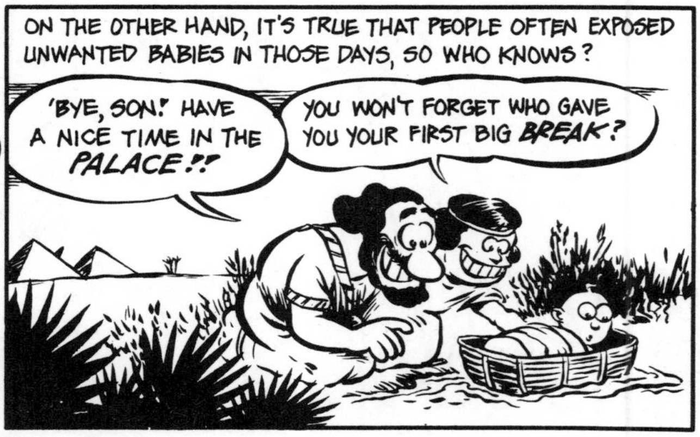
ON THE OTHER HAND, IT'S TRUE THAT PEOPLE OFTEN EXPOSED UNWANTED BABIES IN THOSE DAYS, SO WHO KNOWS?
'BYE, SON! HAVE A NICE TIME IN THE PALACE!!
YOU WON'T FORGET WHO GAVE YOU YOUR FIRST BIG BREAK?

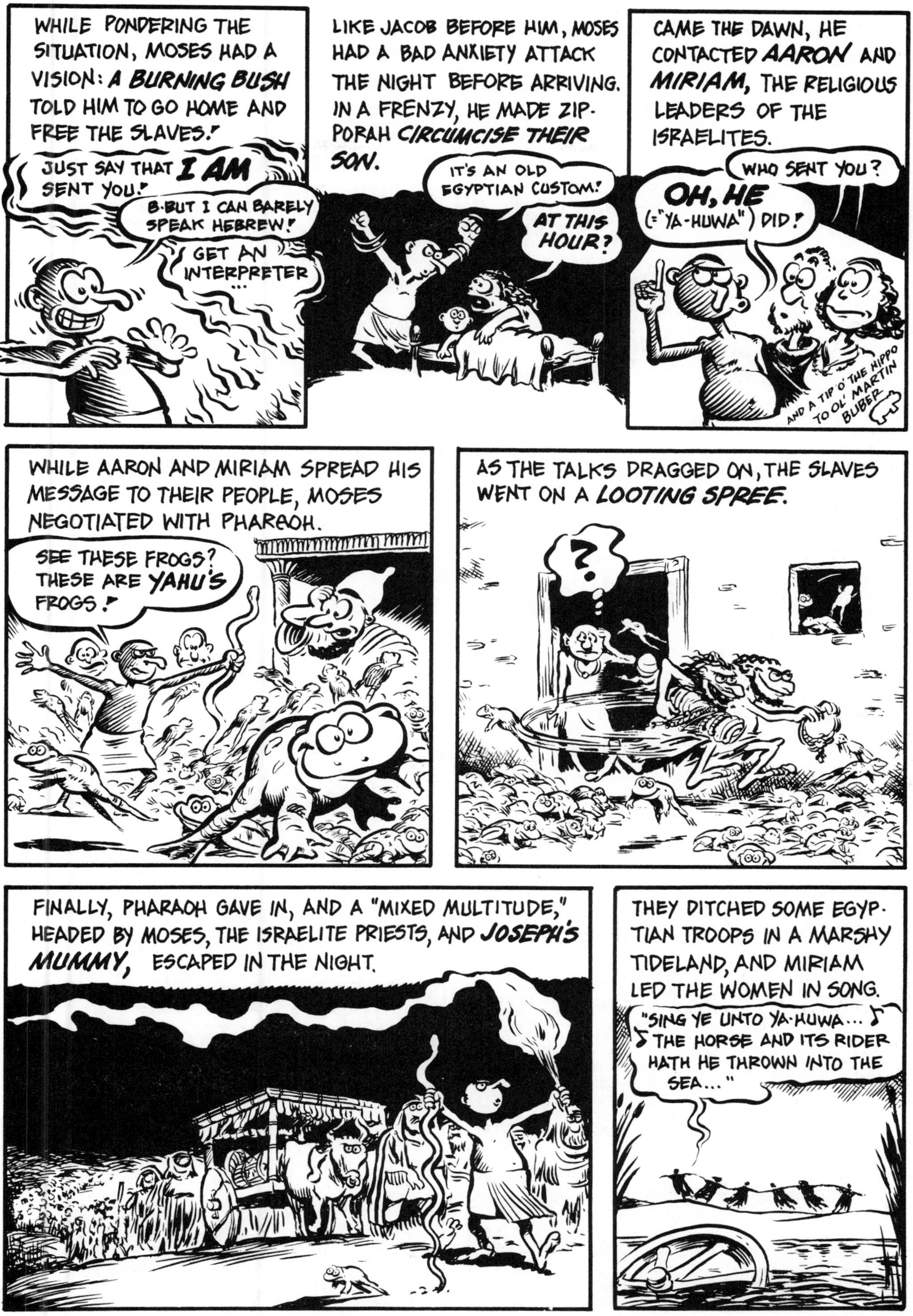
WHILE PONDERING THE SITUATION, MOSES HAD A VISION: A BURNING BUSH TOLD HIM TO GO HOME AND FREE THE SLAVES.
JUST SAY THAT I AM SENT YOU!
B-BUT I CAN BARELY SPEAK HEBREW!
GET AN INTERPRETER ...
LIKE JACOB BEFORE HIM, MOSES HAD A BAD ANXIETY ATTACK THE NIGHT BEFORE ARRIVING. IN A FRENZY, HE MADE ZIP-PORAH CIRCUMCISE THEIR SON.
IT'S AN OLD EGYPTIAN CUSTOM!
AT THIS HOUR?
CAME THE DAWN, HE CONTACTED AARON AND MIRIAM, THE RELIGIOUS LEADERS OF THE ISRAELITES.
WHO SENT YOU?
OH, HE (="YA-HUWA") DID!
AND A TIP O' THE HIPPO TO OL' MARTIN BUBER
WHILE AARON AND MIRIAM SPREAD HIS MESSAGE TO THEIR PEOPLE, MOSES NEGOTIATED WITH PHARAOH.
SEE THESE FROGS? THESE ARE YAHU'S FROGS!
AS THE TALKS DRAGGED ON, THE SLAVES WENT ON A LOOTING SPREE.
?
FINALLY, PHARAOH GAVE IN, AND A "MIXED MULTITUDE," HEADED BY MOSES, THE ISRAELITE PRIESTS, AND JOSEPH'S MUMMY, ESCAPED IN THE NIGHT.
THEY DITCHED SOME EGYP-TIAN TROOPS IN A MARSHY TIDELAND, AND MIRIAM LED THE WOMEN IN SONG.
"SING YE UNTO YA-HUWA... ♪ THE HORSE AND ITS RIDER HATH HE THROWN INTO THE SEA..."

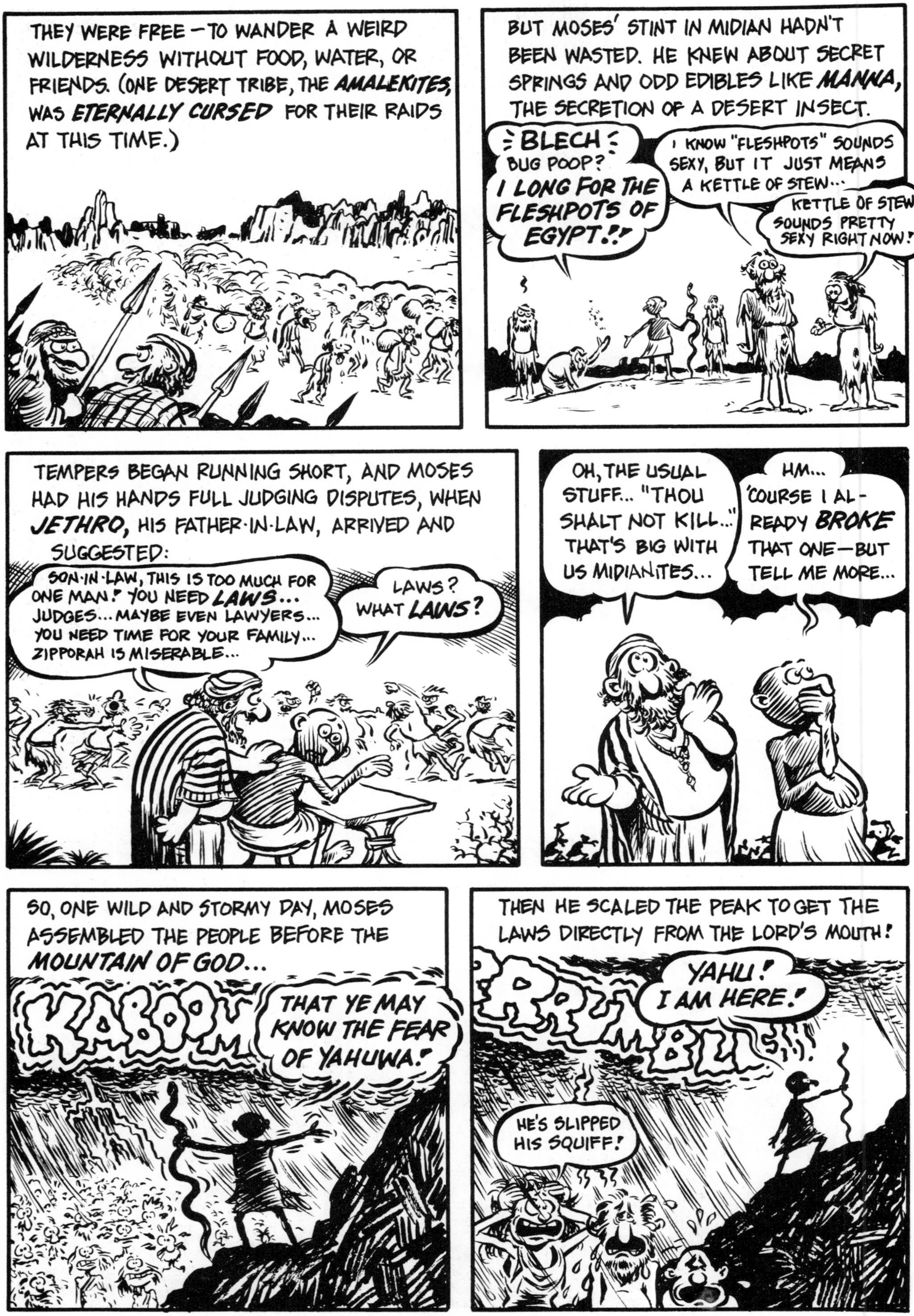
THEY WERE FREE — TO WANDER A WEIRD WILDERNESS WITHOUT FOOD, WATER, OR FRIENDS. (ONE DESERT TRIBE, THE AMALEKITES, WAS ETERNALLY CURSED FOR THEIR RAIDS AT THIS TIME.)
BUT MOSES' STINT IN MIDIAN HADN'T BEEN WASTED. HE KNEW ABOUT SECRET SPRINGS AND ODD EDIBLES LIKE MANNA, THE SECRETION OF A DESERT INSECT.
BLECH BUG POOP? I LONG FOR THE FLESHPOTS OF EGYPT!!
I KNOW "FLESHPOTS" SOUNDS SEXY, BUT IT JUST MEANS A KETTLE OF STEW...
KETTLE OF STEW SOUNDS PRETTY SEXY RIGHT NOW!
TEMPERS BEGAN RUNNING SHORT, AND MOSES HAD HIS HANDS FULL JUDGING DISPUTES, WHEN JETHRO, HIS FATHER-IN-LAW, ARRIVED AND SUGGESTED:
SON-IN-LAW, THIS IS TOO MUCH FOR ONE MAN! YOU NEED LAWS... JUDGES... MAYBE EVEN LAWYERS... YOU NEED TIME FOR YOUR FAMILY... ZIPPORAH IS MISERABLE...
LAWS? WHAT LAWS?
OH, THE USUAL STUFF... "THOU SHALT NOT KILL..." THAT'S BIG WITH US MIDIANITES...
HM... 'COURSE I ALREADY BROKE THAT ONE—BUT TELL ME MORE...
SO, ONE WILD AND STORMY DAY, MOSES ASSEMBLED THE PEOPLE BEFORE THE MOUNTAIN OF GOD...
KABOOM
THAT YE MAY KNOW THE FEAR OF YAHUWA!
THEN HE SCALED THE PEAK TO GET THE LAWS DIRECTLY FROM THE LORD'S MOUTH!
RRUMBLE
YAHU! I AM HERE!
HE'S SLIPPED HIS SQUIFF!

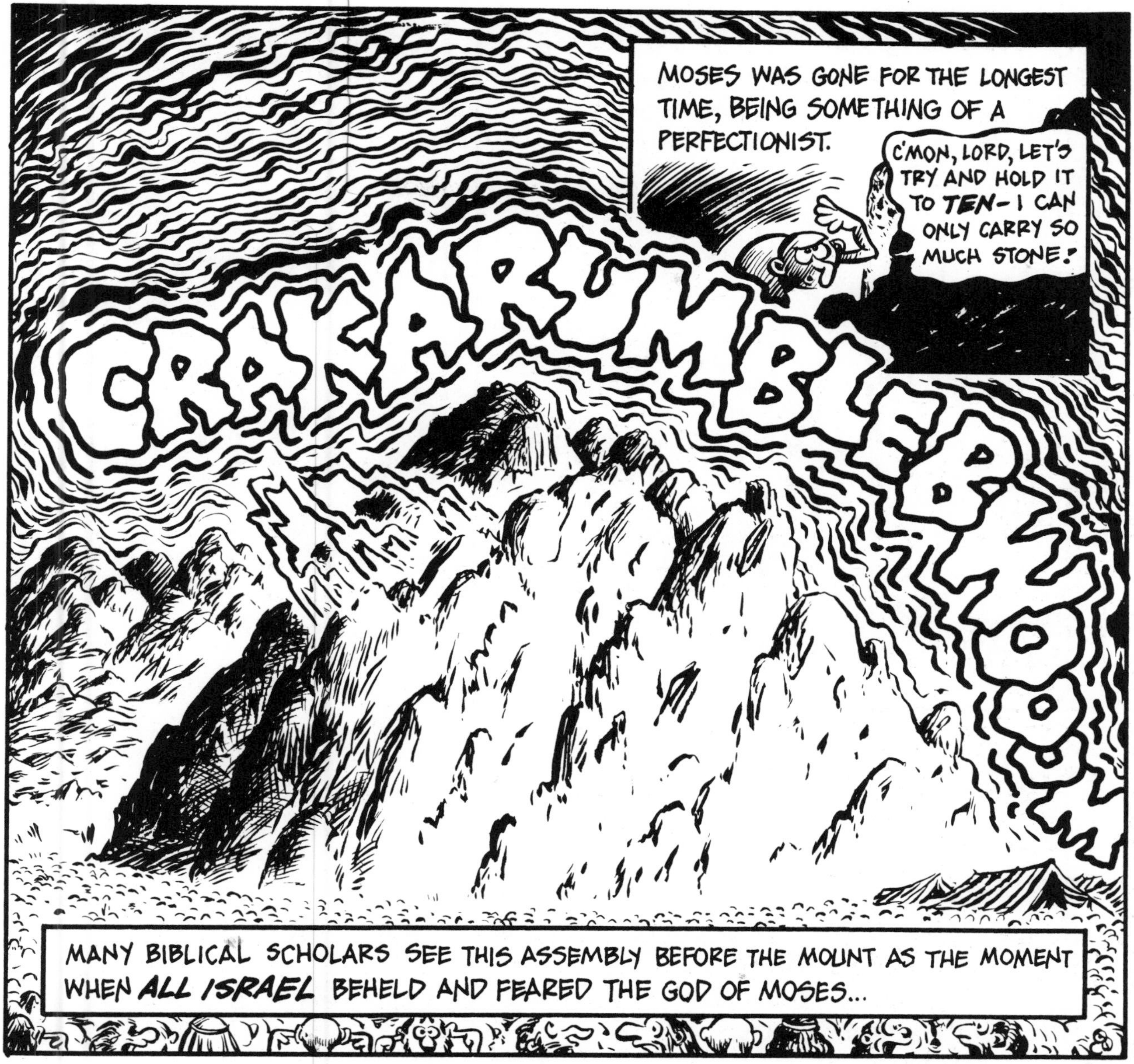
MOSES WAS GONE FOR THE LONGEST TIME, BEING SOMETHING OF A PERFECTIONIST.
C'MON, LORD, LET'S TRY AND HOLD IT TO **TEN**—I CAN ONLY CARRY SO MUCH STONE!
CRAKARUMBLEBWOOOM
MANY BIBLICAL SCHOLARS SEE THIS ASSEMBLY BEFORE THE MOUNT AS THE MOMENT WHEN **ALL ISRAEL** BEHELD AND FEARED THE GOD OF MOSES...

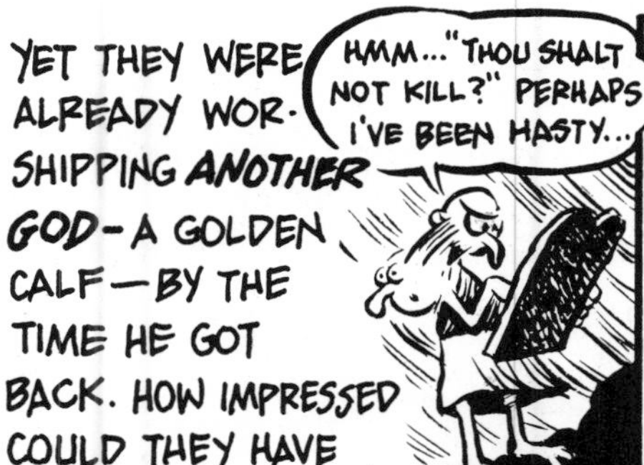
YET THEY WERE ALREADY WOR-SHIPPING **ANOTHER GOD**—A GOLDEN CALF—BY THE TIME HE GOT BACK. HOW IMPRESSED COULD THEY HAVE BEEN?
HMM... "THOU SHALT NOT KILL?" PERHAPS I'VE BEEN HASTY...
O APIS, SAVE US FROM "MOUNTAIN MAN!"

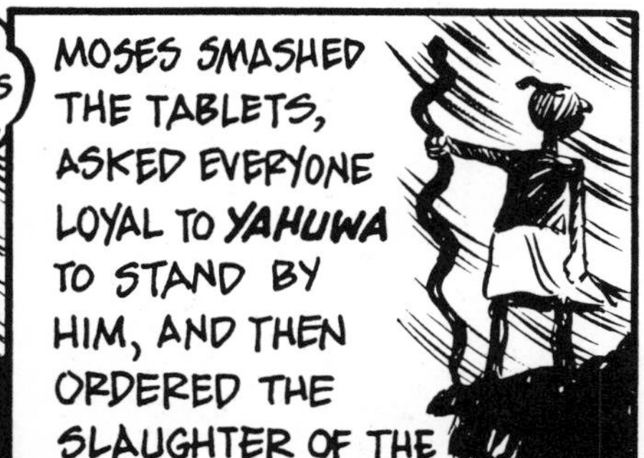
MOSES SMASHED THE TABLETS, ASKED EVERYONE LOYAL TO **YAHUWA** TO STAND BY HIM, AND THEN ORDERED THE SLAUGHTER OF THE CALF-WORSHIPPERS!

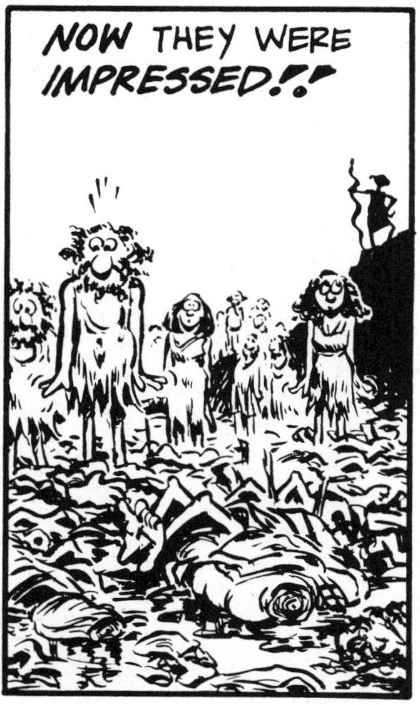
NOW THEY WERE **IMPRESSED!!**

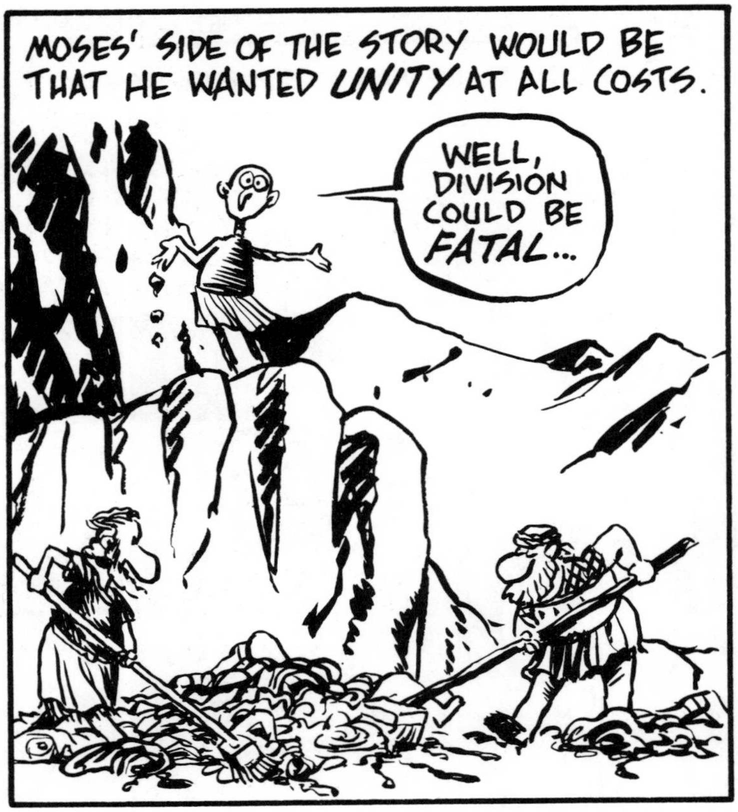
MOSES' SIDE OF THE STORY WOULD BE THAT HE WANTED *UNITY* AT ALL COSTS.
WELL, DIVISION COULD BE *FATAL*...

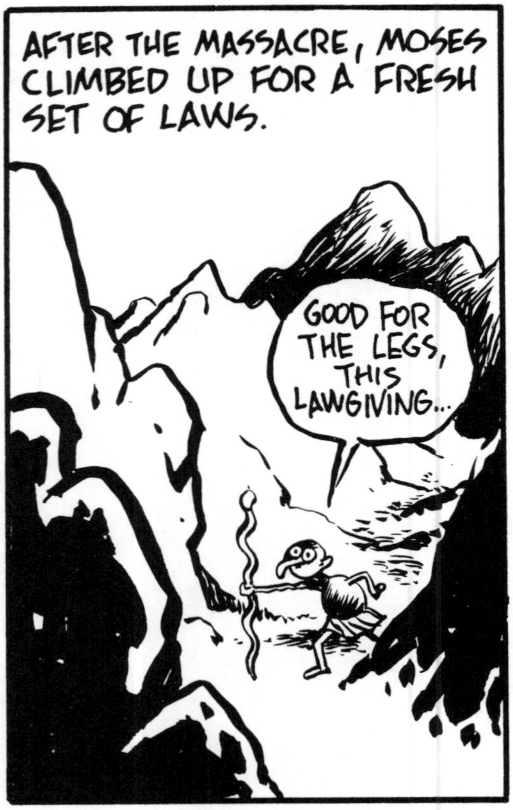
AFTER THE MASSACRE, MOSES CLIMBED UP FOR A FRESH SET OF LAWS.
GOOD FOR THE LEGS, THIS LAWGIVING...

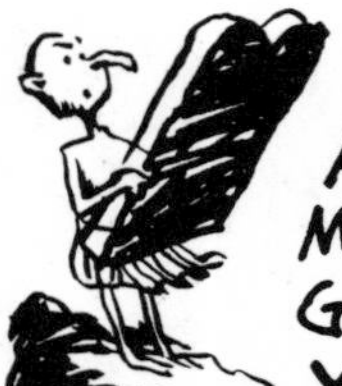

THE VERY *FIRST* COMMANDMENT WAS — NO GODS BEFORE *YAHU*. GOLDEN CALVES WERE *OUT*. GOD'S PRIESTS WOULD BE THE MEN LOYAL TO MOSES AGAINST THE CALF PEOPLE. THE OTHER COMMANDMENTS ARE THE USUAL CIVILIZED RULES AGAINST MURDER, THEFT, AND IMPERTINENCE.

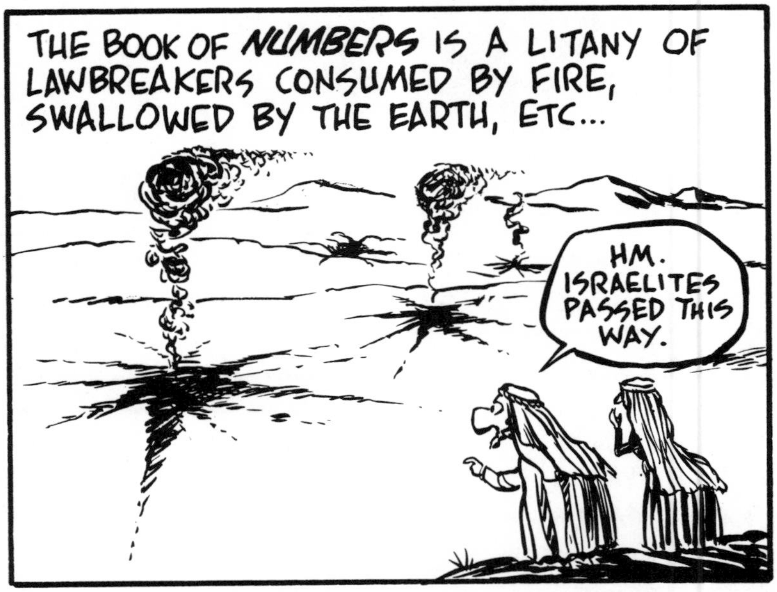
THE BOOK OF *NUMBERS* IS A LITANY OF LAWBREAKERS CONSUMED BY FIRE, SWALLOWED BY THE EARTH, ETC...
HM. ISRAELITES PASSED THIS WAY.

AFTER THE EXODUS, MOSES APPARENTLY KEPT THE EGYPTIAN OBSESSION WITH **CLEANLINESS.** AMONG HIS OTHER LAWS ARE LONG LISTS OF "UNCLEAN" MEATS, BIRDS, AND SEAFOOD, WHICH THE ORTHODOX WILL NOT TOUCH TO THIS DAY!

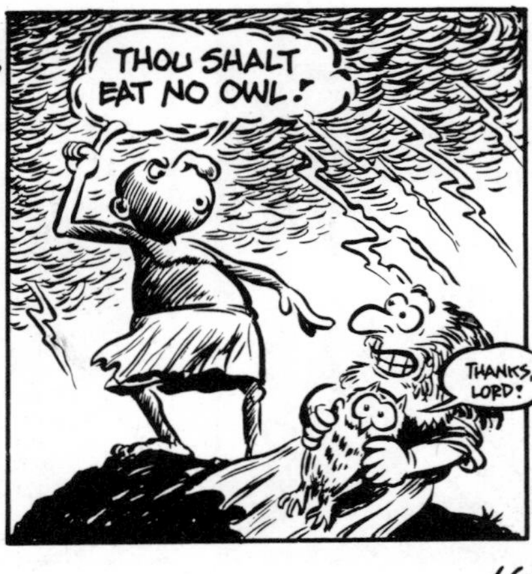
THOU SHALT EAT NO OWL!
THANKS, LORD!

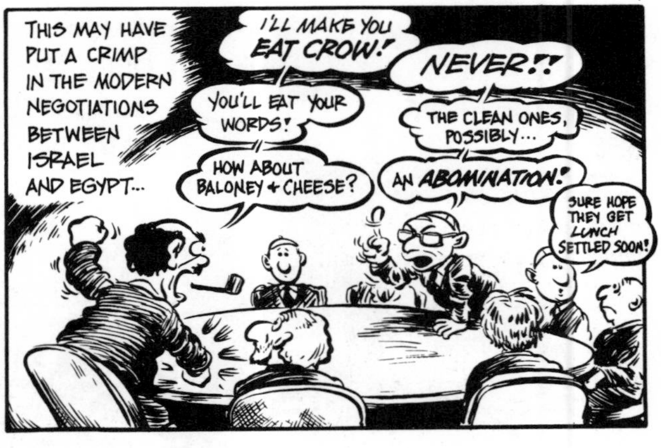
THIS MAY HAVE PUT A CRIMP IN THE MODERN NEGOTIATIONS BETWEEN ISRAEL AND EGYPT...
I'LL MAKE YOU *EAT CROW!*
NEVER!?!
YOU'LL EAT YOUR WORDS!
THE CLEAN ONES, POSSIBLY...
HOW ABOUT BALONEY & CHEESE?
AN *ABOMINATION!*
SURE HOPE THEY GET *LUNCH* SETTLED SOON!

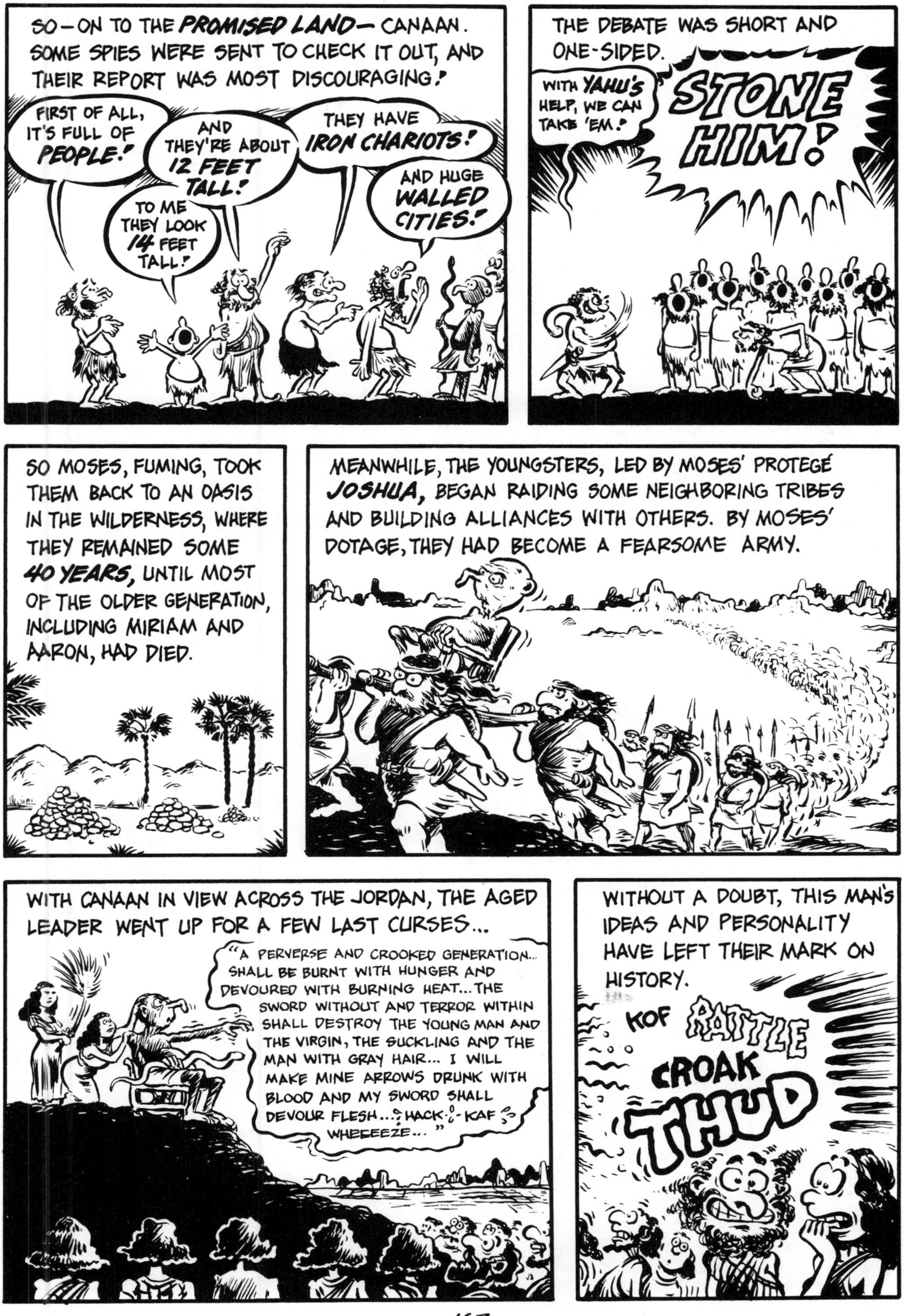
SO — ON TO THE PROMISED LAND — CANAAN. SOME SPIES WERE SENT TO CHECK IT OUT, AND THEIR REPORT WAS MOST DISCOURAGING!
FIRST OF ALL, IT'S FULL OF PEOPLE!
AND THEY'RE ABOUT 12 FEET TALL!
TO ME THEY LOOK 14 FEET TALL!
THEY HAVE IRON CHARIOTS!
AND HUGE WALLED CITIES!
THE DEBATE WAS SHORT AND ONE-SIDED.
WITH YAHU'S HELP, WE CAN TAKE 'EM!
STONE HIM!
SO MOSES, FUMING, TOOK THEM BACK TO AN OASIS IN THE WILDERNESS, WHERE THEY REMAINED SOME 40 YEARS, UNTIL MOST OF THE OLDER GENERATION, INCLUDING MIRIAM AND AARON, HAD DIED.
MEANWHILE, THE YOUNGSTERS, LED BY MOSES' PROTEGÉ JOSHUA, BEGAN RAIDING SOME NEIGHBORING TRIBES AND BUILDING ALLIANCES WITH OTHERS. BY MOSES' DOTAGE, THEY HAD BECOME A FEARSOME ARMY.
WITH CANAAN IN VIEW ACROSS THE JORDAN, THE AGED LEADER WENT UP FOR A FEW LAST CURSES...
"A PERVERSE AND CROOKED GENERATION... SHALL BE BURNT WITH HUNGER AND DEVOURED WITH BURNING HEAT... THE SWORD WITHOUT AND TERROR WITHIN SHALL DESTROY THE YOUNG MAN AND THE VIRGIN, THE SUCKLING AND THE MAN WITH GRAY HAIR... I WILL MAKE MINE ARROWS DRUNK WITH BLOOD AND MY SWORD SHALL DEVOUR FLESH... HACK - KAF WHEEEEZE..."
WITHOUT A DOUBT, THIS MAN'S IDEAS AND PERSONALITY HAVE LEFT THEIR MARK ON HISTORY.
KOF
RATTLE
CROAK
THUD

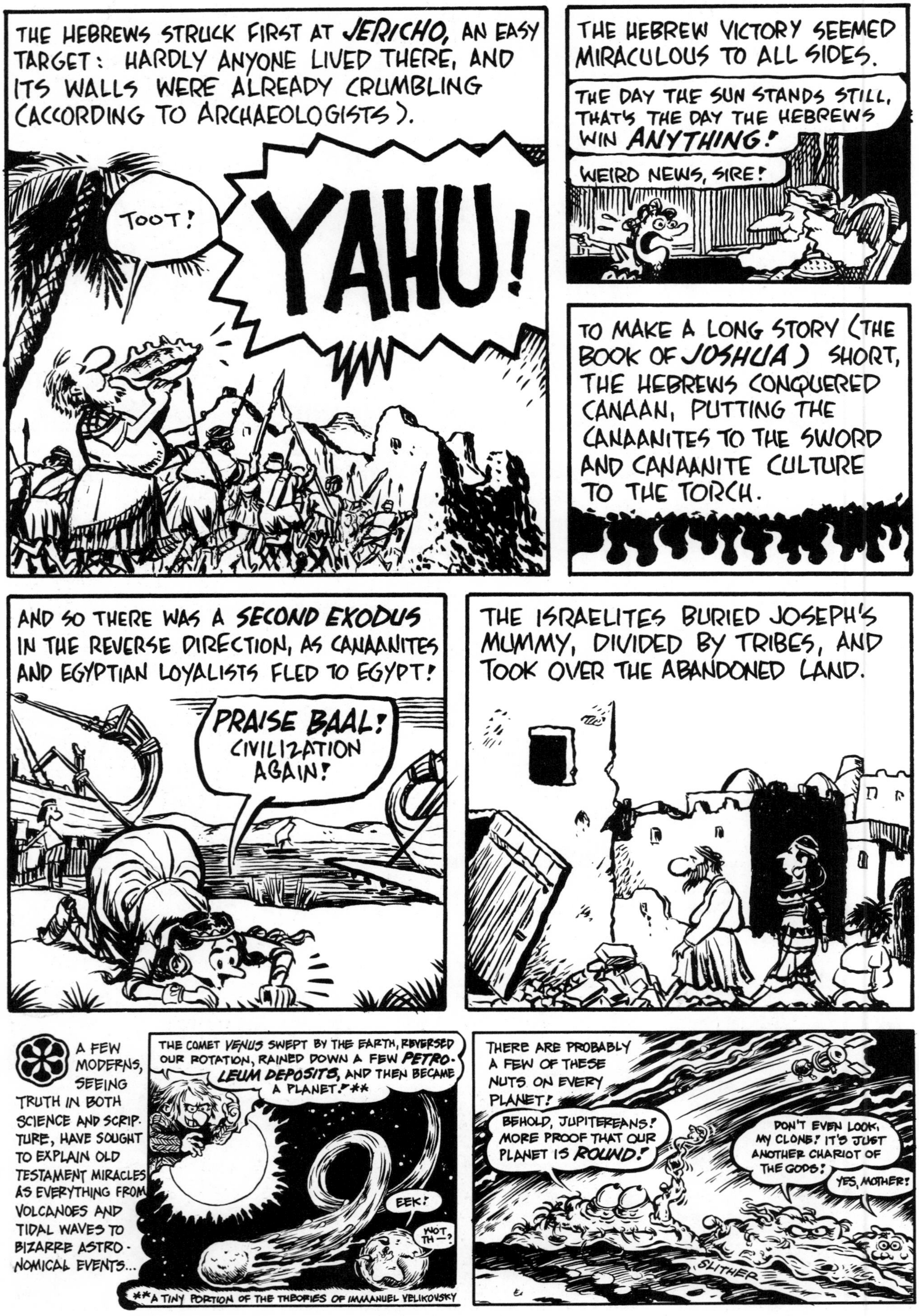
THE HEBREWS STRUCK FIRST AT JERICHO, AN EASY TARGET: HARDLY ANYONE LIVED THERE, AND ITS WALLS WERE ALREADY CRUMBLING (ACCORDING TO ARCHAEOLOGISTS).
TOOT!
YAHU!
THE HEBREW VICTORY SEEMED MIRACULOUS TO ALL SIDES.
THE DAY THE SUN STANDS STILL, THAT'S THE DAY THE HEBREWS WIN ANYTHING!
WEIRD NEWS, SIRE!
TO MAKE A LONG STORY (THE BOOK OF JOSHUA) SHORT, THE HEBREWS CONQUERED CANAAN, PUTTING THE CANAANITES TO THE SWORD AND CANAANITE CULTURE TO THE TORCH.
AND SO THERE WAS A SECOND EXODUS IN THE REVERSE DIRECTION, AS CANAANITES AND EGYPTIAN LOYALISTS FLED TO EGYPT!
PRAISE BAAL! CIVILIZATION AGAIN!
THE ISRAELITES BURIED JOSEPH'S MUMMY, DIVIDED BY TRIBES, AND TOOK OVER THE ABANDONED LAND.
A FEW MODERNS, SEEING TRUTH IN BOTH SCIENCE AND SCRIPTURE, HAVE SOUGHT TO EXPLAIN OLD TESTAMENT MIRACLES AS EVERYTHING FROM VOLCANOES AND TIDAL WAVES TO BIZARRE ASTRONOMICAL EVENTS...
THE COMET VENUS SWEPT BY THE EARTH, REVERSED OUR ROTATION, RAINED DOWN A FEW PETROLEUM DEPOSITS, AND THEN BECAME A PLANET!**
EEK!
WOT, TH—?
THERE ARE PROBABLY A FEW OF THESE NUTS ON EVERY PLANET!
BEHOLD, JUPITEREANS! MORE PROOF THAT OUR PLANET IS ROUND!
DON'T EVEN LOOK, MY CLONE! IT'S JUST ANOTHER CHARIOT OF THE GODS!
YES, MOTHER!
SLITHER
**A TINY PORTION OF THE THEORIES OF IMMANUEL VELIKOVSKY

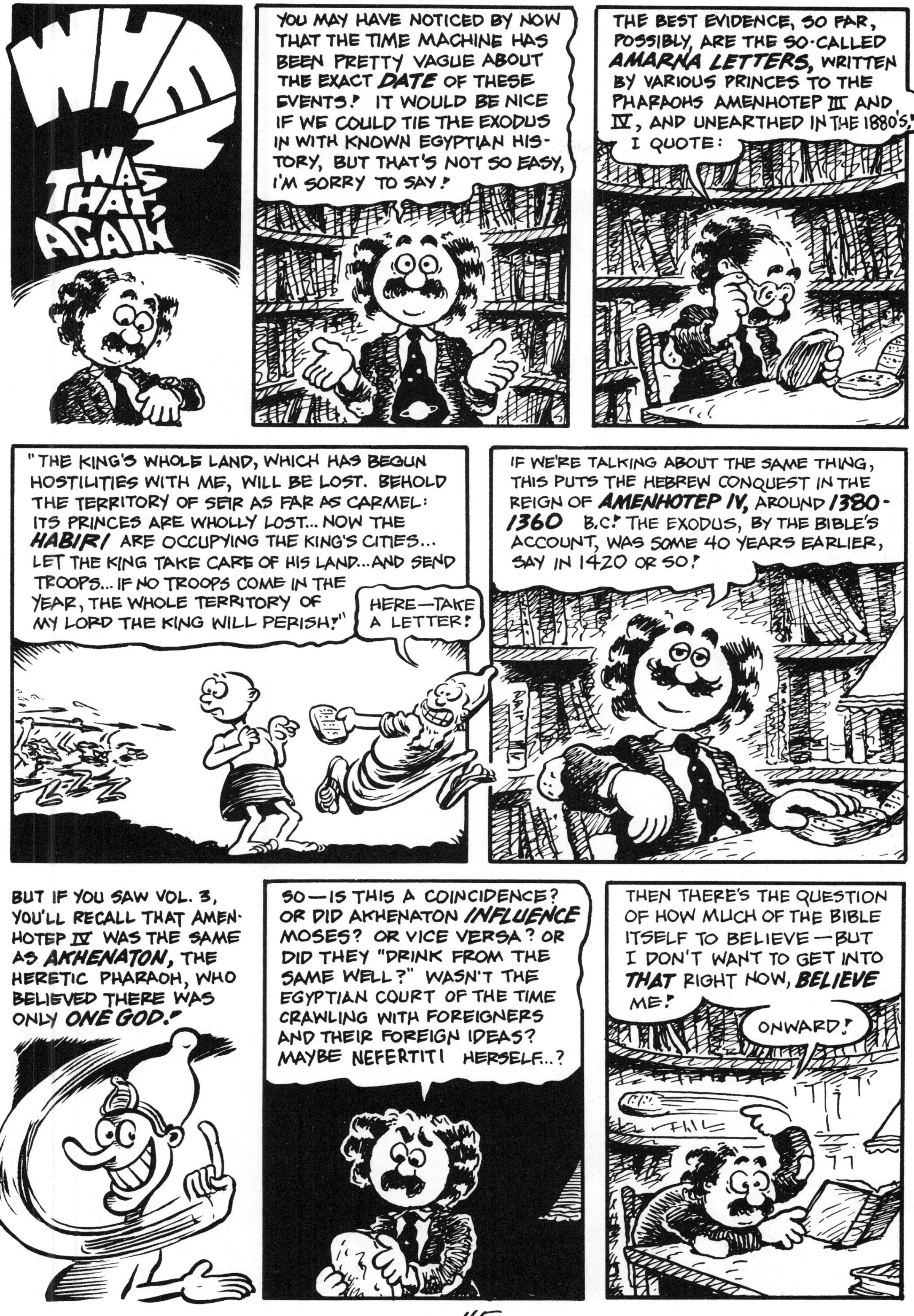
WHO WAS THAT, AGAIN
YOU MAY HAVE NOTICED BY NOW THAT THE TIME MACHINE HAS BEEN PRETTY VAGUE ABOUT THE EXACT *DATE* OF THESE EVENTS! IT WOULD BE NICE IF WE COULD TIE THE EXODUS IN WITH KNOWN EGYPTIAN HISTORY, BUT THAT'S NOT SO EASY, I'M SORRY TO SAY!
THE BEST EVIDENCE, SO FAR, POSSIBLY, ARE THE SO-CALLED ***AMARNA LETTERS,*** WRITTEN BY VARIOUS PRINCES TO THE PHARAOHS AMENHOTEP III AND IV, AND UNEARTHED IN THE 1880'S! I QUOTE:
"THE KING'S WHOLE LAND, WHICH HAS BEGUN HOSTILITIES WITH ME, WILL BE LOST. BEHOLD THE TERRITORY OF SEIR AS FAR AS CARMEL: ITS PRINCES ARE WHOLLY LOST... NOW THE ***HABIRI*** ARE OCCUPYING THE KING'S CITIES... LET THE KING TAKE CARE OF HIS LAND...AND SEND TROOPS... IF NO TROOPS COME IN THE YEAR, THE WHOLE TERRITORY OF MY LORD THE KING WILL PERISH!"
HERE—TAKE A LETTER!
IF WE'RE TALKING ABOUT THE SAME THING, THIS PUTS THE HEBREW CONQUEST IN THE REIGN OF ***AMENHOTEP IV,*** AROUND ***1380-1360*** B.C.! THE EXODUS, BY THE BIBLE'S ACCOUNT, WAS SOME 40 YEARS EARLIER, SAY IN 1420 OR SO!
BUT IF YOU SAW VOL. 3, YOU'LL RECALL THAT AMENHOTEP IV WAS THE SAME AS ***AKHENATON,*** THE HERETIC PHARAOH, WHO BELIEVED THERE WAS ONLY ***ONE GOD!***
SO—IS THIS A COINCIDENCE? OR DID AKHENATON ***INFLUENCE*** MOSES? OR VICE VERSA? OR DID THEY "DRINK FROM THE SAME WELL?" WASN'T THE EGYPTIAN COURT OF THE TIME CRAWLING WITH FOREIGNERS AND THEIR FOREIGN IDEAS? MAYBE NEFERTITI HERSELF...?
THEN THERE'S THE QUESTION OF HOW MUCH OF THE BIBLE ITSELF TO BELIEVE—BUT I DON'T WANT TO GET INTO ***THAT*** RIGHT NOW, ***BELIEVE*** ME!
ONWARD!

JUDGMENT DAYS

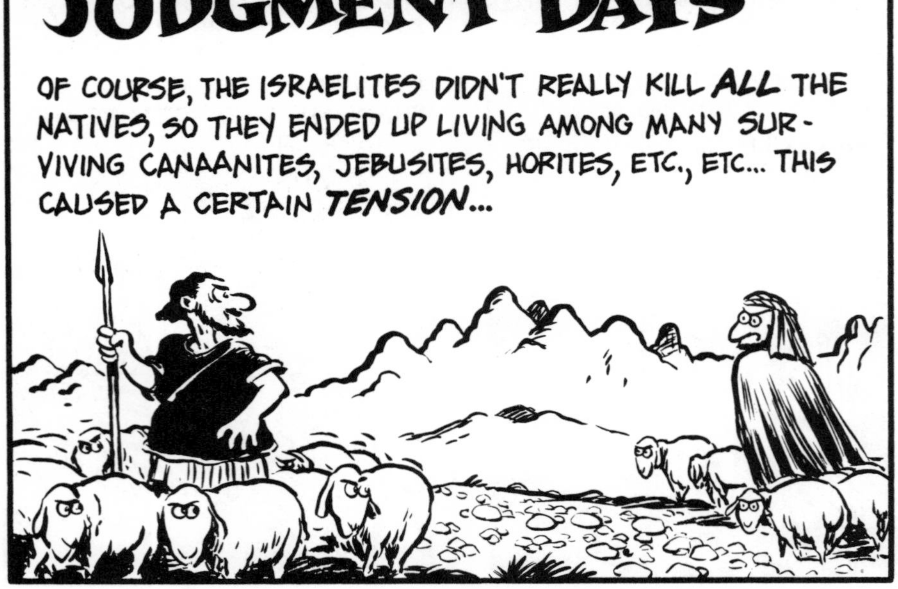
OF COURSE, THE ISRAELITES DIDN'T REALLY KILL ***ALL*** THE NATIVES, SO THEY ENDED UP LIVING AMONG MANY SURVIVING CANAANITES, JEBUSITES, HORITES, ETC., ETC... THIS CAUSED A CERTAIN ***TENSION***...

ESPECIALLY SINCE THE ISRAELITES, AS FORMER OUTCASTS AND SLAVES, ***REJECTED*** SO MANY LOCAL INSTITUTIONS, LIKE IDOLATRY, ART, PERSONAL WEALTH, HORSES AND CHARIOTS —IN THEORY, AT LEAST. IN PRACTICE, THEY WERE NEVER 100% STRICT!

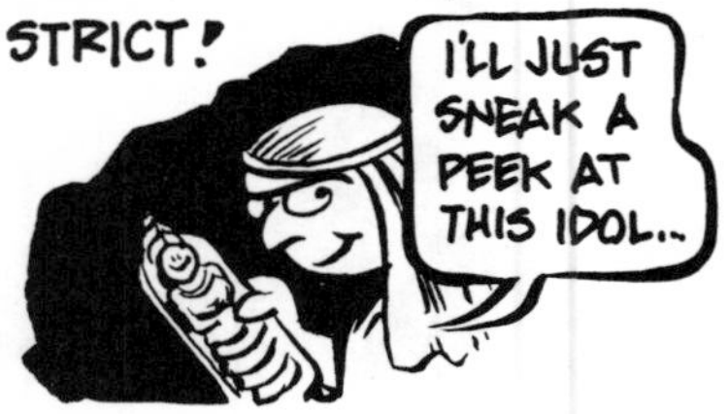
I'LL JUST SNEAK A PEEK AT THIS IDOL...

BUT THEY DEFINITELY FROWNED ON ***KINGS***. WHEN ISRAEL WAS LED BY ANYONE, IT WAS SOMEONE WHO SHOWED UNCOMMON ***JUDGMENT*** IN A CRISIS... SO THESE LEADERS ARE CALLED THE ***JUDGES***.

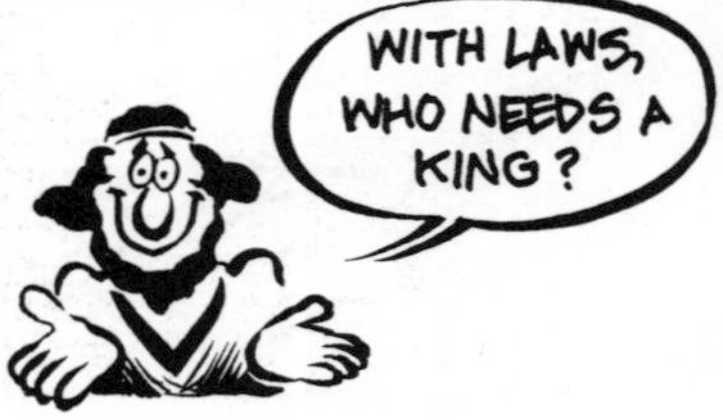
WITH LAWS, WHO NEEDS A KING?

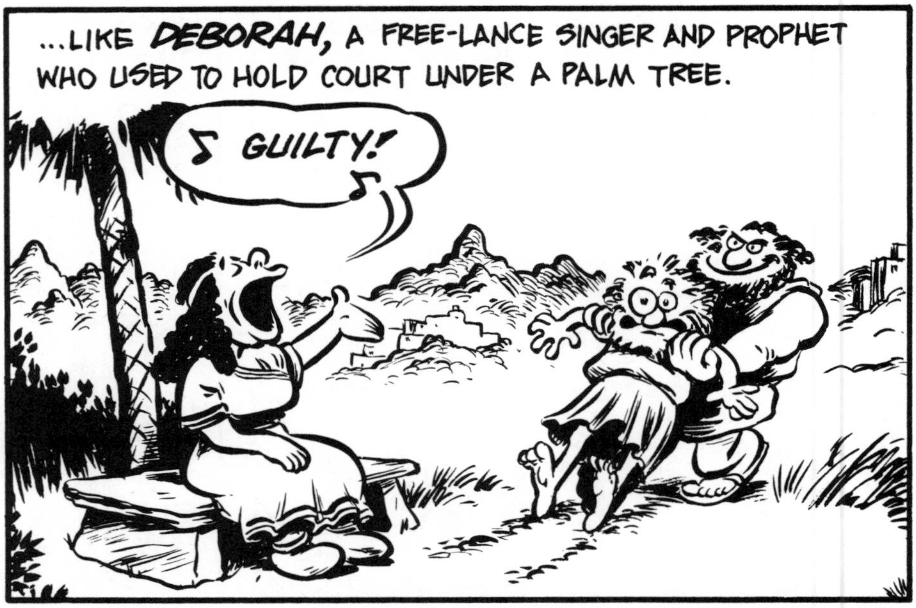
...LIKE ***DEBORAH,*** A FREE-LANCE SINGER AND PROPHET WHO USED TO HOLD COURT UNDER A PALM TREE.
GUILTY!

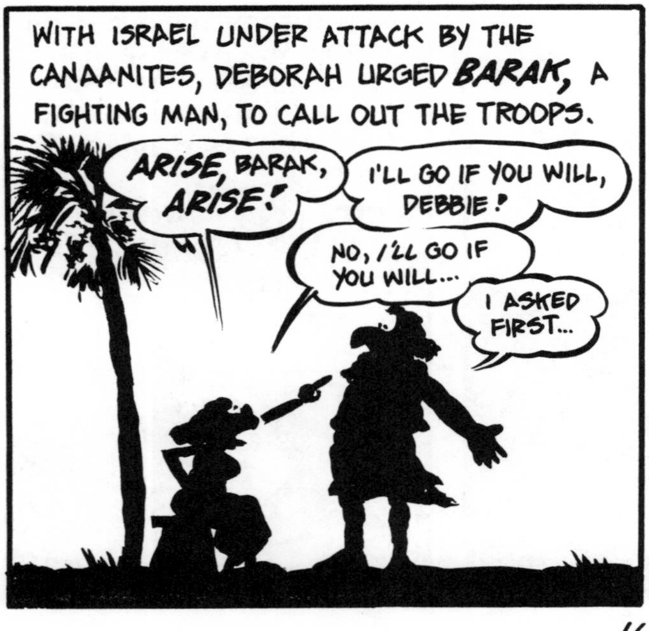
WITH ISRAEL UNDER ATTACK BY THE CANAANITES, DEBORAH URGED ***BARAK,*** A FIGHTING MAN, TO CALL OUT THE TROOPS.
ARISE, BARAK, ARISE!
I'LL GO IF YOU WILL, DEBBIE!
NO, I'LL GO IF YOU WILL...
I ASKED FIRST...

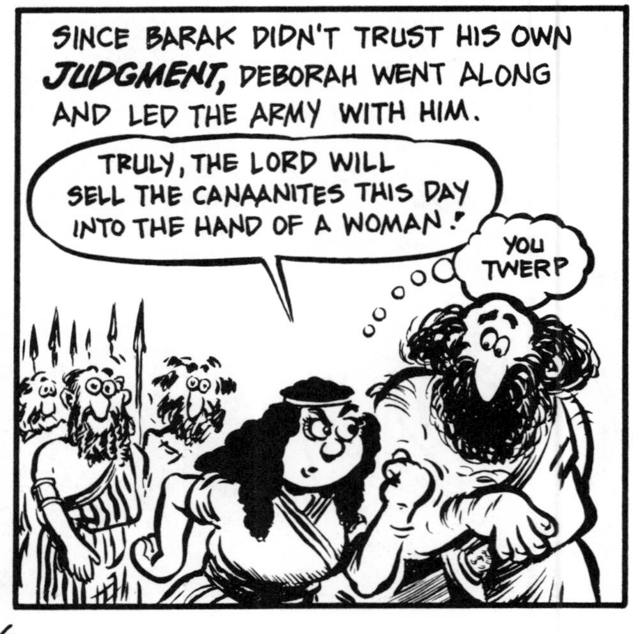
SINCE BARAK DIDN'T TRUST HIS OWN ***JUDGMENT,*** DEBORAH WENT ALONG AND LED THE ARMY WITH HIM.
TRULY, THE LORD WILL SELL THE CANAANITES THIS DAY INTO THE HAND OF A WOMAN!
YOU TWERP

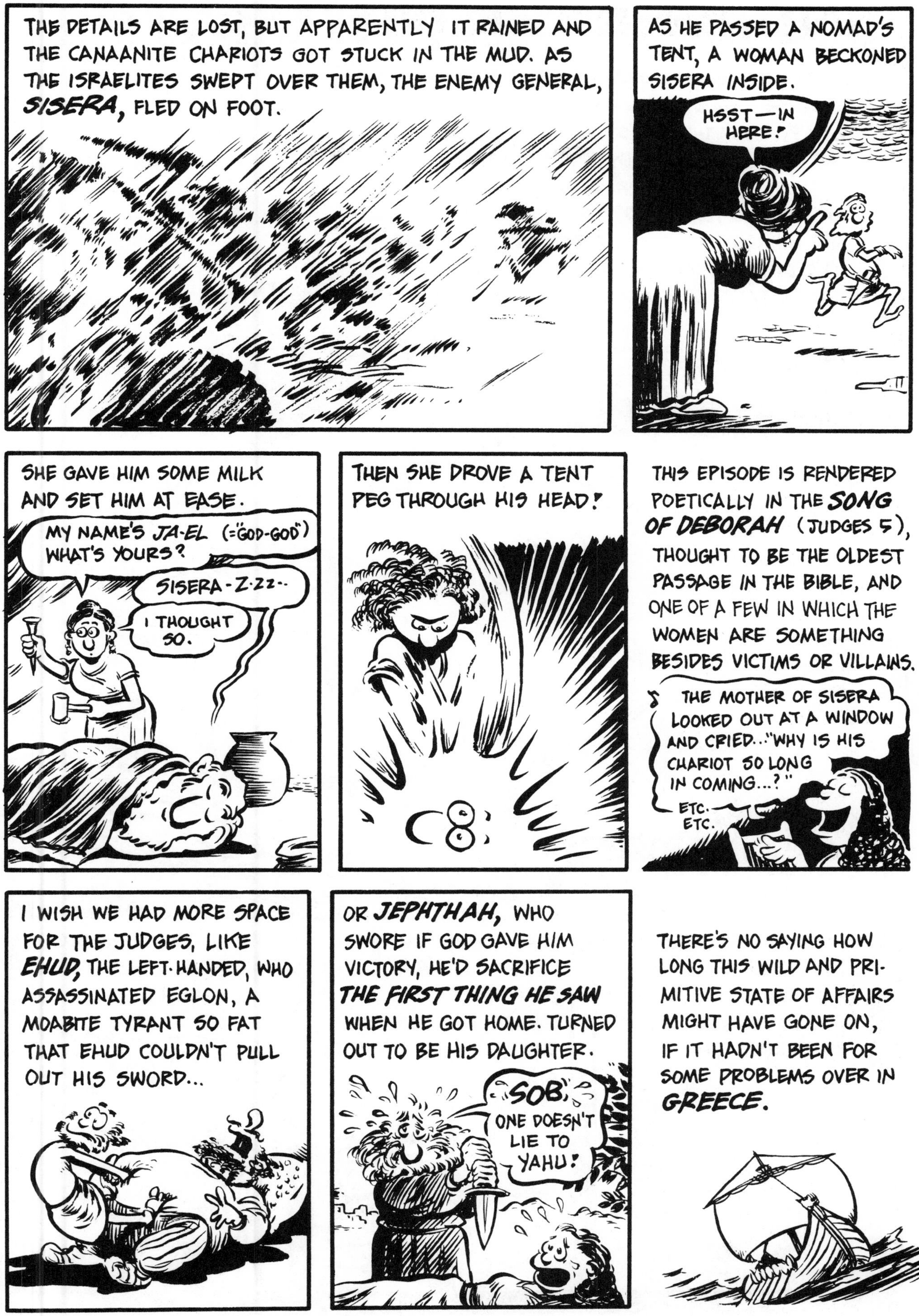
THE DETAILS ARE LOST, BUT APPARENTLY IT RAINED AND THE CANAANITE CHARIOTS GOT STUCK IN THE MUD. AS THE ISRAELITES SWEPT OVER THEM, THE ENEMY GENERAL, SISERA, FLED ON FOOT.
AS HE PASSED A NOMAD'S TENT, A WOMAN BECKONED SISERA INSIDE.
HSST—IN HERE!
SHE GAVE HIM SOME MILK AND SET HIM AT EASE.
MY NAME'S JA-EL (="GOD-GOD") WHAT'S YOURS?
SISERA-Z-ZZ..
I THOUGHT SO.
THEN SHE DROVE A TENT PEG THROUGH HIS HEAD!
THIS EPISODE IS RENDERED POETICALLY IN THE SONG OF DEBORAH (JUDGES 5), THOUGHT TO BE THE OLDEST PASSAGE IN THE BIBLE, AND ONE OF A FEW IN WHICH THE WOMEN ARE SOMETHING BESIDES VICTIMS OR VILLAINS.
THE MOTHER OF SISERA LOOKED OUT AT A WINDOW AND CRIED..."WHY IS HIS CHARIOT SO LONG IN COMING...?" ETC. ETC.
I WISH WE HAD MORE SPACE FOR THE JUDGES, LIKE EHUD, THE LEFT-HANDED, WHO ASSASSINATED EGLON, A MOABITE TYRANT SO FAT THAT EHUD COULDN'T PULL OUT HIS SWORD...
OR JEPHTHAH, WHO SWORE IF GOD GAVE HIM VICTORY, HE'D SACRIFICE THE FIRST THING HE SAW WHEN HE GOT HOME. TURNED OUT TO BE HIS DAUGHTER.
SOB, ONE DOESN'T LIE TO YAHU!
THERE'S NO SAYING HOW LONG THIS WILD AND PRIMITIVE STATE OF AFFAIRS MIGHT HAVE GONE ON, IF IT HADN'T BEEN FOR SOME PROBLEMS OVER IN GREECE.

HERE COME THE PHILISTINES!

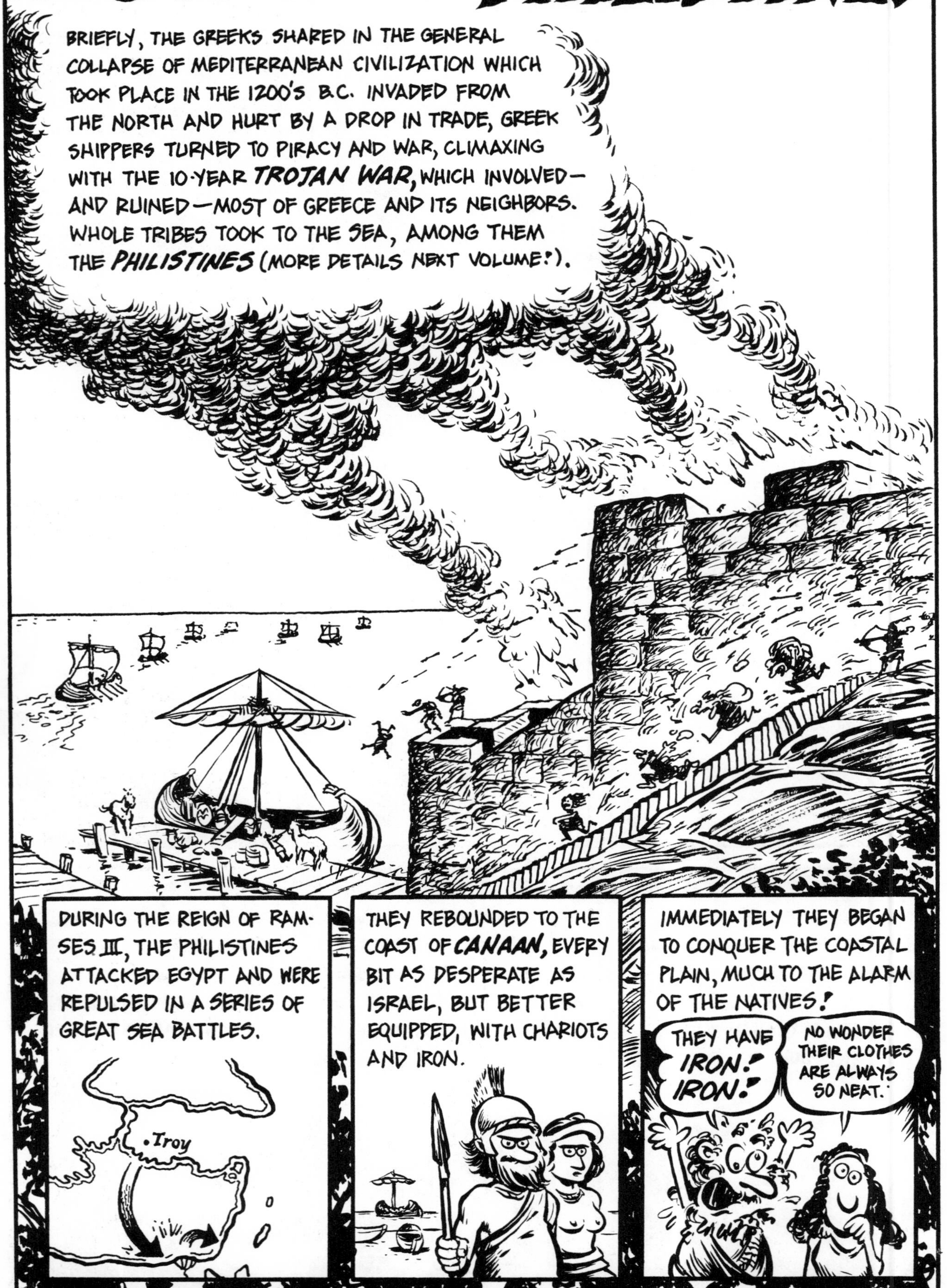
BRIEFLY, THE GREEKS SHARED IN THE GENERAL COLLAPSE OF MEDITERRANEAN CIVILIZATION WHICH TOOK PLACE IN THE 1200'S B.C. INVADED FROM THE NORTH AND HURT BY A DROP IN TRADE, GREEK SHIPPERS TURNED TO PIRACY AND WAR, CLIMAXING WITH THE 10-YEAR TROJAN WAR, WHICH INVOLVED—AND RUINED—MOST OF GREECE AND ITS NEIGHBORS. WHOLE TRIBES TOOK TO THE SEA, AMONG THEM THE PHILISTINES (MORE DETAILS NEXT VOLUME!).
DURING THE REIGN OF RAMSES III, THE PHILISTINES ATTACKED EGYPT AND WERE REPULSED IN A SERIES OF GREAT SEA BATTLES.
Troy
THEY REBOUNDED TO THE COAST OF CANAAN, EVERY BIT AS DESPERATE AS ISRAEL, BUT BETTER EQUIPPED, WITH CHARIOTS AND IRON.
IMMEDIATELY THEY BEGAN TO CONQUER THE COASTAL PLAIN, MUCH TO THE ALARM OF THE NATIVES!
THEY HAVE IRON! IRON!
NO WONDER THEIR CLOTHES ARE ALWAYS SO NEAT.

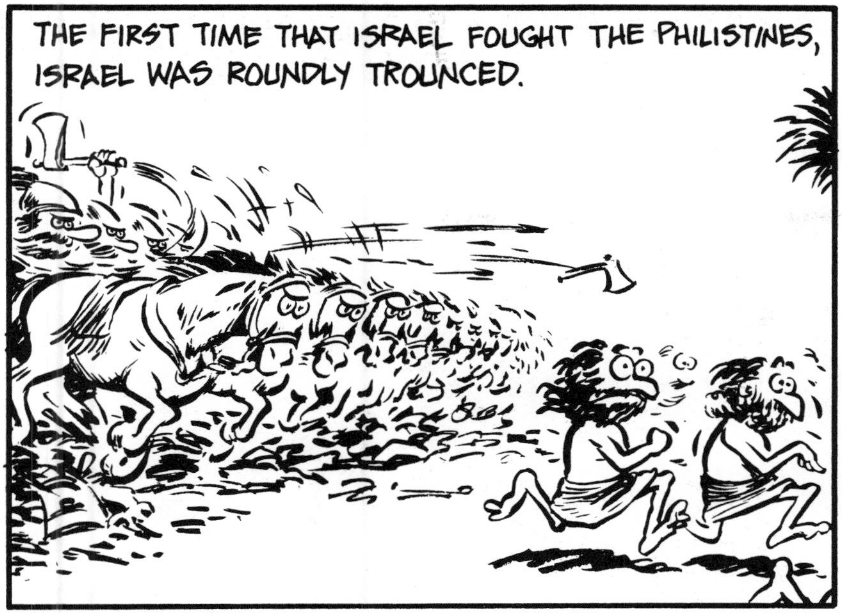
THE FIRST TIME THAT ISRAEL FOUGHT THE PHILISTINES, ISRAEL WAS ROUNDLY TROUNCED.

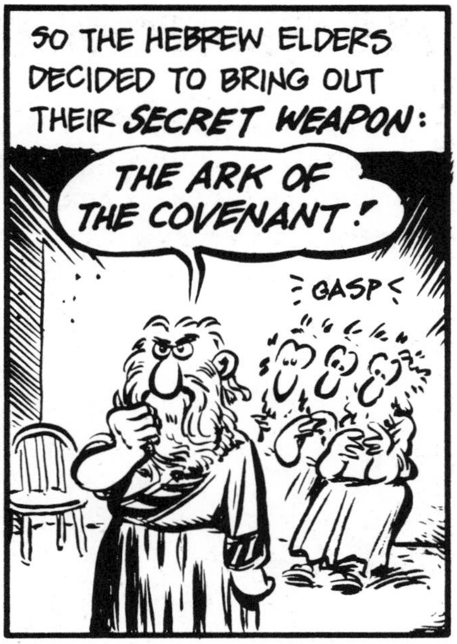
SO THE HEBREW ELDERS DECIDED TO BRING OUT THEIR *SECRET WEAPON*:
THE ARK OF THE COVENANT!
GASP

THE ARK OF THE COVENANT WAS ISRAEL'S MOST SACRED OBJECT! A MASSIVE, ORNATE WOODEN CHEST THAT HAD BEEN WITH JOSHUA AT JERICHO, IT HELD THE LAWS OF MOSES AND MAY EVEN HAVE CARRIED JOSEPH'S MUMMY. THE TROOPS CHEERED—

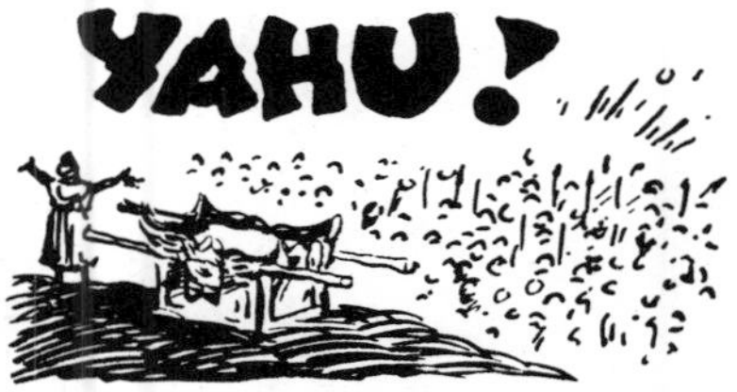
YAHU!

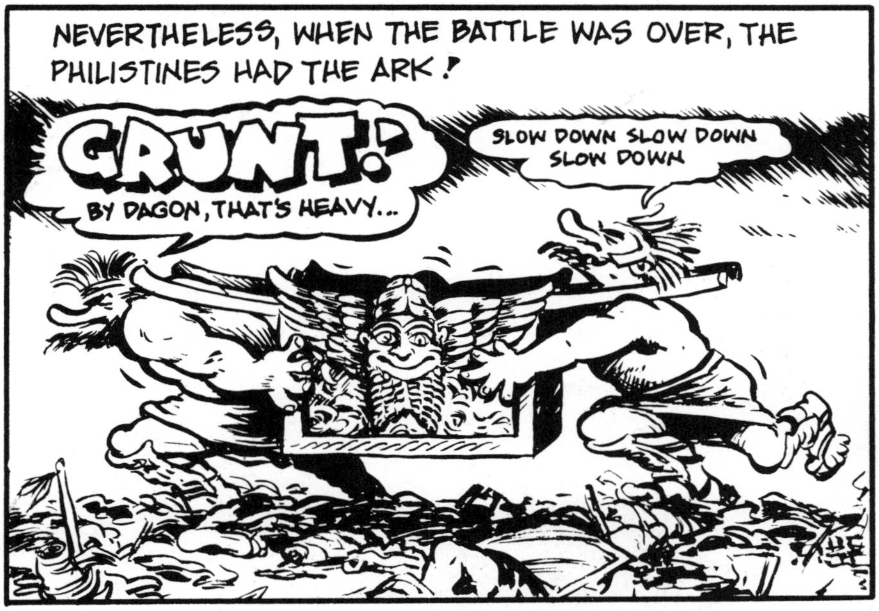
NEVERTHELESS, WHEN THE BATTLE WAS OVER, THE PHILISTINES HAD THE ARK!
GRUNT! BY DAGON, THAT'S HEAVY...
SLOW DOWN SLOW DOWN SLOW DOWN

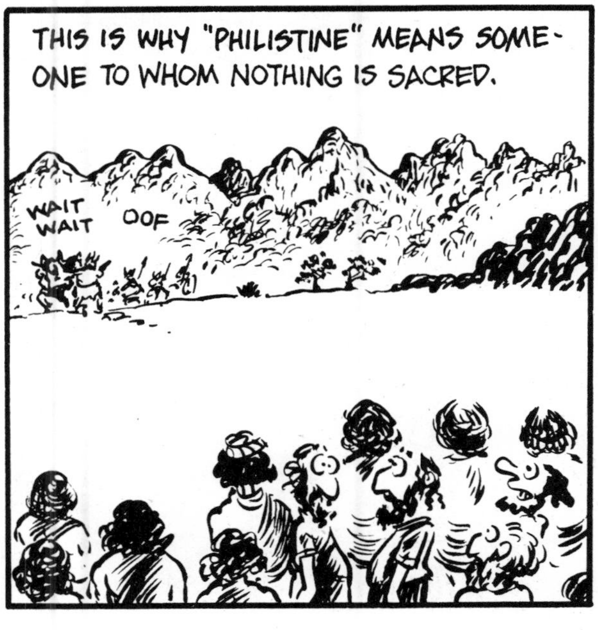
THIS IS WHY "PHILISTINE" MEANS SOME-ONE TO WHOM NOTHING IS SACRED.
WAIT WAIT
OOF

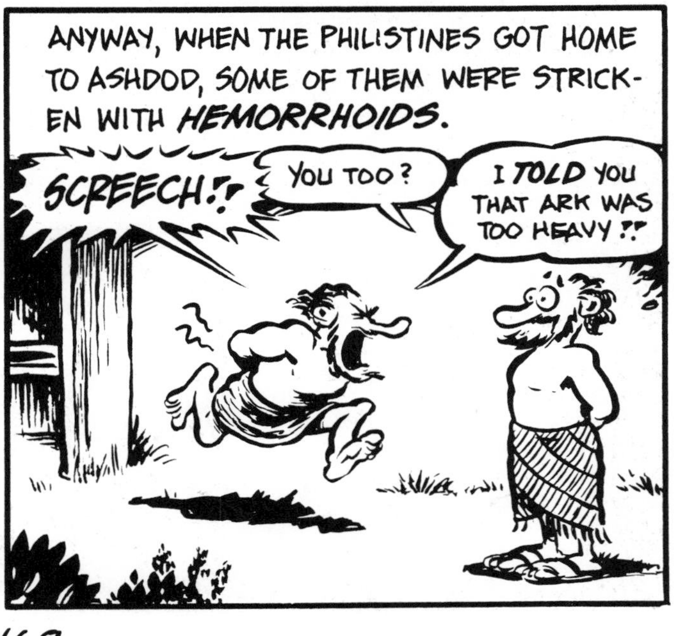
ANYWAY, WHEN THE PHILISTINES GOT HOME TO ASHDOD, SOME OF THEM WERE STRICK-EN WITH *HEMORRHOIDS*.
SCREECH!?!
YOU TOO?
I *TOLD* YOU THAT ARK WAS TOO HEAVY?!

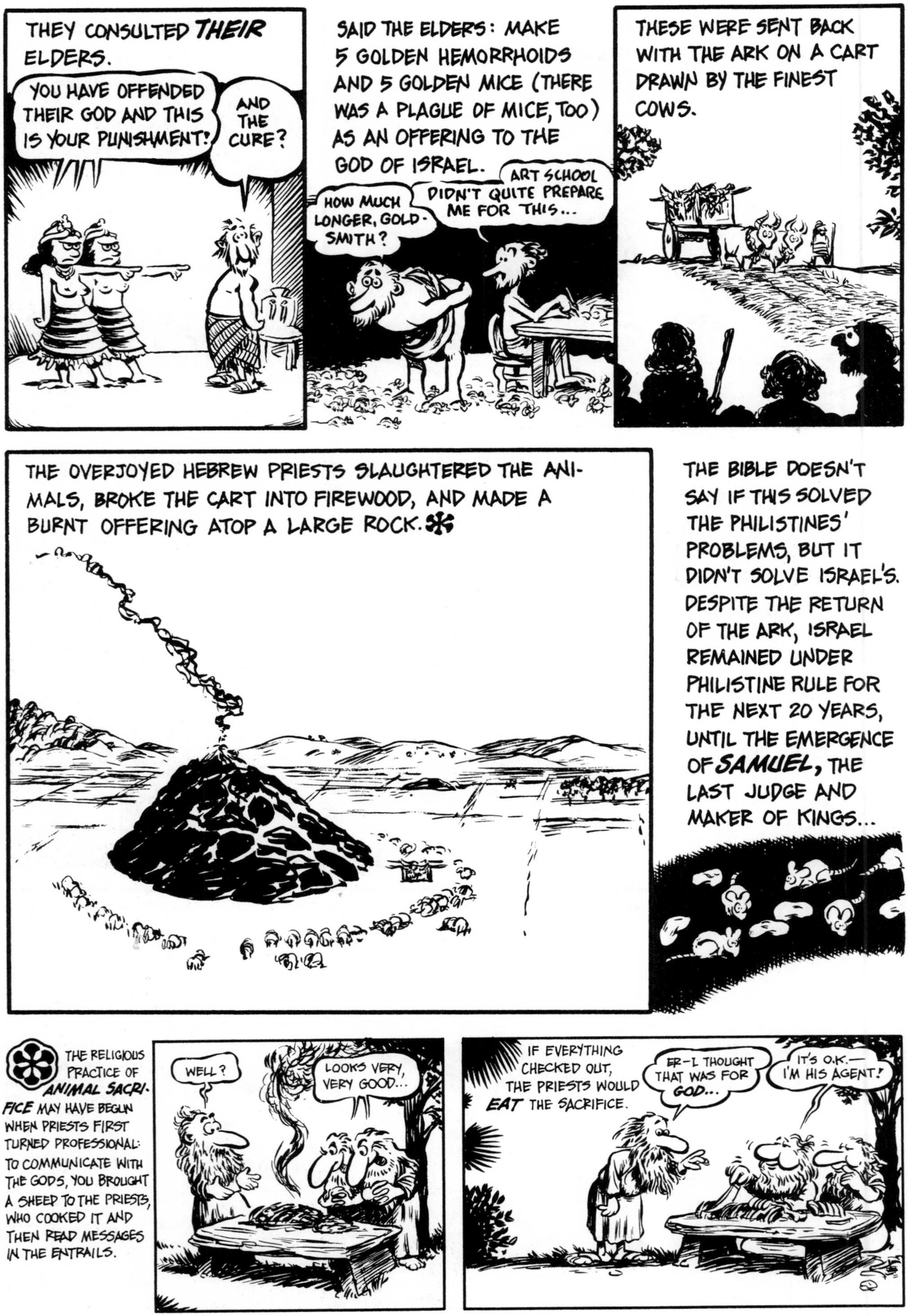
THEY CONSULTED THEIR ELDERS.
YOU HAVE OFFENDED THEIR GOD AND THIS IS YOUR PUNISHMENT!
AND THE CURE?
SAID THE ELDERS: MAKE 5 GOLDEN HEMORRHOIDS AND 5 GOLDEN MICE (THERE WAS A PLAGUE OF MICE, TOO) AS AN OFFERING TO THE GOD OF ISRAEL.
HOW MUCH LONGER, GOLDSMITH?
ART SCHOOL DIDN'T QUITE PREPARE ME FOR THIS...
THESE WERE SENT BACK WITH THE ARK ON A CART DRAWN BY THE FINEST COWS.
THE OVERJOYED HEBREW PRIESTS SLAUGHTERED THE ANIMALS, BROKE THE CART INTO FIREWOOD, AND MADE A BURNT OFFERING ATOP A LARGE ROCK.✻
THE BIBLE DOESN'T SAY IF THIS SOLVED THE PHILISTINES' PROBLEMS, BUT IT DIDN'T SOLVE ISRAEL'S. DESPITE THE RETURN OF THE ARK, ISRAEL REMAINED UNDER PHILISTINE RULE FOR THE NEXT 20 YEARS, UNTIL THE EMERGENCE OF SAMUEL, THE LAST JUDGE AND MAKER OF KINGS...
✻ THE RELIGIOUS PRACTICE OF ANIMAL SACRIFICE MAY HAVE BEGUN WHEN PRIESTS FIRST TURNED PROFESSIONAL: TO COMMUNICATE WITH THE GODS, YOU BROUGHT A SHEEP TO THE PRIESTS, WHO COOKED IT AND THEN READ MESSAGES IN THE ENTRAILS.
WELL?
LOOKS VERY, VERY GOOD...
IF EVERYTHING CHECKED OUT, THE PRIESTS WOULD EAT THE SACRIFICE.
ER—I THOUGHT THAT WAS FOR GOD...
IT'S O.K.— I'M HIS AGENT!

SAMUEL'S STORY BEGAN WHEN A CHILDLESS WOMAN, *HANNAH*, WENT TO TEMPLE AND VOWED INWARDLY:

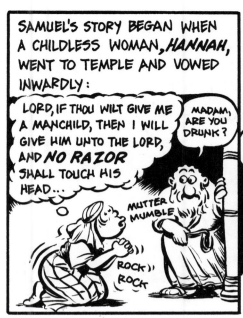

LORD, IF THOU WILT GIVE ME A MANCHILD, THEN I WILL GIVE HIM UNTO THE LORD, AND *NO RAZOR* SHALL TOUCH HIS HEAD...

MADAM, ARE YOU DRUNK?

MUTTER MUMBLE

ROCK ROCK

ELI, THE PRIEST, BLESSED HANNAH; SHE WENT HOME; AND IN TIME HAD A SON, *SAMUEL*, WHOM SHE GAVE BACK TO ELI TO RAISE!

I VOWED, AND HE'S PROBABLY YOURS, ANYWAY!

GROWING TO MANHOOD IN THE TEMPLE, HANNAH'S BOY GOT A REPUTATION AS A PROPHET!

DOOM!

THERE'S JUST SOMETHIN' ABOUT HIM...

IT WAS THE SONS OF ELI WHO HAD DIED GUARDING THE ARK AGAINST THE PHILISTINES, LEAVING ONLY SAMUEL TO JUDGE ISRAEL. WHEN THE TIME WAS RIPE, 20 YEARS LATER, HE CALLED OUT THE TROOPS.

THIS TIME, THE ISRAELITES TROUNCED THE PHILISTINES. (IT PROBABLY RAINED AGAIN.)

SAMUEL BECAME ISRAEL'S LEADER, TRAVELLING FROM PLACE TO PLACE TO SIT IN JUDGMENT.

THE FIRST *CIRCUIT COURT* JUDGE!

IT'S A SHORT CIRCUIT.

THEN, AS SAMUEL GREW OLD, SOME OF THE ELDERS APPROACHED HIM WITH A REQUEST.

SAMUEL, WE WANT A *KING*!!

THE BIBLE DOESN'T GIVE ALL THE REASONS WHY THEY WANTED A KING, BUT WE CAN GUESS.

TIMES HAVE CHANGED: WE'RE A REAL NATION NOW!

OTHER NATIONS HAVE KINGS!

WE NEED SOMEONE TO NEGOTIATE WITH THEM!

THEY THINK PROPHETS ARE TOO WEIRD!

TOO INFLEXIBLE!

TOO HAIRY!

AND WE NEED A REAL ARMY TO FIGHT THOSE PHILISTINES!

WELL?

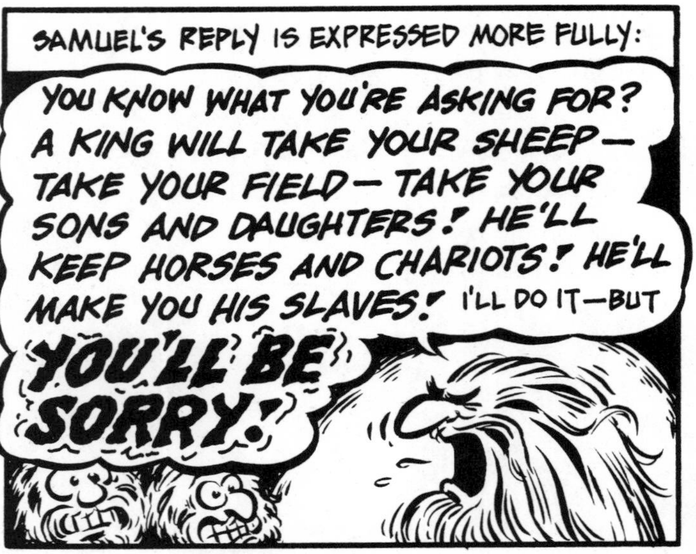
SAMUEL'S REPLY IS EXPRESSED MORE FULLY:
YOU KNOW WHAT YOU'RE ASKING FOR? A KING WILL TAKE YOUR SHEEP— TAKE YOUR FIELD— TAKE YOUR SONS AND DAUGHTERS! HE'LL KEEP HORSES AND CHARIOTS! HE'LL MAKE YOU HIS SLAVES! I'LL DO IT—BUT YOU'LL BE SORRY!

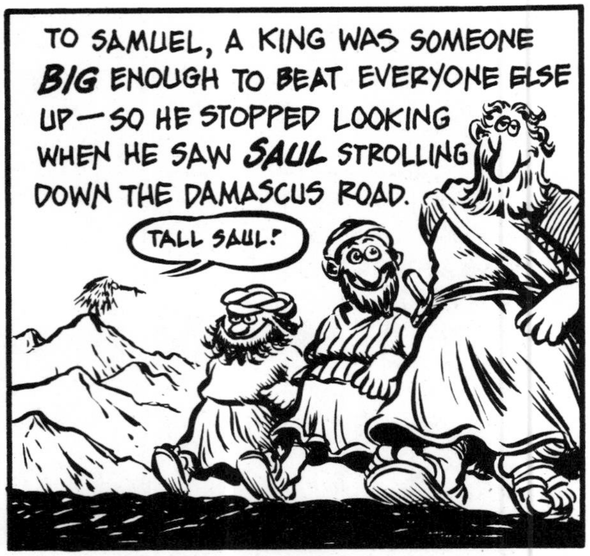
TO SAMUEL, A KING WAS SOMEONE BIG ENOUGH TO BEAT EVERYONE ELSE UP—SO HE STOPPED LOOKING WHEN HE SAW SAUL STROLLING DOWN THE DAMASCUS ROAD.
TALL SAUL!

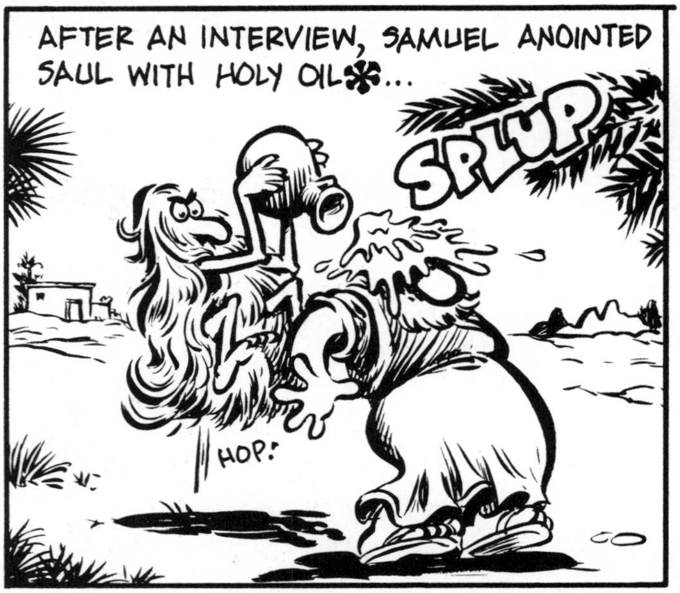
AFTER AN INTERVIEW, SAMUEL ANOINTED SAUL WITH HOLY OIL✽...
SPLUP
HOP!

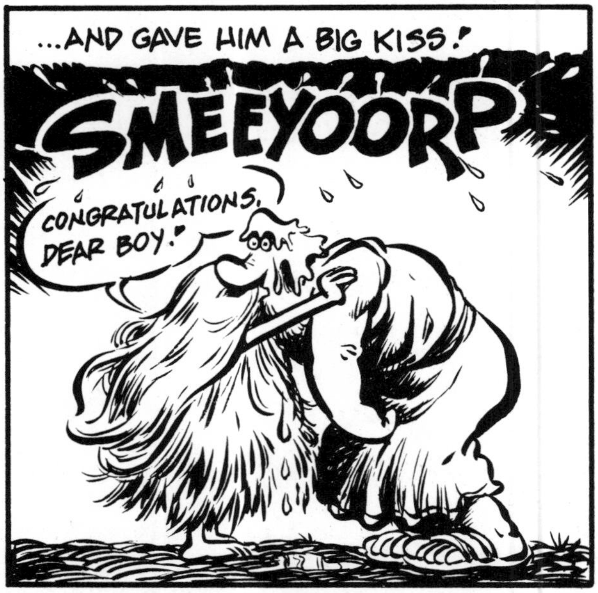
...AND GAVE HIM A BIG KISS!
SMEEYOORP
CONGRATULATIONS, DEAR BOY!

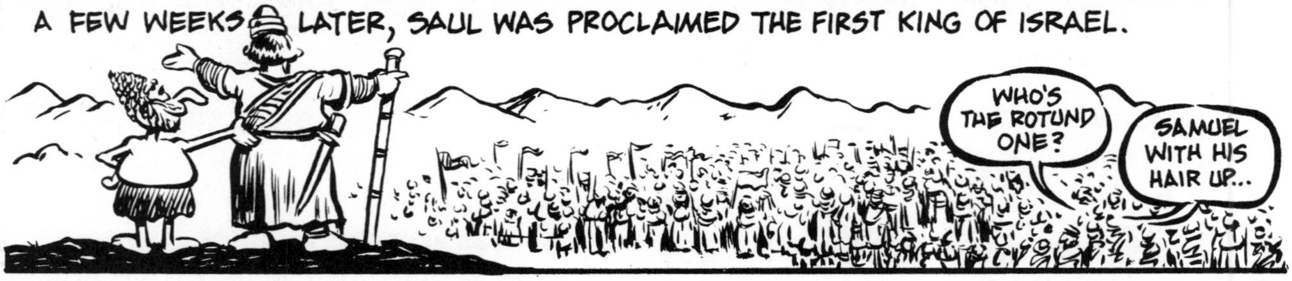
A FEW WEEKS LATER, SAUL WAS PROCLAIMED THE FIRST KING OF ISRAEL.
WHO'S THE ROTUND ONE?
SAMUEL WITH HIS HAIR UP...

✽ THE HEBREW CUSTOM OF POURING OIL ON THE KING'S HEAD IS THOUGHT TO COME FROM AN EGYPTIAN CEREMONY IN WHICH A ROYAL GOVERNOR SWORE LOYALTY TO PHARAOH, THE LIVING GOD.

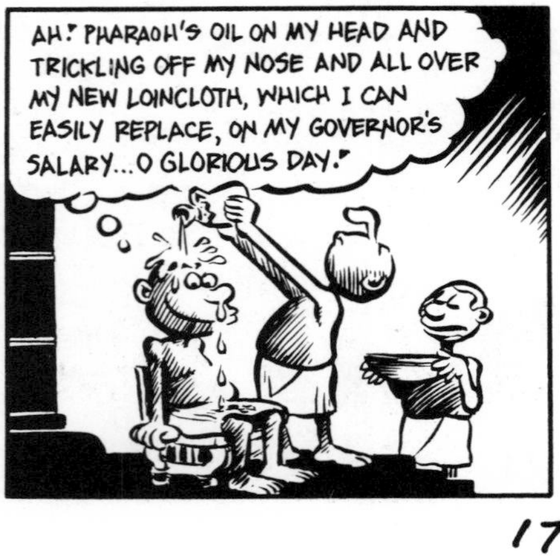
AH! PHARAOH'S OIL ON MY HEAD AND TRICKLING OFF MY NOSE AND ALL OVER MY NEW LOINCLOTH, WHICH I CAN EASILY REPLACE, ON MY GOVERNOR'S SALARY...O GLORIOUS DAY!

IN THE CASE OF THE HEBREWS, THEN, THE ANOINTING DID NOT GIVE THE KING ABSOLUTE POWER, BUT RATHER MEANT THAT HE WAS MERELY *GOD'S GOVERNOR*.

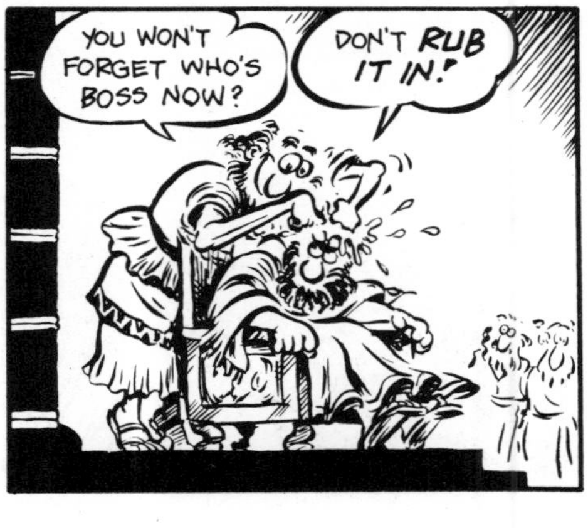
YOU WON'T FORGET WHO'S BOSS NOW?
DON'T RUB IT IN!

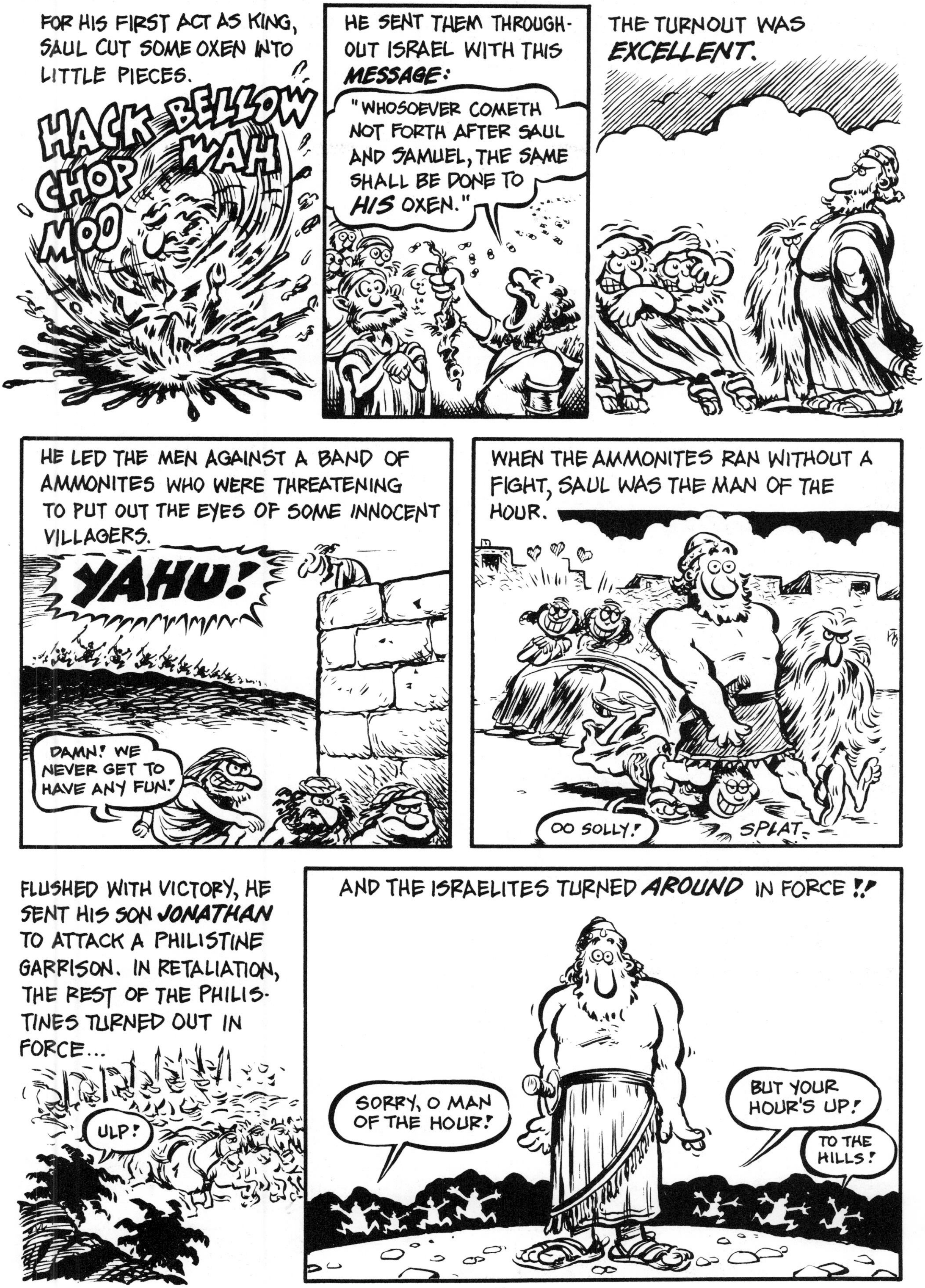
FOR HIS FIRST ACT AS KING, SAUL CUT SOME OXEN INTO LITTLE PIECES.
HACK BELLOW CHOP WAH MOO
HE SENT THEM THROUGH-OUT ISRAEL WITH THIS MESSAGE:
"WHOSOEVER COMETH NOT FORTH AFTER SAUL AND SAMUEL, THE SAME SHALL BE DONE TO HIS OXEN."
THE TURNOUT WAS EXCELLENT.
HE LED THE MEN AGAINST A BAND OF AMMONITES WHO WERE THREATENING TO PUT OUT THE EYES OF SOME INNOCENT VILLAGERS.
YAHU!
DAMN! WE NEVER GET TO HAVE ANY FUN!
WHEN THE AMMONITES RAN WITHOUT A FIGHT, SAUL WAS THE MAN OF THE HOUR.
OO SOLLY!
SPLAT
FLUSHED WITH VICTORY, HE SENT HIS SON JONATHAN TO ATTACK A PHILISTINE GARRISON. IN RETALIATION, THE REST OF THE PHILIS-TINES TURNED OUT IN FORCE...
ULP!
AND THE ISRAELITES TURNED AROUND IN FORCE!!
SORRY, O MAN OF THE HOUR!
BUT YOUR HOUR'S UP!
TO THE HILLS!

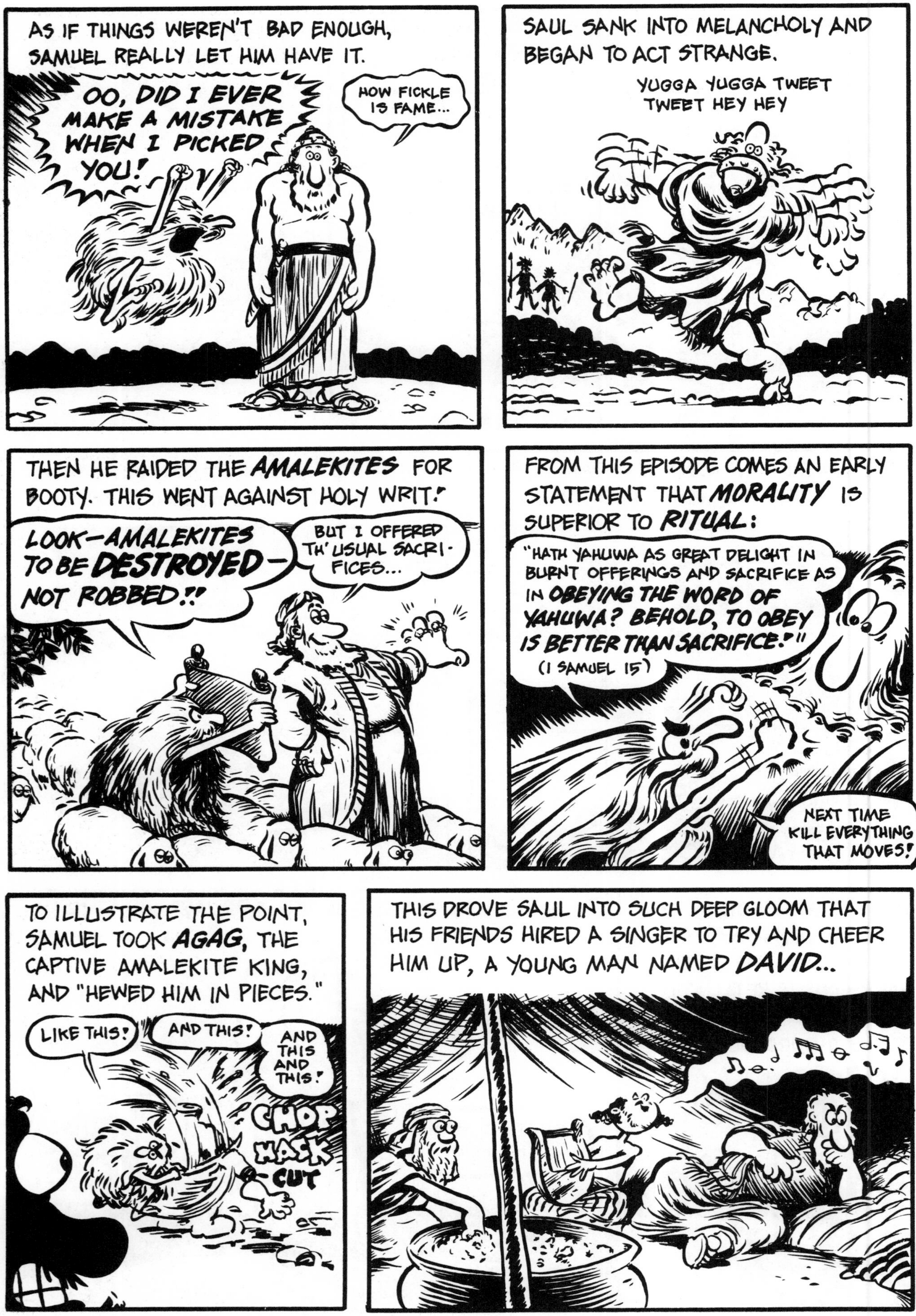
AS IF THINGS WEREN'T BAD ENOUGH, SAMUEL REALLY LET HIM HAVE IT.
OO, DID I EVER MAKE A MISTAKE WHEN I PICKED YOU!
HOW FICKLE IS FAME...
SAUL SANK INTO MELANCHOLY AND BEGAN TO ACT STRANGE.
YUGGA YUGGA TWEET TWEET HEY HEY
THEN HE RAIDED THE AMALEKITES FOR BOOTY. THIS WENT AGAINST HOLY WRIT!
LOOK—AMALEKITES TO BE DESTROYED—NOT ROBBED!!
BUT I OFFERED TH' USUAL SACRIFICES...
FROM THIS EPISODE COMES AN EARLY STATEMENT THAT MORALITY IS SUPERIOR TO RITUAL:
"HATH YAHUWA AS GREAT DELIGHT IN BURNT OFFERINGS AND SACRIFICE AS IN OBEYING THE WORD OF YAHUWA? BEHOLD, TO OBEY IS BETTER THAN SACRIFICE!" (I SAMUEL 15)
NEXT TIME KILL EVERYTHING THAT MOVES!
TO ILLUSTRATE THE POINT, SAMUEL TOOK AGAG, THE CAPTIVE AMALEKITE KING, AND "HEWED HIM IN PIECES."
LIKE THIS!
AND THIS!
AND THIS AND THIS!
CHOP
HACK
CUT
THIS DROVE SAUL INTO SUCH DEEP GLOOM THAT HIS FRIENDS HIRED A SINGER TO TRY AND CHEER HIM UP, A YOUNG MAN NAMED DAVID...

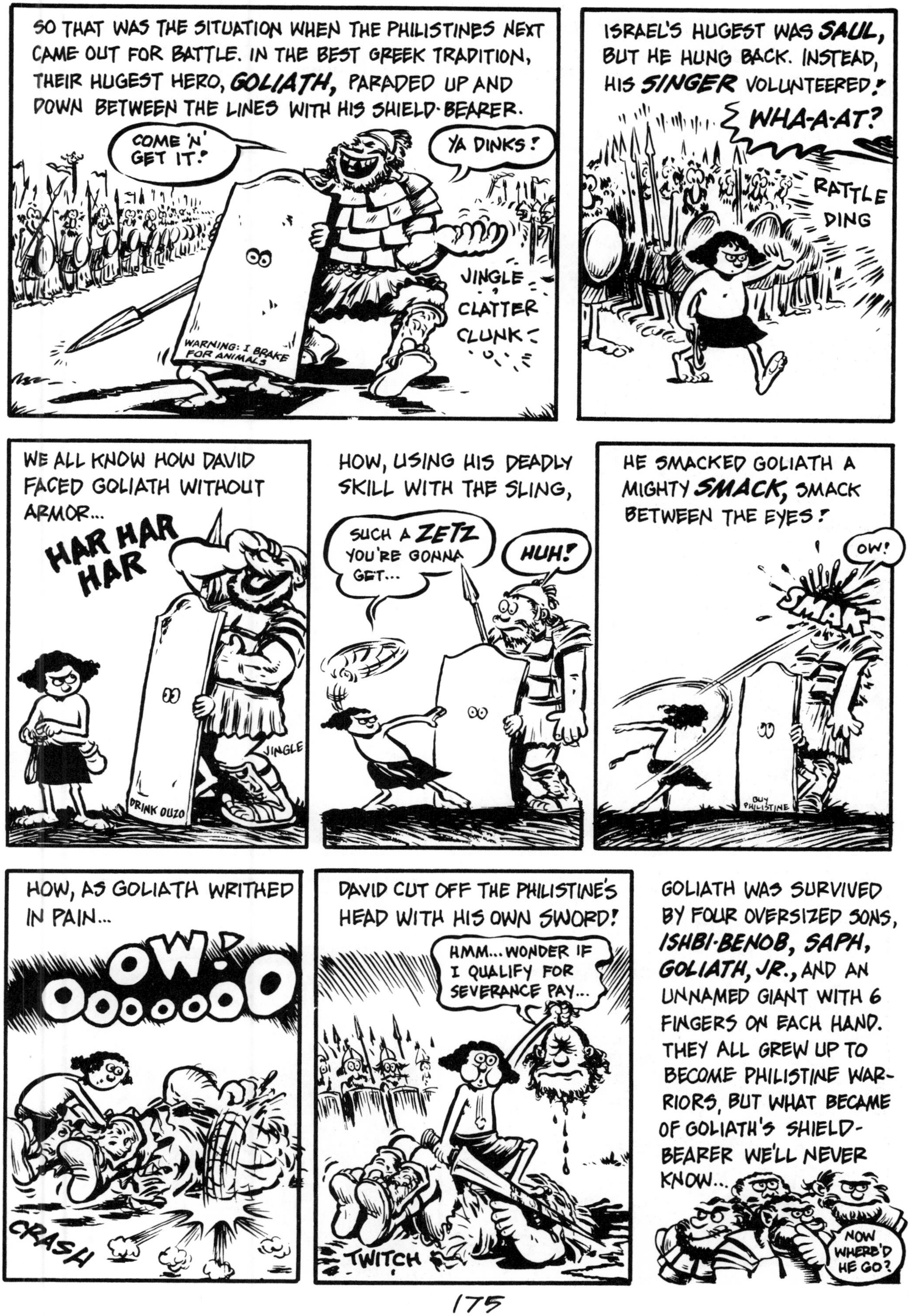
SO THAT WAS THE SITUATION WHEN THE PHILISTINES NEXT CAME OUT FOR BATTLE. IN THE BEST GREEK TRADITION, THEIR HUGEST HERO, GOLIATH, PARADED UP AND DOWN BETWEEN THE LINES WITH HIS SHIELD-BEARER.
COME 'N' GET IT!
YA DINKS!
JINGLE
CLATTER
CLUNK
WARNING: I BRAKE FOR ANIMALS
ISRAEL'S HUGEST WAS SAUL, BUT HE HUNG BACK. INSTEAD, HIS SINGER VOLUNTEERED!
WHA-A-AT?
RATTLE
DING
WE ALL KNOW HOW DAVID FACED GOLIATH WITHOUT ARMOR...
HAR HAR HAR
JINGLE
DRINK OUZO
HOW, USING HIS DEADLY SKILL WITH THE SLING,
SUCH A ZETZ YOU'RE GONNA GET...
HUH!
HE SMACKED GOLIATH A MIGHTY SMACK, SMACK BETWEEN THE EYES!
OW!
SMAK
BUY PHILISTINE
HOW, AS GOLIATH WRITHED IN PAIN...
OW!OOOOOOOO
CRASH
DAVID CUT OFF THE PHILISTINE'S HEAD WITH HIS OWN SWORD!
HMM... WONDER IF I QUALIFY FOR SEVERANCE PAY...
TWITCH
GOLIATH WAS SURVIVED BY FOUR OVERSIZED SONS, ISHBI-BENOB, SAPH, GOLIATH, JR., AND AN UNNAMED GIANT WITH 6 FINGERS ON EACH HAND. THEY ALL GREW UP TO BECOME PHILISTINE WARRIORS, BUT WHAT BECAME OF GOLIATH'S SHIELD-BEARER WE'LL NEVER KNOW...
NOW WHERE'D HE GO?

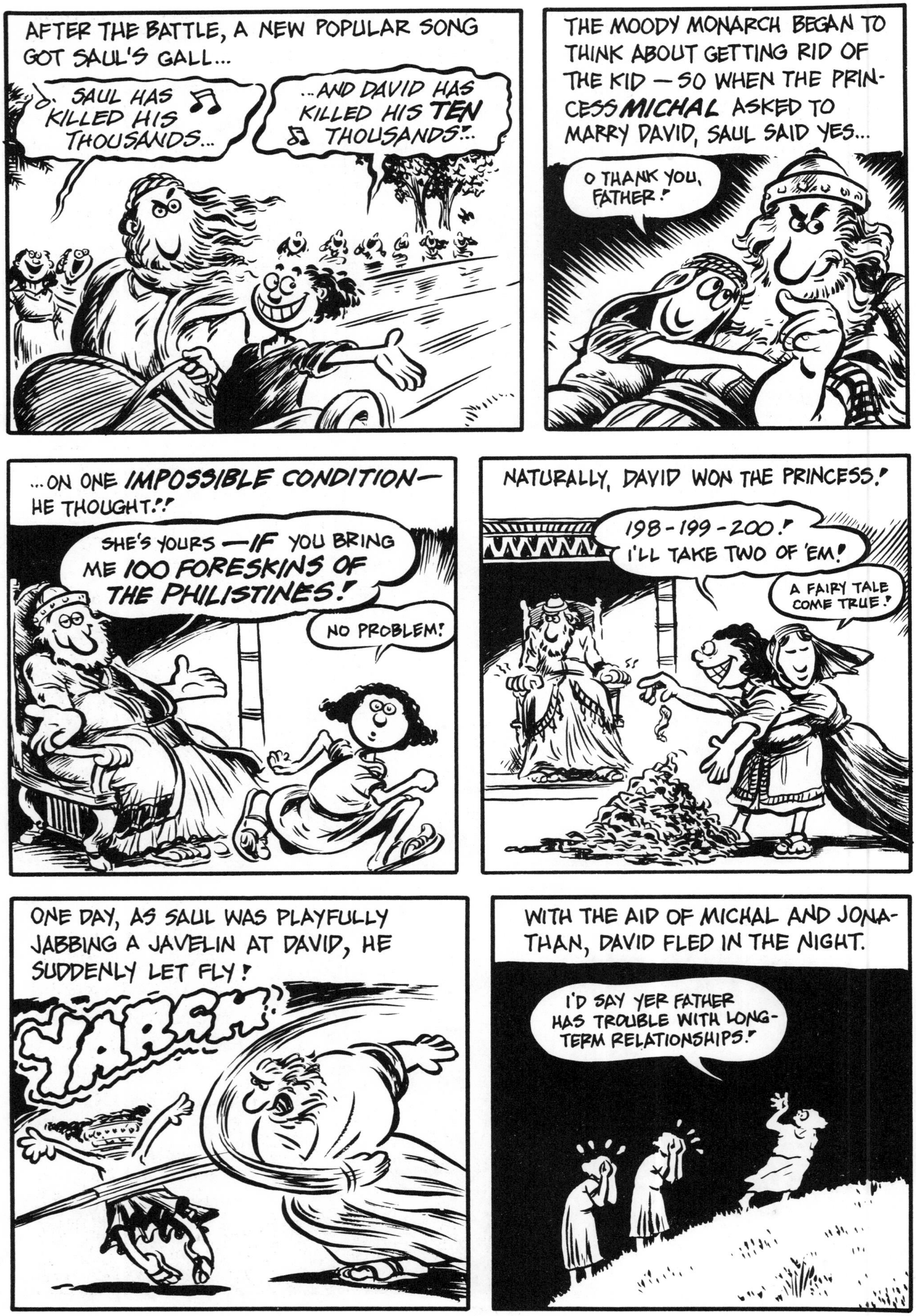
AFTER THE BATTLE, A NEW POPULAR SONG GOT SAUL'S GALL...
SAUL HAS KILLED HIS THOUSANDS...
...AND DAVID HAS KILLED HIS TEN THOUSANDS!..
THE MOODY MONARCH BEGAN TO THINK ABOUT GETTING RID OF THE KID — SO WHEN THE PRIN-CESS MICHAL ASKED TO MARRY DAVID, SAUL SAID YES...
O THANK YOU, FATHER!
...ON ONE IMPOSSIBLE CONDITION— HE THOUGHT!!
SHE'S YOURS —IF YOU BRING ME 100 FORESKINS OF THE PHILISTINES!
NO PROBLEM!
NATURALLY, DAVID WON THE PRINCESS!
198-199-200! I'LL TAKE TWO OF 'EM!
A FAIRY TALE COME TRUE!
ONE DAY, AS SAUL WAS PLAYFULLY JABBING A JAVELIN AT DAVID, HE SUDDENLY LET FLY!
YARRGH!
WITH THE AID OF MICHAL AND JONA-THAN, DAVID FLED IN THE NIGHT.
I'D SAY YER FATHER HAS TROUBLE WITH LONG-TERM RELATIONSHIPS!

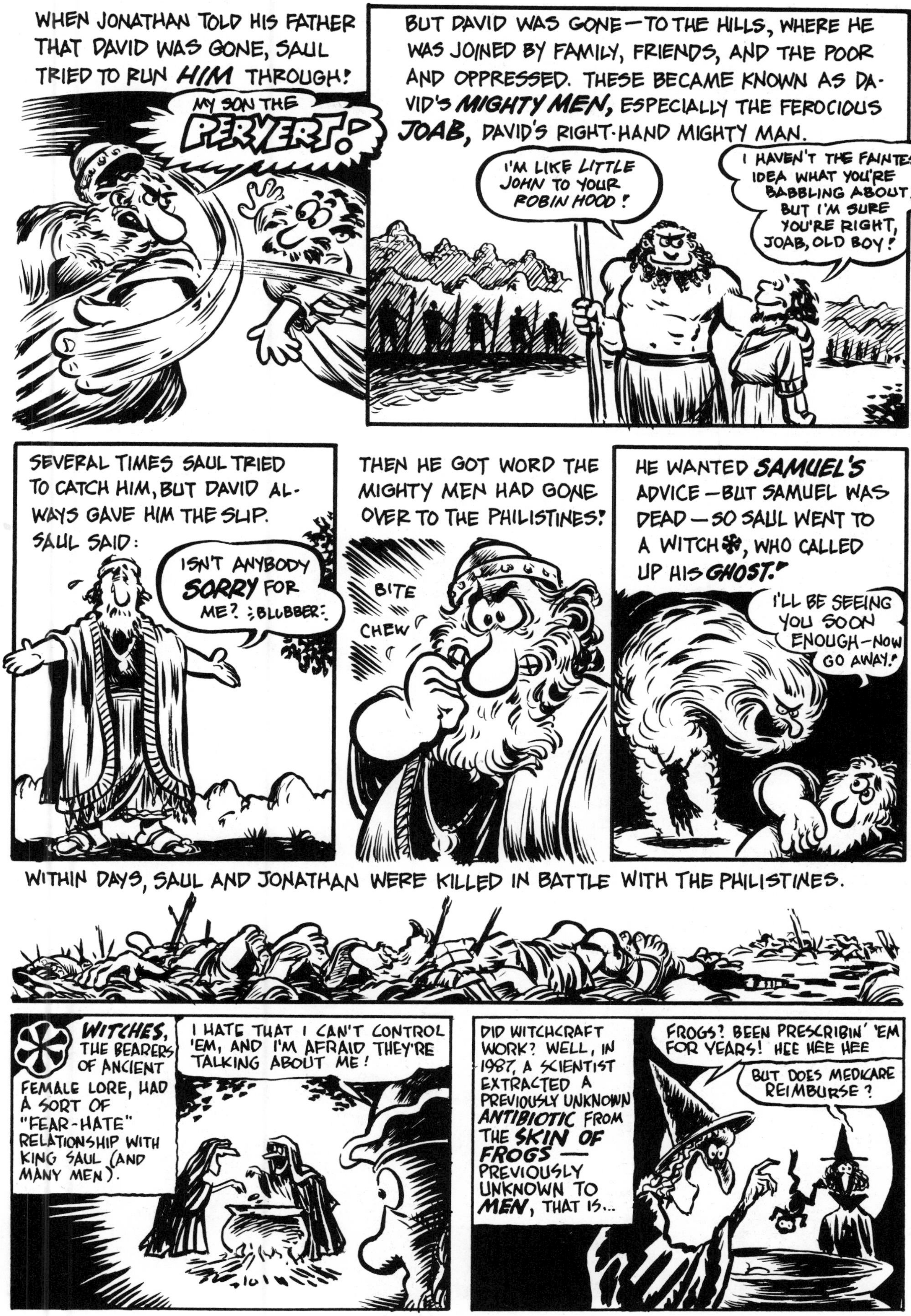
WHEN JONATHAN TOLD HIS FATHER THAT DAVID WAS GONE, SAUL TRIED TO RUN **HIM** THROUGH!
MY SON THE PERVERT!
BUT DAVID WAS GONE—TO THE HILLS, WHERE HE WAS JOINED BY FAMILY, FRIENDS, AND THE POOR AND OPPRESSED. THESE BECAME KNOWN AS DAVID'S **MIGHTY MEN**, ESPECIALLY THE FEROCIOUS **JOAB**, DAVID'S RIGHT-HAND MIGHTY MAN.
I'M LIKE LITTLE JOHN TO YOUR ROBIN HOOD!
I HAVEN'T THE FAINTEST IDEA WHAT YOU'RE BABBLING ABOUT, BUT I'M SURE YOU'RE RIGHT, JOAB, OLD BOY!
SEVERAL TIMES SAUL TRIED TO CATCH HIM, BUT DAVID ALWAYS GAVE HIM THE SLIP. SAUL SAID:
ISN'T ANYBODY **SORRY** FOR ME? :BLUBBER:
THEN HE GOT WORD THE MIGHTY MEN HAD GONE OVER TO THE PHILISTINES!
BITE
CHEW
HE WANTED **SAMUEL'S** ADVICE—BUT SAMUEL WAS DEAD—SO SAUL WENT TO A WITCH✽, WHO CALLED UP HIS **GHOST**.
I'LL BE SEEING YOU SOON ENOUGH—NOW GO AWAY!
WITHIN DAYS, SAUL AND JONATHAN WERE KILLED IN BATTLE WITH THE PHILISTINES.
✽ **WITCHES**, THE BEARERS OF ANCIENT FEMALE LORE, HAD A SORT OF "FEAR-HATE" RELATIONSHIP WITH KING SAUL (AND MANY MEN).
I HATE THAT I CAN'T CONTROL 'EM, AND I'M AFRAID THEY'RE TALKING ABOUT ME!
DID WITCHCRAFT WORK? WELL, IN 1987, A SCIENTIST EXTRACTED A PREVIOUSLY UNKNOWN **ANTIBIOTIC** FROM THE **SKIN OF FROGS**—PREVIOUSLY UNKNOWN TO **MEN**, THAT IS...
FROGS? BEEN PRESCRIBIN' 'EM FOR YEARS! HEE HEE HEE
BUT DOES MEDICARE REIMBURSE?

NOW DAVID LED THE MIGHTY MEN TO **HEBRON,** WHERE THE TRIBE OF **JUDAH** CROWNED HIM KING. THE REST OF ISRAEL FOLLOWED **ISHBAAL,** A SON OF SAUL. THIS SPLIT WAS A TASTE OF THINGS TO COME.

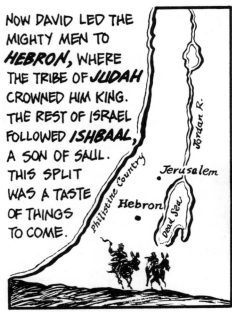

Jordan R.

Philistine Country

Jerusalem

Hebron

Dead Sea

FOR TWO YEARS THE RIVALS BATTLED, AND BIT BY BIT THE MIGHTY MEN GOT THE UPPER HAND. FINALLY, ISHBAAL WAS ASSAS-SINATED IN BED.

THE KILLERS BROUGHT HIS HEAD TO DAVID.

TO THEIR SHOCK, HE ORDERED THEM EXECUTED AND THEIR HANDS AND FEET CUT OFF AND HUNG UP!

WE DON'T GO MURDERING KINGS IN THEIR BEDS!

WAGGLE

AND SO, AT AGE 30 (OR SO) DAVID BECAME KING OF ISRAEL.

FOR HIS CAPITAL, DAVID CHOSE **JERUSALEM,** A HILL TOWN OCCUPIED SINCE 1800 B.C., BY THE JEBUSITES, A PEOPLE WHOM ISRAEL HAD NEVER MANAGED TO CONQUER. IM-PRESSED BY ITS STRONG POSITION, DAVID LED AN ARMY AGAINST JERUSALEM AND TOOK THE CITY.

THEN HE DANCED HALF-NAKED THROUGH THE STREETS, SINGING HYMNS OF VICTORY.

PANT, PUFF

178

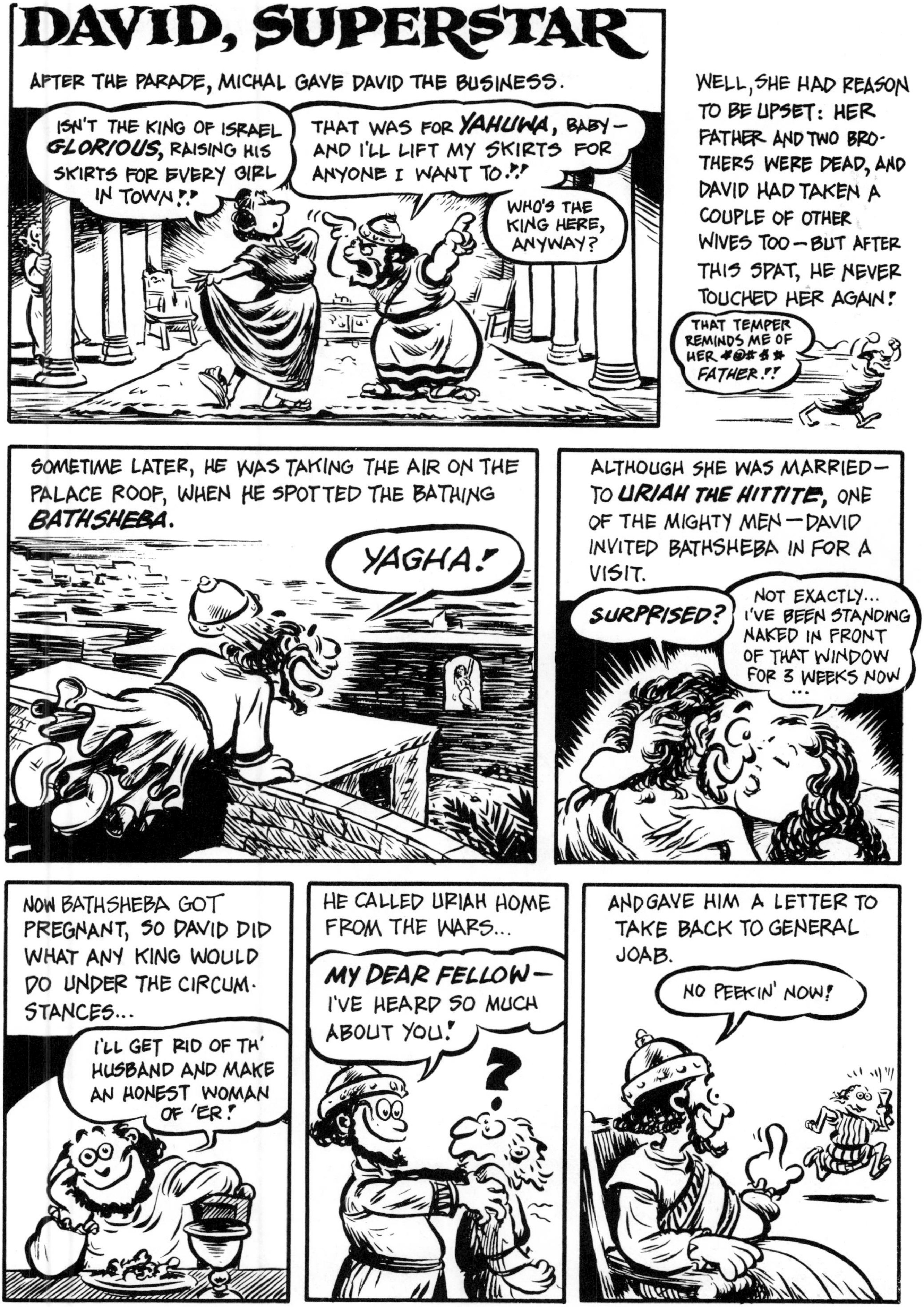
DAVID, SUPERSTAR
AFTER THE PARADE, MICHAL GAVE DAVID THE BUSINESS.
ISN'T THE KING OF ISRAEL GLORIOUS, RAISING HIS SKIRTS FOR EVERY GIRL IN TOWN!?
THAT WAS FOR YAHUWA, BABY— AND I'LL LIFT MY SKIRTS FOR ANYONE I WANT TO!?
WHO'S THE KING HERE, ANYWAY?
WELL, SHE HAD REASON TO BE UPSET: HER FATHER AND TWO BROTHERS WERE DEAD, AND DAVID HAD TAKEN A COUPLE OF OTHER WIVES TOO—BUT AFTER THIS SPAT, HE NEVER TOUCHED HER AGAIN!
THAT TEMPER REMINDS ME OF HER #@#$* FATHER!?
SOMETIME LATER, HE WAS TAKING THE AIR ON THE PALACE ROOF, WHEN HE SPOTTED THE BATHING BATHSHEBA.
YAGHA!
ALTHOUGH SHE WAS MARRIED— TO URIAH THE HITTITE, ONE OF THE MIGHTY MEN—DAVID INVITED BATHSHEBA IN FOR A VISIT.
SURPRISED?
NOT EXACTLY... I'VE BEEN STANDING NAKED IN FRONT OF THAT WINDOW FOR 3 WEEKS NOW...
NOW BATHSHEBA GOT PREGNANT, SO DAVID DID WHAT ANY KING WOULD DO UNDER THE CIRCUMSTANCES...
I'LL GET RID OF TH' HUSBAND AND MAKE AN HONEST WOMAN OF 'ER!
HE CALLED URIAH HOME FROM THE WARS...
MY DEAR FELLOW— I'VE HEARD SO MUCH ABOUT YOU!
?
AND GAVE HIM A LETTER TO TAKE BACK TO GENERAL JOAB.
NO PEEKIN' NOW!

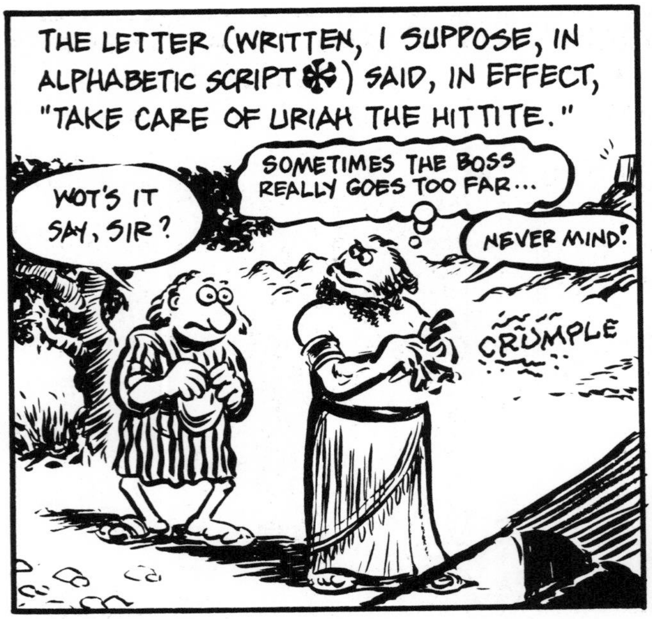
THE LETTER (WRITTEN, I SUPPOSE, IN ALPHABETIC SCRIPT ✿) SAID, IN EFFECT, "TAKE CARE OF URIAH THE HITTITE."
WOT'S IT SAY, SIR?
SOMETIMES THE BOSS REALLY GOES TOO FAR...
NEVER MIND!
CRUMPLE

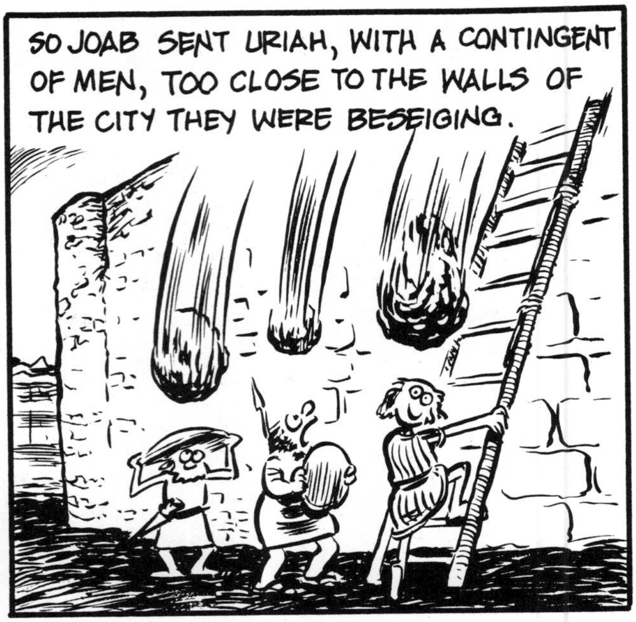
SO JOAB SENT URIAH, WITH A CONTINGENT OF MEN, TOO CLOSE TO THE WALLS OF THE CITY THEY WERE BESEIGING.

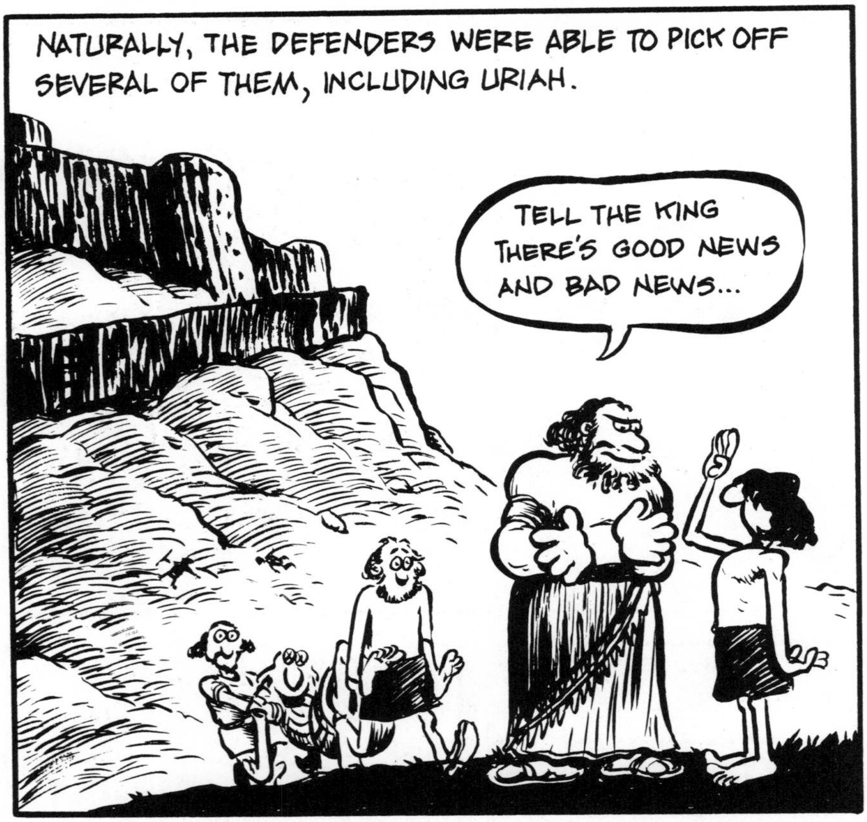
NATURALLY, THE DEFENDERS WERE ABLE TO PICK OFF SEVERAL OF THEM, INCLUDING URIAH.
TELL THE KING THERE'S GOOD NEWS AND BAD NEWS...

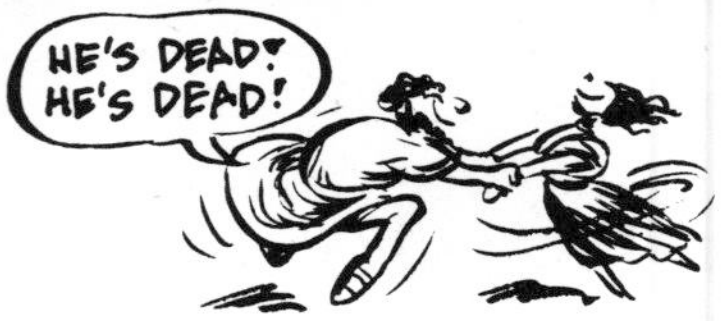
HE'S DEAD! HE'S DEAD!

AFTER A PROPER PERIOD OF MOURNING, DAVID MARRIED BATHSHEBA, BUT THEIR BABY DIED—GOD'S PUNISHMENT, IT WAS SAID. STILL, THEY TRIED AGAIN, AND THE SECOND EFFORT WORKED: A SON THEY NAMED ***SOLOMON.***

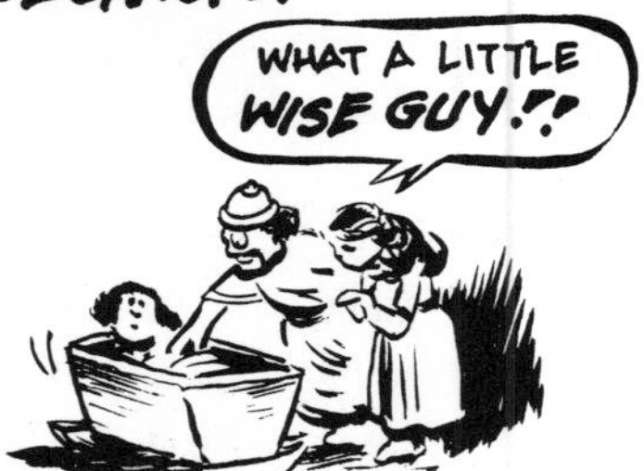
WHAT A LITTLE ***WISE GUY!?!***

✿ THE ***ALPHABET*** WAS INVENTED AT LEAST TWICE IN ANCIENT CANAAN, BUT ALL VERSIONS DIED OUT EXCEPT FOR THE ONE DEVISED BY SEMITIC COPPER MINERS IN THE SINAI. THIS 22-CHARACTER SCRIPT, BASED ON EGYPTIAN ***HIEROGLYPHS***, IS THE ANCESTOR OF ALL MODERN ALPHABETS.

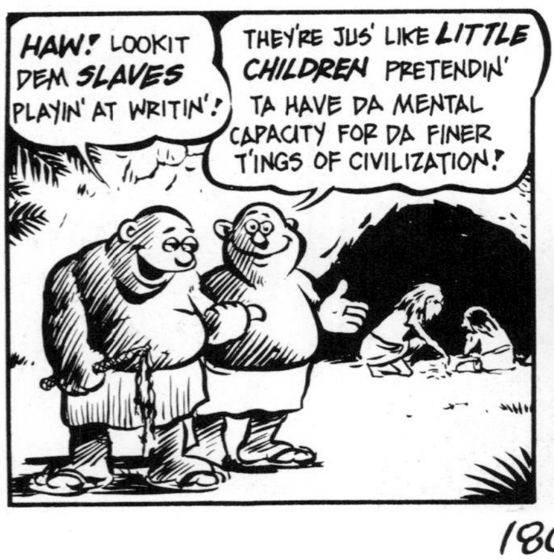
HAW! LOOKIT DEM ***SLAVES*** PLAYIN' AT WRITIN'!
THEY'RE JUS' LIKE ***LITTLE CHILDREN*** PRETENDIN' TA HAVE DA MENTAL CAPACITY FOR DA FINER T'INGS OF CIVILIZATION!

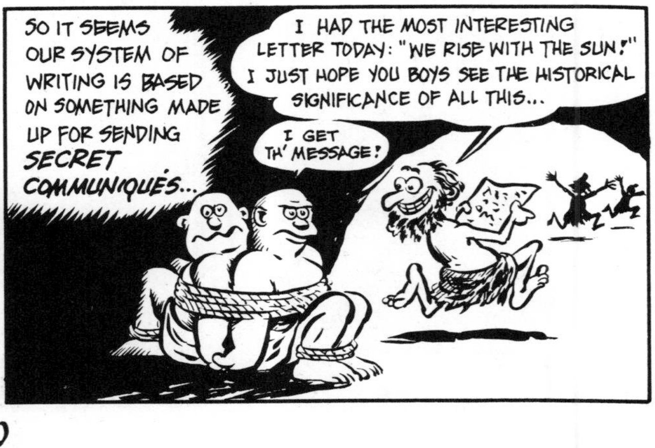
SO IT SEEMS OUR SYSTEM OF WRITING IS BASED ON SOMETHING MADE UP FOR SENDING ***SECRET COMMUNIQUÉS...***
I HAD THE MOST INTERESTING LETTER TODAY: "WE RISE WITH THE SUN!" I JUST HOPE YOU BOYS SEE THE HISTORICAL SIGNIFICANCE OF ALL THIS...
I GET TH' MESSAGE!

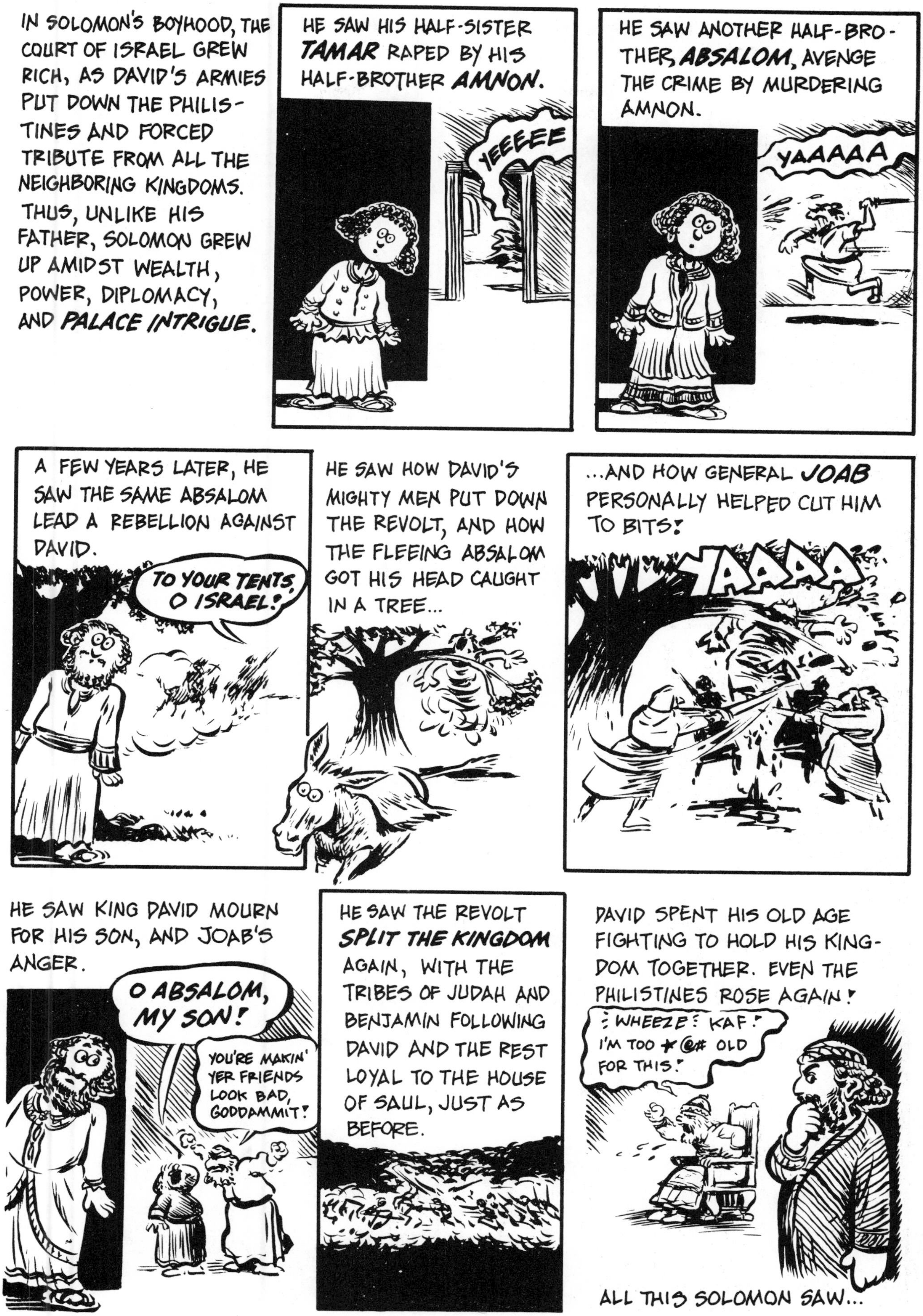
IN SOLOMON'S BOYHOOD, THE COURT OF ISRAEL GREW RICH, AS DAVID'S ARMIES PUT DOWN THE PHILISTINES AND FORCED TRIBUTE FROM ALL THE NEIGHBORING KINGDOMS. THUS, UNLIKE HIS FATHER, SOLOMON GREW UP AMIDST WEALTH, POWER, DIPLOMACY, AND **PALACE INTRIGUE**.
HE SAW HIS HALF-SISTER **TAMAR** RAPED BY HIS HALF-BROTHER **AMNON**.
YEEEEEE
HE SAW ANOTHER HALF-BROTHER, **ABSALOM**, AVENGE THE CRIME BY MURDERING AMNON.
YAAAAA
A FEW YEARS LATER, HE SAW THE SAME ABSALOM LEAD A REBELLION AGAINST DAVID.
TO YOUR TENTS, O ISRAEL!
HE SAW HOW DAVID'S MIGHTY MEN PUT DOWN THE REVOLT, AND HOW THE FLEEING ABSALOM GOT HIS HEAD CAUGHT IN A TREE...
...AND HOW GENERAL **JOAB** PERSONALLY HELPED CUT HIM TO BITS!
YAAAA
HE SAW KING DAVID MOURN FOR HIS SON, AND JOAB'S ANGER.
O ABSALOM, MY SON!
YOU'RE MAKIN' YER FRIENDS LOOK BAD, GODDAMMIT!
HE SAW THE REVOLT **SPLIT THE KINGDOM** AGAIN, WITH THE TRIBES OF JUDAH AND BENJAMIN FOLLOWING DAVID AND THE REST LOYAL TO THE HOUSE OF SAUL, JUST AS BEFORE.
DAVID SPENT HIS OLD AGE FIGHTING TO HOLD HIS KINGDOM TOGETHER. EVEN THE PHILISTINES ROSE AGAIN!
:WHEEZE: KAF! I'M TOO *@# OLD FOR THIS!
ALL THIS SOLOMON SAW...

AS DAVID LAY DYING, RACKED BY CHILLS, HIS ADVISERS TRIED TO WARM HIM UP WITH THE BEAUTY *ABISHAG*, AND HIS SONS BEGAN EYEING THE THRONE...

I DON'T GET IT! THIS NEVER FAILED BEFORE!

ONE, *ADONIJAH* ("LORD JAH") STAGED HIS OWN CORONATION WITHOUT INVITING SOLOMON.

MEANWHILE, BATHSHEBA BEGGED THE DYING KING TO FAVOR HER SON.

AS YOU VALUE *MY* LIFE, LORD!

GURGLEDY

HE SAYS "YES!"

JAB

CLAIMING DAVID'S BLESSING, THE PRIESTS, PROPHETS, AND MIGHTY MEN PROCLAIMED SOLOMON KING AND HELD A HUGE PARADE. AT THE SIGHT, ADONIJAH'S FRIENDS TURNED TAIL!

I'LL TAKE THAT!

ADONIJAH ENDED UP BEGGING FOR MERCY, AND SOLOMON SAID:

"IF HE SHALL SHOW HIMSELF A WORTHY MAN, THERE SHALL NOT A HAIR OF HIM FALL TO EARTH!"

BUT AS SOON AS DAVID DIED, SOLOMON FOUND AN EXCUSE TO PUT HIS RIVAL TO DEATH.

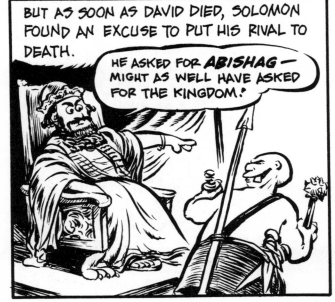

HE ASKED FOR *ABISHAG* — MIGHT AS WELL HAVE ASKED FOR THE KINGDOM!

ADONIJAH'S FRIENDS, TOO, WERE OFFED, INCLUDING OLD GENERAL JOAB, AS HE CLUNG TO THE TABERNACLE ALTAR.

GIVE UP?

POKE!

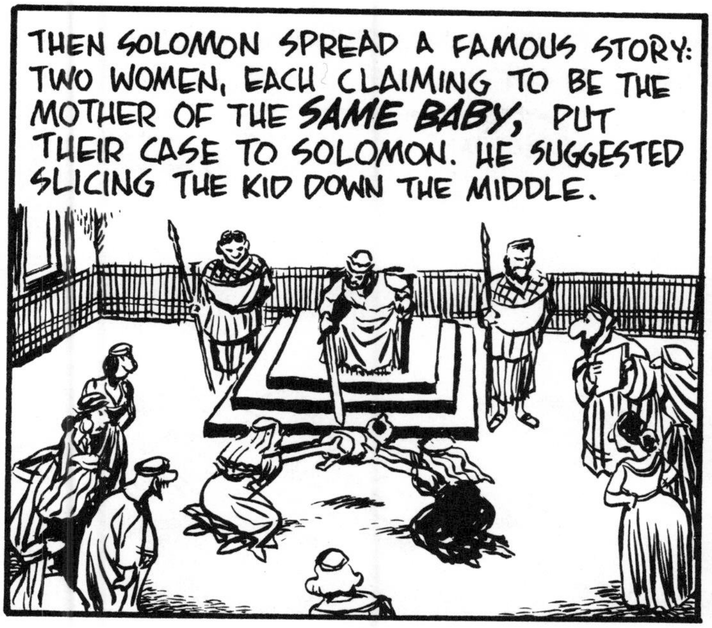
THEN SOLOMON SPREAD A FAMOUS STORY: TWO WOMEN, EACH CLAIMING TO BE THE MOTHER OF THE **SAME BABY,** PUT THEIR CASE TO SOLOMON. HE SUGGESTED SLICING THE KID DOWN THE MIDDLE.

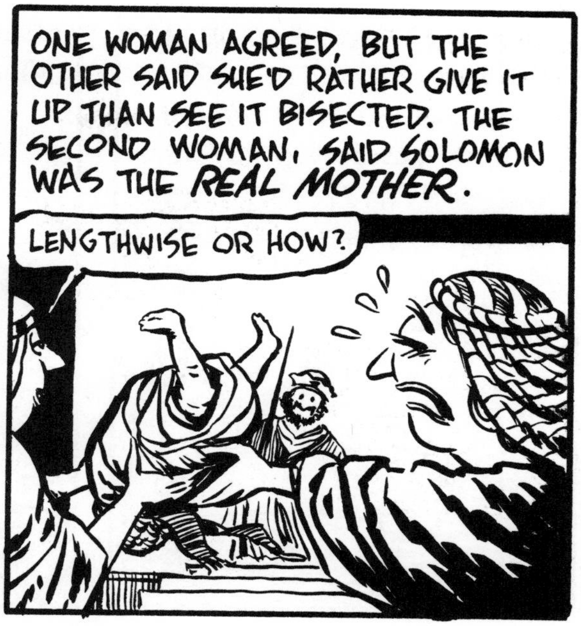
ONE WOMAN AGREED, BUT THE OTHER SAID SHE'D RATHER GIVE IT UP THAN SEE IT BISECTED. THE SECOND WOMAN, SAID SOLOMON WAS THE **REAL MOTHER**.
LENGTHWISE OR HOW?

NOW, SAYS THE BIBLE, SOMETHING **ODD** HAPPENED: ON HEARING THIS INCIDENT, ALL ISRAEL **TREMBLED**. WHY DID THEY TREMBLE?

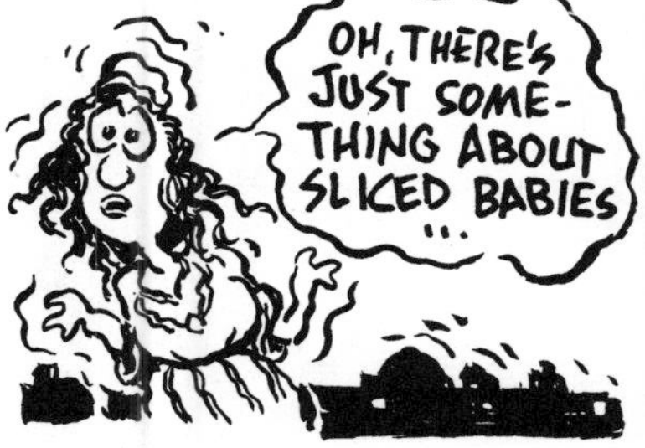
OH, THERE'S JUST SOMETHING ABOUT SLICED BABIES ...

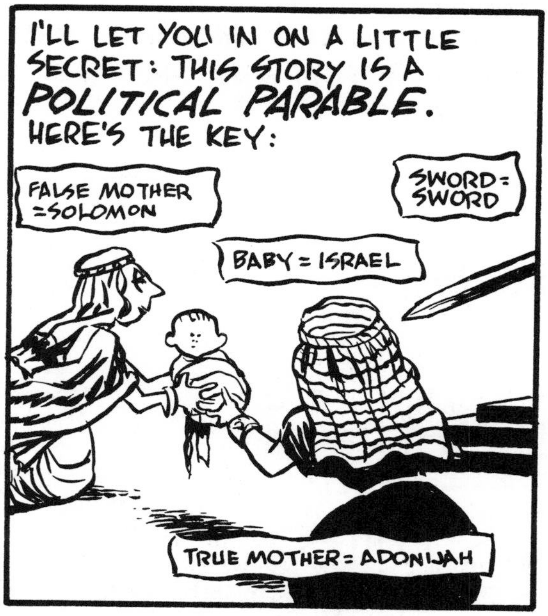
I'LL LET YOU IN ON A LITTLE SECRET: THIS STORY IS A **POLITICAL PARABLE**. HERE'S THE KEY:
FALSE MOTHER =SOLOMON
SWORD= SWORD
BABY = ISRAEL
TRUE MOTHER = ADONIJAH

THE STORY UNLOCKED: SOLOMON, THE **ILLEGITIMATE** HEIR TO THE THRONE, WAS WILLING TO **SPLIT THE KINGDOM** WITH **CIVIL WAR**. ADONIJAH'S FAMILY, THE HOUSE OF SAUL, SHOULD GIVE UP THE THRONE RATHER THAN SEE ISRAEL DIVIDED.

•

NOW DOES THE TREMBLING MAKE SENSE??

SO SOLOMON BECAME ISRAEL'S MOST POWERFUL KING; AND JUST AS SAMUEL HAD FORESEEN, HE LAID HEAVY TAXES, BEEFED UP THE CHARIOTRY, TOOK HUNDREDS OF WIVES, AND WORSHIPPED ALIEN GODS!

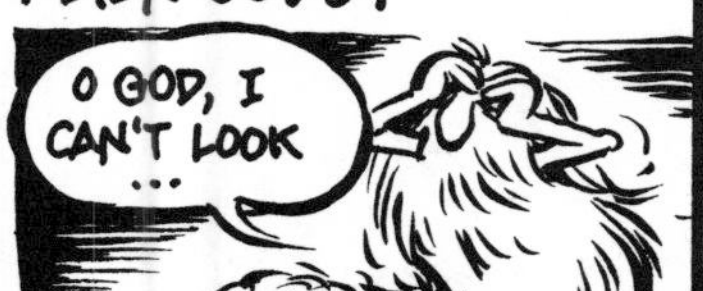
O GOD, I CAN'T LOOK ...

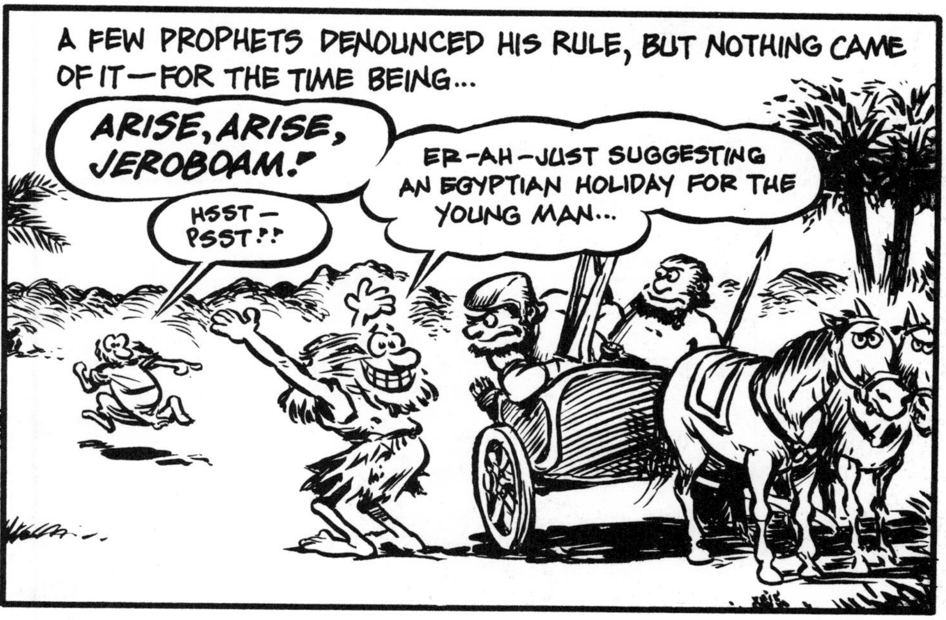
A FEW PROPHETS DENOUNCED HIS RULE, BUT NOTHING CAME OF IT—FOR THE TIME BEING...
ARISE, ARISE, JEROBOAM!
HSST— PSST?!
ER-AH—JUST SUGGESTING AN EGYPTIAN HOLIDAY FOR THE YOUNG MAN...

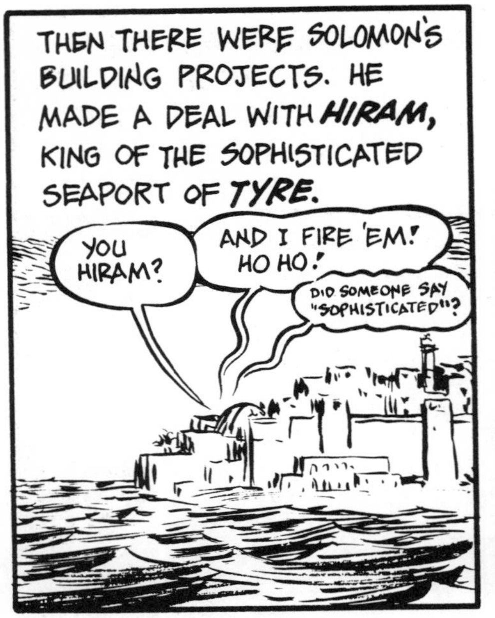
THEN THERE WERE SOLOMON'S BUILDING PROJECTS. HE MADE A DEAL WITH ***HIRAM,*** KING OF THE SOPHISTICATED SEAPORT OF ***TYRE.***
YOU HIRAM?
AND I FIRE 'EM! HO HO!
DID SOMEONE SAY "SOPHISTICATED"!?

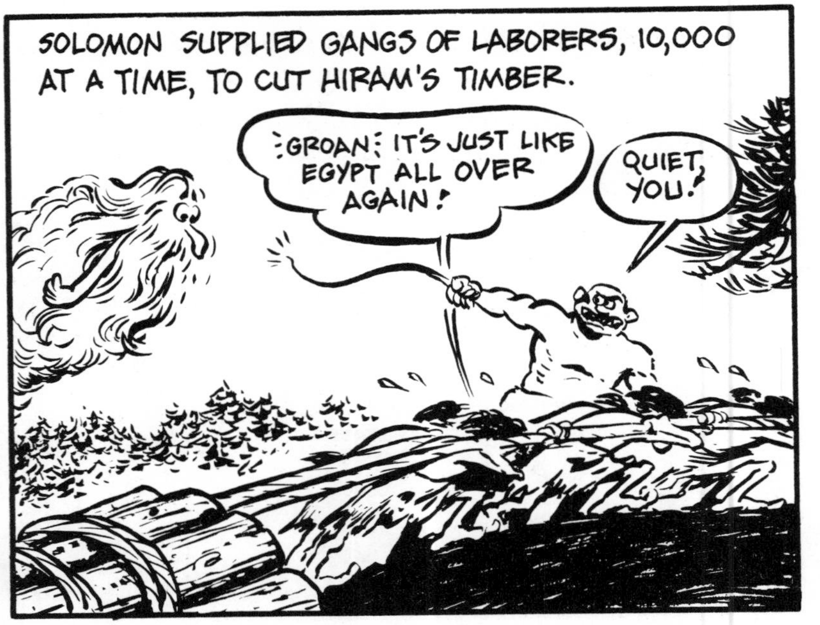
SOLOMON SUPPLIED GANGS OF LABORERS, 10,000 AT A TIME, TO CUT HIRAM'S TIMBER.
:GROAN: IT'S JUST LIKE EGYPT ALL OVER AGAIN!
QUIET, YOU!

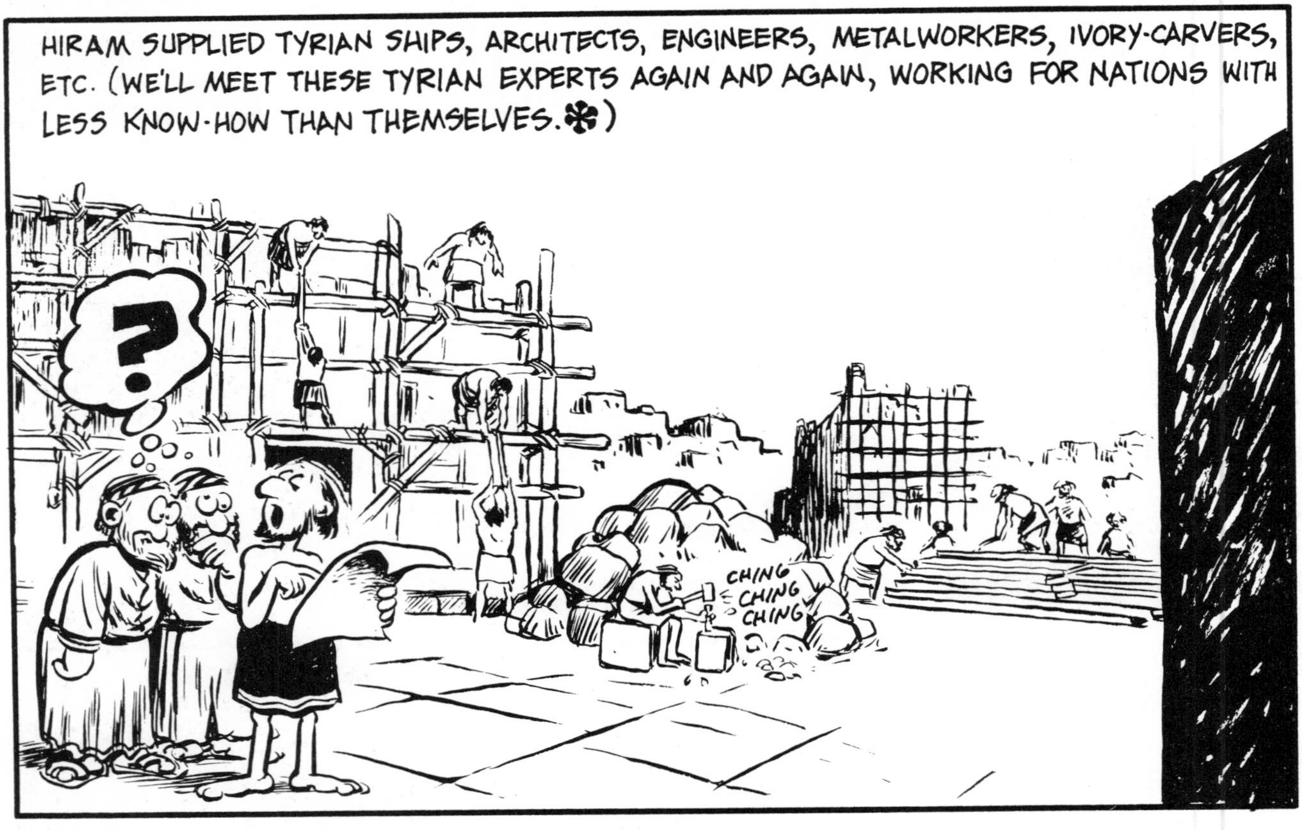
HIRAM SUPPLIED TYRIAN SHIPS, ARCHITECTS, ENGINEERS, METALWORKERS, IVORY-CARVERS, ETC. (WE'LL MEET THESE TYRIAN EXPERTS AGAIN AND AGAIN, WORKING FOR NATIONS WITH LESS KNOW-HOW THAN THEMSELVES. ✽)
?
CHING CHING CHING

✽ ONE MEASURE OF THE SCIENTIFIC ABILITY OF ANCIENT PEOPLES IS HOW ACCURATELY THEY COMPUTED THE VALUE OF ***"PI,"*** THE RATIO OF A CIRCLE'S CIRCUMFERENCE TO ITS DIAMETER, OR 3.14159... THE EGYPTIANS HAD IT AT $^{256}/_{81}$, OR 3.16049..., AND THE BABYLONIANS USED $3\frac{1}{8} = 3.125$.

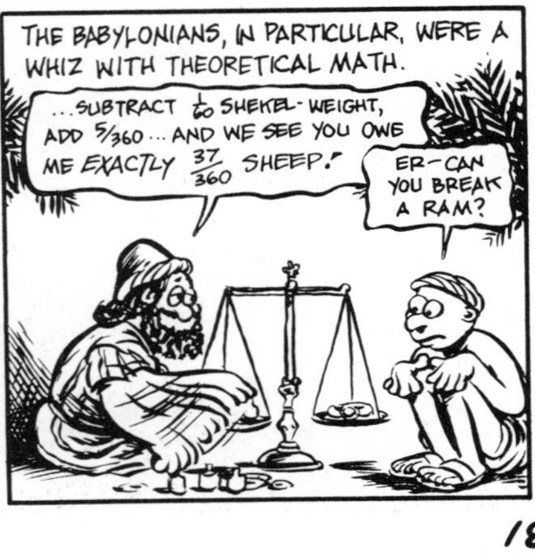
THE BABYLONIANS, IN PARTICULAR, WERE A WHIZ WITH THEORETICAL MATH.
...SUBTRACT 1/60 SHEKEL-WEIGHT, ADD 5/360 ... AND WE SEE YOU OWE ME *EXACTLY* 37/360 SHEEP!
ER-CAN YOU BREAK A RAM?

THE BIBLE, WRITTEN DURING A SLUMP IN EGYPTIAN AND BABYLONIAN CIVILIZATION, MENTIONS A GIANT ROUND CAULDRON AT SOLOMON'S TEMPLE, 30 CUBITS AROUND AND 10 CUBITS ACROSS—GIVING THE BIBLICAL VALUE FOR PI AT EXACTLY **3.**

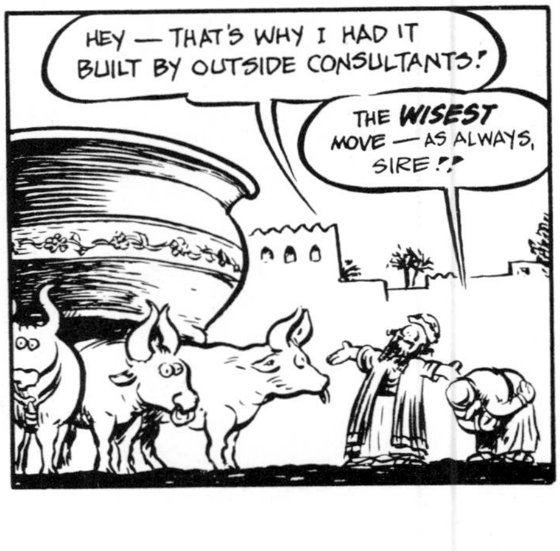
HEY — THAT'S WHY I HAD IT BUILT BY OUTSIDE CONSULTANTS!
THE ***WISEST*** MOVE — AS ALWAYS, SIRE!?

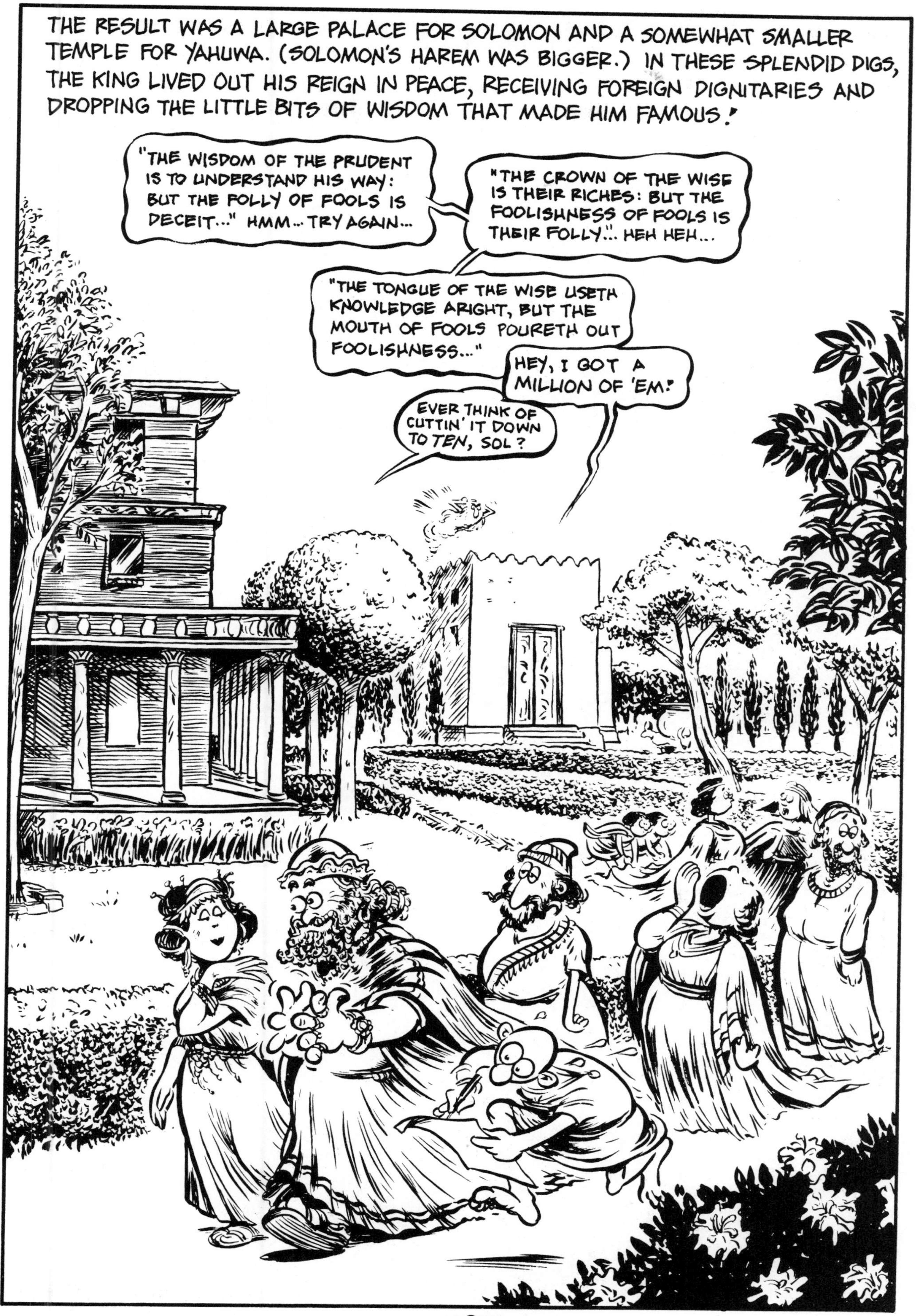
THE RESULT WAS A LARGE PALACE FOR SOLOMON AND A SOMEWHAT SMALLER TEMPLE FOR YAHUWA. (SOLOMON'S HAREM WAS BIGGER.) IN THESE SPLENDID DIGS, THE KING LIVED OUT HIS REIGN IN PEACE, RECEIVING FOREIGN DIGNITARIES AND DROPPING THE LITTLE BITS OF WISDOM THAT MADE HIM FAMOUS!
"THE WISDOM OF THE PRUDENT IS TO UNDERSTAND HIS WAY: BUT THE FOLLY OF FOOLS IS DECEIT..." HMM... TRY AGAIN...
"THE CROWN OF THE WISE IS THEIR RICHES: BUT THE FOOLISHNESS OF FOOLS IS THEIR FOLLY."... HEH HEH...
"THE TONGUE OF THE WISE USETH KNOWLEDGE ARIGHT, BUT THE MOUTH OF FOOLS POURETH OUT FOOLISHNESS..."
HEY, I GOT A MILLION OF 'EM!
EVER THINK OF CUTTIN' IT DOWN TO *TEN*, SOL?

SPLIT KINGDOM

DURING SOLOMON'S REIGN, PROTEST WAS MUTED, BUT AFTER HIS DEATH, PLENTY OF DISGRUNTLED SUBJECTS CAME TO THE CORONATION OF HIS SON *REHOBOAM.*

THEIR SPOKESMAN, *JEROBOAM,* WHO HAD COME OUT OF HIDING IN EGYPT, CONFRONTED THE NEW KING.

I'LL GET TO THE POINT: *ARE YOU GONNA BE AN IMPROVEMENT ON YOUR FATHER?*

AFTER CHECKING WITH HIS ADVISERS, REHOBOAM GAVE THIS MEMORABLE ANSWER:

MY FATHER CHASTISED YOU WITH WHIPS...

I SHALL CHASTISE YOU WITH *SCORPIONS!?*

KITCHY KITCHY KITCHY

TO WHICH JEROBOAM MADE AN EQUALLY MEMORABLE REPLY:

TO YOUR TENTS, O ISRAEL?!?

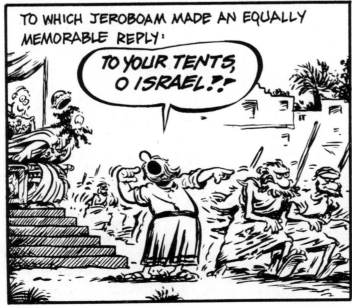

AT FIRST, REHOBOAM DIDN'T TAKE THIS SERIOUSLY, BUT WHEN THEY STONED HIS CHIEF TAX COLLECTOR TO DEATH, HE RETURNED TO JERUSALEM IN A HURRY.

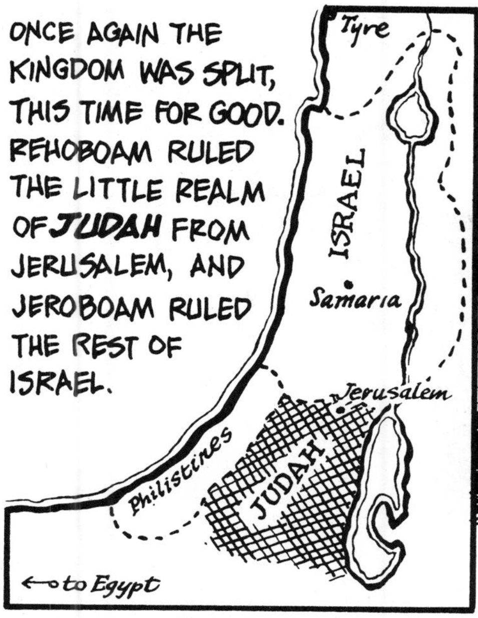
ONCE AGAIN THE KINGDOM WAS SPLIT, THIS TIME FOR GOOD. REHOBOAM RULED THE LITTLE REALM OF JUDAH FROM JERUSALEM, AND JEROBOAM RULED THE REST OF ISRAEL.
Tyre
ISRAEL
Samaria
Jerusalem
Philistines
JUDAH
← to Egypt

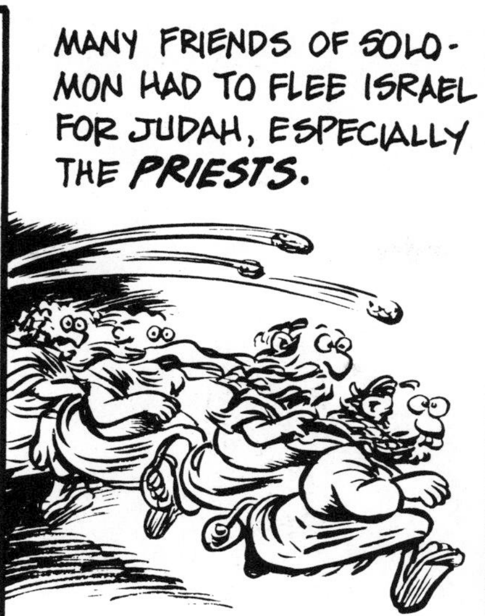
MANY FRIENDS OF SOLOMON HAD TO FLEE ISRAEL FOR JUDAH, ESPECIALLY THE PRIESTS.

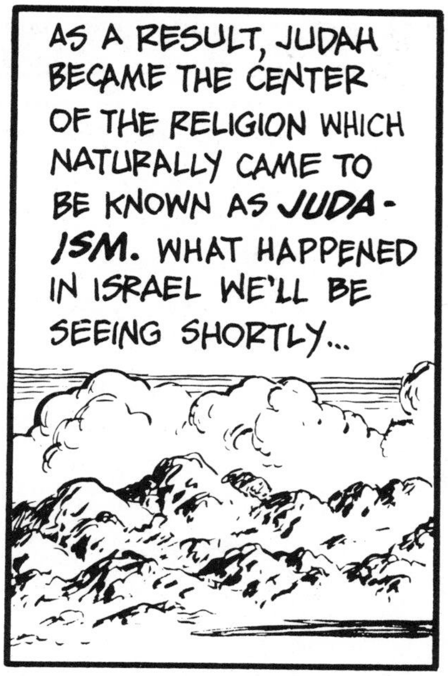
AS A RESULT, JUDAH BECAME THE CENTER OF THE RELIGION WHICH NATURALLY CAME TO BE KNOWN AS JUDAISM. WHAT HAPPENED IN ISRAEL WE'LL BE SEEING SHORTLY...

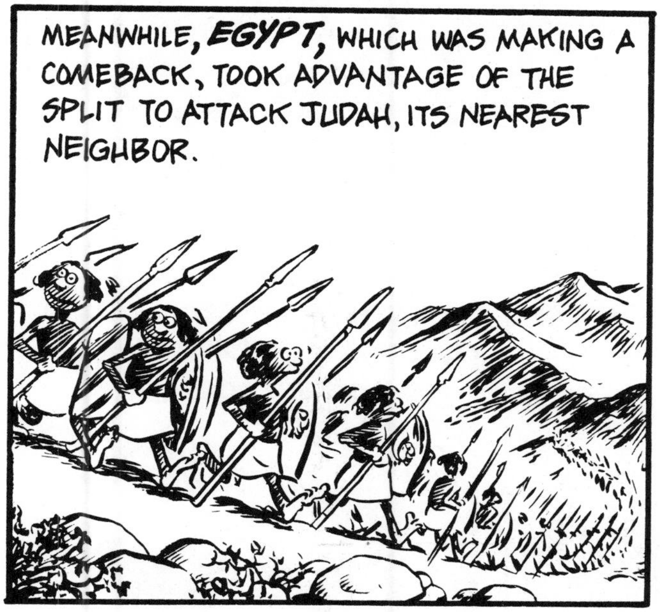
MEANWHILE, EGYPT, WHICH WAS MAKING A COMEBACK, TOOK ADVANTAGE OF THE SPLIT TO ATTACK JUDAH, ITS NEAREST NEIGHBOR.

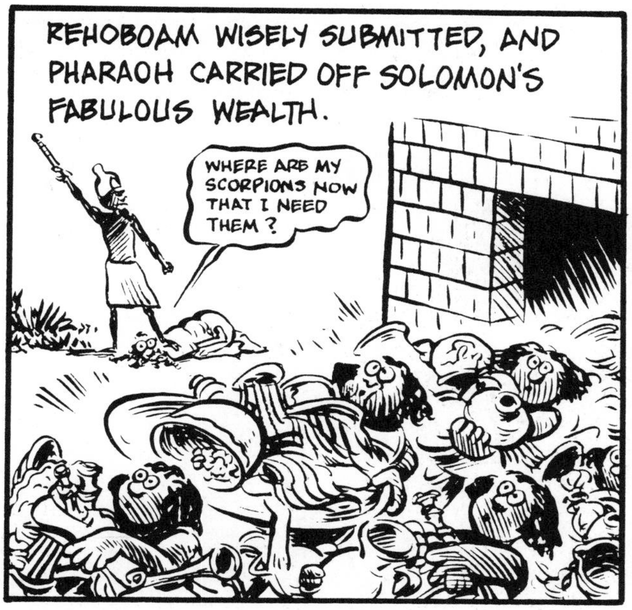
REHOBOAM WISELY SUBMITTED, AND PHARAOH CARRIED OFF SOLOMON'S FABULOUS WEALTH.
WHERE ARE MY SCORPIONS NOW THAT I NEED THEM?

THOUGH POOR, JUDAH DID FAIRLY WELL UNDER EGYPTIAN PROTECTION, AND THE HOUSE OF DAVID RULED WITHOUT INTERRUPTION; BUT IN ISRAEL THINGS WENT LESS SMOOTHLY...

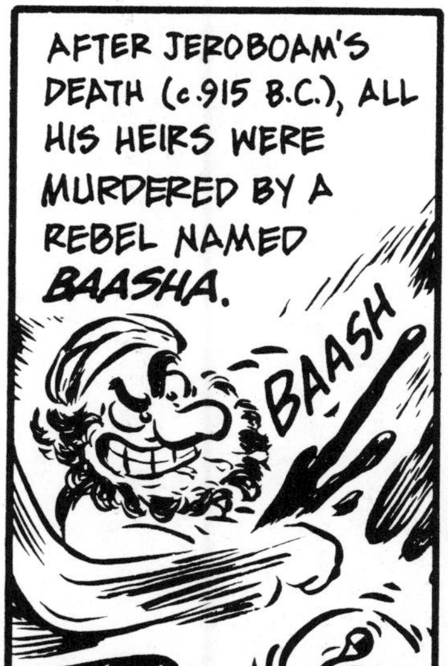
AFTER JEROBOAM'S DEATH (c.915 B.C.), ALL HIS HEIRS WERE MURDERED BY A REBEL NAMED BAASHA.
BAASH

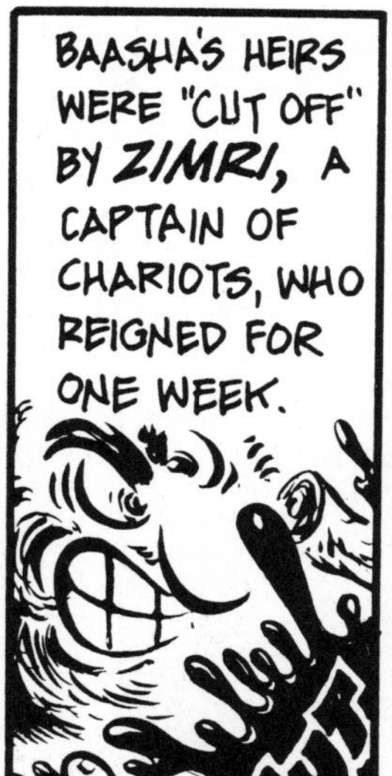
BAASHA'S HEIRS WERE "CUT OFF" BY ZIMRI, A CAPTAIN OF CHARIOTS, WHO REIGNED FOR ONE WEEK.
CUT

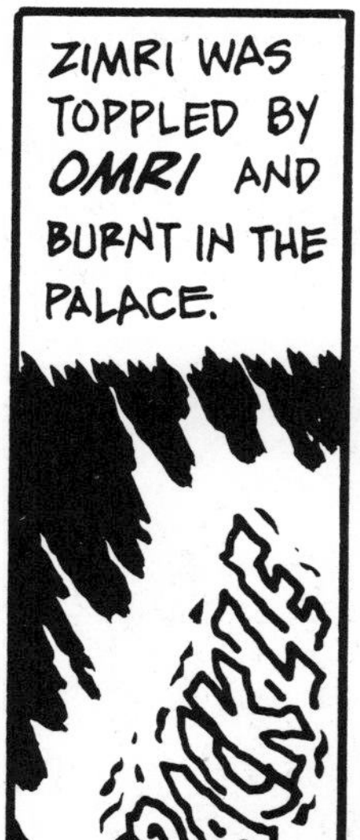
ZIMRI WAS TOPPLED BY OMRI AND BURNT IN THE PALACE.
CRACKLE

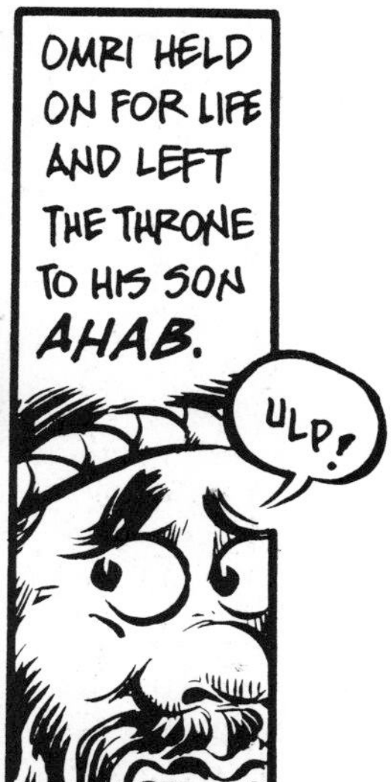
OMRI HELD ON FOR LIFE AND LEFT THE THRONE TO HIS SON AHAB.
ULP!

ASSYRIA RISING

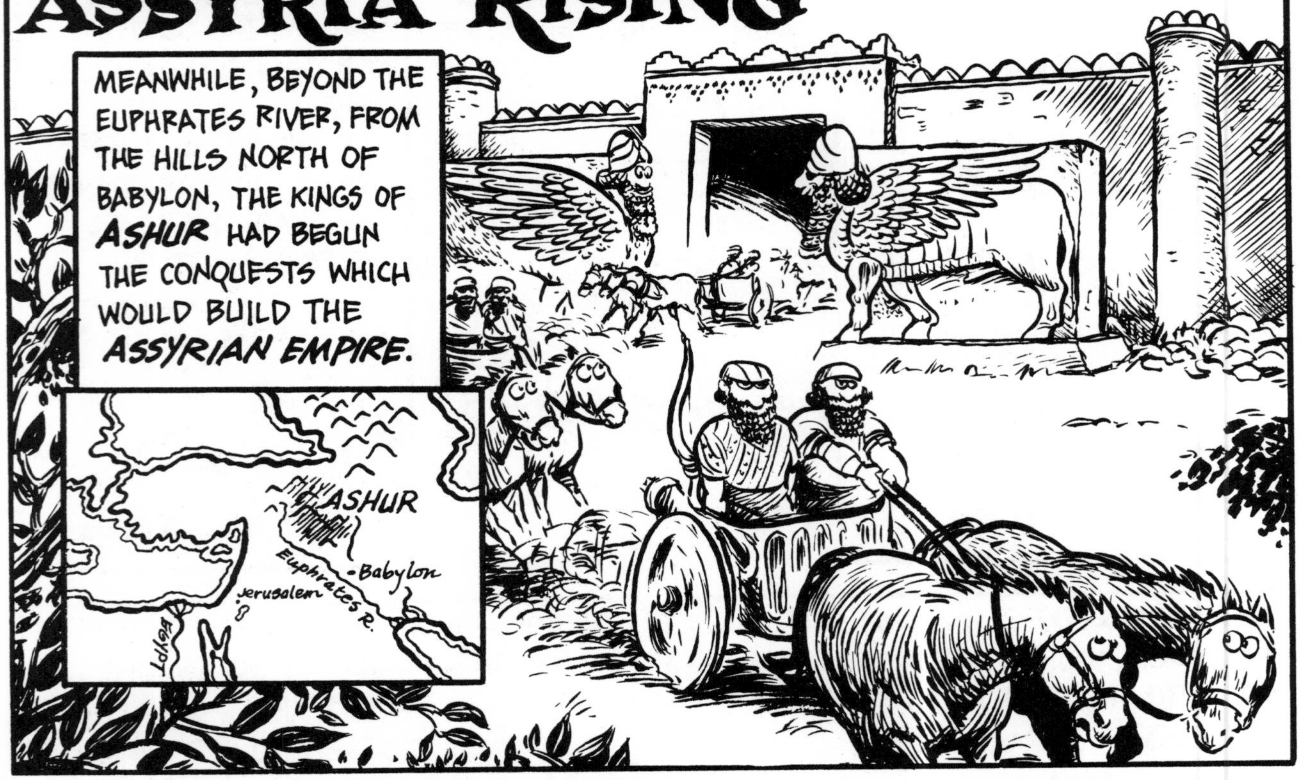
MEANWHILE, BEYOND THE EUPHRATES RIVER, FROM THE HILLS NORTH OF BABYLON, THE KINGS OF ***ASHUR*** HAD BEGUN THE CONQUESTS WHICH WOULD BUILD THE ***ASSYRIAN EMPIRE.***
ASHUR
Babylon
Euphrates R.
Jerusalem
Egypt

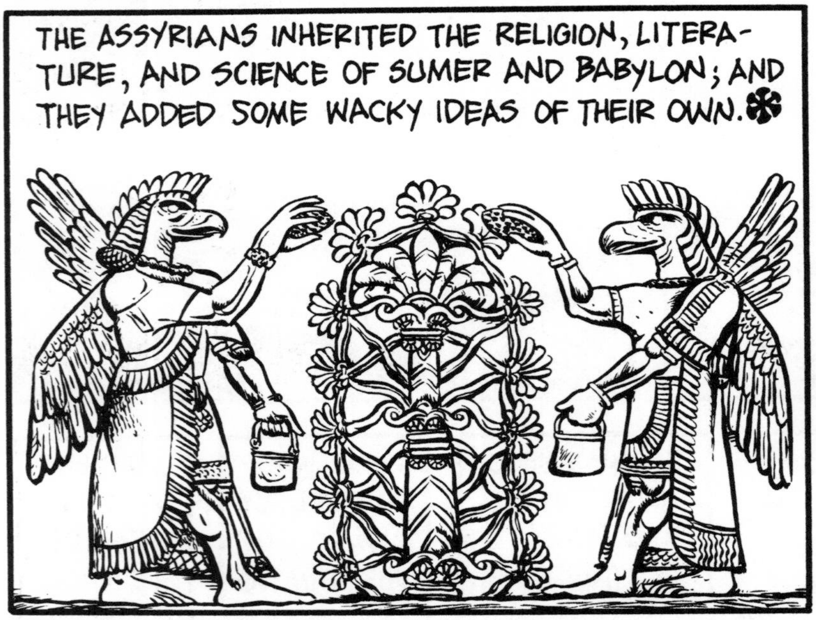
THE ASSYRIANS INHERITED THE RELIGION, LITERATURE, AND SCIENCE OF SUMER AND BABYLON; AND THEY ADDED SOME WACKY IDEAS OF THEIR OWN. ✿

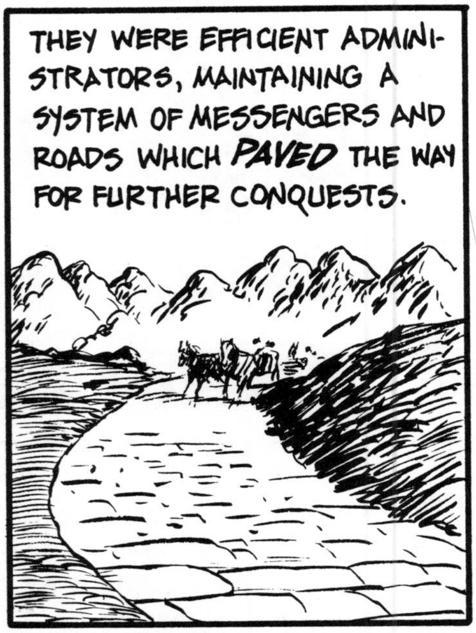
THEY WERE EFFICIENT ADMINISTRATORS, MAINTAINING A SYSTEM OF MESSENGERS AND ROADS WHICH ***PAVED*** THE WAY FOR FURTHER CONQUESTS.

✿ THE ASSYRIAN PRIESTHOOD, ADDICTED TO MUMBO-JUMBO, HAD LET THE PRACTICE OF MEDICINE SLIDE FROM A REASONABLY HIGH LEVEL INTO A MESS OF MAGIC SPELLS AND INCANTATIONS. ONE WONDERS WHAT THEIR ***MEDICAL SCHOOLS*** WERE LIKE...

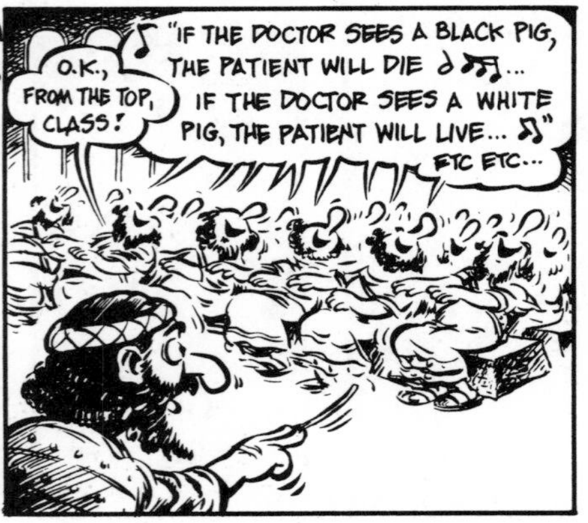
O.K., FROM THE TOP, CLASS!
♪ "IF THE DOCTOR SEES A BLACK PIG, THE PATIENT WILL DIE ♪♫... IF THE DOCTOR SEES A WHITE PIG, THE PATIENT WILL LIVE... ♫"
ETC ETC...

THIS MAY EXPLAIN WHY A SICK ASSYRIAN, INSTEAD OF CONSULTING A DOCTOR, WOULD USUALLY JUST SIT OUTSIDE HIS DOORWAY AND TAKE ADVICE FROM ANYONE WHO CARED TO GIVE IT!

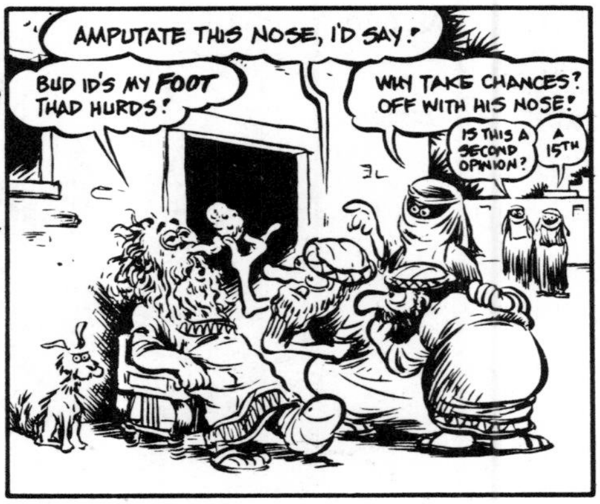
AMPUTATE THIS NOSE, I'D SAY!
BUD ID'S MY ***FOOT*** THAD HURDS!
WHY TAKE CHANCES? OFF WITH HIS NOSE!
IS THIS A SECOND OPINION?
A 15TH

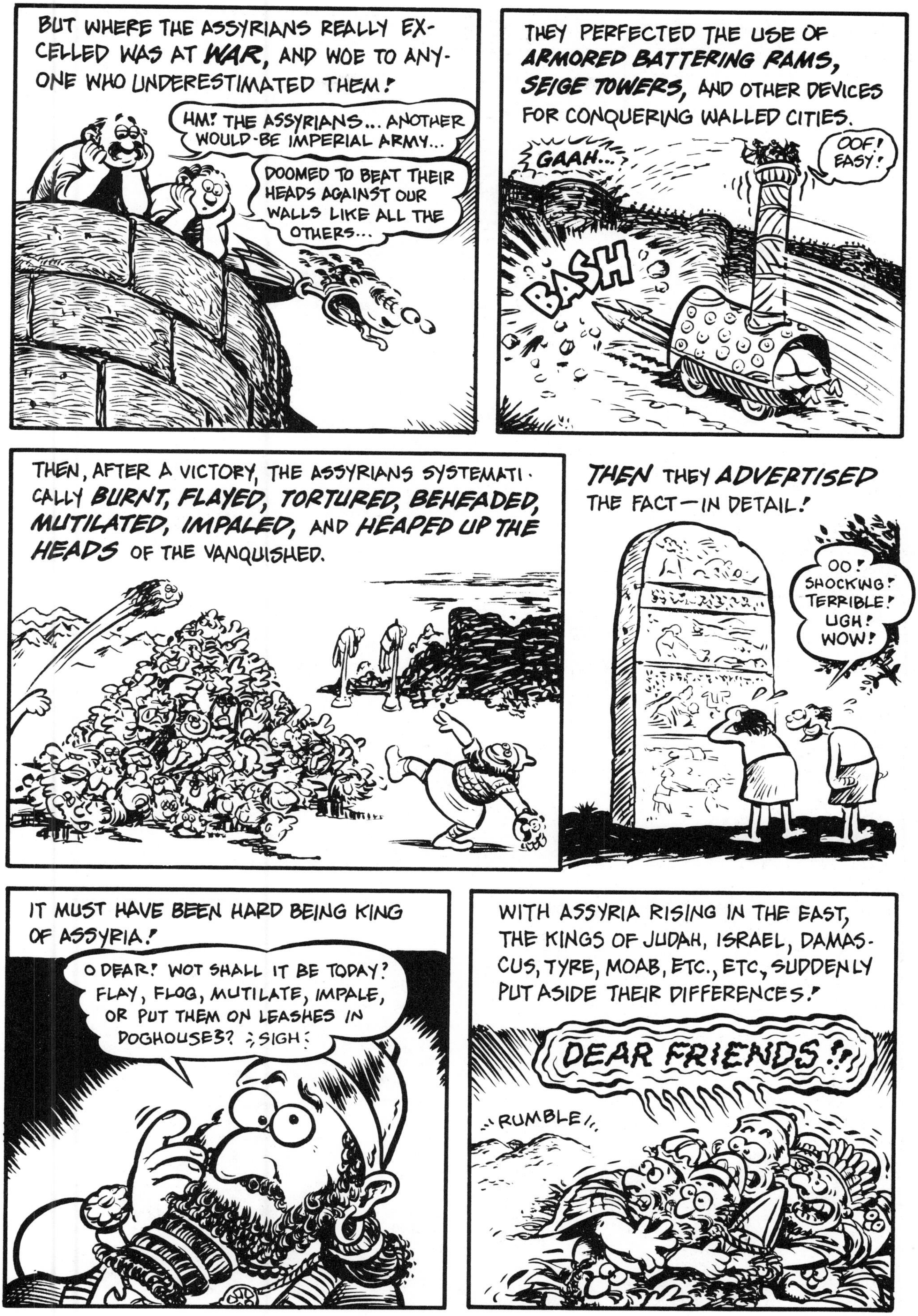
BUT WHERE THE ASSYRIANS REALLY EXCELLED WAS AT WAR, AND WOE TO ANYONE WHO UNDERESTIMATED THEM!
HM! THE ASSYRIANS... ANOTHER WOULD-BE IMPERIAL ARMY...
DOOMED TO BEAT THEIR HEADS AGAINST OUR WALLS LIKE ALL THE OTHERS...
THEY PERFECTED THE USE OF ARMORED BATTERING RAMS, SEIGE TOWERS, AND OTHER DEVICES FOR CONQUERING WALLED CITIES.
GAAH...
OOF! EASY!
BASH
THEN, AFTER A VICTORY, THE ASSYRIANS SYSTEMATICALLY BURNT, FLAYED, TORTURED, BEHEADED, MUTILATED, IMPALED, AND HEAPED UP THE HEADS OF THE VANQUISHED.
THEN THEY ADVERTISED THE FACT—IN DETAIL!
OO! SHOCKING! TERRIBLE! UGH! WOW!
IT MUST HAVE BEEN HARD BEING KING OF ASSYRIA!
O DEAR! WOT SHALL IT BE TODAY? FLAY, FLOG, MUTILATE, IMPALE, OR PUT THEM ON LEASHES IN DOGHOUSES? ;SIGH;
WITH ASSYRIA RISING IN THE EAST, THE KINGS OF JUDAH, ISRAEL, DAMASCUS, TYRE, MOAB, ETC., ETC, SUDDENLY PUT ASIDE THEIR DIFFERENCES!
DEAR FRIENDS!?!
RUMBLE

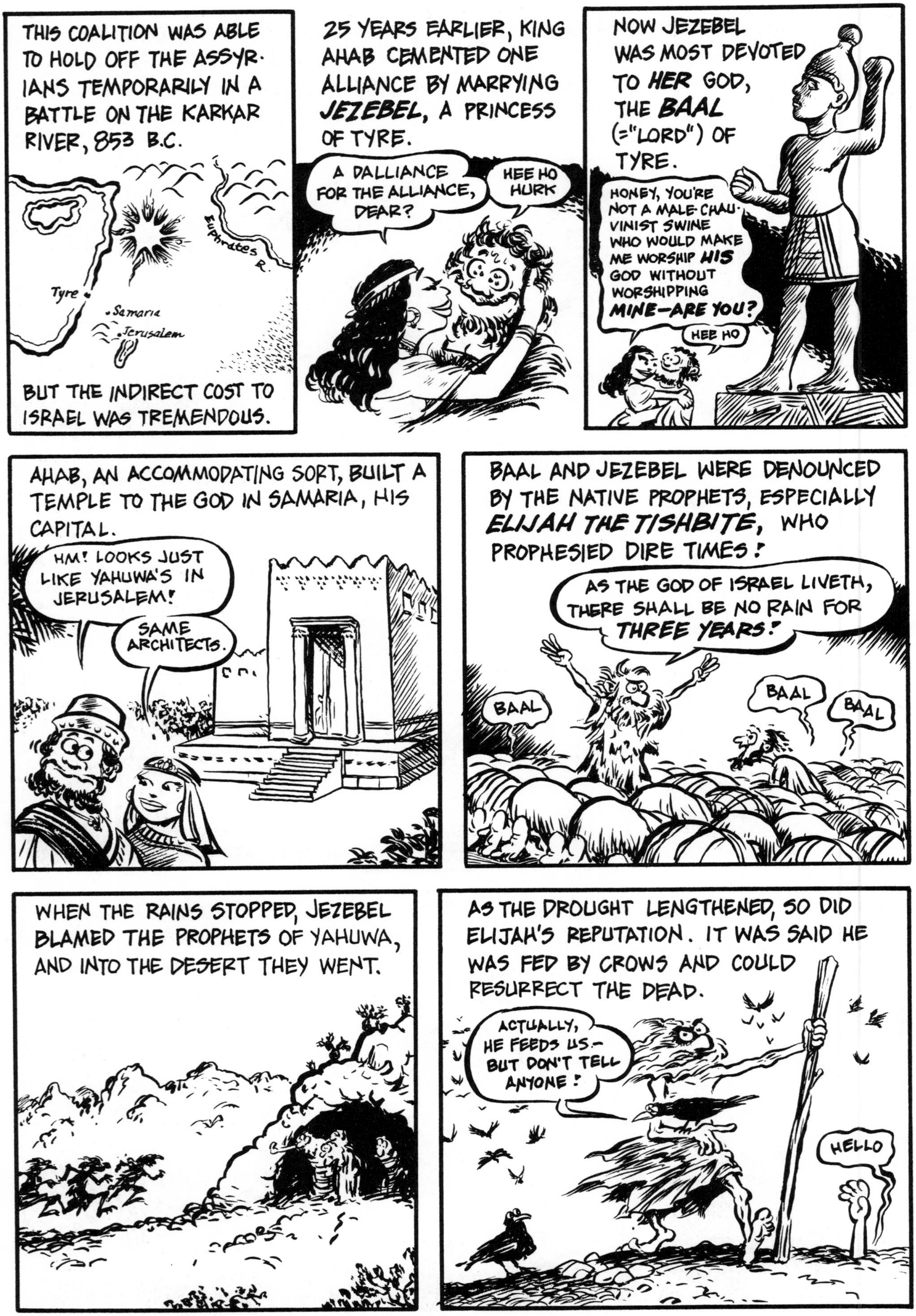
THIS COALITION WAS ABLE TO HOLD OFF THE ASSYRIANS TEMPORARILY IN A BATTLE ON THE KARKAR RIVER, 853 B.C.
Euphrates R.
Tyre
Samaria
Jerusalem
BUT THE INDIRECT COST TO ISRAEL WAS TREMENDOUS.
25 YEARS EARLIER, KING AHAB CEMENTED ONE ALLIANCE BY MARRYING JEZEBEL, A PRINCESS OF TYRE.
A DALLIANCE FOR THE ALLIANCE, DEAR?
HEE HO HURK
NOW JEZEBEL WAS MOST DEVOTED TO HER GOD, THE BAAL (="LORD") OF TYRE.
HONEY, YOU'RE NOT A MALE-CHAUVINIST SWINE WHO WOULD MAKE ME WORSHIP HIS GOD WITHOUT WORSHIPPING MINE—ARE YOU?
HEE HO
AHAB, AN ACCOMMODATING SORT, BUILT A TEMPLE TO THE GOD IN SAMARIA, HIS CAPITAL.
HM! LOOKS JUST LIKE YAHUWA'S IN JERUSALEM!
SAME ARCHITECTS.
BAAL AND JEZEBEL WERE DENOUNCED BY THE NATIVE PROPHETS, ESPECIALLY ELIJAH THE TISHBITE, WHO PROPHESIED DIRE TIMES!
AS THE GOD OF ISRAEL LIVETH, THERE SHALL BE NO RAIN FOR THREE YEARS!
BAAL
BAAL
BAAL
WHEN THE RAINS STOPPED, JEZEBEL BLAMED THE PROPHETS OF YAHUWA, AND INTO THE DESERT THEY WENT.
AS THE DROUGHT LENGTHENED, SO DID ELIJAH'S REPUTATION. IT WAS SAID HE WAS FED BY CROWS AND COULD RESURRECT THE DEAD.
ACTUALLY, HE FEEDS US— BUT DON'T TELL ANYONE!
HELLO

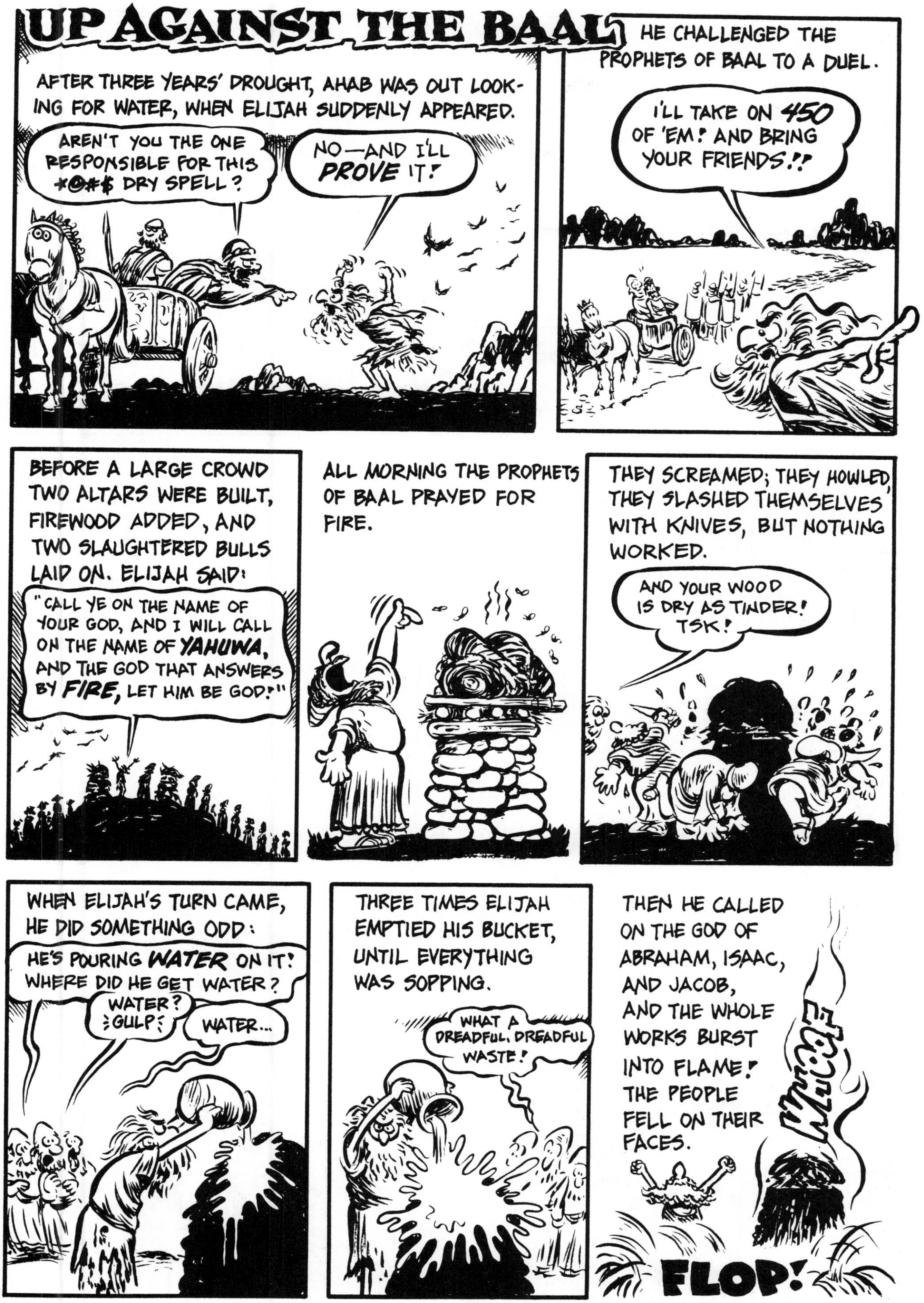

UP AGAINST THE BAAL
AFTER THREE YEARS' DROUGHT, AHAB WAS OUT LOOKING FOR WATER, WHEN ELIJAH SUDDENLY APPEARED.
AREN'T YOU THE ONE RESPONSIBLE FOR THIS *@#$ DRY SPELL?
NO—AND I'LL PROVE IT!
HE CHALLENGED THE PROPHETS OF BAAL TO A DUEL.
I'LL TAKE ON 450 OF 'EM! AND BRING YOUR FRIENDS!!
BEFORE A LARGE CROWD TWO ALTARS WERE BUILT, FIREWOOD ADDED, AND TWO SLAUGHTERED BULLS LAID ON. ELIJAH SAID:
"CALL YE ON THE NAME OF YOUR GOD, AND I WILL CALL ON THE NAME OF YAHUWA, AND THE GOD THAT ANSWERS BY FIRE, LET HIM BE GOD!"
ALL MORNING THE PROPHETS OF BAAL PRAYED FOR FIRE.
THEY SCREAMED; THEY HOWLED, THEY SLASHED THEMSELVES WITH KNIVES, BUT NOTHING WORKED.
AND YOUR WOOD IS DRY AS TINDER! TSK!
WHEN ELIJAH'S TURN CAME, HE DID SOMETHING ODD:
HE'S POURING WATER ON IT! WHERE DID HE GET WATER?
WATER? GULP
WATER...
THREE TIMES ELIJAH EMPTIED HIS BUCKET, UNTIL EVERYTHING WAS SOPPING.
WHAT A DREADFUL, DREADFUL WASTE!
THEN HE CALLED ON THE GOD OF ABRAHAM, ISAAC, AND JACOB, AND THE WHOLE WORKS BURST INTO FLAME! THE PEOPLE FELL ON THEIR FACES.
WHOOF!
FLOP!

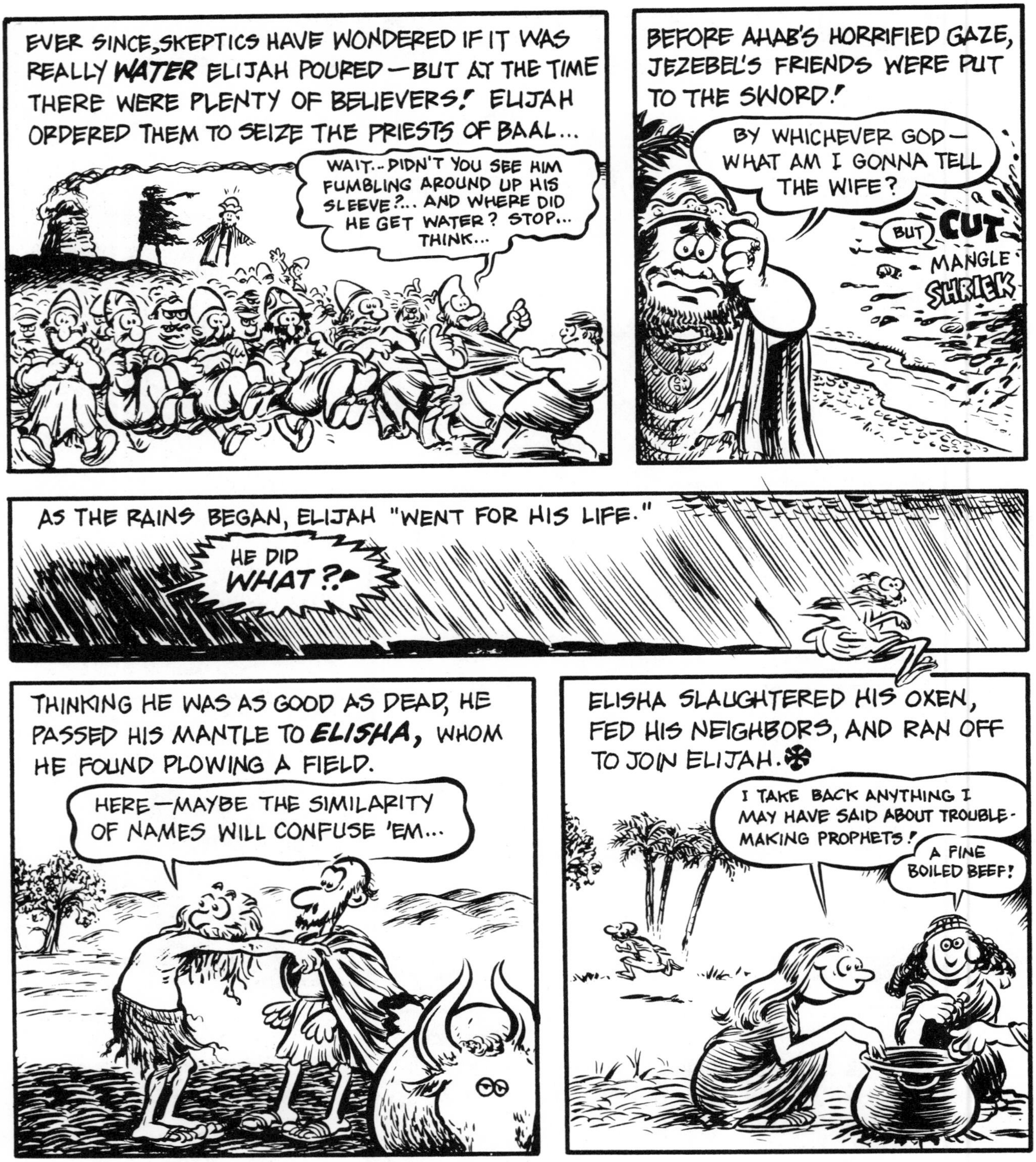
EVER SINCE, SKEPTICS HAVE WONDERED IF IT WAS REALLY WATER ELIJAH POURED—BUT AT THE TIME THERE WERE PLENTY OF BELIEVERS! ELIJAH ORDERED THEM TO SEIZE THE PRIESTS OF BAAL...
WAIT...DIDN'T YOU SEE HIM FUMBLING AROUND UP HIS SLEEVE?... AND WHERE DID HE GET WATER? STOP... THINK...
BEFORE AHAB'S HORRIFIED GAZE, JEZEBEL'S FRIENDS WERE PUT TO THE SWORD!
BY WHICHEVER GOD—WHAT AM I GONNA TELL THE WIFE?
BUT
CUT
MANGLE
SHRIEK
AS THE RAINS BEGAN, ELIJAH "WENT FOR HIS LIFE."
HE DID WHAT?!
THINKING HE WAS AS GOOD AS DEAD, HE PASSED HIS MANTLE TO ELISHA, WHOM HE FOUND PLOWING A FIELD.
HERE—MAYBE THE SIMILARITY OF NAMES WILL CONFUSE 'EM...
ELISHA SLAUGHTERED HIS OXEN, FED HIS NEIGHBORS, AND RAN OFF TO JOIN ELIJAH. ✽
I TAKE BACK ANYTHING I MAY HAVE SAID ABOUT TROUBLE-MAKING PROPHETS!
A FINE BOILED BEEF!

✽ TO SEE THE SOMETIMES STRAINED RELATIONS BETWEEN THE ANCIENT ISRAELITES AND THEIR PROPHETS, WE MIGHT NOTE AN INCIDENT IN THE 2ND BOOK OF *KINGS*, IN WHICH THE PROPHET ELISHA IS MOCKED BY A CROWD OF CHILDREN.

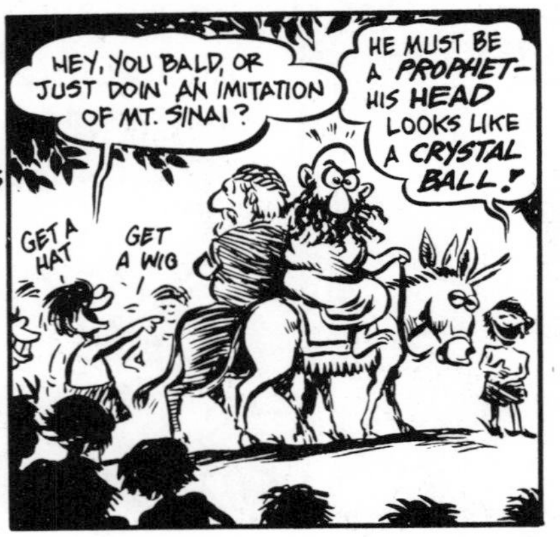
HEY, YOU BALD, OR JUST DOIN' AN IMITATION OF MT. SINAI?
HE MUST BE A PROPHET—HIS HEAD LOOKS LIKE A CRYSTAL BALL!
GET A HAT
GET A WIG!

SO ELISHA "CURSED THEM IN THE NAME OF THE LORD, AND THERE CAME FORTH TWO SHE-BEARS FROM THE WOOD AND TARE FORTY AND TWO CHILDREN OF THEM."
(2 KINGS 2:23-24)

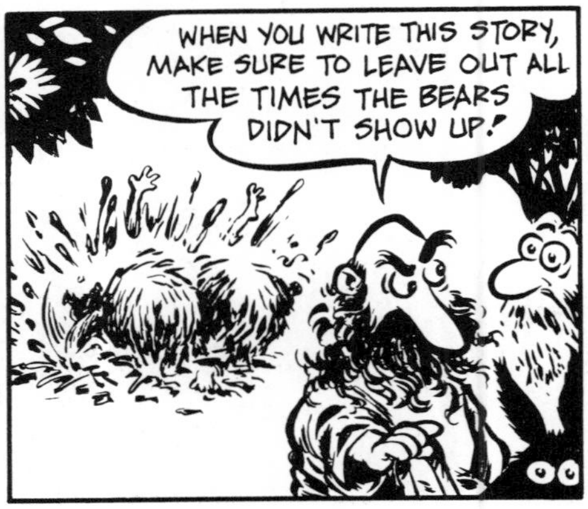
WHEN YOU WRITE THIS STORY, MAKE SURE TO LEAVE OUT ALL THE TIMES THE BEARS DIDN'T SHOW UP!

NOW 15 YEARS PASS... ELIJAH WAS DEAD; AHAB WAS DEAD; AHAB'S SON **JORAM** RULED ISRAEL, AND HIS GRANDSON **AHAZIAH** RULED JUDAH; JEZEBEL STILL LIVED; AND ELISHA, NOW A ROYAL CONSULTANT AND LEADER OF A LARGE BAND OF PROPHETS, DECIDED THE TIME HAD COME FOR A FINAL SOLUTION TO THE BAAL PROBLEM...

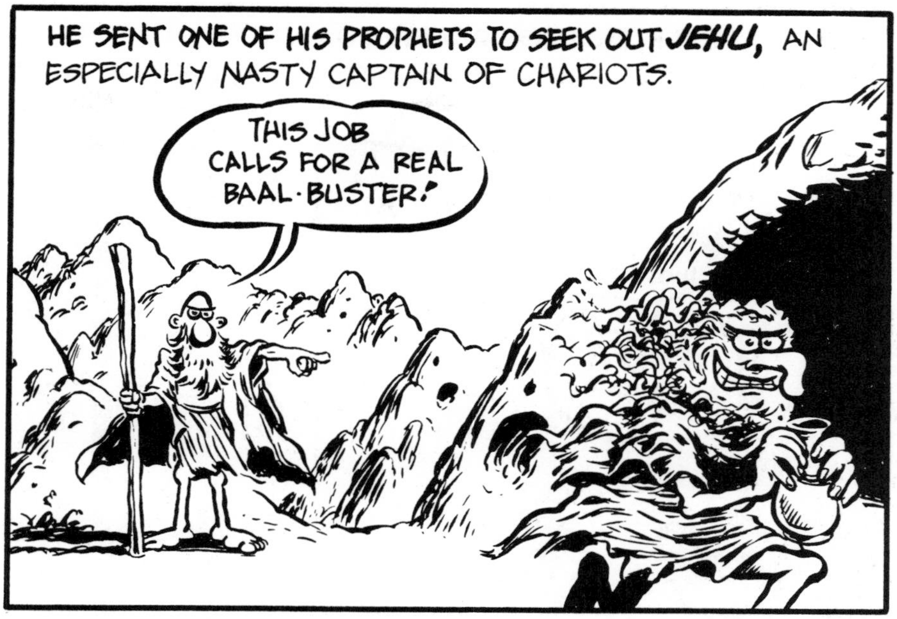
HE SENT ONE OF HIS PROPHETS TO SEEK OUT JEHU, AN ESPECIALLY NASTY CAPTAIN OF CHARIOTS.
THIS JOB CALLS FOR A REAL BAAL-BUSTER!

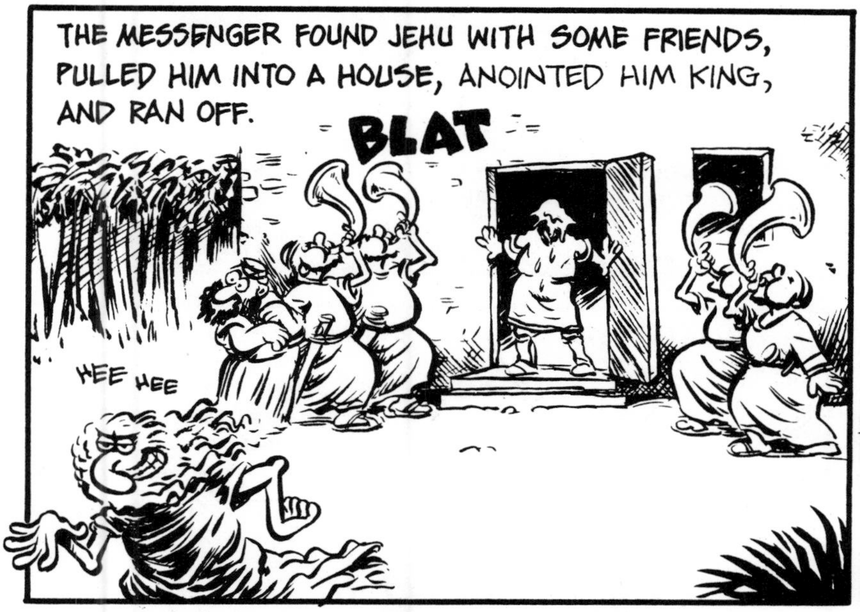
THE MESSENGER FOUND JEHU WITH SOME FRIENDS, PULLED HIM INTO A HOUSE, ANOINTED HIM KING, AND RAN OFF.
BLAT
HEE HEE

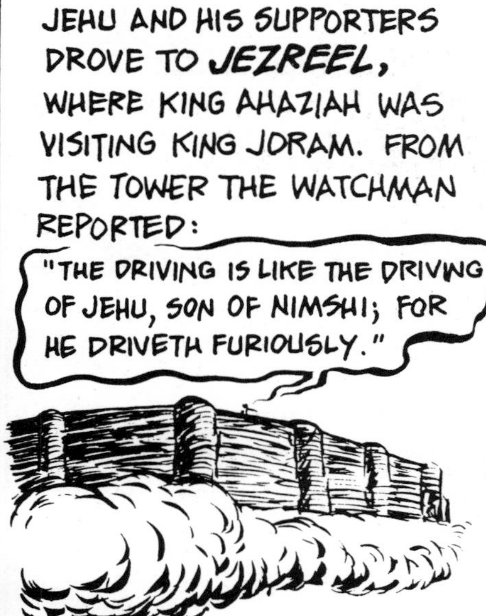
JEHU AND HIS SUPPORTERS DROVE TO JEZREEL, WHERE KING AHAZIAH WAS VISITING KING JORAM. FROM THE TOWER THE WATCHMAN REPORTED:
"THE DRIVING IS LIKE THE DRIVING OF JEHU, SON OF NIMSHI; FOR HE DRIVETH FURIOUSLY."

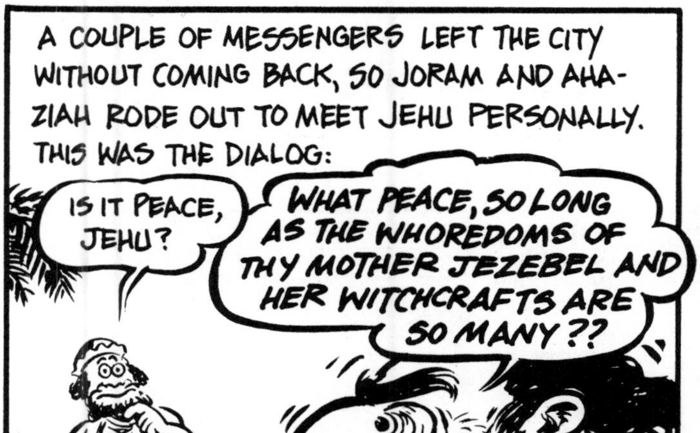
A COUPLE OF MESSENGERS LEFT THE CITY WITHOUT COMING BACK, SO JORAM AND AHAZIAH RODE OUT TO MEET JEHU PERSONALLY. THIS WAS THE DIALOG:
IS IT PEACE, JEHU?
WHAT PEACE, SO LONG AS THE WHOREDOMS OF THY MOTHER JEZEBEL AND HER WITCHCRAFTS ARE SO MANY??

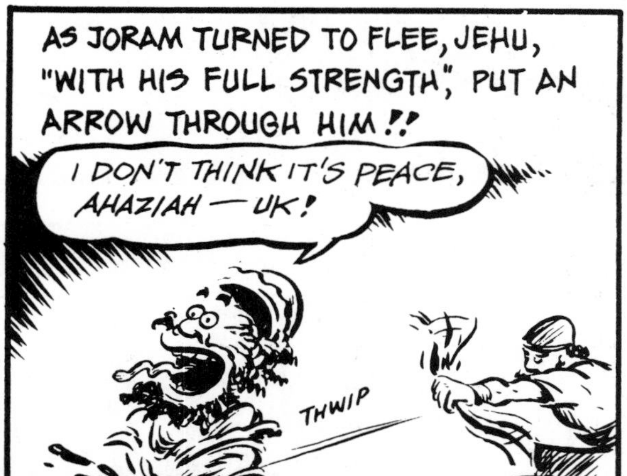
AS JORAM TURNED TO FLEE, JEHU, "WITH HIS FULL STRENGTH", PUT AN ARROW THROUGH HIM!!
I DON'T THINK IT'S PEACE, AHAZIAH — UK!
THWIP
THWOK

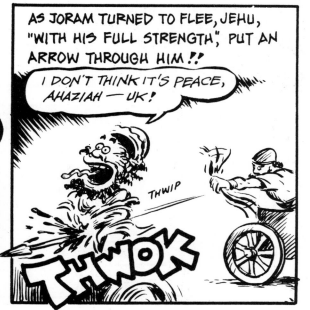

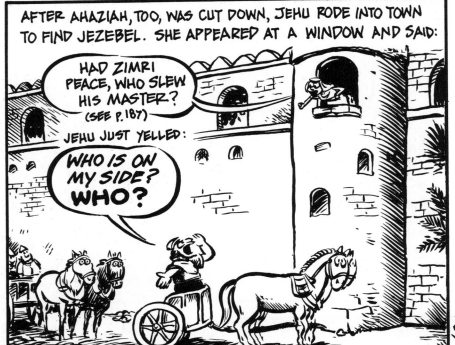

AFTER AHAZIAH, TOO, WAS CUT DOWN, JEHU RODE INTO TOWN TO FIND JEZEBEL. SHE APPEARED AT A WINDOW AND SAID:

HAD ZIMRI PEACE, WHO SLEW HIS MASTER? (SEE P. 187)

JEHU JUST YELLED:

WHO IS ON MY SIDE? WHO?

TWO OR THREE EUNUCHS STUCK OUT THEIR HEADS, AND, AT JEHU'S ORDER, THREW THE OLD QUEEN DOWN.

EEEEEEE

SPLAT

JEHU'S CHARIOTS TRAMPLED HER BODY UNTIL NOTHING WAS LEFT BUT THE HANDS, FEET, AND HEAD.

"THIS IS THE WORD OF YAHUWAH, SPOKEN BY HIS SERVANT ELIJAH THE TISHBITE, SAYING, IN THE PORTION OF JEZREEL SHALL DOGS EAT THE FLESH OF JEZEBEL..."

THEN HE WROTE TO THE ELDERS IN CHARGE OF AHAB'S **70** CHILDREN, CHALLENGING THEM EITHER TO FIGHT OR TO SEND IN THE ROYAL HEADS. THE ELDERS DIDN'T TAKE LONG TO DECIDE.

THE 70 HEADS WERE HEAPED IN TWO PILES AT THE CITY GATE.

≋SIGH≋ I'M JUST NO COMPETITION FOR THE ASSYRIANS...

WHAT WAS THE ORIGIN OF EUNUCHS? ONE THEORY IS THAT FRENZIED DEVOTEES OF ISHTAR WOULD SACRIFICE THEIR OWN ORGANS TO THE SEX GODDESS. ANOTHER IDEA IS THAT KINGS, THINKING OF MEN AS THEIR OXEN, WOULD GELD THEM AS NEEDED.

LOOK ON THE BRIGHT SIDE — NOW YOU'RE 100% AGGRESSION-FREE!

WHATEVER THE CASE, KINGS FOUND THE PLUMP AND PASSIONLESS EUNUCHS USEFUL AT COURT, ESPECIALLY AS **HAREM GUARDS.**

WHAT ARE YOU DOING TO THE EUNUCH?

HONEY, EVEN A **SPAYED CAT** LIKES TO BE SCRATCHED BEHIND THE EARS!!

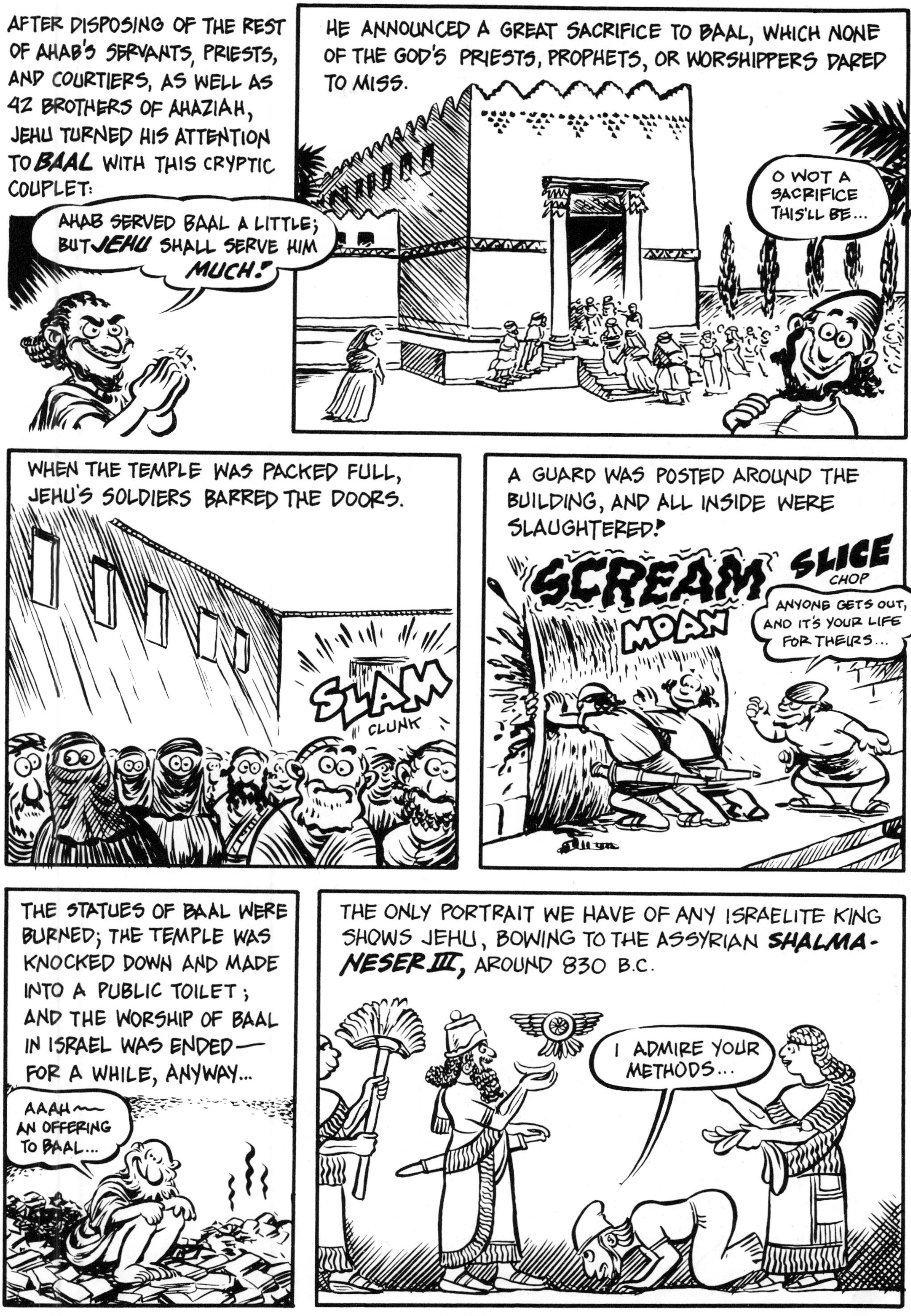
AFTER DISPOSING OF THE REST OF AHAB'S SERVANTS, PRIESTS, AND COURTIERS, AS WELL AS 42 BROTHERS OF AHAZIAH, JEHU TURNED HIS ATTENTION TO BAAL WITH THIS CRYPTIC COUPLET:
AHAB SERVED BAAL A LITTLE; BUT JEHU SHALL SERVE HIM MUCH!
HE ANNOUNCED A GREAT SACRIFICE TO BAAL, WHICH NONE OF THE GOD'S PRIESTS, PROPHETS, OR WORSHIPPERS DARED TO MISS.
O WOT A SACRIFICE THIS'LL BE...
WHEN THE TEMPLE WAS PACKED FULL, JEHU'S SOLDIERS BARRED THE DOORS.
SLAM
CLUNK
A GUARD WAS POSTED AROUND THE BUILDING, AND ALL INSIDE WERE SLAUGHTERED!
SCREAM
SLICE
CHOP
MOAN
ANYONE GETS OUT, AND IT'S YOUR LIFE FOR THEIRS...
THE STATUES OF BAAL WERE BURNED; THE TEMPLE WAS KNOCKED DOWN AND MADE INTO A PUBLIC TOILET; AND THE WORSHIP OF BAAL IN ISRAEL WAS ENDED— FOR A WHILE, ANYWAY...
AAAH— AN OFFERING TO BAAL...
THE ONLY PORTRAIT WE HAVE OF ANY ISRAELITE KING SHOWS JEHU, BOWING TO THE ASSYRIAN SHALMANESER III, AROUND 830 B.C.
I ADMIRE YOUR METHODS...

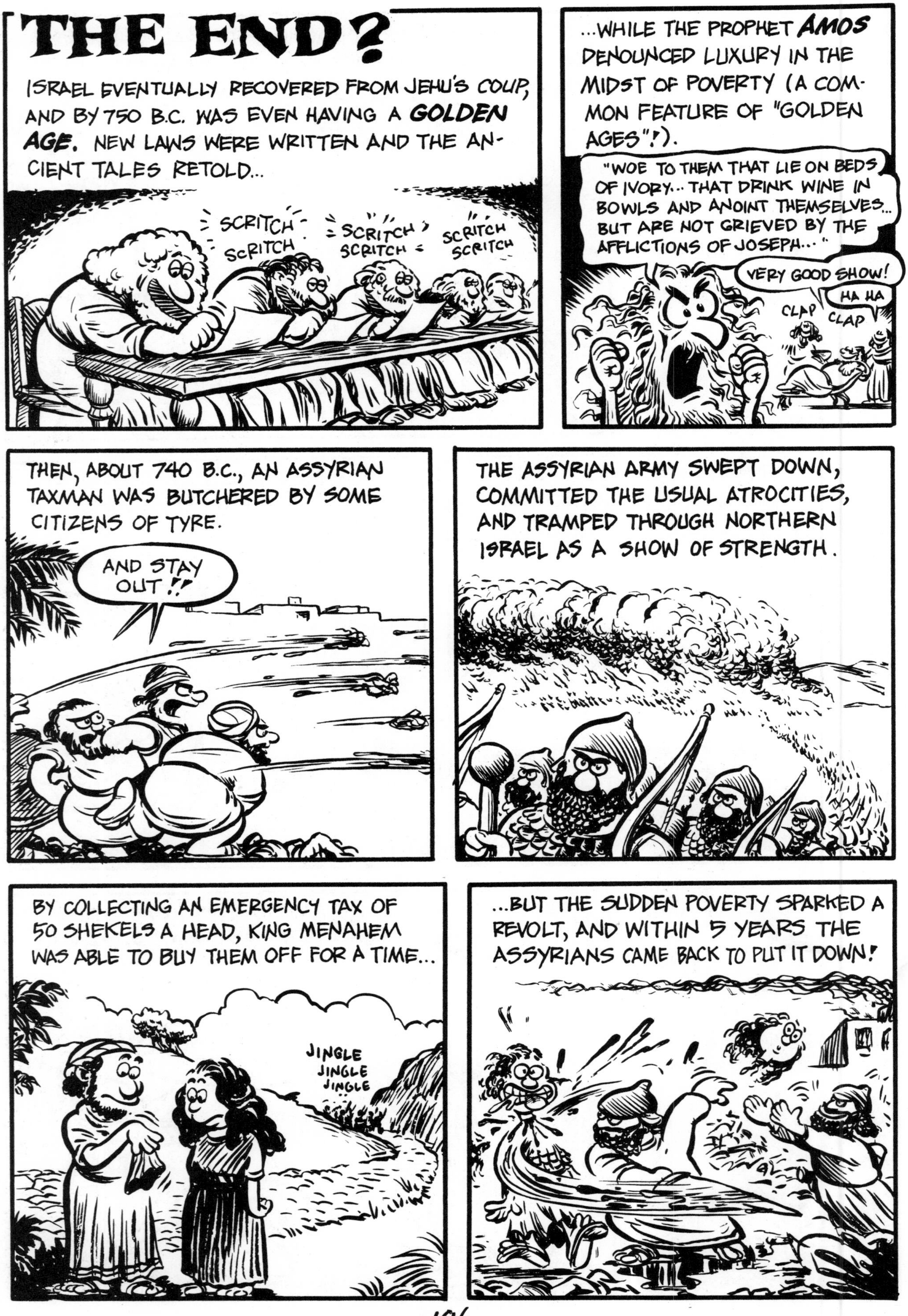
THE END?
ISRAEL EVENTUALLY RECOVERED FROM JEHU'S COUP, AND BY 750 B.C. WAS EVEN HAVING A GOLDEN AGE. NEW LAWS WERE WRITTEN AND THE ANCIENT TALES RETOLD...
SCRITCH SCRITCH
SCRITCH SCRITCH
SCRITCH SCRITCH
...WHILE THE PROPHET AMOS DENOUNCED LUXURY IN THE MIDST OF POVERTY (A COMMON FEATURE OF "GOLDEN AGES"!).
"WOE TO THEM THAT LIE ON BEDS OF IVORY... THAT DRINK WINE IN BOWLS AND ANOINT THEMSELVES... BUT ARE NOT GRIEVED BY THE AFFLICTIONS OF JOSEPH..."
VERY GOOD SHOW!
HA HA
CLAP
CLAP
THEN, ABOUT 740 B.C., AN ASSYRIAN TAXMAN WAS BUTCHERED BY SOME CITIZENS OF TYRE.
AND STAY OUT!!
THE ASSYRIAN ARMY SWEPT DOWN, COMMITTED THE USUAL ATROCITIES, AND TRAMPED THROUGH NORTHERN ISRAEL AS A SHOW OF STRENGTH.
BY COLLECTING AN EMERGENCY TAX OF 50 SHEKELS A HEAD, KING MENAHEM WAS ABLE TO BUY THEM OFF FOR A TIME...
JINGLE JINGLE JINGLE
...BUT THE SUDDEN POVERTY SPARKED A REVOLT, AND WITHIN 5 YEARS THE ASSYRIANS CAME BACK TO PUT IT DOWN!

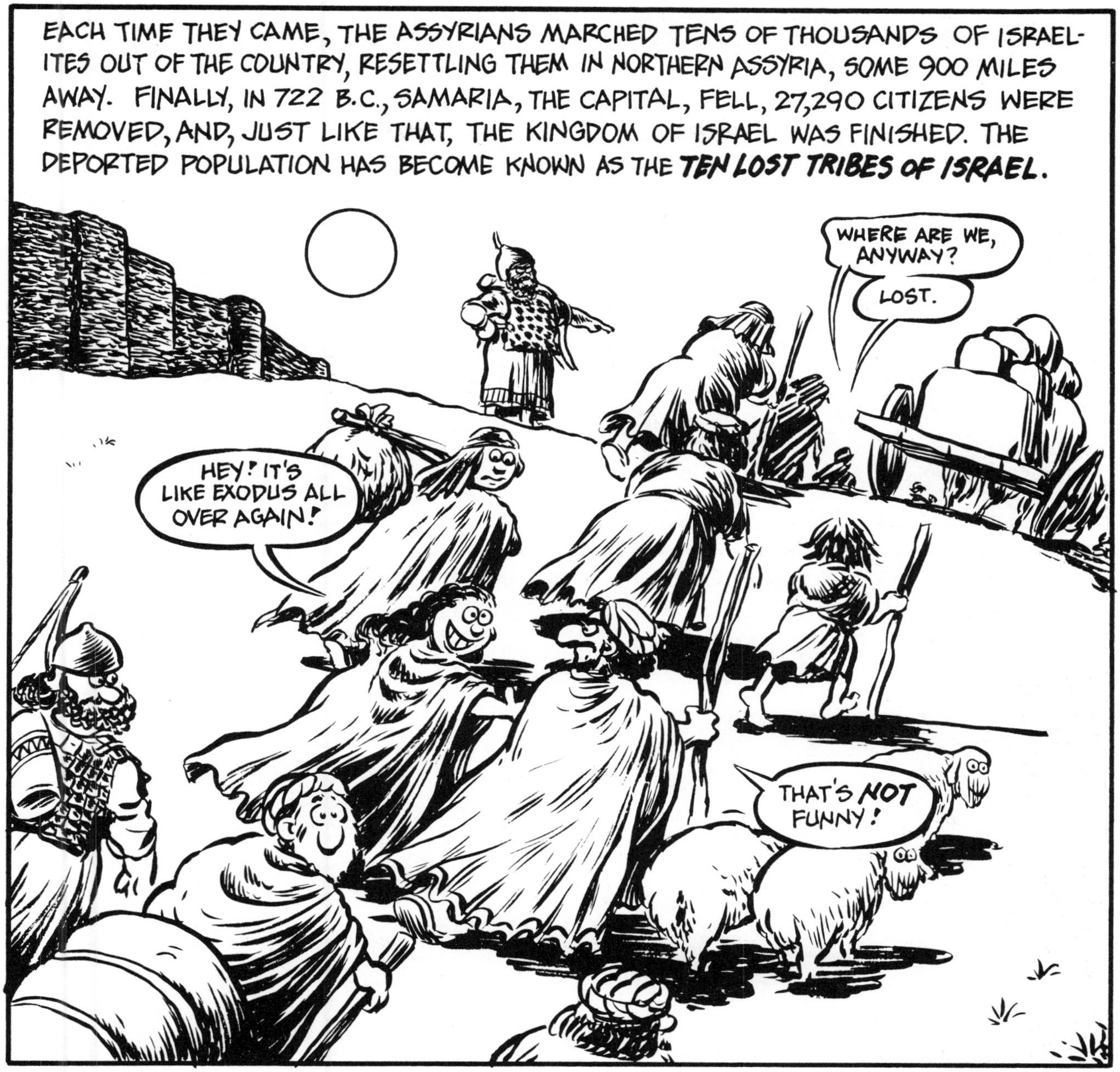
EACH TIME THEY CAME, THE ASSYRIANS MARCHED TENS OF THOUSANDS OF ISRAELITES OUT OF THE COUNTRY, RESETTLING THEM IN NORTHERN ASSYRIA, SOME 900 MILES AWAY. FINALLY, IN 722 B.C., SAMARIA, THE CAPITAL, FELL, 27,290 CITIZENS WERE REMOVED, AND, JUST LIKE THAT, THE KINGDOM OF ISRAEL WAS FINISHED. THE DEPORTED POPULATION HAS BECOME KNOWN AS THE ***TEN LOST TRIBES OF ISRAEL***.
WHERE ARE WE, ANYWAY?
LOST.
HEY! IT'S LIKE EXODUS ALL OVER AGAIN!
THAT'S ***NOT*** FUNNY!

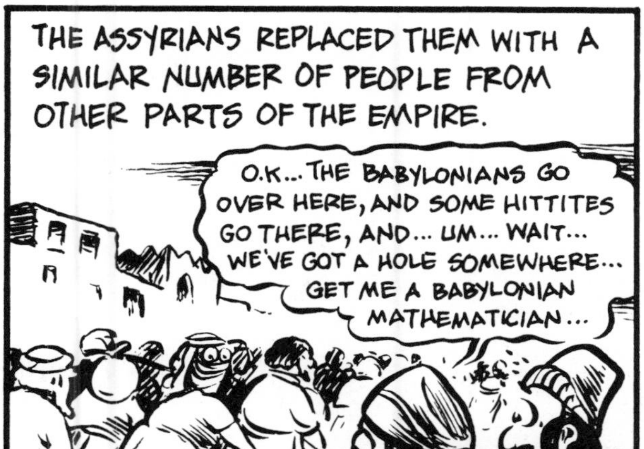
THE ASSYRIANS REPLACED THEM WITH A SIMILAR NUMBER OF PEOPLE FROM OTHER PARTS OF THE EMPIRE.
O.K... THE BABYLONIANS GO OVER HERE, AND SOME HITTITES GO THERE, AND... UM... WAIT... WE'VE GOT A HOLE SOMEWHERE... GET ME A BABYLONIAN MATHEMATICIAN...

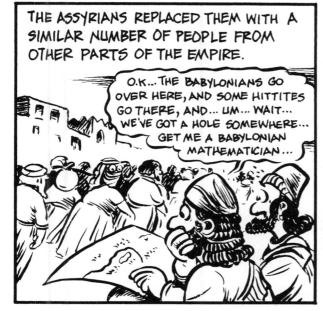

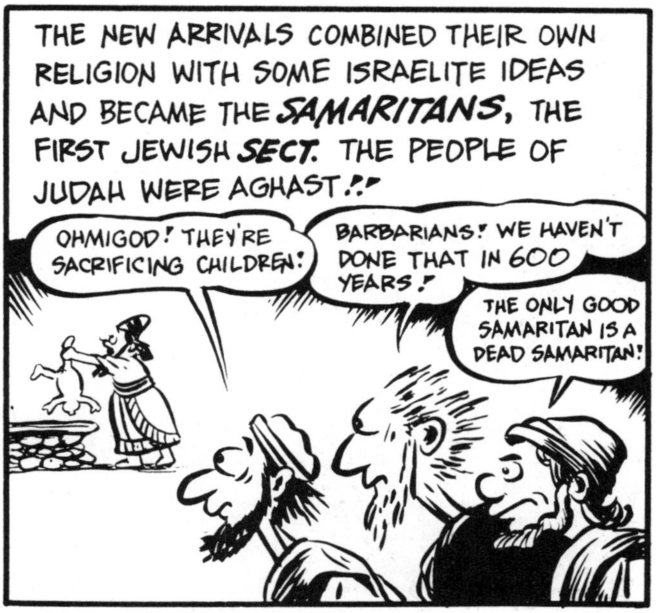
THE NEW ARRIVALS COMBINED THEIR OWN RELIGION WITH SOME ISRAELITE IDEAS AND BECAME THE ***SAMARITANS***, THE FIRST JEWISH ***SECT***. THE PEOPLE OF JUDAH WERE AGHAST!!
OHMIGOD! THEY'RE SACRIFICING CHILDREN!
BARBARIANS! WE HAVEN'T DONE THAT IN 600 YEARS!
THE ONLY GOOD SAMARITAN IS A DEAD SAMARITAN!

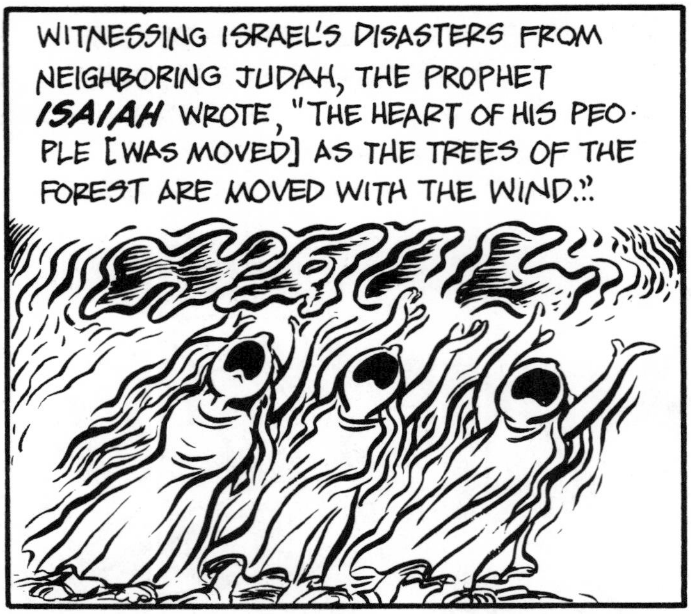
WITNESSING ISRAEL'S DISASTERS FROM NEIGHBORING JUDAH, THE PROPHET ISAIAH WROTE, "THE HEART OF HIS PEOPLE [WAS MOVED] AS THE TREES OF THE FOREST ARE MOVED WITH THE WIND."

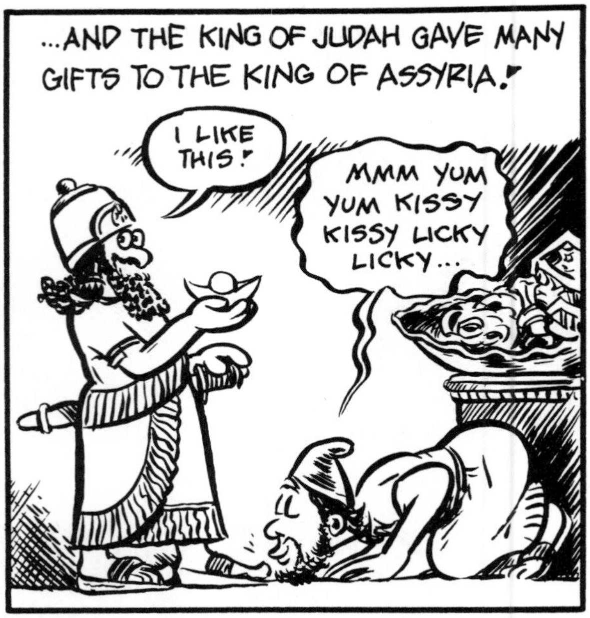
...AND THE KING OF JUDAH GAVE MANY GIFTS TO THE KING OF ASSYRIA!
I LIKE THIS!
MMM YUM YUM KISSY KISSY LICKY LICKY...

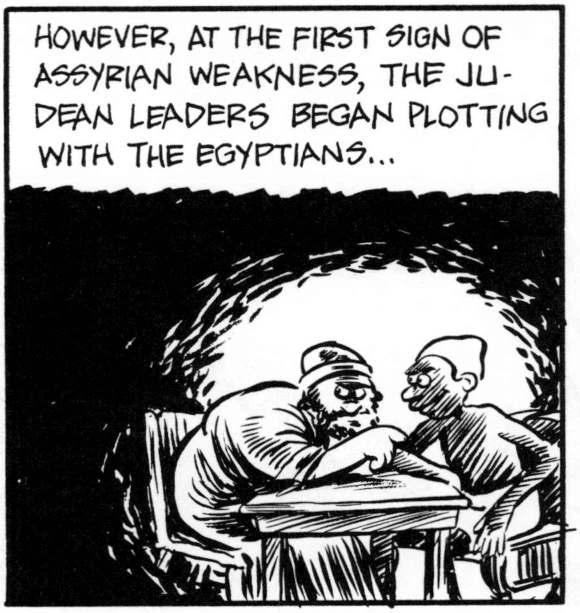
HOWEVER, AT THE FIRST SIGN OF ASSYRIAN WEAKNESS, THE JUDEAN LEADERS BEGAN PLOTTING WITH THE EGYPTIANS...

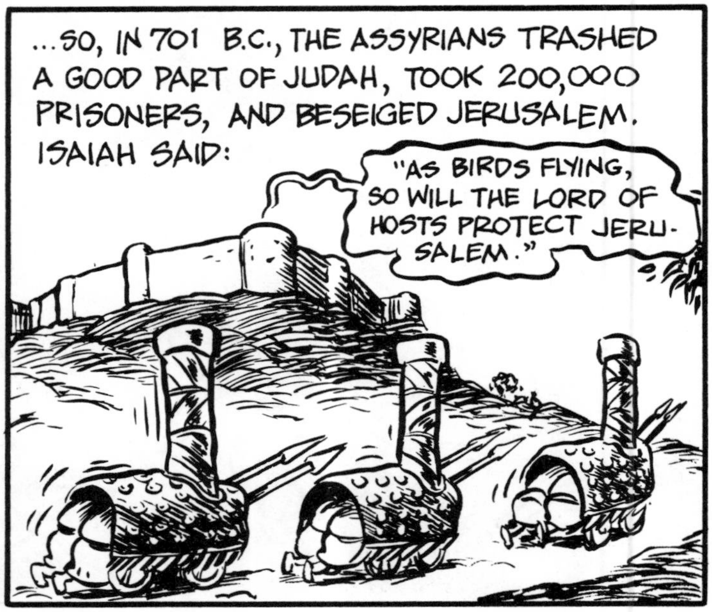
...SO, IN 701 B.C., THE ASSYRIANS TRASHED A GOOD PART OF JUDAH, TOOK 200,000 PRISONERS, AND BESEIGED JERUSALEM. ISAIAH SAID:
"AS BIRDS FLYING, SO WILL THE LORD OF HOSTS PROTECT JERUSALEM."

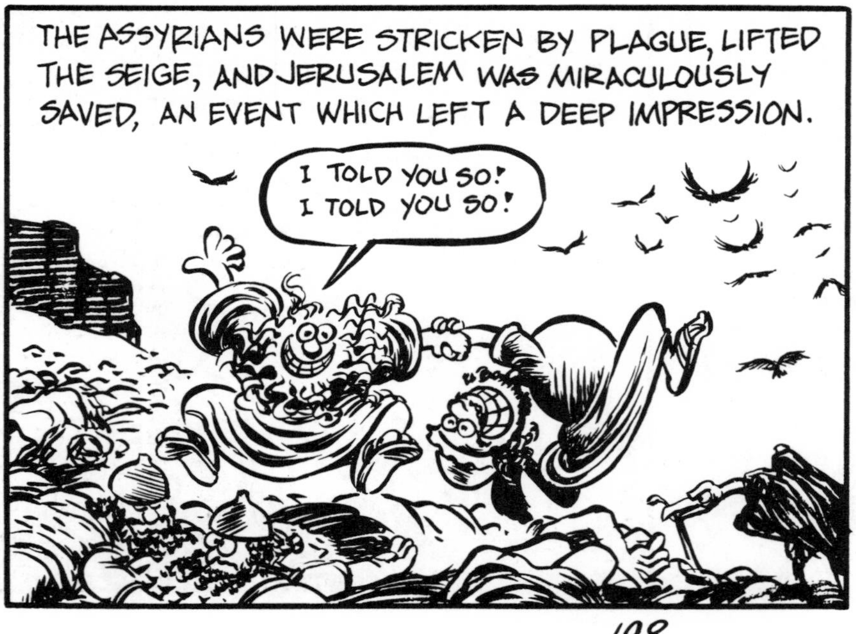
THE ASSYRIANS WERE STRICKEN BY PLAGUE, LIFTED THE SEIGE, AND JERUSALEM WAS MIRACULOUSLY SAVED, AN EVENT WHICH LEFT A DEEP IMPRESSION.
I TOLD YOU SO! I TOLD YOU SO!

BY CAREFULLY CHOOSING ITS ALLIES, THE ALL-BUT-RUINED KINGDOM OF JUDAH MANAGED TO SURVIVE ANOTHER 100 YEARS, ACTUALLY OUTLIVING THE ASSYRIAN EMPIRE, WHICH FELL TO THE BABYLONIANS IN 612 B.C.

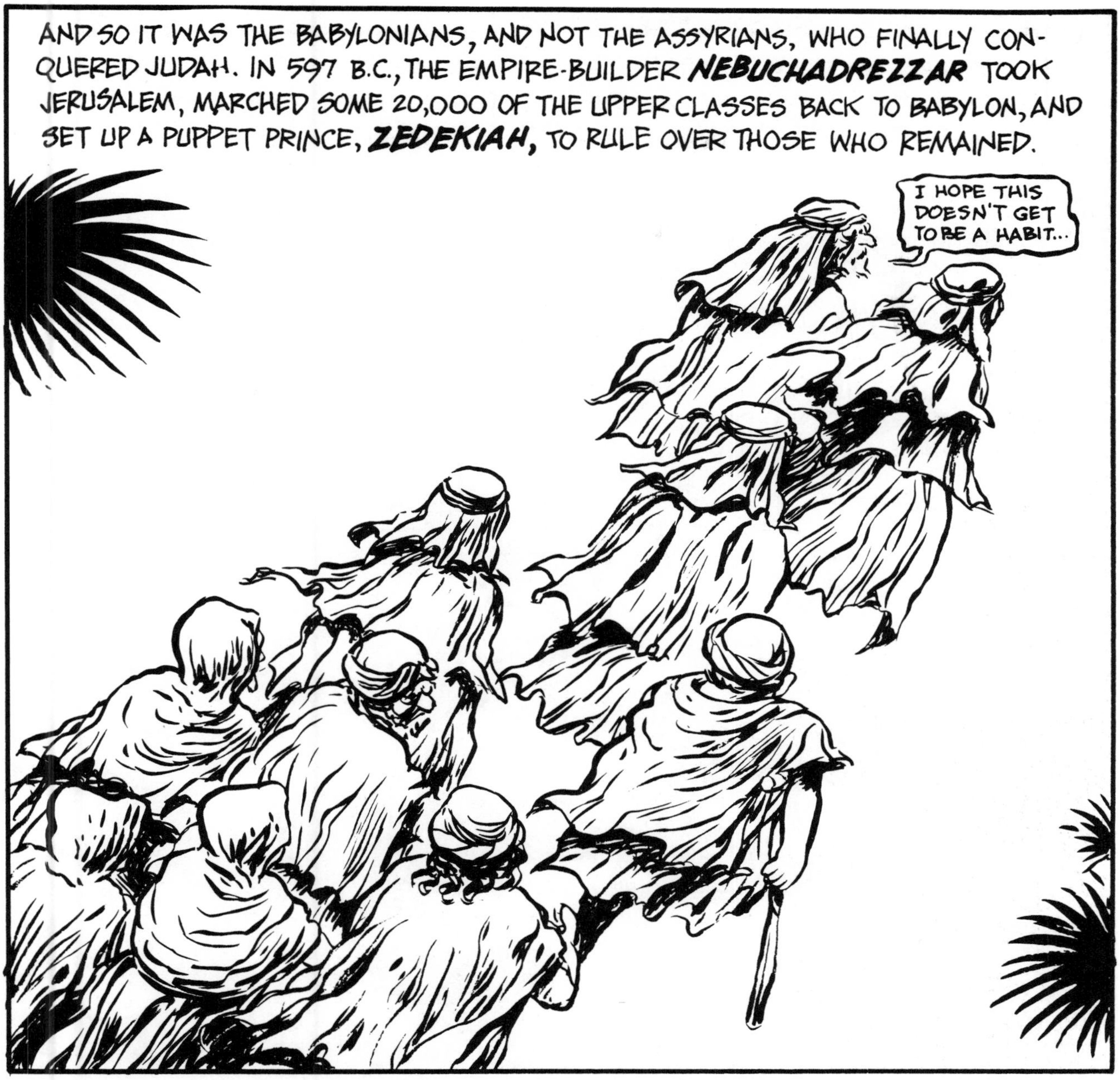
AND SO IT WAS THE BABYLONIANS, AND NOT THE ASSYRIANS, WHO FINALLY CONQUERED JUDAH. IN 597 B.C., THE EMPIRE-BUILDER NEBUCHADREZZAR TOOK JERUSALEM, MARCHED SOME 20,000 OF THE UPPER CLASSES BACK TO BABYLON, AND SET UP A PUPPET PRINCE, ZEDEKIAH, TO RULE OVER THOSE WHO REMAINED.
I HOPE THIS DOESN'T GET TO BE A HABIT...

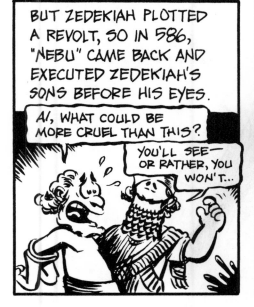

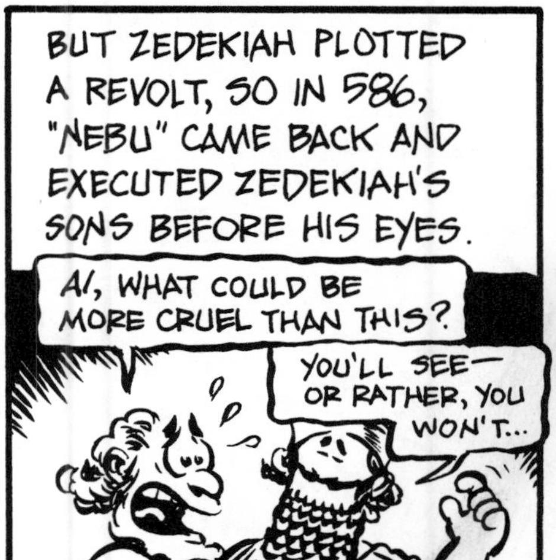
BUT ZEDEKIAH PLOTTED A REVOLT, SO IN 586, "NEBU" CAME BACK AND EXECUTED ZEDEKIAH'S SONS BEFORE HIS EYES.
AI, WHAT COULD BE MORE CRUEL THAN THIS?
YOU'LL SEE— OR RATHER, YOU WON'T...

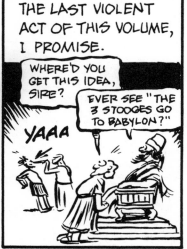

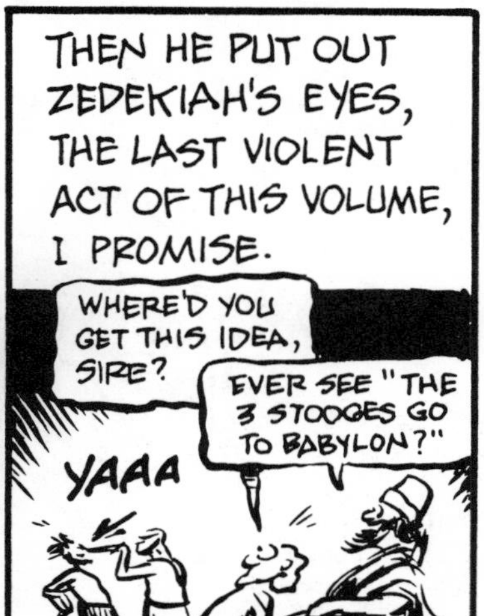
THEN HE PUT OUT ZEDEKIAH'S EYES, THE LAST VIOLENT ACT OF THIS VOLUME, I PROMISE.
WHERE'D YOU GET THIS IDEA, SIRE?
EVER SEE "THE 3 STOOGES GO TO BABYLON?"
YAAA

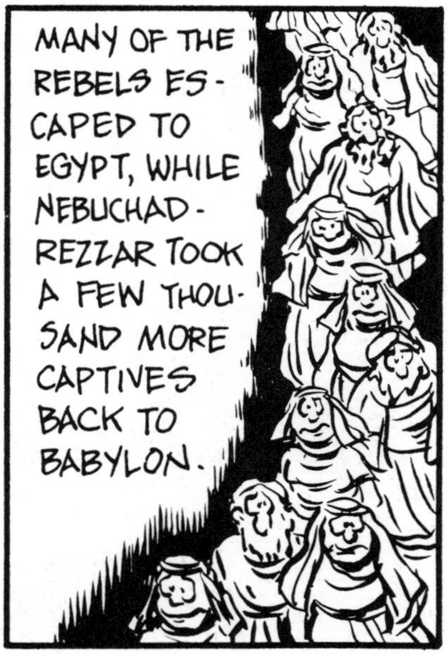
MANY OF THE REBELS ESCAPED TO EGYPT, WHILE NEBUCHADREZZAR TOOK A FEW THOUSAND MORE CAPTIVES BACK TO BABYLON.

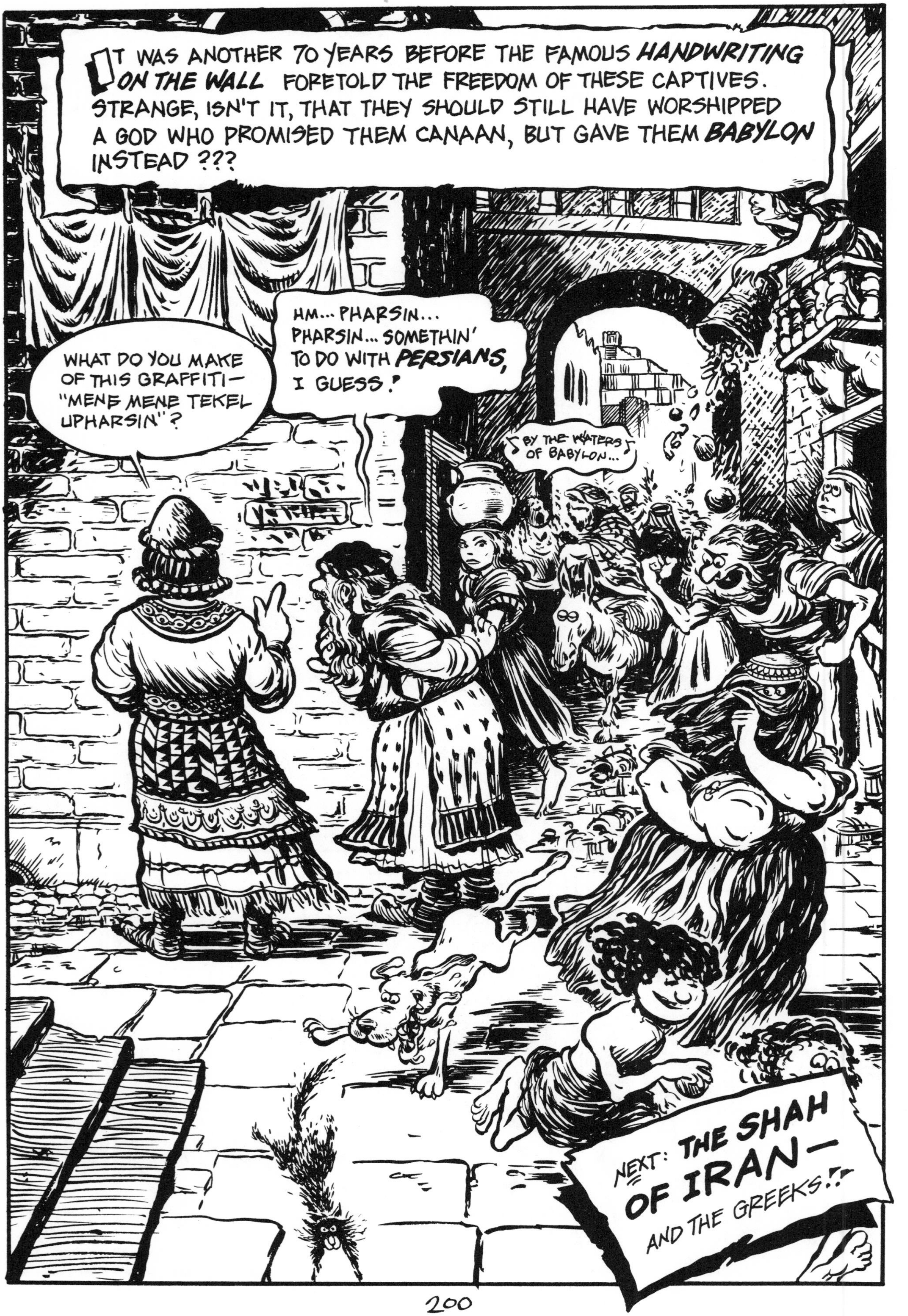
IT WAS ANOTHER 70 YEARS BEFORE THE FAMOUS HANDWRITING ON THE WALL FORETOLD THE FREEDOM OF THESE CAPTIVES. STRANGE, ISN'T IT, THAT THEY SHOULD STILL HAVE WORSHIPPED A GOD WHO PROMISED THEM CANAAN, BUT GAVE THEM BABYLON INSTEAD???
WHAT DO YOU MAKE OF THIS GRAFFITI— "MENE MENE TEKEL UPHARSIN"?
HM... PHARSIN... PHARSIN... SOMETHIN' TO DO WITH PERSIANS, I GUESS.
BY THE WATERS OF BABYLON...
NEXT: THE SHAH OF IRAN— AND THE GREEKS!?

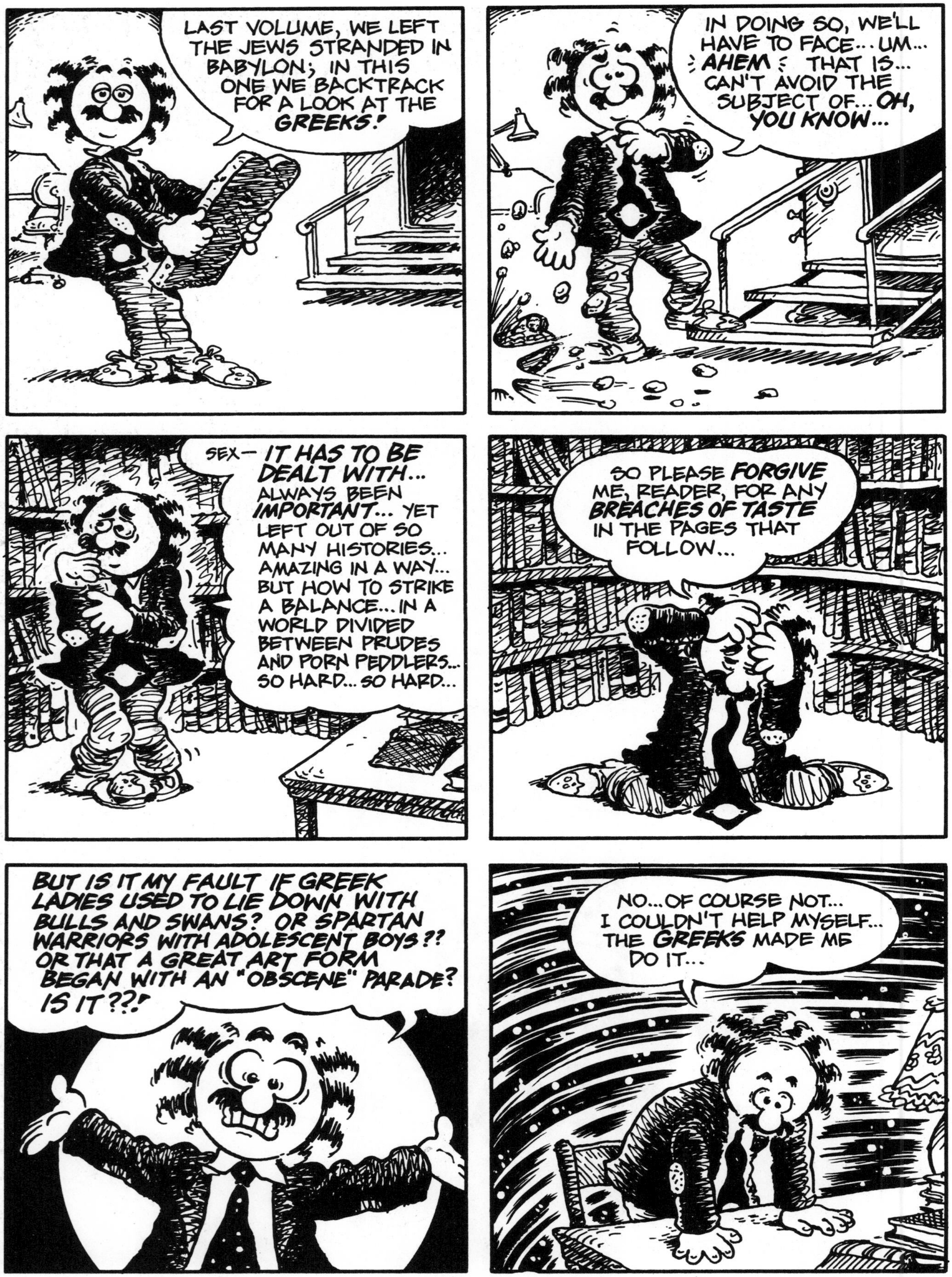
LAST VOLUME, WE LEFT THE JEWS STRANDED IN BABYLON; IN THIS ONE WE BACKTRACK FOR A LOOK AT THE GREEKS!
IN DOING SO, WE'LL HAVE TO FACE... UM... AHEM THAT IS... CAN'T AVOID THE SUBJECT OF... OH, YOU KNOW...
SEX— IT HAS TO BE DEALT WITH... ALWAYS BEEN IMPORTANT... YET LEFT OUT OF SO MANY HISTORIES... AMAZING IN A WAY... BUT HOW TO STRIKE A BALANCE... IN A WORLD DIVIDED BETWEEN PRUDES AND PORN PEDDLERS... SO HARD... SO HARD...
SO PLEASE FORGIVE ME, READER, FOR ANY BREACHES OF TASTE IN THE PAGES THAT FOLLOW...
BUT IS IT MY FAULT IF GREEK LADIES USED TO LIE DOWN WITH BULLS AND SWANS? OR SPARTAN WARRIORS WITH ADOLESCENT BOYS?? OR THAT A GREAT ART FORM BEGAN WITH AN "OBSCENE" PARADE? IS IT??!
NO... OF COURSE NOT... I COULDN'T HELP MYSELF... THE GREEKS MADE ME DO IT...

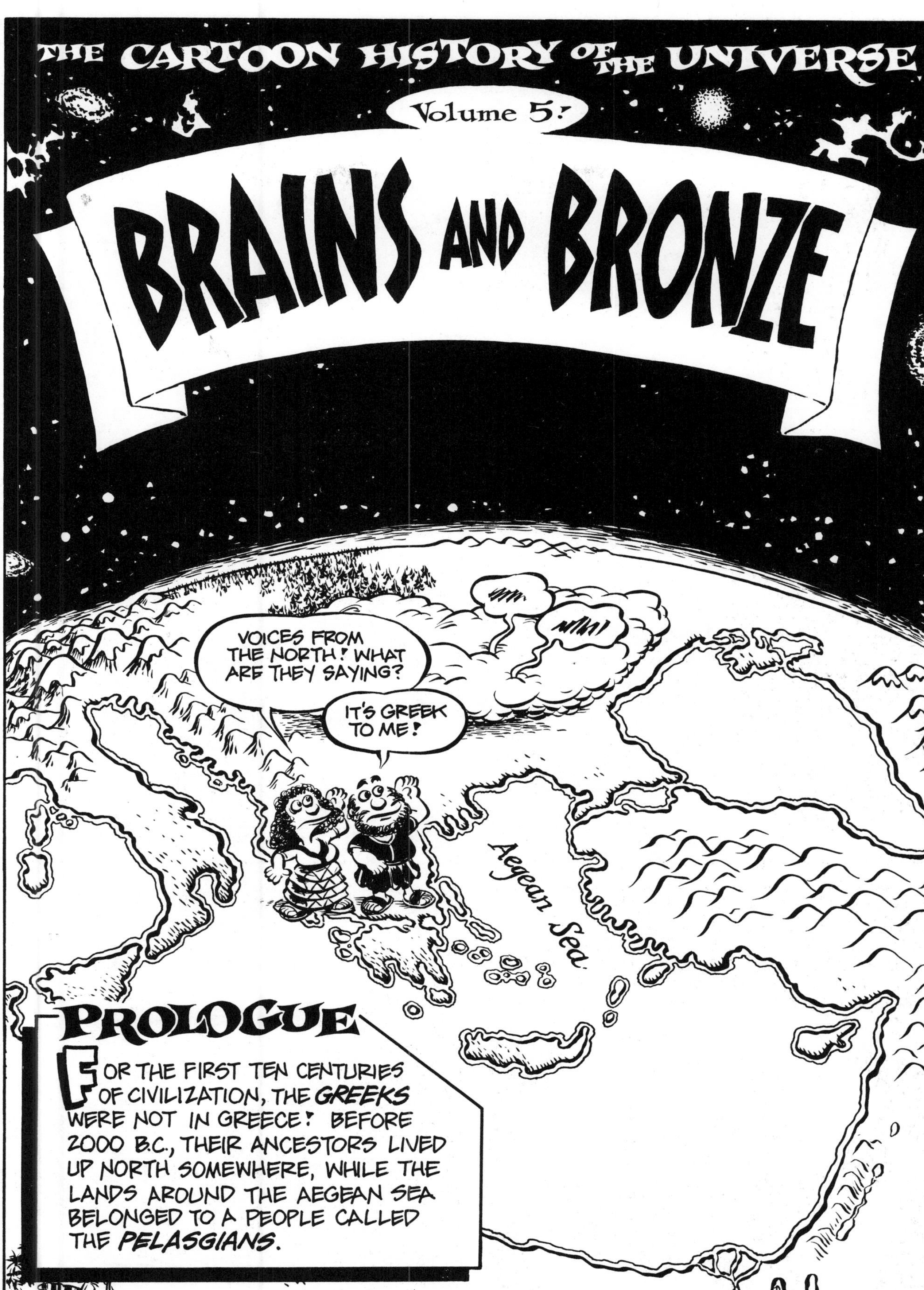
THE CARTOON HISTORY OF THE UNIVERSE
Volume 5:
BRAINS AND BRONZE
VOICES FROM THE NORTH! WHAT ARE THEY SAYING?
IT'S GREEK TO ME!
Aegean Sea
PROLOGUE
FOR THE FIRST TEN CENTURIES OF CIVILIZATION, THE GREEKS WERE NOT IN GREECE! BEFORE 2000 B.C., THEIR ANCESTORS LIVED UP NORTH SOMEWHERE, WHILE THE LANDS AROUND THE AEGEAN SEA BELONGED TO A PEOPLE CALLED THE PELASGIANS.

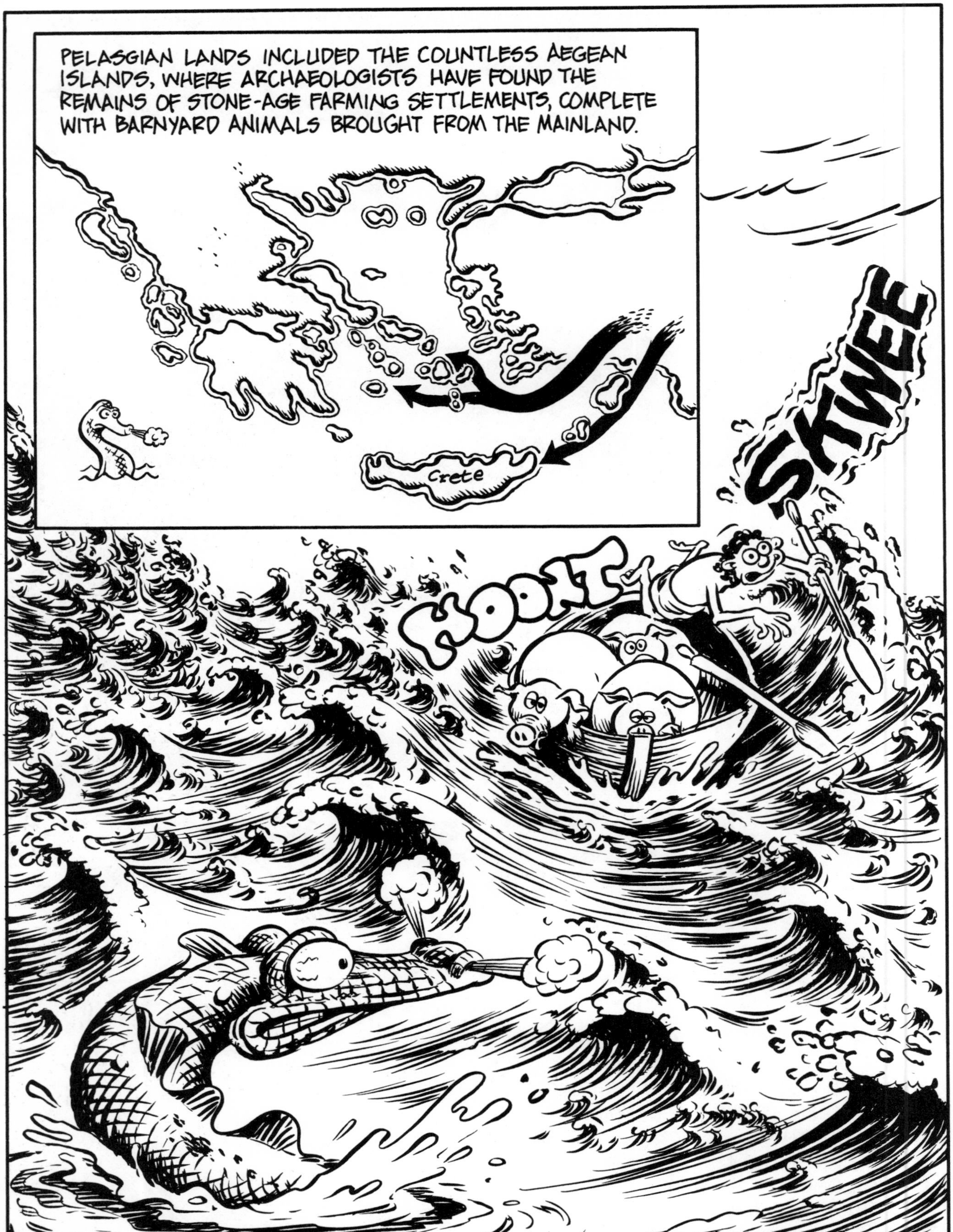
PELASGIAN LANDS INCLUDED THE COUNTLESS AEGEAN ISLANDS, WHERE ARCHAEOLOGISTS HAVE FOUND THE REMAINS OF STONE-AGE FARMING SETTLEMENTS, COMPLETE WITH BARNYARD ANIMALS BROUGHT FROM THE MAINLAND.
Crete
SKWEE
HOONT

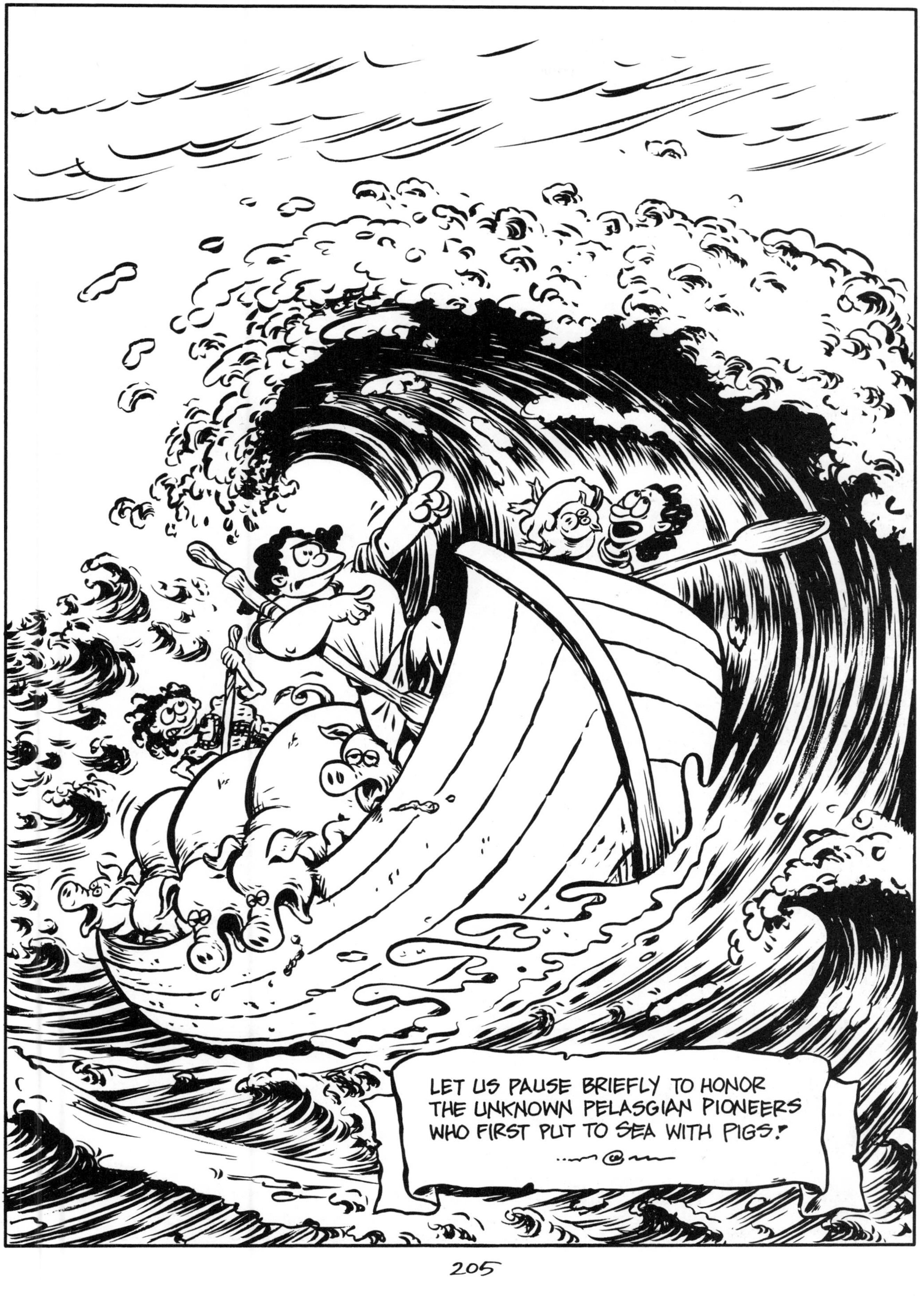
LET US PAUSE BRIEFLY TO HONOR THE UNKNOWN PELASGIAN PIONEERS WHO FIRST PUT TO SEA WITH PIGS!

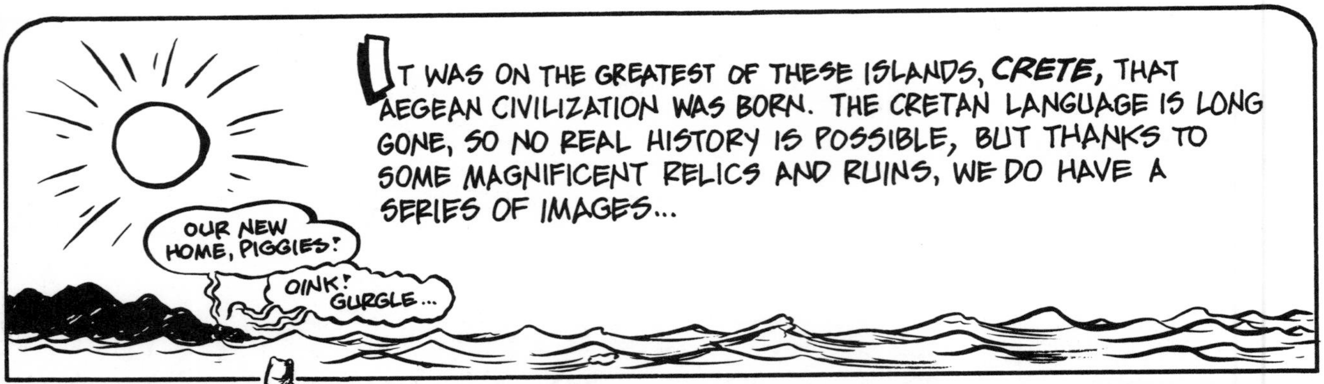
IT WAS ON THE GREATEST OF THESE ISLANDS, ***CRETE,*** THAT AEGEAN CIVILIZATION WAS BORN. THE CRETAN LANGUAGE IS LONG GONE, SO NO REAL HISTORY IS POSSIBLE, BUT THANKS TO SOME MAGNIFICENT RELICS AND RUINS, WE DO HAVE A SERIES OF IMAGES...
OUR NEW HOME, PIGGIES!
OINK! GURGLE...
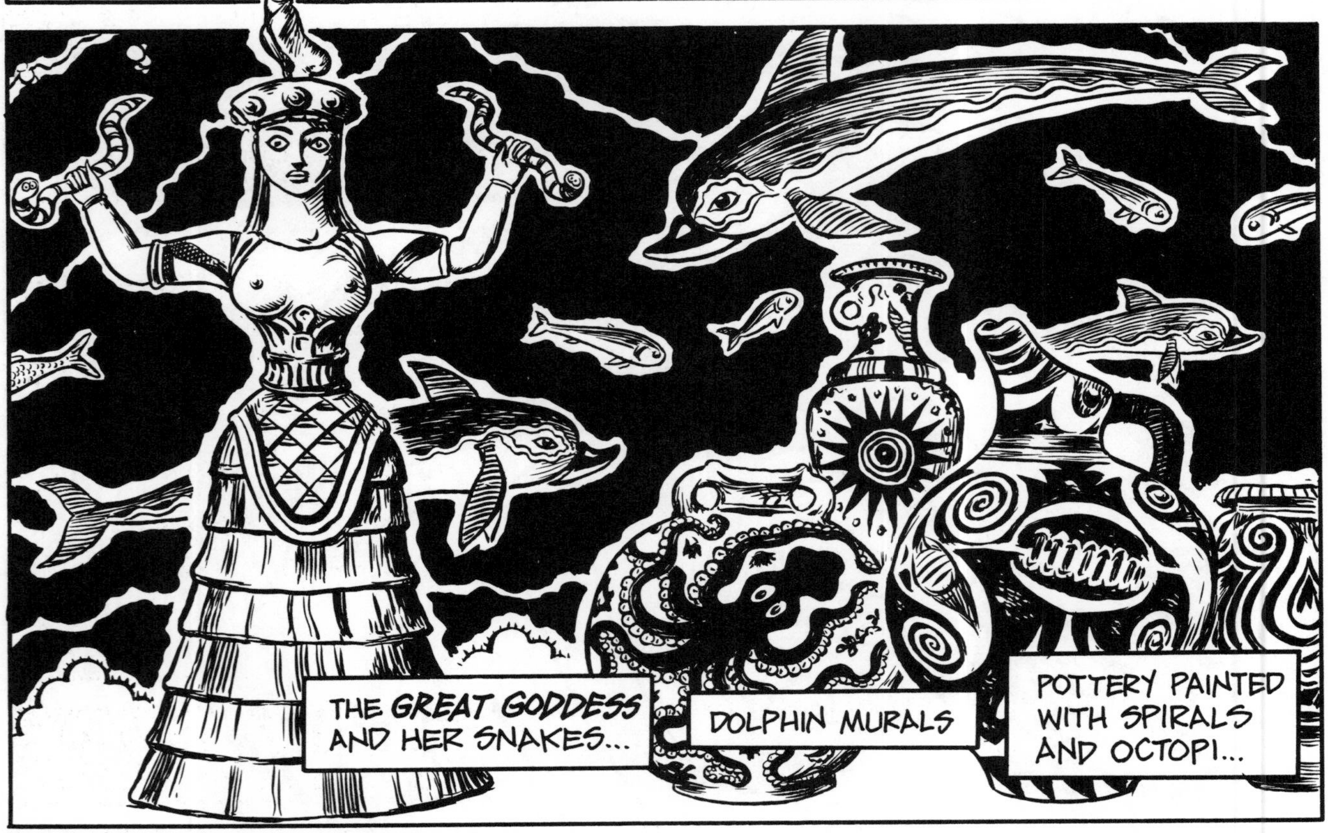
THE ***GREAT GODDESS*** AND HER SNAKES...
DOLPHIN MURALS
POTTERY PAINTED WITH SPIRALS AND OCTOPI...
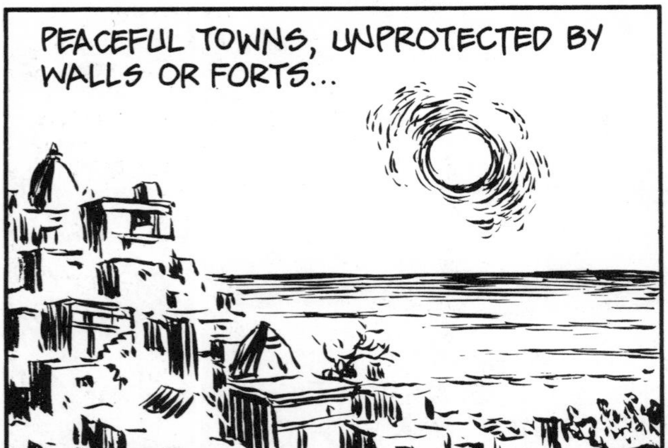
PEACEFUL TOWNS, UNPROTECTED BY WALLS OR FORTS...
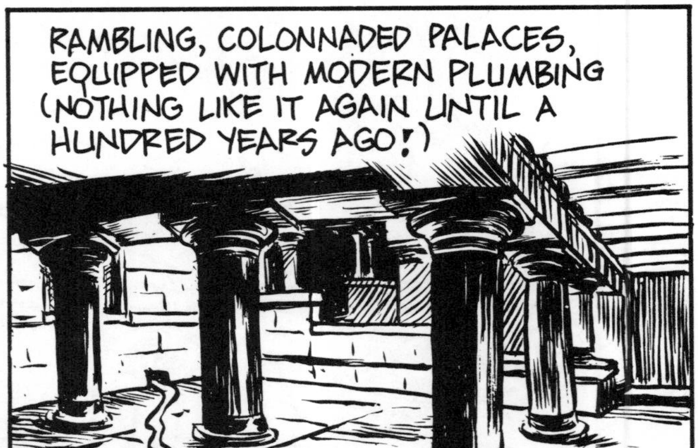
RAMBLING, COLONNADED PALACES, EQUIPPED WITH MODERN PLUMBING (NOTHING LIKE IT AGAIN UNTIL A HUNDRED YEARS AGO!)
KER FLUSH!

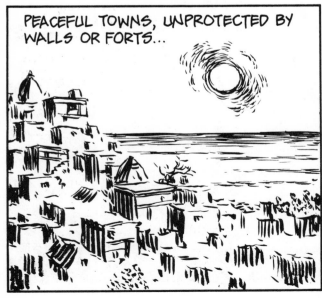

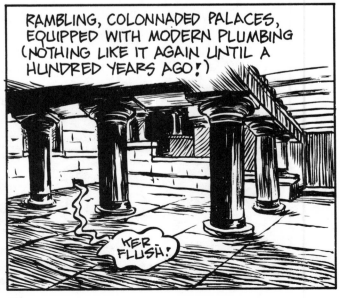

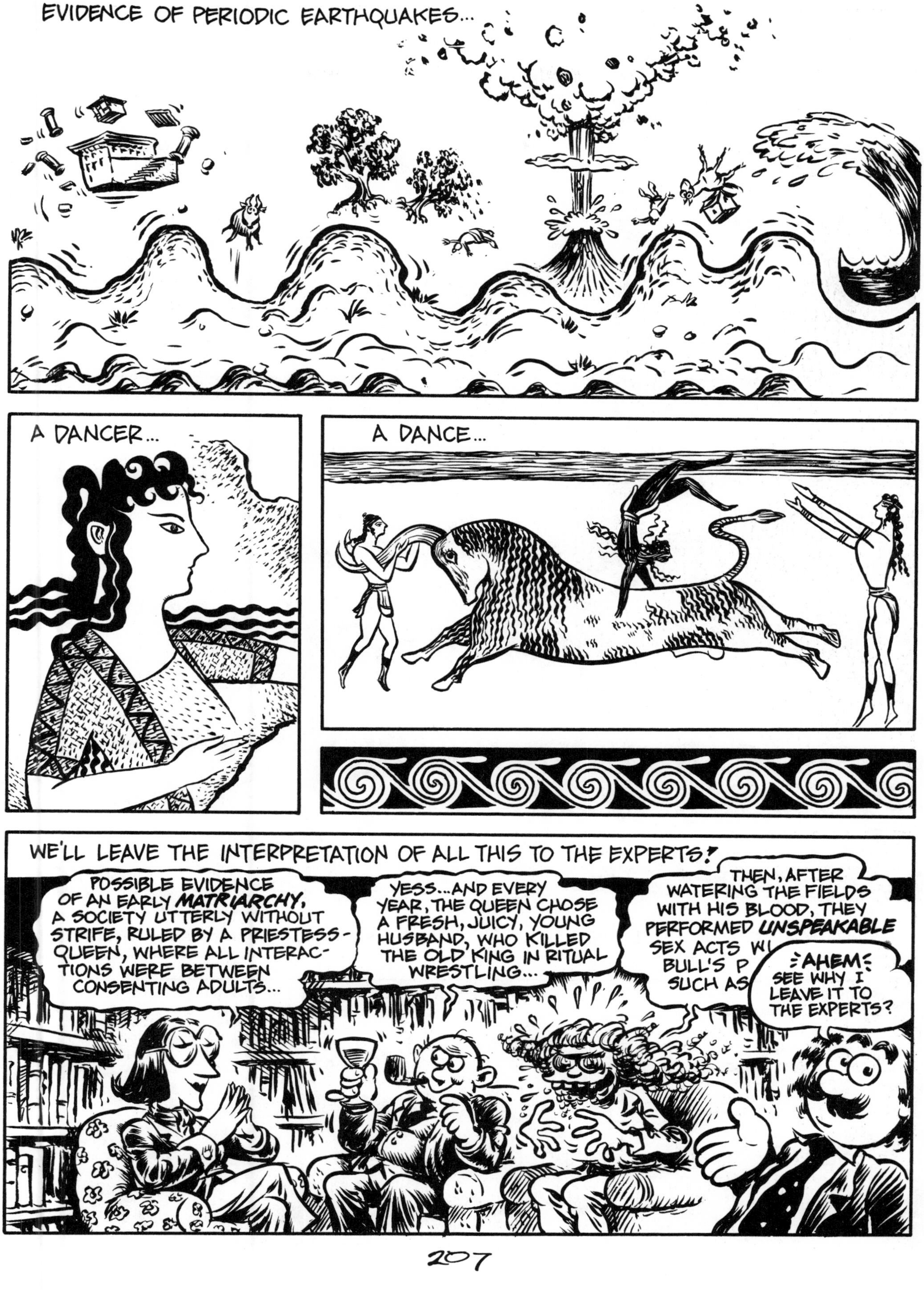
EVIDENCE OF PERIODIC EARTHQUAKES...
A DANCER...
A DANCE...
WE'LL LEAVE THE INTERPRETATION OF ALL THIS TO THE EXPERTS!
POSSIBLE EVIDENCE OF AN EARLY **MATRIARCHY**, A SOCIETY UTTERLY WITHOUT STRIFE, RULED BY A PRIESTESS-QUEEN, WHERE ALL INTERACTIONS WERE BETWEEN CONSENTING ADULTS...
YESS...AND EVERY YEAR, THE QUEEN CHOSE A FRESH, JUICY, YOUNG HUSBAND, WHO KILLED THE OLD KING IN RITUAL WRESTLING...
THEN, AFTER WATERING THE FIELDS WITH HIS BLOOD, THEY PERFORMED **UNSPEAKABLE** SEX ACTS W BULL'S P SUCH AS
AHEM SEE WHY I LEAVE IT TO THE EXPERTS?

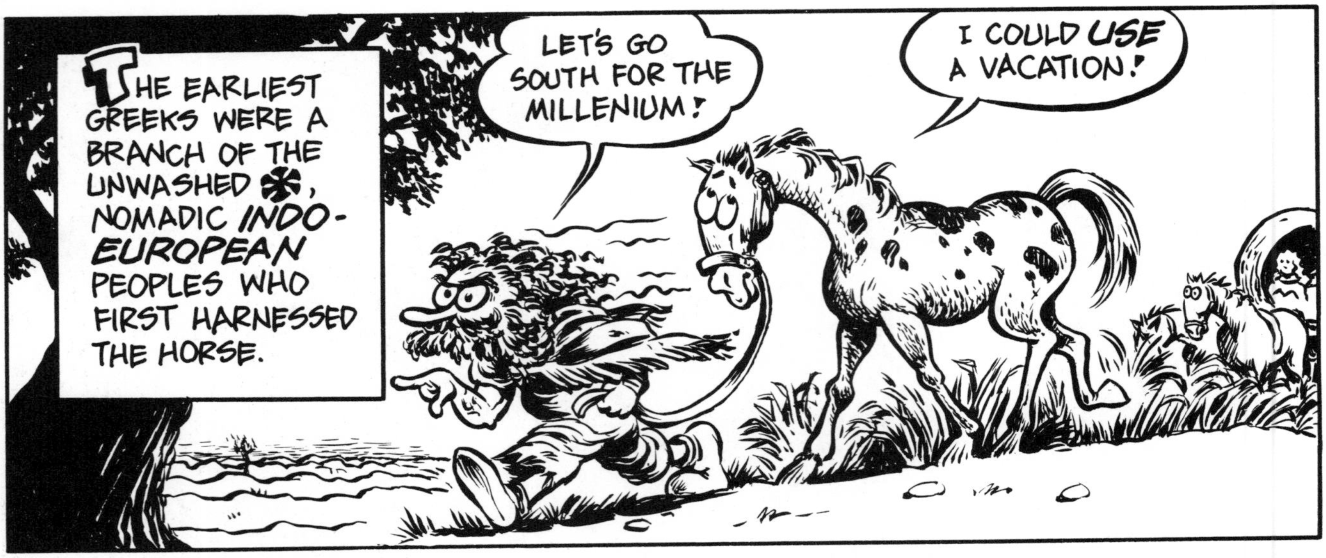
THE EARLIEST GREEKS WERE A BRANCH OF THE UNWASHED ✽, NOMADIC *INDO-EUROPEAN* PEOPLES WHO FIRST HARNESSED THE HORSE.
LET'S GO SOUTH FOR THE MILLENIUM!
I COULD *USE* A VACATION!

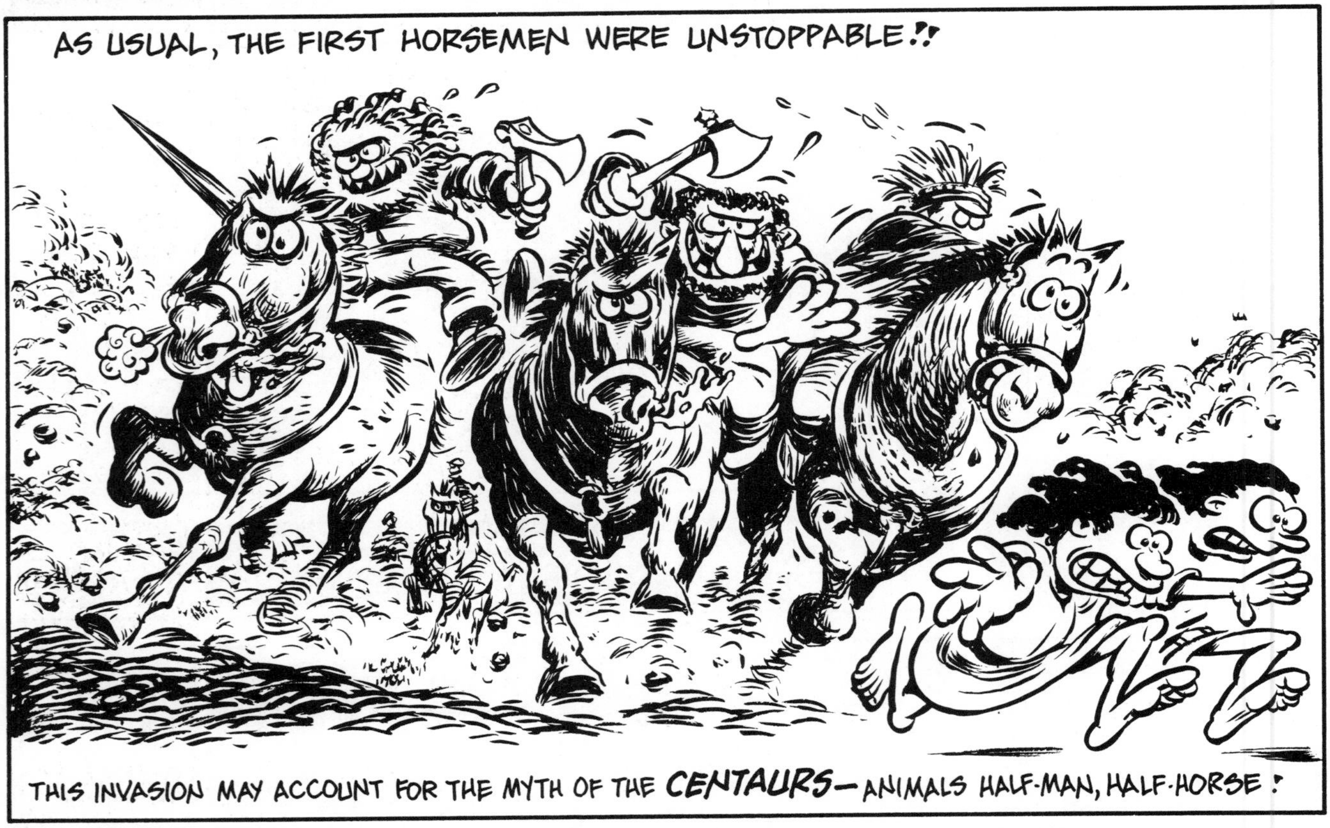
AS USUAL, THE FIRST HORSEMEN WERE UNSTOPPABLE!!
THIS INVASION MAY ACCOUNT FOR THE MYTH OF THE *CENTAURS*— ANIMALS HALF-MAN, HALF-HORSE!

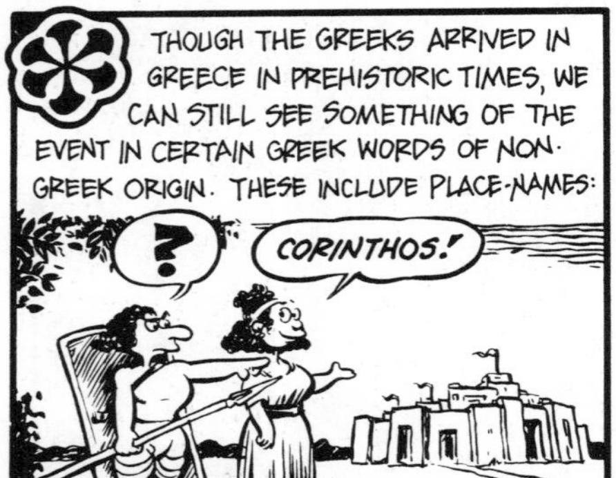
✽ THOUGH THE GREEKS ARRIVED IN GREECE IN PREHISTORIC TIMES, WE CAN STILL SEE SOMETHING OF THE EVENT IN CERTAIN GREEK WORDS OF NON-GREEK ORIGIN. THESE INCLUDE PLACE-NAMES:
?
CORINTHOS!

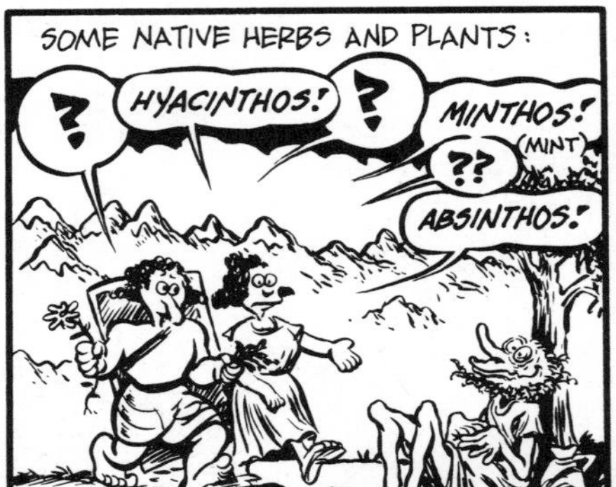
SOME NATIVE HERBS AND PLANTS:
?
HYACINTHOS!
?
MINTHOS! (MINT)
??
ABSINTHOS!

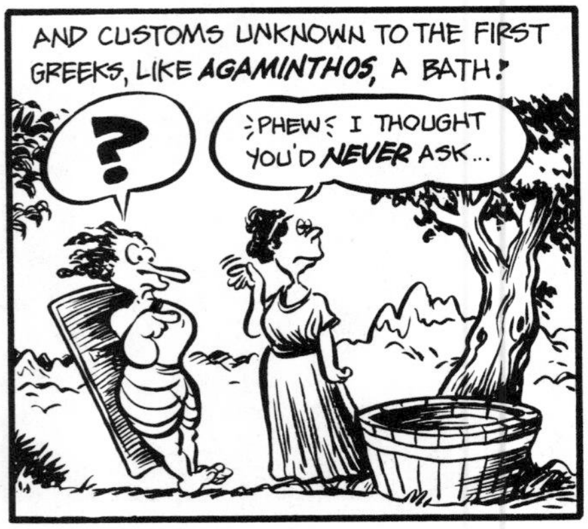
AND CUSTOMS UNKNOWN TO THE FIRST GREEKS, LIKE *AGAMINTHOS*, A BATH!
?
PHEW! I THOUGHT YOU'D *NEVER* ASK...

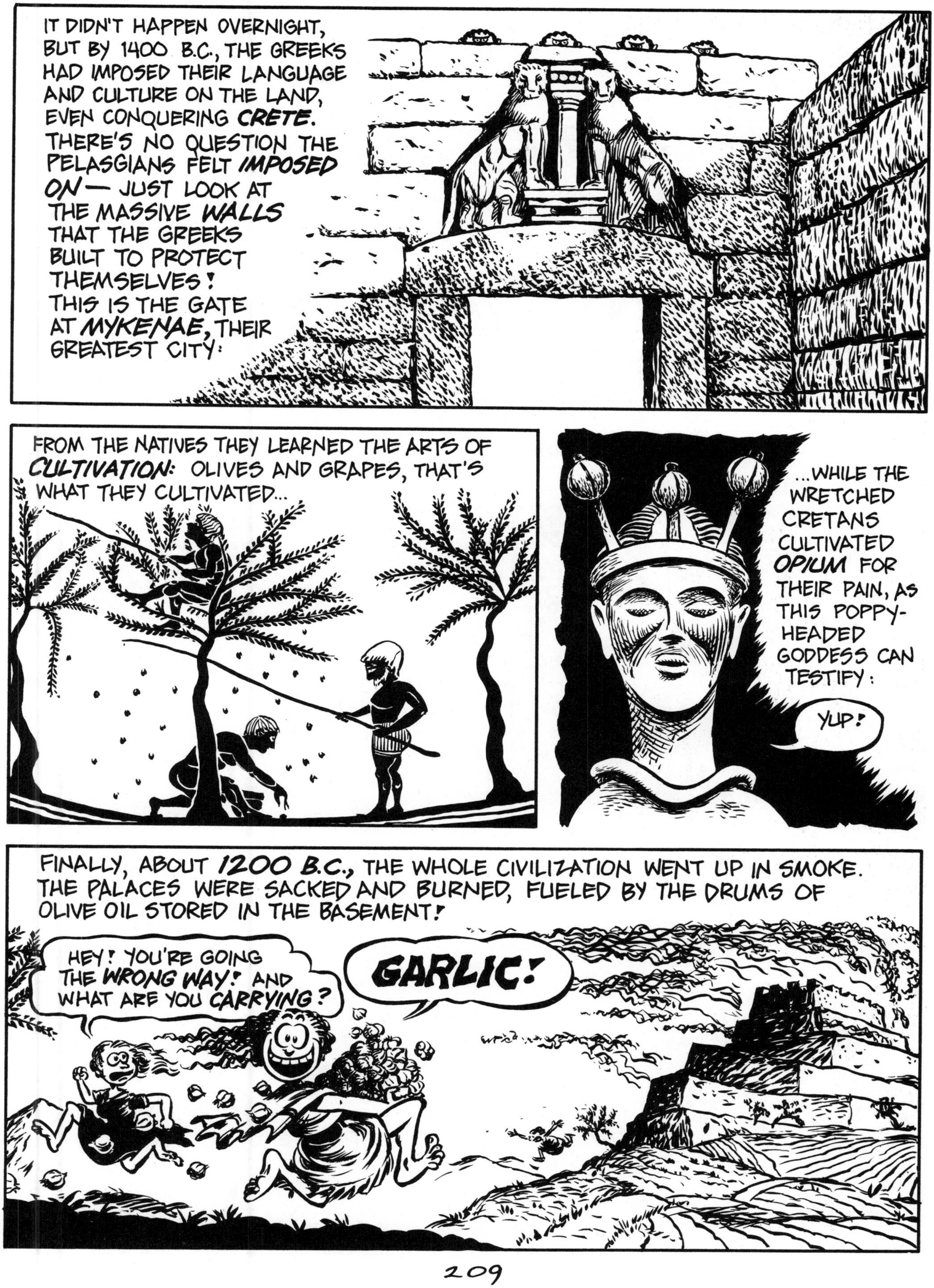
IT DIDN'T HAPPEN OVERNIGHT, BUT BY 1400 B.C., THE GREEKS HAD IMPOSED THEIR LANGUAGE AND CULTURE ON THE LAND, EVEN CONQUERING CRETE. THERE'S NO QUESTION THE PELASGIANS FELT IMPOSED ON— JUST LOOK AT THE MASSIVE WALLS THAT THE GREEKS BUILT TO PROTECT THEMSELVES! THIS IS THE GATE AT MYKENAE, THEIR GREATEST CITY:
FROM THE NATIVES THEY LEARNED THE ARTS OF CULTIVATION: OLIVES AND GRAPES, THAT'S WHAT THEY CULTIVATED...
...WHILE THE WRETCHED CRETANS CULTIVATED OPIUM FOR THEIR PAIN, AS THIS POPPY-HEADED GODDESS CAN TESTIFY:
YUP!
FINALLY, ABOUT 1200 B.C., THE WHOLE CIVILIZATION WENT UP IN SMOKE. THE PALACES WERE SACKED AND BURNED, FUELED BY THE DRUMS OF OLIVE OIL STORED IN THE BASEMENT!
HEY! YOU'RE GOING THE WRONG WAY! AND WHAT ARE YOU CARRYING?
GARLIC!

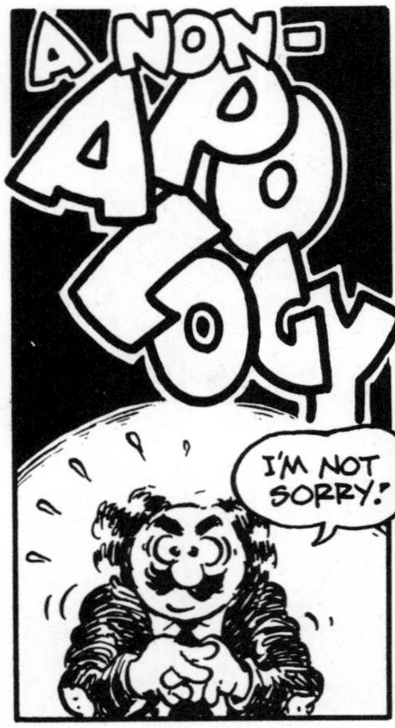
A NON-APOLOGY
I'M NOT SORRY!

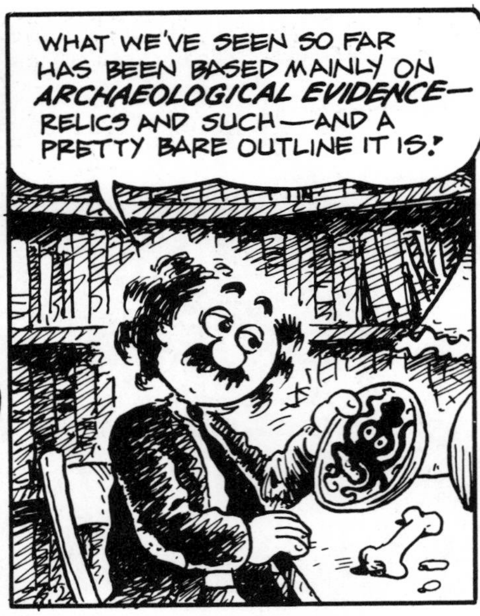
WHAT WE'VE SEEN SO FAR HAS BEEN BASED MAINLY ON ARCHAEOLOGICAL EVIDENCE—RELICS AND SUCH—AND A PRETTY BARE OUTLINE IT IS!

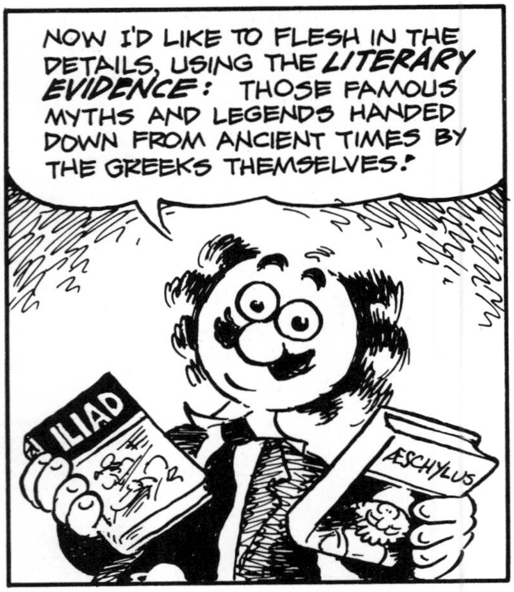
NOW I'D LIKE TO FLESH IN THE DETAILS, USING THE LITERARY EVIDENCE: THOSE FAMOUS MYTHS AND LEGENDS HANDED DOWN FROM ANCIENT TIMES BY THE GREEKS THEMSELVES!
ILIAD
ÆSCHYLUS

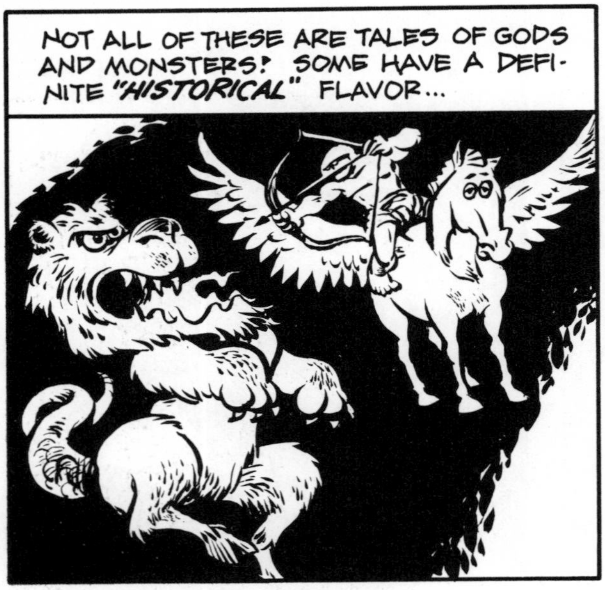
NOT ALL OF THESE ARE TALES OF GODS AND MONSTERS! SOME HAVE A DEFINITE "HISTORICAL" FLAVOR...

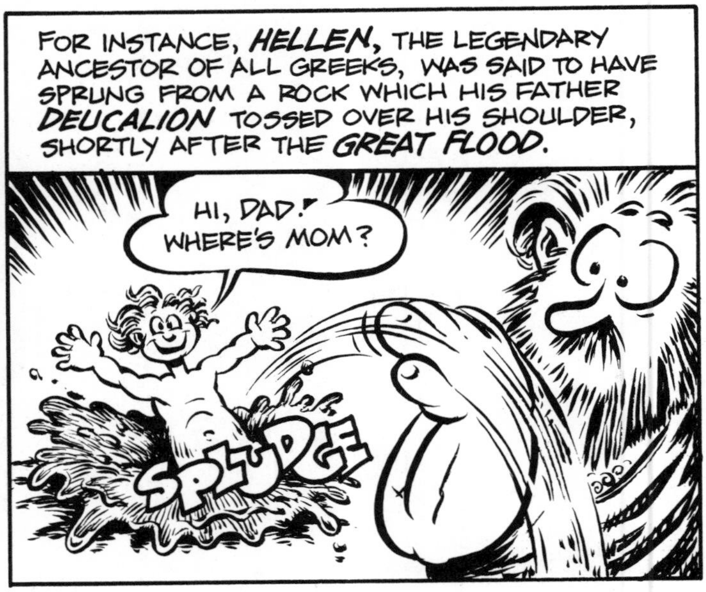
FOR INSTANCE, HELLEN, THE LEGENDARY ANCESTOR OF ALL GREEKS, WAS SAID TO HAVE SPRUNG FROM A ROCK WHICH HIS FATHER DEUCALION TOSSED OVER HIS SHOULDER, SHORTLY AFTER THE GREAT FLOOD.
HI, DAD! WHERE'S MOM?
SPLUDGE

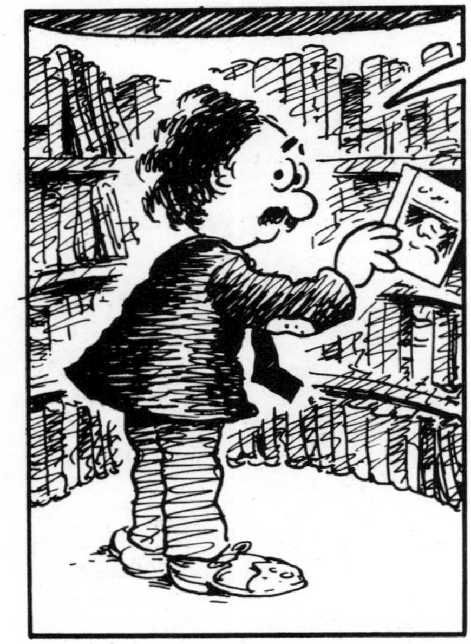

WELL... THAT'S AN ***ORIGIN MYTH***... THEY'RE ALWAYS WEIRD... BUT AS WE APPROACH THE TIME OF ***DECLINE*** AND ***FALL,*** THE LEGENDS GET DOWNRIGHT ***BELIEVABLE!*** AND EVEN IF THEY'RE ***NOT*** TRUE, THEY CAN CERTAINLY TELL US SOMETHING ABOUT THE PEOPLE WHO ***MADE THEM UP!!***

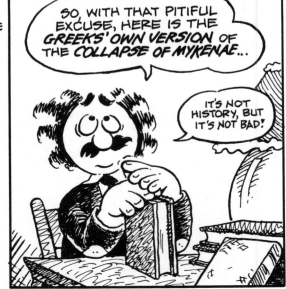

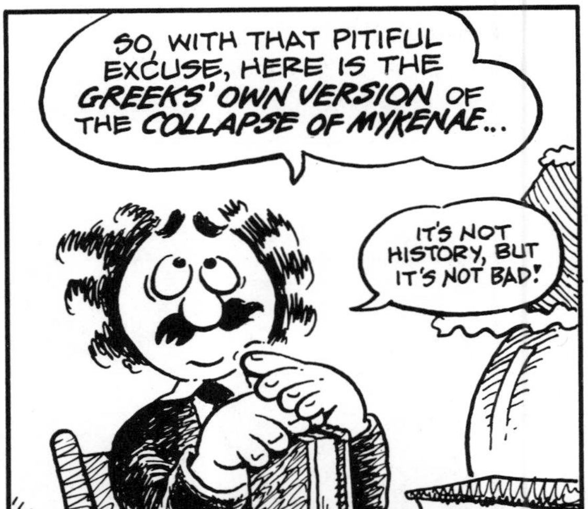
SO, WITH THAT PITIFUL EXCUSE, HERE IS THE GREEKS' OWN VERSION OF THE COLLAPSE OF MYKENAE...
IT'S NOT HISTORY, BUT IT'S NOT BAD!

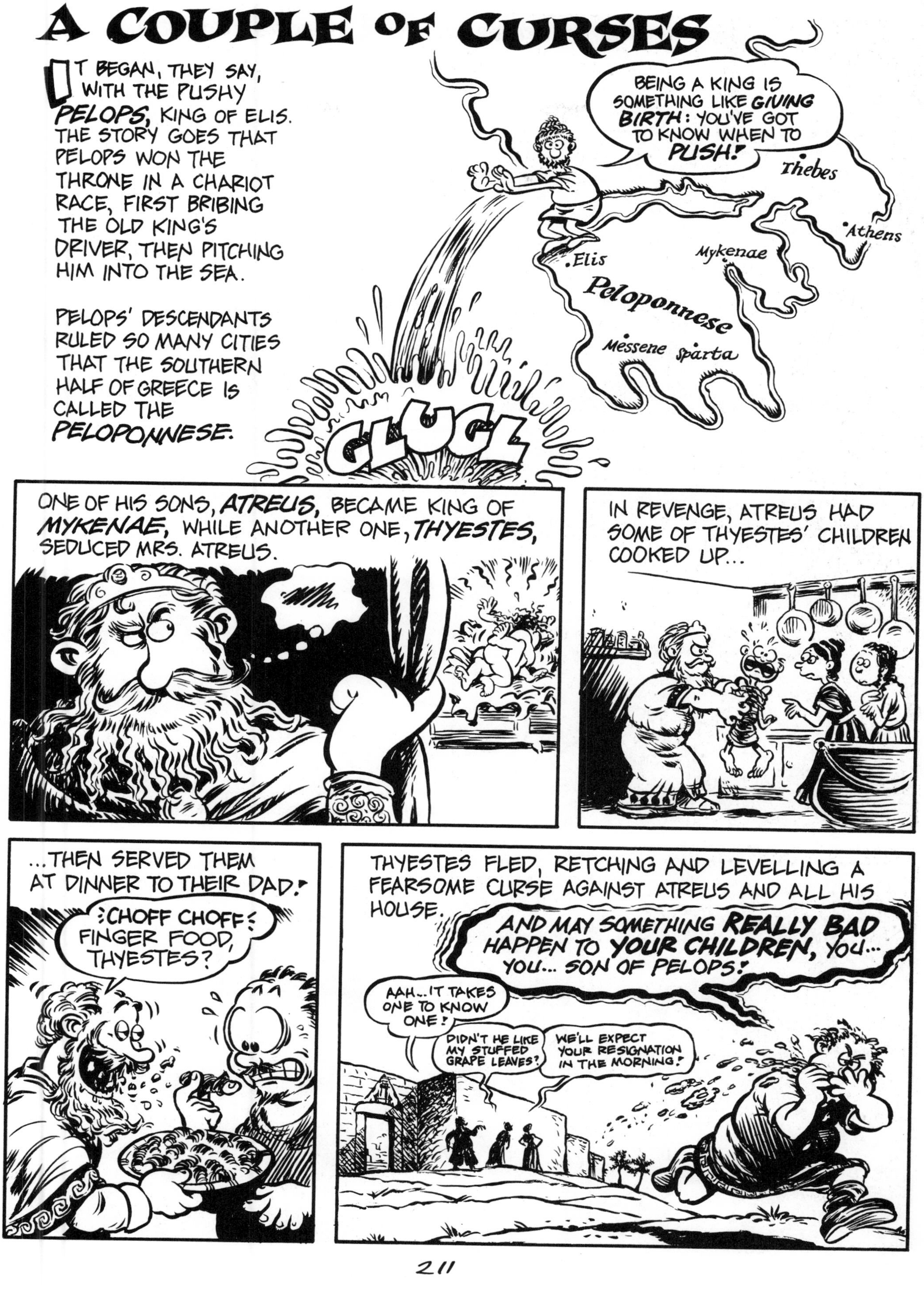

A COUPLE OF CURSES
IT BEGAN, THEY SAY, WITH THE PUSHY PELOPS, KING OF ELIS. THE STORY GOES THAT PELOPS WON THE THRONE IN A CHARIOT RACE, FIRST BRIBING THE OLD KING'S DRIVER, THEN PITCHING HIM INTO THE SEA.
PELOPS' DESCENDANTS RULED SO MANY CITIES THAT THE SOUTHERN HALF OF GREECE IS CALLED THE PELOPONNESE.
BEING A KING IS SOMETHING LIKE GIVING BIRTH: YOU'VE GOT TO KNOW WHEN TO PUSH!
Thebes
Athens
Mykenae
Elis
Peloponnese
Messene
Sparta
GLUGL
ONE OF HIS SONS, ATREUS, BECAME KING OF MYKENAE, WHILE ANOTHER ONE, THYESTES, SEDUCED MRS. ATREUS.
IN REVENGE, ATREUS HAD SOME OF THYESTES' CHILDREN COOKED UP...
...THEN SERVED THEM AT DINNER TO THEIR DAD!
CHOFF CHOFF FINGER FOOD, THYESTES?
THYESTES FLED, RETCHING AND LEVELLING A FEARSOME CURSE AGAINST ATREUS AND ALL HIS HOUSE.
AND MAY SOMETHING REALLY BAD HAPPEN TO YOUR CHILDREN, YOU... YOU... SON OF PELOPS!
AAH... IT TAKES ONE TO KNOW ONE!
DIDN'T HE LIKE MY STUFFED GRAPE LEAVES?
WE'LL EXPECT YOUR RESIGNATION IN THE MORNING!

NOW THE SCENE SHIFTS TO *THEBES*, RULED BY QUEEN *JOCASTA* AND KING *LAIOS*. LAIOS, TOO, LIVED UNDER A CURSE!

ANYTHING I CAN DO TO HELP, DEAR?

NO... IT JUST SEEMS TO GO WITH THE JOB...

YEARS EARLIER, LAIOS HAD BEEN FORCED TO FLEE THEBES AND TAKE REFUGE AT THE COURT OF *PELOPS*. BEFORE RETURNING HOME, FOR SOME REASON, HE *KIDNAPPED* ONE OF PELOPS' SONS AND HENCE THE CURSE—

MAY YOUR **OWN SON** KILL YOU, THEBAN!

SO, WHEN JOCASTA BORE A BABY BOY, THEY SPIKED ITS HEELS AND EXPOSED IT ON THE SLOPES!

THE CHILD WAS RESCUED BY SHEPHERDS AND ADOPTED BY THE KING AND QUEEN OF CORINTH, WHO NAMED HIM *OEDIPUS* (="SWOLLEN FOOT").

*@+!

A LIKELY STORY, YOU SAY? SEE VOL 4, 158.

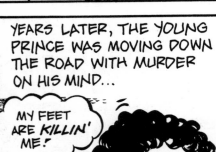

YEARS LATER, THE YOUNG PRINCE WAS MOVING DOWN THE ROAD WITH MURDER ON HIS MIND...

MY FEET ARE *KILLIN'* ME!

AT A CROSSROADS HE HAPPENED TO RUN INTO HIS FATHER, *LAIOS*, WHO WAS COMING HOME FROM *DELPHI*.

OOF!

WATCH IT!

WHO YOU TELLIN' TO WATCH IT?

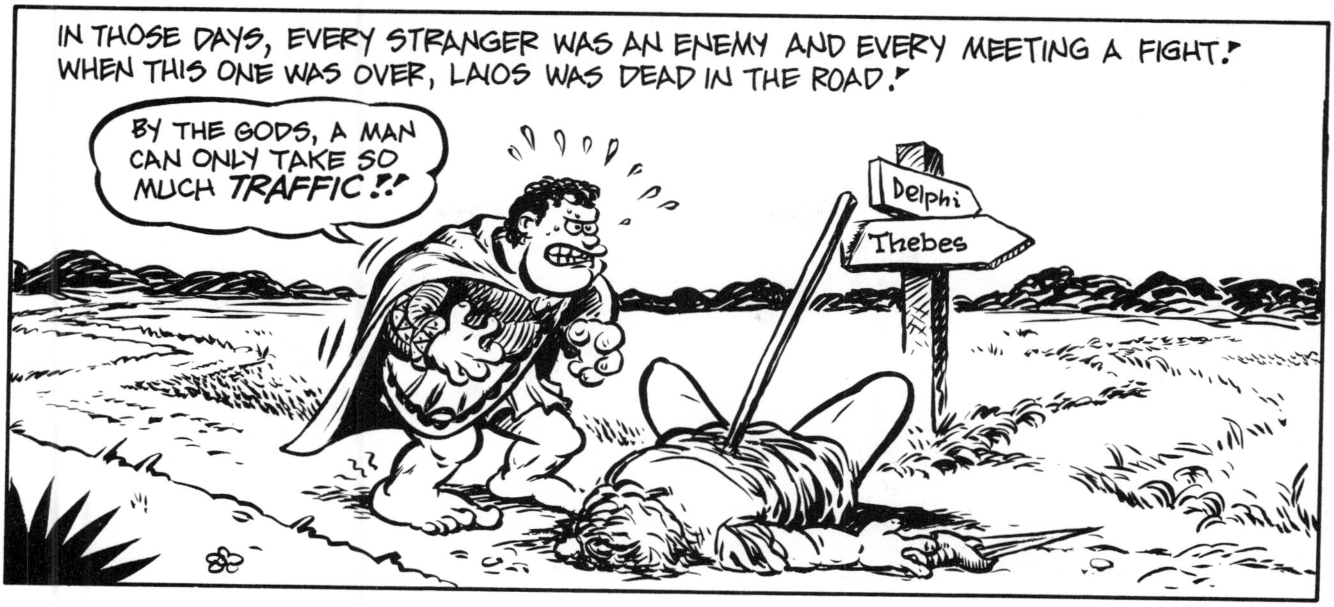
IN THOSE DAYS, EVERY STRANGER WAS AN ENEMY AND EVERY MEETING A FIGHT! WHEN THIS ONE WAS OVER, LAIOS WAS DEAD IN THE ROAD!
BY THE GODS, A MAN CAN ONLY TAKE SO MUCH TRAFFIC!!
Delphi
Thebes

OEDIPUS MOVED ON TO THEBES, FOUND THE POSITION OF KING OPEN, AND, AFTER PASSING A STRANGE QUALIFYING EXAM✻, HE GOT THE JOB—AND JOCASTA, HIS MOTHER, AS WIFE!!

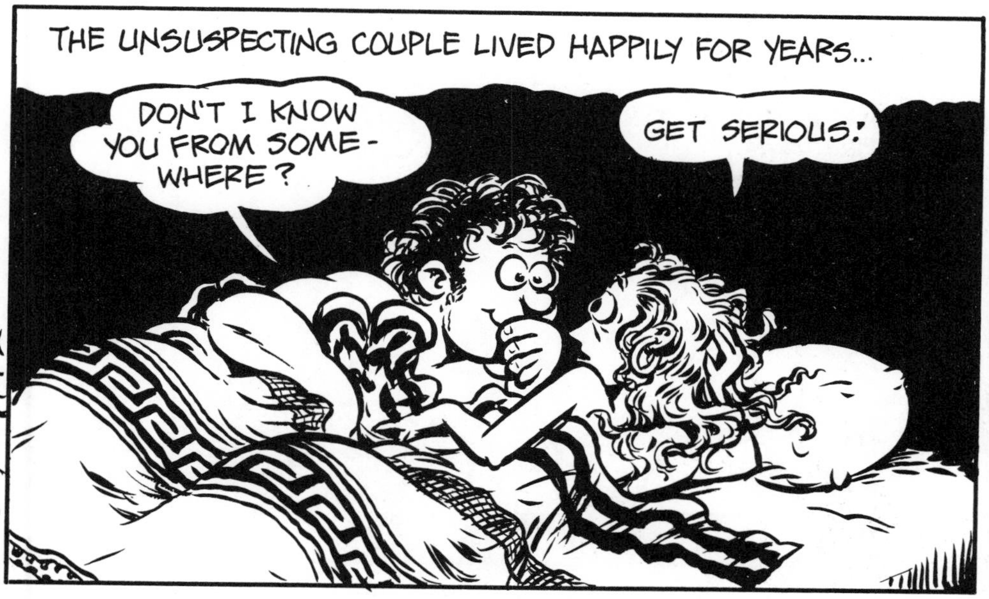
THE UNSUSPECTING COUPLE LIVED HAPPILY FOR YEARS...
DON'T I KNOW YOU FROM SOME-WHERE?
GET SERIOUS!

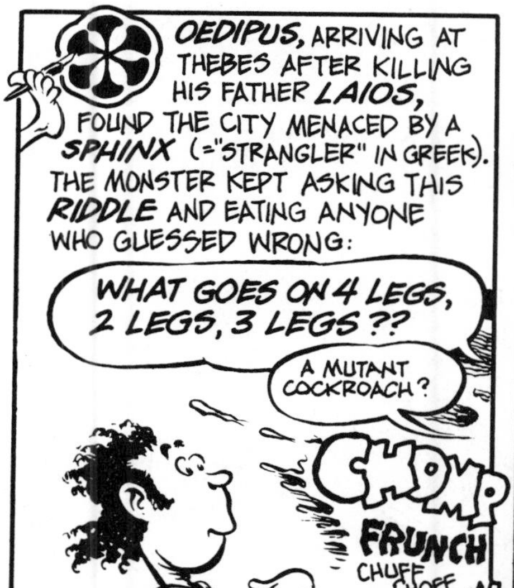
OEDIPUS, ARRIVING AT THEBES AFTER KILLING HIS FATHER LAIOS, FOUND THE CITY MENACED BY A SPHINX (="STRANGLER" IN GREEK). THE MONSTER KEPT ASKING THIS RIDDLE AND EATING ANYONE WHO GUESSED WRONG:
WHAT GOES ON 4 LEGS, 2 LEGS, 3 LEGS??
A MUTANT COCKROACH?
CHOMP
FRUNCH
CHUFF
CHOFF
GRIND
SWALLOW

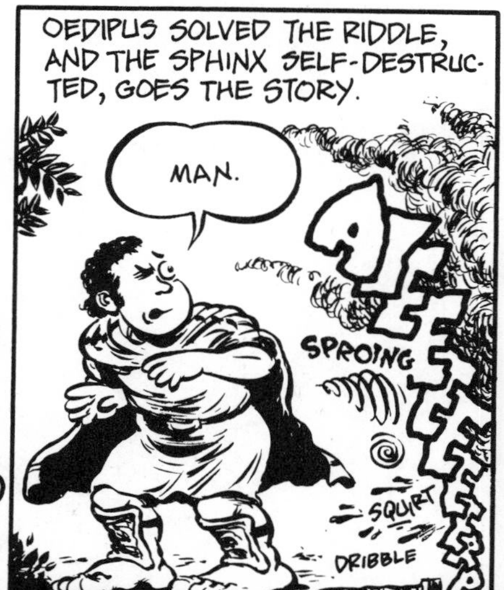
OEDIPUS SOLVED THE RIDDLE, AND THE SPHINX SELF-DESTRUCTED, GOES THE STORY.
MAN.
AIEEEEEEEE
SPROING
SQUIRT
DRIBBLE
BECAUSE MAN CRAWLS DURING INFANCY AND LEANS ON A CANE IN OLD AGE— ED.

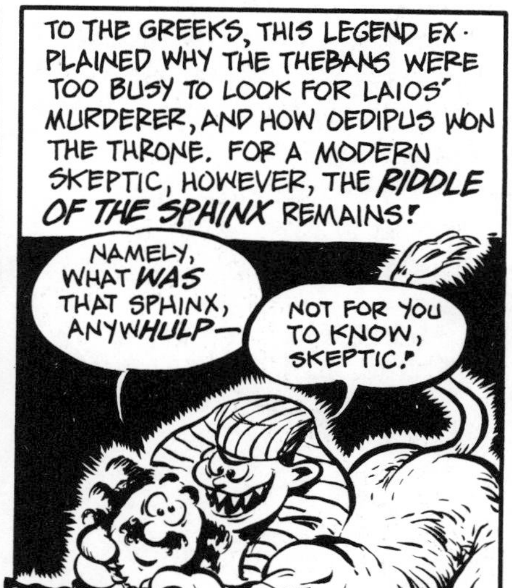
TO THE GREEKS, THIS LEGEND EXPLAINED WHY THE THEBANS WERE TOO BUSY TO LOOK FOR LAIOS' MURDERER, AND HOW OEDIPUS WON THE THRONE. FOR A MODERN SKEPTIC, HOWEVER, THE RIDDLE OF THE SPHINX REMAINS!
NAMELY, WHAT WAS THAT SPHINX, ANYWHULP—
NOT FOR YOU TO KNOW, SKEPTIC!

YEARS PASS... A PLAGUE IS RAGING IN THEBES... EVERY ATTEMPT IS MADE TO APPEASE THE GODS... BUT AFTER ALL THE SHEEP, GOATS, COWS, AND DOVES ARE SACRIFICED, THE PLAGUE RAGES ON, AND OEDIPUS WANTS TO KNOW **WHY...**

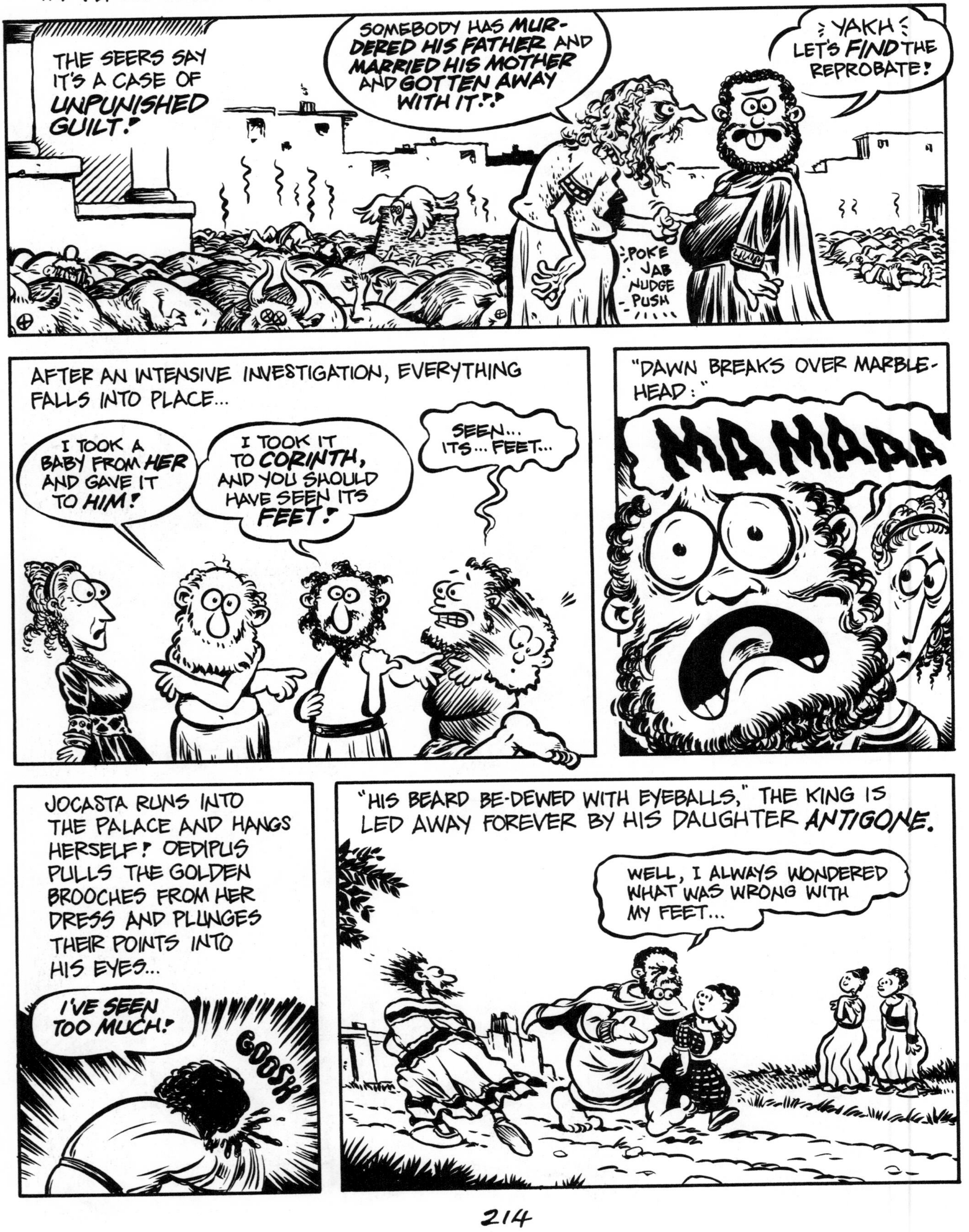

THE SEERS SAY IT'S A CASE OF **UNPUNISHED GUILT!**
SOMEBODY HAS **MURDERED HIS FATHER** AND **MARRIED HIS MOTHER** AND **GOTTEN AWAY WITH IT!!**
YAKH
LET'S **FIND** THE REPROBATE!
POKE
JAB
NUDGE
PUSH
AFTER AN INTENSIVE INVESTIGATION, EVERYTHING FALLS INTO PLACE...
I TOOK A BABY FROM **HER** AND GAVE IT TO **HIM!**
I TOOK IT TO **CORINTH**, AND YOU SHOULD HAVE SEEN ITS **FEET!**
SEEN... ITS... FEET...
"DAWN BREAKS OVER MARBLEHEAD:"
MAMAAA
JOCASTA RUNS INTO THE PALACE AND HANGS HERSELF! OEDIPUS PULLS THE GOLDEN BROOCHES FROM HER DRESS AND PLUNGES THEIR POINTS INTO HIS EYES...
I'VE SEEN TOO MUCH!
GOOSH
"HIS BEARD BE-DEWED WITH EYEBALLS," THE KING IS LED AWAY FOREVER BY HIS DAUGHTER **ANTIGONE.**
WELL, I ALWAYS WONDERED WHAT WAS WRONG WITH MY FEET...

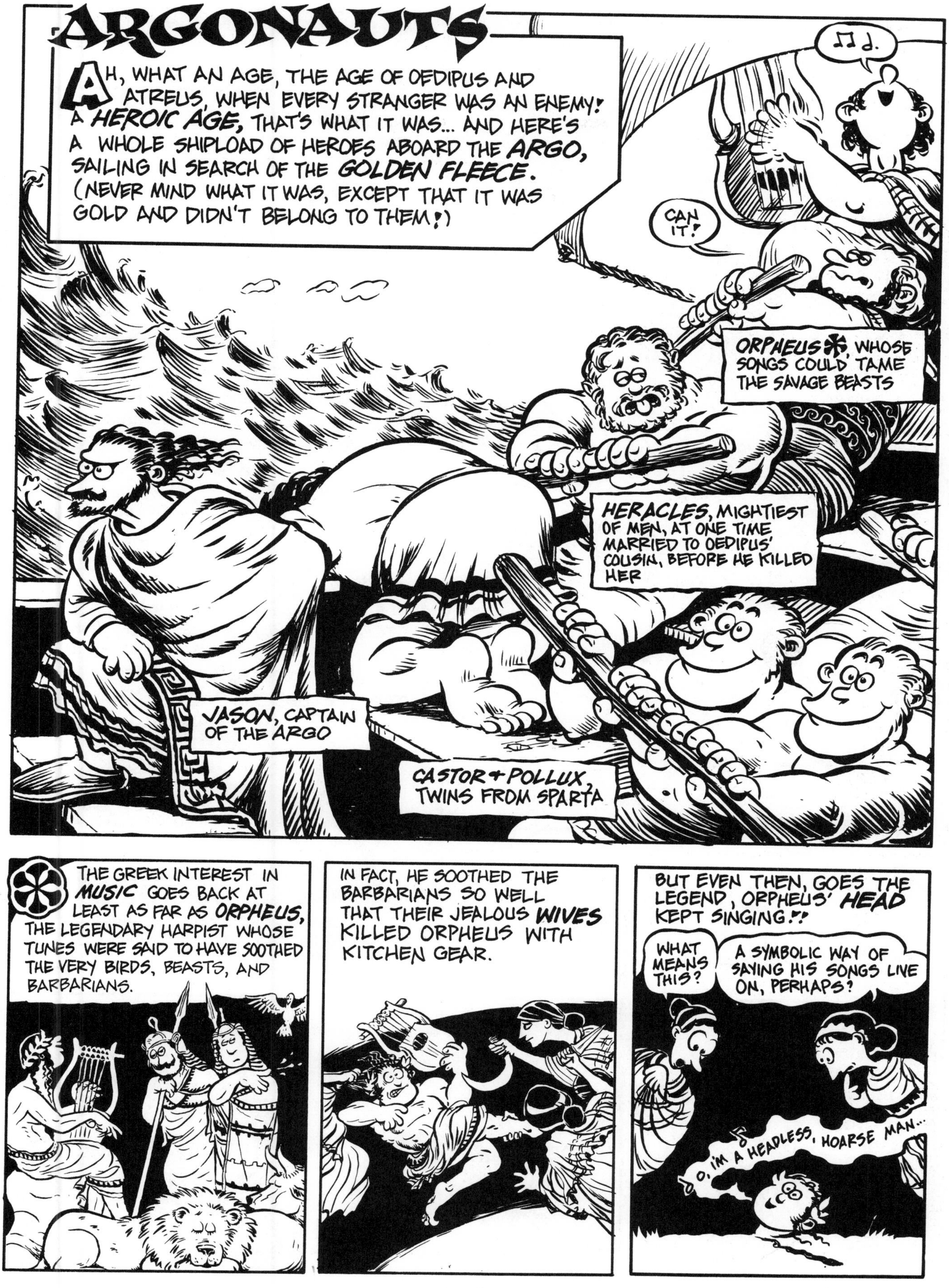
ARGONAUTS
AH, WHAT AN AGE, THE AGE OF OEDIPUS AND ATREUS, WHEN EVERY STRANGER WAS AN ENEMY! A HEROIC AGE, THAT'S WHAT IT WAS... AND HERE'S A WHOLE SHIPLOAD OF HEROES ABOARD THE ARGO, SAILING IN SEARCH OF THE GOLDEN FLEECE. (NEVER MIND WHAT IT WAS, EXCEPT THAT IT WAS GOLD AND DIDN'T BELONG TO THEM!)
CAN IT!
ORPHEUS*, WHOSE SONGS COULD TAME THE SAVAGE BEASTS
HERACLES, MIGHTIEST OF MEN, AT ONE TIME MARRIED TO OEDIPUS' COUSIN, BEFORE HE KILLED HER
JASON, CAPTAIN OF THE ARGO
CASTOR + POLLUX, TWINS FROM SPARTA
THE GREEK INTEREST IN MUSIC GOES BACK AT LEAST AS FAR AS ORPHEUS, THE LEGENDARY HARPIST WHOSE TUNES WERE SAID TO HAVE SOOTHED THE VERY BIRDS, BEASTS, AND BARBARIANS.
IN FACT, HE SOOTHED THE BARBARIANS SO WELL THAT THEIR JEALOUS WIVES KILLED ORPHEUS WITH KITCHEN GEAR.
BUT EVEN THEN, GOES THE LEGEND, ORPHEUS' HEAD KEPT SINGING!!
WHAT MEANS THIS?
A SYMBOLIC WAY OF SAYING HIS SONGS LIVE ON, PERHAPS?
O, I'M A HEADLESS, HOARSE MAN...

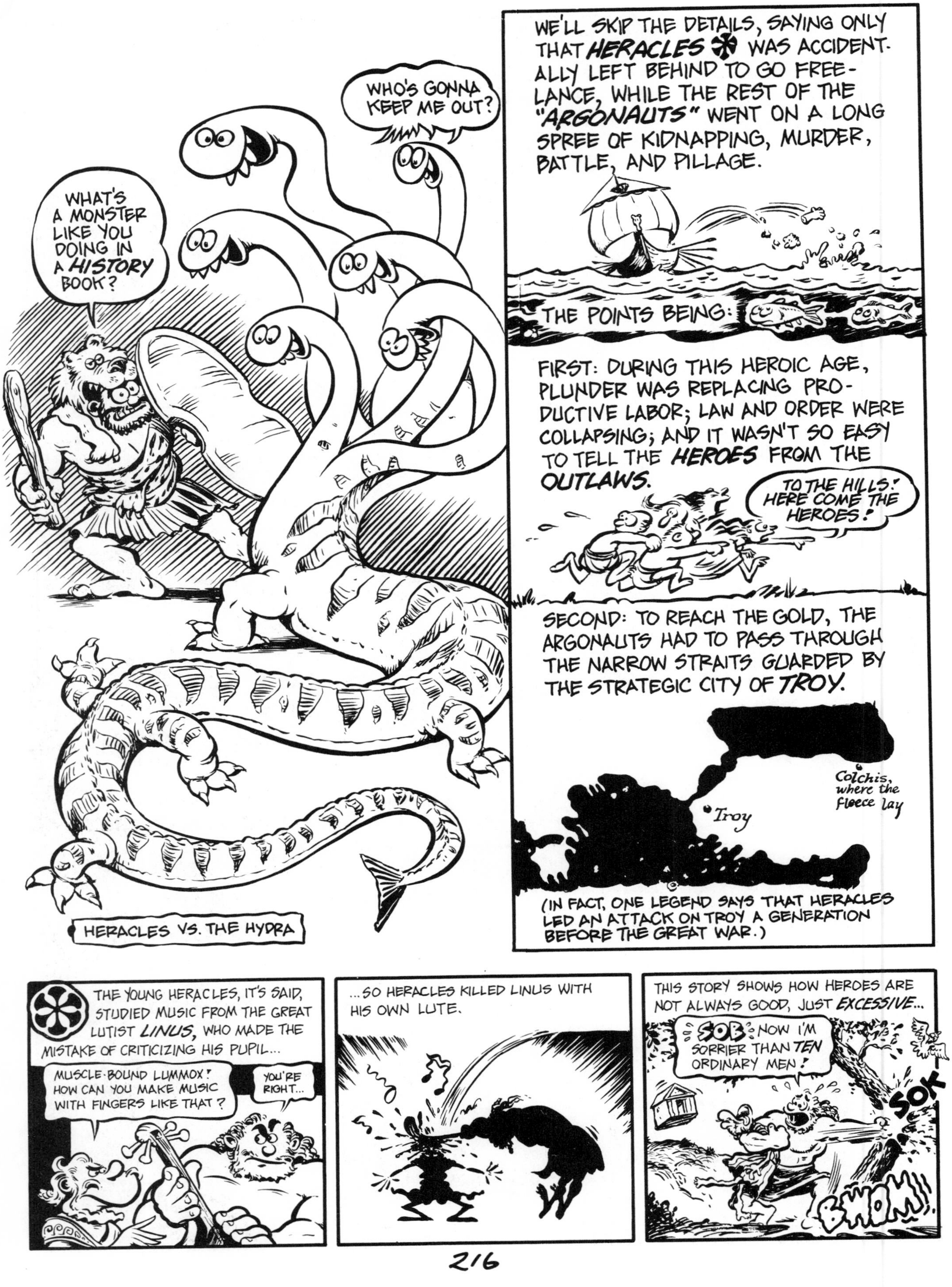
WHAT'S A MONSTER LIKE YOU DOING IN A HISTORY BOOK?
WHO'S GONNA KEEP ME OUT?
HERACLES VS. THE HYDRA
WE'LL SKIP THE DETAILS, SAYING ONLY THAT HERACLES WAS ACCIDENTALLY LEFT BEHIND TO GO FREE-LANCE, WHILE THE REST OF THE "ARGONAUTS" WENT ON A LONG SPREE OF KIDNAPPING, MURDER, BATTLE, AND PILLAGE.
THE POINTS BEING:
FIRST: DURING THIS HEROIC AGE, PLUNDER WAS REPLACING PRODUCTIVE LABOR; LAW AND ORDER WERE COLLAPSING; AND IT WASN'T SO EASY TO TELL THE HEROES FROM THE OUTLAWS.
TO THE HILLS! HERE COME THE HEROES!
SECOND: TO REACH THE GOLD, THE ARGONAUTS HAD TO PASS THROUGH THE NARROW STRAITS GUARDED BY THE STRATEGIC CITY OF TROY.
Colchis, where the Fleece lay
Troy
(IN FACT, ONE LEGEND SAYS THAT HERACLES LED AN ATTACK ON TROY A GENERATION BEFORE THE GREAT WAR.)
THE YOUNG HERACLES, IT'S SAID, STUDIED MUSIC FROM THE GREAT LUTIST LINUS, WHO MADE THE MISTAKE OF CRITICIZING HIS PUPIL...
MUSCLE-BOUND LUMMOX! HOW CAN YOU MAKE MUSIC WITH FINGERS LIKE THAT?
YOU'RE RIGHT...
...SO HERACLES KILLED LINUS WITH HIS OWN LUTE.
THIS STORY SHOWS HOW HEROES ARE NOT ALWAYS GOOD, JUST EXCESSIVE...
SOB! NOW I'M SORRIER THAN TEN ORDINARY MEN!
SOK
BWOM!!

NOW BACK TO ***THEBES...*** OEDIPUS' SONS VIED FOR THE THRONE... ONE, ***ETEOKLES,*** GOT IT, WHILE THE OTHER, ***POLYNIKES,*** ROAMED GREECE IN SEARCH OF ALLIES.

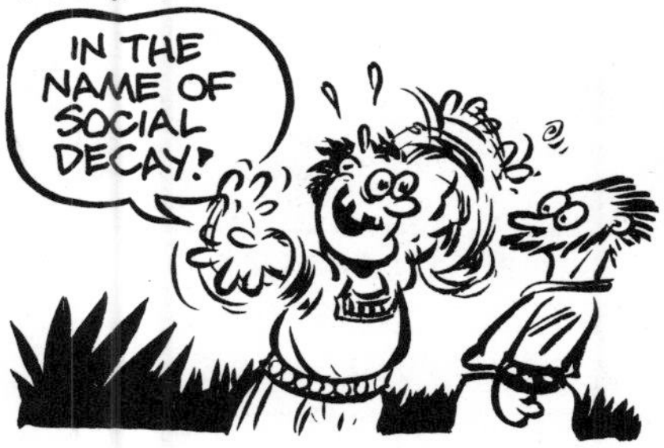
IN THE NAME OF SOCIAL DECAY!

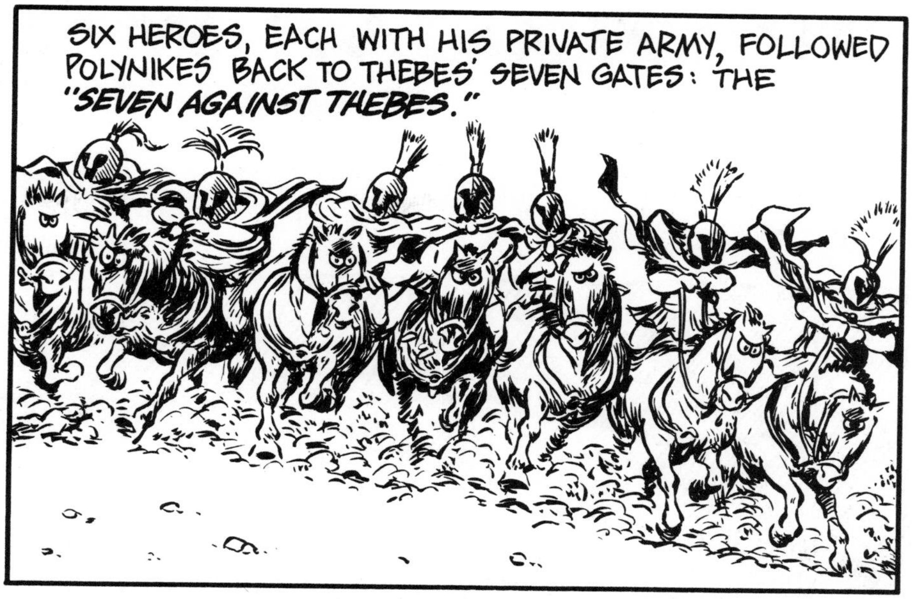
SIX HEROES, EACH WITH HIS PRIVATE ARMY, FOLLOWED POLYNIKES BACK TO THEBES' SEVEN GATES: THE "SEVEN AGAINST THEBES."

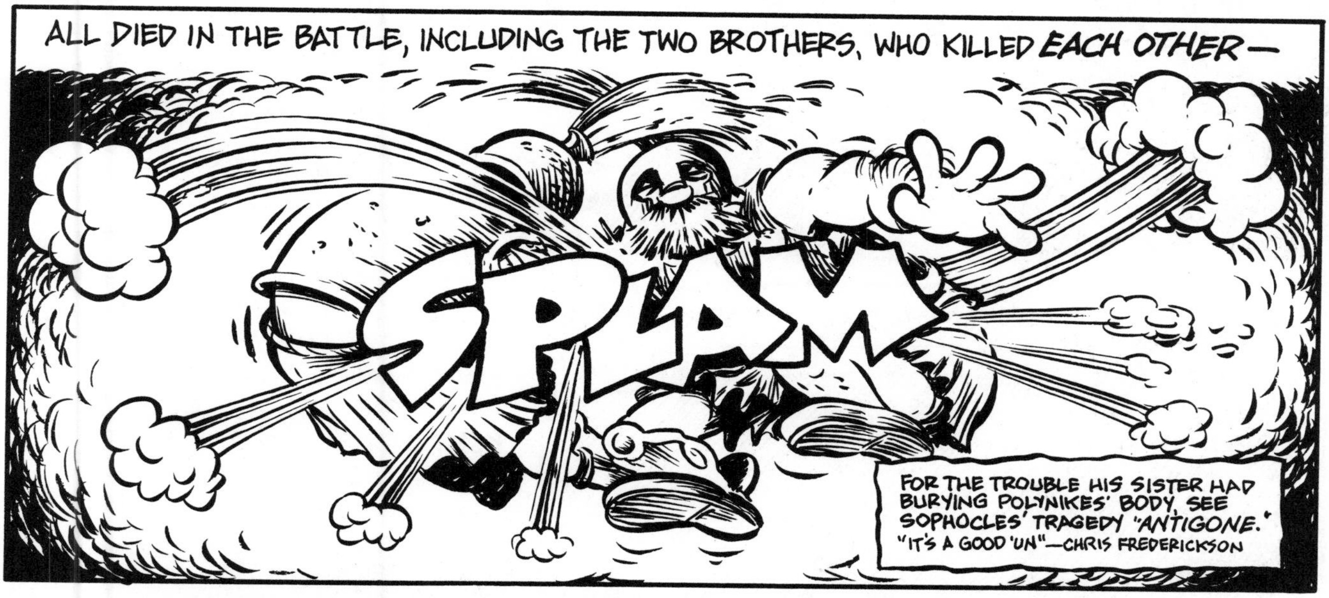
ALL DIED IN THE BATTLE, INCLUDING THE TWO BROTHERS, WHO KILLED EACH OTHER—
SPLAM
FOR THE TROUBLE HIS SISTER HAD BURYING POLYNIKES' BODY, SEE SOPHOCLES' TRAGEDY "ANTIGONE." "IT'S A GOOD 'UN"—CHRIS FREDERICKSON

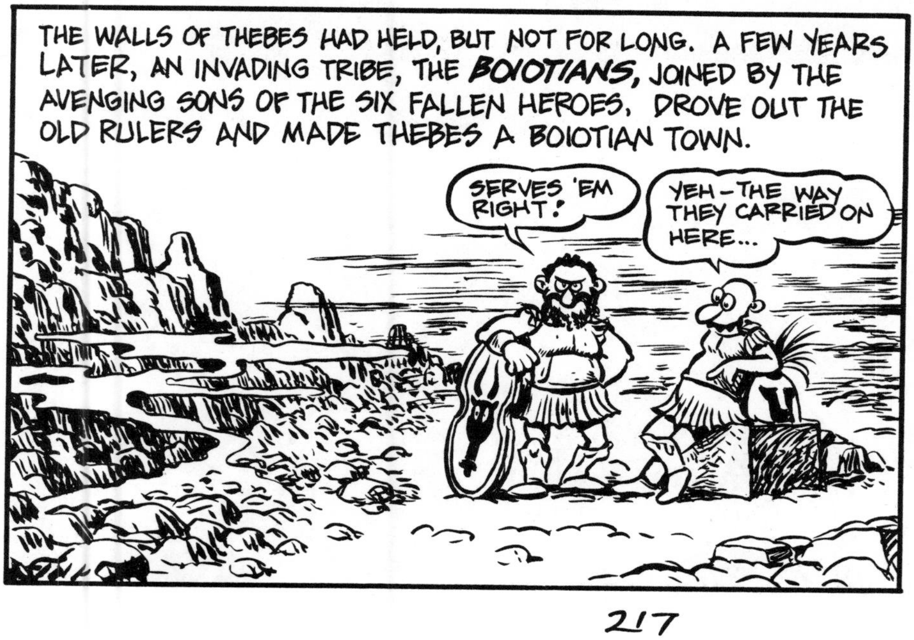
THE WALLS OF THEBES HAD HELD, BUT NOT FOR LONG. A FEW YEARS LATER, AN INVADING TRIBE, THE BOIOTIANS, JOINED BY THE AVENGING SONS OF THE SIX FALLEN HEROES, DROVE OUT THE OLD RULERS AND MADE THEBES A BOIOTIAN TOWN.
SERVES 'EM RIGHT!
YEH—THE WAY THEY CARRIED ON HERE...

THIS SECOND THEBAN WAR, IT TURNED OUT, WAS JUST THE ***PRELIMINARY*** TO THE ***MAIN EVENT.*** SOON, THIS NEW GENERATION OF HEROES WOULD BE AT ***TROY,*** AND THE CURSE AGAINST ATREUS WOULD BE FULFILLED...

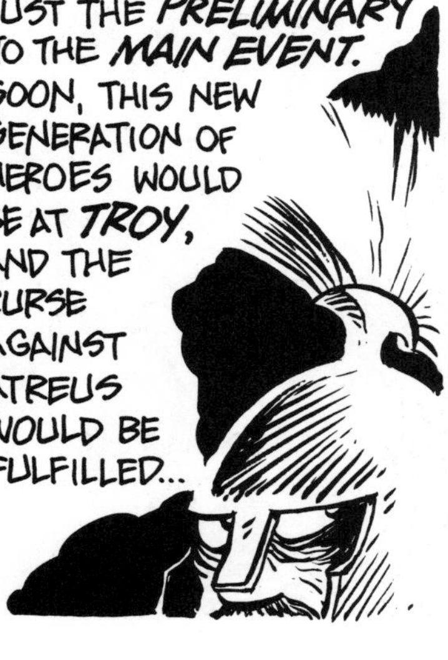

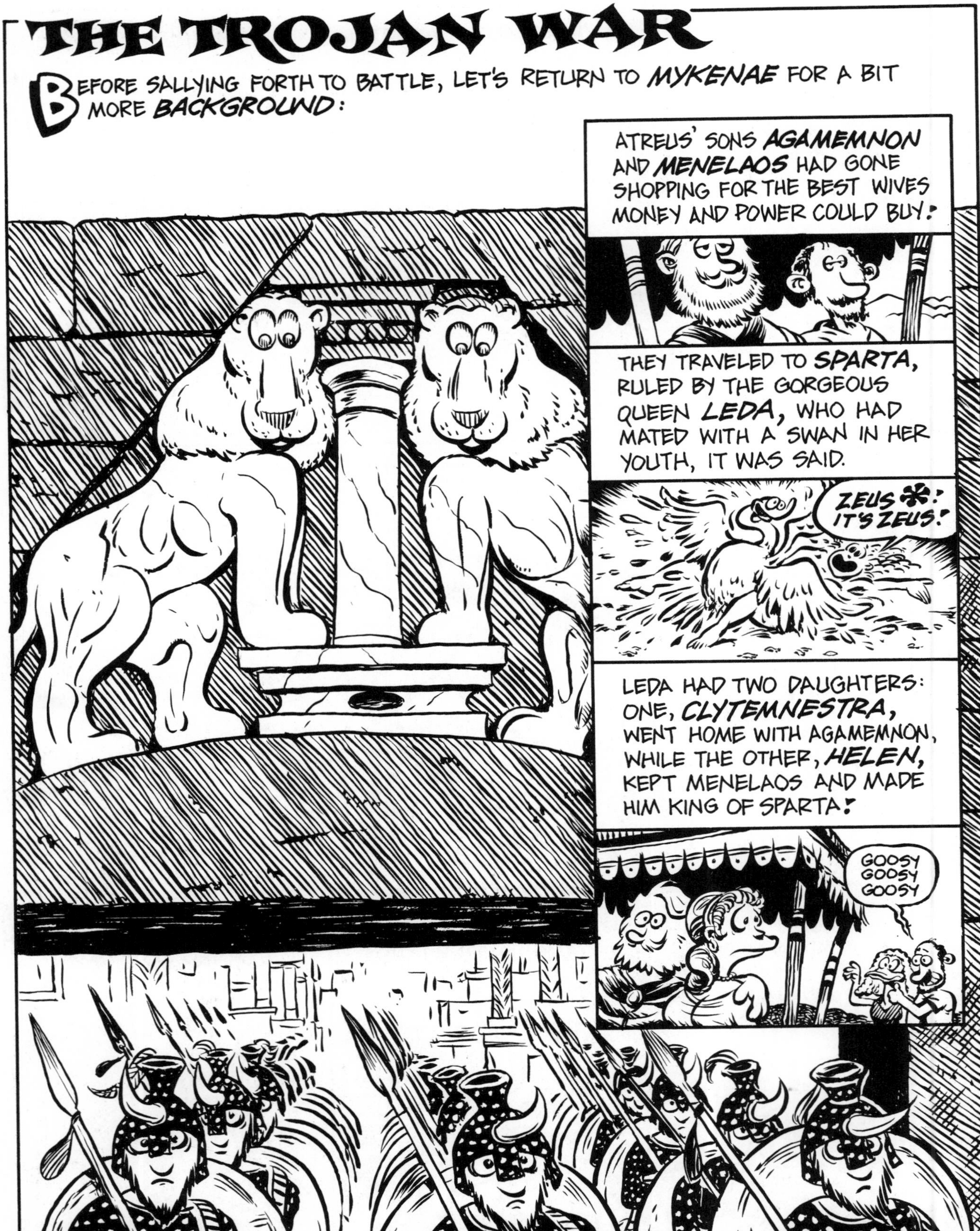
THE TROJAN WAR
BEFORE SALLYING FORTH TO BATTLE, LET'S RETURN TO MYKENAE FOR A BIT MORE BACKGROUND:
ATREUS' SONS AGAMEMNON AND MENELAOS HAD GONE SHOPPING FOR THE BEST WIVES MONEY AND POWER COULD BUY!
THEY TRAVELED TO SPARTA, RULED BY THE GORGEOUS QUEEN LEDA, WHO HAD MATED WITH A SWAN IN HER YOUTH, IT WAS SAID.
ZEUS*! IT'S ZEUS!
LEDA HAD TWO DAUGHTERS: ONE, CLYTEMNESTRA, WENT HOME WITH AGAMEMNON, WHILE THE OTHER, HELEN, KEPT MENELAOS AND MADE HIM KING OF SPARTA!
GOOSY GOOSY GOOSY

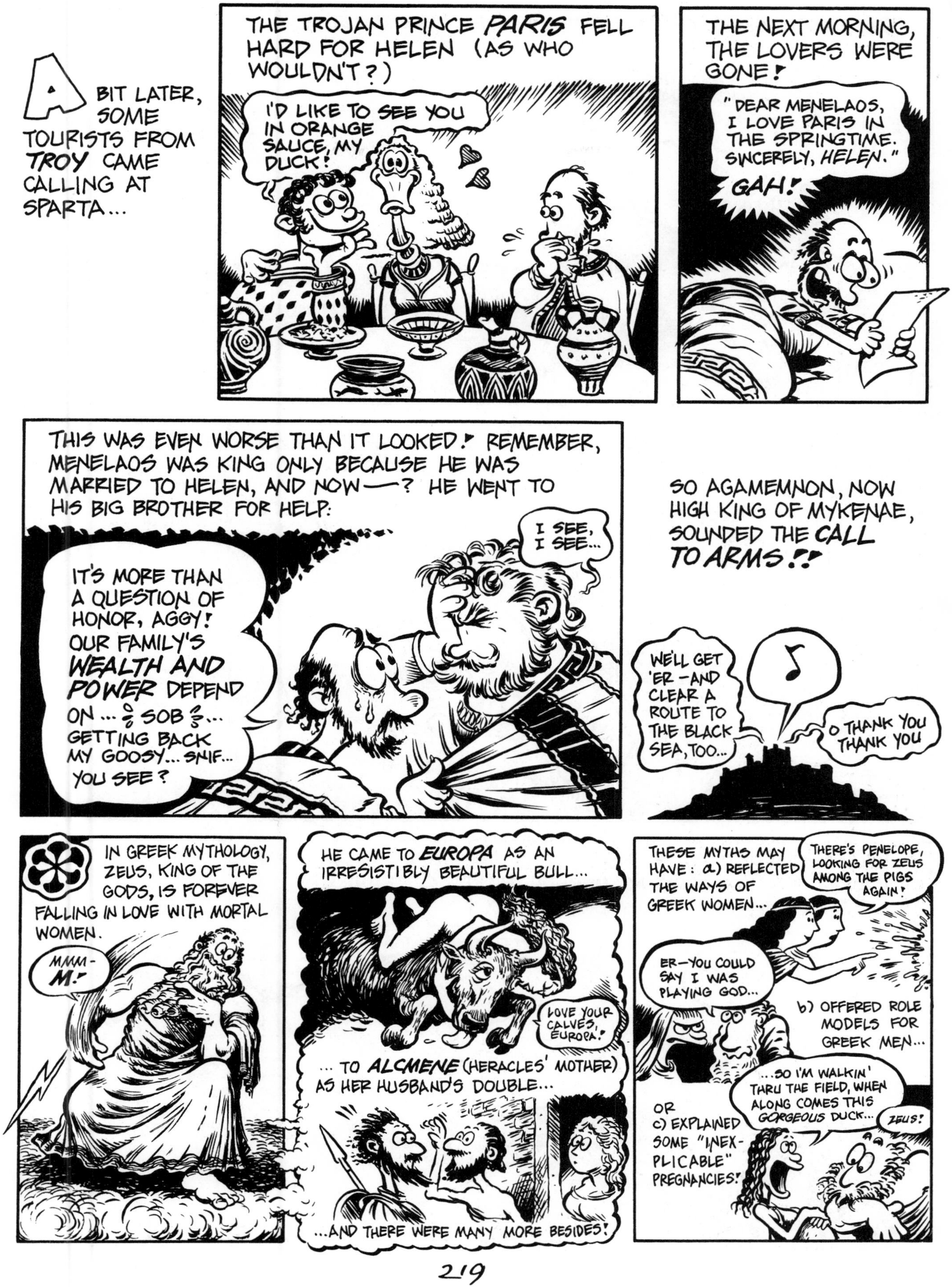
A BIT LATER, SOME TOURISTS FROM TROY CAME CALLING AT SPARTA...
THE TROJAN PRINCE PARIS FELL HARD FOR HELEN (AS WHO WOULDN'T?)
I'D LIKE TO SEE YOU IN ORANGE SAUCE, MY DUCK!
THE NEXT MORNING, THE LOVERS WERE GONE!
"DEAR MENELAOS, I LOVE PARIS IN THE SPRINGTIME. SINCERELY, HELEN."
GAH!
THIS WAS EVEN WORSE THAN IT LOOKED! REMEMBER, MENELAOS WAS KING ONLY BECAUSE HE WAS MARRIED TO HELEN, AND NOW—? HE WENT TO HIS BIG BROTHER FOR HELP:
IT'S MORE THAN A QUESTION OF HONOR, AGGY! OUR FAMILY'S WEALTH AND POWER DEPEND ON... SOB... GETTING BACK MY GOOSY... SNIF... YOU SEE?
I SEE, I SEE...
SO AGAMEMNON, NOW HIGH KING OF MYKENAE, SOUNDED THE CALL TO ARMS!!
WE'LL GET 'ER—AND CLEAR A ROUTE TO THE BLACK SEA, TOO...
♪
O THANK YOU THANK YOU
IN GREEK MYTHOLOGY, ZEUS, KING OF THE GODS, IS FOREVER FALLING IN LOVE WITH MORTAL WOMEN.
MMM-M!
HE CAME TO EUROPA AS AN IRRESISTIBLY BEAUTIFUL BULL...
LOVE YOUR CALVES, EUROPA!
... TO ALCMENE (HERACLES' MOTHER) AS HER HUSBAND'S DOUBLE...
...AND THERE WERE MANY MORE BESIDES!
THESE MYTHS MAY HAVE: a) REFLECTED THE WAYS OF GREEK WOMEN...
THERE'S PENELOPE, LOOKING FOR ZEUS AMONG THE PIGS AGAIN!
ER—YOU COULD SAY I WAS PLAYING GOD...
b) OFFERED ROLE MODELS FOR GREEK MEN...
...SO I'M WALKIN' THRU THE FIELD, WHEN ALONG COMES THIS GORGEOUS DUCK...
ZEUS!
OR c) EXPLAINED SOME "INEX-PLICABLE" PREGNANCIES!

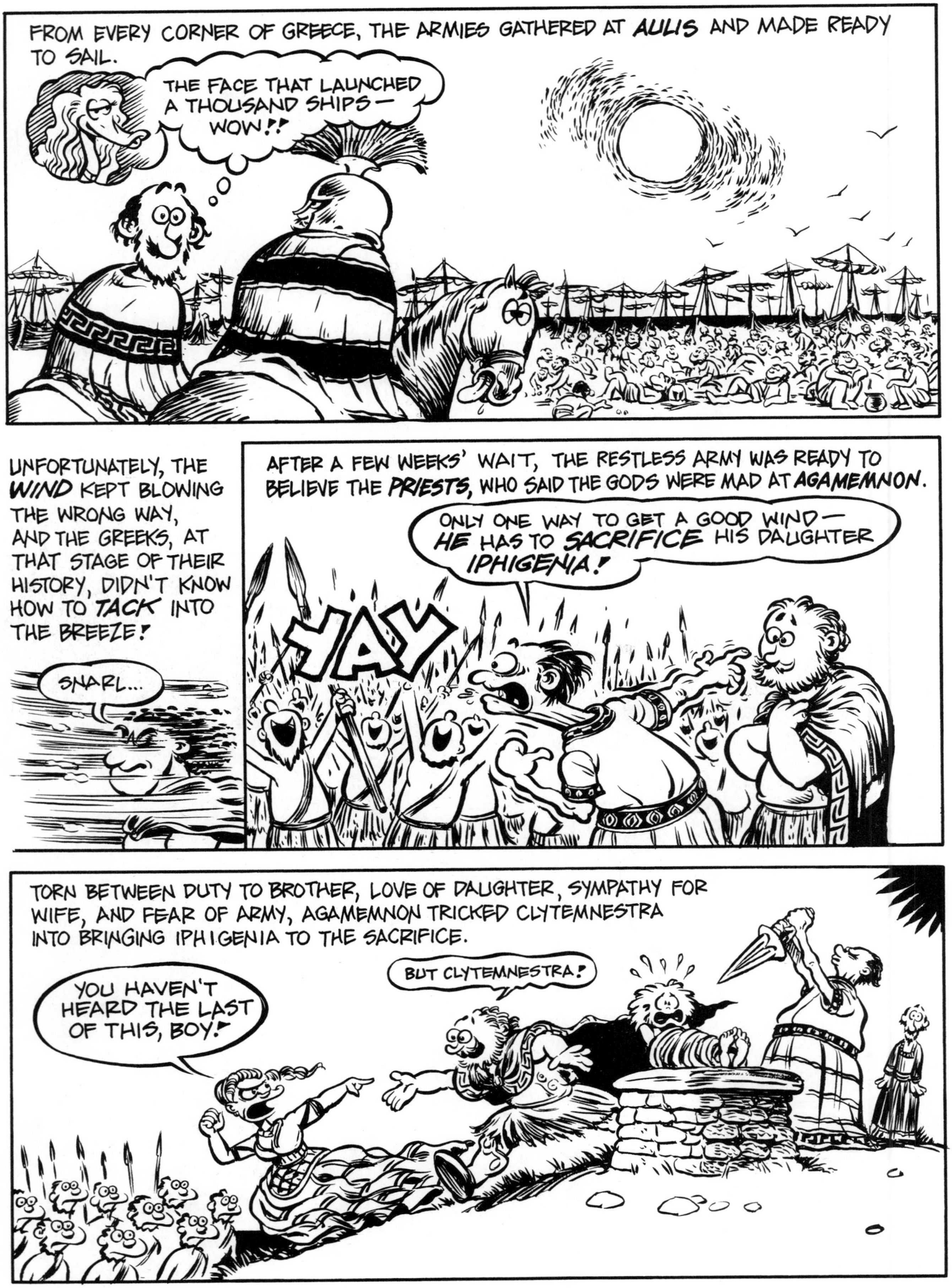
FROM EVERY CORNER OF GREECE, THE ARMIES GATHERED AT AULIS AND MADE READY TO SAIL.
THE FACE THAT LAUNCHED A THOUSAND SHIPS— WOW!!
UNFORTUNATELY, THE WIND KEPT BLOWING THE WRONG WAY, AND THE GREEKS, AT THAT STAGE OF THEIR HISTORY, DIDN'T KNOW HOW TO TACK INTO THE BREEZE!
SNARL...
AFTER A FEW WEEKS' WAIT, THE RESTLESS ARMY WAS READY TO BELIEVE THE PRIESTS, WHO SAID THE GODS WERE MAD AT AGAMEMNON.
ONLY ONE WAY TO GET A GOOD WIND— HE HAS TO SACRIFICE HIS DAUGHTER IPHIGENIA!
YAY
TORN BETWEEN DUTY TO BROTHER, LOVE OF DAUGHTER, SYMPATHY FOR WIFE, AND FEAR OF ARMY, AGAMEMNON TRICKED CLYTEMNESTRA INTO BRINGING IPHIGENIA TO THE SACRIFICE.
YOU HAVEN'T HEARD THE LAST OF THIS, BOY!
BUT CLYTEMNESTRA!

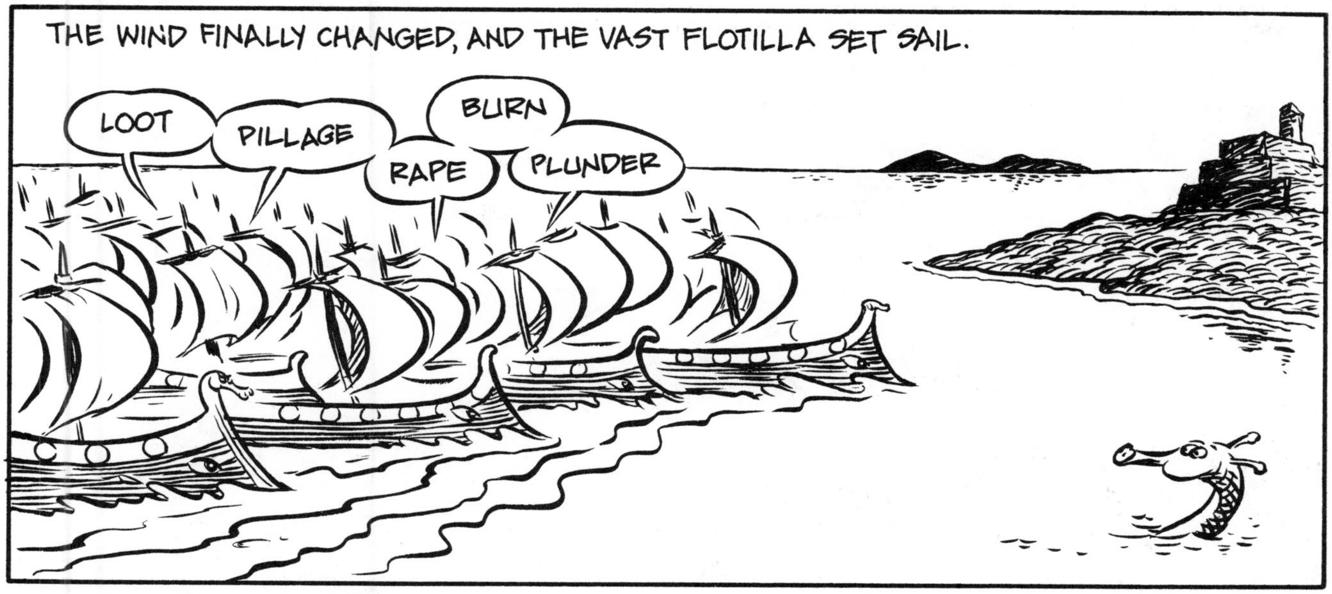
THE WIND FINALLY CHANGED, AND THE VAST FLOTILLA SET SAIL.
LOOT
PILLAGE
RAPE
BURN
PLUNDER

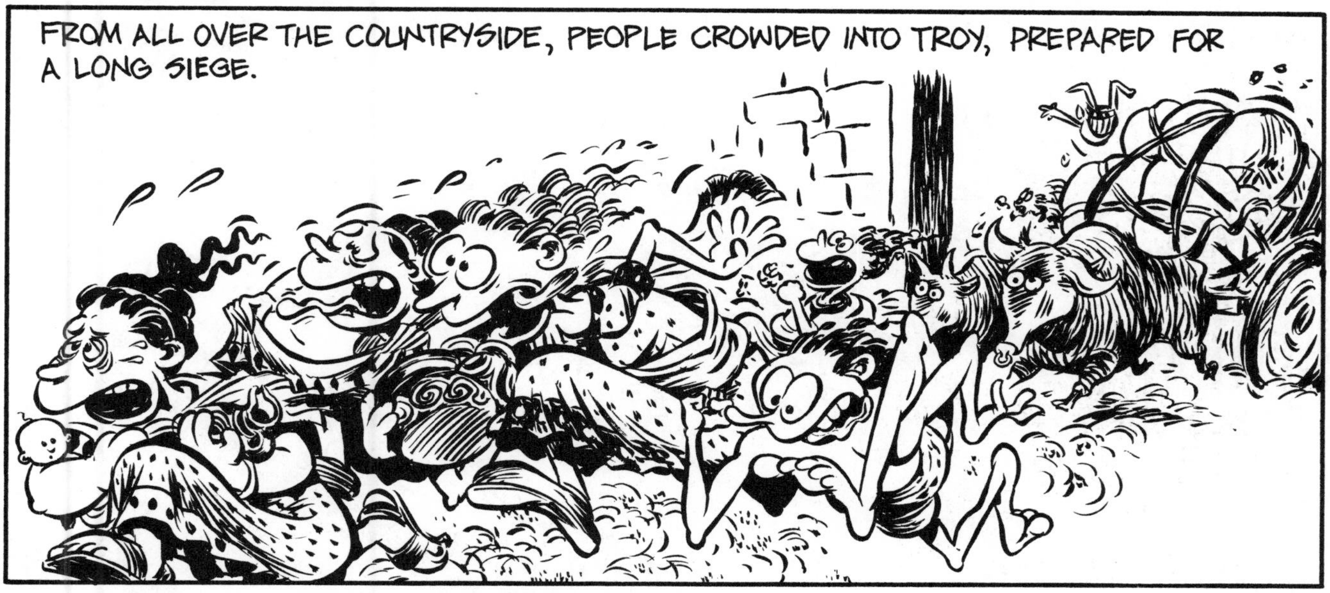
FROM ALL OVER THE COUNTRYSIDE, PEOPLE CROWDED INTO TROY, PREPARED FOR A LONG SIEGE.

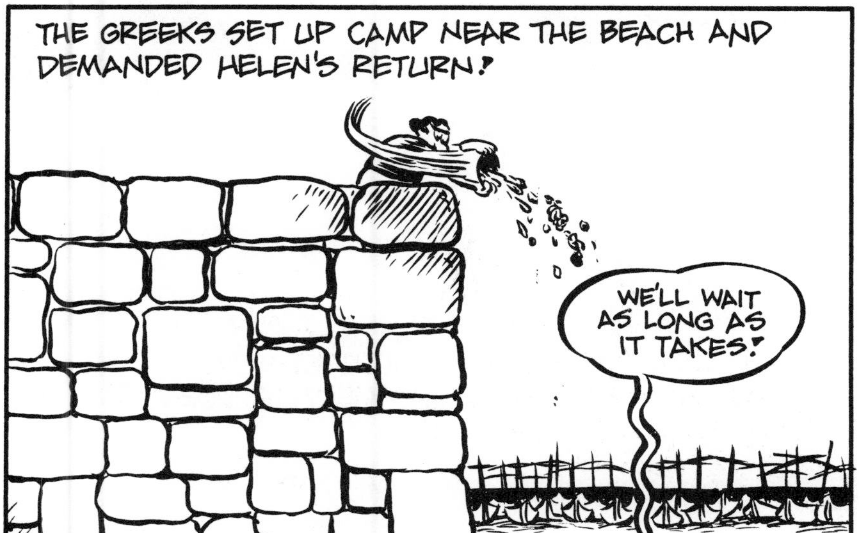
THE GREEKS SET UP CAMP NEAR THE BEACH AND DEMANDED HELEN'S RETURN!
WE'LL WAIT AS LONG AS IT TAKES!

THE TROJANS REFUSED, AND THE WAR BEGAN... AND DRAGGED ON... AND ON... THE GREEKS CAME AND WENT... THE TROJANS HELD OUT... BUT WE GET NO CLEAR PICTURE OF THE ACTION UNTIL THE WAR'S ***NINTH YEAR***, DESCRIBED IN HOMER'S GREAT EPIC, THE ***ILIAD***...

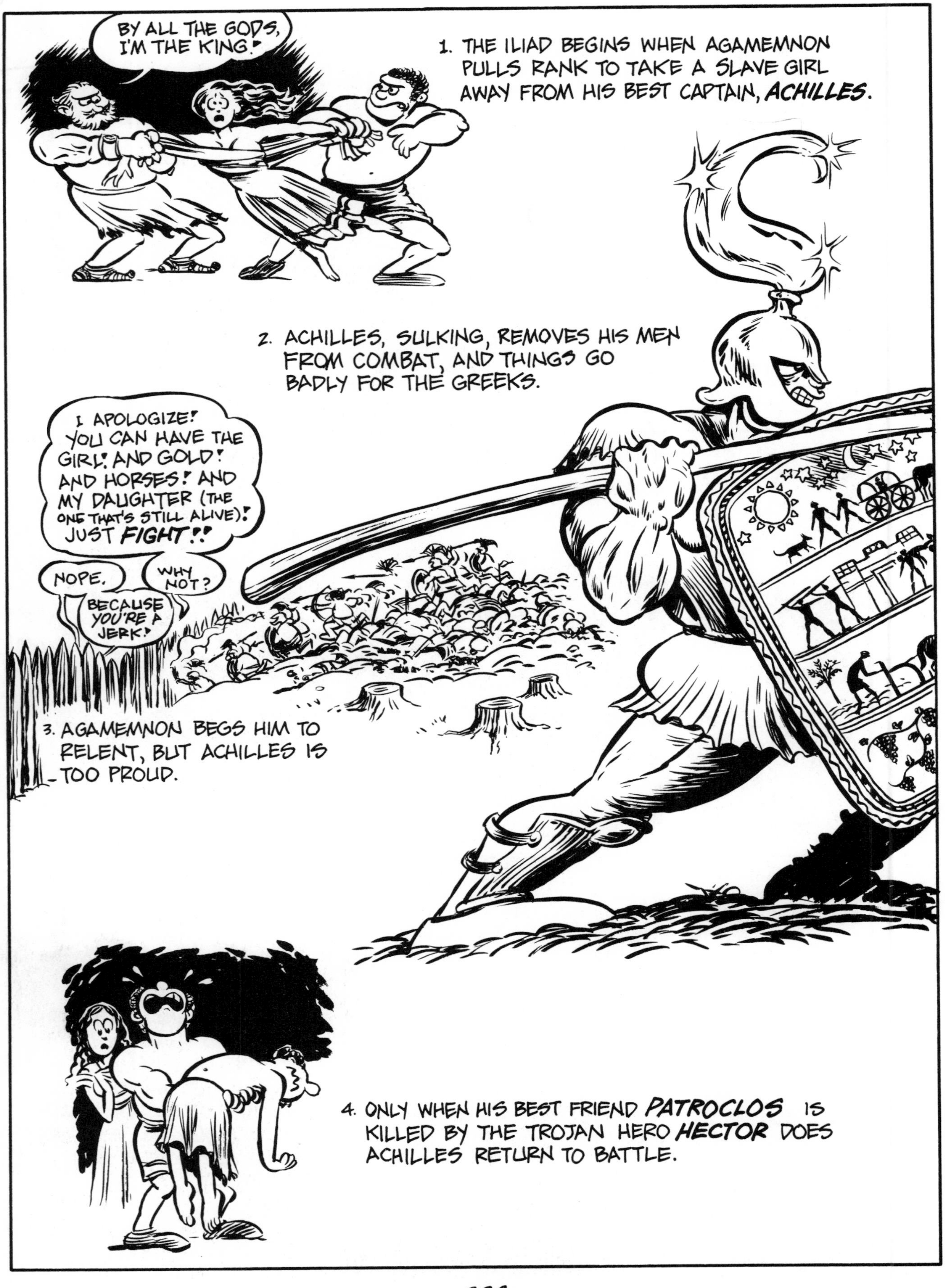
BY ALL THE GODS, I'M THE KING!
1. THE ILIAD BEGINS WHEN AGAMEMNON PULLS RANK TO TAKE A SLAVE GIRL AWAY FROM HIS BEST CAPTAIN, ACHILLES.
2. ACHILLES, SULKING, REMOVES HIS MEN FROM COMBAT, AND THINGS GO BADLY FOR THE GREEKS.
I APOLOGIZE! YOU CAN HAVE THE GIRL! AND GOLD! AND HORSES! AND MY DAUGHTER (THE ONE THAT'S STILL ALIVE)! JUST FIGHT!!
NOPE.
WHY NOT?
BECAUSE YOU'RE A JERK!
3. AGAMEMNON BEGS HIM TO RELENT, BUT ACHILLES IS TOO PROUD.
4. ONLY WHEN HIS BEST FRIEND PATROCLOS IS KILLED BY THE TROJAN HERO HECTOR DOES ACHILLES RETURN TO BATTLE.

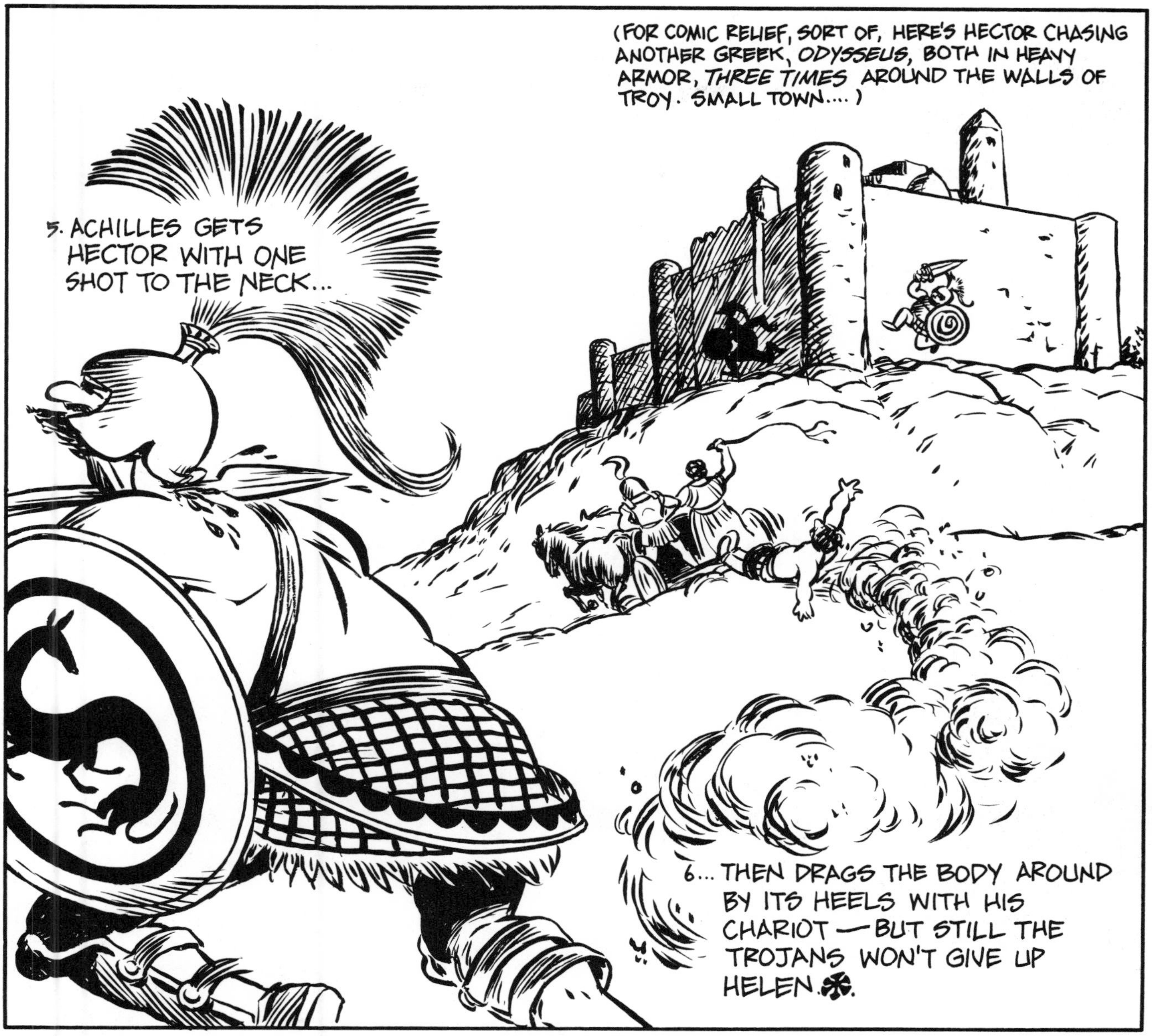
5. ACHILLES GETS HECTOR WITH ONE SHOT TO THE NECK...
(FOR COMIC RELIEF, SORT OF, HERE'S HECTOR CHASING ANOTHER GREEK, ODYSSEUS, BOTH IN HEAVY ARMOR, THREE TIMES AROUND THE WALLS OF TROY. SMALL TOWN....)
6... THEN DRAGS THE BODY AROUND BY ITS HEELS WITH HIS CHARIOT — BUT STILL THE TROJANS WON'T GIVE UP HELEN.

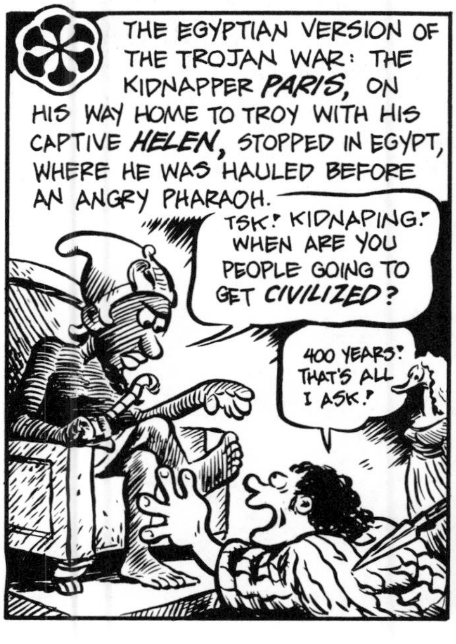
THE EGYPTIAN VERSION OF THE TROJAN WAR: THE KIDNAPPER PARIS, ON HIS WAY HOME TO TROY WITH HIS CAPTIVE HELEN, STOPPED IN EGYPT, WHERE HE WAS HAULED BEFORE AN ANGRY PHARAOH.
TSK! KIDNAPING! WHEN ARE YOU PEOPLE GOING TO GET CIVILIZED?
400 YEARS! THAT'S ALL I ASK!

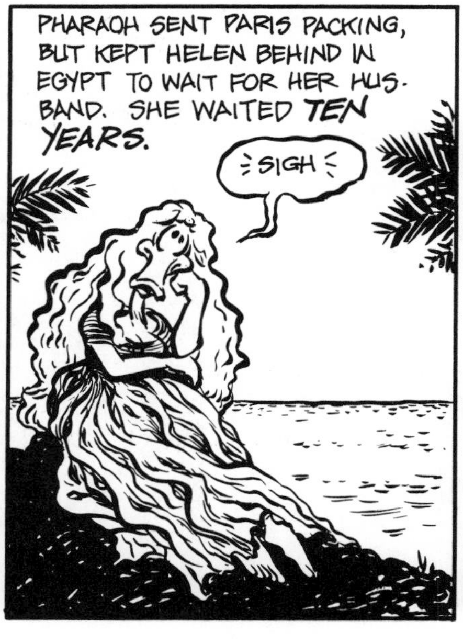
PHARAOH SENT PARIS PACKING, BUT KEPT HELEN BEHIND IN EGYPT TO WAIT FOR HER HUS-BAND. SHE WAITED TEN YEARS.
SIGH

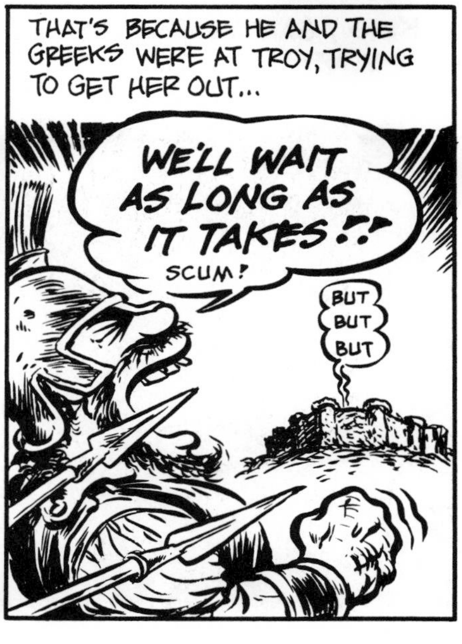
THAT'S BECAUSE HE AND THE GREEKS WERE AT TROY, TRYING TO GET HER OUT...
WE'LL WAIT AS LONG AS IT TAKES!!
SCUM!
BUT BUT BUT

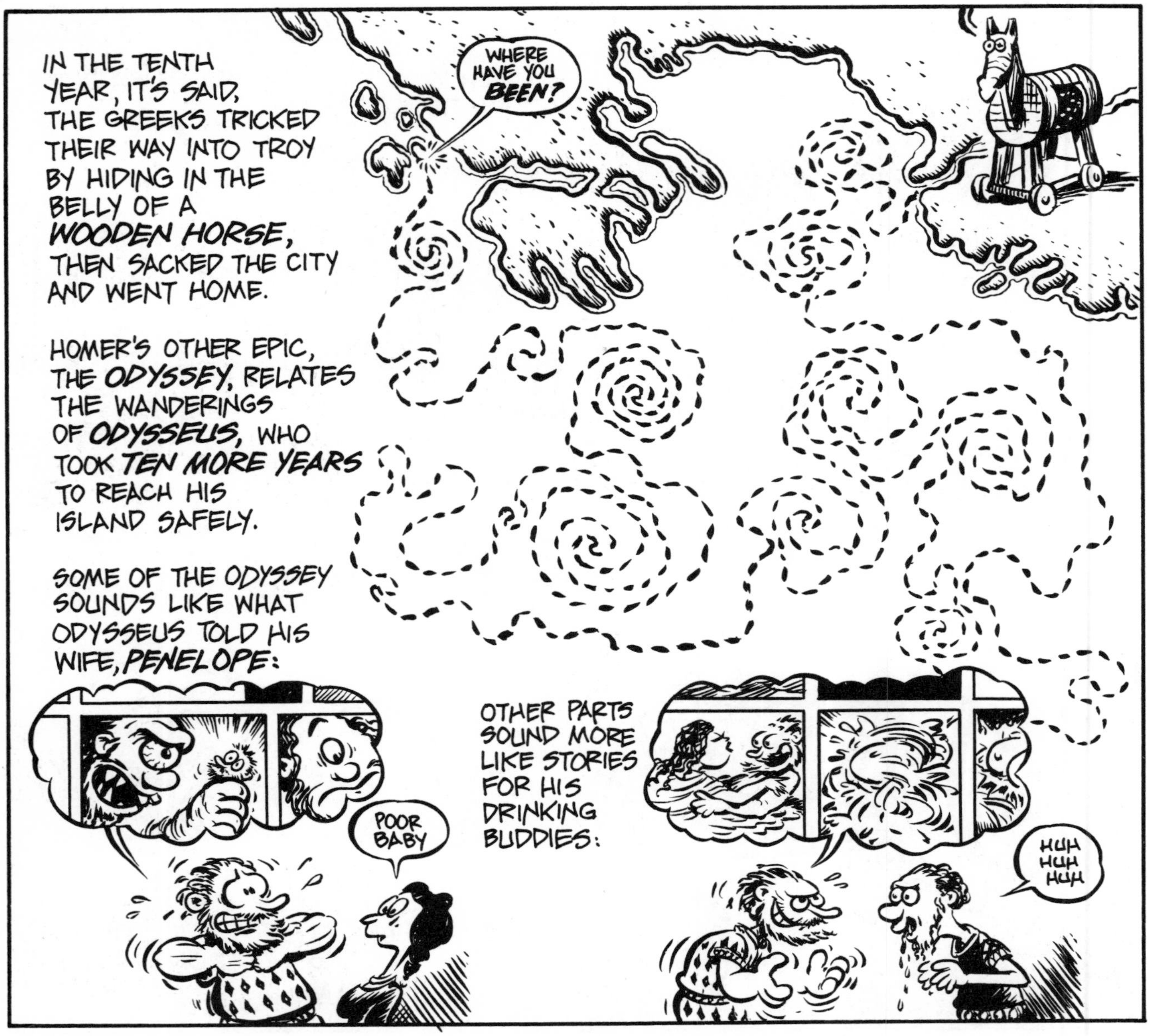
IN THE TENTH YEAR, IT'S SAID, THE GREEKS TRICKED THEIR WAY INTO TROY BY HIDING IN THE BELLY OF A **WOODEN HORSE,** THEN SACKED THE CITY AND WENT HOME.
WHERE HAVE YOU **BEEN?**
HOMER'S OTHER EPIC, THE **ODYSSEY,** RELATES THE WANDERINGS OF **ODYSSEUS,** WHO TOOK **TEN MORE YEARS** TO REACH HIS ISLAND SAFELY.
SOME OF THE ODYSSEY SOUNDS LIKE WHAT ODYSSEUS TOLD HIS WIFE, **PENELOPE:**
POOR BABY
OTHER PARTS SOUND MORE LIKE STORIES FOR HIS DRINKING BUDDIES:
HUH HUH HUH

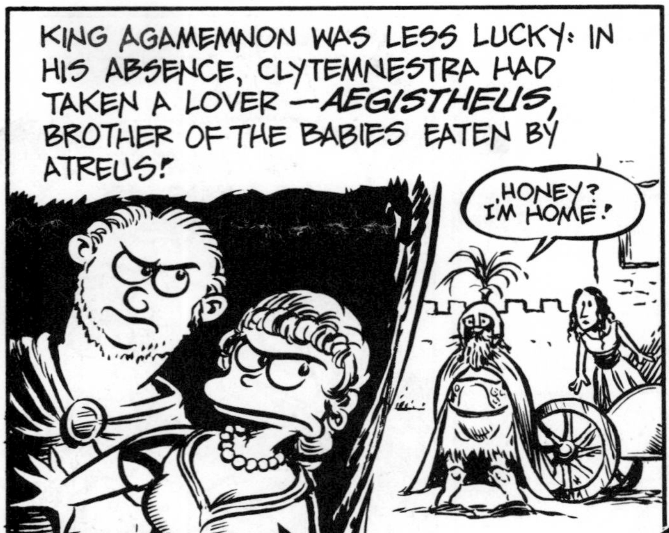
KING AGAMEMNON WAS LESS LUCKY: IN HIS ABSENCE, CLYTEMNESTRA HAD TAKEN A LOVER —**AEGISTHEUS,** BROTHER OF THE BABIES EATEN BY ATREUS!
HONEY? I'M HOME!

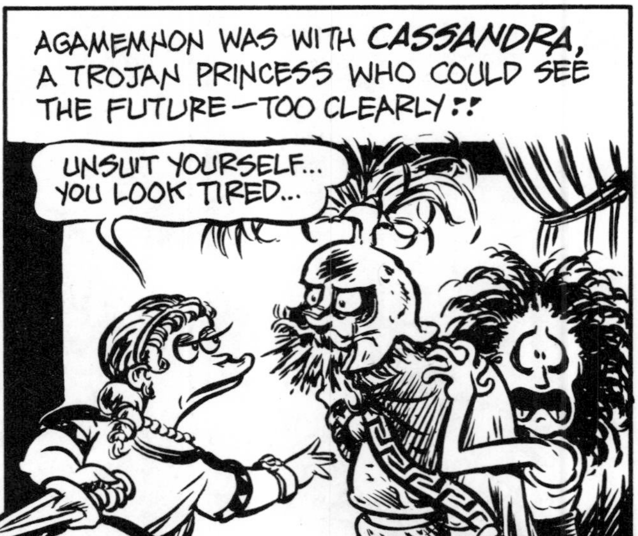
AGAMEMNON WAS WITH **CASSANDRA,** A TROJAN PRINCESS WHO COULD SEE THE FUTURE—TOO CLEARLY!!
UNSUIT YOURSELF... YOU LOOK TIRED...

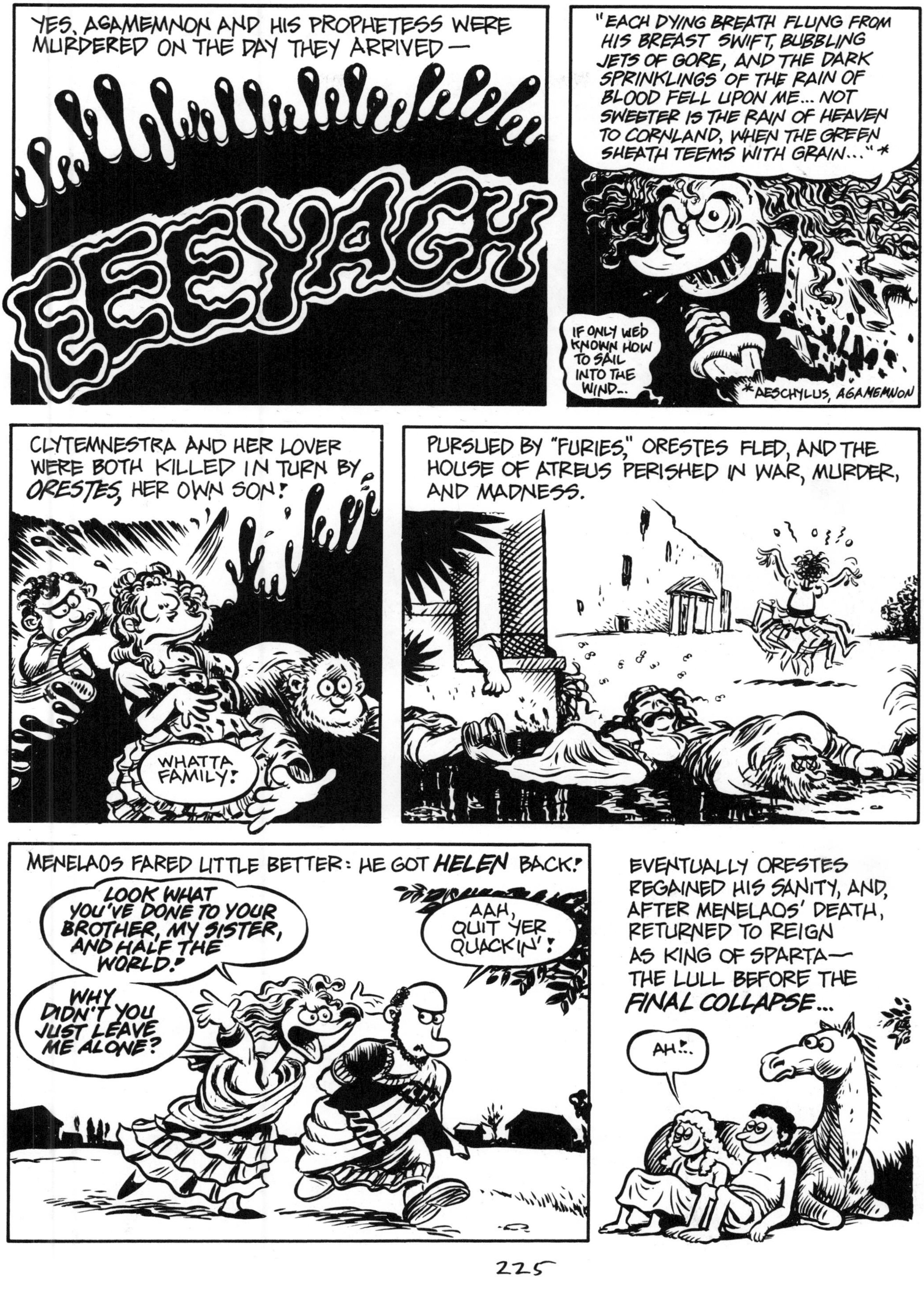
YES, AGAMEMNON AND HIS PROPHETESS WERE MURDERED ON THE DAY THEY ARRIVED—
EEYAGH
"EACH DYING BREATH FLUNG FROM HIS BREAST SWIFT, BUBBLING JETS OF GORE, AND THE DARK SPRINKLINGS OF THE RAIN OF BLOOD FELL UPON ME... NOT SWEETER IS THE RAIN OF HEAVEN TO CORNLAND, WHEN THE GREEN SHEATH TEEMS WITH GRAIN..." *
IF ONLY WE'D KNOWN HOW TO SAIL INTO THE WIND...
*AESCHYLUS, AGAMEMNON
CLYTEMNESTRA AND HER LOVER WERE BOTH KILLED IN TURN BY ORESTES, HER OWN SON!
WHATTA FAMILY!
PURSUED BY "FURIES," ORESTES FLED, AND THE HOUSE OF ATREUS PERISHED IN WAR, MURDER, AND MADNESS.
MENELAOS FARED LITTLE BETTER: HE GOT HELEN BACK!
LOOK WHAT YOU'VE DONE TO YOUR BROTHER, MY SISTER, AND HALF THE WORLD!
WHY DIDN'T YOU JUST LEAVE ME ALONE?
AAH, QUIT YER QUACKIN'!
EVENTUALLY ORESTES REGAINED HIS SANITY, AND, AFTER MENELAOS' DEATH, RETURNED TO REIGN AS KING OF SPARTA— THE LULL BEFORE THE FINAL COLLAPSE...
AH!..

DORIANS AND DARKNESS

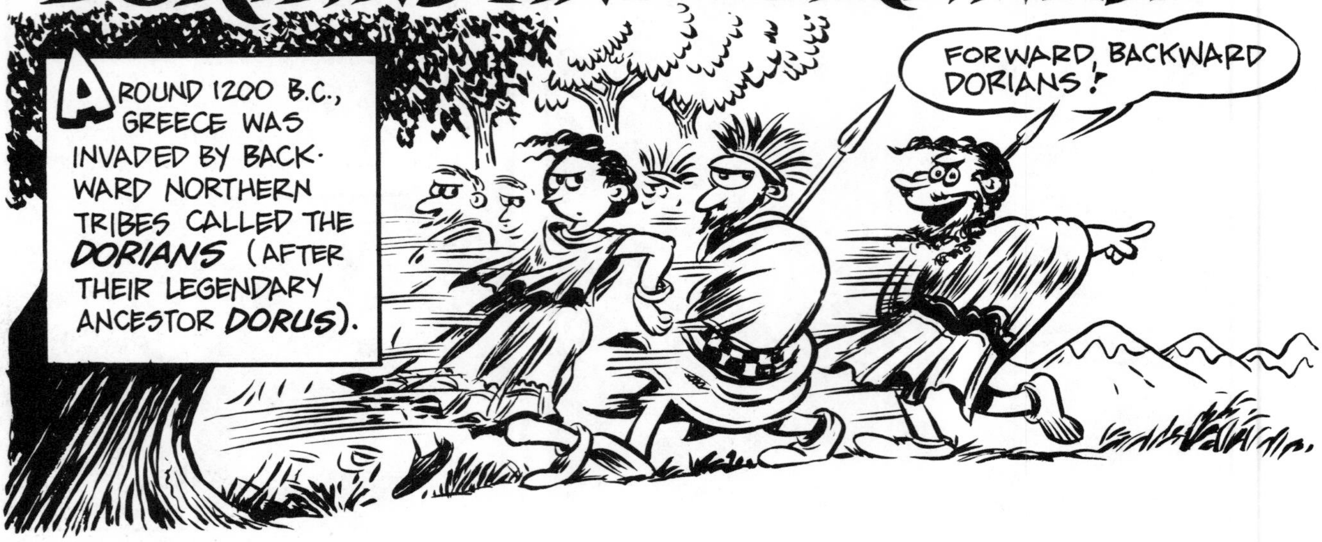
AROUND 1200 B.C., GREECE WAS INVADED BY BACKWARD NORTHERN TRIBES CALLED THE ***DORIANS*** (AFTER THEIR LEGENDARY ANCESTOR ***DORUS***).
FORWARD, BACKWARD DORIANS!

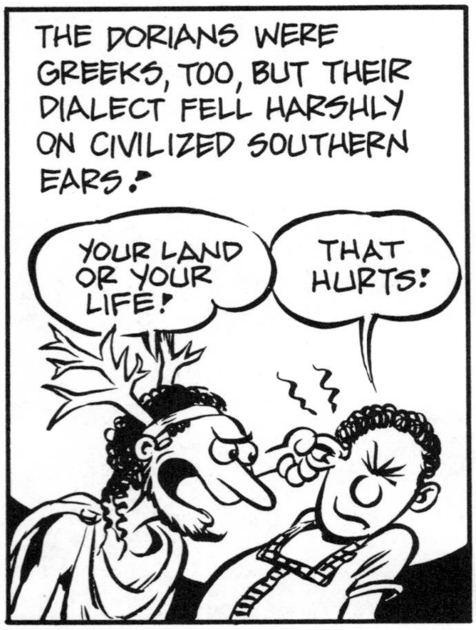
THE DORIANS WERE GREEKS, TOO, BUT THEIR DIALECT FELL HARSHLY ON CIVILIZED SOUTHERN EARS!
YOUR LAND OR YOUR LIFE!
THAT HURTS!

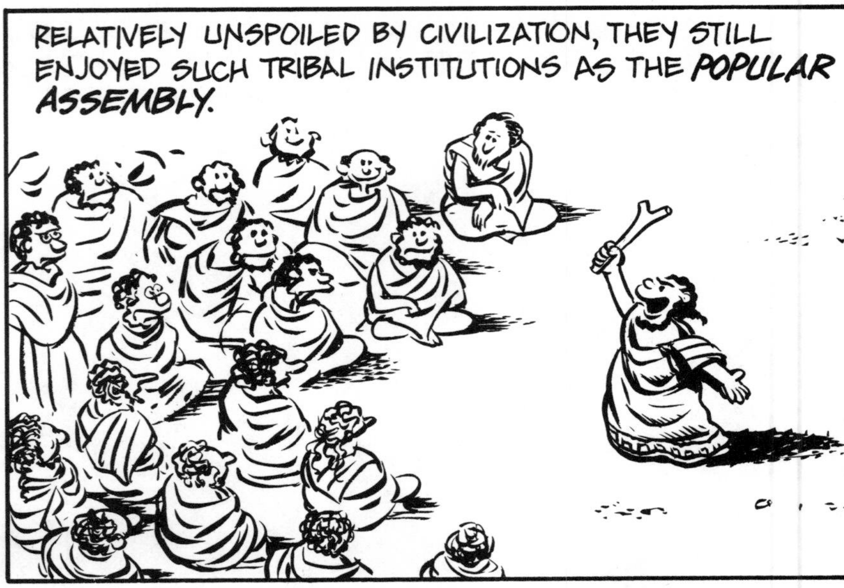
RELATIVELY UNSPOILED BY CIVILIZATION, THEY STILL ENJOYED SUCH TRIBAL INSTITUTIONS AS THE ***POPULAR ASSEMBLY***.

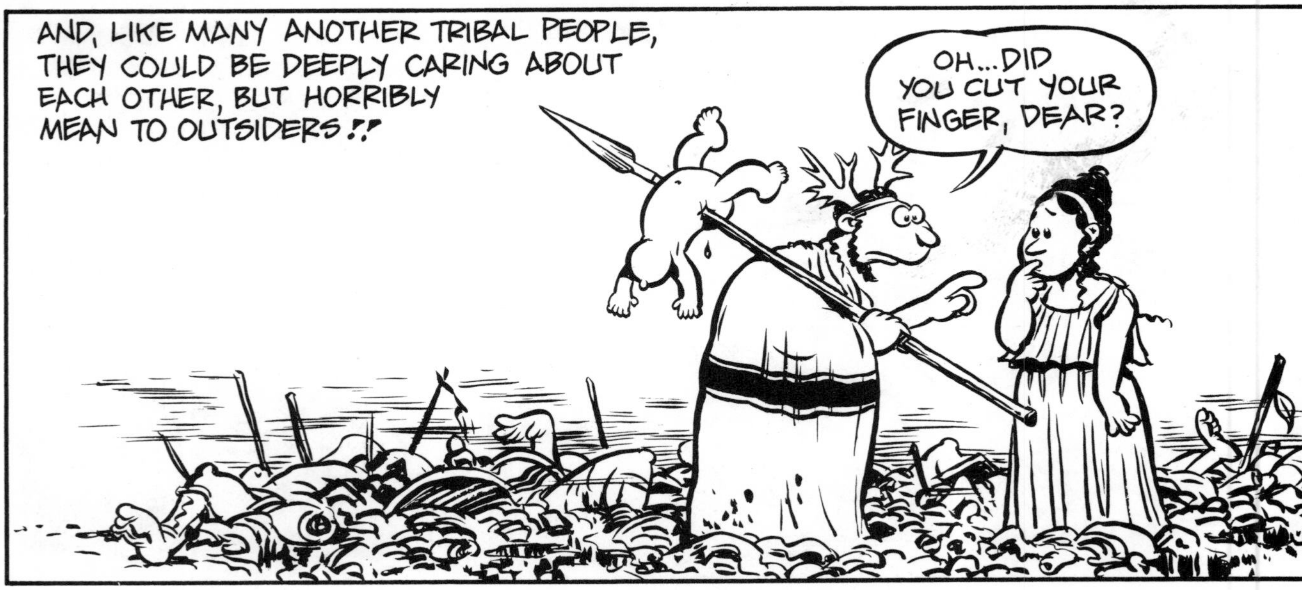
AND, LIKE MANY ANOTHER TRIBAL PEOPLE, THEY COULD BE DEEPLY CARING ABOUT EACH OTHER, BUT HORRIBLY MEAN TO OUTSIDERS!!
OH...DID YOU CUT YOUR FINGER, DEAR?

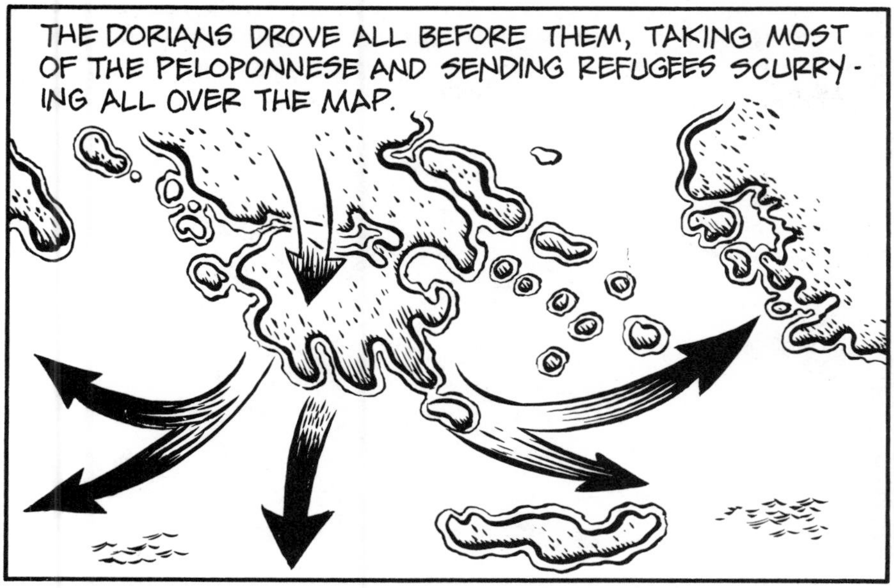
THE DORIANS DROVE ALL BEFORE THEM, TAKING MOST OF THE PELOPONNESE AND SENDING REFUGEES SCURRYING ALL OVER THE MAP.

THERE WERE EXCEPTIONS: THEY COULDN'T CONQUER THE ***ATHENIANS,*** WHO EVER AFTERWARDS CLAIMED TO BE THE TRUE, ORIGINAL GREEKS, OR THE ***ARCADIANS,*** WHO PRESERVED THE WEIRDEST, MOST ANCIENT RELIGIOUS RITES IN THEIR MOUNTAIN STRONGHOLDS.

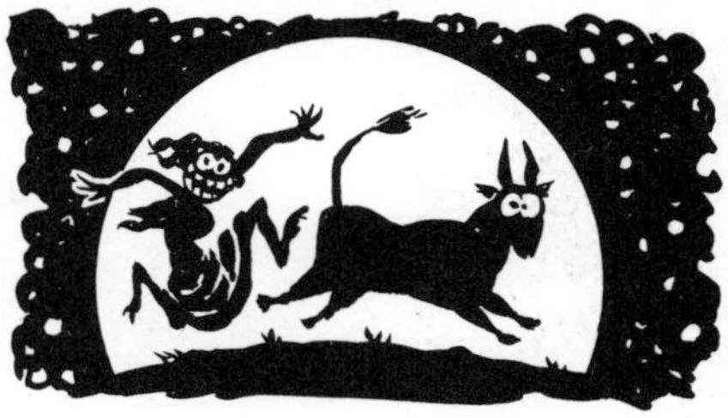

THE DORIAN-DRIVEN PEOPLES ENDED UP IN THE STRANGEST PLACES—BRITAIN, FOR EXAMPLE ... AND WE SAW IN VOL. 4 HOW DESPERATE SEA-RAIDERS ATTACKED EGYPT AND BECAME ISRAEL'S ENEMIES: THE ***PHILISTINES,*** WHICH MAY BE ANOTHER WAY OF SAYING ***PELASGIANS...*** AND ONE OF THESE VOLUMES, WE'LL SEE WHAT ALL THIS HAD TO DO WITH CHINA!

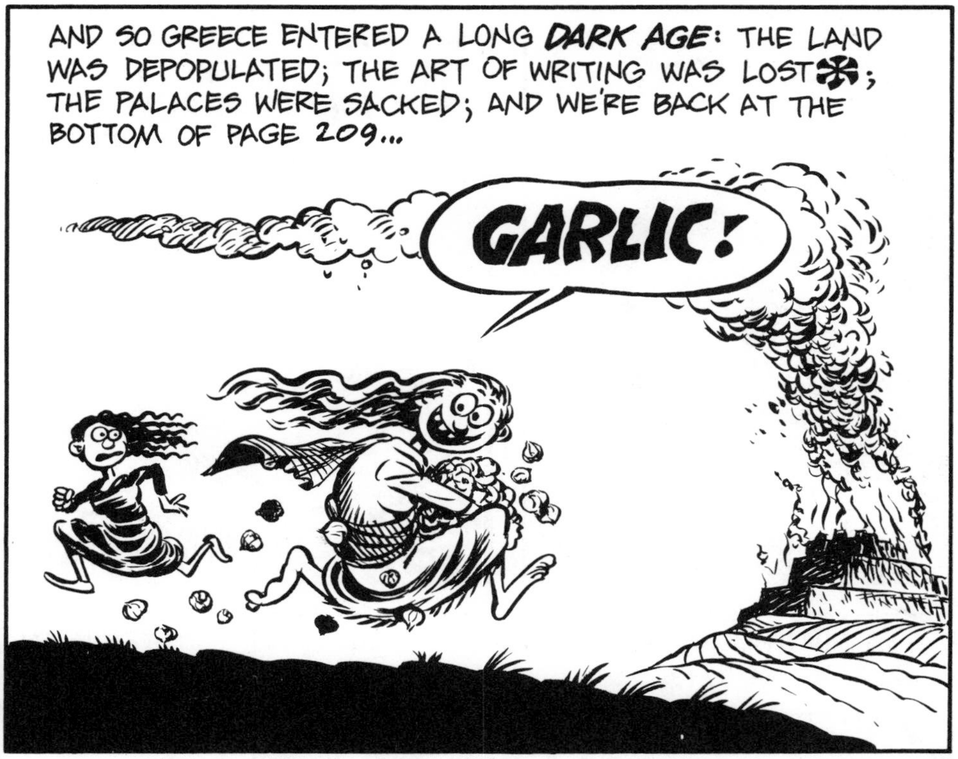
AND SO GREECE ENTERED A LONG ***DARK AGE***: THE LAND WAS DEPOPULATED; THE ART OF WRITING WAS LOST❋; THE PALACES WERE SACKED; AND WE'RE BACK AT THE BOTTOM OF PAGE 209...
GARLIC!

❋ THE EARLY GREEKS HAD A SYSTEM OF WRITING—NOW CALLED ***"LINEAR B"***—BASED ON THE PICTOGRAMS OF CRETE AND USED FOR ONLY ONE PURPOSE: KEEPING THE PALACE ACCOUNTS.

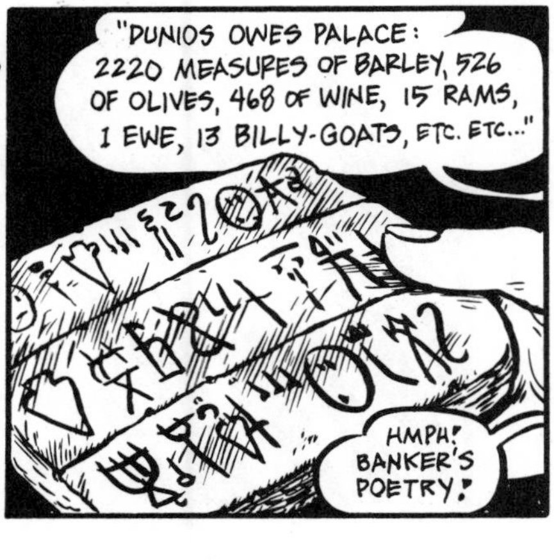
"DUNIOS OWES PALACE: 2220 MEASURES OF BARLEY, 526 OF OLIVES, 468 OF WINE, 15 RAMS, 1 EWE, 13 BILLY-GOATS, ETC. ETC..."
HMPH! BANKER'S POETRY!

WHEN CIVILIZATION COLLAPSED AROUND 1200 B.C., AND THE USE OF LINEAR B WAS COMPLETELY FORGOTTEN, SOME PEOPLE MUST HAVE WELCOMED ***ILLITERACY*** AS ONE OF THE BRIGHT SPOTS OF THE GREEK DARK AGES (1200-800 B.C.)!?

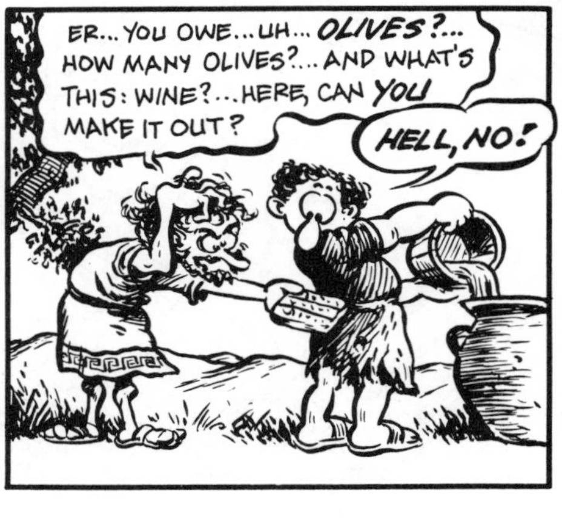
ER... YOU OWE... UH... ***OLIVES?***... HOW MANY OLIVES?... AND WHAT'S THIS: WINE?... HERE, CAN ***YOU*** MAKE IT OUT?
HELL, NO!

FUNNY THINGS, DARK AGES... DESPITE THE POVERTY AND ILLITERACY, IT MAY HAPPEN THAT ***TECHNOLOGY*** ADVANCES ANYWAY—AND THAT'S WHAT HAPPENED IN GREECE WITH ***METAL-WORKING***.

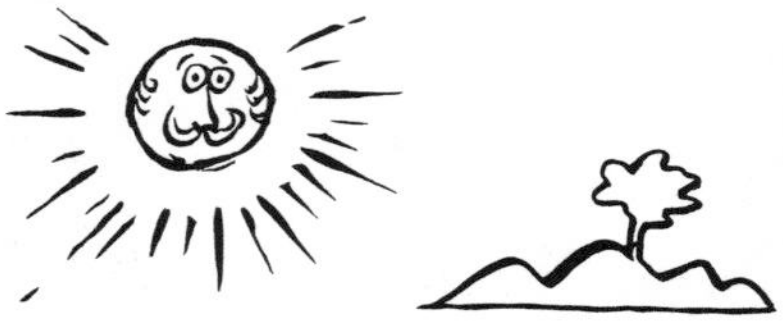

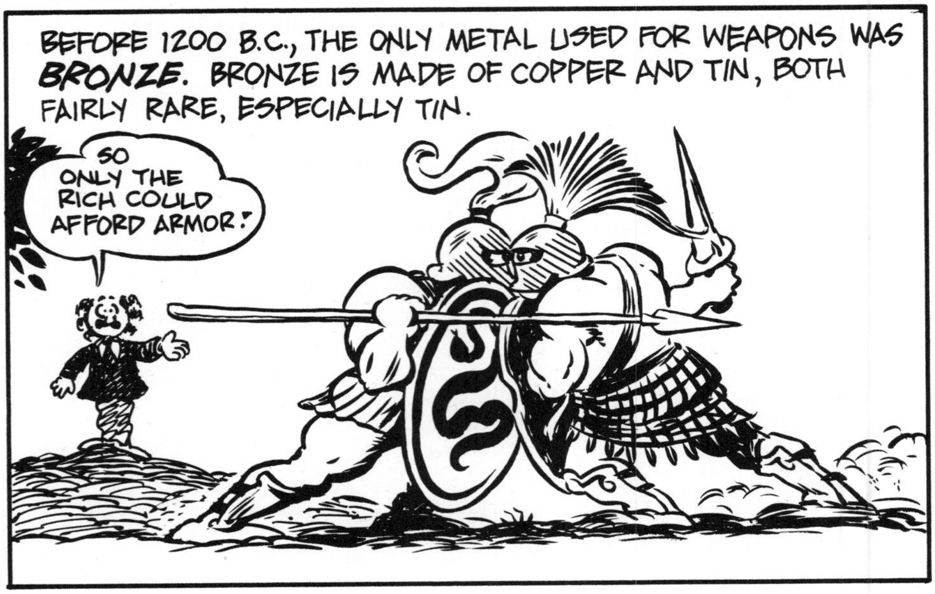
BEFORE 1200 B.C., THE ONLY METAL USED FOR WEAPONS WAS BRONZE. BRONZE IS MADE OF COPPER AND TIN, BOTH FAIRLY RARE, ESPECIALLY TIN.
SO ONLY THE RICH COULD AFFORD ARMOR!

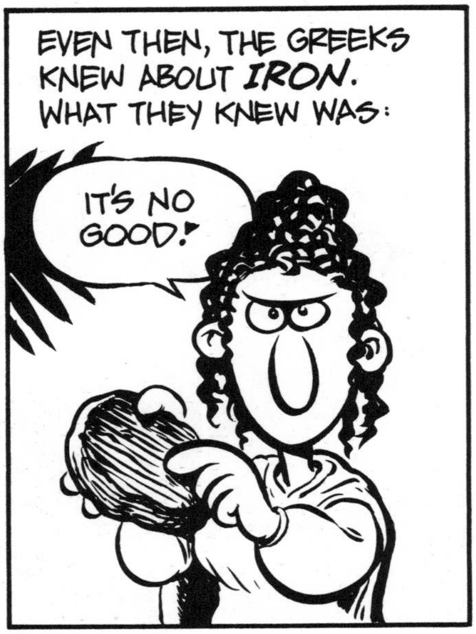
EVEN THEN, THE GREEKS KNEW ABOUT IRON. WHAT THEY KNEW WAS:
IT'S NO GOOD!

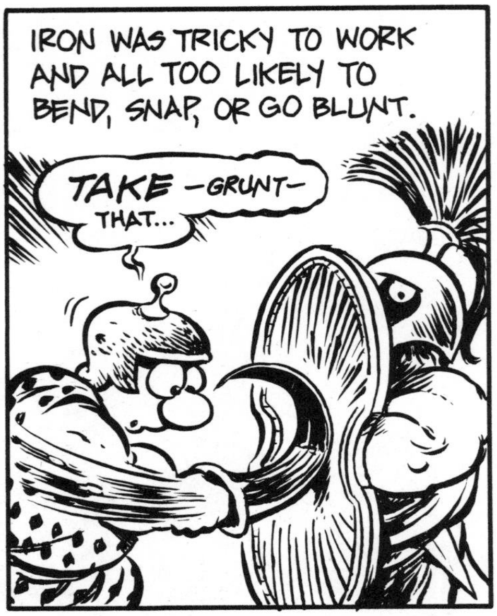
IRON WAS TRICKY TO WORK AND ALL TOO LIKELY TO BEND, SNAP, OR GO BLUNT.
TAKE —GRUNT— THAT...

SO FOR YEARS, THEY USED IT ONLY FOR FARM TOOLS... BUT GRADUALLY THE SECRETS OF IRON-WORKING SPREAD FROM THEIR SOURCE IN ARMENIA, AND SOMETIME DURING THE DARK AGES, GOOD IRON WEAPONS APPEARED IN GREECE.

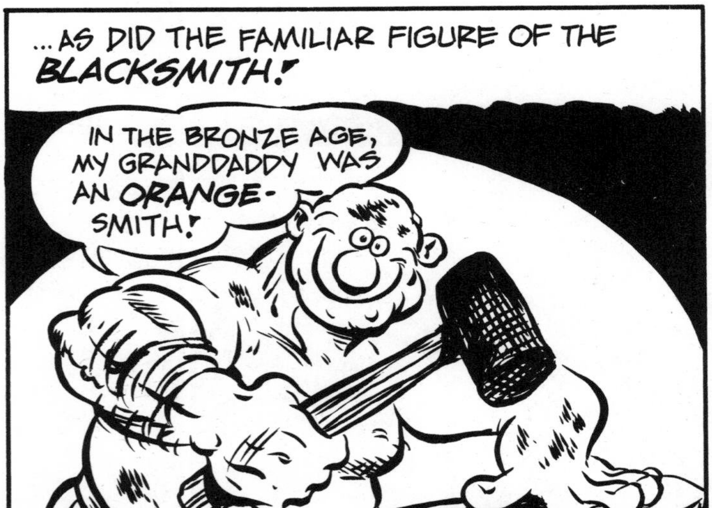
...AS DID THE FAMILIAR FIGURE OF THE BLACKSMITH!
IN THE BRONZE AGE, MY GRANDDADDY WAS AN ORANGE-SMITH!

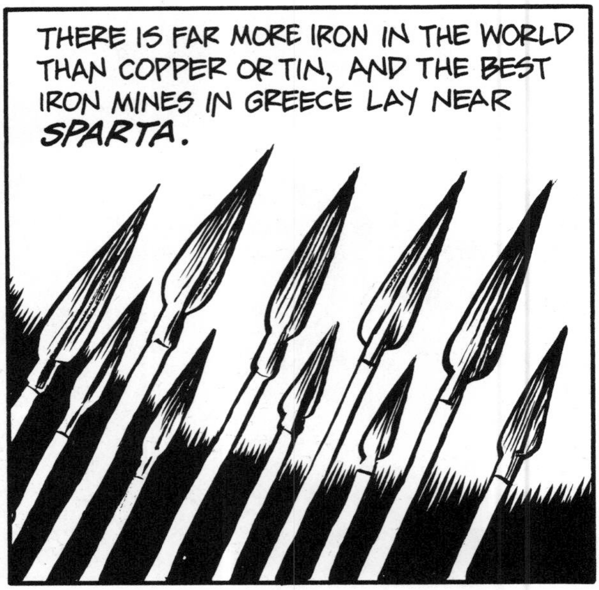
THERE IS FAR MORE IRON IN THE WORLD THAN COPPER OR TIN, AND THE BEST IRON MINES IN GREECE LAY NEAR SPARTA.

IRON CONSTITUTION

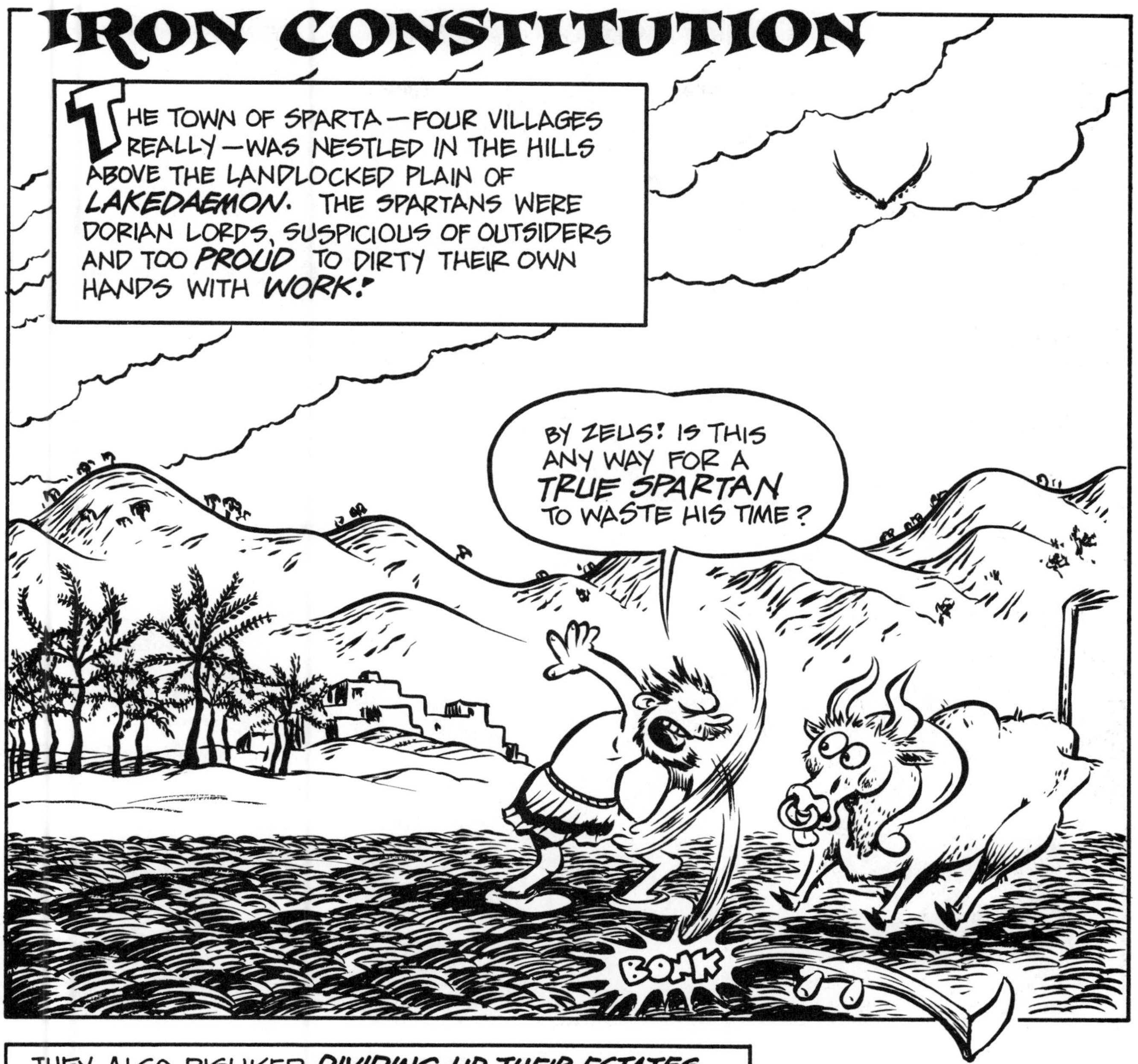
THE TOWN OF SPARTA—FOUR VILLAGES REALLY—WAS NESTLED IN THE HILLS ABOVE THE LANDLOCKED PLAIN OF LAKEDAEMON. THE SPARTANS WERE DORIAN LORDS, SUSPICIOUS OF OUTSIDERS AND TOO PROUD TO DIRTY THEIR OWN HANDS WITH WORK!
BY ZEUS! IS THIS ANY WAY FOR A TRUE SPARTAN TO WASTE HIS TIME?
BONK

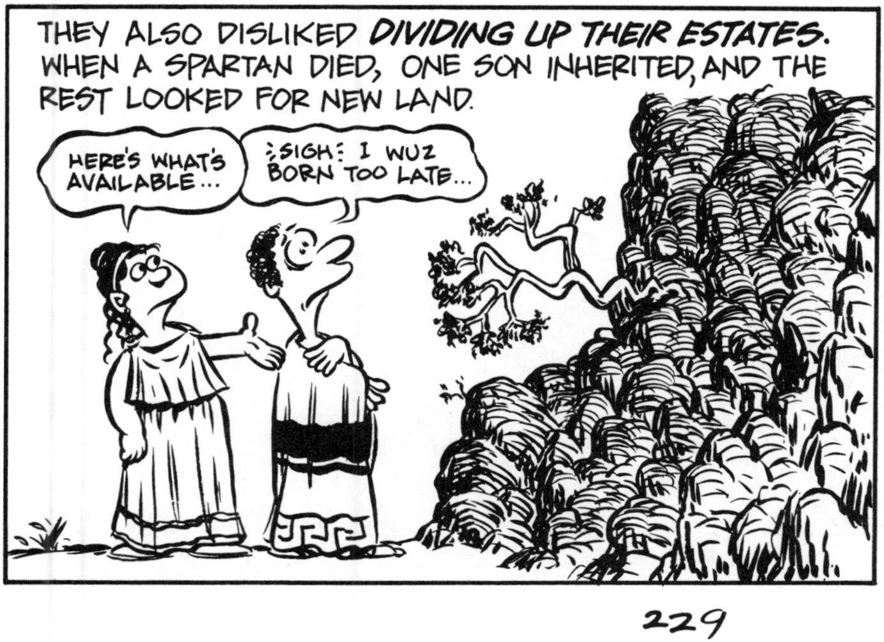
THEY ALSO DISLIKED DIVIDING UP THEIR ESTATES. WHEN A SPARTAN DIED, ONE SON INHERITED, AND THE REST LOOKED FOR NEW LAND.
HERE'S WHAT'S AVAILABLE...
:SIGH: I WUZ BORN TOO LATE...

AS GREECE EMERGED FROM THE DARK AGES, AROUND ***750 B.C.***, THE SPARTANS WERE PREPARING TO SOLVE THEIR TWIN "PROBLEMS"— LABOR AND LAND—BY GOING TO ***WAR***. THEY BEGAN TO DRILL IN THE NEW TACTICS OF THE ***HOPLITE PHALANX***...

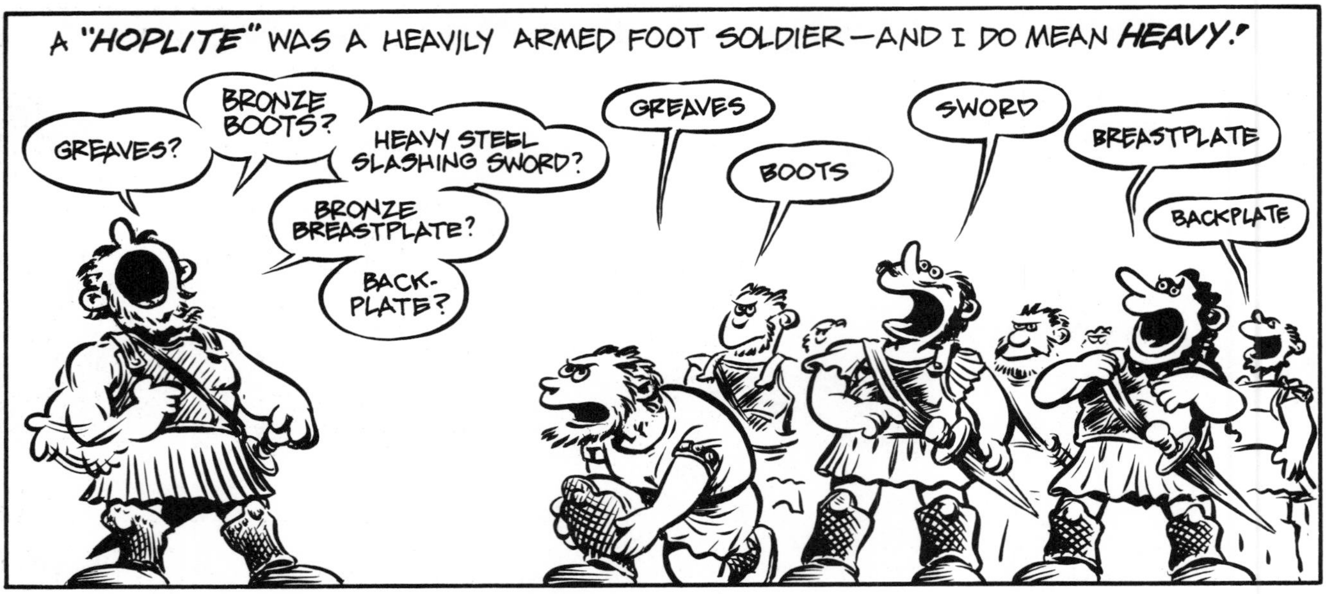
A "HOPLITE" WAS A HEAVILY ARMED FOOT SOLDIER—AND I DO MEAN HEAVY!
GREAVES?
BRONZE BOOTS?
HEAVY STEEL SLASHING SWORD?
BRONZE BREASTPLATE?
BACK-PLATE?
GREAVES
BOOTS
SWORD
BREASTPLATE
BACKPLATE

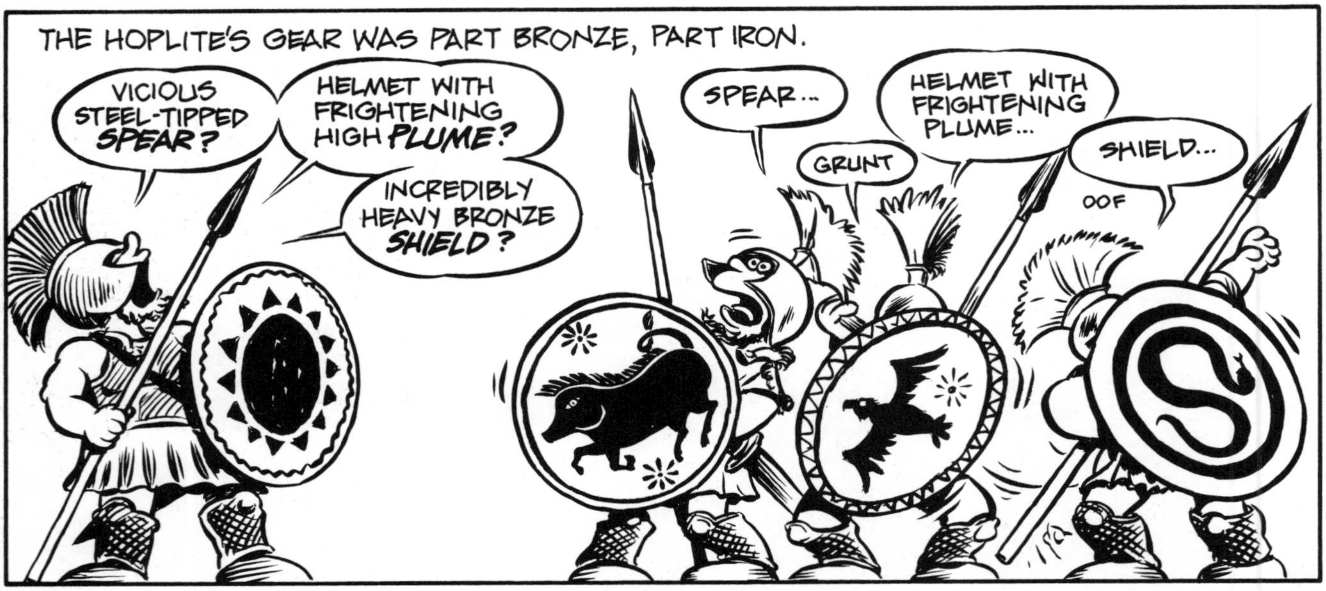
THE HOPLITE'S GEAR WAS PART BRONZE, PART IRON.
VICIOUS STEEL-TIPPED SPEAR?
HELMET WITH FRIGHTENING HIGH PLUME?
INCREDIBLY HEAVY BRONZE SHIELD?
SPEAR...
GRUNT
HELMET WITH FRIGHTENING PLUME...
OOF
SHIELD...

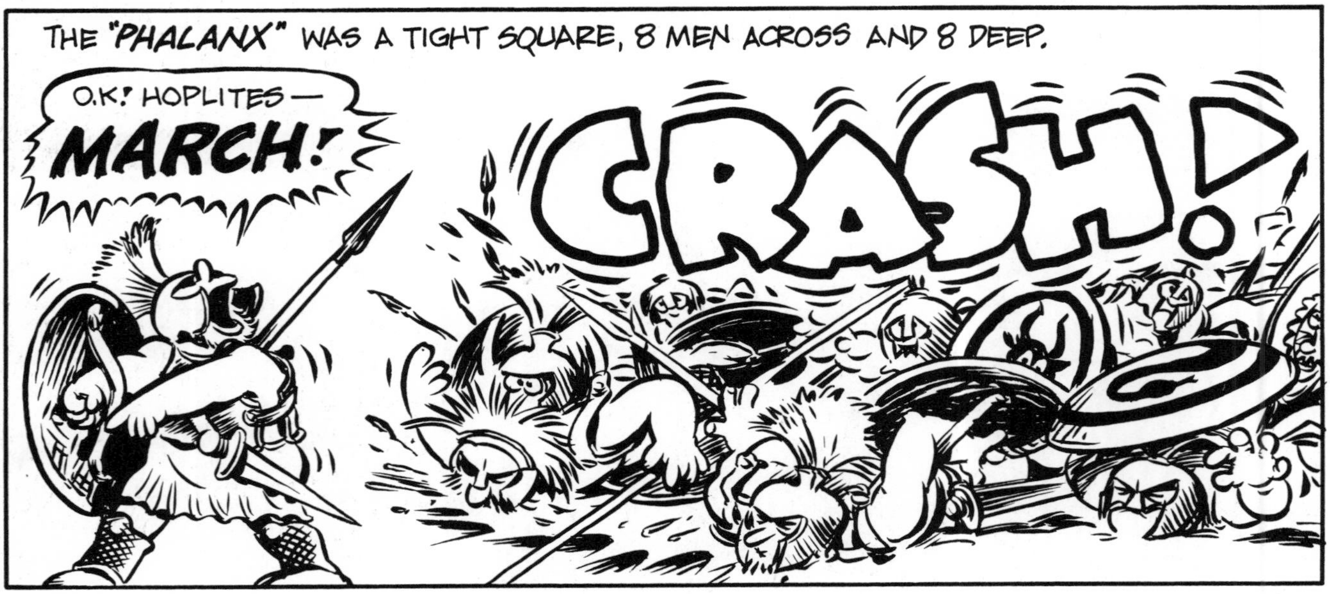
THE "PHALANX" WAS A TIGHT SQUARE, 8 MEN ACROSS AND 8 DEEP.
O.K.! HOPLITES— MARCH!
CRASH!

WELL, PRACTICE MAKES PERFECT, AND SOON THE SPARTANS WERE DOING "LEFT FACE," "RIGHT FACE," "DOUBLE TIME," AND "OVERLAPPING SHIELDS" WITHOUT FALLING DOWN OR STABBING EACH OTHER *TOO* MUCH.

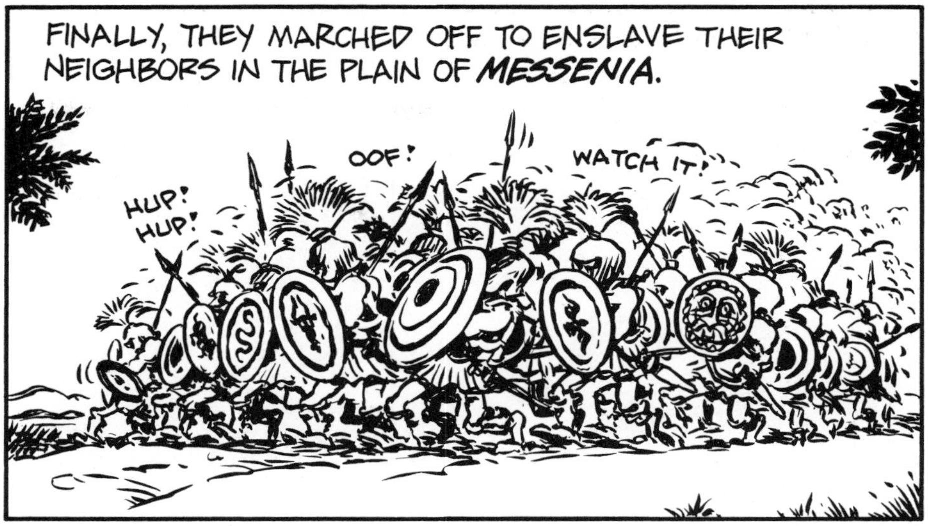
FINALLY, THEY MARCHED OFF TO ENSLAVE THEIR NEIGHBORS IN THE PLAIN OF *MESSENIA*.
HUP! HUP!
OOF!
WATCH IT!

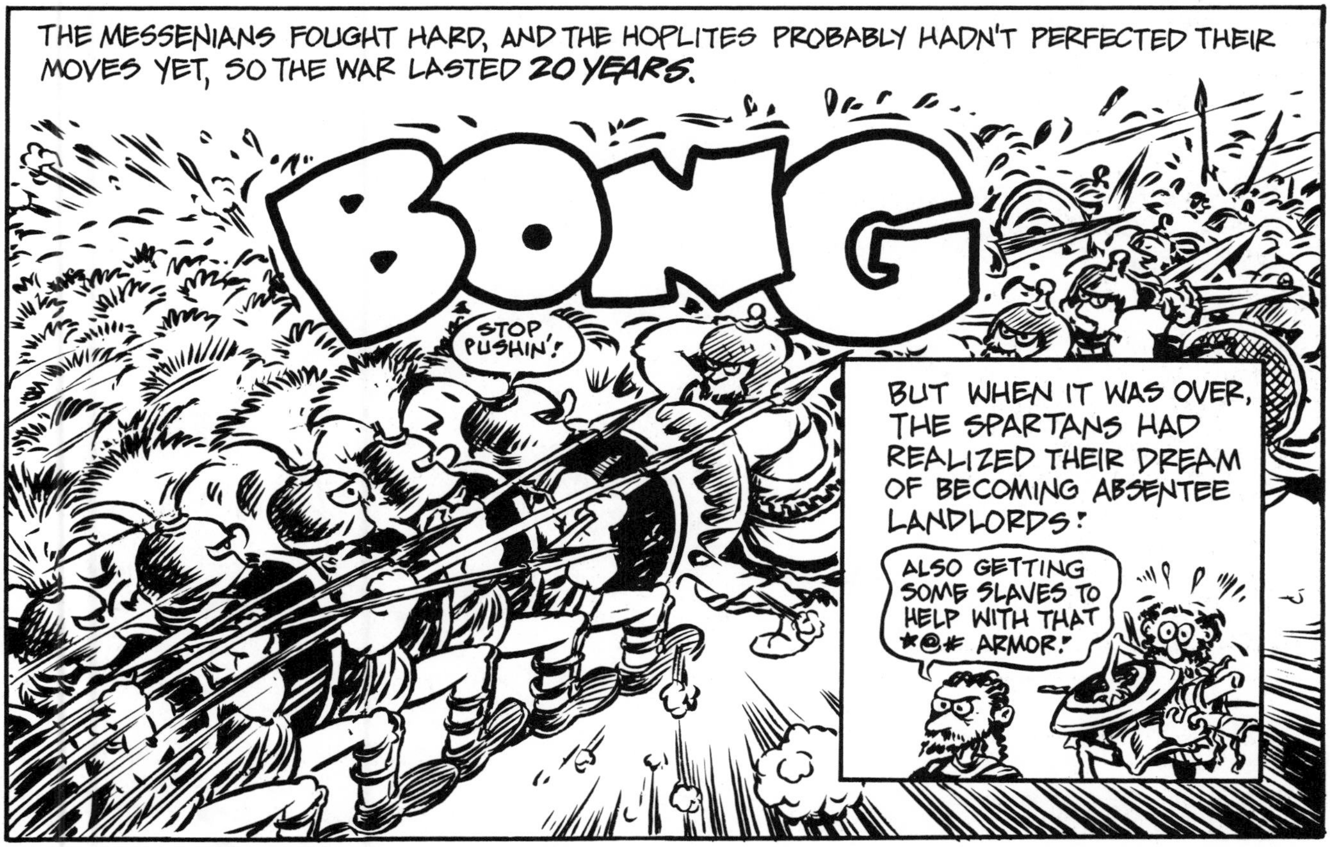
THE MESSENIANS FOUGHT HARD, AND THE HOPLITES PROBABLY HADN'T PERFECTED THEIR MOVES YET, SO THE WAR LASTED *20 YEARS*.
BONG
STOP PUSHIN'!
BUT WHEN IT WAS OVER, THE SPARTANS HAD REALIZED THEIR DREAM OF BECOMING ABSENTEE LANDLORDS!
ALSO GETTING SOME SLAVES TO HELP WITH THAT *@# ARMOR!

WHILE THE SPARTAN MEN WERE AT WAR—WHICH WAS OFTEN—WHAT ABOUT THE SPARTAN **WOMEN?** WELL, DURING SPARTA'S FIRST WAR OF CONQUEST, THE WOMEN MADE SOME **CONQUESTS** TOO—AMONG THE SLAVES WHO REMAINED AT HOME!!

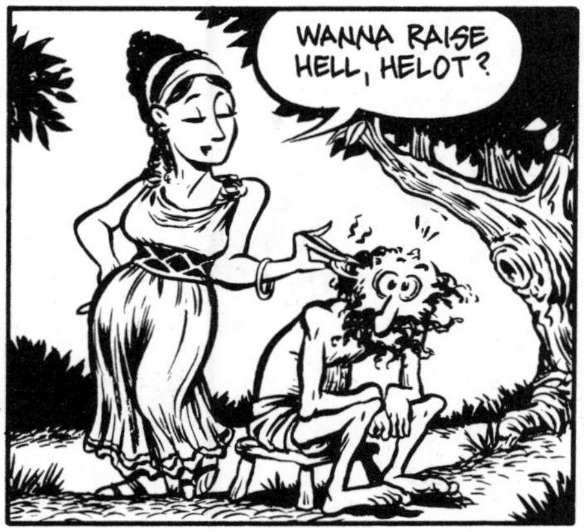
WANNA RAISE HELL, HELOT?

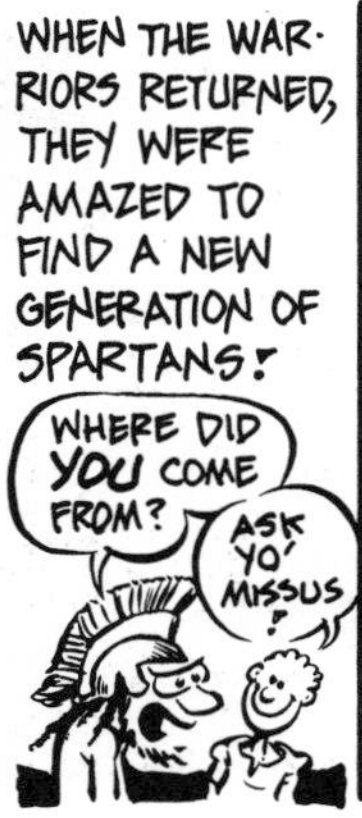
WHEN THE WARRIORS RETURNED, THEY WERE AMAZED TO FIND A NEW GENERATION OF SPARTANS!
WHERE DID *YOU* COME FROM?
ASK YO' MISSUS!

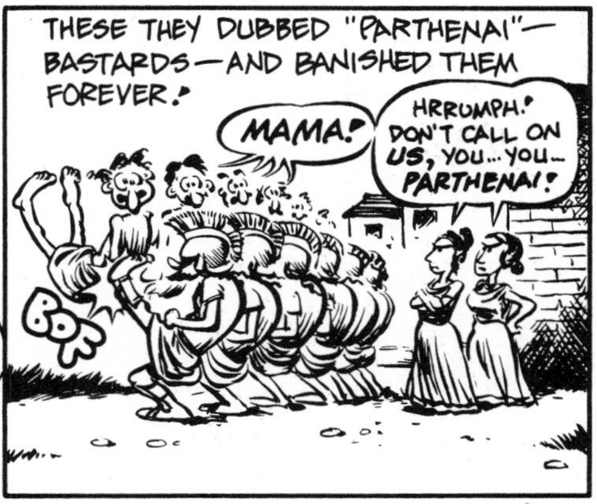
THESE THEY DUBBED "PARTHENAI"—BASTARDS—AND BANISHED THEM FOREVER!
MAMA!
HRRUMPH! DON'T CALL ON *US*, YOU... YOU... *PARTHENAI*!
BOF

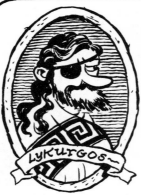

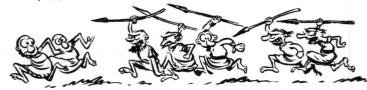

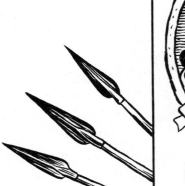

HAVING FREED THEMSELVES FROM DRUDGERY AND TOIL, THE SPARTANS NOW FACED THE JOB OF HOLDING DOWN A LARGE POPULATION OF ***ANGRY SUBJECTS.*** THIS TWISTED THEIR SOCIETY INTO SOME PRETTY ODD SHAPES...

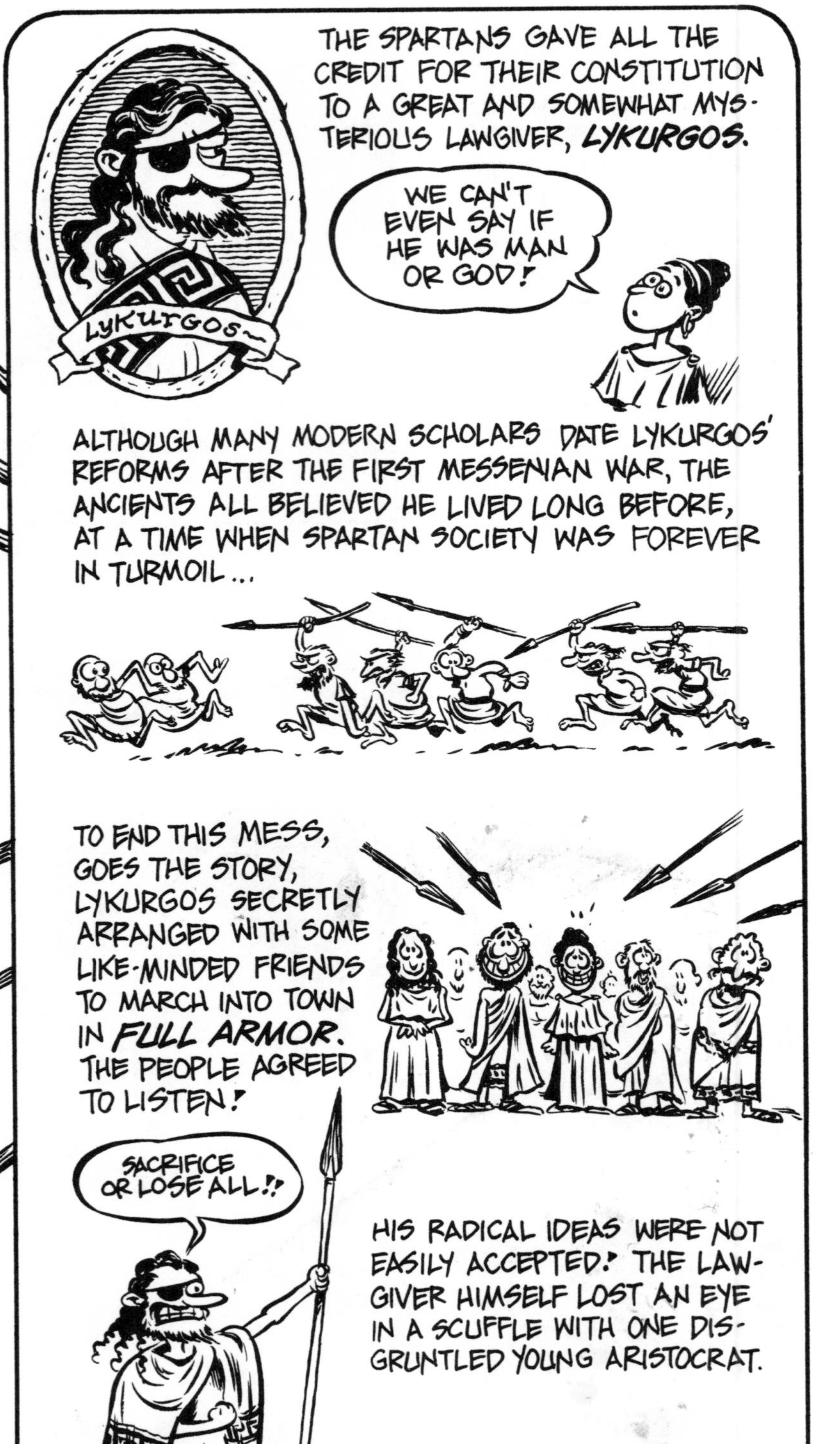

THE SPARTANS GAVE ALL THE CREDIT FOR THEIR CONSTITUTION TO A GREAT AND SOMEWHAT MYSTERIOUS LAWGIVER, LYKURGOS.
LYKURGOS
WE CAN'T EVEN SAY IF HE WAS MAN OR GOD!
ALTHOUGH MANY MODERN SCHOLARS DATE LYKURGOS' REFORMS AFTER THE FIRST MESSENIAN WAR, THE ANCIENTS ALL BELIEVED HE LIVED LONG BEFORE, AT A TIME WHEN SPARTAN SOCIETY WAS FOREVER IN TURMOIL...
TO END THIS MESS, GOES THE STORY, LYKURGOS SECRETLY ARRANGED WITH SOME LIKE-MINDED FRIENDS TO MARCH INTO TOWN IN FULL ARMOR. THE PEOPLE AGREED TO LISTEN!
SACRIFICE OR LOSE ALL!!
HIS RADICAL IDEAS WERE NOT EASILY ACCEPTED! THE LAWGIVER HIMSELF LOST AN EYE IN A SCUFFLE WITH ONE DISGRUNTLED YOUNG ARISTOCRAT.
IT'S HARD TO SAY HOW MUCH SPARTAN CUSTOM BEGAN WITH LYKURGOS, BUT IT'S GENERALLY AGREED HE SET THE TONE, AT LEAST

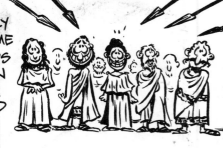

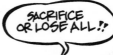

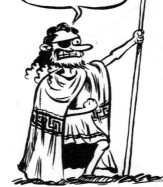

TO GIVE ALL "TRUE SPARTANS" A STAKE IN THE STATE, THE *LAND WAS RE-DIVIDED* AMONG ALL CITIZENS. IT WAS WORKED BY THE *HELOTS*, SERFS WHO "GAVE" HALF THEIR HARVEST TO THE SPARTAN LORDS.

SPARTANS MUST LIVE SIMPLY. *SILVER, GOLD* ✳, AND OTHER FRILLS WERE BANNED: BY LAW, SPARTAN *CEILINGS* WERE FINISHED ROUGHLY, WITH AN AXE!

MY, HOW THE TREES GROW IN CORINTH!

THE *EPHOR*, OR HEAD MAN, WAS ELECTED BY THE *POPULAR ASSEMBLY*. HE PRESIDED OVER A COUNCIL OF 30 OF THE "BEST" MEN, INCLUDING TWO (!) KINGS AT A TIME.

WE'VE BEEN DEVALUED!

EATING AT HOME WAS ABOLISHED. ALL SPARTANS JOINED "MESS CLUBS" AND TOOK THEIR MEALS IN COMMON FOR THE REST OF THEIR LIVES! THIS WAS A HARD LAW TO SWALLOW, THEY SAY...

AND THE *FOOD* IS IMPOSSIBLE!

SPARTAN *WOMEN*, ALWAYS INDEPENDENT— REMEMBER HELEN?— ENJOYED MORE RIGHTS THAN WOMEN ELSEWHERE IN GREECE. THEY DID MILITARY EXERCISES, OWNED PROPERTY, AND *RAN SPARTA* WHILE THE MEN WERE AT WAR (OFTEN!).

COME BACK *WITH* YOUR SHIELD OR *ON* IT!

SO THAT ALL SPARTANS SHOULD KNOW THE LAW, IT WAS *NEVER WRITTEN*, BUT *SUNG* AT FESTIVALS FROM TIME TO TIME.

♪ NEVER FIGHT TOO LONG AGAINST ONE FOE... LEST YOUR TACTICS HE SHOULD COME TO KNOW...

SPLANGA SPLANGA

AND MORE ➤

THE SPARTAN LAWGIVER *LYKURGOS* TOOK ALL GOLD AND SILVER OUT OF CIRCULATION AND REPLACED THEM WITH A CURRENCY OF *IRON*.

THE REAL SOURCE OF OUR STRENGTH!

SPARTA HAD PLENTY OF IRON, SO THIS "MONEY" WASN'T WORTH MUCH: TOO BULKY TO STEAL, POINTLESS TO COUNTERFEIT, AND NOT EVEN PARTICULARLY EASY TO SPEND!

"NO RHETORIC-MASTER, FORTUNE-TELLER, HARLOT-MONGER, JEWELLER, OR ENGRAVER WOULD SET FOOT IN A COUNTRY WHICH HAD NO MONEY."
— PLUTARCH, *LIFE OF LYKURGOS*

✳@# SPARTANS ARE RAISIN' THE UNEMPLOYMENT RATE!

CONSEQUENTLY, SPARTANS REMAINED IMMUNE TO FOREIGN VICES, TRINKETS, AND "MARKETING SKILLS" IN GENERAL!

MONEY?...MONEY? I HAD SOME ONCE, BUT IT'S ALL GONE TO RUST...

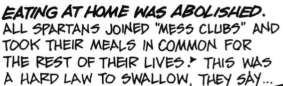

THE SPARTANS PUT ***PHYSICAL FITNESS*** FIRST: SICKLY BABIES WERE EXPOSED TO DIE, AND THE LIVING WEREN'T PAMPERED!

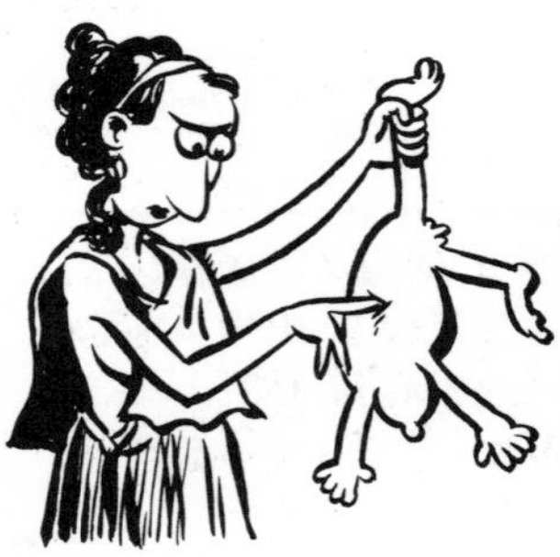

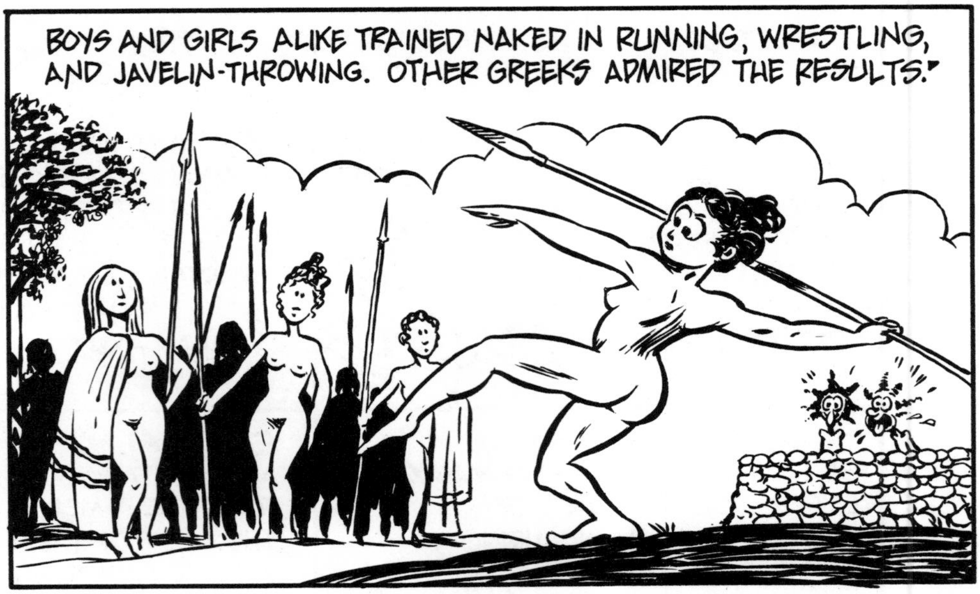
BOYS AND GIRLS ALIKE TRAINED NAKED IN RUNNING, WRESTLING, AND JAVELIN-THROWING. OTHER GREEKS ADMIRED THE RESULTS.

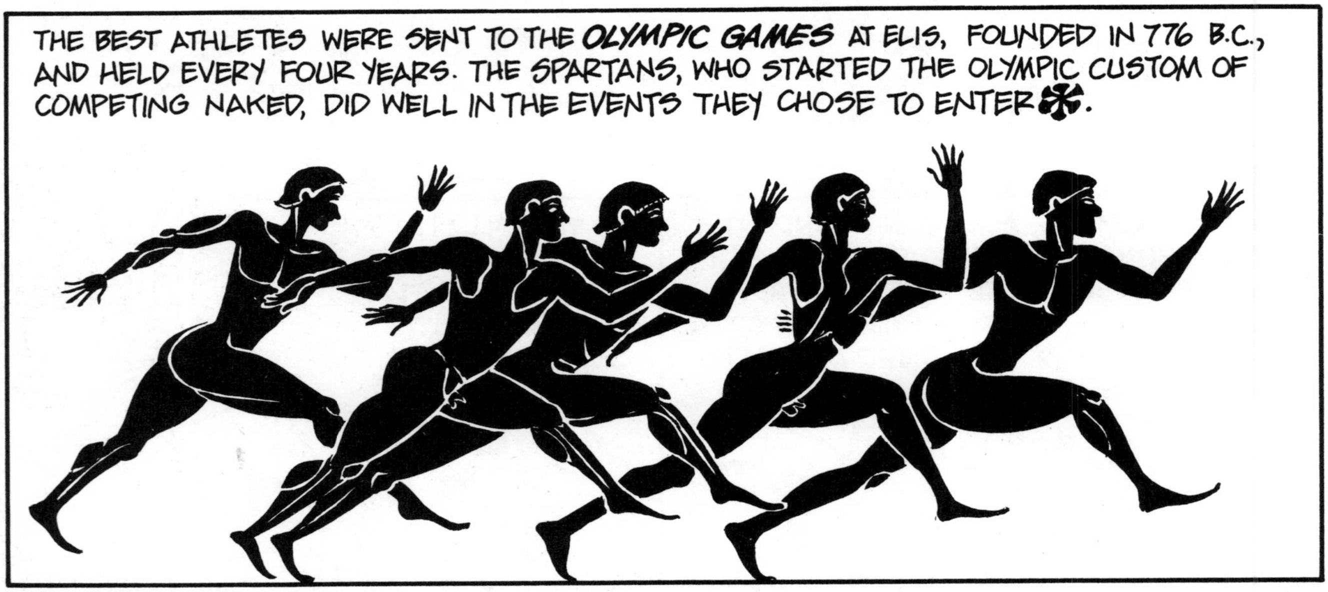
THE BEST ATHLETES WERE SENT TO THE OLYMPIC GAMES AT ELIS, FOUNDED IN 776 B.C., AND HELD EVERY FOUR YEARS. THE SPARTANS, WHO STARTED THE OLYMPIC CUSTOM OF COMPETING NAKED, DID WELL IN THE EVENTS THEY CHOSE TO ENTER ✲.

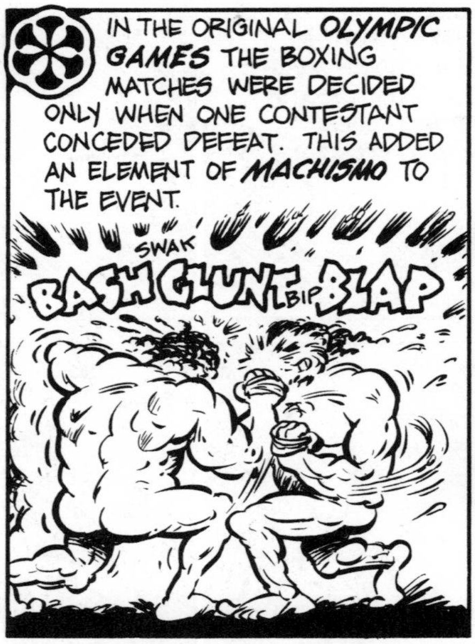
✲ IN THE ORIGINAL OLYMPIC GAMES THE BOXING MATCHES WERE DECIDED ONLY WHEN ONE CONTESTANT CONCEDED DEFEAT. THIS ADDED AN ELEMENT OF MACHISMO TO THE EVENT.
SWAK
BASH CLUNT BIP BLAP

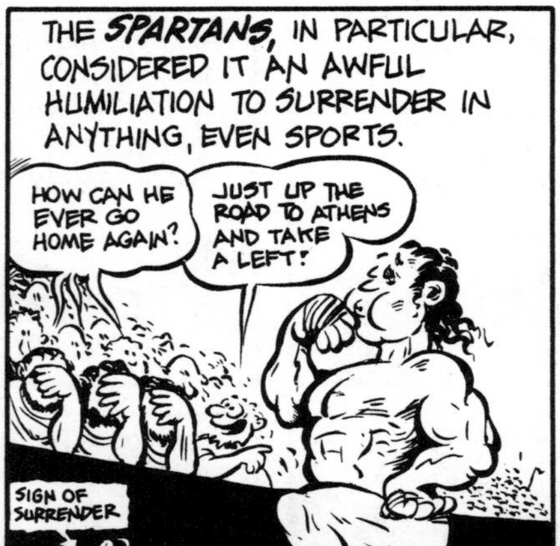
THE SPARTANS, IN PARTICULAR, CONSIDERED IT AN AWFUL HUMILIATION TO SURRENDER IN ANYTHING, EVEN SPORTS.
HOW CAN HE EVER GO HOME AGAIN?
JUST UP THE ROAD TO ATHENS AND TAKE A LEFT!
SIGN OF SURRENDER

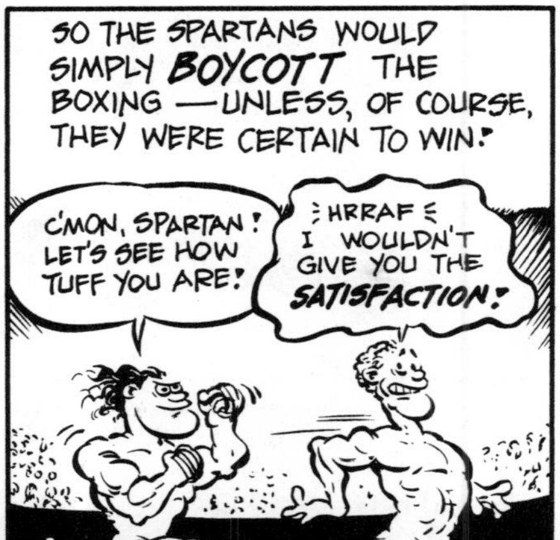
SO THE SPARTANS WOULD SIMPLY BOYCOTT THE BOXING — UNLESS, OF COURSE, THEY WERE CERTAIN TO WIN!
C'MON, SPARTAN! LET'S SEE HOW TUFF YOU ARE!
HRRAF I WOULDN'T GIVE YOU THE SATISFACTION!

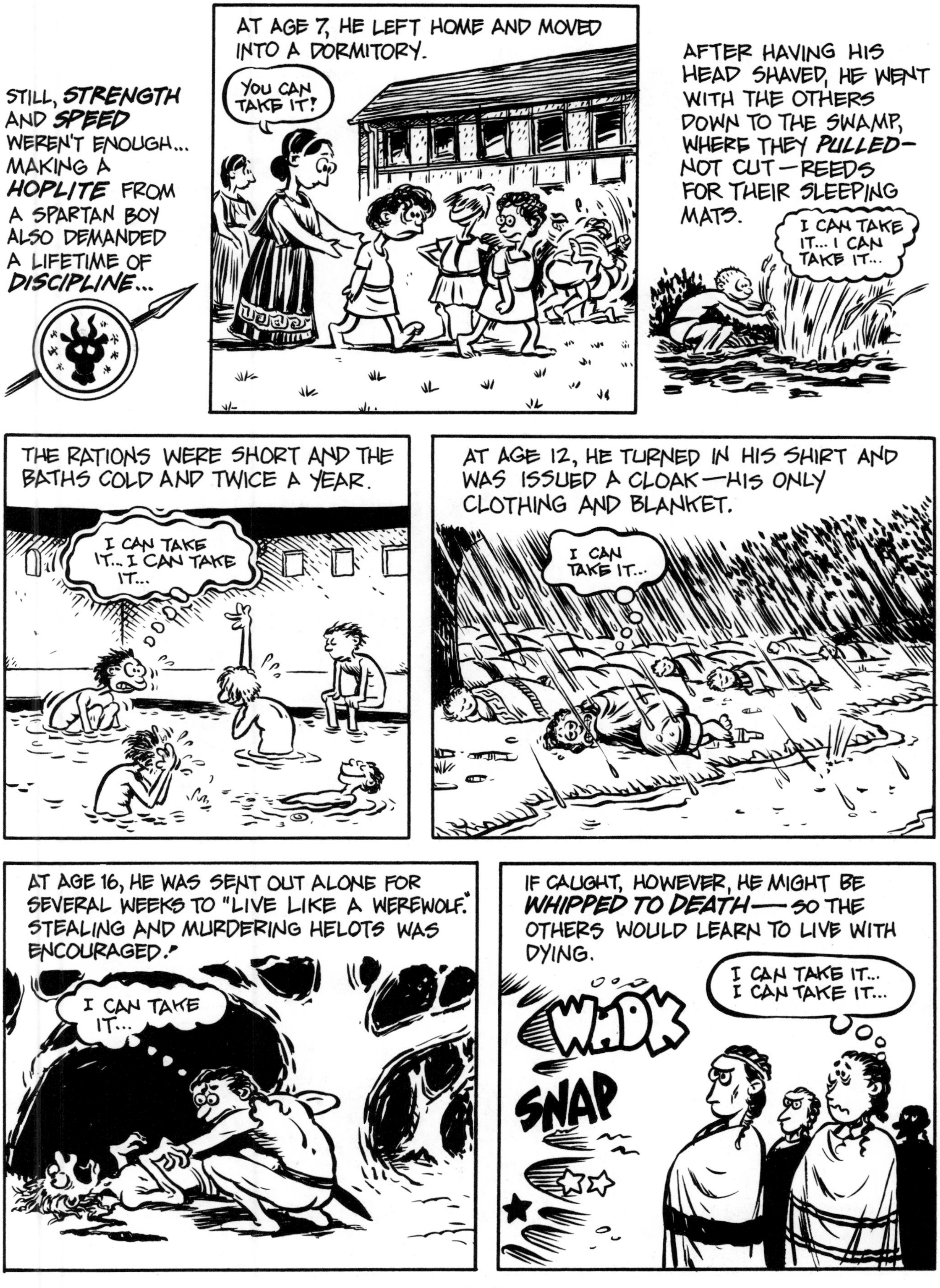
STILL, STRENGTH AND SPEED WEREN'T ENOUGH... MAKING A HOPLITE FROM A SPARTAN BOY ALSO DEMANDED A LIFETIME OF DISCIPLINE...
AT AGE 7, HE LEFT HOME AND MOVED INTO A DORMITORY.
YOU CAN TAKE IT!
AFTER HAVING HIS HEAD SHAVED, HE WENT WITH THE OTHERS DOWN TO THE SWAMP, WHERE THEY PULLED—NOT CUT—REEDS FOR THEIR SLEEPING MATS.
I CAN TAKE IT... I CAN TAKE IT...
THE RATIONS WERE SHORT AND THE BATHS COLD AND TWICE A YEAR.
I CAN TAKE IT... I CAN TAKE IT...
AT AGE 12, HE TURNED IN HIS SHIRT AND WAS ISSUED A CLOAK—HIS ONLY CLOTHING AND BLANKET.
I CAN TAKE IT...
AT AGE 16, HE WAS SENT OUT ALONE FOR SEVERAL WEEKS TO "LIVE LIKE A WEREWOLF." STEALING AND MURDERING HELOTS WAS ENCOURAGED.*
I CAN TAKE IT...
IF CAUGHT, HOWEVER, HE MIGHT BE WHIPPED TO DEATH—SO THE OTHERS WOULD LEARN TO LIVE WITH DYING.
WHOK
SNAP
I CAN TAKE IT... I CAN TAKE IT...

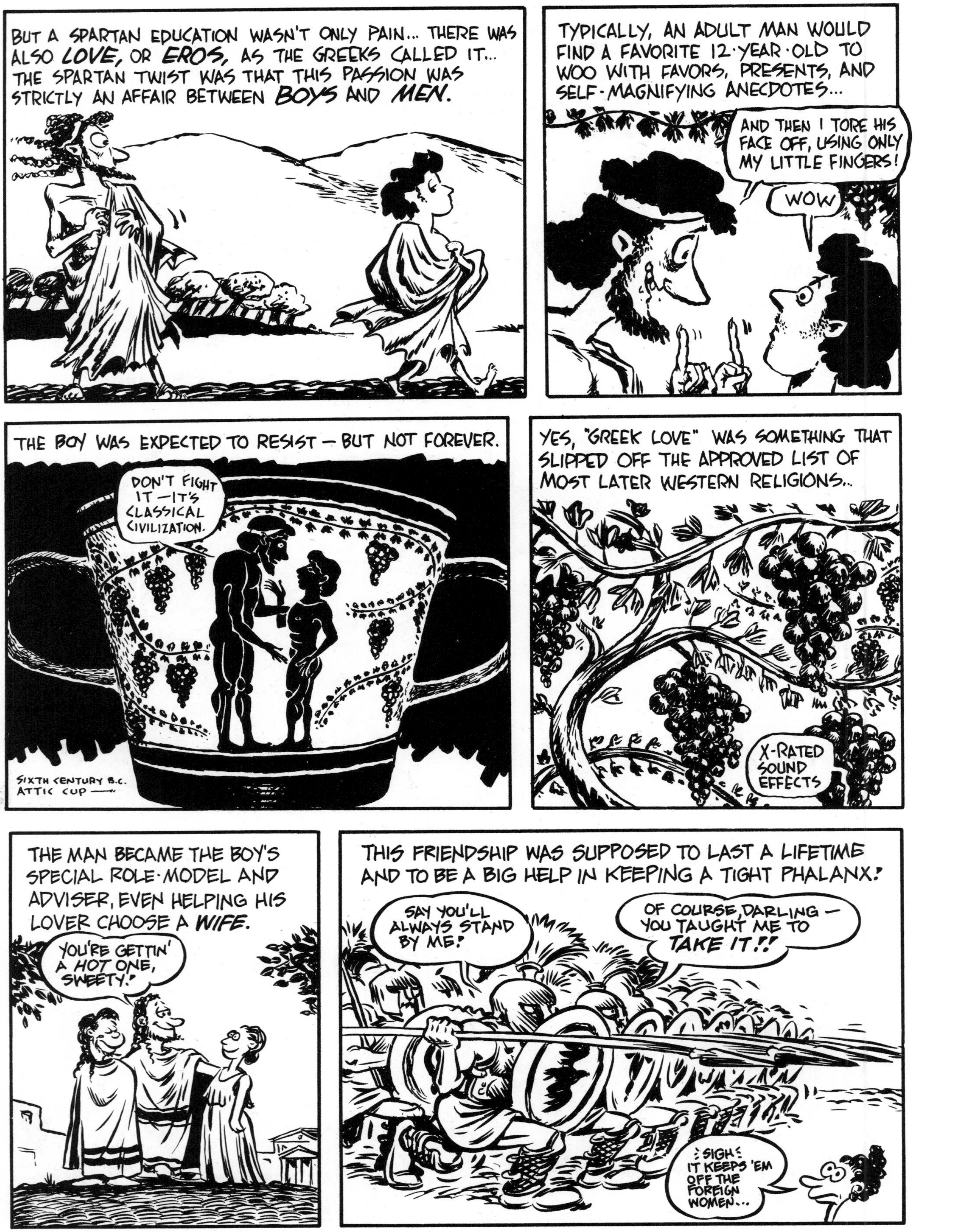
BUT A SPARTAN EDUCATION WASN'T ONLY PAIN... THERE WAS ALSO LOVE, OR EROS, AS THE GREEKS CALLED IT... THE SPARTAN TWIST WAS THAT THIS PASSION WAS STRICTLY AN AFFAIR BETWEEN BOYS AND MEN.
TYPICALLY, AN ADULT MAN WOULD FIND A FAVORITE 12-YEAR-OLD TO WOO WITH FAVORS, PRESENTS, AND SELF-MAGNIFYING ANECDOTES...
AND THEN I TORE HIS FACE OFF, USING ONLY MY LITTLE FINGERS!
WOW
THE BOY WAS EXPECTED TO RESIST — BUT NOT FOREVER.
DON'T FIGHT IT — IT'S CLASSICAL CIVILIZATION.
SIXTH CENTURY B.C. ATTIC CUP
YES, "GREEK LOVE" WAS SOMETHING THAT SLIPPED OFF THE APPROVED LIST OF MOST LATER WESTERN RELIGIONS..
X-RATED SOUND EFFECTS
THE MAN BECAME THE BOY'S SPECIAL ROLE-MODEL AND ADVISER, EVEN HELPING HIS LOVER CHOOSE A WIFE.
YOU'RE GETTIN' A HOT ONE, SWEETY!
THIS FRIENDSHIP WAS SUPPOSED TO LAST A LIFETIME AND TO BE A BIG HELP IN KEEPING A TIGHT PHALANX!
SAY YOU'LL ALWAYS STAND BY ME!
OF COURSE, DARLING — YOU TAUGHT ME TO TAKE IT!!
SIGH IT KEEPS 'EM OFF THE FOREIGN WOMEN...

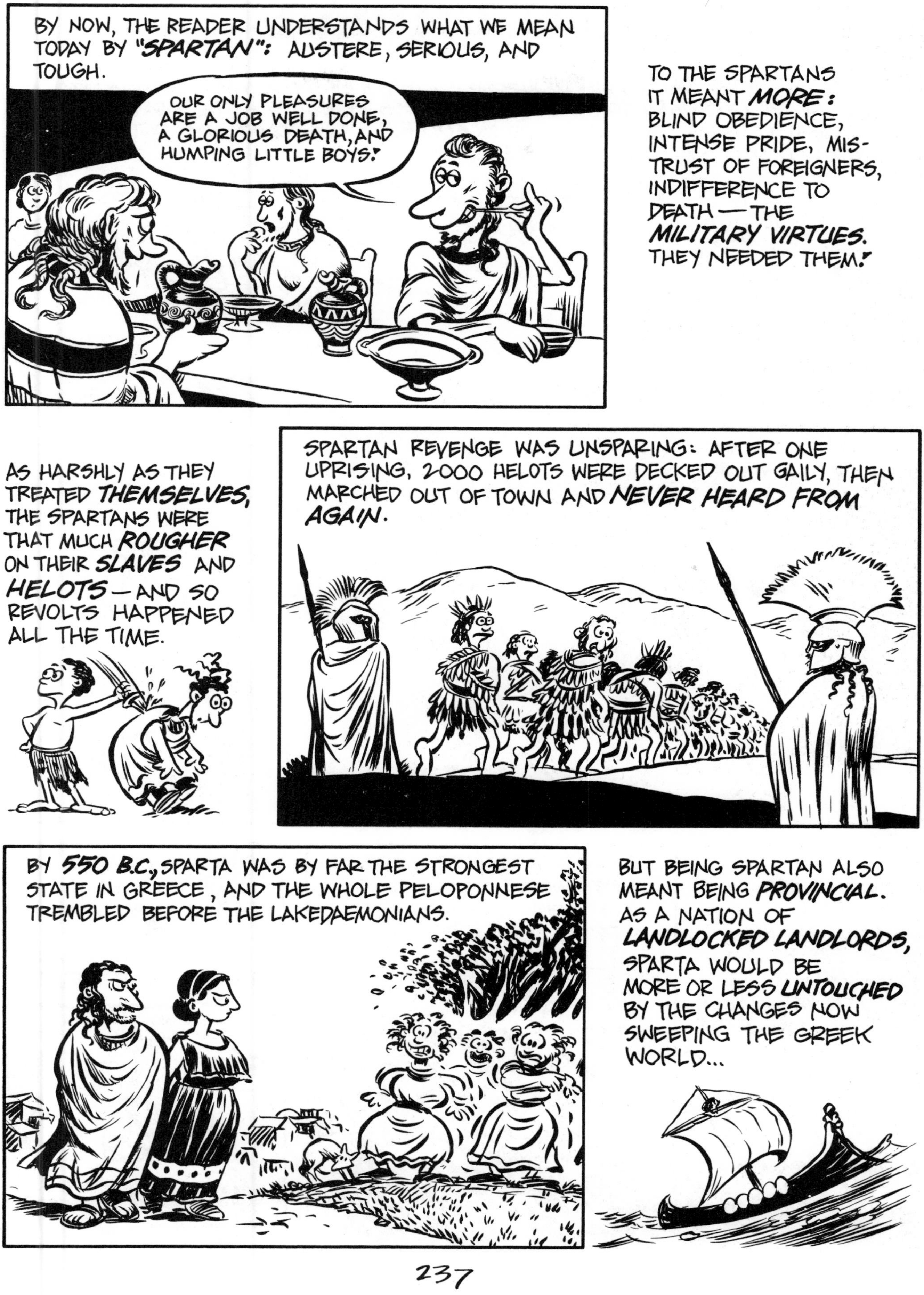
BY NOW, THE READER UNDERSTANDS WHAT WE MEAN TODAY BY "SPARTAN": AUSTERE, SERIOUS, AND TOUGH.
OUR ONLY PLEASURES ARE A JOB WELL DONE, A GLORIOUS DEATH, AND HUMPING LITTLE BOYS!
TO THE SPARTANS IT MEANT MORE: BLIND OBEDIENCE, INTENSE PRIDE, MISTRUST OF FOREIGNERS, INDIFFERENCE TO DEATH — THE MILITARY VIRTUES. THEY NEEDED THEM!
AS HARSHLY AS THEY TREATED THEMSELVES, THE SPARTANS WERE THAT MUCH ROUGHER ON THEIR SLAVES AND HELOTS — AND SO REVOLTS HAPPENED ALL THE TIME.
SPARTAN REVENGE WAS UNSPARING: AFTER ONE UPRISING, 2000 HELOTS WERE DECKED OUT GAILY, THEN MARCHED OUT OF TOWN AND NEVER HEARD FROM AGAIN.
BY 550 B.C., SPARTA WAS BY FAR THE STRONGEST STATE IN GREECE, AND THE WHOLE PELOPONNESE TREMBLED BEFORE THE LAKEDAEMONIANS.
BUT BEING SPARTAN ALSO MEANT BEING PROVINCIAL. AS A NATION OF LANDLOCKED LANDLORDS, SPARTA WOULD BE MORE OR LESS UNTOUCHED BY THE CHANGES NOW SWEEPING THE GREEK WORLD...

SPREADING GREECE

CAUGHT IN THE SAME LAND SQUEEZE AS THE SPARTANS, MANY OTHER GREEKS TURNED **OUTWARD** TO THE **SEA**. LANDLESS PEASANTS BY THE BOATLOAD WENT LOOKING FOR FARMS, AND BY **600 B.C.**, THE COAST WAS DOTTED WITH COUNTLESS GREEK **COLONIES**:

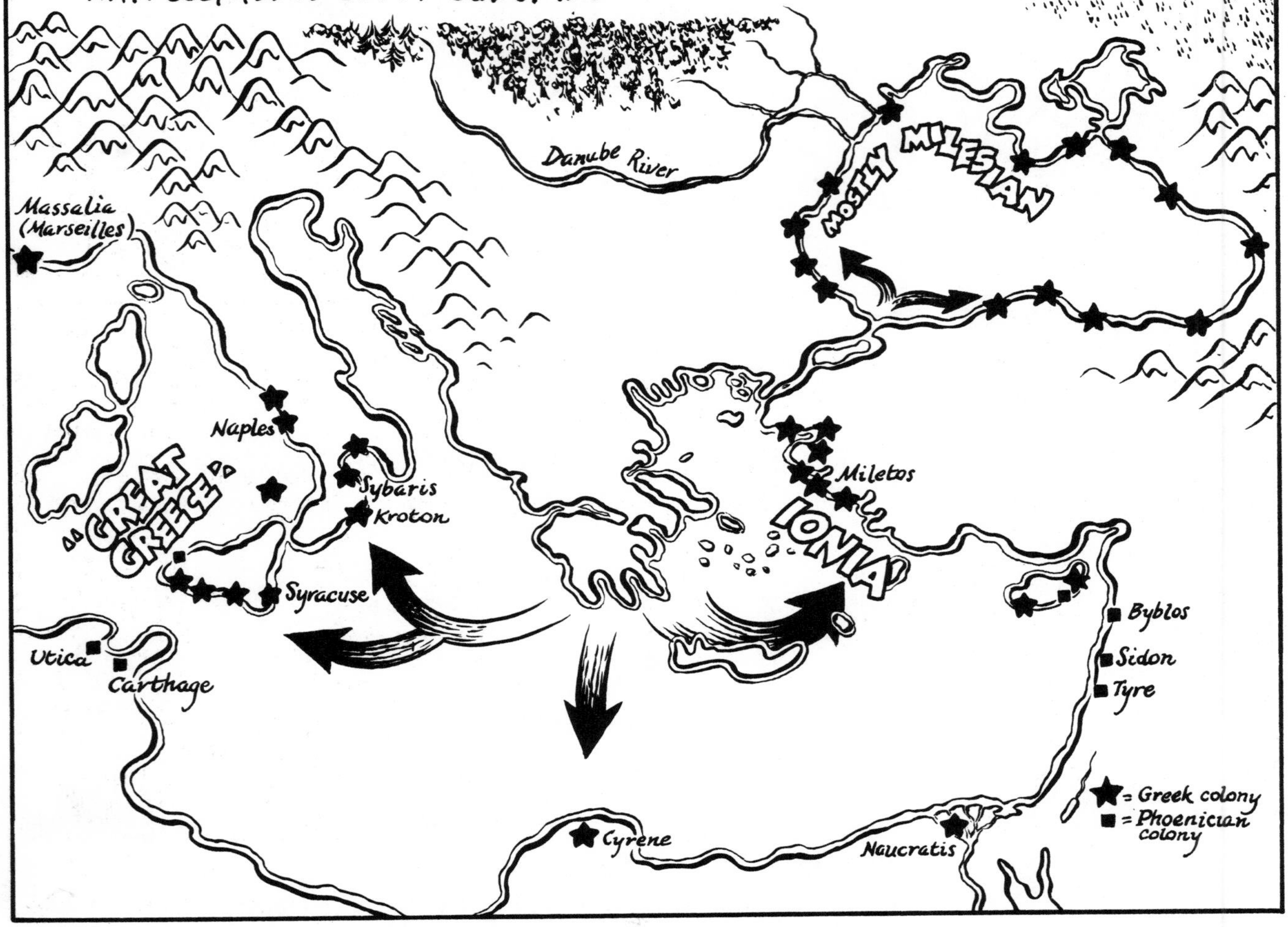

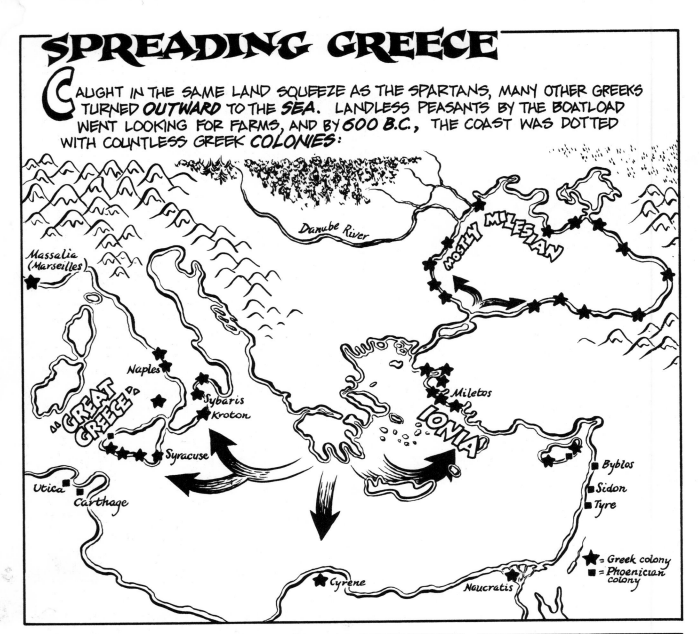

Danube River
MOSTLY MILESIAN
Massalia (Marseilles)
Naples
GREAT GREECE
Sybaris
Kroton
Syracuse
Miletos
IONIA
Utica
Carthage
Byblos
Sidon
Tyre
Cyrene
Naucratis
= Greek colony
= Phoenician colony

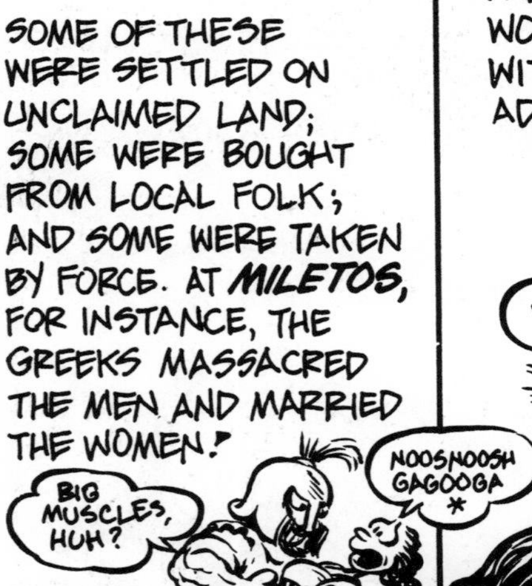

SOME OF THESE WERE SETTLED ON UNCLAIMED LAND; SOME WERE BOUGHT FROM LOCAL FOLK; AND SOME WERE TAKEN BY FORCE. AT **MILETOS**, FOR INSTANCE, THE GREEKS MASSACRED THE MEN AND MARRIED THE WOMEN!
BIG MUSCLES, HUH?
NOOSHNOOSH GAGOOGA *
* "BETWEEN YOUR EARS"

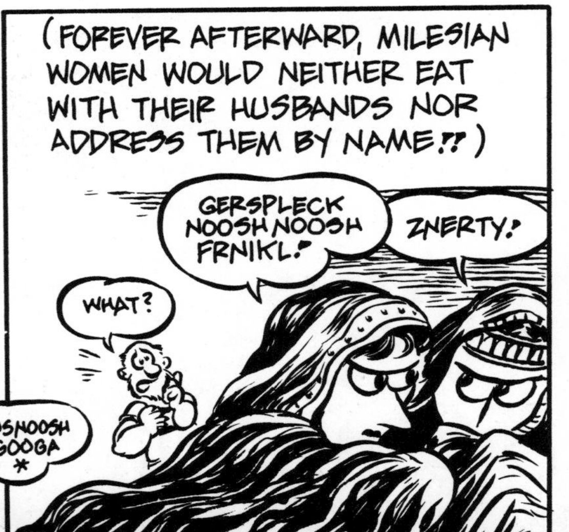

(FOREVER AFTERWARD, MILESIAN WOMEN WOULD NEITHER EAT WITH THEIR HUSBANDS NOR ADDRESS THEM BY NAME!!)
GERSPLECK NOOSHNOOSH FRNIKL!
ZNERTY!
WHAT?

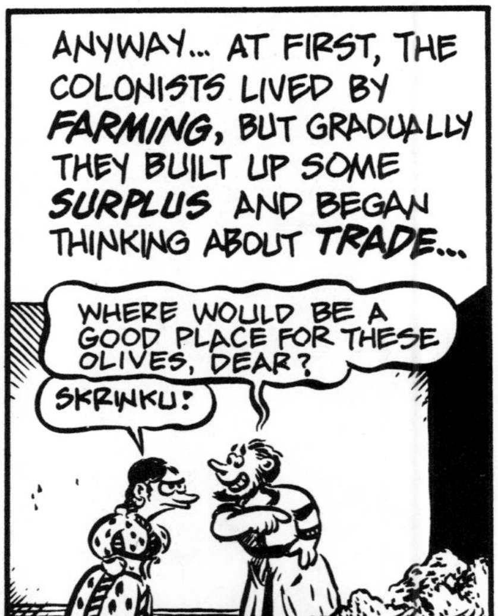

ANYWAY... AT FIRST, THE COLONISTS LIVED BY **FARMING**, BUT GRADUALLY THEY BUILT UP SOME **SURPLUS** AND BEGAN THINKING ABOUT **TRADE**...
WHERE WOULD BE A GOOD PLACE FOR THESE OLIVES, DEAR?
SKRINKU!

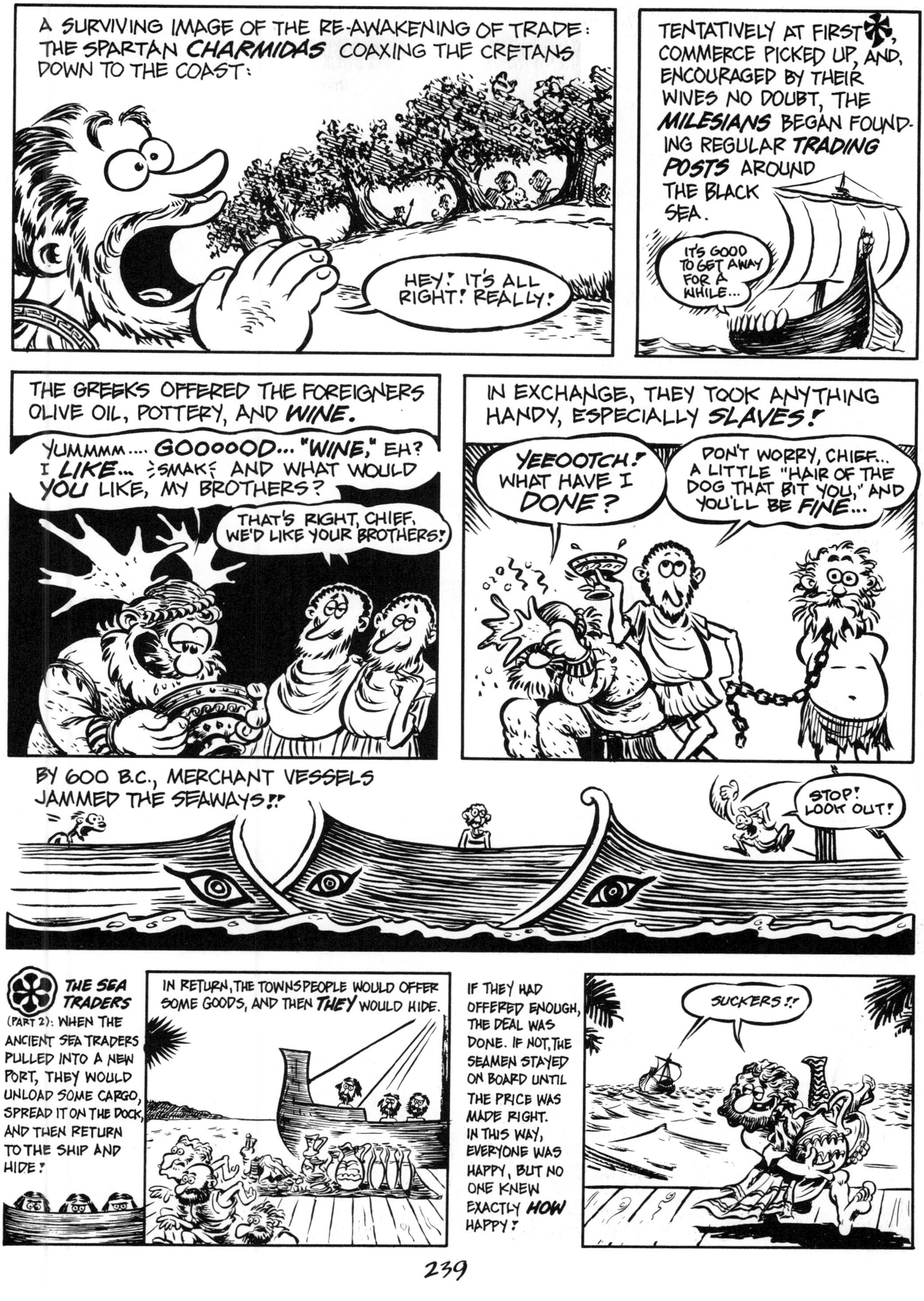
A SURVIVING IMAGE OF THE RE-AWAKENING OF TRADE: THE SPARTAN CHARMIDAS COAXING THE CRETANS DOWN TO THE COAST:
HEY! IT'S ALL RIGHT! REALLY!
TENTATIVELY AT FIRST, COMMERCE PICKED UP, AND, ENCOURAGED BY THEIR WIVES NO DOUBT, THE MILESIANS BEGAN FOUNDING REGULAR TRADING POSTS AROUND THE BLACK SEA.
IT'S GOOD TO GET AWAY FOR A WHILE...
THE GREEKS OFFERED THE FOREIGNERS OLIVE OIL, POTTERY, AND WINE.
YUMMMM.... GOOOOOD... "WINE," EH? I LIKE... SMAK AND WHAT WOULD YOU LIKE, MY BROTHERS?
THAT'S RIGHT, CHIEF, WE'D LIKE YOUR BROTHERS!
IN EXCHANGE, THEY TOOK ANYTHING HANDY, ESPECIALLY SLAVES!
YEEOOTCH! WHAT HAVE I DONE?
DON'T WORRY, CHIEF... A LITTLE "HAIR OF THE DOG THAT BIT YOU," AND YOU'LL BE FINE...
BY 600 B.C., MERCHANT VESSELS JAMMED THE SEAWAYS!!
STOP! LOOK OUT!
THE SEA TRADERS (PART 2): WHEN THE ANCIENT SEA TRADERS PULLED INTO A NEW PORT, THEY WOULD UNLOAD SOME CARGO, SPREAD IT ON THE DOCK, AND THEN RETURN TO THE SHIP AND HIDE!
IN RETURN, THE TOWNSPEOPLE WOULD OFFER SOME GOODS, AND THEN THEY WOULD HIDE.
IF THEY HAD OFFERED ENOUGH, THE DEAL WAS DONE. IF NOT, THE SEAMEN STAYED ON BOARD UNTIL THE PRICE WAS MADE RIGHT. IN THIS WAY, EVERYONE WAS HAPPY, BUT NO ONE KNEW EXACTLY HOW HAPPY!
SUCKERS!!

IN THE COURSE OF THEIR TRAVELS, THE GREEKS SAW WHAT *CIVILIZED LIFE* WAS: NOT MUCH LIKE THEIR OWN!?

I WANT IT!

THEY BEGAN MADLY *BORROWING* IDEAS FROM THE CIVILIZED PEOPLE ACROSS THE SEA, LIKE THE *PHOENICIANS.*

WE'VE ALREADY MET THESE "PHOENICIANS" IN VOL 4—AS THE COASTAL *CANAANITES* OF *TYRE:* PURPLE DYE-MAKERS ("PHOENIX"="PURPLE" IN GREEK), SOLOMON'S ARCHITECTS, JEZEBEL'S RELATIVES, BAAL-WORSHIPPERS, AND, THROUGHOUT THEIR LONG HISTORY, MERCHANT SEAMEN AND COLONIZERS.

YOU PEOPLE HAVE BEEN *AROUND!*

AROUND AFRICA, ACTUALLY!

THE GREEKS LIFTED PHOENICIAN RELIGIOUS IDEAS, SHIPBUILDING TRICKS, AND, MOST IMPORTANT, THEIR *ALPHABET.* ONCE AGAIN, GREECE WAS LITERATE! ✱

WHY, THIS IS SO SIMPLE, A *CHILD* COULD LEARN IT!

GOOD. ARE THERE ANY CHILDREN AROUND WHO CAN TEACH IT TO US?

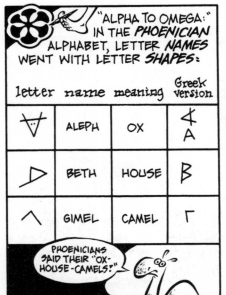

"ALPHA TO OMEGA:" IN THE *PHOENICIAN* ALPHABET, LETTER *NAMES* WENT WITH LETTER *SHAPES:*

letter	name	meaning	Greek version
∀	ALEPH	OX	A
▷	BETH	HOUSE	B
∧	GIMEL	CAMEL	Γ

PHOENICIANS SAID THEIR "OX-HOUSE-CAMELS!"

WHEN THE GREEKS BORROWED THE ALPHABET, THEY ALSO KEPT THE LETTER NAMES, EVEN THOUGH THESE WERE MEANINGLESS IN GREEK.

THIS ONE'S CALLED "ALPHA"—ZEUS KNOWS WHY...

TURN IT OVER... IT MIGHT LOOK LESS LIKE AN OX...

THE PHOENICIAN LETTERS, AS IN SEMITIC ALPHABETS TODAY, WERE ALL *CONSONANTS.* THE GREEKS FELT THE NEED FOR *VOWELS,* AND INVENTED THEM!

HMM... SOMETHING'S *MISSING* HERE...

O?

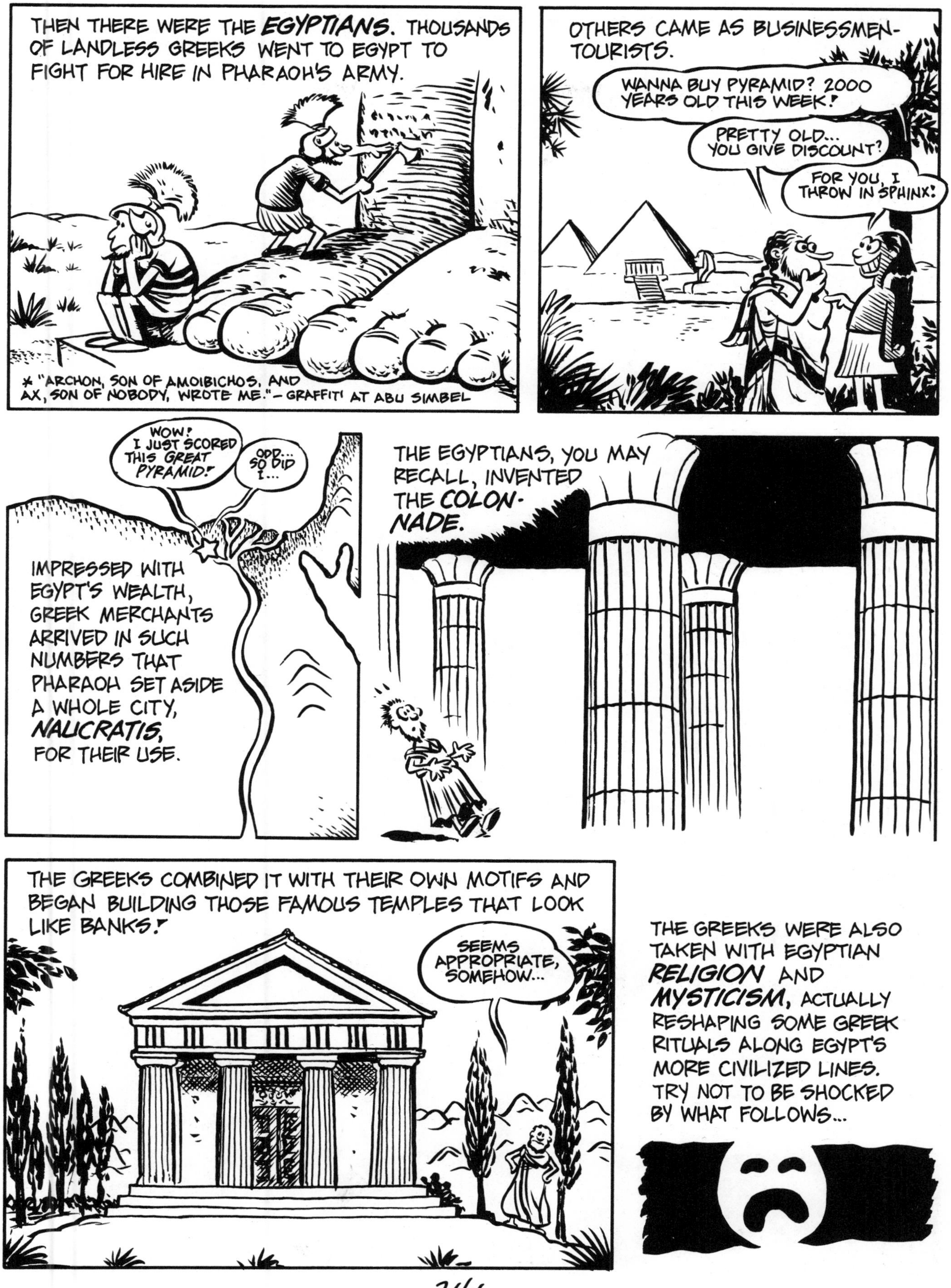
THEN THERE WERE THE EGYPTIANS. THOUSANDS OF LANDLESS GREEKS WENT TO EGYPT TO FIGHT FOR HIRE IN PHARAOH'S ARMY.
* "ARCHON, SON OF AMOIBICHOS, AND AX, SON OF NOBODY, WROTE ME." - GRAFFITI AT ABU SIMBEL
OTHERS CAME AS BUSINESSMEN-TOURISTS.
WANNA BUY PYRAMID? 2000 YEARS OLD THIS WEEK!
PRETTY OLD... YOU GIVE DISCOUNT?
FOR YOU, I THROW IN SPHINX!
WOW! I JUST SCORED THIS GREAT PYRAMID!
ODD... SO DID I...
IMPRESSED WITH EGYPT'S WEALTH, GREEK MERCHANTS ARRIVED IN SUCH NUMBERS THAT PHARAOH SET ASIDE A WHOLE CITY, NAUCRATIS, FOR THEIR USE.
THE EGYPTIANS, YOU MAY RECALL, INVENTED THE COLONNADE.
THE GREEKS COMBINED IT WITH THEIR OWN MOTIFS AND BEGAN BUILDING THOSE FAMOUS TEMPLES THAT LOOK LIKE BANKS!
SEEMS APPROPRIATE, SOMEHOW...
THE GREEKS WERE ALSO TAKEN WITH EGYPTIAN RELIGION AND MYSTICISM, ACTUALLY RESHAPING SOME GREEK RITUALS ALONG EGYPT'S MORE CIVILIZED LINES. TRY NOT TO BE SHOCKED BY WHAT FOLLOWS...

IN THE NORTH OF GREECE, SOME COUNTRY FOLK WORSHIPPED ***DIONYSOS***, GOD OF ***WINE***. THE STORY WENT THAT AS AN INFANT, DIONYSOS WAS ***TORN LIMB FROM LIMB***, THEN MIRACULOUSLY REBORN.

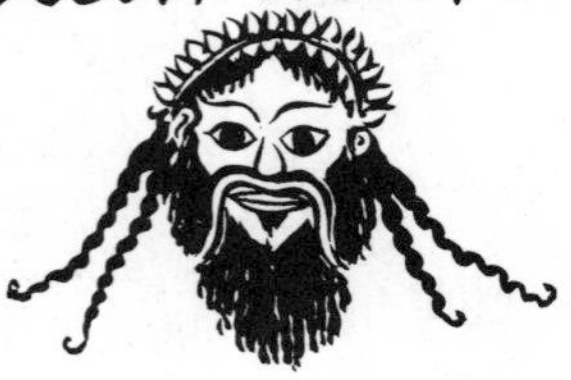

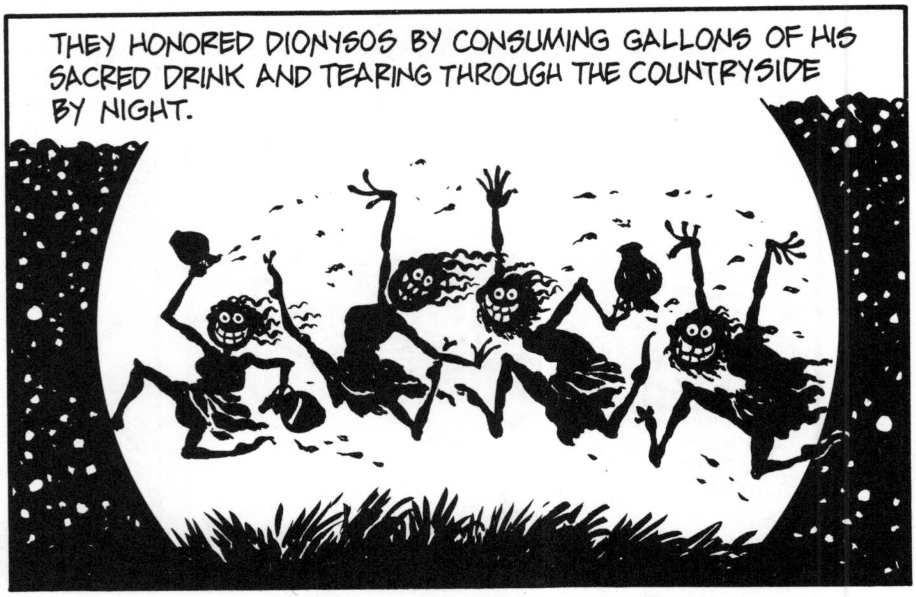
THEY HONORED DIONYSOS BY CONSUMING GALLONS OF HIS SACRED DRINK AND TEARING THROUGH THE COUNTRYSIDE BY NIGHT.

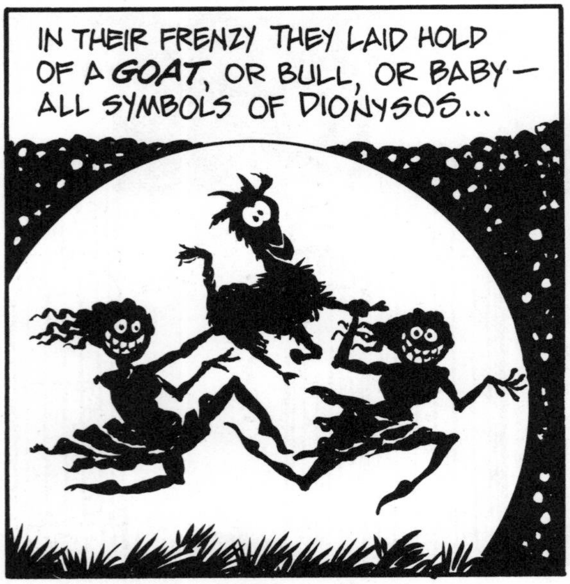
IN THEIR FRENZY THEY LAID HOLD OF A GOAT, OR BULL, OR BABY— ALL SYMBOLS OF DIONYSOS...

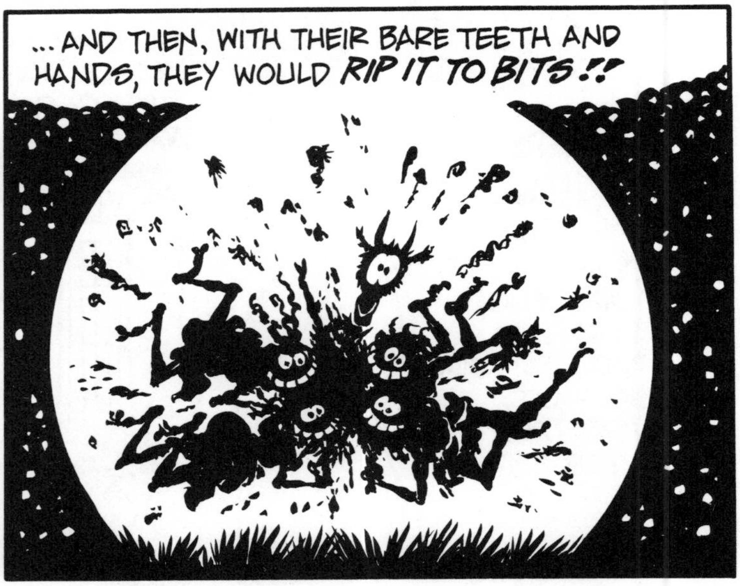
...AND THEN, WITH THEIR BARE TEETH AND HANDS, THEY WOULD RIP IT TO BITS!!

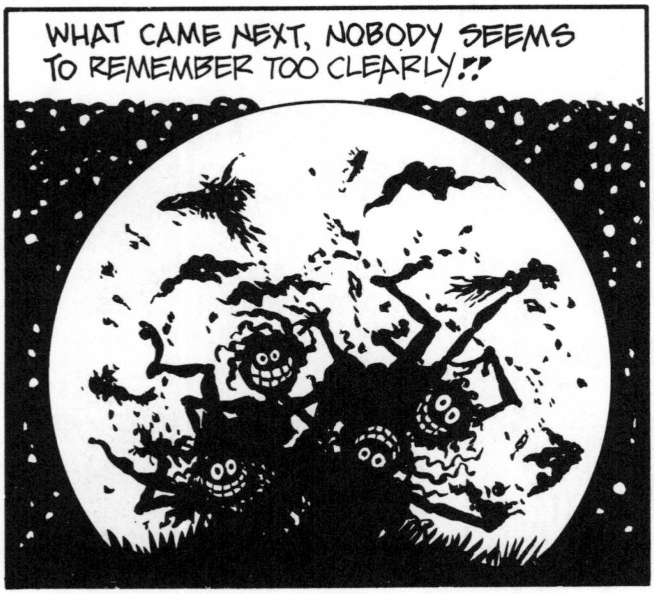
WHAT CAME NEXT, NOBODY SEEMS TO REMEMBER TOO CLEARLY!?

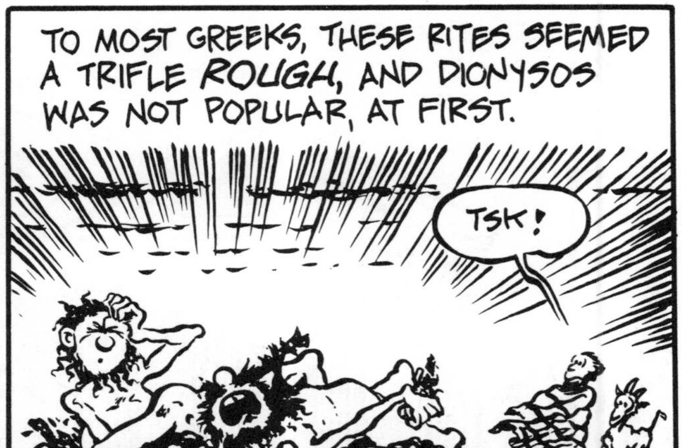
TO MOST GREEKS, THESE RITES SEEMED A TRIFLE ROUGH, AND DIONYSOS WAS NOT POPULAR, AT FIRST.
TSK!

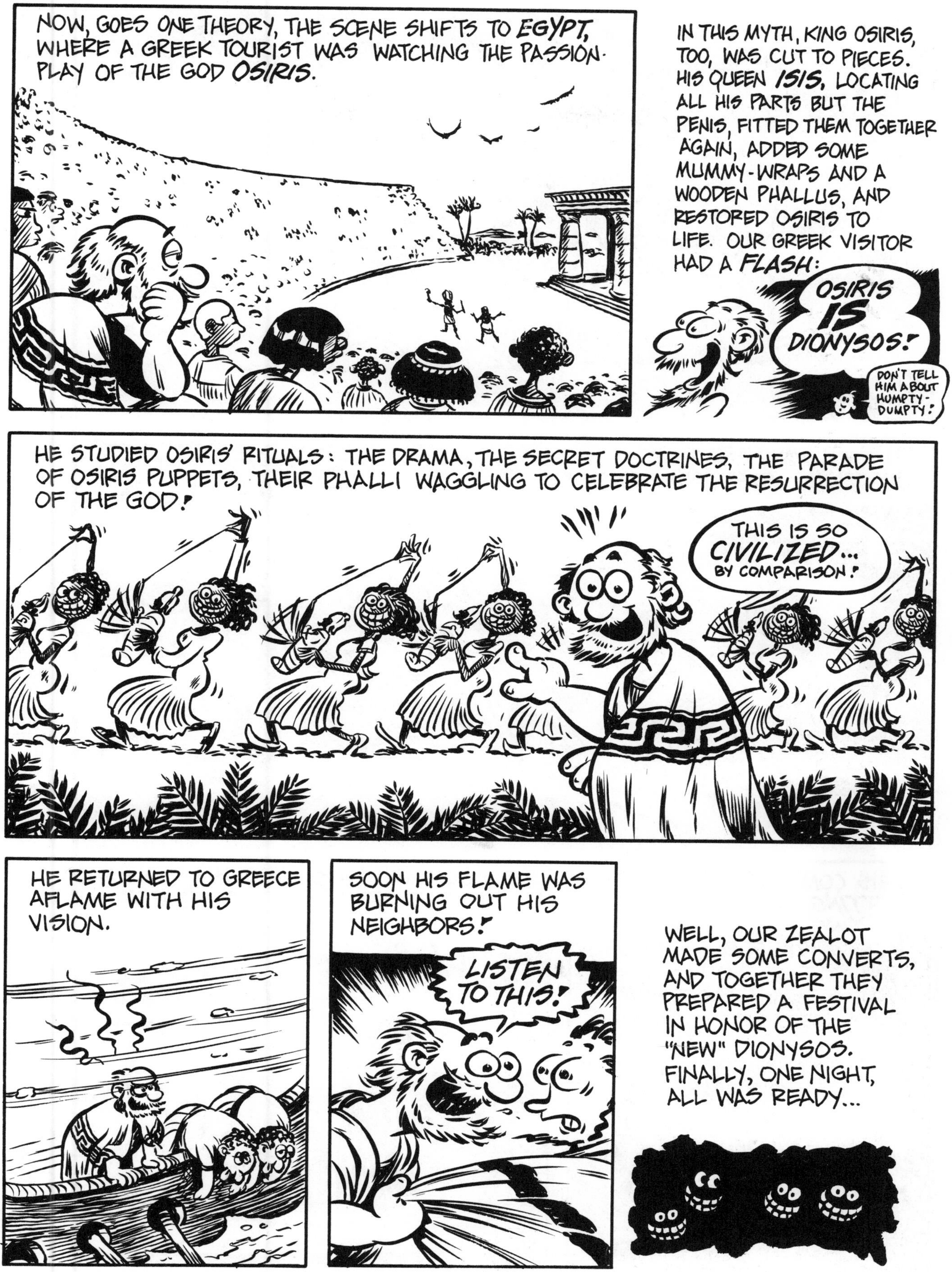
NOW, GOES ONE THEORY, THE SCENE SHIFTS TO *EGYPT*, WHERE A GREEK TOURIST WAS WATCHING THE PASSION-PLAY OF THE GOD *OSIRIS*.
IN THIS MYTH, KING OSIRIS, TOO, WAS CUT TO PIECES. HIS QUEEN *ISIS*, LOCATING ALL HIS PARTS BUT THE PENIS, FITTED THEM TOGETHER AGAIN, ADDED SOME MUMMY-WRAPS AND A WOODEN PHALLUS, AND RESTORED OSIRIS TO LIFE. OUR GREEK VISITOR HAD A *FLASH*:
OSIRIS IS DIONYSOS!
DON'T TELL HIM ABOUT HUMPTY-DUMPTY!
HE STUDIED OSIRIS' RITUALS: THE DRAMA, THE SECRET DOCTRINES, THE PARADE OF OSIRIS PUPPETS, THEIR PHALLI WAGGLING TO CELEBRATE THE RESURRECTION OF THE GOD!
THIS IS SO CIVILIZED... BY COMPARISON!
HE RETURNED TO GREECE AFLAME WITH HIS VISION.
SOON HIS FLAME WAS BURNING OUT HIS NEIGHBORS!
LISTEN TO THIS!
WELL, OUR ZEALOT MADE SOME CONVERTS, AND TOGETHER THEY PREPARED A FESTIVAL IN HONOR OF THE "NEW" DIONYSOS. FINALLY, ONE NIGHT, ALL WAS READY...

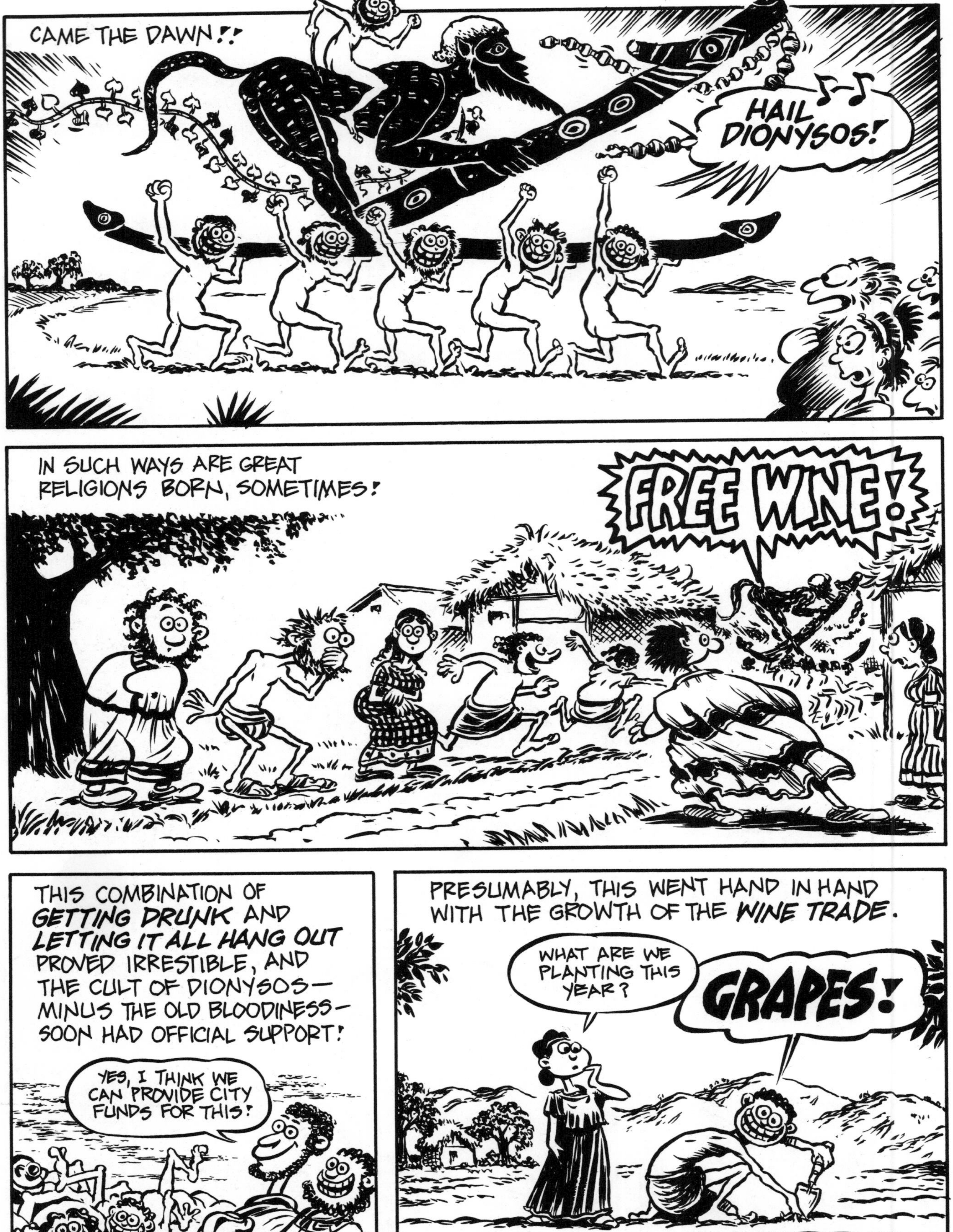
CAME THE DAWN!!
HAIL DIONYSOS!
IN SUCH WAYS ARE GREAT RELIGIONS BORN, SOMETIMES!
FREE WINE!
THIS COMBINATION OF ***GETTING DRUNK*** AND ***LETTING IT ALL HANG OUT*** PROVED IRRESTIBLE, AND THE CULT OF DIONYSOS— MINUS THE OLD BLOODINESS— SOON HAD OFFICIAL SUPPORT!
YES, I THINK WE CAN PROVIDE CITY FUNDS FOR THIS!
PRESUMABLY, THIS WENT HAND IN HAND WITH THE GROWTH OF THE ***WINE TRADE***.
WHAT ARE WE PLANTING THIS YEAR?
GRAPES!

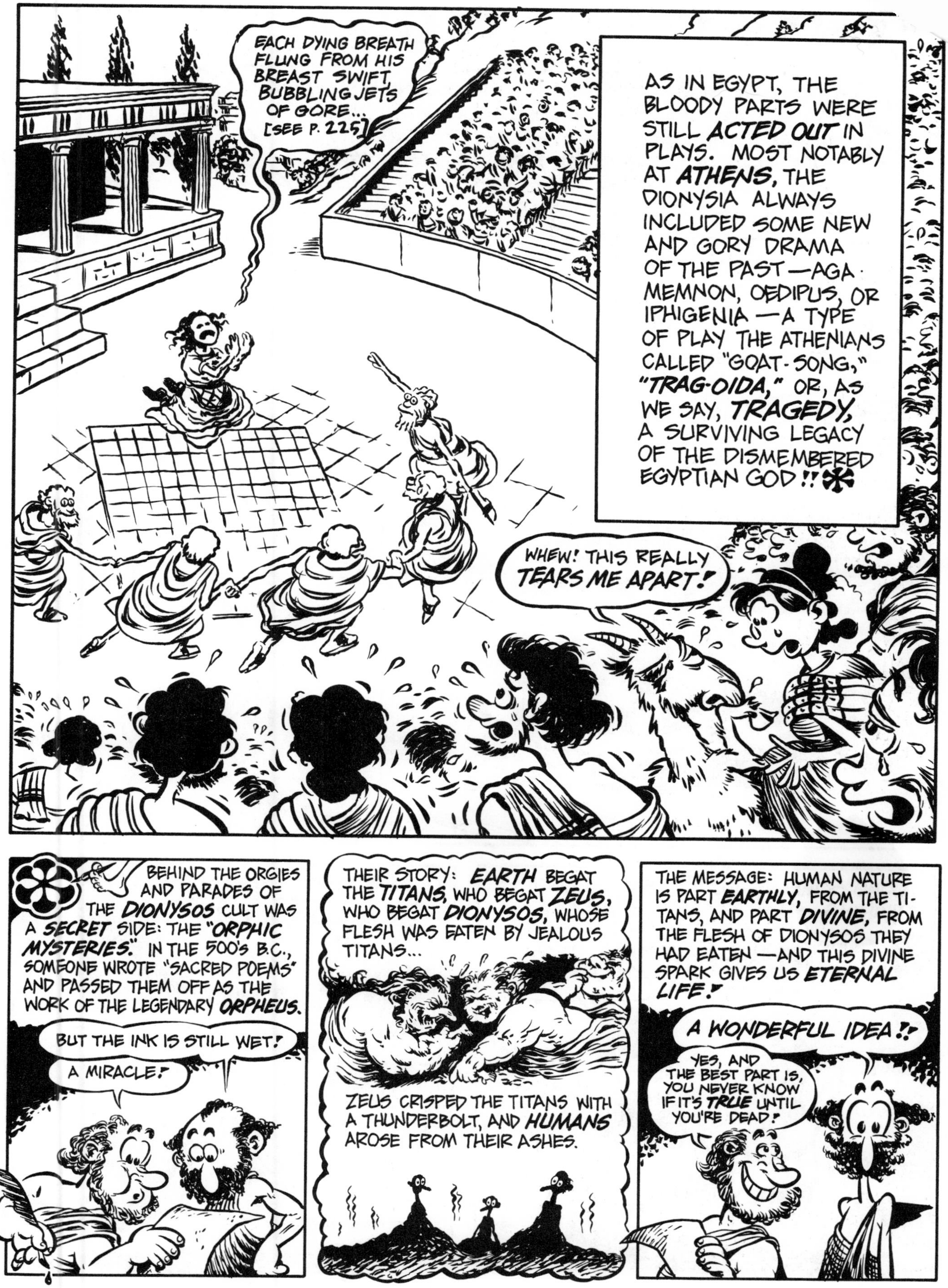
EACH DYING BREATH FLUNG FROM HIS BREAST SWIFT, BUBBLING JETS OF GORE... [SEE P. 225]
AS IN EGYPT, THE BLOODY PARTS WERE STILL ACTED OUT IN PLAYS. MOST NOTABLY AT ATHENS, THE DIONYSIA ALWAYS INCLUDED SOME NEW AND GORY DRAMA OF THE PAST—AGAMEMNON, OEDIPUS, OR IPHIGENIA—A TYPE OF PLAY THE ATHENIANS CALLED "GOAT-SONG," "TRAG-OIDA," OR, AS WE SAY, TRAGEDY, A SURVIVING LEGACY OF THE DISMEMBERED EGYPTIAN GOD!!
WHEW! THIS REALLY TEARS ME APART!
BEHIND THE ORGIES AND PARADES OF THE DIONYSOS CULT WAS A SECRET SIDE: THE "ORPHIC MYSTERIES." IN THE 500'S B.C., SOMEONE WROTE "SACRED POEMS" AND PASSED THEM OFF AS THE WORK OF THE LEGENDARY ORPHEUS.
BUT THE INK IS STILL WET!
A MIRACLE!
THEIR STORY: EARTH BEGAT THE TITANS, WHO BEGAT ZEUS, WHO BEGAT DIONYSOS, WHOSE FLESH WAS EATEN BY JEALOUS TITANS...
ZEUS CRISPED THE TITANS WITH A THUNDERBOLT, AND HUMANS AROSE FROM THEIR ASHES.
THE MESSAGE: HUMAN NATURE IS PART EARTHLY, FROM THE TITANS, AND PART DIVINE, FROM THE FLESH OF DIONYSOS THEY HAD EATEN—AND THIS DIVINE SPARK GIVES US ETERNAL LIFE!
A WONDERFUL IDEA!!
YES, AND THE BEST PART IS, YOU NEVER KNOW IF IT'S TRUE UNTIL YOU'RE DEAD!

"LET'S BE RATIONAL"

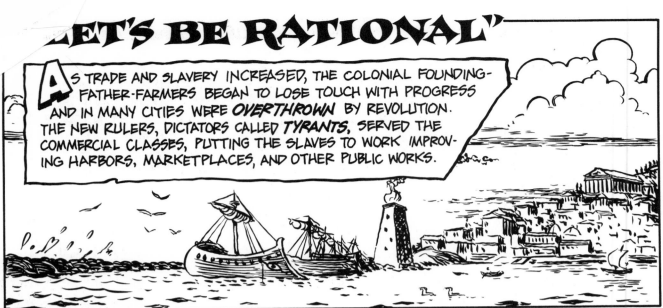

AS TRADE AND SLAVERY INCREASED, THE COLONIAL FOUNDING-FATHER-FARMERS BEGAN TO LOSE TOUCH WITH PROGRESS AND IN MANY CITIES WERE *OVERTHROWN* BY REVOLUTION. THE NEW RULERS, DICTATORS CALLED *TYRANTS*, SERVED THE COMMERCIAL CLASSES, PUTTING THE SLAVES TO WORK IMPROVING HARBORS, MARKETPLACES, AND OTHER PUBLIC WORKS.

THEN, BEGINNING IN *IONIA*, A FUNNY THING HAPPENED! THE TYRANT WAS *THRASYBULOS* OF MILETOS...

HM... HARBOR'S FINISHED... SO'S THE PUBLIC MARKET... BUSINESS IS BOOMING...

SNERTZL

MY PALACE COULDN'T BE POSHER... HOT AND COLD RUNNING WINE... LIVE MUZAK...

SO WHAT'S TO BUY NEXT? I WANT SOMETHING... REALLY... USELESS...

I KNOW! I'LL GET A PHILOSOPHER!!

HIRING SOMEONE JUST TO SIT AROUND THINKING — NOW *THERE* WAS AN IDEA!

WHAT SHOULD I THINK ABOUT?

ANYTHING YOU LIKE!

IT MUST HAVE BEEN HARD AT FIRST!

A *RAISE????* IS THAT ALL YOU CAN THINK OF?! OUT!

OW! CENSORSHIP REARS ITS UGLY FOOT!

THE FIRST SUCCESSFUL THINKER AT MILETOS WAS **THALES** (640-546 B.C.), A PHOENICIAN BY DESCENT.

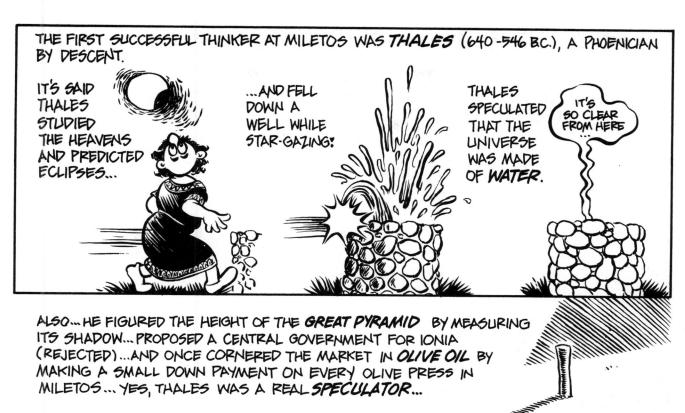

IT'S SAID THALES STUDIED THE HEAVENS AND PREDICTED ECLIPSES...

...AND FELL DOWN A WELL WHILE STAR-GAZING!

THALES SPECULATED THAT THE UNIVERSE WAS MADE OF **WATER**.

IT'S SO CLEAR FROM HERE...

ALSO... HE FIGURED THE HEIGHT OF THE **GREAT PYRAMID** BY MEASURING ITS SHADOW... PROPOSED A CENTRAL GOVERNMENT FOR IONIA (REJECTED)... AND ONCE CORNERED THE MARKET IN **OLIVE OIL** BY MAKING A SMALL DOWN PAYMENT ON EVERY OLIVE PRESS IN MILETOS... YES, THALES WAS A REAL **SPECULATOR**...

THALES' STUDENT **ANAXIMANDER** REJECTED THE IDEA THAT EVERYTHING WAS WATER.

YER ALL WET, TEACH!

HE SUGGESTED THAT THE EARTH HAD **EVOLVED** AND PEOPLE WERE DESCENDED FROM **FISH!**

COUSIN! YOU LOOKED AT FOSSILS!

ANAXIMANDER ALSO BROUGHT THE **SUN DIAL**, A BABYLONIAN GADGET, TO GREECE.

WHAT WAS HAPPENING HERE? THESE IONIANS WERE THEORIZING ABOUT THE COSMOS **WITHOUT MENTIONING THE GODS!?** THIS WAS NOVEL!

"IF ANIMALS, LIKE MEN, COULD PAINT AND MAKE THINGS, HORSES AND OXEN WOULD FASHION THE GODS IN THEIR OWN IMAGE."

SAID ANAXIMANDER'S CONTEMPORARY XENOPHANES

THAT'S NOT TO SAY THE EARLY PHILOSOPHERS WEREN'T RELIGIOUS! CONSIDER **PYTHAGORAS**...

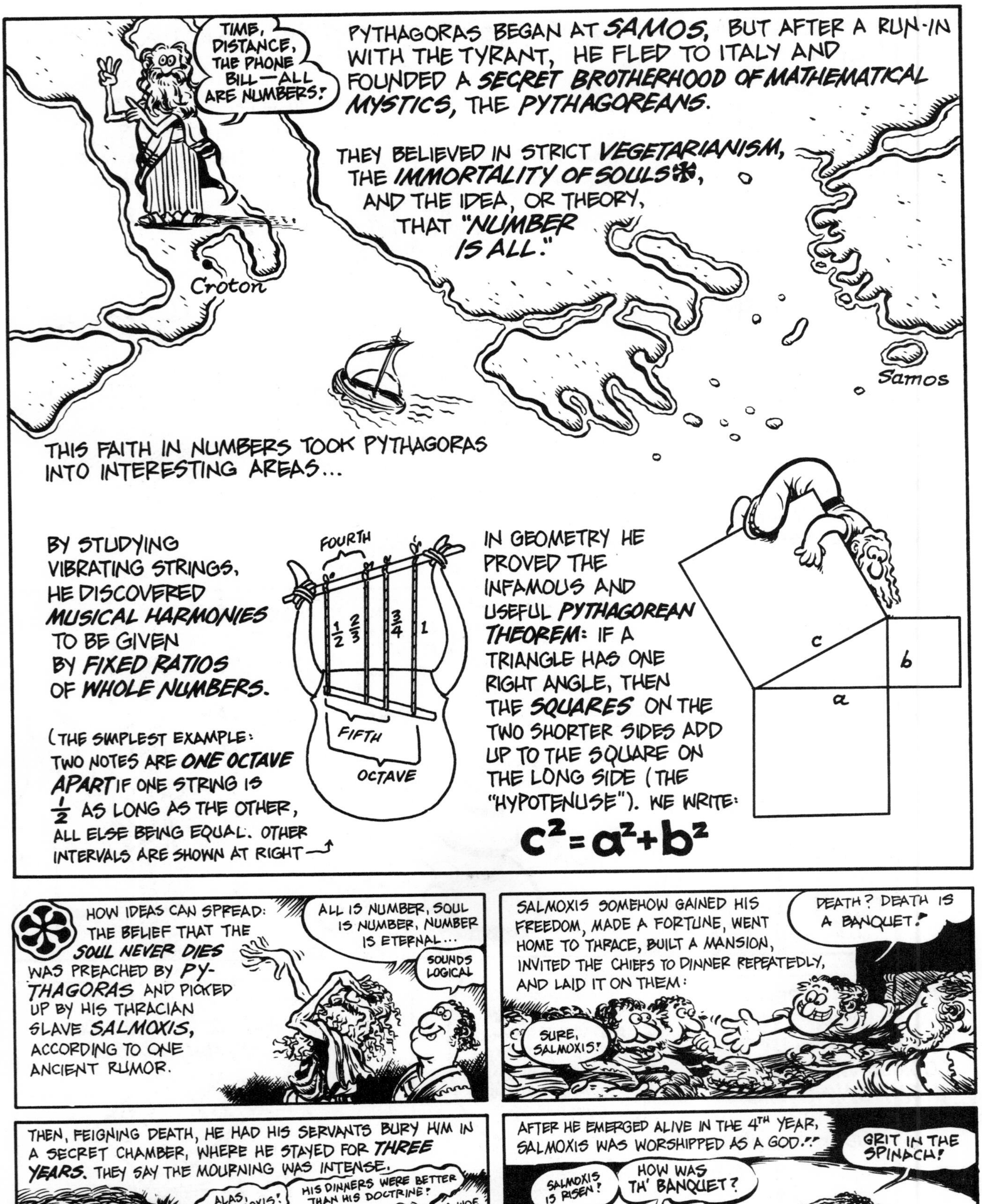
TIME, DISTANCE, THE PHONE BILL—ALL ARE NUMBERS!
PYTHAGORAS BEGAN AT SAMOS, BUT AFTER A RUN-IN WITH THE TYRANT, HE FLED TO ITALY AND FOUNDED A SECRET BROTHERHOOD OF MATHEMATICAL MYSTICS, THE PYTHAGOREANS.
THEY BELIEVED IN STRICT VEGETARIANISM, THE IMMORTALITY OF SOULS✻, AND THE IDEA, OR THEORY, THAT "NUMBER IS ALL."
Croton
Samos
THIS FAITH IN NUMBERS TOOK PYTHAGORAS INTO INTERESTING AREAS...
BY STUDYING VIBRATING STRINGS, HE DISCOVERED MUSICAL HARMONIES TO BE GIVEN BY FIXED RATIOS OF WHOLE NUMBERS.
(THE SIMPLEST EXAMPLE: TWO NOTES ARE ONE OCTAVE APART IF ONE STRING IS 1/2 AS LONG AS THE OTHER, ALL ELSE BEING EQUAL. OTHER INTERVALS ARE SHOWN AT RIGHT
FOURTH
1/2 2/3 3/4 1
FIFTH
OCTAVE
IN GEOMETRY HE PROVED THE INFAMOUS AND USEFUL PYTHAGOREAN THEOREM: IF A TRIANGLE HAS ONE RIGHT ANGLE, THEN THE SQUARES ON THE TWO SHORTER SIDES ADD UP TO THE SQUARE ON THE LONG SIDE (THE "HYPOTENUSE"). WE WRITE:
$c^2 = a^2 + b^2$
c
b
a
✻ HOW IDEAS CAN SPREAD: THE BELIEF THAT THE SOUL NEVER DIES WAS PREACHED BY PYTHAGORAS AND PICKED UP BY HIS THRACIAN SLAVE SALMOXIS, ACCORDING TO ONE ANCIENT RUMOR.
ALL IS NUMBER, SOUL IS NUMBER, NUMBER IS ETERNAL...
SOUNDS LOGICAL
SALMOXIS SOMEHOW GAINED HIS FREEDOM, MADE A FORTUNE, WENT HOME TO THRACE, BUILT A MANSION, INVITED THE CHIEFS TO DINNER REPEATEDLY, AND LAID IT ON THEM:
DEATH? DEATH IS A BANQUET!
SURE, SALMOXIS!
THEN, FEIGNING DEATH, HE HAD HIS SERVANTS BURY HIM IN A SECRET CHAMBER, WHERE HE STAYED FOR THREE YEARS. THEY SAY THE MOURNING WAS INTENSE.
ALAS, SALMOXIS!
HIS DINNERS WERE BETTER THAN HIS DOCTRINE!
O WOE O WOE!
AFTER HE EMERGED ALIVE IN THE 4TH YEAR, SALMOXIS WAS WORSHIPPED AS A GOD!!
SALMOXIS IS RISEN!
HOW WAS TH' BANQUET?
GRIT IN THE SPINACH!

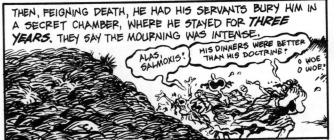

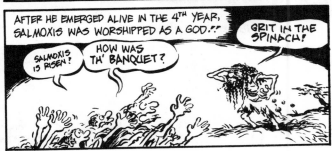

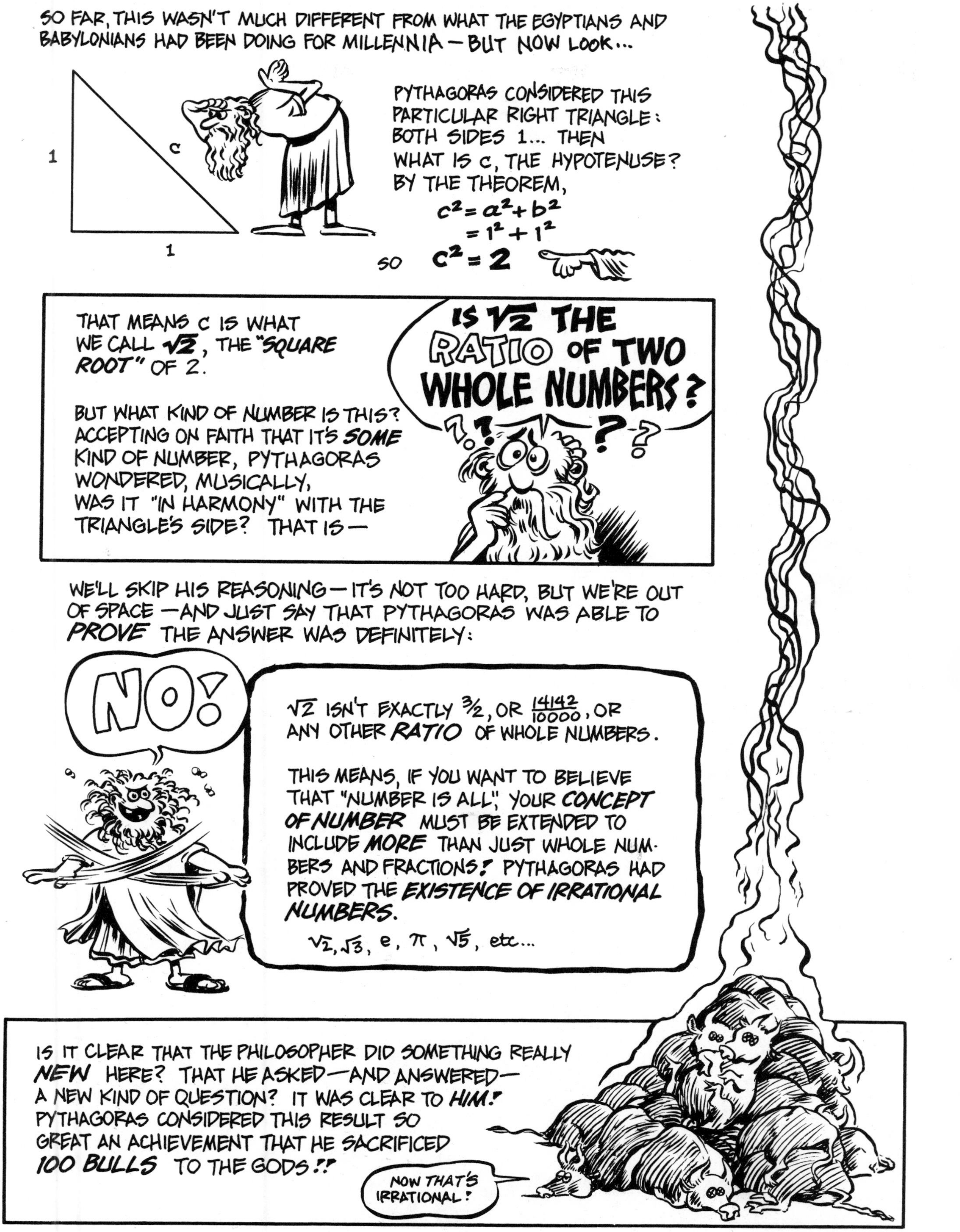
SO FAR, THIS WASN'T MUCH DIFFERENT FROM WHAT THE EGYPTIANS AND BABYLONIANS HAD BEEN DOING FOR MILLENNIA — BUT NOW LOOK...
1
c
1
PYTHAGORAS CONSIDERED THIS PARTICULAR RIGHT TRIANGLE: BOTH SIDES 1... THEN WHAT IS c, THE HYPOTENUSE? BY THE THEOREM,
$c^2 = a^2 + b^2$
$= 1^2 + 1^2$
SO $c^2 = 2$
THAT MEANS c IS WHAT WE CALL $\sqrt{2}$, THE "SQUARE ROOT" OF 2.
BUT WHAT KIND OF NUMBER IS THIS? ACCEPTING ON FAITH THAT IT'S SOME KIND OF NUMBER, PYTHAGORAS WONDERED, MUSICALLY, WAS IT "IN HARMONY" WITH THE TRIANGLE'S SIDE? THAT IS—
IS $\sqrt{2}$ THE RATIO OF TWO WHOLE NUMBERS?
WE'LL SKIP HIS REASONING — IT'S NOT TOO HARD, BUT WE'RE OUT OF SPACE — AND JUST SAY THAT PYTHAGORAS WAS ABLE TO PROVE THE ANSWER WAS DEFINITELY:
NO!
$\sqrt{2}$ ISN'T EXACTLY $3/2$, OR $\frac{14142}{10000}$, OR ANY OTHER RATIO OF WHOLE NUMBERS.
THIS MEANS, IF YOU WANT TO BELIEVE THAT "NUMBER IS ALL," YOUR CONCEPT OF NUMBER MUST BE EXTENDED TO INCLUDE MORE THAN JUST WHOLE NUMBERS AND FRACTIONS! PYTHAGORAS HAD PROVED THE EXISTENCE OF IRRATIONAL NUMBERS.
$\sqrt{2}$, $\sqrt{3}$, e, π, $\sqrt{5}$, etc...
IS IT CLEAR THAT THE PHILOSOPHER DID SOMETHING REALLY NEW HERE? THAT HE ASKED — AND ANSWERED — A NEW KIND OF QUESTION? IT WAS CLEAR TO HIM! PYTHAGORAS CONSIDERED THIS RESULT SO GREAT AN ACHIEVEMENT THAT HE SACRIFICED 100 BULLS TO THE GODS!!
NOW THAT'S IRRATIONAL!

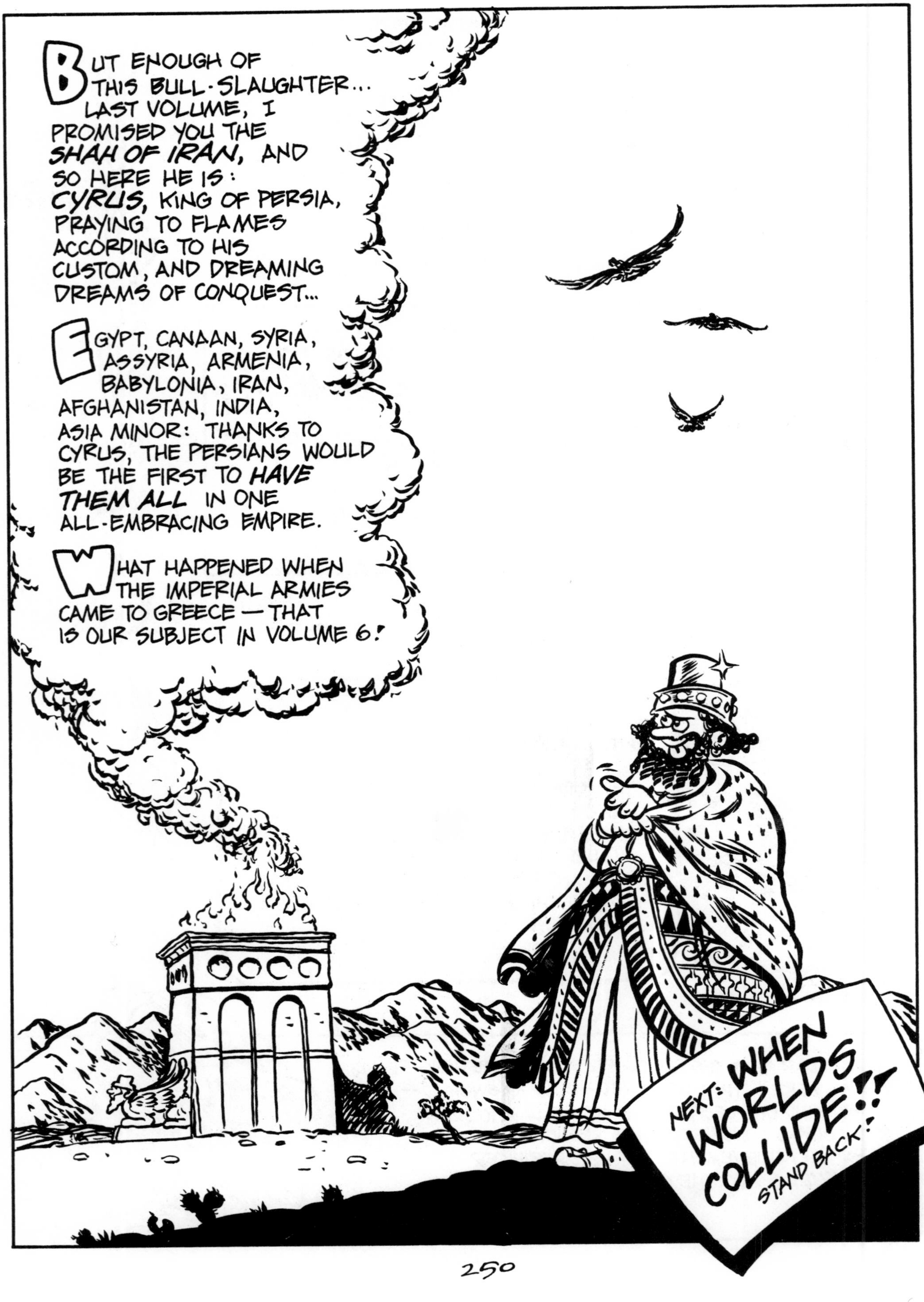
BUT ENOUGH OF THIS BULL-SLAUGHTER... LAST VOLUME, I PROMISED YOU THE SHAH OF IRAN, AND SO HERE HE IS: CYRUS, KING OF PERSIA, PRAYING TO FLAMES ACCORDING TO HIS CUSTOM, AND DREAMING DREAMS OF CONQUEST...
EGYPT, CANAAN, SYRIA, ASSYRIA, ARMENIA, BABYLONIA, IRAN, AFGHANISTAN, INDIA, ASIA MINOR: THANKS TO CYRUS, THE PERSIANS WOULD BE THE FIRST TO HAVE THEM ALL IN ONE ALL-EMBRACING EMPIRE.
WHAT HAPPENED WHEN THE IMPERIAL ARMIES CAME TO GREECE — THAT IS OUR SUBJECT IN VOLUME 6!
NEXT: WHEN WORLDS COLLIDE!!
STAND BACK!

IN THE LAST VOLUME WE MET THE GREEKS: THEIR LEGENDS, CUSTOMS, AND THOUGHT! NOW WE FOCUS ON THEIR GREAT WAR WITH THE *PERSIAN EMPIRE!*

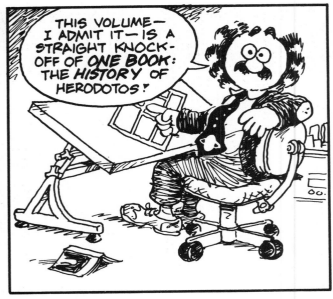

THIS VOLUME— I ADMIT IT— IS A STRAIGHT KNOCK-OFF OF *ONE BOOK:* THE *HISTORY* OF HERODOTOS!

NOWADAYS HISTORIANS *SNEER* AT HERODOTOS!

"THE FATHER OF LIES," THEY CALL HIM!

¡IDIOTS!

WHO AMONG THEM CAN MATCH HIS WEALTH OF DETAIL, HIS UNDERSTANDING OF CHARACTER, HIS LITERARY GIFTS, AND HIS ABILITY TO GIVE THE *FEEL* OF AN ERA WHEN *ORACLES* AND *DREAMS* STILL HAD POWER IN THE WORLD ??

AND THE *BEST* THING ABOUT HERODOTOS: HE MAKES UP ALL THE *DIALOG!*

A HISTORIAN AFTER MY OWN HEART!

SO LET'S RETURN TO A TIME WHEN NEARLY EVERYONE BELIEVED IN PROPHECY AND MAGIC— AND I *DON'T* MEAN 1967...

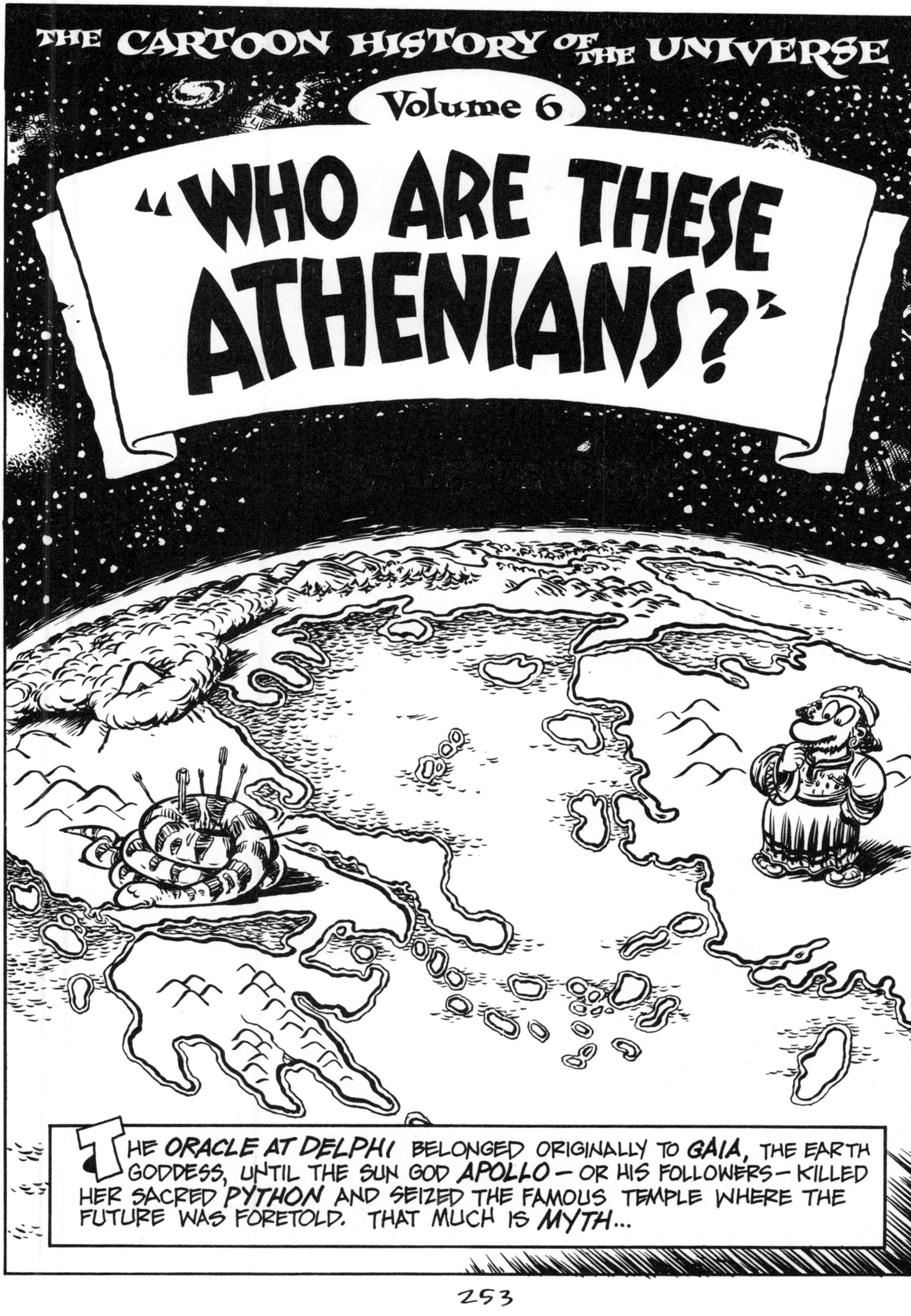
THE CARTOON HISTORY OF THE UNIVERSE
Volume 6
"WHO ARE THESE ATHENIANS?"
THE ORACLE AT DELPHI BELONGED ORIGINALLY TO GAIA, THE EARTH GODDESS, UNTIL THE SUN GOD APOLLO – OR HIS FOLLOWERS – KILLED HER SACRED PYTHON AND SEIZED THE FAMOUS TEMPLE WHERE THE FUTURE WAS FORETOLD. THAT MUCH IS MYTH...

THE RICHES OF CROESOS

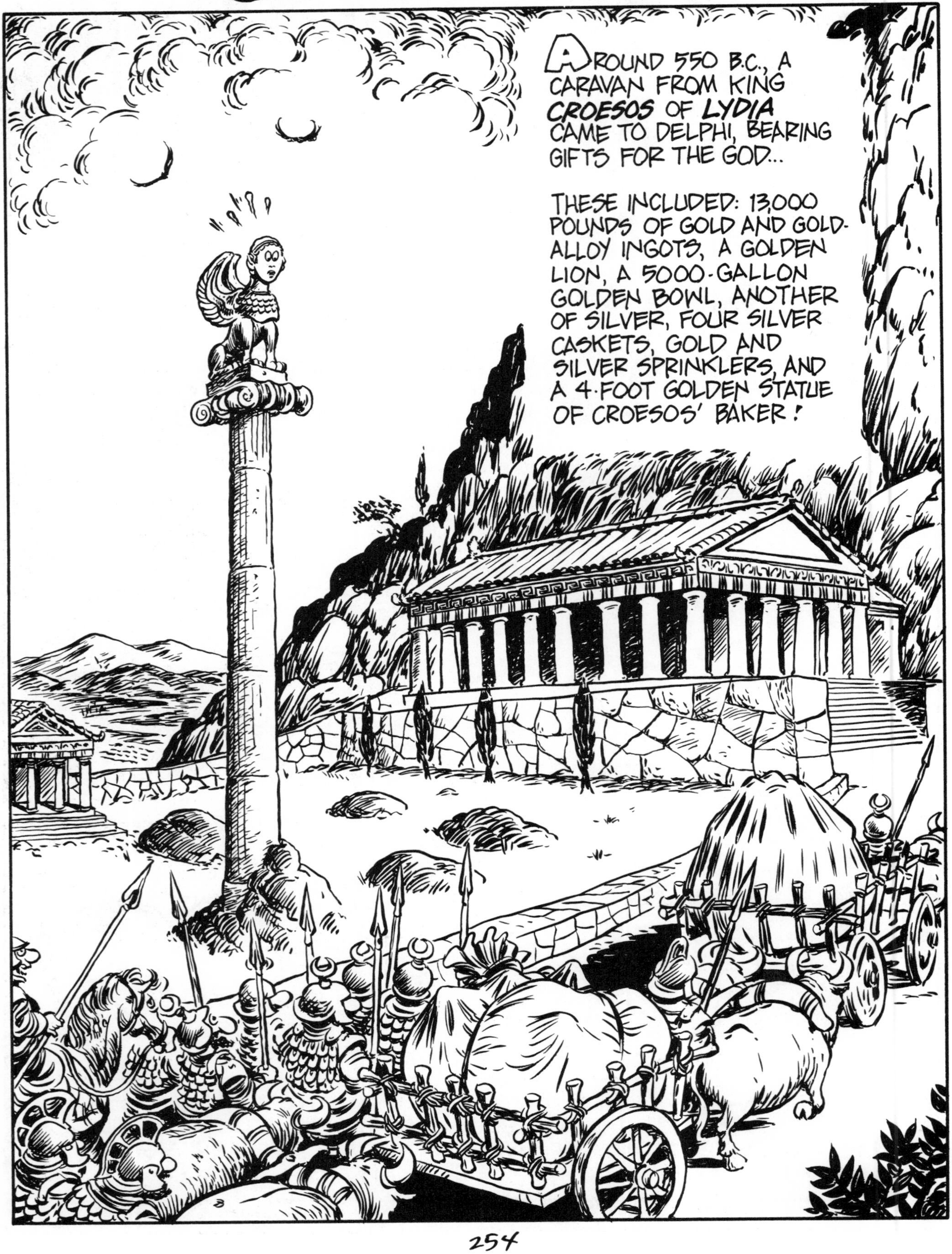
AROUND 550 B.C., A CARAVAN FROM KING CROESOS OF LYDIA CAME TO DELPHI, BEARING GIFTS FOR THE GOD...
THESE INCLUDED: 13,000 POUNDS OF GOLD AND GOLD-ALLOY INGOTS, A GOLDEN LION, A 5000-GALLON GOLDEN BOWL, ANOTHER OF SILVER, FOUR SILVER CASKETS, GOLD AND SILVER SPRINKLERS, AND A 4-FOOT GOLDEN STATUE OF CROESOS' BAKER!

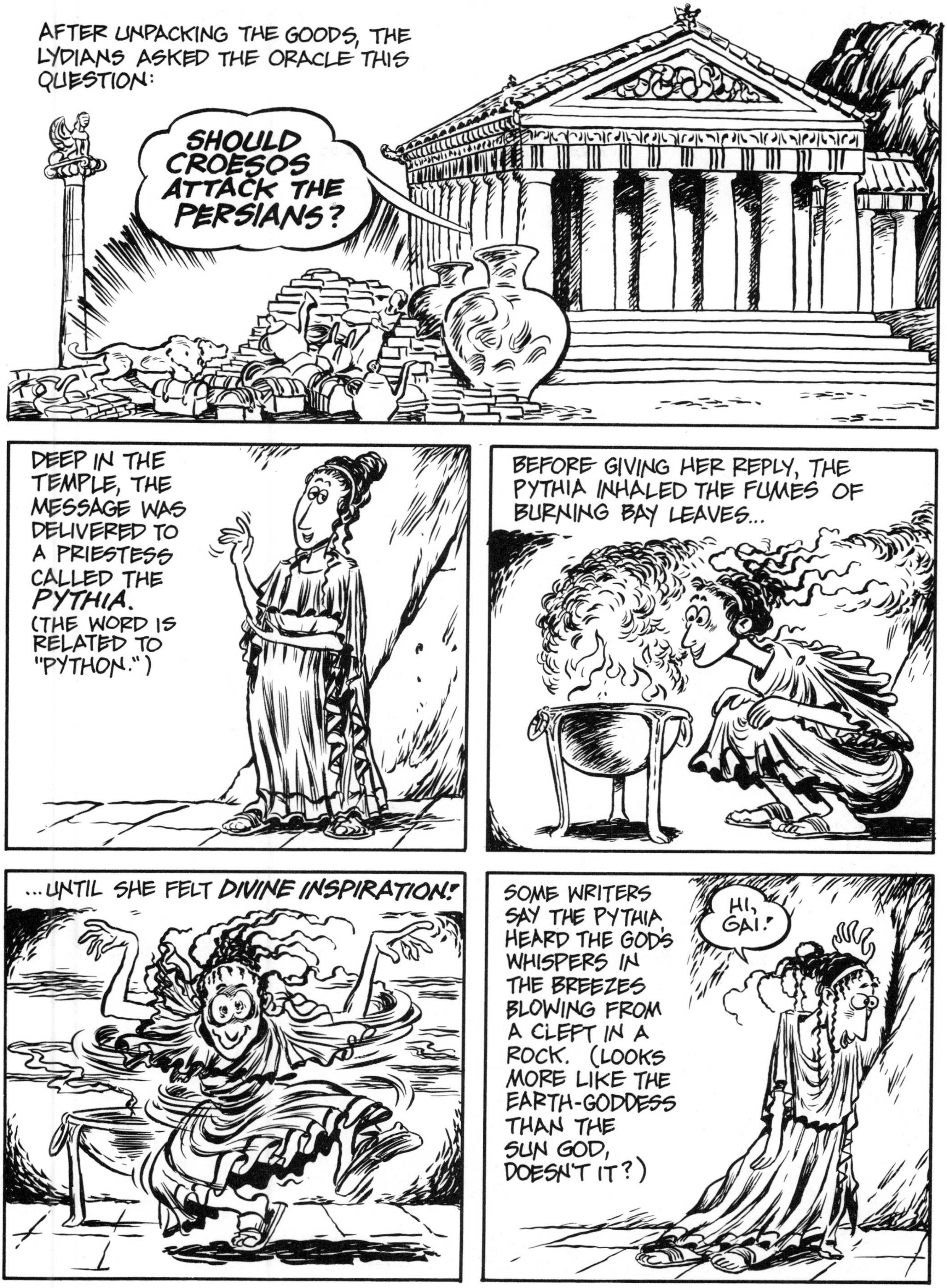
AFTER UNPACKING THE GOODS, THE LYDIANS ASKED THE ORACLE THIS QUESTION:
SHOULD CROESOS ATTACK THE PERSIANS?
DEEP IN THE TEMPLE, THE MESSAGE WAS DELIVERED TO A PRIESTESS CALLED THE *PYTHIA*. (THE WORD IS RELATED TO "PYTHON.")
BEFORE GIVING HER REPLY, THE PYTHIA INHALED THE FUMES OF BURNING BAY LEAVES...
...UNTIL SHE FELT *DIVINE INSPIRATION!*
SOME WRITERS SAY THE PYTHIA HEARD THE GOD'S WHISPERS IN THE BREEZES BLOWING FROM A CLEFT IN A ROCK. (LOOKS MORE LIKE THE EARTH-GODDESS THAN THE SUN GOD, DOESN'T IT?)
HI, GAI!

WHAT'S WEALTH WITHOUT SECURITY?

MEANWHILE, BACK IN LYDIA, CROESOS WAS WORRIED! LORD OF WESTERN ASIA MINOR, INCLUDING THE GREEK CITIES OF *IONIA*, THIS KING WAS *RICH*: HIS FAMILY ✱ HAD *INVENTED* COINAGE...

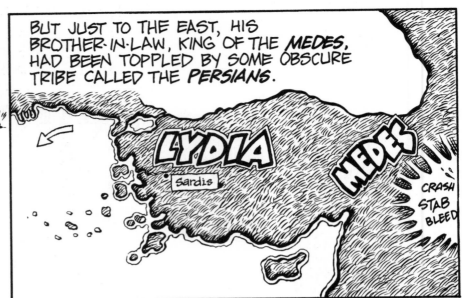

BUT JUST TO THE EAST, HIS BROTHER-IN-LAW, KING OF THE *MEDES*, HAD BEEN TOPPLED BY SOME OBSCURE TRIBE CALLED THE *PERSIANS*.

LYDIA

Sardis

MEDES

CRASH STAB BLEED

CROESOS OWED IT TO HIS BROTHER-IN-LAW TO RETALIATE, BUT HE HAD A LOT TO LOSE, AND SO HE SENT TO DELPHI — AND NERVOUSLY WAITED...

SURE HOPE THE TREASURE ARRIVED IN ONE PIECE...

THE PIRATES HAVE BEEN JUST *AWFUL* LATELY...

WHY DOES EVERYTHING HAVE TO TAKE SIX MONTHS?

BITE

LONG BEFORE COINAGE WAS INVENTED, PEOPLE ALREADY USED GOLD AND SILVER AS A MEDIUM OF EXCHANGE. PRECIOUS METALS ARE RARE AND DURABLE, AND THEY MAKE PRETTY JEWELRY.

BUT HOW TO KNOW IF GOLD WAS GENUINE? YOU HAD TO BITE IT! (PURE GOLD IS SOFT.)

NOW ALL MY CROWNS ARE DENTED!

SO — AROUND 700 B.C., THE LYDIAN KINGS BEGAN STAMPING LUMPS OF GOLD WITH THE ROYAL SEAL, AS A GUARANTEE OF PURITY: THE FIRST COINS.

TODAY OUR COINS ARE BASE ALLOY...OUR DOLLARS ARE PAPER... MONEY MAKES UGLY JEWELRY... ALL THAT'S LEFT IS THE GOVERNMENT GUARANTEE— BUT OF *WHAT*??!

A GUARANTEE TO PRINT MORE MONEY...

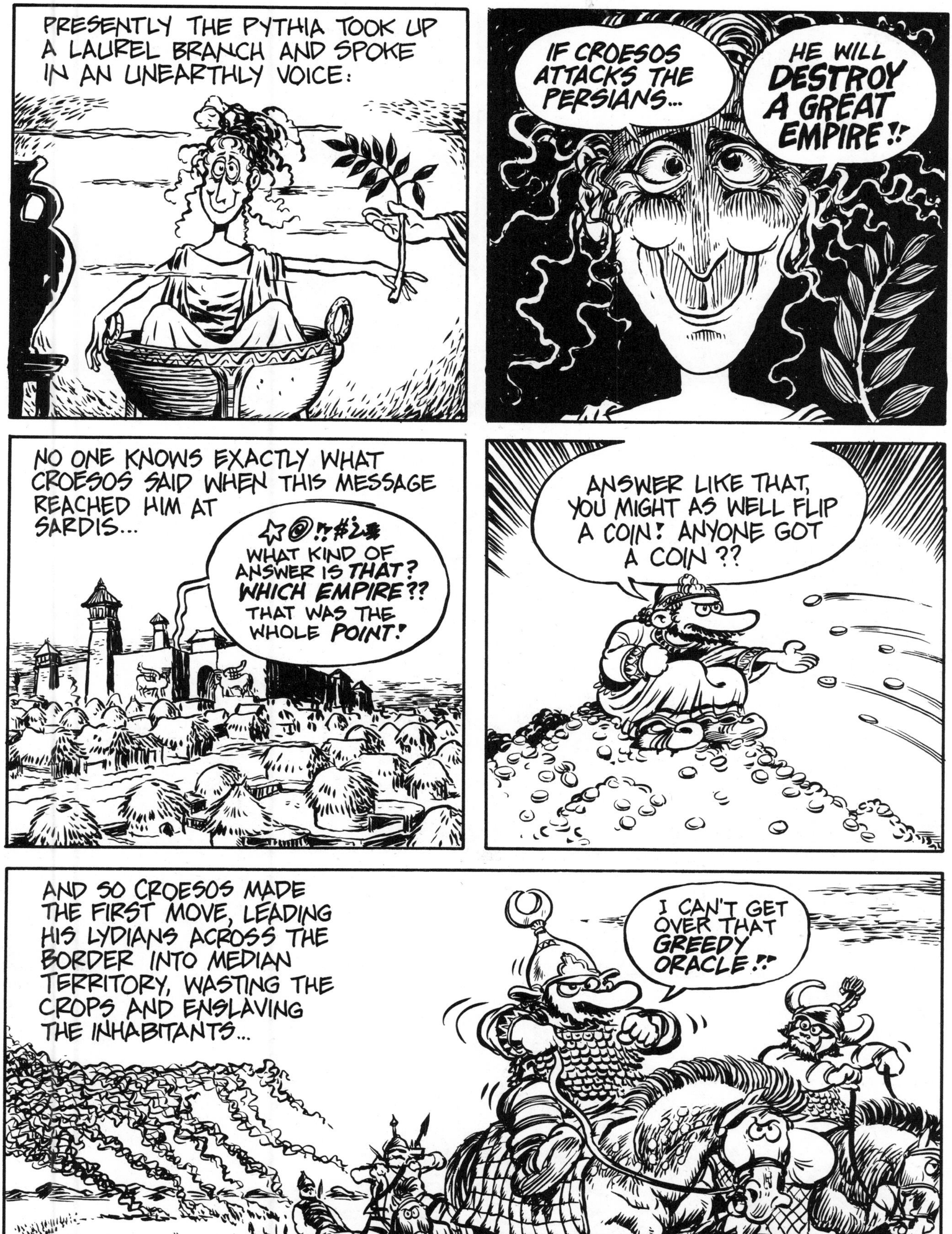
PRESENTLY THE PYTHIA TOOK UP A LAUREL BRANCH AND SPOKE IN AN UNEARTHLY VOICE:
IF CROESOS ATTACKS THE PERSIANS...
HE WILL DESTROY A GREAT EMPIRE!!
NO ONE KNOWS EXACTLY WHAT CROESOS SAID WHEN THIS MESSAGE REACHED HIM AT SARDIS...
WHAT KIND OF ANSWER IS THAT? WHICH EMPIRE?? THAT WAS THE WHOLE POINT!
ANSWER LIKE THAT, YOU MIGHT AS WELL FLIP A COIN! ANYONE GOT A COIN??
AND SO CROESOS MADE THE FIRST MOVE, LEADING HIS LYDIANS ACROSS THE BORDER INTO MEDIAN TERRITORY, WASTING THE CROPS AND ENSLAVING THE INHABITANTS...
I CAN'T GET OVER THAT GREEDY ORACLE!!

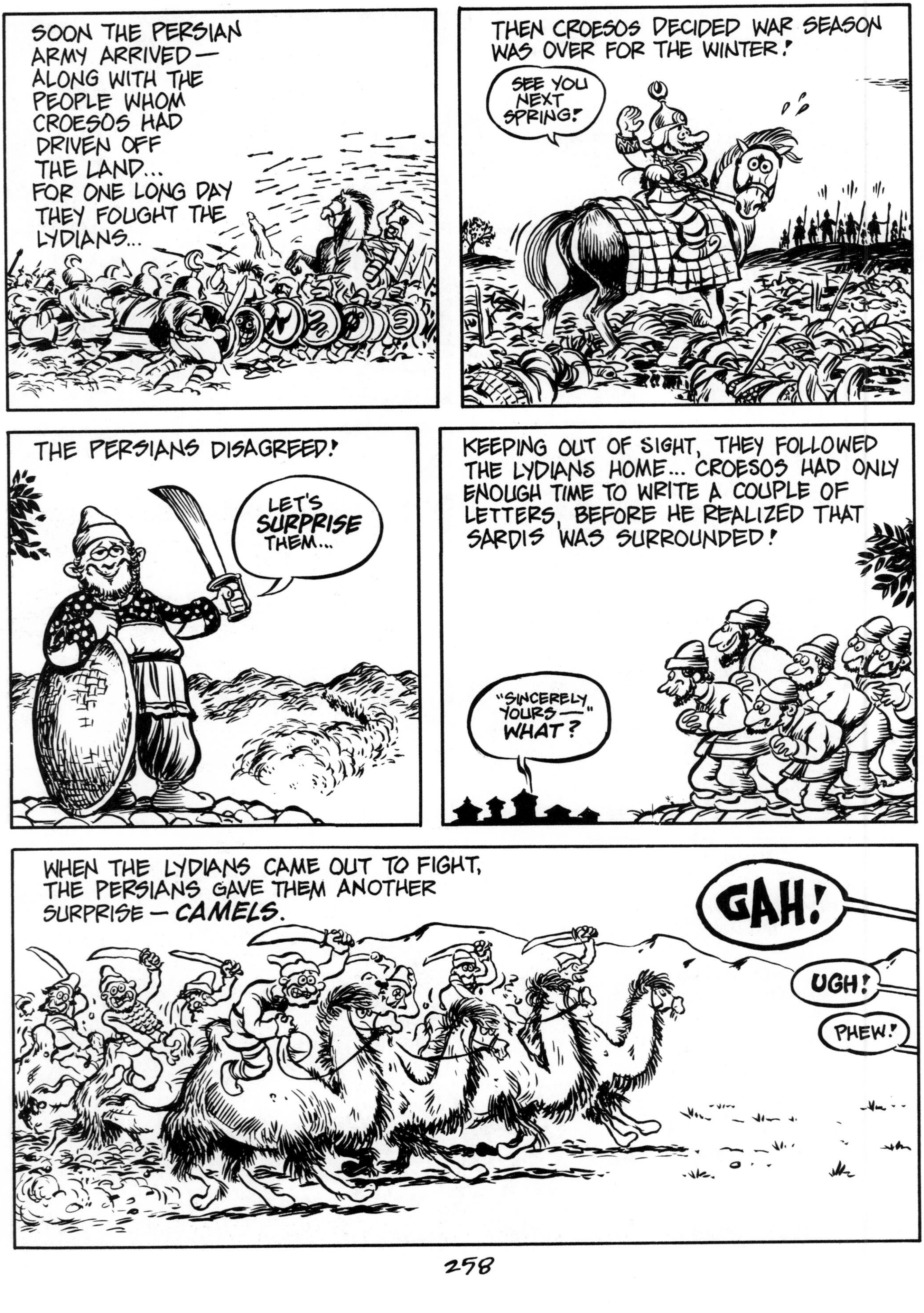
SOON THE PERSIAN ARMY ARRIVED— ALONG WITH THE PEOPLE WHOM CROESOS HAD DRIVEN OFF THE LAND... FOR ONE LONG DAY THEY FOUGHT THE LYDIANS...
THEN CROESOS DECIDED WAR SEASON WAS OVER FOR THE WINTER!
SEE YOU NEXT SPRING!
THE PERSIANS DISAGREED!
LET'S SURPRISE THEM...
KEEPING OUT OF SIGHT, THEY FOLLOWED THE LYDIANS HOME... CROESOS HAD ONLY ENOUGH TIME TO WRITE A COUPLE OF LETTERS, BEFORE HE REALIZED THAT SARDIS WAS SURROUNDED!
"SINCERELY YOURS—" WHAT?
WHEN THE LYDIANS CAME OUT TO FIGHT, THE PERSIANS GAVE THEM ANOTHER SURPRISE — CAMELS.
GAH!
UGH!
PHEW!

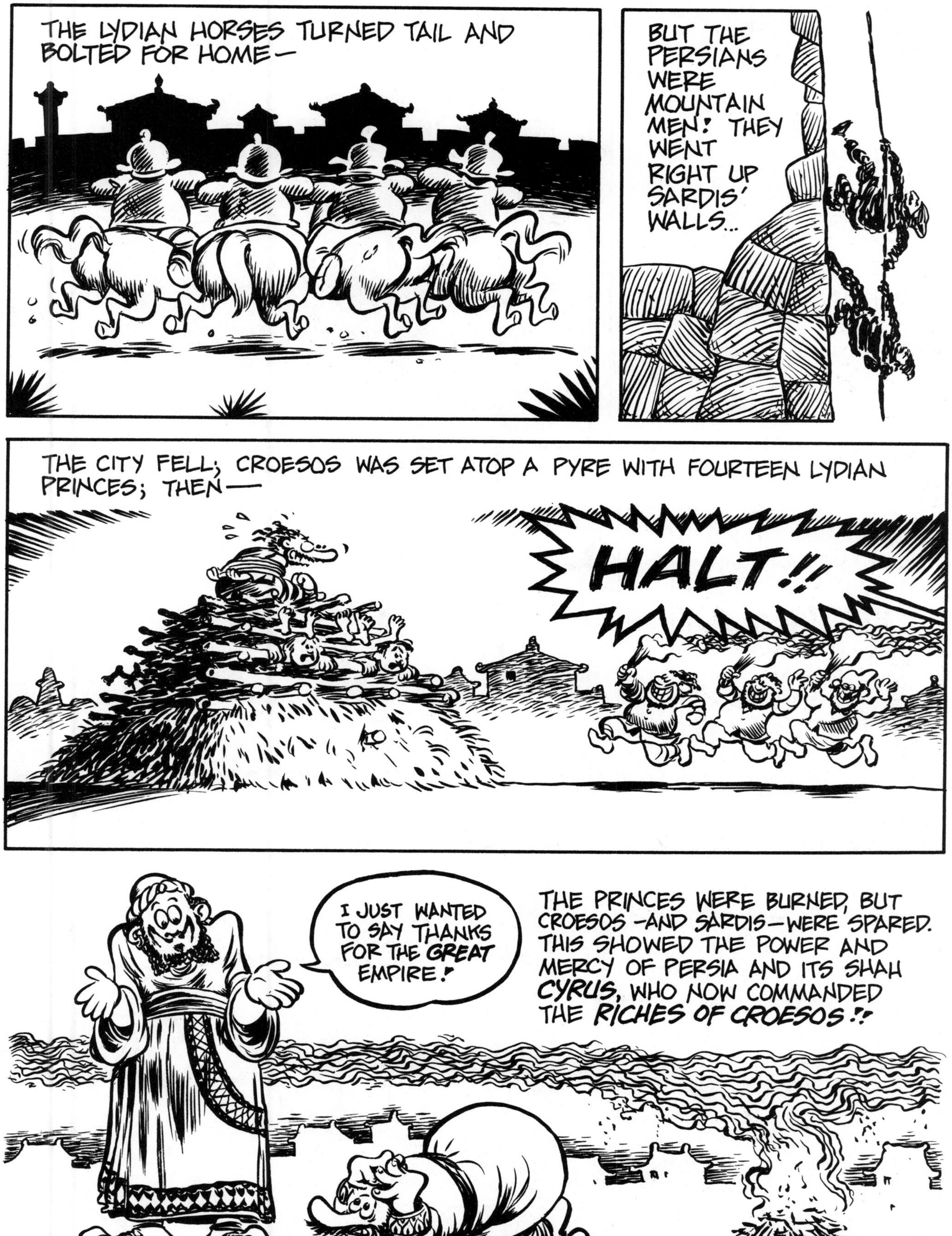
THE LYDIAN HORSES TURNED TAIL AND BOLTED FOR HOME—
BUT THE PERSIANS WERE MOUNTAIN MEN! THEY WENT RIGHT UP SARDIS' WALLS...
THE CITY FELL; CROESOS WAS SET ATOP A PYRE WITH FOURTEEN LYDIAN PRINCES; THEN—
HALT!!
I JUST WANTED TO SAY THANKS FOR THE **GREAT** EMPIRE!
THE PRINCES WERE BURNED, BUT CROESOS —AND SARDIS— WERE SPARED. THIS SHOWED THE POWER AND MERCY OF PERSIA AND ITS SHAH **CYRUS**, WHO NOW COMMANDED THE **RICHES OF CROESOS**!!

"MENE MENE..."

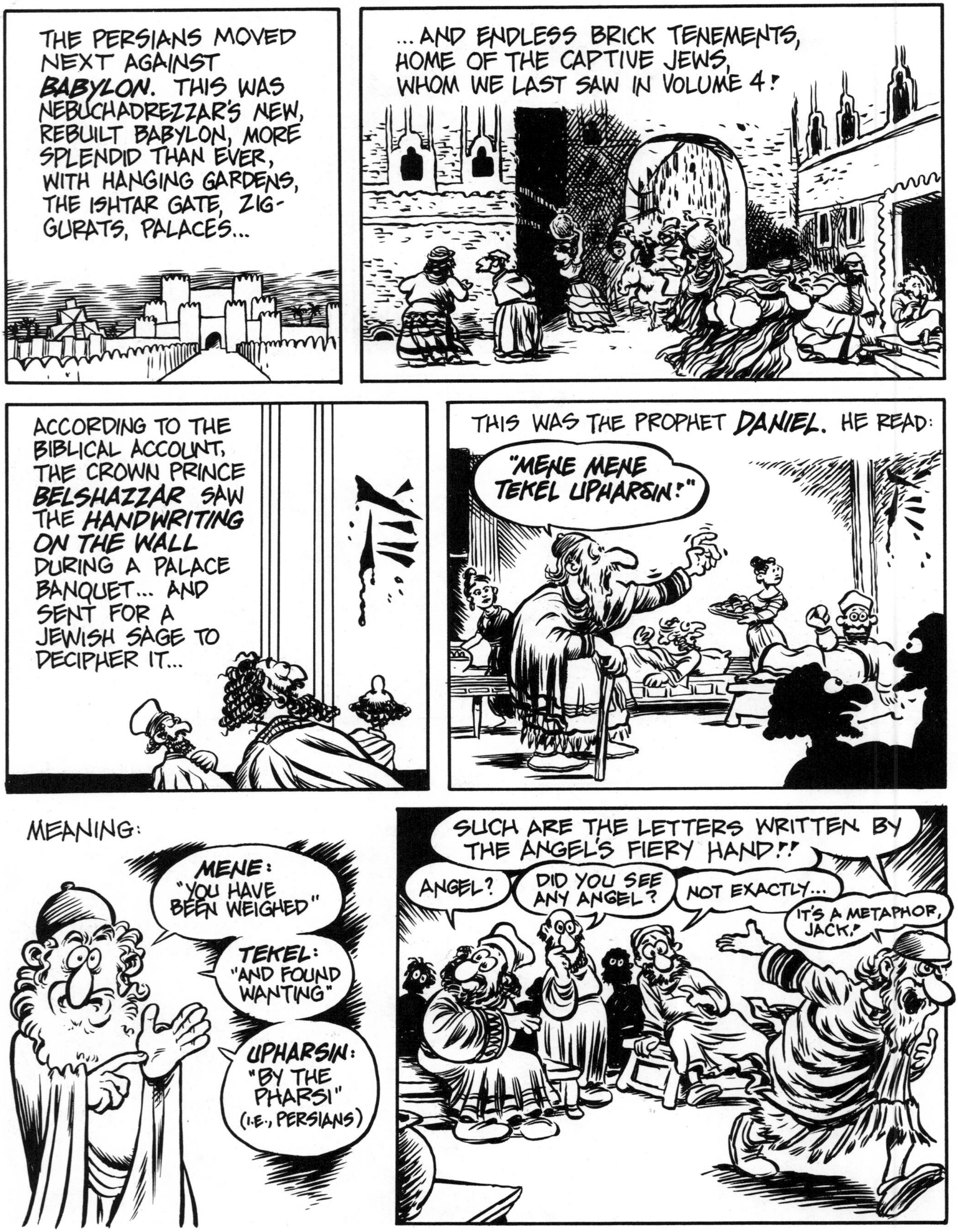
THE PERSIANS MOVED NEXT AGAINST BABYLON. THIS WAS NEBUCHADREZZAR'S NEW, REBUILT BABYLON, MORE SPLENDID THAN EVER, WITH HANGING GARDENS, THE ISHTAR GATE, ZIG-GURATS, PALACES...
...AND ENDLESS BRICK TENEMENTS, HOME OF THE CAPTIVE JEWS, WHOM WE LAST SAW IN VOLUME 4!
ACCORDING TO THE BIBLICAL ACCOUNT, THE CROWN PRINCE BELSHAZZAR SAW THE HANDWRITING ON THE WALL DURING A PALACE BANQUET... AND SENT FOR A JEWISH SAGE TO DECIPHER IT...
THIS WAS THE PROPHET DANIEL. HE READ:
"MENE MENE TEKEL UPHARSIN!"
MEANING:
MENE: "YOU HAVE BEEN WEIGHED"
TEKEL: "AND FOUND WANTING"
UPHARSIN: "BY THE PHARSI" (I.E., PERSIANS)
SUCH ARE THE LETTERS WRITTEN BY THE ANGEL'S FIERY HAND!!
ANGEL?
DID YOU SEE ANY ANGEL?
NOT EXACTLY...
IT'S A METAPHOR, JACK!

UPSTREAM FROM BABYLON CYRUS' MEN DIVERTED THE EUPHRATES RIVER...

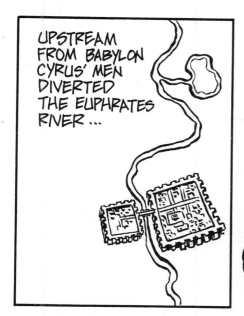

...WADED ALONG THE CITY WALL BY NIGHT...

...AND WERE INSIDE BABYLON'S BRONZE GATES BEFORE THEY COULD BE LOCKED!

THE BIBLE SAYS THE CITY FELL JUST AS BELSHAZZAR'S BANQUET WAS WINDING UP.

MENE MENE TEKEL UPHARSIN!

:BWORP:

THEN, IN ANOTHER GREAT PUBLIC RELATIONS MOVE, CYRUS ALLOWED ALL CAPTIVE PEOPLES TO GO HOME AND PRACTICE THEIR OWN RELIGIONS.

HEY, I WOULDN'T FORCE *MY* RELIGION ON ANYONE!

I CAN BARELY UNDERSTAND IT MYSELF!!

SOME OF THEM SAID THEY'D RATHER *STAY*— THE ORIGIN OF THE IRAQI JEWS...

AH... WE'VE GOT THIS LITTLE IMPORT-EXPORT THING GOING... AND CAN'T REALLY AFFORD TO CLOSE DOWN...

OTHERS RETURNED TO JERUSALEM, WHERE THEY FOUND A WHOLE NEW SET OF INHABITANTS!! (IT'S AN OLD PROBLEM...)

GRRRRR..

A GREAT EMPIRE

SO WHO WERE THESE PERSIANS? ORIGINALLY THEIR FOREBEARS WERE INDO-EUROPEAN NOMADS, KNOWN AS THE *ARYANS*, FROM BEYOND THE CASPIAN SEA.

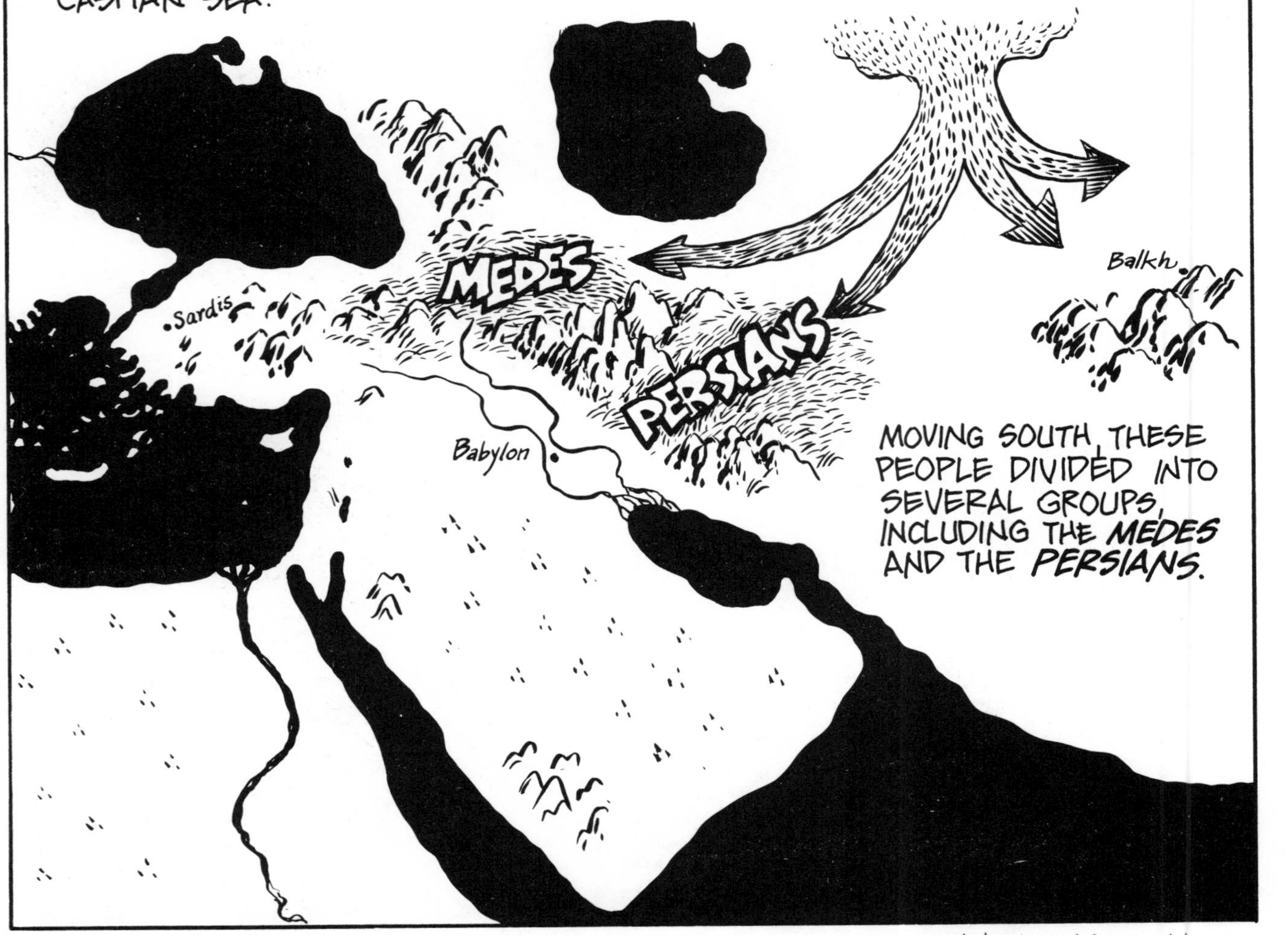

MEDES
Sardis
PERSIANS
Balkh
Babylon

MOVING SOUTH, THESE PEOPLE DIVIDED INTO SEVERAL GROUPS, INCLUDING THE *MEDES* AND THE *PERSIANS*.

THE MEDES, WHO LIVED IN ASSYRIAN TERRITORY, BECAME CIVILIZED EARLY, WHILE THE PERSIANS WERE STILL PRETTY WILD!

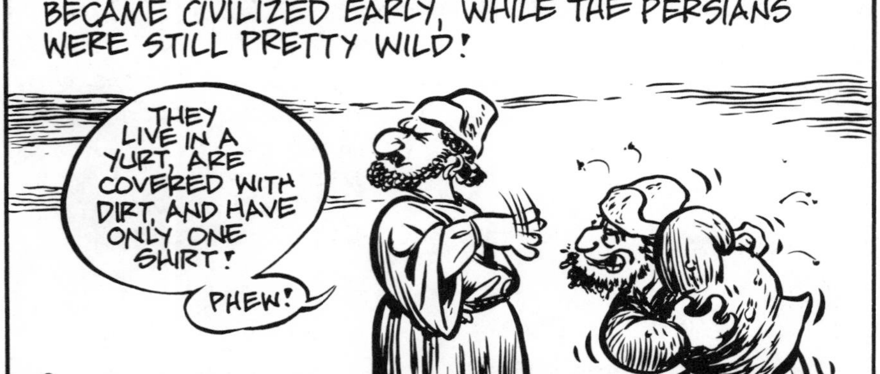

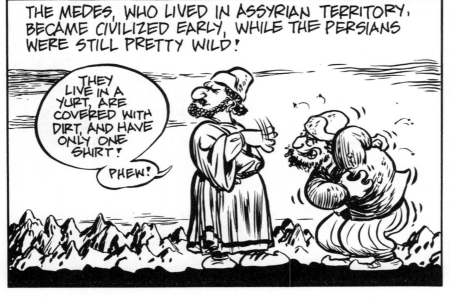

THEY LIVE IN A YURT, ARE COVERED WITH DIRT, AND HAVE ONLY ONE SHIRT!
PHEW!

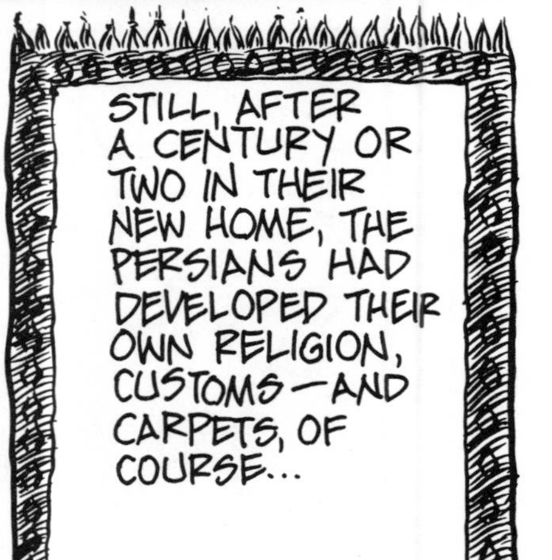

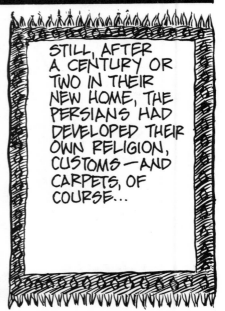

STILL, AFTER A CENTURY OR TWO IN THEIR NEW HOME, THE PERSIANS HAD DEVELOPED THEIR OWN RELIGION, CUSTOMS—AND CARPETS, OF COURSE...

THEIR RELIGION, AS PREACHED BY *ZARATHUSTRA of BALKH*, DIVIDED ALL THINGS INTO TWO PRINCIPLES, *GOOD* AND *EVIL*.

BALKH TODAY

GOOD WAS IDENTIFIED WITH THE *ONE GOD AHURA-MAZDA*, WHO WAS REALIZED IN FIRE, WHILE EVIL WAS *DARKNESS*.

THEIR DEAD WERE NEITHER BURIED NOR CREMATED, BUT SIMPLY EXPOSED TO THE ELEMENTS.

VERY EAGLE-LOGICAL!

THE MINISTERS OF THE FAITH WERE THE *MAGI* ("*MAHG-EE*")— HENCE OUR WORD "MAGIC."

AHA! AHURA-MAZDA!

THE WORST SIN WAS TO TELL A LIE. CRIMINALS ALWAYS CONFESSED!

FEROZ, DID YOU CHOP DOWN THE PEACH TREE?

YES, FATHER!

THEIR HABIT WAS TO RECONSIDER SOBERLY ANY DECISION THEY HAD MADE WHILE DRUNK. AND VICE VERSA.

THIS COULD GO ON AND ON AND ON...

THEIR RETAIL TRADE WAS TIGHTLY CONTROLLED: OF THE GREEK MARKETPLACES, CYRUS SAID,

WHO ARE THESE PEOPLE, WHO HAVE SPECIAL PLACES WHERE THEY GO TO CHEAT EACH OTHER?

AFTER THEIR CONQUESTS, THE PERSIANS BROUGHT HOME EVERY SHRUB AND FLOWER OF THE REALM, PLANTING FORMAL GARDENS CALLED *PAIRIDAEZA*, FROM WHICH WE DERIVE "PARADISE."

THE PERSIAN EMPIRE BEGAN WITH THE CONQUESTS OF ***CYRUS THE GREAT***.

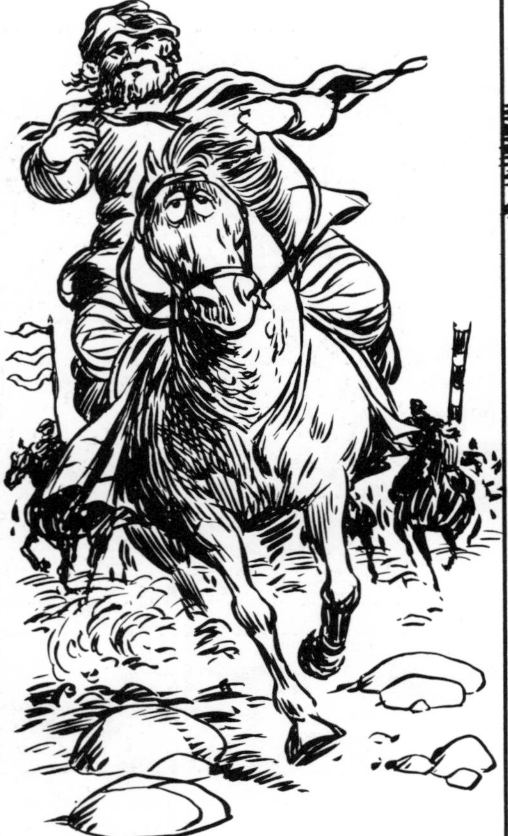

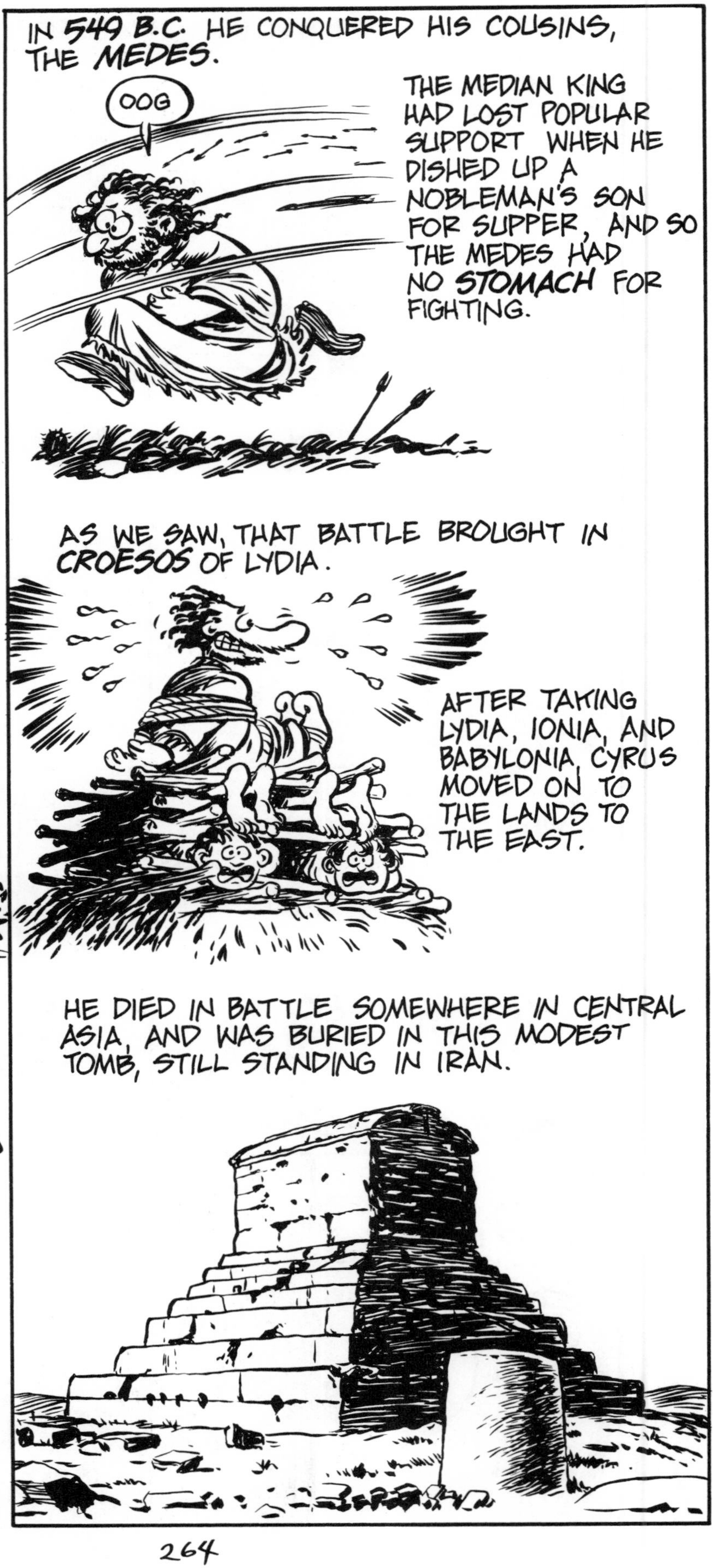
IN **549 B.C.** HE CONQUERED HIS COUSINS, THE **MEDES**.
OOG
THE MEDIAN KING HAD LOST POPULAR SUPPORT WHEN HE DISHED UP A NOBLEMAN'S SON FOR SUPPER, AND SO THE MEDES HAD NO **STOMACH** FOR FIGHTING.
AS WE SAW, THAT BATTLE BROUGHT *IN* ***CROESOS*** OF LYDIA.
AFTER TAKING LYDIA, IONIA, AND BABYLONIA, CYRUS MOVED ON TO THE LANDS TO THE EAST.
HE DIED IN BATTLE SOMEWHERE *IN* CENTRAL ASIA, AND WAS BURIED *IN* THIS *MODEST* TOMB, STILL STANDING IN IRAN.

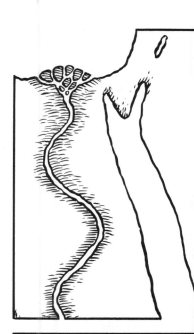

CYRUS' SON **CAMBYSES** ADDED EGYPT TO THE EMPIRE, WENT HORRIBLY INSANE, AND DIED. HIS STORY IS FULL OF ACTION, CRUELTY, AND SOME INTERESTING FACTS ABOUT CROSSING THE ARABIAN DESERT, BUT WE DON'T HAVE ROOM—SORRY! (YOU CAN READ ALL ABOUT IT IN HERODOTOS...)

THIS WAS THE END OF EGYPT'S INDEPENDENCE FOR OVER A THOUSAND YEARS.

SNIF

AFTER CAMBYSES, PERSIA WAS RULED BY TWO **MAGI**, WHO WERE KILLED BY SEVEN ARISTOCRATS.

THE SEVEN MADE A PACT:

THE CROWN GOES TO THE ONE WHOSE **HORSE** NEIGHS FIRST AT **DAWN TOMORROW!**

?

WELL...

ER...

THAT NIGHT A SERVANT SECRETLY VISITED THE **MARES**...

EASY GIRL...

...AND SO **DARIUS** BECAME KING OF PERSIA!!

WHEE UH

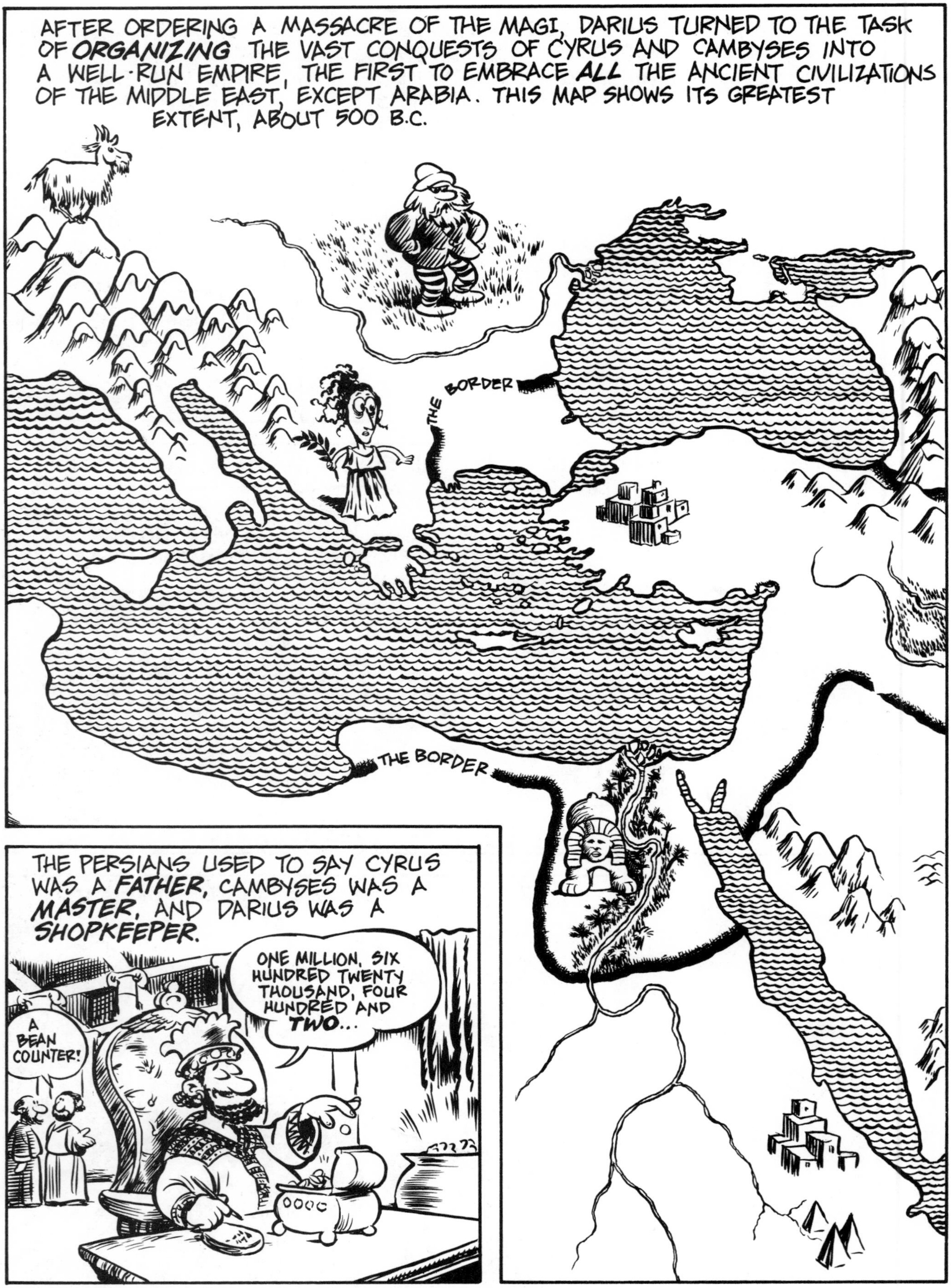
AFTER ORDERING A MASSACRE OF THE MAGI, DARIUS TURNED TO THE TASK OF ORGANIZING THE VAST CONQUESTS OF CYRUS AND CAMBYSES INTO A WELL-RUN EMPIRE, THE FIRST TO EMBRACE ALL THE ANCIENT CIVILIZATIONS OF THE MIDDLE EAST, EXCEPT ARABIA. THIS MAP SHOWS ITS GREATEST EXTENT, ABOUT 500 B.C.
THE BORDER
THE BORDER
THE PERSIANS USED TO SAY CYRUS WAS A FATHER, CAMBYSES WAS A MASTER, AND DARIUS WAS A SHOPKEEPER.
ONE MILLION, SIX HUNDRED TWENTY THOUSAND, FOUR HUNDRED AND TWO...
A BEAN COUNTER!

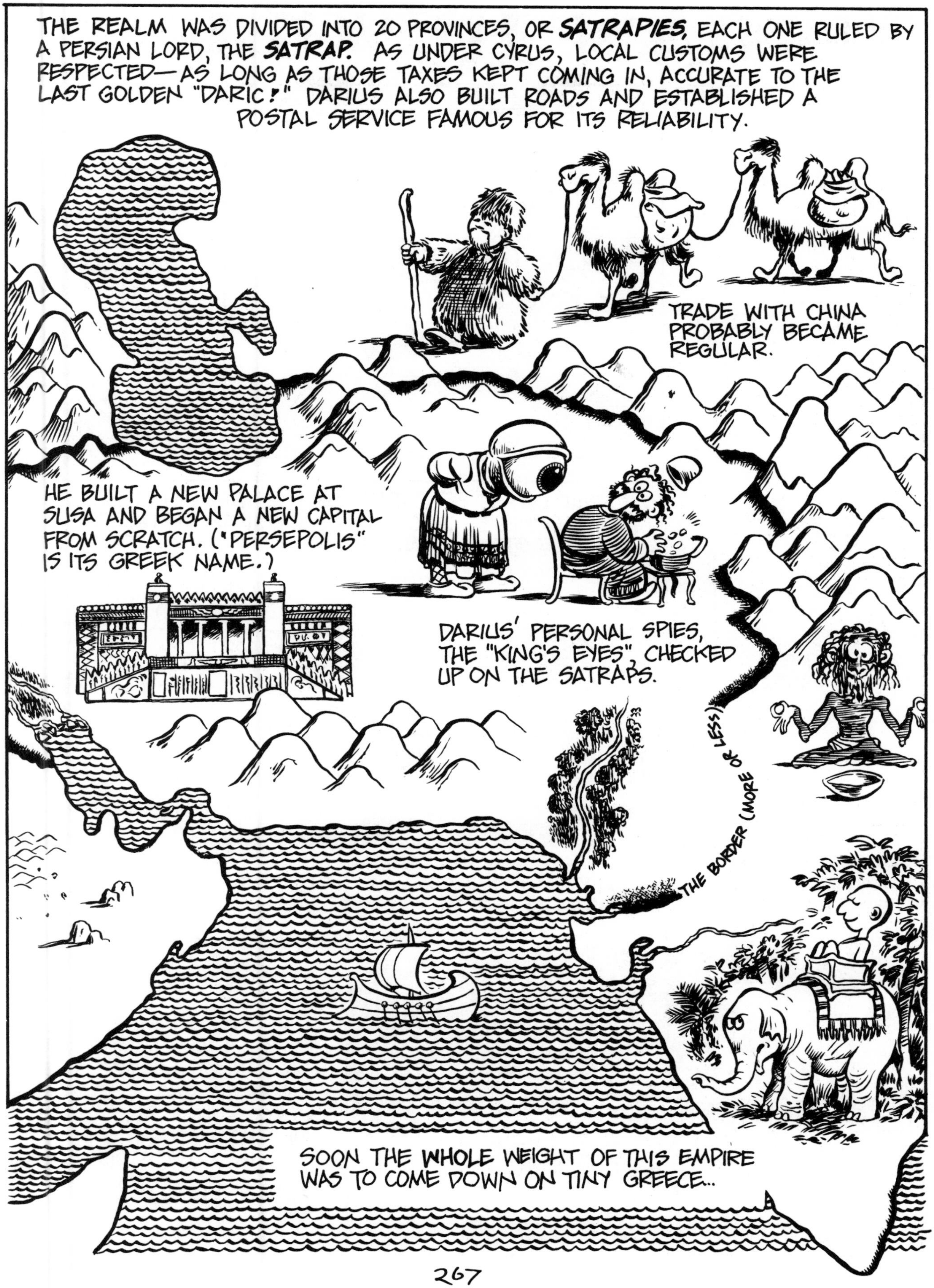
THE REALM WAS DIVIDED INTO 20 PROVINCES, OR **SATRAPIES**, EACH ONE RULED BY A PERSIAN LORD, THE **SATRAP**. AS UNDER CYRUS, LOCAL CUSTOMS WERE RESPECTED—AS LONG AS THOSE TAXES KEPT COMING IN, ACCURATE TO THE LAST GOLDEN "DARIC!" DARIUS ALSO BUILT ROADS AND ESTABLISHED A POSTAL SERVICE FAMOUS FOR ITS RELIABILITY.
TRADE WITH CHINA PROBABLY BECAME REGULAR.
HE BUILT A NEW PALACE AT SUSA AND BEGAN A NEW CAPITAL FROM SCRATCH. ("PERSEPOLIS" IS ITS GREEK NAME.)
DARIUS' PERSONAL SPIES, THE "KING'S EYES", CHECKED UP ON THE SATRAPS.
THE BORDER (MORE OR LESS)
SOON THE **WHOLE** WEIGHT OF THIS EMPIRE WAS TO COME DOWN ON TINY GREECE...

IONIAN REVOLT

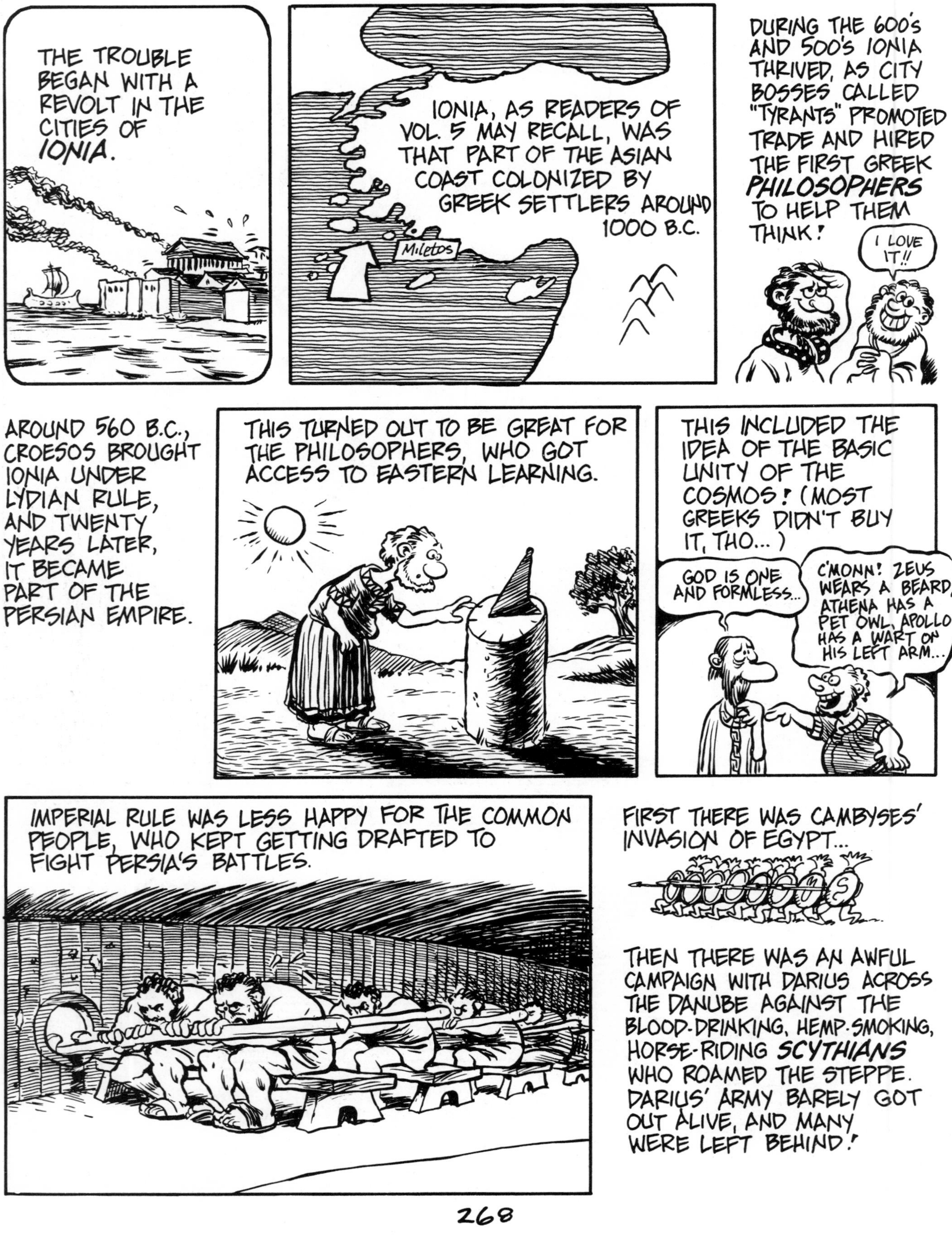

THE TROUBLE BEGAN WITH A REVOLT IN THE CITIES OF *IONIA*.
IONIA, AS READERS OF VOL. 5 MAY RECALL, WAS THAT PART OF THE ASIAN COAST COLONIZED BY GREEK SETTLERS AROUND 1000 B.C.
Miletos
DURING THE 600'S AND 500'S IONIA THRIVED, AS CITY BOSSES CALLED "TYRANTS" PROMOTED TRADE AND HIRED THE FIRST GREEK ***PHILOSOPHERS*** TO HELP THEM THINK!
I LOVE IT!!
AROUND 560 B.C., CROESOS BROUGHT IONIA UNDER LYDIAN RULE, AND TWENTY YEARS LATER, IT BECAME PART OF THE PERSIAN EMPIRE.
THIS TURNED OUT TO BE GREAT FOR THE PHILOSOPHERS, WHO GOT ACCESS TO EASTERN LEARNING.
THIS INCLUDED THE IDEA OF THE BASIC UNITY OF THE COSMOS! (MOST GREEKS DIDN'T BUY IT, THO...)
GOD IS ONE AND FORMLESS...
C'MONN! ZEUS WEARS A BEARD, ATHENA HAS A PET OWL, APOLLO HAS A WART ON HIS LEFT ARM...
IMPERIAL RULE WAS LESS HAPPY FOR THE COMMON PEOPLE, WHO KEPT GETTING DRAFTED TO FIGHT PERSIA'S BATTLES.
FIRST THERE WAS CAMBYSES' INVASION OF EGYPT...
THEN THERE WAS AN AWFUL CAMPAIGN WITH DARIUS ACROSS THE DANUBE AGAINST THE BLOOD-DRINKING, HEMP-SMOKING, HORSE-RIDING ***SCYTHIANS*** WHO ROAMED THE STEPPE. DARIUS' ARMY BARELY GOT OUT ALIVE, AND MANY WERE LEFT BEHIND!

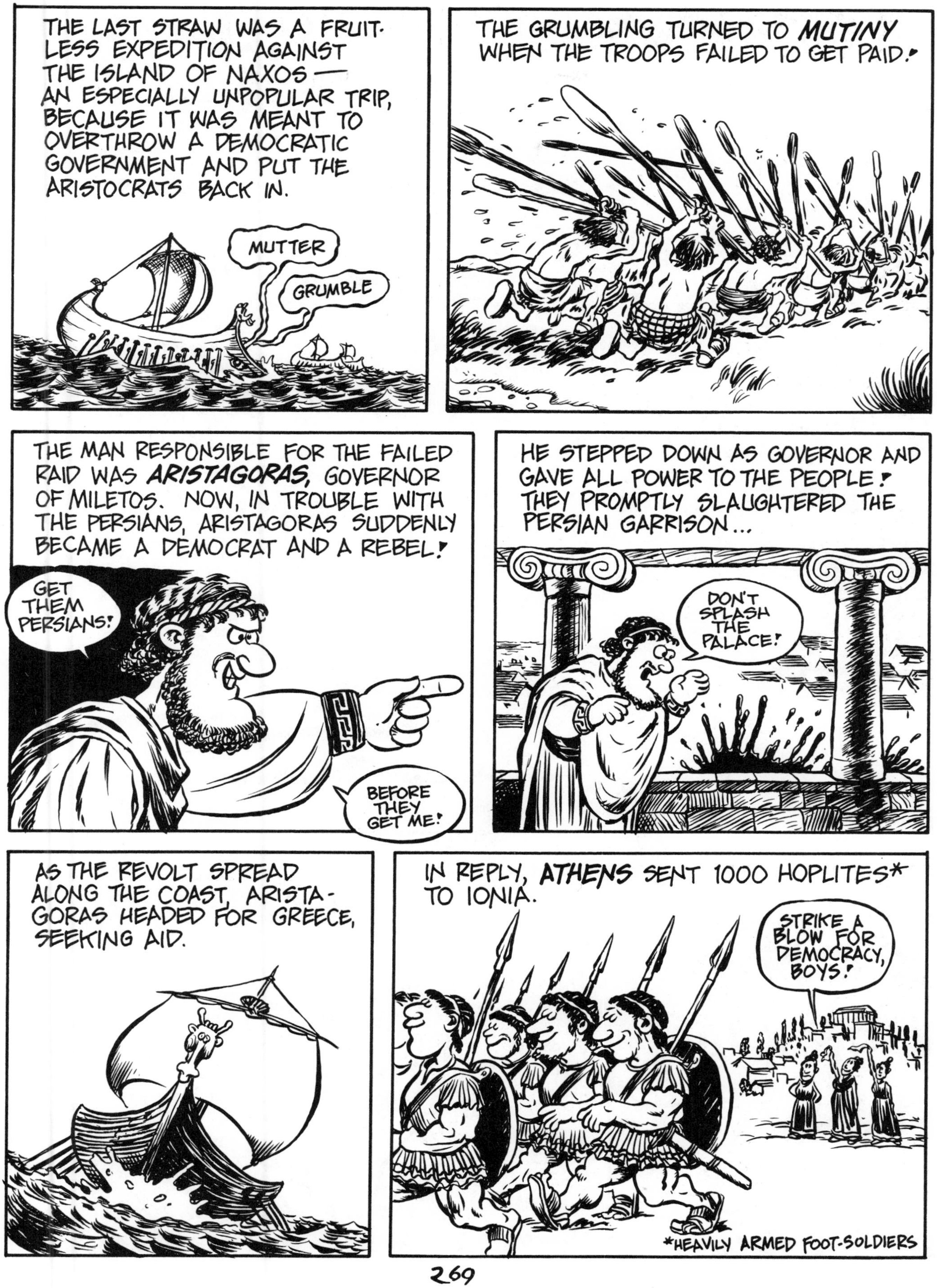
THE LAST STRAW WAS A FRUITLESS EXPEDITION AGAINST THE ISLAND OF NAXOS— AN ESPECIALLY UNPOPULAR TRIP, BECAUSE IT WAS MEANT TO OVERTHROW A DEMOCRATIC GOVERNMENT AND PUT THE ARISTOCRATS BACK IN.
MUTTER
GRUMBLE
THE GRUMBLING TURNED TO ***MUTINY*** WHEN THE TROOPS FAILED TO GET PAID!
THE MAN RESPONSIBLE FOR THE FAILED RAID WAS ***ARISTAGORAS,*** GOVERNOR OF MILETOS. NOW, IN TROUBLE WITH THE PERSIANS, ARISTAGORAS SUDDENLY BECAME A DEMOCRAT AND A REBEL!
GET THEM PERSIANS!
BEFORE THEY GET ME!
HE STEPPED DOWN AS GOVERNOR AND GAVE ALL POWER TO THE PEOPLE! THEY PROMPTLY SLAUGHTERED THE PERSIAN GARRISON...
DON'T SPLASH THE PALACE!
AS THE REVOLT SPREAD ALONG THE COAST, ARISTAGORAS HEADED FOR GREECE, SEEKING AID.
IN REPLY, **ATHENS** SENT 1000 HOPLITES* TO IONIA.
STRIKE A BLOW FOR DEMOCRACY, BOYS!
*HEAVILY ARMED FOOT-SOLDIERS

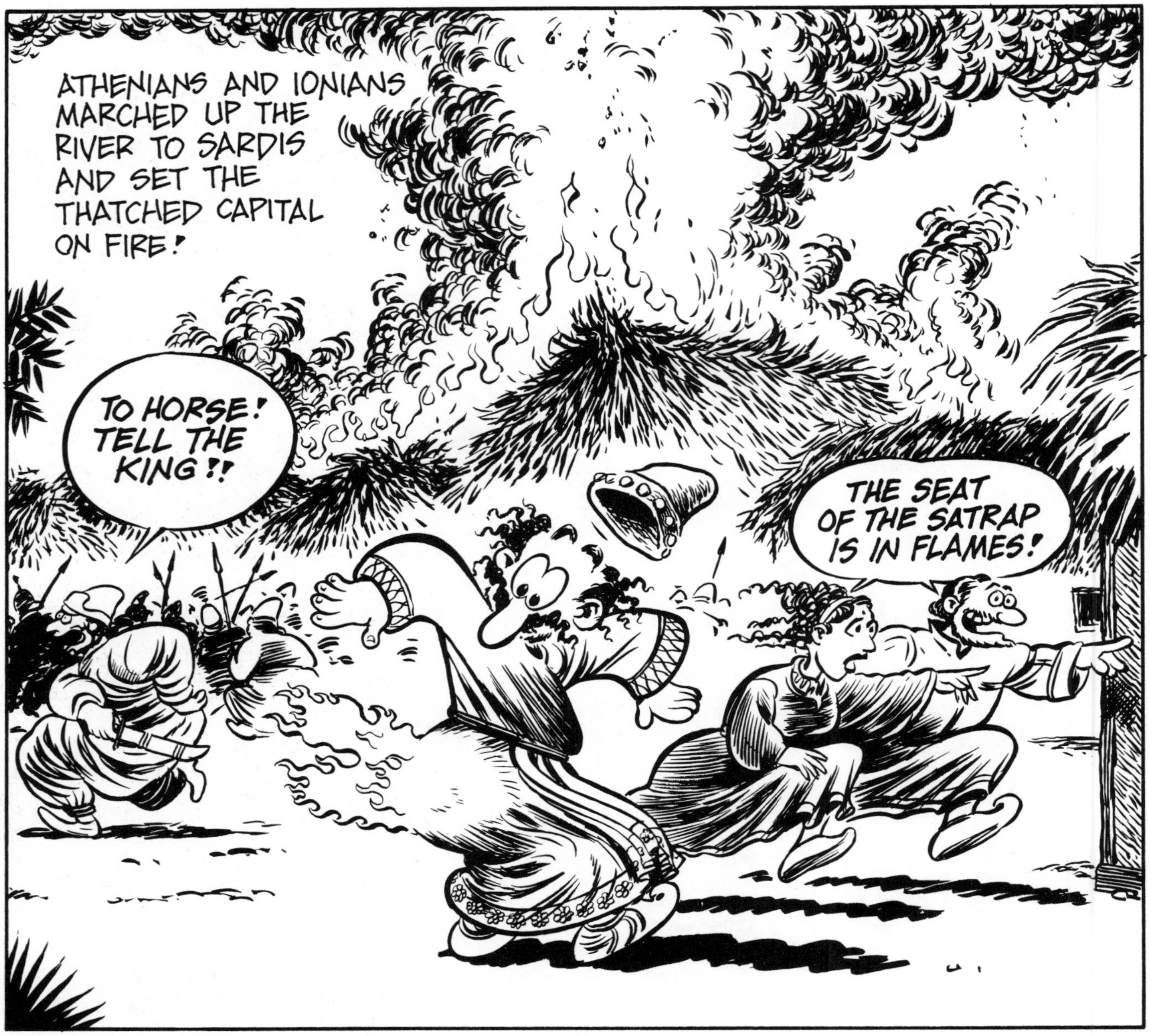
ATHENIANS AND IONIANS MARCHED UP THE RIVER TO SARDIS AND SET THE THATCHED CAPITAL ON FIRE!
TO HORSE! TELL THE KING!!
THE SEAT OF THE SATRAP IS IN FLAMES!

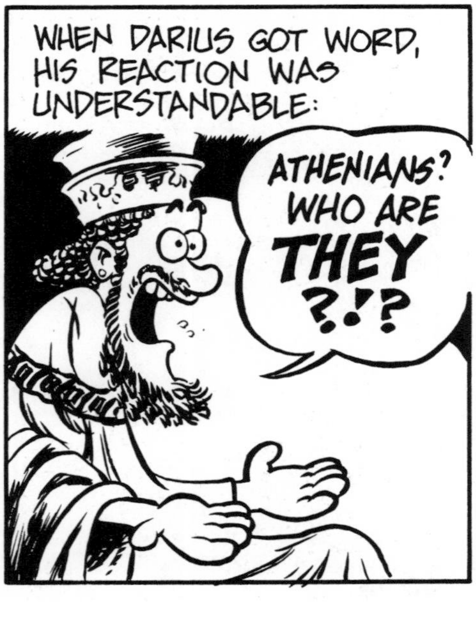
WHEN DARIUS GOT WORD, HIS REACTION WAS UNDERSTANDABLE:
ATHENIANS? WHO ARE THEY ?!?

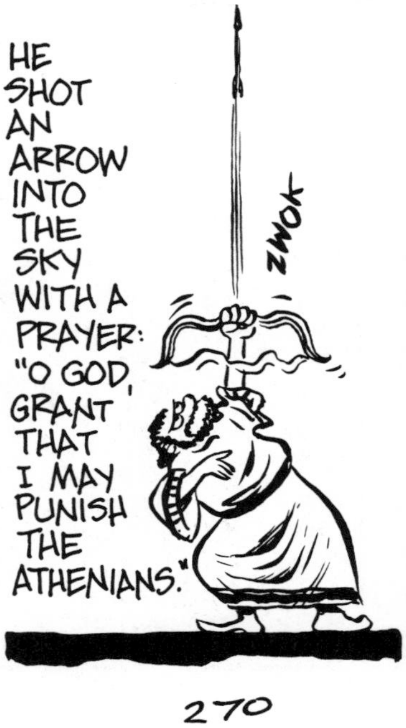
HE SHOT AN ARROW INTO THE SKY WITH A PRAYER: "O GOD, GRANT THAT I MAY PUNISH THE ATHENIANS."
ZWOK

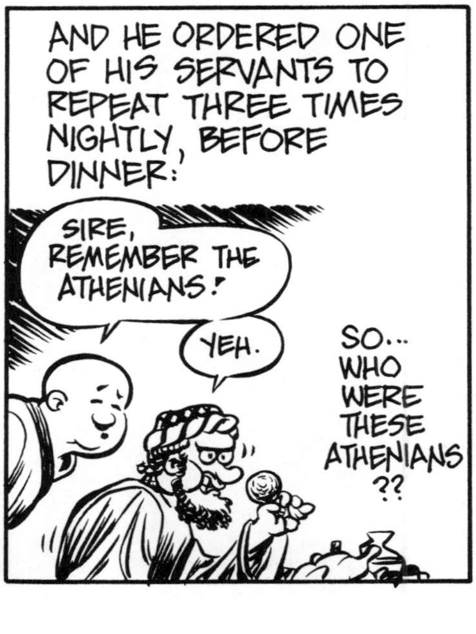
AND HE ORDERED ONE OF HIS SERVANTS TO REPEAT THREE TIMES NIGHTLY, BEFORE DINNER:
SIRE, REMEMBER THE ATHENIANS!
YEH.
SO... WHO WERE THESE ATHENIANS ??

EARLY ATHENS

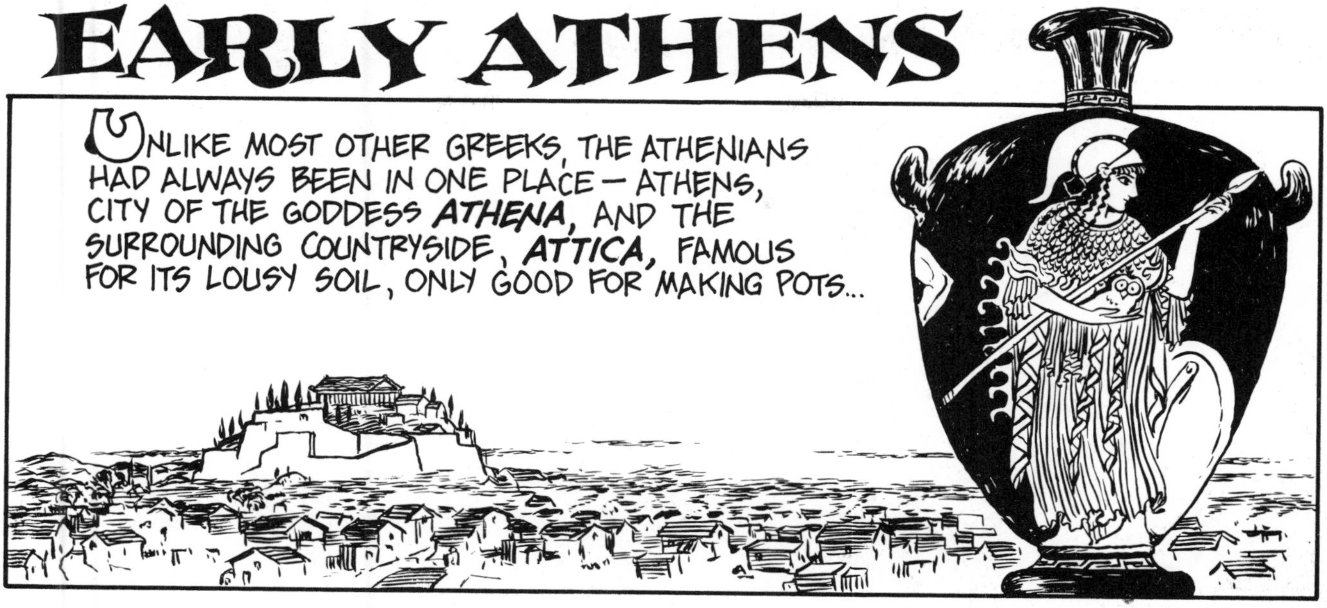
UNLIKE MOST OTHER GREEKS, THE ATHENIANS HAD ALWAYS BEEN IN ONE PLACE — ATHENS, CITY OF THE GODDESS ***ATHENA,*** AND THE SURROUNDING COUNTRYSIDE, ***ATTICA,*** FAMOUS FOR ITS LOUSY SOIL, ONLY GOOD FOR MAKING POTS...

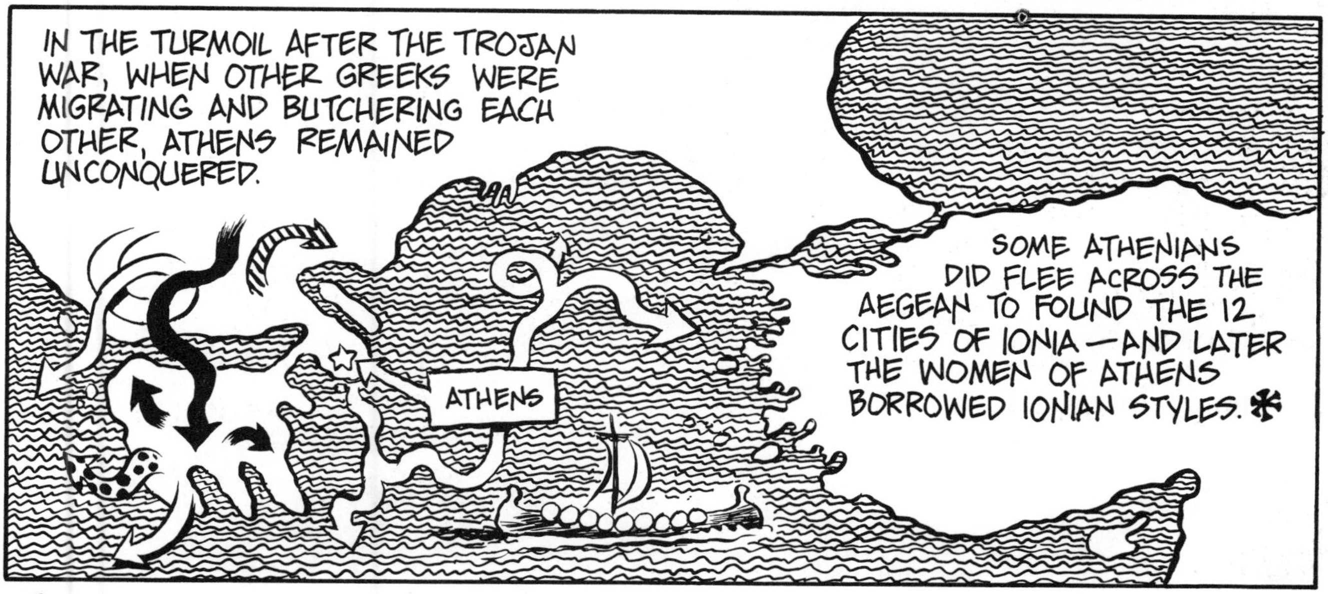
IN THE TURMOIL AFTER THE TROJAN WAR, WHEN OTHER GREEKS WERE MIGRATING AND BUTCHERING EACH OTHER, ATHENS REMAINED UNCONQUERED.
ATHENS
SOME ATHENIANS DID FLEE ACROSS THE AEGEAN TO FOUND THE 12 CITIES OF IONIA — AND LATER THE WOMEN OF ATHENS BORROWED IONIAN STYLES. ✽

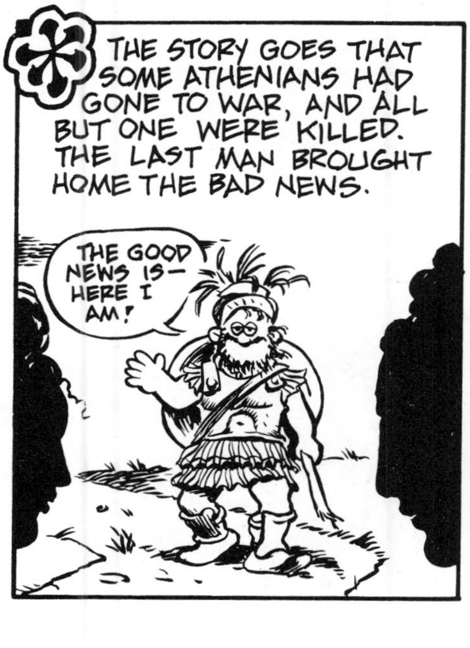
✽ THE STORY GOES THAT SOME ATHENIANS HAD GONE TO WAR, AND ALL BUT ONE WERE KILLED. THE LAST MAN BROUGHT HOME THE BAD NEWS.
THE GOOD NEWS IS— HERE I AM!

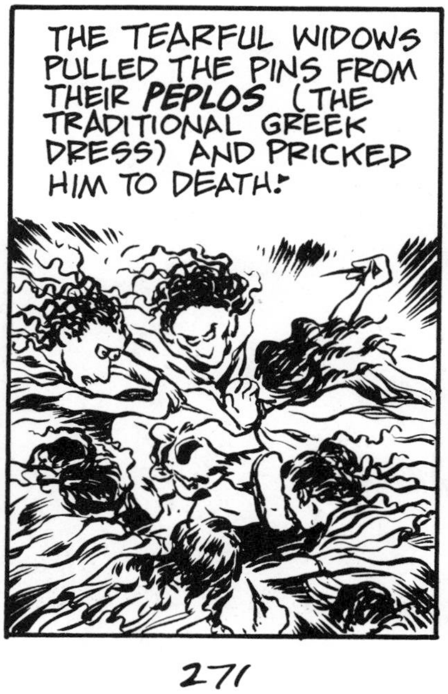
THE TEARFUL WIDOWS PULLED THE PINS FROM THEIR ***PEPLOS*** (THE TRADITIONAL GREEK DRESS) AND PRICKED HIM TO DEATH!

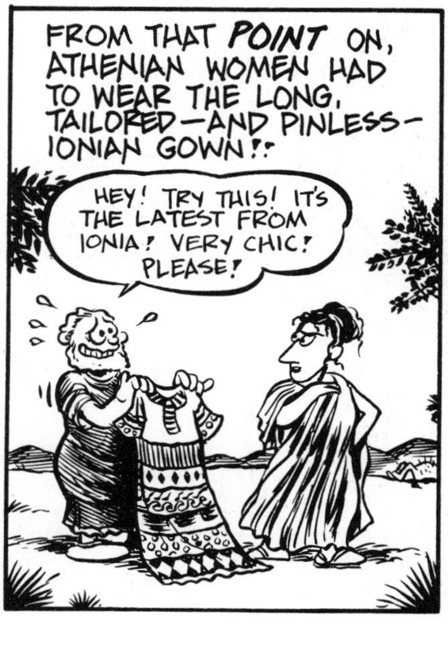
FROM THAT ***POINT*** ON, ATHENIAN WOMEN HAD TO WEAR THE LONG, TAILORED — AND PINLESS — IONIAN GOWN!
HEY! TRY THIS! IT'S THE LATEST FROM IONIA! VERY CHIC! PLEASE!

FOR CENTURIES AFTER THE TROJAN WAR, LIFE IN ATTICA FOLLOWED A DEPENDABLE PATTERN...

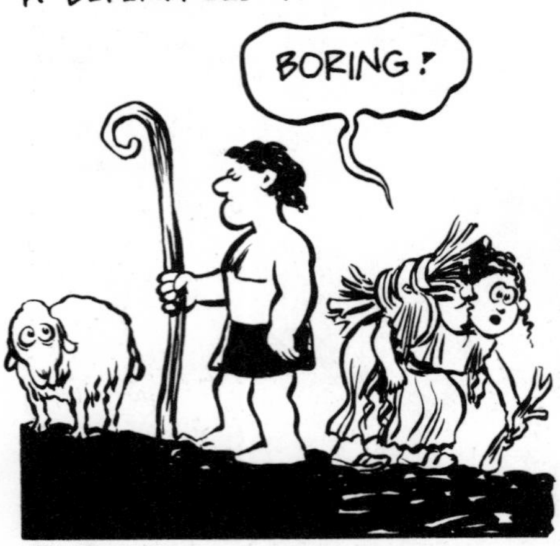
BORING!

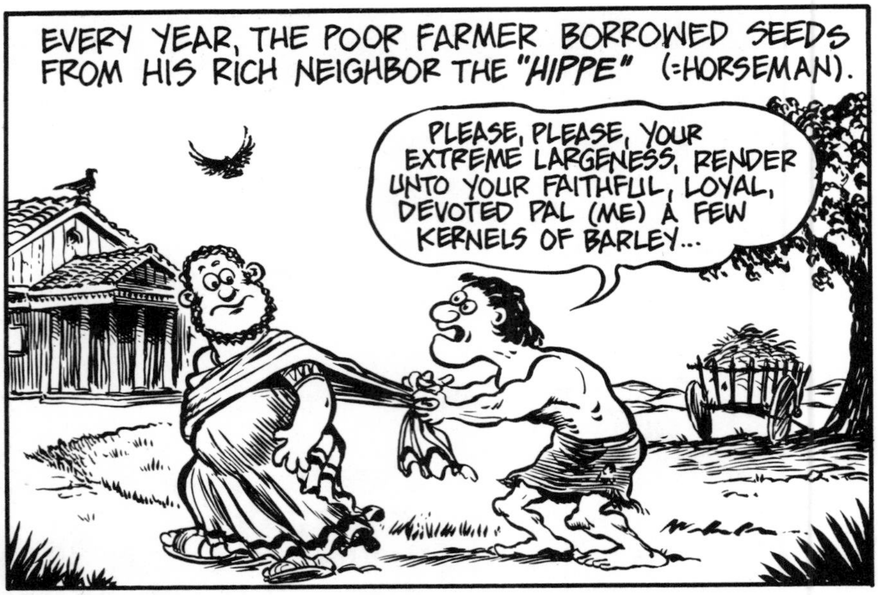
EVERY YEAR, THE POOR FARMER BORROWED SEEDS FROM HIS RICH NEIGHBOR THE "HIPPE" (=HORSEMAN).
PLEASE, PLEASE, YOUR EXTREME LARGENESS, RENDER UNTO YOUR FAITHFUL, LOYAL, DEVOTED PAL (ME) A FEW KERNELS OF BARLEY...

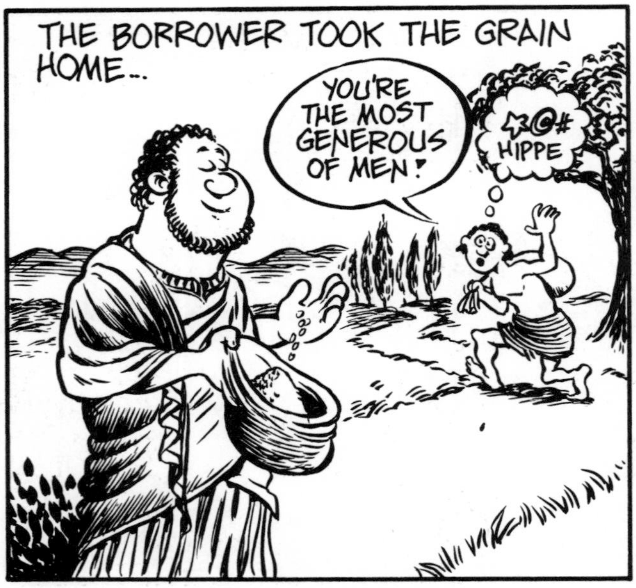
THE BORROWER TOOK THE GRAIN HOME...
YOU'RE THE MOST GENEROUS OF MEN!
%@# HIPPE

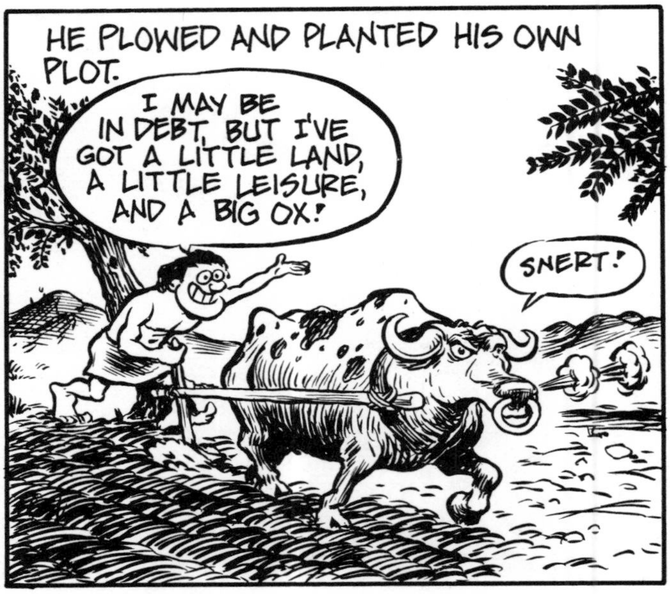
HE PLOWED AND PLANTED HIS OWN PLOT.
I MAY BE IN DEBT, BUT I'VE GOT A LITTLE LAND, A LITTLE LEISURE, AND A BIG OX!
SNERT!

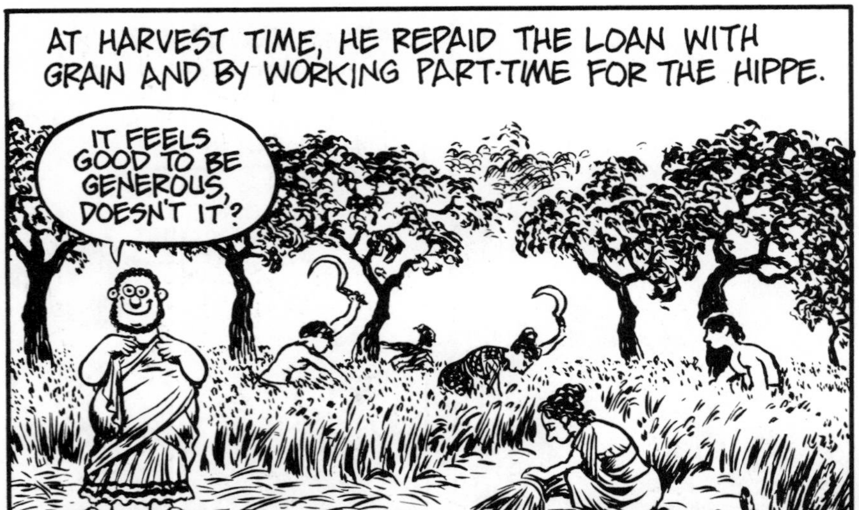
AT HARVEST TIME, HE REPAID THE LOAN WITH GRAIN AND BY WORKING PART-TIME FOR THE HIPPE.
IT FEELS GOOD TO BE GENEROUS, DOESN'T IT?

BUT THESE "DARK AGES" WERE BOUND TO END!! TRADE PICKED UP... ***MONEY,*** THAT LYDIAN INVENTION, FOLLOWED, AND WHERE MONEY GOES, CAN *CONFLICT* BE FAR BEHIND?

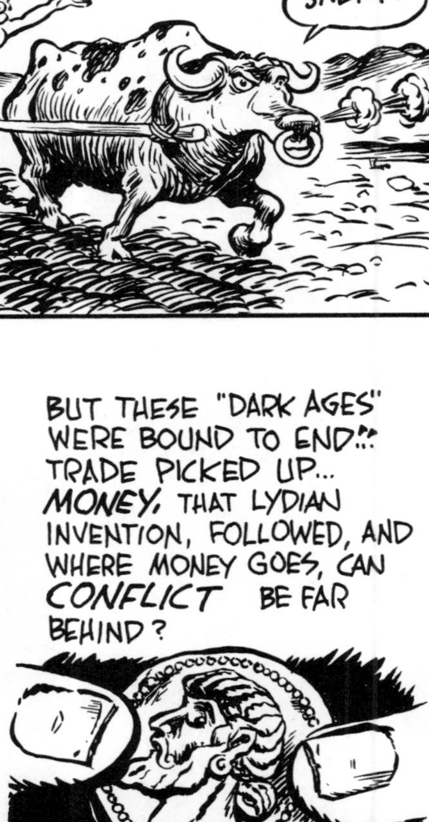

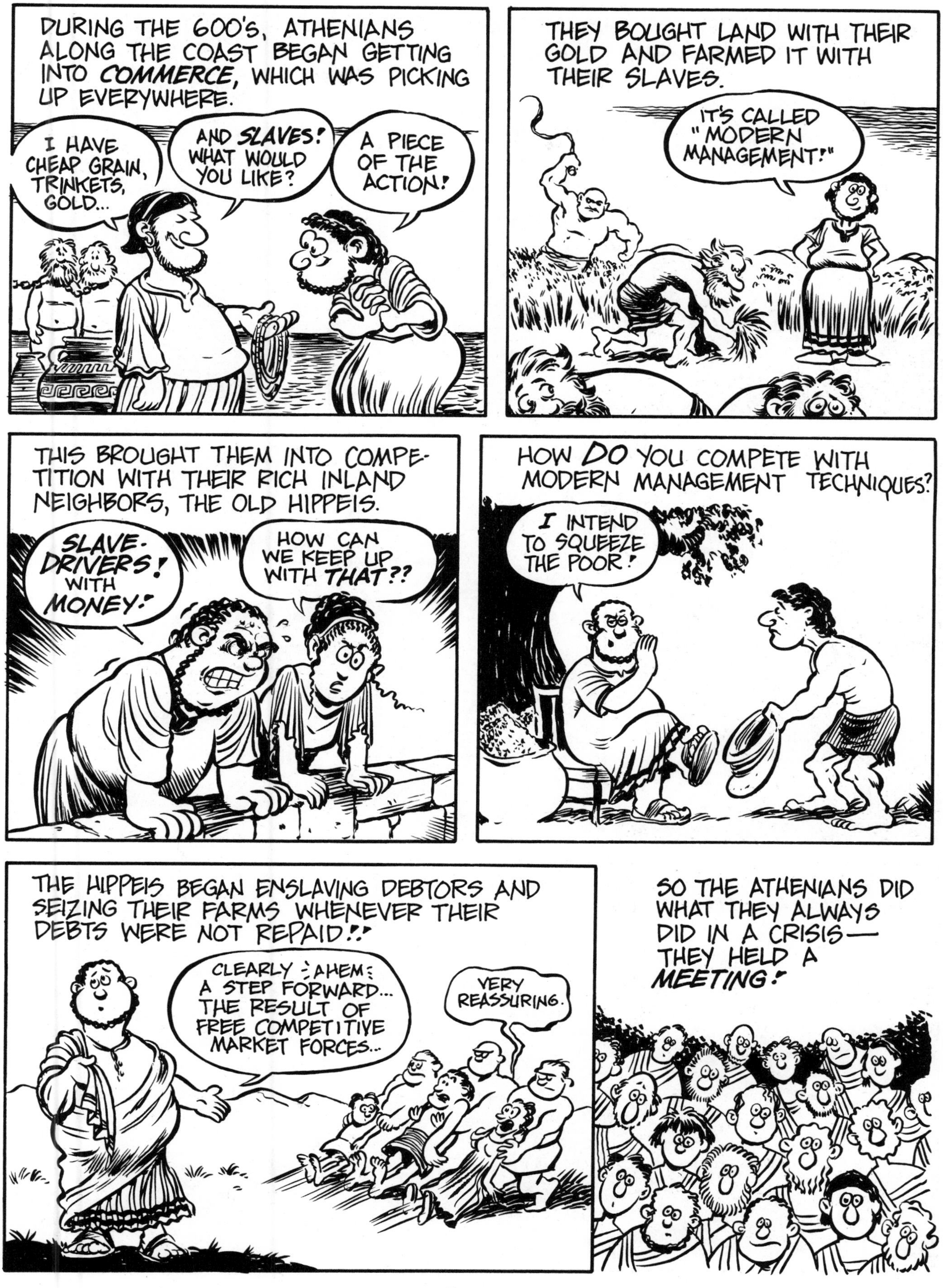
DURING THE 600'S, ATHENIANS ALONG THE COAST BEGAN GETTING INTO COMMERCE, WHICH WAS PICKING UP EVERYWHERE.
I HAVE CHEAP GRAIN, TRINKETS, GOLD...
AND SLAVES! WHAT WOULD YOU LIKE?
A PIECE OF THE ACTION!
THEY BOUGHT LAND WITH THEIR GOLD AND FARMED IT WITH THEIR SLAVES.
IT'S CALLED "MODERN MANAGEMENT!"
THIS BROUGHT THEM INTO COMPETITION WITH THEIR RICH INLAND NEIGHBORS, THE OLD HIPPEIS.
SLAVE-DRIVERS! WITH MONEY!
HOW CAN WE KEEP UP WITH THAT??
HOW DO YOU COMPETE WITH MODERN MANAGEMENT TECHNIQUES?
I INTEND TO SQUEEZE THE POOR!
THE HIPPEIS BEGAN ENSLAVING DEBTORS AND SEIZING THEIR FARMS WHENEVER THEIR DEBTS WERE NOT REPAID!!
CLEARLY :AHEM: A STEP FORWARD... THE RESULT OF FREE COMPETITIVE MARKET FORCES...
VERY REASSURING.
SO THE ATHENIANS DID WHAT THEY ALWAYS DID IN A CRISIS— THEY HELD A MEETING!

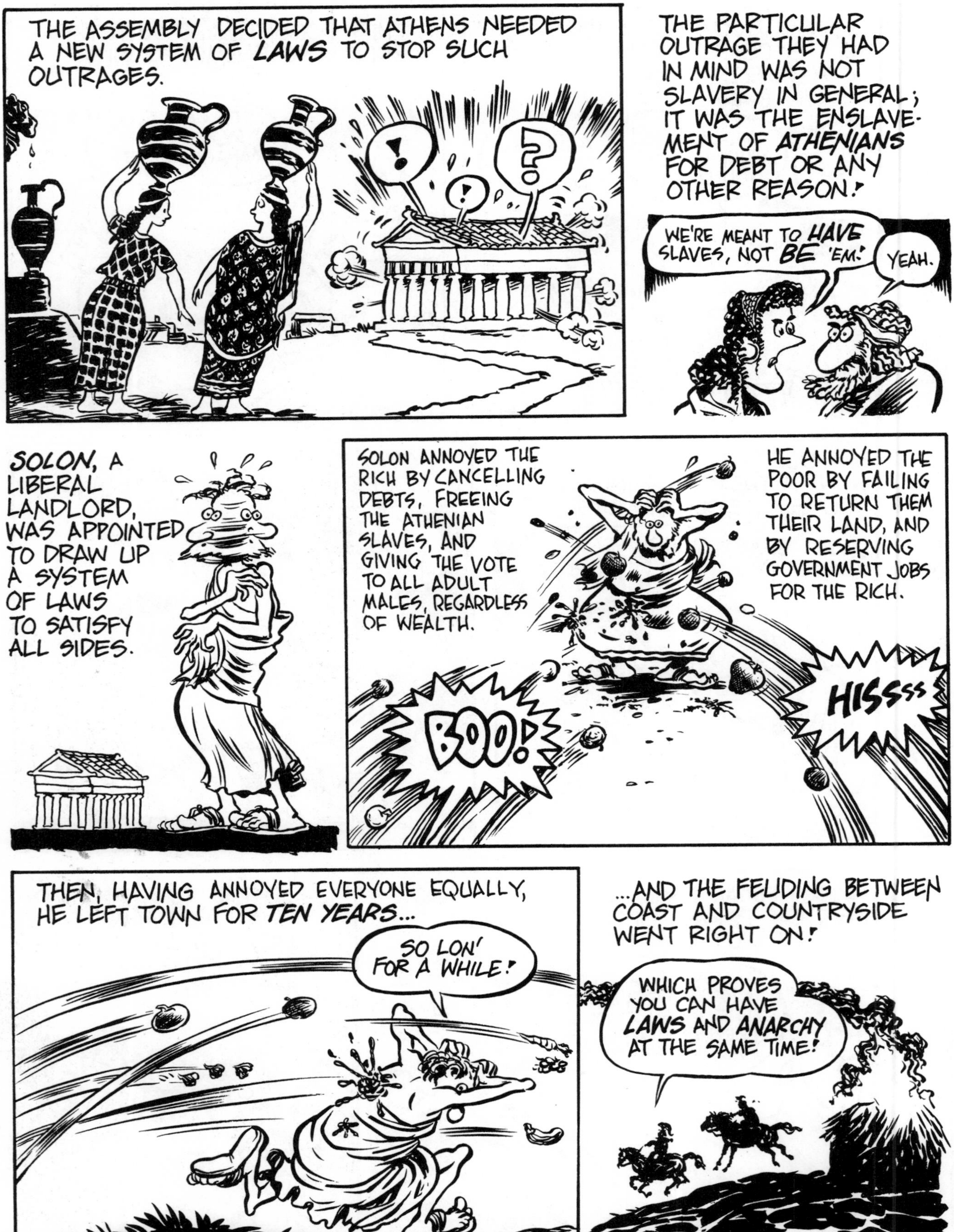

THE ASSEMBLY DECIDED THAT ATHENS NEEDED A NEW SYSTEM OF LAWS TO STOP SUCH OUTRAGES.
!
!
?
THE PARTICULAR OUTRAGE THEY HAD IN MIND WAS NOT SLAVERY IN GENERAL; IT WAS THE ENSLAVEMENT OF ATHENIANS FOR DEBT OR ANY OTHER REASON!
WE'RE MEANT TO HAVE SLAVES, NOT BE 'EM!
YEAH.
SOLON, A LIBERAL LANDLORD, WAS APPOINTED TO DRAW UP A SYSTEM OF LAWS TO SATISFY ALL SIDES.
SOLON ANNOYED THE RICH BY CANCELLING DEBTS, FREEING THE ATHENIAN SLAVES, AND GIVING THE VOTE TO ALL ADULT MALES, REGARDLESS OF WEALTH.
HE ANNOYED THE POOR BY FAILING TO RETURN THEM THEIR LAND, AND BY RESERVING GOVERNMENT JOBS FOR THE RICH.
BOO!
HISSSS
THEN, HAVING ANNOYED EVERYONE EQUALLY, HE LEFT TOWN FOR TEN YEARS...
SO LON' FOR A WHILE!
...AND THE FEUDING BETWEEN COAST AND COUNTRYSIDE WENT RIGHT ON!
WHICH PROVES YOU CAN HAVE LAWS AND ANARCHY AT THE SAME TIME!

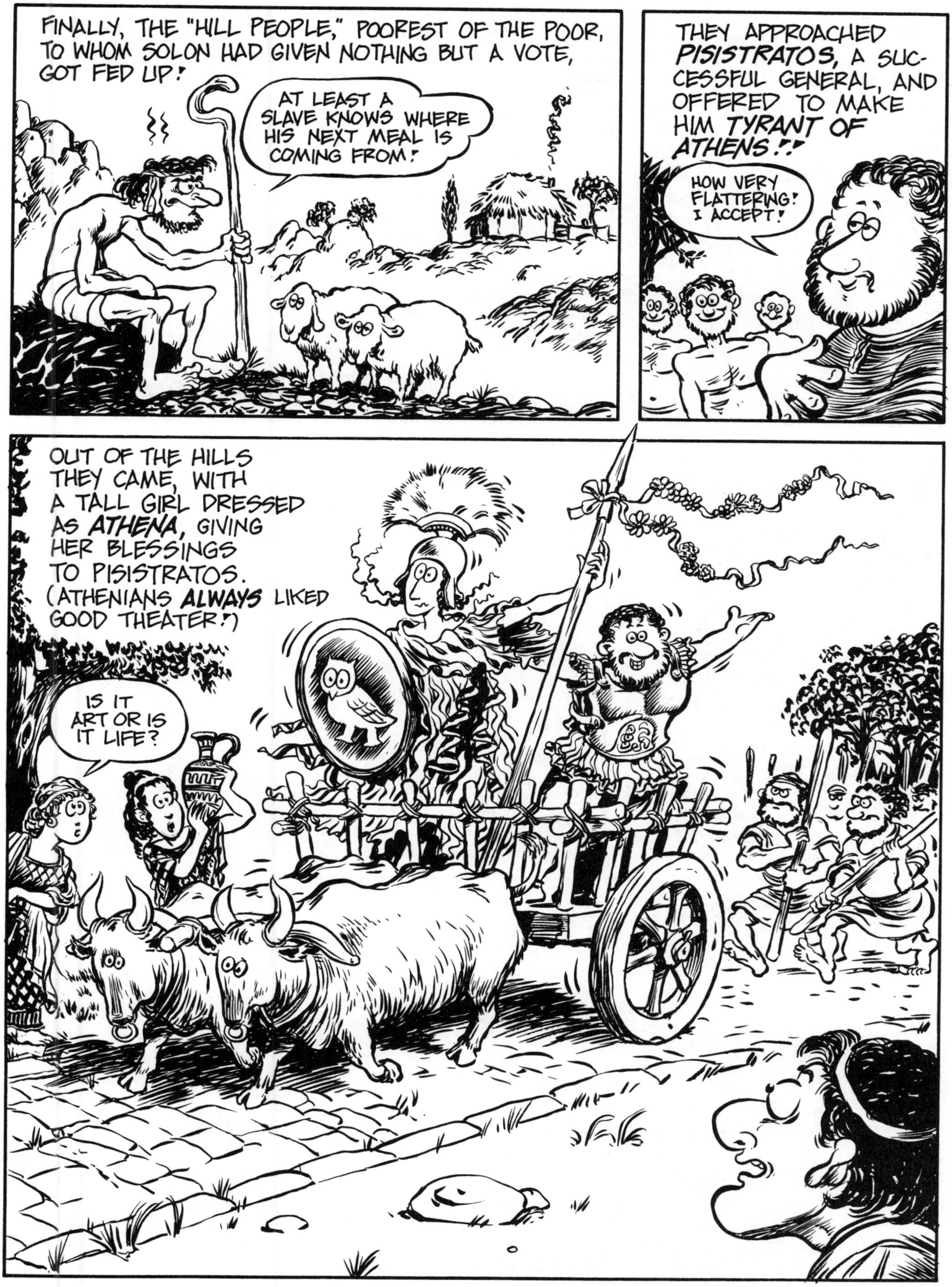
FINALLY, THE "HILL PEOPLE," POOREST OF THE POOR, TO WHOM SOLON HAD GIVEN NOTHING BUT A VOTE, GOT FED UP!
AT LEAST A SLAVE KNOWS WHERE HIS NEXT MEAL IS COMING FROM!
THEY APPROACHED PISISTRATOS, A SUCCESSFUL GENERAL, AND OFFERED TO MAKE HIM TYRANT OF ATHENS!!
HOW VERY FLATTERING! I ACCEPT!
OUT OF THE HILLS THEY CAME, WITH A TALL GIRL DRESSED AS ATHENA, GIVING HER BLESSINGS TO PISISTRATOS. (ATHENIANS ALWAYS LIKED GOOD THEATER!)
IS IT ART OR IS IT LIFE?

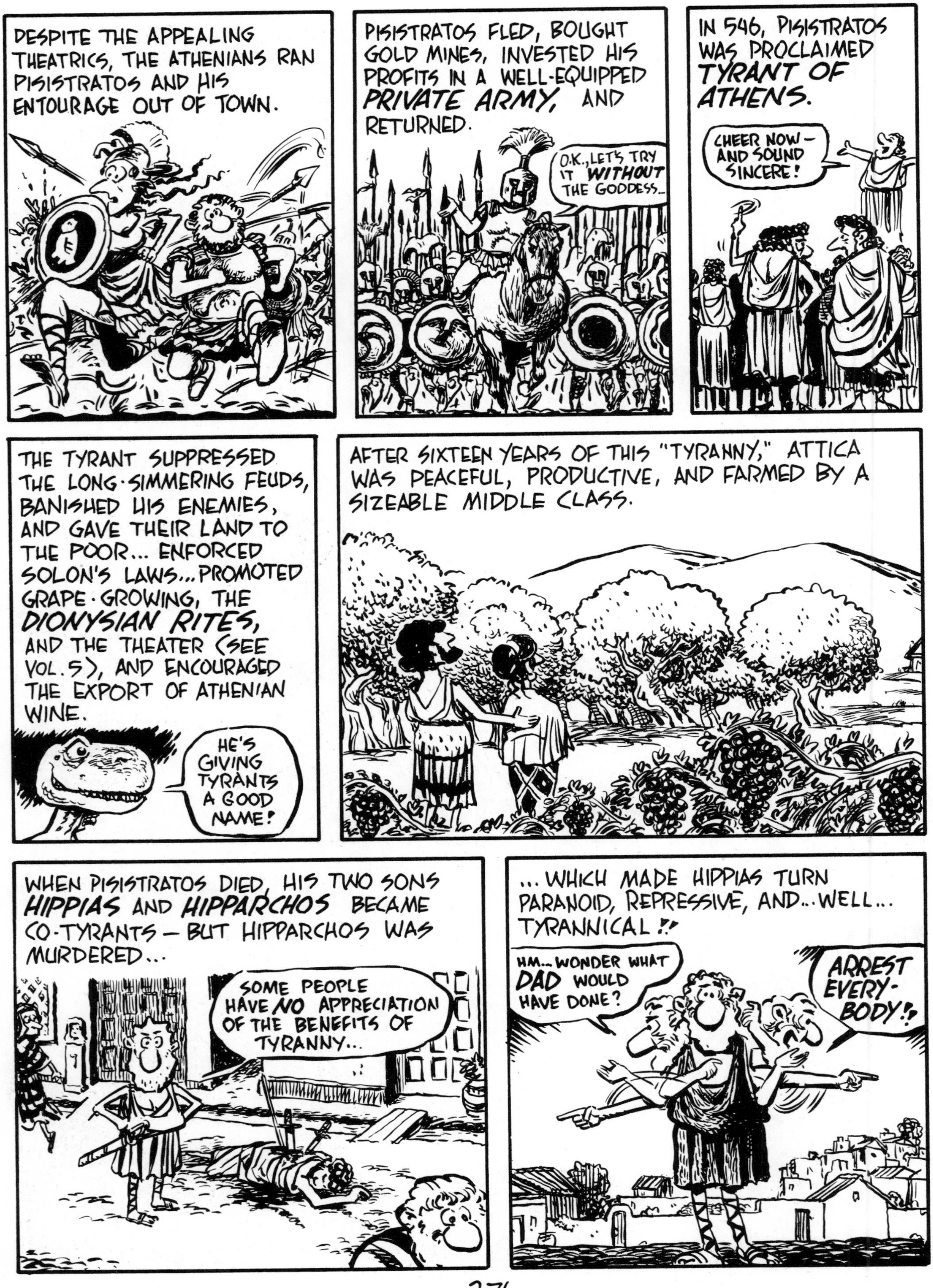
DESPITE THE APPEALING THEATRICS, THE ATHENIANS RAN PISISTRATOS AND HIS ENTOURAGE OUT OF TOWN.
PISISTRATOS FLED, BOUGHT GOLD MINES, INVESTED HIS PROFITS IN A WELL-EQUIPPED PRIVATE ARMY, AND RETURNED.
O.K., LET'S TRY IT WITHOUT THE GODDESS...
IN 546, PISISTRATOS WAS PROCLAIMED TYRANT OF ATHENS.
CHEER NOW— AND SOUND SINCERE!
THE TYRANT SUPPRESSED THE LONG-SIMMERING FEUDS, BANISHED HIS ENEMIES, AND GAVE THEIR LAND TO THE POOR... ENFORCED SOLON'S LAWS... PROMOTED GRAPE-GROWING, THE DIONYSIAN RITES, AND THE THEATER (SEE VOL. 5), AND ENCOURAGED THE EXPORT OF ATHENIAN WINE.
HE'S GIVING TYRANTS A GOOD NAME!
AFTER SIXTEEN YEARS OF THIS "TYRANNY," ATTICA WAS PEACEFUL, PRODUCTIVE, AND FARMED BY A SIZEABLE MIDDLE CLASS.
WHEN PISISTRATOS DIED, HIS TWO SONS HIPPIAS AND HIPPARCHOS BECAME CO-TYRANTS — BUT HIPPARCHOS WAS MURDERED...
SOME PEOPLE HAVE NO APPRECIATION OF THE BENEFITS OF TYRANNY...
...WHICH MADE HIPPIAS TURN PARANOID, REPRESSIVE, AND... WELL... TYRANNICAL!?!
HM... WONDER WHAT DAD WOULD HAVE DONE?
ARREST EVERY-BODY!?!

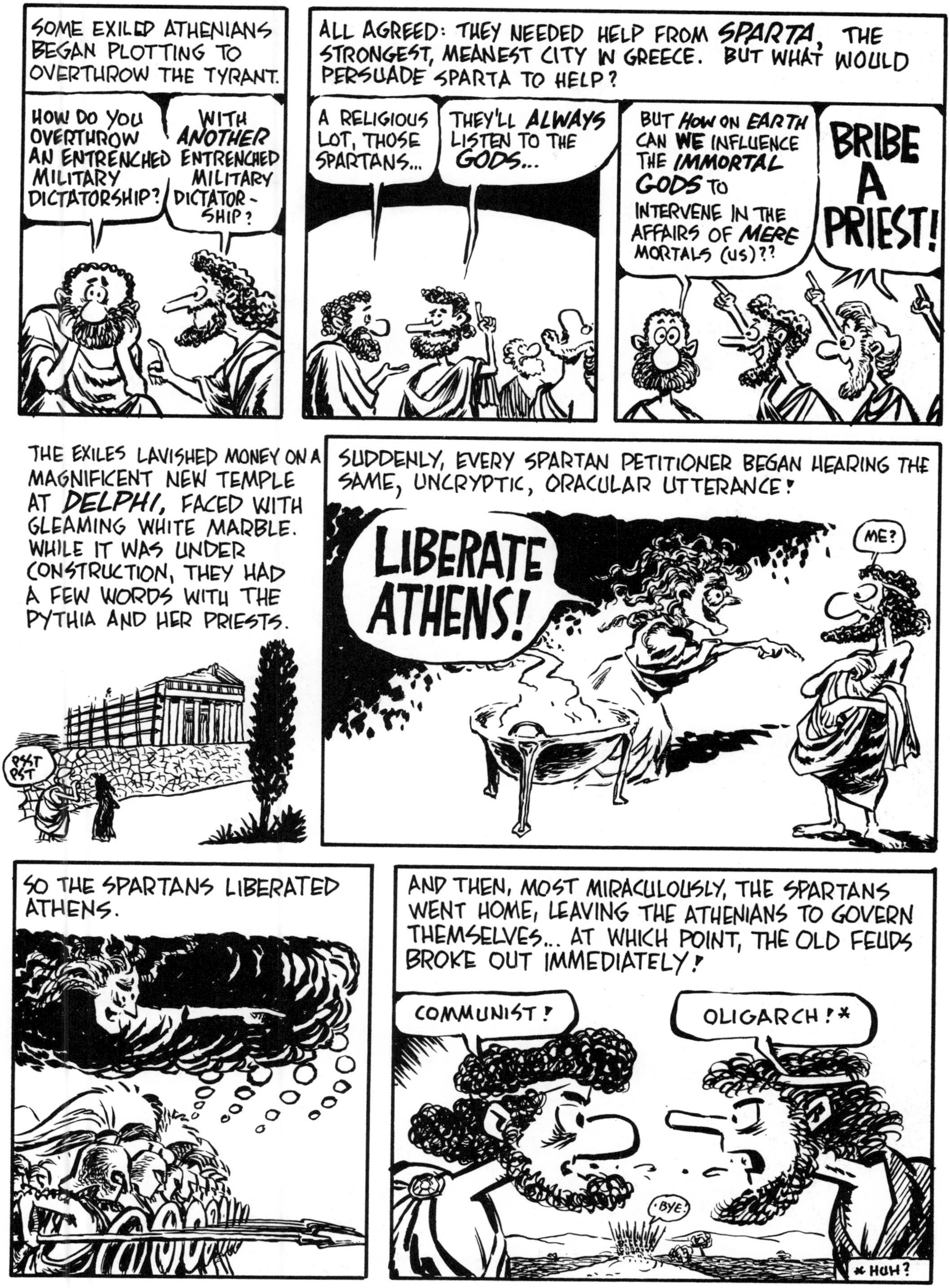
SOME EXILED ATHENIANS BEGAN PLOTTING TO OVERTHROW THE TYRANT.
HOW DO YOU OVERTHROW AN ENTRENCHED MILITARY DICTATORSHIP?
WITH ANOTHER ENTRENCHED MILITARY DICTATOR-SHIP?
ALL AGREED: THEY NEEDED HELP FROM SPARTA, THE STRONGEST, MEANEST CITY IN GREECE. BUT WHAT WOULD PERSUADE SPARTA TO HELP?
A RELIGIOUS LOT, THOSE SPARTANS...
THEY'LL ALWAYS LISTEN TO THE GODS...
BUT HOW ON EARTH CAN WE INFLUENCE THE IMMORTAL GODS TO INTERVENE IN THE AFFAIRS OF MERE MORTALS (US)??
BRIBE A PRIEST!
THE EXILES LAVISHED MONEY ON A MAGNIFICENT NEW TEMPLE AT DELPHI, FACED WITH GLEAMING WHITE MARBLE. WHILE IT WAS UNDER CONSTRUCTION, THEY HAD A FEW WORDS WITH THE PYTHIA AND HER PRIESTS.
PSST PST
SUDDENLY, EVERY SPARTAN PETITIONER BEGAN HEARING THE SAME, UNCRYPTIC, ORACULAR UTTERANCE!
LIBERATE ATHENS!
ME?
SO THE SPARTANS LIBERATED ATHENS.
AND THEN, MOST MIRACULOUSLY, THE SPARTANS WENT HOME, LEAVING THE ATHENIANS TO GOVERN THEMSELVES... AT WHICH POINT, THE OLD FEUDS BROKE OUT IMMEDIATELY!
COMMUNIST!
OLIGARCH!*
BYE!
* HUH?

IT WAS THE USUAL FIGHT: THE ***RICH***, AS USUAL, THOUGHT THE GOVERNMENT WAS THEIRS BY RIGHT... BUT THE LOWER CLASSES, GROWN STRONG UNDER PISISTRATOS, DECLARED ATHENS A ***DEMOCRACY***, RULED BY THE ***POPULAR ASSEMBLY***.

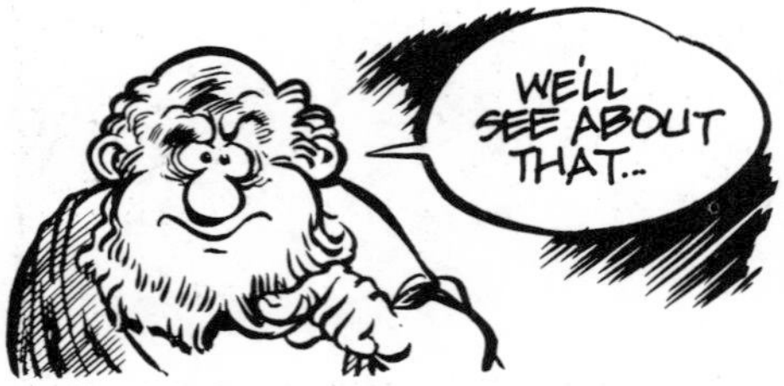
WE'LL SEE ABOUT THAT...

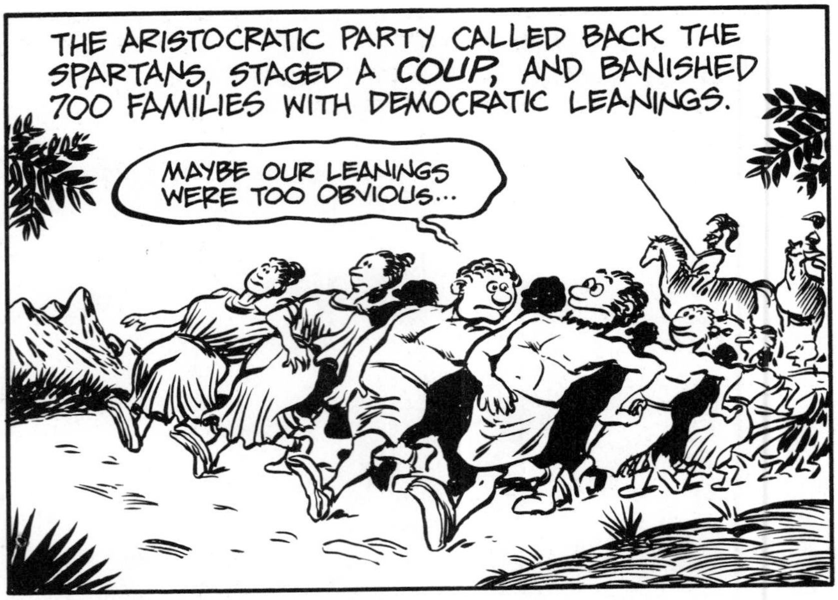
THE ARISTOCRATIC PARTY CALLED BACK THE SPARTANS, STAGED A COUP, AND BANISHED 700 FAMILIES WITH DEMOCRATIC LEANINGS.
MAYBE OUR LEANINGS WERE TOO OBVIOUS...

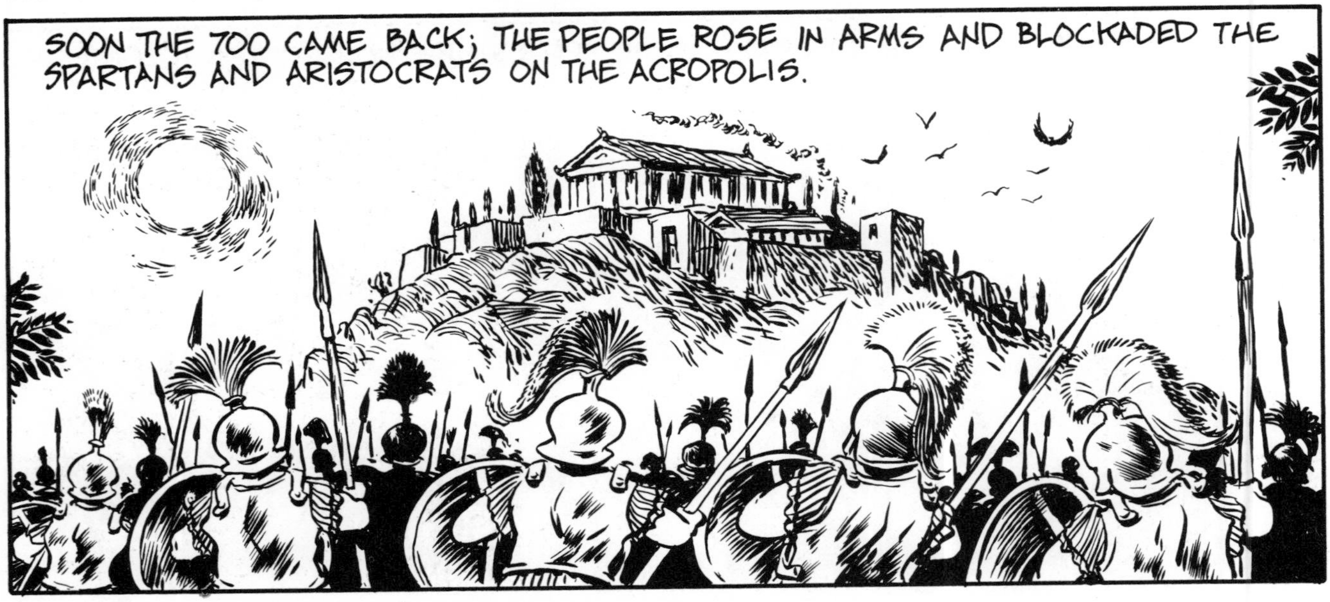
SOON THE 700 CAME BACK; THE PEOPLE ROSE IN ARMS AND BLOCKADED THE SPARTANS AND ARISTOCRATS ON THE ACROPOLIS.

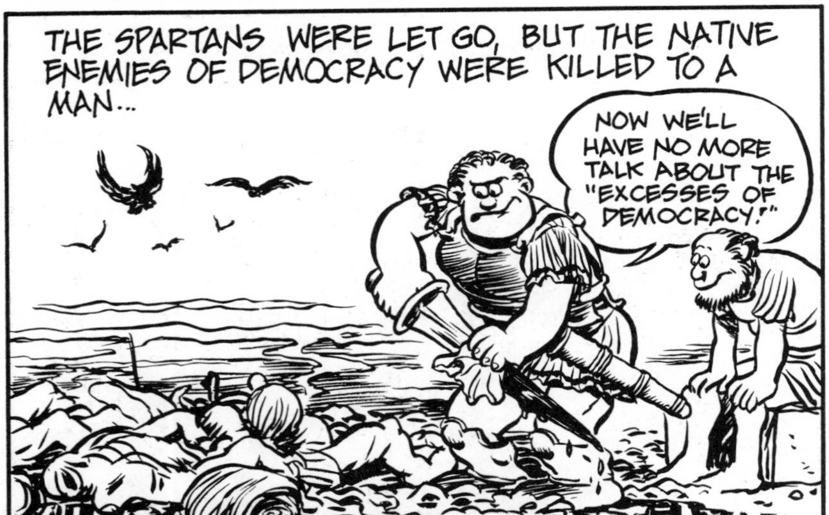
THE SPARTANS WERE LET GO, BUT THE NATIVE ENEMIES OF DEMOCRACY WERE KILLED TO A MAN...
NOW WE'LL HAVE NO MORE TALK ABOUT THE "EXCESSES OF DEMOCRACY!"

THIS BLOODY EVENT, CALLED THE ***ATHENIAN REVOLUTION***, FINALLY ESTABLISHED THE FAMOUS DEMOCRACY. HOW THIS GOVERNMENT WORKED WE'LL LEAVE ASIDE FOR NOW, JUST SAYING THAT, THANKS TO THE TYRANT'S ENFORCEMENT OF SOLON'S LAWS, ATHENS ALREADY HAD AN UNUSUALLY LARGE AND WELL-FED INFANTRY OF ***HOPLITES***.

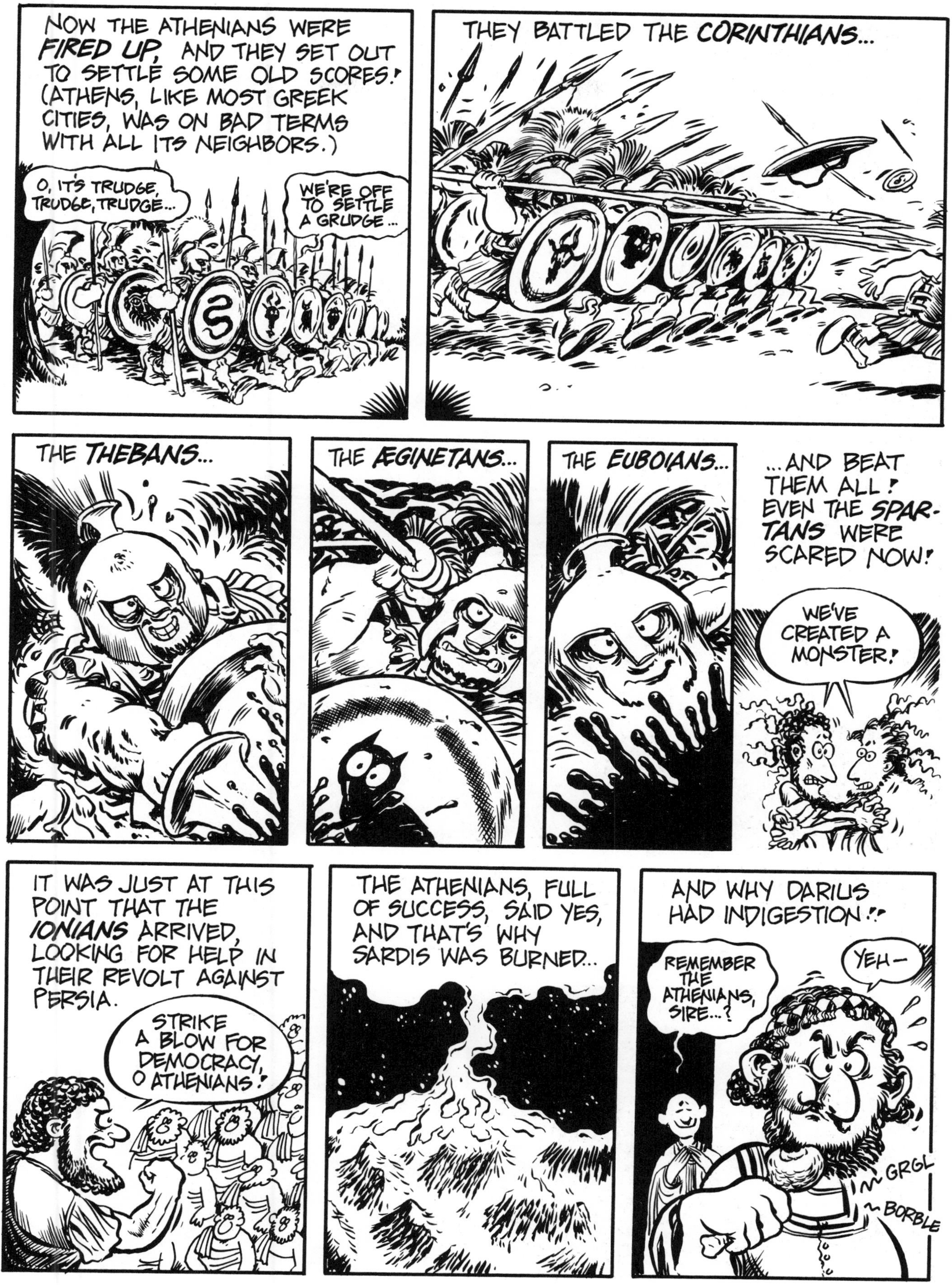
NOW THE ATHENIANS WERE FIRED UP, AND THEY SET OUT TO SETTLE SOME OLD SCORES! (ATHENS, LIKE MOST GREEK CITIES, WAS ON BAD TERMS WITH ALL ITS NEIGHBORS.)
O, IT'S TRUDGE, TRUDGE, TRUDGE...
WE'RE OFF TO SETTLE A GRUDGE...
THEY BATTLED THE CORINTHIANS...
THE THEBANS...
THE ÆGINETANS...
THE EUBOIANS...
...AND BEAT THEM ALL! EVEN THE SPARTANS WERE SCARED NOW!
WE'VE CREATED A MONSTER!
IT WAS JUST AT THIS POINT THAT THE IONIANS ARRIVED, LOOKING FOR HELP IN THEIR REVOLT AGAINST PERSIA.
STRIKE A BLOW FOR DEMOCRACY, O ATHENIANS!
THE ATHENIANS, FULL OF SUCCESS, SAID YES, AND THAT'S WHY SARDIS WAS BURNED...
AND WHY DARIUS HAD INDIGESTION!
REMEMBER THE ATHENIANS, SIRE...?
YEH—
GRGL
BORBLE

MARATHON

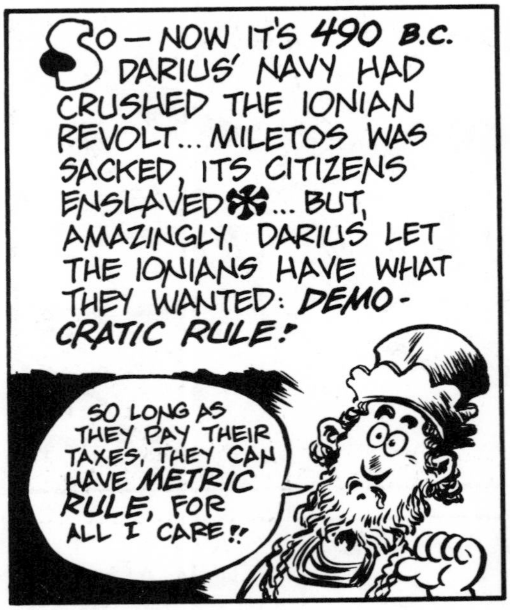
SO—NOW IT'S **490 B.C.** DARIUS' NAVY HAD CRUSHED THE IONIAN REVOLT... MILETOS WAS SACKED, ITS CITIZENS ENSLAVED✽... BUT, AMAZINGLY, DARIUS LET THE IONIANS HAVE WHAT THEY WANTED: ***DEMOCRATIC RULE!***
SO LONG AS THEY PAY THEIR TAXES, THEY CAN HAVE ***METRIC RULE,*** FOR ALL I CARE!!

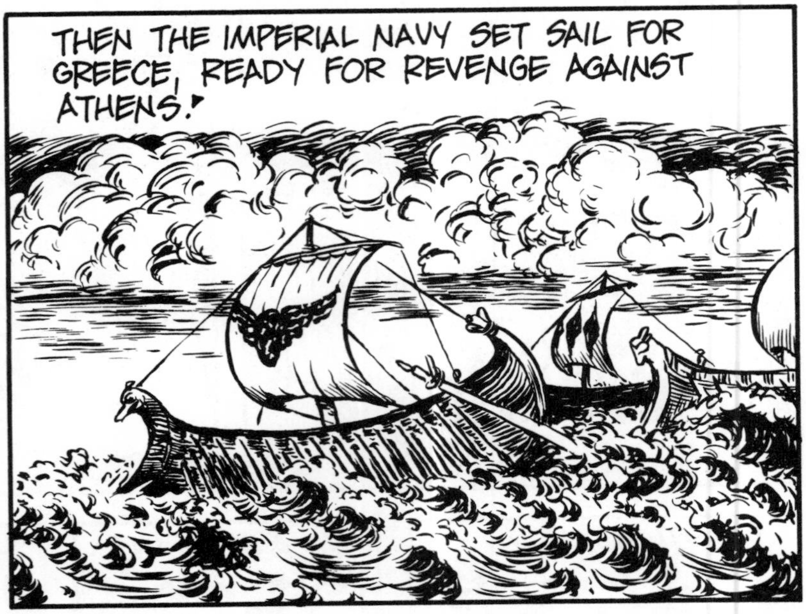
THEN THE IMPERIAL NAVY SET SAIL FOR GREECE, READY FOR REVENGE AGAINST ATHENS!

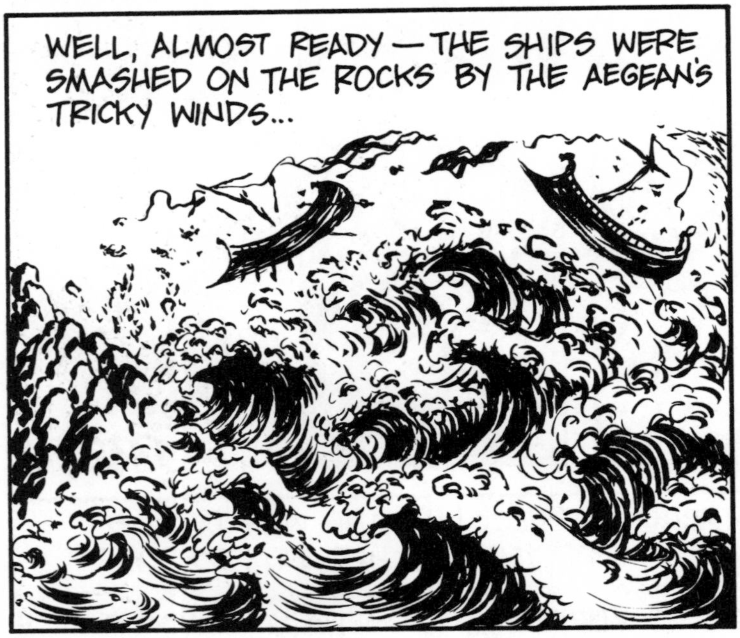
WELL, ALMOST READY—THE SHIPS WERE SMASHED ON THE ROCKS BY THE AEGEAN'S TRICKY WINDS...

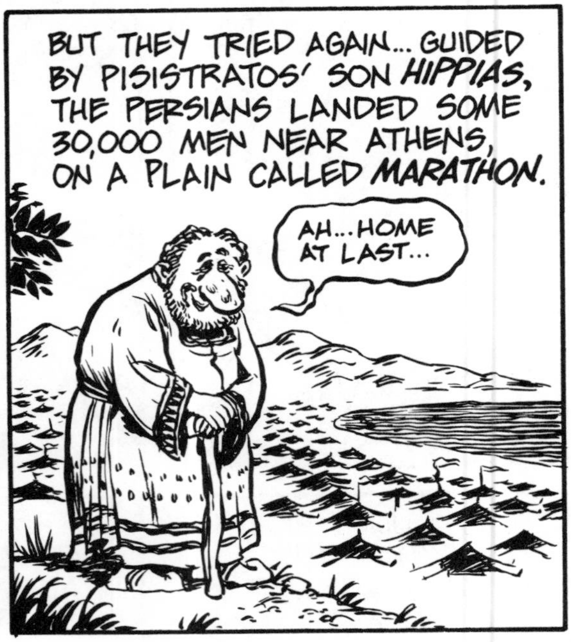
BUT THEY TRIED AGAIN... GUIDED BY PISISTRATOS' SON ***HIPPIAS,*** THE PERSIANS LANDED SOME 30,000 MEN NEAR ATHENS, ON A PLAIN CALLED ***MARATHON.***
AH... HOME AT LAST...

✽ IN THE YEAR 493, THE PLAYWRIGHT ***PHRYNICOS*** WROTE ***THE FALL OF MILETOS,*** AN ACCOUNT OF THE IONIAN REVOLT. SOMETHING IN THIS PLAY ***OFFENDED*** THE ATHENIANS, AND PHRYNICOS WAS ASSESSED A HEAVY FINE.

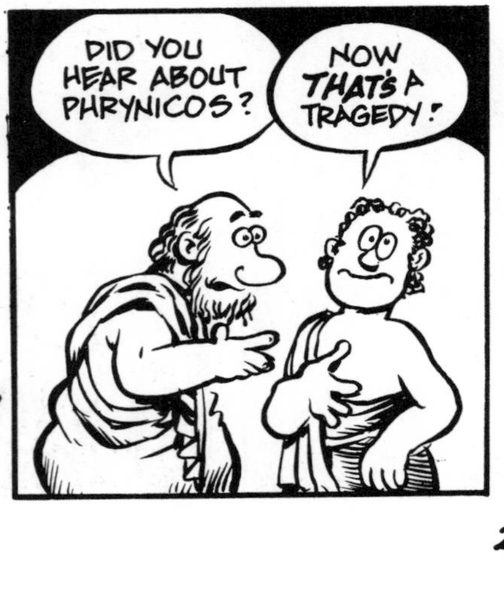
DID YOU HEAR ABOUT PHRYNICOS?
NOW ***THAT'S*** A TRAGEDY!

FROM THEN ON, ATHENIAN TRAGEDIANS ALMOST ALWAYS TOOK THEIR SUBJECTS FROM THE ***MYTHS*** AND ***LEGENDS.***

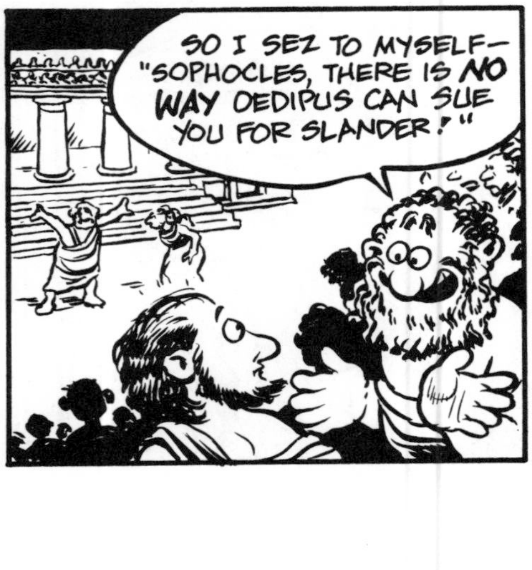
SO I SEZ TO MYSELF—"SOPHOCLES, THERE IS ***NO WAY*** OEDIPUS CAN SUE YOU FOR SLANDER!"

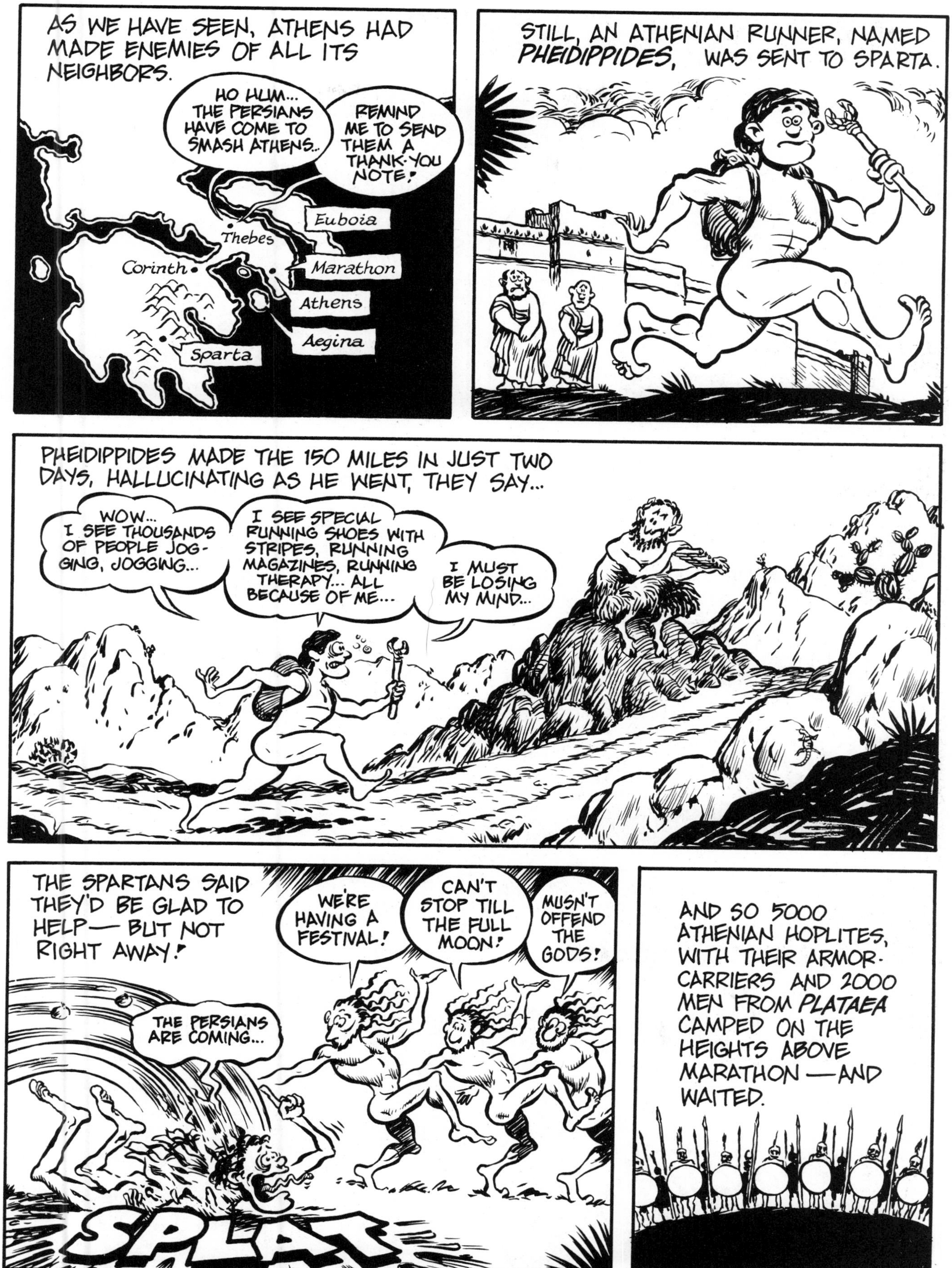
AS WE HAVE SEEN, ATHENS HAD MADE ENEMIES OF ALL ITS NEIGHBORS.
HO HUM... THE PERSIANS HAVE COME TO SMASH ATHENS...
REMIND ME TO SEND THEM A THANK-YOU NOTE!
Euboia
Thebes
Corinth
Marathon
Athens
Aegina
Sparta
STILL, AN ATHENIAN RUNNER, NAMED PHEIDIPPIDES, WAS SENT TO SPARTA.
PHEIDIPPIDES MADE THE 150 MILES IN JUST TWO DAYS, HALLUCINATING AS HE WENT, THEY SAY...
WOW... I SEE THOUSANDS OF PEOPLE JOG-GING, JOGGING...
I SEE SPECIAL RUNNING SHOES WITH STRIPES, RUNNING MAGAZINES, RUNNING THERAPY... ALL BECAUSE OF ME...
I MUST BE LOSING MY MIND...
THE SPARTANS SAID THEY'D BE GLAD TO HELP— BUT NOT RIGHT AWAY!
WE'RE HAVING A FESTIVAL!
CAN'T STOP TILL THE FULL MOON!
MUSN'T OFFEND THE GODS!
THE PERSIANS ARE COMING...
SPLAT
AND SO 5000 ATHENIAN HOPLITES, WITH THEIR ARMOR-CARRIERS AND 2000 MEN FROM PLATAEA CAMPED ON THE HEIGHTS ABOVE MARATHON —AND WAITED.

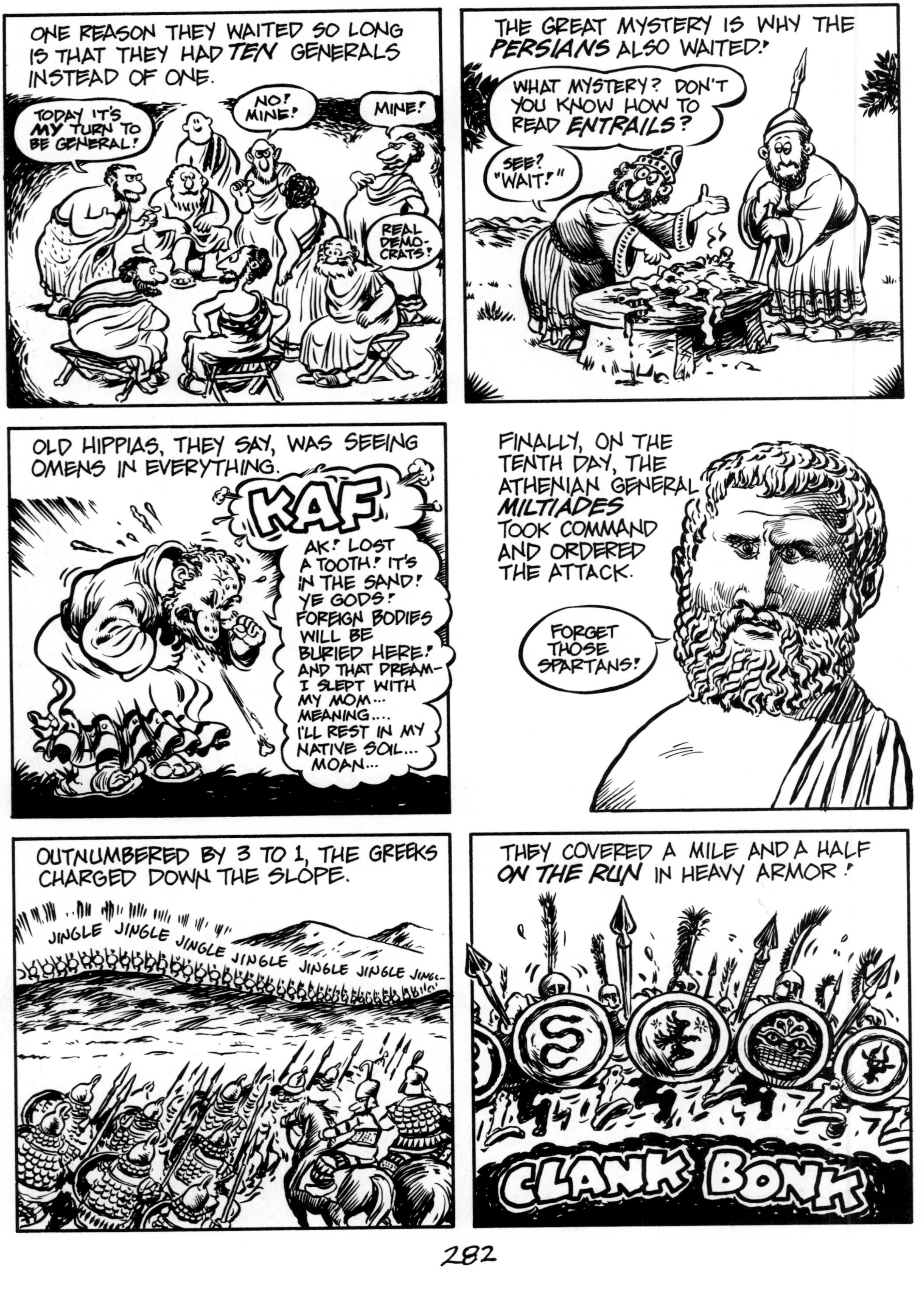
ONE REASON THEY WAITED SO LONG IS THAT THEY HAD TEN GENERALS INSTEAD OF ONE.
TODAY IT'S MY TURN TO BE GENERAL!
NO! MINE!
MINE!
REAL DEMO-CRATS!
THE GREAT MYSTERY IS WHY THE PERSIANS ALSO WAITED!
WHAT MYSTERY? DON'T YOU KNOW HOW TO READ ENTRAILS?
SEE? "WAIT!"
OLD HIPPIAS, THEY SAY, WAS SEEING OMENS IN EVERYTHING.
KAF
AK! LOST A TOOTH! IT'S IN THE SAND! YE GODS! FOREIGN BODIES WILL BE BURIED HERE! AND THAT DREAM- I SLEPT WITH MY MOM... MEANING.... I'LL REST IN MY NATIVE SOIL... MOAN...
FINALLY, ON THE TENTH DAY, THE ATHENIAN GENERAL MILTIADES TOOK COMMAND AND ORDERED THE ATTACK.
FORGET THOSE SPARTANS!
OUTNUMBERED BY 3 TO 1, THE GREEKS CHARGED DOWN THE SLOPE.
JINGLE JINGLE JINGLE JINGLE JINGLE JINGLE JINGL...
THEY COVERED A MILE AND A HALF ON THE RUN IN HEAVY ARMOR!
CLANK BONK

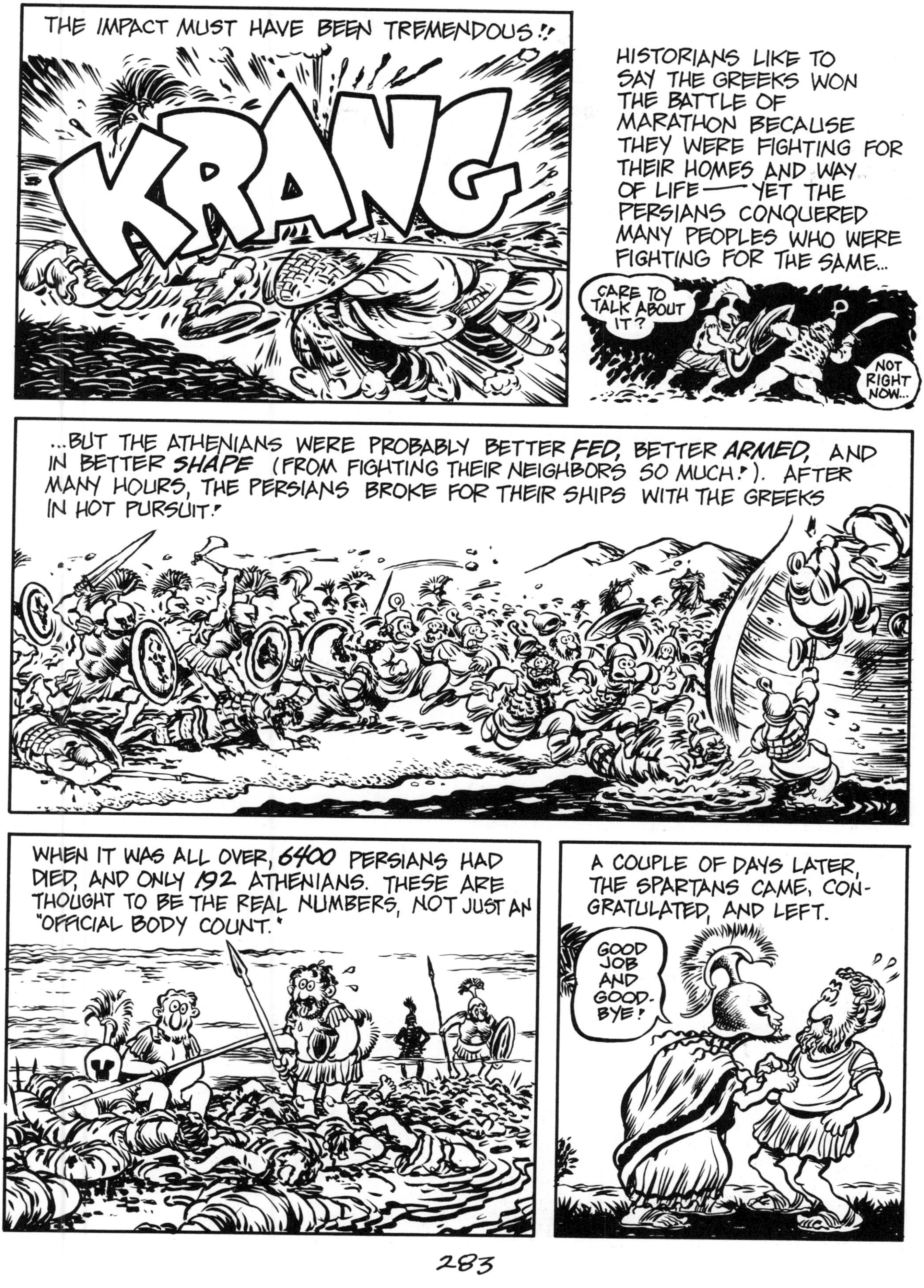
THE IMPACT MUST HAVE BEEN TREMENDOUS!!
KRANG
HISTORIANS LIKE TO SAY THE GREEKS WON THE BATTLE OF MARATHON BECAUSE THEY WERE FIGHTING FOR THEIR HOMES AND WAY OF LIFE — YET THE PERSIANS CONQUERED MANY PEOPLES WHO WERE FIGHTING FOR THE SAME...
CARE TO TALK ABOUT IT?
NOT RIGHT NOW...
...BUT THE ATHENIANS WERE PROBABLY BETTER FED, BETTER ARMED, AND IN BETTER SHAPE (FROM FIGHTING THEIR NEIGHBORS SO MUCH!). AFTER MANY HOURS, THE PERSIANS BROKE FOR THEIR SHIPS WITH THE GREEKS IN HOT PURSUIT!
WHEN IT WAS ALL OVER, 6400 PERSIANS HAD DIED, AND ONLY 192 ATHENIANS. THESE ARE THOUGHT TO BE THE REAL NUMBERS, NOT JUST AN "OFFICIAL BODY COUNT."
A COUPLE OF DAYS LATER, THE SPARTANS CAME, CONGRATULATED, AND LEFT.
GOOD JOB AND GOOD-BYE!

SILVER AND SHIPS

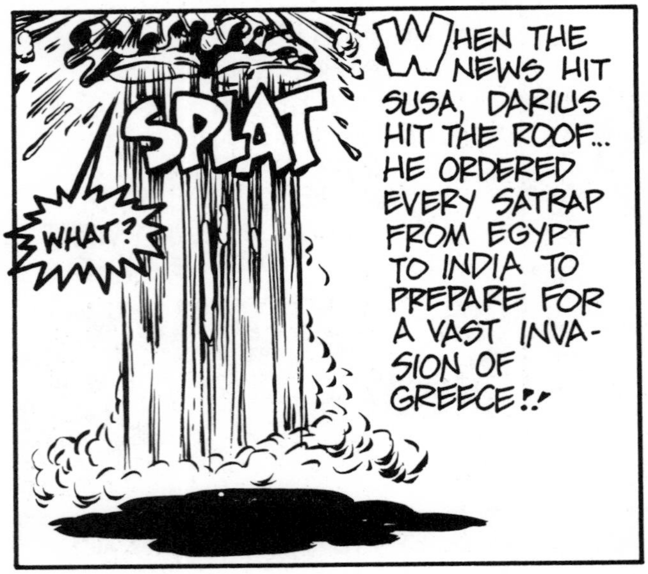
WHEN THE NEWS HIT SUSA, DARIUS HIT THE ROOF... HE ORDERED EVERY SATRAP FROM EGYPT TO INDIA TO PREPARE FOR A VAST INVASION OF GREECE!!
SPLAT
WHAT?

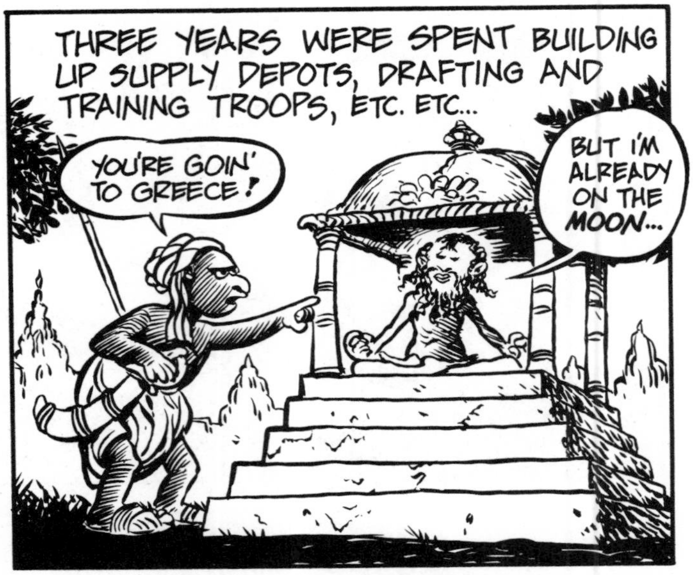
THREE YEARS WERE SPENT BUILDING UP SUPPLY DEPOTS, DRAFTING AND TRAINING TROOPS, ETC. ETC...
YOU'RE GOIN' TO GREECE!
BUT I'M ALREADY ON THE MOON...

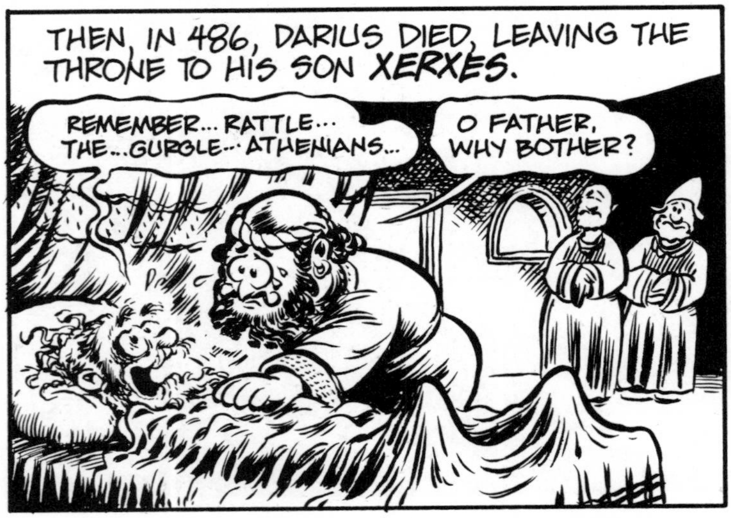
THEN, IN 486, DARIUS DIED, LEAVING THE THRONE TO HIS SON XERXES.
REMEMBER... RATTLE... THE...GURGLE... ATHENIANS...
O FATHER, WHY BOTHER?

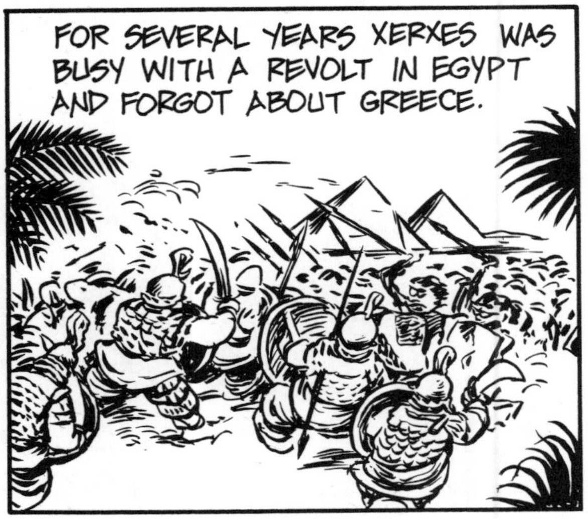
FOR SEVERAL YEARS XERXES WAS BUSY WITH A REVOLT IN EGYPT AND FORGOT ABOUT GREECE.

MEANWHILE, BACK IN ATHENS, MILTIADES, HERO OF MARATHON, WAS ACCUSED OF MISUSE OF PUBLIC FUNDS AND ARRESTED; HE DIED IN JAIL OF GANGRENE, CAUSING THE ATHENIANS TO PONDER THE FICKLENESS OF FATE (AND OTHERS TO PONDER THE FICKLENESS OF ATHENS).

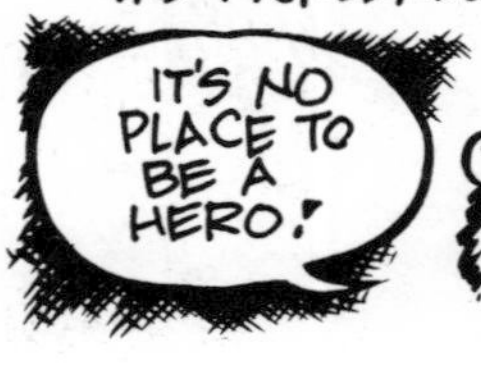
IT'S NO PLACE TO BE A HERO!

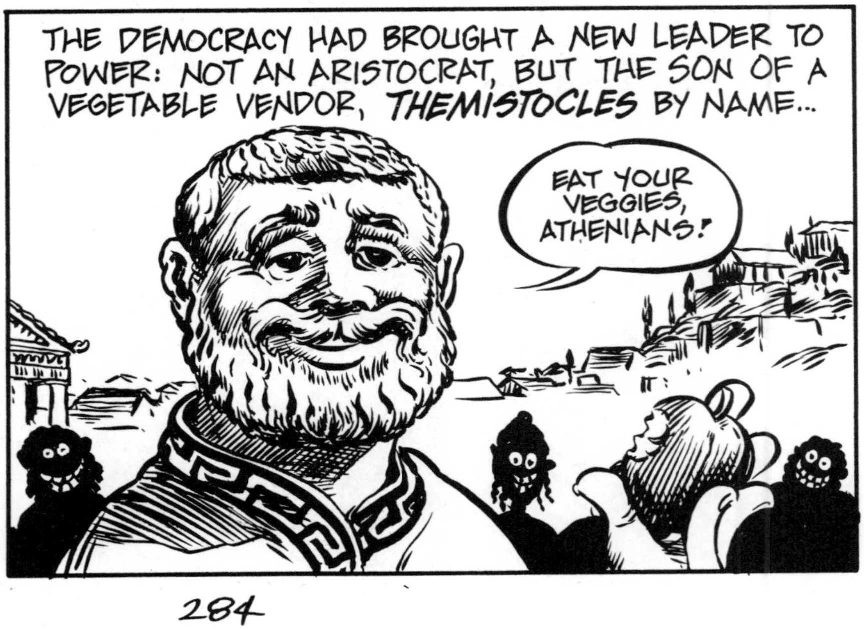
THE DEMOCRACY HAD BROUGHT A NEW LEADER TO POWER: NOT AN ARISTOCRAT, BUT THE SON OF A VEGETABLE VENDOR, THEMISTOCLES BY NAME...
EAT YOUR VEGGIES, ATHENIANS!

NOW IT HAPPENED THAT THE SLAVES WORKING THE ATHENIAN *SILVER MINES* — A MOST AWFUL PLACE, WITH 3-FOOT SHAFTS AND 12-HOUR SHIFTS — HAD STRUCK AN ESPECIALLY RICH VEIN.

SOME PEOPLE WANTED SIMPLY TO DIVIDE UP THE SURPLUS, WHILE THEMISTOCLES PROPOSED TO SPEND IT ON *WARSHIPS.* THEMISTOCLES, WHO HAD *OSTRACIZED* ✱ ALL HIS POLITICAL RIVALS, CARRIED THE VOTE.

WITH WARSHIPS, WE CAN GET ALL THE SILVER WE NEED!

BY THE YEAR *480*, ATHENS HAD GREAT SHIPYARDS AND 200 *TRIREMES* — AS MANY AS THE REST OF GREECE COMBINED.

✱ BATTLESHIPS WITH 3 TIERS OF OARS

✱ UNDER ATHENIAN LAW, IN ANY GIVEN YEAR THE PEOPLE HAD THE RIGHT TO *BANISH ONE CITIZEN* FOR ANY REASON THEY PLEASED, BY MAJORITY VOTE.

WHAD I DO?

NOTHING. WE JUST DON'T *LIKE* YOU VERY MUCH...

THIS WAS CALLED *OSTRACISM*, BECAUSE THE NAMES WERE WRITTEN ON POTSHERDS — "OSTRAKA" IN GREEK.

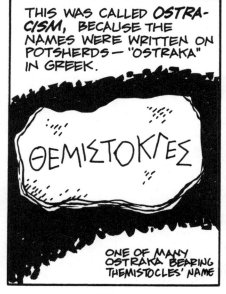

ΘΕΜΙΣΤΟΚΓΕΣ

ONE OF MANY OSTRAKA BEARING THEMISTOCLES' NAME

AFTER *TEN YEARS*, THE OSTRACIZED CITIZEN WAS FREE TO RETURN WITHOUT FURTHER PENALTY.

HEY-Y-Y! WELCOME *HOME!*

IT'S SO NICE TO HAVE YOU BACK TO KICK AROUND!

ACROPOLIS NOW!

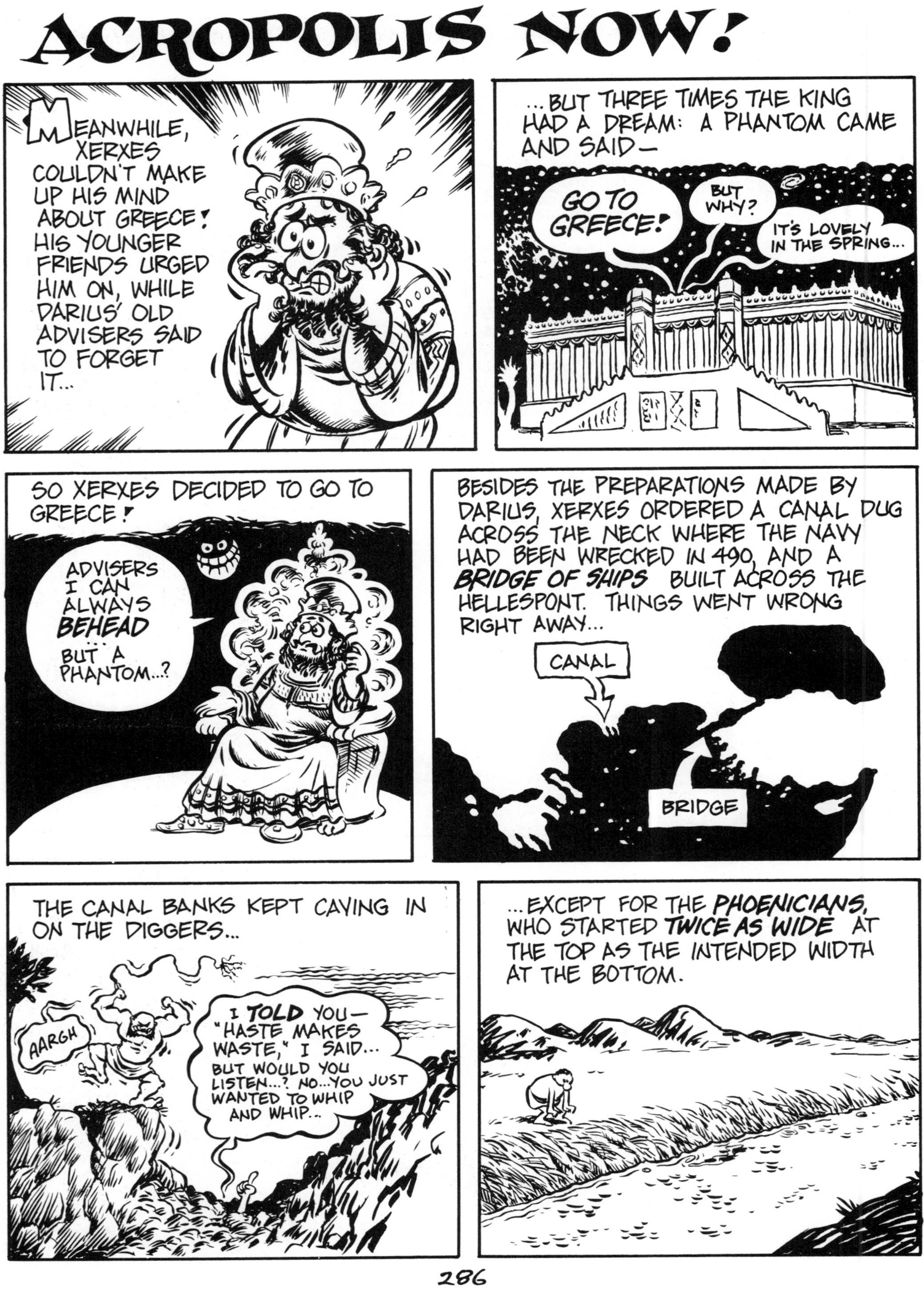

MEANWHILE, XERXES COULDN'T MAKE UP HIS MIND ABOUT GREECE! HIS YOUNGER FRIENDS URGED HIM ON, WHILE DARIUS' OLD ADVISERS SAID TO FORGET IT...
...BUT THREE TIMES THE KING HAD A DREAM: A PHANTOM CAME AND SAID—
GO TO GREECE!
BUT WHY?
IT'S LOVELY IN THE SPRING...
SO XERXES DECIDED TO GO TO GREECE!
ADVISERS I CAN ALWAYS BEHEAD... BUT A PHANTOM...?
BESIDES THE PREPARATIONS MADE BY DARIUS, XERXES ORDERED A CANAL DUG ACROSS THE NECK WHERE THE NAVY HAD BEEN WRECKED IN 490, AND A BRIDGE OF SHIPS BUILT ACROSS THE HELLESPONT. THINGS WENT WRONG RIGHT AWAY...
CANAL
BRIDGE
THE CANAL BANKS KEPT CAVING IN ON THE DIGGERS...
AARGH
I TOLD YOU— "HASTE MAKES WASTE," I SAID... BUT WOULD YOU LISTEN...? NO...YOU JUST WANTED TO WHIP AND WHIP...
...EXCEPT FOR THE PHOENICIANS, WHO STARTED TWICE AS WIDE AT THE TOP AS THE INTENDED WIDTH AT THE BOTTOM.

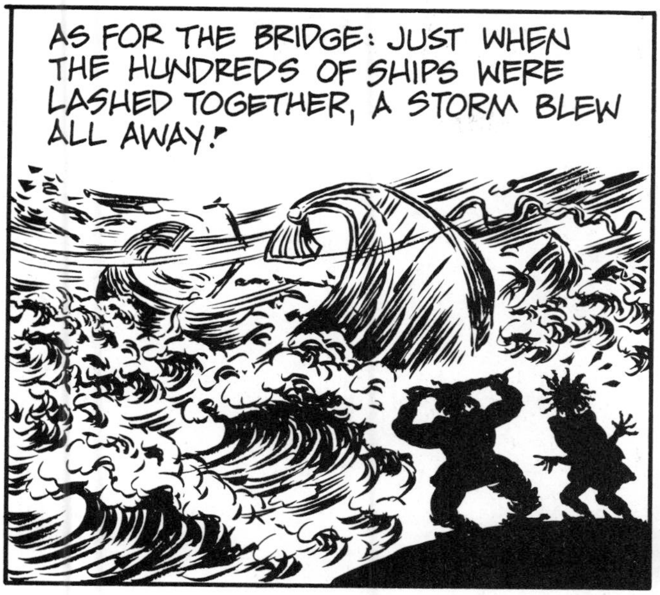
AS FOR THE BRIDGE: JUST WHEN THE HUNDREDS OF SHIPS WERE LASHED TOGETHER, A STORM BLEW ALL AWAY!

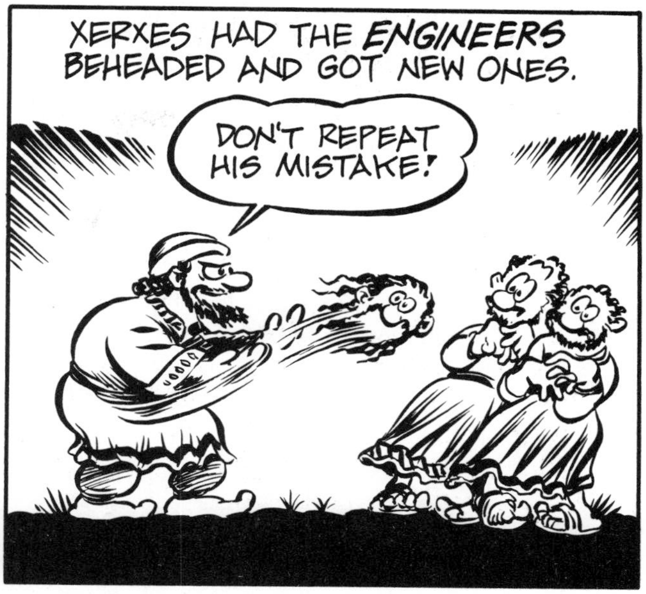
XERXES HAD THE *ENGINEERS* BEHEADED AND GOT NEW ONES.
DON'T REPEAT HIS MISTAKE!

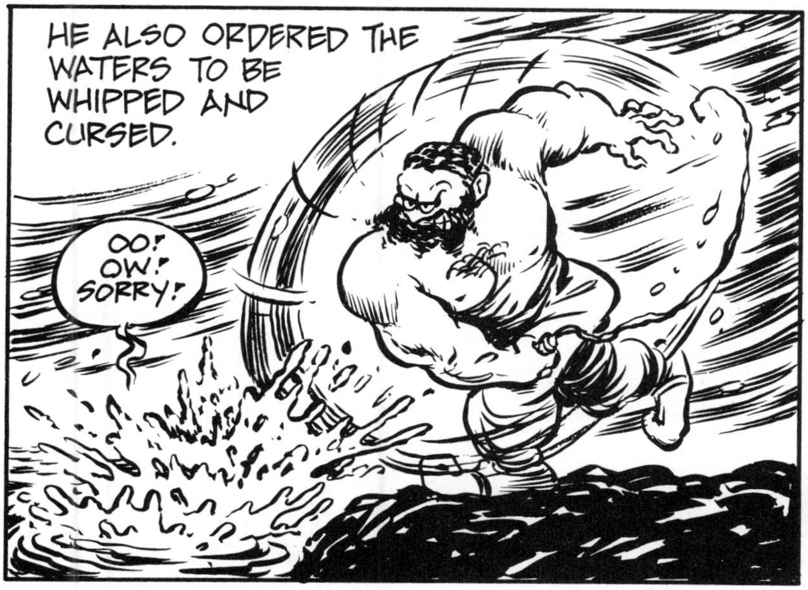
HE ALSO ORDERED THE WATERS TO BE WHIPPED AND CURSED.
OO! OW! SORRY!

THE BRIDGE WAS REBUILT, THE SHIPS ATTACHED BY CABLES OF *LINEN* AND *PAPYRUS* — EACH SOME THREE FEET THICK. IT WAS COVERED WITH PLANKS, THEN WITH DIRT, AND WALLS WERE MADE TO PREVENT THE HORSES FROM SEEING THE WATER AND TAKING FRIGHT.

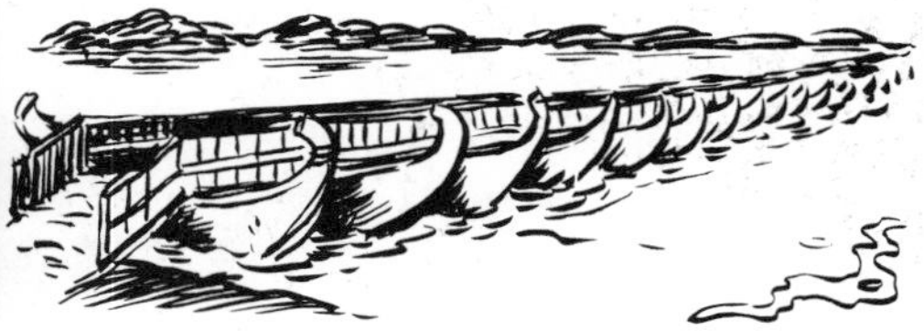

THE ARMY ITSELF WAS IMMENSE: MILLIONS, BY ANCIENT ACCOUNTS, HUNDREDS OF THOUSANDS, ACCORDING TO MODERN HISTORIANS... THEN ADD ON THE COUNTLESS SERVANTS, WIVES, MISTRESSES, CAMP-FOLLOWERS ... AND DON'T FORGET THE PACK ANIMALS... AND IT ALL ADDS UP TO *ONE THING* —

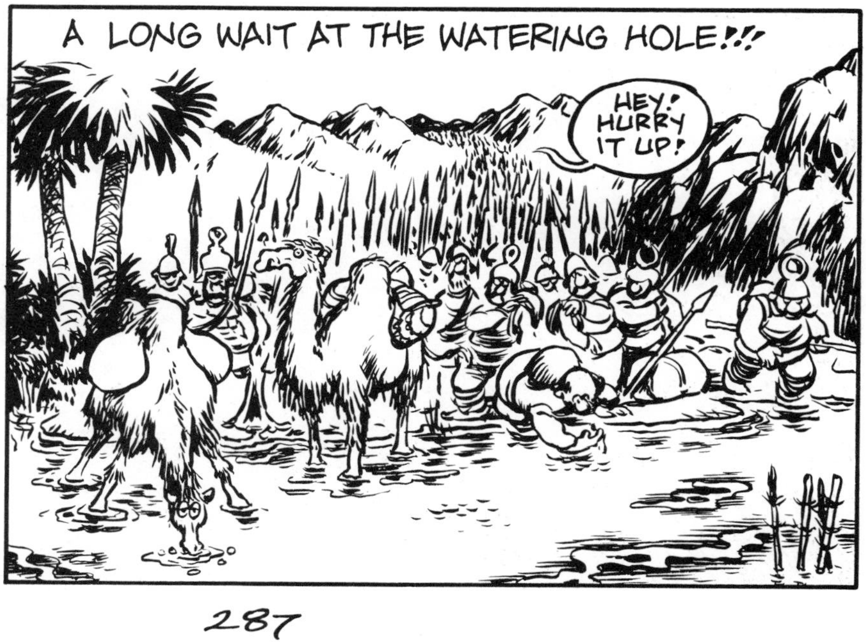
A LONG WAIT AT THE WATERING HOLE!!!
HEY! HURRY IT UP!

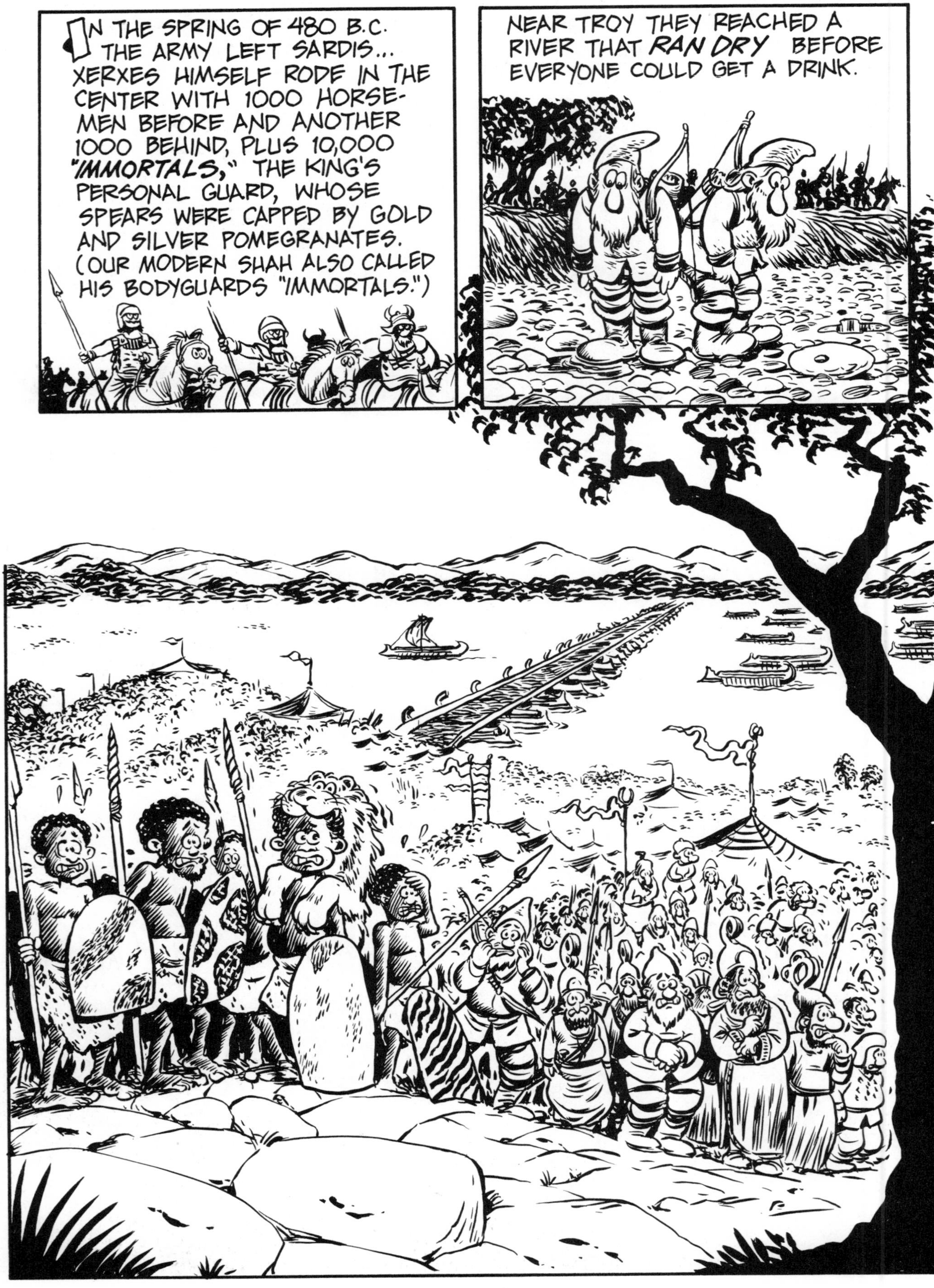
IN THE SPRING OF 480 B.C. THE ARMY LEFT SARDIS... XERXES HIMSELF RODE IN THE CENTER WITH 1000 HORSEMEN BEFORE AND ANOTHER 1000 BEHIND, PLUS 10,000 "IMMORTALS," THE KING'S PERSONAL GUARD, WHOSE SPEARS WERE CAPPED BY GOLD AND SILVER POMEGRANATES. (OUR MODERN SHAH ALSO CALLED HIS BODYGUARDS "IMMORTALS.")
NEAR TROY THEY REACHED A RIVER THAT RAN DRY BEFORE EVERYONE COULD GET A DRINK.

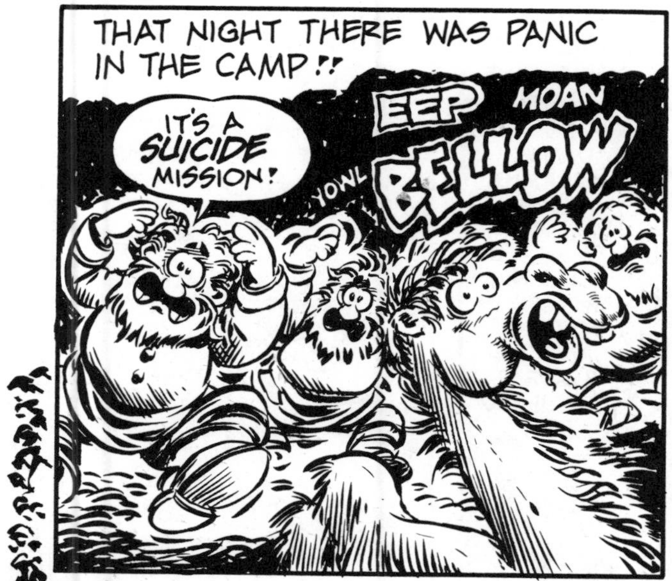
THAT NIGHT THERE WAS PANIC IN THE CAMP!!
IT'S A SUICIDE MISSION!
EEP
MOAN
YOWL
BELLOW

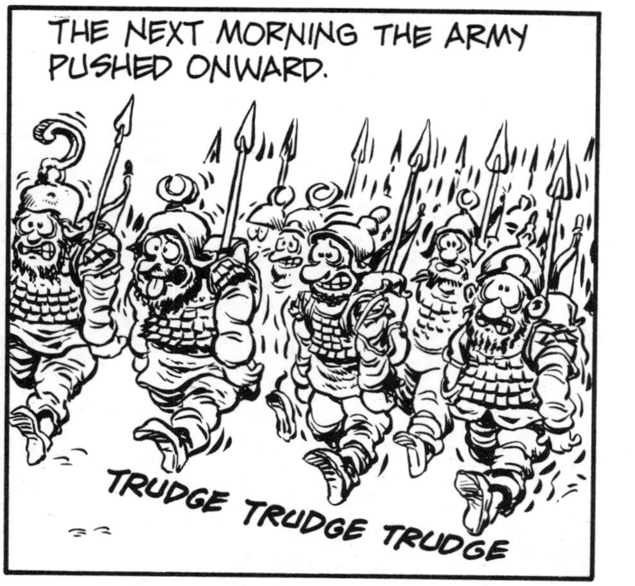
THE NEXT MORNING THE ARMY PUSHED ONWARD.
TRUDGE TRUDGE TRUDGE

WHEN THEY REACHED THE HELLESPONT, XERXES REVIEWED THE TROOPS AND HAD A CONVERSATION WITH HIS OLD UNCLE ***ARTABANUS,*** WHO HAD BEEN AGAINST THIS TRIP ALL ALONG.

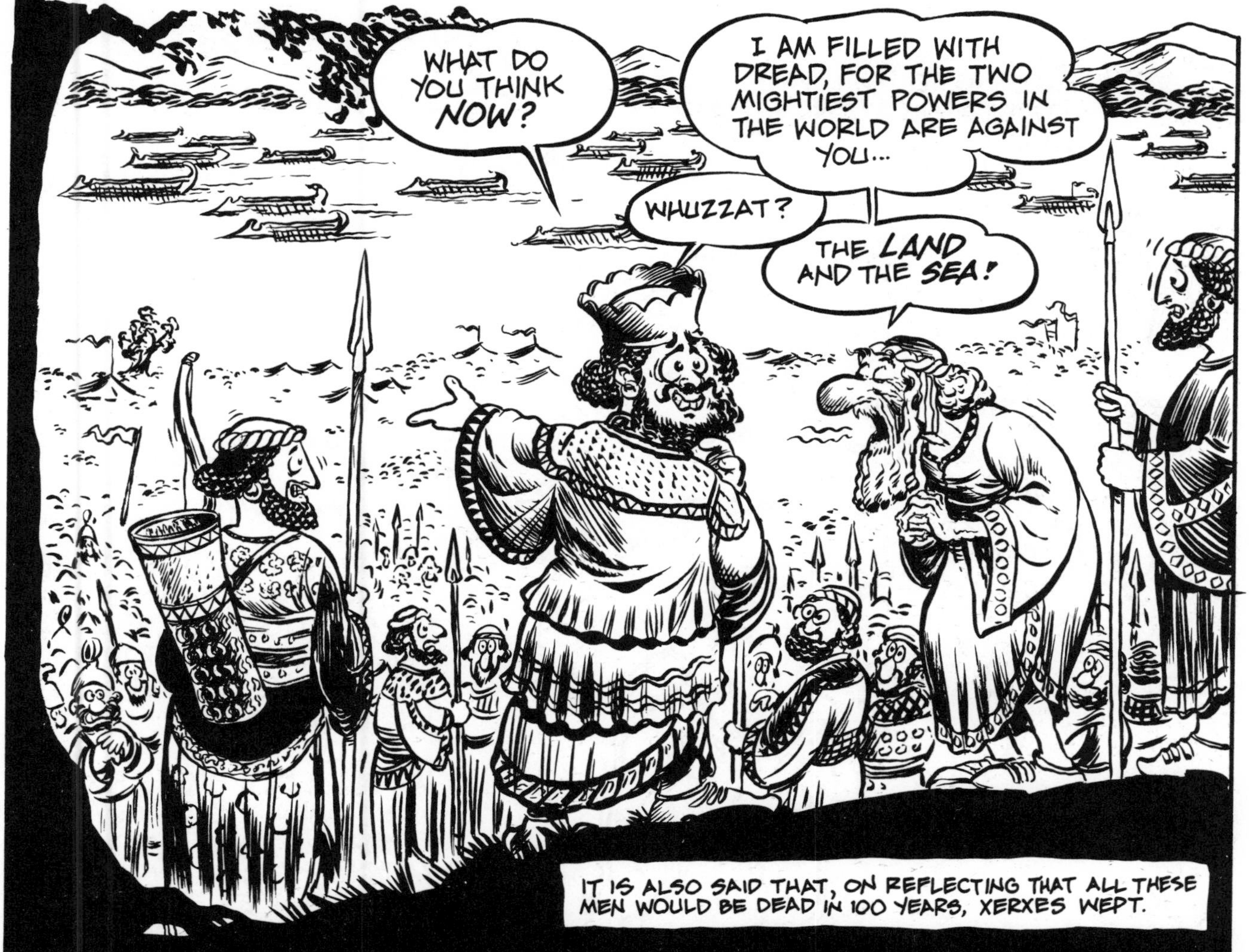
WHAT DO YOU THINK NOW?
I AM FILLED WITH DREAD, FOR THE TWO MIGHTIEST POWERS IN THE WORLD ARE AGAINST YOU...
WHUZZAT?
THE LAND AND THE SEA!
IT IS ALSO SAID THAT, ON REFLECTING THAT ALL THESE MEN WOULD BE DEAD IN 100 YEARS, XERXES WEPT.

AFTER CROSSING THE BRIDGE (WHICH TOOK A **WEEK**), THE ARMY HEADED FOR GREECE, DRINKING RIVERS DRY AND EATING EVERYTHING IN SIGHT.

AT LEAST THEY DIDN'T ASK FOR SECONDS!

BWORP

THE DELPHIC ORACLE WAS FLIPPING OUT! SHE SAID:

"DIVINE SALAMIS, YOU WILL BRING DEATH TO WOMEN'S SONS WHEN THE CORN IS SCATTERED AND THE HARVEST GATHERED IN!"

IN ATHENS, THEMISTOCLES TRIED TO PUT THIS IN THE BEST LIGHT:

SHE SAID "**DIVINE** SALAMIS" — IS THAT SO BAD??

"DIVINE SALAMIS?"

AS IN "HOLY BOLOGNAS?"

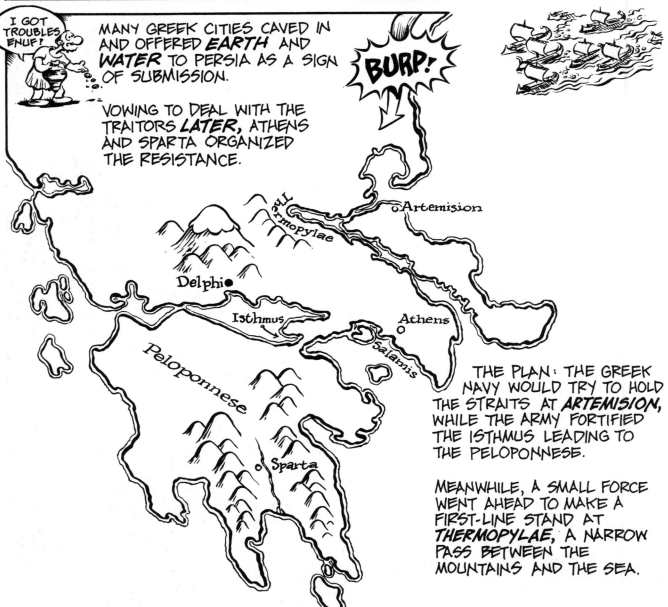

I GOT TROUBLES ENUF!

MANY GREEK CITIES CAVED IN AND OFFERED **EARTH** AND **WATER** TO PERSIA AS A SIGN OF SUBMISSION.

VOWING TO DEAL WITH THE TRAITORS **LATER,** ATHENS AND SPARTA ORGANIZED THE RESISTANCE.

BURP!

Artemision

Thermopylae

Delphi

Isthmus

Athens

Salamis

Peloponnese

Sparta

THE PLAN: THE GREEK NAVY WOULD TRY TO HOLD THE STRAITS AT **ARTEMISION,** WHILE THE ARMY FORTIFIED THE ISTHMUS LEADING TO THE PELOPONNESE.

MEANWHILE, A SMALL FORCE WENT AHEAD TO MAKE A FIRST-LINE STAND AT **THERMOPYLAE,** A NARROW PASS BETWEEN THE MOUNTAINS AND THE SEA.

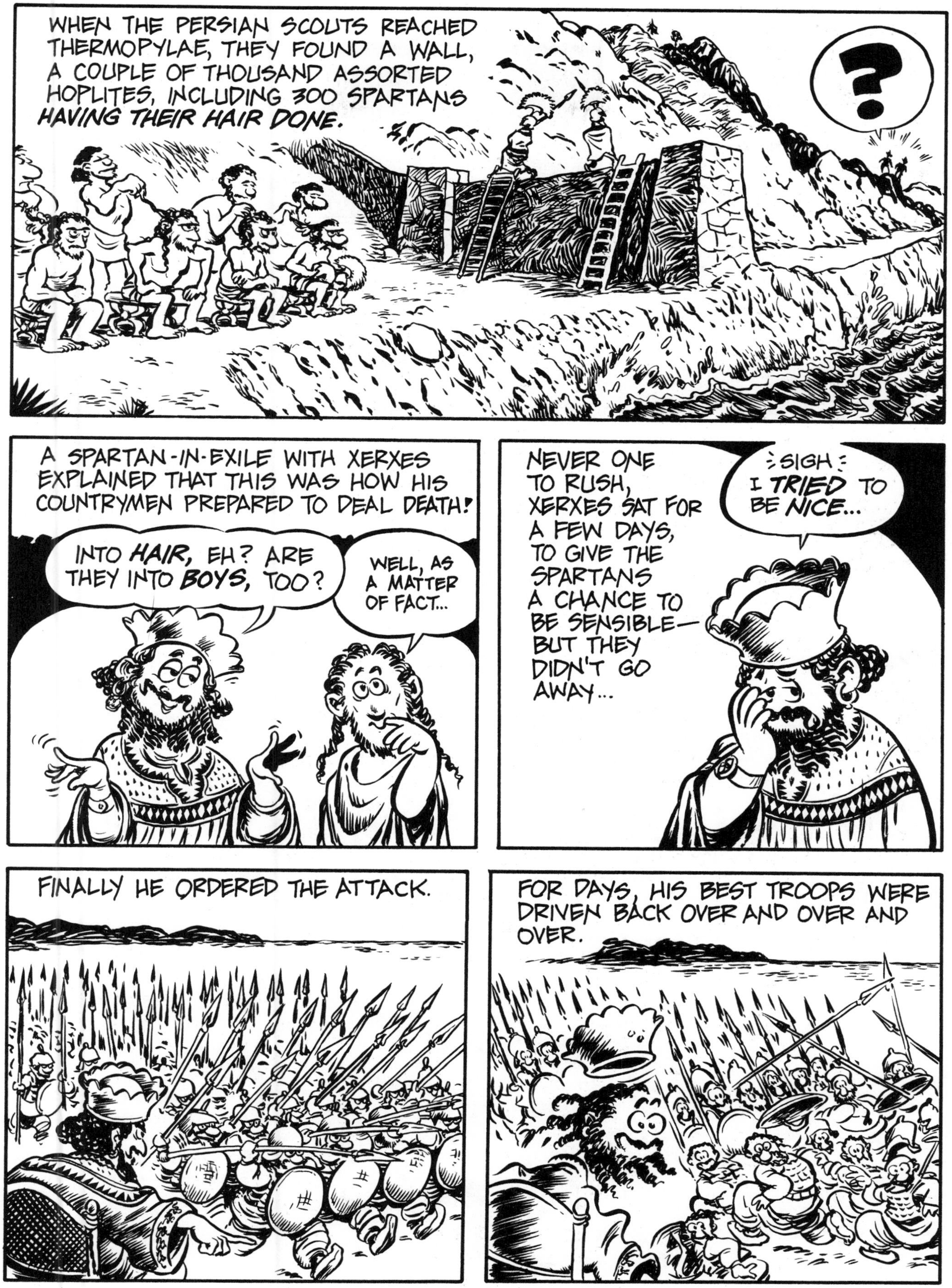
WHEN THE PERSIAN SCOUTS REACHED THERMOPYLAE, THEY FOUND A WALL, A COUPLE OF THOUSAND ASSORTED HOPLITES, INCLUDING 300 SPARTANS *HAVING THEIR HAIR DONE.*
?
A SPARTAN-IN-EXILE WITH XERXES EXPLAINED THAT THIS WAS HOW HIS COUNTRYMEN PREPARED TO DEAL DEATH!
INTO *HAIR,* EH? ARE THEY INTO *BOYS,* TOO?
WELL, AS A MATTER OF FACT...
NEVER ONE TO RUSH, XERXES SAT FOR A FEW DAYS, TO GIVE THE SPARTANS A CHANCE TO BE SENSIBLE— BUT THEY DIDN'T GO AWAY...
SIGH
I *TRIED* TO BE *NICE*...
FINALLY HE ORDERED THE ATTACK.
FOR DAYS, HIS BEST TROOPS WERE DRIVEN BACK OVER AND OVER AND OVER.

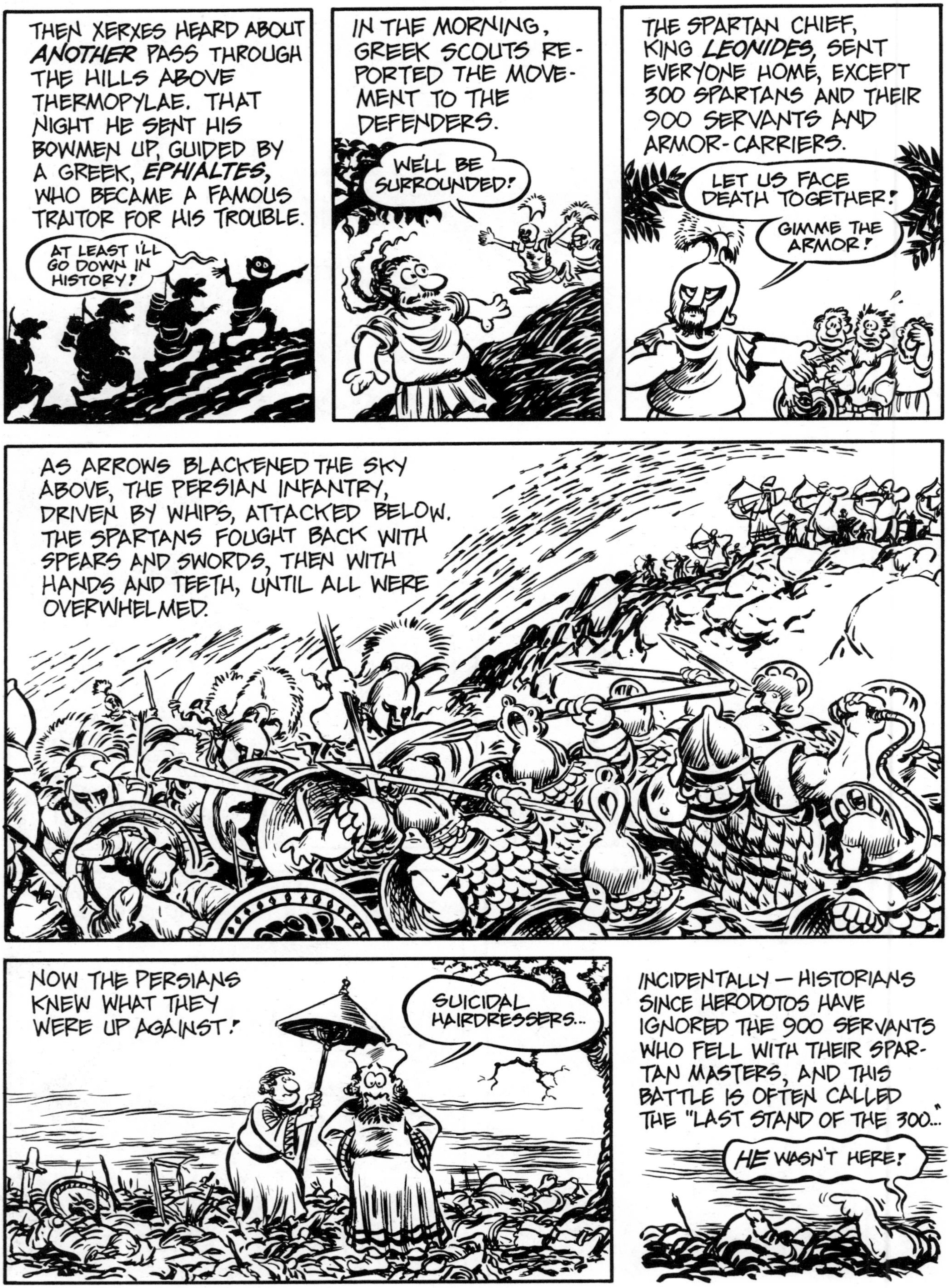
THEN XERXES HEARD ABOUT *ANOTHER* PASS THROUGH THE HILLS ABOVE THERMOPYLAE. THAT NIGHT HE SENT HIS BOWMEN UP, GUIDED BY A GREEK, *EPHIALTES*, WHO BECAME A FAMOUS TRAITOR FOR HIS TROUBLE.
AT LEAST I'LL GO DOWN IN HISTORY!
IN THE MORNING, GREEK SCOUTS REPORTED THE MOVEMENT TO THE DEFENDERS.
WE'LL BE SURROUNDED!
THE SPARTAN CHIEF, KING *LEONIDES*, SENT EVERYONE HOME, EXCEPT 300 SPARTANS AND THEIR 900 SERVANTS AND ARMOR-CARRIERS.
LET US FACE DEATH TOGETHER!
GIMME THE ARMOR!
AS ARROWS BLACKENED THE SKY ABOVE, THE PERSIAN INFANTRY, DRIVEN BY WHIPS, ATTACKED BELOW. THE SPARTANS FOUGHT BACK WITH SPEARS AND SWORDS, THEN WITH HANDS AND TEETH, UNTIL ALL WERE OVERWHELMED.
NOW THE PERSIANS KNEW WHAT THEY WERE UP AGAINST!
SUICIDAL HAIRDRESSERS...
INCIDENTALLY — HISTORIANS SINCE HERODOTOS HAVE IGNORED THE 900 SERVANTS WHO FELL WITH THEIR SPARTAN MASTERS, AND THIS BATTLE IS OFTEN CALLED THE "LAST STAND OF THE 300..."
HE WASN'T HERE!

ON THE SAME DAY AS THE LAND BATTLE, THE NAVIES WERE FIGHTING AT ARTEMISION.

BASH

AFTER SUFFERING HEAVY LOSSES, THE GREEKS WERE FORCED TO RETREAT DOWN THE COAST TO THE ISLAND OF **SALAMIS**, NEAR ATHENS.

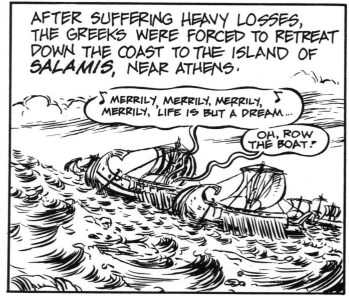

♪ MERRILY, MERRILY, MERRILY, MERRILY, 'LIFE IS BUT A DREAM... ♪

OH, ROW THE BOAT!

THIS MEANT THAT NOTHING NOW STOOD BETWEEN XERXES AND ATHENS...

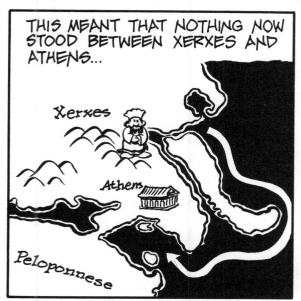

Xerxes

Athens

Peloponnese

...SO NATURALLY, THE ATHENIANS HELD A MEETING! THE QUESTION: STAY AND FIGHT, OR CLEAR OUT OF THE WAY ??

WHAT A QUESTION!

MILTIADES' SON **CIMON** LED A SYMBOLIC PARADE OF YOUNG HIPPEIS, WHO LAID DOWN THEIR HORSES' BRIDLES IN THE TEMPLE— MEANING: DON'T FIGHT WITH CAVALRY, BUT WITH **SHIPS**...

BREAKS MY HEART, REALLY... TO LET THAT NAVY RABBLE GET THE GLORY... BUT LET'S BE REASONABLE...

...SO ATHENS WAS EVACUATED, EXCEPT FOR A FEW DIE-HARDS HOLED UP ON THE ACROPOLIS.

Panel 1

XERXES TOOK HIS TIME GETTING THERE...

WE HAVE TO WASTE THE COUNTRYSIDE VERY, VERY CAREFULLY!

Panel 2

...BUT FINALLY THE IMPERIALS REACHED ATHENS, STORMED THE ACROPOLIS, KILLED THE DIE-HARDS, AND TORCHED THE TEMPLES — MISSION ACCOMPLISHED!!

ARE YOU HAPPY, NOW, DAD??

Panel 3

THEN XERXES JOINED HIS NAVY, WHICH HAD SAILED INTO THE BAY OF PHALERUM, JUST AROUND THE CORNER FROM SALAMIS.

Athens→

Salamis

GREEK NAVY

PERSIAN NAVY

Panel 4

NOW — A WORD ABOUT THE GREEK NAVY: ALTHOUGH NEARLY HALF THE SHIPS WERE FROM *ATHENS*, THE OTHER ALLIES COULDN'T BEAR THE THOUGHT OF TAKING ORDERS FROM AN ATHENIAN...

ESPECIALLY NOT THE PUSHY SON OF A VEGETABLE VENDOR!!

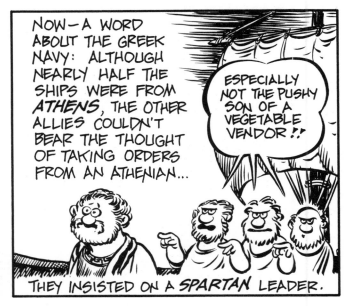

THEY INSISTED ON A *SPARTAN* LEADER.

Panel 5

THEMISTOCLES, THE ATHENIAN ADMIRAL, WENT ALONG, BUT SECRETLY PASSED CASH TO *EURYBIADES*, THE SPARTAN, TO KEEP HIM FRIENDLY.

YOUR HAND, EURYBIADES!

Panel 6

WHEN WORD CAME TO SALAMIS THAT ATHENS WAS BURNED, THE PELOPONNESIANS WANTED TO HEAD SOUTH AGAIN!

YES, A MORE SOUTHERLY POSITION WOULD BE MORE SECURE...

BRAZIL, FOR EXAMPLE...

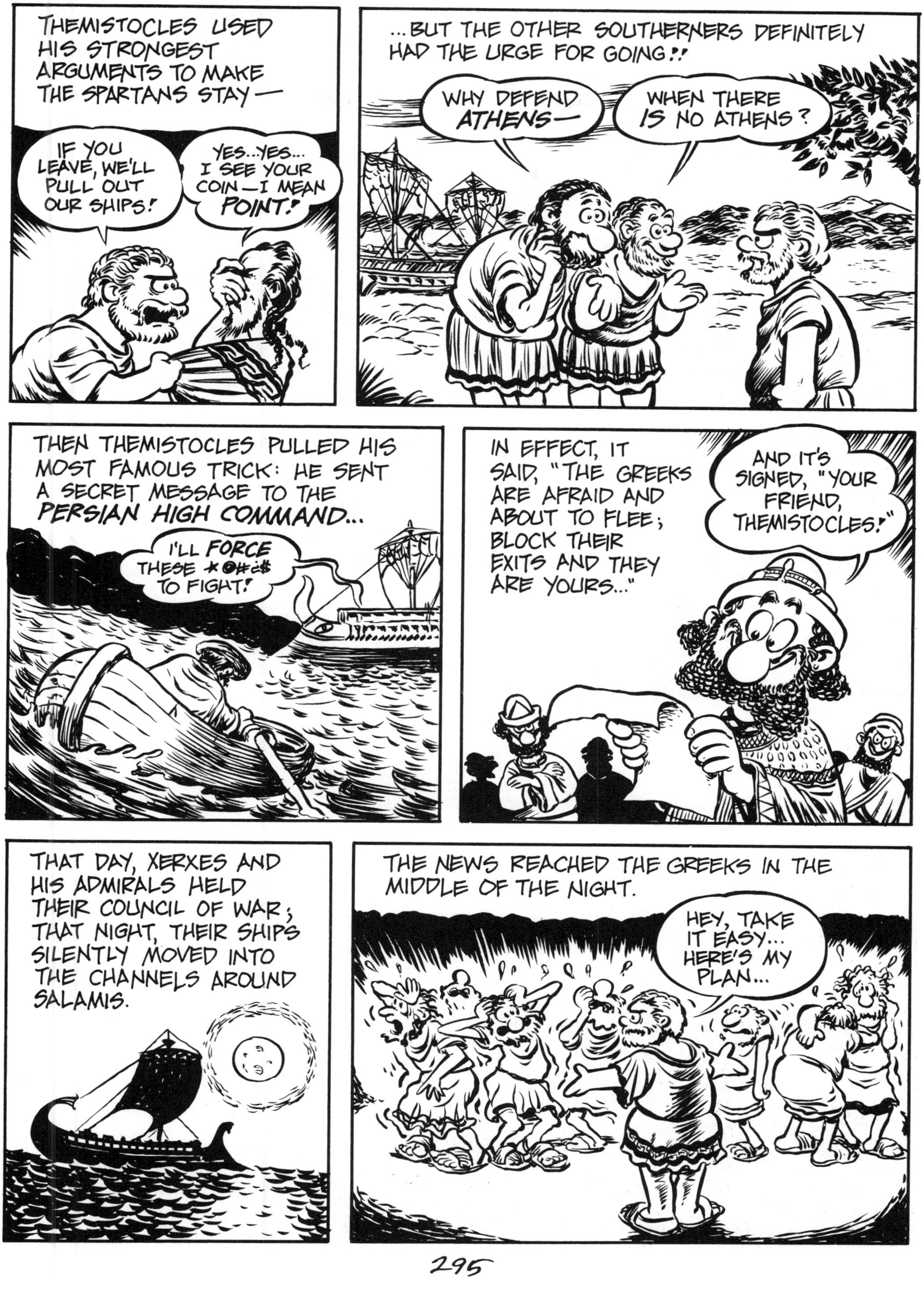

THEMISTOCLES USED HIS STRONGEST ARGUMENTS TO MAKE THE SPARTANS STAY—
IF YOU LEAVE, WE'LL PULL OUT OUR SHIPS!
YES...YES... I SEE YOUR COIN—I MEAN POINT!
...BUT THE OTHER SOUTHERNERS DEFINITELY HAD THE URGE FOR GOING!!
WHY DEFEND ATHENS—
WHEN THERE IS NO ATHENS?
THEN THEMISTOCLES PULLED HIS MOST FAMOUS TRICK: HE SENT A SECRET MESSAGE TO THE PERSIAN HIGH COMMAND...
I'LL FORCE THESE *@#¢$ TO FIGHT!
IN EFFECT, IT SAID, "THE GREEKS ARE AFRAID AND ABOUT TO FLEE; BLOCK THEIR EXITS AND THEY ARE YOURS..."
AND IT'S SIGNED, "YOUR FRIEND, THEMISTOCLES!"
THAT DAY, XERXES AND HIS ADMIRALS HELD THEIR COUNCIL OF WAR; THAT NIGHT, THEIR SHIPS SILENTLY MOVED INTO THE CHANNELS AROUND SALAMIS.
THE NEWS REACHED THE GREEKS IN THE MIDDLE OF THE NIGHT.
HEY, TAKE IT EASY... HERE'S MY PLAN...

AT DAWN THEY ROWED OUT IN SINGLE FILE, FIRST THE SPARTANS, THEN THE ALLIES, AND FINALLY THE 200 ATHENIAN TRIREMES.

XERXES SAT HERE

THESE *TRIREMES*, WITH THREE BANKS OF OARS, WERE HEAVIER AND SLOWER THAN THE PHOENICIAN OR EGYPTIAN SHIPS OF THE IMPERIAL NAVY, BUT STRONG AND EQUIPPED WITH A VICIOUS UNDERWATER "BEAK."

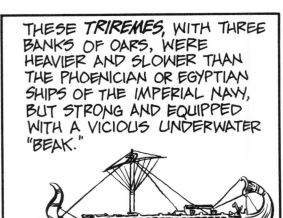

THE PLAN WAS TO DRAW THE ENEMY INTO CONFINED WATERS, SO THE GREEKS CAME ABOUT, FACING FRONT—AND WAITED.

THE IMPERIALS ADVANCED, AND THE GREEKS *BACKED UP*, FORMING A GREAT *U*-SHAPE.

WHEN THEY HAD PRACTICALLY BACKED ONTO THE BEACH, AN IMMENSE SHOUT WENT UP FROM SALAMIS:

STOP BACKING UP! ARE YOU CRAZY?!

AT THIS POINT, THE GREEKS ATTACKED!!

RAM!

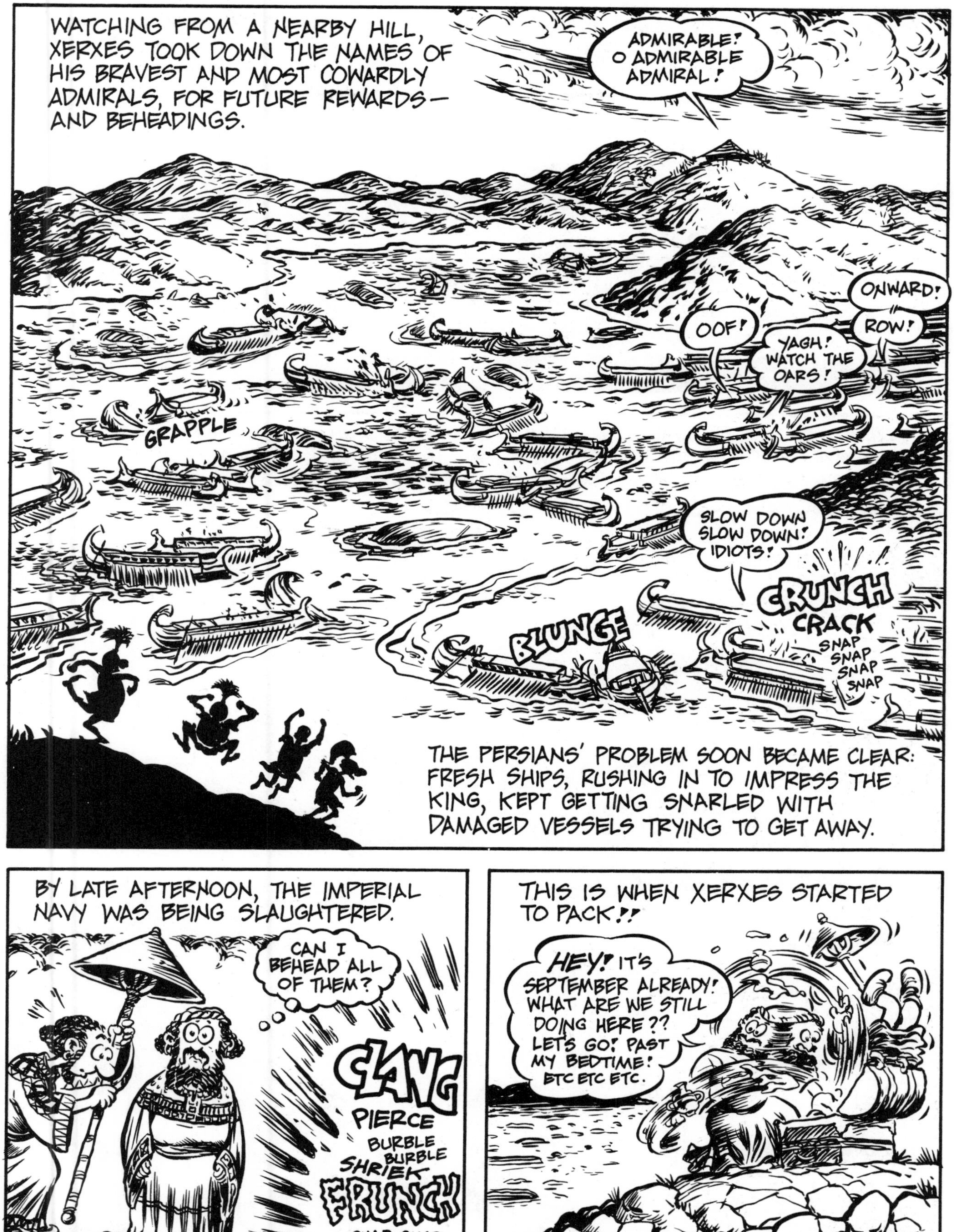
WATCHING FROM A NEARBY HILL, XERXES TOOK DOWN THE NAMES OF HIS BRAVEST AND MOST COWARDLY ADMIRALS, FOR FUTURE REWARDS— AND BEHEADINGS.
ADMIRABLE! O ADMIRABLE ADMIRAL!
ONWARD!
ROW!
OOF!
YAGH! WATCH THE OARS!
GRAPPLE
SLOW DOWN SLOW DOWN! IDIOTS!
CRUNCH
CRACK
SNAP SNAP SNAP SNAP
BLUNGE
THE PERSIANS' PROBLEM SOON BECAME CLEAR: FRESH SHIPS, RUSHING IN TO IMPRESS THE KING, KEPT GETTING SNARLED WITH DAMAGED VESSELS TRYING TO GET AWAY.
BY LATE AFTERNOON, THE IMPERIAL NAVY WAS BEING SLAUGHTERED.
CAN I BEHEAD ALL OF THEM?
CLANG
PIERCE
BURBLE BURBLE
SHRIEK
FRUNCH
SNAP SNAP SNAP
EEYAGH
THIS IS WHEN XERXES STARTED TO PACK!!
HEY! IT'S SEPTEMBER ALREADY! WHAT ARE WE STILL DOING HERE?? LET'S GO! PAST MY BEDTIME! ETC ETC ETC.

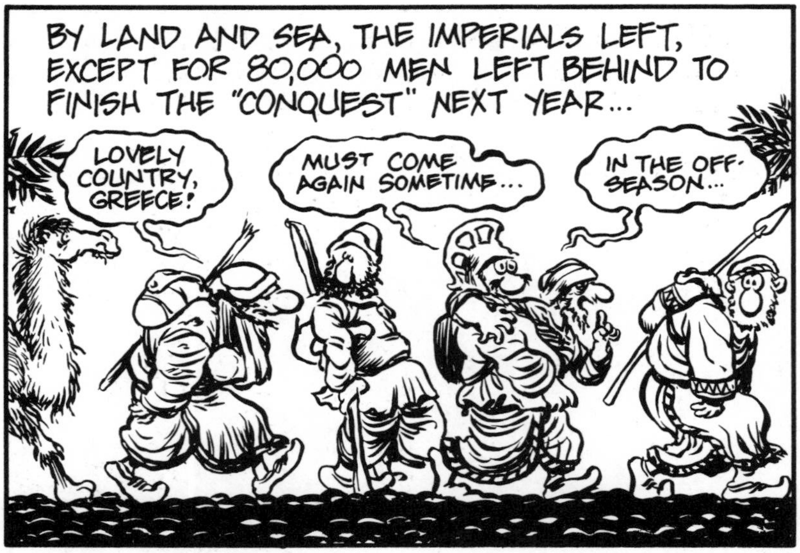
BY LAND AND SEA, THE IMPERIALS LEFT, EXCEPT FOR 80,000 MEN LEFT BEHIND TO FINISH THE "CONQUEST" NEXT YEAR...
LOVELY COUNTRY, GREECE!
MUST COME AGAIN SOMETIME...
IN THE OFF-SEASON...

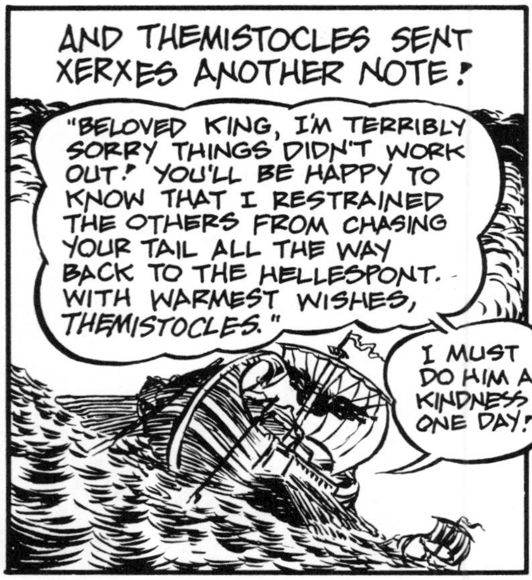
AND THEMISTOCLES SENT XERXES ANOTHER NOTE!
"BELOVED KING, I'M TERRIBLY SORRY THINGS DIDN'T WORK OUT! YOU'LL BE HAPPY TO KNOW THAT I RESTRAINED THE OTHERS FROM CHASING YOUR TAIL ALL THE WAY BACK TO THE HELLESPONT. WITH WARMEST WISHES, THEMISTOCLES."
I MUST DO HIM A KINDNESS ONE DAY!

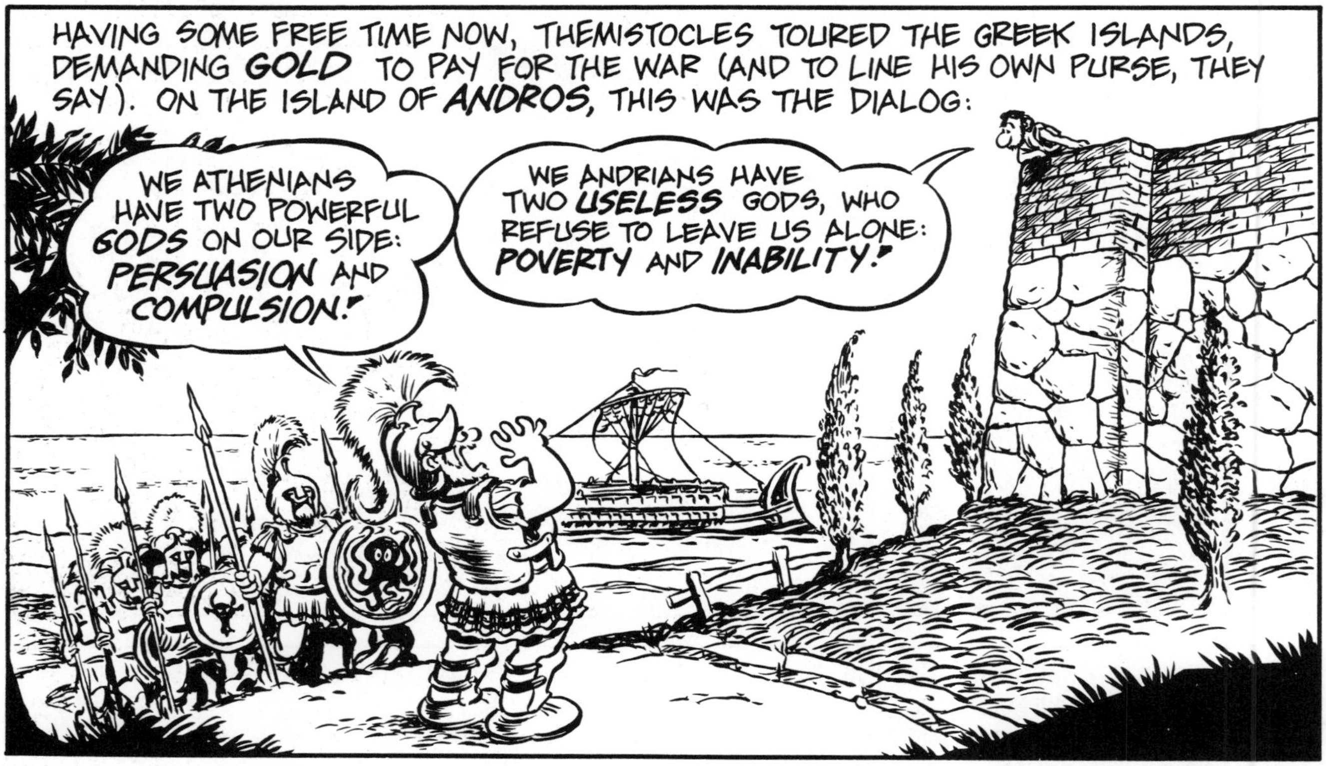
HAVING SOME FREE TIME NOW, THEMISTOCLES TOURED THE GREEK ISLANDS, DEMANDING GOLD TO PAY FOR THE WAR (AND TO LINE HIS OWN PURSE, THEY SAY). ON THE ISLAND OF ANDROS, THIS WAS THE DIALOG:
WE ATHENIANS HAVE TWO POWERFUL GODS ON OUR SIDE: PERSUASION AND COMPULSION!
WE ANDRIANS HAVE TWO USELESS GODS, WHO REFUSE TO LEAVE US ALONE: POVERTY AND INABILITY!

FINALLY, THE COMMANDERS WHO HAD FOUGHT AT SALAMIS MET TO DIVIDE THE LOOT AND AWARD A PRIZE TO THE ***MOST VALIANT MAN*** OF THE CAMPAIGN. IN THE VOTING, IT SEEMS, EVERYONE PUT ***HIMSELF*** FIRST AND ***THEMISTOCLES*** SECOND—AND SO NO PRIZE WAS GIVEN!!

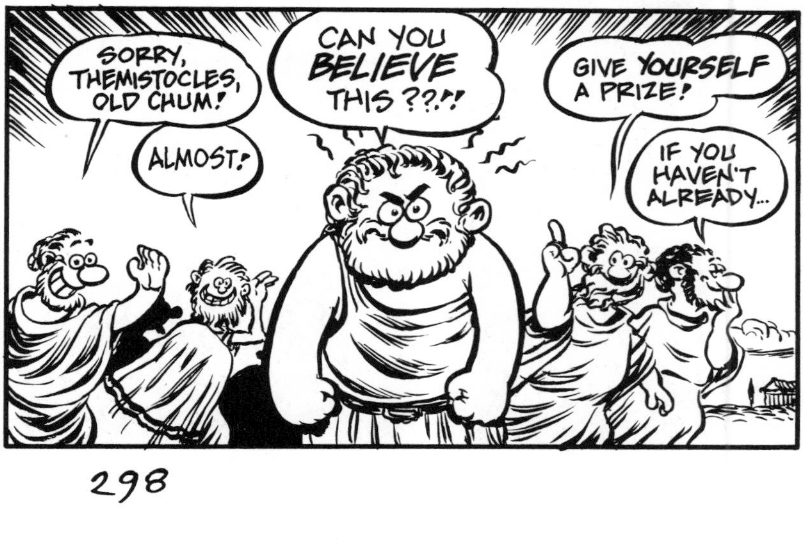
SORRY, THEMISTOCLES, OLD CHUM!
ALMOST!
CAN YOU BELIEVE THIS??!!
GIVE YOURSELF A PRIZE!
IF YOU HAVEN'T ALREADY...

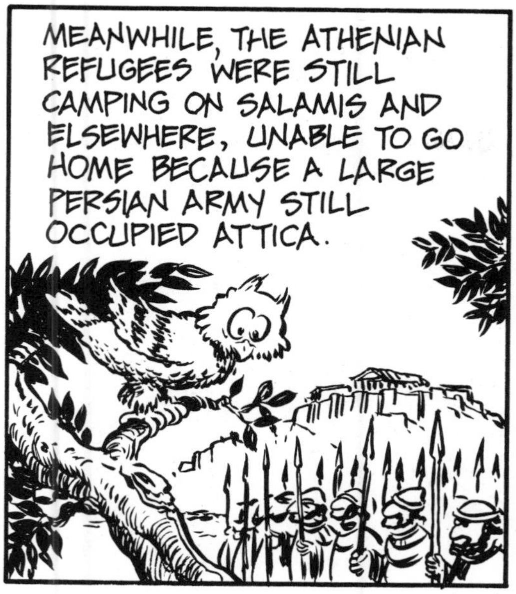
MEANWHILE, THE ATHENIAN REFUGEES WERE STILL CAMPING ON SALAMIS AND ELSEWHERE, UNABLE TO GO HOME BECAUSE A LARGE PERSIAN ARMY STILL OCCUPIED ATTICA.

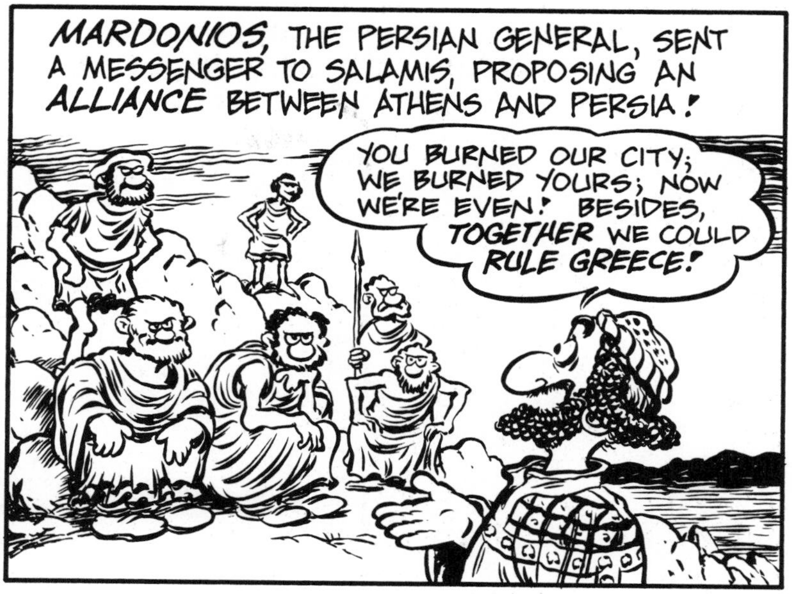
MARDONIOS, THE PERSIAN GENERAL, SENT A MESSENGER TO SALAMIS, PROPOSING AN ALLIANCE BETWEEN ATHENS AND PERSIA!
YOU BURNED OUR CITY; WE BURNED YOURS; NOW WE'RE EVEN! BESIDES, TOGETHER WE COULD RULE GREECE!

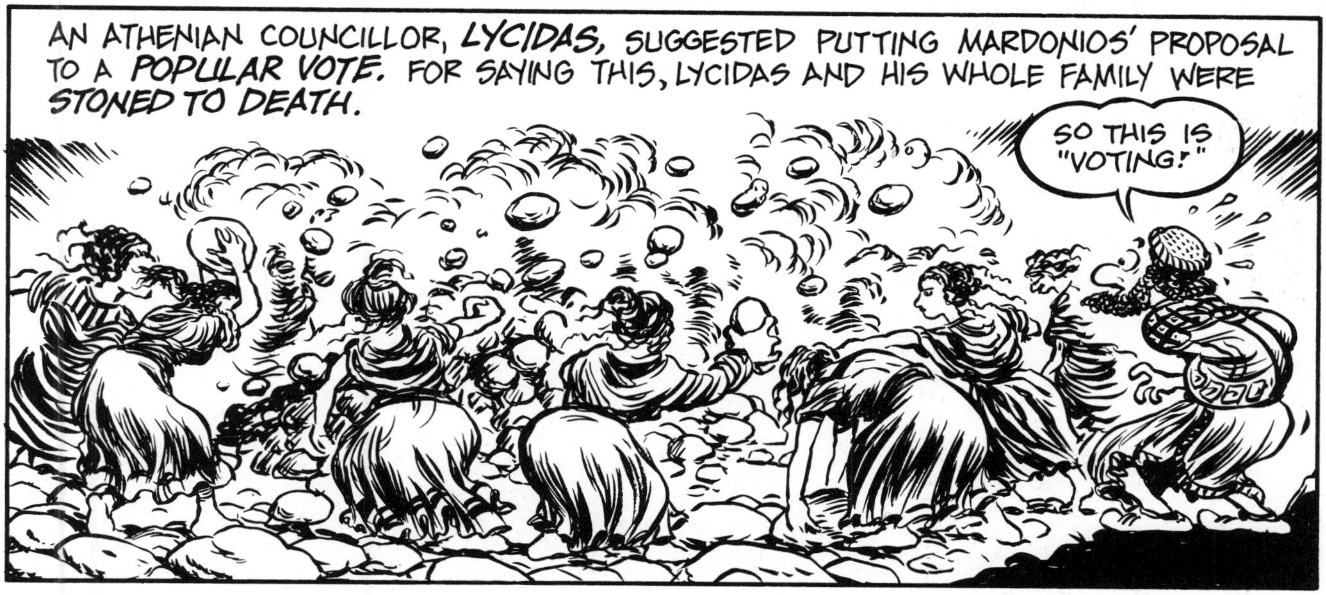
AN ATHENIAN COUNCILLOR, LYCIDAS, SUGGESTED PUTTING MARDONIOS' PROPOSAL TO A POPULAR VOTE. FOR SAYING THIS, LYCIDAS AND HIS WHOLE FAMILY WERE STONED TO DEATH.
SO THIS IS "VOTING!"

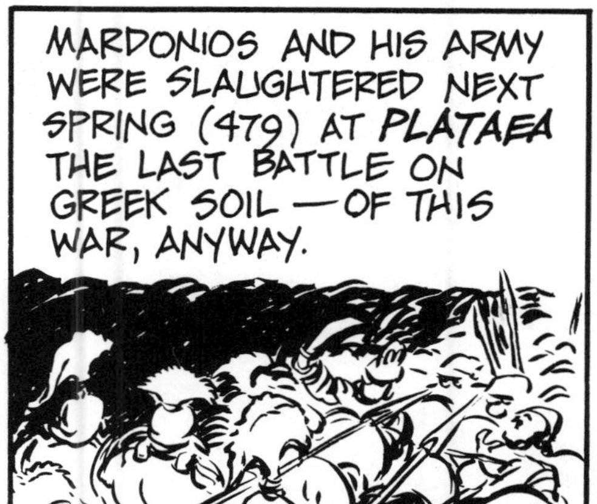
MARDONIOS AND HIS ARMY WERE SLAUGHTERED NEXT SPRING (479) AT PLATAEA THE LAST BATTLE ON GREEK SOIL — OF THIS WAR, ANYWAY.

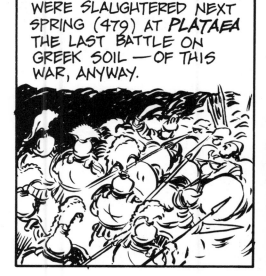

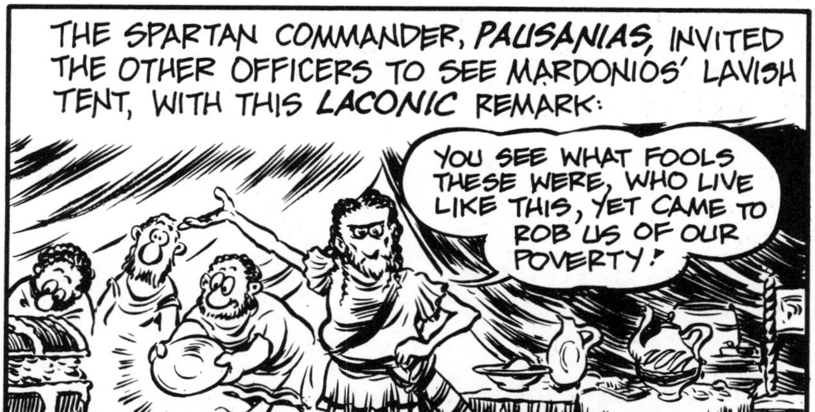
THE SPARTAN COMMANDER, PAUSANIAS, INVITED THE OTHER OFFICERS TO SEE MARDONIOS' LAVISH TENT, WITH THIS LACONIC REMARK:
YOU SEE WHAT FOOLS THESE WERE, WHO LIVE LIKE THIS, YET CAME TO ROB US OF OUR POVERTY!

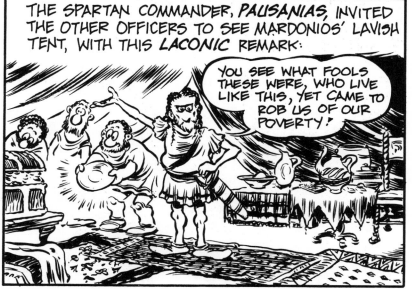

AND SO GREECE WAS SAVED...

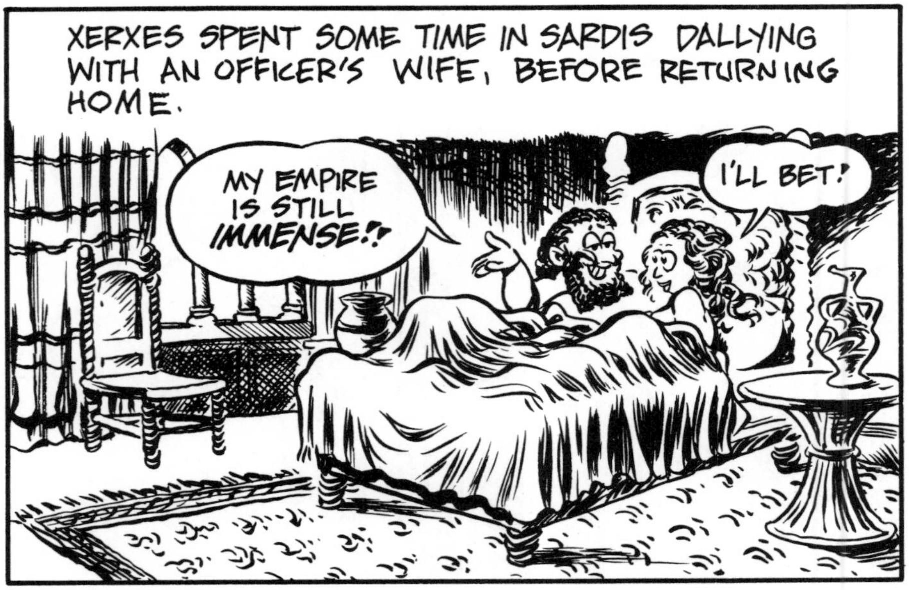
XERXES SPENT SOME TIME IN SARDIS DALLYING WITH AN OFFICER'S WIFE, BEFORE RETURNING HOME.
MY EMPIRE IS STILL ***IMMENSE!?***
I'LL BET!

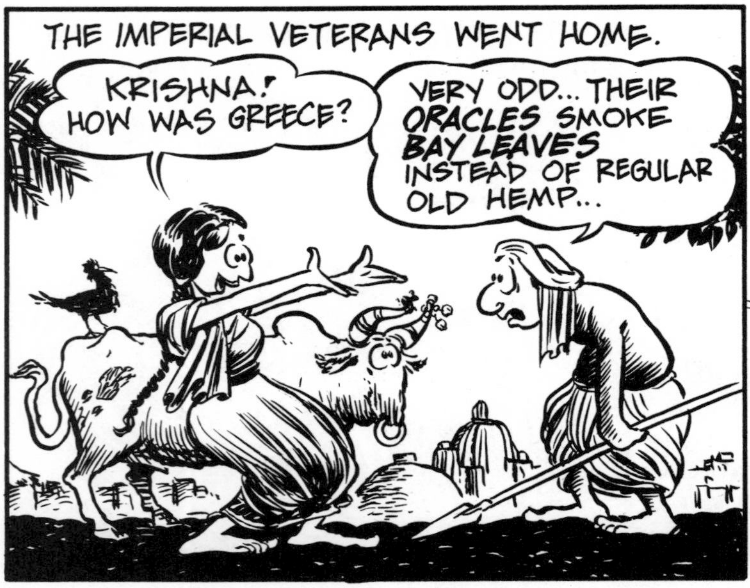
THE IMPERIAL VETERANS WENT HOME.
KRISHNA! HOW WAS GREECE?
VERY ODD... THEIR ***ORACLES*** SMOKE ***BAY LEAVES*** INSTEAD OF REGULAR OLD HEMP...

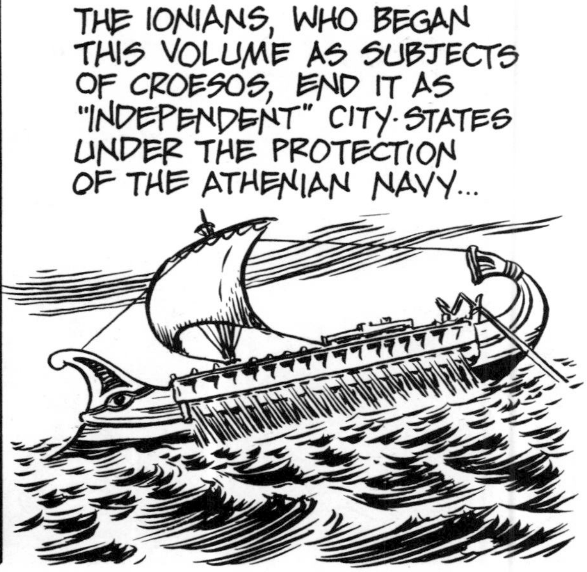
THE IONIANS, WHO BEGAN THIS VOLUME AS SUBJECTS OF CROESOS, END IT AS "INDEPENDENT" CITY-STATES UNDER THE PROTECTION OF THE ATHENIAN NAVY...

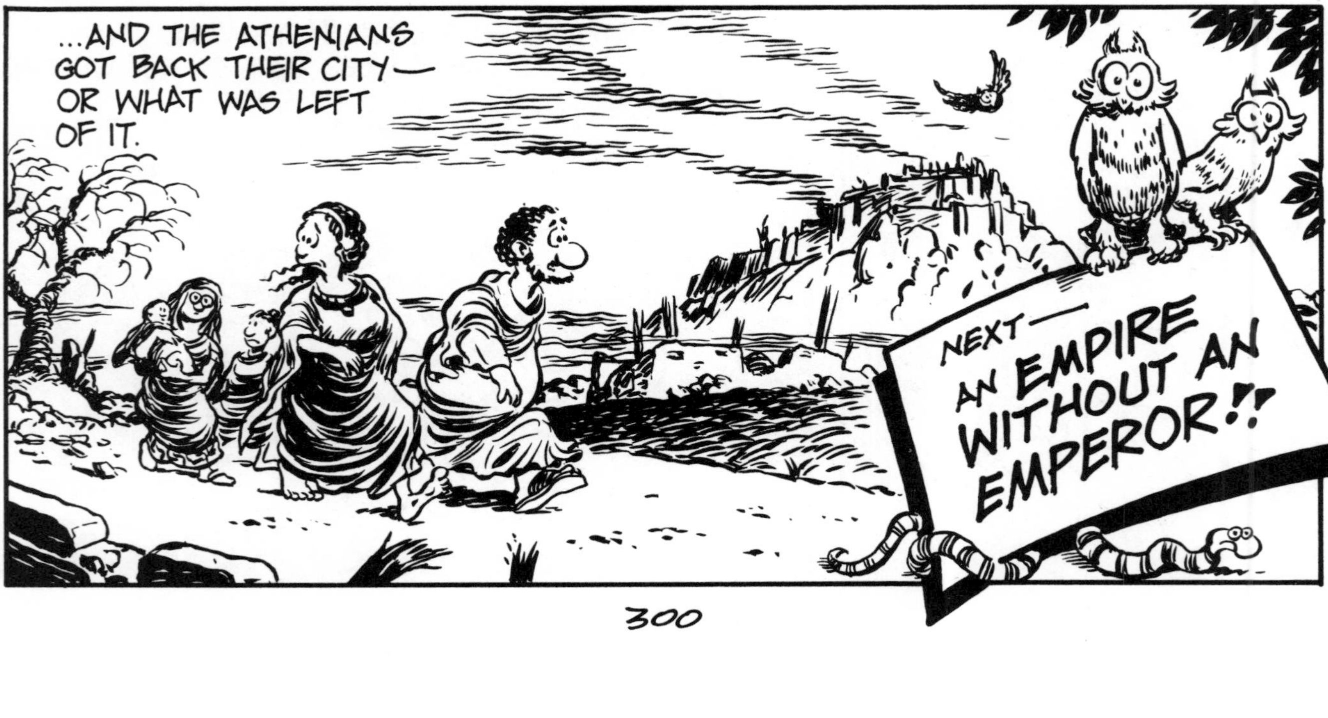
...AND THE ATHENIANS GOT BACK THEIR CITY— OR WHAT WAS LEFT OF IT.
NEXT— AN **EMPIRE WITHOUT AN EMPEROR!?**

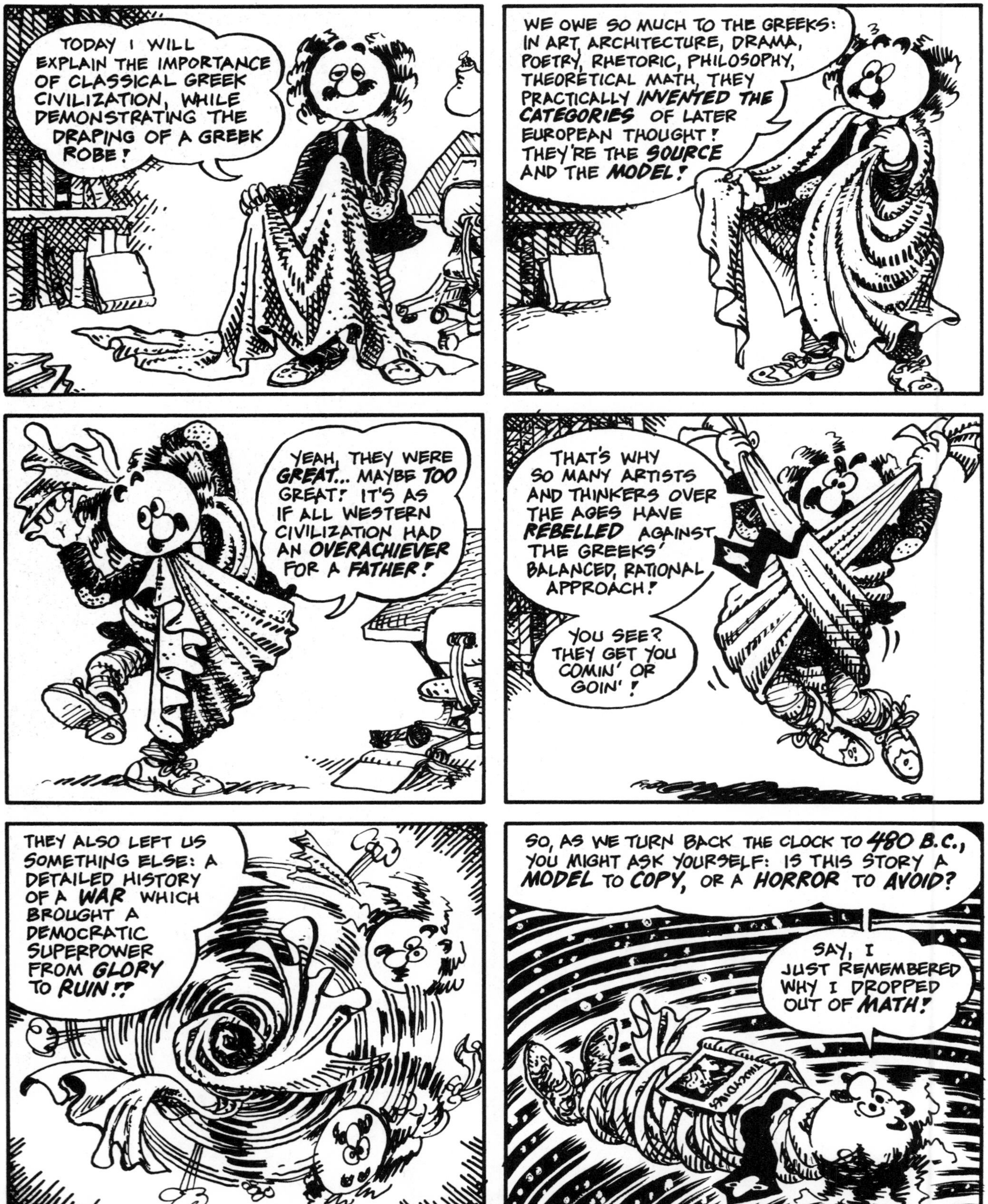
TODAY I WILL EXPLAIN THE IMPORTANCE OF CLASSICAL GREEK CIVILIZATION, WHILE DEMONSTRATING THE DRAPING OF A GREEK ROBE!
WE OWE SO MUCH TO THE GREEKS: IN ART, ARCHITECTURE, DRAMA, POETRY, RHETORIC, PHILOSOPHY, THEORETICAL MATH, THEY PRACTICALLY **INVENTED THE CATEGORIES** OF LATER EUROPEAN THOUGHT! THEY'RE THE **SOURCE** AND THE **MODEL**!
YEAH, THEY WERE **GREAT**... MAYBE **TOO** GREAT! IT'S AS IF ALL WESTERN CIVILIZATION HAD AN **OVERACHIEVER** FOR A **FATHER**!
THAT'S WHY SO MANY ARTISTS AND THINKERS OVER THE AGES HAVE **REBELLED** AGAINST THE GREEKS' BALANCED, RATIONAL APPROACH!
YOU SEE? THEY GET YOU COMIN' OR GOIN'!
THEY ALSO LEFT US SOMETHING ELSE: A DETAILED HISTORY OF A **WAR** WHICH BROUGHT A DEMOCRATIC SUPERPOWER FROM **GLORY** TO **RUIN**!?
SO, AS WE TURN BACK THE CLOCK TO **480 B.C.**, YOU MIGHT ASK YOURSELF: IS THIS STORY A **MODEL** TO **COPY**, OR A **HORROR** TO **AVOID**?
SAY, I JUST REMEMBERED WHY I DROPPED OUT OF **MATH**!

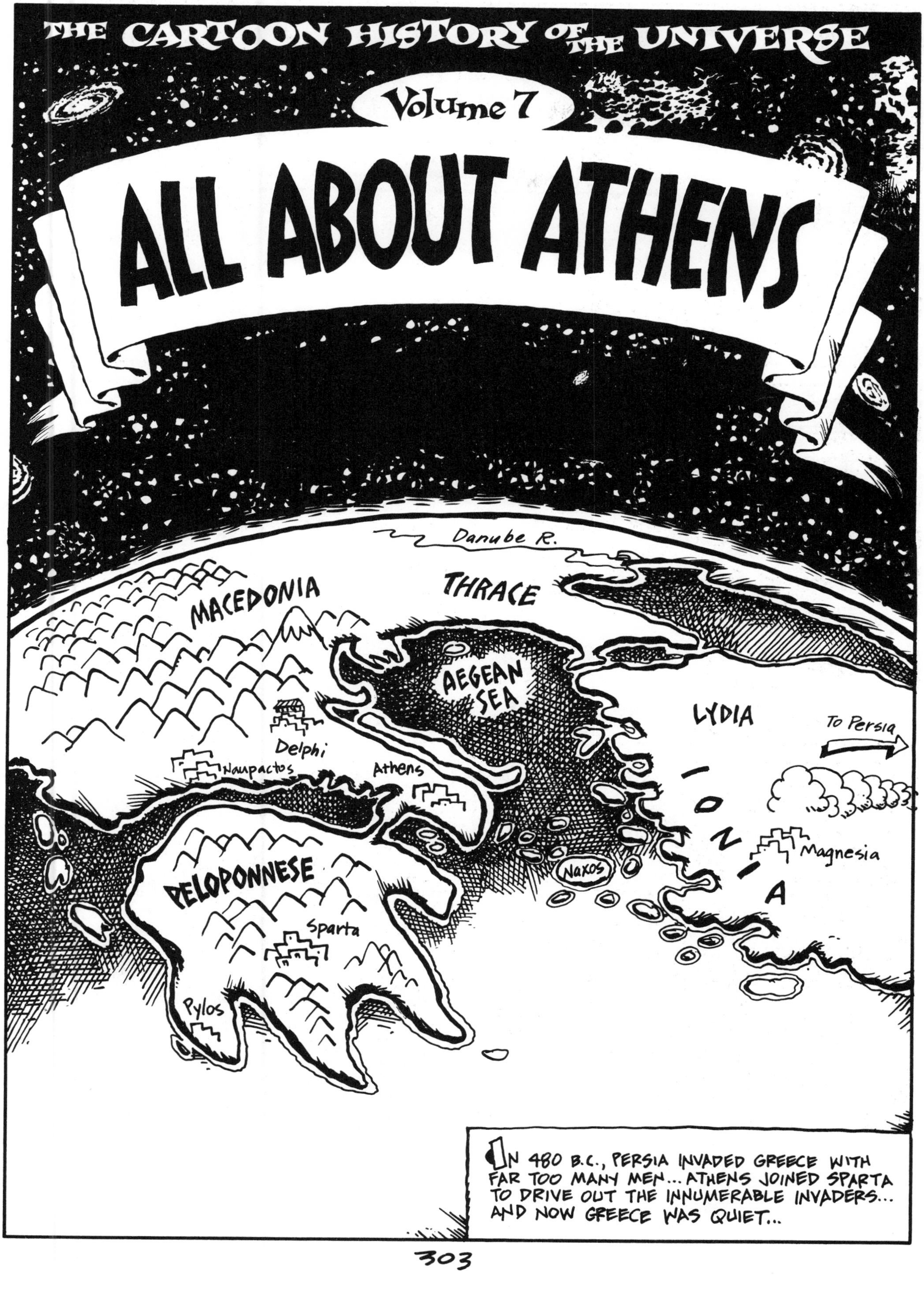
THE CARTOON HISTORY OF THE UNIVERSE
Volume 7
ALL ABOUT ATHENS
Danube R.
THRACE
MACEDONIA
AEGEAN SEA
LYDIA
To Persia
Delphi
Naupactos
Athens
IONIA
Magnesia
Naxos
PELOPONNESE
Sparta
Pylos
IN 480 B.C., PERSIA INVADED GREECE WITH FAR TOO MANY MEN... ATHENS JOINED SPARTA TO DRIVE OUT THE INNUMERABLE INVADERS... AND NOW GREECE WAS QUIET...

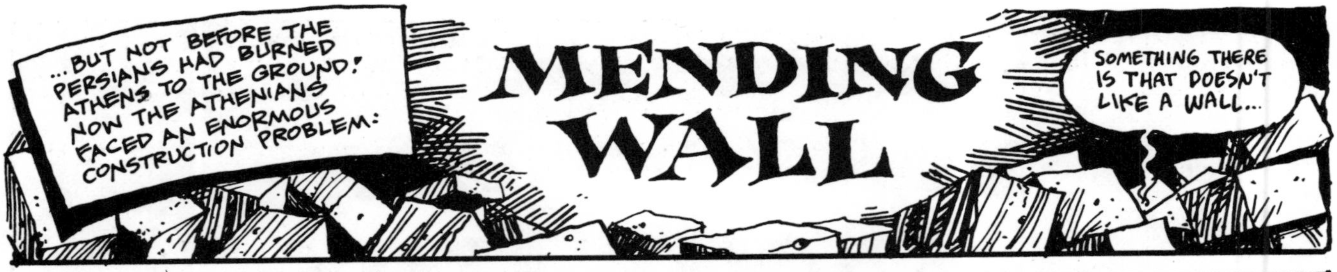
...BUT NOT BEFORE THE PERSIANS HAD BURNED ATHENS TO THE GROUND! NOW THE ATHENIANS FACED AN ENORMOUS CONSTRUCTION PROBLEM:
MENDING WALL
SOMETHING THERE IS THAT DOESN'T LIKE A WALL...

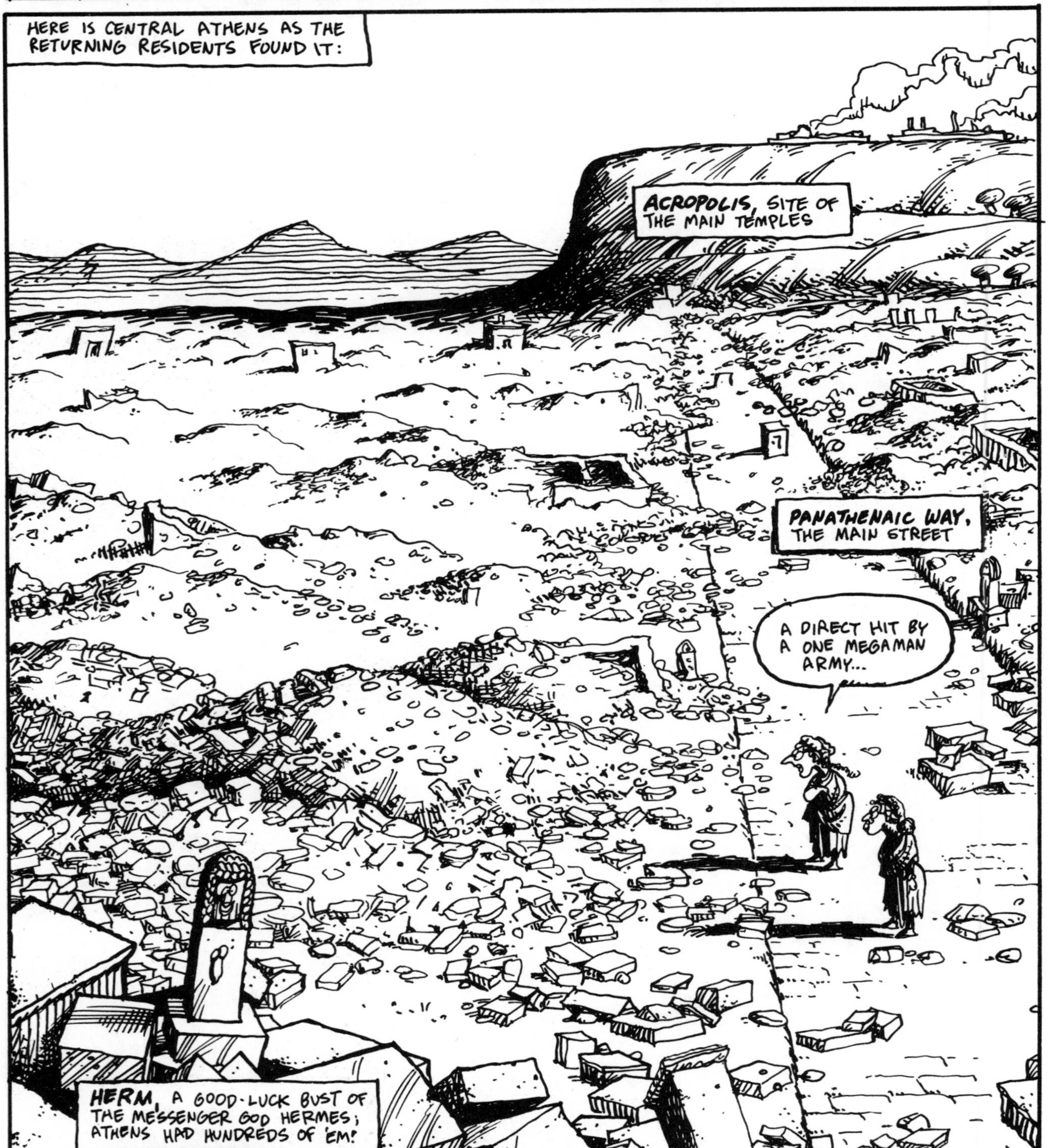
HERE IS CENTRAL ATHENS AS THE RETURNING RESIDENTS FOUND IT:
ACROPOLIS, SITE OF THE MAIN TEMPLES
PANATHENAIC WAY, THE MAIN STREET
A DIRECT HIT BY A ONE MEGAMAN ARMY...
HERM, A GOOD-LUCK BUST OF THE MESSENGER GOD HERMES; ATHENS HAD HUNDREDS OF 'EM!

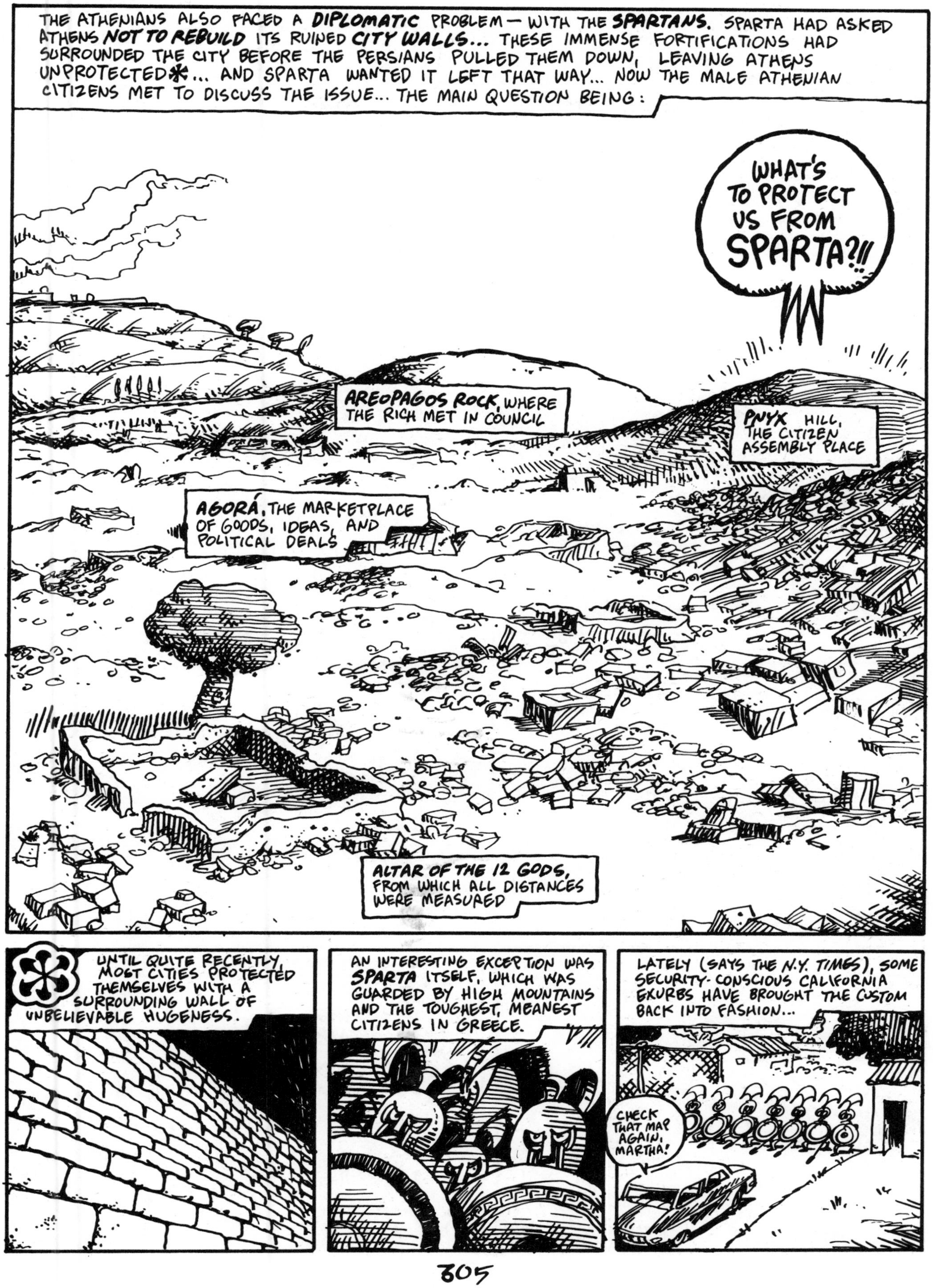
THE ATHENIANS ALSO FACED A DIPLOMATIC PROBLEM — WITH THE SPARTANS. SPARTA HAD ASKED ATHENS NOT TO REBUILD ITS RUINED CITY WALLS... THESE IMMENSE FORTIFICATIONS HAD SURROUNDED THE CITY BEFORE THE PERSIANS PULLED THEM DOWN, LEAVING ATHENS UNPROTECTED✻... AND SPARTA WANTED IT LEFT THAT WAY... NOW THE MALE ATHENIAN CITIZENS MET TO DISCUSS THE ISSUE... THE MAIN QUESTION BEING:
WHAT'S TO PROTECT US FROM SPARTA?!!
AREOPAGOS ROCK, WHERE THE RICH MET IN COUNCIL
PNYX HILL, THE CITIZEN ASSEMBLY PLACE
AGORÁ, THE MARKETPLACE OF GOODS, IDEAS, AND POLITICAL DEALS
ALTAR OF THE 12 GODS, FROM WHICH ALL DISTANCES WERE MEASURED
✻ UNTIL QUITE RECENTLY, MOST CITIES PROTECTED THEMSELVES WITH A SURROUNDING WALL OF UNBELIEVABLE HUGENESS.
AN INTERESTING EXCEPTION WAS SPARTA ITSELF, WHICH WAS GUARDED BY HIGH MOUNTAINS AND THE TOUGHEST, MEANEST CITIZENS IN GREECE.
LATELY (SAYS THE N.Y. TIMES), SOME SECURITY-CONSCIOUS CALIFORNIA EXURBS HAVE BROUGHT THE CUSTOM BACK INTO FASHION...
CHECK THAT MAP AGAIN, MARTHA!

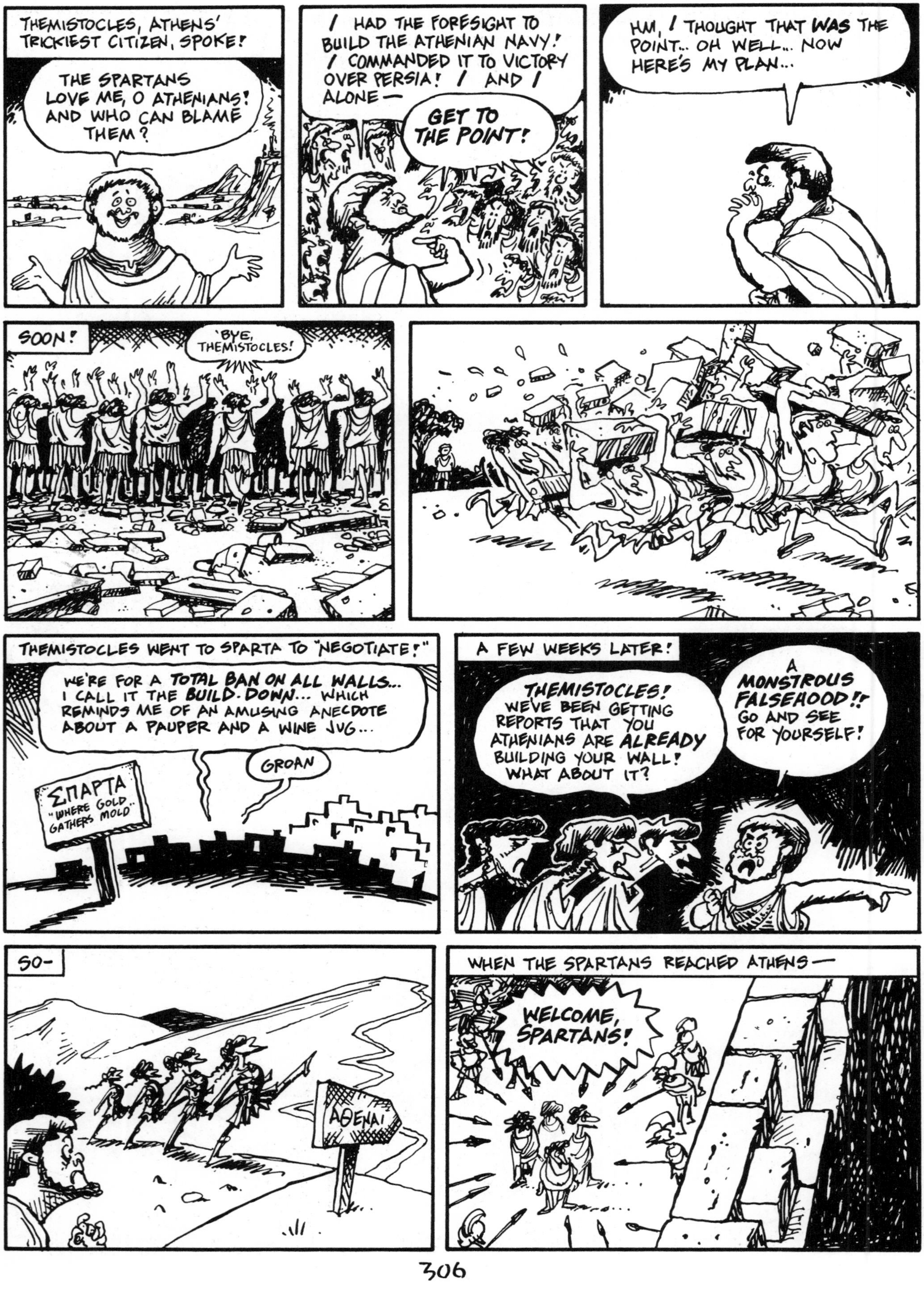
THEMISTOCLES, ATHENS' TRICKIEST CITIZEN, SPOKE!
THE SPARTANS LOVE ME, O ATHENIANS! AND WHO CAN BLAME THEM?
I HAD THE FORESIGHT TO BUILD THE ATHENIAN NAVY! I COMMANDED IT TO VICTORY OVER PERSIA! I AND I ALONE—
GET TO THE POINT!
HM, I THOUGHT THAT **WAS** THE POINT... OH WELL... NOW HERE'S MY PLAN...
SOON!
'BYE, THEMISTOCLES!
THEMISTOCLES WENT TO SPARTA TO "NEGOTIATE!"
WE'RE FOR A **TOTAL BAN ON ALL WALLS**... I CALL IT THE **BUILD-DOWN**... WHICH REMINDS ME OF AN AMUSING ANECDOTE ABOUT A PAUPER AND A WINE JUG...
GROAN
ΣΠΑΡΤΑ "WHERE GOLD GATHERS MOLD"
A FEW WEEKS LATER!
THEMISTOCLES! WE'VE BEEN GETTING REPORTS THAT YOU ATHENIANS ARE **ALREADY** BUILDING YOUR WALL! WHAT ABOUT IT?
A **MONSTROUS FALSEHOOD!!** GO AND SEE FOR YOURSELF!
SO-
ΑΘΕΝΑΙ
WHEN THE SPARTANS REACHED ATHENS—
WELCOME, SPARTANS!

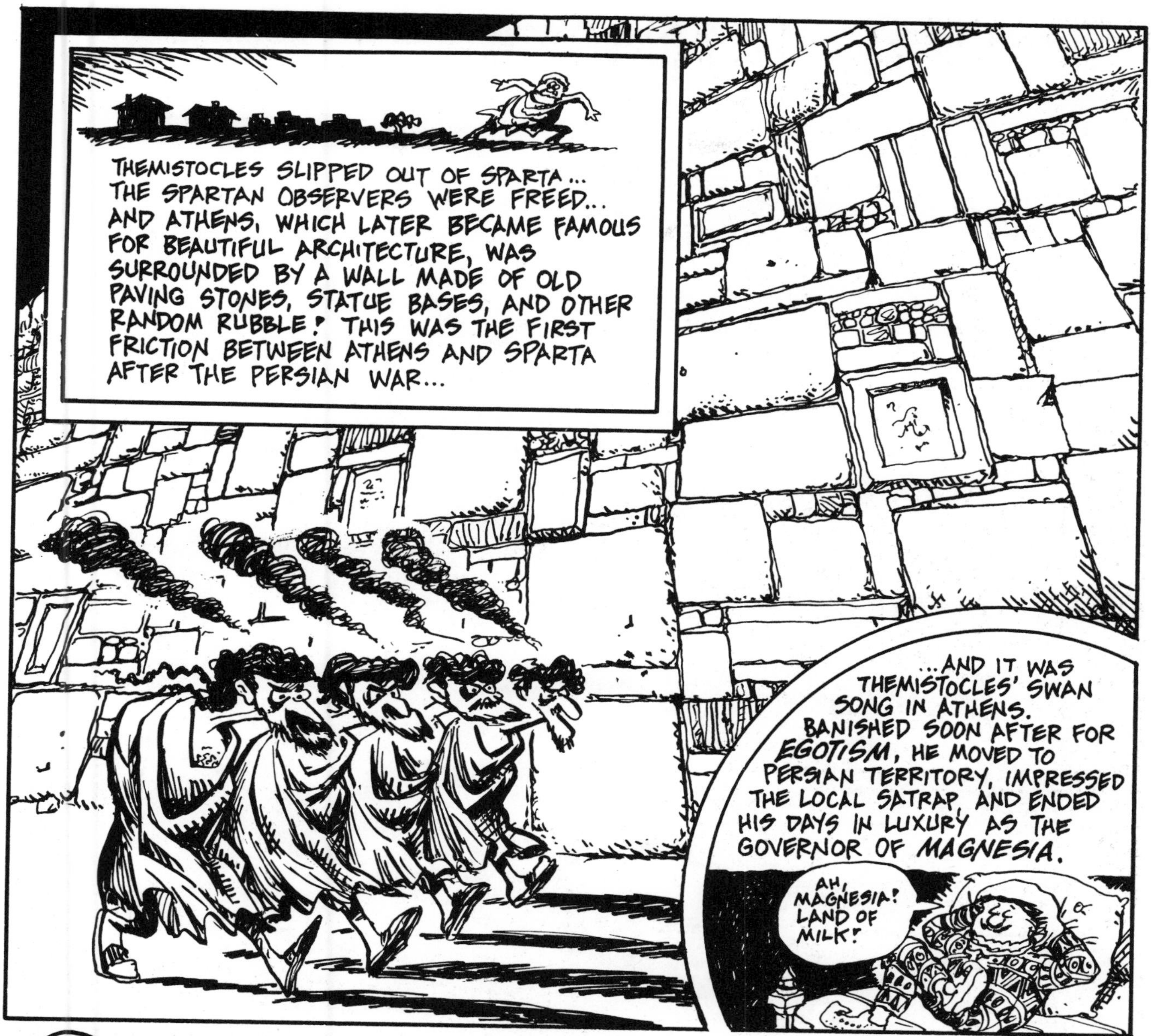
THEMISTOCLES SLIPPED OUT OF SPARTA... THE SPARTAN OBSERVERS WERE FREED... AND ATHENS, WHICH LATER BECAME FAMOUS FOR BEAUTIFUL ARCHITECTURE, WAS SURROUNDED BY A WALL MADE OF OLD PAVING STONES, STATUE BASES, AND OTHER RANDOM RUBBLE! THIS WAS THE FIRST FRICTION BETWEEN ATHENS AND SPARTA AFTER THE PERSIAN WAR...
...AND IT WAS THEMISTOCLES' SWAN SONG IN ATHENS. BANISHED SOON AFTER FOR EGOTISM, HE MOVED TO PERSIAN TERRITORY, IMPRESSED THE LOCAL SATRAP, AND ENDED HIS DAYS IN LUXURY AS THE GOVERNOR OF MAGNESIA.
AH, MAGNESIA! LAND OF MILK!

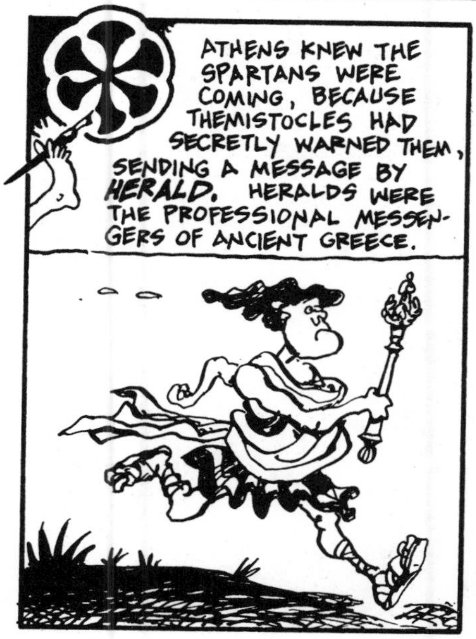
ATHENS KNEW THE SPARTANS WERE COMING, BECAUSE THEMISTOCLES HAD SECRETLY WARNED THEM, SENDING A MESSAGE BY HERALD. HERALDS WERE THE PROFESSIONAL MESSENGERS OF ANCIENT GREECE.

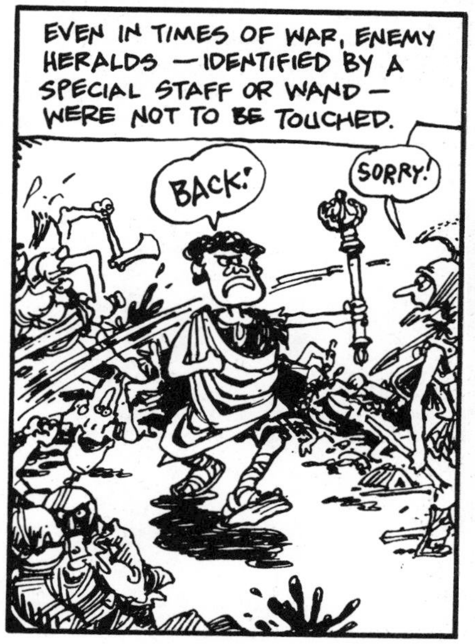
EVEN IN TIMES OF WAR, ENEMY HERALDS —IDENTIFIED BY A SPECIAL STAFF OR WAND— WERE NOT TO BE TOUCHED.
BACK!
SORRY!

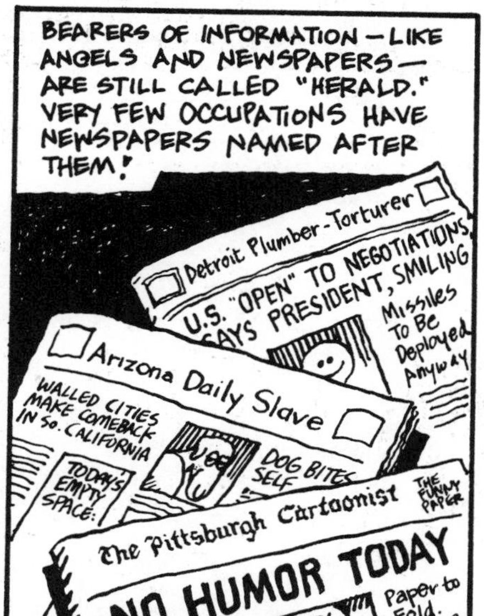
BEARERS OF INFORMATION—LIKE ANGELS AND NEWSPAPERS— ARE STILL CALLED "HERALD." VERY FEW OCCUPATIONS HAVE NEWSPAPERS NAMED AFTER THEM!
Detroit Plumber-Torturer
U.S. "OPEN" TO NEGOTIATIONS, SAYS PRESIDENT, SMILING
Missiles To Be Deployed Anyway
Arizona Daily Slave
WALLED CITIES MAKE COMEBACK IN So. CALIFORNIA
DOG BITES SELF
TODAY'S EMPTY SPACE:
The Pittsburgh Cartoonist
THE FUNNY PAPER
NO HUMOR TODAY
SOB!
Paper to Fold. Get it?

WOOD & IRON

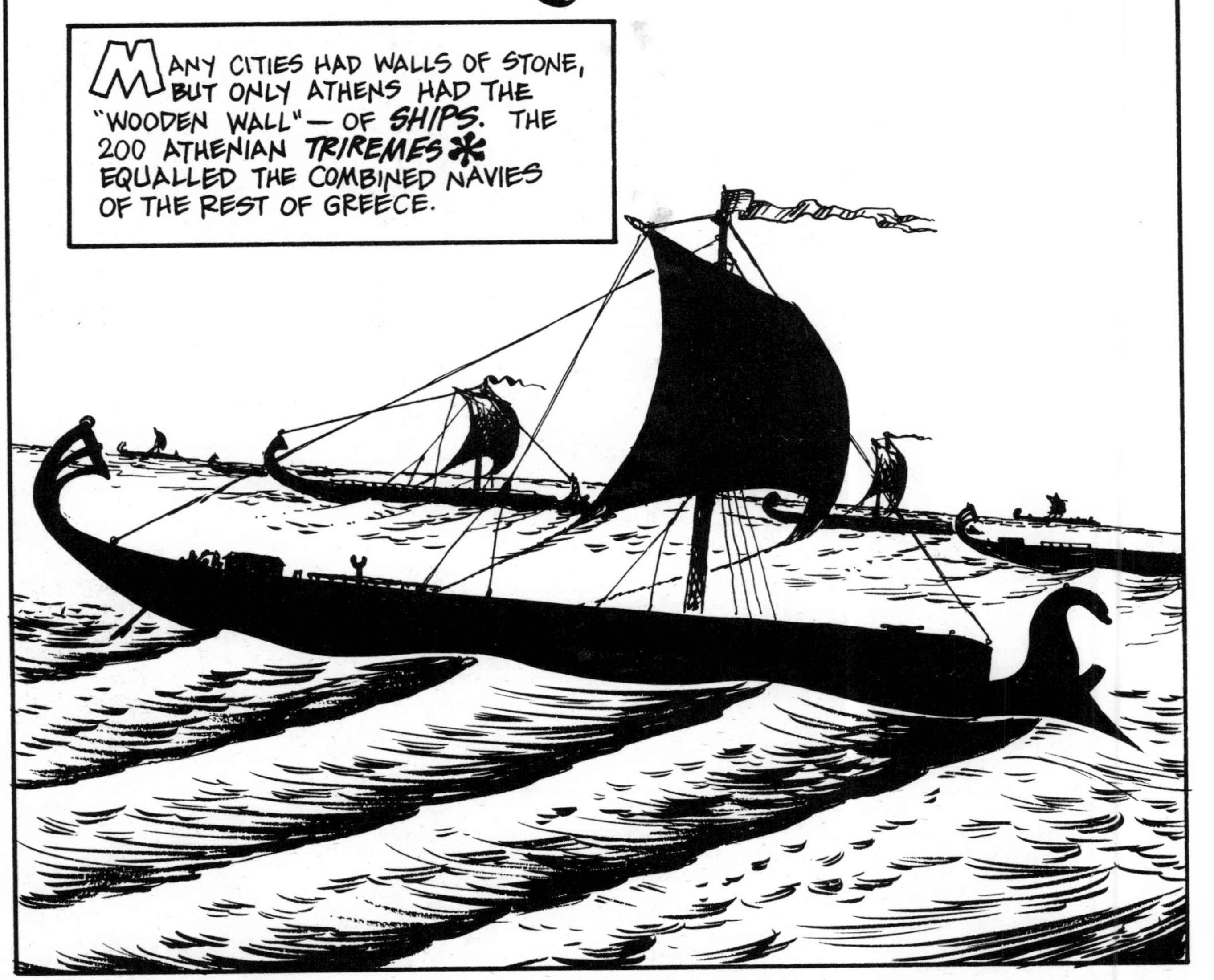
MANY CITIES HAD WALLS OF STONE, BUT ONLY ATHENS HAD THE "WOODEN WALL"—OF SHIPS. THE 200 ATHENIAN TRIREMES* EQUALLED THE COMBINED NAVIES OF THE REST OF GREECE.

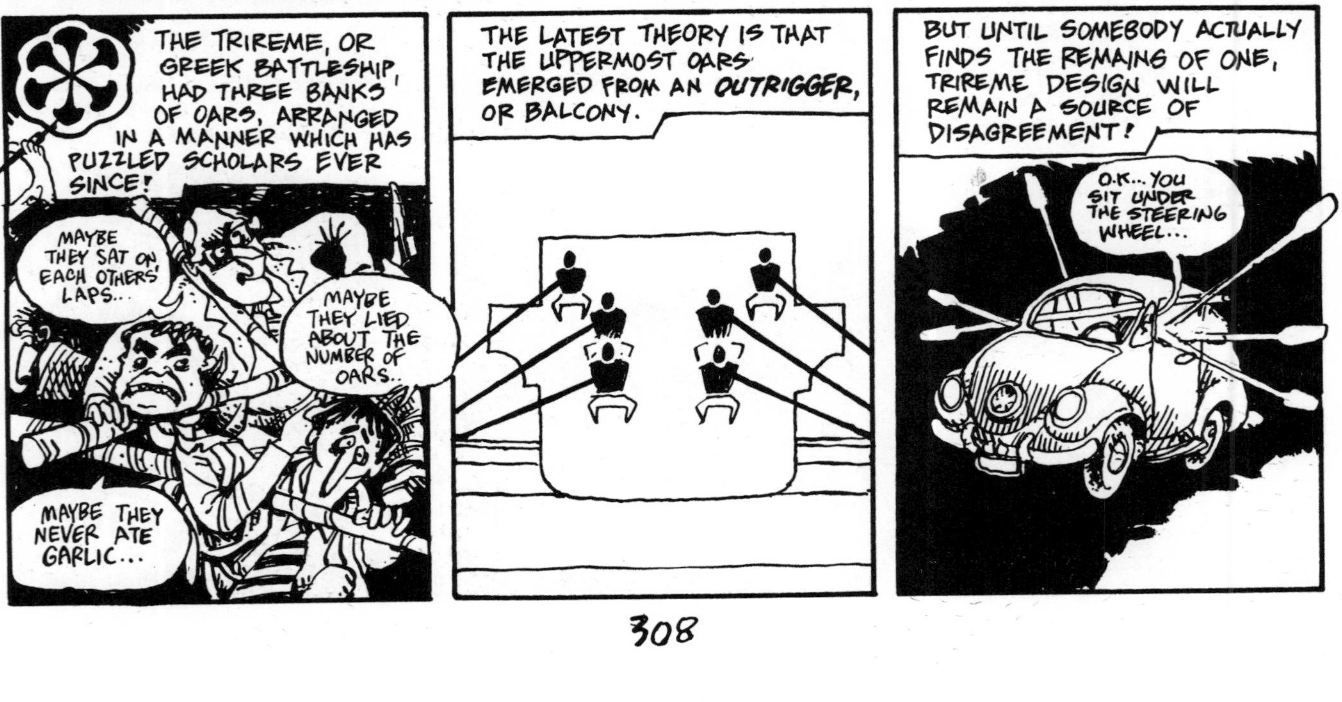
* THE TRIREME, OR GREEK BATTLESHIP, HAD THREE BANKS OF OARS, ARRANGED IN A MANNER WHICH HAS PUZZLED SCHOLARS EVER SINCE!
MAYBE THEY SAT ON EACH OTHERS' LAPS...
MAYBE THEY LIED ABOUT THE NUMBER OF OARS..
MAYBE THEY NEVER ATE GARLIC...
THE LATEST THEORY IS THAT THE UPPERMOST OARS EMERGED FROM AN OUTRIGGER, OR BALCONY.
BUT UNTIL SOMEBODY ACTUALLY FINDS THE REMAINS OF ONE, TRIREME DESIGN WILL REMAIN A SOURCE OF DISAGREEMENT!
O.K... YOU SIT UNDER THE STEERING WHEEL...

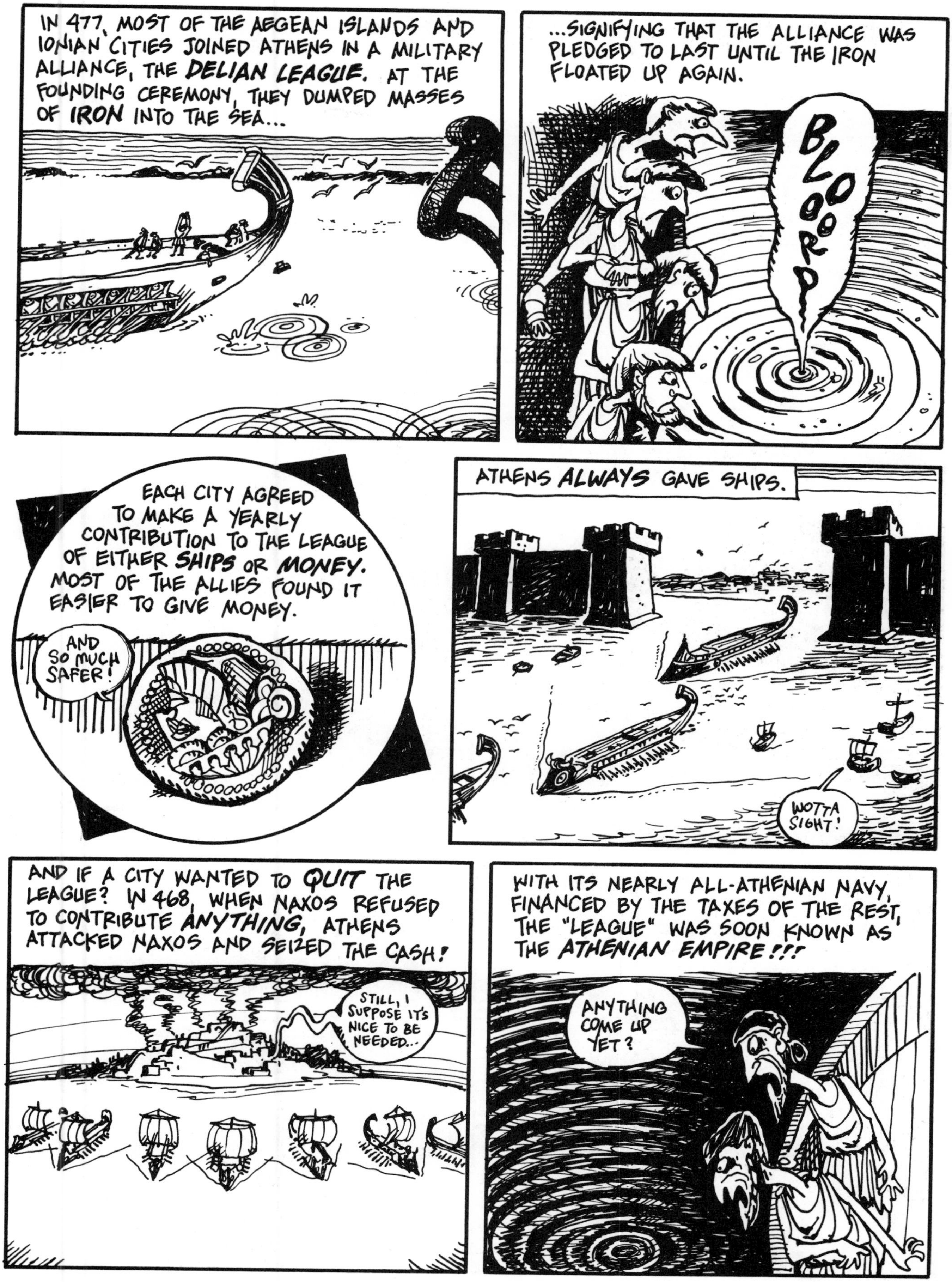
IN 477, MOST OF THE AEGEAN ISLANDS AND IONIAN CITIES JOINED ATHENS IN A MILITARY ALLIANCE, THE DELIAN LEAGUE. AT THE FOUNDING CEREMONY, THEY DUMPED MASSES OF IRON INTO THE SEA...
...SIGNIFYING THAT THE ALLIANCE WAS PLEDGED TO LAST UNTIL THE IRON FLOATED UP AGAIN.
BLOOORP
EACH CITY AGREED TO MAKE A YEARLY CONTRIBUTION TO THE LEAGUE OF EITHER SHIPS OR MONEY. MOST OF THE ALLIES FOUND IT EASIER TO GIVE MONEY.
AND SO MUCH SAFER!
ATHENS ALWAYS GAVE SHIPS.
WOTTA SIGHT!
AND IF A CITY WANTED TO QUIT THE LEAGUE? IN 468, WHEN NAXOS REFUSED TO CONTRIBUTE ANYTHING, ATHENS ATTACKED NAXOS AND SEIZED THE CASH!
STILL, I SUPPOSE IT'S NICE TO BE NEEDED...
WITH ITS NEARLY ALL-ATHENIAN NAVY, FINANCED BY THE TAXES OF THE REST, THE "LEAGUE" WAS SOON KNOWN AS THE ATHENIAN EMPIRE!!!
ANYTHING COME UP YET?

IN LATER, UNHAPPIER TIMES, MORE THAN A FEW ATHENIANS LOOKED BACK AT THE 470'S AS THE "GOOD OLD DAYS," WHEN THE ALLIES WERE LOYAL, SPARTA WAS FRIENDLY, AND RICH CITIZENS RULED THE STATE!

I THOUGHT THIS WAS A DEMOCRACY!

IT IS... I CAN VOTE FOR ANY RICH MAN I WANT TO...

WE CAN CATCH A GLIMPSE OF THE GOOD LIFE IN THE GOOD OLD DAYS FROM PLUTARCH'S PORTRAIT OF **KIMON**, THE LEADING CITIZEN OF THE TIME.

OK... THIS OVER HERE... NO, WAIT...

KIMON, AN EASY GOING SORT, ENJOYED HUNTING, DRINKING, AND PARTYING WITH HIS FRIENDS.

HA HA!

HOO HA!

HO HO!

HAR HAR!

HE SHARED THE FAMILY ESTATE WITH HIS SISTER **ELPINIKE**, WHO IN SOME RESPECTS WAS MORE INTERESTING THAN HE WAS.

ER... FELLOWS...

SHE HAD LOVE AFFAIRS WITH SEVERAL OF KIMON'S FRIENDS, MOST NOTABLY THE ARTIST **POLYGNOTOS**.

HE PUT HER FACE ON A PUBLIC MURAL, "THE TROJAN WOMEN."

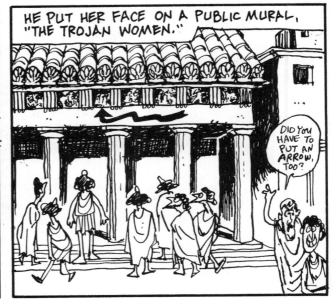

DID YOU HAVE TO PUT AN ARROW, TOO?

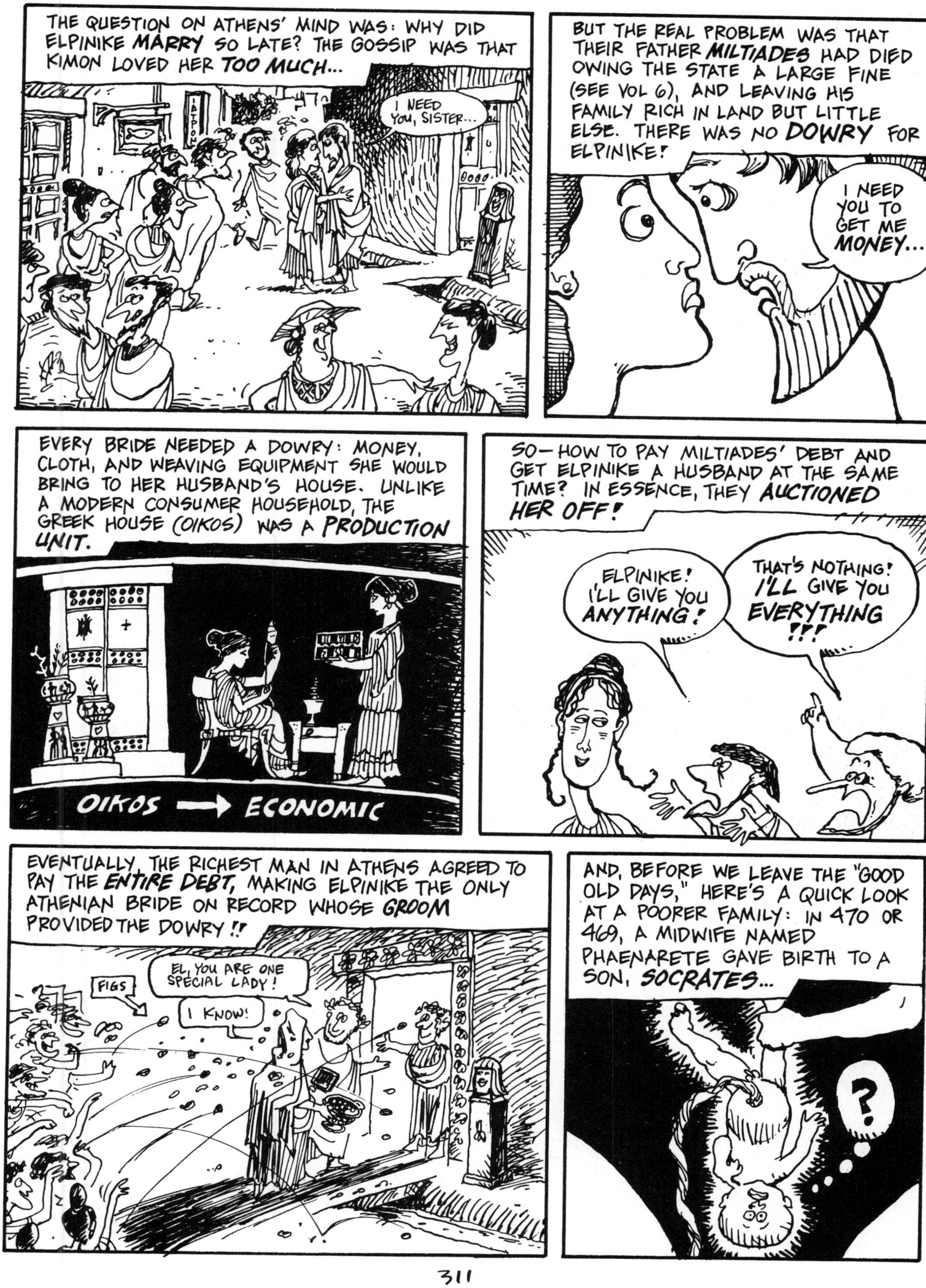
THE QUESTION ON ATHENS' MIND WAS: WHY DID ELPINIKE MARRY SO LATE? THE GOSSIP WAS THAT KIMON LOVED HER TOO MUCH...
I NEED YOU, SISTER...
IATPON
BUT THE REAL PROBLEM WAS THAT THEIR FATHER MILTIADES HAD DIED OWING THE STATE A LARGE FINE (SEE VOL 6), AND LEAVING HIS FAMILY RICH IN LAND BUT LITTLE ELSE. THERE WAS NO DOWRY FOR ELPINIKE!
I NEED YOU TO GET ME MONEY...
EVERY BRIDE NEEDED A DOWRY: MONEY, CLOTH, AND WEAVING EQUIPMENT SHE WOULD BRING TO HER HUSBAND'S HOUSE. UNLIKE A MODERN CONSUMER HOUSEHOLD, THE GREEK HOUSE (OIKOS) WAS A PRODUCTION UNIT.
OIKOS → ECONOMIC
SO—HOW TO PAY MILTIADES' DEBT AND GET ELPINIKE A HUSBAND AT THE SAME TIME? IN ESSENCE, THEY AUCTIONED HER OFF!
ELPINIKE! I'LL GIVE YOU ANYTHING!
THAT'S NOTHING! I'LL GIVE YOU EVERYTHING!!!
EVENTUALLY, THE RICHEST MAN IN ATHENS AGREED TO PAY THE ENTIRE DEBT, MAKING ELPINIKE THE ONLY ATHENIAN BRIDE ON RECORD WHOSE GROOM PROVIDED THE DOWRY!!
FIGS
EL, YOU ARE ONE SPECIAL LADY!
I KNOW!
AND, BEFORE WE LEAVE THE "GOOD OLD DAYS," HERE'S A QUICK LOOK AT A POORER FAMILY: IN 470 OR 469, A MIDWIFE NAMED PHAENARETE GAVE BIRTH TO A SON, SOCRATES...
?

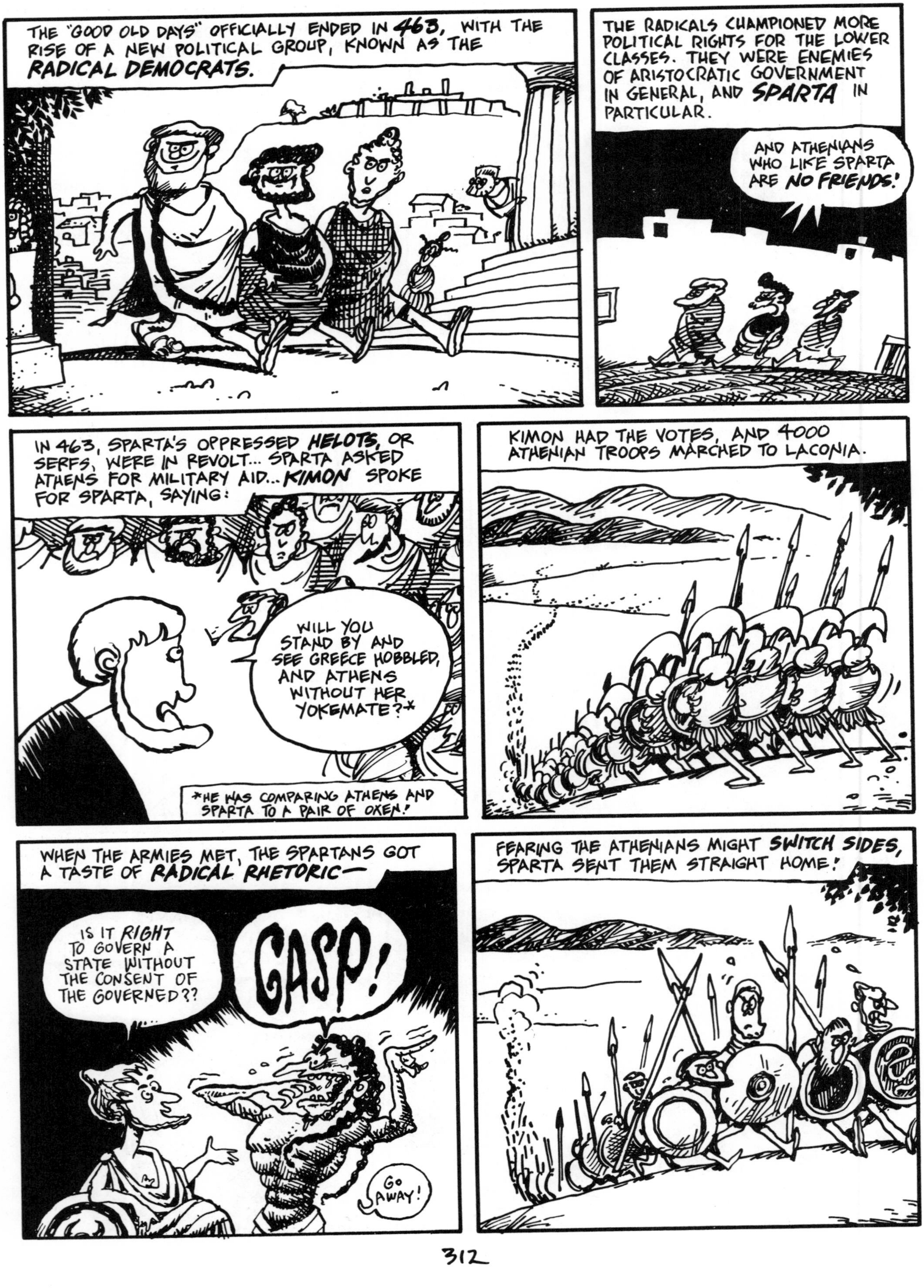
THE "GOOD OLD DAYS" OFFICIALLY ENDED IN 463, WITH THE RISE OF A NEW POLITICAL GROUP, KNOWN AS THE RADICAL DEMOCRATS.
THE RADICALS CHAMPIONED MORE POLITICAL RIGHTS FOR THE LOWER CLASSES. THEY WERE ENEMIES OF ARISTOCRATIC GOVERNMENT IN GENERAL, AND SPARTA IN PARTICULAR.
AND ATHENIANS WHO LIKE SPARTA ARE NO FRIENDS!
IN 463, SPARTA'S OPPRESSED HELOTS, OR SERFS, WERE IN REVOLT... SPARTA ASKED ATHENS FOR MILITARY AID... KIMON SPOKE FOR SPARTA, SAYING:
WILL YOU STAND BY AND SEE GREECE HOBBLED, AND ATHENS WITHOUT HER YOKEMATE?*
*HE WAS COMPARING ATHENS AND SPARTA TO A PAIR OF OXEN!
KIMON HAD THE VOTES, AND 4000 ATHENIAN TROOPS MARCHED TO LACONIA.
WHEN THE ARMIES MET, THE SPARTANS GOT A TASTE OF RADICAL RHETORIC—
IS IT RIGHT TO GOVERN A STATE WITHOUT THE CONSENT OF THE GOVERNED??
GASP!
GO AWAY!
FEARING THE ATHENIANS MIGHT SWITCH SIDES, SPARTA SENT THEM STRAIGHT HOME!

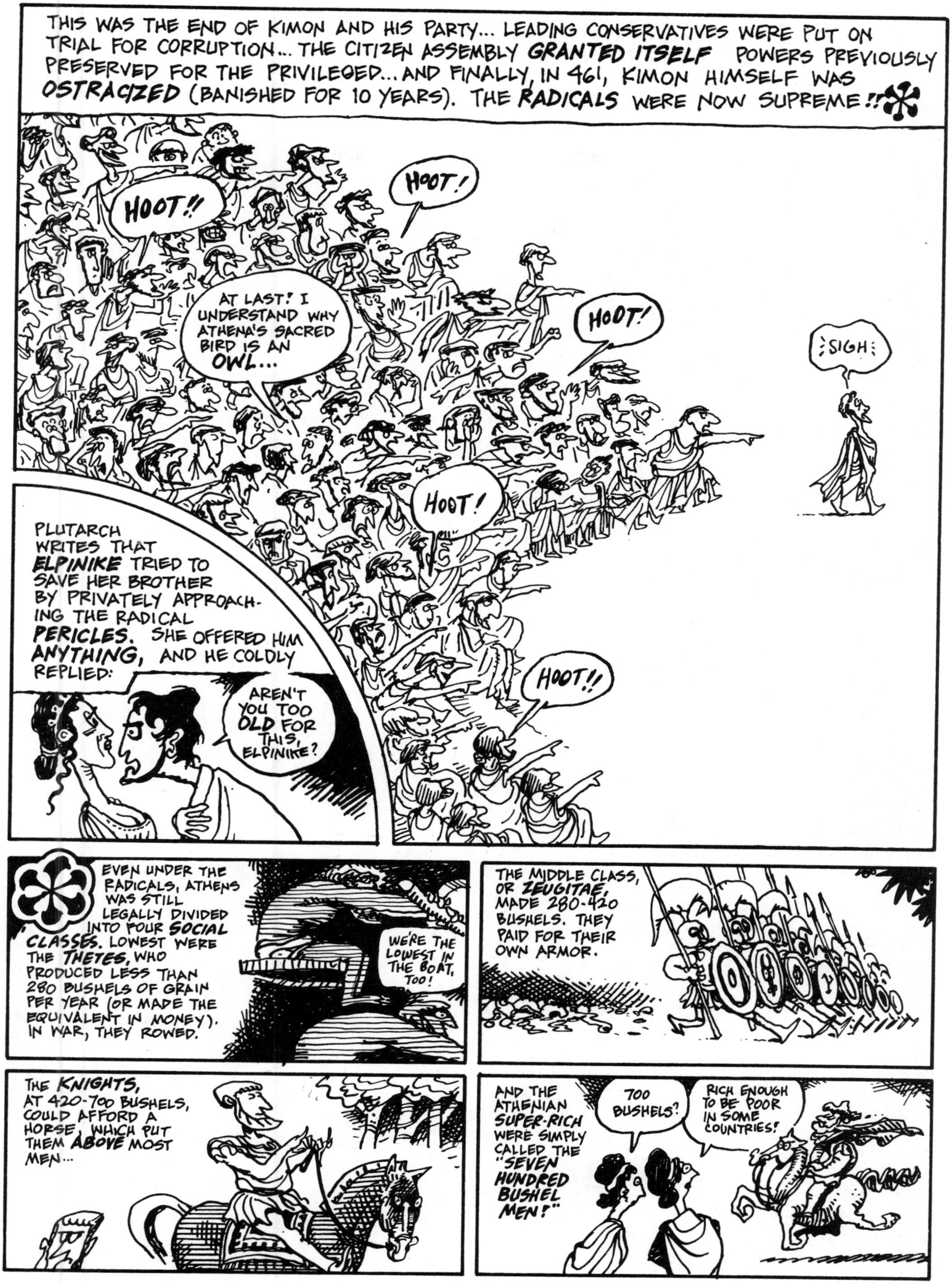
THIS WAS THE END OF KIMON AND HIS PARTY... LEADING CONSERVATIVES WERE PUT ON TRIAL FOR CORRUPTION... THE CITIZEN ASSEMBLY GRANTED ITSELF POWERS PREVIOUSLY PRESERVED FOR THE PRIVILEGED... AND FINALLY, IN 461, KIMON HIMSELF WAS OSTRACIZED (BANISHED FOR 10 YEARS). THE RADICALS WERE NOW SUPREME!!
HOOT!!
HOOT!
AT LAST! I UNDERSTAND WHY ATHENA'S SACRED BIRD IS AN OWL...
HOOT!
SIGH
HOOT!
HOOT!!
PLUTARCH WRITES THAT ELPINIKE TRIED TO SAVE HER BROTHER BY PRIVATELY APPROACHING THE RADICAL PERICLES. SHE OFFERED HIM ANYTHING, AND HE COLDLY REPLIED:
AREN'T YOU TOO OLD FOR THIS, ELPINIKE?
EVEN UNDER THE RADICALS, ATHENS WAS STILL LEGALLY DIVIDED INTO FOUR SOCIAL CLASSES. LOWEST WERE THE THETES, WHO PRODUCED LESS THAN 280 BUSHELS OF GRAIN PER YEAR (OR MADE THE EQUIVALENT IN MONEY). IN WAR, THEY ROWED.
WE'RE THE LOWEST IN THE BOAT, TOO!
THE MIDDLE CLASS, OR ZEUGITAE, MADE 280-420 BUSHELS. THEY PAID FOR THEIR OWN ARMOR.
THE KNIGHTS, AT 420-700 BUSHELS, COULD AFFORD A HORSE, WHICH PUT THEM ABOVE MOST MEN...
AND THE ATHENIAN SUPER-RICH WERE SIMPLY CALLED THE "SEVEN HUNDRED BUSHEL MEN!"
700 BUSHELS?
RICH ENOUGH TO BE POOR IN SOME COUNTRIES!

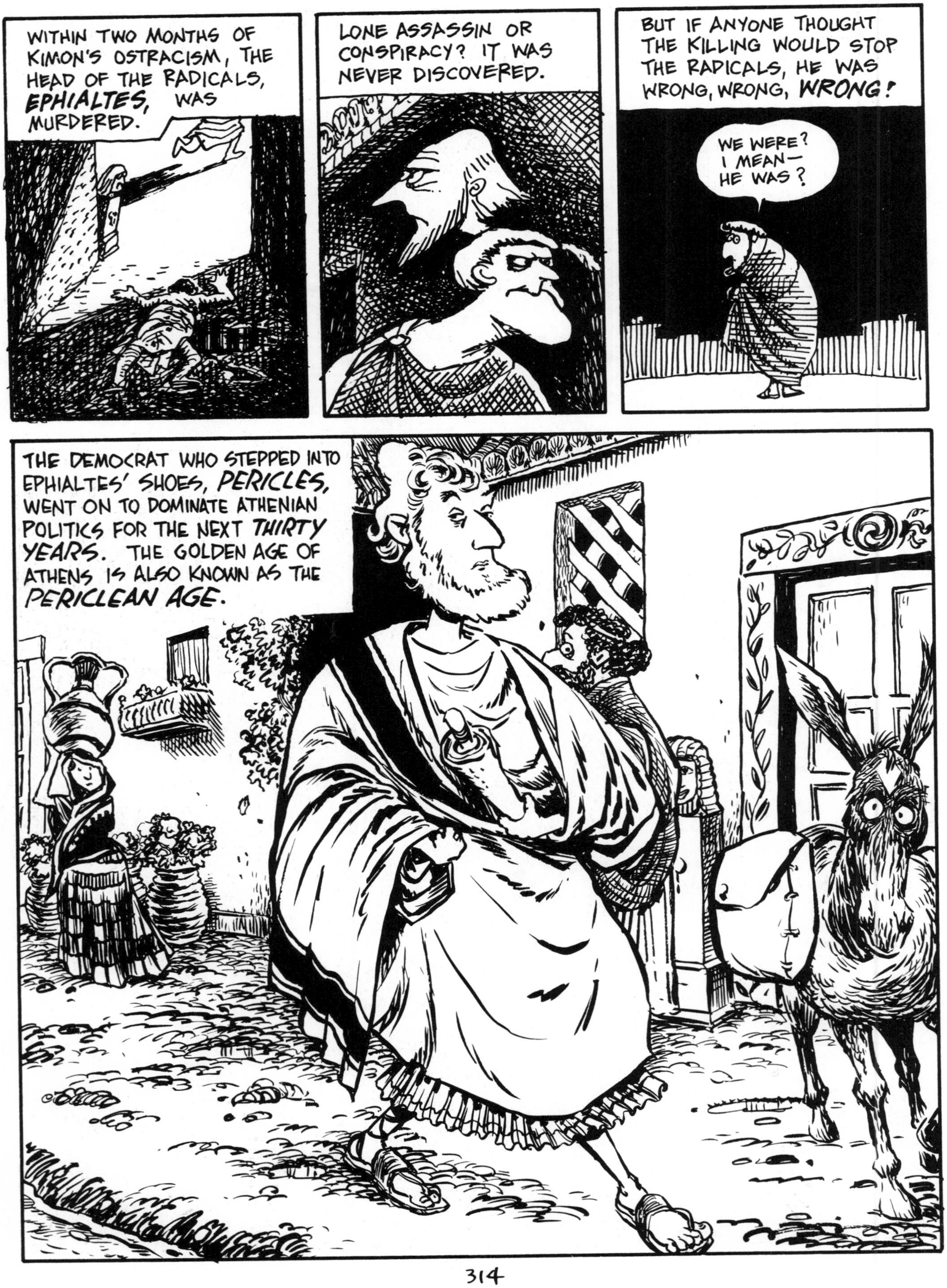
WITHIN TWO MONTHS OF KIMON'S OSTRACISM, THE HEAD OF THE RADICALS, EPHIALTES, WAS MURDERED.
LONE ASSASSIN OR CONSPIRACY? IT WAS NEVER DISCOVERED.
BUT IF ANYONE THOUGHT THE KILLING WOULD STOP THE RADICALS, HE WAS WRONG, WRONG, WRONG!
WE WERE? I MEAN— HE WAS?
THE DEMOCRAT WHO STEPPED INTO EPHIALTES' SHOES, PERICLES, WENT ON TO DOMINATE ATHENIAN POLITICS FOR THE NEXT THIRTY YEARS. THE GOLDEN AGE OF ATHENS IS ALSO KNOWN AS THE PERICLEAN AGE.

Panel 1 (top left): INCORRUPTIBLE, CALM, REMOTE, ENDOWED WITH GREAT FORESIGHT, SHREWD, TOUGH, AND A THUNDEROUS SPEAKER, PERICLES WAS CALLED THE **OLYMPIAN**, AFTER MOUNT OLYMPUS, HOME OF THE GODS.

SO PERICLES IS LIKE A GOD?

NO... HIS *HEAD* IS LIKE A *MOUNTAIN!*

Panel 2 (top right): HE ALSO HAD SEVERAL OTHER NICK-NAMES, BECAUSE AN ACCIDENT OF BIRTH HAD LEFT HIM WITH A *POINTED HEAD*.

SQUILL HEAD!! SQUILL HEAD!!

ZIPPY THE GREEK!

Panel 3 (middle left): HE *LIVED* FOR *POLITICS*, EVERY DAY WALKING THE SAME ROUTE TO THE AGORÁ, OR MARKETPLACE.

AH, ZEUS, HEAD OF THE GODS!

"FROM HIS HUGE GALLERY OF A PATE HE SENDS FORTH TROUBLE FOR THE STATE."

Panel 4 (middle right): BUT AT HOME— HIS WIFE (WHO WAS ALSO HIS COUSIN ✱) DIVORCED HIM, AND HIS SONS LONGED FOR LUXURY!

PHAUGH! *ZEUS* HAS A BAD MARRIAGE, TOO!

Panel 5 (bottom left): ACCORDING TO AN OLD ATHENIAN LAW, *DAUGHTERS* COULD NOT BE *HEIRS.* PROPERTY, LIKE THE FAMILY NAME, WENT TO THE SONS.

EVEN IF THEY'RE LAZIER, STUPIDER, AND LESS DESERVING THAN THEIR SISTERS!

Panel 6 (bottom middle): AND IF THERE WERE NO SONS?

O WOE! WOE!

Panel 7 (bottom right): TO KEEP THE FORTUNE IN THE FAMILY, THE DAUGHTER MUST MARRY HER *CLOSEST MALE RELATIVE.* THIS MAY EXPLAIN PERICLES' UNHAPPY MARRIAGE!

⌇GROWL⌇ DUTY IS DUTY!

AND THEY WONDER WHY WE WAIL AT FUNERALS..

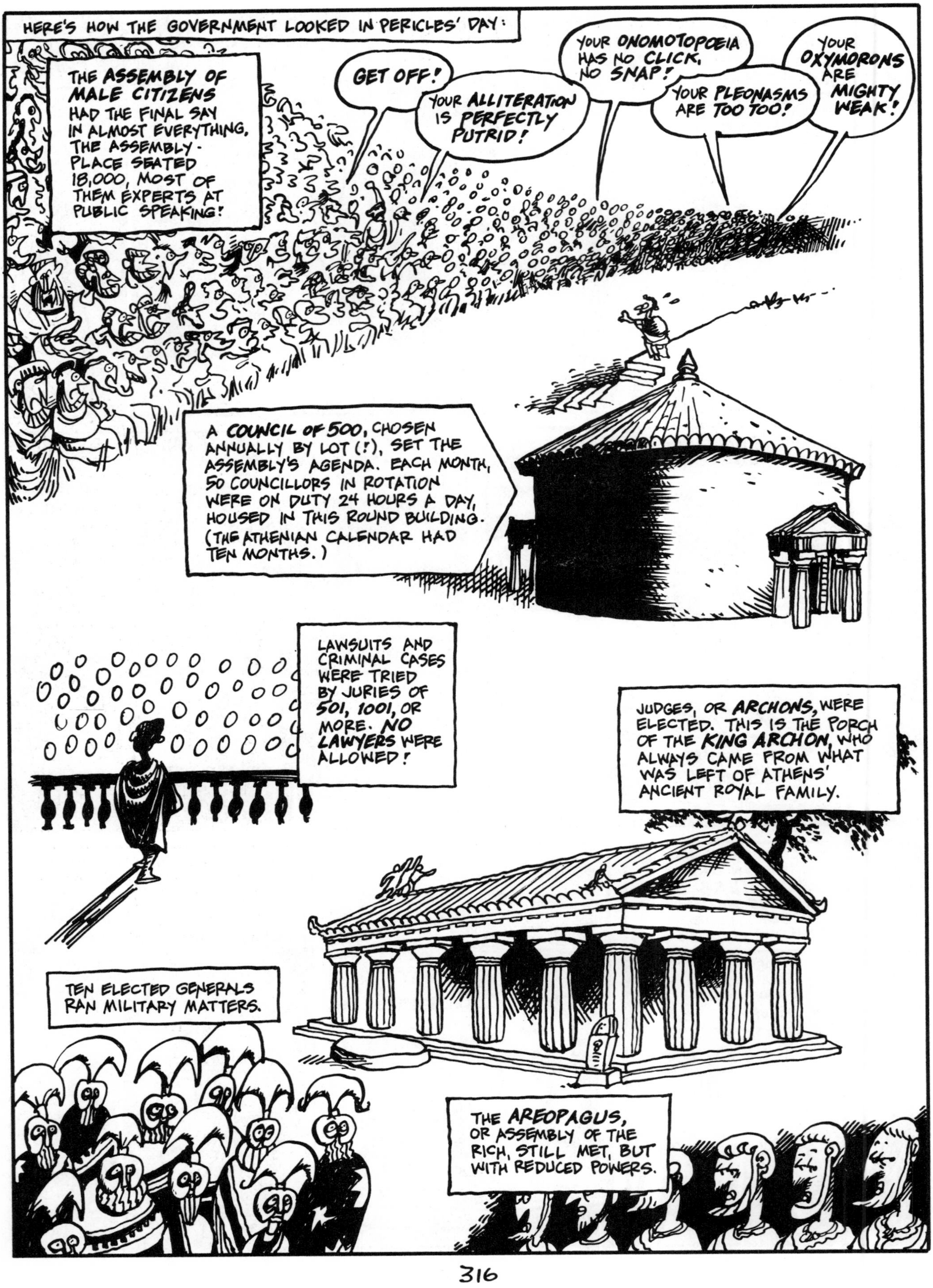
HERE'S HOW THE GOVERNMENT LOOKED IN PERICLES' DAY:
THE ASSEMBLY OF MALE CITIZENS HAD THE FINAL SAY IN ALMOST EVERYTHING. THE ASSEMBLY-PLACE SEATED 18,000, MOST OF THEM EXPERTS AT PUBLIC SPEAKING!
GET OFF!
YOUR ALLITERATION IS PERFECTLY PUTRID!
YOUR ONOMOTOPOEIA HAS NO CLICK, NO SNAP!
YOUR PLEONASMS ARE TOO TOO!
YOUR OXYMORONS ARE MIGHTY WEAK!
A COUNCIL OF 500, CHOSEN ANNUALLY BY LOT (!), SET THE ASSEMBLY'S AGENDA. EACH MONTH, 50 COUNCILLORS IN ROTATION WERE ON DUTY 24 HOURS A DAY, HOUSED IN THIS ROUND BUILDING. (THE ATHENIAN CALENDAR HAD TEN MONTHS.)
LAWSUITS AND CRIMINAL CASES WERE TRIED BY JURIES OF 501, 1001, OR MORE. NO LAWYERS WERE ALLOWED!
JUDGES, OR ARCHONS, WERE ELECTED. THIS IS THE PORCH OF THE KING ARCHON, WHO ALWAYS CAME FROM WHAT WAS LEFT OF ATHENS' ANCIENT ROYAL FAMILY.
TEN ELECTED GENERALS RAN MILITARY MATTERS.
THE AREOPAGUS, OR ASSEMBLY OF THE RICH, STILL MET, BUT WITH REDUCED POWERS.

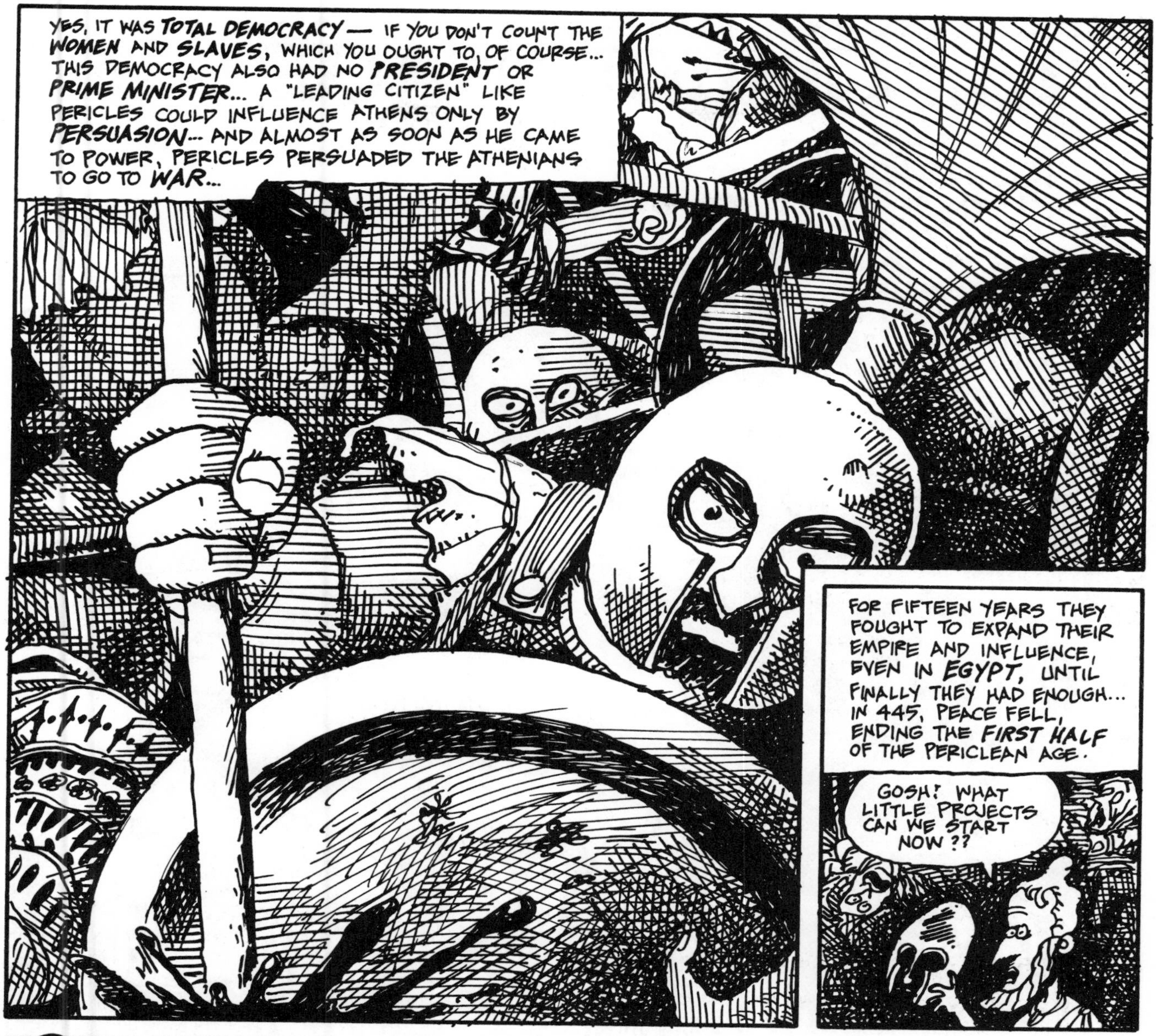
YES, IT WAS TOTAL DEMOCRACY — IF YOU DON'T COUNT THE WOMEN AND SLAVES, WHICH YOU OUGHT TO, OF COURSE... THIS DEMOCRACY ALSO HAD NO PRESIDENT OR PRIME MINISTER... A "LEADING CITIZEN" LIKE PERICLES COULD INFLUENCE ATHENS ONLY BY PERSUASION... AND ALMOST AS SOON AS HE CAME TO POWER, PERICLES PERSUADED THE ATHENIANS TO GO TO WAR...
FOR FIFTEEN YEARS THEY FOUGHT TO EXPAND THEIR EMPIRE AND INFLUENCE, EVEN IN EGYPT, UNTIL FINALLY THEY HAD ENOUGH... IN 445, PEACE FELL, ENDING THE FIRST HALF OF THE PERICLEAN AGE.
GOSH! WHAT LITTLE PROJECTS CAN WE START NOW??

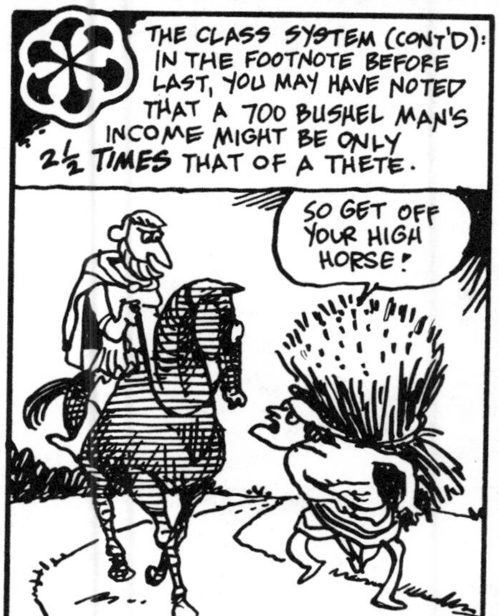
THE CLASS SYSTEM (CONT'D): IN THE FOOTNOTE BEFORE LAST, YOU MAY HAVE NOTED THAT A 700 BUSHEL MAN'S INCOME MIGHT BE ONLY 2½ TIMES THAT OF A THETE.
SO GET OFF YOUR HIGH HORSE!

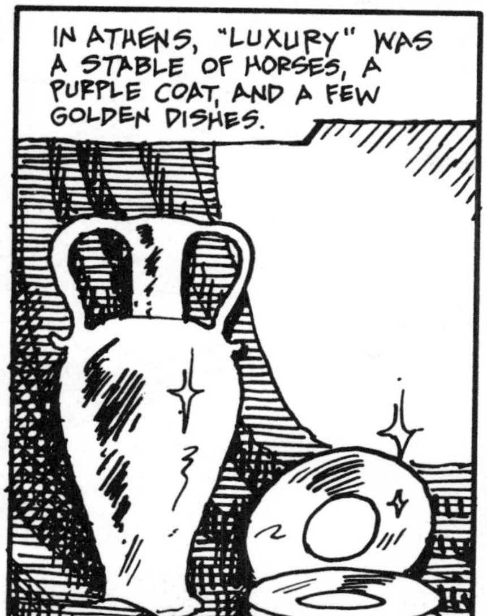
IN ATHENS, "LUXURY" WAS A STABLE OF HORSES, A PURPLE COAT, AND A FEW GOLDEN DISHES.

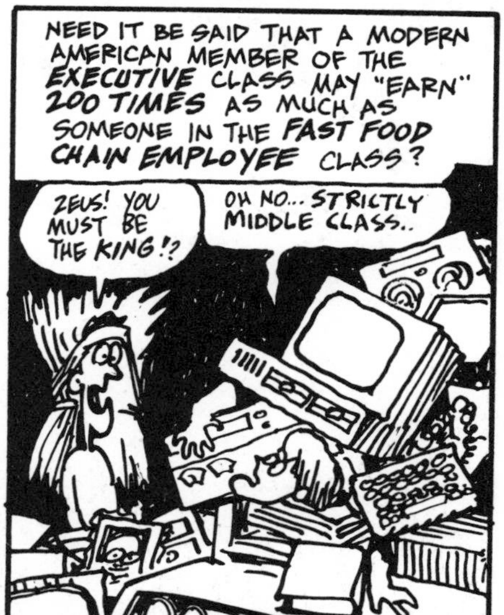
NEED IT BE SAID THAT A MODERN AMERICAN MEMBER OF THE EXECUTIVE CLASS MAY "EARN" 200 TIMES AS MUCH AS SOMEONE IN THE FAST FOOD CHAIN EMPLOYEE CLASS?
ZEUS! YOU MUST BE THE KING!?
OH NO... STRICTLY MIDDLE CLASS..

THE GOLDEN AGE

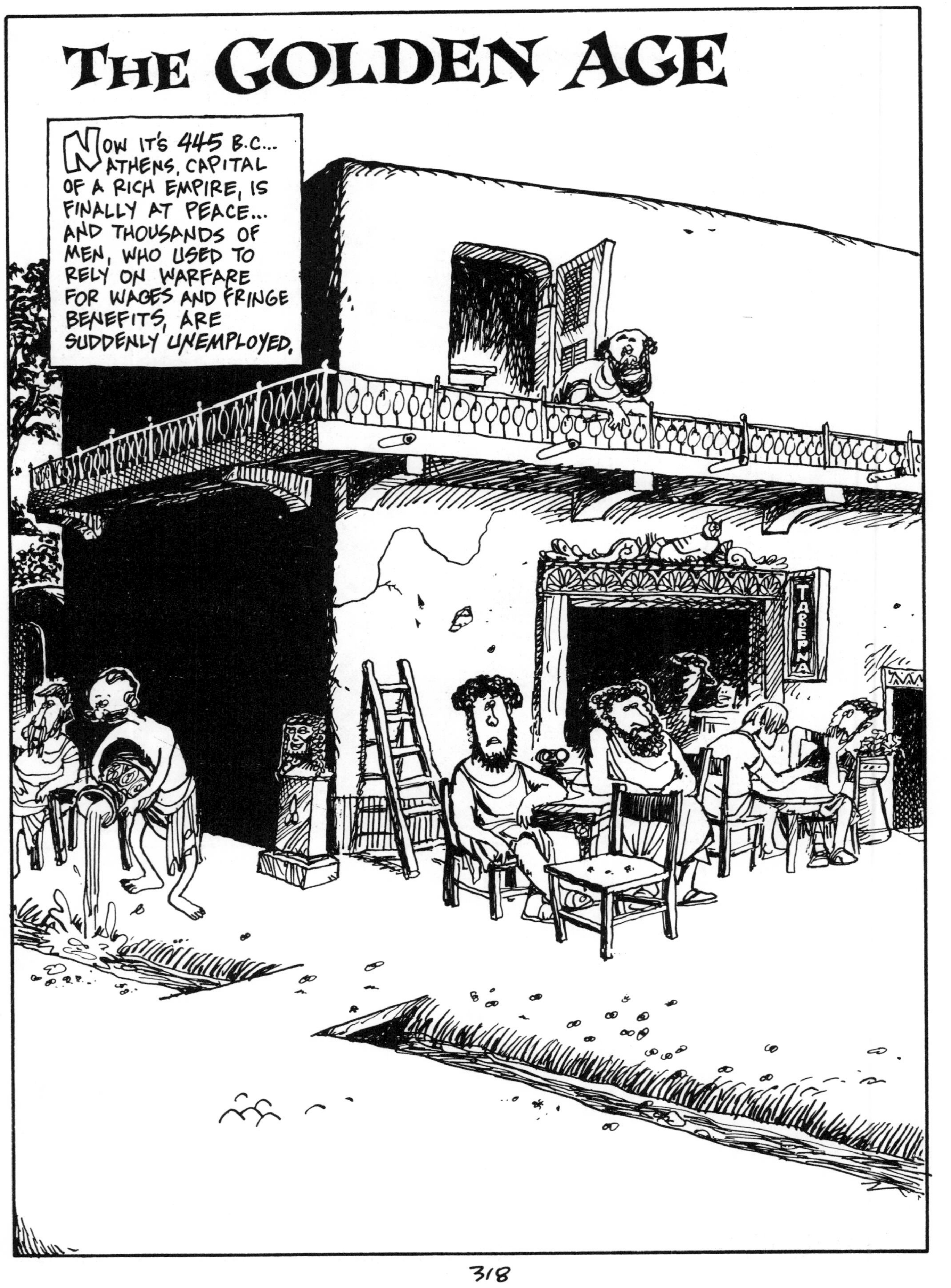
NOW IT'S 445 B.C... ATHENS, CAPITAL OF A RICH EMPIRE, IS FINALLY AT PEACE... AND THOUSANDS OF MEN, WHO USED TO RELY ON WARFARE FOR WAGES AND FRINGE BENEFITS, ARE SUDDENLY UNEMPLOYED.
TABEPNA

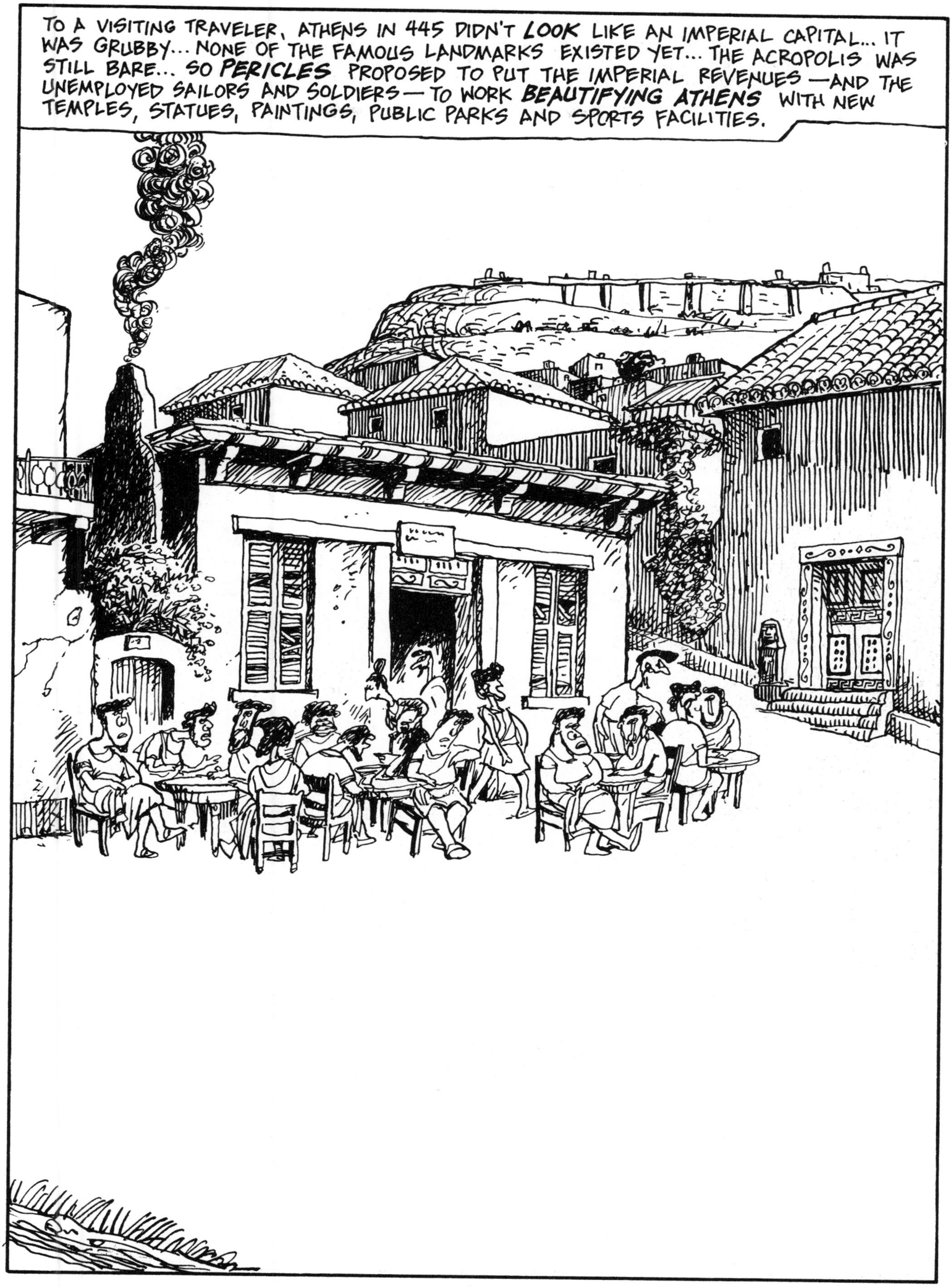
TO A VISITING TRAVELER, ATHENS IN 445 DIDN'T **LOOK** LIKE AN IMPERIAL CAPITAL... IT WAS GRUBBY... NONE OF THE FAMOUS LANDMARKS EXISTED YET... THE ACROPOLIS WAS STILL BARE... SO **PERICLES** PROPOSED TO PUT THE IMPERIAL REVENUES —AND THE UNEMPLOYED SAILORS AND SOLDIERS— TO WORK **BEAUTIFYING ATHENS** WITH NEW TEMPLES, STATUES, PAINTINGS, PUBLIC PARKS AND SPORTS FACILITIES.

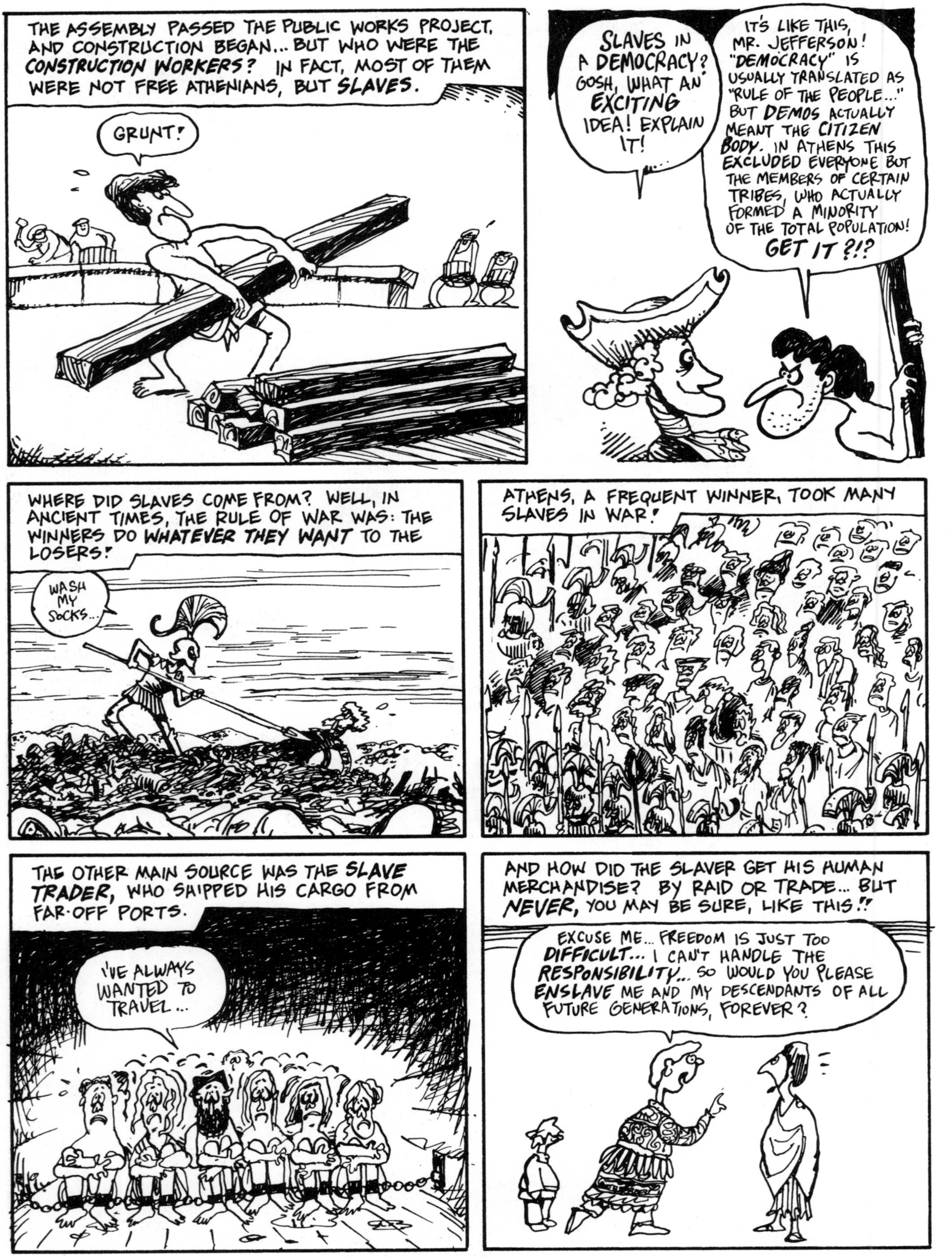
THE ASSEMBLY PASSED THE PUBLIC WORKS PROJECT, AND CONSTRUCTION BEGAN... BUT WHO WERE THE CONSTRUCTION WORKERS? IN FACT, MOST OF THEM WERE NOT FREE ATHENIANS, BUT SLAVES.
GRUNT!
SLAVES IN A DEMOCRACY? GOSH, WHAT AN EXCITING IDEA! EXPLAIN IT!
IT'S LIKE THIS, MR. JEFFERSON! "DEMOCRACY" IS USUALLY TRANSLATED AS "RULE OF THE PEOPLE..." BUT DEMOS ACTUALLY MEANT THE CITIZEN BODY. IN ATHENS THIS EXCLUDED EVERYONE BUT THE MEMBERS OF CERTAIN TRIBES, WHO ACTUALLY FORMED A MINORITY OF THE TOTAL POPULATION! GET IT?!?
WHERE DID SLAVES COME FROM? WELL, IN ANCIENT TIMES, THE RULE OF WAR WAS: THE WINNERS DO WHATEVER THEY WANT TO THE LOSERS!
WASH MY SOCKS...
ATHENS, A FREQUENT WINNER, TOOK MANY SLAVES IN WAR!
THE OTHER MAIN SOURCE WAS THE SLAVE TRADER, WHO SHIPPED HIS CARGO FROM FAR-OFF PORTS.
I'VE ALWAYS WANTED TO TRAVEL...
AND HOW DID THE SLAVER GET HIS HUMAN MERCHANDISE? BY RAID OR TRADE... BUT NEVER, YOU MAY BE SURE, LIKE THIS!!
EXCUSE ME... FREEDOM IS JUST TOO DIFFICULT... I CAN'T HANDLE THE RESPONSIBILITY... SO WOULD YOU PLEASE ENSLAVE ME AND MY DESCENDANTS OF ALL FUTURE GENERATIONS, FOREVER?

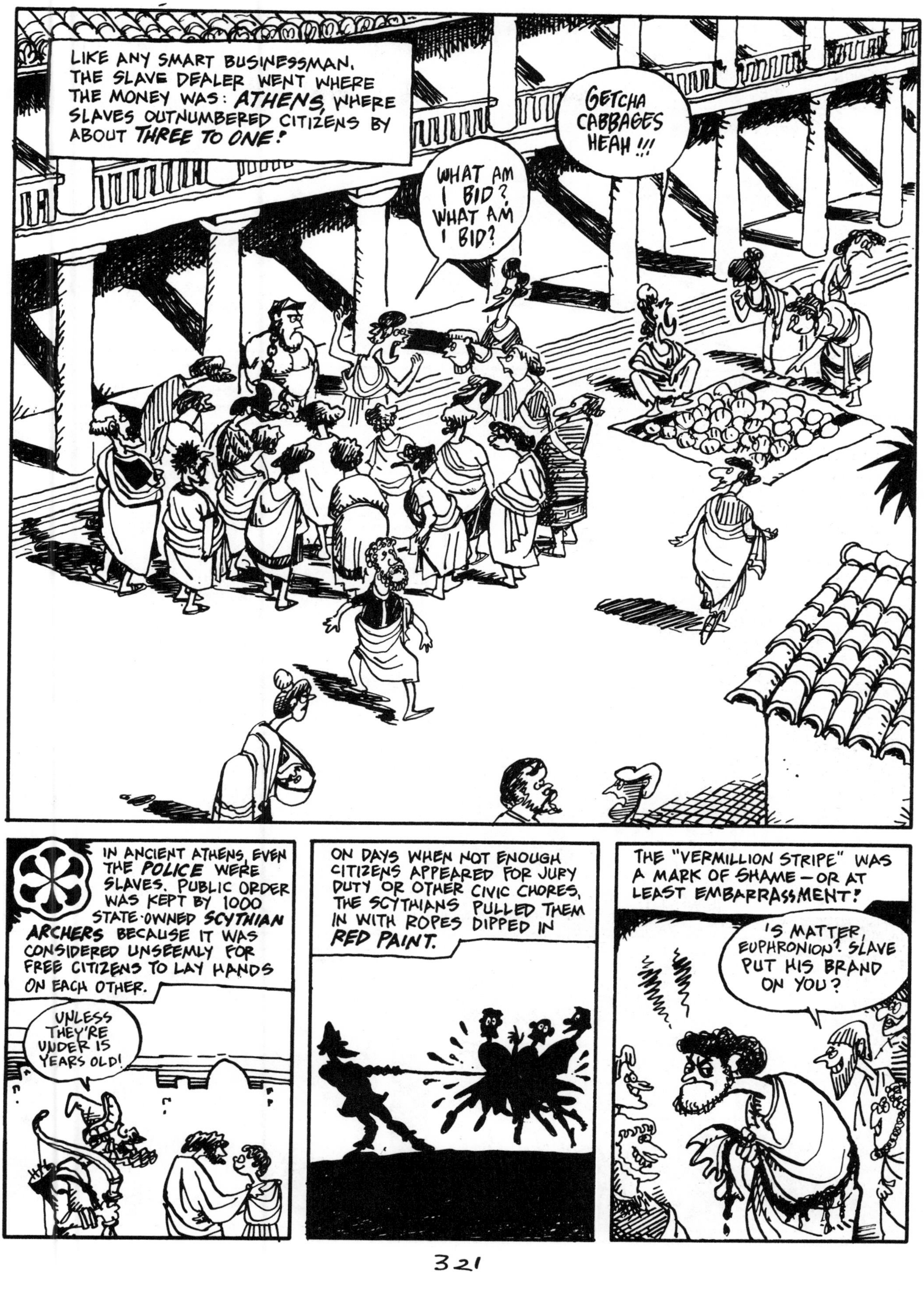
LIKE ANY SMART BUSINESSMAN, THE SLAVE DEALER WENT WHERE THE MONEY WAS: ATHENS, WHERE SLAVES OUTNUMBERED CITIZENS BY ABOUT THREE TO ONE!
GETCHA CABBAGES HEAH !!!
WHAT AM I BID? WHAT AM I BID?
IN ANCIENT ATHENS, EVEN THE POLICE WERE SLAVES. PUBLIC ORDER WAS KEPT BY 1000 STATE-OWNED SCYTHIAN ARCHERS BECAUSE IT WAS CONSIDERED UNSEEMLY FOR FREE CITIZENS TO LAY HANDS ON EACH OTHER.
UNLESS THEY'RE UNDER 15 YEARS OLD!
ON DAYS WHEN NOT ENOUGH CITIZENS APPEARED FOR JURY DUTY OR OTHER CIVIC CHORES, THE SCYTHIANS PULLED THEM IN WITH ROPES DIPPED IN RED PAINT.
THE "VERMILLION STRIPE" WAS A MARK OF SHAME—OR AT LEAST EMBARRASSMENT!
'S MATTER, EUPHRONION? SLAVE PUT HIS BRAND ON YOU?

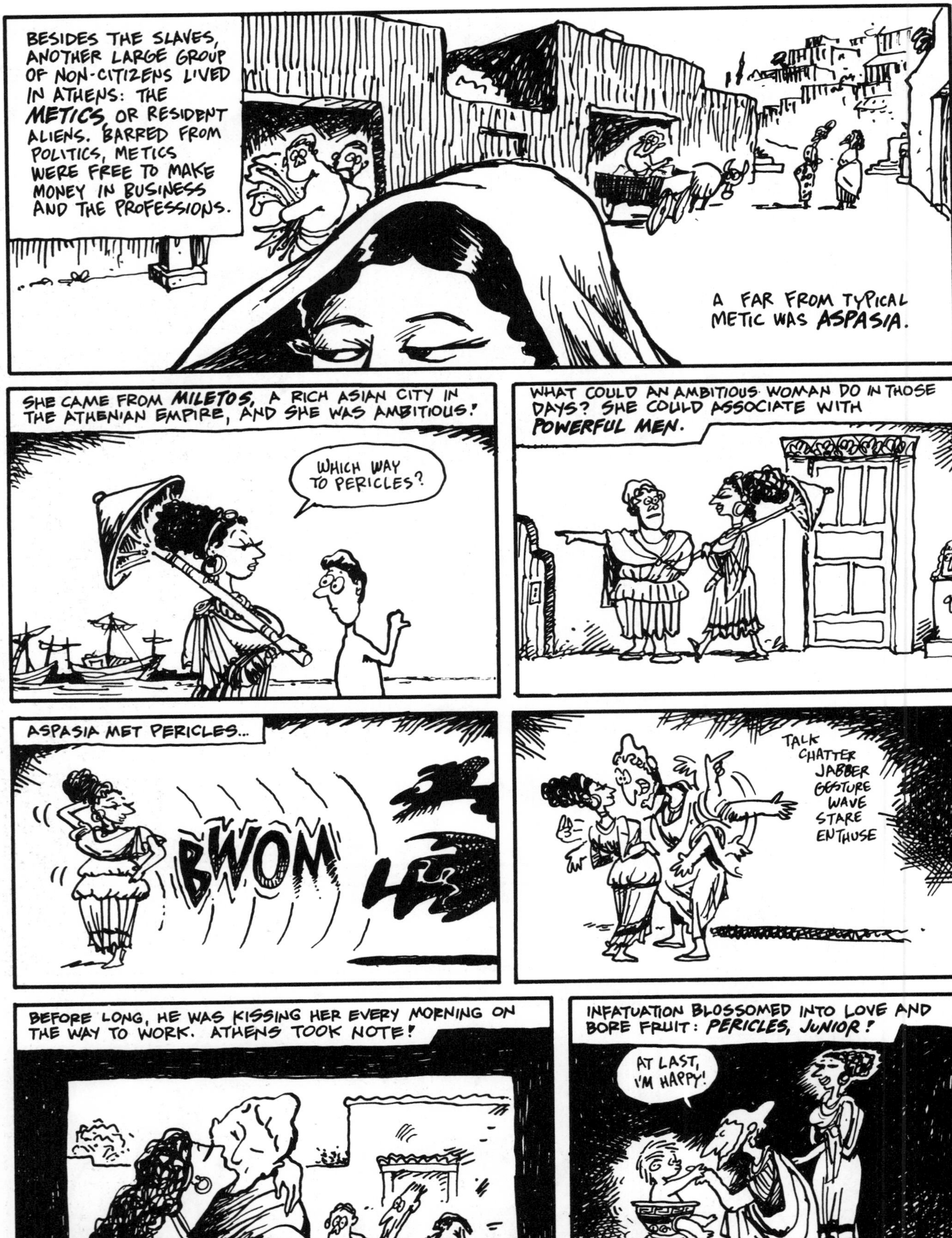
BESIDES THE SLAVES, ANOTHER LARGE GROUP OF NON-CITIZENS LIVED IN ATHENS: THE **METICS**, OR RESIDENT ALIENS. BARRED FROM POLITICS, METICS WERE FREE TO MAKE MONEY IN BUSINESS AND THE PROFESSIONS.
A FAR FROM TYPICAL METIC WAS **ASPASIA**.
SHE CAME FROM **MILETOS**, A RICH ASIAN CITY IN THE ATHENIAN EMPIRE, AND SHE WAS AMBITIOUS!
WHICH WAY TO PERICLES?
WHAT COULD AN AMBITIOUS WOMAN DO IN THOSE DAYS? SHE COULD ASSOCIATE WITH **POWERFUL MEN**.
ASPASIA MET PERICLES...
BWOM
TALK
CHATTER
JABBER
GESTURE
WAVE
STARE
ENTHUSE
BEFORE LONG, HE WAS KISSING HER EVERY MORNING ON THE WAY TO WORK. ATHENS TOOK NOTE!
INFATUATION BLOSSOMED INTO LOVE AND BORE FRUIT: ***PERICLES, JUNIOR*!**
AT LAST, I'M HAPPY!

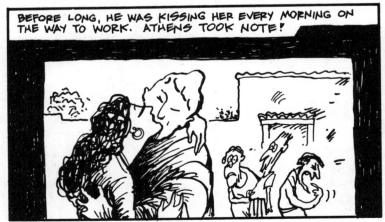

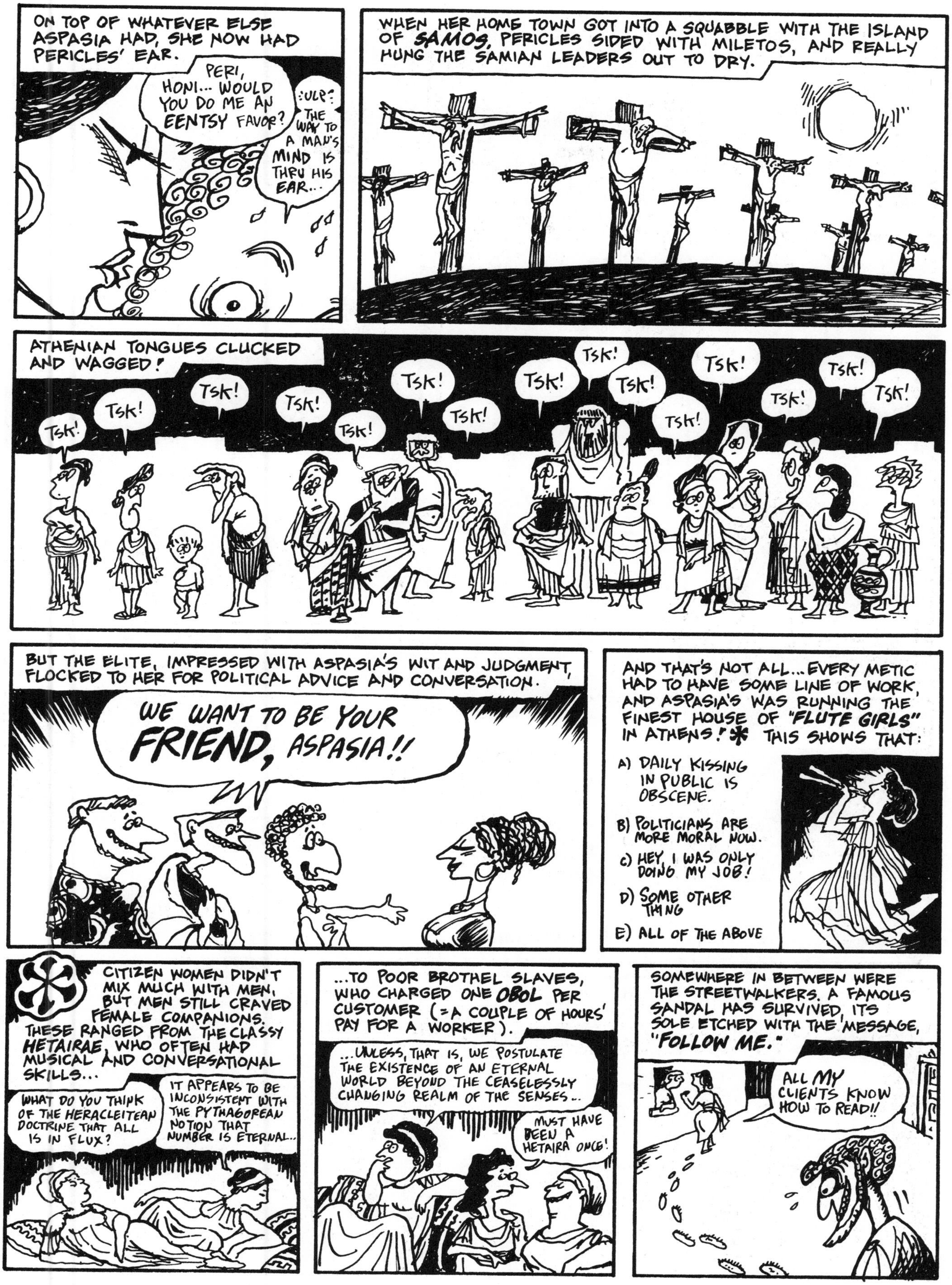

ON TOP OF WHATEVER ELSE ASPASIA HAD, SHE NOW HAD PERICLES' EAR.
PERI, HONI... WOULD YOU DO ME AN EENTSY FAVOR?
:ULP:
THE WAY TO A MAN'S MIND IS THRU HIS EAR...
WHEN HER HOME TOWN GOT INTO A SQUABBLE WITH THE ISLAND OF SAMOS, PERICLES SIDED WITH MILETOS, AND REALLY HUNG THE SAMIAN LEADERS OUT TO DRY.
ATHENIAN TONGUES CLUCKED AND WAGGED!
TSK! TSK! TSK! TSK! TSK! TSK! TSK! TSK! TSK! TSK! TSK! TSK! TSK! TSK! TSK!
BUT THE ELITE, IMPRESSED WITH ASPASIA'S WIT AND JUDGMENT, FLOCKED TO HER FOR POLITICAL ADVICE AND CONVERSATION.
WE WANT TO BE YOUR FRIEND, ASPASIA!!
AND THAT'S NOT ALL... EVERY METIC HAD TO HAVE SOME LINE OF WORK, AND ASPASIA'S WAS RUNNING THE FINEST HOUSE OF "FLUTE GIRLS" IN ATHENS! * THIS SHOWS THAT:
A) DAILY KISSING IN PUBLIC IS OBSCENE.
B) POLITICIANS ARE MORE MORAL NOW.
C) HEY, I WAS ONLY DOING MY JOB!
D) SOME OTHER THING
E) ALL OF THE ABOVE
* CITIZEN WOMEN DIDN'T MIX MUCH WITH MEN, BUT MEN STILL CRAVED FEMALE COMPANIONS. THESE RANGED FROM THE CLASSY HETAIRAE, WHO OFTEN HAD MUSICAL AND CONVERSATIONAL SKILLS...
WHAT DO YOU THINK OF THE HERACLEITEAN DOCTRINE THAT ALL IS IN FLUX?
IT APPEARS TO BE INCONSISTENT WITH THE PYTHAGOREAN NOTION THAT NUMBER IS ETERNAL...
...TO POOR BROTHEL SLAVES, WHO CHARGED ONE OBOL PER CUSTOMER (= A COUPLE OF HOURS' PAY FOR A WORKER).
...UNLESS, THAT IS, WE POSTULATE THE EXISTENCE OF AN ETERNAL WORLD BEYOND THE CEASELESSLY CHANGING REALM OF THE SENSES...
MUST HAVE BEEN A HETAIRA ONCE!
SOMEWHERE IN BETWEEN WERE THE STREETWALKERS. A FAMOUS SANDAL HAS SURVIVED, ITS SOLE ETCHED WITH THE MESSAGE, "FOLLOW ME."
ALL MY CLIENTS KNOW HOW TO READ!!

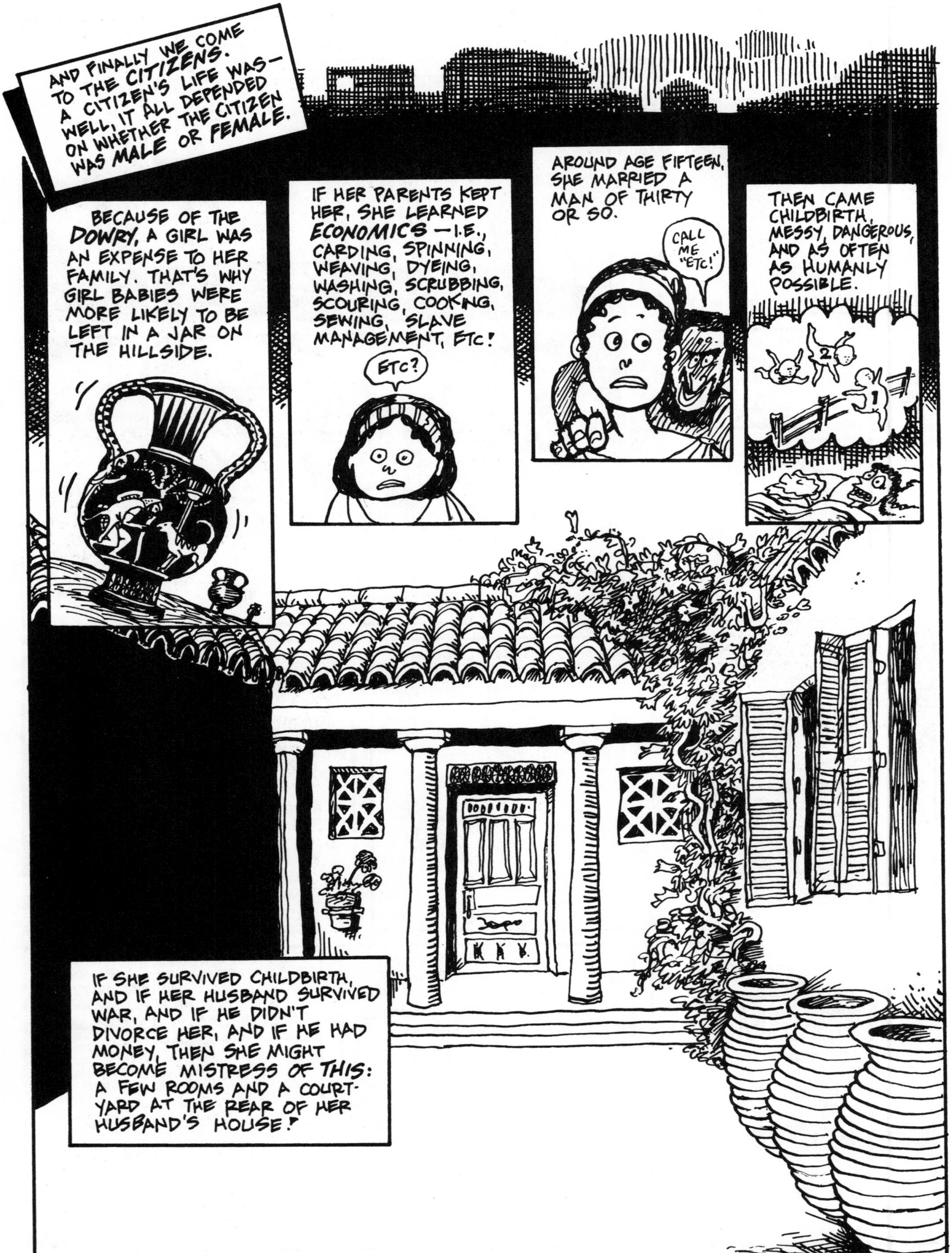
AND FINALLY WE COME TO THE CITIZENS. A CITIZEN'S LIFE WAS— WELL, IT ALL DEPENDED ON WHETHER THE CITIZEN WAS MALE OR FEMALE.
BECAUSE OF THE DOWRY, A GIRL WAS AN EXPENSE TO HER FAMILY. THAT'S WHY GIRL BABIES WERE MORE LIKELY TO BE LEFT IN A JAR ON THE HILLSIDE.
IF HER PARENTS KEPT HER, SHE LEARNED ECONOMICS — I.E., CARDING, SPINNING, WEAVING, DYEING, WASHING, SCRUBBING, SCOURING, COOKING, SEWING, SLAVE MANAGEMENT, ETC!
ETC?
AROUND AGE FIFTEEN, SHE MARRIED A MAN OF THIRTY OR SO.
CALL ME "ETC!"
THEN CAME CHILDBIRTH, MESSY, DANGEROUS, AND AS OFTEN AS HUMANLY POSSIBLE.
2
1
IF SHE SURVIVED CHILDBIRTH, AND IF HER HUSBAND SURVIVED WAR, AND IF HE DIDN'T DIVORCE HER, AND IF HE HAD MONEY, THEN SHE MIGHT BECOME MISTRESS OF THIS: A FEW ROOMS AND A COURTYARD AT THE REAR OF HER HUSBAND'S HOUSE!

THE MALE CITIZENS WERE FREE TO CREATE CLASSICAL CULTURE, THANKS TO THE HARD WORK OF THE WOMEN, METICS, AND SLAVES.

FREE TO TALK POLITICS ENDLESSLY...

FREE TO SPIN OUT PHILOSOPHICAL SPECULATION AT MARATHON DRINKING PARTIES...

I SHAY TH' *SUN* IS A *HOT ROCK* BIGGER THAN THE PELOPONNESE!!

HA HA HAW HAW

"SYMPOSIUM" = DRINKING TOGETHER

IN THE AGE OF PERICLES, THIS SMALL GROUP, ABOUT 40,000 MEN, PRODUCED SEVERAL OF HISTORY'S GREATEST ARTISTS, WRITERS, AND THINKERS!

LIKE *WHO?*

DON'T FORCE ME TO FLATTER MYSELF...

THE PLAYWRIGHT *SOPHOCLES* (496-406) PERFECTED THE ART OF *TRAGEDY*, SETTING THE STAGE FOR ALL LATER WESTERN DRAMA.

IN THIS SCENE, OEDIPUS, YOU DISCOVER THAT YOUR WIFE IS REALLY YOUR MOTHER, WHILE THE CHORUS TAPS OUT ITS LITTLE DANCE!

THE SCULPTOR *PHIDIAS* (500-c.430) WAS THE MOST FAMOUS IN ANCIENT GREECE. BEFORE PHIDIAS, STATUES WERE STIFF. AFTERWARD, THEY GREW OVER-WIGGLY.

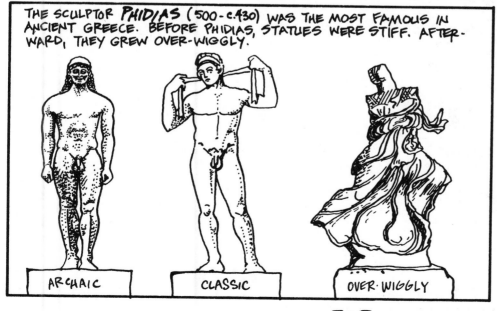

ARCHAIC

CLASSIC

OVER-WIGGLY

WHAT DID THESE ARTISTS HAVE IN COMMON? BALANCED PROPORTIONS, PURITY OF EXPRESSION, RESTRAINT IN ORNAMENTATION, EMOTION TEMPERED BY REASON... THESE ARE THE ELEMENTS OF THE *CLASSIC STYLE*, WHICH ATTAINED PERFECTION IN A *SINGLE BUILDING*...

THE FAMOUS ATHENIAN HOG SLAUGHTERHOUSE?

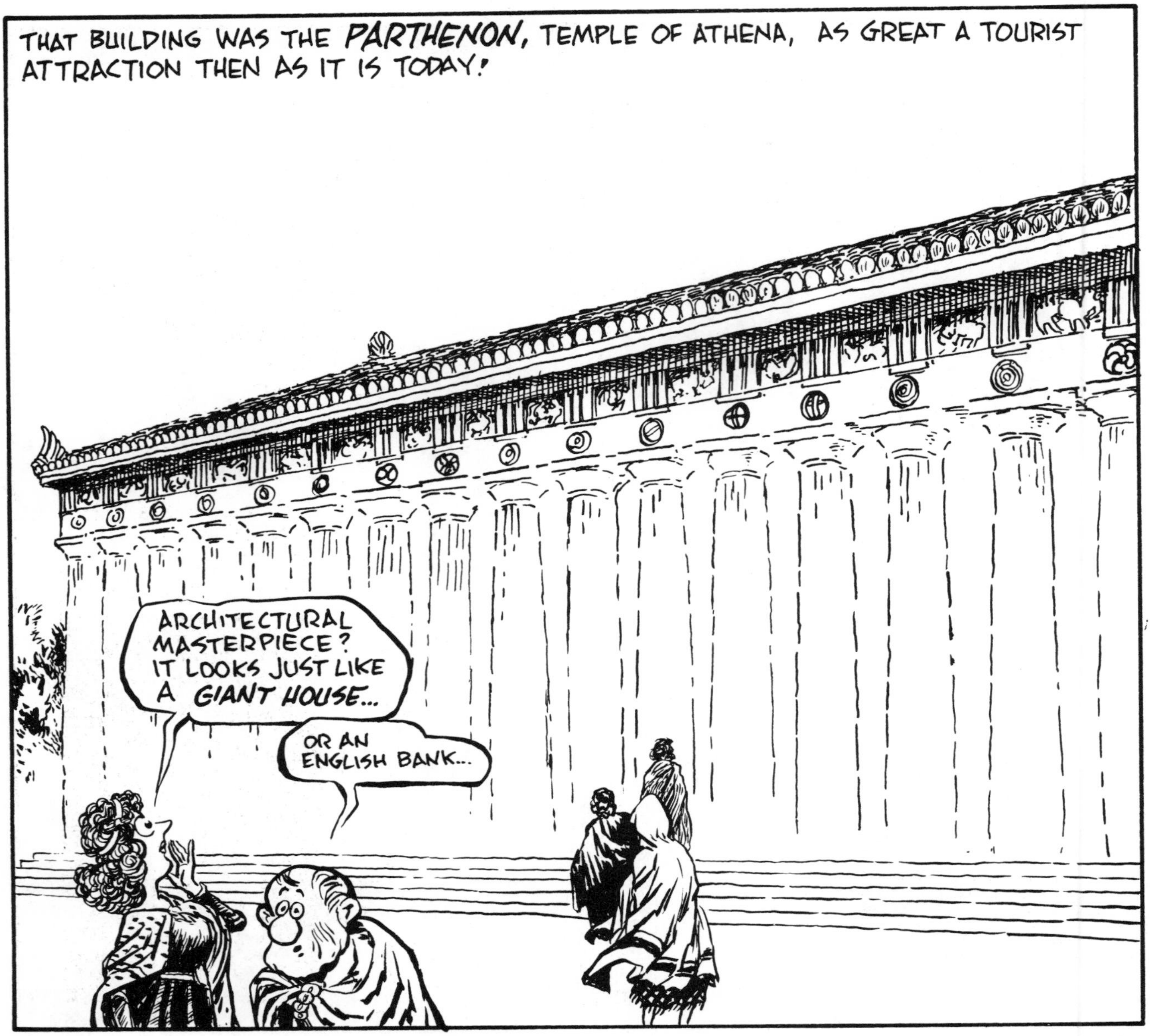
THAT BUILDING WAS THE *PARTHENON,* TEMPLE OF ATHENA, AS GREAT A TOURIST ATTRACTION THEN AS IT IS TODAY!
ARCHITECTURAL MASTERPIECE? IT LOOKS JUST LIKE A *GIANT HOUSE...*
OR AN ENGLISH BANK...

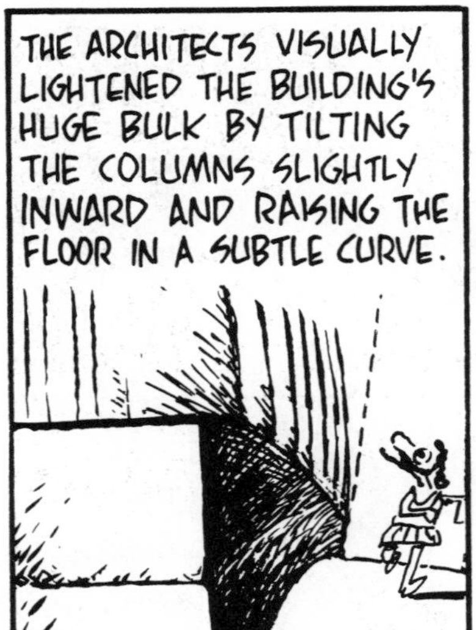
THE ARCHITECTS VISUALLY LIGHTENED THE BUILDING'S HUGE BULK BY TILTING THE COLUMNS SLIGHTLY INWARD AND RAISING THE FLOOR IN A SUBTLE CURVE.

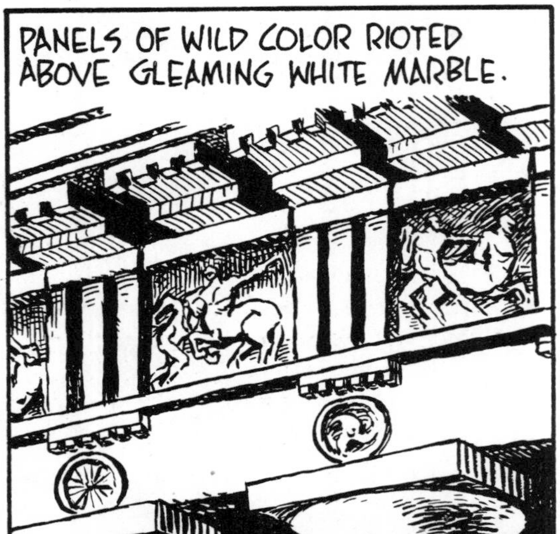
PANELS OF WILD COLOR RIOTED ABOVE GLEAMING WHITE MARBLE.

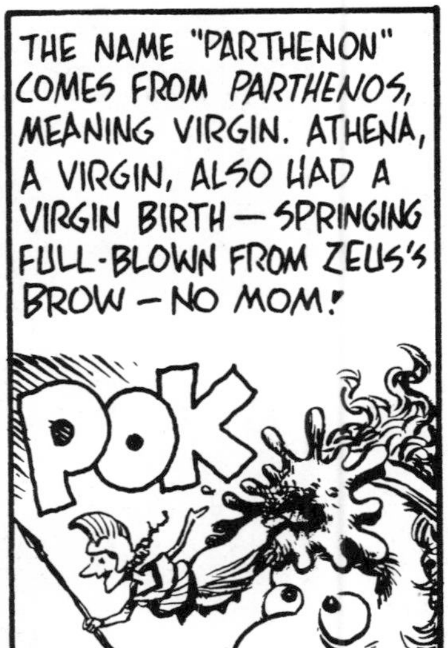
THE NAME "PARTHENON" COMES FROM *PARTHENOS,* MEANING VIRGIN. ATHENA, A VIRGIN, ALSO HAD A VIRGIN BIRTH — SPRINGING FULL-BLOWN FROM ZEUS'S BROW — NO MOM!
POK

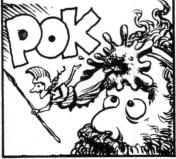

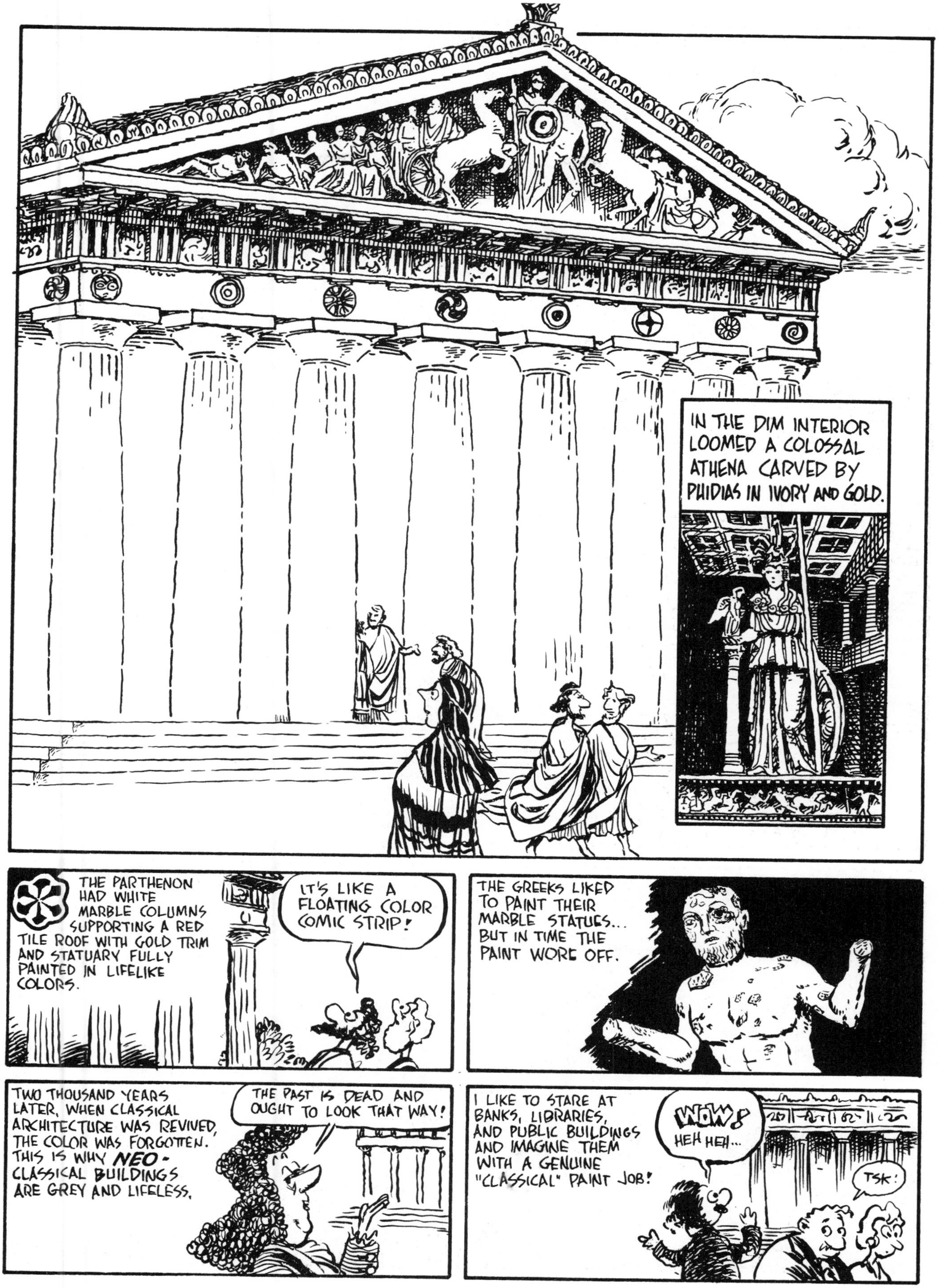

IN THE DIM INTERIOR LOOMED A COLOSSAL ATHENA CARVED BY PHIDIAS IN IVORY AND GOLD.
THE PARTHENON HAD WHITE MARBLE COLUMNS SUPPORTING A RED TILE ROOF WITH GOLD TRIM AND STATUARY FULLY PAINTED IN LIFELIKE COLORS.
IT'S LIKE A FLOATING COLOR COMIC STRIP!
THE GREEKS LIKED TO PAINT THEIR MARBLE STATUES... BUT IN TIME THE PAINT WORE OFF.
TWO THOUSAND YEARS LATER, WHEN CLASSICAL ARCHITECTURE WAS REVIVED, THE COLOR WAS FORGOTTEN. THIS IS WHY NEO-CLASSICAL BUILDINGS ARE GREY AND LIFELESS.
THE PAST IS DEAD AND OUGHT TO LOOK THAT WAY!
I LIKE TO STARE AT BANKS, LIBRARIES, AND PUBLIC BUILDINGS AND IMAGINE THEM WITH A GENUINE "CLASSICAL" PAINT JOB!
WOW! HEH HEH...
TSK!

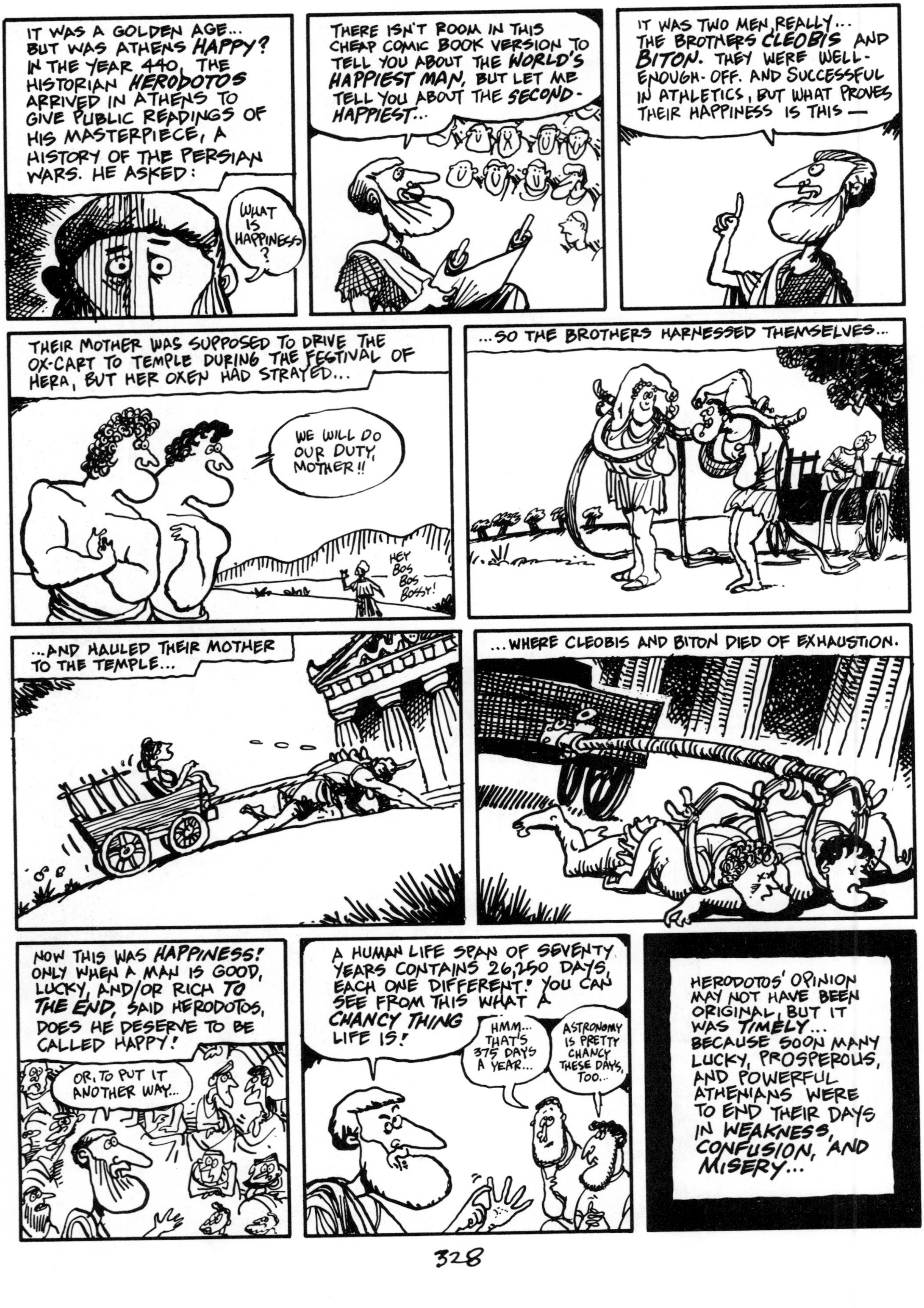

IT WAS A GOLDEN AGE... BUT WAS ATHENS HAPPY? IN THE YEAR 440, THE HISTORIAN HERODOTOS ARRIVED IN ATHENS TO GIVE PUBLIC READINGS OF HIS MASTERPIECE, A HISTORY OF THE PERSIAN WARS. HE ASKED:
WHAT IS HAPPINESS?
THERE ISN'T ROOM IN THIS CHEAP COMIC BOOK VERSION TO TELL YOU ABOUT THE WORLD'S HAPPIEST MAN, BUT LET ME TELL YOU ABOUT THE SECOND-HAPPIEST...
IT WAS TWO MEN, REALLY... THE BROTHERS CLEOBIS AND BITON. THEY WERE WELL-ENOUGH-OFF. AND SUCCESSFUL IN ATHLETICS, BUT WHAT PROVES THEIR HAPPINESS IS THIS —
THEIR MOTHER WAS SUPPOSED TO DRIVE THE OX-CART TO TEMPLE DURING THE FESTIVAL OF HERA, BUT HER OXEN HAD STRAYED...
WE WILL DO OUR DUTY, MOTHER!!
HEY BOS BOS BOSSY!
...SO THE BROTHERS HARNESSED THEMSELVES...
...AND HAULED THEIR MOTHER TO THE TEMPLE...
...WHERE CLEOBIS AND BITON DIED OF EXHAUSTION.
NOW THIS WAS HAPPINESS! ONLY WHEN A MAN IS GOOD, LUCKY, AND/OR RICH TO THE END, SAID HERODOTOS, DOES HE DESERVE TO BE CALLED HAPPY!
OR, TO PUT IT ANOTHER WAY...
A HUMAN LIFE SPAN OF SEVENTY YEARS CONTAINS 26,250 DAYS, EACH ONE DIFFERENT! YOU CAN SEE FROM THIS WHAT A CHANCY THING LIFE IS!
HMM... THAT'S 375 DAYS A YEAR...
ASTRONOMY IS PRETTY CHANCY THESE DAYS, TOO...
HERODOTOS' OPINION MAY NOT HAVE BEEN ORIGINAL, BUT IT WAS TIMELY... BECAUSE SOON MANY LUCKY, PROSPEROUS, AND POWERFUL ATHENIANS WERE TO END THEIR DAYS IN WEAKNESS, CONFUSION, AND MISERY...

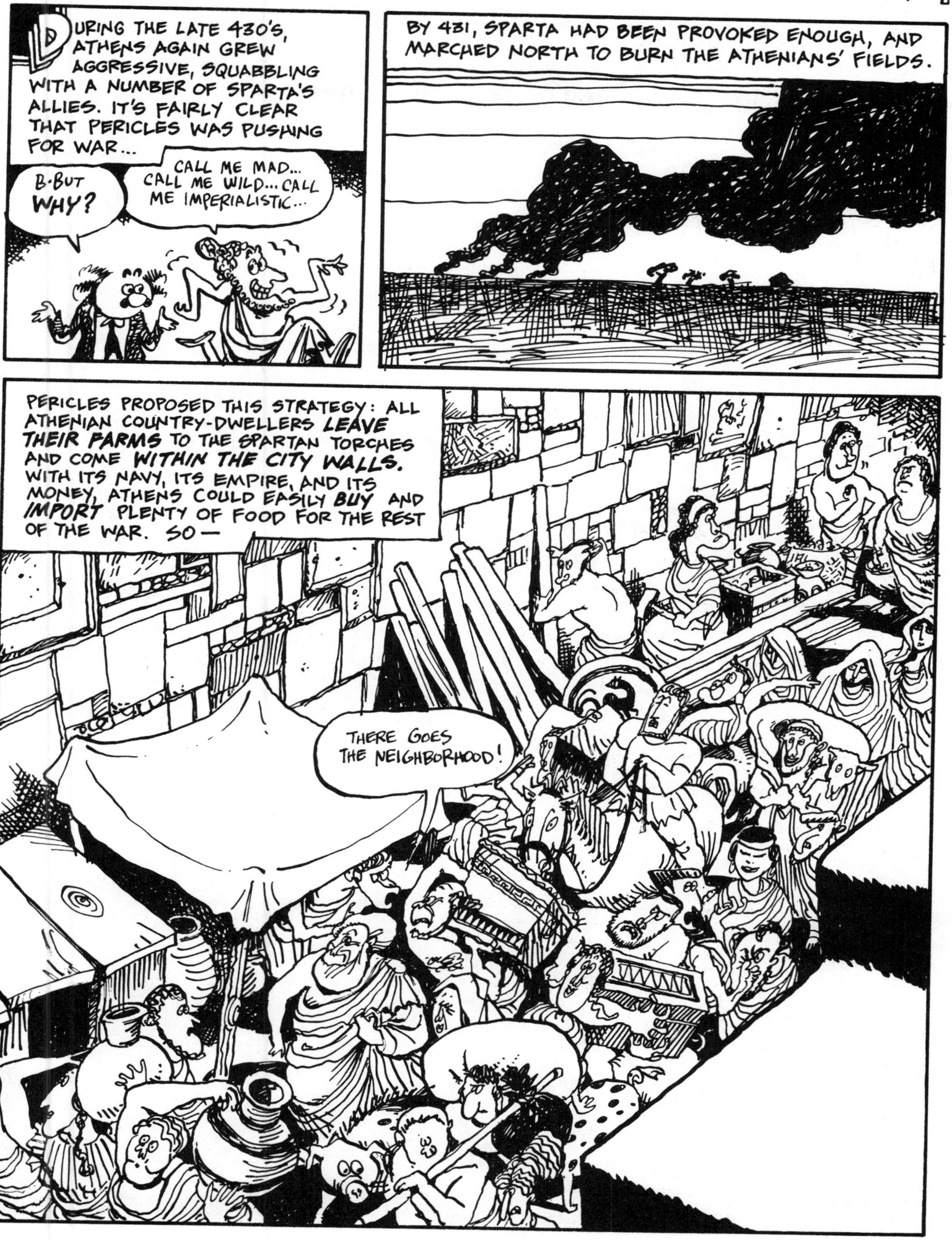
DURING THE LATE 430'S, ATHENS AGAIN GREW AGGRESSIVE, SQUABBLING WITH A NUMBER OF SPARTA'S ALLIES. IT'S FAIRLY CLEAR THAT PERICLES WAS PUSHING FOR WAR...
B-BUT WHY?
CALL ME MAD... CALL ME WILD... CALL ME IMPERIALISTIC...
BY 431, SPARTA HAD BEEN PROVOKED ENOUGH, AND MARCHED NORTH TO BURN THE ATHENIANS' FIELDS.
PERICLES PROPOSED THIS STRATEGY: ALL ATHENIAN COUNTRY-DWELLERS LEAVE THEIR FARMS TO THE SPARTAN TORCHES AND COME WITHIN THE CITY WALLS. WITH ITS NAVY, ITS EMPIRE, AND ITS MONEY, ATHENS COULD EASILY BUY AND IMPORT PLENTY OF FOOD FOR THE REST OF THE WAR. SO—
THERE GOES THE NEIGHBORHOOD!

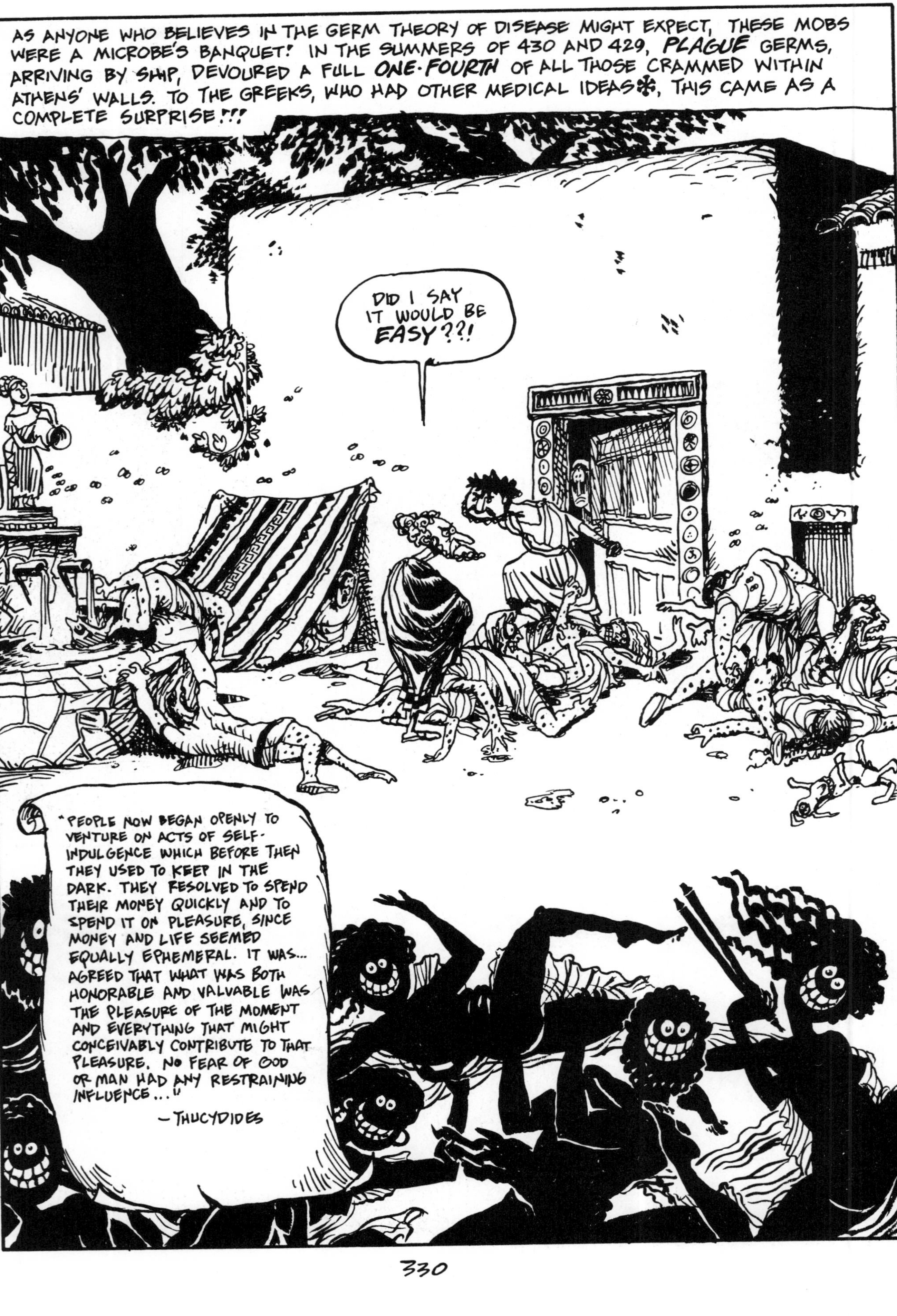
AS ANYONE WHO BELIEVES IN THE GERM THEORY OF DISEASE MIGHT EXPECT, THESE MOBS WERE A MICROBE'S BANQUET! IN THE SUMMERS OF 430 AND 429, PLAGUE GERMS, ARRIVING BY SHIP, DEVOURED A FULL ONE-FOURTH OF ALL THOSE CRAMMED WITHIN ATHENS' WALLS. TO THE GREEKS, WHO HAD OTHER MEDICAL IDEAS*, THIS CAME AS A COMPLETE SURPRISE!!!
DID I SAY IT WOULD BE EASY??!
"PEOPLE NOW BEGAN OPENLY TO VENTURE ON ACTS OF SELF-INDULGENCE WHICH BEFORE THEN THEY USED TO KEEP IN THE DARK. THEY RESOLVED TO SPEND THEIR MONEY QUICKLY AND TO SPEND IT ON PLEASURE, SINCE MONEY AND LIFE SEEMED EQUALLY EPHEMERAL. IT WAS... AGREED THAT WHAT WAS BOTH HONORABLE AND VALUABLE WAS THE PLEASURE OF THE MOMENT AND EVERYTHING THAT MIGHT CONCEIVABLY CONTRIBUTE TO THAT PLEASURE. NO FEAR OF GOD OR MAN HAD ANY RESTRAINING INFLUENCE..."
—THUCYDIDES

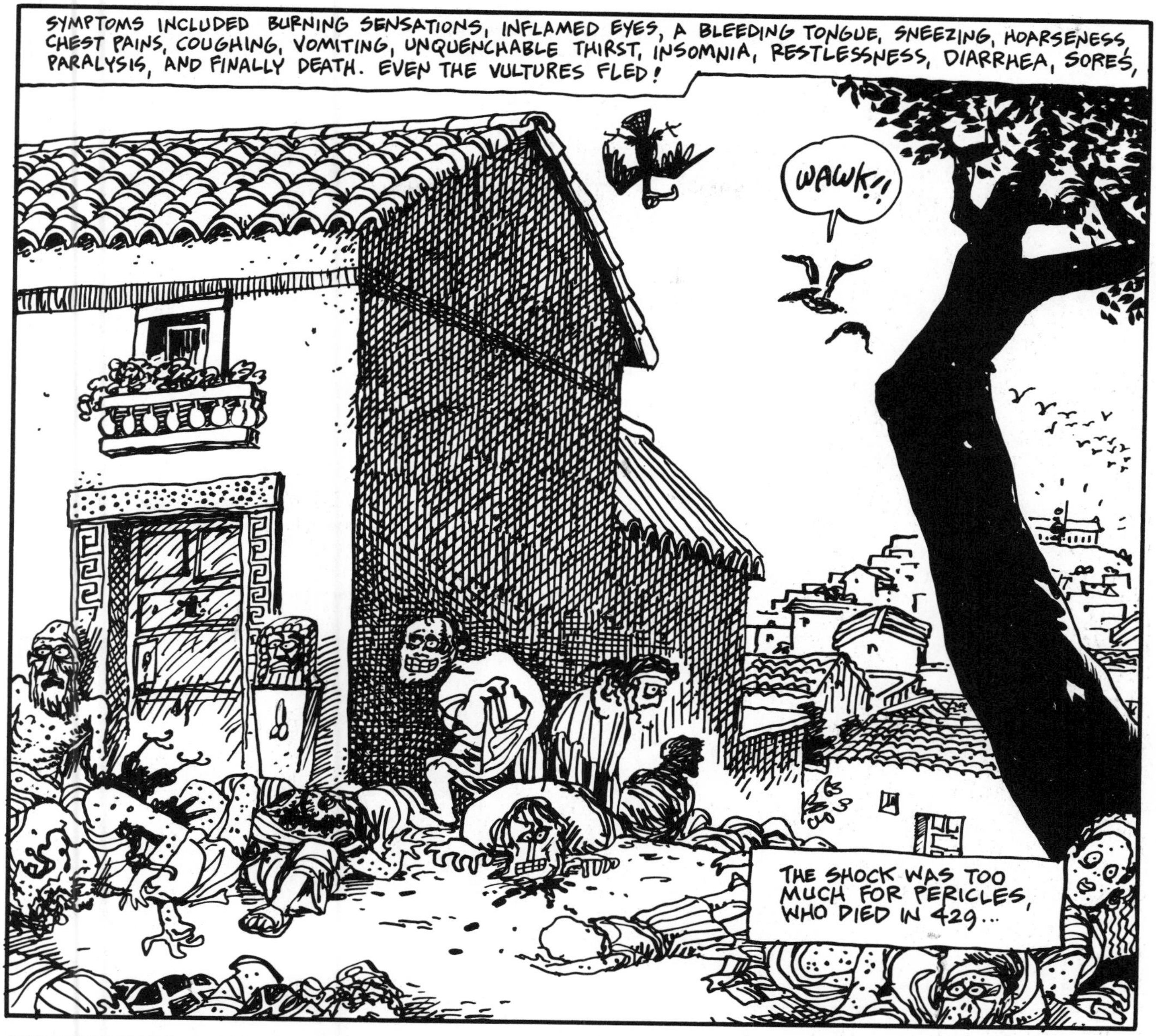
SYMPTOMS INCLUDED BURNING SENSATIONS, INFLAMED EYES, A BLEEDING TONGUE, SNEEZING, HOARSENESS, CHEST PAINS, COUGHING, VOMITING, UNQUENCHABLE THIRST, INSOMNIA, RESTLESSNESS, DIARRHEA, SORES, PARALYSIS, AND FINALLY DEATH. EVEN THE VULTURES FLED!
WAWK!!
THE SHOCK WAS TOO MUCH FOR PERICLES, WHO DIED IN 429...

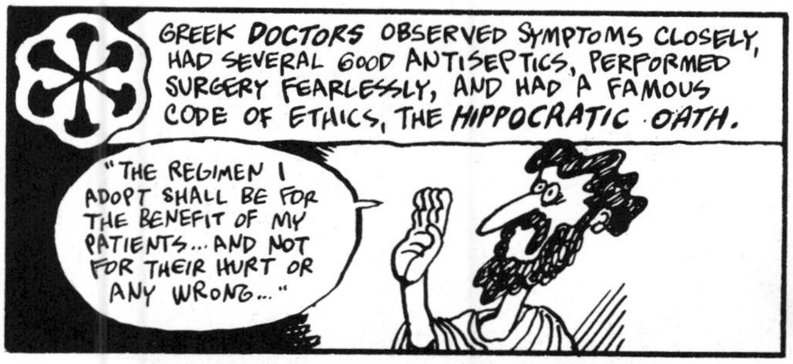
GREEK DOCTORS OBSERVED SYMPTOMS CLOSELY, HAD SEVERAL GOOD ANTISEPTICS, PERFORMED SURGERY FEARLESSLY, AND HAD A FAMOUS CODE OF ETHICS, THE HIPPOCRATIC OATH.
"THE REGIMEN I ADOPT SHALL BE FOR THE BENEFIT OF MY PATIENTS... AND NOT FOR THEIR HURT OR ANY WRONG..."

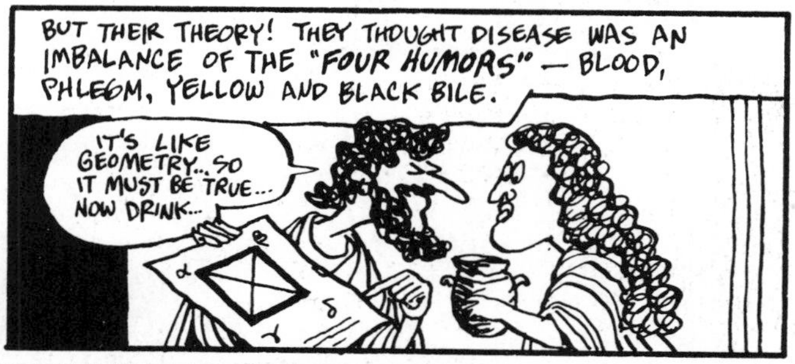
BUT THEIR THEORY! THEY THOUGHT DISEASE WAS AN IMBALANCE OF THE "FOUR HUMORS" — BLOOD, PHLEGM, YELLOW AND BLACK BILE.
IT'S LIKE GEOMETRY... SO IT MUST BE TRUE... NOW DRINK...

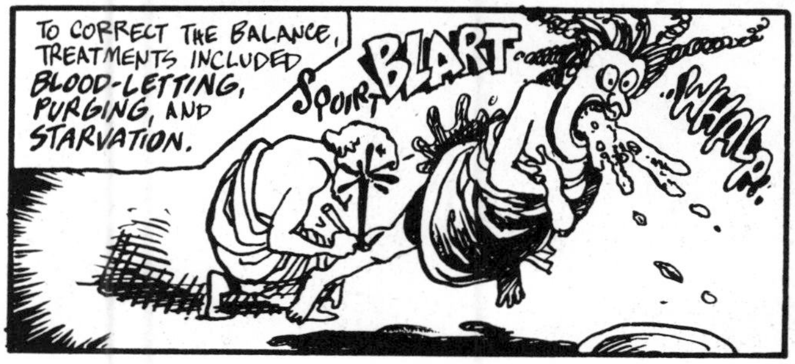
TO CORRECT THE BALANCE, TREATMENTS INCLUDED BLOOD-LETTING, PURGING, AND STARVATION.
SPOIRT
BLART

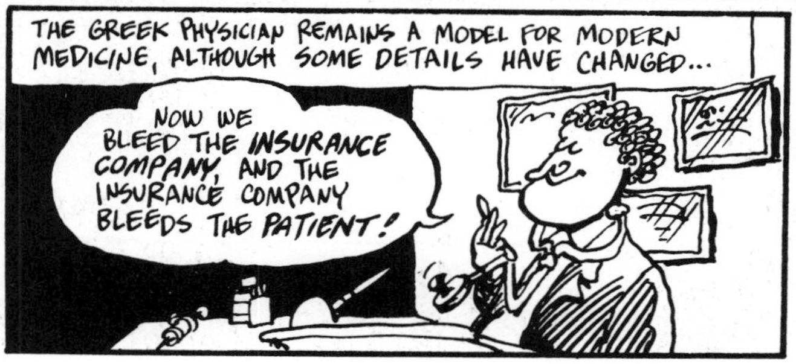
THE GREEK PHYSICIAN REMAINS A MODEL FOR MODERN MEDICINE, ALTHOUGH SOME DETAILS HAVE CHANGED...
NOW WE BLEED THE INSURANCE COMPANY, AND THE INSURANCE COMPANY BLEEDS THE PATIENT!

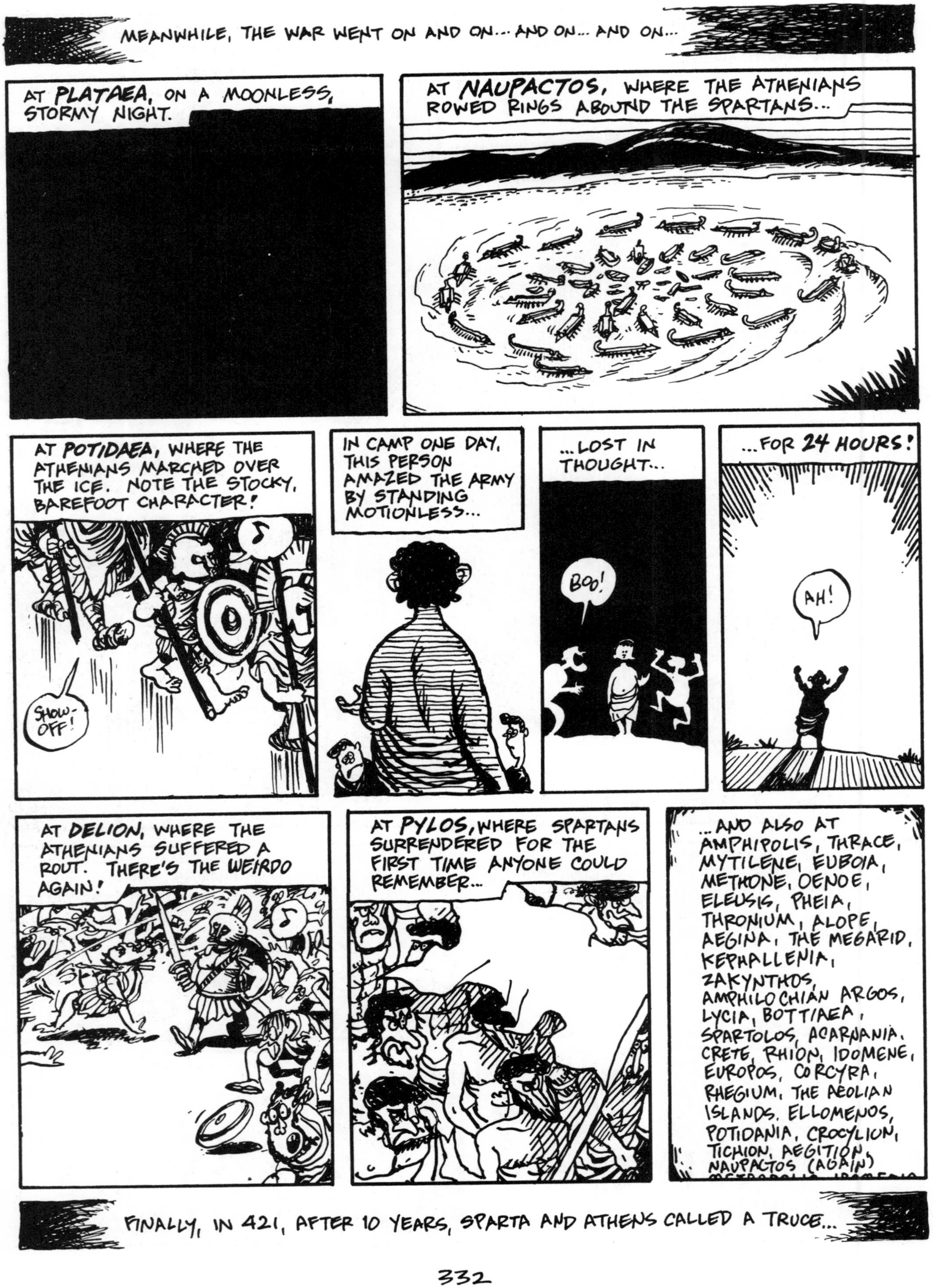
MEANWHILE, THE WAR WENT ON AND ON... AND ON... AND ON...
AT PLATAEA, ON A MOONLESS, STORMY NIGHT.
AT NAUPACTOS, WHERE THE ATHENIANS ROWED RINGS ABOUND THE SPARTANS...
AT POTIDAEA, WHERE THE ATHENIANS MARCHED OVER THE ICE. NOTE THE STOCKY, BAREFOOT CHARACTER!
SHOW-OFF!
IN CAMP ONE DAY, THIS PERSON AMAZED THE ARMY BY STANDING MOTIONLESS...
...LOST IN THOUGHT...
BOO!
...FOR 24 HOURS!
AH!
AT DELION, WHERE THE ATHENIANS SUFFERED A ROUT. THERE'S THE WEIRDO AGAIN!
AT PYLOS, WHERE SPARTANS SURRENDERED FOR THE FIRST TIME ANYONE COULD REMEMBER...
...AND ALSO AT AMPHIPOLIS, THRACE, MYTILENE, EUBOIA, METHONE, OENOE, ELEUSIS, PHEIA, THRONIUM, ALOPE, AEGINA, THE MEGARID, KEPHALLENIA, ZAKYNTHOS, AMPHILOCHIAN ARGOS, LYCIA, BOTTIAEA, SPARTOLOS, ACARNANIA, CRETE, RHION, IDOMENE, EUROPOS, CORCYRA, RHEGIUM, THE AEOLIAN ISLANDS, ELLOMENOS, POTIDANIA, CROCYLION, TICHION, AEGITION, NAUPACTOS (AGAIN)
FINALLY, IN 421, AFTER 10 YEARS, SPARTA AND ATHENS CALLED A TRUCE...

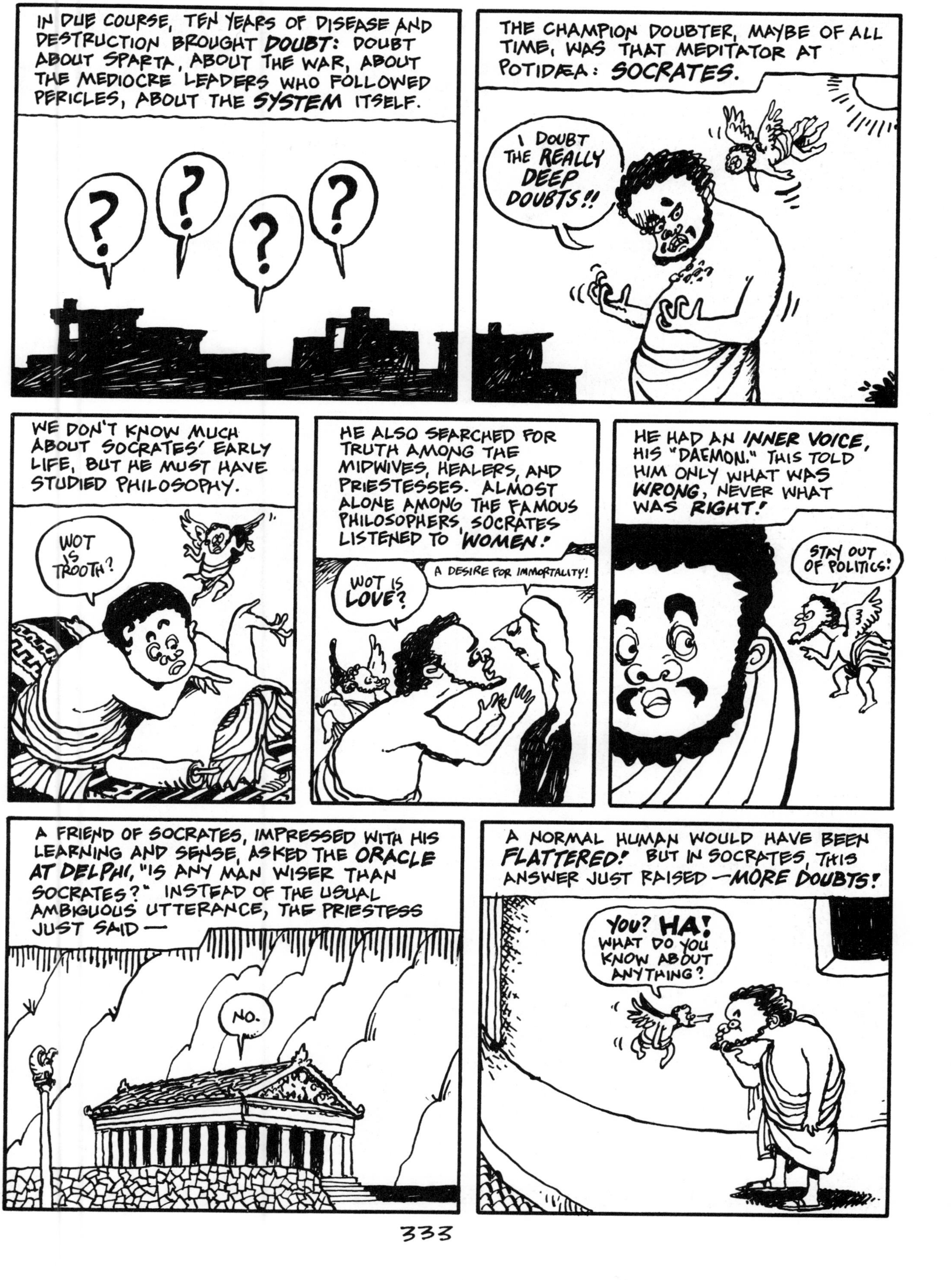
IN DUE COURSE, TEN YEARS OF DISEASE AND DESTRUCTION BROUGHT DOUBT: DOUBT ABOUT SPARTA, ABOUT THE WAR, ABOUT THE MEDIOCRE LEADERS WHO FOLLOWED PERICLES, ABOUT THE SYSTEM ITSELF.
?
?
?
?
THE CHAMPION DOUBTER, MAYBE OF ALL TIME, WAS THAT MEDITATOR AT POTIDÆA: SOCRATES.
I DOUBT THE REALLY DEEP DOUBTS!!
WE DON'T KNOW MUCH ABOUT SOCRATES' EARLY LIFE, BUT HE MUST HAVE STUDIED PHILOSOPHY.
WOT IS TROOTH?
HE ALSO SEARCHED FOR TRUTH AMONG THE MIDWIVES, HEALERS, AND PRIESTESSES. ALMOST ALONE AMONG THE FAMOUS PHILOSOPHERS, SOCRATES LISTENED TO WOMEN!
WOT IS LOVE?
A DESIRE FOR IMMORTALITY!
HE HAD AN INNER VOICE, HIS "DAEMON." THIS TOLD HIM ONLY WHAT WAS WRONG, NEVER WHAT WAS RIGHT!
STAY OUT OF POLITICS!
A FRIEND OF SOCRATES, IMPRESSED WITH HIS LEARNING AND SENSE, ASKED THE ORACLE AT DELPHI, "IS ANY MAN WISER THAN SOCRATES?" INSTEAD OF THE USUAL AMBIGUOUS UTTERANCE, THE PRIESTESS JUST SAID—
NO.
A NORMAL HUMAN WOULD HAVE BEEN FLATTERED! BUT IN SOCRATES, THIS ANSWER JUST RAISED—MORE DOUBTS!
YOU? HA! WHAT DO YOU KNOW ABOUT ANYTHING?

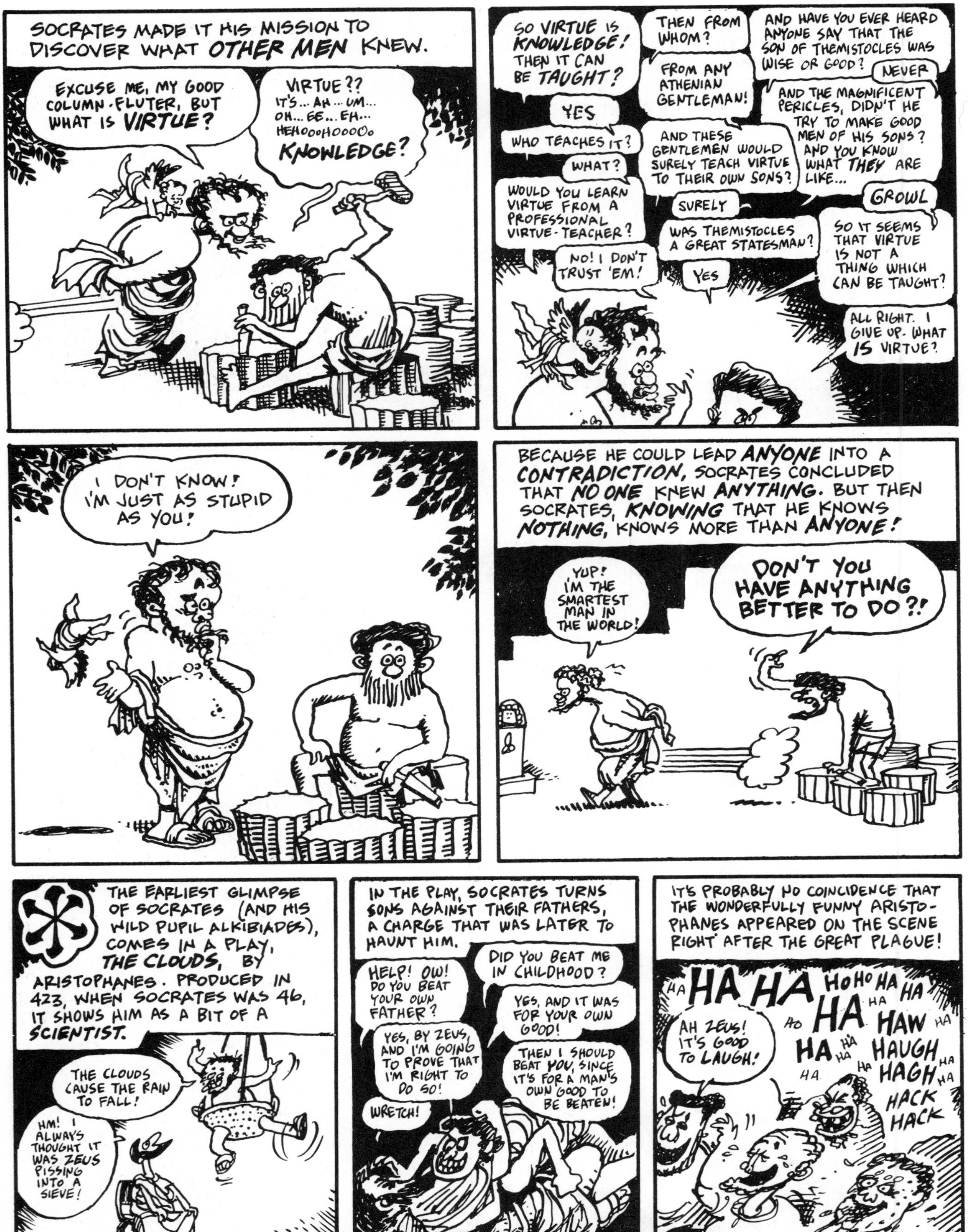

SOCRATES MADE IT HIS MISSION TO DISCOVER WHAT OTHER MEN KNEW.
EXCUSE ME, MY GOOD COLUMN-FLUTER, BUT WHAT IS VIRTUE?
VIRTUE?? IT'S... AH... UM... OH... EE... EH... HEHOOOHOOOOO KNOWLEDGE?
SO VIRTUE IS KNOWLEDGE! THEN IT CAN BE TAUGHT?
YES
WHO TEACHES IT?
WHAT?
WOULD YOU LEARN VIRTUE FROM A PROFESSIONAL VIRTUE-TEACHER?
NO! I DON'T TRUST 'EM!
THEN FROM WHOM?
FROM ANY ATHENIAN GENTLEMAN!
AND THESE GENTLEMEN WOULD SURELY TEACH VIRTUE TO THEIR OWN SONS?
SURELY
WAS THEMISTOCLES A GREAT STATESMAN?
YES
AND HAVE YOU EVER HEARD ANYONE SAY THAT THE SON OF THEMISTOCLES WAS WISE OR GOOD?
NEVER
AND THE MAGNIFICENT PERICLES, DIDN'T HE TRY TO MAKE GOOD MEN OF HIS SONS? AND YOU KNOW WHAT THEY ARE LIKE...
GROWL
SO IT SEEMS THAT VIRTUE IS NOT A THING WHICH CAN BE TAUGHT?
ALL RIGHT. I GIVE UP. WHAT IS VIRTUE?
I DON'T KNOW! I'M JUST AS STUPID AS YOU!
BECAUSE HE COULD LEAD ANYONE INTO A CONTRADICTION, SOCRATES CONCLUDED THAT NO ONE KNEW ANYTHING. BUT THEN SOCRATES, KNOWING THAT HE KNOWS NOTHING, KNOWS MORE THAN ANYONE!
YUP! I'M THE SMARTEST MAN IN THE WORLD!
DON'T YOU HAVE ANYTHING BETTER TO DO?!
THE EARLIEST GLIMPSE OF SOCRATES (AND HIS WILD PUPIL ALKIBIADES), COMES IN A PLAY, THE CLOUDS, BY ARISTOPHANES. PRODUCED IN 423, WHEN SOCRATES WAS 46, IT SHOWS HIM AS A BIT OF A SCIENTIST.
THE CLOUDS CAUSE THE RAIN TO FALL!
HM! I ALWAYS THOUGHT IT WAS ZEUS PISSING INTO A SIEVE!
IN THE PLAY, SOCRATES TURNS SONS AGAINST THEIR FATHERS, A CHARGE THAT WAS LATER TO HAUNT HIM.
HELP! OW! DO YOU BEAT YOUR OWN FATHER?
YES, BY ZEUS, AND I'M GOING TO PROVE THAT I'M RIGHT TO DO SO!
WRETCH!
DID YOU BEAT ME IN CHILDHOOD?
YES, AND IT WAS FOR YOUR OWN GOOD!
THEN I SHOULD BEAT YOU, SINCE IT'S FOR A MAN'S OWN GOOD TO BE BEATEN!
IT'S PROBABLY NO COINCIDENCE THAT THE WONDERFULLY FUNNY ARISTOPHANES APPEARED ON THE SCENE RIGHT AFTER THE GREAT PLAGUE!
HA HA HA HO HO HA HA HA HA HA HAW HA HA HA HA HAUGH HA HA HAGH HA HACK HACK
AH ZEUS! IT'S GOOD TO LAUGH!

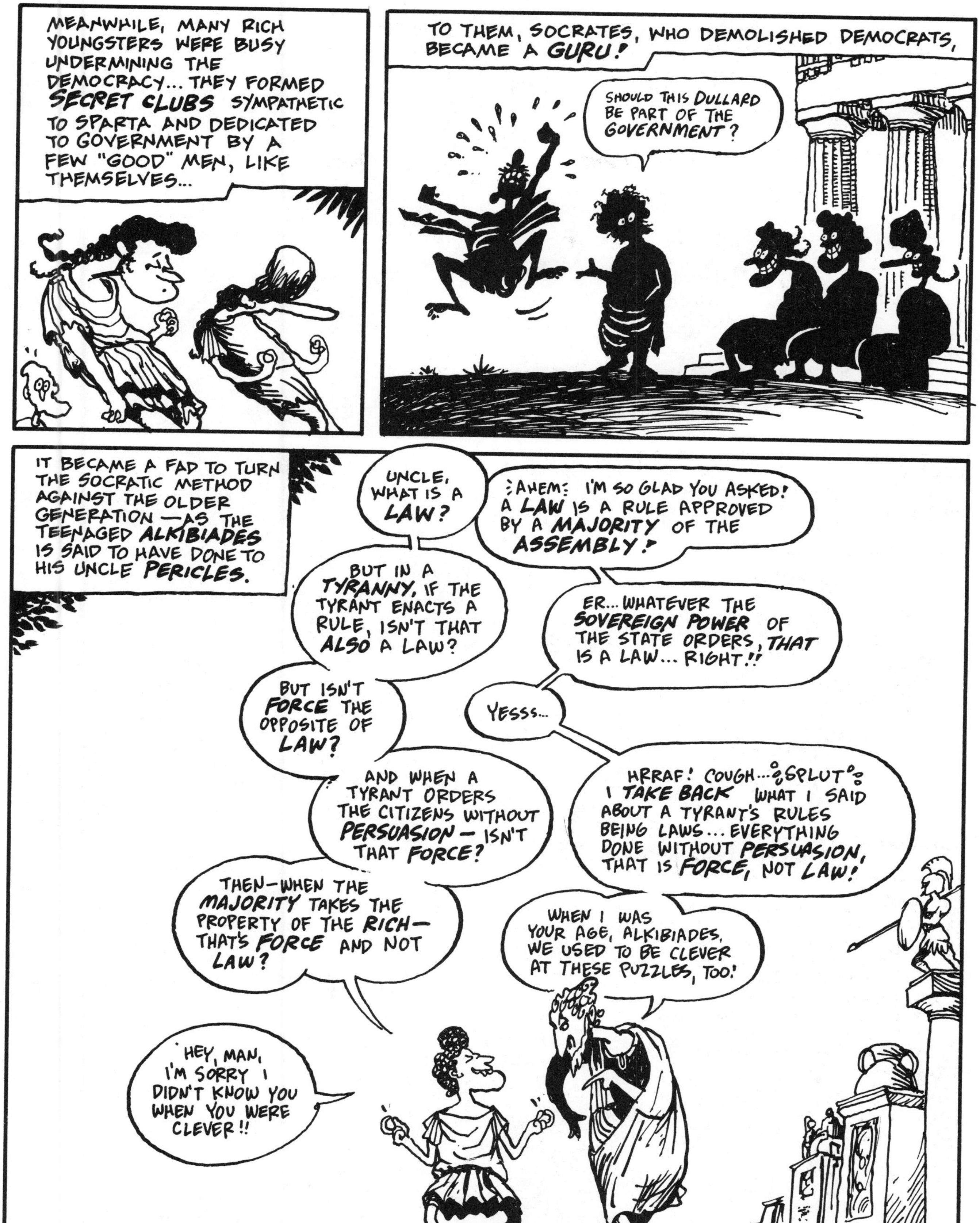

MEANWHILE, MANY RICH YOUNGSTERS WERE BUSY UNDERMINING THE DEMOCRACY... THEY FORMED SECRET CLUBS SYMPATHETIC TO SPARTA AND DEDICATED TO GOVERNMENT BY A FEW "GOOD" MEN, LIKE THEMSELVES...
TO THEM, SOCRATES, WHO DEMOLISHED DEMOCRATS, BECAME A GURU!
SHOULD THIS DULLARD BE PART OF THE GOVERNMENT?
IT BECAME A FAD TO TURN THE SOCRATIC METHOD AGAINST THE OLDER GENERATION —AS THE TEENAGED ALKIBIADES IS SAID TO HAVE DONE TO HIS UNCLE PERICLES.
UNCLE, WHAT IS A LAW?
:AHEM: I'M SO GLAD YOU ASKED! A LAW IS A RULE APPROVED BY A MAJORITY OF THE ASSEMBLY!
BUT IN A TYRANNY, IF THE TYRANT ENACTS A RULE, ISN'T THAT ALSO A LAW?
ER... WHATEVER THE SOVEREIGN POWER OF THE STATE ORDERS, THAT IS A LAW... RIGHT!!
BUT ISN'T FORCE THE OPPOSITE OF LAW?
YESSS...
AND WHEN A TYRANT ORDERS THE CITIZENS WITHOUT PERSUASION — ISN'T THAT FORCE?
HRRAF! COUGH... SPLUT I TAKE BACK WHAT I SAID ABOUT A TYRANT'S RULES BEING LAWS... EVERYTHING DONE WITHOUT PERSUASION, THAT IS FORCE, NOT LAW!
THEN—WHEN THE MAJORITY TAKES THE PROPERTY OF THE RICH— THAT'S FORCE AND NOT LAW?
WHEN I WAS YOUR AGE, ALKIBIADES, WE USED TO BE CLEVER AT THESE PUZZLES, TOO!
HEY, MAN, I'M SORRY I DIDN'T KNOW YOU WHEN YOU WERE CLEVER!!
(FROM XENOPHON'S MEMORABILIA)

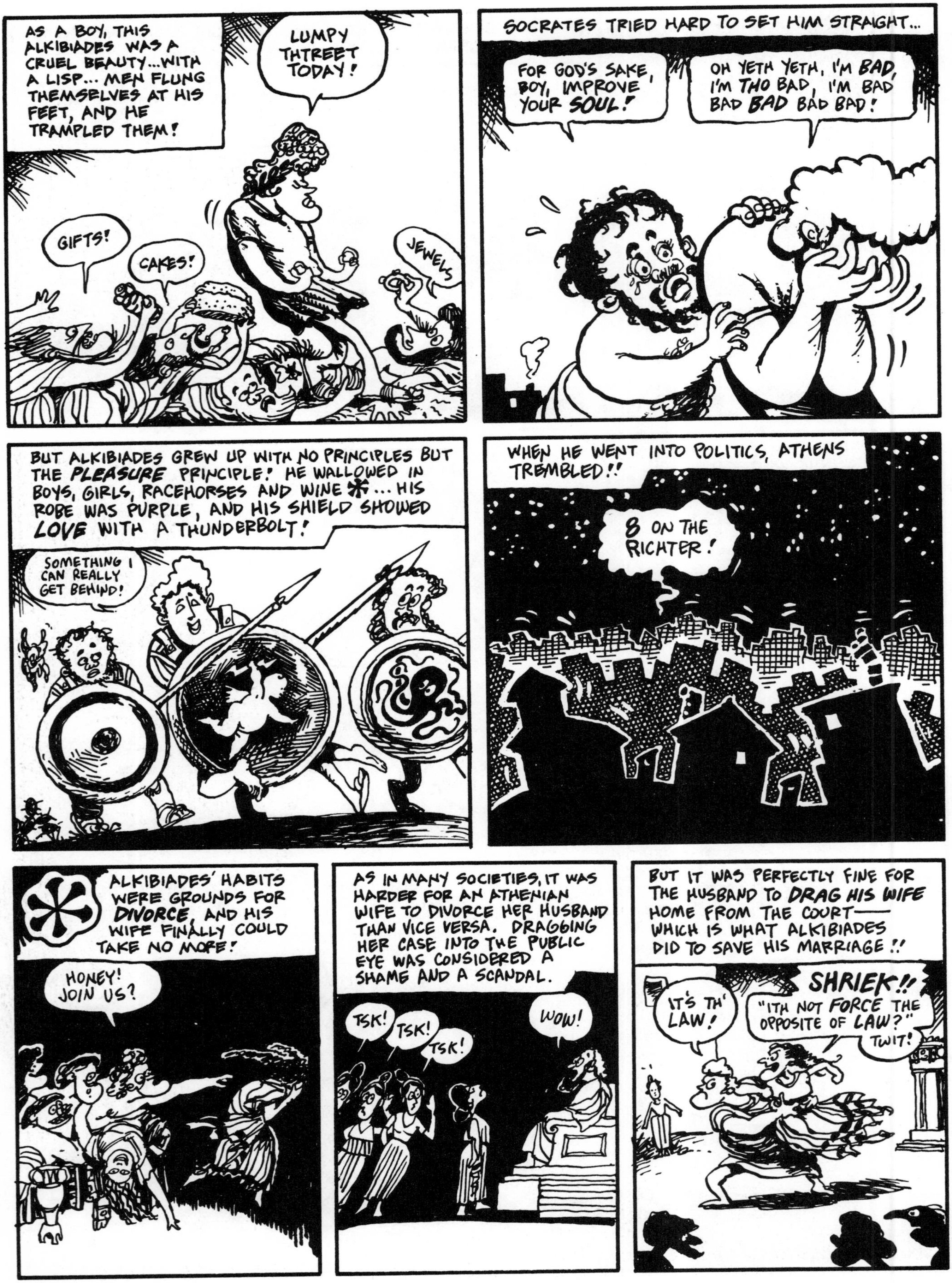
AS A BOY, THIS ALKIBIADES WAS A CRUEL BEAUTY...WITH A LISP... MEN FLUNG THEMSELVES AT HIS FEET, AND HE TRAMPLED THEM!
LUMPY THTREET TODAY!
GIFTS!
CAKES!
JEWELS
SOCRATES TRIED HARD TO SET HIM STRAIGHT...
FOR GOD'S SAKE, BOY, IMPROVE YOUR SOUL!
OH YETH YETH, I'M BAD, I'M THO BAD, I'M BAD BAD BAD BAD BAD!
BUT ALKIBIADES GREW UP WITH NO PRINCIPLES BUT THE PLEASURE PRINCIPLE! HE WALLOWED IN BOYS, GIRLS, RACEHORSES AND WINE ✱... HIS ROBE WAS PURPLE, AND HIS SHIELD SHOWED LOVE WITH A THUNDERBOLT!
SOMETHING I CAN REALLY GET BEHIND!
WHEN HE WENT INTO POLITICS, ATHENS TREMBLED!!
8 ON THE RICHTER!
✱ ALKIBIADES' HABITS WERE GROUNDS FOR DIVORCE, AND HIS WIFE FINALLY COULD TAKE NO MORE!
HONEY! JOIN US?
AS IN MANY SOCIETIES, IT WAS HARDER FOR AN ATHENIAN WIFE TO DIVORCE HER HUSBAND THAN VICE VERSA. DRAGGING HER CASE INTO THE PUBLIC EYE WAS CONSIDERED A SHAME AND A SCANDAL.
TSK!
TSK!
TSK!
WOW!
BUT IT WAS PERFECTLY FINE FOR THE HUSBAND TO DRAG HIS WIFE HOME FROM THE COURT— WHICH IS WHAT ALKIBIADES DID TO SAVE HIS MARRIAGE!!
SHRIEK!!
IT'S TH' LAW!
"ITH NOT FORCE THE OPPOSITE OF LAW?"
TWIT!

FIVE YEARS PASS
...

AFTER FIVE YEARS OF PEACE, *ALKIBIADES*, NOW BIG IN POLITICS, CALLED ON ATHENS TO RESUME THE WAR. HE PROPOSED TO ADD *SICILY* TO THE ATHENIAN EMPIRE.

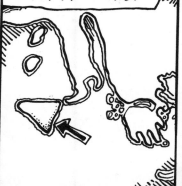

A HUGE FLEET OF 200 TRIREMES WAS OUTFITTED TO INVADE SICILY.

LOOK YONDER! ALKIBIADES' FLAGSHIP!

THE LOVE BOAT!

BUT THERE WAS ALSO A *VERY UNHAPPY* ANTI-WAR PARTY WHICH INCLUDED THE YOUNG NEO-CONSERVATIVES AND MANY OLD VETERANS.

ONE MORNING, THE PLANNING WAS INTERRUPTED BY A STUNNING ACT OF *SABOTAGE* AND *BLASPHEMY*: IN THE NIGHT, SOMEONE HAD DISFIGURED ALMOST EVERY *HERM* IN TOWN!

OUCH!

MORE THAN ANYTHING ELSE, THIS REVEALED WHAT ATHENS HAD BECOME: IMPOTENT, ITS FAITH IN THE GODS ERODED, AND PREY TO CONSPIRACIES OF MEN WHO DID THEIR WORK BY NIGHT... BUT *WHO DID IT??!!*

337

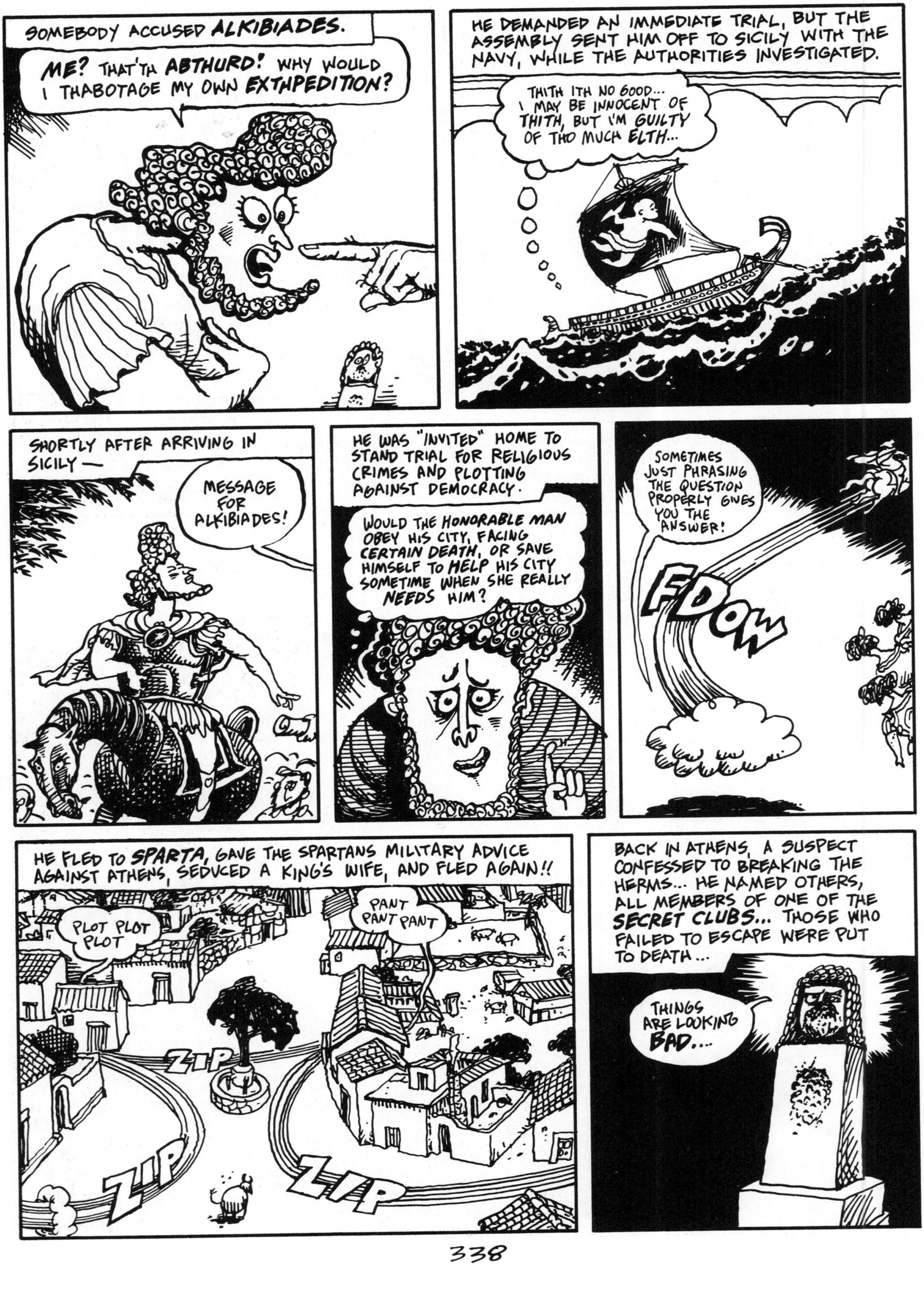
SOMEBODY ACCUSED ALKIBIADES.
ME? THAT'TH ABTHURD! WHY WOULD I THABOTAGE MY OWN EXTHPEDITION?
HE DEMANDED AN IMMEDIATE TRIAL, BUT THE ASSEMBLY SENT HIM OFF TO SICILY WITH THE NAVY, WHILE THE AUTHORITIES INVESTIGATED.
THITH ITH NO GOOD... I MAY BE INNOCENT OF THITH, BUT I'M GUILTY OF THO MUCH ELTH...
SHORTLY AFTER ARRIVING IN SICILY —
MESSAGE FOR ALKIBIADES!
HE WAS "INVITED" HOME TO STAND TRIAL FOR RELIGIOUS CRIMES AND PLOTTING AGAINST DEMOCRACY.
WOULD THE HONORABLE MAN OBEY HIS CITY, FACING CERTAIN DEATH, OR SAVE HIMSELF TO HELP HIS CITY SOMETIME WHEN SHE REALLY NEEDS HIM?
SOMETIMES JUST PHRASING THE QUESTION PROPERLY GIVES YOU THE ANSWER!
FDOW
HE FLED TO SPARTA, GAVE THE SPARTANS MILITARY ADVICE AGAINST ATHENS, SEDUCED A KING'S WIFE, AND FLED AGAIN!!
PLOT PLOT PLOT
PANT PANT PANT
ZIP
ZIP
ZIP
BACK IN ATHENS, A SUSPECT CONFESSED TO BREAKING THE HERMS... HE NAMED OTHERS, ALL MEMBERS OF ONE OF THE SECRET CLUBS... THOSE WHO FAILED TO ESCAPE WERE PUT TO DEATH...
THINGS ARE LOOKING BAD...

THEN CAME DEFEAT, REVOLUTION, AND COLLAPSE....

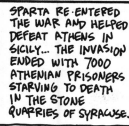

SPARTA RE-ENTERED THE WAR AND HELPED DEFEAT ATHENS IN SICILY... THE INVASION ENDED WITH 7000 ATHENIAN PRISONERS STARVING TO DEATH IN THE STONE QUARRIES OF SYRACUSE.

IN 411, THE SECRET CLUBS OVERTHREW DEMOCRACY IN ATHENS... THERE WERE PLOTS AND COUNTERPLOTS.

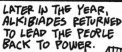

LATER IN THE YEAR, ALKIBIADES RETURNED TO LEAD THE PEOPLE BACK TO POWER.

PARTY!

SOON HE DIS-GRACED HIMSELF AGAIN... THIS TIME, HE FLED TO PERSIAN PROTECTION!

ZOW

THE WAR AGAINST SPARTA DRAGGED ON...

BROKE AND EXHAUSTED, ATHENS KEPT BATTLING.

THEIR FINAL DEFEAT WAS AT AEGISPOTOMAI, WHERE SPARTA KILLED ALL PRISONERS.

THE PORTS OF ATHENS WERE BLOCKADED.

IN 404, THE STARVING ATHENIANS SURRENDERED UNCONDITIONALLY, AND THE SPARTANS MARCHED IN.

...AND ALKIBIADES, IN BED WITH HIS MISTRESS, WAKES UP TO SHOUTING AND THE SMELL OF SMOKE...

HEE! HA! HO!

WRAPPING HIS NIGHTSHIRT AROUND HIS ARM AS A SHIELD, HE LEAPS THROUGH THE FLAMES, AND IS CUT DOWN BY PERSIAN ARROWS.

THIRTY TYRANTS

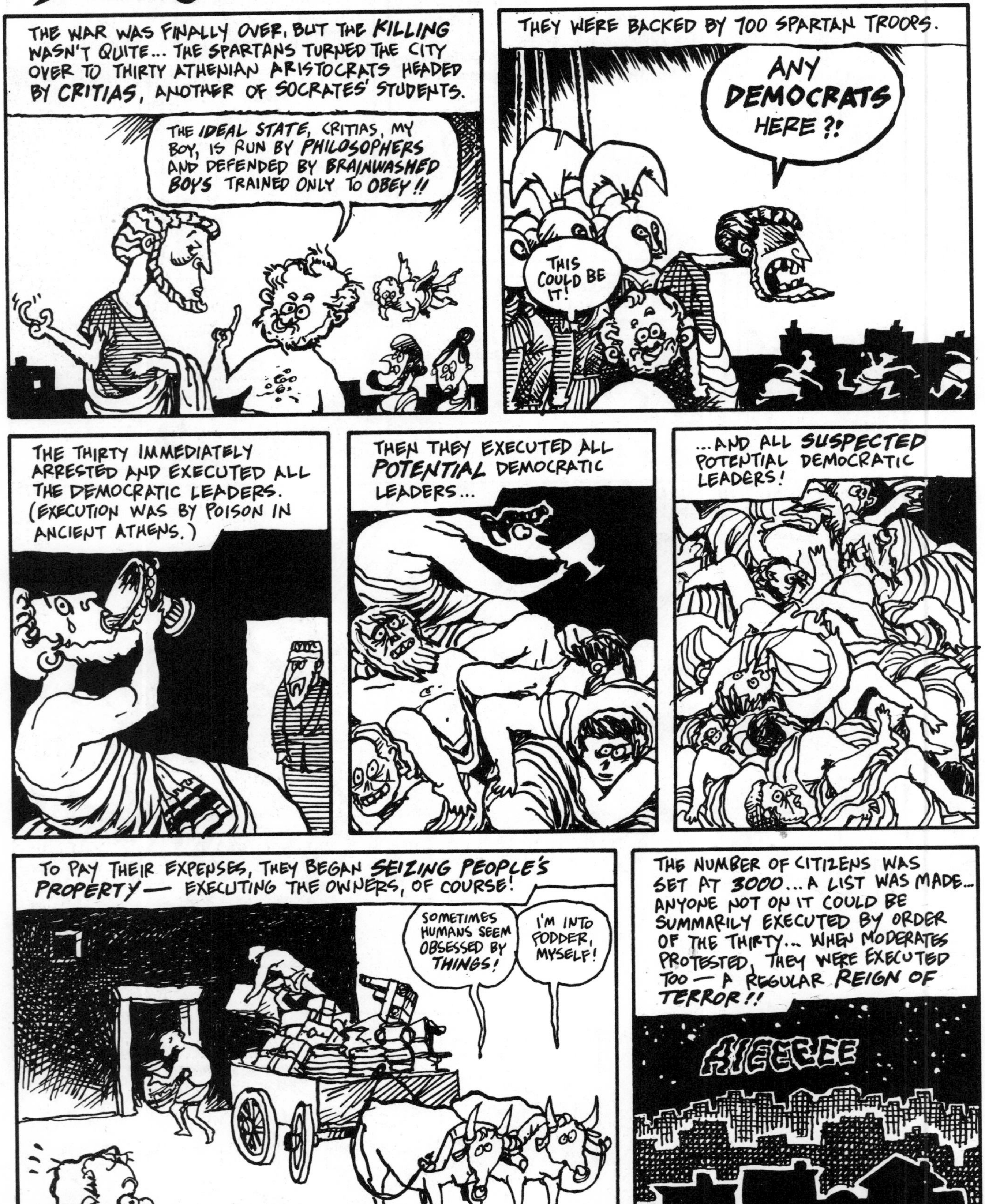

THE WAR WAS FINALLY OVER, BUT THE KILLING WASN'T QUITE... THE SPARTANS TURNED THE CITY OVER TO THIRTY ATHENIAN ARISTOCRATS HEADED BY CRITIAS, ANOTHER OF SOCRATES' STUDENTS.
THE IDEAL STATE, CRITIAS, MY BOY, IS RUN BY PHILOSOPHERS AND DEFENDED BY BRAINWASHED BOYS TRAINED ONLY TO OBEY!!
THEY WERE BACKED BY 700 SPARTAN TROOPS.
ANY DEMOCRATS HERE?!
THIS COULD BE IT!
THE THIRTY IMMEDIATELY ARRESTED AND EXECUTED ALL THE DEMOCRATIC LEADERS. (EXECUTION WAS BY POISON IN ANCIENT ATHENS.)
THEN THEY EXECUTED ALL POTENTIAL DEMOCRATIC LEADERS...
...AND ALL SUSPECTED POTENTIAL DEMOCRATIC LEADERS!
TO PAY THEIR EXPENSES, THEY BEGAN SEIZING PEOPLE'S PROPERTY— EXECUTING THE OWNERS, OF COURSE!
SOMETIMES HUMANS SEEM OBSESSED BY THINGS!
I'M INTO FODDER, MYSELF!
THE NUMBER OF CITIZENS WAS SET AT 3000... A LIST WAS MADE... ANYONE NOT ON IT COULD BE SUMMARILY EXECUTED BY ORDER OF THE THIRTY... WHEN MODERATES PROTESTED, THEY WERE EXECUTED TOO— A REGULAR REIGN OF TERROR!!
AIEEEEE

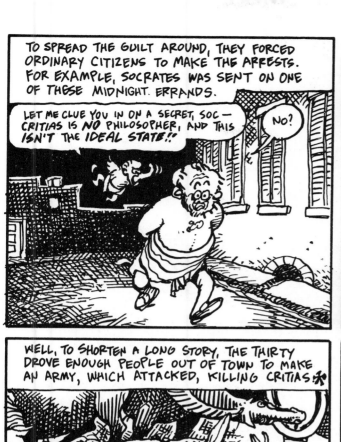

TO SPREAD THE GUILT AROUND, THEY FORCED ORDINARY CITIZENS TO MAKE THE ARRESTS. FOR EXAMPLE, SOCRATES WAS SENT ON ONE OF THESE MIDNIGHT ERRANDS.

LET ME CLUE YOU IN ON A SECRET, SOC— CRITIAS IS *NO* PHILOSOPHER, AND THIS *ISN'T* THE *IDEAL STATE!!*

No?

BUT HE JUST WENT HOME.

ISN'T IT JUST A *LITTLE* LIKE THE IDEAL STATE, TO PLUNDER, AND MURDER?

GET INSIDE!!

WELL, TO SHORTEN A LONG STORY, THE THIRTY DROVE ENOUGH PEOPLE OUT OF TOWN TO MAKE AN ARMY, WHICH ATTACKED, KILLING CRITIAS.✱

CLANK

THE REST OF THE THIRTY FLED... ARISTOCRATS AND COMMON PEOPLE MADE PEACE... AND WITH SPARTA'S PERMISSION, DEMOCRACY WAS RESTORED — AGAIN!!

NO HARD FEELINGS?!

NO... I'M NUMB!

THE TYRANT CRITIAS IS LINKED TO THE ATLANTIS LEGEND BY PLATO'S DIALOG CRITIAS, WRITTEN MANY YEARS LATER. (PLATO WAS CRITIAS' COUSIN.)

I'LL PORTRAY THE DUDE IN A MELLOWER MOOD...

IN THE DIALOG, CRITIAS TELLS THE STORY OF THE LOST CIVILIZATION.

"ATLANTIS... WAS AN ISLAND, LARGER THAN *LIBYA* AND *ASIA*, AND WHEN SUNK BY AN EARTHQUAKE, BECAME AN IMPASS- ABLE BARRIER OF *MUD* TO VOYAGERS..."

THE LEGEND MAY BE LOOSELY BASED ON THE VOLCANIC ERUPTION WHICH BLEW AWAY 3/4 OF THE ISLAND OF *THERA* AROUND 1200 B.C.

MANY CULTURES HAVE THESE LEGENDS—

ONCE UPON A TIME, SOME FISH WERE STRANDED ON LAND! NOW THEY WALK! THEY FLY!

HA!

341

THE DEATH OF SOCRATES

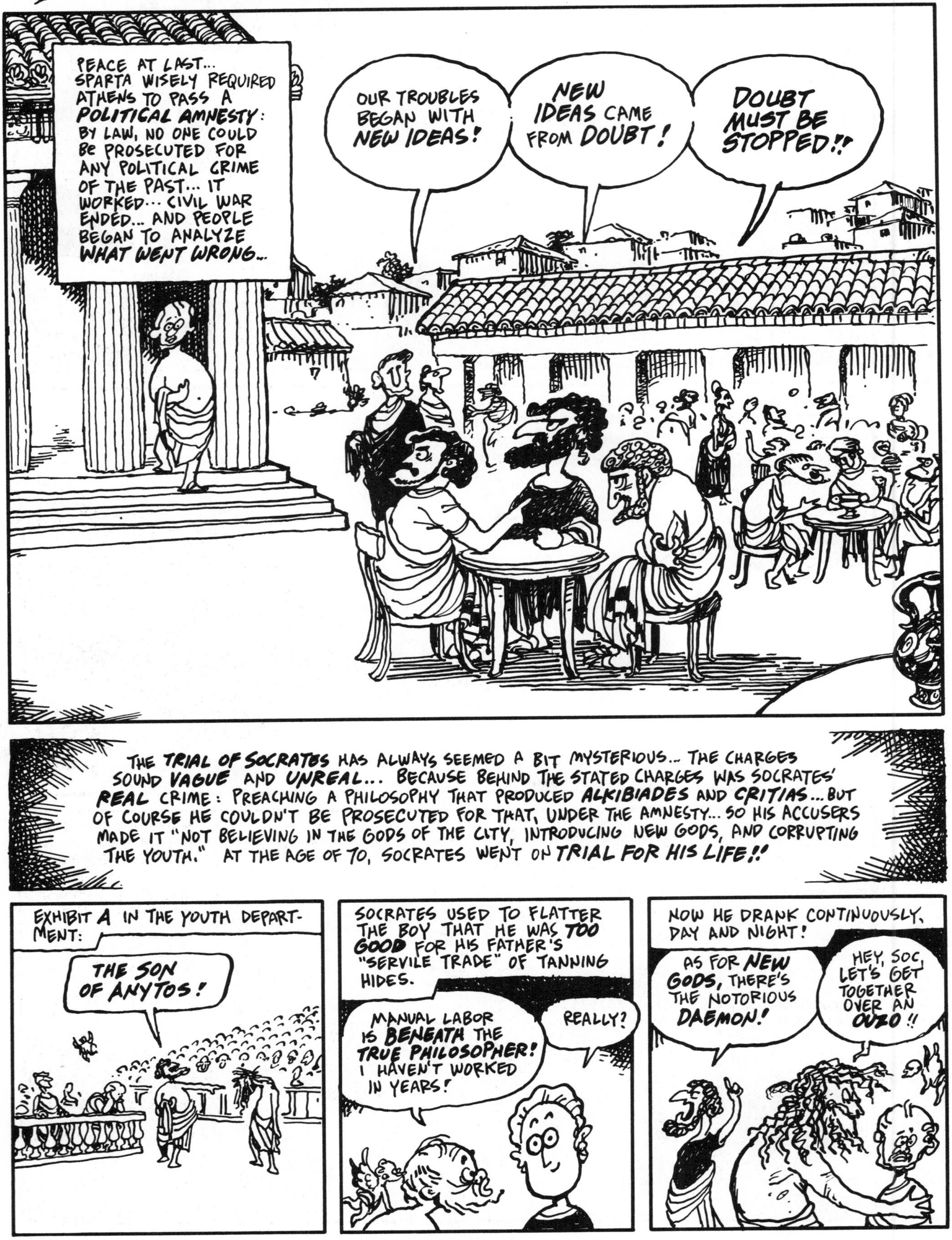

PEACE AT LAST... SPARTA WISELY REQUIRED ATHENS TO PASS A POLITICAL AMNESTY: BY LAW, NO ONE COULD BE PROSECUTED FOR ANY POLITICAL CRIME OF THE PAST... IT WORKED... CIVIL WAR ENDED... AND PEOPLE BEGAN TO ANALYZE WHAT WENT WRONG...
OUR TROUBLES BEGAN WITH NEW IDEAS!
NEW IDEAS CAME FROM DOUBT!
DOUBT MUST BE STOPPED!!
THE TRIAL OF SOCRATES HAS ALWAYS SEEMED A BIT MYSTERIOUS... THE CHARGES SOUND VAGUE AND UNREAL... BECAUSE BEHIND THE STATED CHARGES WAS SOCRATES' REAL CRIME: PREACHING A PHILOSOPHY THAT PRODUCED ALKIBIADES AND CRITIAS... BUT OF COURSE HE COULDN'T BE PROSECUTED FOR THAT, UNDER THE AMNESTY... SO HIS ACCUSERS MADE IT "NOT BELIEVING IN THE GODS OF THE CITY, INTRODUCING NEW GODS, AND CORRUPTING THE YOUTH." AT THE AGE OF 70, SOCRATES WENT ON TRIAL FOR HIS LIFE!!
EXHIBIT A IN THE YOUTH DEPARTMENT:
THE SON OF ANYTOS!
SOCRATES USED TO FLATTER THE BOY THAT HE WAS TOO GOOD FOR HIS FATHER'S "SERVILE TRADE" OF TANNING HIDES.
MANUAL LABOR IS BENEATH THE TRUE PHILOSOPHER! I HAVEN'T WORKED IN YEARS!
REALLY?
NOW HE DRANK CONTINUOUSLY, DAY AND NIGHT!
AS FOR NEW GODS, THERE'S THE NOTORIOUS DAEMON!
HEY, SOC, LET'S GET TOGETHER OVER AN OUZO!!

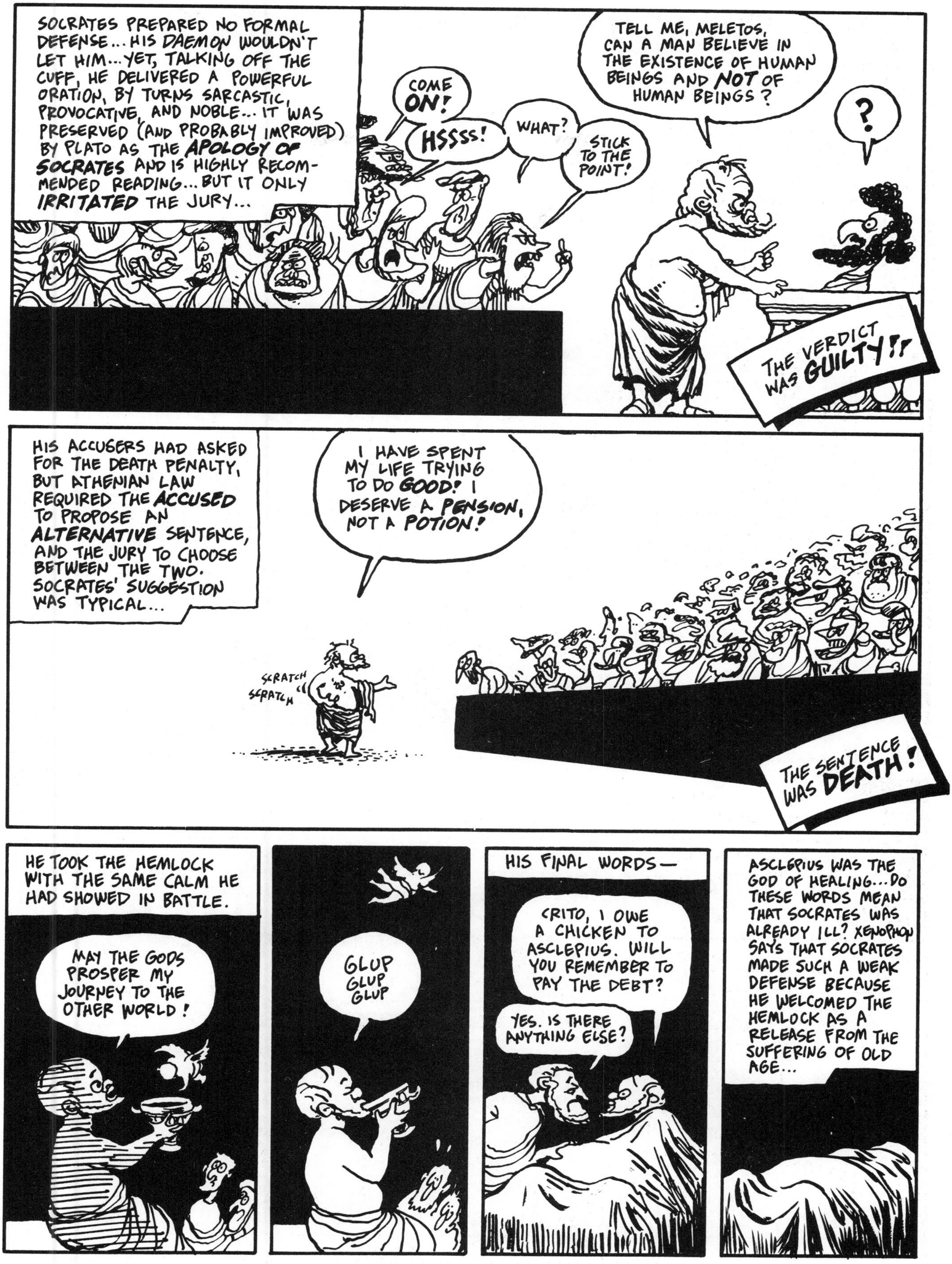
SOCRATES PREPARED NO FORMAL DEFENSE... HIS DAEMON WOULDN'T LET HIM... YET, TALKING OFF THE CUFF, HE DELIVERED A POWERFUL ORATION, BY TURNS SARCASTIC, PROVOCATIVE, AND NOBLE... IT WAS PRESERVED (AND PROBABLY IMPROVED) BY PLATO AS THE APOLOGY OF SOCRATES AND IS HIGHLY RECOMMENDED READING... BUT IT ONLY IRRITATED THE JURY...
COME ON!
HSSSS!
WHAT?
STICK TO THE POINT!
TELL ME, MELETOS, CAN A MAN BELIEVE IN THE EXISTENCE OF HUMAN BEINGS AND NOT OF HUMAN BEINGS?
?
THE VERDICT WAS GUILTY!!
HIS ACCUSERS HAD ASKED FOR THE DEATH PENALTY, BUT ATHENIAN LAW REQUIRED THE ACCUSED TO PROPOSE AN ALTERNATIVE SENTENCE, AND THE JURY TO CHOOSE BETWEEN THE TWO. SOCRATES' SUGGESTION WAS TYPICAL...
I HAVE SPENT MY LIFE TRYING TO DO GOOD! I DESERVE A PENSION, NOT A POTION!
SCRATCH SCRATCH
THE SENTENCE WAS DEATH!
HE TOOK THE HEMLOCK WITH THE SAME CALM HE HAD SHOWED IN BATTLE.
MAY THE GODS PROSPER MY JOURNEY TO THE OTHER WORLD!
GLUP GLUP GLUP
HIS FINAL WORDS—
CRITO, I OWE A CHICKEN TO ASCLEPIUS. WILL YOU REMEMBER TO PAY THE DEBT?
YES. IS THERE ANYTHING ELSE?
ASCLEPIUS WAS THE GOD OF HEALING... DO THESE WORDS MEAN THAT SOCRATES WAS ALREADY ILL? XENOPHON SAYS THAT SOCRATES MADE SUCH A WEAK DEFENSE BECAUSE HE WELCOMED THE HEMLOCK AS A RELEASE FROM THE SUFFERING OF OLD AGE...

PHILOSOPHY BECOMES ACADEMIC

BID FAREWELL TO FIFTH-CENTURY ATHENS! GONE IS THE EMPIRE!* GONE IS THE GOLDEN AGE! GONE ARE KIMON, ELPINIKE, PERICLES, ASPASIA, THE SONS OF PERICLES, AESCHYLOS, SOPHOCLES, PHIDIAS, ALKIBIADES, AND ESPECIALLY SOCRATES!

KIND OF DULL WITHOUT THE PEST AROUND...

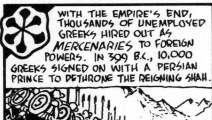

WITH THE EMPIRE'S END, THOUSANDS OF UNEMPLOYED GREEKS HIRED OUT AS MERCENARIES TO FOREIGN POWERS. IN 399 B.C., 10,000 GREEKS SIGNED ON WITH A PERSIAN PRINCE TO DETHRONE THE REIGNING SHAH.

DEFEATED IN BATTLE, THEIR OFFICERS WERE INVITED TO A PERSIAN BANQUET AND MURDERED.

THE TERRIFIED, LEADERLESS SOLDIERS HELD A MEETING TO DISCUSS THEIR PROSPECTS.

WE'RE SUNK.

WE'RE NOT.

WE MIGHT BE.

SOMEBODY SNEEZED.

SNIZ!

TO THE GREEKS, THIS WAS AN OMEN SENT FROM THE GODS! THEY ALL FELL TO THEIR KNEES.

NEVER ARGUE WITH AN OMEN...

A SINGLE SNEEZE GAVE THEM THE COURAGE TO BATTLE BACK TO GREECE!

HOW DO YOU KNOW WHEN SOMETHING'S AN OMEN? TO ME IT WAS JUST AN ITCHY NOSE!

WHEN 10,000 MEN DROP, YOU CAN BE FAIRLY SURE...

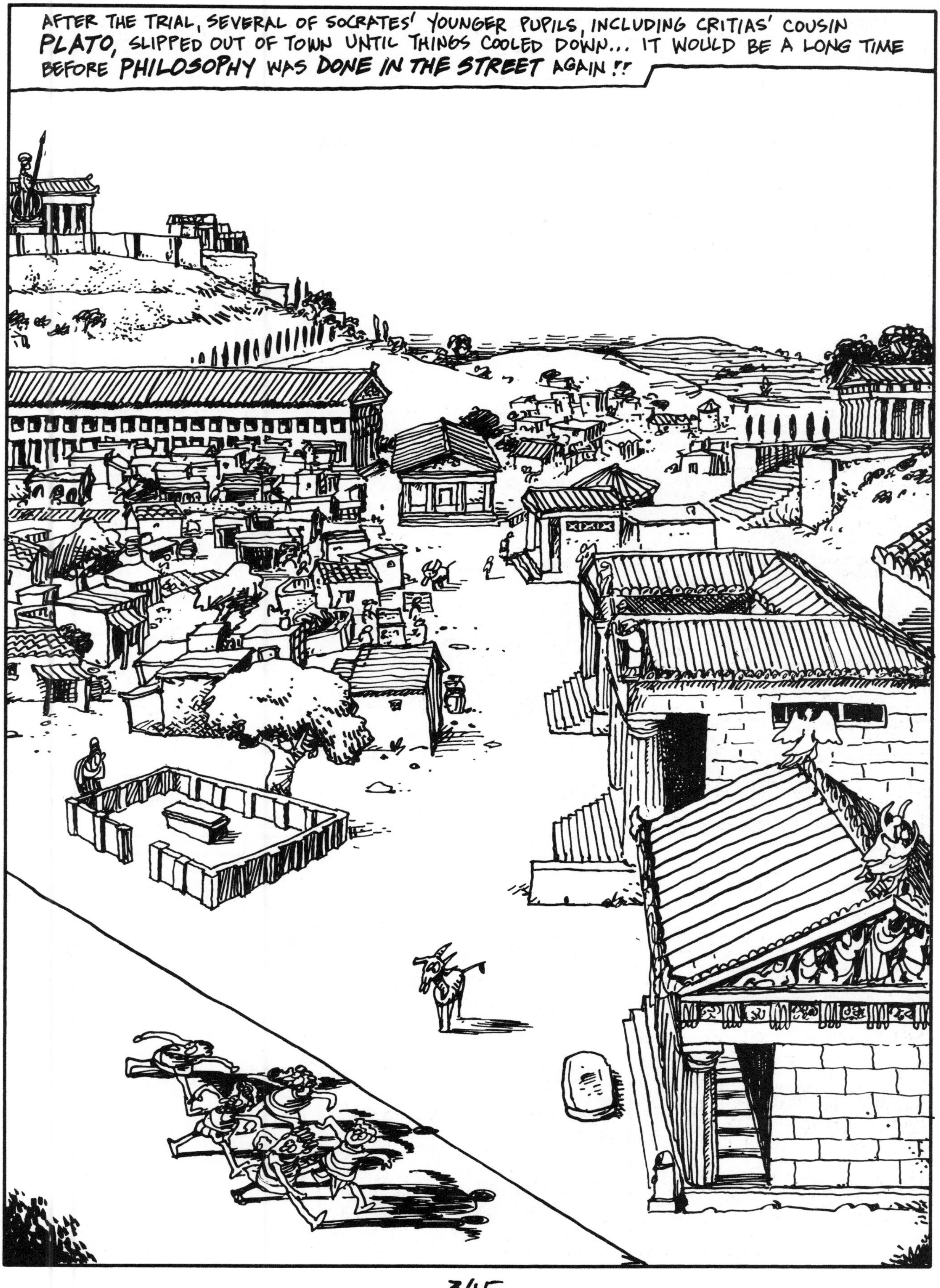
AFTER THE TRIAL, SEVERAL OF SOCRATES' YOUNGER PUPILS, INCLUDING CRITIAS' COUSIN **PLATO**, SLIPPED OUT OF TOWN UNTIL THINGS COOLED DOWN... IT WOULD BE A LONG TIME BEFORE **PHILOSOPHY** WAS **DONE IN THE STREET** AGAIN!!

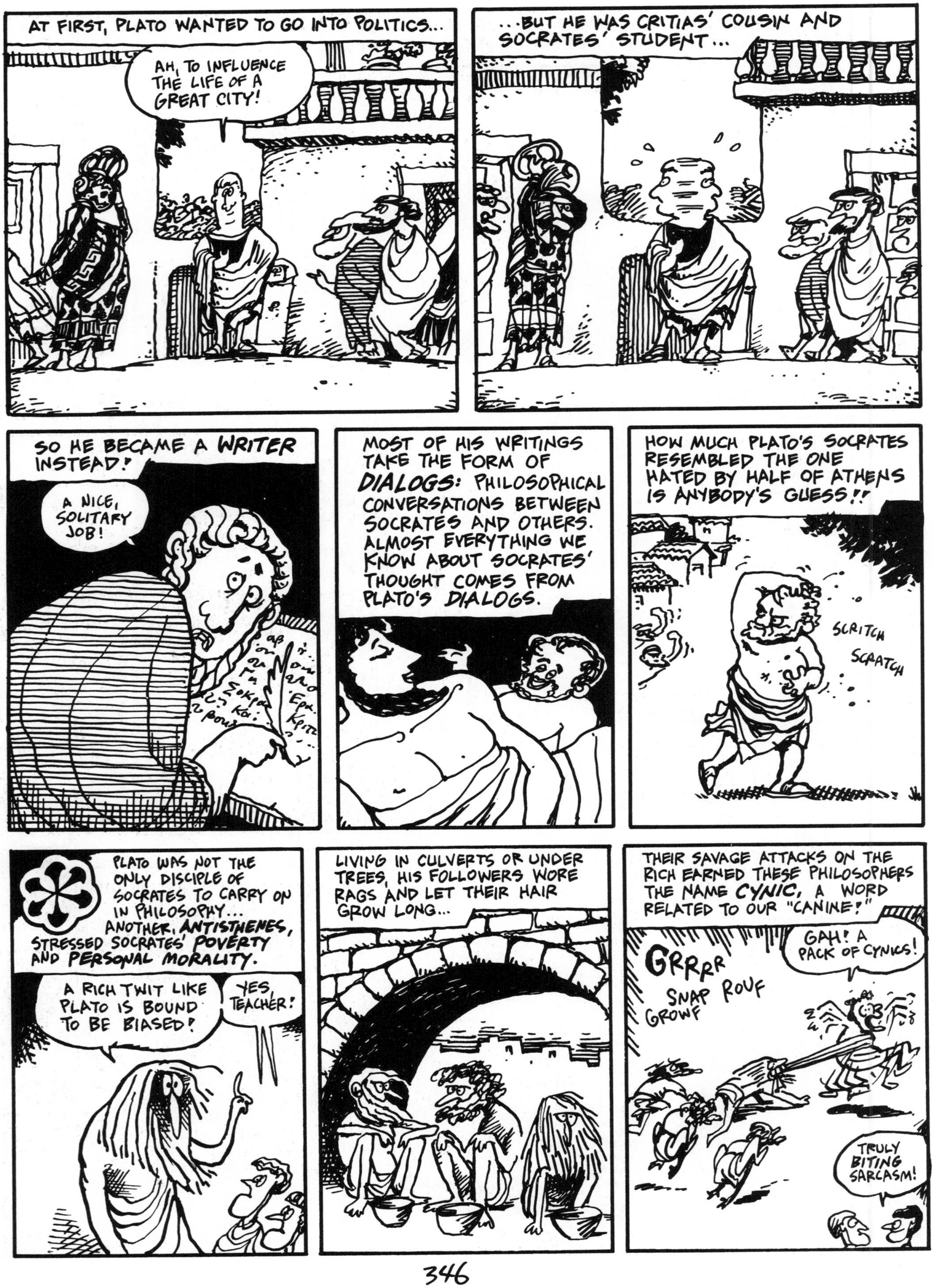
AT FIRST, PLATO WANTED TO GO INTO POLITICS...
AH, TO INFLUENCE THE LIFE OF A GREAT CITY!
...BUT HE WAS CRITIAS' COUSIN AND SOCRATES' STUDENT...
SO HE BECAME A WRITER INSTEAD!
A NICE, SOLITARY JOB!
MOST OF HIS WRITINGS TAKE THE FORM OF DIALOGS: PHILOSOPHICAL CONVERSATIONS BETWEEN SOCRATES AND OTHERS. ALMOST EVERYTHING WE KNOW ABOUT SOCRATES' THOUGHT COMES FROM PLATO'S DIALOGS.
HOW MUCH PLATO'S SOCRATES RESEMBLED THE ONE HATED BY HALF OF ATHENS IS ANYBODY'S GUESS!!
SCRITCH
SCRATCH
PLATO WAS NOT THE ONLY DISCIPLE OF SOCRATES TO CARRY ON IN PHILOSOPHY... ANOTHER, ANTISTHENES, STRESSED SOCRATES' POVERTY AND PERSONAL MORALITY.
A RICH TWIT LIKE PLATO IS BOUND TO BE BIASED!
YES, TEACHER!
LIVING IN CULVERTS OR UNDER TREES, HIS FOLLOWERS WORE RAGS AND LET THEIR HAIR GROW LONG...
THEIR SAVAGE ATTACKS ON THE RICH EARNED THESE PHILOSOPHERS THE NAME CYNIC, A WORD RELATED TO OUR "CANINE!"
GRRRR
SNAP ROUF
GROWF
GAH! A PACK OF CYNICS!
TRULY BITING SARCASM!

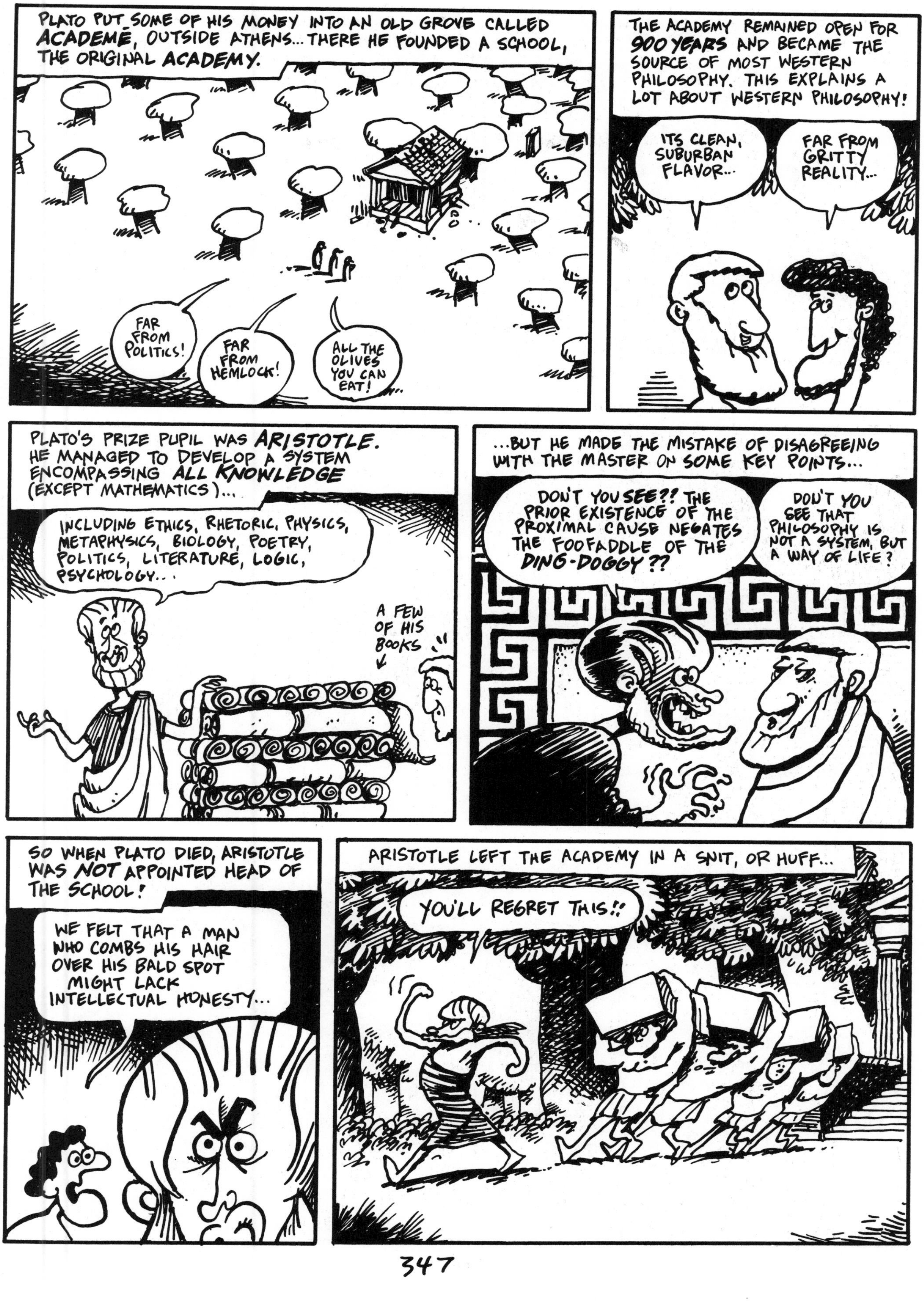
PLATO PUT SOME OF HIS MONEY INTO AN OLD GROVE CALLED ACADEME, OUTSIDE ATHENS... THERE HE FOUNDED A SCHOOL, THE ORIGINAL ACADEMY.
FAR FROM POLITICS!
FAR FROM HEMLOCK!
ALL THE OLIVES YOU CAN EAT!
THE ACADEMY REMAINED OPEN FOR 900 YEARS AND BECAME THE SOURCE OF MOST WESTERN PHILOSOPHY. THIS EXPLAINS A LOT ABOUT WESTERN PHILOSOPHY!
ITS CLEAN, SUBURBAN FLAVOR...
FAR FROM GRITTY REALITY...
PLATO'S PRIZE PUPIL WAS ARISTOTLE. HE MANAGED TO DEVELOP A SYSTEM ENCOMPASSING ALL KNOWLEDGE (EXCEPT MATHEMATICS)...
INCLUDING ETHICS, RHETORIC, PHYSICS, METAPHYSICS, BIOLOGY, POETRY, POLITICS, LITERATURE, LOGIC, PSYCHOLOGY...
A FEW OF HIS BOOKS
...BUT HE MADE THE MISTAKE OF DISAGREEING WITH THE MASTER ON SOME KEY POINTS...
DON'T YOU SEE?? THE PRIOR EXISTENCE OF THE PROXIMAL CAUSE NEGATES THE FOOFADDLE OF THE DING-DOGGY??
DON'T YOU SEE THAT PHILOSOPHY IS NOT A SYSTEM, BUT A WAY OF LIFE?
SO WHEN PLATO DIED, ARISTOTLE WAS NOT APPOINTED HEAD OF THE SCHOOL!
WE FELT THAT A MAN WHO COMBS HIS HAIR OVER HIS BALD SPOT MIGHT LACK INTELLECTUAL HONESTY...
ARISTOTLE LEFT THE ACADEMY IN A SNIT, OR HUFF...
YOU'LL REGRET THIS!!

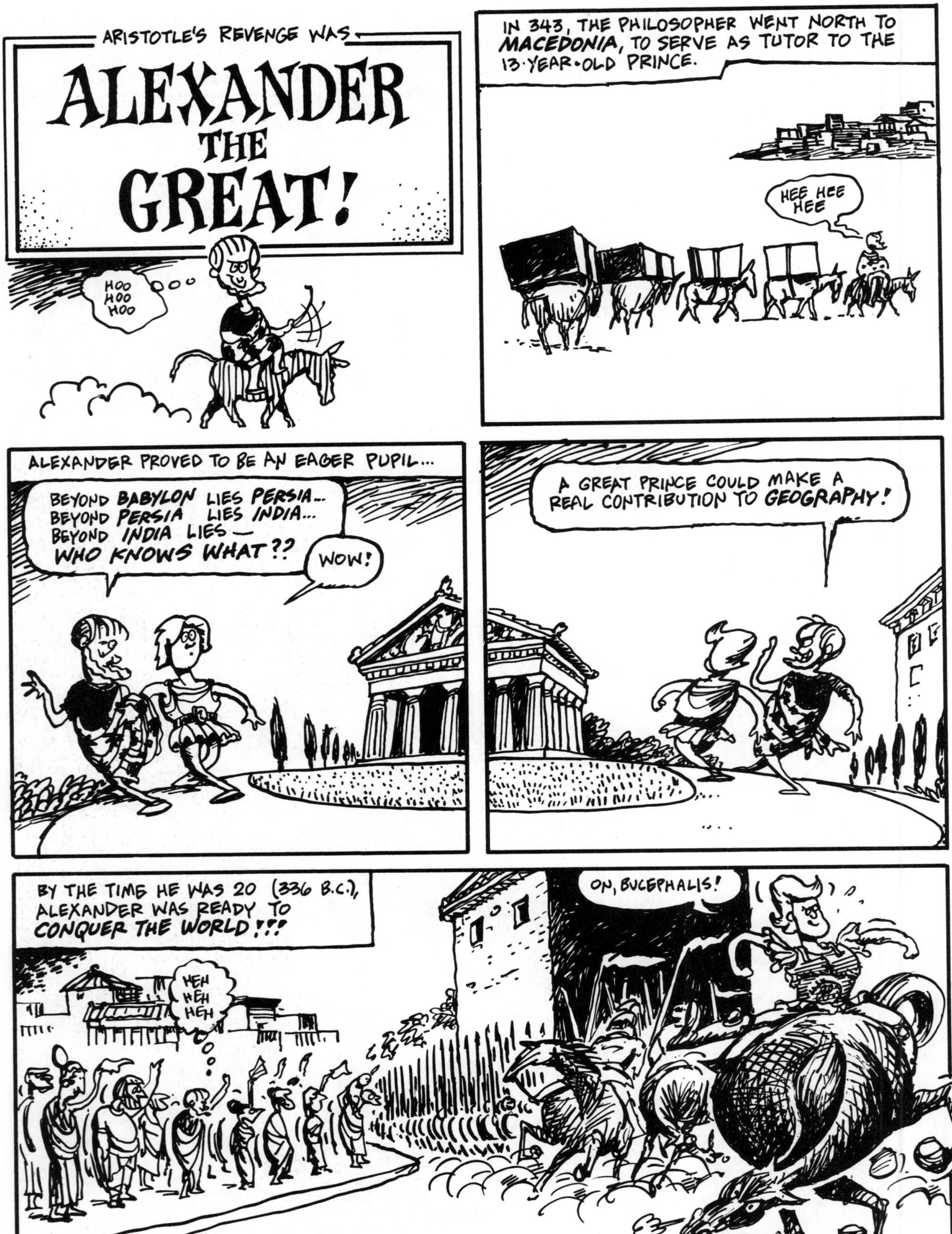

ARISTOTLE'S REVENGE WAS
ALEXANDER THE GREAT!
HOO HOO HOO
IN 343, THE PHILOSOPHER WENT NORTH TO MACEDONIA, TO SERVE AS TUTOR TO THE 13-YEAR-OLD PRINCE.
HEE HEE HEE
ALEXANDER PROVED TO BE AN EAGER PUPIL...
BEYOND BABYLON LIES PERSIA... BEYOND PERSIA LIES INDIA... BEYOND INDIA LIES— WHO KNOWS WHAT??
WOW!
A GREAT PRINCE COULD MAKE A REAL CONTRIBUTION TO GEOGRAPHY!
BY THE TIME HE WAS 20 (336 B.C.), ALEXANDER WAS READY TO CONQUER THE WORLD!?!
HEH HEH HEH
ON, BUCEPHALIS!

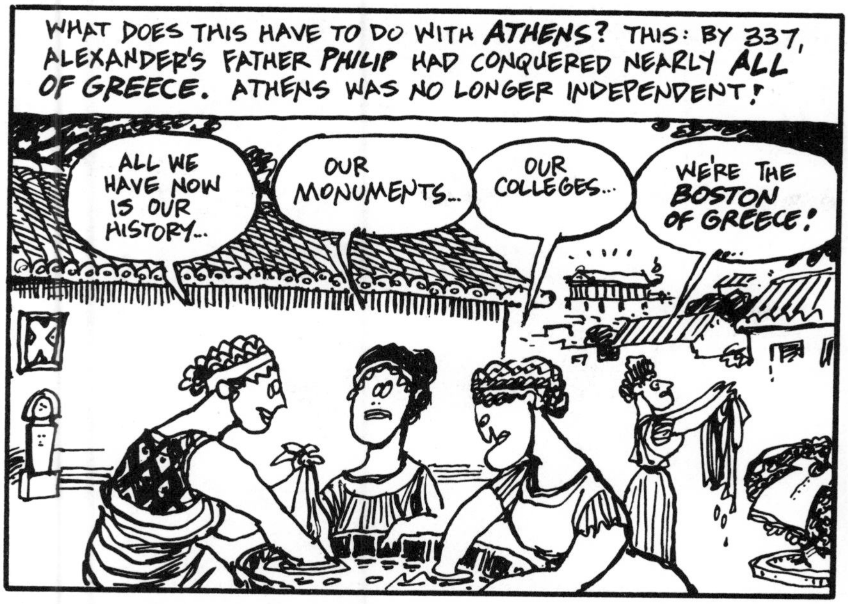
WHAT DOES THIS HAVE TO DO WITH ATHENS? THIS: BY 337, ALEXANDER'S FATHER PHILIP HAD CONQUERED NEARLY ALL OF GREECE. ATHENS WAS NO LONGER INDEPENDENT!
ALL WE HAVE NOW IS OUR HISTORY...
OUR MONUMENTS...
OUR COLLEGES...
WE'RE THE BOSTON OF GREECE!

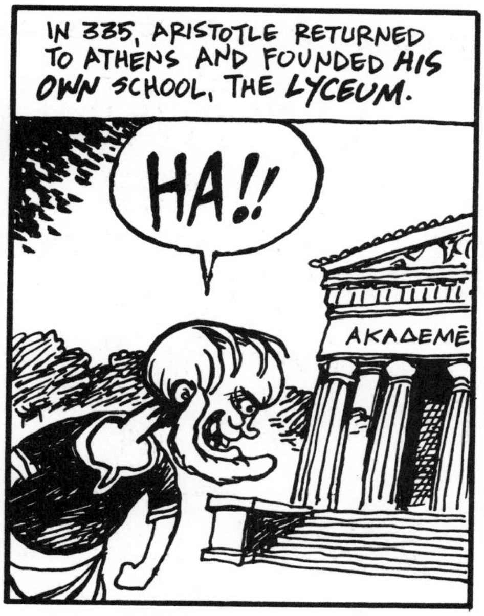
IN 335, ARISTOTLE RETURNED TO ATHENS AND FOUNDED HIS OWN SCHOOL, THE LYCEUM.
HA!!
AKADEME

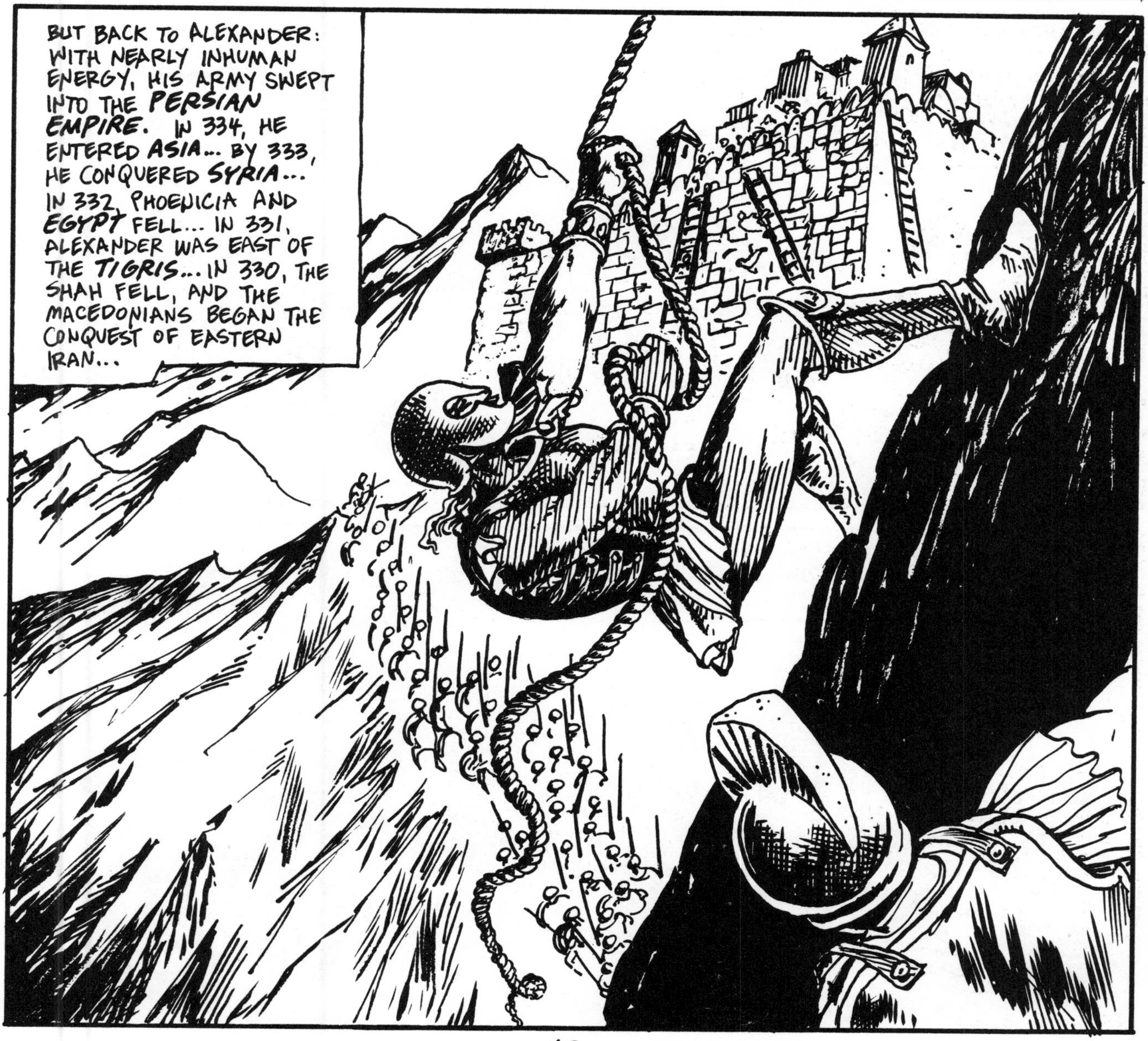
BUT BACK TO ALEXANDER: WITH NEARLY INHUMAN ENERGY, HIS ARMY SWEPT INTO THE PERSIAN EMPIRE. IN 334, HE ENTERED ASIA... BY 333, HE CONQUERED SYRIA... IN 332, PHOENICIA AND EGYPT FELL... IN 331, ALEXANDER WAS EAST OF THE TIGRIS... IN 330, THE SHAH FELL, AND THE MACEDONIANS BEGAN THE CONQUEST OF EASTERN IRAN...

FOR THREE AWFUL YEARS THEY TRAMPED AROUND THE MOUNTAINS OF CENTRAL ASIA.

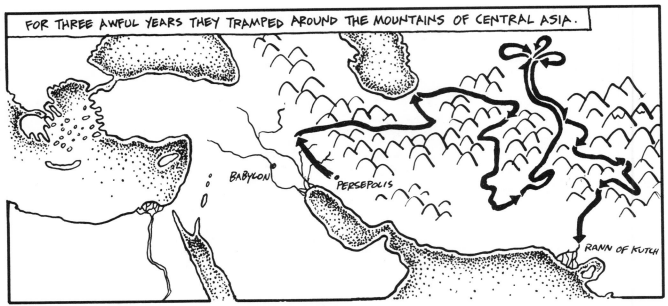

BABYLON

PERSEPOLIS

RANN OF KUTCH

EMERGING AT KASMIR, THEY MARCHED DOWN THE JHELUM TOWARD THE RANN OF KUTCH... AND WERE GREETED BY **ARMORED ELEPHANTS.**

GOSH! ONE NEVER TIRES OF ENCOUNTERING NOVELTIES!

FURTHER THAN THIS THE ARMY REFUSED TO GO, DESPITE ALEXANDER'S COMMANDS!

MEN! THINK OF THE NOVELTIES YET TO BE SEEN!

RIGHT!

THE INVADERS TURNED BACK... LET'S LET THEM GO... LET'S STAY AND EXPLORE THIS WONDERFUL COUNTRY OF ELEPHANTS, THE JHELUM, AND THE RANN OF KUTCH!!

NEXT INDIA!

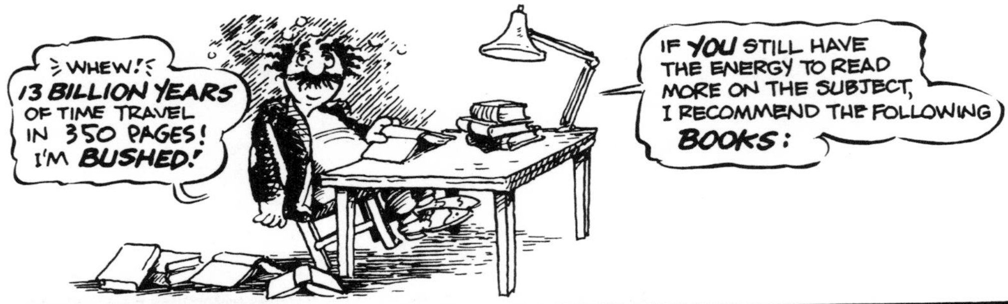
WHEW! 13 BILLION YEARS OF TIME TRAVEL IN 350 PAGES! I'M BUSHED!
IF YOU STILL HAVE THE ENERGY TO READ MORE ON THE SUBJECT, I RECOMMEND THE FOLLOWING BOOKS:

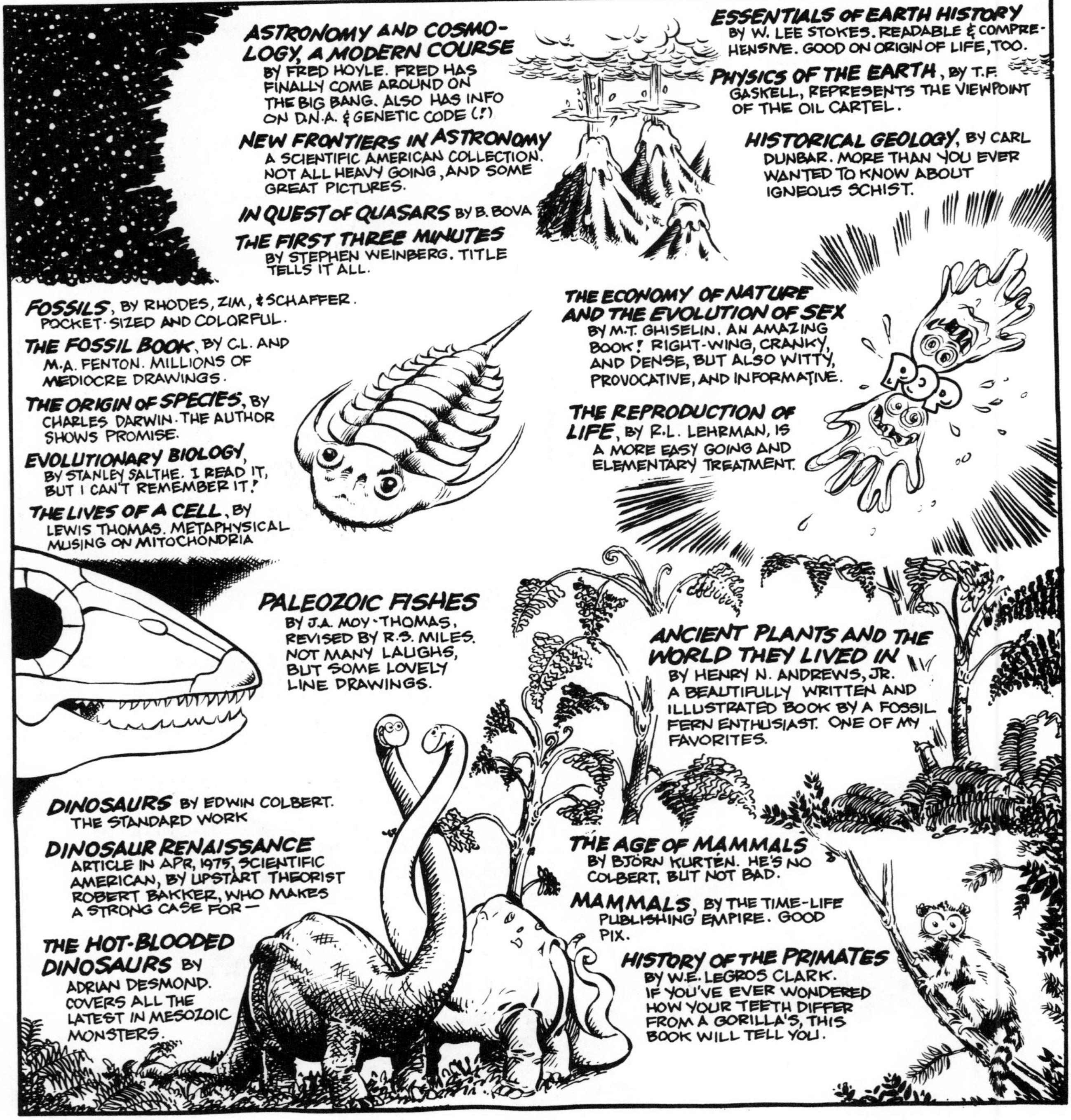
ASTRONOMY AND COSMOLOGY, A MODERN COURSE BY FRED HOYLE. FRED HAS FINALLY COME AROUND ON THE BIG BANG. ALSO HAS INFO ON D.N.A. & GENETIC CODE (!)
NEW FRONTIERS IN ASTRONOMY A SCIENTIFIC AMERICAN COLLECTION. NOT ALL HEAVY GOING, AND SOME GREAT PICTURES.
IN QUEST OF QUASARS BY B. BOVA
THE FIRST THREE MINUTES BY STEPHEN WEINBERG. TITLE TELLS IT ALL.
ESSENTIALS OF EARTH HISTORY BY W. LEE STOKES. READABLE & COMPREHENSIVE. GOOD ON ORIGIN OF LIFE, TOO.
PHYSICS OF THE EARTH, BY T.F. GASKELL, REPRESENTS THE VIEWPOINT OF THE OIL CARTEL.
HISTORICAL GEOLOGY, BY CARL DUNBAR. MORE THAN YOU EVER WANTED TO KNOW ABOUT IGNEOUS SCHIST.
FOSSILS, BY RHODES, ZIM, & SCHAFFER. POCKET-SIZED AND COLORFUL.
THE FOSSIL BOOK, BY C.L. AND M.A. FENTON. MILLIONS OF MEDIOCRE DRAWINGS.
THE ORIGIN OF SPECIES, BY CHARLES DARWIN. THE AUTHOR SHOWS PROMISE.
EVOLUTIONARY BIOLOGY, BY STANLEY SALTHE. I READ IT, BUT I CAN'T REMEMBER IT!
THE LIVES OF A CELL, BY LEWIS THOMAS. METAPHYSICAL MUSING ON MITOCHONDRIA
THE ECONOMY OF NATURE AND THE EVOLUTION OF SEX BY M.T. GHISELIN. AN AMAZING BOOK! RIGHT-WING, CRANKY, AND DENSE, BUT ALSO WITTY, PROVOCATIVE, AND INFORMATIVE.
THE REPRODUCTION OF LIFE, BY R.L. LEHRMAN, IS A MORE EASY GOING AND ELEMENTARY TREATMENT.
POP
PALEOZOIC FISHES BY J.A. MOY-THOMAS, REVISED BY R.S. MILES. NOT MANY LAUGHS, BUT SOME LOVELY LINE DRAWINGS.
ANCIENT PLANTS AND THE WORLD THEY LIVED IN BY HENRY N. ANDREWS, JR. A BEAUTIFULLY WRITTEN AND ILLUSTRATED BOOK BY A FOSSIL FERN ENTHUSIAST. ONE OF MY FAVORITES.
DINOSAURS BY EDWIN COLBERT. THE STANDARD WORK
DINOSAUR RENAISSANCE ARTICLE IN APR, 1975, SCIENTIFIC AMERICAN, BY UPSTART THEORIST ROBERT BAKKER, WHO MAKES A STRONG CASE FOR—
THE HOT-BLOODED DINOSAURS BY ADRIAN DESMOND. COVERS ALL THE LATEST IN MESOZOIC MONSTERS.
THE AGE OF MAMMALS BY BJÖRN KURTÉN. HE'S NO COLBERT, BUT NOT BAD.
MAMMALS, BY THE TIME-LIFE PUBLISHING EMPIRE. GOOD PIX.
HISTORY OF THE PRIMATES BY W.E. LEGROS CLARK. IF YOU'VE EVER WONDERED HOW YOUR TEETH DIFFER FROM A GORILLA'S, THIS BOOK WILL TELL YOU.

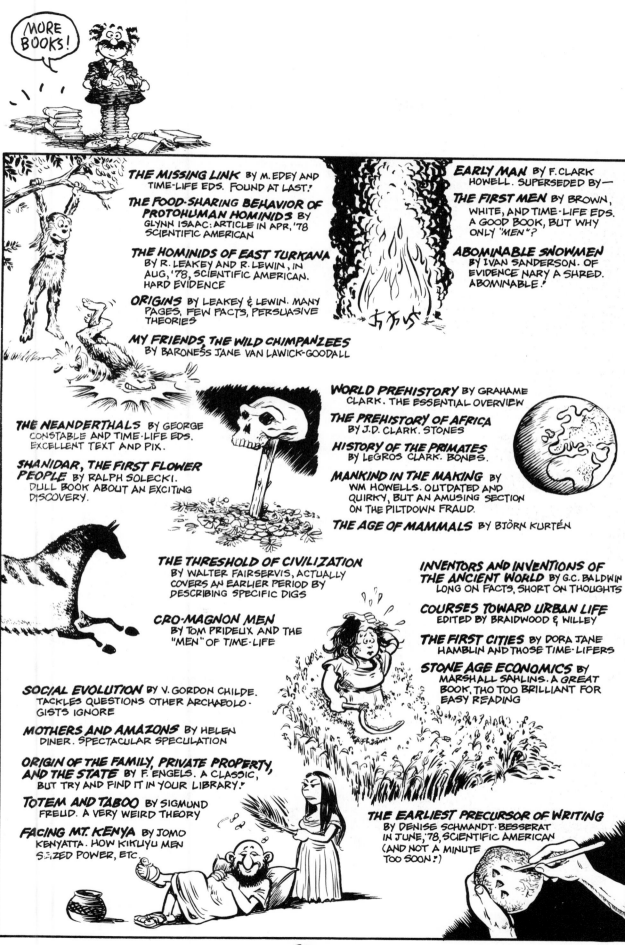

MORE BOOKS!

THE MISSING LINK BY M. EDEY AND TIME-LIFE EDS. FOUND AT LAST!

THE FOOD-SHARING BEHAVIOR OF PROTOHUMAN HOMINIDS BY GLYNN ISAAC: ARTICLE IN APR, '78 SCIENTIFIC AMERICAN

THE HOMINIDS OF EAST TURKANA BY R. LEAKEY AND R. LEWIN, IN AUG, '78, SCIENTIFIC AMERICAN. HARD EVIDENCE

ORIGINS BY LEAKEY & LEWIN. MANY PAGES, FEW FACTS, PERSUASIVE THEORIES

MY FRIENDS, THE WILD CHIMPANZEES BY BARONESS JANE VAN LAWICK-GOODALL

EARLY MAN BY F. CLARK HOWELL. SUPERSEDED BY—

THE FIRST MEN BY BROWN, WHITE, AND TIME-LIFE EDS. A GOOD BOOK, BUT WHY ONLY *"MEN"*?

ABOMINABLE SNOWMEN BY IVAN SANDERSON. OF EVIDENCE NARY A SHRED. ABOMINABLE!

THE NEANDERTHALS BY GEORGE CONSTABLE AND TIME-LIFE EDS. EXCELLENT TEXT AND PIX.

SHANIDAR, THE FIRST FLOWER PEOPLE BY RALPH SOLECKI. DULL BOOK ABOUT AN EXCITING DISCOVERY.

WORLD PREHISTORY BY GRAHAME CLARK. THE ESSENTIAL OVERVIEW

THE PREHISTORY OF AFRICA BY J.D. CLARK. STONES

HISTORY OF THE PRIMATES BY LEGROS CLARK. BONES.

MANKIND IN THE MAKING BY WM HOWELLS. OUTDATED AND QUIRKY, BUT AN AMUSING SECTION ON THE PILTDOWN FRAUD.

THE AGE OF MAMMALS BY BJÖRN KURTÉN

THE THRESHOLD OF CIVILIZATION BY WALTER FAIRSERVIS, ACTUALLY COVERS AN EARLIER PERIOD BY DESCRIBING SPECIFIC DIGS

CRO-MAGNON MEN BY TOM PRIDEUX AND THE "MEN" OF TIME-LIFE

INVENTORS AND INVENTIONS OF THE ANCIENT WORLD BY G.C. BALDWIN LONG ON FACTS, SHORT ON THOUGHTS

COURSES TOWARD URBAN LIFE EDITED BY BRAIDWOOD & WILLEY

THE FIRST CITIES BY DORA JANE HAMBLIN AND THOSE TIME-LIFERS

STONE AGE ECONOMICS BY MARSHALL SAHLINS. A *GREAT* BOOK, THO TOO BRILLIANT FOR EASY READING

SOCIAL EVOLUTION BY V. GORDON CHILDE. TACKLES QUESTIONS OTHER ARCHAEOLOGISTS IGNORE

MOTHERS AND AMAZONS BY HELEN DINER. SPECTACULAR SPECULATION

ORIGIN OF THE FAMILY, PRIVATE PROPERTY, AND THE STATE BY F. ENGELS. A CLASSIC, BUT TRY AND FIND IT IN YOUR LIBRARY!

TOTEM AND TABOO BY SIGMUND FREUD. A VERY WEIRD THEORY

FACING MT. KENYA BY JOMO KENYATTA. HOW KIKUYU MEN SEIZED POWER, ETC.

THE EARLIEST PRECURSOR OF WRITING BY DENISE SCHMANDT-BESSERAT IN JUNE, '78, SCIENTIFIC AMERICAN (AND NOT A MINUTE TOO SOON!)

WHOOF MORE BOOKS THAN EVER! GUESS I'LL TAKE 'EM BACK TO THE LIBRARY SO YOU CAN HAVE A LOOK AT 'EM!

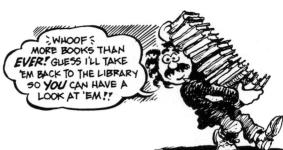

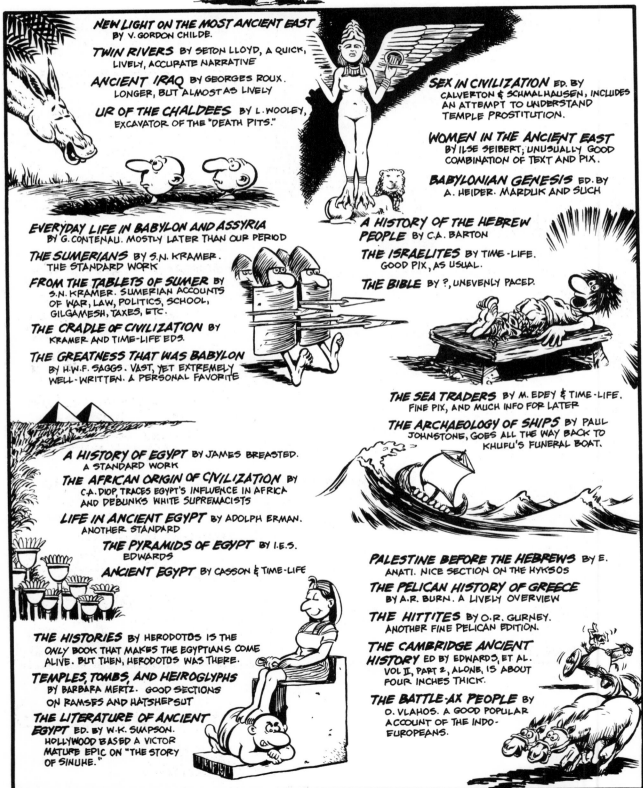

NEW LIGHT ON THE MOST ANCIENT EAST BY V. GORDON CHILDE.

TWIN RIVERS BY SETON LLOYD, A QUICK, LIVELY, ACCURATE NARRATIVE

ANCIENT IRAQ BY GEORGES ROUX. LONGER, BUT ALMOST AS LIVELY

UR OF THE CHALDEES BY L. WOOLEY, EXCAVATOR OF THE "DEATH PITS."

SEX IN CIVILIZATION ED. BY CALVERTON & SCHMALHAUSEN, INCLUDES AN ATTEMPT TO UNDERSTAND TEMPLE PROSTITUTION.

WOMEN IN THE ANCIENT EAST BY ILSE SEIBERT; UNUSUALLY GOOD COMBINATION OF TEXT AND PIX.

BABYLONIAN GENESIS ED. BY A. HEIDER. MARDUK AND SUCH

EVERYDAY LIFE IN BABYLON AND ASSYRIA BY G. CONTENAU. MOSTLY LATER THAN OUR PERIOD

THE SUMERIANS BY S.N. KRAMER. THE STANDARD WORK

FROM THE TABLETS OF SUMER BY S.N. KRAMER. SUMERIAN ACCOUNTS OF WAR, LAW, POLITICS, SCHOOL, GILGAMESH, TAXES, ETC.

THE CRADLE OF CIVILIZATION BY KRAMER AND TIME-LIFE EDS.

THE GREATNESS THAT WAS BABYLON BY H.W.F. SAGGS. VAST, YET EXTREMELY WELL-WRITTEN. A PERSONAL FAVORITE

A HISTORY OF THE HEBREW PEOPLE BY C.A. BARTON

THE ISRAELITES BY TIME-LIFE. GOOD PIX, AS USUAL.

THE BIBLE BY ?, UNEVENLY PACED.

THE SEA TRADERS BY M. EDEY & TIME-LIFE. FINE PIX, AND MUCH INFO FOR LATER

THE ARCHAEOLOGY OF SHIPS BY PAUL JOHNSTONE, GOES ALL THE WAY BACK TO KHUFU'S FUNERAL BOAT.

A HISTORY OF EGYPT BY JAMES BREASTED. A STANDARD WORK

THE AFRICAN ORIGIN OF CIVILIZATION BY C.A. DIOP, TRACES EGYPT'S INFLUENCE IN AFRICA AND DEBUNKS WHITE SUPREMACISTS

LIFE IN ANCIENT EGYPT BY ADOLPH ERMAN. ANOTHER STANDARD

THE PYRAMIDS OF EGYPT BY I.E.S. EDWARDS

ANCIENT EGYPT BY CASSON & TIME-LIFE

THE HISTORIES BY HERODOTOS IS THE ONLY BOOK THAT MAKES THE EGYPTIANS COME ALIVE. BUT THEN, HERODOTOS WAS THERE.

TEMPLES, TOMBS, AND HEIROGLYPHS BY BARBARA MERTZ. GOOD SECTIONS ON RAMSES AND HATSHEPSUT

THE LITERATURE OF ANCIENT EGYPT ED. BY W.K. SIMPSON. HOLLYWOOD BASED A VICTOR MATURE EPIC ON "THE STORY OF SINUHE."

PALESTINE BEFORE THE HEBREWS BY E. ANATI. NICE SECTION ON THE HYKSOS

THE PELICAN HISTORY OF GREECE BY A.R. BURN. A LIVELY OVERVIEW

THE HITTITES BY O.R. GURNEY. ANOTHER FINE PELICAN EDITION.

THE CAMBRIDGE ANCIENT HISTORY ED BY EDWARDS, ET AL. VOL II, PART 2, ALONE, IS ABOUT FOUR INCHES THICK.

THE BATTLE-AX PEOPLE BY O. VLAHOS. A GOOD POPULAR ACCOUNT OF THE INDO-EUROPEANS.

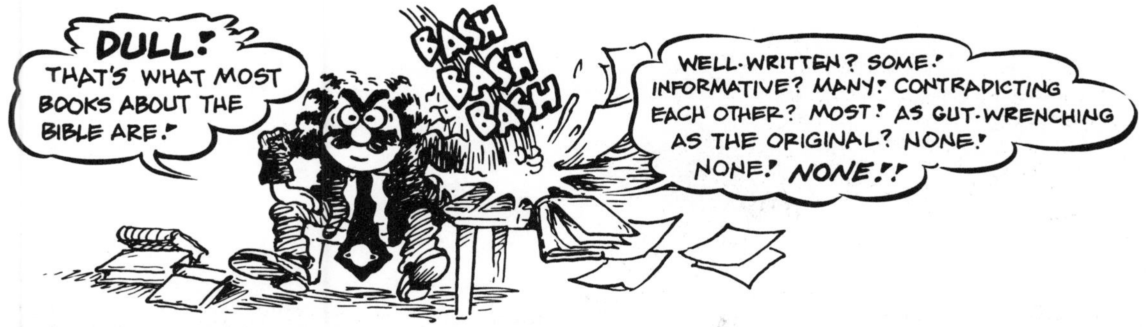
DULL! THAT'S WHAT MOST BOOKS ABOUT THE BIBLE ARE!
BASH BASH BASH
WELL-WRITTEN? SOME! INFORMATIVE? MANY! CONTRADICTING EACH OTHER? MOST! AS GUT-WRENCHING AS THE ORIGINAL? NONE! NONE! NONE!!

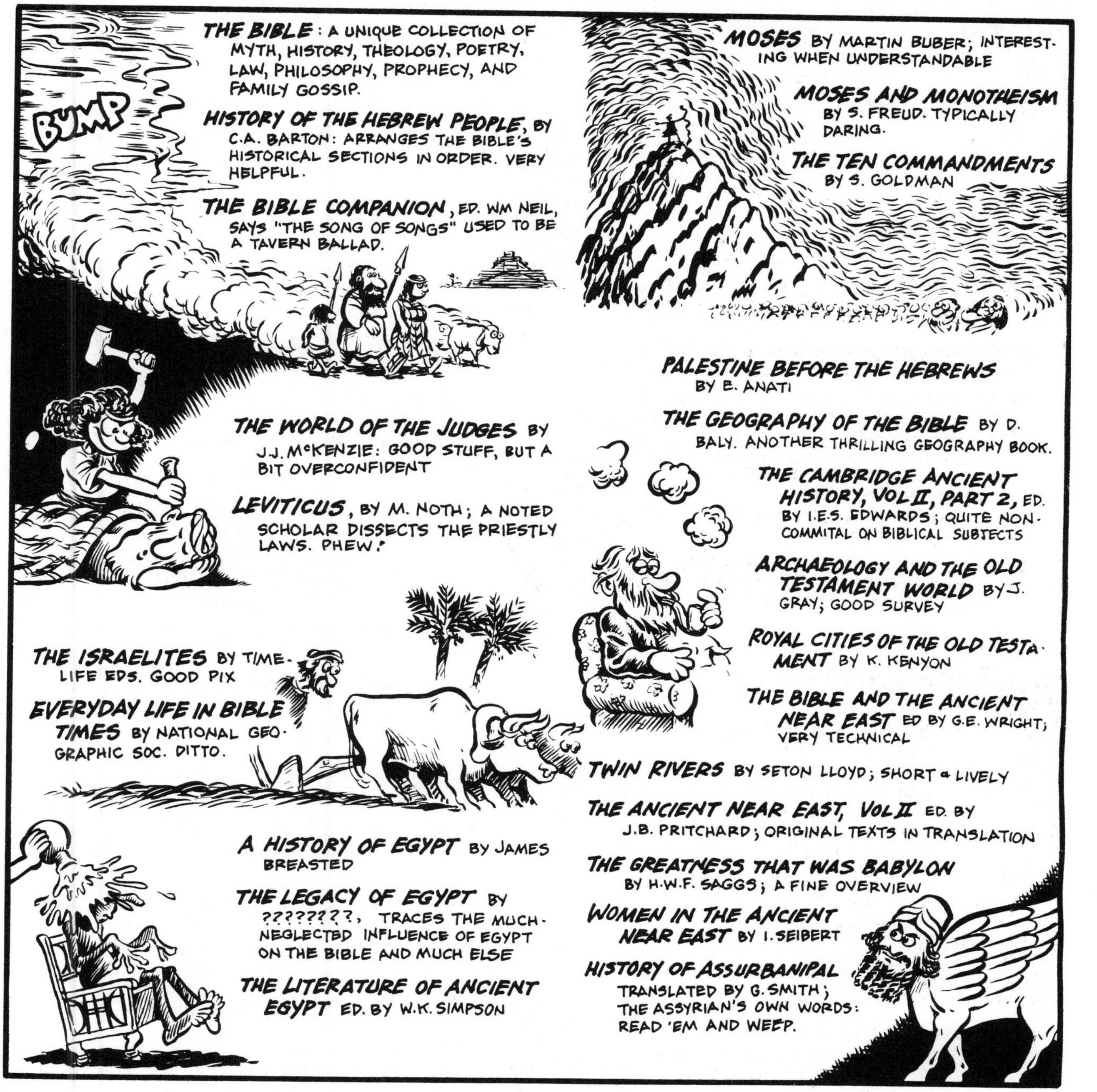
THE BIBLE: A UNIQUE COLLECTION OF MYTH, HISTORY, THEOLOGY, POETRY, LAW, PHILOSOPHY, PROPHECY, AND FAMILY GOSSIP.
BUMP
HISTORY OF THE HEBREW PEOPLE, BY C.A. BARTON: ARRANGES THE BIBLE'S HISTORICAL SECTIONS IN ORDER. VERY HELPFUL.
THE BIBLE COMPANION, ED. WM NEIL, SAYS "THE SONG OF SONGS" USED TO BE A TAVERN BALLAD.
MOSES BY MARTIN BUBER; INTERESTING WHEN UNDERSTANDABLE
MOSES AND MONOTHEISM BY S. FREUD. TYPICALLY DARING.
THE TEN COMMANDMENTS BY S. GOLDMAN
THE WORLD OF THE JUDGES BY J.J. McKENZIE: GOOD STUFF, BUT A BIT OVERCONFIDENT
LEVITICUS, BY M. NOTH; A NOTED SCHOLAR DISSECTS THE PRIESTLY LAWS. PHEW!
PALESTINE BEFORE THE HEBREWS BY E. ANATI
THE GEOGRAPHY OF THE BIBLE BY D. BALY. ANOTHER THRILLING GEOGRAPHY BOOK.
THE CAMBRIDGE ANCIENT HISTORY, VOL II, PART 2, ED. BY I.E.S. EDWARDS; QUITE NON-COMMITAL ON BIBLICAL SUBJECTS
ARCHAEOLOGY AND THE OLD TESTAMENT WORLD BY J. GRAY; GOOD SURVEY
THE ISRAELITES BY TIME-LIFE EDS. GOOD PIX
EVERYDAY LIFE IN BIBLE TIMES BY NATIONAL GEOGRAPHIC SOC. DITTO.
ROYAL CITIES OF THE OLD TESTAMENT BY K. KENYON
THE BIBLE AND THE ANCIENT NEAR EAST ED BY G.E. WRIGHT; VERY TECHNICAL
TWIN RIVERS BY SETON LLOYD; SHORT & LIVELY
A HISTORY OF EGYPT BY JAMES BREASTED
THE LEGACY OF EGYPT BY ????????, TRACES THE MUCH-NEGLECTED INFLUENCE OF EGYPT ON THE BIBLE AND MUCH ELSE
THE LITERATURE OF ANCIENT EGYPT ED. BY W.K. SIMPSON
THE ANCIENT NEAR EAST, VOL II ED. BY J.B. PRITCHARD; ORIGINAL TEXTS IN TRANSLATION
THE GREATNESS THAT WAS BABYLON BY H.W.F. SAGGS; A FINE OVERVIEW
WOMEN IN THE ANCIENT NEAR EAST BY I. SEIBERT
HISTORY OF ASSURBANIPAL TRANSLATED BY G. SMITH; THE ASSYRIAN'S OWN WORDS: READ 'EM AND WEEP.

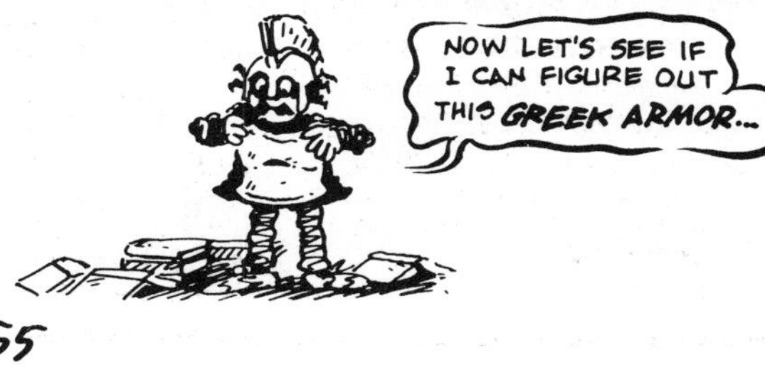
NOW LET'S SEE IF I CAN FIGURE OUT THIS GREEK ARMOR...

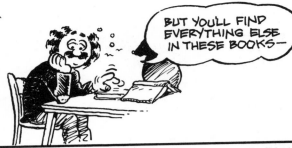

I CAN'T RECALL WHERE THAT STORY ABOUT PYTHAGORAS CAME FROM—IT'S JUST OLD MATH LORE...
BUT YOU'LL FIND EVERYTHING ELSE IN THESE BOOKS—

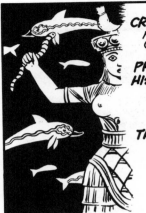

CRETE AND MYCENAE BY S. MARINATOS. LOVELY PHOTOS OF CRETAN ART

PROBLEMS IN ANCIENT HISTORY, VOL 1, ED D. KAGAN. THE PROBLEM WITH ALL HISTORY IS THAT THE EXPERTS DISAGREE ABOUT EVERYTHING!

THE BATTLE-AX PEOPLE BY O. VLAHOS

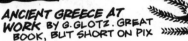

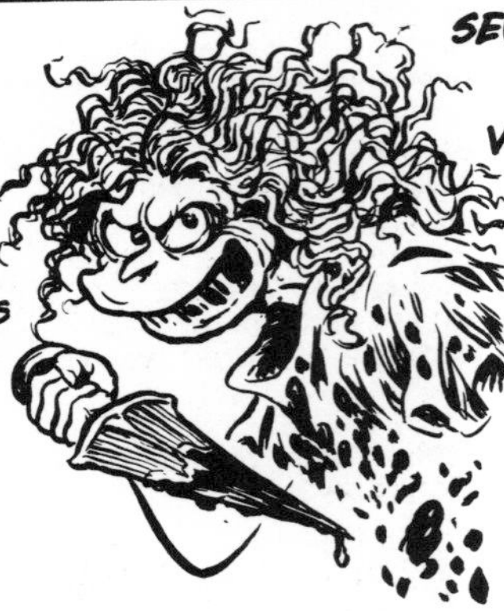

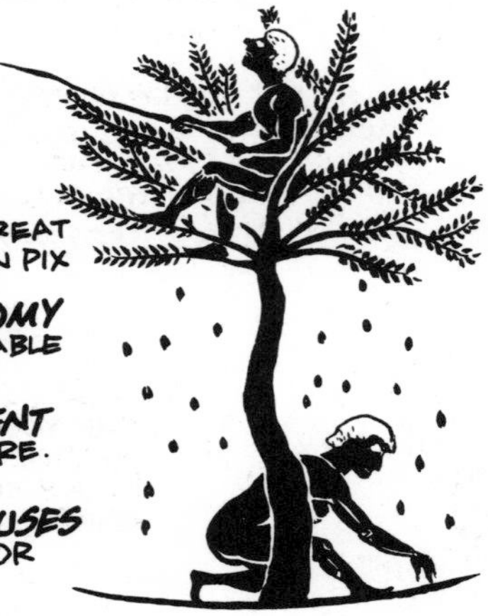

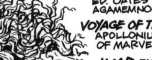

SEVEN FAMOUS GREEK PLAYS ED. OATES AND O'NEILL. AGAMEMNON, OEDIPUS, ETC.

VOYAGE OF THE ARGO BY APOLLONIUS OF RHODES. FULL OF MARVELS.

ILIAD BY HOMER. THE FIRST GREAT NOVEL.

ODYSSEY BY HOMER. THE FIRST GREAT "WESTERN."

OXFORD COMPANION TO CLASSICAL LITERATURE ED P. HARVEY. FITS IT ALL TOGETHER!

ALSO: THE FILM **IPHIGENIA**, DIRECTED BY M. CACOYANNIS, AFTER EURIPIDES

ANCIENT GREECE AT WORK BY G. GLOTZ. GREAT BOOK, BUT SHORT ON PIX

THE ANCIENT ECONOMY BY M. FINLEY. READABLE AND ENLIGHTENING

DAILY LIFE IN ANCIENT GREECE BY R. FLACIERE. ATHENS MOSTLY

ANCIENT GREEK HOUSES BY B.C. RIDER. FLOOR PLANS ONLY!

PHALLOS: A SYMBOL AND ITS HISTORY IN THE MALE WORLD BY TH. VANGAARD. GOOD INSIGHTS INTO BABOONS

ORPHEUS AND GREEK RELIGION BY W.K.C. GUTHRIE. EXCELLENT, THO SOMETIMES DIFFICULT

THE GOLDEN BOUGH BY J. FRAZER. A 1-VOLUME ABRIDGEMENT OF THE IMMENSE CLASSIC ON MAGIC AND RELIGION

THE ORIGIN AND EARLY FORM OF GREEK TRAGEDY BY G. ELSE. THE "GREAT MAN" THEORY

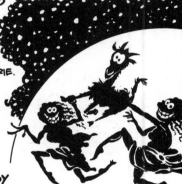

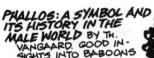

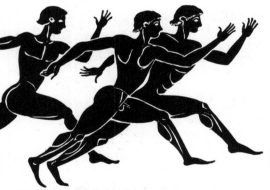

EARLY SPARTA BY G.L. HUXLEY

LIVES OF THE NOBLE GREEKS AND ROMANS BY PLUTARCH. THE LIFE OF LYKURGOS INCLUDES MANY GOOD STORIES OF LIFE IN SPARTA.

OLYMPIA BY L. DREES. AN ILLUSTRATED, DETAILED, GUSHY ACCOUNT OF THE OLYMPIC GAMES

WEAPONS BY E. TUNIS. GOOD PIX

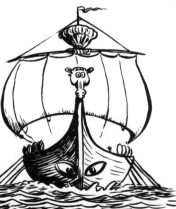

THE PELICAN HISTORY OF GREECE BY A.R. BURN. LIVELY, CONCISE, GOOD DETAILS

THE HISTORIES BY HERODOTOS. JUST GREAT! I PLAN TO STEAL MOST OF IT FOR VOL. 6!

THE CAMBRIDGE ANCIENT HISTORY, VOL III ED. BURY, COOK, ADCOCK. THICK & FLAVORLESS AS A BEAN SANDWICH

WHAT HAPPENED IN HISTORY BY V.G. CHILDE. METAL, TRADE, AND SOCIAL LIFE

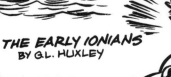

THE EARLY IONIANS BY G.L. HUXLEY

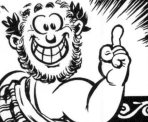

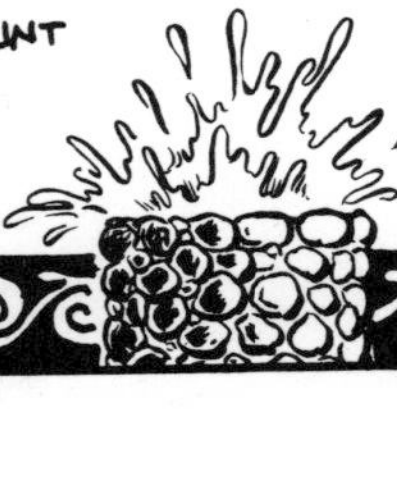

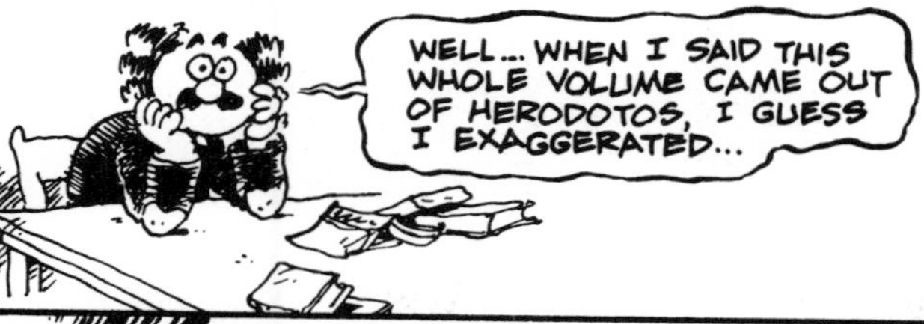
WELL... WHEN I SAID THIS WHOLE VOLUME CAME OUT OF HERODOTOS, I GUESS I EXAGGERATED...

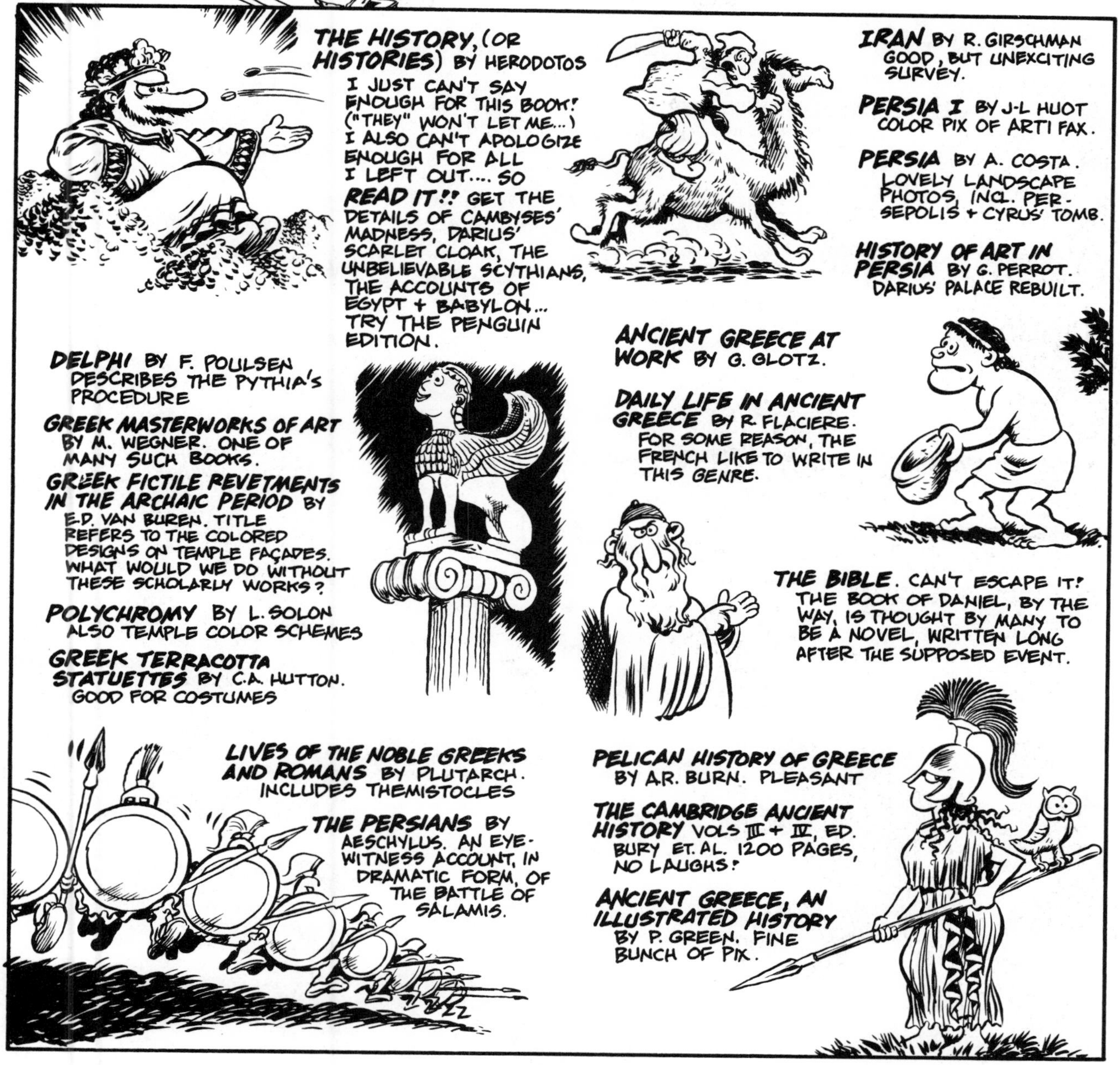
THE HISTORY, (OR HISTORIES) BY HERODOTOS
I JUST CAN'T SAY ENOUGH FOR THIS BOOK! ("THEY" WON'T LET ME...) I ALSO CAN'T APOLOGIZE ENOUGH FOR ALL I LEFT OUT.... SO READ IT!! GET THE DETAILS OF CAMBYSES' MADNESS, DARIUS' SCARLET CLOAK, THE UNBELIEVABLE SCYTHIANS, THE ACCOUNTS OF EGYPT + BABYLON... TRY THE PENGUIN EDITION.
IRAN BY R. GIRSCHMAN
GOOD, BUT UNEXCITING SURVEY.
PERSIA I BY J-L HUOT
COLOR PIX OF ARTI FAX.
PERSIA BY A. COSTA.
LOVELY LANDSCAPE PHOTOS, INCL. PERSEPOLIS + CYRUS' TOMB.
HISTORY OF ART IN PERSIA BY G. PERROT.
DARIUS' PALACE REBUILT.
DELPHI BY F. POULSEN
DESCRIBES THE PYTHIA'S PROCEDURE
GREEK MASTERWORKS OF ART BY M. WEGNER. ONE OF MANY SUCH BOOKS.
GREEK FICTILE REVETMENTS IN THE ARCHAIC PERIOD BY E.D. VAN BUREN. TITLE REFERS TO THE COLORED DESIGNS ON TEMPLE FAÇADES. WHAT WOULD WE DO WITHOUT THESE SCHOLARLY WORKS?
POLYCHROMY BY L. SOLON
ALSO TEMPLE COLOR SCHEMES
GREEK TERRACOTTA STATUETTES BY C.A. HUTTON.
GOOD FOR COSTUMES
ANCIENT GREECE AT WORK BY G. GLOTZ.
DAILY LIFE IN ANCIENT GREECE BY R. FLACIERE.
FOR SOME REASON, THE FRENCH LIKE TO WRITE IN THIS GENRE.
THE BIBLE. CAN'T ESCAPE IT! THE BOOK OF DANIEL, BY THE WAY, IS THOUGHT BY MANY TO BE A NOVEL, WRITTEN LONG AFTER THE SUPPOSED EVENT.
LIVES OF THE NOBLE GREEKS AND ROMANS BY PLUTARCH. INCLUDES THEMISTOCLES
THE PERSIANS BY AESCHYLUS. AN EYE-WITNESS ACCOUNT, IN DRAMATIC FORM, OF THE BATTLE OF SALAMIS.
PELICAN HISTORY OF GREECE BY A.R. BURN. PLEASANT
THE CAMBRIDGE ANCIENT HISTORY VOLS III + IV, ED. BURY ET. AL. 1200 PAGES, NO LAUGHS!
ANCIENT GREECE, AN ILLUSTRATED HISTORY BY P. GREEN. FINE BUNCH OF PIX.
ZZZ

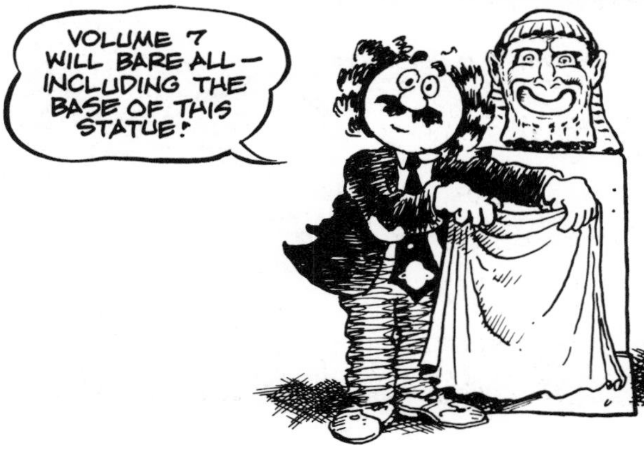
VOLUME 7 WILL BARE ALL — INCLUDING THE BASE OF THIS STATUE!

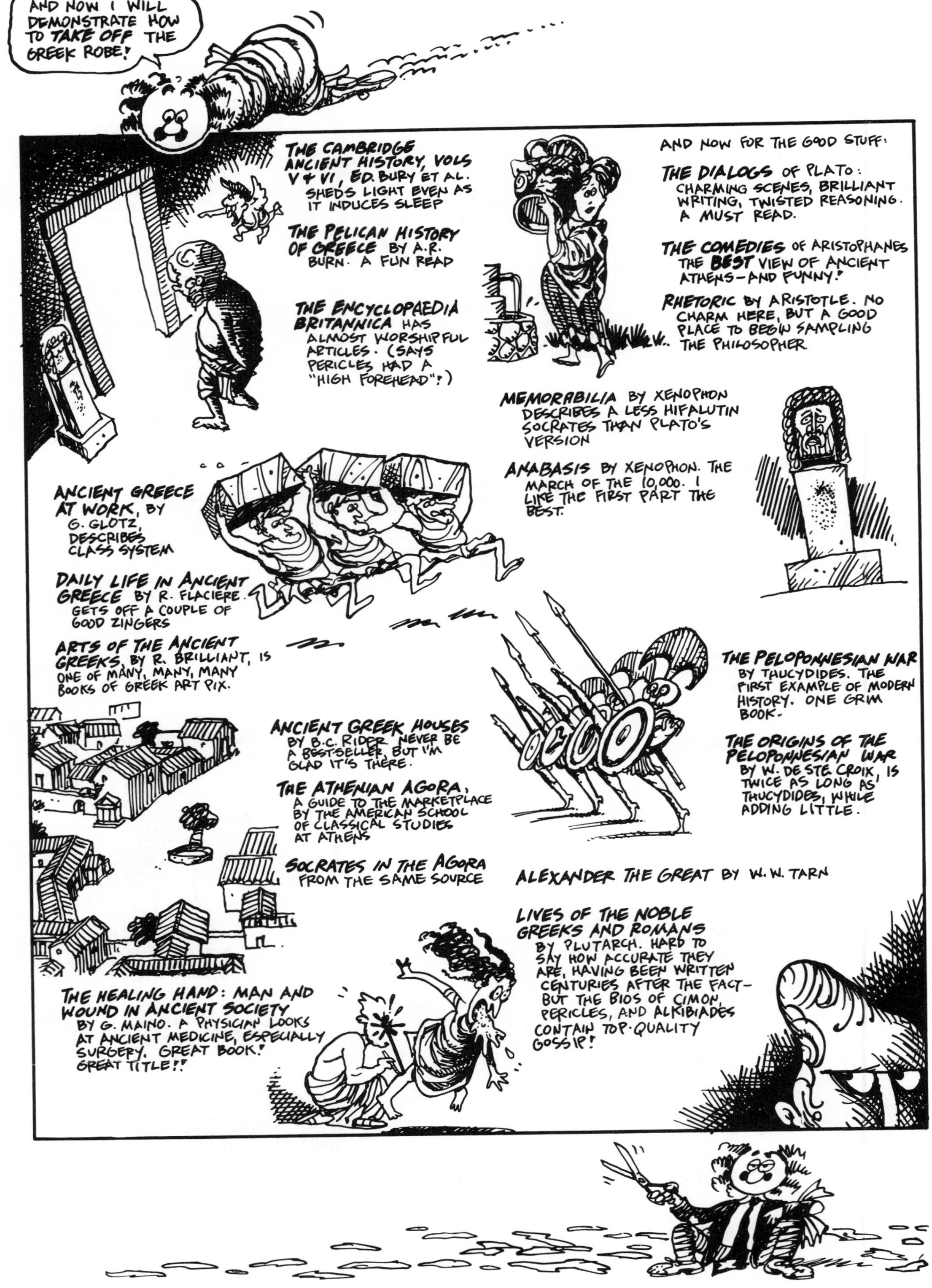
AND NOW I WILL DEMONSTRATE HOW TO TAKE OFF THE GREEK ROBE!
THE CAMBRIDGE ANCIENT HISTORY, VOLS V & VI, ED. BURY ET AL. SHEDS LIGHT EVEN AS IT INDUCES SLEEP
THE PELICAN HISTORY OF GREECE BY A.R. BURN. A FUN READ
THE ENCYCLOPAEDIA BRITANNICA HAS ALMOST WORSHIPFUL ARTICLES. (SAYS PERICLES HAD A "HIGH FOREHEAD"!)
AND NOW FOR THE GOOD STUFF:
THE DIALOGS OF PLATO: CHARMING SCENES, BRILLIANT WRITING, TWISTED REASONING. A MUST READ.
THE COMEDIES OF ARISTOPHANES THE BEST VIEW OF ANCIENT ATHENS—AND FUNNY!
RHETORIC BY ARISTOTLE. NO CHARM HERE, BUT A GOOD PLACE TO BEGIN SAMPLING THE PHILOSOPHER
MEMORABILIA BY XENOPHON DESCRIBES A LESS HIFALUTIN SOCRATES THAN PLATO'S VERSION
ANABASIS BY XENOPHON. THE MARCH OF THE 10,000. I LIKE THE FIRST PART THE BEST.
ANCIENT GREECE AT WORK, BY G. GLOTZ, DESCRIBES CLASS SYSTEM
DAILY LIFE IN ANCIENT GREECE BY R. FLACIERE. GETS OFF A COUPLE OF GOOD ZINGERS
ARTS OF THE ANCIENT GREEKS, BY R. BRILLIANT, IS ONE OF MANY, MANY, MANY BOOKS OF GREEK ART PIX.
THE PELOPONNESIAN WAR BY THUCYDIDES. THE FIRST EXAMPLE OF MODERN HISTORY. ONE GRIM BOOK.
ANCIENT GREEK HOUSES BY B.C. RIDER NEVER BE A BEST-SELLER, BUT I'M GLAD IT'S THERE.
THE ORIGINS OF THE PELOPONNESIAN WAR BY W. DE STE. CROIX, IS TWICE AS LONG AS THUCYDIDES, WHILE ADDING LITTLE.
THE ATHENIAN AGORA, A GUIDE TO THE MARKETPLACE BY THE AMERICAN SCHOOL OF CLASSICAL STUDIES AT ATHENS
SOCRATES IN THE AGORA FROM THE SAME SOURCE
ALEXANDER THE GREAT BY W. W. TARN
LIVES OF THE NOBLE GREEKS AND ROMANS BY PLUTARCH. HARD TO SAY HOW ACCURATE THEY ARE, HAVING BEEN WRITTEN CENTURIES AFTER THE FACT—BUT THE BIOS OF CIMON, PERICLES, AND ALKIBIADES CONTAIN TOP-QUALITY GOSSIP!
THE HEALING HAND: MAN AND WOUND IN ANCIENT SOCIETY BY G. MAINO. A PHYSICIAN LOOKS AT ANCIENT MEDICINE, ESPECIALLY SURGERY. GREAT BOOK! GREAT TITLE!!

LARRY GONICK HAS NO BIOGRAPHY
ASIDE FROM STUDYING MATH AT HARVARD,
LIVING IN ARIZONA, MASSACHUSETTS, INDIA,
AND CALIFORNIA, WORKING IN PHARMACOLOGY
LABS, PROGRAMMING COMPUTERS, SWIMMING LAPS,
GOING TO THE LIBRARY, AND WATCHING SPORTS
ON T.V., HE DOES NOTHING EXCEPT DRAW CARTOONS
ALL DAY.

HE LIVES IN SAN FRANCISCO WITH HIS
WIFE AND TWO DAUGHTERS. THEIR HOUSE SEEMS
TO GET SMALLER EVERY DAY.